UNDERSTANDING INSURANCE LAW
Second Edition

Robert H. Jerry, II

Professor and Herff Chair of Excellence in Law

Cecil C. Humphreys School of Law

The University of Memphis

LEGAL TEXT SERIES

1996

MATTHEW◆BENDER

Questions About This Publication

For questions about the Editorial Content appearing in this volume or reprint permission, please call:

Mark Wasserman, J.D. at 1–800–424–0651 (ext.270)

Outside the United States and Canada please call .... (212) 967–7707
For assistance with shipments, billing or other customer service matters, please call:

Customer Service Department 1–800–533–1646

Jerry, Robert H. 1953-
    Understanding insurance law / Robert H. Jerry, II. — 2nd ed. p. cm.
    — (Legal text series)
    Includes index.
    ISBN 0-8205-2467-0 (softcover)
    1. Insurance law—United States. I. Title. II. Series.
KF1164.J47 1996
346.73'086—dc20
[347.30686]

MATTHEW BENDER & CO.
11 PENN PLAZA, NEW YORK, NY 10001 212-661-5050
201 MISSION STREET, SAN FRANCISCO, CA 94105 415-908-3200
1275 BROADWAY, ALBANY, NY 12201 518-462-3331

(Matthew Bender & Co., Inc.)   (Pub.837)

"To Lisa, John, Jim & Beth"

PREFACE TO THE SECOND EDITION

In the preface to this book's first edition, I began with the observation that "[f]ew subjects as important as insurance law are so neglected by American law schools and law students. There are signs, however, that this may be changing." Eight years later it is apparent that much has changed. Teaching materials, casebooks, and scholarly writing on insurance law in monographs and periodicals are much more abundant. The Association of American Law Schools now has a Section on Insurance Law, which facilitates interaction among academics with teaching and research interests in insurance law. From my vantage point, enrollment in insurance law courses continues to increase. Indeed, it appears that students and legal educators have come to understand what practitioners have known for years — insurance law is an extremely important subject; indeed, it is difficult even to imagine a legal transaction or event that does not implicate insurance in some way.

Because the substance of insurance law is so vast, the aims of this book must be modest. My purpose is to present in one volume a substantive and analytic survey of the topics one is likely to find covered in a law school course in insurance law. To the extent judges and lawyers also find this work to be helpful, I am gratified. But my principle objective is to make the substance of insurance law accessible to the student and to the general practitioner unfamiliar with the subject.

Much of this book is necessarily descriptive. But I intend that the text also provide perspective — sometimes historical, sometimes economic, sometimes political. I firmly believe that viewing the law through different prisms helps to make today's student a better lawyer tomorrow. Also, I do not hesitate in this text to offer my own critical assessment of insurance law doctrines and the directions of their evolution, but I will strive to make clear where description ends and my own opinion begins.

Because this book's emphasis is on the basics, no effort is made to annotate the field comprehensively. That chore is left to the writers and editors of the several specialized and multivolume treatises, with which anyone undertaking serious research in the subject must become familiar. Accordingly, this book identifies only the leading cases and law review articles for most topics. For topics where no "leading case" exists, the book has citations to representative cases that might serve as the springboard for locating cases relevant to the particular problem in a particular jurisdiction.

Any writer in any field stands on the shoulders of many outstanding scholars whose work preceded his or her own. Thus, if there is any merit in my suggestions about insurance law, I must give much credit to the "senior scholars" of insurance law, such as Robert Keeton, Spencer Kimball, Edwin Patterson, and William Vance, each of whom did path-breaking work in this field. I have also benefited from the work of outstanding scholars at other law schools whose careers are more contemporaneous with my own. And there is a younger group of insurance law scholars who

PREFACE

have published some splendid work. Because I dare not risk leaving anyone off a list, I will let the footnotes of this text identify the people to whom I refer, and I submit that the list will still be incomplete.

There are several people to whom I owe special thanks. I am grateful to my friend Peter Maxfield for giving me the idea to write a basic text on the fundamentals of insurance law. Several of my colleagues at The University of Memphis have read portions of the second edition and have saved me from making mistakes: June Entman; Amanda Esquibel; Ernest Lidge; Paulette Delk; Lars Gustafsson; and Robert Cox. Special thanks go to Charles Silver of the University of Texas for his advice and suggestions on section 114. Likewise, I remember with appreciation those who gave similar assistance as I wrote the first edition: Emeric Fischer, David Snively, Kim Dayton, and Beth Kravetz. Mistakes that remain are mine alone. I received invaluable research assistance from several University of Memphis law students: Michael Elsner; Jason Massie; Bill Burns; Teresa Newsom; and Bryan Rosenstiel. Likewise, I recall with appreciation the research assistance provided by a number of University of Kansas law students who helped with the first edition: Scott Young, Charles Scanlon, Kevin Engels, Susan Hunt, Brian Doerr, and Jerry Capps. I am grateful to the endowment for the Herbert Herff Chair of Excellence in Law at The University of Memphis and to the University of Kansas School of Law Research Fund for giving these present and former students financial support for their considerable efforts. I am also grateful to Clark Kimball, my editor at Matthew Bender, whose reading of both editions has made this book better. Many thanks are also owed my secretary at The University of Memphis, Karol Usmani, for completing with skill and good humor many of the tedious tasks required to get this manuscript ready for publication. Last but not least, I owe thanks to the students in my insurance law classes at The University of Memphis and the University of Kansas; their questions — and my concern about what they might ask — have helped me acquire insights that I would not otherwise have discovered.

There are others whose support has been indispensable. I am privileged to serve as the first permanent holder of the Herbert Herff Chair of Excellence in Law at The University of Memphis; I am gratified that my work is deemed worthy of the generous support of the Herff endowment. I also recall with appreciation the encouragement of many colleagues at the University of Kansas, my former academic home and the place where most of my academic career, at least until now, has been spent. Although my five years' service as dean of that law school delayed this second edition, I do not regret the time spent in that particular service, notwithstanding the inevitable costs to my teaching and research.

Finally, I am grateful to my wife Lisa for her love and patience through all the years during which the editions of this book were written. Since the first edition, Lisa and I have welcomed three wonderful children into our lives. I sometimes wonder whether the first edition would even have been written if John, Jim, and Beth had joined our household a few years earlier. Regardless, they, too, have made some sacrifices to enable me to prepare the second edition. I also recall Lisa's contribution in yet another way to this book: her willingness to edit most of the first edition of this book before my publisher saw it improved the text in ways that survive into the second edition.

I sincerely hope the readers of this book find it helpful to their understanding of insurance law. As always, I invite their suggestions, criticisms, and comments.

Cecil C. Humphreys School of Law

The University of Memphis
Memphis, Tennessee

April 1996

TABLE OF CONTENTS

PART A
WHAT IS INSURANCE LAW?

Chapter 1. What Is Insurance?

PART B
ESTABLISHING THE CONTRACTUAL RELATIONSHIP

Chapter 3. Contract Formation

Chapter 4. The Insurable Interest Requirement

Chapter 5. Scope of Obligations: Persons and Interests Protected

PART C
PERFORMING THE CONTRACTUAL OBLIGATIONS

Chapter 7. The Insured's Duty to Pay Premiums

Chapter 8. The Mechanics of Claim Presentation

Chapter 10. Excuses for the Insurer's Nonperformance

Chapter 11. The Additional Duties in Third-Party Insurance

PART D
SOME REMAINING MATTERS

Chapter 12. Group Insurance

Chapter 13. Automobile Insurance

(Pub.837)

Chapter 14. Reinsurance

(Matthew Bender & Co., Inc.)

SECTION CORRELATION TABLES FOR FIRST AND SECOND EDITIONS

To the maximum extent possible, the Table of Contents to the second edition of Understanding Insurance Law has not been changed. Thus a cite to a specific section of the first edition will usually correlate to discussion of the same topic in the second edition, and vice versa. In some parts of the book, however, reorganization to incorporate recent developments or to improve the presentation of the material has necessitated some changes in how the sections are numbered. To assist the user of this text who wishes to compare the discussion in the first edition (or the user of the first edition who wishes to find discussion of the same subject in the second edition), the following tables identify changes in the organization of the second edition. Sections not listed in the following two tables discuss the same subject in both the first and second editions of Understanding Insurance Law.

Table I

The first column identifies the section in the first edition, and the second column identifies the section in the second edition where discussion of the first edition's subject can be found:

1st Edition	2d Edition
13A[e]	13A[f]
13D[a]	13A[e]
25G[a]	25G[d][2]
25G[b]	25G[a]
25G[c]	25G[b]
35[c][2][ii]	35[c][2][iii]
43[a]	44[b]
43[b]	44[a]
43[c]	44[c]
44	45
45[a]	43
45[b]-[f]	47[a]-[e]
52A[d][2]	52A[d][3]
52A[d][3]	52A[d][4]
52B[b][1]	52B[c]
52B[b][2]	52B[d]
63B	63C
63C	63B
64[a]	64[b]
64[b]	64[a][1]
64[c]	64[a][2]
65[a]	65[b]
65[b]	65[c]
65[c]	65[d]
65[d]	65[e]
65[e]	65[f]
65[f]	65[g]

(Matthew Bender & Co., Inc.)

Table II

The first column identifies a section in the second edition, and the second column identifies the section in the first edition where discussion of the second edition's subject can be found:

(Matthew Bender & Co., Inc.)

INTRODUCTION

§ 1 Why Study Insurance Law?

The importance of insurance to our nation and planet is obvious. Justice Black wrote in *United States v. South-Eastern Underwriters Association:* [1] "Perhaps no modern commercial enterprise directly affects so many persons in all walks of life as does the insurance business. Insurance touches the home, the family, and the occupation or the business of almost every person in the United States." [2] Professors Harnett and Thornton began their article on the insurable interest doctrine by stating: "The creation and enforcement of insurance contracts impinge at every turn upon the public interest and vitally affect the social and economic welfare of individuals." [3] Professor Kimball simply but profoundly observed in his influential article on insurance regulation: "Insurance is a small world that reflects the purposes of the larger world outside it." [4] If insurance plays such a significant role in our economic and social lives, the legal rules regulating the insurance industry definitely merit careful analysis and study.

Indeed, it is difficult even to imagine an event or transaction that does not involve insurance in some way. Thus, lawyers in virtually every kind of practice need at least a basic understanding of insurance law principles. A lawyer who organizes commercial transactions must appraise the risks of the transaction and make recommendations about whether these risks should be — or can be — insured. A lawyer counseling an individual or a firm about financial planning must think about the possible needs for insurance for various contingencies. A lawyer prosecuting or defending a claim for personal injury or property damage is routinely concerned with whether the claimant will succeed in reaching insurance proceeds for a covered loss. These kinds of issues surface repeatedly in any general practice of law, and, for some lawyers, these issues absorb every hour of every day.

Beyond the enormous practical implications of the subject, insurance law challenges both the student and practitioner to think about broad societal values and norms. For example, a person contemplating a new business activity or enterprise may decide whether to undertake it based on his or her ability to insure the risks involved. The extent to which the rules of insurance law support or discourage the underwriting of the risk may determine whether the contemplated business initiative even occurs. Thus, insurance law is highly relevant to important questions concerning the kinds and amount of economic activity our society should encourage. To take another example, one underlying rationale of tort law is that holding individuals responsible for their intentional and negligent conduct deters certain kinds of behavior deemed repugnant or undesirable by society as a whole. To what extent is this rationale defeated by allowing individuals to insure against the consequences

---

[1] 322 U.S. 533 (1943).

[2] 322 U.S. at 540.

[3] Bertram Harnett & John V. Thornton, *Insurable Interest in Property: A Socio-Economic Reevaluation of a Legal Concept,* 48 Colum. L. Rev. 1162 (1948).

[4] Spencer L. Kimball, *The Purpose of Insurance Regulation: A Preliminary Inquiry in the Theory of Insurance Law,* 45 Minn. L. Rev. 471, 524 (1961).

(Matthew Bender & Co., Inc.)   (Pub.837)

of their negligent conduct? Tort law also seeks to compensate the victims of tortious conduct. To what extent is this objective frustrated by preventing the insurability of intentional acts? What constitutes an "intentional act" is a perplexing question regardless of its context. Insurance law's distinction between intentional and unintentional acts tells us something about how our society attempts to achieve the goals of tort law — and perhaps something about how strongly our society feels about these goals. Insurance law principles tell us something about our society's attitudes on racial and gender equality, concentrations of economic power and capital, and resource allocation. Those interested in the economic theory of law will find in insurance law virtually endless food for thought. Insurance law often portends new legal theories for achieving fairness in the broader context of the law of promissory obligations. The study of recent developments in insurance law thus provides a glimpse of how commercial transactions generally might be regulated in the future.

Insurance is the primary mechanism by which economic actors in our society transfer risk and distribute loss. It is still fair to assert that insurance law receives inadequate emphasis in most law school curricula notwithstanding a markedly increased interest in the subject during the past ten years. Tort law enjoys the status of a required first-year course at virtually all law schools, but the law of tort liability is a relatively minor system for transferring risk and distributing loss in the United States and many other nations. Indeed, for the insurance scholar, tort law is simply a special kind of insurance. Contract law, the study of which is also required in the first year of virtually all law school degree programs, facilitates the ordering of our society by making some promises enforceable and therefore worthy of reliance. The primary object of an insurance contract is to *trade* risk for the ultimate purpose of distributing it, but every contract that is the product of a bargained-for exchange involves, like an insurance contract, an allocation of risk. Thus, one might view every contract emerging from the bargaining process as involving a subsidiary contract of insurance, where risk is allocated as part of the consideration.

Last but not least, another reason to study insurance law is the interesting nature of the subject.[5] This is true of virtually any subject in the law, once one has committed sufficient energy to have control of the subject's fundamentals. Insurance law, however, is often unfairly stereotyped as an activity primarily involving the probing of the fine print in thick stacks of documents. Of course, the close reading of contract language is an important part of insurance law. But the individual embarking upon the study of insurance law with the misconception that nothing more is involved is likely to be pleasantly surprised.

---

[5] At the reception following the wedding of one of my students, I met a group of attorneys from a large Kansas City law firm. Upon learning my occupation, one of the group asked me what subjects I teach, and I responded "insurance law and banking law." The fellow yelled to one of his colleagues standing nearby, "Hey, John, come over here; I've finally met someone more boring than you are." In an act of self-defense, I raised the issue of gender discrimination in insurance rating, and the boring subject of insurance law consumed a major portion of the evening's remaining conversation.

(Matthew Bender & Co., Inc.)   (Pub.837)

§ 2 The Outline of This Book

The premise of this book's organization is that insurance law is best understood if its legal principles are arranged according to the various stages in the life of a contract. An insurance policy is, after all, a contract between insurer and insured. Like any contract, an insurance contract is formed, performed, and sometimes breached. Many issues of contract formation, performance, and nonperformance are the same regardless of the type of insurance involved. It is true that individual lines of insurance sometimes have peculiar rules with unique applications, but this book emphasizes the commonality of rules in the different lines and breaks out the individual lines of insurance only when specialized attention is essential to a proper understanding of the principles.

In Part A, this book considers the question "what is insurance law." Chapter 1 addresses the narrower question "what is insurance." This chapter considers a definition of insurance, briefly sketches the history of insurance, examines the meaning of the phrase "business of insurance," and explores the various ways of classifying insurance. Chapter 2 gives the rest of the answer to the question "what is insurance law" by examining legislative and judicial sources of insurance law. This chapter discusses the uncertain boundary between state and federal regulation of insurance, state statutory and administrative regulation, and various techniques of judicial regulation.

In Part B, this book considers issues germane to the establishment of the contractual relationship between insurer and insured. Chapter 3 explores the process of contract formation. This chapter discusses, for example, the mechanics of offer and acceptance, the insurance binder, the effect of delivery of the policy, and the role of the broker or agent in contract formation. Chapter 4 is devoted to the insurable interest requirement. Chapter 5 examines the scope of obligations created as to persons and interests protected when the formation process is successfully completed. Subjects covered in this chapter include the rights of life insurance beneficiaries, rights of assignees, partial interests in property, and related subjects. Chapter 6 continues the discussion of the scope of obligations created with reference to the risks covered. This chapter principally focuses upon the nature of coverage, explicit and implicit limitations upon coverage, and causation issues.

In Part C, this book considers issues relevant to the performance of contractual obligations. Chapter 7 discusses the insured's duty to pay premiums. Chapter 8 explores the mechanics of claims presentation, including notice of loss, proof of loss, and disposition of claims. Chapter 9 examines the insurer's duty to pay proceeds, including problems in measuring the amount of loss, subrogation, and overlapping coverages. Chapter 10 is devoted to excuses for the insurer's nonperformance, such as the insured's breach of warranty, misrepresentation, and concealment. Chapter 11 is devoted to the additional duties in liability insurance, such as the insured's duty to cooperate and the insurer's duties to defend and settle.

Finally, in Part D, this book examines a few topics that defy easy categorization. Chapter 12 discusses special problems in group insurance, Chapter 13 is devoted to special issues in automobile insurance, and Chapter 14 considers issues in reinsurance.

§ 3 Sources for Further Study

Anyone currently writing about insurance law stands on the shoulders of many excellent thinkers and writers. The following list of insurance sources is not exhaustive, but it does identify many of the significant or widely-used insurance law works.

[a] Multivolume Treatises: General

John A. Appleman & Jean Appleman, *Insurance Law and Practice* (orig. ed. 1941 by John A. Appleman; rev. ed. by Jean Appleman) (West) (approximately 60 volumes)

George I. Couch, *Couch on Insurance Second* (2d rev. ed 1984; 2d ed. by R. Anderson; rev. by M. Rhodes) (Lawyer's Co-operative/Bancroft-Whitney) (approximately 30 volumes)

[b] Multivolume Treatises: Specialized

Bertram Harnett, *Responsibilities of Insurance Agents and Brokers* (originally published in 1974 and updated annually) (Matthew Bender; 2 volumes)

Rowland H. Long, *The Law of Liability Insurance* (originally published in 1966, and updated annually) (Matthew Bender; 4 volumes)

Pat Magarick & Ken Brownlee, *Casualty Insurance Claims* (4th ed. 1995) (Clark Boardman Callaghan; 3 volumes)

Irvin E. Schermer, *Automobile Liability Insurance* (2d rev. ed. 1989) (Clark Boardman; 3 volumes)

Alan I. Widiss, *Uninsured and Underinsured Motorist Insurance* (originally published in 1982 and updated annually) (Anderson Publishing Co.; 3 volumes)

Allan D. Windt, *Insurance Claims and Disputes: Representation of Insureds and Insurers* (3d ed. 1995) (Shepard's/McGraw-Hill; 2 volumes)

Business Insurance: Law & Practice Guide (1989) (Matthew Bender; 3 volumes)

No-Fault and Uninsured Motorist Automobile Insurance (originally published in 1986, and updated annually) (Matthew Bender; 4 volumes)

[c] One-Volume Treatises: General

Kenneth S. Abraham, *Distributing Risk: Insurance, Legal Theory, and Public Policy* (1986) (Yale University Press)

John F. Dobbyn, *Insurance Law in a Nutshell* (3d ed. 1996) (West)

Robert E. Keeton & Alan I. Widiss, *Insurance Law: A Guide to Fundamental Principles, Legal Doctrines, and Commercial Practices* (Student ed. 1988; this is an updated edition of Robert E. Keeton's 1971 one-volume treatise) (West)

Edwin W. Patterson, *Essentials of Insurance Law: An Outline of Legal Doctrines in Their Relations to Insurnace Practices* (2d ed. 1985) (reproduction of 2d ed. 1957) (McGraw-Hill)

William R. Vance, *Handbook on the Law of Insurance* (3d ed. Anderson 1951) (West)

[d] One-Volume Treatises: Specialized

Kenneth S. Abraham, *Environmental Liability Insurance Law* (1991) (Prentice-Hall)

Buist M. Anderson, *Anderson on Life Insurance* (1991) (Little-Brown)

Stephen S. Ashley, *Bad Faith Actions: Liability and Damages* (1984) (Callaghan)

Charles W. Carnahan, *Conflict of Laws and Life Insurance Contracts* (1958) (Dennis)

Robert F. Cushman, Bruce Roznowski & William E. Simpson, eds., *Prosecuting and Defending Insurance Claims* (1989) (John Wiley & Sons)

William F. Meyer, *Life and Health Insurance Law* (1972) (Lawyer's Co-operative/Bancroft-Whitney)

Mark C. Rahdert, *Covering Accident Costs: Insurance, Liability, and Tort Reform* (1995) (Temple University Press)

William M. Shernoff, Sanford M. Gage, & H. Levine, *Insurance Bad Faith Litigation* (1984) (Matthew Bender)

Grayden S. Staring, *Law of Reinsurance* (1993) (Clark Boardman)

Jeffrey W. Stempel, *Interpretation of Insurance Contracts: Law and Strategy for Insurers and Policyholders* (1994) (Little, Brown & Co.)

Dennis J. Walls, *Litigation and Prevention of Insurer Bad Faith* (2d ed. 1994) (Shepard's/McGraw-Hill)

M. Woodroof, J. Fonseca, & A. Squillante, *Automobile Insurance and No-Fault Law* (1974) (Lawyer's Co-operative/Bancroft-Whitney)

Tod I. Zuckerman & Mark C. Raskoff, *Environmental Insurance Litigation: Law and Practice* (1992) (Shepard's/McGraw-Hill)

[e] Casebooks

Kenneth S. Abraham, *Insurance Law and Regulation: Cases and Materials* (2d ed. 1995) (Foundation Press)

Emeric Fischer & Peter N. Swisher, *Principles of Insurance Law* (2d ed. 1994) (Matthew Bender)

Roger C. Henderson, *Insurance Law: Cases & Materials* (1989) (Michie)

Spencer L. Kimball, *Cases and Materials on Insurance Law* (1992) (Little-Brown)

Alan I. Widiss, *Insurance: Materials on Fundamental Principles, Legal Doctrines, and Regulatory Acts* (1989) (West)

Kenneth H. York, John W. Whelan, & Leo P. Martinez, *Insurance Law: Cases, Materials, and Problems* (3d ed. 1994) (West)

William F. Young & Eric M. Holmes, *Insurance: Cases and Materials* (2d ed. 1985) (Foundation Press)

[f]　Case Reporting Services and Other Research Aids

Litigation Research Group, *Insurance Litigation Reporter*

Prentice-Hall, Inc., *Insurance Guide*

Annotated insurance policy forms, published by the Tort and Insurance Practice Section, American Bar Association, and the Defense Research Institute

National Association of Insurance Commissioners: Model Laws, Regulations, and Guidelines (1985; updated regularly)

Bureau of National Affairs, Inc., *Insurance Coverage Litigation Report* (commencing publication in September 1995)

Mealy's Insurance Law Reports (weekly case summaries on various insurance law subjects)

[g]　Periodicals

Defense Counsel Journal (formerly *Insurance Counsel Journal*) (published by International Association of Defense Counsel, formerly the International Association of Insurance Counsel)

Tort & Insurance Law Journal (formerly *Forum*) (published by the Tort and Insurance Practice Section, American Bar Association)

The Brief (published by the Tort and Insurance Practice Section, American Bar Association)

Insurance Law Journal (published until 1980 by Commerce Clearing House, at which time the journal was terminated)

Journal of Insurance Regulation (published by the National Association of Insurance Commissioners)

[h]　One-Volume Works on the Insurance Industry and the Insurance Business

John D. Long & Davis W. Gregg, *Property and Liability Insurance Handbook* (1965) (Richard D. Irwin, Inc.)

S. Huebner, K. Black, & R. Cline, *Property and Liability Insurance* (3d ed. 1982) (Prentice-Hall)

Judith K. Mintel, *Insurance Rate Litigation: A Survey of Judicial Treatment of Insurance Ratemaking and Insurance Rate Regulation*(1983) (Huebner)

C. Galloway & J. Galloway, *Handbook of Accounting for Insurance Companies* (1986) (McGraw-Hill)

Muriel L. Crawford, *Law and the Life Insurance Contract* (7th ed. 1993) (Richard D. Irwin, Inc.)

Mark S. Dorfman, *Introduction to Insurance* (3d ed. 1987) (Prentice-Hall)

Barry D. Smith et al., *Property and Liability Insurance Principles* (2d ed. 1994) (IIA)

Michael G. Collins, *Introduction to Insurance* (3d ed. 1988) (St Mut)

Albert H. Mowbray, Ralph H. Blanchard, & Arthur C. Williams, Jr., *Insurance: Its Theory and Practice in the United States* (6th ed. 1979) (Krieger)

Emmett J. Vaughan, *Fundamentals of Risk and Insurance* (6th ed. 1992) (John Wiley & Sons)

David L. Bickelhaupt, *General Insurance* (11th ed. 1983) (Richard D. Irwin, Inc.)

Spencer L. Kimball, *Insurance and Public Policy: A Study in the Legal Implementation of Social and Economic Public Policy, Based on Wisconsin Records 1835-1959* (1990) (reproduction of 1960 ed. of University of Wisconsin Press) (Bks Demand)

Spencer L. Kimball & Herbert S. Denenberg, eds., *Insurance, Government, and Social Policy: Studies in Insurance Regulation* (1981) (reprint of 1969 ed.)(Richard D. Irwin, Inc.)

[i] Other Written Materials

Concise handbooks with insurance statistics are the following:

The Fact Book 1994: Property and Casualty Insurance Facts (1994) (Insurance Information Institute; published annually)

Life Insurance Fact Book 1994 (American Council of Life Insurance; published annually)

The Alliance of American Insurers annually publishes a collection of insurance policies, forms, and endorsements commonly used by many insurers in the United States. Occasionally, this book quotes the language from a policy form contained in Alliance of American Insurers, *The Insurance Professionals' Policy Kit: A Collection of Sample Insurance Forms*, hereafter cited as *Policy Kit*. In the preparation of the second edition of this text, the 1994-1995 edition of *Policy Kit* has been used.

The National Insurance Law Service ("NILS") publishes several reference works on insurance law. The volume titled *National Index of Insurance Laws* contains an index, arranged by insurance subject, with citations to each state's statutes, regulations, bulletins, and attorney general opinions on the indexed subject. A researcher who wants to know what every state's law says on a particular matter can save much time by consulting this index. The volume is updated annually. NILS also publishes an index to insurance periodicals, the *National Insurance Law Review* (which reprints insurance-related articles from other journals), and a guidebook on reinsurance law, among other works.

[j] Electronic Data Resources

Since the late 1970s, every law student is taught the fundamentals of research using Westlaw and Lexis/Nexis, and this information is available to law practitioners as well. Each service provides detailed information on how to use the electronic databases to perform legal research, including research in insurance files that have been created in each database. The materials available through Westlaw and Lexis/Nexis are extraordinarily vast, and the research techniques are extremely powerful. For more information, one should refer to the materials made available by each service.

In the 1990s, the Internet has become a tremendous source of information for anyone equipped with a personal computer and a modem, and on-line databases are a rich source of information about insurance and insurance law. As of late 1995, one of the significant on-line resources for information concerning insurance and risk management is RISKNet, created by Dr. James R. Garven. As of this writing, RISKNet access is free of charge, and its subscribers include over 1,200 insurance professionals, risk managers, attorneys, and academics around the world. It is a constant source of dialogue about current issues in the insurance business generally and sometimes insurance law specifically.

To access RISKNet (as well as other on-line resources), one needs a personal computer, a modem, Internet access, and a world-wide-web browser. For law students, many law school or university student computing laboratories provide what is needed to access RISKNet. It is also helpful before accessing RISKNet to have some understanding of how the world-wide-web works. RISKNet is available through the Legal Domain Network ("LDN"), which can be accessed at the following address:

> http://www.kentlaw.edu/lawnet/lawnet.html

That address will lead the user to the LDN's directory, through which the user can access not only RISKNet but a vast number of law-related on-line resources. To bypass this opening page and go directly to RISKNet, one can use the following address:

> http://www.kentlaw.edu/cgi-bin/ldn news/- T + law.listserv.risknet

That page provides users with the ability to do keyword searches on the RISKNet database. Also, for those who wish to participate in the discussion on RISKNet, the FAQ (i.e., 'frequently asked questions') link at the top of that page provides users with the ability to subscribe on-line (subscriptions are screened to insure that participants use the database for its stated purposes). The FAQ link is also available at the following address:

> http://www.kentlaw.edu/cgi-bin/faq/law.listserv.risknet

The information provided here about RISKNet is current as of late 1995. In the event this information should become obsolete, updated information about RISKNet will be available from Dr. Garvin at the following address:

> risknet info@risknet.com

Computer-research technology is ever-changing, but its importance and future expansion is unquestionable.

PART A

WHAT IS INSURANCE LAW?

(Matthew Bender & Co., Inc.)

(Pub.837)

CHAPTER 1

WHAT IS INSURANCE?

§ 10   Defining Insurance

[a]   The Nature of Risk

Life is uncertain. We cannot predict with confidence what the future holds. Events are not completely random, but few events are absolutely certain. Every person is certain to die sometime in the future, but the time of death cannot be predicted with certainty. Accidents occur; indeed, if the times at which accidents occur could be predicted with certainty, steps would be taken to prevent many of them. People make promises every day, and the recipients of the promises expect the promises to be kept. Yet, a chance always exists, due either to events outside the promisor's control or to the fact that people sometimes change their minds, that a promise will not be performed.

The inherent uncertainty of events can be described in terms of chance or probability. In insurance, this uncertainty is normally described in terms of *risk*. For every human at a given age, a risk of death exists; the amount of risk is measured on actuarial tables. Every time an automobile is operated, a risk exists that an accident causing injury might occur; the amount of risk is a function of several factors, including the skill of the vehicle's driver, the number of miles driven, the geographic location of the vehicle, and the age and safety features of the vehicle. A risk exists that a building or home will be destroyed by fire or weather; based on the experience of other buildings of similar age, materials, and location, the risk of a particular structure suffering damage can be measured. That earthquakes, including some serious ones, will occur in some heavily populated areas of the United States in the next fifty to one hundred years is certain; but the precise times of these occurrences are unknown.[1]

[b]   Coping with Risk

People make judgments about risk every day. Before engaging in an activity, an individual will make some sort of calculation, perhaps instinctively, about the activity's probable benefits and costs. After making this calculation, a person might decide not to engage in the activity — although inaction entails risks of its own which must be evaluated. However, if a decision is made to proceed with the activity, the individual might choose to take certain steps to manage the risk of incurring costs.

---

[1] The foregoing risks are examples of *negative,* or undesirable, risks. But risk can be *positive,* in the sense that the risk is a beneficial one. For example, if a person has a one-in-100 chance of winning a contest, a chance of gain or benefit exists, rather than a chance of loss. The chance of obtaining a benefit is a positive risk.

(Matthew Bender & Co., Inc.)   (Pub.837)

People cope with risk in various ways. One way to attempt to manage risk is *to limit the probability of loss*. For example, many industries utilize complex, dangerous machinery, which place the employees who use them at some risk. However, the probability that an employee will lose a finger or hand in a cutting machine is reduced if guards or other safety devices are used around the cutting device. Similarly, brick buildings are less likely to catch fire than wood buildings. Thus, a builder might choose to use masonry rather than wood in a given structure so as to limit the probability of loss.

Another way to cope with risk is *to limit the effects of loss*. For example, passengers in automobiles are at risk of injury through accidents. If an accident occurs and the passenger is wearing a seat belt, the passenger is less likely to suffer injury; if an injury is suffered, it is likely to be less severe. Thus, to limit the effects of an accident should it occur, many people choose to "buckle up," thereby limiting the effects of loss. Similarly, buildings are subject to a risk of fire, regardless of the construction materials used. To limit the effects of a fire should it occur, many building owners install sprinkler systems. A sprinkler system will not prevent a fire, but it will limit the effect of a fire should one occur.

Diversification is a particularly important way of limiting the effects of loss. For example, individuals who invest in the stock market expect to make money, but they are also at risk of losing money. To minimize the risk that a sharp decline in the value of one stock will decimate the investor's assets, most investors own a wide variety of the stocks. Through this strategy, losses in one stock are much more likely to be offset by profits in other stocks; if fortunate, the investor will show a net profit from the total portfolio. (Of course, diversification also limits the chance, or "risk," that the investor will benefit from a sharp increase in the value of one stock.) Similarly, the shirt manufacturer who is uncertain whether a new supplier of cloth will provide goods of adequate quality may choose to diversify by placing its order for cloth with several suppliers, thereby minimizing the risk that the entire batch of cloth ordered for a particular job will fail to meet the manufacturer's specifications.

Sometimes people cope with risk through *self-insurance*. For example, a restaurant owner, cognizant of the possibility that a patron may contract food poisoning, is likely to take substantial preventive measures to limit the risk of such an occurrence. After taking such steps, a remote risk nonetheless exists that a customer might be poisoned. The owner may calculate that such an event will rarely occur and may conclude that if it does occur the damages associated with the event could easily be paid from the owner's assets. Alternatively, the owner may choose to set aside a portion of each year's profits into a reserve fund designated to pay the loss should it occur. In either case, the owner chooses to bear the risk. This is, in effect, self-insurance.

Sometimes, after weighing potential benefits and costs of a particular activity, and after taking appropriate steps, if any, to minimize the probability or extent of loss, the individual may choose to engage in the activity without doing anything further with regard to the risk. Thus, some people choose to *ignore* risk. For example, the tightrope walker may purchase special shoes to reduce the risk of falling and may install a safety net to minimize the amount of loss should a fall occur, but if the performer proceeds with the walk, the performer has decided both to assume the risk that remains and to bear the costs of loss should the injury materialize. The performer is not self-insuring, because the performer has no assets to compensate for suffering a loss of life, which is one of the risks. Rather, the performer is choosing to ignore the risk.

In situations where risk cannot be managed sufficiently through preventive measures or through steps that reduce the effects of loss, and where assumption of the risk is not feasible, people usually cope with risk by *transferring* it to someone else. This approach to coping with risk is discussed in the next subsection.

[c]   The Economics of Transferring and Distributing Risk

[1]   The Value of Transferring Risk

An individual's attitude toward risk is influenced by several factors, including the probability of loss, the potential magnitude of the loss, and the person's ability to absorb the loss.

With respect to loss, people are either risk preferring, risk neutral, or risk averse. Imagine forcing several individuals to choose between a fifty percent chance of losing $1000 (which computes to an "expected loss" of $500)[2] or a certainty of losing $500. Some people are *risk preferring:* these people would choose to forego the certain loss in the hope of incurring no loss, despite the equal probability of suffering a large loss. In the same situation, many people are *risk neutral,* that is, indifferent to the alternatives. A substantial group of people are *risk averse:* this group would choose to lose $500 with certainty instead of confronting the fifty percent chance of losing twice as much.

As the potential magnitude of loss increases, most people become more risk averse.[3] This is true even though the probability of loss declines. Thus, when confronted with a one in 10,000 chance of losing $10,000 (an expected loss of $1) and the prospect of losing $1 with certainty, many people previously indifferent would prefer to lose $1 with certainty to avoid the possibility, albeit a remote one, of suffering a substantial loss. However, the more wealth a person has, the less likely it is that the person will be averse to risk: a multimillionaire is more likely to be indifferent toward the choice of losing $1 with certainty and confronting the one-in-10,000 chance of losing $10,000.[4]

---

[2] An "expected loss" is the magnitude of the loss, should it materialize, times the probability that it will occur. Thus, if someone has a one in two chance of losing $500, the expected loss is $250. If the chance of losing $500 is one in ten, the expected loss is $50.

[3] This discussion assumes rational behavior. Sometimes people behave irrationally and ignore risks. E.g., Ray v. Federated Guar. Life Ins. Co., 381 So. 2d 847 (La. Ct. App. 1980) (insured, insane and under delusion that he possessed supernatural powers, held his head under water in bathtub and drowned).

[4] With respect to moderate beneficial risks, many people are risk preferring. For example, lotteries operated by state governments have been successful because large numbers of people prefer moderate amounts of risk: when faced with the choice of retaining one dollar in the pocket and exchanging that dollar for a one-in-a-million chance of winning several thousand

When people are averse to the risk of a loss, they are usually willing to pay someone else to assume the risk. For example, assume that X has a one-in-100 chance of suffering a loss of $1000 (an expected loss of $10). Since X is risk averse, X is willing to pay $15 to someone else, Y, in exchange for Y's promise to reimburse X for X's loss, should X incur it. In other words, the value to X of having the risk assumed by someone else is $15. If 99 people similarly situated to X reach the same agreement with Y, Y will receive $1500 (100 times $15), and Y will have to pay one person the sum of $1000 (since if 100 people each have a one-in-100 chance of suffering the loss, the probabilities indicate that one person probably will suffer the loss).Y earns a profit of $500, which increases Y's satisfaction. Also, the satisfaction of X and each of the 99 similarly situated people is enhanced, because each of them transfers to someone else the risk to which they were averse.

In this illustration, X and the others entered into agreements with Y to transfer risk for a price. X and the others were *insureds* and Y was the *insurer;* each of the 100 insureds entered into an *insurance contract* with Y. A *market* existed in which X and Y could meet, and in which X could transfer and Y could assume risk for a price. X placed a value on having the risk transferred, and X received this value when Y assumed the risk. Also, Y benefitted by assuming the risk of many people similarly situated to X and by *pooling* these risks together, so that each individual's risk could be *distributed* across the pool. The $15 which Y charged X was the *insurance premium.* Based on the loss experience of the pool and statistical probabilities, Y knew that collecting $15 from each insured very likely would be adequate to cover the losses of all the insureds, plus provide Y a reasonable return for putting itself at risk. An insurance contract has a variety of economic implications, a few of which are discussed in the next subsection.

[2] Economic Effects of the Transfer and Distribution of Risk

The illustration in the foregoing section demonstrates several aspects of the economic impact of a contract of insurance. Most obviously, X completely eliminated the risk by transferring it to Y for a price. This transfer has value for X, since X desired to be free of the risk and this objective was achieved. Moreover, the transaction had value to Y, since Y, by dealing in risk on a large scale, could earn a profit. If the costs and benefits of the transaction are viewed in this way, it can be said that since the satisfaction of both parties was improved, the transaction was a desirable one; indeed, society as a whole would be better off if a large number of similar, mutually beneficial transactions would occur.[5]

However, total elimination of risk can have undesirable side effects. If X's risk is completely eliminated through transfer to Y, X might have less incentive to take

---

dollars, many people are willing to trade the dollar for the small chance of winning the large prize. However, when faced with the prospect of receiving $500 with certainty and a 50 percent chance of receiving $1000, many people would be indifferent, and many others would be risk averse, in that they would prefer $500 with certainty rather than face a 50 percent chance of getting nothing.

[5] For excellent discussions of the economics of risk and insurance, see Ejan MacKaay, *The Economics of Information and Law* 173–80 (1982), and A. Michael Polinsky, *An Introduction to Law and Economics* 53–58 (2d ed., 1989).

measures that prevent the loss from occurring or minimize the effect of loss once it occurs. Thus, the existence of insurance can have the perverse effect of increasing the probability of loss. For example, if a mechanic knows that in the event his or her tools are stolen the insurer will reimburse the loss in full, the mechanic may be less likely to suffer the inconvenience of putting tools in a locked storage area at the end of each working day. This phenomenon is called *moral hazard.*

The theoretically ideal response to the problem of moral hazard would be for the insurer to monitor the insured's behavior and adjust the premium based on the extent to which the insured takes adequate steps to safeguard his or her property. If such measurements were possible, the insurance would be priced in exact conformity with the amount of risk being transferred to the insurer. For obvious reasons, however, monitoring the behavior of each insured is not feasible. Even if the prospect of having a third party constantly inquiring into one's behavior were acceptable, the administrative costs of such a system would be prohibitive.

To deal with the moral hazard phenomenon, in most insurance transactions the insured retains some responsibility for the risk through either a *deductible* or *coinsurance.* With a deductible, the insured bears any loss up to some stated amount, with the insurer bearing the rest. (In homeowner's or automobile insurance, a common deductible is in the range of $100 to $500.) With coinsurance, the insured bears some stated percentage of the loss regardless of its amount, with the insurer bearing the rest. Thus, in the foregoing example, the mechanic-insured has an incentive to preserve his or her own property because the mechanic will bear some portion of any loss.

Requiring the insured to bear a portion of the loss is not a totally satisfactory solution for the risk averse person. On balance, however, that solution is the best one. To compensate for the moral hazard phenomenon, premiums would have to be much higher if all of the mechanic's risk were transferred; the insured benefits in the long run by paying lower premiums while simultaneously taking some measures that prevent loss or limit its effects.

Another economic effect of an insurance contract devolves from practical limitations inherent in the process by which the fee charged the insured is computed. The amount of the fee, or premium, should equal the insured's expected loss (e.g., a one-in-five probability of losing $100 computes to an expected loss of $20) plus a share of the insurer's administrative costs.[6] However, because life is uncertain, calculating each person's expected loss with absolute precision is impossible. Indeed, the expenses involved in calculating each person's expected loss would be enormous; to cover these administrative costs, premiums would be exorbitant. Moreover, if such predictions were possible on an individual basis, insurance would not be necessary, since each person would know when loss would occur and then would take all necessary preventive measures, thereby eliminating the value of transferring risk.

Because of the complete impracticality of individual rating, insurers group similar risks together and charge each member of the group the same premium. Insurers

---

[6] In the case of stock company (see § 13B[a], *infra*), the insurer's administrative costs should include an allowance for a reasonable profit.

will subdivide insureds into distinct groups as long as the cost of measuring the differentiating factor is less than the premium reduction the insurer can offer members of a differentiated, better-risk group. To illustrate, assume that smokers on the average have a shorter lifespan than nonsmokers. This distinction could be the basis for an insurer offering nonsmokers lower cost life insurance than smokers. However, making the distinction will involve some administrative and investigative costs. Some of these costs will result from attempting to control factors that will tend to make the smoker-nonsmoker distinction inaccurate, such as problems with the trustworthiness of the data (applicants who know they can secure a lower premium will have a tendency to understate their smoking habits), the uncertainty over whether a person who has quit smoking has a different life expectancy than either a nonsmoker or a presently-active smoker, and the possible differential impact of different amounts of daily smoking. If the cost of accurately distinguishing smokers from nonsmokers exceeds the premium reduction that could be offered nonsmokers, insurers will not make the distinction, since the insurer is likely to lose more smoking customers to insurers who do not make the distinction than the insurer will gain in new non-smoking customers.

From the foregoing emerges another observation. At a certain point in any risk classification scheme, further subdivision of the group becomes too expensive relative to the benefits gained. Thus, it is inevitable that within the same group some insureds will be better risks than others, even though all members of the group pay the same premium. In fact, any group will have a higher proportion of less desirable risks, since more applications for the insurance will tend to come from those who get a better bargain. This phenomenon is called *adverse selection.* Insurers and regulators must take into account the existence of adverse selection when deciding upon the scope of coverage and the premiums to be charged for the coverage.

The concept of risk and an understanding of its economic significance provide the cornerstone for a useful definition of insurance.

[d] A Definition

All contracts either expressly or implicitly allocate risk in one way or another.[7] For example, in contract drafting, language of condition is used to allocate risk. If the parties agree that A will purchase B 's house on the condition that A is able to obtain financing, B bears the risk that financing will be available to A. If financing is unavailable to A, A has no duty to buy the house. In the absence of such a condition, A bears the risk that financing will not be available, because A would still be obligated to buy the house even if financing is not found. Although conditioning

---

[7] This discussion focuses on the use of a voluntarily created contract as a means of transferring risk. It should also be noted that at times the law *involuntarily* transfers risk. Ordinarily, the law leaves the risk of loss on the party unfortunate enough to suffer the loss. Thus, if Smith suffers an injury while building bookshelves at home, Smith bears the risk of loss. However, if Smith is an *employee* who is injured while building shelves for Smith's *employer,* the statutory law of workers' compensation will shift the loss to the employer; thus, the risk of loss caused by the employee's loss is borne by the employer. This, too, is a transfer of risk, but the transfer is involuntary. The employer, who now bears the risk, may choose to transfer this risk to an insurer by taking out a policy of workers' compensation insurance.

A 's duty to purchase the house upon the availability of suitable financing transfers risk from *A* to *B,* this does not mean that the contract between *A* and *B* is a contract of insurance. Insurance contracts have additional characteristics.

In the illustration in the previous subsection concerning the contract between *X* and *Y,* the contract not only *transferred* but also *distributed* risk. When *Y* assumed *X* 's risk of loss as well as the risk of 99 other persons, *Y* was able to distribute the risk across a large group of persons possessing similar risks. The characteristic of risk distribution sets insurance contracts apart from other kinds of contracts. It can be said, then, that *a contract of insurance is an agreement in which one party (the insurer), in exchange for a consideration provided by the other party (the insured), assumes the other party's risk and distributes it across a group of similarly situated persons, each of whose risk has been assumed in a similar transaction.*

Like any attempted definition of insurance, the foregoing definition does not always yield a clear answer to the question of whether a particular contract is a contract of insurance. However, the definition does identify the factors most important for distinguishing insurance contracts from contracts that transfer risk but do not constitute insurance.

§ 11 A Brief Historical Overview

In his influential article on insurance law published over three decades ago, Professor Spencer Kimball observed that "[i]nsurance is a small world that reflects the purposes of the larger world outside it."[1] To extend upon his observation, the insurance business and principles of insurance law have evolved symbiotically with changing economic conditions. Thus, one's understanding of a substantial portion of modern insurance law principles can be aided by exploring their historical roots.[2]

A number of ancient societies, including those of the Egyptians, Chinese, Greeks, Romans, Hindus, Hebrews, and Christians, had primitive insurance arrangements. Within these societies were religious or social groups whose secondary purposes included giving assistance from a common fund to the group's injured, impaired, or otherwise disadvantaged members. Traces of commercial insurance have been identified in the Code of Hammurabi, the Hindu Laws of Manu, and in the laws of the ancient Greeks.

---

[1] Spencer Kimball, *The Purpose of Insurance Regulation: A Preliminary Inquiry in the Theory of Insurance Law,* 45 Minn. L. Rev. 471, 524 (1961).

[2] The discussion in this section draws heavily upon several sources: William R. Vance, *Handbook on the Law of Insurance* § 2, at 9–27 (3d ed., B. Anderson, 1951); W. Winter, *Marine Insurance: Its Principles and Practice* 11–22 (1929); Edwin W. Patterson, *The Insurance Commissioner in the United States* 513–37 (1927); George Clayton, *British Insurance* (1971); John G. Day, *Economic Regulation of Insurance in the United States* 3–49 (1970); Prudential Insurance Company of America, *The Documentary History of Insurance: 1000 B.C.–1875 A.D.* (1915); Irving Pfeffer, *The Early History of Insurance,* Annals (Summer, 1966), *reprinted in* Kailin Tuan, ed., 1 *Modern Insurance: Theory and Education* 3–16 (1972); F. Oviatt, *Historical Study of Fire Insurance in the United States,* Annals (1905), *reprinted in* Tuan, *supra,* at 40–60.

One of the more important ancient practices was devised by the Babylonians, whose civilization thrived some three thousand years before the common era. The Babylonians developed what would later to known as the contract of "bottomry": money or goods would be loaned, either for interest or for interest plus a share of to-be-earned profits, to a borrower, on the understanding that the borrower's obligation to pay the interest (or interest and profits) would be eliminated if certain accidents occurred that prevented the earning of profits, such as if the vessel carrying the goods sank. The "contract of bottomry" was adopted by the Phoenicians, the Greeks, and later the Romans, and it has been argued that the Romans deserve credit for modifying bottomry into the insurance contract as it is commonly understood today.[3]

A significant commercial practice of insurance did not emerge, however, until the Middle Ages. Trade among the more prosperous medieval states was conducted primarily by sea; shippers and merchants were quick to appreciate the beneficial aspects of insurance in dispersing the risk of marine travel. At the beginning of the twelfth century, a small, but vigorous insurance business existed in the maritime states of Italy. Insurance was introduced to England in the mid-thirteenth century by merchants from northern Italy known as the "Lombards." The Lombards founded trading houses in London; in fact, London's "Lombard Street" today marks the place where these houses were located. During the fourteenth and fifteenth centuries, a period of flourishing commerce, the practice of insuring maritime risks spread throughout Europe and England. By 1677, Lombard Street had become established as the center for insurance transactions.[4]

Although the insurance trade grew during the sixteenth and seventeenth centuries, the English lacked a customary, uniform, or organized way of conducting the insurance business. Insuring was accomplished privately by individuals, many of whom were merchants themselves; a considerable part of this business was conducted at an inn on Tower Street in London known as "Lloyd's Coffee House." Interestingly, the simple fact that Lloyd's was a popular resort for merchants and shippers engaged in international trade had much to do with the emergence of a systematic way of conducting the insurance business. By 1688, it was customary for a person interested in obtaining insurance on a particular vessel or cargo to go to Lloyd's and circulate among those present a slip of paper upon which was written a description of a vessel or cargo, the identity or nature of the captain and crew, the voyage contemplated, and the amount of insurance desired. Anyone interested in insuring the vessel or cargo would write beneath the description their name or initials, followed by the amount for which that person was willing to be held liable in the event of a loss. The term "underwriter" evolved from this practice. In 1692, Lloyd's moved to Lombard Street.

The system of individual, private underwriting brought considerable wealth to many, but even at this early time the benefits of using a corporation combining the

---

[3] See G. Clayton, *supra,* at 14-19.

[4] The discussion which follows necessarily greatly compresses much history. For a detailed discussion of the development of insurance in England, see G. Clayton, *supra* note 2, at 34-142.

assets of many individuals to underwrite claims were widely appreciated. In 1720, those who favored the corporate method of underwriting persuaded Parliament, over the objection of the private underwriters at Lloyd's, to charter two corporations for the writing of insurance, the London Assurance Corporation and the Royal Exchange Assurance Corporation, and to grant these companies a monopoly on corporate underwriting. As it turned out, however, the business of the two corporations grew slowly, and the stifling of other corporate efforts due to Parliament's grant of a monopoly allowed the business of the private underwriters at Lloyd's to flourish. In 1769 the underwriters at Lloyd's formed an organized society with rules and regulations governing the business of underwriting. These underwriters moved to premises in the Royal Exchange; in 1779 the "Lloyd's Policy" form was adopted by the society as the standard form for marine insurance. Parliament in 1795 made this form the standard for England, and this form, with minor changes, still remains the standard one.

As the foregoing discussion indicates, the first significant commerce was maritime, and early insurance developed largely in this setting. Other lines of the insurance business were slower to develop. About fifteen years after the London fire of 1666, an informal organization for the purpose of insuring against loss by fire opened in the rear of the Royal Exchange, and in 1710 the first and oldest of all fire insurance companies, the Sun Fire Office, was founded. However, the institution of fire insurance was not greeted as favorably as marine insurance, for even at this early time the link between arson and insurance concerned the public. Nevertheless, by the last half of the nineteenth century, the benefits of fire insurance were widely accepted, and the fire insurance industry grew rapidly.

Other lines of insurance were also slow to develop. It was not until 1706 that an enduring effort to market life insurance occurred, and the first organization formed for insuring against loss of life, the Equitable Assurance Society of London, was not founded until 1762. Accident insurance did not appear until 1849, when the Railway Passengers' Assurance Company was established in London to insure against loss caused by railway accidents. Seven years later, the company broadened its scope to cover accidents of all kinds.

In many respects, the development of insurance in the United States paralleled developments in England. In the early years of the colonies, insurance on American risks was normally placed with English underwriters, but a few efforts were made to organize the American market. During the final years of the colonial period, insurance offices were opened in Philadelphia, New York, and other port cities. The first fire insurance company, a mutual company called the "Philadelphia Contributionship for Insuring Houses from Loss by Fire," was established in Philadelphia in 1752; Benjamin Franklin was one of its first directors. The first American insurance corporation was chartered in 1792 in Philadelphia, and this company does business today as the Insurance Company of North America. Seventeen more companies received charters by 1803.

Accident insurance was marketed shortly after 1860 to cover risks associated with travel by railroad. Although a mutually owned life insurance plan was created in 1759 for Presbyterian ministers in Pennsylvania, it was not until after the Civil War that life insurance was sold in the United States on a widespread basis. Health and disability insurance did not appear until the turn of the twentieth century.

Except for a few notable periods, the twentieth century has predominantly been a period of growing commerce and heightened prosperity. The insurance industry has prospered along with the economic growth of this period. At the end of 1992, the insurance industry had assets exceeding $2.4 trillion. As of 1994, there were more than 6,000 insurance companies operating in the United States. Premiums in the United States for all kinds of insurance totaled nearly $700 billion in 1992, almost $3000 for every person in the country.[5] By any measure, the insurance industry is today one of the most important in this country and, indeed, the world.[6]

§ 12   The "Business of Insurance"

A dispute over what constitutes insurance is most likely to occur when state regulatory authorities attempt to exercise jurisdiction over an enterprise on the ground that the activities constitute the "business of insurance" and therefore are subject to state regulation.

[a]   State Statutory Definitions

To determine the reach of state regulation, legislatures have sometimes enacted statutory definitions of insurance. For example, section 22 of the California Insurance Code defines insurance as a "contract whereby one undertakes to indemnify another against loss, damage, or liability arising from a contingent or unknown event."[1] If applied literally, such definitions would cause numerous relationships not normally characterized as insurance transactions to be subjected to state regulation.

---

[5] Insurance Information Institute, *The Fact Book 1994: Property/Casualty Insurance Facts* 5 (1994). Premium receipts in 1992 were $227.5 billion for the property/casualty industry, and $216.5 billion for the life insurance and annuity area. Health insurance premiums, including premiums charged by commercial insurers, Blue Cross and Blue Shield plans, self-insureds, and HMOs, were $255.5 billion in 1991. *Id.* at 5. If only health insurance written by commercial insurers is included, total U.S. premiums would equal $486.8 billion. *Id.* at 18.

[6] Total premiums in the world for life, non-life, and commercial health insurance totaled $1.414 trillion in 1991. The United States accounted for 34.4% of the total world premiums, and the United States and Japan together accounted for 54.2% of the total world premium. *Id.* at 18-19.

[1] Cal. Ins. Code § 22. The West Virginia statute is also broad: "Insurance is a contract whereby one undertakes to indemnify another or to pay a specified amount upon determinable contingencies." W. Va. Code § 33-1-1. The Kentucky statute is narrower by virtue of its use of the term "risks," a business term of art, but it is broad in reaching every surety relationship: " 'Insurance' is a contract whereby one undertakes to pay or indemnify another as to loss from certain specified contingencies or perils called 'risks,' or to pay or grant a specified amount of determinable benefit or annuity in connection with ascertainable risk contingencies, or to act as surety." Ky. Rev. Stat. § 304.1-030. The California statute was analyzed in detail in Title Ins. Co. of Minn. v. State Board of Equalization, 842 P.2d 121 (Cal. 1992) (en banc).

As a result, in situations where the issue is whether an insurance contract is involved, courts have interpreted the statutes to make clear that the existence of indemnification in the relationship, without more, does not establish conclusively that insurance is involved.

One of the leading cases is *Jordan v. Group Health Association,*[2] a 1939 District of Columbia Circuit Court of Appeals decision. The issue in *Jordan* was whether state insurance statutes applied to group health plans, where medical services are provided as needed in exchange for the payment of a monthly fee. In holding that the association was *not* engaged in the business of insurance, the court stated:

> That an incidental element of risk distribution or assumption may be present should not outweigh all other factors. If attention is focused only on that feature, the line between insurance or indemnity and other types of legal arrangement and economic function becomes faint, if not extinct. This is especially true when the contract is for the sale of goods or services on contingency. But obviously it was not the purpose of the insurance statutes to regulate all arrangements for assumption or distribution of risk. That view would cause them to engulf practically all contracts, particularly conditional sales and contingent service agreements. The fallacy is in looking only at the risk element, to the exclusion of all others present or their subordination to it. The question turns, not on whether risk is involved or assumed, but on whether that or something else to which it is related in the particular plan is its principal object and purpose.[3]

Jordan gave birth to what is now called the "principal object and purpose" test. As applied, this test requires courts to inquire into the nature of the contractual relationship. Not surprisingly, results in the cases are diverse. In *California Physician's Service v. Garrison,*[4] the California Supreme Court considered whether a group health plan constitutes insurance. Following the logic of *Jordan,* the court stated in holding that the doctors' group was not subject to state laws regulating insurance:

> Absence or presence of assumption of risk or peril is not the sole test to be applied in determining [the plan's] status. The question more broadly, is whether looking at the plan of operation as a whole, "service" rather than "indemnity" is its principal object and purpose. . . . Certainly the objects and purposes of the corporation organized and maintained by the California physicians have a wide scope in the field of social service. Probably there is no more impelling need than that of adequate medical care on a voluntary, low-cost basis for persons of small income. The medical profession unitedly is endeavoring to meet that need. Unquestionably this is "service" of a high order and not "indemnity."[5]

---

[2] 107 F.2d 239 (D.C.Cir. 1939).

[3] 107 F.2d at 247–48.

[4] 172 P.2d 4 (Cal. 1946).

[5] 172 P.2d at 16. Courts, perhaps sensitive to society's need to promote alternative methods of distributing health care, have usually been supportive of medical groups' arguments that they are not engaged in the business of insurance when the question is whether the group

In *Transportation Guaranty Co. v. Jellins,* a 1946 California decision, the court considered whether truck maintenance contracts under which the contractor agreed to garage the trucks, service them, procure insurance for them, and make necessary mechanical repairs constituted insurance. The court held that service predominated in these contracts and that the arrangement was not insurance. In a recent Ohio case,[6] the court held that a vehicle protection plan which extended the sellers' and manufacturers' warranties and covered repairs necessitated by mechanical breakdowns of defective parts did not constitute insurance, and the court explicitly declared irrelevant the fact that the coverage was offered by an entity that neither manufactured nor sold the vehicle.[7] Similar results have been reached in other cases.[8]

In some situations, the insurance elements of the contract have been found to predominate. In another Ohio case, the court held that an automobile maintenance contract, where the contractor promised to make all necessary repairs and

---

is subject to state regulation. See, e.g., New Mexico Life Ins. Guar. Ass'n v. Moore, 596 P.2d 260, (N.M. 1979); Huff v. St. Joseph's Mercy Hospital of Dubuque Corp., 261 N.W.2d 695 (Iowa 1978). This same logic may explain the result in Poznik v. Massachusetts Medical Professional Ins. Ass'n, 628 N.E.2d 1 (Mass. 1994), where the court held that legislatively-created non-profit joint underwriting association created to make medical malpractice insurance more accessible was not engaged in the "business of insurance," even though it issued policies, underwrote insurance, collected premiums, adjusted claims, and paid losses, because it was not in the business of making a profit and assumed no risk of loss in light of the fact that losses in excess of premiums collected would be distributed among participating physicians and hospitals. Different results from the foregoing are possible when the question shifts to whether federal antitrust law applies to the group. See Anglin v. Blue Shield of Va., 693 F.2d 315 (4th Cir. 1982) (operators of prepaid health care plans could be considered insurers for some purposes, and therefore entitled to immunity from federal antitrust law under the McCarran-Ferguson Act).

[6] Griffin Systems, Inc. v. Ohio Dep't of Ins., 575 N.E.2d 803 (Ohio 1991).

[7] 575 N.E.2d at 808.

[8] See, e.g., GAF Corp. v. County Sch. Bd. of Washington Cty., Va., 629 F.2d 981 (4th Cir. 1980) (roofing supplier's guarantee to repair leaks caused by defects in product and faulty workmanship did not constitute a contract of insurance); Boyle v. Orkin Exterminating Co., 578 So. 2d 786 (Fla. Dist. Ct. App. 1991) (lifetime termite damage guarantee is not contract of insurance); Truta v. Avis Rent A Car System, Inc., 238 Cal. Rptr. 806 (Cal. Ct. App. 1987) (collision damage waiver does not constitute insurance); Rayos v. Chrysler Credit Corp., 683 S.W.2d 546, (Tex. Ct. App. 1985) (five-year/50,000-mile warranty is not a contract of insurance); Cole Bros. & Hart v. Haven, 7 N.W. 383 (Iowa 1880) (promise of seller of lightning rods to pay all damages caused by lightning to building upon which rods were erected is not insurance); Evans & Tate v. Premier Refining Co., 120 S.E. 553 (Ga. Ct. App. 1923) (seller of automobile lubricant who promises to replace broken gears of users of the lubricant is not in business of insurance). The Supreme Court of Ohio has made fine distinctions on this issue. Compare State ex rel. Herbert v. Standard Oil Co., 35 N.E.2d 437 (Ohio 1941) (warranty on new tires promising to repair or to substitute new tires at a reduced price if damaged by reason of faulty construction or materials, but excluding damage from other causes is not insurance) with State ex rel. Duffy v. Western Auto Supply Co., 16 N.E.2d 256 (Ohio 1938) (guarantee which purported to indemnify owner of tires against all road hazards that may make tires unfit for service constituted insurance).

replacements for a period of one year, constituted insurance.[9] In an Arizona case, the court held that a contract to replace television picture tubes, which failed as a result of manufacturing defects after the manufacturer's warranty had expired, constituted insurance. The fact that the contractor was neither the seller nor the manufacturer was important to the decision.[10] In an Arkansas case, a used car dealer's "debt-cancellation contracts," which could be purchased for a weekly or monthly fee and which provided that the dealership would discharge the car buyer's outstanding debt on a vehicle purchased and financed through the dealer in the event the vehicle were wrecked, totaled, or stolen without the buyer's fault, constituted insurance.[11] Again, other cases are in accord with these decisions.[12]

Many of these cases are extremely difficult to reconcile. Each of the contracts involved a transfer and distribution of risk. Literally applying a statutory definition in such cases points toward holding the contracts to be within the field of permissible state regulation. Few people, however, would contend that all warranties, for example, should be swept within the ambit of insurance regulation. Moreover, most people would recognize that the contemporary marketing practices for many products involve the offer at the point of sale of "extended" protection by some separate entity against failure of the product, and it makes little sense to deter such warranty arrangements under the reasoning that such contracts resemble insurance and must be regulated as such. Extended warranty arrangements can, of course, lead to consumer abuse, and the problems of the insolvent, nowhere-to-be-found warrantor are ever-present. If one concludes that governmental regulation of these practices is needed, the opposing view might urge that the state insurance department is the most appropriate agency to undertake it.

Unfortunately, no test that has been articulated thus far provides easy answers in all cases. The "principal object and purpose" test simply provides a starting place for probing whether indemnity or service predominates in a particular transaction. Asking whether the business practice at issue involves "one or more of the evils"

---

[9] Mein v. U.S. Car Testing Co., 184 N.E.2d 489 (Ohio Ct.App. 1964). See also People v. American Motor Club, Inc., 520 N.Y.S.2d 383 (N.Y. Sup. Ct. 1987) (prepaid collision contract that obligated seller to repair damaged vehicle regardless of cost and for which buyer paid annual fee plus service charge constituted contract of insurance); Griffin Systems, Inc. v. Washburn, 505 N.E.2d 1121 (Ill. App. Ct. 1987) (automobile parts replacement plan constituted insurance, and not service or warranty).

[10] Guaranteed Warranty Corp. v. State ex rel. Humphrey, 533 P.2d 87 (Ariz. Ct. App. 1975).

[11] Douglass v. Dynamic Enterprises, 869 S.W.2d 14 (Ark. 1994).

[12] See, e.g., Schoepflin v. Tender Loving Care Corp., 631 So. 2d 909 (Ala. 1993)(new car mechanical failure service contract constituted "insurance" and breach of contract could serve as basis for bad faith tort claim); Ollendorff Watch Co. v. Pink, 17 N.E.2d 676 (N.Y. 1938) (watch company that promised to replace customer's watches lost through burglary or robbery within one year of purchase was engaged in insurance business); Continental Auto Club, Inc. v. Navarre, 60 N.W.2d 180 (Mich. 1953) (automobile club providing various services, such as towing, bail bond, etc., constitutes business of insurance); Ware v. Heath, 237 S.W.2d 362 (Tex. Ct. App. 1951) (building and loan association providing for release of debt in event of death of debtor is engaged in insurance business).

that state insurance statutes were designed to regulate is problematic when an old regulatory regimen is compared against a novel, innovative business arrangement. Asking whether risk transference and distribution are "central and relatively important" instead of being "merely incidental" may sweep too broadly when applied to third-party extended warranty arrangements.[13]

In the final analysis, many analysts will return to the *Jordan* test and ask a simple question: What is the principal object of the contract? Is it indemnity, or is it something else, such as service? If the principal object of the contract is indemnity, the contract constitutes "insurance" and is therefore within the scope of state regulation.

[b]   The McCarran-Ferguson Act Definition

The term "business of insurance" is the guidepost to demarcating federal and state control of the insurance industry. Section 2(a) of the McCarran-Ferguson Act, 15 U.S.C. § 1012, provides: "The business of insurance, and every person engaged therein, shall be subject to the laws of the several States which relate to the regulation or taxation of such business." According to section 2(b) of the Act, "No Act of Congress shall be construed to invalidate, impair, or supersede any law enacted by any State for the purpose of regulating the business of insurance, or which imposes a fee or tax upon such business, unless such Act specifically relates to the business of insurance. . . ." Thus, the term "business of insurance" separates the field of state regulation from the zone of federal regulation: to the extent the states regulate the business of insurance, the federal government is preempted from instituting its own scheme of regulation — unless Congress chooses to reenter the field by enacting a statute "specifically relating" to the business of insurance.

The federal-state allocation of the power to regulate the insurance industry is discussed in a later section.[14]

[c]   Self-Insurance as the "Business of Insurance"

Is self-insurance the "business of insurance"? At first glance, the answer would seem to be no; deciding to retain risk and not transfer it to a third party should not transform the party deciding to retain risk into an insurer. An essential aspect of an insurance contract is the transfer of risk, and this does not occur when a party self-insures. This answer is consistent with the holdings of most courts that have considered the question.[15] It follows from this answer that a risk-retention program should not constitute "other insurance" for the purpose of an insurance policy that requires the exhaustion of "other insurance" before the coverage of the policy is applicable.[16] Similarly, a self-insured lessor who undertakes to defend both lessee

---

[13] These tests were suggested by then-Professor and now-Judge Keeton twenty-five years ago. Robert E. Keeton, *Insurance Law* 552 (3d ed. 1971).

[14] See § 21, *infra*.

[15] See, e.g., State v. Continental Cas. Co., 879 P.2d 1111 (Idaho 1994); Budget Rent A Car Systems, Inc. v. Taylor, 626 So. 2d 976 (Fla. Dist. Ct. App. 1993).

[16] See State v. Continental Cas. Co., 879 P.2d 1111 (Idaho 1994); Annot., *Self-Insurance Against Liability As Other Insurance Within Meaning of Liability Insurance Policy*, 46 A.L.R.4th 707 (1986).

and lessor against a third-party's claim is not the lessee's insurer and owes no continuing duty to defend the lessee after lessor reaches a settlement with the third-party of the third-party's claim against the lessor.[17] A self-insured employer, in the absence of a private contract with its employee or a statutory duty, would have no obligation to defend the employee who allegedly injured a third party while operating its employer's vehicle within the scope of employment.[18]

For some purposes, however, the "first-glance" answer is problematic. The statutory framework for compensating victims of automobile accidents in most states contemplates that drivers and owners of motor vehicles will have certain minimum levels of financial resources that can be used to compensate victims of the negligent operation of motor vehicles. These statutes typically recognize that a person or corporation with sufficient wealth can opt out of any requirement to purchase liability insurance; in other words, self-insurance that meets certain standards can satisfy the obligation to get liability insurance. If one views the self-insurance as constituting the equivalent of the liability insurance that would otherwise have been obtained, it is a short step to holding that the self-insured has some obligations of a liability insurer, particularly when those obligations are necessary to further the purposes of the statutory framework for accident victim compensation.[19]

This last observation is illustrated by *Hillegass v. Landwehr*,[20] a 1993 Wisconsin case. Landwehr and Bain, an employee of Burlington Air Express, drove a company car on a personal trip. While Landwehr, who had his own liability insurance policy, was operating the vehicle, he was involved in a collision with another car that injured the plaintiff. Burlington was self-insured, and it argued that Landwehr's insurer, whose coverage purported to be excess over other valid and collectible insurance, provided the primary coverage. The court disagreed, concluding that Burlington could not escape both the expense of premium payments and the possibility of being held liable as a primary insurer simply by deciding to retain the risk. Thus, the court concluded that "other insurance" included both third-party contractual insurance and self-insurance.[21]

§ 13   Classification of Insurance

At first glance, insurance law appears to be a highly structured subject. Secondary materials often focus on discrete areas, and researchers using indexes to such materials must often look beyond the heading "insurance" to some subset of the subject, such as "casualty insurance," "liability insurance," or "property insurance." In large measure, this truncated structure is a byproduct of the manner in which the

---

[17] Budget Rent A Car Systems, Inc. v. Taylor, 626 So. 2d 976 (Fla. Dist. Ct. App. 1993).

[18] Overbaugh v. Strange, 867 P.2d 1016 (Kan. 1994).

[19] See generally Annot., *Applicability of Uninsured Motorist Statutes to Self-Insurers*, 27 A.L.R.4th 1266 (1983).

[20] 499 N.W.2d 652 (Wis. 1993).

[21] 499 N.W.2d at 655-56. In a footnote, the court summarized the split among jurisdictions that had considered this issue and reported that most of the dozen or so courts with authority on the issue had held that self-insurance did not constitute insurance.

(Matthew Bender & Co., Inc.)

insurance business evolved. Historically, the business of insurance developed along different *lines* that corresponded to various kinds of risks being covered. For example, the line of marine insurance developed and was relatively mature before other lines, such as life and health insurance, had even emerged. Insurance companies tended to specialize in one line; sometimes government regulation prevented them from writing in some other line. As a result, the business of insurance became compartmentalized according to the kind of risk insured. Simultaneously, principles of law evolved for each of these different lines, which institutionalized a number of demarcations that persist in the substantive law of insurance to this day. Understanding modern insurance law is considerably more difficult without some comprehension of the ways in which insurance is classified.

In addition to the traditional method of classifying insurance according to the kind of risk covered, insurance is sometimes classified according to other criteria, such as the nature of the insurer and the nature of the marketing process. These divisions have had less influence on the substantive content of insurance law, but understanding their nature is also helpful to one's understanding of the subject.

The following sections examine the various approaches to classifying insurance.

§ 13A Classification by Nature of the Risk

Historically, statutory regulation of the insurance business as well as insurer specialization in particular lines has resulted in three major categories of insurance: marine and inland marine, life, and fire and casualty.

[a] Marine and Inland Marine

Marine insurance descends directly from the underwriting that occurred in Lloyd's Coffee House three centuries ago. Marine insurance, as marketed today, is a form of "all-risk" insurance (meaning, the insurance covers all forms of loss not specifically excluded) that insures ships and their cargoes against "perils of the sea." Marine insurance is normally written on shipping in international waters.

Insurers of marine risks found it natural to extend their business to other areas of property insurance. In fact, the extension of marine insurance to inland risks was inevitable. Transporting a good from New York to London involves some nonmarine travel: the goods must move from a warehouse in New York to the ship and from the ship in London to a warehouse. These "over-land" risks were not covered by the traditional policy of marine insurance, and thus a new insurance product had to be devised: *inland marine insurance.* Initially, this line of insurance covered ships and cargoes in inland waterways, such as rivers, canals, and lakes; it is from this extension that the category took its name "inland marine." However, inland marine insurers later expanded their business to cover goods that were subjected to other kinds of transportation risks and ultimately to goods that were capable of being moved. With time, the term "marine" came be understood to apply both to marine and inland marine policies, and marine insurers also undertook to insure carriers for their liability to those whose goods they carried. Thus, modern marine insurance has several branches: transportation insurance for goods in transit; instrumentalities of transportation insurance (for bridges, tunnels, piers, etc.); insurance for the vessels on which persons or goods are transported; bailees' customers policies; personal and commercial floaters (for movable personal or business property); insurance for loss due to the unavailability of a particular vessel or conveyance; and insurance protecting a carrier against liability to those who ship their goods.[1]

[b] Life Insurance

The second major traditional category of insurance is *life insurance*. In essence, life insurance is a contract under which the insurer promises to pay proceeds upon the death of the person whose life is insured. Historically, however, the life insurance line has also included personal insurance of other varieties, such as health insurance and accident insurance. Sometimes annuities are categorized in this line.

[1] Term versus Whole-Life

Hundreds of different kinds of life insurance policies are marketed today, but basically all of these policies fall into one of two categories: *term* or *whole-life*.

Term insurance is essentially pure insurance. The insured purchases coverage for a specified duration and the designated beneficiary collects the proceeds only if the insured dies within the specified term. Some policies allow the insured to renew the policy at the end of the term, but a term policy with a renewal option is usually more expensive. Term insurance, unlike whole-life insurance, does not have a savings component that enables the insured to get some money back should the insured decide to "cash" the policy before death. With term insurance, as the insured ages, either the amount of the premium increases or the amount of coverage declines; this is because as a person ages, the risk of death increases.

Whole-life insurance (sometimes also called "ordinary life") is really two things in one: it is a policy of term insurance *and* a savings plan. Part of every premium covers the cost of the insurance, and the remainder goes into the savings component of the product. In the early years, very little of the premium goes into savings, but in later years a bigger proportion enters savings. The amount of the savings is called the policy's "cash value" or "surrender value." Anytime the insured desires (after an initial period of normally two or three years but before the insured's death), the insured can borrow against the cash value at a designated interest rate or cash the policy and receive the "surrender value." Should the insured die after withdrawing part of the cash value, that portion of the cash value withdrawn is not available to the insured's beneficiary in the form of proceeds.

Whole-life insurance is more expensive than term insurance because part of the premium goes into the savings component of the product. However, the premium does not increase over time (nor does the amount of proceeds payable at death decline), which is sometimes viewed as an advantage. Thus, whole-life insurance is sometimes described as insurance written for a fixed amount on a person's life for a fixed premium. In reality, however, the cost of the term insurance portion of

---

[1] See National Association of Insurance Commissioners, *Model Laws, Regulations and Guidelines,* at 690–1 (1984) ("Nationwide Inland Marine Definition"); Solomon S. Huebner, Kenneth Black, Jr., & Robert Cline, *Property and Liability Insurance* 152 (3d ed. 1982).

the whole-life product does increase with time: as the insured ages, the policy's cash value increases, meaning that the difference between the policy's face value (which is what the insurer will pay should the insured die while the policy is in force and before the cash value has been borrowed) and its cash value — which difference is actually the term insurance portion of the product — declines. Thus, as the insured ages, less term insurance is provided each year while the premium remains the same, which means the effective cost of the insurance component of the product increases.

Both term and whole-life insurance is marketed under a variety of names, and some products blend the two concepts into one policy. Yet all life insurance products can be described by reference to term or whole-life definitions. The variations on these two products usually involve how the insured pays for the coverage or how the benefits are calculated.

With respect to term life insurance, there are a couple of variations worth noting. "Credit insurance" is a form of coverage for debtors: if the insured debtor dies or becomes disabled before a debt (such as a loan to purchase a home secured by a mortgage) is discharged, the insurer discharges the debt or makes the periodic payments on the debt. Thus, the insurance is virtually the same as term life insurance with, perhaps, a disability endorsement: as the debt is paid down (and the insured simultaneously ages), the amount of coverage declines while the premium remains level. No cash values accumulate as the insurance remains in force. If the debt is paid early, most statutes require unearned premiums to be refunded to the debtor. If the insured dies while the amount of insurance in force exceeds the amount of the debt, the usual result is for the amount of proceeds exceeding the amount of the debt to be refunded to the insured's estate. Usually, the insurance is marketed on a group basis: for example, a lending institution (such as a bank) may have a master policy with an insurer, and the coverage is made available to the lender's debtors as a way to ensure that the debt is paid.[2]

Another variation of term life insurance is "deposit term insurance."[3] This kind of policy is essentially a blend of whole-life and term insurance. The coverage looks like renewable term coverage with a large first-year premium; the premium drops in the second year, and then slowly increases over time, all while the amount of coverage remains the same. Thus, the first premium includes a deposit that in essence sets up a small cash value. This deposit is forfeited if the policy is allowed to lapse before the term expires. If the policy is kept in force for the length of the term, the deposit plus interest is returned to the insured. If the insured dies before the end of the term, the face amount of the policy plus the deposit is paid to the beneficiary. Also, the policy has various conversion options at the end of each term.

Most whole-life products are very similar, with the main differences being in the ways premiums or benefits are calculated. In the archetype whole-life policy,

---

[2] The Uniform Consumer Credit Code ("UCCC") regulates to some extent the use of term insurance to secure debt; for example, the UCCC provides that the amount of credit life insurance sold cannot exceed the amount of the debt and requires certain disclosures to the insured.

[3] Uniform Consumer Credit Code (1974 Act) §§ 2.401, 3.201, 3.203 (at 7A U.L.A. 1 (1985)).

sometimes also called "straight life" or "ordinary life," the insured pays premiums for a lifetime or until the insured reaches a specific age, such as 65, or maybe even 100 (which for most people equates to paying premiums for a lifetime); if the insured lives to the designated age, the cash value finally equals the face value, the policy is terminated, and the insured receives the accumulated cash value in a lump sum.

If the insured desires to pay for the policy on an accelerated basis, the insured might purchase a "limited-payment life" policy. Under the limited-payment life arrangement, the insured pays premiums for a set number of years in the foreseeable future or until some pre-planned event (such as retirement). The extreme version of limited-payment life is "single premium life," where the entire cost of the policy is paid in one lump sum. The supposed advantage of limited payment life is that the premium payments are ordinarily completed prior to retirement, but the premiums are considerably larger. A disadvantage is that if the insured dies while still paying premiums, the insured paid "too much" for the insurance protection, since equal coverage could have been purchased at a much lower price.

The Tax Reform Act of 1986 curtailed many tax advantages but left intact the special tax-deferred buildup of savings for life insurance.[4] This led to an increased number of investments in single-premium life insurance.[5] This did not escape Congress's attention, and changes in the Internal Revenue Code in 1988[6] began to close the door on the tax-avoidance features of this kind of policy. The IRS has issued an interim rule[7] which limits the tax-sheltering ability of the single-premium life insurance policy. It seems unlikely that these kinds of policies will retain their advantageous tax treatment.

Because whole life is more expensive than term, many young people are unable to afford whole life insurance immediately. To assist these buyers, some insurers offer variations on whole-life that reduce the size of the premium in the policy's early years. In a "graded premium" whole-life policy, the premium increases in the first five years, and remains level thereafter. This arrangement simply redistributes the premiums across the life of the policy; the level premium subsequent to year five will be slightly higher than whole-life policies without the graded premium feature. In some similar policies, the premiums are set at a lower, but flat level for the first three or five years of the policy, and then jump to a higher level where they remain for the life of the policy.

"Endowment life insurance" is essentially limited-payment life insurance. Under such a policy, the insured pays premiums until some specified age at which time

---

[4] Generally, the cash value of a whole-life policy is not taxable until the policy is surrendered. Also, the cash value can be borrowed at low interest without paying income taxes. Because the Tax Reform Act of 1986 cut back many tax shelters, single-premium life was vigorously marketed as a means to get tax-deferred earnings and tax-free access to earnings and principal.

[5] See generally Radie Bunn & Edward Graves, *Single Premium Life Insurance,* 16 Tax Management Compensation Planning Journal 205 (1988).

[6] IRC § 7702 was amended by the Technical & Miscellaneous Revenue Act of 1988, 102 Stat. 3342.

[7] Interim Rule 49,356, Standard Federal Tax Reporter (1995).

an "endowment" exists — the policy's cash value equals the face value. At maturity, the insured may have the option either to take the entire cash value in a lump sum or to have the cash value paid back in the form of an annuity. The emphasis in this product is on creating a fund that will support the insured during his or her retirement years. Functionally, this product is very similar to an annuity or retirement plan, except that some insurance greater than the cash value is provided in the early years of the policy.

There are other kinds of whole life policies, but each involves the same two elements: a combination of term insurance and a savings plan.[8]

For young people who are unable to afford whole-life insurance even when premiums are reduced in the policy's early years, some insurers offer "convertible term" insurance. In essence, convertible term insurance gives the insured the option at some designated time in the future to convert the policy to whole life by agreeing to pay thereafter the regular whole life premium charged individuals of the attained age.

An alternative approach to conversion is to allow the term policy to be turned into whole life if the insured pays the difference between what the premiums on the term insurance were and what premiums on a whole life policy would have cost, plus interest. Conversion is expensive, but what the insured obtains with convertible term is insurance against the risk that the insured might become uninsurable in the future and therefore be unable to acquire whole life insurance.

During the last decade, insurers, in order to become more competitive with other financial institutions, began marketing a variant of whole-life insurance called "universal life." Many kinds of universal life insurance policies exist, but the typical contract operates as follows. The insurer credits the insured's premium to a "cash-value account." Each month, the insurer deducts from this account the cost of the insurance protection, which (as with other kinds of insurance) increases as the insured ages. The remainder of the account accumulates with interest. A minimum interest rate is guaranteed by the insurer, but typically the insurer pays a rate competitive with other financial instruments (such as United States Treasury bills). Normally the insured can modify the amount of the death benefit and change the timing of premium payments to respond to changing economic conditions.

In actuality, universal life is a more sophisticated and in some respects improved whole life policy. As with whole life, the insured can withdraw the cash value entirely (upon surrender of the insurance coverage); unlike whole life, the insured can withdraw portions of the account, which is a major advantage of universal life, as well as alter the premium levels from time to time and the timing of payments. Some universal life policies operate like whole life in the following sense: when the insured dies, the beneficiaries receive only the policy's face amount. The other kind of universal life policy, which is more expensive, pays the beneficiaries both

---

[8] For a more complete discussion on the various kinds of life insurance plans available, see Editors of Consumers Reports, *The Consumers Union Report on Life Insurance* (1977). Also, some financial guides contain good, short summaries of the kinds of insurance products available. E.g., Jane Bryant Quinn, *Everyone's Money Book* 366–466 (1979).

the face amount of the policy and the accumulated cash value upon the insured's death. Although universal life is an intensively marketed alternative to whole life insurance, it does not vary the whole life policy's basic formula: part of the premium pays for a policy of term insurance, and the remainder is deposited in some sort of savings account, from which the insured can make withdrawals prior to his or her death. However, with universal life, it is better to think of the savings account as an investment in the insurance company.

"Variable life" is a more recent evolution of the universal life policy, and is essentially identical to universal life insurance except in one respect. The cash value account, unlike universal life where the insurer pays a stated rate of interest on the cash value, is invested in instruments of the insured's choice, such as stocks, bonds, money market funds, or a combination of such instruments. This allows the insured to increase the level of investment risk, thereby (hopefully) increasing the return. If the investments do poorly and the cash value declines below the amount needed to pay the insurance premium, the insured is required to contribute additional sums to the account in order to maintain the insurance protection.[9] The basic assumption underlying variable life policies is that over the long term alternative investments, like the stock market, will consistently outperform other kinds of investments without undue risk. There are still further variations on the universal-variable theme; some insurers market "flexible premium variable" or "variable-universal life" insurance, which typically denotes a policy that combines most of the features of universal and variable life.

As of 1993, universal or variable insurance products constituted about 16.7 percent of all life insurance in force, but this figure is destined to increase. Of all new policies purchased in 1993, 20 percent were universal or variable products, and these accounted for 27 percent of the face value of all policies sold during the year. Whole-life (including the variable and universal policies) insurance constitutes about 62 percent of all non-group, non-industrial life insurance in force, but when group insurance (about 90 percent of which is term) and credit life is added to the mix, term insurance constitutes about 63 percent of all life insurance in force in the United States.[10]

[2] Other Categories of Life Insurance

A few other types of life insurance merit brief mention. *Industrial life insurance* refers to a kind of life insurance that is written in small amounts and for which the insured pays small, frequently assessed (often weekly) sums. Often the ostensible purpose of the policy is to pay for burial expenses in the event of the insured's death. The policy is typically marketed through the agent's direct solicitation, and the agent often collects the premiums in a personal visit. The insurance normally has a distinctive pattern of clauses, such as a "facility of payment" clause that allows the insurer to pay the proceeds upon death of the insured to anyone who appears to be

---

[9] For concise explanations of universal life insurance, see Randall L. Shaw, *Universal Life Insurance: How It Works,* 71 A.B.A. J. 68 (Feb. 1985); Alan Lazarescu & Harold Leff, *Universal Life Insurance: Legal, Regulatory and Actuarial Aspects,* 17 Forum 1000 (1982).

[10] The 1993 data comes from American Council of Life Insurance, *1994 Life Insurance Fact Book* 12, 16, 20, 27 (1994).

(Matthew Bender & Co., Inc.)

entitled to the proceeds, prohibitions on assignments, an absence of loan provisions and settlement options, and the absence of a suicide limitation. Physical examinations usually are not required, but misrepresentations about the applicant's health are fully contestable. Although the policies are designed to be easy to administer, the high costs of marketing the policies and collecting premiums make the price of industrial life insurance much higher than other available kinds of insurance. Ironically, purchasers of industrial life are predominantly low-income individuals. Parents are sometimes encouraged to purchase such policies on the lives of their children, even though the chance of a child's death is highly remote and the children's long-run welfare probably would be enhanced if the parents insured their own lives, naming the children as beneficiaries. Because industrial life insurance is expensive to market and a relatively poor value, it is slowly disappearing from the marketplace.[11]

Sometimes a distinction is drawn between *participating* and *nonparticipating* life insurance. A participating policy is one in which dividends based upon company earnings are paid by the company to the policyholder. The dividends usually are held in a fund for the insurer or are used to pay part of the premium. A nonparticipating policy is one on which no dividends are paid. A more ancient kind of participatory policy is the *tontine* policy. A tontine insurance policy differs from a traditional dividend-earning whole life policy in that the dividends are put in a large fund that is payable, upon the expiration of a designated period, to the surviving policyholders. Due to their highly speculative nature, tontine policies are seldom written today.

When the phrase "mutual life insurance" is used, the reference is to a participating policy sold by a mutual insurance company. Basically, the insured under a mutual life insurance policy pays a premium slightly larger than the expected loss plus administrative expenses. If the company's loss experience is lower than expected, the excess of the insureds' premiums over that which is necessary to pay claims and administrative expenses is returned to the insured in the form of a dividend. Thus, the holder of a mutual life insurance policy "participates" in the carrying of the risk. If the company's loss is lower than expected, the insured conceivably could pay less for the insurance than would the holder of a "non-participating" policy, a distinction discussed above. As one would expect, most participating policies are written by mutual companies and most non-participating policies are written by stock companies. The distinction between stock and mutual companies is discussed in more detail in a subsequent section.[12]

References to *burial insurance* appear from time to time in materials about insurance. Sometimes life, health, accident, disability, or other kinds of insurance policies will provide for the payment of funeral expenses in the event of the insured's death. The term burial insurance when used to refer to these kinds of coverages has no special significance. However, sometimes people have formed an association under

---

[11] In 1993, industrial life insurance accounted for less than 0.2 percent ($2.2 billion) of all life insurance in force in the United States, which reflects a significant decline from 2.3% in 1973. American Council of Life Insurance *1994 Life Insurance Factbook* 20, 32 (1994).

[12] See § 13B[a], *infra*.

which each member contributes a small sum on a periodic basis to pay the burial expenses of anyone in the association who dies. In fact, among the earliest examples of insurance failures are burial societies that assessed their members on a pro rata basis for the expenses of burying a deceased member: as the young members realized they were bearing a disproportionate share of the losses, they would gradually drop out of the association, leaving only higher risk, older members in the group. This phenomenon, now described as the principle of adverse selection,[13] ultimately led to the disintegration of many early societies.[14] Where burial societies comply with state statutes regulating the business of insurance, their contracts are valid.[15] However, many such groups organize without making any effort to obtain a license or otherwise comply with state laws. In these situations, where courts have had occasion to consider the validity of the contracts issued by the societies, courts have uniformly held the schemes unlawful and the individual contracts void.[16]

[3] Annuities

An annuity is a contract between a financial institution (such as an insurer) and an individual under which the institution, in exchange for the individual's prior payment, promises to make periodic payments to the individual for a stated period of time. Pensions, for example, are essentially annuity contracts: the employee (or the employer on the employee's behalf) makes contributions to a fund, and upon the employee's retirement (or other designated time) the fund makes monthly payments to the employee until some time in the future (such as, for example, the end of a term of years or the date of the employee's death).

Although annuities are sometimes categorized within the broad category "life insurance," an annuity serves a distinctly different purpose than a life insurance policy. People normally purchase contracts of life insurance to provide security against the risk of a premature death. Frequently there are others who depend upon the insured for support; sometimes there is a long-term debt (such as a bank's loan to purchase a house which is secured by a mortgage on the house) upon which the insured's estate would default in the absence of life insurance. Should the insured die prematurely, those who depend on the insured would be disadvantaged, or the creditor might foreclose on the security for the loan. To eliminate the risk of these events occurring due to premature death, an individual purchases life insurance. In many respects, an annuity is the opposite of a life insurance policy: an annuity is insurance against the risk of a long life. Should an individual live a long time past his or her working years, this person might run short of resources and might become a burden on others. To avoid the risks attendant upon living an unexpectedly long life, an individual purchases an annuity.

---

[13] See § 10[c], *supra*.

[14] The demise of the actuarially unsound burial societies was an influential factor in the development of industrial life insurance. See Malvin E. Davis, *Industrial Life Insurance in the United States* 3-5 (1944).

[15] E.g., Peterson v. Smith, 196 So. 505 (Miss. 1940); Mississippi Benefit Ass'n v. Majure, 29 So. 2d 110 (Miss. 1947); State ex rel. Kuble v. Capitol Benefit Ass'n, 21 N.W.2d 890 (Iowa 1946).

[16] E.g., State v. Willett, 86 N.E. 68 (Ind. 1908); State ex rel. Landis v. DeWitt C. Jones Co., 147 So. 230 (Fla. 1933).

The role that annuities play in protecting against the risk of a long life is starkly illustrated by the use of annuities in settling tort suits where large amounts of damages have been awarded or are likely to be awarded. Suppose it is forecasted that the sum of money needed to compensate a victim of a tort for loss of income over a lifetime, future medical and rehabilitation expenses, and other long term costs is five million dollars. To settle a dispute, the parties may agree that the defendant, instead of paying five million dollars presently, will purchase an annuity that promises to pay the victim a sum of money each month, adequate to compensate for expenses, for a lifetime. The price of such an annuity would be considerably less than five million dollars, yet the plaintiff would be fully compensated.[17]

The fact that an annuity is virtually the opposite of a life insurance policy has resulted in most courts characterizing an annuity as an "investment" instead of as "insurance."[18]

Life insurance at least has the characteristic that upon the payment of the first premium the insurer becomes obligated to pay a large sum to the insured's beneficiaries should the insured die. In this respect, life insurance has a characteristic akin to "indemnity": the insurer will reimburse the insured's beneficiaries for the loss caused by the insured's death. With an annuity, the underwriter assumes no obligation to reimburse a large sum upon some contingency. Instead, if the insured dies before reaching a given age, the annuity holder may forfeit contributions or the

---

[17] This is simply an application of the principle of valuing money over time. The insurer receives a lump sum upon the purchase of the annuity, but most of this sum is invested and earns interest. The insurer can afford to pay proceeds exceeding the lump sum because the total proceeds are less than the lump sum plus earned interest. This operates in liability and property insurance as well; a portion of insurers' total income is interest earned on premiums.

That insurers value money relative to time is illustrated nicely by a unique retroactive policy a consortium of insurers sold MGM Grand Hotels, Inc. in 1981. The policy, sold for $39 million, purported to provide $170 million in coverage for claims arising from the deaths of 85 people and injuries to about 1,000 others from a 1980 hotel fire in Las Vegas. The insurers reasoned that they could invest the $39 million during the lengthy litigation process and ultimately earn a profit. See *MGM Grand to Cover Hotel Fire Claims With $170 Million Retroactive Insurance*, Wall St. J., Feb. 11, 1981, at 4., col. 1. The presumed advantage to MGM was the "differential tax treatment of the insurance premium—deducted early by MGM, but taken into income later by the insurers." Mark J. Roe, *Bankruptcy and Mass Tort*, 84 Colum. L. Rev. 846, 922 n. 110 (1984). Whether either the insured or the insurers gained the benefits they sought is questionable. The parties were soon embroiled in litigation over the insurers' obligations; the insurers countered that MGM was settling victims' claims for excessive amounts. The litigation was eventually settled. See David Lauter, *MGM Cases Still Smoldering; Settlement Fund Reaches $140M; Hotel Battles Insurers*, Nat'l L.J., May 23, 1983, p. 7; Rich Arthurs, *MGM Settlement Uncorks the Champagne*, Legal Times, Apr. 8, 1985, p. 4.

[18] E.g., NationsBank v. Variable Annuity Life Ins. Co., 115 S.Ct. 810 (1995) (fixed annuities); Securities & Exchange Comm'n v. Variable Annuity Life Ins. Co. of America, 359 U.S. 65 (1959) (variable annuities); Mercy v. Olsen, 672 S.W.2d 196 (Tenn. 1984); In re Rhodes' Estate, 94 N.Y.S.2d 406 (N.Y. 1950). For an thought-provoking critique of this line of authority, see Spencer L. Kimball, *Reflections on the Meaning of" 'Insurance,"* 2 Int'l J. of Ins. Law 226 (1995).

annuity holder's designated beneficiary may receive a sum equal to the deceased's contributions (perhaps with interest). In these respects, an annuity has no "indemnity" characteristic, and the arrangement appears more like an investment which may or may not prove profitable.[19] Certainly, annuities have purposes distinct from those of life insurance contracts, and they raise different regulatory problems. Yet the underlying objective of an annuity contract is no different from that of any other kind of insurance: an individual confronts a risk (in this case, the risk of a long life), and the individual is willing to pay an insurer to assume that risk. In annuities and insurance generally, the consumer receives a valuable benefit: security in knowing that he or she is protected from a substantial risk.

Most people believe that the ideal insurance package is one that provides protection against both the risk of premature death and the risk of a long life. Thus, many people purchase life insurance and simultaneously make contributions toward an annuity.

[4] Life Insurance and Taxes

Full discussion of the ramifications of life insurance for federal or state income tax liabilities, or federal estate or state death tax liabilities is beyond the scope of this text. But the importance of life insurance to tax planners should not be overlooked. For purposes of the federal income tax, amounts received under a life insurance contract paid on account of the death of the insured are excluded from gross income. Assuming a life insurance contract meets certain tests,[20] it does not matter if the proceeds represent the death benefit, the increased value of the policy due to investment, or a return of premiums paid.[21]

Thus, life insurance can be an important tool for individuals who wish to avoid income taxes as their wealth accumulates. If a policy is surrendered and the accumulated cash value is returned to the insured, this is a taxable event,[22] but the benefit to the insured is that the cash value accumulates on a tax-free basis, and the taxable event can be timed to occur when the insured's marginal income tax rate is lower (as is likely to be the case if the insured allows the cash value to accumulate until the insured's retirement years). Of course, there are other financial planning tools that offer similar advantages; each individual must carefully evaluate, usually with expert assistance, which of these possibilities is best suited to his or her own needs.

---

[19] See Metropolitan Police Retiring Ass'n, v. Tobriner, 306 F.2d 775 (D.C. Cir. 1962) (association of employees who receive upon retirement a payback of their contributions to the association plus interest is not engaged in business of insurance).

[20] For policies issued after 1984, the policy must qualify as a life insurance contract under applicable state law and meet either a cash value accumulation test or a guideline premium/cash value corridor test. I.R.C. § 7702. Special rules apply to universal life policies issued before 1985. See I.R.C. § 101(f).

[21] I.R.C. § 101.

[22] See I.R.C. § 72(g). Generally speaking, the insured pays taxes on the proceeds received exceeding premiums paid; the precise calculation depends on whether the insured receives the cash value in a lump sum or as an annuity.

(Matthew Bender & Co., Inc.)

Life insurance left in force until the insured's death can also be an important estate planning tool. As federal law now stands, only a small percentage of the populace will have a federal estate tax liability; because most Americans have some kind of life insurance in force, it is clear that most Americans have life insurance for the purpose of either protecting their beneficiaries from the economic costs of their own deaths (e.g., lost income or even the expenses of the funeral) or creating an estate that can be passed to heirs. But for those individuals with large estates (i.e., in excess of the unified gift tax-estate tax credit of $600,000), life insurance — if several requirements are met[23] — can provide cash, on a tax-free basis, at a time a tax liability is created on account of the insured's death. Further information on this important, and increasingly complicated, subject can be found elsewhere.[24]

[c] Fire and Casualty Insurance

Fire insurance normally includes coverage for loss caused by hostile fire.[25] Also, fire insurance companies often write insurance in the so-called "allied lines" that protect against loss through lightning, explosion, earthquake, water, wind, hail, rain, collision, riot, and civil commotion.

Casualty insurance is primarily concerned with the insured's legal liability for injuries to others or for damage to other persons' property. Casualty insurance also embraces, however, workers' compensation insurance; credit insurance; fidelity and surety bonds; accident and health; disability; insurance against loss by burglary, robbery, or theft; insurance for damage to property; collision insurance; and a number of other discrete areas, such as plate glass, and boiler and machinery insurance.[26]

A few of the foregoing subcategories of casualty insurance merit further explanation. *Workers' compensation insurance* is the key ingredient of the workers' compensation system, which now exists in all states. Workers' compensation statutes replace the common law tort action with a system of absolute liability for injury or death suffered by an employee in an employment-related activity.[27] The

---

23 Under I.R.C. § 2042, life insurance proceeds are included in a decedent's estate if either (1) the proceeds are payable to the decedent's estate, regardless of whether the decedent has an ownership interest in the policy, or (2) the decedent possessed any "incident of ownership" over the applicable policy at the time of his or her death. Also, I.R.C. § 2035 provides that if a decedent owns a policy on his or her life and dies within three years of transferring the policy to someone else, the policy proceeds are fully includible in the decedent's estate. By negative implication, if the tests of § 2042 or § 2035 are not triggered, life insurance proceeds are not included in the decedent's estate.

24 See, e.g., 5 Boris Bittker & Lawrence Lokken, *Federal Taxation of Income, Estates and Gifts*, 2d ed., 127-1 to 127-31 (1993); Richard Stephens, et al., *Federal Estate and Gift Taxation*, 2d ed., ¶ 4.15 (1991); Craig Hampton, *Survivorship Life Insurance* (1994).

25 The distinction between a "hostile" fire and a "friendly" fire is discussed in § 66, *infra*.

26 Casualty insurance, however, has sometimes been defined more broadly. One definition treated casualty insurance as embracing all forms of legal liability, disability and medical care insurance, and selected kinds of property insurance. Clarence A. Kulp & J. Hall, *Casualty Insurance* 15–16 (1968).

27 For additional information about worker's compensation, see Arthur Larson, *The Law of Workmen's Compensation* (1972).

employee's compensation is funded by insurance paid for by the employer (unless the employer can qualify under the applicable state law as a self-insurer). Insurers typically sell employers a package of coverage sometimes referred to as "Workers' Compensation and Employers' Liability Insurance Policy." This contract protects the employer against financial loss caused when the employer is legally responsible for an employee's occupational injury or disease and when the employer has tort liability not preempted by the state workers' compensation statute. The insurer agrees to pay all compensation or other benefits required by the employer by the workers' compensation law and to pay on the insured's behalf all sums that the insured might become legally obligated to pay as damages because of injury (or death) of an employee in the course of employment.

Suretyship is the practice of one person agreeing to guarantee the debts or obligations of another. A surety bond is essentially a promise, evidenced by a writing, to a creditor that one person or company (the surety) will pay the debt or perform the obligation of some other person (the obligee) should that person fail to pay or perform. Surety bonds are commonly used in construction; for example, a contractor may require a subcontractor to post a bond to secure the subcontractor's performance. A fidelity bond is a special, but common kind of suretyship: the surety agrees to pay any loss suffered by an employer (or firm, etc.) caused by the dishonesty of an employee (or officer, etc.) In effect, the surety guarantees an individual's honest performance of some duty. Fidelity bonds are commonly used in banks and other financial institutions, corporations, and a variety of other commercial settings.

The creation of a suretyship relationship, in and of itself, does not involve insurance. It is simply one person agreeing to guarantee the obligation of another. However, when an organization is created to enter into a large number of suretyship relationships in exchange for payments made by people seeking the guarantees, the enterprise is engaged in a risk transference and distribution activity, which potentially becomes an insurance business subject to regulation by the states.

The accident and health category is so broad that its classification as a subcategory of casualty insurance seems inappropriate. Accident and health coverages have closely related purposes. *Accident insurance* reimburses the insured for pecuniary loss suffered as a result of injuries sustained in an accident. *Health insurance* reimburses the insured for pecuniary loss arising out of disease-related illness. In both kinds of insurance, the insured is reimbursed for medical and hospital expenses and, in the case of accident insurance and sometimes health insurance, earnings lost as a result of the incapacity.

Accident and health coverages are often combined in the same policy, thereby protecting the insured from loss from either kind of disability. Also, accident insurance is frequently offered as a supplement to life insurance. If death is caused by accident, many life policies pay "double indemnity" (meaning proceeds twice the amount of the policy's face value); the cost of this additional coverage is relatively low. Accident insurance is also provided with other coverages, most prominently with automobile insurance. Various kinds of specialized health insurance exist. "Major medical" is expanded coverage for catastrophic medical expenses.

(Matthew Bender & Co., Inc.)

Hospitalization insurance is widely marketed, as are various other kinds of supplementary coverages. "Blue Cross and Blue Shield" are well-known words in the health insurance field. Blue Cross is a hospitalization insurance system under which member hospitals receive reimbursement for the services rendered by them to an insured patient. Blue Shield is a similar plan offered to reimburse physicians and other health care providers for medical and surgical services rendered member patients.

[d] Other Kinds of Insurance

At least two other kinds of insurance exist that are normally regarded as being outside the three traditional categories. *Title insurance* is insurance against defects in legal title to property. For example, the seller of a house may agree to provide the buyer with a policy of title insurance. When giving the buyer a deed to the premises, the seller will warrant that the seller possesses good title; if this warranty is not fulfilled, the insurer agrees to defend the insured's (buyer's) claim of title and to reimburse the insured for any damages suffered as a result of some third party's successful claim against the title to the property. Title insurance, then, is basically insurance against the risk of incomplete information about someone's legal rights. The event carrying the potential to produce loss is a subsequent assertion of a claim of right against the property.

Reinsurance is a form of insurance for insurance companies. Frequently, the insurer underwriting the consumer's risk (sometimes called the "primary" or "direct" insurer) transfers a part of the assumed risk to some other insurance company (the "reinsurer.") The reinsurer agrees to reimburse the primary insurer for its losses according to some agreed-upon formula. The reinsurer might also agree to reimburse the primary insurer for some of its administrative expenses in adjusting claims. The reinsurer, in exchange for assuming a portion of the risk, receives a premium from the primary insurer.

The objective of reinsurance is very similar to that of primary insurance: the insurer, like the consumer, desires to eliminate part of its risk by transferring it to another party. By entering into a reinsurance contract, the insurer reduces its potential liability, and this enables the insurer to write more insurance directly to consumers. Reinsurance also provides the insurer with protection from catastrophic losses. For example, the individual losses caused by a hurricane may be small, but in combination such losses could be more than the insurer could absorb. Even though the consumer is rarely aware of the existence of a reinsurance contract, reinsurance is an extremely important way of dispersing risk. This subject is discussed in later sections.[28]

[e] First-Party versus Third-Party Insurance

Another way of distinguishing among different kinds of insurance involves the distinction between first-party and third-party insurance. In first-party insurance, the

---

[28] For an overview of reinsurance, see § 140, *infra;* Graydon S. Staring, *Law of Reinsurance* (1993); R. Gastel and S. Mooney, *Reinsurance: Fundamentals and Current Issues* (1983).

contract between the insurer and the insured indemnifies the insured for a loss suffered directly by the insured. Property insurance, for example, is first-party insurance; the damage to the property is an immediate, direct diminution of the insured's assets. The proceeds are paid to the insured to redress the insured's loss. Liability insurance, on the other hand, is sometimes described as third-party insurance because the interests protected by the contract are ultimately those of third parties injured by the insured's conduct. For example, if the insured negligently causes injury to a third party, the third party will possess a claim against the insured. If this claim is reduced to a judgment, the insured will suffer a loss; the insured's loss, however, is "indirect" in the sense that the third party suffers the "direct" loss. The liability insurer will reimburse the insured for any liability the insured may have to the third party, but in the event of payment, the insured merely serves as a conduit for transmission of the proceeds from the insurer to the third party. Thus, it is sometimes said that liability insurance is actually designed to protect unknown third parties.

All insurance except liability insurance can be fairly thought of as first-party insurance. In life insurance, the insured ordinarily designates a beneficiary to receive the proceeds of the policy, but this does not mean that the insurance is third-party. The loss is suffered by the insured; it is the insured whose life is lost. Unless the owner of the policy chooses to create third-party rights in a beneficiary, it is the insured's estate that receives the proceeds. Health insurance is somewhat uneasily categorized under this framework. Frequently, the health insurer pays the provider of health care services (e.g., the hospital or doctor) directly, rather than paying the proceeds to the insured. But the loss — the illness and its expenses — is suffered directly by the insured. The health care provider suffers a "loss" in a sense when it provides medical care, but the insurance is designed, first and foremost, not to help health care providers but to help individuals who incur medical bills. The health care provider is similarly situated to the auto repair shop that fixes the insured's automobile damaged by a falling tree: the insurer may pay the auto repair shop directly, but this does not mean the insurance is for the benefit of the auto repair shop.

The first-party versus third-party insurance distinction assists in understanding the concept of "no-fault" insurance. No-fault insurance is essentially the substitution of first-party insurance for tort liability. The victim of a tort, instead of looking to the tortfeasor and the tortfeasor's insurer for reimbursement, looks to his or her own insurer for first-party protection. First-party insurance is compulsory, and victims lose the right to sue the tortfeasor for small losses under a 'pure' no-fault scheme. In essence, the term "no-fault" is used to describe a system where the victim recovers for the victim's own loss from the victim's own insurer, without regard to the fault of the third party or the victim's own contributory fault. The no-fault concept is discussed in more detail in a later section.[29]

[f] A Trend Toward Reclassification?

Historically, insurers undertook to issue insurance only in one of the distinct categories of risk. This was not entirely a voluntary choice, as statutes in most states

---

[29] See § 132, *infra.*

confined insurers to writing insurance in only one line. Over time, however, these restrictions were removed, and many insurers commenced what was called "multiple line" underwriting, meaning the writing of insurance in all lines except life. Eventually, these insurers were allowed to add life insurance to their lines, resulting in what was known as "all-line" underwriting.[30]

Today, with the practice of multiple-line and all-line underwriting, the prospective insured can often deal with one company and one agent to meet all of his or her insurance needs. Thus, from the consumer's vantage point, distinguishing among lines is not important. Few consumers think about or need worry about the traditional distinctions among various lines. For example, the automobile is a device which has shown itself capable of injuring as well as being damaged in many ways. The insured, however, need not deal with different companies to get the diverse coverage needed. Instead, the insured can obtain all the necessary coverages relevant to the automobile in one policy: insurance for personal injury or death arising out of the automobile's use, for liability to third parties, and for damage to the automobile itself, whether or not the automobile is being used at the time.

If the risk-based classification of insurance has outlived its usefulness and is now given respect largely because of tradition, it is fair to ask whether a reclassification of the insurance business is now appropriate. Indeed, a reappraisal of the traditional classification scheme might enhance the subject's clarity.

A modernized classification scheme could recognize four categories of insurance: marine, personal, property, and liability. Marine insurance, understood as the insurance of the risks involved in international shipping, has an ancient heritage, which renders it a branch of the business truly unique unto itself. Personal insurance would include life, health, and accident insurance — all of which are designed to protect personal interests. Property insurance would include all insurance intended to indemnify the insured for damage to the insured's property interests, including some insurance now marketed under the rubric of inland marine insurance and casualty insurance. Finally, liability insurance would include all insurance designed to reimburse the insured for any liability the insured might incur to a third party.

The historical demarcations cannot be ignored, and they need to be understood because they will be with us for some time, particularly among those who are engaged in the insurance trade itself. But categorizing insurance into four principal areas — marine, property, personal, and liability — could provide a more accurate picture of the real differences between the kinds of coverage available, and hopefully will aid one's understanding of the subject.

§ 13B   Classification By Nature of the Insurer

No generally accepted method of categorizing insurers currently exists. Nevertheless, insurers are organized and conduct their business in different ways, and it is possible to classify insurers by reference to some of these distinctions.

---

[30] See generally David L. Bickelhaupt & John H. Magee, *General Insurance* 577–603 (8th ed. 1970).

Some insurers are designed to generate profit for their owners, while others are established on a not-for-profit basis. There are basically two kinds of for-profit insurers: stock companies and Lloyd's syndicates. The other kinds of insurers are typically operated on a not-for-profit basis: mutual companies, fraternal benefit organizations, and mutual assessment organizations.

[a] Stock versus Mutual Companies

A *stock company* is a corporation, organized like any other corporation, that sells insurance. The owners of the corporation are the stockholders, who need not be policyholders. The stockholders, as in any corporation, supply the capital, pay all losses (up to the value of their stock), and take the profits.[1]

Unlike a stock company, a *mutual company* is owned by the policyholders.[2] Most mutual companies are incorporated under state statutes providing specifically for their existence. Each member pays a premium in advance, usually in an amount slightly larger than what is necessary to cover that individual's expected loss plus a fair share of administrative expenses. Depending on the company's losses and expenses and the amount of interest earned on the reserves, the company may refund a portion of the premium to the policyholder at the end of the year in the form of a dividend. The supposed advantage of a mutual company is that if losses are lower than anticipated, the insured's refund will enable the insured to obtain insurance at a lower rate than anticipated. Some mutuals, however, have the option to assess the members for sums (usually not exceeding the amount of the premium) necessary to cover unanticipated large losses. With a stock company, these additional losses would be absorbed by the stockholders.

Most property and liability insurance in the U.S. is sold by stock companies. As of 1993, about 95 percent of all life insurance companies were stock companies, but the mutual companies are older and larger, and account for almost 37 percent of all life insurance in force.[3]

[b] Lloyd's Syndicates

Lloyd's syndicates literally date to the underwriters who gathered at Lloyd's Coffee House in London in the 1600s.[4] Currently, Lloyd's has about 26,000 underwriting members; most of these are nonprofessional investors known as "Names," and a few are full-time insurance underwriters. The Names have joined to form syndicates, each of which has as few as two or three but perhaps as many as a few thousand members. The syndicates (currently there are about 200 of them)

---

[1] See 18 APPLEMAN §§ 10001–10018, at 1–78 (1945).

[2] See *id.,* §§ 10041–10070, at 79–184.

[3] American Council of Life Insurance, *1994 Life Insurance Fact Book* 109 (1994).

[4] For a good summary of how Lloyd's functions, see Thomas W. Wilson, ch., *How Lloyd's Functions: A Primer on Operations* (1994) (Practising Law Institute: Course Handbook Series No. A4-4459). For a good summary of Lloyd's history, its current problems, and proposed changes, see Daborah A. Tompkinson, ch., *Challenge At Lloyd's* (1994) (Practising Law Institute: Course Handbook Series No. A4- 4459); Eileen Dacey, ch., *The Future of Lloyd's and the Global Insurance Market* (1993) (Practising Law Institute: Course Handbook Series No. A-679).

subscribe on behalf of their members to cover risks or percentages of risks. The liability of a Name depends on his or her percentage share of the syndicate, but each Name is personally liable without limit for the syndicate's losses. Thus, to become a Name, an individual (corporations cannot become Names) must have substantial means; currently, a British Name must have net worth exceeding 250,000 (roughly $450,000), and an American Name must have net worth exceeding $1 million; also, each Name must restate his or her wealth annually.[5] A syndicate or group of syndicates is managed by an underwriting agency, which employs a management staff, maintains a "box" on the floor of the Lloyd's exchange, and staffs the box with a representative of the agency.

In England, the broker is considered the agent of the customer for most purposes, including the obtaining of insurance. At Lloyd's, the insurance underwriting process begins when a broker licensed by Lloyd's approaches an underwriter in a box in the "Room" (the Lloyd's headquarters in London) and presents on what is called the "slip" the details of the risk. (If a non-Lloyd's broker is attempting to place the insurance, that broker must work through a Lloyd's broker.) The broker negotiates with the underwriter over both the terms of the insurance and the premium. Once the parties agree upon the terms and the premium, the underwriter indicates on the slip, alongside the underwriter's initials, the percentage of the risk the underwriter's syndicate is willing to cover. The underwriter who initially structures the deal is known as the "lead underwriter." The broker retains the slip, and then approaches various boxes in the Room and asks underwriters in these boxes to consider subscribing their syndicates for a percentage of the risk. Subsequent underwriters might decide to subscribe upon new or changed conditions of the insurance package; ultimately the broker must secure the agreement of all prior subscribers to the changed or new terms. The broker continues with this process until the risk is completely subscribed. The syndicates are then provided with copies of the slip. The broker's policy department prepares a written policy; it is forwarded to an office at Lloyd's which checks the policy for form and content and ultimately sends the policy to the insured. In the meantime, the broker may provide the insured with a letter stating that the insurance is in force.

The method by which Lloyd's, a self-regulated institution, is managed has undergone much change since the early 1980s. A 1982 act of Parliament created the "Council of Lloyd's," an oversight body that supplemented the prior, entirely internal management system. In 1991, the Chairman at Lloyd's appointed a task force to consider the competitive position of Lloyd's in the world insurance market. The 1992 report of this Task Force (called the "Rowland Report" after the name of the chair of the Task Force) recommended many changes at Lloyd's, some of which have been implemented.

Pursuant to a reorganization initiated in 1993, as of 1995 the 14-member Council (which reflects a reduction in the Council's membership by one-half) is composed of six "working" Names (Names who actively participate in underwriting at Lloyd's), four "external" Names (unlike working Names, the "outside" or "external"

---

[5] See Danial Bianca, "Understanding Lloyd's," in Eileen Dacey, ch., *The Future of Lloyd's, supra,* pp. 37-8. For discussion of how one becomes a Name, see Wilson, *supra.*

Names are simply passive investors in the market), and four "nominated members," whose appointments must be approved by the Governor of the Bank of England. The working Names elect the Chairman of Lloyd's, who oversees the Council and the "Market Board," which oversees Lloyd's business development. The "Regulatory Board," which is chaired by a nominated member and is composed of the eight members of the Council who are not working Names, is responsible for enforcing Lloyd's system of self-regulation.[6]

In October 1993, a very significant change was approved at Lloyd's: the admission of corporate capital into the market. This was prompted by the departure of Names from Lloyd's due to heavy losses in the late 1980s arising out of Hurricane Hugo, the San Francisco earthquake, the Piper Alpha oil rig leak, and the Exxon Valdez oil tanker spillage, losses which reduced the capacity at Lloyd's by about twenty percent. This change could mark the end of Lloyd's most distinctive feature, unlimited personal liability, as investors turn to the protection of the corporate form. Also, as corporate Names become more important to Lloyd's, the passive investor will become less common; corporate Names are certain to insist upon more of a role in how the business of Lloyd's is conducted. Individual Names continue to have unlimited liability, but in January 1993, a "stop-loss" program was implemented for these persons' protection. Under this significant innovation which is applicable to every Name, Names are protected against very large losses through what is in effect an insurance plan funded by contributions made by all Names.

An issue that has been problematic for Lloyd's (and U.S. insurers as well) has been the "long tail" on many claims. (The term "tail" refers to the length of time between an event which produces a loss, such as an exposure to a dangerous substance, and the manifestation of the injury resulting from the exposure, which can occur years later.) If a policy covers "occurrences" that "occur" during the policy's term,[7] and if "occurrence" is defined as when the injury or damage is manifested, the result is that the insurer provides coverage for a loss that is compensated at 1995's higher prices, even though the policy providing coverage was purchased and paid for with dollars collected when premiums were much lower and when the large liabilities of the 1990s were not anticipated. Under Lloyd's three-year accounting system, if liabilities cannot be assessed three years after the coverage year in question, a syndicate must leave its books open. The Names remain liable for losses until the account year closes; the upshot, then, is that no profits can be distributed for the year in question until much later.[8]

---

[6] Biaca, *supra,* at 35-42.

[7] For a more detailed discussion of occurrence policies, see § 65, *infra.*

[8] For more detail, see Bianca, *supra,* at 43-44. Corporate capital cannot be attracted to participate in such a system unless assurances can be given that new corporate investors will not indirectly pay for the losses of prior years. Thus, Lloyd's has created a wholly-owned company, "NewCo.," which will be a reinsurance company and which will take on all outstanding liabilities of Lloyd's from 1985 and before. NewCo. will be capitalized by all syndicates with pre-1986 policies, and it is hoped that this initiative will "ring-fence" (a term-of-art used to describe how NewCo. will confine the seemingly unbounded liabilities) all pre-1986 liabilities.

The recent problems at Lloyd's[9] have also spawned lawsuits where Names have sought to circumvent the unlimited liability they assumed.[10] About 4000 Names have sued their agents and others on account of losses arising out of the practice in a small number of syndicates of repeatedly reinsuring the same risk — the so-called "London Market Excess spiral."[11] In the United States, some Names have sought rescission of their contracts with Lloyd's syndicates on account of alleged fraud and violations of securities laws. These efforts have been unsuccessful, as courts have uniformly held that the proper forums for adjudicating or arbitrating these claims are in England, as specified in the contracts pursuant to which the plaintiffs in these cases became Names.[12]

To summarize, Lloyd's of London is a distinctive institution, and it will remain so. Nevertheless, Lloyd's is currently undergoing changes that will alter forever some of the fundamental characteristics of the institution.[13]

In the United States, insurance exchanges modeled on Lloyd's of London have not played a major role in the insurance marketplace. In the 1980s, three exchanges modeled on Lloyd's were established in the United States, but only one, the Illinois Insurance Exchange, survived to the 1990s.[14] The Illinois Insurance Exchange, which opened in Chicago in 1982, initially emphasized reinsurance in high-technology fields, and eventually developed a reputation for creating insurance for unusual risks. With gross premiums in the $200-$250 million range,[15] this exchange has not yet achieved its ambitions of becoming a major player in the market. The New York Insurance Exchange, organized in 1980, dealt principally in reinsurance, but this exchange collapsed in 1988.[16] In early 1983, the Insurance Exchange of the Americas opened in Miami, with aspirations to secure a substantial portion of the premium volume of Latin America. After an initial period of rapid growth, this exchange fell victim to lack of capitalization and substantial losses. The Exchange shut down operations in 1987, was placed in receivership by the Florida Insurance

---

9 See Nicholas Sinfield, "The Future of Lloyd's is Assured," in Dacey, *supra,* at 193-94.

10 See Stephen Lewis & Clifford Chance, *The "Names" Litigation* (1994) (Practising Law Institute: Course Handbook Series No. A4-4459).

11 See Sinfield, *supra,* at 188-89.

12 Bonny v. Society of Lloyd's, 3 F.3d 156 (7th Cir. 1993), *cert. denied,* 114 S.Ct. 1059 (1994); Roby v. Corporation of Lloyd's, 996 F.2d 1353 (2d Cir. 1993), *cert. denied,* 114 S.Ct. 385 (1994); Riley v. Kingsley Underwriting Agencies, Ltd., 969 F.2d 953 (10th Cir.), cert. denied, 113 S.Ct. 658 (1992).

13 For a series of articles on the "remaking" of Lloyd's, see Bus. Ins., Aug. 28, 1995, at 3-50.

14 The differences between Lloyd's of London and the American exchanges, as well as regulatory issues raised by the American exchanges, are discussed in Stevens, *Legal Structures of Insurance Exchanges,* 17 Forum 887 (1982). See also Gabay, *The New York Insurance Exchange,* 15 Forum 618 (1981).

15 The Exchange's gross premiums of $204.8 million in 1989 compared to $9.5 billion written by Lloyd's. *Insurance Exchange Here Seeking Clout in a Risky Business,* Chicago Tribune, July 15, 1990, at Bus.-1. Gross premiums were $142.4 million during the first six months of 1994. *USA: Illinois Insurance Future Prove Popular,* Reinsurance, Oct. 4, 1994, at 7.

16 *USA: A Colossus in Crisis—Reinsurance Sector,* Reinsurance, Oct. 4, 1994, at 29.

Department in 1987, and was liquidated in 1988.[17] Whether insurance exchanges will ever play a major role in the American market is doubtful. The failure of two of the three United States exchanges and the highly-publicized recent problems at Lloyd's is likely to make American investors wary of the exchange model for the foreseeable future, at least on this side of the Atlantic.

[c]   Fraternal Benefit Organizations

A *fraternal benefit organization ("FBO")*, sometimes called a mutual benefit society, is an organization that, although created for other social and benevolent purposes, provides insurance benefits, typically life insurance, to its members.[18] In this arrangement, each individual member helps insure the others and is insured by them. Fraternities, lodges, and employee's associations are examples of the kinds of organizations that provide this kind of insurance. Fraternal life insurance developed in the late-nineteenth century at about the same time industrial life insurance developed. For a time in this early period, the amount of insurance written by FBOs actually exceeded the amount sold by commercial insurers. The advent of group life insurance, however, provided a superior mechanism for offering low-cost coverage, and this development essentially halted the rapid of growth of fraternal life insurance. Yet since World War II the amount of fraternal life insurance in force has grown steadily, and as of 1993 approximately $215 billion of such insurance was in force, which accounted for 1.5 percent of all life insurance in the United States. FBOs usually receive favored regulatory and tax treatment, but a large number of failures of such bodies in recent years has resulted in closer examination of the their underwriting activities.

[d]   Other Private Insurance Entities

Two kinds of insurance enterprises deserve mention, even though both are very small parts of the insurance marketplace. In 1907, Massachusetts passed a law authorizing mutual savings banks to sell life insurance to residents or persons working in the state. Similar laws were passed in New York in 1938 and Connecticut in 1941.[19] Because the insurance is sold over-the-counter and without the use of agents, this kind of insurance is typified by low expenses and low costs to consumers. The amount of coverage that can be purchased is limited,[20] and the total amount of insurance in force is small — only $40.5 billion in 1993, or less that 0.3 percent of all life insurance in force in the United States. However, sales have been increasing in recent years; the amount of savings bank insurance in force increased 7.8 percent in 1993 over the prior year.[21]

---

[17] *Another Insurance Exchange Member Falls,* South Florida Bus. J., May 27, 1991, at 1; *Insurance Exchange Remains on the Ropes,* Miami Herald, Nov. 16, 1987, at Bus.-19.

[18] See 18 APPLEMAN §§ 10141–10153, at 268–692 (1945).

[19] For a more detailed discussion of this history, see Solomon S. Huebner & Kenneth Black, Jr., *Life Insurance* 558-62 (10th ed. 1982).

[20] The limits are as follows: Connecticut, $100,000 ($200,000 for group term); New York, $50,000 ($350,000 for group term); Massachusetts, $500,000. American Council of Life Insurance, *1994 Life Insurance Fact Book* 122 (1994).

[21] *Id.* at 122.

An *insurance exchange,* sometimes called a "reciprocal association" or "mutual assessment organization," is an association of individuals or persons who join together for the purpose of providing insurance among themselves.[22] Not to be confused with the Lloyd's model of "insurance exchange," the reciprocal association acts through a person or corporation serving as attorney-in-fact for the organization. A classic example of such an association is the burial society, which first came into existence over two hundred years ago. A group of individuals would agree to form an association and charge each of the members a pro rata share of the expenses associated with the burial of a deceased member. Through this arrangement, the risk of incurring expenses at death would be spread among the association's membership. Insurance exchanges today constitute a de minimis portion of the insurance market.

[e] Government Insurance

Although insurance in the United States is typically provided through private sources, federal or state government sometimes provides insurance. To that extent, it is appropriate to classify insurance into two broad categories: private and governmental.

Government's largest and most important role as an insurer is in the area of health insurance. Medicare is a federal program of health insurance available to social security and railroad retirement recipients who are over the age of 65 or who are disabled.[23] A premium is charged annually, and the coverage is limited by deductibles and coinsurance. Medicare has two parts; the first, "Part A," is the Hospital Insurance ("HI") program, and it is financed through payroll taxes.[24] The second, "Part B," is the Supplementary Medical Insurance ("SMI") program, which covers physicians' services and related health care expenses.[25] Medicare is administered by the Health Care Financing Administration of the Department of Health and Human Services, but private insurers are involved in the program's administration, principally by processing claims and paying out benefits. During 1995, Congress debated, and the Republican majorities in the Senate and House appeared likely to approve, sweeping changes in the Medicare program. The extent to which President Clinton and the Democratic congressional leadership, who opposed the Republican proposals, would be able to modify the Republican proposals was uncertain.

---

[22] See *id.,* §§ 10121–10125, at 224–240.

[23] For a concise summary of the Medicare program, see Barry R. Furrow et al., *Health Law* 560-602 (1995).

[24] Part A covers inpatient hospital care, subject to limitations for the number of days of care, for any "spell of illness." 42 U.S.C. § 1395d(a). Covered services include semiprivate accommodations, nursing services, drugs, supplies, dianostic or therapeutic items or services normally furnished by the hospital to inpatients, etc. 42 U.S.C. § 1395x(b). Part A also covers some home health services, 42 U.S.C. § 1395x(m), and some post-hospital-stay services rendered in a "skilled nursing facility." 42 U.S.C. § 1395d(a)(2). Part A does not cover physician's services.

[25] Among the many services and procedures covered in Part B are physician's services, services (e.g., drugs) normally administered in a physician's office, outpatient diagnostic services, home dialysis, ambulance services when necessary, some vaccinations, prosthetic devices, etc. 42 U.S.C. § 1395x(q), (s)(1) through (s)(14).

It is sometimes said that the government's two main health insurance programs are Medicare and Medicaid. Medicaid, however, is technically not an insurance plan, although it superficially appears to operate as such. Medicaid is a cooperative federal-state program jointly financed by state and federal governments, with federal financial support provided to participating states that choose to provide medical assistance to low-income persons. Participation in the Medicaid program by the states is optional, but once a state decides to participate it must comply with federal statutory and regulatory requirements. In fact, all states decided to participate, although as of 1995 about a dozen states had obtained waivers that allow them to operate different, but approved kinds of medical assistance programs for the indigent. The federal Medicaid requirements include mandates as to payment levels, who must be allowed to participate, and the minimum categories of services that must be provided to eligible persons. Medicaid is not "risk-spreading" in the sense of insurance. In contrast, even though Medicare is not actuarially sound and requires a subsidy funded through a payroll tax on all workers regardless of age, it does possess many of the normal incidents of insurance.

For members of the Armed Forces, the federal government has historically played a role in insurance, either as a provider or arranger of coverage. At the outset of World War I, private carriers were unwilling to provide life and accident insurance to members of the military due to the hazards of military service. Therefore, during the war, Congress passed a special statute[26] to make life and accident coverage available to those in the military service. The insurance was provided directly by the federal government to the insured. Immediately before World War II, a similar program was created under the title "National Service Life Insurance." In 1965, Congress created a program called "Servicemen's Group Life Insurance." This program, administered by life insurance companies under contract with the government, is now used to provide coverage for members of the armed forces.[27] SGLI resembles group insurance, where the government owns the master policy, the serviceperson is the certificate holder, and a private enterprise assumes the risk.

Federal insurance programs also exist in other areas. In 1938, Congress enacted the Federal Crop Insurance Act.[28] In this statute, Congress created the Federal Crop Insurance Corporation and authorized it to enter into contracts for crop insurance.[29] The stated purpose of the Act is "to promote the national welfare by improving the economic stability of agriculture through a sound system of crop insurance."[30] The National Flood Insurance Act of 1968[31] was designed to provide insurance to property owners in flood-prone areas where it was previously unavailable. Under the statutory framework, if a state or local governmental body enters the program and agrees to pay premiums, individual property owners within those areas may purchase flood insurance. In 1950, Congress passed the Federal Deposit Insurance

[26] War Risk Insurance Act, Oct. 6, 1917, *as amended,* 38 U.S.C. §§ 400 *et seq.*
[27] See 38 U.S.C. §§ 765 et seq.
[28] 7 U.S.C. §§ 1501–1520.
[29] 7 U.S.C. § 1508.
[30] 7 U.S.C. § 1502.
[31] 42 U.S.C. §§ 4001–4128.

(Matthew Bender & Co., Inc.)

Act.[32] The Federal Deposit Insurance Corporation, which was created by the Act, provides insurance for deposits in banks that belong to the Federal Reserve System.[33] The Federal Housing Administration, which operates under the authority of the National Housing Act of 1934,[34] implements a variety of loan and mortgage insurance programs. A significant aspect of the many functions of the FHA is to insure mortgages on one- to four-family dwellings, single-family dwellings damaged in major disasters, and property improvement loans.[35] Under the Price-Anderson Act of 1957,[36] the federal government provides excess liability coverage for damage caused by nuclear power-generation accidents. Two governmental agencies provide insurance against risks encountered by private businesses engaged in foreign trade. The Export-Import Bank, an agency of the United States created by an act of Congress, insures United States businesses that export goods overseas against the political risks of doing business in foreign countries.[37] The Overseas Private Investment Corporation provides coverage against property loss due to expropriation of assets by a foreign government, war or insurrection, and the inability to convert dollars into local currency.[38] Under the Urban Growth and New Community Development Act,[39] the federal government directly offers crime insurance to urban residential and business properties unable to obtain the coverage at affordable rates.

In each of these areas, Congress made a judgment that private insurance markets were unable to make needed insurance available at a reasonable cost. In other words, federal intervention in the private market was thought essential to remedying the inadequacies of the private market. Although few would argue that some federal role is needed in some situations and useful in others as a method of promoting national priorities, some aspects of the federal role are controversial. For example, the federal subsidy of flood insurance has arguably encouraged over- development of some flood plains, leading to enormous losses when serious flooding does occur, such as in 1993 and 1995 in the Mississippi and Missouri Rivers' basins. It is unlikely, however, that the federal role as an insurance provider will diminish, even if changes are made in some areas. It is likely, for example, that some federal role will eventually be created to assist private markets in preparing for the huge losses that would accompany a catastrophic earthquake or hurricane, an event which could occur at any time and which will certainly occur sometime in the future. Although a comprehensive federal program of health insurance for all Americans seems less likely after the failure of the President Clinton's proposal in 1994, continued worsening of the problems of health care access and affordability could one day resurrect interest in a more expansive federal role.

---

[32] 12 U.S.C. §§ 1811–1832.

[33] 12 U.S.C. § 1814(b), 1821(f).

[34] 24 C.F.R. § 200.1.

[35] 24 C.F.R. § 200.5.

[36] 42 U.S.C. § 2210.

[37] 12 U.S.C. § 635.

[38] 22 U.S.C. § 2191.

[39] 42 U.S.C. § 4501.

§ 13C Classification by Nature of Marketing

The process by which insurance products are marketed to consumers also provides a basis for classifying insurance. The principal marketing distinction distinguishes *group policies* from *individual policies*. The process by which insurance policies are marketed to individuals usually proceeds in five steps: (i) the insurer's solicitation of the application; (ii) the application; (iii) the issuance of a binder; (iv) insurer evaluation of the risk; and (v) issuance of the policy. This process is discussed in more detail in a later section.[1] At the end of the process, one policy is issued to one individual.

The term *group insurance* refers to an insurance plan under which a number of persons are provided coverage under a single policy issued to a single party with whom the persons are affiliated, such as an employer or an association. The single party (often called the "group representative") who negotiates the insurance with the insurer is issued a "master policy," which sets forth all of the terms and conditions of the insurance. The persons who actually receive the coverage (often called "certificate holders") are normally issued "certificates" that describe the essential features of the coverage.

Group insurance is widely used in the life and health insurance lines. As of 1993, 40 percent of all life insurance[2] and approximately 90 percent of all health insurance[3] was sold on a group basis. However, only a de minimus portion of the market for liability and property insurance is sold to groups. Several explanations exist for this uneven distribution of group insurance, but one is of overarching significance: the tax advantages provided employers and employees when life and health insurance is made a fringe benefit are not available for property and liability insurance.

Employers who provide life and health insurance to their employees can deduct the cost of the insurance as a business expense, something which is not possible with ordinary salary. Thus, providing an employee an extra dollar's worth of life or health insurance costs the employer less than providing the employee with an extra dollar of salary, and this gives employers an incentive to load compensation packages more heavily with health and life insurance. Moreover, these fringe benefits are, for the most part, excluded from the employee's taxable income, which causes employees to be more interested in receiving the benefits. In the opinion of many experts, the tax subsidy causes overutilization of health insurance, meaning that many Americans now have more and better health insurance plans than they would optimally desire in the absence of the subsidy. This phenomenon, it is argued, has led directly to the overutilization of some health care services, which has in turn inflated the costs of health care, with the perverse effects of making health care less affordable for many Americans and further increasing the demand for better health insurance to pay the higher costs (which in turn further fuels the upward spiral in health care costs). Although the political hurdles in reducing the tax subsidy are formidable

---

[1] See § 30, *infra.*

[2] American Council of Life Insurance, *1994 Life Insurance Fact Book* 28 (1994).

[3] See Office of Technology Assessment, *Medical Testing and Health Insurance* 3 (1988) (placing figure at between 85 and 90 percent).

(eliminating the subsidy, as some have suggested, is probably a political impossibility), some narrowing of the subsidy may well occur in the future.

Even absent a tax subsidy, however, it is probable that life and health insurance would be favored by employers and therefore offered to employees on a group basis simply because these risks are more directly related to the employment relationship. Indeed, this logical nexus may be part of the reason the favored tax treatment for life and health insurance was created in the first place. Another important consideration involves claims processing. The administrative attention needed to settle claims in the property and liability lines is much greater than what is required in life and health insurance. To the extent a greater need exists for individual attention to claims and coverage, the benefits of group insurance are diminished. For these reasons, group insurance is not likely to become as pervasive in the property and liability lines as it is in life and health insurance.

Group insurance raises a number of interesting legal issues, and many of these are discussed in later sections.[4]

---

[4] See §§ 120–26, *infra*.

CHAPTER 2

SOURCES OF INSURANCE LAW

§ 20 The Rationale for Regulation: Generally

For most of the twentieth century, the proposition that government should regulate the insurance industry has been assumed with few, if any, second thoughts. During the 1980s, however, some government officials, industry representatives, and consumer advocates urged significant deregulation of certain aspects of the insurance business.[1] The debate over the proper mix of government regulation and free competition in the business of insurance has continued into the 1990s, and will no doubt continue for the foreseeable future. To understand the debate, it is helpful first to analyze the theoretical justifications for insurance regulation.

The American economy, heavily influenced by the doctrine of laissez faire, is predicated on the assumption that an unregulated marketplace is the norm. Advocates of government intervention in the marketplace have the burden to demonstrate that an unregulated marketplace cannot achieve important public objectives. A variety of justifications for government intervention have been offered and accepted in assorted settings; at least five of these are relevant to the insurance industry.[2]

One rationale for regulation is the inability of the marketplace to deal with *excessive competition*. In its classic formulation, this rationale claims that excessive competition in some industries leads to unacceptably low prices, which drives firms out of business. If only one or two firms survive, those firms are then able to exact unfair advantages in the marketplace. In the insurance industry, excessive competition, it is feared, could lead to insurer insolvencies. Of course, in many industries good reasons exist for allowing less efficient, unprofitable firms to perish. However, the failure of an insurance company due to excessive competition has potentially severe consequences. Insureds commonly invest substantial sums of money in insurance policies that promise annuities for retirement, payments to dependents

---

[1] See, e.g., Staff, National Association of Insurance Commissioners, *Monitoring Competition: A Means of Regulating the Property and Liability Insurance Business,* vol. 1, at 65 (1974); Conference Board, *Insurance Deregulation: Issues and Perspectives* (1982).

[2] In addition to the five justifications discussed below, the following justifications are sometimes offered for government regulation: the need to control monopoly power; the need to control windfall profits; the need to correct for externalities; the need to alleviate scarcity; and the need to redistribute wealth. For further discussion of the theory of regulation and justifications for it, see generally Stephen Breyer, *Regulation and Its Reform* (1982).

upon death, or compensation for loss of property and harm to other interests. Consequently, the bankruptcy of an insurer can cause substantial hardship and suffering for insureds and their beneficiaries. One way to cope with insurer insolvency is to require surviving insurers to assume the obligations of the insolvent insurer. However, this approach, for all its merit, cannot promise insureds complete protection. Thus, most states regulate the rates insurers charge for insurance so as to eliminate the possibility of destructive competition.[3] These statutes reflect an unwillingness to trust an unsupervised marketplace with the responsibility of protecting the substantial reliance of insureds upon insurers.

A second rationale for regulation is to compensate for *inadequate information.* For a free market to function effectively, participants in the market need information with which to evaluate competing products. Information itself can be viewed as a commodity, for which there is a supply and a demand; in many industries, the market for information does not function perfectly. In the insurance industry, it is argued, information is scarce and not easily obtainable. Insureds lack easy access to information about the future solvency of insurers. Similarly, the consumer has few ways to compare the quality of service that alternative companies might provide before purchasing a policy.[4] Insurance contracts are complicated; the consumer is often baffled by their content. Comparing the value of alternative products is extremely difficult for the average consumer. Consumers as a class have an interest in acquiring information, but no satisfactory way exists for consumers to share the costs of acquiring it. When the amount of information in the marketplace is inadequate, competition is imperfect: consumers are unable to choose the best product for themselves, and sometimes they may even choose worthless products.

Government regulation requiring disclosure of information to either the consumer or a government agency acting as the consumer's proxy can compensate for deficient information in the marketplace. Also, government regulation to maintain insurer solvency and to promote fair claims processing practices can theoretically eliminate the need for consumers to search for information. By requiring the text of insurance policies to contain clear language, government regulation presumably can compensate for a lack of consumer comprehension of the substance of policies. Regulation aimed at encouraging or requiring cost disclosures can increase the ability of consumers to compare alternative products. In fact, most state insurance departments have a public information office, whose avowed purpose is to increase the public's access to information.

Unequal bargaining power is sometimes used as a justification for regulation. The assumption that the most efficient allocation of resources will occur in a free market depends upon, among other things, a roughly equal balance of power between buyers and sellers. If prices (and wages) are to perform their resource-allocating tasks, markets must operate freely. If one party has disproportionate market power, that

---

[3] For further discussion, see § 22[b], *infra.*

[4] One of the few sources of information comparing the service provided by insurance companies is the Consumers Union, which periodically publishes data in the periodical *Consumer Reports* about consumer experiences; the data is accumulated through questionnaires submitted by subscribers of the magazine.

party may be able to impede the free movement of society's resources, ultimately leading to a misallocation of resources. Regulation, it is argued, can improve the balance of power, thereby improving the efficiency of markets. In the insurance setting, the justification is predicated upon the alleged need to protect consumers — both private citizens and small businesses — from being pressured to enter into ill-advised contracts with large insurance companies. Aiding the party who suffers from a lack of bargaining power has been a pervasive theme in contract cases for many years, but the favoritism for the weaker party appeared even earlier in insurance litigation.

A fourth justification for regulation can best be described as *paternalism*. Even when information about alternatives is fully and freely available in the marketplace, it is sometimes argued that consumers nevertheless make irrational decisions and that government regulation is therefore required. The paternalism rationale is frequently controversial, for it often pits notions of "individual freedom of choice" against "the common good." The debate over laws recently enacted in many states to require all occupants of automobiles to wear seat belts is a good example. For one person, a mandatory seat belt helmet law is necessary to force changes in behavior patterns by those who otherwise would make an irrational choice not to protect themselves (and the general public, in the sense that the public incurs many of the costs of injuries that could have been prevented through seat belt use) against a significant risk. For another person, a mandatory seat belt law is an invasion by government into an area where personal choice should be paramount.[5]

In insurance, an analogous debate exists over state "anti-rebate" laws, which prohibit insurance agents from rebating a portion of their commissions to insureds.[6] Proponents of the laws argue that agents perform a valuable service for consumers by providing information about alternative insurance choices. It is argued that agents would not perform these services unless adequately compensated; allowing consumers to negotiate with agents for rebates of the agents' commissions will reduce agents' compensation and their incentive to supply necessary information to consumers. This argument, of course, presumes that consumers will make irrational decisions if agents are not allowed to assist them with their choices.[7] Stated otherwise, the paternalism rationale presumes that government knows what is good for consumers better than the consumers do themselves. The paternalism rationale's assumption that consumers behave irrationally is inconsistent with the free market's assumption of rational consumer behavior and with principles of free choice, but

---

[5] Another good example is the debate over laws enacted in some states and considered in others that would require motorcyclists and their passengers to wear helmets. The issues are similar, although the cost-benefit analysis is somewhat murkier because of the argument by those opposing mandatory helmet laws that helmets impair peripheral vision and thereby increase accident frequency.

[6] Commissions are paid by the insurer to the agent; the commission is typically a percentage of the premium paid by the insured to the insurer.

[7] For discussion of anti-rebate statutes, see Robert H. Jerry, II & Reginald R. Robinson, *Statutory Prohibitions on the Negotiation of Insurance Agent Commissions: Substantive Due Process Review Under State Constitutions,* 51 Ohio St. L. J. 773 (1990); Annot., *Insurance Anti-Rebate Statutes: Validity and Construction,* 90 A.L.R.4th 213 (1994).

much government regulation — including insurance regulation — is based on the paternalism rationale.

A fifth justification for government regulation is the need to achieve *important social objectives*. Sometimes the free market simply fails to achieve objectives highly valued by society. For example, all states have some kind of statute or regulation prohibiting discrimination of various sorts in insurance. Because certain kinds of unacceptable discrimination would exist in a free market, government regulation is deemed necessary to promote egalitarian values. The automobile is the focal point for a plethora of societal concerns, and a major concern is compensating victims of accidents. The free market has proved unable to provide what our society deems minimally necessary, and our society has resorted to government regulation: most states require operators of vehicles to maintain a specified amount of liability insurance or to demonstrate financial responsibility if involved in an accident, and many states require each owner of a vehicle to purchase minimum levels of first-party personal injury protection. Occasionally, the government actually provides insurance not otherwise available in the open market. In these situations, a judgment is made that an efficient market is not society's only goal; sometimes government regulation is necessary — even if the market is efficient — to achieve other social values.

When any of the foregoing rationales is invoked to justify insurance regulation, a simultaneous judgment is made that the unregulated market has failed to achieve or is incapable of achieving important public objectives: the market cannot control excessive competition; the market cannot make needed information widely available; the market cannot reasonably accommodate unequal bargaining power; consumers behave irrationally notwithstanding the existence of a free market; or the market cannot achieve important social objectives. Where the presumption favoring a free market is rebutted successfully, government regulation occurs.

Regulation of the insurance industry occurs most overtly through legislation. However, the obviousness of statutory regulation sometimes obscures the role that courts play in regulating the insurance industry through the process of case-by-case adjudication. Subsequent sections explore both modes of regulation.

§ 21   Legislative Regulation: State versus Federal Control

[a]   The Origins of the McCarran-Ferguson Act

In the late eighteenth and early nineteenth centuries, the insurance industry was relatively undeveloped. During this period, regulation occurred primarily through the restrictions in each corporate charter granted by state legislatures.[1] The states,

---

[1] For example, the 1794 charter granted the Insurance Company of North America, the first insurance corporation in the United States, prohibited the company from engaging in other businesses, required that the deposits be placed in the Bank of Pennsylvania, limited the company's investment in real estate, and specified minimum amounts of liquid assets to be kept in reserve to pay losses. John G. Day, *Economic Regulation of Insurance in the United States* 4 (1970).

realizing the industry's revenue potential, also taxed insurers and their agents. The reporting requirements developed to implement tax laws probably made it easier for the states to insist upon detailed reporting in connection with later, more vigorous regulation.[2] With the advent of general incorporation statutes in the early nineteenth century, the practice of granting specific charters for insurance companies fell into disuse.[3]

However, at the time states enacted general incorporation legislation, many states also passed legislation governing the establishment of insurance companies. These statutes imposed requirements similar to those contained in a typical insurer's corporate charter. Insurers were required to make periodic reports to a state official, avoid certain kinds of investments, and maintain certain minimum levels of capitalization and reserves.[4] States often imposed more onerous burdens on out-of-state insurers.[5]

Insurers were inclined to view the patchwork system of state regulation as burdensome, and by the 1860s insurers were urging Congress to adopt national standards that would make insurers federal institutions analogous to banks. As part of an effort to encourage federal supplantation of state regulation, a number of New York insurance companies in the mid-1860s set up a case they hoped would invalidate the system of state regulation. Paul, a Virginia resident, was appointed by these companies as their agent. He applied for a Virginia license, but refused to deposit bonds with the state treasurer as required by state law. Paul was not granted a license, but he proceeded to sell a policy of insurance to a Virginia resident anyway, and he was convicted for violating the Virginia licensing statute. The Virginia Supreme Court affirmed his conviction. Paul challenged his conviction in the United States Supreme Court on the grounds that Virginia's stricter requirements for foreign insurers violated the Privileges and Immunities Clause of the United States Constitution,[6] that the federal commerce power allowed regulation of insurers, and that this power resided exclusively with the federal government.[7]

In 1869, the Supreme Court rejected Paul's arguments, thereby dashing the hopes of insurers interested in promoting federal regulation. The Court held in *Paul v. Virginia*[8] that a corporation is not a citizen within the meaning of the Privileges and Immunities Clause. More importantly, the Court held that "issuing a policy of insurance is not a transaction of commerce," which was tantamount to placing the business of insurance outside the constitutional authority of Congress. Under this ruling, to which the Court adhered for seventy-five years,[9] individual states retained the authority to regulate insurance companies.

---

[2] Edwin W. Patterson, *The Insurance Commissioner in the United States* 524–30 (1927); Day, note 1, *supra*, at 5.

[3] Day, note 1, *supra*, at 5.

[4] *Id.* at 6.

[5] *Id.* at 7.

[6] U.S. Const., art. IV, § 2.

[7] Day, note 1, *supra*, at 15.

[8] 75 U.S. (8 Wall.) 168, 183 (1869).

[9] See, e.g., New York Life Ins. Co. v. Deer Lodge County, 231 U.S. 495, 508 (1913); Hooper v. California, 155 U.S. 648, 655 (1895).

The insurance industry grew with the rest of the country; as the business became bigger and more complex, the public urged more rigorous state regulation. By 1900, most states had some kind of licensing procedure for companies and agents. However, abuses in the life insurance industry soon attracted the public's attention. These practices included the payment of excessively large commissions to agents, the making of false representations about future dividends, the waste of company assets on lobbying activities and the inability of many companies to account for related expenditures, nepotism in the hiring of insurance company employees, and other practices where company officials abused their positions for personal gain.

Public concern led to an investigation by a New York legislative committee led by Senator William W. Armstrong. In 1906, the Armstrong Committee issued a lengthy report, which led to the enactment of remedial legislation in New York. Among other changes, the New York law required detailed year-end reporting by insurers, ordered the allocation of policy dividends to insureds, abolished tontine insurance, limited the amount of new business the insurer could write each year, and imposed strict regulations on agent commissions.[10]

By 1919, thirty-six states had separate insurance departments vested with the exclusive task of administering regulatory statutes.[11] By 1930, insurance departments in most states were given greater authority to collect information from insurers and were also charged with the responsibility of preserving insurer solvency. The departments were also authorized to review insurers' business decisions on reserve levels, valuation of assets, and investments. In addition, regulators were given some authority over policy forms and unfair trade practices, such as rebating, misrepresentation, twisting, and discrimination.[12]

By 1944, state insurance regulation was relatively comprehensive in all areas but ratemaking.[13] Although about two-thirds of the states had adopted rate regulation in some form, the scope of state regulation was uneven, and the degree of enforcement of the regulatory schemes varied widely. Notwithstanding the existence of statutes in most states, in 1944 "insurance ratemaking was as yet largely uncontrolled in the United States."[14]

In the early 1940s, the Attorney General of Missouri, frustrated with the ineffectiveness of state ratemaking regulation and hoping to encourage federal involvement, sought a determination in federal court that the business of insurance constituted interstate commerce subject to the antitrust laws. He obtained an indictment against the South-Eastern Underwriters Association, an association of 198 stock fire insurance companies in six states, its officers, and its member companies.

---

[10] See generally H. Roger Grant, *Insurance Reform: Consumer Action in the Progressive Era* (1979).

[11] Patterson, note 2, *supra,* at 536–37; Day, note 1, *supra,* at 10.

[12] Spencer L. Kimball, *Insurance and Public Policy* 121–28 (1960).

[13] Day, note 1, *supra,* at 18. For additional discussion of state regulation of ratemaking, see § 22[b], *infra.*

[14] Spencer L. Kimball & Ronald N. Boyce, *The Adequacy of State Insurance Rate Regulation: The McCarran-Ferguson Act in Historical Perspective,* 56 Mich. L. Rev. 545, 552 (1958).

The indictment charged the defendants with violating the Sherman Act by agreeing to fix rates and boycotting nonmembers. The district court dismissed the indictment on the authority of *Paul v. Virginia,* ruling that insurance was not interstate commerce. In 1944, however, the Supreme Court reversed the dismissal in a four-to-three decision. *United States v. South-Eastern Underwriters Association*[15] overruled the longstanding principle of *Paul v. Virginia* and held that insurance transactions were subject to federal regulation under the Commerce Clause. This decision removed the constitutional impediment to federal regulation of the insurance industry.

Ironically, by 1944, the insurance industry preferred the generally lax regulation of the state authorities. Moreover, the industry was concerned that federal antitrust laws might be applied in a way that prohibited the pooling of actuarial data, a practice central to the ratemaking process. For other reasons, too, the industry feared both the potential havoc that federal antitrust regulation might create and the uncertainties inherent in substituting federal for state regulation. The industry knew that the Court's holding in *SEUA* regarding the scope of the Commerce Clause could not be overturned. Therefore, the industry rallied behind legislation proposed by the National Association of Insurance Commissioners to limit the impact of *SEUA.* This proposal was enacted by Congress and was called the McCarran-Ferguson Act.[16]

[b]   The Substance of the McCarran-Ferguson Act

In section 1 of the McCarran-Ferguson Act, Congress stated the underlying policy of the statute as one favoring state regulation of the insurance business:

> Congress declares that the continued regulation and taxation by the several States of the business of insurance is in the public interest, and that silence on the part of the Congress shall not be construed to impose any barrier to the regulation or taxation of such business by the several States.

If the industry's motivation for proposing the statute is to be credited, Congress presumably favored state regulation because of the states' closer proximity to the kinds of problems needing regulation and because of concern over the effect of supplanting existing structures of state regulation with untested, yet-to-be devised federal structures.

The operative language of the Act appeared in section 2:

> (a) The business of insurance, and every person engaged therein, shall be subject to the laws of the several States which relate to the regulation or taxation of such business.

> (b) No Act of Congress shall be construed to invalidate, impair, or supersede any law enacted by any State for the purpose of regulating the business of insurance, or which imposes a fee or tax upon such business, unless such Act specifically relates to the business of insurance: *Provided,* That after June 30, 1948, [the Sherman Act of 1890, the Clayton Act of 1914, and the Federal Trade

---

[15] 322 U.S. 533 (1944).

[16] 15 U.S.C. §§ 1011 et seq. For an overview of the statute, its history, and its interpretation, see Linda M. Lent, *McCarran-Ferguson in Perspective,* 48 Ins. Counsel J. 411 (1981).

Commission Act of 1914] shall be applicable to the business of insurance to the extent that such business is not regulated by State law.

Section 3(b) of the statute stated that the Sherman Act would apply to some insurer activities regardless of whatever regulation the states might enact: "Nothing contained in this chapter shall render the said Sherman Act inapplicable to any agreement to boycott, coerce, or intimidate, or act of boycott, coercion, or intimidation." Section 4 similarly ensured the supremacy of three labor statutes: "Nothing contained in this chapter shall be construed to affect in any manner the application to the business of insurance of the . . . National Labor Relations Act, or . . . the Fair Labor Standards Act of 1938, or . . . the Merchant Marine Act, 1920."

Given the background of the passage of the McCarran-Ferguson Act, the statute's purpose was clear. As the Supreme Court soon explained, "[o]bviously Congress' purpose was broadly to give support to the existing and future state systems for regulating and taxing the business of insurance. . . . [I]ts purpose was evidently to throw the whole weight of its power behind the state systems."[17]

[c] The Effects of the McCarran-Ferguson Act

In essence, the McCarran-Ferguson Act gave supremacy to state regulation of the business of insurance to the extent the states chose to occupy the regulatory field. Accordingly, shortly after the Act was passed, state insurance commissioners and representatives of the industry collaborated in an effort to draft and propose state legislation to occupy the areas exempted from federal regulation. The NAIC and an organization created by the NAIC composed of representatives of the industry drafted model rate regulation and fair trade practices statutes. The model ratemaking legislation reflected the beliefs that concerted ratemaking was essential to insurer solvency and that such joint activity should proceed under state supervision. By 1950, some form of rate regulation had been adopted in every state.

The states were somewhat slower to enact unfair trade practices legislation. In the mid-1950s, the Federal Trade Commission initiated inquiries into unsavory practices in the advertising of accident and health insurance. Concern about possible federal intervention encouraged the states to act, and by 1963, unfair trade practices statutes were adopted in all the states. This legislation, as enacted in most states, empowered the state insurance commissioner to issue cease and desist orders for misrepresentations and false advertising, for defamation, boycotts, coercion, and intimidation, for issuing false financial statements, providing stock options and advisory board contracts, and unfairly discriminating in life insurance, annuities, accident, and health insurance, and for rebating.

---

[17] Prudential Ins. Co. v. Benjamin, 328 U.S. 408, 429–30 (1946). The evolution of the Supreme Court's interpretation of the statute is described and analyzed in Spencer L. Kimball & Barbara P. Heaney, *Emasculation of the McCarran-Ferguson Act: A Study of Judicial Activism,* 1985 Utah L. Rev. 1. For a discussion of the Supreme Court's decisions in the cases considering whether annuities constitute insurance or investments, and the concomitant ramifications for the scope of state regulatory authority, see Spencer L. Kimball, *Reflections on the Meaning of "Insurance,"* 2 Int'l J. of Ins. Law 226 (1995).

The process repeated itself in the 1960s and early 1970s when public concern over automobile insurance rates led to a Department of Transportation inquiry. With the prospect of federal intervention looming, a majority of the states enacted some kind of no-fault statute; in about half of these states, the statutory changes reformed the tort system with respect to compensation of victims of auto accidents.

To summarize, the McCarran-Ferguson Act's principal effect was to favor state regulation of the business of insurance. To the extent the states chose to regulate, federal regulation was preempted. The states, taking advantage of Congress' invitation to preempt its exercise of the commerce power, enacted comprehensive statutory schemes regulating the business of insurance. Nevertheless, numerous areas exist where the demarcation between the state's rightful authority and federal power is not clear. As discussed in the next section, in many respects, the demarcation between state and federal regulation is at best uneasy.

[d] Current Status of the State-Federal Accommodation

Generally speaking, the McCarran-Ferguson Act gives state insurance statutes supremacy over federal laws, but this statement is subject to significant qualification. The Act does not give the states supremacy over *all* the activities of insurance companies; activities of insurers not within the "business of insurance" are subject to the full reach of Congress' authority under the Commerce Clause. Thus, many activities of insurers are subject to "paramount federal regulation" where the "business of insurance" is not involved.[18] Insurance companies must comply with federal tax laws, many of the filing and disclosure requirements of the securities laws, and federal labor laws. Moreover, Congress' decision in the McCarran-Ferguson Act to give state statutes primacy over Congress' exercise of its commerce power does not limit the applicability of the Equal Protection Clause.[19] Notwithstanding this hefty array of potential federal regulation, the insurance industry remains the largest American industry to escape significant federal regulation.

Nevertheless, the period since *South-Eastern Underwriters* and the enactment of the McCarran-Ferguson Act has been at best a period of uneasy accommodation of state and federal authority. The reasons for this tension can be found in ambiguities in the McCarran-Ferguson Act itself. In deciding whether an insurer's activity is exempt from federal regulation by virtue of the existence of a paramount state regulatory statute, the McCarran-Ferguson Act requires that one or more questions be answered:

(1) Is the challenged activity of the insurer within the "business of insurance" that the Act purports to exempt from federal regulation? The phrase "business of

---

[18] See Securities and Exchange Comm'n v. National Securities, Inc., 393 U.S. 453, 459–60 (1969). For a discussion of whether the Fair Housing Act, Title VIII of the Civil Rights Act of 1968, 42 U.S.C. §§ 2601–3619, applies to the insurance industry (specifically the denial of insurance coverage which may have the effect of making housing unavailable to the applicant), see Leo J. Jordan, *Property Insurance and Fair Housing,* 18 Forum 223 (1983).

[19] See Metropolitan Life Ins. Co. v. Ward, 470 U.S. 869 (1985). In *Ward,* the Court declared invalid a domestic preference tax statute, which favored domestic insurers, under the Equal Protection Clause.

insurance" appears in each of the substantive sections of the Act,[20] but the term is left undefined. If this question is answered in the negative, the inquiry need not proceed because the activity will have no special exemption from federal law.

(2) If the challenged activity is within the "business of insurance," is the federal statute sought to be applied to the activity one that "specifically relates" to the business of insurance? The "specifically relates to" exception in the main clause of section 2(b) (prior to the proviso) contemplates that federal legislation regulating the business of insurance, if specific enough, can override state legislation. Thus, if this question is answered affirmatively, the insurer's activity enjoys no protection from federal regulation, and the analysis ends.

(3) If the challenged activity is within the "business of insurance" and the federal statute sought to be applied is not one that "specifically relates" to the business of insurance, is the federal statute one that operates "to invalidate, impair, or supersede" a state law enacted "for the purpose of regulating the business of insurance"? The McCarran-Ferguson Act in section 2(b) prohibits construing an Act of Congress in a way that invalidates, impairs, or supersedes such a state law. If an Act is construed otherwise, or if the purpose of the state law is determined not to be regulating the business of insurance, the federal and state regulatory schemes can operate side by side.

(4) If it is a federal antitrust statute that is sought to be applied to the challenged activity, is the challenged insurer activity "regulated" by state law? The proviso in section 2(b) expressly contemplates that only if the challenged activity is "regulated" by state law does the McCarran-Ferguson Act proscribe federal antitrust regulation.

(5) If it is the Sherman Act that is sought to be applied to the challenged activity, does the challenged activity involve an "agreement to boycott, coerce, or intimidate" or an "act of boycott, coercion, or intimidation"? If so, in accordance with the language of section 3(b), the McCarran-Ferguson Act does not protect the activity from a challenge under the Sherman Act.

In the following subsections, each of the foregoing five questions is discussed.

[1] The "Business of Insurance"

The uneasy accommodation between state and federal authority in insurance regulation is due in large measure to the absence of a definition in the McCarran-Ferguson Act of the "business of insurance." This important phrase is the touchstone for determining whether federal regulation has been preempted by the states. During the three decades after the Act became law, only three Supreme Court decisions considered the meaning of the phrase.[21] However, in two decisions in 1979 and 1982, *Group Life & Health Insurance Co. v. Royal Drug Co.*[22] and *Union Labor*

---

[20] The only section of the Act in which the phrase "business of insurance" does not appear is section 5, which simply defines the term "state."

[21] See Securities and Exchange Comm'n v. National Securities, Inc., 393 U.S. 453 (1969); Securities and Exchange Comm'n v. Variable Annuity Life Ins. Co., 359 U.S. 65 (1959); Federal Trade Comm'n v. National Cas. Co., 357 U.S. 560 (1958).

[22] 440 U.S. 205 (1979). See generally Robert P. Rothman, Comment, *Definition of "Business of Insurance" Under the McCarran-Ferguson Act After Royal Drug,* 80 Colum. L. Rev. 1475 (1980).

Life Insurance Co. v. Pireno,[23] the Supreme Court articulated and refined a three-part test for determining whether an insurer's activity is within the business of insurance.

Under the *Royal Drug-Pireno* test, three questions must be asked when determining whether an insurer's activity constitutes the "business of insurance": (1) Does the activity involve the underwriting or spreading of risk? (2) Does the activity involve an integral part of the insurer-insured relationship? (3) Is the activity limited to entities within the insurance industry? The Court in *Pireno* stated that none of these tests is necessarily determinative, thereby indicating that a challenged insurer activity must be evaluated against all three criteria.

To satisfy the first part of the test, the insurer's activity must both transfer and distribute risk. This test was based in part on the Court's decision in *SEC v. Variable Annuity Life Insurance Co. of America,* a 1959 decision in which the Court held that the sale of variable-annuity contracts was beyond the scope of the business of insurance.[24] The plurality opinion stated that "absent some guarantee of fixed income, the variable annuity places all of the investment risks on the annuitant, none on the company. . . . But we conclude that the concept of 'insurance' involves some investment risk-taking on the part of the company,"[25] and none was found in the case.[26] Both *Royal Drug* and *Pireno* also indicated that the transfer of risk must be accompanied by an element of risk spreading: "[U]nless there is some element of spreading the risk more widely, there is no underwriting of risk."[27]

To satisfy the second part of the test, the insurer's activity must relate to an integral part of the contract between insurer and insured.[28] This part of the test was based on the Court's holding in *SEC v. National Securities, Inc.*[29] In *National Securities,* the SEC brought an action under federal securities laws seeking to enjoin the merger of two insurance companies. The trial court refused the SEC's request for a preliminary injunction, and shortly thereafter the shareholders and the Arizona Director of Insurance approved the merger. The SEC then amended its complaint to seek to unwind the merger. The District Court dismissed the complaint, holding in part that the SEC's action was barred by section 2(b) of the McCarran-Ferguson Act. The Court of Appeals affirmed, but the Supreme Court reversed. The Court stated that section 2(b) was designed to protect from impairment, invalidation, or preemption by congressional action state laws concerned with the relationship between the insurance company and its policyholders:

> Congress was concerned with the type of state regulation that centers around the contract of insurance. . . . The relationship between insurer and insured, the type of policy which could be issued, its reliability, interpretation, and

---

[23] 458 U.S. 119 (1982).

[24] 359 U.S. at 71–73.

[25] 359 U.S. at 71.

[26] 359 U.S. at 73.

[27] 440 U.S. at 214 n.12.

[28] *Pireno,* 458 U.S. at 128; *Royal Drug,* 440 U.S. at 215–16.

[29] 393 U.S. 453 (1969).

enforcement — these were the core of the "business of insurance." Undoubtedly, other activities of insurance companies relate so closely to their status as reliable insurers that they too must be placed in the same class. But whatever the exact scope of the statutory term, it is clear where the focus was — it was on the relationship between the insurance company and the policyholder. Statutes aimed at protecting or regulating this relationship, directly or indirectly, are laws regulating the "business of insurance."[30]

In *Royal Drug,* the Court refined the *National Securities* standard. The Court noted that in a broad sense "every business decision made by an insurance company has some impact on its reliability, its ratemaking, and its status as a reliable insurer. . . ." Such a view of section 2(b) would be too broad, the Court reasoned, since the statutory language "exempts the 'business of insurance' and not the 'business of insurance companies.' " Under this refinement of *National Securities,*[31] a refinement later reaffirmed in *Pireno,* an insurer's activity having only an "indirect" effect on the reliability of the insurer or on the insurer-insured relationship does not qualify as the "business of insurance."

To satisfy the third part of the *Royal Drug-Pireno* test, it is necessary to show that the challenged insurer activity is limited to entities within the insurance industry. The Court in *Royal Drug* looked to the legislative history of the McCarran-Ferguson Act and concluded that "the primary concern of both representatives of the insurance industry and the Congress was that cooperative ratemaking efforts be exempt from the antitrust laws."[32] Since the exemption's only purpose was to insulate conduct by industry actors from antitrust attack, the Court concluded that the exemption did not extend to activities involving parties outside the insurance industry.[33]

When applying this three-part test to the activities of insurers in both *Royal Drug* and *Pireno,* the Court concluded that the insurers did not enjoy antitrust immunity under section 2(b) of the McCarran-Ferguson Act. *Royal Drug* involved the following situation: Blue Shield, a Texas insurer, offered policies entitling insureds to purchase prescription drugs for $2 each from any pharmacy that participated in a "Pharmacy Agreement" with Blue Shield. Insureds could purchase prescription drugs from "nonparticipating" pharmacies, but the insureds would not have the benefit of the discounted price. All pharmacies in Texas were invited to sign the "Pharmacy Agreement," under which the pharmacy would be required to sell prescription drugs to Blue Shield's policyholders for $2 each and would be reimbursed by Blue Shield only for their costs. As a practical matter, only pharmacies that could profitably sell prescription drugs for less than a $2 markup could participate in the plan.

---

[30] 393 U.S. at 460.

[31] The opinion in *National Securities,* before discussing the importance of the insurer-policyholder relationship, actually made the same point: "The statute did not purport to make the States supreme in regulating all the activities of insurance *companies;* its language refers not to the persons or companies who are subject to state regulation, but to laws 'regulating the *business* of insurance.' " *National Securities, supra,* 393 U.S. at 459.

[32] 440 U.S. at 221.

[33] 440 U.S. at 231.

Owners of nonparticipating pharmacies sued Blue Shield and several participating pharmacies under section 1 of the Sherman Act, contending that the defendants had conspired to fix the retail prices of prescription drugs through the Pharmacy Agreements. The district court granted a summary judgment to Blue Shield and the other defendants, holding that the Agreements constituted the "business of insurance" within section 2(b) of the McCarran-Ferguson Act and that as such the Agreements were exempt from attack under the federal antitrust laws. The Second Circuit reversed, and the Supreme Court affirmed the reversal, holding that the Agreements were not the "business of insurance" and therefore were subject to scrutiny under the Sherman Act.

The Court reasoned that the Agreements did not satisfy the first test, since the Agreements "are merely arrangements for the purchase of goods and services by Blue Shield. . . . Such cost-savings arrangements may well be sound business practice, and may well inure ultimately to the benefit of policyholders in the form of lower premiums, but they are not the 'business of insurance.' "[34] As for the second test, the Court rejected Blue Shield's contention that the Agreements were integrally related to the "reliability, interpretation, and enforcement" of the policies.[35] And, since the Agreements involved parties outside the industry, the Court concluded that the Agreements did not meet the third test.[36]

Pireno involved an arrangement whereby a health insurer obtained professional advice from a peer review committee of a state chiropractic association. Under the agreement between the insurer and the association, upon the insurer's request the association would determine whether a policyholder's claim for reimbursement of the cost of chiropractic treatment involved reasonably necessary services and fair charges, thereby coming within the coverage of the insurer's policy. Plaintiff, an individual chiropractor, brought an action claiming that the arrangement violated section 1 of the Sherman Act in that it was a conspiracy to fix the prices that chiropractors would be allowed to charge for their services. The district court granted a summary judgment for the defendants on the ground that the insurer's use of peer review was part of the "business of insurance" exempted under section 2(b) of the McCarran-Ferguson Act. The Second Circuit reversed, holding that the arrangement did not satisfy the requirements of *Royal Drug*. The Supreme Court affirmed the Second Circuit.

Justice Brennan, writing for the six-justice majority, reasoned that the first prong of the three-part test was not met because the peer review process did not "spread" or "underwrite" risk. The process occurred only *after* the risk had been transferred. As for the second part of the test, the Court reasoned that the peer review process was not an integral part of the relationship between insurer and insured. Rather, the process was a separate arrangement between the insurer and parties outside the business of insurance; although peer review might assist the insurer in knowing which claims are within coverage, the Court thought this "a matter of indifference to the policyholder, whose only concern is *whether* his claim is paid, not *why* it is

---

[34] 440 U.S. at 214.
[35] 440 U.S. at 216.
[36] 440 U.S. at 224.

paid." As for the third factor, the Court observed that the peer review practices involved entities outside the insurance industry — practicing chiropractors. Accordingly, the insurer's activity, which was alleged to restrain competition in the market for chiropractic services, was not immune from antitrust scrutiny under section 2(b) of the McCarran-Ferguson Act.

The Supreme Court's decisions in *Royal Drug* and *Pireno* left several matters unresolved. In particular, confusion existed about the meaning of Justice Brennan's conclusion in applying the first prong of the test in *Pireno* that insurer activities after the transfer of the risk are not the business of insurance. Applied literally, the time that the policy is issued is when the risk is transferred from insured to insurer; if that were so, all aspects of the insurer's performance of its contract, including such activities as settling claims and paying proceeds, do not constitute the "business of insurance." Such a conclusion would vitiate the "business of insurance" antitrust exemption. Fortunately, this problem with *Royal Drug* and *Pireno* was clarified in the Court's 1993 decision in *United States Department of the Treasury v. Fabe*,[37] where a majority of the court stated:

> There can be no doubt that the actual performance of an insurance contract falls within the "business of insurance" as we understood that phrase in *Pireno* and *Royal Drug*. To hold otherwise would be mere formalism. The Court's statement in Pireno that the "transfer of risk from insured to insurer is effected by means of a contract between the parties . . . and . . . is complete at the time the contract is entered" . . . presumes that the insurance contract in fact will be enforced. Without performance of the terms of the insurance policy, there is no risk transfer at all.[39]

Fabe provides a more plausible construction of the first prong of the test; it is more cogent to view the completion of contract performance as the moment risk is transferred, and it would seem to follow that contract performance is not completed until the extent of the loss has been determined and the insured's claim settled. Yet such a construction would have pointed toward a different outcome in *Pireno* because the peer review process challenged in that case was part of the claims settlement process.

Additional confusion exists over the first prong's insistence that an activity, to constitute the business of insurance, must involve a significant transfer of risk from the policyholder to the insurer. This insistence has the potential to except from the business of insurance activities long thought safe from federal regulation. For example, it could be argued that cooperative ratemaking and pooling of loss data neither "directly" involve the insurer-insured relationship nor involve the transfer and distribution of risk. Similarly, it is arguable that other kinds of state regulation — such as supervision over the advertising and marketing of policies and the licensing of agents and companies — do not transfer or distribute risk and do not constitute an "integral part" of the relationship between insurer and insured. If the first prong of the *Royal Drug-Pireno* test is applied literally, these activities fall outside the

---

[37] 113 S.Ct. 2202 (1993).

[39] *Id.* at 2209 (quoting *Pireno*, 458 U.S. at 130).

business of insurance, even though they are precisely the kinds of activities that Congress sought to leave to state regulation.[40] Subsequent lower court decisions did not, however, apply the test so literally,[41] and other courts held other activities that would not pass muster under a technical reading of the statute safe from federal preemption.[42]

Although the ambiguity was not immediately apparent, the explanation in *Royal Drug* of the third prong, that "an exempt entity forfeits antitrust exemption by acting in concert with nonexempt parties,"[43] became the basis of an argument by plaintiffs in *Hartford Fire Insurance Co. v. California*[44] that defendant domestic insurers forfeited their antitrust exemption when they acted in concert with foreign insurers. The argument's logic was that the foreign insurers were already beyond the regulatory jurisdiction of the states (a point the *Hartford Fire* opinion would explicitly leave undecided) and therefore not the beneficiaries of section 2(b)'s exemption, and thus were "nonexempt" parties for the purpose of the third prong's test. In a unanimous portion of the *Hartford Fire* opinion, the Court clarified this aspect of *Royal Drug* and explained that domestic insurers do not lose their McCarran-Ferguson antitrust exemption "simply because they agreed or acted with foreign reinsurers."[45]

With so much ambiguity persisting after the decisions in *Royal Drug* and *Pireno*, there was some hope that the Supreme Court would bring clarity to the Act in its 1993 decision in *United States Department of the Treasury v. Fabe*.[46] Although, as noted above, *Fabe* cleared some of the air, considerable ambiguity survived the decision. In *Fabe*, the United States in proceedings under Ohio law to liquidate an insolvent insurer asserted priority under federal bankruptcy law on claims asserted as the obligee on various surety bonds. The Ohio Superintendent of Insurance, the liquidator appointed in state court, brought a declaratory judgment action seeking to establish that priority in the liquidation proceeding was controlled by Ohio law, which ranked the federal priority lower. The basis for the Superintendent's claim was that the state statute regulated the "business of insurance," and was therefore not preempted by the federal statute by virtue of section 2(b) of the McCarran-Ferguson Act. In a 5-4 decision with Justice Blackmun writing for the majority, the

---

[40] In this respect, the *Royal Drug-Pireno* test may overrule a portion of *National Securities,* where the Court stated: "Certainly the fixing of rates is part of this business; that is what *South-Eastern Underwriters* was all about. The selling and advertising of policies . . . and the licensing of companies and their agents . . . are also within the scope of the statute." 393 U.S. at 460.

[41] See, e.g., Owens v. Aetna Life & Cas. Co., 654 F.2d 218 (3d Cir.), cert. denied, 454 U.S. 1092 (1981); Proctor v. State Farm Mut. Auto. Ins. Co., 675 F.2d 308 (D.C.Cir. 1982), cert. denied, 459 U.S. 839 (1982).

[42] See, e.g., Steinberg v. Guardian Life Ins. Co., 486 F. Supp. 122 (E.D.Pa 1980) (insurer-agent relationships); Federal Trade Comm'n v. American Hosp. and Life Ins. Co., 357 U.S. 560 (1958) (advertising).

[43] 440 U.S. at 231.

[44] 113 S.Ct. 2891 (1993).

[45] 113 S.Ct. at 2903.

[46] 113 S.Ct. 2202 (1993).

Court held that the Ohio priority statute was not preempted to the extent it protected policyholders, but it was not a statute enacted for the purpose of regulating the business of insurance to the extent it was designed to further the interests of creditors rather than policyholders. Under this test, the preference in the Ohio statute for expenses in administering the insolvency proceeding was reasonably necessary to protect policyholders, and therefore took priority. However, the preferences conferred upon employees and other general creditors were "too tenuous" a connection to the ultimate aim of insurance, and therefore did not escape preemption.[47]

Justice Kennedy, writing for the dissent, did not agree that the activity in question — liquidation of an insolvent insurer — constituted the "business of insurance." As the dissenting opinion observed, liquidating an insurer does not involve protecting or regulating the relationship between insurer and policyholder or the spreading or underwriting of risk: "This is not the regulation of the business of insurance, but the regulation of creditors' rights in an insolvency proceeding."[48] The majority, however, extending from its recognition that contract performance is a part of the "business of insurance," reasoned that carrying out the enforcement of insurance contracts by ensuring the payment of policyholder claims despite an intervening insolvency constituted the "business of insurance."[49] Yet, as the dissent observed, once an insurer is bankrupt, no business of insurance transpires; no new contracts are written, and no existing policies are settled. The "ongoing business" of insurance is not involved, and the Ohio statute simply disburses an insolvent insurer's assets in an equitable manner.[50]

Fabe illustrates how difficult it is to define the state-federal accommodation a half-century after the enactment of McCarran-Ferguson. The question confronted in the case was relatively straightforward: whether the Ohio priority statute was a law "enacted for the purpose of regulating the business of insurance" within section 2(b) of the McCarran-Ferguson Act. Five members of the Supreme Court said yes, concluding that dissolving an insurer and terminating its business, along with deciding which policyholders will ultimately be paid on their claims, constitutes the "business of insurance." Four members of the Court said no, reasoning that dissolving an insolvent insurer and ranking the priorities of creditors (including policyholders) does not involve the "business of insurance," given that the insurer has ceased to function as an ongoing concern. With the Supreme Court splitting so closely on such a basic issue, it seems inevitable that much confusion will persist in the future over the scope of the business of insurance, and that the answers may change depending upon who is appointed to the Court in future years.

[2] The "Specifically Relates" Exception

The main clause of section 2(b) (prior to the proviso) contains a broadly phrased exception from the McCarran-Ferguson Act's effect of giving primacy to state regulation: where a federal statute "specifically relates" to the business of insurance,

---

[47] 113 S.Ct. at 2204.
[48] 113 S.Ct. at 2214.
[49] 113 S.Ct. at 2209.
[50] 113 S.Ct. at 2214.

the federal statute may be allowed to supersede a state statute regulating the business of insurance. The "specifically relates to" exception has not been particularly troublesome for courts.[51]

An example of the kind of statute that "specifically relates" to the business of insurance is section 4 of the McCarran-Ferguson Act, where Congress specified that nothing in the Act would prevent federal labor laws from applying to the business of insurance. Congress, in effect, repealed section 2(b) insofar as federal labor law is concerned. Thus, section 2(b)'s "specifically relates" clause states expressly what would have been implicit anyway — that in the future Congress might enact regulatory statutes and expressly apply these statutes to the business of insurance. At the same time, the language makes clear that any statute Congress might enact in the future regulating interstate commerce will not apply to the business of insurance absent a specific expression of congressional intent that the statute so applies.[52]

[3]   The Existence of a Conflict Between Federal and State Law

The language of section 2(b) that precludes federal preemption of state regulation is the phrase "to invalidate, impair, or supersede": if the federal statute would operate "to invalidate, impair, or supersede" a state law enacted "for the purpose of regulating the business of insurance," the federal law will not operate at all. However, if the federal statute does not conflict with the state statute, both statutes will operate side by side.

Applying this standard requires a dual inquiry. First, is the state law sought to be given primacy over a federal law one that was enacted for the purpose of regulating the business of insurance? In *SEC v. National Securities*,[53] the Supreme Court held that state laws intended to regulate either directly or indirectly the insurer-insured relationship are laws regulating the business of insurance.[54] Statutes within a state's insurance code are almost always intended to regulate the business of insurance.[55] In applying the language of the main clause (before the proviso) of

---

[51] One reason the issue has not been troublesome is that it is relatively easy to avoid. In Arizona Governing Committee v. Norris, 463 U.S. 1073 (1983), the Court explicitly left open the question whether Title VII specifically relates to the business of insurance within the meaning of the McCarran-Ferguson Act by observing that it was applying Title VII to employers, not to insurance companies, and therefore was not superseding any law applicable to the insurance business. 463 U.S. at 1087 n. 17.

[52] See Barnett Bank of Marion Cty. v. Gallagher, 43 F.3d 631 (11th Cir. 1995)(provisions of National Bank Act authorizing national banks in some locations to be agents for insurers do not specifically relate to the business of insurance); Cochran v. Paco, Inc., 606 F.2d 460 (5th Cir. 1979) (Truth in Lending Act does not specifically relate to the business of insurance).

[53] 393 U.S. 453 (1969).

[54] 393 U.S. at 460.

[55] But see United Services Auto. Ass'n v. Muir, 792 F.2d 356 (3d Cir. 1986), *cert. denied sub nom.*, Grode v. United Services Auto Ass'n, 479 U.S. 1031 (1987) (provision of state insurance code designed to prevent competition between banks and insurers is not regulation of business of insurance); Tingle v. Pacific Mutual Ins. Co., 996 F.2d 105 (5th Cir. 1993) (misrepresentation statute in insurance code not business of insurance and therefore preempted by ERISA).

section 2(b), courts have generally held that statutes of general applicability only incidentally regulating insurance companies do not entitle an insurer's challenged activity to McCarran-Ferguson Act immunity.[56]

The second part of the inquiry is whether a conflict exists between the federal and state statutes.[57] The federal statute sought to be applied will be denied operative effect only if it invalidates, impairs, or supersedes the state statute regulating the business of insurance. For purposes of deciding whether federal law overrides state law under ordinary Supremacy Clause analysis, a conflict exists when the state's law "stands as an obstacle to the accomplishment and execution of the full purposes and objectives of Congress."[58] By analogy, if the federal law, when applied, would obstruct the accomplishment and execution of the state's objective of regulating the business of insurance, the federal law must yield to the state law.[59] Dual or duplicative regulation, or the mere existence of an overlap, is not a conflict.[60]

Although this framework is easily stated, it is more difficult to apply. At the outset, it is important to recognize that because the inquiry has dual aspects, not every conflict between federal and state law gives supremacy to state law. If a state law is not intended to regulate the business of insurance, but is instead intended to

Confusion surrounds, however, state insurance regulation and the preemptive effect of the Employment Retirement Income Security Act ("ERISA"), §§ 29 U.S.C. 1001–1381. For additional discussion, see § 24[e], *infra*.

56 E.g., Hart v. Orion Ins. Co., 453 F.2d 1358 (10th Cir. 1971) (state arbitration code); Hamilton Life Ins. Co. v. Republic Nat'l Life Ins. Co., 408 F.2d 606 (2d Cir. 1969) (state arbitration code); Securities and Exchange Comm'n v. Republic Nat'l Life Ins. Co., 378 F. Supp. 430 (S.D. N.Y. 1974) (dictum). But see Washburn v. Corcoran 643 F. Supp. 554 (S.D. N.Y. 1986) (McCarran-Ferguson Act barred application of Federal Arbitration Act to matter concerning liquidation of insurer).

57 Whether a conflict exists is ultimately a question of constitutional proportions. The Supremacy Clause of the United States Constitution, Art. VI, cl. 2, provides that "the laws of the United States . . . shall be the supreme Law of the Land; . . . any Thing in the Constitution or Laws of any State to the Contrary notwithstanding." In the McCarran-Ferguson Act, Congress adopted a law expressly saving state legislation from the preemptive effect of the Supremacy Clause. See Securities and Exchange Comm'n v. National Securities, Inc., 393 U.S. 453 (1969) (McCarran-Ferguson Act protects some of Arizona's regulatory activities from "normal operations of the Supremacy Clause.") The power to "suspend" the Supremacy Clause is contained in the Clause itself, since a saving statute establishes as the law of the United States that state law is supreme. It is thus federal law that any state statute regulating the business of insurance has primacy over a federal statute that would, if applied, invalidate, impair, or supersede the state statute. Federal statutes supersede state statutes when Congress exercises its commerce power so as to preempt an entire field of regulation or when a conflict exists between federal and state law.

58 Jones v. Rath Packing Co., 430 U.S. 519, 525–26 (1977).

59 This does not violate the Supremacy Clause, since that clause ordains that federal law is supreme — and federal law in this instance ordains that state law is supreme.

60 See National Association for the Advancement of Colored People v. American Family Mut. Ins. Co., 978 F.2d 287 (7th Cir. 1992) (Fair Housing Act does not conflict with Wisconsin insurance regulation, which meant NAACP could challenge alleged redlining by insurer as a form of racial discrimination).

regulate, for example, securities transactions (i.e., the relationship between a stockholder in the insurance company and the corporate entity), an inconsistent federal law that regulates securities transactions will not yield to the state law, since the state law, though in conflict, does not regulate the "business of insurance."

A difficult problem is presented if one concludes, for example, that state regulation of the stockholder-corporation relationship is part of an effort to regulate the business of insurance, perhaps because regulating the payment of dividends to stockholders or approving acquisitions of domestic insurers through tender offers is necessary to ensure enough reserves to maintain the viability of policies held by the company's policyholders.[61] From such a conclusion, it follows that inconsistent federal securities regulation would impair state regulation of the business of insurance and that insurers should be immune from inconsistent aspects of federal securities law. Such a conclusion would no doubt be favored by some insurers, but the result could deprive stockholders of some protections and benefits they receive under federal securities laws.

[4]   Federal Antitrust Law and State Regulation

Determining whether state law has primacy over federal law is particularly complex in the antitrust area because the insurance industry's exemption from the antitrust laws is not total.[62] Section 2(b)'s proviso states that "after June 30, 1948, . . . the Sherman Act, and . . . the Clayton Act, and . . . the Federal Trade Commission Act, . . . shall be applicable to the business of insurance to the extent that such business *is not regulated by State Law*." The proviso raises a question as to whether a state statute "regulates" an aspect of the business of insurance sufficiently to prevent Congress or its delegate (such as, for example, the Federal Trade Commission) from intervening in the area.

This question is analogous to the question raised by the language of the main clause of section 2(b): under that provision, a state statute achieves primacy over federal law only if it were "enacted by [a] State for the purpose of regulating the business of insurance." As noted above, state insurance codes meet this test and thus override inconsistent federal laws, but courts have generally held that state statutes of general applicability that only incidentally regulate insurance companies do not

---

[61] Under the Supreme Court's decisions in *Royal Drug* and *Pireno* on the meaning of the "business of insurance," which as the text demonstrates are vulnerable to criticism, such a conclusion is probably incorrect. The insurer's relationship with its stockholders does not involve the underwriting or spreading of risk and the stockholders are presumably entities outside the insurance industry. As such, the insurer's relationship with its stockholders — even when the relationship has a direct effect upon the viability of insurance policies and thus a direct tie to the policyholder-insurer relationship — is probably not the business of insurance. Such a conclusion goes beyond *Securities and Exchange Comm'n v. National Securities, Inc.*, 393 U.S. 453 (1969), where the Court, in allowing the federal and state regulatory schemes to coexist, stopped short of concluding that the federal securities laws superseded state regulation. For further discussion, see § 21[d], *supra*.

[62] For an overview of antitrust and insurance generally, see Insurance Industry Committee, Section of Antitrust Law of the American Bar Association, *The Insurance Antitrust Handbook* (1995).

override federal laws. However, in applying the language of the proviso of section 2(b), courts have been more willing to treat statutes of general applicability, such as corporation codes, general business and professional codes, and state antitrust laws, as laws that regulate the business of insurance. In these cases, state legislatures are assumed to have made a judgment about the extent to which insurers should be regulated when the general state statutes were enacted. Using general statutes in this way allows the challenged insurer activity to acquire immunity from federal regulation without the state taking definite, overt efforts to regulate the insurer-insured relationship.[63]

Another difficulty in the language of the proviso is the extent to which a state must have effective regulation to avoid the application of federal antitrust law. At one extreme, the mere existence of a state statute could be enough to constitute state regulation that preempts federal regulation. Alternatively, a court might look behind the form of the statute to determine the extent to which it is actually enforced by state officials; unless meaningful enforcement exists, it could be said that the state is not "regulating" the area. The Supreme Court has not clearly spoken on this issue. In *Federal Trade Commission v. National Casualty Co.,*[64] the Supreme Court held that the area of deceptive advertising was sufficiently regulated by the states because appropriate statutes had been enacted. The Court limited this holding, however, by suggesting that in a future case a distinction might be made between the mere existence of a statute and the effectiveness of its enforcement.[65] Lower courts have generally been inclined to interpret the section 2(b) proviso's preemptive effect on federal regulation more broadly, and thus have afforded primacy to a reasonably comprehensive state statutory scheme authorizing state regulation of some facet of the insurance business.[66] However, it is likely that Congress intended the antitrust exemption to be available only when effective state regulation, rather than a mere pretense of regulation, exists.[67] One matter is clear: the exemption, when it does

---

[63] See California League of Independent Ins. Producers v. Aetna Cas. & Sur. Co., 175 F. Supp. 857 (N.D. Cal. 1959) (California statute authorizing cooperation between insurance companies in ratemaking held sufficient regulation over relationship of insurance agents and insurers to preempt agents' action claiming violation of Sherman Act because insurance companies agreed to decrease the rate of commissions); Manasen v. California Dental Services, 424 F. Supp. 657 (N.D. Cal. 1976), *rev'd on other grounds,* 638 F.2d 1152 (9th Cir. 1979) (in suit by dentists against corporation providing prepaid dental plans, state antitrust law, corporation code and business and professions code are sufficient to constitute state regulation of business of insurance). See Steven Koch, Note, *McCarran-Ferguson Act Immunity from the Truth in Lending Act and Title VII,* 48 U. Chi. L. Rev. 730, 750 (1981).

[64] 357 U.S. 560 (1958).

[65] Although involving state-action immunity and not McCarran-Ferguson immunity, this distinction was explicitly recognized and applied by the Court in Federal Trade Comm'n v. Ticor Title Ins. Co., 504 U.S. 621 (1992).

[66] See Ohio AFL-CIO v. Insurance Rating Bd., 451 F.2d 1178 (6th Cir. 1971), *cert. denied,* 409 U.S. 917 (1972); Steinberg v. Guardian Life Ins. Co. of Am., 486 F. Supp. 122, 124 (E.D.Pa. 1980); California League of Independent Ins. Producers v. Aetna Cas. & Sur. Co., 175 F. Supp. 857, 860 (N.D. Cal. 1959).

[67] For excellent discussions of this point, see Larry O. Carlson, *The Insurance Exemption from the Antitrust Laws,* 57 Tex. L. Rev. 1127, 1140–61 (1979); Kimball & Boyce, note 14, *supra,* at 570–75.

exist, only operates to protect insurer activity that either occurs or has its effect in the state seeking to apply its own regulatory scheme. In *FTC v. Travelers Health Ass'n*,[68] the Supreme Court held that one state's regulation cannot provide an exemption for insurer activity occurring beyond its borders.[69] The upshot of this holding is that regulatory activity in one or even a few states is not sufficient to create immunity for the challenged activity in all other states or in states where no regulation exists.

[5] The Boycott, Coercion, and Intimidation Exception

If one seeks to subject a insurer's activity to Sherman Act scrutiny, the Sherman Act will apply — even if the insurer's activity constitutes the "business of insurance" and even if state law regulates it — if the activity involves a boycott, coercion, or intimidation. Section 3(b) of the McCarran-Ferguson Act provides that nothing in the Act "shall render the Sherman Act inapplicable to any agreement to boycott, coerce, or intimidate, or any act of boycott, coercion, or intimidation." The meaning of the statute is not self-evident on its face. The principal ambiguity, on which the legislative history is not helpful, is whether the section 3(b) exception to the McCarran-Ferguson Act's scheme of giving primacy to state law pertains only to insurer activity against other insurers or more broadly to insurer activity affecting policyholders and the general public.

The Supreme Court has spoken to the meaning of "boycott" in section 3(b) on two occasions. In 1978, the Court decided *St. Paul Fire & Marine Insurance Co. v. Barry*,[70] in which it held that the boycott exception extends to insurer activities affecting parties outside the industry, a conclusion which narrows the domain of state primacy. In *Barry*, Rhode Island physicians had refused to accept an unfavorable change in their malpractice policies. Other malpractice insurers in the state refused to insure the physicians. The physicians sued the insurers for violating the Sherman Act, and the insurers successfully moved to dismiss the antitrust claim on the ground that it was barred by the McCarran-Ferguson Act. The court of appeals reversed, holding that the complaint stated a claim within the 'boycott' exception of section 3(b). Thus, the issue before the court was whether the boycott exception applies to disputes between policyholders and insurers.

The insurers argued that the term "boycott" refers only to combinations or restraints that target competitors of the boycotters as the objects of the refusal to deal. Because the insurers' alleged refusal to deal did not target other insurers, it was argued that the section 3(b) exception did not apply.[71] But the Court observed

---

[68] 362 U.S. 293 (1960).

[69] In *Travelers Health*, the insurer operated a mail order business throughout the country from its Nebraska office, even though licensed only in Nebraska and Virginia. The FTC issued a cease and desist order against the making of certain statements in the advertisement. The Court held that the FTC's jurisdiction could be preempted by the state regulation of the place where the improper activity had its effect, i.e., where the advertising was received. However, Nebraska's unfair advertising statute could not reach beyond Nebraska's authority; therefore, the FTC ruling was sustained.

[70] 438 U.S. 531 (1978).

[71] 438 U.S. at 533.

that in the labor-boycott cases, which provided necessary context for the meaning of the "boycott," it was not essential that the boycotters and the ultimate targets be in competition with each other. The Court concluded that

> [w]hatever other characterizations are possible, petitioners' conduct fairly may be viewed as "an organized boycott" . . . of St. Paul's policyholders. . . . This agreement did not simply fix rates or terms of coverage; it effectively barred St. Paul's policyholders from all access to alternative sources of coverage and even from negotiating for more favorable terms elsewhere in the market.[72] Having found that the "conduct in question accords with the common understanding of a boycott,"[73] the Court concluded that the alleged conduct fell within the section 3(b) exception. In elaborating upon the scope of the holding, the Court described the defendants' conduct as a refusal to deal on any terms,[74] and pointed out that "conduct by individual actors falling short of concerted activity is simply not a 'boycott' within § 3(b),"[75] and that it was not holding "all concerted activity violative of the Sherman Act [to be] within § 3(b)."[76]

Barry left the scope of the section 3(b) exception unclear. Read broadly, the Court's holding seemed to give standing to members of the public to challenge a rate agreed upon by a group of insurers and subsequently approved by the state on the ground that the insurers had concertedly refused to deal with the public on terms other than their agreed-upon price.[77] This was the concern articulated by the dissent. If this broad reading was intended by the majority, the section 3(b) exception would swallow up all of section 2, thereby exposing insurers to antitrust liability generally.[78] Such a reading would not seem likely, but the fact that the Court's opinion in *Barry* did not foreclose the mere asking of the question revealed the ambiguity of the holding.

In 1993, the Court decided *Hartford Fire Insurance Co. v. California*,[79] a case in which 19 states and numerous private parties brought antitrust suits against domestic insurers, domestic and foreign reinsurers, and insurance brokers on account of their alleged agreement to boycott general liability insurers that used nonconforming forms. The district court granted the defendants' motion to dismiss on the ground, inter alia, that defendants had antitrust immunity under section 2(b) of the McCarran-Ferguson Act. The court of appeals reversed, basing part of its decision on the conclusion that most of the alleged conduct fell within the section 3(b) exception. In an opinion complicated by the fact that different majorities joined the separate opinions of Justices Souter and Scalia, the Court elaborated upon the issues confronted two decades earlier in *Barry*.

---

[72] 438 U.S. at 544.

[73] 438 U.S. at 544.

[74] 438 U.S. at 544.

[75] 438 U.S. at 555.

[76] 438 U.S. at 555.

[77] Cf. Blue Shield of Virginia v. McCready, 457 U.S. 465 (1982) (consumer has standing to assert antitrust violation based on alleged conspiracy between Blue Shield and psychiatric society to exclude psychologists from receiving compensation under health insurance plans).

[78] Carlson, note 67, *supra,* at 1168.

[79] 113 S.Ct. 2891 (1993).

Although the Court split 5-4 on the section 3(b) issue, the majority and dissenting opinions did have some common ground, as Justice Souter explained. First, "only those refusals to deal involving the coordinated action of multiple actors constitute § 3(b) boycotts."[80] This much had been said in *Barry*. Second, a section 3(b) boycott need not involve an "absolute refusal to deal." As was the situation in *United States v. South-Eastern Underwriters Ass'n*,[81] a concerted refusal to deal with competitors to attempt to force non-member insurers into conspiracies would fit the definition.[82] Third, "a § 3(b) boycott need not entail unequal treatment of the targets of the boycott and its instigators."[84] Fourth, concerted activity, although essential to a boycott, is not by itself sufficient to establish a "boycott" under section 3(b). Some kind of "enforcement activity," i.e., a concerted effort to obtain objectives through the additional exercise of some kind of power or leverage.[85] Where the majority and dissenters parted company was over the issue of what degree of additional conduct besides concerted behavior was required to create a section 3(b) boycott.

Four justices joined Justice Scalia's analysis of the section 3(b) exception. In explaining the meaning of the term "boycott," Justice Scalia rejected the view hat a boycott requires an absolute refusal to deal on any terms. Although such conduct definitely constitutes a boycott, a boycott exists in "less absolute" circumstances; that is, a concerted refusal to deal on specified terms may (or may not) be a boycott.[86] Justice Scalia explained that a boycott may be "conditional" in the sense that a refusal to deal may offer the target the chance of renewed dealings when the target acquiesces in the boycotters' demands. In addition, a boycott may be "partial," as when the boycott involves a refusal to deal in some, but not all transactions with the target.[87] Justice Scalia distinguished a conditional boycott from a "concerted agreement to seek particular terms in particular transactions";[88] the latter does not involve coercion because it simply involves an announcement of an intent not to deal except upon particular terms. However, if the concerted agreement is expanded into a refusal to deal with the target on unrelated transactions or for unrelated purposes in an attempt to coerce acquiescence on the specified terms, the conduct becomes a boycott (although perhaps only a "partial boycott" if the parties seeking to impose terms continued to deal with the targets on some transactions).[89] Under

---

[80] 113 S.Ct. at 2903.

[81] 322 U.S. 533 (1944).

[83] 113 S.Ct. at 2903-04.

[84] 113 S.Ct. at 2904.

[85] 113 S.Ct. at 2904.

[86] See 113 S.Ct. at 2912.

[87] 113 S.Ct. at 2912.

[88] 113 S.Ct. at 2911.

[89] 113 S.Ct. at 2911. Under this framework, *Barry* was correctly decided, according to Justice Scalia, because the refusal of the St. Paul's competitors (three other insurers) to deal with St. Paul's customers involved a condition unrelated to the contracts in question: to deal with the three insurers, one could not have been a St. Paul customer. 113 S.Ct. at 2914. However, Justice Powell's language in *Barry* that a boycott is a refusal to deal on any terms, see St. Paul Fire & Marine Ins. Co. v. Barry, 438 U.S. 531, 544 (1978), while correct, is too narrow because a section 3(b) boycott can be a refusal to deal on specified terms (which necessarily includes a willingness to deal on some terms).

Justice Scalia's reasoning, the mere refusal of reinsurers to provide reinsurance if the language of underlying primary policies were not changed would not be a boycott; instead, it was simply a concerted announcement of an intent not to deal except upon particular terms. However, the complaints contained sufficient allegations of "boycott" to sustain the relevant counts of the complaint against a motion to dismiss.[90]

Four Justices, including Justice Souter who wrote the dissent to Justice Scalia's opinion, found the majority's definition of "boycott" to be too narrow. After a detailed analysis of the pleadings in the case, Justice Souter concluded that the majority's decision that 'boycott' encompasses just those refusals to deal that are 'unrelated' or 'collateral' to the objective sought by those refusing to deal" was "at odds with our own description of our Sherman Act cases in *Barry*."[91]

After *Hartford Fire*, it is fair to say that the scope of the section 3(b) exception is better understood than in years past, but the precise meaning of "boycott" as that term is used in section 3(b) remains elusive, and as a practical matter this means that future development of the meaning of "boycott" in future litigation is inevitable.[92]

[6] The Future of the State-Federal Accommodation

If one thing is clear, it is that the extent to which the McCarran-Ferguson Act gives primacy to state regulation is unclear. Commentators have suggested new frameworks to clarify and refine the existing body of law.[93] In recent years, Congress has considered proposals to amend the McCarran-Ferguson Act.[94] Those advocating changes in the Act contend that making the insurance industry subject to federal antitrust law would promote competition in the industry, thereby

---

[90] 113 S.Ct. at 2917.

[91] 113 S.Ct. at 2908.

[92] In October 1994, the insurers and insurer organizations reached an out-of-court settlement with the attorney generals and several private plaintiffs. Under the agreement, the defendants will contribute $36 million to create an institute which will provide risk-management education, technical services, and a public entity insurance database for local government agencies. Also, the ISO will be reorganized so that it is controlled by persons in the insurance industry but not executives of large insurance companies. For a spirited discussion of the disputed fact issues in the *Hartford Fire* litigation, compare Ian Ayres & Peter Siegelman, *The Economics of the Insurance Antitrust Suits: Toward an Exclusionary Theory*, 63 Tul. L. Rev. 971 (1989), with George Priest, *The Antitrust Suits and the Public Understanding of Insurance*, 63 Tul. L. Rev. 999 (1989).

[93] See, e.g., Alan M. Anderson, *Insurance and Antitrust Law: The McCarran-Ferguson Act and Beyond*, 25 Wm. & Mary L. Rev. 81 (1983); G. Keith Nedrow, *The McCarran Controversy: Insurance and the Antitrust Law*, 12 Conn. L. Rev. 205 (1980); Steven Koch, Note, *McCarran-Ferguson Act Immunity from the Truth in Lending Act and Title VII*, 48 U. Chi. L. Rev. 730 (1981); see also Earl W. Kintner, Joseph P. Bauer, & Michael J. Allen, *Application of the Antitrust Laws to the Activities of Insurance Companies: Heavier Risks, Expanded Coverage, and Greater Liability*, 63 N.C. L. Rev. 431 (1985).

[94] See, e.g., Ruth Gastel, ed., *Antitrust*, Insurance Information Institute Reports (Nov. 1994) (discussing 1994 proposals and reactions to them); *Insurance Competition Improvement Act, S. 2474*, Hearing before the Subcomm. on Antitrust, Monopoly and Business Rights of the Senate Comm. on the Judiciary, 96th Cong., 2d Sess. (May 29, 1980).

benefiting consumers and society generally. Whatever the merit of this position, amending or repealing the McCarran-Ferguson Act would have effects beyond anti-trust law because the Act saves state regulation from federal preemption in other areas as well.[95]

The fundamental question underlying this discussion is what kind of accommoda-tion between federal and states interests *should* exist in the regulation of insurance. Until the 1980s, the primacy of the state role was sometimes questioned, but never seriously. The liability insurance crisis of the mid-1980s, when prices escalated and many businesses and municipalities found themselves without coverage for some important kinds of risk, and highly visible failures of some large insurance companies during the late 1980s and early 1990s led to unprecedented scrutiny of the state regulatory system, a scrutiny which has continued into the mid-1990s. In an era when the proper relationship of the federal and state governments is vigorously debated, the precise direction of changes in the uneasy accommodation is extremely difficult to predict. However, recent political trends suggest that any substantial shift of state responsibility to the federal level is unlikely.

[e]   State-Federal Accommodation Issues Arising Under ERISA

In the Employee Income Retirement Security Act of 1974 ("ERISA"),[96] Congress created one of the knottiest problems of statutory interpretation imaginable. Justice Blackmun's observation in *Metropolitan Life Insurance Co. v. Massachusetts*,[97] that the two preemption sections of the statute "perhaps are not a model of legislative drafting"[98] must rank as one of the great judicial understatements of all time. Unfortunately, this complexity cannot be ignored; ERISA has an impact on an enormous number of questions relating to group insurance plans, and the relationship of ERISA to the McCarran-Ferguson Act says a great deal about the accommodation of federal and state interests in insurance regulation.

ERISA is a comprehensive federal regulatory scheme for employee benefit (i.e., pension and welfare) plans, which are defined as a plan, fund, or program maintained or established by an employer "for the purpose of providing for its participants or their beneficiaries, through the purchase of insurance or otherwise,"[99] certain fringe benefits, including "medical, surgical, or hospital care or benefits."[100] ERISA artic-ulates a variety of requirements relating to participation, funding, and vesting of benefits in benefit plans,[101] and creates uniform standards for reporting, disclosure,

---

[95] See Group Life & Health Ins. Co. v. Royal Drug Co., 440 U.S. 205, 218 n.18 (1979) ("the *primary* purpose of the McCarran-Ferguson Act was to preserve state regulation of the activities of insurance companies. . . . The question in the present case, however, is one under the quite different *secondary* purpose of the McCarran-Ferguson Act — to give insurance companies only a limited exemption from the antitrust laws.")

[96] 29 U.S.C. § 1001 et seq.

[97] 471 U.S. 741 (1985).

[98] 471 U.S. at 739.

[99] 29 U.S.C. § 1002(1). The "or otherwise" contemplates that some employee pension or welfare plans may be self-funded, i.e. self-insured.

[100] 29 U.S.C. § 1002(3).

[101] 29 U.S.C. §§ 1051-1086.

and fiduciary duties.[102] As numerous courts have subsequently observed, it was the clear intention of Congress to occupy the field of regulation of employee benefit plans, to the exclusion of even consistent state regulation.[103] In an effort to make this preemptive effect clear, ERISA's drafters created an express preemption provision in section 514 of the statute,[104] which was itself composed of three inter-related directives.

The first directive in section 514, the "preemption clause," stated that the provisions of ERISA "shall supersede any and all State laws insofar as they may now or hereafter relate to any employee benefit plan."[105] The key phrase in the preemption clause is "relate to": the state law in question must "relate to" the employee benefit plan for ERISA's preemption to apply, and state statutes which do not "relate to" such plans can be applied without regard to ERISA.

Yet ERISA's drafters desired to preserve in the states the authority to regulate some areas in which the states enjoyed primacy. Thus, the second directive in section 514, the "saving clause," stated that "except as provided in [the deemer clause, the third directive], nothing in this subchapter shall be construed to exempt or relieve any person from any law of any State which regulates insurance, banking, or securities."[106] The saving clause, both in its language and intent, shadows the McCarran-Ferguson Act, even though the precise relationship between the saving clause and McCarran-Ferguson is not clear. As stated in *Metropolitan Life*,[107] "[t]he ERISA saving clause, with its similarly worded protection of 'any law of any State which regulates insurance,' appears to have been designed to preserve the McCarran-Ferguson Act's reservation of the business of insurance to the States. The saving clause and the McCarran-Ferguson Act serve the same federal policy and utilize similar language to define what is left to the States." This federal policy gives primacy to state regulation of the business of insurance.[108]

As the language of the saving clause anticipates, the "deemer clause," the third directive in section 514, modifies the savings clause by providing that "[n]either an employee benefit plan . . . nor any trust established under such a plan, shall be deemed to be an insurance company or other insurer, bank, trust company, or investment company or to be engaged in the business of insurance or banking for purposes of any law of any State purporting to regulate insurance companies,

---

[102] 29 U.S.C. §§ 1021-31, 1101-14.

[103] Metropolitan Life Insurance Co. v. Massachusetts, 471 U.S. 741, 739 (1985); Tri-State Machine, Inc. v. Nationwide Life Ins. Co., 33 F.3d 309, 312 (4th Cir. 1994); Custer v. Pan American Life Ins. Co., 12 F.3d 410, 418 (4th Cir. 1993).

[104] 29 U.S.C. § 1144.

[105] ERISA § 514(a), 29 U.S.C. § 1144(a).

[106] ERISA § 514(b)(2)(A), 29 U.S.C. § 1144(b)(2)(A).

[107] 471 U.S. 741 at 744 n.21 (1985).

[108] See Wolfson v. Mutual Benefit Life Ins. Co., 51 F.2d 141 (8th Cir. 1995)(claim for life insurance benefits under ERISA plan was properly stayed because insurer was subject of pending state rehabilitation proceeding in state court); Stuart Circle Hospital Corp. v. Aetna Health Management, 995 F.2d 500 (4th Cir.), *cert. denied,* 114 S.Ct. 579 (1993) (state statute regulating mandatory providers of health care saved from ERISA preemption).

insurance contracts, banks, trust companies, or investment companies."[109] The deemer clause has the effect of prohibiting a state from regulating self-insured employee benefit plans under the reasoning that such plans constitute the "business of insurance." The distinction the deemer clause seeks to draw is between the business of insurance companies, which is regulated by state law notwithstanding ERISA, and the business of employee benefit plans, which are subject to exclusive federal regulation even though self-insured plans resemble traditional insurance in many respects.

The three directives in section 514 of ERISA are complex in their own right. When this complexity is combined with a wide variety of state law, both statutory and decisional, relating to insurance (and group insurance in particular), it is not surprising that courts have been presented with a broad range of issues requiring evaluation of where the federal-state boundary should be located when insurance is one of the benefits in an employee benefit plan.

The first significant Supreme Court case[110] to consider the ERISA preemption issue was *Shaw v. Delta Air Lines*,[111] a 1983 decision. At issue in *Shaw* were two New York statutes, one of which prohibited discrimination in employee benefit plans on the basis of pregnancy and the other which required employers to pay sick-leave benefits to employees who could not work due to pregnancy. The Court held that the state laws "related to" an employee benefit plan because, relying on *Black's Law Dictionary,* the statutes had a "connection with or reference to" such a plan, and Congress's intent to give the phrase "relates to" a broad meaning meant no preemption analysis was necessary.[112]

The scope of ERISA preemption received further elucidation two years later in *Metropolitan Life Insurance Co. v. Massachusetts*,[113] At issue was a Massachusetts law that required insureds to provide certain mental health benefits. The insurer challenged the statute on the grounds that the mandated benefits statute was a health law, not an insurance law, and was therefore not saved from ERISA preemption by the savings clause. The Court rejected this argument and held that the statute was saved from preemption. The Court explained that mandated benefits statutes are within the ambit of traditional insurance laws and had been considered regulation of the "business of insurance" under judicial interpretations of the McCarran-Ferguson Act.[114] Significantly, the holding in *Metropolitan Life* created, as the Court itself explicitly recognized, a distinction between insured employee benefit plans and uninsured (or self-insured) employee benefit plans: the former are subject

---

[109] ERISA § 514(b)(2)(B), 29 U.S.C. § 1144(b)(2)(B).

[110] In Alessi v. Raybestos-Manhattan, Inc., 451 U.S. 504 (1981), the Court held that ERISA preempted a New Jersey statute that prohibited reducing pension benefits by an amount equal to any workers' compensation award for which a retiree was eligible. The Court reasoned that the statute eliminated a method for calculating pension benefits that federal law permitted, but the Court did not probe ERISA's preemption language in detail.

[111] 463 U.S. 85 (1983).

[112] 463 U.S. at 96-97.

[113] 471 U.S. 741 (1985).

[114] 471 U.S. at 743-44.

to indirect state regulation when the savings clause allows insurance laws to be applied, but the latter are immune from state regulation. But the Court said this was a distinction created by Congress, ordained by Congress's decision to save state insurance regulation from ERISA preemption.[115]

Metropolitan Life left unresolved the question of what other kinds of state laws, in addition to mandated benefit statutes, "relate to" employee benefit plans but are nevertheless saved from preemption under the savings clause. This question would not remain unaddressed for long; in an important 1987 decision, the Court considered whether state laws regulating an insurance company's handling of claims for ERISA benefits are saved from preemption. In *Pilot Life Insurance Co. v. Dedeaux*,[116] Dedeaux, who had injured his back at work, was covered for long-term disability benefits under his employer's ERISA plan. The plan was insured under a policy issued by Pilot Life, which had the authority to decide and process claims. Dedeaux received benefits for two years after the accident, but for the next three years the insurer allegedly terminated and reinstated benefits several times. Dedeaux sued Pilot Life for tortious breach of contract, breach of fiduciary duties, and fraud, and sought damages for emotional distress and punitive damages. The insurer argued that ERISA preempted Dedeaux's common law bad faith claims, and the district court agreed. The Fifth Circuit reversed, but the Supreme Court agreed with the district court and held Dedeaux's claims preempted.[117]

In sorting through the preemption issue, the Court first observed that it was apparent that Dedeaux's claims "relate[d] to" an employee benefit plan and therefore fell within the preemption clause in section 514(a).[118] This led to the next step, an analysis of the effect of the savings clause. Here the Court called upon its prior decisions defining "business of insurance" under the McCarran-Ferguson Act,[119] and reasoned that the phrase "regulates insurance" in the savings clause requires that a state statute must "not just have an impact on the insurance industry, but must be specifically directed toward that industry."[120] The Court concluded that the law of bad faith has its roots in general principles of tort and contract law, not laws that regulate insurance as such. Moreover, the Court observed that under the three-factor test for "business of insurance" under the McCarran-Ferguson Act,[121] the common law of bad faith does not affect the spreading of policyholder risk, an essential element of the "business of insurance." Similarly, although the common law of bad faith has a connection to the relationship between insurer and insured, another of the three-factor requirements, the relationship is "attenuated at best," unlike the situation in *Metropolitan Life*: the law of bad faith "is therefore no more 'integral' to the insurer-insured relationship than any State's general contract law is integral to a contract made in that state."[122] Thus, the court concluded that the savings clause did not protect Dedeaux's bad faith claims from ERISA preemption.

---

[115] 471 U.S. at 747.
[116] 481 U.S. 41 (1987).
[117] 481 U.S. at 43-44.
[118] 418 U.S. at 47.
[119] 481 U.S. at 48 (discussing *Union Labor Life Ins. Co. v. Pireno,* 458 U.S. 119 (1982).
[120] 481 U.S. at 50.
[121] See § 21[d], *supra.*
[122] 481 U.S. at 51.

Finally, the court evaluated Dedeaux's common law claims in light of what it characterized as ERISA's comprehensive civil enforcement scheme, and concluded that "the deliberate care with which ERISA's civil enforcement remedies were drafted and the balancing of policies embodied in its choice of remedies argue strongly for the conclusion that ERISA's civil enforcement remedies were intended to be exclusive."[123] after which the ERISA[124] preemption section was modeled and which displaced all state law actions pertaining to violations of contracts between employers and labor organizations.[125]

The immediate effect of *Pilot Life* is to preempt bad faith law with respect to insurance provided as part of an employee benefit plan. This effect is a substantial one; because most health insurance, much life insurance, and some disability insurance are provided as fringe benefits in the employment setting, insureds in these situations cannot assert insurers' bad faith performance of their contract obligations, and can only claim those remedies specifically provided by ERISA. This development, perhaps more than any other, moderated what was in the 1970s and early 1980s a seemingly explosive growth in insurer bad faith liability.[126] By the same token, however, preemption of state claims where ERISA provides no remedy means that some plan participants or their beneficiaries who bring certain kinds of state actions (such as wrongful death actions) may have no remedy at all.[127]

Given prior Supreme Court holdings recognizing the broad preemptive effect of ERISA to secure the objective of national uniformity in the regulation of employee benefit plans, the result in *Pilot Life* is not surprising. But the result was hardly inevitable. The Court could have held that national uniformity requires preempting state laws that regulate the actual performance by insurers of claim processing obligations (i.e., whether an insurer could deny a claim), but that national uniformity does not require uniform remedies for insurers' breach of their obligations once the law of ERISA has answered the question of whether the insurer acted properly.

Also, there was no necessary reason for the Court relying on the McCarran-Ferguson Act's definition of "business of insurance" to help define the scope of "insurance" in the ERISA preemption statute, given that the language in the two statutes is not precisely the same and thus could be given different interpretations, particularly since McCarran-Ferguson and ERISA are very different statutes. This alternative analysis would have upheld Dedeaux's right to seek a remedy for bad faith breach under Mississippi law if he could have established Pilot Life's failure to adhere to its ERISA obligations.

---

[123] 481 U.S. at 54. The Court found support for this conclusion in section 301 of the Labor-Management Relations Act,

[124] 29 U.S.C. § 185.

[125] 481 U.S. at 55-56.

[126] For more discussion of this point, see Kenneth Abraham, *The Natural History of the Insurer's Liability for Bad Faith,* 72 Tex. L. Rev. 1295 (1994).

[127] See Tolton v. American Biodyne, Inc., 48 F.3d 937 (6th Cir. 1995) (rejecting bad faith claim); Kuhl v. Lincoln National Health Plan, 999 F.2d 298 (8th Cir. 1993)(no remedy for plaintiff alleging husband's death resulted in delayed authorization for surgery); Settles v. Golden Rule Ins. Co., 927 F.2d 505 (10th Cir. 1991) (no remedy for wrongful death action against ERISA health plan).

Moreover, there is some danger in using the "business of insurance" definition as developed in the cases applying the McCarran-Ferguson Act to decide the scope of ERISA preemption. For example, it has been held that a state statute defining what constitutes misrepresentation on an insurance application is preempted by ERISA because the statute does not "effect a spreading of policyholder risk," one of the three requirements of the *Royal Drug-Pireno* test.[128] This kind of analysis means that a broad range of what has traditionally been considered the regulation of the business of insurance could be preempted by ERISA. This result would be troubling, because state statutes, like the misrepresentation statutes, are aimed directly at the business of insurance, unlike, for example, statutes of general applicability that might happen to touch in some way upon the affairs of insurers.[129]

To put this discussion in its broader context, what is at stake is whether state law or federal law will be paramount in the regulation of insurance which is provided as part of an employee benefit plan. Congress's intent, as the Court has recognized, is to establish a uniform regulatory system that relieves plan administrators from the burdens of dealing with conflicting state regulations. To the extent remedies available to plan participants differ from state to state, the calculations of plan benefit levels in light of anticipated liabilities will vary from state to state, which is burdensome for employee benefit plans that are multi-state in their operations.[130] With these concerns apparently in mind, the Supreme Court in *Pilot Life* came down firmly on the side of favoring federal law.

Pilot Life, notwithstanding its substantial impact, did not resolve all preemption issues under ERISA. In 1990, the Supreme Court decided *FMC Corp. v. Holliday*,[131] in which it held that a Pennsylvania statute disallowing subrogation against a person's recovery arising out of an auto accident was preempted by ERISA. In this case, Holliday received reimbursement from a self-funded employee benefit plan for a portion of her medical expenses arising out of an auto accident. Her tort claim against the driver of the auto in which she was injured was settled, and the employer gave notice that it would seek reimbursement for the amounts it had paid for her medical expenses. Holliday refused reimbursement under the reasoning that the state anti-subrogation statute prevented the employer from exercising a subrogation right. The Court observed initially that the anti-subrogation statute "relate[s] to" an employee benefit plan.[132] Applying the *Shaw* "connection with or reference to" test, the Court found in the text of the Pennsylvania statute itself a reference to benefit plans.[133] The Court also found a connection between the statute and the plan in the fact that the Pennsylvania statute would have an impact on costs in Pennsylvania dissimilar to impacts in other states, and this differentiation "would complicate the

---

[128] See Tingle v. Pacific Mut. Ins. Co., 996 F.2d 105 (5th Cir. 1993).

[129] See Anderson v. Humana, Inc., 24 F.2d 889 (7th Cir. 1994) (employee's state claim against HMO sponsor alleging violation of state consumer fraud act for failure to disclose certain information held preempted by ERISA). See generally Annot., *Coverage of Insurance Transactions Under State Consumer Protection Statutes*, 77 A.L.R.4th 991 (1990).

[130] See FMC Corp. v. Holliday, 498 U.S. 52 (1990).

[131] 498 U.S. 52 (1990).

[132] 498 U.S. at 58.

[133] 498 U.S. at 59.

administration of nationwide plans, producing inefficiencies that employers might offset with decreased benefits."[134] The Court then observed that the statute was clearly protected by the savings clause, as the anti-subrogation statute was a direct regulation of the insurance industry.[135] Having reached this conclusion, the anti-subrogation statute would not be preempted unless the deemer clause took the statute outside the reach of the saving clause, and this required the Court to interpret the deemer clause for the first time.

The Court read the deemer clause "to exempt self-funded ERISA plans from state laws that 'regulat[e] insurance' within the meaning of the saving clause."[136] Accordingly, the deemer clauses' prohibition on states deeming an employee benefit plan to be an insurer has the effect of relieving self-funded ERISA plans from state laws "purporting to regulate insurance."[137] The Court explained the situation in this way:

> As a result, self-funded ERISA plans are exempt from state regulation insofar as that regulation "relate[s] to" the plans. State laws directed toward the plans are preempted because they relate to an employee benefit plan but are not "saved" because they do not regulate insurance. State laws that directly regulate insurance are "saved" but do not reach self-funded employee benefit plans because the plans may not be deemed to be insurance companies . . . On the other hand, employee benefit plans that are insured are subject to indirect state insurance regulation. An insurance company that insures a plan remains an insurer for purposes of state laws "purporting to regulate insurance" after application of the deemed clause. The insurance company is therefore not relieved from state insurance regulation. The ERISA plan is consequently bound by state insurance regulations insofar as they apply to the plan's insurer.[138] By this view, the deemer clause is at least as broad as the saving clause, except that the saving clause has the "independent effect of protecting state insurance regulation of insurance contracts purchased by employee benefit plans."[139]

The Court's reasoning rejected a view of the deemer clause that would have exempted from the saving clause only state insurance regulations that are pretexts for impinging on "core ERISA concerns"; the Court was unwilling to open the door to litigation over what is a "core" ERISA concern. Also, this reasoning rejected an alternative view of the deemer clause that would have exempted from the saving clause only state law or regulations that deem plans to be insurers only for the purposes of state laws that apply to insurance as a business (such as laws relating to licensing or capitalization requirements). On this point, the Court concluded that the clear language of section 514 would not permit an interpretation that the deemer clause was directed only to laws governing the business of insurance; instead, the

---

[134] 498 U.S. at 60.
[135] 498 U.S. at 61.
[136] 498 U.S. at 61.
[137] 498 U.S. at 61.
[138] 498 U.S. at 61.
[139] 498 U.S. at 64.

deemer clause's reference to "insurance contracts" seemed anomalous if the deemer clause had been intended only to refer to the business of insurance companies. Thus, *Holliday* carried forward the Court's view that Congress intended ERISA preemption to have a very broad sweep. Also, as Justice Stevens pointed out, the Court carried forward the distinction between insured and self-funded employee benefit plans, so that in Pennsylvania a self-insured plan would have a right to enforce a subrogation clause against an injured employee but an insured plan would not have that same right. In Justice Stevens's view, if Congress had intended such an irrational result, it would have said so more explicitly in section 514.[140]

This broad view of preemption was left intact by the 1993 decision in *John Hancock Mutual Life Insurance Co. v. Harris Trust & Savings Bank,*[141] where the Court held that a group annuity contract between insurer and the trustee of the employer's retirement plan did not qualify for the full measure of ERISA's guaranteed benefit policy exclusion, which meant that the insurer was subject to ERISA's fiduciary obligations.[142] To get to this result, the Court concluded that the plan's deposits were not exempt from ERISA's regulation simply because they were placed in an insurer's general account. State insurance law regulates those accounts, but because this regulation does not conflict with ERISA regulation of the trustee's fiduciary duties, dual regulation under ERISA and state law is possible, and therefore should occur.[143] Although no state law was preempted, ERISA was nevertheless given a broad range of operation, which Justice Thomas claimed in dissent "disrupts nearly 20 years of settled expectations" of the insurance industry and buyers of their group annuities.[144]

It was not until the Court decided *New York State Conference of Blue Cross & Blue Shield Plans v. Travelers Insurance Co.* in 1995 that there was a hint about the location of possible limits on the scope of ERISA preemption. In *New York State Conference,* commercial health insurers and their trade associations challenged a New York statute that required hospitals to collect surcharges from patients covered by a commercial insurer but not from patients insured by a Blue Cross/Blue Shield plan, and subjected certain HMOs to surcharges varying with the number of Medicaid patients enrolled. The insurers argued that the surcharges "relate[d] to" employee benefit plans and thus were preempted by ERISA. The Second Circuit agreed with the insurers; giving close attention to the prior Supreme Court decisions, the Second Circuit concluded that the surcharges, which were intended to increase the costs of some commercial insurance and HMOs in order to make the Blue Cross/Blue Shield plans more attractive[145] and that this "purpose[ful] interference with

---

[140] 498 U.S. at 66 (Stevens, J., dissenting).

[141] 114 S.Ct. 517 (1993).

[142] 114 S.Ct. at 529.

[143] 114 S.Ct. at 525.

[144] 114 S.Ct. at 531, 537.

[145] To put the case in context, commercial insurers and HMOs screened out many poor risks, leaving those risks to the Blue Cross/Blue Shield plans, which in turn had become more expensive and therefore less competitive, to the detriment of those individuals enrolled in the Blue Cross/Blue Shield plans. The surcharges were intended to reduce the comparative advantage the commercial insurers and HMOs enjoyed.

the choices that ERISA plans make for health care coverage . . . is sufficient to constitute [a] 'connection with' ERISA plans [triggering ERISA preemption]."[146] In the Third Circuit, however, a contrary decision had been reached, and the court there had held that New Jersey's similar statute did not trigger ERISA preemption.[147] In *New York State Conference,* the Supreme Court in a unanimous opinion written by Justice Souter reversed the Second Circuit's decision, holding that the New York surcharge statute did not "relate to" an employee benefit plan.[148]

To have held otherwise would have disrupted New York's (and other states') efforts to manage a crisis in health care access and affordability in circumstances where it is apparent that, in the wake of the failure of the Clinton health care reform proposal and the absence of support in Congress for any alternative plan, no federal solution is near. In fact, the Court justified its result by noting that finding ERISA preemption would have "displace[d] general health care regulation" by states, something Congress could not have intended.[149] But the tension between this result and prior decisions involving ERISA preemption is apparent. Under the "connection with or reference to" tests of *Shaw,* the Second Circuit's decision was entirely plausible. The surcharges affected plan costs, and could well affect a plan administrator's choice of alternative health care packages for plan participants; this, it would seem, amounts to an ample predicate for finding ERISA preemption, given the broad sweep of section 514 recognized in prior decisions. But the Court thought the New York surcharge statute to be different. The effects on plan costs did not "function as a regulation of an ERISA plan itself" because commercial insurers and HMOs could continue to offer more attractive plans notwithstanding the surcharge, and plan administrators could still choose which plans to purchase. Also, the surcharges did not preclude uniform interstate benefit packages or uniform administrative practices.[150] The Court explained that "cost-uniformity was almost certainly not an object of pre-emption, just as laws with only an indirect economic effect on the relative costs of various health insurance packages in a given State are a far cry form those 'conflicting directives' from which Congress meant to insulate ERISA plans."[151] But the Court left open the possibility that in some future case "acute, albeit indirect, economic effects" might "force an ERISA plan to adopt a certain scheme of substantive coverage or effectively restrict its choice of insurers, and that such a state law might indeed be pre-empted under § 514."[152] This part of the decision, as a practical matter, modified the *Shaw* test, making "acute economic effects" a new, or at least supplemental, test for ERISA preemption in circumstances where the connection of the state law to the ERISA plan is not apparent on its face.

To what extent *New York State Conference* marks a reversal of past ERISA preemption jurisprudence is difficult to assess. At a minimum, the Court's decision

[146] 115 S.Ct. at 1676, quoting 14 F.3d at 719.

[147] United Wire, Metal and Machine Health and Welfare Fund v. Morristown Memorial Hosp., 995 F.2d 1179, *cert. denied,* 114 S.Ct. 382 (1993).

[148] 115 S.Ct. at 1676.

[149] 115 S.Ct. at 1680.

[150] 115 S.Ct. at 1678.

[151] 115 S.Ct. at 1680.

[152] 115 S.Ct. at 1683.

invites states to impose surcharges — which are, in effect, taxes — on some health care providers, which would affect the costs of some employee benefit plans, but anti-tax sentiment endemic to politics in the 1990s suggests this ramification is unlikely to materialize. *New York State Conference* suggests that regulating the quality of benefits provided is a field left to the states.[153] This suggests, for example, that malpractice actions against health care providers are subject to state regulation and are not preempted by ERISA.[154] In addition, the decision invites states to consider more active regulation of health benefit plans. Because the decision upholds a state regulatory role, one can view the decision as consistent with the political winds of the mid-1990s, which tend to support taking some regulatory roles from Washington and giving those roles to the states.

If one grants that the decision in *New York State Conference* is an appropriate accommodation of federal and state regulatory interests (in this instance, the federal interest in regulating pension plans and the state interest in regulating health care costs) and if one accepts the premise that indirect economic effects like those in *New York State Conference* are insufficient to trigger ERISA preemption, then it would seem fair to revisit *Pilot Life* and ask whether the indirect economic effects associated with subjecting insurers (and concomitantly employee benefit plans) to differing remedial schemes (as distinguished from differing standards for finding liability) in different states are sufficiently "acute" to justify the broad ERISA preemption approved there. In other words, if *New York State Conference* marks some degree of reversal in the trend of upholding broad ERISA preemption, the unanswered question is how much of a retrenchment the Court is willing to countenance. One must look to future ERISA preemption cases, and there are sure to be some because ERISA preemption litigation shows no sign of abatement, for an answer to this question and for illumination of this extraordinarily complex and uncertain area.

§ 22 The State Regulatory Framework: Statutory Controls

Because each state separately regulates the business of insurance, the statutory law of each state is the starting point for sketching the legislative regulatory framework. The sheer volume of this statutory law precludes a detailed discussion of it in this book. However, a number of generalizations are possible. When compared to state commercial legislation, state insurance legislation is extremely disorganized. There is nothing in state insurance law that even comes close to the unifying influence of the Uniform Commercial Code. In fact, few states have insurance "codes" in the ordinary sense of the term. Most state insurance "codes" are a hodge-podge of many independently drafted and enacted provisions. In fact, Professor Kimball once described state insurance statutes as a "rubbish heap without parallel in the law-making of modern man."[1] Yet in discrete areas of statutory

---

[153] 115 S.Ct. at 1678-79.

[154] See Dukes v. U.S. Healthcare, Inc., 57 F.3d 350 (3d Cir. 1995); Pacificare of Okla., Inc. v. Burrage, 59 F.3d 151 (10th Cir. 1995).

[1] Spencer L. Kimball, *Unfinished Business in Insurance Regulation,* 1969 Wis. L. Rev. 1019.

regulation, a surprising degree of uniformity exists from state to state. This is due primarily to two factors. First, many states have enacted model acts promulgated by the National Association of Insurance Commissioners. This has resulted in substantial uniformity in many state statutes. Second, and more important, the purposes of the statutory schemes are virtually identical. As a result, many state insurance statutes are similar in both content and wording.[2]

[a] Objectives of State Regulation

Although the larger objectives of insurance regulation are to prevent destructive competition, compensate for inadequate information, relieve unequal bargaining power, and assist consumers incapable of rationally acting in their best interests, the *articulated* objectives of state legislative regulation are essentially fourfold: (1) ensuring that consumers are charged fair and reasonable prices for insurance products; (2) protecting the solvency of insurers; (3) preventing unfair practices and overreaching by insurers; and (4) guaranteeing the availability of coverage to the public.

To a large extent, these objectives overlap. For example, in regulating rates, the first and second objectives overlap: it is important not only that a fair price be charged for the risk assumed but also that a sufficiently high price be charged to maintain insurers' solvency. Similarly, the first and third objectives overlap: unfair prices may be related to an unfair practice of discriminating against particular groups.

To some extent, these objectives are contradictory. For example, the second and fourth objectives are sometimes difficult to achieve simultaneously: charging a premium sufficiently high to maintain adequate reserves may result in coverage not being affordable for certain segments of the population. To some extent, the first and third objectives are inconsistent: eliminating discrimination in insurance rating is potentially at odds with setting a fair or reasonable rate, since insurance rates should be a function of risk; however, due to the expense of risk evaluation, an unbounded effort to categorize and subdivide risks in search of the fair rate would eventually lead to prohibitively expensive rates.

In the following subsections, the principal legislative methods of achieving these objectives are identified and discussed in light of the identified goals of regulation.

[b] Rate Regulation

The current methods of rate regulation in the states are somewhat diverse. These methods are easier to understand if viewed from a historical perspective.

---

[2] For an excellent overview of state regulation, see Jonathan Macey & Geoffrey Miller, *Costly Policies: State Regulation and Antitrust Exemption in Insurance Markets* 76-110 (1993), which was a draft of an article the authors subsequently published as *The McCarran-Ferguson Act of 1945: Reconceiving the Federal Role of Insurance Regulation*, 68 N.Y.U.L.Rev. 13 (1993). A good collection of essays on the subject can be found in Francine Semaya & Vincent Vitkowskey, eds., *The State of Insurance Regulation* (1991) (published by Tort and Insurance Practice Section, American Bar Association).

During the last half of the nineteenth century, some insurers in the fire and casualty lines set their rates in concert to avoid what were perceived to be the destructive consequences of competition.[3] However, the general public, concerned about excessive rates, viewed insurer cooperation with great suspicion. The outgrowth of this suspicion and of the public's general hostility to trusts, large corporations, and other accumulations of wealth prompted the enactment in many states of "anti-compact legislation." The underlying premise of these statutes was that competition in the insurance industry would best serve the public's needs. The Supreme Court upheld the validity of these statutes,[4] and by 1913 twenty-three states had enacted such laws.[5] However, these laws were relatively easy to circumvent and were usually not seriously enforced.

Whatever force the anti-compact laws possessed was ultimately negated by legislation enacted in many states authorizing joint ratemaking under the supervision of state regulatory authorities. In 1909, Kansas became the first state to enact such a statute: the Kansas law prohibited rate discrimination, required the filing of rates and rating plans with the State Insurance Superintendent, and authorized the Superintendent to alter the filed rate if it were inadequate or excessive. In 1911 the Merritt Committee, charged by the New York legislature with the task of investigating fire insurance rating, recommended that New York enact a statute supervising joint ratemaking and requiring each insurer to join a supervised rating bureau. The NAIC made a substantially identical recommendation in 1914. The Merritt Committee and the NAIC did not go so far as to suggest authorizing insurance commissioners to alter filed rates (unless the rates were discriminatory), but they might have been reluctant to do so only because the Supreme Court, which had a challenge to the Kansas statute under consideration, had not yet announced its decision upholding the states' authority to fix insurance rates.[6]

By 1944, approximately thirty-three states had adopted rate regulation in some form; only twelve states continued to rely on anti-compact legislation.[7] However, both the scope of state regulation and the extent of enforcement of the statutory schemes varied widely. In addition, the interstate character of the business of insurance made regulation by the individual states largely ineffective.[8] The Missouri

---

[3] Cooperative ratemaking emerged in these lines largely because of highly cyclical losses throughout the nineteenth century, which culminated in the disastrous Chicago and Boston fires of 1871 and 1872. Kimball & Boyce, note 14 (§ 21), *supra,* at 548.

[4] *Id.* at 550.

[5] *Id.*

[6] German Alliance Ins. Co. v. Lewis, 233 U.S. 389 (1914). The Insurance Department in New York, in implementing the legislation enacted pursuant to the Merritt Committee's recommendation, insisted on approving rates in advance even though it lacked explicit authority to do so under the New York statute. Staff, National Association of Insurance Commissioners, note 1 (§ 20), *supra,* at 19.

[7] Day, note 1 (§ 21), *supra,* at 21.

[8] About 18 states regulated fire insurance rates, about 36 states had laws on worker's compensation insurance, about ten states regulated automobile insurance rates, and two states regulated general liability insurance rates. For life, accident, and health insurance, competition and legal reserve requirements were the only modes of regulation. In the states that had some

Attorney General's frustration with the pattern of ineffective enforcement led to the *SEUA* decision in 1944, which removed impediments to federal regulation. This decision resulted in the enactment of the McCarran-Ferguson Act in 1945,[9] which gave supremacy to state regulation of the business of insurance.

In an effort to occupy the regulatory field, by 1951 virtually all states had adopted with minor variations model fire and casualty rate-regulation legislation that had been drafted through cooperative efforts of the NAIC and industry representatives. These statutes allowed concerted ratemaking under the supervision of a state regulatory authority. Rating bureaus, essentially cooperative ratesetting enterprises, could exist if licensed by a state agency, but insurers could also file rates independently of a bureau.[10] Also, any member of a bureau could deviate from the bureau's rate with the Commissioner's approval after a hearing; an approved deviation would be valid for one year. Rates, whether filed by a bureau or independently by an insurer, had to be supported by adequate data. "Excessive, inadequate or unfairly discriminatory rates" were prohibited. Most states followed the model bills' "prior approval" approach under which rates filed with the state insurance department would not become effective until 15 days after filing; if not disapproved before the 15-day period expired, the rates were deemed to have been approved and went into effect.[11] A number of so-called "file and use" states provided that the rates became effective upon filing but could be disapproved within a stated period.[12]

---

form of insurance rate regulation, most states required the filing of rates and rating plans. At least five of these states required prior approval of the rates by the insurance department, while the others only allowed the insurance department to disapprove the rates. In Texas the Department actually fixed or made the rates, but in most states the power to fix or alter rates was limited. Day, note 1 (§ 21), *supra,* at 21–22; Kimball & Boyce, note 14 (§ 21), *supra,* at 547–50.

[9] See § 21, *supra.*

[10] The bureaus exist for the most part only in the fields of fire, casualty, and inland marine insurance. In life, health, and accident insurance, rates ordinarily have been made by each insurer separately rather than through a rating organization. Robert E. Keeton, *Insurance Law* 561–62 (1971).

[11] United States Department of Justice, *The Pricing and Marketing of Insurance* 22 (1977). A few states authorized the insurance department to fix rates. Staff, National Association of Insurance Commissioners, note 1 (§ 20), *supra,* at 24 n. 63. The prior approval approach, which most states follow, comes in two formats: (a) the rate does not become effective until approved by the Insurance Department; (b) the rate becomes effective unless disapproved by the Department within a specified period of time. Both prior approval approaches differ from the "file and use" approach, under which a rate becomes effective immediately upon filing, although it is subject to disapproval by affirmative action of the Department within a specified period of time. Some file and use statutes require bureau members to adhere to the bureau's filings, while other such statutes treat the bureau's filings as advisory only. About one-third of the states have experimented with some kind of no-file or other similar "open competition" system, where the law makes no requirement that a rate be approved by or perhaps even filed with the Department. *Id.* at 58 (chart categorizing the law of each state).

[12] Day, note 1 (§ 21), *supra,* at 27–28; Kimball & Boyce, note 14 (§ 21), *supra,* at 556. Practical difficulties soon developed in the states following the prior approval approach, largely because the bureaus were entitled to a hearing before the state insurance department

The prior approval ratemaking format remains the most popular in the states, despite the fact that many states have modified their rate regulation legislation and have moved toward systems that rely more extensively on competition to set rates. Approximately thirty states have some kind of prior approval statute, and about fifteen utilize a "file and use" approach. A few others appear to have "use and file" statutes, meaning that the rates can be used immediately and need not be filed until some future date, and fewer than five states have no-file, "open competition" systems.[13] The predominance of prior approval statutes does not mean that market forces are insubstantial in the setting of rates. If filed rates reflect the market and if few rates are challenged in the regulatory process, actual rates would closely reflect market conditions.

In recent years, state regulation of insurance rates has spawned considerable controversy, particularly in areas where high insurance rates have touched the public's nerves. The most notorious circumstances involves California's Proposition 103, approved by the voters of California in 1988.[14] Proposition 103 made several dramatic changes in California insurance law and regulation: the anti-rebate statute was repealed; the state antitrust exemption for insurance companies was repealed; prior approval of rates was mandated; banks were allowed to sell insurance; and an immediate twenty percent reduction in automobile, homeowner, commercial, and municipality rates was mandated, with rates being frozen for one year while individual insurers were given the opportunity to demonstrate that they should be exempted from this regulation on the grounds that the reforms substantially threatened their insolvency. Shortly after Proposition 103 was approved, insurers challenged its constitutionality. In 1989, the California Supreme Court held that the mandatory twenty percent rebate could often be unconstitutionally confiscatory and that the one-year freeze on rate increases unless an insurer could show the substantial threat of insolvency was unconstitutional on its face. The court then directed the California department of insurance to develop an alternative rebate system.[15] The department did so, and ordered insurers to refund millions of dollars of premiums. Insurers then challenged the validity of the rate regulations and the validity of one

---

any time an insurer wanted to deviate from a bureau's established rate. Some insurers resigned from bureaus for this reason, but a substantial number tried to arrange "partial subscriptions" to the bureaus. These insurers tried to remain in their bureaus for some lines of insurance but act independently for other lines. The bureaus and their full subscribers, apprehensive of the increased competition that would accompany more independent filings, resisted the efforts of the insurers seeking partial membership. The net effect of these complications was that those insurers seeking to deviate from the bureau rates encountered substantial delays, and the competition that might have occurred from independent filings and deviations from bureau rates that might have occurred was suppressed. In 1962, the NAIC, responding in part to Congressional hearings inquiring into rating practices, amended its model rating laws and removed many procedural impediments to competitive ratemaking.

[13] See National Association of Insurance Commissioners, *Model Insurance Laws, Regulations and Guidelines* 775-19 (1994). Given the complexity of the statutes and the possibly different interpretations of them by different readers, these numbers are necessarily only estimates.

[14] Proposition 103 is codified at Cal. Ins. Code § 1861.

[15] See Calfarm Ins. Co. v. Deukmejian, 771 P.2d 1247 (Cal. 1989).

insurer's rebate liability. In a 1994 decision, the California Supreme Court upheld the regulations and the rollback order,[16] thus setting the stage for a refund of premiums which, with interest, could total in excess of $1 billion. As of mid-1995, many insurers were balking at making the refunds, and the tension between the new California insurance commissioner and the insurance industry (which had generally supported his candidacy and had hoped for a more sympathetic regulatory approach than that conducted by his predecessor) was growing.[17]

California, however, was not the only state where major reforms occurred, even though California's reforms have been the most widely publicized by far. Pennsylvania also adopted singificant insurance reform legislation in 1990,[18] and Texas enacted a number of pro-consumer reforms in 1991, including substantial deregulation of property and casualty rates.[19]

Rate approval is an extremely complicated undertaking. Striking the appropriate balance between an excessive rate and a rate sufficient to prevent insurer insolvency is not an easy task. Similarly, striking the balances appropriate to preventing discrimination among insureds can be difficult. This has prompted many to wonder whether public regulation of rates can improve significantly, if at all, upon the operation of market forces. A definitive answer to this question may not be possible, and the issue may be on the political agenda for some time to come.

[c] Insurer Solvency

Obviously, rate regulation has a direct relationship to the objective of insurer solvency. However, other state statutes also seek to secure insurer solvency. The modern era of solvency regulation dates to the 1960s, when a wave of insurer insolvencies developed primarily among companies writing substandard auto insurance.[20] In the immediate aftermath of these insolvencies, the NAIC proposed model statutes to create guaranty associations. These statutes create an association of insurers to satisfy the obligations of insolvent insurers through assessments on insurers doing business in the state.[21] In effect, these statutes create a safety net for insureds who happen to do business with a financially unstable insurer.[22] The NAIC also created a centralized database and early warning system to help identify troubled insurance companies in the early 1970s, and in 1989 the NAIC created a working group to help identify potentially troubled companies of national significance.[23]

---

[16] See 20th Century Ins. Co. v. Garamendi, 878 P.2d 566 (Cal. 1994)(en banc), *cert. denied,* 115 S.Ct. 1106 (1995).

[17] See *California Insurer Rebate Tension Rises,* Bus. Ins. (May 22, 1995), p. 28.

[18] Pa. Stat. Ann. 40 § 1171.1.

[19] Tex. Ins. Code Ann. § 21.28(c).

[20] Earl Pomeroy, "State Insurance Regulation: A Blueprint for the Future," in Tort and Insurance Practice Section, ABA, *The State Of Insurance Regulation* 9 (1991).

[21] See National Association of Insurance Commissioners, note 13, *supra,* at 520–1 (Life and Health Insurance Guaranty Association Model Act); at 540–1 (Post-Assessment Property and Liability Insurance Guaranty Association Model Act).

[22] Annot., *What Constitutes Insolvency of Insurance Company Justifying State Dissolution Proceedings and the Like,* 17 A.L.R.4th 16 (1982).

[23] See NAIC, Services to NAIC Members 18 (Feb. 1992).

Another important aspect of solvency regulation are those statutes that provide for periodic examinations of insurers and audits of their annual reports. By investigating detailed accounting information submitted by insurers, state regulators, working with the NAIC, seek to determine whether insurers doing business in the state have the financial ability to meet their commitments. The examination-audit statutes dovetail with the licensing statutes: state regulators will only license an insurer to do business in the state if it appears that the insurer is a financially stable institution. The financial requirements for insurers to obtain a license vary greatly in the different states.

Several other kinds of statutes have as a predominant purpose the protection and furtherance of insurer solvency. For example, all states have statutes prescribing the kinds of investments insurers are allowed to make. Similar statutes regulate the methods by which insurer assets are valued, so that a true picture of the insurer's financial health is available.[24] All states have statutes that require insurers to create as a liability on their balance sheets a "reserve" thought adequate to provide a fund to meet policy obligations as they are incurred. Most states have adopted statutes or regulations that regulate insurer holding company systems; this regulation is intended to ensure that those who control or seek to acquire control of insurers will not manage the insurer contrary to the interests of policyholders.[25]

---

[24] One of the significant developments in this area is the advent of risk-based capital formulas to evaluate insurer strength. As life insurers sought to compete with high-interest-paying institutions in the 1980s, some insurers made excessively high interest commitments and invested in higher-risk assets and real estate ventures in order to support their high commitments. To better assess insurer solvency by taking into account the risk of assets and liabilities, in 1992 the NAIC approved a Life Risk-Based Capital Formula that was used for the first time for 1993 annual statements filed by life insurers in 1994. See Bernard Webb & Claude Lilly, *Raising the Safety Net: Risk- Based Capital for Life Insurance Companies* (1994). In 1993, the NAIC approved risk-based capital requirements for the property-casualty industry, and the first annual reports of insurers under the new requirements occurred in 1995. *Using Capital Adequacy Models*, Best's Review (Dec. 1994), at 21.

[25] See National Association of Insurance Commissioners, note 12, *supra,* at 440–1 (Insurance Holding Company System Regulatory Act). There is a substantial debate over whether portions of this statute allowing the Insurance Commissioner to approve takeovers of domestic insurers is unconstitutional. See John M. Sheffey, *The Unconstitutionality of State Insurance Takeover Statutes: An Unfortunate But Not Necessarily Final Result,* 69 Minn. L. Rev. 821 (1985); Susan Webster, Note, *State Regulation of Tender Offers for Insurance Companies after Edgar v. Mite,* 51 Fordham L. Rev. 943 (1983). In Edgar v. Mite, 457 U.S. 624 (1982), five justices held a state corporate anti-takeover statute, which is similar in some respects to the insurance statutes, unconstitutional on Commerce Clause grounds, and a plurality held the statute preempted by the Williams Act, 15 U.S.C. §§ 78m(d)–(e), 78n(d)–(f). See Christopher Keele, Note, *State Insurance Takeover Acts: A Constitutional Analysis After Edgar v. Mite,* 59 Ind. L. J. 255 (1984). Courts which have confronted the issue have taken different positions on the constitutionality of the state holding company acts, but the weight of opinion is that the statutes are constitutional or federal courts should abstain from the determination. Three decisions upheld the state acts against Commerce Clause attack in 1989. See Hoylake Investments Ltd. v. Washburn, 723 F. Supp. 42 (N.D. Ill. 1989) (Illinois holding company act); Hoylake Investments Ltd. v. Bell, 723 F. Supp. 576 (D.Kan. 1989) (Kansas holding company act); Hoylake Investments Ltd. v. Gallinger, 722 F. Supp. 573

[d] Unfair Practices and Insurer Overreaching

It became clear at an early time that insurance companies were capable of taking advantage of poorly informed consumers. Thus, much early statutory law (and judicial case law) was designed to equalize the relationship between insurer and insured.

Specific problems were often met with specific solutions. In the nineteenth century, some states enacted statutes providing that no condition in an application for insurance would be valid unless specifically stated in the policy itself. These statutes were designed to prevent insurers from relying on obscure conditions outside the text of the policy that purported to relieve the insurer of liability in certain circumstances.[26] Throughout most of the nineteenth century, it was assumed that an insured who discontinued his premium payments under a whole-life insurance policy forfeited any equity he had previously accumulated. However, statutes enacted in many states in the late nineteenth and early twentieth centuries required the insurer to provide some sort of minimum cash surrender value in the event of default after a specified period of time.[27] The rule of contract law that allowed a party to void a contract upon the other party's breach of a warranty provision, regardless of the provision's materiality, worked great hardship on many policyholders. Thus, statutes enacted in many states around the turn of the century declared that no policy would be voided for breach of warranty unless that fact warranted was material or was intentionally misrepresented.[28] Statutes like these remain in force in many states today.

The enactment of the McCarran-Ferguson Act provided an impetus for additional state legislative efforts. Hoping to preempt federal regulation, state legislatures took steps to regulate the bargaining relationship between the insurer and the applicant.[29] In the late 1940s and early 1950s, each of the states enacted statutes to prohibit such practices as false or misleading advertising, misrepresentation of a competitor's product, and failing to pay valid claims.[30] Most of these statutes authorize the state

---

(D.Ariz. 1989) (Arizona holding company act). The opposite result was reached in another case, Alleghany Corp. v. Pomeroy, 700 F. Supp. 460 (D.N.D. 1988), but this decision was reversed by the Eighth Circuit under the reasoning that the district court should have abstained under the *Younger* doctrine. Alleghany Corp. v. Pomeroy, 898 F.2d 1314 (8th Cir. 1990). See also Alleghany Corp. v. McCartney, 896 F.2d 1138 (8th Cir. 1990) (Nebraska federal district court acted properly in dismissing on abstention grounds action challenging constitutionality of Nebraska holding company act). The Seventh Circuit took a different position on the abstention issue, but this decision was ultimately vacated by the U.S. Supreme Court. Alleghany Corp. v. Haase, 896 F.2d 1046 (7th Cir. 1990), *vacated and remanded with instructions to dismiss complaint,* 499 U.S. 933 (1991). Before its decision was vacated, the Seventh Circuit had held that suits challenging the Wisconsin and Indiana holding company acts could proceed and the district courts were not required to abstain.

[26] See William R. Vance, *Vance on Insurance* 38 (3d ed. Anderson 1951).

[27] *Id.* at 608–09.

[28] See *id.* at 39.

[29] Section 1(b) of the McCarran-Ferguson Act, 15 U.S.C. § 1012(b), provided that after a three-year period, federal antitrust laws would apply to the business of insurance "to the extent that such business is not regulated by State law."

[30] See § 21[c], *supra.*

insurance commissioner to commence an investigation into alleged unfair trade practices and to issue cease and desist orders where such practices are occurring.

Today, to combat overreaching and unfairness in the marketplace, considerable attention is given to increasing the availability of, and access to, information.[31] Economists have long observed that full and free information is a prerequisite to a competitive, efficient market. One important source of information for consumers in the insurance business is advertising. Advertising, by making consumers aware of available products and the alternatives, both promotes distribution of coverage and enhances product competition. Inaccurate advertising, however, has an equal potential for frustrating the public interest by encouraging unnecessary and incorrect purchases. Thus, much modern regulation can fairly be described as "truth-in-advertising" regulation.[32]

Under the reasoning that a consumer who understands his or her rights and obligations under a contract is less likely to be the victim of sharp practices and is more likely to purchase a useful product, statutes in some states mandate minimum standards for language used in policies, often using "reading ease tests" to determine whether the policy's language is sufficiently "plain."[33] Insurance commissioners usually have the express authority to disapprove forms that are obscure, misleading, or unclear.[34] In fire insurance, regulation of forms is especially rigid: each state mandates the exact wording for the standard fire insurance contract.

All states have statutes empowering state regulatory officials to license agents and brokers.[35] As with most licensing schemes, the policy underlying the regulation is

---

[31] In recent years, considerable attention has been given to making more information available about the price of insurance at the point of sale. See National Association of Insurance Commissioners, note 13, *supra*, at 580–1 ("Life Insurance Disclosure Model Regulation"); Symposium, *Regulation of Life Cost Disclosure and Market Conduct*, 13 J. of Ins. Reg. 397 (1995); Spencer L. Kimball & Mark S. Rapaport, *What Price "Price Disclosure"? The Trend to Consumer Protection in Life Insurance*, 1972 Wis. L. Rev. 1025; Joseph M. Belth, *Price Disclosure in Life Insurance*, 1972 Wis. L. Rev. 1054.

[32] See, e.g., National Association of Insurance Commissioners, note 13, *supra*, at 570–1 ("Rules Governing the Advertising of Life Insurance"; enacted either by statute or regulation in approximately 23 states).

[33] *See id.* at 575-1. The Model Life and Health Insurance Policy Language Simplification Model Act requires the text of an insurance policy to achieve "a minimum score of 40 on the Flesch reading ease test" or an equivalent score on a comparable test. *Id.* at 575-3. See also Mass. Gen. Laws Ann. ch. 175, § 2B. Whether such statutes achieve their purpose is a matter of considerable doubt. See Skariat, *Readable Policies,* 21 For the Defense 17 (Jan. 1980). The enormous complexity of the task of making contracts comprehensible to consumers is discussed in Jeffrey Davis, *Protecting Consumers from Overdisclosure and Gobbledygook: An Empirical Look at the Simplification of Consumer-Credit Contracts,* 63 Va. L. Rev. 841 (1977).

[34] This authority to disapprove forms can also be used in many states to disapprove forms with excessive rates, with rates that endanger the insurer's solvency, and with clauses that violate any statute, regulation, or "are otherwise contrary to law."

[35] See National Association of Insurance Commissioners, note 13, *supra,* at 850–1 ("Unauthorized Insurers Model Statute.") See generally 1 B. Harnett, *Responsibilities of Insurance Agents and Brokers,* §§ 5.06–5.11, at 5-28 to 5-558.2 (1986).

to ensure the competency and honesty of those who provide services for the public. Also, the threat of license revocation can be used to deter overreaching and unfair practices. Similarly, all states have statutes that provide for the licensing of each insurance company doing business within the state and that explicitly empower state regulatory officials to enjoin the activities of insurers not authorized to do business in the state.[36]

Most statutes on insurer overreaching are aimed at the marketing practices of insurers and their agents. Claims processing is regulated legislatively by statutes that assess penalties for delays in paying claims.[37] Also, a number of states have statutes that impose penalties against an insurance company that refuses to pay a claim, forces the insured to sue the insurer to recover, and subsequently loses the insured's suit.[38]

All states have some procedure by which the insurance department can receive consumer complaints. Some legitimate complaints will fall within an area where the department has the authority to investigate and give relief. However, even if the department lacks authority to resolve a complaint or it is otherwise inappropriate for the department to take specific action, which will often be the case, the procedure for merely receiving the complaint may provide considerable benefit to the consumer. Such procedures are an important method of transmitting information to consumers about insurance statutes and regulations, consumer rights, and available remedies. Sometimes the consumer's complaint is unfounded or based on a misconception of some sort, and a department staff person can educate the consumer about the situation. Sometimes the staff person might make an inquiry to the company involved on the consumer's behalf, and thereby obtain a resolution of the grievance through a process much like mediation. Occasionally, the staff person's inquiry may signal to the insurer that an unfair practice has been discovered, and this development may cause the company to reverse or modify its position. At other times, the staff person may simply advise the person about how one secures relief through the judicial process. In each of these ways, the consumer complaint procedures help to provide relief for unfair trade practices.

[e]   Coverage

States regulate the coverage of insurance policies in a number of ways. The most pervasive kind of coverage regulation seeks to increase the amount of coverage that insureds possess, perhaps even by mandating the purchase of coverage. For example, all states have financial responsibility statutes for owners of automobiles, and these statutes effectively require owners of automobiles to have liability insurance or the financial wherewithal to pay for losses they cause. In about one-half the states, liability insurance is compulsory. The public policy underlying these statutes is to

---

[36] See generally 16 APPLEMAN §§ 8631–8653 (1981).

[37] See § 99, *infra*.

[38] See, e.g., Fla. Stat. Ann. § 627.428 (allowing attorney's fees for insured who prevails); Or. Rev. Stat. § 743.114 (allowing attorney's fees for insured who prevails); Tenn. Code Ann. § 56-7-105 (if insured prevails, insurer must pay loss plus interest plus penalty of 25% of the liability plus attorney fees not exceeding 12.5% of the award).

ensure that adequate funds will exist to reimburse individuals who suffer physical injury or economic loss in automobile accidents.[39]

Legislatures commonly specify the content of insurance policies, and this has obvious effects on coverage. For example, some statutes mandate that health policies cover the insured's dependents from the moment of birth.[40] Statutes in some states prohibit insurers from offsetting increased social security benefits in group disability income policies.[41] In a few states, statutes limit insurers' use of genetic information to make risk or premium classifications.[42]

States also regulate coverage by prescribing rules for access to insurance. For example, all states have some kind of so-called "residual market plan" through which automobile insurance is sold to people unable to obtain insurance in the voluntary market. The most common mechanism in the states is the "assigned risk" plan, under which insurers doing business in a state are required to insure some portion of otherwise uninsurable risks.[43]

At first glance, increasing coverage through regulation may seem to be a good thing. But whenever an insurer is required to increase coverage, the insurer's costs must rise, which often must be followed by an increase in rates. This consequence can run counter to the objective of keeping rates fair and reasonable; also, if a certain kind of insurance becomes more expensive because the coverage is broader, fewer people may be able to afford it.

Occasionally, states use regulation of coverage to achieve objectives unrelated altogether to the business of insurance. For example, statutes in a few states require all insurers doing business in the state to exclude from health insurance policies coverage for abortions.[44] In such states, coverage for abortions typically may be obtained by purchasing a separate, optional rider for which a separate premium must be paid.[45] A similar statute prohibits state governmental bodies from providing state employees with health insurance covering abortions.[46] The apparent purpose of such

---

[39] See Tomai-Minogue v. State Farm Mutual Auto. Ins. Co., 770 F.2d 1228 (4th Cir. 1985); Nationwide Mutual Ins. Co. v. Roberts, 134 S.E.2d 654 (N.C. 1964).

[40] See National Association of Insurance Commissioners, note 13, *supra,* at 130–1 (Model Newborn Children Bill; endorsed but not adopted by the NAIC).

[41] See *id.* at 380-1 (Model Regulation to Prohibit the Offset of Increased Social Security Benefits in Group Disability Income Policies; two states have statutes and 13 states have regulations).

[42] See, e.g., Tenn. Code Ann. § 56-7-207 (sickle-cell anemia and hemoglobin-C); Fla. Stat. Ann. § 626.9707 (sickle-cell anemia with respect to disability insurance); Md. Ann. Code art. 48A, § 223 (sickle-cell, hemoglobin-C, Tay-Sachs, and any genetic trait which is "harmless within itself.")

[43] See, e.g., Virginia Farm Bureau Mut. Ins. Co. v. Saccio, 133 S.E.2d 268 (Va. 1963) (explaining how one such plan operates).

[44] See, e.g., R.I. Gen. Laws § 36-12-2.1; Idaho Code 41-3934; Ky. Rev. Stat. Ann. § 304.5-160.

[45] See, e.g., Mo. Rev. Stat. § 376.805; Pa. Stat. Ann., tit. 18, § 3215(e) (declared unconstitutional; see note 47, *infra*); R.I.G.L. § 27-18-28 (declared unconstitutional; see note 47, *infra*).

[46] See, e.g., Neb. Ins. Code § 44-1615.01; Pa. Stat. Ann., tit. 18, § 3215(d); R.I.G.L. § 36-12-2.1 (declared unconstitutional; see note 47, *infra*).

statutes is to use the insurance mechanism to regulate abortion. From one viewpoint, the statutes are designed to make abortions more difficult to obtain, thereby impairing a woman's constitutional right. From another viewpoint, the statutes are designed to protect the interests of individuals who oppose abortion: without the legislation, a portion of the insurance premium of consumers who oppose abortion is used to pay for abortions of other insureds; with the legislation, those who wish insurance coverage for abortions must purchase the coverage, without cross-subsidization by consumers who oppose abortion. In two cases, statutes that limit insurance coverage for abortions have been held unconstitutional as impermissible burdens on a woman's constitutional right to an abortion.[47]

[f] Deregulation: A Realistic Alternative?

Beginning in the mid-1970s, a broad-based "deregulation" movement gained momentum,[48] and this movement continues to have vitality in the mid-1990s. With respect to many sectors of the economy it is widely perceived that government regulation has failed and that deregulation, where tried, has been successful.

Deregulation of the insurance industry has its proponents, but the voices of those who prefer some measure of regulation are strong. For example, some recommendations urge elimination of barriers to alternative ways of marketing insurance. To be specific, savings banks might be encouraged to market life insurance in larger numbers.[49] Others recommend that commercial banks be allowed to engage in the insurance business. Obviously, banks who desire to enter insurance markets urge deregulation and the elimination of barriers to their entry. Most insurers, however, would prefer that banks not enter insurance markets; thus, most insurers favor regulation of banks that limits their ability to function as insurers. Most insurance agents desire to be free to compete for clients and premiums, but most agents support anti-rebating laws[50] pursuant to which government, through regulation, prohibits agents or brokers and consumers from negotiating the size of the agent's

---

[47] See National Education Ass'n of Rhode Island v. Garrahy, 598 F. Supp. 1374 (1984), aff'd, 779 F.2d 790 (3d Cir. 1986); American College of Obstetricians and Gynecologists v. Thornburgh, 737 F.2d 283 (3d Cir. 1984). *American College* was affirmed by the United States Supreme Court, but the ruling on the constitutionality of the insurance statute issue was not before the Court. Thornburgh v. American College of Obstetricians and Gynecologists, 476 U.S. 747, 749 (1986).

[48] Four successive Presidents — Nixon, Ford, Carter, and Reagan — made regulatory reform a top priority, and the appropriate scope of federal regulation was an agenda item for both the Bush and Clinton administrations. In 1975, the Securities and Exchange Commission ordered an end to the fixing of brokerage fees by the national securities exchanges. In 1978, the airline industry was substantially deregulated, and deregulation occurred in the trucking industry in 1980. See generally Leonard W. Weiss and M. Klass, *Case Studies in Regulation: Revolution and Reform* (1981). For surveys of issues in insurance regulation, see Douglas Caddy, *Legislative Trends in Insurance Regulation* (1986); Banks McDowell, *The Crisis in Insurance Regulation* (1994).

[49] Savings banks in New York, Massachusetts, and Connecticut are authorized by state law to sell life insurance. See § 13B[d], *supra.*

[50] See § 22[a], *supra.*

commission. Not surprisingly, whether one favors regulation or deregulation depends on how one perceives the benefits of regulation or the absence of regulation.

Most of the discussion of the relative merit of regulation and deregulation has occurred with respect to the rates charged for insurance. During the 1950s, most rate regulation was concerned with insurers' setting adequate minimum rates in order to avoid the effects of cutthroat competition.[51] In the 1960s and 1970s, two contrasting views of rate regulation developed. One view favored greater reliance on competition to set rates.[52] This viewpoint urged that the costs of performing rate regulation garnered no benefits, suggesting that relying on competition to set rates would work as well, if not better, and all of the expense of rate regulation would be saved or put to other superior uses.[53] During the 1970s, a number of states experimented with reliance upon competition to set rates, and it appeared that increased reliance on competition led neither to "cutthroat competition" nor to weakening the solidity of insurers' financial health. Indeed, some evidence suggested that rate regulation did not correlate with financial health and that both profits and rates tended to be more stable where competition was encouraged.[54]

In complete contrast to the pro-competition movement, the paramount concern in some states, particularly with respect to auto insurance, became "affordability of coverage and suppression of rate increases in the face of rising claim costs."[55] In these states, the momentum shifted in favor of more, not less, rate regulation for the purpose of maintaining consumer access to coverage at reasonable prices.[56] Proposition 103 in California was the most notorious of the rate-rollback voter initiatives; although clearly pro-consumer in its orientation, Proposition 103 contemplated increased rate regulation after a period in which California had moved toward more deregulation.[57] Thus, in the 1990s, two distinct views of the

---

[51] Scott E. Harrington, *Rate Suppression,* 59 J. of Risk & Ins. 185 (1992).

[52] See Stewart W. Kemp, *Insurance and Competition,* 17 Idaho L. Rev. 547 (1981) (discusses proposed federal legislation to promote competition in insurance; concludes that competition in insurance takes many forms, that more price competition will be beneficial, but that total deregulation is not appropriate); John G. Day, *Changing Attitudes About Insurance Regulation,* 14 Forum 744 (1979). For an effective statement of the case favoring deregulation, see Stelzer & Alpert, "Benefits and Costs of Insurance Deregulation," in N. Weber, ed., *Insurance Deregulation: Issues and Perspectives* 6–13 (1982).

[53] See, e.g., Zack Stamp, *A Modest Proposal: Repeal of State Rating Laws,* 91 Best's Rev.-Prop./Cas. Ins. Ed. 45 (Jan. 1991) (citing Palmer Belvue Corp. study showing that "a property/casualty insurance market whose pricing is left to the market rather than regulated by the government returns more value to consumers.")

[54] See, e.g., United States Dep't of Justice, *The Pricing and Marketing of Insurance* 36–60 (1977). These findings suggested that establishing or augmenting guaranty funds would be sufficient to provide reasonable safeguards against insurer insolvency; thus, rate regulation would be at best a superfluous — and perhaps even a counterproductive — activity. *Id.* at 61–75.

[55] Harrington, *supra* note 51.

[56] For more discussion, see Orin S. Kramer, *Rate Suppression, Rate-of-return Regulation, and Solvency,* 10 J. of Ins. Reg. 523 (1992).

[57] For further discussion of Proposition 103, see § 22[a], *supra.*

appropriate governmental role continue to evolve: one view appeals to anti-government populist notions to expunge the government's regulatory role, while another appeals to anti-insurer populist notions to increase the government's regulatory role. Thus, it would be a mistake to assume that populist sentiments always support deregulation. It may be that popular sentiment runs more in favor of changing whatever regulatory scheme happens to be in place at any given time, at least in sectors of the economy that have been dominated historically by large, prominent firms, rather than in favor of any particular regulatory philosophy.

If deregulation were to occur on a widespread basis, insurance rates should more accurately reflect the costs of assuming the risk. It would be difficult, to say the least, for any government regulator to improve upon the accuracy of a price set for a product in a competitive, fair marketplace. In a free market, insurers will compete for the low-risk members of any particular class, thereby driving down their rates. As classifications are drawn more narrowly, higher rates will exist for higher-risk pools of insureds. Although individuals with higher risks may be disadvantaged by the higher rates presented them in a deregulated market, insurers will have less incentive to engage in discriminatory marketing practices (such as redlining, which is the practice of drawing territorial boundaries for rating purposes to the detriment of low-income or minority groups), which tend to arise when insurers are compelled to insure higher-risk individuals (or groups) or to insure higher-risk individuals (or groups) at the same rate charged to people with lower risks.[58]

Total deregulation, however, may not be desirable. Our regulatory system operates on the premise that a certain amount of "cross-subsidization" is appropriate in insurance markets. Cross-subsidization describes a rate structure where a lower-risk group pays a slightly inflated price in order to subsidize a higher-risk group. For example, if gender discrimination in annuities were deemed inappropriate, it would be necessary for men — who on the average constitute a lower risk than women due to their shorter average life expectancy — to pay as a group more than the total costs they impose on the insurance pool; in this way, men as a group would subsidize women as a group, who would pay less as a group than the total costs they impose on the system. In health insurance, healthy people tend to pay premiums disproportionately higher than the value of their risk; this is for the benefit of the less healthy, many of whom could not afford premiums adjusted to reflect their expected consumption of health care services. A proponent of deregulation might respond, however, that a choice to transfer income from one group to another should be made in the legislative process, where duly elected representatives can articulate the relevant public policies, instead of in the rate-making process by an administrator exercising delegated authority.

---

[58] An issue has arisen in a number of recent cases as to whether the Fair Housing Act, 42 U.S.C. §§ 3601 et seq., prohibits redlining practices in the property and casualty insurance industry. As of this writing, a split exists in the federal circuit court decisions, making it possible that the U.S. Supreme Court will speak to this issue in some future case. Compare Nationwide Mut. Ins. Co. v. Cisneros, 52 F.3d 1351 (6th Cir. 1995) (Act prohibits redlining); NAACP v. American Family Mut. Ins. Co., 978 F.2d 287 (7th Cir. 1992) (Act prohibits redlining), with Mackey v. Nationwide Ins. Cos., 724 F.2d 419 (4th Cir. 1984) (Act does not apply to underwriting practices of insurance companies).

Finally, it is worth noting that much of the debate over the appropriateness of continued regulation in the insurance industry occurs in the context of considering whether the McCarran-Ferguson Act's antitrust exemption should be repealed. If the exemption were repealed, insurers would presumably be able to share raw experience data with each other for the purpose of setting actuarially sound rates, but insurers would not be able to set rates jointly, to pool administrative expense data, or to share experience data in a manner that suggests what the ultimate rates should be.[59]

§ 23 State Regulation: Administrative Controls

Although American government, both at the state and federal levels, is often described as a tripartite system of legislative, executive, and judicial regulation, some observers describe American government as a "four-branch" system, with administrative agencies constituting the additional regulatory authority.[1] Actually, the only authority of administrative agencies is that which is delegated to them by the legislative branch. However, these delegations are often very broad, and thus administrative agencies constitute an important mode of regulation in their own right.

[a] The Department of Insurance

All states have some sort of office that is charged with the duty of administering the state's regulatory insurance laws.[2] In most states, the office is called the "Department of Insurance," and the official who heads the Department is usually called the "Insurance Commissioner." In about two-thirds of the states, the Department is a separate regulatory entity; in the remaining states, the insurance agency is a part of some other state department, such as a "Department of Insurance and Banking" or a "Corporation Commission." In a majority of the states, the Commissioner is appointed by and serves at the pleasure of the governor. In about half the remaining states, the Commissioner is appointed by some other governmental entity, and in the other half the Commissioner is elected by the public-at-large.[3]

The Department of Insurance exercises authority delegated to it by the legislature. The primary responsibility of the Insurance Commissioner is to protect the public, and to that end the authority of the Commissioner is usually stated broadly. As an implementer of law, the Commissioner makes "law" in a broad sense.[4]

---

[59] See Stelzer & Alpert, note 52, *supra*, at 12; Shenefield, "Competition and the Insurance Industry: The New Frontier of Deregulation," in Weber, note 52, *supra*, at 14–19.

[1] See Lawrence Freedman, *Power and Politics in America* 119 (1971).

[2] For a general discussion of the powers of state insurance commissioners, see 19 APPLEMAN §§ 10391–10436 (1982).

[3] See United States Comptroller General, *Report to the Congress of the United States: Issues and Needed Improvements in State Regulation of the Insurance Business* 16 (1979). The Commissioner is elected in twelve states. Sara Marley, *High Turnover Among Regulators,* Bus. Ins., Dec. 5, 1994.

[4] For a brief but incisive analysis of the role of the typical Insurance Commissioner, see Kenneth S. Abraham, *Distributing Risk: Insurance, Legal Theory, and Public Policy* 38–41 (1986).

Administering and applying a statute inevitably requires interpreting its substance and designing procedural rules for implementation of the substantive standards. As any administrative lawyer knows, the substantive and procedural rules generated in the administrative process have a tangible effect on the conduct of regulated parties.

[b] National Association of Insurance Commissioners

The National Association of Insurance Commissioners (NAIC), an association of the chief insurance regulatory officials of the fifty states, the District of Columbia, and the territories, was organized in 1871, shortly after the Supreme Court's decision in *Paul v. Virginia* made it clear that the states had the exclusive authority to regulate the insurance business. The NAIC, through its staff and various committees currently headquartered in Kansas City, Missouri, proposes model laws and regulations for possible adoption by the states, studies problems of insurance regulation, gathers and distributes information on regulatory matters, and maintains financial data for the purpose of detecting insurer insolvency at an early stage.[5] The proceedings of the NAIC's regular biannual meetings are published; these volumes serve as an important source of research information. The NAIC has no legal authority, but it does provide a "coordinating influence" on the regulation of the insurance industry by the several states.[6]

For years, the NAIC was a relatively modest operation, but it has grown significantly in recent years along with some of the regulatory problems its work addresses. From the early 1980s through the early 1990s, the size of the NAIC's budget quadrupled. Yet the size of the NAIC remains small when compared with some insurance department budgets and the total budgets for all state insurance departments combined.[7] The growth in the presence of the NAIC occurred in the wake of the liability insurance crisis of the mid-1980s and the failure of a number of large insurance companies in the late 1980s and early 1990s. At the same time, the highly- publicized problems of the failed insurers, which occurred in the wake of a huge, expensive bailout of the ineptly-regulated savings and loan industry, prompted considerable scrutiny of the NAIC and the entire system of state regulation.

In response to those who criticized the rigor of state solvency regulation and advocated a greater federal presence in this area, the NAIC initiated an accreditation

---

[5] Of particular importance in this regard is the work of the NAIC's Securities Valuation Office. This office values, using uniform criteria, the securities held in virtually every U.S. insurer's portfolio.

[6] For example, the NAIC develops and provides all state insurance departments with the form on which insurers file their annual statements. The annual statements provide a major portion of the statistical data regarding the insurance business. United States Comptroller General, note 3, *supra*, at 23.

[7] In 1993, the NAIC had a budget of approximately $25.2 million (NAIC 1993 Annual Report, p. 27), compared to total insurance department expenditures in the U.S. of approximately $646 million (based on an NAIC survey of state insurance departments). *The NAIC: Too Little, Too Late?* Bus. Ins., Dec. 7, 1992, at 3. The projected NAIC budget for 1996 is approximately $40.75 million. *Belt-tightening in '96 for NAIC,* Bus. Ins., Dec. 18, 1995, at 3.

process in 1990 as a way to encourage states to enact a core set of NAIC model solvency regulation laws and to maintain certain minimum standards of solvency regulation. Although more than thirty states by 1994 had obtained accreditation, the program has proved to be one of the NAIC's more controversial activities. Battles between the NAIC and some state insurance departments (such as Vermont) and the suspension of New York's accreditation, which was followed by the New York legislature's enactment of a statute that would impose retaliatory fines on companies domiciled in other states that acted against New York insurers because of the suspension, have received considerable publicity.[8] Even though the uniformity created by the accreditation process arguably validates the view that some kind of minimal federal regulation is appropriate, the initiative has had the support of most state regulators.

[c] How Effective Is State Regulation?

As might be expected, a consensus on the effectiveness of state regulation of the insurance business does not exist. Those who are critical of leaving the regulation of such an important industry to state officials make several arguments. First, the business of insurance is truly interstate in character and therefore requires coordinated national policy; therefore, the present system should be supplanted with a regulatory framework administered by a national agency. Second, the financial requirements for insurers are absurdly low, exemplifying a parochial attitude that sets regulatory objectives at a level that the weakest insurers can meet. Third, requiring insurers to deal with fifty separate regulatory entities is grossly inefficient.[9] Fourth, better, more competent regulation will occur at the national level, since many state insurance departments are underfunded and understaffed and since state regulators are more likely to identify with the interests of the industry instead of consumers. Although it is sometimes suggested that state regulation is cheaper than federal regulation, the total amount spent in the states on insurance regulation approximates the combined total of the budgets of the Securities and Exchange

---

[8] See *State legislators slam NAIC*, Bus. Ins., Mar. 6, 1995, at 1.

[9] State laws taxing foreign insurers illustrate the potential difficulties inherent in regulation by fifty separate entities. Virtually all jurisdictions have so-called "retaliatory statutes" which substitute the general tax laws of a foreign insurer's home state for the general tax laws of the state in which the insurer is doing business when the foreign insurer's home state's laws are more burdensome than the laws of the state in which the business is occurring. In *Western & Southern Life Ins. Co. v. State Bd. of Equalization*, 451 U.S. 648 (1981), the Supreme Court held that the McCarran-Ferguson Act removed any Commerce Clause restriction upon the power of the states to tax the insurance business. However, the Equal Protection Clause does apply, and it is essential that the discrimination between foreign and domestic corporations bear a rational relationship to a legitimate state purpose. The Court held in *WSLI* that California's purpose of deterring other states from imposing discriminatory or excessive taxes on California insurers was a legitimate state purpose that the California legislature could have rationally believed would be promoted by the retaliatory tax. However, in *Metropolitan Life Ins. Co. v. Ward*, 470 U.S. 869 (1985), the Court held that an Alabama statute imposing a substantially lower gross premium tax rate on domestic insurers, with the apparent and illegitimate purpose of attempting to promote the insurance business within Alabama, violated the Equal Protection Clause.

Commission and the Federal Trade Commission, two large federal agencies with broad authority over financial and trade regulation matters.[10] When this relatively large sum is spread among the states — each state must regulate all of the insurance companies that do business within the state's boundaries — a picture of spreading an excessively large sum of money too thin begins to emerge. Fifth, state legislatures, lacking adequate staffs and severely constrained in the amount of time that can be devoted to legislating, are incapable of evaluating subtleties of the business of insurance; hence, state legislatures and their delegates are more vulnerable to the pressure of special interests able to marshal information needed for law writing. Nor is it likely that the state insurance commissioner will intercede on the consumer's behalf. The regulator with a consumer-oriented perspective is unlikely to be "rewarded" by the public with another job upon the end of his tenure; but the regulator who fails to promote the industry's interests is likely to be denied employment in the industry upon leaving his office.[11]

On the other hand, the continued existence of the system is evidence that state regulation has substantial support. Advocates of state regulation make several points. First, the existence of a state regulatory framework has a definite advantage over a nonexistent federal regulatory framework whose effectiveness and approach is unknown. Second, state regulation is arguably more innovative, since regulatory experiments are more likely to occur when the impact is confined, unlike a national system of regulation. Third, in the same vein, the adverse effects of poor regulation are confined to a few states; inept regulation at the federal level would have national consequences, and the savings and loan crisis of the late 1980s is offered as prime evidence. Fourth, states having no need for a federal program should not be burdened with them. For example, under the current system, if one state needs a special program to deal with high-risk drivers, other states need not go along; but under a national system, all states would presumably participate in the program, whether necessary to the state or not. Fifth, it is doubtful that insurance issues generally would attract the amount of congressional oversight they deserve. Sixth, the criticism that regulation in some states is ineffective is not a serious one. Most underwriting is done by companies licensed in a handful of states with solid regulatory records. The advocates of continued state insurance regulation also make the same arguments offered for preferring state regulation generally: state government officials are closer to the people; a federal insurance administrator would be a minor appointee in the federal bureaucracy; lobbying groups have more effect at the federal level; and a federal regulatory agency would be subject to more temptation to change social policy than a state agency.[12]

---

[10] See United States Comptroller General, note 3, *supra*, at 36; see also U.S. General Accounting Office, *Insurance Departments: Trends in Resources and Workloads in Delaware, North Carolina, and Ohio* (Jan. 1987).

[11] The classic studies and commentaries on this issue are United States Comptroller General, note 3, *supra;* Jon S. Hanson & Thomas E. Obenberger, *Mail Order Insurers: A Case Study in the Ability of the States to Regulate the Insurance Business,* 50 Marq. L. Rev. 175 (1966); Spencer L. Kimball, Symposium, *Insurance Regulation,* 1969 Wis. L. Rev. 1019.

[12] For the classic articulations of the case favoring continued state regulation, see Spencer L. Kimball, "The Case for State Regulation of Insurance," in S. Kimball & Herbert S.

Whatever the merit of these competing views, recent political trends suggest that more regulation will be entrusted to the states in the future, not less.

§ 24   Case Studies in Regulation

[a]   The Controversy over Gender-Based Rating

In the context of the debate over the proper accommodation of federal and state government regulation rests a significant, well-publicized issue: whether the use of gender in setting insurance premiums and payments should be prohibited. Examination of this issue sheds light on the nature of insurance, the extent to which regulation is appropriate, and the boundary between federal and state regulation.

[1]   Gender and Risk

The statistical evidence is undeniable: men, on the average, pose different risks for insurers than do women, on the average. For example, statistics show that women as a group live longer than men as a group. Currently, the average female's life expectancy is about seven years longer than that of the average male. At every age, the incidence of death is higher for males than for females. Therefore, life insurance is more expensive for men than for women because men on the average have shorter lives and consequently have less opportunity to make periodic payments of premiums. Conversely, women usually pay more for annuities than do men (and if men and women make equal contributions, men usually receive higher monthly benefits). This is because men constitute a lower risk for an annuity provider (since they do not live as long to collect the annuity); if men are a lower risk, men should be able to purchase the annuity at a lower cost (or else receive a greater monthly benefit).

In health and disability insurance, because of maternity costs women as a group present more of a risk to insurers than do men as a group. Thus, women often pay more than men for the same health and disability insurance coverage. In automobile insurance, young men have significantly more automobile accidents than young women; men as a group have twice as many fatal automobile accidents as do women as a group. Therefore, men — particularly young men — usually pay more for automobile insurance than women.

In these settings, gender is a low-cost way to differentiate risks. If equally accurate and cheaper methods of measuring risk were available, insurers would be spurred by competition to use them. Similarly, if a more accurate method of measuring risk were available at the same cost, insurers would use that alternative as well. It is not surprising, then, that many insurers have contended for a number of years that they should be allowed to use gender when calculating the price to be charged or the benefits to be provided in certain kinds of insurance.

Denenberg, eds., *Insurance, Government, and Social Policy: Studies in Insurance Regulation* 411–434 (1969); Trowbridge, *The Superiority of State Regulation*, in Weber, note 52 (§ 22), *supra*, at 20–22.

[2] The Supreme Court's Title VII Cases and Their Reach

The use of gender-distinct tables to calculate annuity premiums and benefits was challenged in a number of cases in the 1970s and early 1980s. The first of these cases to reach the Supreme Court was *Los Angeles Department of Water & Power v. Manhart.*[1] For many years, the Department administered a retirement plan for its employees funded by employer and employee contributions. After studying mortality tables and reviewing its own experience, the Department concluded that its female employees on the average lived a few years longer than its male employees. As a result, the cost of a retirement pension for an average female exceeded the cost of the same pension for an average male. The reason for the disparity was simple: the average female employee lived longer to collect benefits. Therefore, the Department required female employees to make monthly contributions about 15 percent higher than those of comparably situated male employees. Since the contributions were deducted from the employees' paychecks, the Department's female employees had less take-home pay than the male employees.

In 1973, Manhart and four other female employees of the Department brought a class action suit on behalf of all of the Department's past and present female employees against the Department for requiring females to make larger contributions than males to receive identical monthly retirement benefits. The plaintiffs claimed that this plan discriminated against women in violation of Title VII of the Civil Rights Act of 1964, which makes it an unlawful employment practice "to discriminate against any individual with respect to his compensation, terms, conditions, or privileges of employment, because of such individual's race, color, religion, sex or national origin."[2]

When the *Manhart* case reached the Supreme Court in 1978, the Court ruled that even though women as a class live longer than men, the Department's practice of requiring females to make larger contributions to its pension plan than the males violated the Civil Rights Act. The Court reasoned that the Act protects *individuals* and that requiring individual women to pay more than individual men for an equal benefit violated federal law.

Five years later, the Supreme Court faced a similar question in *Arizona Governing Committee v. Norris:*[3] whether Title VII also prohibits an employer from providing its employees with a retirement plan that, although funded by equal contributions from males and females, provides men a higher monthly benefit than women. The Court, following the logic of *Manhart,* held in *Arizona Governing Committee* that the employer which provided such a plan violated Title VII.

Under the logic of these two Supreme Court decisions, it is a violation of Title VII for an employer to provide its employees any kind of insurance fringe benefit — whether a retirement plan, a life insurance policy, or an automobile insurance

---

[1] 435 U.S. 702 (1978).

[2] 42 U.S.C. § 2000e-2(a)(1).

[3] 463 U.S. 1073 (1983).

policy — unless identical benefits are provided to both men and women and unless contributions, if any, are the same for both genders.[4]

These two decisions, however, do not require insurance companies to offer their products to the public on a unisex basis. Insurers are free to sell, and private individuals are free to buy, annuities and insurance policies that give different benefits to men and women or that charge men and women different prices. Thus, although an employer may not lawfully provide the employee with an insurance policy whose benefits or contributions are calculated with reference to gender, the employer can give the employee a sum of money, and the employee can use the money to purchase an insurance policy whose price or benefits are calculated according to gender-distinct tables.

[3]   The Proposed Federal Legislation

In most sessions of Congress since 1980, legislation has been introduced that would prohibit discrimination in insurance on the basis of race, color, religion, sex, or national origin. Such proposals typically address discrimination in both the writing and sale of insurance policies and annuities. Also, and most controversially, such proposals would prohibit insurers' using gender-based mortality tables or any other form of gender-based grouping in setting insurance premiums and benefits. In other words, "equalization" of existing insurance contracts of similarly situated males and females would be mandated, and this would occur either by equalizing premiums on contracts with identical coverages or by equalizing coverages on policies with identical premiums. If existing contracts are not abrogated, any attempt to equalize existing policies retroactively would have to occur by increasing the lower coverage to equal the higher and not reducing the higher coverage. To say the least, this proposed legislation raises many provocative questions.

[4]   Is Gender-Based Rating Discriminating or Discriminatory?

One of the questions raised by a proposed ban on gender-distinct rating is whether it is "unfair" to price insurance according to gender. Supporters of the "group perspective" say no: insurance is inherently "discriminating" because the purpose of insurance is to divide a group of potential insureds into smaller categories and price each group according to its risk. Thus, persons with a history of heart disease should pay more for life insurance than persons without that affliction, persons in high risk occupations should pay more for life insurance than college professors, and so on. By this analysis, charging women the same as men for life insurance would be "discriminatory" to women, since women are lower risks than men for this kind of insurance.

Advocates of the "individual perspective" argue yes: it is unfair and "discriminatory" to price insurance according to gender. This viewpoint contends that with respect to certain traits people should be treated the same even if actuarial tables

---

[4] See also Hillesland v. Paccar, Inc., 722 P.2d 1239 (Or. Ct. App. 1986) (holding that employer's health plan discriminated against plaintiff on basis of gender, because package of benefits relating to maternity and pregnancy she received as married female employee was less comprehensive than package of benefits a married male employee received, in violation of Title VII and state law).

and other risk-measuring devices indicate differences. For example, black-americans on the average have a shorter life expectancy than whites, but, because our society views racial discrimination with repugnance, no one contends that black-americans should pay more for life insurance or receive a premium reduction for annuities. Our society also values treating people equally without regard to differences in religious beliefs: if evidence were produced showing that Catholics have a shorter lifespan than non-Catholics, no one would seriously suggest that Catholics pay more for life insurance or receive a premium reduction for annuities. According to proponents of the individual perspective, insurers should not be allowed to use gender to set insurance benefits and premiums any more than they should be allowed to use race, color, national origin, or religion.

Ultimately, choosing between the individual perspective and the group perspective requires making a judgment about what "equality" means in this context. The maxim that equal things should be treated alike and different things should be treated differently is unhelpful, for it does not explain how to determine whether things are alike or different: when distinguishing fruits from vegetables, apples and oranges are alike, but when distinguishing citrus fruits from other kinds of fruits, apples and oranges are different. Without a supplementary standard that describes whether for a particular purpose things are alike or dissimilar, the term equality is nearly meaningless.

For some purposes people should be treated alike, and for some purposes people should be treated differently. Everyone agrees that for the purpose of deciding who is entitled to vote in elections, all people (at least those aged 18 or older) should be treated equally regardless of income. However, most people agree that for the purpose of deciding who should pay for some government programs, income is a relevant characteristic: our society has decided that the poor should have some tax exemptions that are not available to the wealthy. Everyone agrees that for the purpose of deciding who is entitled to a public education, physical disability is not relevant; but for the purpose of deciding who gets a driver's license, everyone agrees that some physical disabilities — such as lack of sight — are highly relevant. Essentially, the question confronting our society is whether gender is a relevant, permissible characteristic for deciding how much insurance should cost (or how much coverage should be provided). Those adhering to the individual perspective on the meaning of equality contend that gender is an irrelevant, impermissible criterion for insurance rating. Proponents of the group perspective argue the contrary and suggest that our society should be satisfied in the insurance setting with an understanding of equality that treats groups — but not necessarily individuals — equally.

The choice between the individual and the group perspective raises one other related issue: what is a fair "cross-subsidy" in insurance? Whenever different risks are put into the same pool and are assessed the same premium, insureds with lower risks subsidize insureds with higher risks. This is called a "cross-subsidy," and it is inevitable to some extent in any insurer's risk pool because of adverse selection. Because any pool of insureds will have a disproportionate number of higher-risk insureds, the pool's higher risks are necessarily subsidized by the pool's lower risks who stand to collect, on average, less in proceeds per dollar of premium paid than the higher risks. Also, cross-subsidies are sometimes deliberately created. For example, if a program of national health insurance were implemented in which all insureds paid the same premium for the same benefits, massive cross-subsidies would occur; in simple terms, the infirm would be subsidized by the healthy. Returning to the issue of gender, if all persons were charged the same premiums for the same amount of insurance regardless of gender, some cross-subsidies between men and women would be created depending on the kind of insurance involved. (For example, in annuities, a cross-subsidy would be created in favor of women; in life insurance, a cross-subsidy would be created in favor of men.) Realizing that some cross-subsidies are inevitable in insurance, the question raised by the proposed mandated use of gender-neutral tables in insurance is whether the additional cross-subsidies created between the genders are desirable. How one answers this question depends in large measure on one's assessment of the relative fairness of the individual versus the group perspective.

[5] State versus Federal Regulation

Although not obvious at first glance, the issue of gender discrimination in insurance raises a regulatory question of some significance. Justice Powell in his dissent in *Arizona Governing Committee* suggested that the McCarran-Ferguson Act's explicit reservation of regulation of the business of insurance to the states was relevant to determining the meaning of Title VII's prohibitions on discrimination in the employer-employee setting.[5] By interpreting Title VII as disallowing the use of gender in pricing insurance provided as a fringe benefit in the employer-employee setting, Justice Powell believed that the Court usurped the states' authority to decide how risk should be spread, a central aspect of the business of insurance.[6] Justice Marshall, writing for the majority, rejected Justice Powell's contention, reasoning that the Court's holding only pertained to an employment practice and not to an insurance practice; states would remain free to regulate the insurance business as they saw fit.[7]

---

[5] 463 U.S. at 1079 nn. 5–6.

[6] Many articles have been published on this issue. See, e.g., Lea Brilmayer, Richard W. Hekeler, Douglas Laycock & Teresa A. Sullivan, *Sex Discrimination in Employer-Sponsored Insurance Plans: A Legal and Demographic Analysis,* 47 U. Chi. L. Rev. 505 (1980); George J. Benston, *The Economics of Gender Discrimination in Employee Fringe Benefits: Manhart Revisited,* 49 U. Chi. L. Rev. 489 (1982); Lea Brilmayer, Douglas Laycock & Teresa A. Sullivan,*The Efficient Use of Group Averages as Nondiscrimination: A Rejoinder to Professor Benston,* 50 U. Chi. L. Rev. 222 (1983); George J. Benston, *Discrimination and Economic Efficiency in Employee Fringe Benefits: A Clarification of Issues and a Response to Professors Brilmayer, Laycock, and Sullivan,* 50 U. Chi. L. Rev. 250 (1983); Robert H. Jerry, II & Kyle B. Mansfield, *Justifying Unisex Insurance: Another Perspective,* 34 Am. U. L. Rev. 329 (1985); Spencer L. Kimball, *Reverse Sex Discrimination: Manhart,* 1979 Am. B. Found. Res. J. 85; George Rutherglen, *Sexual Equality in Fringe-Benefit Plans,* 65 Va. L. Rev. 199 (1979); Paula Sharp, Comment, *Insurance as a Public Accommodation: Challenging Gender-based Actuarial Tables at the State Level,* 15 Colum. Hum. Rts. L. Rev. 227 (1984). See generally Kenneth S. Abraham, *Efficiency and Fairness in Insurance Risk Classification,* 71 Va. L. Rev. 403 (1985).

[7] 463 U.S. at 1087–88 n.17.

That *Manhart* and *Arizona Governing Committee* affect the "business of insurance" is undeniable. Nearly half of all life insurance and a substantial portion of health insurance is sold on a group basis, and most of this is provided in the employment setting. Under the rationale of the Supreme Court's holdings, these insurance products must be rated according to unisex tables — and this would seem to be true even if state legislatures were to require that insurers employ gender-distinct tables in insurance rating.[8]

Of course, state legislatures are free to specify whether gender can be used to rate insurance. In California, after the *Manhart* case was decided, the legislature enacted a statute requiring insurers to use differentials based on gender for ordinary life insurance and individual annuities.[9] In four states, automobile insurance cannot be rated according to gender.[10] In 1985, a Montana statute requiring all insurance sold in the state to have rates and benefits calculated according to gender-neutral tables took effect.[11]

If the criteria to be used in rating insurance are specified by the federal government, obviously the states' role in regulating the business of insurance is diminished. However, the business of insurance has never been immune from all federal regulation; indeed, insurers are not entitled to violate federal civil rights statutes. Mandating individual equality in insurance would simply be an extension of this country's federal civil rights laws, to which insurers are already subject and which state regulators cannot frustrate.

[6] Unisex Insurance and Its Effect on the Marketplace

Another question raised by proposals to prohibit gender-distinct rating is whether such a requirement would result in unacceptable market distortions. As a preliminary

---

[8] After the *Manhart* decision, the California legislature enacted a statute requiring differentials based on gender for ordinary life insurance (not ordinarily sold on a group basis) and individual annuities. West's Ann. Cal. Ins. Code § 790.03(f). Under the logic of the *National Securities* case discussed in § 21[d], *supra,* a state legislature could not circumvent federal civil rights policy by requiring employers to provide different fringe benefits to men and women, meaning, insurance products whose values are calculated by using gender-distinct tables.

[9] See note 8, *supra.*

[10] Hawaii Rev. Stat. § 294-33; Mass. Ann. Laws ch. 175E, § 4(d); Mich. Comp. Laws Ann. § 500.2027(c); N.C. Gen. Stat. § 58-124.19(4). For more discussion, see Stephen Ryan, Note, *The Elimination of Gender Discrimination in Insurance Pricing: Does Automobile Insurance Rate Without Sex?,* 61 Notre Dame L. Rev. 748 (1986).

[11] See Mont. Code Ann. § 49-2-309. In 1988, the Massachusetts Commissioner of Insurance issued regulations prohibiting life insurers from using race, color, religion, sex, marital status, or national origin to price life insurance. 211 Code Mass. Regs. §§ 35.00 et seq. (1987). The regulations were challenged in *Telles v. Commissioner of Ins.,* 574 N.E.2d 359 (Mass. 1991), by female residents who had purchased life insurance policies, male resident who had purchased policies on the lives of female family members, and two insurance companies. The Massachusetts Supreme Court vacated the regulations on the ground that the Commissioner lacked authority to issue them, "as they are in direct conflict with several statutes which expressly permit the very type of risk classification involved in this case." 574 N.E.2d at 360.

inquiry, it is helpful to consider the potential effect on the marketplace of the Supreme Court's decisions in *Manhart* and *Norris*.

Assuming rational consumer behavior, the effect of *Manhart* and *Norris,* in the absence of across-the-board use of unisex rating, is ironic. Consider this simple application of some basic economic principles: Suppose a man (M) and woman (W) are the same age; they work for the same employer and receive the same fringe benefits; assume also that tax considerations are irrelevant. M and W have the option either to take their pension contributions in a lump sum at retirement or in the form of an annuity. M's and W's best prediction is that they will live to the average life expectancies for their genders. If M and W are husband and wife and desire to maximize their joint lifetime income, W should elect the employer-provided annuity — since that annuity is calculated on merged actuarial tables that understate her life expectancy and therefore provide her with a larger annuity than she would obtain in the open market. M should elect the lump-sum payment and use this sum to purchase an annuity in the open market where annuities are calculated on a gender-distinct basis and which provide him with larger monthly benefits than he would obtain under merged tables.

Now, follow the secondary effects of M and W's choices, if repeated by all other similarly situated insureds. Due to the principle of adverse selection, most insureds opting for the employer's retirement plan's benefits will be women, and open-market annuity groups will be dominated by men. Over time, because men will die sooner on the average, the monthly benefits provided under the open market annuity will eventually exceed those provided by the employer's annuity; simultaneously, as the employer's plan becomes heavily utilized by women, who on the average tend to live longer, the benefits paid out on a monthly basis per retiree will begin to decline. Eventually, the benefits provided in the employer's annuity will be the same as those that were provided to women when gender-distinct tables were used. Similarly, the benefits provided under open-market annuities will approximate those offered to men under the employer's plan when gender-distinct tables were used. In short, market forces will lead to the "discrimination" about which the proponents of the individual perspective complained.

One way to eliminate these distortions is to require all annuities (and, necessarily, all insurance policies) to be priced without regard to gender. However, if either less accurate or more costly risk-measuring devices are substituted for gender, overall administrative costs will rise, which must be reflected in the price of insurance to consumers. Available evidence suggests that these costs will be relatively moderate, but a consensus on whether society is willing to pay these costs for unisex rating has yet to emerge.

Implementing unisex rating would also affect the distribution of wealth. Whenever one group is required to pay more for a product and another group's payment is reduced, some redistribution of wealth will occur. In annuities, wealth will be distributed from men as a group to women as a group. Interestingly, many individuals will feel no effect: those who are married and who opt for the "joint-survivor option" (the annuity is paid out to the annuity holder and his or her beneficiary as long as *either* lives) will not be affected by the change to unisex rating.

Joint survivor benefits are already calculated according to what are, in effect, merged tables. Young women will pay more for automobile insurance, but they will pay less for health insurance; for young men, the effects are precisely the opposite. Are these changes desirable? The total costs to society as a whole from unisex rating would be moderate in the sense that our society can easily afford them.[12] The question is whether our society *desires* to incur these costs to achieve the goal of "individual equality without regard to gender" in insurance. This is, like the other choices inherent in the unisex rating controversy, a matter for the Congress to determine.

[b]   AIDS and Insurance Underwriting

Acquired Immune Deficiency Syndrome (AIDS) is one of the most serious health afflictions in history. First recognized in 1981,[13] AIDS actually refers to a condition caused by a viral infection known as the Human Immunodeficiency Virus ("HIV.") The virus invades cells (known as "T-cells") that enable a person's immune system to function; the interference with the immune system leaves the HIV-infected person unable to resist disease, and eventually the person dies of one or more other infections that afflict persons with AIDS. Over 400,000 cases of AIDS had been diagnosed in the U.S. and its territories through June 1994, with more than 243,000 of these cases progressing to death.[14] Estimates of the incidence of HIV infection are less precise, but most experts believe that between one and two million Americans are afflicted with HIV, representing one out of every 250 Americans, and perhaps as many as 10 million people worldwide.[15] Barring a breakthrough in

---

[12] The Comptroller General estimated that the one-time-only administrative costs of implementing unisex insurance on a prospective basis would be approximately $485 million, less than two percent of the total administrative costs for the industry in one year. Comptroller General of the United States, *Economic Implications of the Fair Insurance Practices Act,* Report to Sen. Orrin G. Hatch et al., Appendix I, at 27–28 (Apr. 6, 1984). The Comptroller General was less certain about the redistributive effects of unisex rating, but was nonetheless confident that these effects would be less than the administrative costs. *Id.* at 24–27.

Retroactive gender equality would be another matter. The Comptroller estimated that the "topping up" costs in the pension field would strain the reserves of many insurance companies and could in the short term lead to some insolvencies. *Id.* at 4, 17–18. In a case affecting the retirement funds of many college and university faculty in the country, the Second Circuit approved of retroactive unisex rating where the insurer promised only a very modest rate of return on certain contributions and the retroactive rating would not result in returns below the guaranteed rate. The court conceded that males as a class would be adversely affected by the decision, with the value of their pensions being reduced by about 8% and with women's pensions enjoying an equal increase in income. See Spirt v. TIAA, 735 F.2d 23 (2d Cir.), *cert. denied,* 469 U.S. 881 (1984).

[13] Current evidence suggests that HIV may have been spreading in sub-Saharan Africa for as long as 200 years. It was not until recently that enough people were infected to reach the critical mass needed to cause an epidemic. Henry P. Kaplan, "The HIV-Infected Healthcare Worker," in 1 *Health Law Practice Guide,* ch. 10 (1994). For a succinct background and bibliography of the illness and its legal ramifications, see Mark Rothstein, *Medical Screening and the Employee Health Cost Crisis Information* 81-94 (1989).

[14] Centers for Disease Control and Prevention, *HIV/AIDS Surveillance Report 1994;* 6 (no.1), (hereafter "CDC Report") at 5, 14.

[15] See Rothstein, *supra* note 13, at 81.

the treatment of the virus,[16] it appears that one hundred percent of HIV-positive individuals will progress to clinical AIDS, which is fatal in all cases. Estimates of the costs of treating AIDS patients vary, but a conservative estimate is $80,000 in lifetime costs per AIDS patient,[17] which would place total costs to the health care system in the range of billions of dollars. No matter what dimension is used to describe the impact of AIDS, it is clear that AIDS remains an extraordinarily serious world-wide problem, one of unprecedented scope in this century.

No cure or vaccine for HIV or AIDS is expected soon, but because it is now known that HIV is transmitted in only a few specific ways, the primary assault on AIDS is through preventing further spread of the virus that causes it.[18] HIV is transmitted through unprotected heterosexual or homosexual intercourse, by sharing unsterilized syringes used in intravenous drug injections, by receiving certain HIV-infected body fluids (such as blood via transfusion, through sexual contact, or otherwise; semen; a mother's milk via a breast-fed newborn, etc.), or by receiving a tainted organ or tissue transplant. Health-care workers are also exposed to such risks as cuts during surgery and needle sticks, which makes HIV an occupational hazard for the health-care professions.[19] A non-infected person's casual contact with an HIV-infected person (such as through kissing, sharing eating utensils, etc.) does not transmit HIV. About 60 percent of all reported AIDS cases involve men who have had sex with other men,[20] but in many parts of the world AIDS is a heterosexual phenomenon, and in the United States the most significant increase in HIV-infection is occurring as a result of heterosexual sexual activity.[21] Once infected with HIV, the human body requires a period of time to develop antibodies. Current methods of testing for the illness identify the antibodies, so there is a period

---

[16] Sadly, such a breakthrough is unlikely. "Rapid mutation, a long period during which the virus exists in a latent form escaping the immune response, and the ability of the virus to move through the body in CD 4+ lymphocytes and macrophages make the disease impossible to cure, chronically infectious, and difficult to produce a vaccine against." Kaplan, *supra* note 13, at 10-2.

[17] Kaplan, *supra* note 13, at 90.

[18] See Larry Gostin, *A Decade of a Maturing Epidemic: An Assessment and Directions for Future Public Policy,* 5 Notre Dame J.L. Ethics & Pub. Pol'y 7, 11-27 (1990).

[19] Kaplan, *supra* note 13, at 10-4. Through June 1994, 42 health care workers in the U.S. were documented as having developed AIDS through occupational exposure to HIV-infected blood, and an addition 88 health care workers may have been infected through an occupational transmission of the virus. *CDC Report* at 15.

[20] *CDC Report* at 8. About 25 percent of all AIDS cases involve intravenous drug users, and about seven percent of all AIDS cases resulted from heterosexual contact. *Id.* As of 1991, the incident of infection for HIV in the U.S. population is approximately 0.8% for heterosexuals, 3.2% for intravenous drug users, and 6.2% for gay men. Kaplan, *supra* note 13, at 10-3.

[21] From 1991 to 1992, persons with AIDS who were infected with HIV through heterosexual transmission accounted for the largest proportionate increase in reported AIDS cases in the U.S. From 1985 to 1993, the proportion of persons with AIDS who reported heterosexual contact with a partner at risk for or with documented HIV infection increased from 1.9 percent to 9.0 percent. Center for Disease Control and Prevention, *Morbidity and Mortality Weekly Report* (Mar. 11, 1994).

of time (which can range, apparently, from one to six months) after infection when a person will not test positive on an HIV-antibody test.[22] Thereafter, an HIV-positive person will remain asymptomatic for a period of time, usually ranging from seven to ten years. At that point, one or more symptoms will begin to appear (the initial symptoms are minor, and are often incorrectly attributed to a cold, the flu, or fatigue), but eventually the symptoms will be sufficiently serious and long-term that the collapse of the body's immune system is apparent and the diagnosis of AIDS is possible.[23]

The AIDS crisis raises a diverse set of legal issues,[24] and several of these issues are directly relevant to insurance law.[25] Probably the most prominent of these issues involves to what extent insurers should be allowed to screen or test for HIV during underwriting.

Since the 1980s, almost all life and health insurers have attempted to screen applicants for AIDS.[26] Only open enrollment plans, such as those insurance plans offered to all employees within a certain period of the first date of employment, do not screen or test for AIDS. Normally, open enrollment plans involve large employers and large risk pools, which distribute the costs of AIDS-related claims across a very large base. The logic of large-group underwriting is that which underlies insurance rating generally: The insurer has an interest in keeping higher risks out of its pools of insureds. Moreover, the adverse selection potential with respect to HIV-infection and AIDS is apparent: Upon a positive diagnosis, the afflicted person knows that he or she will have significant health care expenses in the future prior to his or her certain death, and this person has a strong incentive to seek insurance as a means to deal with these future costs.

Typically, the application itself asks whether the applicant has ever tested positive on an HIV-antibody test and whether the applicant has symptoms characteristic of AIDS. Applicants whose answers reveal any stage of HIV infection are almost always rejected for coverage.[27] Also, because insurers who market policies through agents rely to some extent on their agents to make judgments in the field about

---

[22] See Kaplan, *supra* note 13, at 81; see generally Steven Eisenstat, *An Analysis of the Rationality of Mandatory Testing for the HIV Antibody: Balancing the Governmental Public Health Interests with the Individual's Privacy,* 52 U. Pitt. L. Rev. 327 (1991).

[23] See Kaplan, *supra* note 13, at 10-5 to 10-8.

[24] See generally Robert Jarvis, et al., *AIDS Law in a Nutshell* (1991).

[25] For an excellent summary of the issues and a discussion of each, see Alan I. Widiss, *To Insure or Not to Insure Persons Infected with the Virus that Causes AIDS,* 77 Iowa L. Rev. 1617 (1992). For a now-dated but nevertheless useful summary of alternative sides of the issues involving AIDS and underwriting, see Benjamin Schatz, *The AIDS Insurance Crisis: Underwriting or Overreaching?,* 100 Harv. L. Rev. 1782 (1987); Karen Clifford & Russel Iuculano, AIDS and Insurance: *The Rationale for AIDS-Related Testing,* 100 Harv. L. Rev. 1806 (1987).

[26] Randall R. Bovbjerg, *AIDS and Insurance: How Private Health Coverage Relates to HIV/AIDS Infection and to Public Programs,* 77 Iowa L. Rev. 1561, 1585 (1992).

[27] *Id.* at 1585 (citing Jill Eden, Laurie Mount & Lawrence Miike, Office of Technology Assessment, Staff Paper No. 2, *AIDS and Health Insurance: An OTA Survey* (Washington, D.C., Feb. 1988), at 30, 37, 40).

whether an applicant should be insured, it is probable (although no data is known to exist about this practice) that agents informally screen out individuals whom they believe are likely to generate significant costs for the insurer, and that this results in some individuals who are at risk for AIDS (and some individuals who are not, due to over-inclusive assumptions and stereotyping about the illness) being denied insurance.

In addition to questions that raise directly the possibility of HIV infection, the insurer may also seek from the applicant additional information that is thought to be relevant to whether an applicant is at risk for AIDS. Questions on the application may inquire into whether the applicant has any history of drug abuse, infection with a sexually transmitted disease, blood transfusions, and other conditions which are related to the risk of HIV-infection. Although some insurers have asked questions about the applicant's sexual orientation, living arrangements, or financial affairs (such as who the applicant has named as a beneficiary on life insurance policies in force), this practice is very controversial, and violates a recommendation of the National Association of Insurance Commissioners.[28] Insurers' queries into an applicant's sexual preferences violate many peoples' sensibilities, and as a result, some insurers have used the location of the applicant's residence and type of employment as a proxy for a direct question about sexual orientation, notwithstanding the highly indirect link between these factors and whether a person is afflicted with the HIV virus. Whenever an applicant's answers trigger the insurer's underwriting concerns, the insurer may require that the applicant be tested for the HIV antibody.

Except for a short period after initial infection, the presence of the HIV antibody is easily identifiable through blood testing, and the factors which make an individual at risk for AIDS are generally readily identifiable. Because the costs to a health insurer of an AIDS-afflicted person are large over that person's lifetime, health insurers have a purely economic interest in screening for the presence of the virus and excluding these persons from the risk pools. Also, because AIDS afflicts adolescent and young adults in disproportionate numbers, life insurers have a similar economic interest. The intensity of the insurers' interest is heightened by the fact that adolescent and young adults have traditionally been the healthiest groups in our society, thus making them particularly desirable as prospective insureds. In other words, AIDS has created an incentive for insurers to intensify their underwriting for groups that traditionally have required relatively less underwriting.

The effects of this intensified underwriting in health insurance are particularly significant. To the extent the insurer succeeds in identifying those who have a higher risk of contracting AIDS, the insurer will charge what may be an unaffordable premium or perhaps limit coverage entirely. If an employer's group is identified as being disproportionately risky for AIDS due to the presence of one or more infected or high-risk individuals, the cost to the employer of providing the coverage to employees will go up, which may cause the employer to purchase a policy with less

---

28 See National Ass'n of Ins. Comm'rs, "Medical/Lifestyle Questions and Underwriting Guidelines," in I NAIC, *Model Laws, Regulations & Guidelines* 60-1 (1995) ("No question shall be used which is designed to establish the sexual orientation of the applicant.")

generous coverage, to drop the coverage altogether, or to seek to remove the individuals causing this increase in premium or loss of coverage from the employer's work force. In the end, the AIDS victim, the person who needs the coverage most, is the person most likely to lose coverage or perhaps even his or her employment. The options that remain, such as expensive coverage through a high-risk pool (even if one exists) or spending down one's personal assets in order to qualify for Medicaid, are problematic.

In the early 1980s when the contours of the AIDS epidemic were becoming better understood and insurers began to adjust their underwriting, whether insurers should even be allowed to test for the HIV antibody was a hotly debated issue. Some urged prohibitions on testing under the reasoning that it discriminated unfairly against individuals infected with HIV, that insurers could not guarantee the privacy of test results to the considerable detriment of afflicted individuals, and that at-risk individuals would be discouraged from learning more about their health status under the reasoning that if they learned they were infected, they would lose the ability to answer "I don't know" to an insurer's question on an application about whether they have the virus.[29] Those who urged prohibiting testing for HIV also noted that insurers do not seek to exclude all insureds who are at risk for or who suffer from cancer or serious heart conditions. Thus, the industry's efforts to avoid covering HIV-related illnesses struck some as a manifestation of discrimination against gay men, even though AIDS is not a gay disease and is not limited to men, because the largest single group of HIV-infected persons are gay men who have had a same-gender sexual experience.

Whether insurers could maintain confidentiality about the medical condition of applicants who have or are at-risk for HIV infection has been a matter of particular concern. Insurers do not, of course, routinely disclose applicants' medical information upon any third party's request, but applicants and insureds do not enjoy an absolute right to confidentiality of such information either. In the case of AIDS, widespread misunderstanding about the nature of the disease and numerous instances of intolerance for and discrimination against AIDS victims made the stakes with respect to the confidentiality issue quite high.

In 1980, the NAIC promulgated the "Insurance Information and Privacy Protection Model Act,"[30] which has among its purposes "limit[ing] the disclosure of information collected in connection with insurance transactions."[31] The model act, which has been adopted in about fifteen states, recognizes that an insurer can disclose information about an individual upon that individual's express written authorization.[32] But the act also contemplates disclosure in numerous other circumstances, including disclosure to another insurer for the purpose of detecting or preventing material misrepresentation or material nondisclosure in connection with insurance transactions, or to enable another insurer "to perform its function in connection with an insurance transaction involving an individual."[33] This contemplates, as is the

---

[29] See Widiss, *supra* note 25, at 1644-52.

[30] IV NAIC, *Model Laws, Regulations & Guidelines* 670-1 (1992).

[31] *Id.*, Preamble, at 670-1.

[32] *Id.*, § 13(A), at 670-15.

[33] *Id.*, § 13(C), at 670-16.

practice today, widespread sharing of information about insurance applicants among insurers; thus, the information underlying a negative underwriting decision by one insurer is readily accessible to other insurers. Also, many insurers participate in the Medical Information Bureau, a databank with information collected by participating companies and which can be accessed by any participating insurer.[34]

The arguments about the negative consequences of HIV testing were persuasive to many, and during the 1980s administrative or legislative actions in a few jurisdictions banned the use of AIDS screening tests in insurance underwriting.[35] These limitations were vigorously resisted by the insurance industry, which asserted an interest in controlling the amount of risk in their pools of insureds. By the mid-1990s, most states did not prohibit testing or the use of test results but instead regulated various aspects of AIDS testing, such as by prescribing testing protocols, regulating the confidentiality of test results, and requiring notice and consent for testing.[36] Moreover, the NAIC recommended in 1986 that states adopt guidelines that would forbid life and health insurers from inquiring into an applicant's sexual orientation or using sexual orientation in the underwriting process. The proposed guidelines also condemned the use of factors such as gender, marital status, living arrangements, occupation, beneficiary, medical history, and zip code or other territorial identifiers as substitutes for questions about an applicant's sexual orientation.[37]

___

[34] The Medical Information Bureau ("MIB") is an association of approximately 750 health insurers which maintains a national computer network to provide a "confidential interchange of underwriting information among its members as an alert against fraud." Medical Information Bureau, *MIB Fact Sheet* (Jan. 1990), at 1 (cited in Alan Widiss, *To Insure or Not To Insure Persons Infected With the Virus That Causes AIDS,* 77 Iowa L. Rev. 1617, 1735 (1992)). Estimates indicate that the network has files on 11 million Americans and Canadians, and member-insurers write between 90 and 95 percent of all health insurance in force. See Russell S. Burnside, Note, *The Electronic Communications Privacy Act of 1986: The Challenge of Applying Ambiguous Statutory Language to Intricate Telecommunication Technologies,* 13 Rut. Comp. & Tech. L. J. 451 n. 27 (1987).

[35] For example, in 1987 the Massachusetts Commissioner of Insurance promulgated a regulation prohibiting or restricting testing of prospective insureds for exposure to the AIDS virus, but the Massachusetts Supreme Court later held that the Commissioner lacked the authority to promulgate the regulation. Life Ins. Ass'n of Mass. v. Commissioner of Ins., 530 N.E.2d 168 (Mass. 1988). The New York Superintendent of Insurance issued a regulation prohibiting health insurers from requiring a test for the HIV antibody or to provide information about prior testing. This regulation was later struck down on the ground that the Superintended lacked the authority to issue it. Health Ins. Ass'n of America v. Corcoran, 551 N.Y.S.2d 615 (N.Y. App. 1990), *aff'd,* 565 N.E.2d 1264 (N.Y. 1990). A District of Columbia statute prohibiting discrimination based on the results of AIDS testing was upheld in the face of a claim of unconstitutionality, American Council of Life Ins. v. District of Columbia, 645 F. Supp. 84 (D.D.C. 1986), but the law was modified in 1989 to allow some testing.

[36] By 1995, approximately 40 states had some kind of statute or regulation on the use of AIDS tests in insurance. See National Ass'n of Ins. Comm'rs, "Medical/Lifestyle Questions and Underwriting Guidelines,' in I NAIC, *Model Laws, Regulations & Guidelines* 60-3 to 60-7 (1995).

[37] National Ass'n of Ins. Comm'rs, "Medical/Lifestyle Questions and Underwriting Guidelines,' in I NAIC, *Model Laws, Regulations & Guidelines* 60-1 (1995). For further discussion,

Questions on insurance applications seeking information about an applicant's HIV-testing history, as well as questions about the applicant's other personal characteristics, have effects beyond giving the insurer the information it needs to make an underwriting decision. The mere presence of the questions probably deters some individuals, particularly persons who know or suspect they are HIV-positive, from following through with their applications. More importantly, answering such a question falsely will give the insurer the opportunity to assert misrepresentation as a defense to coverage,[38] although in life insurance the incontestability clause will take away the insurer's defense within two years after the date of the application.[39]

Although misrepresentation is frequently invoked by insurers in defending against claims to coverage in a variety of contexts, the law of misrepresentation is not mechanical. Many cases are fact-intensive; how the elements of the defense apply in particular cases are often arguable; and the costs of litigating the defense can be significant. The unavoidable ambiguity in the law of misrepresentation (and to some extent in the law applying incontestability clauses as well) probably encourages insurers to administer blood tests to applicants. In other words, blood tests may be viewed by insurers as a more efficient and effective way of controlling moral hazard (i.e., controlling the amount of risk in the insurers' pool of insureds) than simple reliance by insurers on the misrepresentation defense.

Beyond the efforts of insurers to control who is admitted into their risk pools, standard policy language can limit coverage for AIDS, just as it can for other conditions. For example, a clause that excludes from coverage pre-existing conditions (or imposes a waiting period until pre-existing conditions are eligible for coverage) denies coverage for HIV-related illnesses equally with other conditions. Specific exclusions for HIV/AIDS conditions seem to be rare, but a few insurance plans have included them, and at least one other has imposed lifetime caps on AIDS benefits.[40]

Whether these limitations can be imposed in the employment setting raises a distinct set of issues because of legislative regulation of the employment relationship. For example, the Americans with Disabilities Act ("ADA"),[41] which was intended to establish a comprehensive prohibition of discrimination based on disability, prohibits an employer subject to the provisions of the act from refusing to employ HIV-positive individuals who are otherwise qualified for the positions

see Comment, *Prohibiting the Use of the Human Immunodeficiency Virus Antibody Test by Employers and Insurers,* 25 Harv. J. Leg. 275 (1988).

[38] See § 102, *infra*; Waxse v. Reserve Life Ins. Co., 809 P.2d 533 (Kan. 1991) (insured did not misrepresent his condition when failing to disclose prior positive test for HIV); Annot., *Rescission or Cancellation of Insurance Policy for Insured's Misrepresentation or Concealment of Information Concerning Human Immunodeficiency Virus (HIV), Acquired Immunodeficiency Syndrome (AIDS), or Related Health Problems,* 15 A.L.R.5th 92 (1993).

[39] See § 104B, *infra*; see Blue Cross & Blue Shield of Ga., Inc. v. Sheehan, 450 S.E.2d 228 (Ga.App. 1994) (incontestability clause barred insurer's effort to rescind health insurance policy where insured committed fraud on application by denying he was HIV-positive).

[40] Randall R. Bovbjerg, *AIDS and Insurance: How Private Health Coverage Relates to HIV/AIDS Infection and to Public Programs,* 77 Iowa L. Rev. 1561, 1595 (1992).

[41] 42 U.S.C. §§ 12101-12213.

they seek.[42] This invites the question as to whether an employer who is barred by the ADA from refusing to hire an otherwise qualified HIV-positive prospective employee can restrict employee benefits (e.g., life, disability, and health insurance) to that same person on account of the same disability. The ADA requires employers to provide the same benefits to employed disabled persons as are provided other employees, but this requirement is subject to two caveats.

First, the ADA, by its own terms, may not be construed to prohibit or restrict insurers (or entities that administer employee benefit plans) from underwriting, classifying, or administering risks.[43] Even though insurers and administrators of benefit plans can discriminate between high-risk and low-risk individuals, it does not necessarily follow that employers can provide to employees insurance plans that discriminate against HIV-afflicted persons or AIDS victims. As discussed earlier,[44] Title VII prohibits *employers* from providing gender-distinct insurance even though the insurance industry is free to create and sell such products. The Equal Employment Opportunity Commission has filed determination letters and is involved in some lawsuits in which it is asserting that benefit modifications singling out HIV or AIDS violate the ADA.[45] At least one court has approved that position.[46] Even if the ADA provides a safe harbor to some employer-provided insurance plans, employers who operate self-funded employee benefits plans are not insurers and therefore cannot claim the benefit of the ADA's protection of the risk-classifying and underwriting activities of insurers.

Second, the ADA does not prevent an employer from conditioning benefits on sound actuarial requirements that are not intended as a subterfuge to evade the purposes of the Act.[47] Thus, it would appear, and the EEOC apparently agrees, that pre-existing condition clauses and other clauses that preclude coverage for persons infected at the beginning of the coverage's effective date are not rendered invalid by the ADA. As for an employer that seeks to reduce benefits to all employees in response to the costs associated with one or more cases of AIDS in the employer's workforce, the tension is apparent: reducing benefits is arguably consistent with

---

[42] See Jeffrey A. Mello, *Limitations of the Americans with Disabilities Act in Protecting Individuals with HIV from Employment Discrimination,* 19 Seton Hall Legis. J. 73 (1994); Laura Pincus, *The Americans with Disabilities Act: Employers' New Responsibilities to HIV-Positive Employees,* 21 Hofstra L. Rev. 561 (1993).

[43] 42 U.S.C. § 12201(c)(1).

[44] See § 24[a][2], *supra.*

[45] See EEOC, *Interim Enforcement Guidance on the Application of the Americans with Disabilities Act to Disability Based Distinction in Employer Provided Health Insurance* (June 8, 1993). For a more detailed discussion of this issue, see Jonathan Mook, *Expanding ADA Coverage to Employee Benefit Plans,* 20 Employee Relations L.J. 571 (1995); Patrick Morgan, Comment, *Applicability of ADA Non-Discrimination Principles to Self-Insured Health Plans: Do "Aids Caps" Violation the Law?,* 11 J. Contemp. Health L. & Pol'y 221 (1994) (arguing that the EEOC regulations limiting aids caps in self-insured plans will ultimately be held invalid).

[46] See Carparts Distribution Center, Inc. v. Automotive Wholesalers' Ass'n of New England, 37 F.3d 12 (1st Cir. 1994).

[47] 42 U.S.C. § 12201(c).

sound actuarial principles, but seems at odds with the purposes of the ADA. As noted above, the EEOC takes the position that AIDS-specific exclusions or caps are not permitted by the ADA.

But the situation is more complicated than that. Another statute relevant to this issue is the Employee Retirement and Income Security Act ("ERISA"),[48] which regulates employee benefit plans and generally supersedes state laws relating to such plans. Although the analysis is complicated, as interpreted by courts ERISA does not give employees vested rights to particular coverages in health insurance plans. Therefore, HIV-positive persons and AIDS victims lack rights to insist upon coverage for their afflictions under ERISA.[49] In *McGann v. H & H Music Co.*,[50] the Fifth Circuit held that an employer did not violate ERISA when it substituted for an insurance plan that provided $1 million in medical benefits a self-funded plan that limited benefits for AIDS-related claims to $5,000. In holding that the employee, whose affliction with AIDS was the reason the employer switched plans, had no entitlement to the benefits under the plan in force when he first learned he carried the HIV virus, the court recognized an employer's right to modify a health benefits plan for its employees even when motivated by a desire to reduce coverage of (that is, to avoid the costs associated with the illness of) a particular employee.

Whether this interpretation of ERISA is correct can be reasonably debated.[51] Regardless, *McGann* preceded the ADA, so whether the holding of the case survives the mandates of the ADA is an open question. In any event, because the Supreme Court's interpretation of the preemptive scope of ERISA leaves self-insured health plans immune from state regulation and ERISA itself does not impose substantive requirements on the content of health plans, employers have an incentive to self-insure in order to preserve the option to exclude coverage for high-risk or expensive medical claims. This, however, only invites a question discussed earlier: whether such exclusions comport with the requirements of the ADA.

All of these complex questions, however, pale when a more fundamental question is raised. If the application of a person seeking life insurance is denied because the applicant is identified as HIV-positive, the person loses a contractual opportunity. With respect to health insurance, the ramifications are very different. Whether insured or not, AIDS patients will not go without health care, and the costs of these services must be absorbed somewhere in the system, whether in the form of a provider write-off, government subsidy, or distribution through an insurance mechanism. If the costs of health care for AIDS victims are not distributed through an insurance mechanism, the question becomes whether the costs will be distributed across all patients of the provider writing-off the care, or across the entire taxpaying public. The lifetime per-patient costs of AIDS are high. Even though former employees have some rights to purchase continuing coverage under COBRA,[52] and

---

[48] 29 U.S.C. §§ 1001-1461.

[49] See Widiss, *supra*, at 1696-1706.

[50] 946 F.2d 401 (5th Cir. 1991), *cert. denied*, 113 S.Ct. 482 (1992).

[51] For a thoughtful discussion of this issue and a critique of McCann, see James R. Bruner, Note, *Aids and Erisa Preemption: The Double Threat*, 41 Duke L.J. 1115 (1992).

[52] See § 64[c], *infra*.

high risk pools provide some help in those states which have created them,[53] these mechanisms, even when viewed in combination with Medicare and Medicaid, fall far short of providing a coordinated, comprehensive solution to the problem of the uninsured AIDS victim.

The 1994 debate on health care reform and the changing political winds in Washington suggest that the likelihood of the enactment of a national health insurance program that guarantees coverage and health care access to all citizens, including AIDS victims, is low. Moreover, there seems to be no particular interest in developing a narrowly-tailored program, either at the federal or state level, that would provide special support for AIDS victims (perhaps to the exclusion of victims of other illnesses).[54] Thus, there is no obvious solution on the horizon that reconciles the insurer's legitimate desire to separate higher-risk insureds from lower-risk insureds for the purpose of charging the higher-risk insureds more or not providing coverage to them at all, and society's desire to ensure that those afflicted with AIDS receive the care they need.

[c] Genetic Screening and Insurance Underwriting

Because insurers have an economic incentive in distinguishing among insureds in setting coverage and premiums whenever it is cost-effective for them to do so,[55] any technology with significant power to predict an individual's future health status is of great interest to insurers. Technological developments of the 1990s portend a revolution in how life, health, and disability insurers conduct their business.

The Human Genome Initiative ("HGI") refers to a massive research project, commenced in 1991 and coordinated by the National Institute for Health, which seeks to construct a map of the human genome, the chromosomal material (i.e., DNA) where human genes reside and which define many individual physical characteristics.[56] Mutations in genes can also contribute to the development of certain diseases. One of the goals of HGI, the most ambitious cooperative biologic research project in history, is to develop within fifteen years a detailed genetic map of the human genome, which at some time in the future would make evaluation of the genome of any particular person relatively easy and inexpensive. Achievement of this goal would facilitate — indeed, could make certain — the diagnosis of a person's disease or his or her susceptibility to certain diseases, and could help lead to cures for some of humankind's most serious afflictions.[57] Already, the

---

[53] See § 22[e], *supra.*

[54] Except for the support provided in Medicare for end-stage renal disease, see 42 U.S.C. § 426-1 and federal programs relating to black-lung disease, see 30 U.S.C. §§ 901-942, there is no major governmentally-provided program that provides for the victims of a particular illness.

[55] See § 10[c], *supra.*

[56] For a detailed history of HGI, see Robert Mullon Cook-Degan, *Origins of the Human Genome Project,* 5 Risk: Health, Safety & Env't 97 (1994). For more detail on the methodology of gene mapping, see Victor A. McKusick, "The Human Genome Project: Plans, Status, and Applications in Biology and Medicine," in George Annas and Sherman Elias, eds., *Gene Mapping: Using Law and Ethics as Guides,* 18 (1992).

[57] See generally C. Thomas Caskey, *Presymptomatic Diagnosis: A First Step Toward Genetic Health Care,* 262 Science 48 (Oct. 1, 1993). The new knowledge generated by HGI

identification of many genes that correlate with certain diseases, such as cystic fibrosis, neurofibromatosis, Huntington's disease, sickle cell anemia, hemochromatosis, phenylketonuria (PKU), and other illnesses, is common.[58]

For some diseases, such as Huntington's, identification of the mutant gene that causes the disease offers the afflicted person nothing but the knowledge that he or she will suffer a premature death from a disease for which there is no cure. This is of some benefit to the person, of course, for it may affect the person's decisions about whether to have children or to marry,[59] whether to take out a long-term mortgage, and what other financial arrangements the person should make in light of the diminution in the person's expected longevity. With respect to other diseases, knowledge that the person will have the disease might lead the person to make adjustments in his or her lifestyle which will postpone the onset of the disease or reduce its severity. Indeed, HGI will probably usher in an entirely new kind of medical care — preemptive therapy.[60] Experts indicate that probably about 4,000 diseases are genetic in origin;[61] thus, the potential of HGI to affect diagnosis, treatment, and prevention of much illness is enormous.

Despite the great promise of HGI, there are reasonable grounds for raising concerns about the impact of the new technology as well. Prenatal diagnosis of fetal conditions can aid treatments, but has other social and ethical ramifications when the information is used to terminate pregnancies.[62] To the extent genetic markers correlate — or are thought to correlate, even if they do not in all cases — to cognitive ability, behavior, and disabilities, the implications for how children are educated in the nation's schools are potentially dramatic.[63] When genetic data is linked with

---

has already caused physicians to ponder the difficult questions of when to order screening, to what extent some kinds of screening should be routine, what constitutes appropriate clinical practice, etc. See Benjamin Wilford & Norman Fost, *The Introduction of Cystic Fibrosis Carrier Screening into Clinical Practice: Policy Considerations,* 70 Milbank Quarterly 629 (Dec. 22, 1992).

[58] Jon Beckwith, *Foreword: The Human Genome Initiative: Genetics' Lightning Rod,* 17 Am. J of Law & Med. 1, 2-8 (1991).

[59] Normally, this disease appears after the person reaches 35 years of age. Huntington's being one of the few diseases that is caused by a dominant gene, meaning that the presence of the gene in either parent will cause the gene to be present in the offspring, the disease is easily passed across generations. See Robert K. Ausman & Dean E. Snyder, 4 *Medical Library: Lawyer's Edition* 151 (1989).

[60] See Caskey, *supra* note 57.

[61] See Kaplan, *supra* note 13, at 76.

[62] See generally Vicki G. Norton, Comment, *Unnatural Selection: Non-therapeutic Preimplantation Genetic Screening and Proposed Regulation,* 41 UCLA L. Rev. 1581 (1994); Abby Lippman, *Prenatal Genetic Testing and Screening: Constructing Needs and Reinforcing Inequities,* 17 Am. J. of Law & Med. 15 (1991); John Robertson, "Genetic Alteration of Embryos: The Ethical Issues," in Aubrey Milunsky & George J. Annas, eds., *Genetics and the Law III,* at 115 (1985); Aubrey Milunsky, "Prenatal Diagnosis: New Tools, New Problems," in Milunsky & Annas, *id.,* at 335.

[63] See generally Delores James, *The Human Genome Initiative: Implications for the Comprehensive School Health Program,* 64 J. of School Health 80 (1994); Dorothy Nelkin & Laurence Tancredi, *Classify and Control: Genetic Information in the Schools,* 17 Am. J. of Law & Med. 51 (1991).

racial and ethnic differences, the potential for exacerbating discrimination is acute.[64] The possible accumulation of vast amounts of genetic data about individuals has implications for privacy, employees in the workplace, and the eligibility of some people for jobs.[65]

Genetic testing has obvious insurance implications as well.[66] Like the situation with HIV testing, a major concern for some is the confidentiality of test results. If a person has had a genetic test, the results of the test become a part of that person's medical record. If that person should later apply for an insurance product involving individual underwriting (e.g., life insurance not sold in a group setting), he or she will sign a release giving the insurer access to those medical records. At that point, the genetic test not only will become known to the insurer but also will become a part of that person's record at the Medical Information Bureau ("MIB"), an organization sponsored by insurers that maintains medical data on applicants and makes that data accessible to all insurers which sponsor the Bureau.[67] Although the MIB promises to maintain the confidentiality of this information, the possibility that this confidentiality could be compromised is always present. Furthermore, one reason to have a genetic test performed is to help a biological relative in the diagnosis of an illness or his or her risk for illness, or to help the person tested and his or her spouse make a choice about whether to have children. If the results of such tests become a part of the person's permanent medical record, the act of helping a third party may have negative repercussions on the person's ability to acquire insurance in the future. At the margin, this may deter some people from having tests performed that would directly or indirectly benefit third parties.[68]

An even more significant ramification of genetic screening for insurance involves the impact of the technology on insurers' ability to distinguish among different degrees of risk, and the secondary effects of this ability on the cost and availability of insurance to some persons. If testing were available at low cost, insurers could identify many kinds of susceptibilities to particular diseases much more easily, and

---

[64] See Patricia A. King, "The Past as Prologue: Race, Class, and Gene Discrimination," in George Annas and Sherman Elias, eds., Gene Mapping: Using Law and Ethics as Guides 94 (1992).

[65] Genetic tests do not, of course, have entirely negative uses in the workplace. In demonstrating a person's susceptibility to certain diseases, tests can be used to caution individuals against taking certain kinds of jobs where the employee is exposed to conditions that increase the risk of a disease to which the employee is already susceptible. Gostin, *supra*, at 111. See generally Lori B. Andrews & Ami S. Jaeger, *Confidentiality of Genetic Information in the Workplace*, 17 Am. J. of Law & Med. 75 (1991); Larry Gostin, *Genetic Discrimination: The Use of Genetically Based Diagnostic and Prognostic Tests by Employers and Insurers*, 17 Am. J. of Law & Med. 109 (1991); Ruth Macklin, "Privacy and Control of Genetic Information," in George Annas and Sherman Elias, eds., *Gene Mapping: Using Law and Ethicd as Guides* 157 (1992).

[66] For a general summary of these implications, see Roberta M. Berry, *The Human Genome Project and the End of Insurance,* 7 U. Fla. J. L. & Pub. Pol'y —(1995); T. H. Cushing, *Should There Be Genetic Testing in Insurance Risk Classification?* 60 Def. Couns. J. 249 (1993).

[67] See note 34, *supra*.

[68] See Cushing, *supra* note 66, at 259.

insurance premiums could be adjusted accordingly. Health insurers might choose not to insure individuals who are at risk for particular conditions, and it is not folly to imagine such information being kept in a database and later being used to affect the availability of insurance to the biological children of persons who have tested positive for certain conditions. Life insurers would certainly be expected to charge more to persons whose genetic markers indicate that the person will have or is likely to have at some later time a life-shortening disease. Disability insurers would decline to underwrite individuals who have genetic markers indicating that illness will prematurely prevent such persons from performing the ordinary requirements of his or her job. As discussed earlier, the American with Disabilities Act is relevant to how employers treat disabled employees, but the ADA does not prevent the application of sound actuarial principles to eligibility for benefits, such as insurance.[69]

To understand the potential impact of genetic screening on underwriting, one might reflect on insurance's role as a leveler of the playing field: risk is distributed across a large group of persons who pay the same for identical coverage, and those who suffer losses are subsidized by those who do not. But uncertainty is an essential ingredient of this formula. The uncertainty that any particular person will suffer a loss provides a basis for pooling a large number of similarly-situated persons, whose risks are simultaneously transferred to the insurer and distributed across the entire pool.[70] This is possible because of the statistical near-certainty that in the large group only a small, random number will actually suffer the loss, notwithstanding the near-total uncertainty as to whether any particular person will suffer a loss. When it is certain that a *particular* person will suffer a loss, the principle of fortuity is lost, and insurers are not at all interested in providing coverage; when the amount of an expected loss equals the total loss that would result, the premium to be charged must equal the amount of the loss, and there is no utility in having an insurance transaction.

Despite insurance's tendency to level the playing field when a large number of insureds is involved, insurers attempt to establish multiple playing fields when it is possible to divide one group of insureds into different sub-groups. In other words, insurers seek to offer sub-groups of a larger pool lower-cost insurance if they have lower risks relative to other groups, provided the cost of distinguishing among the sub-groups does not exceed the discount that can be offered to the lower risk sub-group. Stated otherwise, all other things remaining equal, less uncertainty causes more division into sub-groups with different coverages and different premiums. HGI suggests a future ability to predict illness, disease, and life expectancy with greater certainty; in a world with powerful genetic screening technology, each individual might face a different insurance price based upon his or her genetic map.

In such a world, those who have "bad genes" could lack access to the insurance coverage they need. This kind of world would call into question fundamental

---

[69] See notes 41-48, *supra.*

[70] Professor Richard Epstein has offered the excellent example of the risk of being struck by a meteor. This risk is unpredictable, affects all people equally, does not induce adverse selection, and no one has more or less information about the likelihood of the event. Richard Epstein, *The Legal Regulation of Genetic Discrimination: Old Responses to New Technology,* 74 B.U. L. Rev. 1, 8-9 (1994).

assumptions about insurance, and would raise provocative questions. For example, should everyone have a right to health care (i.e., health insurance) regardless of his or her health needs? Or should market forces be allowed to operate, which means those who are healthier (and therefore less likely to consume health care services) pay less for health insurance, and those in greatest need pay more, which would cause some people to go without care? At one level, it is argued that people should not pay more (or less) for insurance on account of factors they cannot control (such as race or gender).[71] But what, then, about genetic screening? We do not control the composition of our genetic material; thus, should a person whose genes reveal he or she will contract a life-shortening disease by the time he or she reaches middle-age pay the same for health insurance as someone who is healthy and otherwise expects to achieve his or her full life expectancy?[72] These questions are difficult ones, and may ultimately require a broad-scale re-examination of the role of insurance in our society.

[d] A Concluding Thought on the Nature of Insurance

The questions raised in the foregoing case studies on gender-based rating, AIDS and underwriting, and developments in genetic screening require, in the final analysis, reconsideration of the role of insurance in a complex society which simultaneously values economic liberty, wealth, welfare for the disadvantaged, entrepreneurial activity, egalitarianism, and fairness. Clearly, there is much at stake. Maximizing access to insurance (and in the case of health insurance, this means, for many people, health care) is a goal that cannot be perfectly reconciled with the economic forces that underlie the operation of insurance markets. This paradox will require our society to grapple in future years with two fundamentally opposed notions of what insurance really is. Should, on the one hand, insurance be viewed as a product to be purchased and sold in predominately unregulated markets, where access to insurance is a function of a person's risk and ability to pay? In this paradigm, insurance will be unavailable to many people, sometimes people with high risks and great needs. Sometimes the absence of insurance will reduce the amount of commercial activity, and therefore wealth generation, that would otherwise occur. Or, on the other hand, should insurance be viewed as a public good, where access is an entitlement and the costs are spread across the widest groups possible, perhaps even the entire population in some instances? In this paradigm, government, either as facilitator or insurer, plays a much greater role in our lives, but certain values are furthered (and some costs incurred) that are beyond the reach (or effects) of unregulated, or partially regulated, markets. To some extent, this dichotomy is already apparent in the debate over health care reform and the issue of whether health insurance should become a national program.[73] These issues are certain to be with us for many years to come.

---

[71] See § 24[a], *supra*.

[72] For the perspective that genetic screening should be banned, see Joseph M. Miller, Comment, *Genetic Testing and Insurance Classification: National Action Can Prevent Discrimination Based on the "Luck of the Genetic Draw,"* 93 Dick. L. Rev. 729 (1989).

[73] For a thoughtful discourse on this question in the context of health insurance, see Deborah A. Stone, *The Struggle for the Soul of Health Insurance,* 18 J. Health Pol., Pol'y & L. 287 (1993).

§ 25   Judicial Regulation

When one thinks of "government regulation," what usually comes to mind are the statutes enacted by legislatures and the activities of administrative agencies exercising power delegated by legislatures. This view is accurate but incomplete: courts, through the development and application of common law principles in case-by-case adjudication and by the interpretation and application of state statutes in the course of such adjudication, also perform a regulatory function. Over the last several decades, courts have faced a steady stream of litigated controversies allowing them to apply and sometimes create principles of law pertinent to the insurance business.

Viewing the subject matter of insurance law broadly, the legislature clearly functions as the most important lawmaker in the field. The legislature sets policy; it is the branch of government that possesses the authority to create the entities to implement that policy. Courts, however, must wait for cases to arrive before them, and the case-or-controversy doctrine limits courts to the narrow issues presented by these cases. Thus, the judiciary, by its nature, is not well suited to articulating broad policies. Yet when courts dispose of claims, they play an extremely important role in the regulatory process.

[a]   Courts as Regulators

As discussed in greater detail in the following sections, when courts decide a case, they apply rules to a particular fact situation and announce a decision that operates retroactively on the parties. Thus, if an insurer has denied coverage and the court decides that the policy's language provides coverage, the insurer is prevented in future cases from taking the position that the policy provides no coverage. Also, if the insurer's denial of coverage damaged the interests of the insured, the insurer may be required to compensate the insured for reasonably foreseeable losses suffered by the insured as a consequence of the insurer's breach. Other insurers, who are not parties to the litigation in which the rule on coverage was articulated and applied, are technically not bound by the court's decision. However, these insurers will ordinarily adjust their conduct to comply with the court's ruling, for they are now on notice that in future cases that might come before that court the conduct condemned in the decided case will not be tolerated.

Thus, courts play an important role in regulating the business of insurance. When courts interpret contract language, or decide cases through application of thedoc- trines of waiver or estoppel, or determine coverage questions through application of the reasonable expectations doctrine, or experiment with the rapidly evolving duty of good faith and fair dealing, courts are affecting conduct of companies and individuals not parties to litigation and therefore are regulating the business of insurance.

[b]   The Interplay Between Legislative and Judicial Regulation

The two regulatory modes, legislative and judicial, are not entirely distinct. Occasionally cases arise that call into question the interaction of these two modes. The issue is usually articulated in one of two ways: (1) whether a statutory scheme regulating some aspect of the insurance business gives a consumer a private cause of action for damages when an insurer's activity allegedly violates the statute; and (2) whether a statutory scheme delegating regulatory authority to an administrator preempts judicially recognized remedies.

During the 1980s a prominent line of cases debated the issue of whether a consumer has a private right of action against an insurer under state statutes based on the NAIC's model act titled "An Act Relating to Unfair Methods of Competition and Unfair and Deceptive Acts and Practices in the Business of Insurance." This model act has been adopted always in substance and sometimes verbatim in all states. The question raised was whether the legislatures which enacted them intended to give new legal rights to private parties or merely intended the statutes to be a mechanism for administrative enforcement for the benefit of the public at large. In a highly-publicized decision in California, *Royal Globe Insurance Co. v. Superior Court*,[1] it was held that under California's statute in some circumstances the defendant's liability insurer owed a duty to settle not only to the defendant-insured but also to the plaintiff who owned the claim against the insured, and that the statute created a private right of action in both the defendant-insured and the plaintiff. Although the decision had virtually no following outside California,[2] the decision (until it was overruled by the same court nine years later in *Moradi-Shalal v. Fireman's Fund Ins. Cos.*[3]) had a significant impact on claims settlement practices. The decision granted the plaintiff in a tort suit against an insured-defendant a potential claim against the insured's liability carrier anytime the insurer rejected a settlement offer made by the plaintiff. This threat no doubt caused many liability

---

[1] 592 P.2d 329 (Cal. 1979).

[2] Courts in almost all other jurisdictions confronting the issue refused to follow the *Royal Globe* analysis. See, e.g., McWhirter v. Fire Ins. Exch., 878 P.2d 1056 (Okla. 1994); Herrig v. Herrig, 844 P.2d 487 (Wyo. 1992); Gunny v. Allstate Ins. Co., 830 P.2d 1335 (Nev. 1992); Morris v. American Family Mut. Ins. Co., 386 N.W.2d 233 (Minn. 1986); Patterson v. Globe Am. Cas. Co., 685 P.2d 396 (N.M.Ct.App. 1984); Seeman v. Liberty Mut. Ins. Co., 322 N.W.2d 35 (Iowa 1982); Dunrite Auto Body & Motor Works, Inc. v. Liberty Mut. Ins. Co., 590 N.Y.S.2d 152 (N.Y. App. 1992); Scroggins v. Allstate Ins. Co., 393 N.E.2d 718 (Ill. App. Ct. 1979). West Virginia recognizes a private cause of action in the plaintiff, Jenkins v. J.C. Penney Cas. Ins. Co., 280 S.E.2d 252 (W.Va. 1981), but a portion of this opinion prohibiting joinder of the insurer with the insured in the same action was overruled in State ex rel. State Farm Fire & Cas. Co. v. Madden, 451 S.E.2d 721 (W.Va. 1994). For most courts analyzing this issue, it has been important that the state statutes generally prohibit unfair claims settlement practices that occur with sufficient frequency to constitute "a general business practice." This language suggests that to have a remedy, it is necessary to demonstrate more than one incident in violation of the statute, and is indicative of a legislative intent to give a remedy to the authorized government regulator, not to a private party. See, e.g., White v. Uniguard Mut. Ins. Co., 730 P.2d 1014 (Idaho 1986); Mead v. Burns, 509 A.2d 11 (Conn. 1986); Klaudt v. State Farm Mut. Auto. Ins. Co., 658 P.2d 1065 (Mont. 1983); Salois v. Mutual of Omaha Ins. Co., 581 P.2d 1349 (Wash. 1978); Ceshker v. Bankers Commercial Life Ins. Co., 558 S.W.2d 102 (Tex. Ct. App. 1977). In Kentucky, where the legislature in 1988 amended the statute to remove the requirement that the frequency indicate a general business practice, the statute has been held to create a private right of action. See State Farm Mut. Auto. Ins. Co. v. Reeder, 763 S.W.2d 116 (Ky. 1989).

[3] 758 P.2d 58 (Cal. 1988)(en banc).

insurers to settle cases filed against their insureds that would not have been settled but for the potential third-party bad faith claim, and this added expense inevitably fueled an increase of some unknown magnitude in premiums paid by all insureds. The important point to be drawn here, however, does not involve the flawed logic of *Royal Globe*, a case which attracted an enormous amount of attention when decided but which now appears destined only for discussion in footnotes; rather, the important point is that judicial interpretation of legislative enactments can have an enormous impact on how the business of insurance is conducted.

The same phenomenon — the interplay between legislative and judicial regulation — is apparent in courts' assessment of whether the mere existence of state statutory regulation affects the scope of remedies traditionally afforded by the common law. Of course, legislatures are free to alter common law rules by specific legislative pronouncements. However, in a number of instances, the mere existence of legislative regulation has affected the substance of the common law.

For example, under the common law, a broker who undertakes to secure insurance for a consumer is that person's agent. Most courts would probably hold that the common law imposes a fiduciary duty on the broker to take reasonable steps to investigate the solvency of insurers from whom the broker is purchasing policies for his clients. Under the common law, if the broker places insurance in a company that later becomes insolvent, the duty would be breached if the broker knew or should have known of the ensuing insolvency.[4] However, a California court has held that since the legislatures have directed state insurance departments to investigate the solvency of companies, brokers have no obligation to perform this function.[5] Similarly, although many states have recognized a tort of bad faith in the first-party insurance setting, the third-party insurance setting, or in both, some state courts have declined to recognize the tort on the ground that the existence of state regulation eliminates the need for it.[6]

In deciding whether a private right of action exists under a statute or whether a statute preempts common law actions, the critical determination for the court is the legislature's intent. The legislature, within the limits of its own constitutional authority, has the power to eliminate or modify common law rules and rights based upon those rules and to create new causes of action. The difficulty is that the legislature frequently does not speak with clarity, and the courts are then faced with the sometimes demanding task of determining legislative intent.

§ 25A Contract Interpretation

One of the most common methods of judicial regulation is *interpretation*. Interpretation is sometimes described as a process by which one determines the

---

[4] See Sternoff Metals Corp. v. Vertecs Corp., 693 P.2d 175 (Wash. Ct. App. 1984).

[5] See Wilson v. All Service Ins. Corp., 153 Cal. Rptr. 121 (Cal. Ct. App. 1979).

[6] See, e.g., Spencer v. Aetna Life & Cas. Ins. Co., 611 P.2d 149 (Kan. 1980); A.A.A. Pool Service & Supply, Inc. v. Aetna Cas. & Sur. Co., 395 A.2d 724 (R.I. 1978); Farris v. U.S. Fid. and Guar. Co., 587 P.2d 1015 (Or. 1978); Debolt v. Mutual of Omaha, 371 N.E.2d 373 (Ill. App. Ct. 1978).

meaning the parties gave the language they chose to put in their contract. Determining the intent of the parties is usually what courts say they are doing when they interpret a contract's language. However, it is important to realize that *courts interpret contract language;*[1] thus, the process of interpretation is whatever courts do in particular cases. In practice, the criteria employed by courts to determine a contract's meaning are diverse. Thus, a more accurate definition of interpretation is the following: *Interpretation is the process by which a court determines the meaning that it will give the language used by the parties in a contract.*

[a]   Kinds and Causes of Imprecision in Contracts

To understand why disputes arise over a contract's meaning, it is helpful to distinguish three different kinds of imprecision in insurance policies: imprecise language; ambiguous organization; and ambiguity created by extrinsic information.[2]

Professor Farnsworth has articulated a framework by which at least three different types of *imprecise language* can be categorized. One kind of imprecision is *vagueness.* A word is vague if it is imprecise in marginal applications. For example, consider an automobile insurance policy that limits the insurer's liability to "$20,000 each occurrence." The insured's car crosses the median on a multi-lane interstate highway, hits one car in the passing lane, and then slides several hundred feet before hitting a second car in the driving (righthand) lane. Has there been one occurrence or two?[3] If there had been one impact, the term "occurrence" would have presented no difficulty, but the word is imprecise in marginal applications.

Another type of imprecise language is *ambiguity of term.* A term is ambiguous if it has multiple appropriate meanings which cause its use in a particular context to be unclear. Unlike vagueness, a common problem in contracts, examples of disputes over terms with multiple appropriate meanings are relatively rare. To illustrate, suppose an insurer purports to insure a cargo being shipped via a vessel named the "*Tiger,*" but, unknown to the insurer, two vessels are named "*Tiger*"; the shipper means one "*Tiger*" and the insurer means the other.[4] If a loss is suffered by the insured and the insurer denies coverage, the dispute would be caused by ambiguity of term.

Ambiguity of syntax, the third category of imprecise language, involves imprecision of grammatical structure. This kind of ambiguity is very common in contract language generally. For example, an insurance agent is entitled to a commission on

---

[1] Although the question of what meaning is attached to a term by a party is a question of fact, the meaning of words themselves is ordinarily treated as a proper subject for judicial notice. Thus, questions of interpretation of contract documents are ordinarily treated as questions of law for decision by the judge rather than the jury. *Restatement (Second) of Contracts* § 212, comment d (1981).

[2] For a general discussion of imprecision, see E. Allan Farnsworth, *Contracts* 479–80 (1982); E. Allan Farnsworth, *Meaning in the Law of Contracts,* 76 Yale L.J. 939 (1967).

[3] See Liberty Mut. Ins. Co. v. Rawls, 404 F.2d 880 (5th Cir. 1968) (two occurrences); Olsen v. Moore, 202 N.W.2d 236 (Wis. 1972) (one occurrence).

[4] This hypothetical is based on the famous case of Raffles v. Wichelhaus, 2 H. & C. 906, 159 Eng.Rep. 375 (Excheq. 1864), where the question was whether the purchaser breached the contract by failing to pay for goods shipped by one of the vessels named *Peerless.*

renewal premiums paid after termination of his agency, subject to the company's right to "withhold five per cent from the renewal commissions provided herein as a service and collection fee." Might the insurer withhold an amount equal to five percent of the "renewal premiums" collected by the company or is it limited to withholding five percent of the "renewal commissions"?[5] This ambiguity is caused by the imprecision in the structure of the phrases. Although ambiguity of syntax is prevalent in many kinds of contracts, it is relatively rare in insurance policies, probably because such contracts are so carefully scrutinized by insurers. Nevertheless, this kind of ambiguity occasionally surfaces. For example, a medical insurance policy promises to pay for expenses incurred due to any "disease of organs of the body not common to both sexes." Is the insured covered for expenses incurred due to a fibroid tumor of the uterus? The disease can occur in any organ of either sex; the disease occurred in an organ not common to both sexes.[6] The words of the policy are relatively precise; the problem is one of syntax.

The second major category of imprecision in insurance policies is *ambiguity of organization.* At times, a policy's structure is such that it misleads or fails to inform the insured about the nature of the coverage. This is commonly a ground of contention with respect to exclusionary clauses, which may be inconspicuous because they are isolated from the coverage clauses which they limit, are in fine print, or are otherwise difficult to locate.[7]

The third major category of imprecision in insurance policies is *ambiguity created by extrinsic information.* The insured normally receives written and oral information from the insurer and the insurer's representative, such as brochures, certificates, applications, and oral explanations of forms and coverage. Sometimes this extrinsic information is inconsistent with or contradicts the written terms of the policy, thereby creating an ambiguity that must be resolved through techniques of interpretation.[8]

---

[5] See Wabash Life Ins. Co. v. Hacker, 164 N.E.2d 666 (Ind. Ct. App. 1960).

[6] See Business Men's Assur. Ass'n v. Read, 48 S.W.2d 678 (Tex. Ct. App. 1932) (coverage exists). This example is used in Farnsworth, note 2, *supra,* 76 Yale L.J. at 954.

[7] E.g., State Farm Mut. Auto. Ins. Co. v. Bogart, 717 P.2d 449 (Ariz. 1986) (giving effect to nonstandard other insurance clause at end of policy conditions in small-print boilerplate, the effect of which was not clear without consulting definitions section in separate part of policy, would defeat insured's reasonable expectations); Commercial Union Assur. Cos. v. Gollan, 394 A.2d 839 (N.H. 1978) (exclusion in small type and far apart did not adequately advise insured of nature of exclusion); Atwood v. Hartford Acc. & Indem. Co., 365 A.2d 744 (N.H. 1976) (completed operations exclusion clause "buried amidst thirteen others" and defined elsewhere in policy did not give "fair notice" to the insured that loss was not covered, when first page would lead him to believe it was); Paramount Properties Co. v. Transamerica Title Ins. Co., 463 P.2d 746 (Cal. 1970) (termination provision in fine print on second page was not "conspicuous"); Gerhardt v. Continental Ins. Cos., 225 A.2d 328 (N.J. 1966) (coverages on front page and exclusions on separate page did not adequately inform insured about scope of coverage).

[8] See, e.g., Fritz v. Old Am. Ins. Co., 354 F. Supp. 514 (S.D. Tex. 1973) (insured receives coverage due to advertisement suggesting that coverage began when application was deposited in the mail, notwithstanding language in policy suggesting otherwise); Craver v. Union Fid. Life Ins. Co., 307 N.E.2d 265 (Ohio Ct.App. 1973) (insurer bound by content of advertising copy); North Am. Acc. Ins. Co. v. Anderson, 100 F.2d 452 (10th Cir. 1938)

In any case in which a dispute arises over imprecision in an insurance policy, the problem probably could have been avoided if the organization, the terms, the syntax, or the extrinsic information had been more carefully prepared. Why is it, then, that such disputes arise? Some of the same observations that can be made about other kinds of contracts are pertinent to insurance contracts.

Parties do not always anticipate future changes in the context in which the contract language must operate. For example, an insurance policy covers the insured for injuries suffered while operating a "motor vehicle," which is defined as "a self-propelled device upon which any person is or may be transported upon a public highway." When drafted, the intent of the clause is to cover injuries suffered while riding in or on an automobile, truck, tractor, motorcycle, or other similar device. If the insured is injured while operating a motorized bicycle propelled partially by human effort on the pedals and partially by a small, lawnmower-sized motor, is the insured covered?[9] Had the insurer foreseen the development of "minibikes," the contract's language might have been adjusted to eliminate the vagueness.

Sometimes parties to contracts deliberately choose to ignore potentially difficult subjects. For example, liability insurance policies are not very specific on the obligations of insurers to defend an insured in circumstances where claims are made against the insured both within and outside coverage or where the insured desires the defense to be conducted in a particular way.[10] Drafting elaborate policy provisions to deal with these circumstances would be extremely difficult; the mere presence of such provisions would attract the attention of, and perhaps would confuse and alarm, many insureds. Rather than attempt to draft such provisions and incur the costs associated with insureds' confusion, insurers have opted to leave the policy forms in general language and to deal with the troublesome conflicts on a case-by-case basis. Of course, considerable case law has developed with regard to the duty of defense, and the principles in these cases serve, in effect, as "implied terms" of the contract.

In addition to the causes of imprecision endemic to any contract, circumstances unique to the insurance industry lead to imprecision. Many contracts of insurance are intended to cover future events of unknown nature and origin; as a result, these contracts must be written in general terms. Because of this inherent generality, it is often possible to give multiple interpretations to insurance contract language in specific fact settings.

Furthermore, the near-universal reliance in the insurance business on standardized forms, though a highly beneficial practice, does lead to some imprecision. When standardized forms are used in multiple jurisdictions, the industry is sometimes unable to respond to discrete differences in judicial attitudes toward the forms in

---

(application describes insured's occupation as "office duties only" but policy describes occupation as involving "office and traveling duties.")

[9] Cf. Farmers Ins. Exch. v. Galvin, 216 Cal. Rptr. 844 (Cal. Ct. App. 1984) (moped is not a vehicle); Kresyman v. State Farm Mut. Auto. Ins. Co., 623 P.2d 524 (Kan.Ct.App. 1981) (minibike is a motor vehicle for which insurance is required; later superseded by statute).

[10] The issues that arise in these circumstances are discussed in §§ 111[d] and 114[d], *infra*.

the various jurisdictions. Also, a standardized form cannot guarantee standardization in how the forms are interpreted. It is inevitable, then, that inconsistencies will arise in the scope of coverage provided by the same form in different jurisdictions. Because courts interpret policies in a light highly favorable to the insured, insurers inevitably find themselves providing coverage for events they thought were excluded. When a form appears to have outlived its usefulness, the forms are revised, sometimes in a deliberate effort to counteract broad judicial interpretations of the scope of coverage or narrow interpretations of the scope of exclusions. Eventually, another judicial decision will interpret the form more broadly than the insurer anticipated, and this will cause the cycle of insurer redrafting and judicial reinterpretation to repeat itself.

Even so, the benefits of standardization far outweigh the disadvantages. At the cost of limiting consumer choice, standardization allows enormous economies to be achieved. The transaction costs of negotiating the substantive content of each insurance policy sold would be incalculable; avoiding these costs makes insurance affordable and more widely available. Also, standardization enables insurers to manage risk: by defining the risks assumed on a uniform basis, the insurer is spared the need to calculate the price of assuming the risk on an individualized basis.

Sometimes courts interpret the language of policies to achieve a result that supposedly compensates for the unequal bargaining power between insurer and insured. These pro-insured results prompt insurers to modify the forms in an effort to clarify the scope of coverage. Sometimes, then, the complexities of insurance policy language simply reflect the efforts of the industry to deal with judicial decisions — which resulted in the first place from what the courts perceived to be imprecise language.

[b] General Principles of Contract Interpretation

The principal rule of contract interpretation, it is often said, is to determine the intention of the parties.[11] The difficulty with this rule is that the parties will often disagree over the meaning of a term or phrase and will argue over whose understanding of the meaning should control. Thus, it often becomes necessary for a court to interpret the term or phrase. Unfortunately, however, judicial opinions show many different approaches to interpretation, and the absence of a "consensus methodology" means that results in particular cases are often difficult to predict. Moreover, when courts interpret language in insurance contracts, it is not uncommon to find evidence of special rules that have no obvious counterpart in the law of contract interpretation.

Part of the difficulty is rooted in two irreconcilable views of contract interpretation, each of which has its virtues and its following. Under the interpretive approach championed by Professor Williston and followed in the *Restatement (First) of Contracts,* evidence extrinsic to the writing can be examined for the purpose of determining a document's meaning only if the language in the writing is unclear. Whether the language is unclear is decided as a question of law before extrinsic evidence is considered. In other words, the court looks to the four corners of the

---

[11] E.g., Purcell v. Allstate Ins. Co., 310 S.E.2d 530 (Ga. Ct. App. 1983).

document; if the intention of the parties devolving from the four corners is "clear," then the court cannot rewrite the contract by considering the actual words or the meaning given those words by the parties during the contract's negotiation.

The "four-corners" approach to contract interpretation, with its emphasis on the language of the policy, arguably provides increased certainty for the insurer. Judicial decisions are more predictable, insurers are more confident about how their policies will be interpreted, coverage questions can be more quickly resolved, and costs can be reduced (both in administration of policies and in litigation) and these savings redound to the consumer's benefit.[12] Also, the four-corners approach finds support in a theory of contract that expects parties to take care of themselves, and that instructs parties not to expect judicial relief from their bargains in circumstances where the parties agreed to plain language and should have understood, if they had taken the time to think about the matter, that they would be held to the objectively reasonable meaning of the words they used, notwithstanding the fact that they possessed other expectations.

The rigidity of the four-corners approach, particularly in circumstances where it appears that the parties both meant something different than the objectively reasonable, plain meaning of their words, led to an alternative interpretative approach, one of whose early champions was Professor Corbin. To these critics, whose view of interpretation prevails in the *Restatement (Second) of Contracts*, a literal, uncompromising application of the four-corners approach ignores the nature of the contract formation process and often leads to unsound results. Under this approach, words lack meaning in and of themselves; words have meaning only because of the assumptions users and readers of words bring to them, and this is true even when a judge looks at a word or phrase and declares that the words have a "plain meaning." If words need external referents to give them content, it follows that these referents — i.e., the extrinsic evidence — should be considered whenever a question of interpretation of words arises, and this requires asking the parties what they meant when they used particular words. This does not mean, of course, that a particular interpretation will be selected based simply on what the user says the words means; instead, an objective theory applies in most cases of disagreement over meaning, and the court inquires into what party A knew or had reason to know about party B's understanding of the meaning of the words. In most cases the court will prefer the understanding of the party who had less reason to know what the other party understood.[13]

Arizona cases provide an illustration of a court moving from a four-corners rigidity to a more functional approach. In *State Farm Insurance Co. v. Gibbs,*[14] the Arizona Court of Appeals concluded, based upon its review of the four corners of

---

[12] See Standard Venetian Blind Co. v. American Empire Ins., 469 A.2d 563 (Pa. 1983).

[13] Professor Swisher has identified an over-arching "duality" in insurance law, which he describes as a competition between "formalism" and "functionalism." Interpretation is one of a number of examples he offers to illustrate this duality. See Peter N. Swisher, *Judicial Rationales in Insurance Law: Dusting Off the Formal for the Function,* 52 Ohio St. L. J. 1037 (1991).

[14] 678 P.2d 459 (Ariz. Ct. App. 1984).

the agreement, that the insurer and insured clearly expressed an intent that the automobile liability policy exclude from coverage all claims the named insured or his relatives might make against any permissive driver covered under the omnibus clause of the policy. The Arizona Supreme Court criticized *Gibbs* in *Darner Motor Sales, Inc. v. Universal Underwriters Insurance Co.*:[15]

> We cannot pretend that Mr. Gibbs, presumably an average person, had any idea that the policy contained such a clause, or, had he understood its ramifications, would have intended that his premium dollars should be used to protect the entire world except the members of the Gibbs family. Gibbs' intention would probably have been exactly contrary. To support this fiction regarding the insured's intention the court creates a second — that Gibbs bargained, for a lower premium, to get a policy with such an exclusion. The use of the second fiction requires yet a third — that for a higher premium, one could induce State Farm to change its standard auto policy and delete the named insured exclusion. Such a negotiation might be possible for IBM, bargaining to insure its fleet. It defies belief to attribute such power to any ordinary customer. . . . The assumptions made are contrary to common knowledge of the manner in which the great bulk of insurance is transacted. We believe the time has come to remove insurance law from the land of make-believe.[16]

But cases like *Darner Motor Sales* do not enjoy unanimous support. Others would argue that the time has come to put insurance law back on more predictable footings.[17] When courts find an ambiguity in circumstances where the insured claims he or she expected coverage but the insurer believed otherwise, the finding of ambiguity extends potentially to all cases where the words are used, and this expands the pool of covered risks beyond that which the insurer intended. These increased costs associated with increased risks raise the price of coverage for everyone. This is inefficient because some insureds, arguably, would have preferred narrower coverage consistent with a "plain meaning" and do not want to pay for the extra coverage created by the interpretive process. To the extent it is impossible to predict which cases will lead to a finding of ambiguity and expanded coverage, insurers cannot price policies with precision, and this inflates costs. And if all words are potentially ambiguous or vague, which is probably the case, the range of judicial discretion is very broad and the uncertainty of the scope of coverage is very great.

The issue is complicated further in insurance law by the widespread use of stan-dardized forms, and it is with respect to these kinds of contracts that the departure of the *Restatement (Second) of Contracts* from the narrow interpretative approach approved in the *Restatement (First)* is most apparent. Section 211 of the new *Re-statement,* a section that had no counterpart in the original *Restatement,* observes that insurance contracts are almost always standardized and acknowledges that con-sumers are not expected to and do not desire "to understand or even to read the standard terms."[18] Such contracts are treated as integrated agreements under the

---

[15] 682 P.2d 388 (Ariz. 1984).

[16] 682 P.2d at 393 n.6.

[17] See, e.g., David S. Miller, Note, *Insurance as Contract: The Argument for Abandoning the Ambiguity Doctrine,* 88 Colum. L. Rev. 1849 (1988).

[18] *Restatement (Second) of Contracts* § 211, comment b (1981).

parol evidence rule with respect to terms contained in the writing,[19] but "[w]here the other party has reason to believe that the party manifesting such assent would not do so if he knew that the writing contained a particular term, the term is not part of the agreement."[20] In addressing the issue of unfair surprise to the insured from contract language drafted by the insurer, this section repudiates the four-corners approach to contract interpretation in the standardized agreement setting and essentially approves a doctrine of "reasonable expectations":

> Although customers [insureds] typically adhere to standardized agreements and are bound by them without even appearing to know the standard terms in detail, they are not bound to unknown terms which are beyond the range of reasonable expectation. . . . a party [insured] who adheres to the other party's [the insurer's] standard terms does not assent to a term if the other party has reason to believe that the adhering party would not have accepted the agreement if he had known that the agreement contained the particular term.[21]

Since a term of an insurance contract might operate to exclude coverage, coverage can be created where none exists by the letter of the agreement by concluding that the term is "beyond the range of reasonable expectation." Only a few courts have explicitly addressed the role of section 211 of the *Restatement (Second)* in the insurance setting,[22] but it seems inevitable that section 211 will attain greater prominence in future years. The nature of the reasonable expectations doctrine, with which section 211 is closely aligned, is discussed in more detail in a later section.[23]

To attempt to synthesize this discussion, general principles of contract interpretation seem to be capable of organization as follows. First, where competing claims are made about the meaning of a contract, one must determine whether an ambiguity exists. Just because one party to a contract (in insurance disputes, normally the insured) contends that a contract is ambiguous does not mean that an ambiguity exists, nor that the contract might reasonably be interpreted in accordance with whatever the party asserts.[24] But courts are not uniform in the methodology by which the determination of the existence of ambiguity is made. The four-corners of the contract, if clear and explicit, may be the beginning and end of the analysis.[25]

---

[19] *Id.*, § 211(1). See Bolle v. Hume, 619 A.2d 1192, 1197 (D.C. 1993).

[20] *Id.*, § 211(3).

[21] *Id.* § 211, comment f (1981).

[22] See Darner Motor Sales, Inc. v. Universal Underwriters Ins. Co., 682 P.2d 388 (Ariz. 1984). In Collins v. Farmers Ins. Co. of Oregon, 822 P.2d 1146 (Or. 1991) (en banc), the majority of a divided court used a formalistic approach to deny coverage in the face of a dissenting opinion that preferred the approach of section 211.

[23] See § 25D, *infra*.

[24] In insurance specifically, some cases are correctly decided in favor of the insurer on the ground that the insured's proposed interpretation of policy language is utterly untenable and unfounded. E.g., Allstate Ins. Co. v. Ellison, 757 F.2d 1042 (9th Cir. 1985) (applying Alaska law); Fortune v. Wong, 702 P.2d 299 (Haw. 1985).

[25] See AIU Ins. Co. v. Superior Court, 799 P.2d 1253 (Cal. 1990)(en banc); Washington v. Savoie, 634 So. 2d 1176 (La. 1994); Monarch Cortland, a Div. of Monarch Machine Tool Co., Inc. v. Columbia Cas. Co., 626 N.Y.S.2d 426 (N.Y.Sup. 1995); Bickerton, Inc. v. American States Ins. Co., 898 S.W.2d 595 (Mo. Ct. App. 1995); Boos v. National Fed. of State High School Ass'ns, 889 P.2d 797 (Kan.App. 1995); Gredig v. Tennessee Farmers Mut. Ins. Co., 891 S.W.2d 909 (Tenn. Ct. App. 1994).

Other courts will evaluate any relevant extrinsic evidence to decide whether an ambiguity exists.[26]

If an ambiguity exists, the ambiguity must be clarified. Who decides this issue? Traditionally interpretation has been the function of the court, not the jury.[27] Although indications exist that more questions of interpretation will be sent to the jury in the future,[28] most courts are reluctant to submit a question of interpretation to the jury, instead preferring to hold on to this discretion. Again, the question of who should interpret is part and parcel of the discord over interpretive methodology. If interpretation depends only on the four corners of a writing, juries are not needed; judges are fully capable of looking at words and determining whether their meaning is plain or not. But if interpretation depends on an assessment of evidence extrinsic to the writing, that role properly belongs, it would seem, to the jury. But under the reasoning that interpretation is a question of "law," courts usually retain the issue for their own determination.

In resolving an ambiguity, a court must initially assess the two competing interpretations offered by the parties for the term or phrase in question and decide which is to be preferred. As a general rule a court will prefer the meaning of the party who has less reason to know or less knowledge about what the other party understood the term to mean.[29] But this general rule is problematic in circumstances where neither party is offering a reasonable meaning of words or there is no basis in the manifestations of the parties for preferring one party's meaning over the other party's. Indeed, if neither party may be urging a reasonable meaning, it becomes tempting to abandon the functional approach and search for a meaning inherent in words themselves, rather than in how the parties use them, and this draws one closer to the four-corners approach. Fortunately, there are rules which have emerged and evolved through the centuries that courts have used either to decide what constitutes a "plain meaning" or to break ties when there is no basis for preferring one side's proffered meaning over another's. These rules include the following:[30]

> (1) in choosing among alternative meanings, the meaning that operates against the drafter is generally preferred;
>
> (2) if the purpose of the parties can be determined, that purpose is given great weight;

---

26 See, e.g., Monsanto Co. v. International Ins. Co., 652 A.2d 36 (Del. 1994); Ruggles v. Ruggles, 860 P.2d 182 (N.M. 1993); Sims v. Honda Motor Co., 623 A.2d 995 (Conn. 1993); Nahom v. Blue Cross and Blue Shield of Ariz., Inc., 885 P.2d 1113 (Ariz. Ct. App. 1994).

27 See West Bend Mut. Ins. Co. v. Iowa Iron Works, Inc., 503 N.W.2d 596, 598 (Iowa 1993); Parsons v. Bristol Development Co., 62 Cal.2d 861, 402 P.2d 839 (1965) (according to Justice Traynor, interpretation is "solely a judicial function . . . unless the interpretation turns upon the credibility of extrinsic evidence.")

28 See *Restatement (Second) of Contracts* § 212(2) (interpretation of integrated agreement is question of law unless it depends on credibility or choice to be drawn from extrinsic evidence); E. Allan Farnsworth, *Contracts* 536–38 (2d ed. 1990).

29 See *Restatement (Second) of Contracts* § 201 (1981).

30 See generally *Restatement (Second) of Contracts,* §§ 202, 203, 206, 207 (1981); 3 *Corbin on Contracts* §§ 532–560 (1960).

(3) a writing is interpreted as a whole, and separate writings that are part of the same transaction are interpreted together;

(4) where language has a generally understood meaning, the language is given that meaning;

(5) technical terms are given their technical meaning when used in a transaction within the technical field;

(6) where an agreement involves repeated performances, any course of performance acquiesced in by the other party is given great weight in interpreting the agreement;

(7) terms of an agreement are, whenever possible, interpreted as being consistent with each other;

(8) whenever possible, terms should be interpreted in a way that gives them effect or relevance in their setting;

(9) interpretations that make a contract legal are favored over those that make it illegal;

(10) specific terms have greater weight than general terms;

(11) separately negotiated or added terms are given greater weight than standardized terms;

(12) express terms have greater weight than terms implied by course of performance, course of dealing, or usage of the trade;

(13) in choosing among alternative meanings, a meaning that promotes the public interest is favored over one that does not.

Where the general principle of preferring the meaning of the party with the least knowledge about what the other side understands fails to point toward a factor which provides a basis for preferring one party's view over another's, the above-listed "rules of interpretation" provide a way to break the impasse. For example, the important principle that calls for interpreting agreements against the drafter provides a way to shift the calculus in favor of one of the parties where there is otherwise no basis for preferring one party's view over the other's.

[c]   Interpretation of Insurance Contracts

The rules of general contract interpretation discussed in the foregoing section are applicable to any contract. Some courts have said that insurance contracts are to be construed like any other contract, and nothing more is required.[31] But most decisions are fairly read as putting insurance contracts in a different category, and applying some kind of heightened review or alternative interpretive principles.

To take an important example, the oft-repeated phrase that insurance policies are to be construed against the insurer[32] amounts to no more than a statement that a

---

[31] See, e.g., Eli Lilly & Co. v. Home Ins. Co., 482 N.E.2d 467 (Ind. 1985); Standard Venetian Blind Co. v. American Empire Ins. Co., 469 A.2d 563 (Pa. 1983); Insurance Co. of N. Am. v. Adkisson, 459 N.E.2d 310 (Ill. App. Ct. 1984); Parris and Son, Inc. v. Campbell, 196 S.E.2d 334 (Ga. Ct. App. 1973); Brown v. Equitable Life Ins. Co., 211 N.W.2d 431 (Wis. 1973).

[32] See, e.g., Goucher v. John Hancock Mut. Life Ins. Co., 324 A.2d 657 (R.I. 1974).

contract is to be construed against the drafter. To this extent, the interpretive approach is no different from what transpires with garden-variety contracts. Similarly, the "reasonable expectations doctrine" by some formulations is only a rule of interpretation: when two interpretations exist as to what an insured might expect a policy to mean, and one is inapt or absurd while the other is reasonable, the reasonable one is selected.[33] Some interpretations of insurance policies can be explained easily as applications of the rule that when parties attach different meanings to a word or phrase, the meaning of the party with less reason to understand the other side's meaning is to be preferred. It may simply be the case that in insurance transactions, the insurer — the party with more experience and knowledge — typically has more reason to understand that the insured will attach a different meaning to words; when insureds usually win, it is not because insurance policies are a special category of contracts but is because the general rule of contract interpretation is usually pro-insured when standardized forms are involved. *Vlastos v. Sumitomo Marine & Fire Insurance Co. (Europe), Ltd.,*[34] a 1983 Third Circuit decision, is illustrative. At issue in *Vlastos* was the meaning of a warranty under which the insured promised "that the 3rd floor [of her building] is occupied as Janitor's residence." At the time of the fire which destroyed the building, the janitor occupied only a portion of the third floor, with the remainder being occupied by a massage parlor. The insurer argued that the insured breached the warranty because the third floor was not exclusively occupied by the janitor. However, the court reasoned that the insured could have reasonably assumed that the reason the insurer desired a full-time janitor on the premises was to take care of fire hazards and other problems quickly and to deter prowlers and vandals. Whether a janitor occupied an entire floor or only part of a floor was not relevant to these purposes. The insurer contended that the purpose of the warranty was to ensure that a higher-risk tenant would not occupy a portion of the third floor. However, because the insurer had not insisted upon particular uses of other floors of the building and because the insurer had not informed the insured of this purpose, it was not reasonable to expect the insured to understand this to be the purpose of the warranty. The court held that the warranty meant only that a janitor resided on the third floor, not that there be no other occupancy of that floor.[35] One way to view the holding in *Vlastos* is that the insured had a reasonable understanding of the ambiguous clause and no reason to know the insurer's narrower understanding, while the insurer had reason to know that the insured would not share the insurer's understanding. Under these circumstances, the court was correct in favoring the understanding of the insured.

Although the notion that an insurance contract should be interpreted by reference to the principles that govern the interpretation of any contract is alive and well, it is also clear that many decisions cannot be explained cogently by reference to ordinary principles of contract interpretation. In these cases, courts have either explicitly or implicitly recognized that insurance policies have special characteristics

---

[33] See, e.g., Moss v. Mid-America Fire and Marine Ins. Co., 647 P.2d 754, 761 (Idaho 1982); for more discussion, see § 25D, *infra.*

[34] 707 F.2d 775 (3d Cir. 1983).

[35] 707 F.2d at 779.

and must be construed with reference to special, perhaps unique standards.[36]
Professor James Fischer has described the rules of insurance contract interpretation
as ones that "build on general rules applicable to all contracts" but which "are. . .
more than simple extensions of the basic rules of contract" and which "often have
a significant twist."[37] Further, he identifies three rules of insurance contract
interpretation found in some cases that have no contract law counterpart: coverage
terms are interpreted liberally while exclusions are interpreted narrowly; insurance
policies are to be interpreted consistently with a layperson's understanding; if
possible, policies are to be construed so to achieve the purpose of providing
indemnity.[38]

All of this adds up to a decidedly pro-insured bias in insurance policy interpretation, and invites the question as to whether giving insurance policies special
treatment is appropriate. It is fair to assert that the public's apparent desire for
simplicity and greater certainty in legal matters is likely to be reflected in more
formalistic court decisions where the interpretive inquiry is confined to the four
corners of writings.[39] This approach would probably constrain to some extent the
ability of insureds to recover in some coverage cases, would be consistent with the
public's more pro-business, anti-plaintiff attitudes, but would be inconsistent with
populist antagonisms toward, and distrust, of enterprises with large accumulations
of capital, such as insurance companies. But the pro-insured thrust of interpretation
principles in insurance is so well entrenched that a dramatic change is highly
unlikely, and the preference given insureds in insurance policy interpretation is
likely to be with us for some time to come.

[d] The Role of Drafting History

Because a great many insurance policies are standardized forms, any form's
drafting history can be a fertile source of information regarding what the insurer (or
the insurance industry, or, more specifically, the drafters) meant by particular terms.
In litigation over pollution coverage in particular, insurers and policyholders have
thoroughly researched the tiniest minutiae about the circumstances of the drafting
of the various standardized phrases that have been used through the years in
commercial liability forms. This has led in recent years to much argument over the
appropriate role of drafting history in the interpretation of standardized policy
language.

Most courts considering the issue have held that evidence of the drafting history
of standardized forms and other available interpretive materials (such as, for

---

[36] See generally E. Neil Young, John R. Lewis & J. Finlay Lee, *Insurance Contract
Interpretation: Issues and Trends,* 1975 Ins. L.J. 71; Spencer L. Kimball & Werner
Pfennigstorf, *Legislative and Judicial Control of the Terms of Insurance Contracts: A
Comparative Study of American and European Practice,* 39 Ind. L.J. 675, 699–704 (1964).

[37] James M. Fischer, *Why Are Insurance Contracts Subject to Special Rules of Interpretation?: Text versus Context,* 24 Ariz. St. L.J. 995, 1002-03 (1992).

[38] *Id.* at 1004.

[39] Professor Fischer describes this as a "preference for text over context" and a preference
for "neutral rules that would give greater effect to the literal terms of the contract." *Id.* at
1065.

example, speeches of insurance executives at the time forms were being changed, essays and articles by drafters or members of drafting committees, etc.) are relevant to the meaning of disputed policy language.[40] Some courts, however, had declared drafting history irrelevant, usually under the reasoning that the history cannot be used to create ambiguities in what is otherwise clear, unambiguous language.[41] Other courts have been reluctant to let industry interpretations of policy language found in the drafting history be "the last word on the extent of coverage."[42]

Before drafting history can be considered, the parol evidence rule must first be addressed. As discussed earlier,[43] parol evidence (e.g., drafting history) can be admitted to interpret a contract, but if there is no ambiguity there is nothing to interpret. The four-corners approach to contract interpretation asks first whether a contract is ambiguous on its face; if there is no ambiguity, there is nothing to interpret, and parol evidence (e.g., drafting history) is irrelevant. Courts that follow a less-mechanical approach and look at all of the circumstances to determine whether policy language is ambiguous may find the drafting history to be highly relevant.

Even if the parol evidence rule does not bar examination of drafting history, further difficulties may remain. What a drafter (usually an individual or committee) meant may or may not be the same as what a corporate insurer meant when it used the form and issued the policy, although it stands to reason that industry customs and understandings are relevant to determining any particular insurer's understanding; and where an objective standard is used, an industry-wide understanding may be dispositive on what a reasonable insurer should understand in the circumstances. In circumstances where the insurer offers a particular interpretation of language, the fact that a drafting committee or a member of the drafting group thought the words meant what the insurer now asserts they mean is prima facie evidence that the insurer's proffered interpretation is reasonable. On the other hand, if a drafter wrote the words with an entirely different meaning in mind than what the insurer now urges, the drafting history can be hurtful to the insurer (but helpful to the insured). In short, in some situations drafting history can be very informative, even if it must be viewed with caution.

---

[40] See, e.g., New Castle Cty. v. Hartford Acc. & Indem. Co., 933 F.2d 1162, 1169, 1196-98 (3d Cir. 1991), cert. denied, 113 S.Ct. 1846 (1993); Montrose Chem. Corp. of Cal. v. Admiral Ins. Co., 897 P.2d 1 (Cal. 1995); Fireman's Fund Ins. Co. v. Aetna Cas. & Sur. Co., 273 Cal. Rptr. 431 (Cal. Ct. App. 1990) ("where two insurers dispute the meaning of identical standard form policy language—the meaning attached to the provisions by the insurance industry is, at minimum, relevant"); Union Pac. Resources Co. v. Aetna Cas. & Sur. Co., 894 S.W.2d 401 (Tex. Ct. App. 1994) (refusal to allow insured to engage in discovery on drafting history was error); Hoechst Celanese Corp. v. National Union Fire Ins. Co. of Pittsburgh, Pa., 623 A.2d 1128 (Del.Super.Ct. 1992)(discovery into drafting history would be permitted).

[41] See, e.g., Anderson v. Minnesota Ins. Guar. Ass'n, 520 N.W.2d 155 (Minn.App. 1994), rev'd on other grounds, 534 N.W.2d 706 (Minn. 1995); Sylvester Bros. Dev. Co. v. Great Cent. Ins. Co., 480 N.W.2d 368 (Minn.App. 1992).

[42] See American Star Ins. Co. v. Insurance Co. of the West, 284 Cal. Rptr. 45 (Cal. Ct. App. 1991). Compare ACL Technologies, Inc. v. Northbrook Prop. & Cas. Ins. Co., 22 Cal. Rptr.2d 206 (Cal. Ct. App. 1993) (drafting history not admissible for purpose of interpreting 1973 pollution exclusion in CGL).

[43] See § 25A[b], supra.

§ 25B   Judicial Interpretation of Statutory Requirements

Statutes and administrative regulations often specify the language that insurance policies must contain. Despite the best efforts of the legislature, however, these requirements do not eliminate all uncertainty about the scope of coverage. In many cases, courts are asked to decide what the legislature intended when it prescribed coverage.

For example, the Rhode Island legislature enacted a statute (as did many states) requiring that the uninsured motorist coverage of all automobile liability insurance policies issued in the state provide coverage for insureds who suffer loss as a result of "hit-and-run motor vehicles."[1] The term "hit" was not defined. The following question was soon confronted: if an insurer provides coverage for loss caused by a "hit and run vehicle whose operator or owner cannot be identified and which hits: a. You or any family member . . .," is the insured covered when she is run off the road by an unknown vehicle but no physical contact with that vehicle occurs? In *Pin Pin H. Su v. Kemper Insurance Companies/American Motorists Insurance Co.,*[2] the court interpreted the statutory language "hit and run" as "merely a shorthand colloquial expression that is designed to describe a motorist who has caused, or contributed by his negligence to, an accident and flees the scene without being identified."[3] By this reasoning, the insurer's attempt to limit the scope of coverage to hit-and-run accidents involving physical contact was contrary to the policy and language of the statute, and the insured was entitled to coverage, assuming the insured could "prove by a fair preponderance of the evidence that his or her injuries resulted from the negligence of an unidentified motorist."[4]

Numerous other cases present the kind of dispute confronted in *Pin Pin H. Su.*[5] The common pattern is that the legislature articulates a state public policy and attempts to promote this policy by mandating the scope of insurance coverage. That the state has the authority to compel private insurers to do business in accordance with the prescribed policy forms is clear. However, a provision sometimes appears in the policy which differs, or appears to differ, from the statutory requirements. A court may be asked to decide what the legislature has mandated and whether the insurer's provision varies from this mandate. The court's decision on these questions will determine the scope of coverage, which demonstrates yet again the role that courts play in regulating the business of insurance.

---

[1] R.I. Gen. Laws § 27-7-2.1 (1971). For further discussion of the hit-and-run issue in uninsured motorist insurance, see § 133[d], *infra.*

[2] 431 A.2d 416 (R.I. 1981).

[3] *Id.* at 419. Not all courts agree. See § 133[d], *infra.*

[4] *Id.* at 419.

[5] See, e.g., Metz v. Universal Underwriters Ins. Co., 513 P.2d 922 (Cal. 1973) (liability policy's exclusion of vehicles "while rented to others" conflicts with the mandated coverage of permissive users; superseded by statute: see Premier Ins. Co. v. MacDonald, Krieger & Bowyer, Inc., 210 Cal. Rptr. 458 (Cal. Ct. App. 1985)); DeWitt v. Young, 625 P.2d 478 (Kan. 1981) (household and garage shop exclusion held inconsistent with minimum coverages required by Kansas statutes); Allstate Ins. Co. v. United States Fid. & Guar. Co., 619 P.2d 329 (Utah 1980) ("named driver" exclusion contained in automobile liability policy held void as to minimum level of liability coverage required under state statute).

§ 25C   Insurance Policies as Adhesion Contracts

In the classical model, contracts are freely negotiated by parties with roughly equivalent bargaining power. However, the classical model is far removed from the reality of the insurance business. Professor Williston described it this way:

> [Insurance contracts are drafted] with the aid of skillful and highly paid legal talent, from which no deviation desired by an applicant will be permitted. The established underwriter is magnificently qualified to understand and protect its own selfish interests. In contrast, the applicant is a shorn lamb driven to accept whatever contract may be offered on a "take-it-or-leave-it" basis if he wishes insurance protection.[1]

Professor Williston's description is fundamentally accurate, at least with respect to insurance in the non-commercial setting (i.e., insurance marketed to individual consumers). Although the insured can choose from a variety of available coverages, the insured cannot negotiate the substance of the contract with the insurer. The policy's provisions, even if mandated by statute or regulation, are drafted by industry experts. The insured is confronted with a "take or leave" choice. In many transactions, the insured will not even see the policy he purchased until after the first premium is paid. This sort of transaction is what Professor Kessler referred to as the "adhesion contract." The term "adhesion contract" is essentially a description of the manner by which the contract is formed: one party having superior bargaining power imposes its choice of terms on the other party.[2]

In the adhesion setting, a higher probability exists that the party with less bargaining power will be subjected to oppressive, unjust or unexpected provisions. But labeling insurance contracts as adhesion contracts does not guarantee that courts will employ any particular interpretative techniques. In the usual case, when a contract is recognized as being "adhesive," courts are more active in policing the bargain to counterbalance the potential detriment to the weaker parties. One way courts police the bargain is to adhere strictly to the tenet of interpretation that all ambiguities should be construed against the insurer.[3] In addition to utilizing techniques of interpretation, courts have invoked doctrines such as waiver, estoppel, reformation, and rescission to protect insureds. These doctrines create, in effect, rights for the insured that do not exist in the language of the policy.

---

[1] 7 Samuel Williston, *A Treatise on the Law of Contracts* § 900, at 19–20 (3d ed. W. Jaeger 1973). See also Prudential Ins. Co. v. Lamme, 425 P.2d 346 (Nev. 1967).

[2] If insurers competed with each other on both price and coverage terms, this imbalance would be of less concern. Presumably competition over terms would yield optimal terms being offered at an efficient price. However, the benefits of standardization (benefits which redound to the aid of consumers, it must be noted) preclude negotiation of coverage terms in most settings in which insurance is marketed.

[3] See, e.g., Sturla, Inc. v. Fireman's Fund Ins. Co., 684 P.2d 960 (Haw. 1984). As Judge Hand stated in Gaunt v. John Hancock Mut. Life Ins. Co., 160 F.2d 599, 602 (2d Cir.), *cert. denied*, 331 U.S. 849 (1947). ("Insurers who seek to impose upon words of common speech an esoteric significance intelligible only to their craft, must bear the burden of any resulting confusion.")

Illustrative of decisions where courts have recognized the adhesive character of the insurance contract and employed pro-insured interpretive techniques to create rights in the insured despite clear policy language to the contrary is *Ponder v. Blue Cross of Southern California.* [4] The insured was diagnosed as having temporomandibular joint disease, a disease of the joint where the jaw meets the skull. The disease is treated by medical doctors or oral surgeons, or both; in the insured's case, an oral surgeon treated the insured with nonsurgical methods, but eventually surgery was required. Blue Cross denied coverage under an exclusion for "Dental Care" which explicitly mentioned "treatment for or prevention of temporomandibular joint syndrome." The trial court granted a summary judgment for Blue Cross on the ground that the contract's language excluding coverage of temporomandibular joint syndrome was unambiguous. The appeals court reversed. First, the court reasoned that the insured would reasonably expect the policy to cover the costs of treatment for such an illness; in those circumstances, the insurer has "a special burden . . . to highlight exclusions which an ordinary insured might not expect to be in a health insurance contract." [5] Blue Cross, however, failed to make the exclusion "conspicuous," because of the exclusion's "placement, its fine print and the density of the entire contract." [6] Second, as an independent ground for its decision, the court reasoned that "an exclusion in an adhesion contract of insurance must be expressed in words which are 'plain and clear.' " [7] This required, in the court's view, more than terms that are unambiguous and precise; it also requires "understandability." The exclusion failed to pass this test because of its "undefined technical terminology" which was "not calculated to be part of the working vocabulary of average lay persons." [8]

All of these rules are potentially subject to change when one leaves the personal, non-commercial setting and enters the commercial, business setting. [9] When a small, family-owned business with no or few employees is the insured, it may be that the process through which insurance is sold is no less adhesive than that involving individual insureds. At some point, however, the sophistication of the insured increases to the point that the substance of the policy is negotiated, and perhaps even drafted, by the insured or on behalf of the insured by sophisticated agents, risk managers, or lawyers. In these circumstances, it is arguable that the pro-insured interpretive rules that emerge out of the adhesive nature of personal insurance should not apply when a policy of business insurance is involved. [10]

---

[4] 193 Cal. Rptr. 632 (Cal. Ct. App. 1983). Compare Cairns v. Grinnell Mut. Reins. Co., 398 N.W.2d 821 (Iowa 1987) (employing pro-insured presumption, but finding no ambiguity and reaching judgment for insurer).

[5] 193 Cal. Rptr. at 632, 639.

[6] *Id.* at 643.

[7] *Id.* at 640.

[8] *Id.* at 643.

[9] See Slottow v. American Cas. Co. of Reading, Pa., 1 F.3d 912, 919 (9th Cir. 1993) ("What might be acceptable behavior between two large corporations butting heads in the marketplace looks quite different when there is a substantial difference in economic power or sophistication between the parties.")

[10] See Barry R. Ostrager & Thomas R. Newman, *Handbook on Insurance Coverage Disputes* 26-36 (7th ed. 1994).

Sometimes courts stretch the techniques of interpretation so far beyond their normal zones of application that the results cannot be cogently rationalized by resort to traditional doctrines. During the last twenty-five years or so, some courts have applied a doctrine which helps explain the results in these cases — the doctrine of reasonable expectations.

§ 25D   The Doctrine of Reasonable Expectations

It is impossible to say exactly when the doctrine of reasonable expectations emerged. Contract interpretation principles frequently strive to ascertain what parties "intended" words to mean — and it is only a short step to the statement that words should be interpreted in accordance with what the parties "expected" the words to mean. If this were all that the reasonable expectations doctrine meant, the doctrine would only merit brief discussion. As it has developed, however, the doctrine goes much further.[1]

One of the early cases to articulate a broader version of a "reasonable expectations" principle was *Kievit v. Loyal Protection Life Insurance Company,*[2] a 1961 New Jersey decision. The insured in *Kievit* purchased an accident policy providing coverage for loss "resulting directly and independently of all other causes from accidental bodily injuries" but excluding loss "resulting from or contributed to by any disease or ailment." The insured's disability was caused in part by Parkinson's disease, which developed at the same time that the insured's accident occurred. The court concluded that the insured's disability was covered, notwithstanding the policy's rather plain content: "When members of the public purchase policies of insurance they are entitled to the broad measure of protection necessary to fulfill their reasonable expectations."[3] After *Kievit,* many courts endorsed the premise that insurance policies should be enforced in accordance with the insured's reasonable expectations,[4] but there was no consensus in the sense in which the terminology was being used. Under one formulation, the doctrine required that insurance contracts provide the coverage that the insured reasonably believed was being purchased.[5] Under another formulation, the doctrine required that insurance

---

[1] The most complete recent discussion of the doctrine's current status is Roger C. Henderson, *The Doctrine of Reasonable Expectations in Insurance Law After Two Decades,* 51 Ohio St. L.J. 823 (1990). Other discussions of the doctrine are cited there.

[2] 170 A.2d 22 (N.J. 1961). See also Gaunt v. John Hancock Mut. Life Ins. Co., 160 F.2d 599, 601 (2d Cir.), *cert. denied,* 331 U.S. 849 (1947) (understanding of persons "utterly unacquainted with the niceties of life insurance" as to meaning of phrase controls, not understanding of underwriters).

[3] 170 A.2d at 24.

[4] See, e.g., Estrin Constr. Co. v. Aetna Cas. & Sur. Co., 612 S.W.2d 413 (Mo. Ct. App. 1981) ("Knowledge that coverage and exclusion provisions exist in an insurance policy . . . does not preclude a reasonable expectation that the exclusion does not nullify the dominant purpose of the transaction. . . . The law . . . protects expectations *objectively* reasonable, as consonant with the purpose of the standard contract. . . ..")

[5] See C&J Fertilizer, Inc. v. Allied Mut. Ins. Co., 227 N.W.2d 169, 176 (Iowa 1975); Collister v. Nationwide Life Ins. Co., 388 A.2d 1346 (Pa. 1978), *cert. denied,* 439 U.S. 1039 (1978).

contracts provide the coverage that a reasonable person in the place of the insured would expect after reading the policy.[6] Numerous other courts used reasonable expectations simply as a rule of interpretation.[7] These courts typically insisted upon the existence of an ambiguity as a predicate to the doctrine's application. Under this formulation, which continues to have a strong following today, the doctrine meant only that if ambiguities existed in the contract the ambiguities would be resolved in accordance with the reasonable expectations of the insured.[8]

In a prescient two-part article published in 1970,[9] Professor (now Judge) Keeton recognized that it was very difficult to reconcile the results in a large number of insurance law cases with the traditional doctrines used to reach those results. He suggested, however, that two principles explained what would otherwise appear as a large number of unusual insurance law cases: (1) an insurer will be denied any unconscionable advantage in an insurance transaction; and (2) "the objectively reasonable expectations of applicants and intended beneficiaries regarding the terms of insurance contracts will be honored even though painstaking study of the policy provisions would have negated those expectations."[10] This formula "suggests that an individual can have reasonable expectations of coverage that arise from some source *other* than the policy language itself, and that such an extrinsic expectation can be powerful enough to override any policy provisions no matter how clear."[11] In the words of one court, "If a policy is so construed that a reasonable man in the position of the insured would not attempt to read it, the insured's reasonable expectations will not be delimited by the policy language, regardless of the clarity of one particular phrase, among the Augean stable of print."[12] As articulated by Professor Keeton, the doctrine of reasonable expectations is more than a rule of

---

[6] Ingram v. Continental Cas. Co., 451 S.W.2d 177 (Ark. 1970).

[7] See, e.g., Richards v. Hanover Ins. Co., 299 S.E.2d 561 (Ga. 1983); Gowing v. Great Plains Mut. Ins. Co., 483 P.2d 1072 (Kan. 1971); Simon v. Continental Ins. Co., 724 S.W.2d 210 (Ky. 1987).

[8] See Silk v. Flat Top Constr., Inc., 453 S.E.2d 356 (W.Va. 1994); Wellcome v. Home Ins. Co., 849 P.2d 190 (Mont. 1993) (expectation contrary to clear language of policy is not 'objectively reasonable'); State ex rel. Farmers Ins. Exch. v. District Court of Ninth Judicial Dist., Cty. of Teton, 844 P.2d 1099 (Wyo. 1993); State v. Signo Trading Intern., Inc., 612 A.2d 932 (N.J. 1992); Farmers Ins. Exch. v. Young, 832 P.2d 376 (Nev. 1992); Keenan v. Industrial Indem. Co. of the Northwest, 738 P.2d 270 (Wash. 1987); Allstate Ins. Co. v. Ellison, 757 F.2d 1042 (9th Cir. 1985) (applying Alaska law); Auto-Owners Ins. Co. v. Jensen, 667 F.2d 714 (8th Cir. 1981) (applying Minnesota law); Sturla v. Fireman's Fund Ins. Co., 684 P.2d 960 (Haw. 1984).

[9] Robert E. Keeton, *Insurance Law Rights At Variance With Policy Provisions: Part One*, 83 Harv. L. Rev. 961 (1970); Robert E. Keeton, *Insurance Law Rights At Variance With Policy Provisions: Part Two*, 83 Harv. L. Rev. 1281 (1970).

[10] *Id.*, Part One, at 967.

[11] See Mark C. Rahdert, *Reasonable Expectations Reconsidered*, 18 Conn. L. Rev. 323, 335 (1986).

[12] Storms v. United States Fid. & Guar. Co., 388 A.2d 578, 580 (N.H. 1978). See also Aetna Ins. Co v. State Motors, Inc., 244 A.2d 64, 67 (N.H. 1968) ("it is fair to interpret the policy in the light of what a more than casual reading of the policy would reveal to an ordinarily intelligent insured.")

construction. Indeed, the existence of an ambiguity in the policy is not a predicate for the doctrine's application, unlike the ordinary principles of contract interpretation.[13] Courts in at least sixteen states have purported to adopt Professor Keeton's formulation of the doctrine, although only in about ten of these states do the courts' decisions clearly demonstrate that the court understood the doctrine as Professor Keeton articulated it and meant to embrace it, as opposed to approving a weaker version of the doctrine.[14] In his thoughtful, comprehensive analysis of the status of the doctrine,[15] Professor Henderson concludes that the doctrine does have a clearly demarcable core of meaning:

> Although the form of the doctrine of reasonable expectations may not be fully fixed yet in all jurisdictions, and may never be, a doctrinal core has been identified by some of the courts that have viewed the doctrine as creating rights at variance with unambiguous policy language. As a consequence, one may predict with considerable confidence that courts in the remaining jurisdictions will recognize these developments and that any confusion over the nature of the doctrine itself will rapidly dissipate.[16]

Professor Henderson makes clear that the parameters of the doctrine are not precise and that the principle itself is undergoing continued evolution, like any new common law principle. As a result, there is no uniformity with regard to the circumstances in which the doctrine is invoked. Professor Abraham recognized this in his earlier article on the doctrine:

> The courts have employed the expectations principle in cases where the insured's expectation of coverage was probably real and reasonable. They have also employed it where an expectation of coverage was less probable but the policy's denial of coverage seemed unfair. Finally, they have relied on the principle even where an expectation of coverage was improbable and the denial of coverage would not appear unfair. In short, the judicial concept of an "expectation" of coverage is not a monolithic one.[17]

Indeed, only one circumstance routinely appears in the reasonable expectations cases: the insured is an ordinary, unsophisticated consumer, possessing an understanding of only the most rudimentary aspects of the coverage. Thus, the reasonable expectations doctrine is used by courts to protect consumers, not to adjust a commercial relationship between parties with roughly equal bargaining power. Beyond this simple observation, however, generalizations are more difficult.

Even if the core of the doctrine is now better understood, it has not followed that all courts have been eager to approve this core. Critics of the doctrine, as articulated by Professor Keeton, reject the premise on which it rests — that clear language in a policy can be superseded by extrinsic evidence. Also, some find it troublesome

---

[13] See, e.g., Gordinier v. Aetna Cas. & Sur. Co., 742 P.2d 277 (1987); Sparks v. St. Paul Ins. Co., 495 A.2d 406 (N.J. 1985).

[14] These cases are catalogued and analyzed in detail in Henderson, *supra* note 1, at 828-34.

[15] *Id.*

[16] *Id.*, at 838.

[17] Kenneth S. Abraham, *Judge-Made Law and Judge-Made Insurance: Honoring the Reasonable Expectations of the Insured,* 67 Va. L. Rev. 1151, 1153 (1981).

that the doctrine strips insurers of their power to draft contract language in a way that regulates the risks the insurer assumes, thereby leading to unacceptable levels of uncertainty.[18] Thus, some courts have rejected altogether the doctrine of reasonable expectations in favor of the traditional rules of interpretation recognized in contract law,[19] or having once approved the doctrine, have narrowed its scope in subsequent cases.[20]

Indeed, in circumstances where the insurer did nothing to encourage the insured's expectation, had no reason to know of its existence, and did not fail to take prudent steps that would have clarified the situation, the critics' objection is difficult to fault. Likewise, in circumstances where the insured failed through reasonable, available means to inform himself or herself of a limitation on coverage, it is understandable why a court might be reluctant to invoke the doctrine to create a right in the insured at variance with the language of the policy. These are situations, however, where the doctrine is not likely to be applied. It does not follow from the mere fact that an insured has an expectation of coverage that the insured's expectation is reasonable, and the situations just noted are likely to be cases in which the insured's expectation will be deemed unreasonable.

This implies that the doctrine of reasonable expectations is not unbounded, and that the doctrine's contours are found precisely where Professor Keeton "discovered" the doctrine — in the more traditional doctrines with which lawyers and judges are more familiar and comfortable.[21] When the insured's expectation is created by some kind of ambiguity or vagueness in the policy's language, syntax, or organization, something like the doctrine of *contra proferentum* (construe the writing against the drafter) is operating.[22] When the insured's expectation comes from some assertion by an agent of the insurer or through the insurer's advertising, something like the doctrine of misrepresentation or deceit is operating.[23] When the insured's

---

[18] See Stephen Ware, Comment, *A Critique of the Reasonable Expectations Doctrine,* 56 U. Chi. L. Rev. 1461 (1989); Squires, *A Skeptical Look at the Doctrine of Reasonable Expectations,* 6 Forum 252 (1971).

[19] Courts in some states have refused to embrace the doctrine. See, e.g., Alf v. State Farm Fire and Cas. Co., 850 P.2d 1272 (Utah 1993) (stating that prior opinion in Allen v. Prudential Prop. & Cas. Co., 839 P.2d 757 (Utah 1992), which held doctrine inapplicable in absence of ambiguity, repudiated the doctrine in all its forms); American Family Mut. Ins. Co. v. Elliot, 523 N.W.2d 100 (S.D. 1994); Robbins Auto Parts, Inc. v. Granite State Ins. Co., 435 A.2d 507 (N.H. 1981); Menke v. Country Mut. Ins. Co., 401 N.E.2d 539 (Ill. 1980). Courts in at least two states have retracted their earlier approval of the reasonable expectations doctrine. See Hallowell v. State Farm Mut. Auto. Ins. Co., 443 A.2d 925 (Del. 1982); Casey v. Highlands Ins. Co., 600 P.2d 1387 (Idaho 1979).

[20] See Cincinnati Ins. Co. v. Hopkins Sporting Goods, Inc., 522 N.W.2d 837 (Iowa 1994) (the doctrine is inapplicable where nothing in the policy is subject to misunderstanding by the ordinary layperson and the insurer has done nothing to foster the expectation); Weedo v. Stone-E-Brick, Inc., 405 A.2d 788 (N.J. 1979).

[21] See Abraham, note 17, *supra,* at 1175–77; Rahdert, note 11, *supra,* at 325–44.

[22] See Jostens, Inc. v. Northfield Ins. Co., 527 N.W.2d 116 (Minn. Ct. App. 1995)(if a reasonable expectation exists, it must come from policy language; held nothing in policy language supported insured's expectation).

[23] See Cincinnati Ins. Co. v. Hopkins Sporting Goods, Inc., 522 N.W.2d 837 (Iowa 1994) (if nothing in policy is subject to misunderstanding by ordinary layperson, doctrine does not

expectation is grounded in an assumption that coverage for the loss in question would exist given the amount of premium charged, something like the doctrine of unconscionability is operating. When the insured's expectation is part and parcel of the insured's sudden surprise and dismay at the absence of coverage, something like the doctrine of mistake is operating. When the insured's expectation comes from the insurer's invitation to the insured to place trust in the insurer that the insured's coverage needs will be satisfactorily met, something like an estoppel or reliance theory is operating.[24]

Although the doctrine of reasonable expectations has a recognizable core, the manner in which the doctrine is applied by courts depends to a large extent on the circumstances of particular cases. Some of the factors which appear to influence the manner of the doctrine's application are summarized below.[25]

First, although the doctrine as articulated by Professor Keeton speaks to the "objectively reasonable" expectations of the insured, the extent to which an insured actually, subjectively expects coverage is relevant. If the insured cannot persuasively claim a subjective expectation of coverage, this is problematic for, and perhaps fatal to, the insured's case. This consideration is well-known in contract law: even though contract law is predominately an objective system, one who actually knows what the other party means by an expression should not be allowed to demand a performance from the other party inconsistent with that knowledge. Thus, if the insured clearly understood that no coverage would be provided, the insured should not anticipate coverage under the reasonable expectations doctrine. By the same token, if a subjective expectation is patently unreasonable under all the circumstances, no coverage exists.[26] The insured may be able to retrieve his or her position somewhat if the insurer knew that the insured's subjective expectations exceeded the letter of the policy and the insurer did not take steps to clarify the situation.

The notion that the insured's actual or subjective understanding of coverage may limit his or her ability to assert coverage based on reasonable expectations may have particular force when a sophisticated insured or an insured advised by sophisticated agents (e.g., risk managers, brokers, lawyers) negotiates the language of the policy.[27] One can argue, and some courts have held, that pro-insured interpretive rules, including the doctrine of reasonable expectations, do not apply where the insured has

---

apply in absence of special circumstances attributable to insurer that fostered insured's expectation).

24 See Barth v. Coleman, 878 P.2d 319 (N.M. 1994) ("transaction dynamics" can create reasonable expectation). If the insured's expectations cannot be connected to one or more of these more familiar anchors, it is probable that the insured's expectations are idiosyncratic or come from something extrinsic to the relationship of insurer and insured, and these independent expectations are of doubtful reasonableness.

25 See Kenneth S. Abraham, *Distributing Risk: Insurance, Legal Theory, and Public Policy* 119-22 (1986); Henderson, *supra* note 1, at 838.

26 See, e.g., Hawaiian Ins. and Guar. Co., Ltd. v. Brooks, 686 P.2d 23 (Haw. 1984); Allstate Ins. Co. v. Ellison, 757 F.2d 1042 (9th Cir. 1985).

27 For a thorough assessment of this issue, see Jeffrey W. Stempel, *Reassessing the "Sophisticated" Policyholder Defense in Insurance Coverage Litigation*, 42 Drake L. Rev. 807 (1993).

greater sophistication.[28] The implication, of course, is that such an insured cannot actually, subjectively expect coverage contrary to the policy's language.

Second, the extent to which the insurer knew or should have known that a reasonable person in the insured's shoes would have expected coverage is relevant. Although the Keeton formulation by its terms does not suggest this is a relevant circumstance, this factor is part and parcel of the various anchors for the doctrine outlined above, for each involves some circumstance or fact that suggested coverage and which the insurer failed to clarify or explain. Unlike the first factor, this second factor is essentially an objective inquiry: a person is entitled to rely upon a reasonable understanding of manifestations of the other party, in this case the insurer. For example, the insured may not receive adequate notice of an unusual or unexpected term of the policy or a provision limiting apparent coverage; whatever the insured thinks, the insurer should have known that this omission could lead to an expectation of coverage. In some circumstances, enforcing the insured's objectively reasonable expectations will be the equivalent of the imposition of a duty on the insurer to inform the insured about the extent of the coverage: if the insurer should know that a reasonable person would not have anticipated a limitation on coverage, the insurer should inform the insured of the gap in coverage, thereby negating an otherwise reasonable expectation and alerting the insured of the need to take other steps to protect his or her interests.

The importance of this factor in some cases is explicitly recognized by section 211 of the *Restatement (Second) of Contracts*. Section 211 provides that standardized written agreements are enforceable (i.e., are adopted as an integration with respect to the terms in the writing) without regard to knowledge or understanding of the terms where a party to the agreement has reason to believe that similar writings are regularly used to embody terms of the same kind. Subsection (3) provides an exception, however, in circumstances where the other party (here, the insurer) has "reason to believe" that the party manifesting assent to the agreement (here, the insured) would not do so if that party knew the writing contained a particular term; in that event, the particular term is not part of the agreement (i.e., is unenforceable). To apply this exception, one asks what the insurer had "reason to believe." Taken literally, this exception turns the Keeton formulation on its head, because the Keeton test inquires about the reasonable beliefs of the insured, not the insurer.[29] If the drafters of section 211 intended its literal application in this context, the section has failed of its purpose, given that the Keeton formulation has clearly survived section 211. Perhaps section 211 might brake the momentum of the doctrine of reasonable expectations in some jurisdictions, but a better bet is that the doctrine of reasonable expectations will be viewed as eclipsing section 211, and that section 211's exception will be recognized as one of the circumstances relevant to, but not decisive upon, the determination of whether the reasonable expectations doctrine should be invoked.

---

[28] See Barry R. Ostrager & Thomas R. Newman, *Handbook on Insurance Coverage Disputes* 26-36 (7th ed. 1994).

[29] Henderson, *supra* note 1, at 848.

Third, the extent to which the insured through a reasonable effort could have gained an understanding of the situation is relevant. If the insured could read and understand the policy and had sufficient time to do so, but failed to take steps that would have clarified the situation, the insured's claim is weaker. This does not mean that the insured has a duty to read the policy in every case, for in some circumstances neither custom nor good sense requires a painstaking review of insurance provisions. Also, what is a "reasonable effort" will vary with the circumstances: the effort to be expected from a commercial enterprise should differ from that of an individual consumer. But the extent to which the insured could have reasonably obtained an understanding of clear language is likely to influence a court asked to invoke the doctrine.

Although the contours of the doctrine of reasonable expectations are explicable, the fact remains that courts have considerable discretion when applying the doctrine. The tradeoff for tolerating this discretion and the equity that comes with it is some degree of unpredictability in outcomes. Yet, as is true in most legal settings, unpredictability is often the price of obtaining fairness. By applying the doctrine of reasonable expectations, courts exercise a powerful regulatory tool. Insurers dislike unpredictability and understandably so: it is the business of insurers to achieve certainty by pooling what are for the insureds uncertain events. But insurers that train their agents to deal with insureds in good faith, promote sensitivity to the needs of their customers, encourage full disclosure of information rather than the minimal amount necessary to complete the sale, and strive for clarity in the language of their policies reduce the risk that the insurer will fail to satisfy the reasonable expectations of their insureds.

§ 25E Waiver and Estoppel

[a] The Terminology

The term "waiver" has been used in so many different ways by courts that the term today has virtually no meaning. Professor Murray, in discussing the meaning of waiver in contract law generally, listed numerous confusing and contradictory definitions of the term by courts and observed that "a word so used is of no assistance in deciding cases, and it may be positively misleading."[1] As Professor Murray suggests, from one perspective the doctrine of waiver is fraught with mischief. Predicting how the doctrine will be applied in a particular case can be extremely difficult. Yet from the perspective of a court that needs a principle on which to rest a particular result, the doctrine of waiver can be of considerable assistance in deciding cases. In other words, the doctrine has considerable potential for flexible application by courts to achieve justice in particular situations where other doctrines seem inappropriate.[2]

---

[1] John E. Murray, *Murray on Contracts* 382 (2d ed. 1974).

[2] The Murray treatise should not be read as disagreeing with the foregoing. In the third edition of the treatise, the passage quoted in the text accompanying the preceding footnote is omitted, but the passage retains the very good presentation of the varied meanings given by courts to the term "waiver." See John E. Murray, *Murray on Contracts* 627-28 (3d ed. 1990).

Though many different definitions of waiver have been offered, perhaps the best is that a waiver is an intentional, voluntary relinquishment of a known right. Negligence or mistake is usually an insufficient basis for finding a waiver.[3] It is not essential that the waiver be bargained for in the sense that a contractual promise must be supported by a consideration. Even if a waiver needed a contractual foundation, the reliance of a party on the waiver would ordinarily constitute a suitable substitute for a consideration.

Whatever the doctrine of waiver is, the doctrine of estoppel is closely related to it. The doctrine of estoppel essentially requires two elements: an actual misrepresentation and detrimental reliance.[4] Misrepresentations, when they occur, are often attributable to the activities of agents, who mislead the insured as to the nature of the coverage. The insured must rely on this misrepresentation in some way. The essential difference between a waiver and an estoppel is that a waiver involves some sort of relinquishment while an estoppel involves a misrepresentation or inducement. One treatise describes the difference as follows:

> Waiver arises by the act of one party; estoppel by operation of law. Waiver depends upon knowledge of the insurer; estoppel upon a prejudicial change of position by the insured. While they may coexist, they are not identical in connotation. The term estoppel is broader than that of waiver, and may embrace it within its scope, in certain instances, since an insurer, after waiving certain rights, would be estopped thereafter to insist upon them. The converse is not true, as an estoppel need not be founded upon a waiver.[5]

[b] Common Uses of the Doctrines

Because the substance of the doctrines of waiver and estoppel are imprecise, courts often use these doctrines to justify results that seem fair in particular cases. Under the doctrine of waiver, limitations on liability and exclusions to coverage in insurance policies have been ignored. Insurers have been held to waive deadlines for giving notice of claims, filing proof of loss, paying premiums, and performing other acts required of the insured.[6] In the usual fact pattern, the insurer acts in recognition of the validity of the insurance, while knowing that a ground exists upon which the policy can be voided.[7] Sometimes waiver is express, as when the insurer or its agent affirmatively states that the insurer will not rely on a particular circumstance contrary to the terms of the policy to deny its obligations under the policy. More often, the waiver is implied from the circumstances. For example, if the insurer accepts a premium for future coverage with knowledge that the insured has already breached a warranty, the insurer has not expressly waived the breach of warranty but a court may nevertheless imply a waiver in the circumstances. The insurer's mere

---

[3] See generally 16B APPLEMAN § 9081 (1981); 7 COUCH 2d § 35:249 (1985).

[4] See generally 16B APPLEMAN § 9081 (1981); 7 COUCH 2d § 35:250 (1985).

[5] 16B APPLEMAN § 9081, at 497 (1981), *quoted in* Knapke v. Grain Dealers Mut. Ins. Co., 196 N.W.2d 737 (Wis. 1972).

[6] See, e.g., Annot., *Insurer's Acceptance of Defaulted Premium Payment or Defaulted Payment on Premium Note, as Affecting Liability for Loss Which Occurred During Period of Default,* 7 A.L.R.3d 414 (1966).

[7] See Gilbert Frank Corp. v. Federal Ins. Co., 457 N.Y.S.2d 494 (N.Y. App. Div. 1983).

silence in the face of a circumstance or situation is usually an insufficient basis for implying a waiver. However, if the circumstances suggest that the insurer in fairness should "speak" upon learning of the circumstance or situation, a waiver might be implied despite the insurer's silence.

Insurers have been estopped to deny liability in circumstances where insurer action or inaction has induced the insured to pursue activities contrary to the insured's best interests. For example, insurers have sometimes induced insureds not to obtain other insurance by misrepresenting the validity of existing insurance. When the insurer subsequently denied the validity of the existing insurance, courts have estopped the insurer to deny the coverage. If an insurer delivers a policy to the insured with knowledge of an innocent misstatement in the policy, courts have held the insurer estopped to deny coverage because of the insured's reliance on the delivery. Sometimes insurance agents have negligently misrepresented the scope of coverage, and courts have held the insurer estopped to deny the existence of coverage as represented. In many of these cases, the utilization by courts of the doctrine of estoppel is simply a way of stating that the court has concluded that the insured should recover. In some of the cases, both waiver and estoppel are used to explain the result, without making any particular distinction between the doctrines.

In short, the application of the doctrines of waiver and estoppel is basically left to the discretion of judges. Accordingly, these doctrines are powerful tools for courts to use in their efforts to regulate the business of insurance.

[c]   Limitations on the Doctrines

The waiver and estoppel doctrines have far-reaching potential, but both are subject to some limitations. First, neither the insurer nor insured can waive a right that exists for a broader, public purpose. For example, the insurable interest doctrine is designed to protect the public's interest in reducing the incentive for an insured to destroy property or lives intentionally and to prevent the use of insurance contracts as subterfuges for gambling. Accordingly, most courts hold that an insurer cannot waive the insurable interest requirement.[8] Similarly, statutes sometimes give insureds rights, such as the right to notice before certain kinds of policies, usually those mandated for the public's benefit, are canceled. Rights of this sort are ordinarily not subject to waiver by insureds.[9]

Second, the parol evidence rule operates in some situations to constrict the effect of the waiver doctrine. The parol evidence rule prevents a party from offering evidence of prior or concurrent representations or agreements to contradict a writing intended by the parties as a complete and exclusive statement of their agreement. Thus, the insurer or insured who wishes to argue that the other party waived a right prior to the formation of the contract evidenced by the written policy may meet the

---

[8] See § 45, *infra*.

[9] See Charleston Cty. School Dist. v. State Budget and Control Bd., 437 S.E.2d 6 (S.C. 1993) (insured could not waive appraisal right given by statute); Adams v. Aetna Cas. & Sur. Co., 574 So. 2d 1142 (Fla. Dist. Ct. App. 1991) (insured's failure to respond to options for uninsured motorist coverage did not waive right to statutory limit of coverage). For further discussion, see § 62A[c], *infra*.

parol evidence rule. Related to the parol evidence rule is the "no-oral-modification" clause sometimes contained in an application or a policy, which purports to prevent the representatives of insurers from waiving or modifying terms or requirements of the policy. These clauses are enforced by some courts to some extent, and they operate to reduce the impact of the waiver doctrine.

Third, some courts have held that the doctrines of waiver and estoppel cannot be used to expand the *coverage* of policies, which is to be distinguished from using the doctrine to prevent rescission of a policy or a defense to a claim within coverage.[10] In the case of estoppel, this limitation is tantamount to a rejection of contract law's doctrine of promissory estoppel. In this same vein, some courts in insurance cases limit estoppel to misrepresentations of existing fact, as opposed to a promise of future action. Under this limitation, an insurer's promise to give future notice of the nonpayment of a premium will not give rise to an estoppel if the insurer fails to perform as promised. Only if the insurer did not intend to perform in the future at the time of making the promises — which is tantamount to misrepresenting the insurer's present intent — would an estoppel be recognized.

Fourth, estoppel typically requires that the insured detrimentally rely on the act or representation of the insurer. If the insured has knowledge of the basis for the claimed estoppel (such as, for example, if the insurer misrepresents that the policy is in force but the insured knows that the policy is not in force) the insured has no reliance and cannot utilize estoppel.

§ 25F Implied Warranty

The Iowa Supreme Court, borrowing from commercial law, has articulated a doctrine of "implied warranty" in the insurance setting. In *C & J Fertilizer, Inc. v. Allied Mutual Insurance Co.,*[1] the insured's premises were burglarized but the burglars extracted the goods without making any marks or damage on the exterior of the premises.[2] Citing a policy provision which defined burglary as the "felonious abstraction of insured property from within the premises by a person making felonious entry therein by actual force and violence, of which force and violence there are visible marks . . . [on] the exterior of the premises at the place of such entry," the insurer denied coverage. In a five-four decision, the Iowa Supreme Court held for the plaintiff on the grounds of unconscionability and reasonable expectations. Three members of the majority also opined that the insured should prevail on the ground that the insurer breached an implied warranty of fitness. These judges identified the broad purpose of the contract as "merchandized protection" and then reasoned that the language of the contract was inconsistent with that broad purpose, thereby constituting a breach of the implied warranty of fitness.

The contours of this relatively recent theory are far from clear. For example, under some circumstances, a warranty confers a cause of action on one not in privity with

---

[10] See § 61[a], *infra.*

[1] 227 N.W.2d 169 (Iowa 1975).

[2] For further discussion of the visible marks requirement, see § 62B[b], *infra.*

the maker of the warranty. To what extent should an insurance policy confer rights on third parties? If a medical insurer failed to provide benefits to an insured, would the doctor who treated the insured have a cause of action against the insurer? Also, confusion exists in warranty law as to whether contract remedies or tort remedies are appropriate in particular cases. The question of the proper theory of remedy is also controversial and confusing in insurance law; embracing implied warranty law and its uncertainties in insurance law would only add to the confusion.[3] The theory's advantages over others available to courts for resolving disputes between insureds and insurers are not obvious. It is perhaps for these reasons that two other courts have declined to adopt it.[4] Nevertheless, *C&J Fertilizer* illustrates the potentially wide sweep of the judiciary's regulatory authority: one of the assets of the common law system (which is sometimes viewed as a detriment) is its ability to adapt to changing circumstances through the evolution of new theories.

§ 25G Insurers' Liability for Bad Faith

One of the most significant recent developments in insurance law is the recognition that insurers can be held liable in tort for bad faith performance of their duties to insureds. The tort duty contemplates that insurers must deal fairly with insureds and conduct their affairs in good faith. Although this duty has strong connections to the implied duty of good faith and fair dealing found in all contracts, the tort duty has developed its own characteristics, even if the contract duty has significantly influenced bad faith in tort. Indeed, "good faith" and "bad faith" remain elusive concepts with no universally accepted definition. Despite these uncertainties, the use of "good faith" and "bad faith" as standards to test the propriety of insurers' conduct gives courts and juries considerable flexibility in adjusting the relative interests of insurers and insureds. These tests have regulatory significance as well; when an insurer is held liable for bad faith conduct in particular circumstances, other insurers are likely to adjust their conduct so as not to suffer the same fate. Thus, the law of bad faith, like the doctrines of waiver, estoppel, and reasonable expectations, is a means by which courts regulate the insurer-insured relationship.[1]

---

[3] See William M. Lashner, Note, *A Common Law Alternative to the Doctrine of Reasonable Expectations in the Construction of Insurance Contracts*, 57 N.Y.U. L. Rev. 1175, 1182–83 (1982); Joan I. Milstein, Casenote, 64 Geo. L.J. 987 (1976).

[4] See Bartley v. National Union Fire Ins. Co., 824 F. Supp. 624 (N.D. Tex. 1992); Nielsen v. United Services Auto. Ass'n, 612 N.E.2d 526 (Ill. App. Ct. 1993).

[1] Scholarly writing on the subject of bad faith is voluminous. Three treatises have been published on the subject of good faith and fair dealing; a considerable portion of the text of these treatises concerns the duty of good faith in the insurance setting. See Stephen S. Ashley, *Bad Faith Actions: Liability and Damages* (1984); William M. Shernoff, Sanford M. Gage, & H. Levine, *Insurance Bad Faith Litigation* (1984); Dennis J. Walls, *Litigation and Prevention of Insurer Bad Faith* (2d ed. 1994). For a collection of 19 articles and essays with citations to other scholarly writings, see *Symposium on the Law of Bad Faith in Contract and Insurance*, 72 Tex. L. Rev. 1203 (1994).

[a] The Early History of Bad Faith

Exactly what constitutes bad faith conduct by an insurer is not easily stated. As a starting point, the *Restatement (Second) of Contracts* is helpful. Section 205 asserts that every contract imposes upon each party a duty of good faith and fair dealing in the contract's performance and enforcement,[2] but the *Restatement* is less clear about what constitutes good faith performance. In comment a to section 205, the *Restatement* drafters provide this explanation:

> Good faith is defined in Uniform Commercial Code § 1-201(19) as "honesty in fact in the conduct or transaction concerned." "In the case of a merchant" Uniform Commercial Code § 2-103(1)(b) provides that good faith means "honesty in fact and the observance of reasonable commercial standards of fair dealing in the trade." The phrase "good faith" is used in a variety of contexts, and its meaning varies somewhat with the context. Good faith performance or enforcement of a contract emphasizes faithfulness to an agreed common purpose and consistency with the justified expectations of the other party; it excludes a variety of types of conduct characterized as involving "bad faith" because they violate community standards of decency, fairness or reasonableness. The appropriate remedy for a breach of the duty of good faith also varies with the circumstances.[3]

But the *Restatement* itself wrote on a more elaborate history of the meaning of "good faith" in contract law.[4]

For many years, courts had used the maxim that a party to a contract should conduct itself consistent with notions of "good faith and fair dealing" in a variety of ways. In many of its applications, good faith placed limits on the discretion of parties during contract performance. For example, if X and Y have a contract and X's duty is conditioned on satisfaction with Y's performance, the possibility exists that X may seek relief from the contract's obligations by claiming that Y's performance was not satisfactory, when in truth it was. To limit the potential unfairness in this situation, courts used the concept of good faith: X's duty to perform is excused only if X's nonsatisfaction is based upon a good faith assessment of Y's performance. Another example is the situation where one party is entitled to designate a contract term, such as the price or the place of delivery. The party is not free to designate any possible contract term but must instead make a good faith choice of term. These cases stopped short of imposing a *duty* on the parties to exercise good faith in contract performance. Instead, if, in a contract between X and Y, Y fails to exercise good faith, that failure operates as the nonoccurrence of a condition to X's duty to perform, which has the effect of excusing X's duty; X is not given an affirmative remedy for Y's lack of good faith.

The concept of good faith was used in a slightly different way in the famous case *Wood v. Lucy, Lady Duff-Gordon,*[5] a staple of most contract law casebooks. Under

---

[2] *Restatement (Second) of Contracts* § 205 (1981).

[3] *Id.*, comment a.

[4] For a more detailed discussion of this history, see Robert H. Jerry, II, *The Wrong Side of the Mountain: A Comment on Bad Faith's Unnatural History,* 72 Tex. L. Rev. 1317 (1994).

[5] 118 N.E. 1082 (N.Y. 1918).

the agreement, Lucy gave Wood the exclusive right, subject to her approval, to place her endorsements on the fashions designed by others. She was to receive one-half of all profits derived from contracts he made. Wood alleged that she placed her endorsement on some fashions without his knowledge and withheld the profits. Lucy defended on the ground that her promise was not supported by a consideration, in that Wood did not obligate himself to do anything. Judge Cardozo found in the parties' agreement an implied promise made by Wood, arising out of the exclusive nature of the agency, to use his best efforts to place Lucy's endorsements. This promise was essentially an obligation to perform in good faith, and it provided the basis for finding the consideration that enabled Lucy's promise to be enforced. Had the agent failed to fulfill his duty to use best efforts to promote the objects of the agency relationship, Lucy would have had a claim against Wood for breach of contract.

Because the language of good faith was not unknown to courts, it is not surprising that good faith found its way into some early insurance cases in which courts referred to good faith and fair dealing as a duty owed by the insurer to the insured. Thus, in *Brassil v. Maryland Casualty Co.,*[6] a 1914 New York case, the court allowed the insured under a liability policy to recover his expenses of prosecuting an appeal that the insurer had refused to take from a judgment against the insured:

> It is enough to say that it would be a reproach to the law if there were no remedy for so obvious a wrong as was inflicted upon this plaintiff. His rights . . . go deeper than the mere surface of the contract written for him by the defendant. Its stipulations imposed obligations based upon those principles of fair dealing which enter into every contract. Even defendant has invoked [in its answer] this implied obligation of good faith and fair dealing not expressed in the written terms of its written contract. . . . If [it were plaintiff's duty to deal fairly and in good faith with defendant,] it was not less the correlative obligation of the defendant to "deal fairly and in good faith" with him.[7]

Although a smattering of insurance cases in later years acknowledged the implied duty of good faith and fair dealing that every insurer owed its insureds,[8] it was not until the 1950s and 1960s that good faith and fair dealing began to play a significant role in insurer-insured litigation.

[b] Bad Faith in Third-Party Insurance

A series of decisions in California ignited the evolution of the tort of bad faith. In *Brown v. Guarantee Insurance Co.,*[9] a 1957 decision, an appeals court reversed a trial court's dismissal of the insured's complaint alleging that the insurer "did not exercise the good faith required of it by law" when it refused to settle a $15,000 damage claim arising out of an automobile accident for $5,000, the amount of the

---

[6] 104 N.E. 622 (N.Y. 1914).

[7] 104 N.E. at 624.

[8] E.g., American Mut. Liab. Ins. Co. v. Cooper, 61 F.2d 446 (5th Cir. 1932); Boling v. New Amsterdam Cas. Co., 46 P.2d 916 (Okla. 1935); Hilker v. Western Auto. Ins. Co., 231 N.W. 257, *adhered to on rehearing,* 235 N.W. 413 (Wis. 1931).

[9] 319 P.2d 69 (Cal. Ct. App. 1957).

policy limits. The court reasoned that good faith was the best of the alternative ways to describe the obligation of an insurer who, under the provisions of a liability insurance policy, undertakes to defend the insured and enters into settlement negotiations on the insured's behalf. A year later, the California Supreme Court decided in *Comunale v. Traders & General Insurance Co.*[10] that the failure of the insurer "to consider [the insured's] interest in having the suit against him compromised by a settlement within the policy limits" constituted a breach of the "implied covenant of good faith and fair dealing," a promise implied "in every contract that neither party will do anything which will injure the right of the other to receive the benefits of the agreement."[11]

Thus, good faith became the standard by which courts drew a line between an insurer's satisfaction and nonsatisfaction of its obligations to its insured in settlement negotiations. And it was not surprising that good faith was invoked for this purpose. Obviously, an insurer defending an insured against a third-party's claim is not obligated to accept every settlement offer made by that third party; some settlement offers are unreasonable and should be rejected. But failure to accept a settlement offer that any reasonable insurer would accept could have dire consequences for an insured if the case were tried and a judgment for the plaintiff in excess of policy limits resulted. Good faith provided a way to explain the circumstances in which the insurer would be liable for failing to act responsibly in dealing with the settlement of claims against insureds; the insurer that subordinated the insured's interests to its own and thereby caused injury to the insured would be liable for bad faith performance of the contract.

Subsequent cases linked bad faith performance with tort law. In 1967, the California Supreme Court held in *Crisci v. Security Insurance Co.*[12] that breaching the covenant of good faith and fair dealing in the settlement context constituted a tort. The insurer declined an offer to settle the plaintiff's claim against the insured within the policy limits; ultimately a judgment well in excess of the policy limits was entered against the insured. In upholding the insured's judgment against the insurer, the court observed that liability is imposed against an insurer who "unwarrantedly refuses an offered settlement where the most reasonable manner of disposing of the claim is by accepting the settlement . . . not for a bad faith breach of the contract but for failure to meet the duty to accept reasonable settlements, a duty included within the implied covenant of good faith and fair dealing."[13] *Comunale* had stated that the action for breach of the duty to settle lies in both contract and tort, but the court there had been concerned mainly with the contract aspects of the action. *Crisci* reaffirmed *Comunale's* assertion that the duty sounds in both contract and tort,[14] but the court affirmed an award to the insured for her mental suffering, thereby firmly establishing the availability of tort-based remedies for breach of the duty to settle.[15] This was the most important consequence of

---

[10] 328 P.2d 198 (Cal. 1958).

[11] 328 P.2d at 200.

[12] 426 P.2d 173 (Cal. 1967).

[13] 426 P.2d at 176–17.

[14] 426 P.2d at 178 n.3.

[15] 426 P.2d at 178–79.

Crisci's holding that the breach of the duty to settle sounded in tort: it made available the broader remedial powers of tort law — a broader range of consequential damages, damages for mental anguish, and the possibility of punitive damages.

The primary motivation for recognizing tort duties in third-party insurance was the apparent inadequacy of contract remedies to compensate insureds and deter insurers from elevating their own interests above their insureds. For example, suppose a plaintiff offers to settle a claim against the insured for the policy limits. The insurer might prefer to try the case and hope for a zero-dollar judgment; the possibility of a very large judgment means little to the insured if the insurer's exposure is capped at the policy limits. The insured, of course, would prefer the settlement offer be accepted to avoid the risk of incurring a judgment in excess of policy limits, for which excess the insured would be personally responsible. By making the insurer liable in tort for all damages caused the insured by failing to act reasonably to protect the insured's interests, courts hoped to encourage insurers to fulfill their obligations to their insureds.

With the benefit of hindsight, many commentators now contend that courts were too quick to embrace tort remedies as the way to encourage insurers to fulfill their responsibilities and failed to appreciate the full potential of contract remedies to address insurer misconduct.[16] Contract remedies applied flexibly could go far toward fully compensating the aggrieved insured. If an insurer unjustifiably refuses to accept a reasonable settlement offer, it is a foreseeable consequence of the insurer's conduct that a judgment might be entered in excess of the policy limits. If the duty to settle is treated as a subsidiary element of the contractually based duty to defend, the excess judgment would still be the insurer's responsibility under contract law's remedial scheme.

To proponents of the bad faith tort, contract law's remedial scheme suffers from a major weakness. Contract law offers no compensation in the usual case for mental anguish, which the insured frequently endures when the insurer's conduct or neglect places an insured's financial well-being in jeopardy. Similarly, contract law generally does not award punitive damages absent an independent tort. Proponents of the tort argue that without the deterrence provided with broader remedies, insurers will have insufficient incentives to protect the interests of their insureds adequately.[17]

However one assesses that debate, the recognition of a tort remedy for the insurer's bad faith nonperformance of the insurance contract was in some respects

[16] See, e.g., William Powers, Jr., *Border Wars,* 72 Tex. L. Rev. 1209, 1231 (1994); Mark Gergen, *A Cautionary Tale About Contractual Good Faith in Texas,* 72 Tex. L. Rev. 1235, 1274 (1994); Gregory S. Crespi, *Good Faith and Bad Faith in Contract Law: Reflections on A Cautionary Tale and Border Wars,* 72 Tex. L. Rev. 1277, 1289 (1994); Robert H. Jerry, II, *The Wrong Side of the Mountain: A Comment on Bad Faith's Unnatural History,* 72 Tex. L. Rev. 1317, 1342-43 (1994); Alan O. Sykes, *Judicial Limitations on the Discretion of Liability Insurers to Settle or Litigate: An Economic Critique,* 72 Tex. L. Rev. 1345, 1348 (1994).

[17] For discussion of emotional distress recoveries in insurance, see Annot., *Liability of Insurer, or Insurance Agent or Adjuster, for Infliction of Emotional Distress,* 6 A.L.R.5th 297 (1992).

a logical extension of one well-settled line of cases. Tort actions for breach of contract have been recognized in situations where the contract creates a relationship in which the law imposes special duties on one of the parties — such as innkeeper-guest, attorney-client, common carrier-passenger, and bailor-bailee. Although contract law if more flexibly applied would have been able to redress the interests injured by acts or neglects in these relationships,[18] this was not the course that the law took. Instead, courts imposed liability in tort in these situations because of the public interest aspects and other special circumstances inherent in these relationships.[19] That many courts would add the insurer-insured relationship to the list was hardly surprising.

There are indications, however, that the tide may be turning. One of the most important may be a recent decision of the California Supreme Court which described bad faith as being linked to contractual obligations, not tort duties. In *Waller v. Truck Insurance Exchange,*[20] the court held that if there is no potential for coverage under a policy and hence no breach of the duty to defend, there is no available action for bad faith.[21] Interestingly, the court anchored the potential wrong in contract law: in the absence of a potential for coverage and a duty to defend,

> there can be no action for breach of the implied covenant of good faith and fair dealing because the covenant is based on the contractual relationship between the insurer and insured. . . . The legal principle is based on general contract law and the long-standing rule "that neither party will do anything which will injure the right of the other to receive the benefits of the agreement" . . . In sum, the covenant is implied as a supplement to the express contractual covenants, to prevent a contracting party from engaging in conduct that frustrates the other party's rights to the benefits of the agreement.[22]

It would be premature to assert in the 1990s that the law of bad faith is evolving into a contract doctrine and that tort principles no longer define its character. But it would be correct to assert that bad faith currently enjoys the status of a mature, relatively fully-developed doctrine, and that this may invite reassessment of the assumptions on which the doctrine rests.

[c]   Bad Faith in First-Party Cases

As the law of bad faith matured in third-party insurance, insureds began to assert claims for insurers' bad faith performance of their obligations under first-party insurance contracts. This extension from third-party to first-party insurance reached

[18] See Robert H. Jerry, II, *Remedying Insurers' Bad Faith Contract Performance: A Reassessment,* 18 Conn. L. Rev. 271, 310–13 (1986).

[19] See Rawlings v. Apodaca, 726 P.2d 565 (Ariz. 1986); Seaman's Direct Buying Service, Inc. v. Standard Oil Co. of California, 686 P.2d 1158, 1166 (Cal. 1984).

[20] 1995 WL 516406 (Cal. 1995).

[21] For a different point of view and a holding that the plaintiff's bad faith claim does not depend on the existence of coverage, see Republic Ins. Co. v. Stoker, 867 S.W.2d 74 (Tex. Ct. App. 1993).

[22] *Id.,* slip op. at 21.

fruition in the California Supreme Court's decision in *Gruenberg v. Aetna Insurance Co.*, a decision which embraced and solidified prior California precedents in the third-party setting:[23]

> The duty of an insurer to deal fairly and in good faith with its insured is governed by our decisions in *Crisci* [[24]] . . . and *Comunale* [[25]]. . . . We explained that this duty, the breach of which sounds in both contract and tort, is imposed because "[t]here is an implied covenant of good faith and fair dealing in every contract [including insurance policies] that neither party will do anything which will injure the right of the other to receive the benefits of the agreement."
>
> In those two cases, we considered the duty of the insurer to act in good faith and fairly in handling the claims of third persons against the insured, described as a "duty to accept reasonable settlements"; in the case before us we consider the duty of an insurer to act in good faith and fairly in handling the claim of an insured, namely a duty not to withhold unreasonably payments due under a policy. . . . That responsibility . . . is the obligation, deemed to be imposed by the law, under which the insurer must act fairly and in good faith in discharging its contractual responsibilities. Where in so doing, it fails to deal *fairly and in good faith* with its insured by refusing, without proper cause, to compensate its insured for a loss covered by the policy, such conduct may give rise to a cause of action in tort for breach of an implied covenant of good faith and fair dealing.[26]

A number of courts followed California's lead in the first-party setting, and today courts in about half the states adhere to the rule that the insurer who breaches the duty of good faith and fair dealing, either in the third-party setting or in the first-party setting, is liable to the insured in tort for the damages sustained as a result of the breach.[27] The Arizona Supreme Court summarized the rationale for recognizing the tort in *Rawlings v. Apodaca*[28] as follows:

> The breach of contractual covenants ordinarily sounds in contract. However, because of the special relationship between an insurer and its insured, the insured may maintain an action to recover tort damages if the insurer, by an intentional act, also breaches the implied covenant by failing to deal fairly and honestly with its insured's claim or by failing to give equal and fair consideration to the insured's interests.[29]

Not all courts agreed with the extension of the tort of bad faith from the third-party to the first-party setting. These courts typically emphasized the fiduciary relationship

---

[23] 510 P.2d 1032 (Cal. 1973).

[24] 66 Cal.2d 425, 426 P.2d 173, 58 Cal. Rptr. 13 (1967).

[25] 50 Cal.2d 654, 328 P.2d 198 (1958).

[26] 510 P.2d at 1036-37 (emphasis in original).

[27] For a detailed discussion of this issue and a survey of the cases, see Roger C. Henderson, *The Tort of Bad Faith in First-Party Insurance Transactions: Refining the Standard of Culpability and Reformulating the Remedies by Statute,* 26 U. Mich. J. L. Ref. 1 (1992).

[28] 726 P.2d 565 (Ariz. 1986).

[29] 726 P.2d at 579.

inherent in the third-party setting when the insurer undertakes the defense of the insured against a third party's claim, a relationship not present in the first-party relationship. For these courts, the fiduciary relationship was the key element justifying tort remedies for the insurer's bad faith performance of its contractual obligations: the insured in the third-party setting needs a weapon against the insurer who, having assumed the obligation to protect the insured's interests, might choose to subordinate the insured's interests; but in first-party insurance, the weapon is not needed because all the aggrieved insured need do when the insurer fails to give relief for the injury to the insured's interests is to sue the insurer on the policy.[30]

[d] Current Contours of Bad Faith

When the law of bad faith emerged in the 1960s and expanded throughout the 1970s and 1980s, it commanded considerable attention. By the 1990s, it is fair to say that bad faith law has reached the status of a mature, reasonably settled legal doctrine, and that the "probability of substantial doctrinal expansion . . . is low."[31] Yet the law of bad faith still has considerable power, particularly in the view of insurers who have been stung with very large judgments for bad faith performance of their obligations.[32] One of the most significant developments affecting the law of bad faith is the recognition of ERISA's preemptive effects, a topic discussed in the next subsection.

[1] ERISA Preemption

As discussed in an earlier section,[33] the U.S. Supreme Court's 1987 decision in *Pilot Life Insurance Co. v. Dedeaux*[34] held that section 514 of the Employee Retirement Income Security Act of 1974 (ERISA)[35] preempts certain state common law tort and contract claims when an insured employee benefit plan is involved, and makes the ERISA remedial scheme exclusive. Because most health insurance, much life insurance, and some disability insurance are provided through employee benefit plans, this decision means that insurers providing such plans may not be sued for bad faith performance of their obligations under the policies. ERISA provides no equivalent remedy, so the Supreme Court's decision in *Pilot Life* wipes out much of the law of the bad faith. Bad faith claims concerning insurance that is not part

---

[30] See, e.g., A & E Supply Co. v. Nationwide Mut. Fire Ins. Co., 798 F.2d 669 (4th Cir. 1986), *cert. denied,* 479 U.S. 1091 (1987); *Kewin v. Massachusetts Mut. Life Ins. Co.,* 295 N.W.2d 50 (Mich. 1980); *Farris v. United States Fid. & Guar. Co., 587 P.2d 1015 (Or. 1978); Duncan v. Andrew Cty. Mut. Ins. Co., 665 S.W.2d 13 (Mo. Ct. App. 1983).*

[31] Kenneth S. Abraham, *The Natural History of the Insurer's Liability for Bad Faith,* 72 Tex. L. Rev. 1295, 1295 (1994).

[32] Some of these are mentioned in Douglas R. Richmond, *An Overview of Insurance Bad Faith Law and Litigation,* 25 Seton Hall L. Rev. 74, 75-6 nn. 2-5 (1994) ($425 million judgment against consortium of European insurers; $12.3 million judgment against health insurer that denied bone marrow transplant as 'experimental'; $2.1 million in compensatory and $100 million in punitives against insurer that denied $20,000 underinsured motorist claim).

[33] See § 21[e], *supra.*

[34] 481 U.S. 41 (1987).

[35] 29 U.S.C. § 1144.

of an employee benefit plan can still be made. The upshot is that virtually all property and liability insurance, as well as any personal insurance not provided as a fringe benefit to an employee, fall outside the scope of the rule in *Pilot Life*.

Yet where the tort of bad faith is available, it is likely that bad faith breach is routinely added as a count to most insureds' claims against insurers under the reasoning that the count adds a premium to the settlement value of any complaint. Because the potential recoveries under a bad faith count, if proved, are potentially unbounded, the possibility that the tort of bad faith over-deters insurer behavior — even with the existence of ERISA preemption — cannot be casually dismissed.

[2] Nature of Misbehavior Required to Constitute Bad Faith

In the insurance context the descriptions of what constitutes "bad faith" conduct are diverse.[36] Generally speaking, mere negligence on the part of the insurer is usually not enough to constitute bad faith.[37] Negligence combined with something else (such as the insurer's awareness at some point while handling the claim that the claim was probably covered) is sometimes enough to constitute bad faith; this may amount to a "gross negligence" or "reckless disregard" standard.[38] An insurer that opts to deny a debatable claim is not acting in bad faith; but an insurer that denies a claim that is not "fairly debatable" is probably acting in bad faith.[39] Failure to handle a claim in a manner that would alleviate the insured's hardship without impairing the insurer's interests in circumstances where the insurer is aware of the insured's dire straits is probably bad faith.[40]

The shorthand descriptions of what constitutes bad faith vary from jurisdiction to jurisdiction. One court stated that "bad faith requires an extraordinary showing of disingenuous or dishonest failure to carry out a contract."[41] Another said that bad faith is "affirmative misconduct, without good faith defense, in a malicious, dishonest, or oppressive attempt to avoid liability."[42] Another court ruled that an insurer fails to exercise good faith in claims processing "where its refusal to pay the claim is not predicated upon circumstances that furnish reasonable justification therefore."[43] A different court stated that bad faith requires showing the absence

---

[36] For a more detailed discussion, see Douglas R. Richmond, *An Overview of Insurance Bad Faith Law and Litigation,* 25 Seton Hall L. Rev. 74, 96-103 (1994).

[37] See Anderson v. Continental Ins. Co., 271 N.W.2d 368 (Wis. 1978).

[38] See Jessen v. National Excess Ins. Co., 776 P.2d 1244 (N.M. 1989); Aetna Cas. & Sur. Co. v. Day, 487 So. 2d 830 (Miss. 1986).

[39] See Clark-Peterson Co. v. Independent Ins. Associates, 514 N.W.2d 912 (Iowa 1994); Erie Ins. Co. v. Hickman, 622 N.E.2d 515, 520 (Ind. 1993); Palmer by Diacon v. Farmers Ins. Exch. 861 P.2d 895 (Mont. 1993); Rawlings v. Apodaca, 726 P.2d 565 (Ariz. 1986).

[40] See Silberg v. California Life Ins. Co., 521 P.2d 1103 (Cal. 1974); Sparks v. Republic National Life Ins. Co., 647 P.2d 1127 (Ariz. 1982).

[41] Gordon v. Nationwide Mut. Ins. Co., 285 N.E.2d 849, 854 (N.Y. 1972).

[42] First Maine Ins. Co. v. Booth, 876 S.W.2d 255 (Ark. 1994).

[43] Zoppo v. Homestead Ins. Co., 644 N.E.2d 397, 400 (Ohio 1994), *reconsideration denied,* 644 N.E.2d 1589 (Ohio 1995), *petition for cert. filed,* 63 USLW 3834 (May 16, 1995) (No. 94-1880). Compare Centennial Ins. Co. v. Liberty Mut. Ins. Co., 404 N.E.2d 759, 762 (Ohio 1980) ("bad faith, although not susceptible of concrete definition, embraces more than bad judgment or negligence. It imports a dishonest purpose, moral obliquity, conscious

of a "reasonably legitimate or arguable reason" for the insurer's refusal to pay a claim.[44] Yet another court explained that to show bad faith, the insured must show an "absence of a reasonable basis for denying benefits of the policy and [the insurer's] knowledge or reckless disregard of the lack of a reasonable basis for denying the claim."[45] Although these articulations have much in common, a close reading of each would find grounds for distinctions among them.

Occasionally courts have attempted very elaborate explanations of what constitutes bad faith. For example, the Michigan Supreme Court has described bad faith conduct in the third-party setting as the "arbitrary, reckless, indifferent, or intentional disregard of the interests of the person owed a duty."[46] In the same decision, the court listed several supplemental factors that can be considered in determining the presence of bad faith in a third-party setting, such as failure to keep the insured informed of developments that could affect the insured's interests, failure to inform the insured of settlement offers, failure to solicit a settlement offer or to initiate settlement negotiations when warranted in the circumstances, rejecting reasonable settlement offers within the policy limits, attempting to coerce an involuntary contribution from the insured to a settlement within policy limits, failing to properly investigate the plaintiff's claim, disregarding the advice of an adjustor or attorney, refusing to settle a case within the policy limits following an excessive verdict when the chances of reversal on appeal are slight, and failing to take an appeal following a verdict in excess of the policy limits where reasonable grounds for such an appeal exist.[47] Yet these factors are less an explanation of what sort of act or neglect rises to the level of bad faith as it is a cataloging of the kinds of situations in which the insurer may act in bad faith. Deciding whether to appeal an adverse judgment or whether to reject a plaintiff's settlement offer or how much investigation to do each involves questions of judgment, and these factors do not help assess the reasonableness of the exercise of judgment in individual cases.

One difficulty presented by the wide variance in terminology used to describe what constitutes bad faith is an uncertainty about when bad faith conduct is sufficient to justify an award of punitive damages. In tort law generally, the tort itself is insufficient to justify punitive damages, but if the tort is accompanied by some kind of egregious, wanton misconduct a punitive award may be appropriate. With the tort of bad faith, the rhetoric of egregious, extreme misbehavior is used to distinguish mere poor or negligent claims handling, which ordinarily will not constitute tortious conduct under the tort of bad faith, from bad faith claims handling which is actionable. Under general tort law rules, merely showing that the tort of bad faith has occurred is not, in and of itself, equivalent to establishing a right to punitive

---

wrongdoing, breach of a known duty through some ulterior motive or ill will partaking of the nature of fraud.")

[44] Insurance Co. of N. Am. v. Citizensbank of Thomasville, 491 So. 2d 880 (Ala. 1986).

[45] Anderson v. Continental Ins. Co., 271 N.W.2d 368, 376-77 (Wis. 1978).

[46] Commercial Union Ins. Co. v. Liberty Mut. Ins. Co., 393 N.W.2d 161, 164 (Mich. 1986).

[47] 393 N.W.2d at 165–66. For a similar listing, see Brown v. Guarantee Ins. Co., 319 P.2d 69 (Cal. Ct. App. 1958).

damages, as a number of courts have recognized.[48] But if the tort of bad faith requires something more than mere negligence, what kind of "something more" is needed to establish a right to punitive damages? This question has no obvious, easy answer, and this means that the boundary between good faith and bad faith conduct is elusive. Because the tort of bad faith defies easy definition, it will continue to evolve on a case-by-case basis.[49] As certain kinds of insurer conduct are successfully challenged in the adjudicative process, the good faith duty will become easier to describe, but its exact contours will probably never be articulated precisely.

[3] Statutory Penalties and Related Remedies

In many jurisdictions, statutes exist that authorize a court to award attorneys fees, costs, or a statutory penalty to an insured who prevails in an action against against an insurer for failure to pay a claim.[50] These statutes have been held by some courts to provide the exclusive remedy for an insurer's bad faith conduct.[51] They are intended to benefit the insured by leveling the playing field; for example, to the extent an insurer decides to deny a first-party claim under the reasoning that even if the insurer loses at trial the damages will be no greater than what the insurer would have paid if it had performed under the contract, the prospect that the successful insured will recover attorneys fees reduces the insurer's incentive to engage in this kind of behavior.

[4] Reverse Bad Faith

Because the duty of good faith and fair dealing recognized in section 205 of the *Restatement (Second) of Contracts* is owed by all parties to a contract, it is hardly frivolous to ask whether insureds owe a duty of good faith to insurers, and whether insureds can be liable in some sense to insurers for bad faith conduct. Few insurers, of course, would perceive a benefit in instigating litigation against insureds to recover damages for insureds' bad faith conduct. Such suits would cost insurers much goodwill, even if insureds did not file counterclaims in every such case. But the concept of insureds' bad faith conduct could be used as a defense to an insured's claim under a policy, and it is possible to imagine insurers asserting an insured's bad faith as a setoff to the insured's recovery under comparative fault principles.

Although the possibility of reverse bad faith has interested commentators,[52] the

---

[48] See, e.g., Rocanova v. Equitable Life Assur. Soc'y, 634 N.E.2d 940 (N.Y. 1994); Erie Ins. Co. v. Hickman, 622 N.E.2d 515, 520 (Ind. 1993).

[49] See generally Henderson, *supra* note 1, at 40-49.

[50] See, e.g., Kan. Stat. Ann. § 40-256; La. Stat. Ann. § 22-658; Mo. Stat. § 375.420; Wyo. Stat. § 26-15- 124(c); Annot., *What Constitutes Bad Faith on Part of Insurer Rendering It Liable for Statutory Penalty Imposed for Bad Faith in Failure to Pay, or Delay in Paying, Insured's Claim,* 33 A.L.R.4th 579 (1984).

[51] See, e.g., Howell v. Southern Heritage Ins. Co., 448 S.E.2d 275 (Ga. Ct. App. 1994); Stump v. Commercial Union, 601 N.E.2d 327 (Ind. 1992); Spencer v. Aetna Life & Cas. Ins. Co., 611 P.2d 149 (Kan. 1980).

[52] The most thorough and comprehensive discussion of the subject to date is Ellen Smith Pryor, *Comparative Fault and Insurance Bad Faith,* 72 Tex. L. Rev. 1505 (1994). Most commentators have endorsed the doctrine, see, e.g., Douglas R. Richmond, *Insured's Bad Faith as Shield or Sword: Litigation Relief for Insurers?,* 77 Marq. L. Rev. 41 (1993); Patrick

only cases to adopt the doctrine of reverse bad faith have been decided in California.[53] Clearly, one of the hurdles to the widespread recognition of the doctrine is the absence of anything owed by insured to insurer that resembles a fiduciary duty, unlike the duty which runs from insurer in the insured in the third-party setting and which arguably exists in spirit in the first-party setting. Bad faith will probably continue to be viewed as a one-way street in favor of the insured under the reasoning that the insured needs protection but the insurer does not, notwithstanding the untidy nature of this logic. If the law of bad faith undergoes any significant doctrinal change in the future, it is more likely that courts will narrow the insured's remedy for bad faith by recognizing its contractual heritage, rather than by expanding and complicating the law of bad faith through the grant to insurers of a weapon to be used against insureds.

§ 25H   Reformation

Reformation is an extraordinary equitable remedy used in situations where the written agreement in some material respects is inconsistent with the actual agreement of the parties. Either fraud, mistake, or an accident may cause the writing to fail to reflect the parties' agreement. The remedy of reformation rewrites the contract so that it conforms to what the parties intended. Because reformation has the potential to accomplish what courts often disdain — writing the agreement for the parties — courts apply the remedy with great caution.

Several principles have been articulated by courts to describe the limitations of the remedy. Reformation is not available for cases where no writing exists, or where the parties prepare a writing but do not intend it to express their final agreement.[1] Nor is reformation a means for inserting terms in a contract to which the parties never assented.[2] As a corollary of this principle, it is often said that reformation is not available in an instance of unilateral mistake. In the unilateral mistake situation, one of the parties intends to be bound to the contract as written. Reformation is not available unless *both* parties executed a writing that failed to reflect their agreement. Rescission or restitution may be available for a unilateral mistake, but reformation

E. Shipstead & Scott S. Thomas, *Comparative and Reverse Bad Faith: Insured's Breach of Implied Covenant of Good Faith and Fair Dealing as Affirmative Defense or Counterclaim,* 23 Tort & Ins. L. J. 215 (1987), but there are voices on the other side, see, e.g., D. Douglas Brothers, *The Defense of Comparative Bad Faith: A Practitioner's Viewpoint,* 72 Tex. L. Rev. 1565 (1994).

[53] See, e.g., Fleming v. Safeco Ins. Co. of Am., 206 Cal. Rptr. 313 (Cal. Ct. App. 1984); Sorensen v. Allred, 169 Cal. Rptr. 441 (Ct.App. 1980). Other cases have considered the doctrine, but have either disapproved it, see Stephens v. Safeco Ins. Co. of Am., 852 P.2d 565 (Mont. 1993); Tokles & Son, Inc. v. Midwestern Indem. Co., 605 N.E.2d 936 (Ohio 1992), or stopped short of adopting it or rendering holdings about it, see Alexander Underwriters General Agency, Inc. v. Lovett, 357 S.E.2d 258 (Ga. Ct. App. 1987); Jessen v. National Excess Ins. Co., 776 P.2d 1244 (N.M. 1989).

[1] See, e.g., Shurtz v. Jost, 674 S.W.2d 244 (Mo. Ct. App. 1984).

[2] See, e.g., Setzer v. Old Republic Life Ins. Co., 126 S.E.2d 135 (N.C. 1962).

is not.[3] However, reformation may be available for unilateral mistake if fraud or inequitable conduct by one party caused the other party's mistake.[4] Reformation is only used when the evidence is clear and convincing that the parties expressed agreement and an intention to be bound to the terms the court is asked to enforce.[5] This standard, which goes beyond the preponderance standard, is necessary because reformation requires the court to disregard the parol evidence rule.[6]

In insurance, reformation is most often granted in situations where through oversight a provision is inadvertently not stricken from the standardized form even though the parties agreed on what the policy would contain.[7] But the doctrine nevertheless affords considerable discretion to courts, and therefore has considerable potential to assist insureds.[8]

§ 251   The Policing Effect of the Absent Policy Defense

If the insured has not received or otherwise been provided with a copy of the policy, the insured may be ignorant of coverage or obligations the insured may have as a prerequisite to maintaining the coverage.[1] If the insurer is responsible for the insured's lack of information, it follows that the insured may be relieved of a number of obligations, such as the duty to read the policy, the duty to give prompt notice of loss, the duty to forward promptly any claims made against the insured, etc.

---

[3] See, e.g., Evans v. Hartford Life Ins. Co., 704 F.2d 1177 (10th Cir. 1983); Watson v. United States Fid. & Guar. Co., 427 F.2d 1355 (9th Cir. 1970); Harlach v. Metropolitan Prop. and Liability Ins. Co., 602 A.2d 1007, 1010 (Conn. 1992); Estate of Blakely v. Federal Kemper Life Assur. Co., 640 N.E.2d 961, 966 (Ill. App. Ct. 1994).

[4] Jelsma v. Acceptance Ins. Co., 446 N.W.2d 725, 727 (Neb. 1989).

[5] See, e.g., Evans v. Hartford Life Ins. Co., 704 F.2d 1177 (10th Cir. 1983); Moyer v. Title Guar. Co., 177 A.2d 714 (Md. 1962); Cincinnati Ins. Co. v. Fred S. Post, Jr., Co., 747 S.W.2d 777, 781 (Tenn. 1988); Estate of Blakely v. Federal Kemper Life Assur. Co., 640 N.E.2d 961 (Ill. App. Ct. 1994); Earl Williams Constr. Co. v. Thornton & Brooks, Inc., 501 So. 2d 1037 (La. Ct. App. 1987).

[6] For further discussion of the equitable remedy of reformation, see 3 *Corbin on Contracts* §§ 614–15 (1960).

[7] See, e.g., Leithauser v. Hartford Fire Ins. Co., 124 F.2d 117 (6th Cir. 1942); Parchen v. Chessman, 142 P. 631 (Mont. 1914); New York Life Ins. Co. v. Rak, 173 N.E.2d 603 (Ill. App. Ct.), *aff'd,* 180 N.E.2d 470 (Ill. 1961); Ohio Farmers Ins. Co. v. Clinton Cty. Nat'l Bank & Trust Co., 220 N.E.2d 381 (Ohio 1964).

[8] See, e.g., L.Z. Gentry v. American Motorist Ins. Co., 867 P.2d 468 (Okla. 1994) (where constructive fraud induced applicant to agree to contract, policy may be reformed to conform to representations of parties); Jelsma v. Acceptance Ins. Co., 446 N.W.2d 725 (Neb. 1989) (reformation may be granted where through mistake of insurer's agent the policy fails to express the contract as intended by the parties); Washington v. Montgomery Ward Life Ins. Co., 640 So. 2d 822 (La. Ct. App. 1994) (where agent knows insured's true intention as to desired coverage, insurer is bound by agent's knowledge, and policy will be reformed to conform to original intention).

[1] See generally Annot., *Insurer's Duty, and Effect of Its Failure, to Provide Insured or Payee With Copy of Policy or Other Adequate Documentation of Its Terms,* 78 A.L.R.4th 9 (1990).

Moreover, policy limitations or exclusions may be negated if the insured lacked an opportunity to see the restrictions and it was not unreasonable for the insured to expect coverage in the circumstances. In short, where the insured does not know the content of the policy because the insurer has not given the insured a copy of it, there is much potential for mitigation of limitations on or defenses to coverage.

Kippen v. Farm Bureau Mutual Insurance Co.,[2] a 1988 North Dakota case, is instructive. Janice Kippen was injured when she was struck by a motor vehicle owned and operated by a third party. The third party had liability insurance with limits of $50,000. Janice's husband, Carlyle, was an employee of North Dakota Farm Bureau; he was provided a company car for business and personal use. This vehicle was insured by a policy issued by Farm Bureau Mutual, which included $1 million of underinsured motorist coverage. Although Carlyle was listed as a named insured on the policy, he never received a copy of the policy, a certificate of insurance, a declarations sheet, or any other notification of the policy's existence.

Unaware of the Farm Bureau coverage, the Kippens settled their claim with the third party for the policy limits and issued the tortfeasor a general release. When they thereafter learned of the underinsurance coverage, they filed a claim for benefits; this claim, however, was denied by the insurer on the ground that the insured had failed to give prompt notice and had not secured the company's consent before settling with the tortfeasor. In the Kippens' action against the insurer, the court held that the insurer had a duty "to provide notice of coverage and relevant provisions to a named insured,"[3] and that the failure of the insurer to provide the insured with a copy of the policy excused the insured's noncompliance with the policy's provisions regarding prompt notice and the necessity of securing the insurer's consent before settling claims that might jeopardize the insurer's subrogation rights. The court explained: "[U]nder the undisputed facts of this case, it would be unconscionable to allow Farm Bureau Mutual to avoid coverage because of the Kippens' failure to give notice to, and obtain consent of, an unknown insurer."[4] Other courts have reached holdings consistent with *Kippen.*[5]

If the insured understands the nature of the coverage and the requirements of the policy without having seen or been given a copy of the policy, it would seem that the insurer's failure to provide a copy of the policy might have no consequence. In *Kippen*, the court met this argument by noting that underinsured coverage was not required in North Dakota during the relevant time period, and thus there was no basis

---

[2] 421 N.W.2d 483 (N.D. 1988).

[3] 421 N.W.2d at 485.

[4] 421 N.W.2d at 486.

[5] See, e.g., Wayne Chem., Inc. v. Columbus Agency Serv. Corp., 426 F. Supp. 316 (N.D. Ind.), *modified on other grounds,* 567 F.2d 692 (7th Cir. 1977); Farmers Ins. Exch. v. Call, 712 P.2d 231 (Utah 1985); Breeding v. Massachusetts Indem. & Life Ins. Co., 633 S.W.2d 717 (Ky. 1982); Safeco Ins. Co. v. Dairyland Mut. Ins. Co., 446 P.2d 568 (Wash. 1968); Rucks v. Old Republic Life Ins. Co., 345 So. 2d 795 (Fla. Dist. Ct. App. 1977); Gardner v. League Life Ins. Co., 210 N.W.2d 897 (Mich. Ct. App. 1973). See also Sears Mort. Corp. v. Rose, 634 A.2d 74 (N.J. 1993) (despite duty of insurer to supply insured with copy of policy, title insurer need not supply a copy of title commitment to customer if customer's attorney applies for policy).

for holding that the insured should know that he had access to such coverage.[6] It would seem that a breach of this duty should not automatically give rise to coverage; but if the duty is breached and the insured cannot reasonably be expected to understand one of his or her obligations under the policy, the insured should not lose coverage on account of a failure to comply with the policy's requirements.[7]

---

[6] 421 N.W.2d at 486. But the court went further and announced that "even if a statute is sufficient to place the insured on notice of the existence of coverage, that does not alleviate the insurer's primary duty to provide a copy of the policy or other documentation of the terms of coverage."

[7] *Id.*

PART B

ESTABLISHING THE CONTRACTUAL RELATIONSHIP

(Pub.837)

CHAPTER **3**

CONTRACT FORMATION

§ 30   The Process of Contract Formation: An Overview

To create a valid, enforceable promissory obligation, several requirements must be met. These requirements are usually fulfilled through a set of exchanged communications; in the insurance business, these communications occur in a customary, expected sequence. With respect to the marketing of individual policies of insurance, the process of forming a contract typically involves five steps: (1) initial contact between the applicant and an intermediary; (2) submission of the application; (3) issuance of the binder; (4) investigation by the insurer; and (5) delivery of the policy. The process in commercial insurance is similar, although depending on the type of coverage a temporary binder might not be issued. Group insurance policies involve more parties and are more complex, and the process of forming the package of tripartite contractual relationships is more involved. In all of these situations, however, the requirements to form a valid, enforceable contractual obligation are the same.

In this section, the usual process for marketing individual policies will be sketched; subsequent sections will examine the legal requirements for forming a contract against the backdrop of this process.

The first step in the process of forming an insurance contract is the *initial contact between the consumer and the intermediary.* Either the insurer's agent or a broker with limited authority to represent the insurer will somehow come into contact with the prospective insured.[1] Sometimes the consumer will initiate the contact, perhaps in response to an advertisement by the intermediary or perhaps by using the telephone book. The initial contact often involves a face-to-face meeting between the insurer's representative and the consumer, but mass marketing techniques have proliferated in recent years. Newspaper circulars, mailings, and telephone solicitations are common ways of encouraging applications from consumers for insurance. During this preapplication period, which may involve more than one communication, the intermediary typically will explain what the insurer might provide in the way of a product. Simultaneously, the prospective applicant will communicate to the intermediary what he or she expects by way of coverage. In some circumstances, the intermediary will attempt to persuade the prospective insured that certain

---

[1] See § 35, *supra.*

coverages are important or necessary to the well-being of the applicant. Sometimes the consumer will have discussions with several agents or brokers, shopping for the best coverage at the lowest price.

If after the initial contact the consumer desires the insurance that the intermediary is marketing, the transaction will proceed to the second step: *the submission of an application*. The application is normally a form prepared by the insurer and supplied to the applicant through the intermediary. On the application, the consumer will be asked to make certain representations regarding a number of matters relevant to the risk. Often the intermediary fills out the form for the applicant, asking the applicant for information in response to certain questions on the form and then putting the applicant's oral responses in the appropriate spaces. In the process of asking for the information, the intermediary will often interpret or explain the nature of the requests by the insurer. After the form is filled out, the applicant will be asked to sign it. A prudent intermediary should give the applicant an opportunity to read over the form to determine the accuracy of the information on it, but this is not always done. The intermediary will then take the executed application and send it to the insurer. The application will usually be accompanied by the applicant's payment of the first premium.

At the time the intermediary takes the insured's application, the intermediary, if he or she has the authority to do so, may issue a *binder*. The binder (or "conditional receipt") will form a temporary contract of insurance between the insurer and the applicant immediately upon the submission of the application; the formal policy documents will not be created and issued until a later date. The binder is ordinarily evidenced by a written memorandum, but it can be oral. Ordinarily the binder specifies that the insured is covered in accordance with the terms of the formal policy (which the applicant has not seen) until such time as the insurer makes a decision on whether to underwrite the risk. If the insurer decides to assume the risk, a policy will be issued dated as of the day of the application. If the risk is declined, the temporary insurance terminates and the applicant's first premium payment, if any, is returned. Binders can raise difficult factual and legal questions, many of which are explored in a later section.[2]

After the application is submitted (and perhaps the binder issued), the insurer will *evaluate the application*. The purpose of the evaluation, which is typically orchestrated at the insurer's home office, is to enable the insurer to determine whether it desires to assume the risk. The information the insurer uses in the evaluation process normally goes beyond the data the applicant provides. Many insurers maintain inspection departments, whose sole purpose is to gather information for the insurer about risks. Other insurers employ outside firms to do this work. These departments or firms will investigate the applicant's property, attempt to determine the applicant's financial or employment status, or gather any information the insurer deems relevant to the question of whether the applicant would be a satisfactory insured. Insurers also subscribe to "bureau lists" or "association lists," which are centralized indexes of applicants who have been refused insurance, have had frequent losses, or are poor risks for other reasons. Insurers sometimes utilize financial reference

---

[2] See § 33, *infra*.

services and credit agencies to provide underwriting information. In automobile insurance, the insurer may check the applicant's driving record. In life insurance, the insurer may require the applicant to obtain a medical examination, the results of which will be reviewed by the insurer.

If, after investigation, the insurer decides to assume the risk, it will *issue the policy*. The insurer will deliver, usually through the mail but sometimes directly through the intermediary, the formal contract documents to the insured. The policy's effective date will be stated on the face of the document; this date is ordinarily retroactive to the date of application. Most of the documents will be standardized forms, typically fairly lengthy and rather complex. Of course, a contract might not be formed, for instead of issuing a policy the insurer might choose to reject the application. In such a case, the insurer will so notify the applicant and return the first premium payment, if any.

The following sections elaborate upon specific aspects of the process of forming an insurance contract. Particular attention is given to the legal requirements for forming a valid, enforceable contract.

§ 31 The Legal Requirements for Forming a Contract

A contract is a "promise or a set of promises for the breach of which the law gives a remedy, or the performance of which the law in some way recognizes as a duty."[1] An insurance policy is essentially a contract between insurer and insured. In most insurance transactions, promises are exchanged by insurer and insured in the form of an agreement, a manifestation of mutual assent between two or more parties. To create an enforceable agreement, it is necessary that the parties (1) complete successfully the mechanics of offer and acceptance, (2) give consideration to each other to support the other party's promise, (3) possess capacity to contract, (4) satisfy any applicable writing requirement, and (5) contract for a purpose that is not contrary to public policy.

[a] Offer and Acceptance

To form a contract, the parties must manifest to each other their intent to be bound. Under the classical model of contract formation, the mutual assent of the parties is expressed through the mechanics of offer and acceptance. The offeror manifests assent to be bound by inviting another person, the offeree, to make some sort of expression indicating acceptance of the terms on which the offeror invites a contract. When the acceptance is given by the offeree in the manner invited by the offeror, a contract is formed. The same mutual assent requirement in contract law applies to contracts of insurance.[2]

In insurance contract formation, the *applicant* usually makes the offer.[3] As is the

---

[1] *Restatement (Second) of Contracts* § 1 (1981).

[2] See, e.g., Lindsay Ins. Agency v. Mead, 508 N.W.2d 820 (Neb. 1993); Golden Eagle Ins. Co. v. Foremost Ins. Co., 25 Cal. Rptr.2d 242 (Cal. Ct. App. 1993).

[3] See, e.g., G.P. Enterprises, Inc. v. Jackson Nat'l Life Ins. Co., 509 N.W.2d 780 (Mich. Ct. App. 1993); Louisiana Commercial Bank v. Georgia Intern. Life Ins. Co., 618 So. 2d 1091 (La. Ct. App. 1993); Robertson v. Life Ins. Co. of Georgia, 396 S.E.2d 35 (Ga. Ct. App. 1990).

situation with many consumer transactions, the insurer prepares the form on which the consumer makes the offer to the insurer. Then, the insurer is free, within whatever limits may be imposed by statutory law, to accept or reject the offer. Although retaining the power to accept or reject the applicant's offer is an advantage for the insurer, during the time that the insurer is considering how to respond to the applicant's offer the applicant is free to revoke the offer without any liability to the insurer. The ability to revoke an offer prior to acceptance is a basic rule of contract law. As a practical matter, the rule is of little consequence in insurance law since statutes or regulations typically allow the applicant a period of time (usually ten days) after a policy is delivered to rescind the insurance contract and receive a full refund of any premium paid in advance.[4] These statutes and regulations give consumers a power they do not possess at common law: the power to void a contract after the mechanics of offer and acceptance have been completed.

If the insurer responds to the applicant's offer with an insurance policy different from the terms of the policy that the applicant sought, the insurer has made a counteroffer to the applicant.[5] To illustrate, the applicant usually applies for a life insurance policy of a stated face value and premium. (If these terms are missing, the contract is likely to be too indefinite to be enforced).[6] It may be, however, that results of the applicant's medical examination prevent the insurer from accepting the applicant's offer. The insurer may respond by offering coverage of the same face value but at a higher premium. The insurer's counteroffer terminates the applicant's offer and creates in the applicant the power to form a contract by accepting the insurer's offer. Also, the applicant is free to reject the insurer's counteroffer, just as any offeree is free to reject the offer made by another party.

Contract formation is usually evaluated according to *objective* standards. Thus, when *A* makes an invitation to *B*, whether this invitation amounts to an offer depends on what *B* would reasonably understand *A* means in the circumstances. *A's* unstated subjective intentions are irrelevant (unless *B* knows or has reason to know those intentions). Normally, the applicant for insurance would not be reasonable in thinking that the insurance agent who solicits an application is making an offer to the applicant on behalf of the company which the applicant can accept merely by submitting an application. In the usual transaction, the agent is likely to advise the applicant in one way or another that the company reserves the right to accept or reject the application. Also, the application itself is likely to state in language not easily overlooked by the applicant that no binding relationship is created simply by filling out the application.

However, because contracts are formed by reference to objective tests, in some circumstances it is possible for the insurer to make the offer to the consumer, which the consumer then accepts simply by filling out an application. For example, in several cases where the insurer has made a mass mailing to numerous individuals soliciting applications, courts have held that a reasonable person would believe that

---

[4] See, e.g., Ill. Stat., ch. 173, § 975; Pa. Stat. tit. 40, § 752; Neb. Ins. Code § 44-710.8.

[5] See Lindsay Ins. Agency v. Mead, 508 N.W.2d 820, 826 (Neb. 1993); Kopff v. Economy Radiator Service, 838 S.W.2d 449 (Mo. Ct. App. 1992).

[6] See Simmons v. All Am. Life Ins. Co., 838 P.2d 1088, 1090 (Or.App. 1992).

responding to the advertisement by sending in an application formed a contract.[7] Similarly, an applicant who purchases a policy of air-travel insurance from a vending machine in an airport forms a contract as soon as the application is deposited in the machine: the company makes the offer to all who pass by the machine, and the applicant accepts the offer by submitting an application.[8]

If the applicant makes the offer to the insurer, the acceptance occurs when the offeree manifests to the offeror its intent to be bound. Technically, this occurs at the moment the manifestation is dispatched by the offeree (such as the moment the envelope containing the policy is deposited in the mailbox for delivery to the insured). However, the terms of the offer, even if prepared by the insurer, can specify the moment at which the acceptance becomes effective. Thus, the offer — made by the consumer but prepared for the consumer by the insurer — might provide that the acceptance becomes effective upon approval of the application in the home office, or the successful completion of a medical examination by the applicant, or upon delivery of the policy to the applicant. Such requirements are tested according to objective standards, but they are ordinarily valid requirements.[9] Even the possession of the applicant's first premium payment will not cause a contract to be formed if the requirements set forth in the policy for making a valid acceptance have not been met. Of course, in the event the application is rejected, the insurer must return any premium payment to the applicant, but the insurer's possession of the premium will not prevent the insurer from rejecting the application.

Whether an insurance contract is a unilateral or bilateral contract is, surprisingly enough, a subject of some disagreement. Although an insurance contract could theoretically be structured in either form, insurance contracts are usually bilateral. In bilateral contracts, each party gives a promise to the other: the insured promises to pay premiums and perform other duties in the event of a loss in exchange for the insurer's promise to pay proceeds if the loss occurs. However, some commentators have said that insurance contracts are unilateral, not bilateral.[10] A unilateral contract is a contract in which only one side makes a promise. Usually, the offeror makes a promise to do something if the offeree gives a return performance; in this situation, the contract is not formed until the complete performance is given by the offeree, although the offeror is bound to an implied contract not to revoke its offer once the offeree begins to give the return performance. Conceptually, it is difficult to view insurance contracts as unilateral contracts in which the applicant makes the offer of a promise, since the contract under this theory is not formed until the end of the insurer's performance — which is the end of the policy's term — which is when the coverage, and hence the contract, terminates.

---

7 E.g., Fritz v. Old Am. Ins. Co., 354 F. Supp. 514 (S.D. Tex. 1973); Klos v. Mobil Oil Co., 259 A.2d 889 (N.J. 1969); Riordan v. Automobile Club of N.Y., 472 N.Y.S.2d 811 (N.Y. Sup. Ct. 1979); Metts v. Central Standard Life Ins. Co., 298 P.2d 621 (Cal. Ct. App. 1956).

8 See § 32[e], *infra.*

9 E.g., Killpack v. National Old Line Ins. Co., 229 F.2d 851 (10th Cir. 1956); Gray v. Great Am. Reserve Ins. Co., 495 So. 2d 602 (Ala. 1986); Whitmire v. Colonial Life & Acc. Ins. Co., 323 S.E.2d 843 (Ga. Ct. App. 1984).

10 See, e.g., Janice Greider, Muriel Crawford & William Beadles, *Law and the Life Insurance Contract* 34 (6th ed. 1989).

The disposition of some courts and commentators to describe insurance contracts as unilateral contracts comes from the fact that an insured has no continuing obligation to make premium payments: if the insured declines to pay a premium when due, the insurer's only recourse is to cancel the policy. The insurer cannot sue the insured for a premium payment not paid when due. Thus, it is said that the contract is unilateral since the insured makes no promise to do anything. Actually, it would be more accurate to say that the insurance contract is a "reverse unilateral contract" where the offeror offers an immediate performance in exchange for the offeree's promise: the applicant's offer is "this premium payment is yours now if you promise to pay proceeds in the event a covered loss occurs." The obvious difficulty is that the performance — the act of turning over a sum of money — very much resembles a promise to make a payment: "I promise to turn this money over to you if you promise to pay proceeds in the event a covered loss occurs." Perhaps it is better to view an insurance contract as a bilateral contract that has "become unilateral" by full performance on one side — the insured's payment of the premium in advance.

The student who labors through this theoretical quagmire will be disappointed by the following revelation: whether an insurance contract is categorized as bilateral, unilateral, reverse unilateral, or bilateral-become-unilateral has no apparent practical significance. However the offer-acceptance process is described, the result upon the successful completion of this process is a promise for the breach of which the law will give a remedy — in short, a contract.

[b] Consideration

The consideration requirement is not problematic in most insurance transactions. The essence of the consideration doctrine is that each party to a contract must give something of legal value to the other party; a promise not supported by consideration is not enforceable. The largest group of promises rendered unenforceable by the consideration doctrine are promises to make a gift. If an insurance contract is viewed as a bilateral contract, the consideration supporting the insured's promise to pay premiums is the insurer's promise to pay proceeds if certain events occur, and the consideration supporting the insurer's conditional promise to pay proceeds is the insured's promise to pay premiums and to perform other duties in the event of a loss. Thus, a consideration problem could exist in an insurance contract only if the insurer fails to receive something of value from the insured — either the insured's promise to pay premiums or the actual payment of premiums in exchange for the insurer's promise of coverage. This is something the insurer is not likely to overlook. Moreover, if the insurer seeks to justify its nonperformance by claiming that the consideration doctrine has not been met, it is probable that the insured's reliance on the insurer's promise will be enough to make the insurer's promise enforceable.

[c] Capacity

The capacity requirement rarely presents any difficulty in insurance matters. Under the rules of contract law, contracts are voidable at the option of infants (those under eighteen years of age) and the mentally incompetent (in many circumstances). Those who are under the influence of drugs or who are intoxicated at the time of contracting will be able to invalidate a contract unless the other contracting party had no knowledge or reason to know of the impairment. Persons under guardianship have no power to contract at all. These principles of contract law are fully applicable to insurance transactions; there is nothing unique about these applications in the insurance context.

In a few states, statutory law alters the common law capacity rules in insurance contracts. For example, an Illinois statute eliminates the right of an infant aged fifteen years or older to rescind a life, health, or accident insurance policy taken out on his or her own life for the benefit of the applicant or an immediate family member.[11]

[d] The Writing Requirement

The general rule of the Anglo-American legal system is that oral contracts are enforceable, unless the contract falls into a special category in which a writing must exist (or have existed at one time) before the agreement can be enforced. It has been held that oral insurance contracts need be sufficiently specific to show the parties' mutual assent on certain core terms, including the subject matter, the risk insured against, the premium, the duration of coverage, policy limits, and identities of the parties.[12] If the oral contract meets this test (or whatever similar test is applied in a particular jurisdiction), the oral contract is enforceable, assuming there is no separate requirement that the contract be in writing.

With respect to contracts generally, almost all states have adopted writing requirements for specified types of contracts. In most of these states, the requirements are set forth in statutes modeled on section 4 of the 1677 English Statute of Frauds.[13] The 1677 statute specified five kinds of contracts that had to be in writing to be enforced. Insurance contracts were not one of the five categories, and the five traditional categories have very little relevance to most insurance transactions. Only two categories even have potential significance.

The "suretyship provision" of the statute requires a contract to answer for the "debt, default, or miscarriage" of another to be in writing. A guaranty agreement, whereby G promises C to pay D's debt to C, is within this provision and therefore must be in writing. Early cases held that the contracts of guaranty and surety companies were unenforceable without a writing, but most courts now interpret such agreements as contracts to indemnify the creditor against loss or damage from the debtor's nonperformance, rather than contracts to perform the original debtor's obligation. So construed, an oral contract of guaranty insurance is not unenforceable under the statute of frauds.[14]

---

[11] Ill. Rev. Stat. ch. 73, § 854.

[12] See Rabb v. Public Nat'l Ins. Co., 243 F.2d 940, 944 (6th Cir. 1957); Gulf Ins. Co. v. Grisham, 613 P.2d 283 (Ariz. 1980); Overton v. Washington Nat'l Ins. Co., 260 A.2d 444 (R.I. 1970). Compare Boston Camping Distributor Co. v. Lumbermens Mut. Cas. Co., 282 N.E.2d 374 (Mass. 1972) (consumer's testimony that he told agent he wanted "insurance coverage from A to Z, second to none" and agent said he would comply does not show making of contract).

[13] 29 Charles II, c. 3 (1677).

[14] See generally 2 *Corbin on Contracts* §§ 384–88 (1950).

The "one-year provision" requires contracts that cannot be performed within a year to be in writing. Many insurance contracts can be performed within a year and thus fall outside the statute. In life insurance, it is possible that the insured might die and the insurer perform its undertakings within a year. Much casualty insurance is written for terms of one year or less, meaning that the contracts can be performed within a year and therefore need not be in writing. Furthermore, to the extent either of the parties has the right to terminate the contract prior to the passing of a year, the contract is one of uncertain duration and therefore need not be in writing.[15] However, if an insurer provided an insured with a multi-year insurance policy without aggregate policy limits[16] with neither party having the right to cancel, such an agreement would be within the statute and would need to be in writing to be enforceable. Similarly, if an agent promised to renew a policy of insurance each year for the next three years, such a promise could not be performed within a year and therefore would need to be in writing.

Although few insurance contracts are unenforceable because of their failure to satisfy the five-category statute of frauds, a few states have adopted specific statutes of frauds for insurance contracts. These statutes provide that insurance contracts are enforceable only if written.[17] In addition, a number of states, including New York and California, have added a category to the traditional five-category statute that is broad enough to prohibit the enforcement of oral life insurance contracts.[18] The California statute, for example, requires "an agreement which by its terms is not to be performed during the lifetime of the promisor" to be in writing. When one takes out a life insurance policy on one's own life and agrees to pay the premiums, the agreement is not to be performed during the promisor's lifetime, since only upon the insured's death will the contract be performed.

Whether statutes of frauds generally serve any useful purpose has long been the subject of considerable debate.[19] Parliament repealed the English statute in 1954; in the United States, the statutes are being eroded by judicial recognition of broad exceptions to the traditional categories, liberal attitudes regarding the kinds of writings that will satisfy the statutes, and increased use of estoppel as a means to excuse noncompliance with the statutes. In insurance, oral contracts serve a useful purpose in situations where the exposure to a risk is imminent but the person seeking insurance has delayed commencing the application process in time to reduce the agreement to writing. Yet enforcing oral insurance contracts allows an agent to assist

---

[15] *Restatement (Second) of Contracts* § 130, comment b, illustration 6 (1981).

[16] Aggregate limits restrict the insurer's liability in any given policy term to the set amount. If the policy contains only limits per occurrence, the possibility of unlimited occurrences during the policy period makes the insurer's obligation inexhaustible.

[17] See, e.g., Mass. Gen. Laws Ann. ch. 175, § 177C; Conn. Gen. Stat. § 38-92f.

[18] See Cal. Civ. Code § 1624; N.Y. Gen. Oblig. Laws § 5-701.

[19] See, e.g., Robert Braucher, *The Commission and the Law of Contracts,* 40 Cornell L.Q. 696 (1955); Vold, *The Application of the Statute of Frauds under the Uniform Sales Act,* 15 Minn. L. Rev. 391 (1931); Karl N. Llewellyn, *What Price Contract?—An Essay in Perspective,* 40 Yale L.J. 704 (1931); Hugh E. Willis, *The Statute of Frauds—A Legal Anachronism,* 3 Ind. L.J. 528 (1928).

a friend by providing testimony that an oral contract was formed prior to the loss; this is precisely the kind of fraud that the statutes of frauds are intended to prevent.

[e] Public Policy

It is a basic principle of contract law that illegal contracts or contracts contrary to public policy will not be enforced. Insurance contracts are, of course, neither illegal nor per se contrary to public policy. Yet the public policy theme runs throughout insurance law, often in the rubric of specific rules that have the effect of invalidating insurance contracts under specific circumstances. For example, an insurance contract under which the insurer promises to indemnify the insured for loss to property caused by the insured's own arson would be contrary to public policy and unenforceable. A basic insurance law rule is that an insurance contract procured on the life of another by a person who at the time of contracting intends to murder the insured is void.[20] This rule obviously serves important public policies; it could as easily be said that a contract procured under such circumstances contravenes public policy and is therefore void.

From time to time, courts have also used the public policy rationale to invalidate insurance contracts that cover property that is unlawful to possess, such as gambling devices and illegal drugs.[21] Some courts have also extended this holding to goods or buildings not unlawful in and of themselves but which are used to perpetuate an unlawful activity, but the decisions are far from uniform.[22] It is clear that one who insures a partial interest in property (such as a mortgagee) and who is not participating in an illegal use of the property can recover under the insurance if the property is lost or damaged.[23] In a Minnesota case the court invalidated provisions of a professional liability policy that purported to insure an attorney for forfeiture of attorney fees for breach of a fiduciary duty, where the breach consisted of nondisclosure of matters material to the client's interests and trust, on the ground that the provisions were contrary to public policy.[24] In contrast to the Minnesota case, a federal district court in Georgia rejected an insurer's effort to deny coverage on public policy grounds. The insured sought coverage under two liability policies for the expenses incurred in defending and settling claims that the insured had discriminated against minority employees. The court denied the insurer's motion to

---

[20] For more discussion see § 52A[e], *infra.*

[21] See, e.g., Northwest Amusement Co. v. Aetna Cas. & Sur. Co., 107 P.2d 110 (Or. 1940) (slot machines); Mount v. Waite, 7 Johns. (N.Y.) 434 (1811) (lottery tickets).

[22] See, e.g., Vos v. Albany Mut. Fire Ins. Co., 253 N.W. 549 (Minn. 1934) (policy on barn containing a still void); Fidelity & Deposit Co. v. Moore, 3 F.2d 652 (D.C.Or. 1925), *appeal dismissed,* 272 U.S. 317 (1926); but see Boston Ins. Co. v. Read, 166 F.2d 551 (10th Cir. 1948) (recovery allowed under fire policy on building used for illegal sale of liquor); Brown v. New Jersey Ins. Co., 14 P.2d 272 (Or. 1932) (insurance recovery allowed for loss of fake whiskey labels during Prohibition Era).

[23] See, e.g., Goelet v. National Sur. Co., 164 N.E. 101 (N.Y. 1928); Montana Auto Finance Corp. v. British & Federal Fire Underwriters of Norwich Union Fire Ins. Soc'y, 232 P. 198 (Mont. 1924).

[24] See Perl v. St. Paul Fire & Marine Ins. Co., 345 N.W.2d 209 (Minn. 1984).

dismiss the insured's complaint, holding that the policy's coverage for the insured's liability for racially discriminatory practices was not contrary to public policy.[25]

Although, as discussed above, public policy can play a role in determining whether an insurance policy is valid, public policy is more often consulted for the purpose of determining the scope of coverage. For example, it is common for insurance policies to exclude coverage for losses caused intentionally by the insured.[26] A court's perception of public policy is very important to determining the scope of the exclusion.[27] On the issue of whether liability insurance covers an insured's liability for punitive damages, courts' perception of public policy is very important.[28] It is common for accidental death and dismemberment policies to require the death or severance to occur within a certain number of days (usually 90 or 120) after the injury-causing incident. The insurer's purpose is to avoid paying coverage for loss due to non-accidental causes, which are more likely to be the reason for a death or dismemberment as time passes after an accident. But the limitation has the potential to encourage death or dismemberment in circumstances where the insured's on-going fight to retain life or limb is about to exceed the 90- or 120-day restriction after which coverage is lost. A court's perception of public policy will determine how the limitation is interpreted or whether it is even enforced.[29] In these situations and others, a court's view of what public policy requires can be crucial to the resolution of an insurance dispute.

§ 32   Some Troublespots in the Process of Contract Formation

The classic model of contract formation envisions parties with equal bargaining power and perfect information negotiating over the terms of their bargain and ultimately striking a mutually beneficial arrangement. In the real world, this model is frequently — and perhaps usually — an inaccurate description of the process of contract formation. In insurance, this model rarely describes the process of contract formation accurately. Instead, contract formation in most insurance transactions is a process that resembles the classic model in some respects and is otherwise riddled with troublespots. Several of the significant troublespots are explored in this section.

[a]   Insurer's Delay in Responding to the Application

During the period that the insurer has the application under consideration, the applicant is at risk. In the absence of a temporary binder,[1] the applicant has no

---

[25] See Union Camp Corp. v. Continental Cas. Co., 452 F. Supp. 565 (S.D. Ga. 1978). See also Solo Cup Co. v. Federal Ins. Co., 619 F.2d 1178 (7th Cir.), *cert. denied,* 449 U.S. 1033 (1980). See generally Steven L. Willborn, *Insurance, Public Policy, and Employment Discrimination,* 66 Minn. L. Rev. 1003 (1982); Robert L. Pratter & Joanne A. Baker, *The Status of Personal Liability and Comprehensive General Liability Insurance Coverage of Civil Rights Damages,* 48 Ins. Counsel J. 259 (1981).

[26] For further discussion, see §§ 63-63C, *infra.*

[27] See § 63C, *infra.*

[28] See § 65[g], *infra.*

[29] See § 64[a][2], *infra.*

[1] See § 33, *infra.*

coverage. If the insurer has issued the applicant a binder, the applicant is still at risk because the insurer might decline to provide the coverage, and if in the meantime some event renders the applicant a higher risk, the applicant will have even more difficulty obtaining insurance, given the applicant's duty to correct representations on an application that become incorrect prior to the policy's issuance, not to mention the difficulties for the applicant should he or she seek coverage elsewhere. Because of these concerns, some jurisdictions impose upon the insurer a duty to respond promptly to an application for insurance. In these jurisdictions, an insurer unreasonably late in responding to an application loses the right to reject it.[2]

This result is sometimes explained by resort to contract doctrine: retaining the premium and failing to reject the application constitutes acceptance of the applicant's offer.[3] Curiously, it is the insurer's retention of the premium payment which for many courts has been the crucial factor in deciding whether to recognize the insurer's duty not to delay acting upon the application.[4] As explained in *Gorham v. Peerless Life Insurance Co.,*[5] "there appears to be a distinction drawn where the applicant paid the initial premium at the time the application was signed. Delay in acting on the application, along with retention of the premium, . . . is inconsistent with a rejection of risk."[6]

The foregoing analysis, however, departs substantially from contract law's view of the mechanics of offer and acceptance. Except in rare situations, silence in response to an offer does not operate as an acceptance. One of those rare situations where silence is effective to close a contract is where the offeree who fails to respond to the offer nevertheless exercises dominion over offered property. This exception

---

[2] See Talbot v. Country Life Ins. Co., 291 N.E.2d 830 (Ill. App. Ct. 1973); Huberman v. John Hancock Mut. Life Ins. Co., 492 So. 2d 416 (Fla. Dist. Ct. App. 1986); William L. Prosser, *Delay in Acting on an Application for Insurance,* 3 U. Chi. L. Rev. 39 (1935). See generally Annot., *Liability of Insurer for Damages Resulting From Delay in Passing Upon an Application for Life Insurance,* 1 A.L.R.4th 1202 (1980); Annot., *Liability of Insurer for Damages Resulting From Delay in Passing Upon Application for Health Insurance,* 18 A.L.R.4th 1115 (1982). Of course, a court might hold that the delay in a given case was not unreasonable. See, e.g., Megee v. U.S. Fidelity & Guar. Co., 391 A.2d 189 (Del. 1978); Redmond v. National Union Fire Ins. Co., 403 So. 2d 810 (La. Ct. App. 1981). At least one court has held that if the insurer would have rejected the applicant anyway for a good reason, the insurer's delay in responding to the application is not tortious. See Life & Cas. Ins. Co. v. Central Steel Products, Inc., 709 S.W.2d 830 (Ky. Ct. App. 1985).

[3] See, e.g., Cartwright v. Maccabees Mut. Life Ins. Co., 247 N.W.2d 298 (Mich. 1976).

[4] See Megee v. United States Fidelity & Guar. Co., 391 A.2d 189 (Del. 1978)(if no premium is paid, insurer does not have duty to act promptly on application); Thomas v. Life Ins. Co., 55 So. 2d 705 (La. 1951)(because unreasonable delay in retaining premium might deprive applicant from applying elsewhere for insurance, insurer has tort duty not to delay acting on application); Preferred Accident Ins. Co. v. Stone, 58 P. 986, 987 (Kan. 1899)(insurer could not retain premium and hold application in abeyance); Hill v. Chubb Life Am. Ins. Co., 870 P.2d 1133 (Ariz. Ct. App. 1993)(citing additional cases), *rev'd,* 894 P.2d 701 (Ariz. 1995).

[5] 118 N.W.2d 306 (Mich. 1962).

[6] 118 N.W.2d at 309.

could apply where the insurer has applied the applicant's advance premium payment to its own uses.[7]

But the mere possession of a premium payment (as distinct from the exercise of dominion over or use of a premium), when coupled with language in the offer indicating that acceptance is not effective until home-office approval or some other event, should not by itself be sufficient to constitute the act of acceptance which forms a binding legal relationship.[8] A check in the amount of the first premium payment submitted along with an application for insurance is more like a deposit that accompanies an offer, a mere symbol of the applicant's serious interest in seeking a contract with the insurer. Should the applicant choose to revoke the offer (i.e., the application), the advance premium payment would be returned in full to the applicant.

Moreover, the notion that the advance premium payment prevents the applicant from seeking insurance elsewhere[9] is wrong. The applicant is free to apply to other companies for insurance, although such an applicant is vulnerable, having made multiple offers, to be being bound on several policies of life insurance at once. This is an insufficient basis for imposing a duty to act promptly upon the insurer.[10]

If the duty to act promptly is a contract-based duty, the analysis should proceed along the following lines. First, if the insurer explicitly promises to respond to the application within a certain period of time,[11] the insurer may be contractually bound to act within that time. Although such a promise might appear to be an unenforceable gratuitous promise, the facts of particular cases may show the applicant's detrimental reliance on the promise (e.g., by taking medical examinations, providing information, or refraining from dealing with other insurers) which would make the promise to act without delay binding on the basis of detrimental reliance. Second, even in the absence of an explicit promise, courts could find a promise implicit in the circumstances, again made enforceable by the insured's detrimental reliance. Once such a contract to act promptly is formed, the contract is breached as soon as the reasonable time for acting on the application expires, and any loss subsequently occurring that would have been covered if the insurer had acted without undue delay is a foreseeable damage resulting from the insurer's breach of the contract to act on the application without unreasonable delay.

An alternative explanation for the insurer's liability for undue delay in responding to the application is estoppel: the insurer, because of its delay in responding to the

---

[7] See Snyder v. Redding Motors, 280 P.2d 811 (Cal. Ct. App. 1955).

[8] See Cohran v. Liberty Mutual Ins. Co., 368 S.E.2d 751 (Ga. 1988) (insured's counteroffer accompanied by premium check was not accepted by insurer's silence).

[9] See Thomas v. Life Ins. Co., 55 So. 2d 705 (La. 1951).

[10] See State Farm Life Ins. Co. v. Bass, 605 So. 2d 908 (Fla. Dist. Ct. App. 1992)(insurer owes duty to act on application within reasonable time even if premium was not submitted along with application).

[11] For example, in Hill v. Chubb Life Am. Ins. Co., 894 P.2d 701 (Ariz. 1995), the application agreement stated that the applicant would be informed of the insurer's action "within 60 days or be given the reason for the delay." The court said that summary judgment had been inappropriately entered for the insurer and remanded the case for consideration of the plaintiff's contract claim based on the 60-day clause.

application, is estopped to assert noncoverage by denying that it accepted the application.[12] This, of course, resembles the contract-based liability described above that is grounded in detrimental reliance and promissory estoppel. But estoppel is sometimes used as an independent, free-standing doctrine to achieve equity in appropriate cases. One of the elements of estoppel, however, is reliance, and establishing reliance, whether the applicant seeks to invoke equitable or promissory estoppel, may be difficult for some insureds alleging that the insurer has delayed too long in responding to the application. For many courts, estoppel is merely a rationalization for a prejudged conclusion, and it provides little guidance to insurers desiring to know how much delay is reasonable in particular circumstances.

Yet another explanation of the insurer's liability is waiver: by delaying its response to the application, the insurer waives its reliance on the general rule that silence does not constitute acceptance. This theory, like the estoppel theory, is also vague at the margins. Moreover, the insurer's delay in responding to an application does not possess the quality of a knowing, voluntary relinquishment of a right which typifies most waivers.

Most jurisdictions that adhere to the principle that the insurer's excessive delay in responding to an application prevents rejection rationalize the result by reference to tort doctrine. The relationship of insurer and insured, which is affected with the public interest, gives rise to a duty on the insurer's part to respond to the application without unreasonable delay.[13] Establishing a tortious breach of the duty requires that the applicant demonstrate the insurer's negligence in responding to the application. This burden can be carried by showing that the insurer failed to take steps in response to the application that a reasonable insurer would have taken in similar circumstances.

The leading case for the proposition that the insurer can be liable in tort for negligent delay in responding to an application is *Duffie v. Bankers' Life Association*,[14] a 1913 Iowa Supreme Court decision. The applicant, who was qualified in all respects under the insurer's underwriting standards, paid the first premium and submitted the application in accordance with all of the insurer's procedures. The insurer's agent, however, negligently mislaid the application. The application was not forwarded to the insurer until after the applicant had died; the applicant's death was approximately one month after the application was submitted. The applicant's widow, suing as the beneficiary designated in the application, alleged that the insurer's negligence deprived her of benefits to which she would have been entitled had the application been processed normally. The court held that the widow was entitled to recover:

---

[12] E.g., Moore v. Palmetto State Life Ins. Co., 73 S.E.2d 688 (S.C. 1952); Wille v. Farmers Equitable Ins. Co., 232 N.E.2d 468 (Ill. App. Ct. 1967); Combined Am. Ins. Co. v. Parker, 377 S.W.2d 213 (Tex. Ct. App. 1964).

[13] E.g., Travelers Ins. Co. v. Anderson, 210 F. Supp. 735 (W.D. S.C. 1962); Continental Life & Acc. Co. v. Songer, 603 P.2d 921 (Ariz. 1979); Hinds v. United Ins. Co., 149 S.E.2d 771 (S.C. 1966); Republic Nat'l Life Ins. Co., v. Chilcoat, 368 P.2d 821 (Okla. 1961); Duffie v. Bankers' Life Ass'n, 139 N.W. 1087 (Iowa 1913); Davis and Landry v. Guaranty Income Life Ins. Co., 442 So. 2d 621 (La. Ct. App. 1983).

[14] 139 N.W. 1087 (Iowa 1913).

[T]he [insurer] holds and is acting under a franchise from the state. The legislative policy, in granting this, proceeds on the theory that chartering such association is in the interest of the public to the end that indemnity on specific contingencies shall be provided those who are eligible and desire it, and for their protection the state regulates, inspects, and supervises their business. Having solicited applications for insurance, and having so obtained them and received payment of the fees or premiums exacted, they are bound either to furnish the indemnity the state has authorized them to furnish or decline so to do within such reasonable time as will enable them to act intelligently and advisedly thereon, or suffer the consequences flowing from their neglect so to do.[15]

The rule articulated in *Duffie* has been followed in a number of subsequent decisions,[16] but it has been rejected in some jurisdictions. For example, in *Savage v. Prudential Life Insurance Co.,*[17] a 1929 Mississippi decision, the court, in rejecting *Duffie,* stated:

The fact that the insurance companies are granted a franchise to do business in this state does not and should not impose upon them the duty to consider promptly all who offer to them the risk of insuring their lives, no more than would be required of a bank to lend money promptly to all who should make application and suffer loss while the bank was negligent in determining whether or not it would accept the offer and enter into a contract.[18]

A number of jurisdictions agree with the reasoning of *Savage* and refuse to impose a tort duty on the insurer to give a prompt response to the insured's application,[19] although most of these cases appear to involve situations where no premium payment accompanied the application.

To summarize, the case law tends to protect the applicant in circumstances where the insurer unreasonably delays in acting on an application, but the decisions are far from uniform.

[b]   The Insured's Duty to Read the Policy

Because the mutual assent requirement in contract formation is objective rather than subjective, there is no requirement that a party intend or comprehend the

---

[15] 139 N.W. at 1090.

[16] See, e.g., Werthman v. Catholic Order of Foresters, 133 N.W.2d 104 (Iowa 1965); Mann v. Policyholders' Nat'l Life Ins. Co., 51 N.W.2d 853 (N.D. 1952); Carney Through Carney v. Lone Star Life Ins. Co., 540 So. 2d 415 (La. Ct. App. 1989); Independent Life and Acc. Ins. Co. v. McKenzie, 503 So. 2d 376 (Fla. Dist. Ct. App. 1987).

[17] 121 So. 487 (Miss. 1929).

[18] 121 So. at 489.

[19] See, e.g., Worden v. Farmers State Co., Inc., 349 N.W.2d 37 (S.D. 1984); Hayes v. Durham Life Ins. Co., 96 S.E.2d 109 (Va. 1957); Zayc v. John Hancock Mut. Life Ins. Co., 13 A.2d 34 (Pa. 1940) ("Mere delay, however great, in acting on an application does not give rise to an action either in contract or in tort"); Protective Life Ins. Co. v. Robinson, 387 S.E.2d 603 (Ga. Ct. App. 1989); Life & Cas. Ins. Co. v. Central Steel Products, Inc., 709 S.W.2d 830 (Ky. Ct. App. 1985).

consequences of his or her actions. If a party makes a statement that the other reasonably understands as manifesting an intent to be bound, the party will be held to the consequences flowing from that statement. Consistently with the objective theory of contract, courts have often held that a party is not entitled to relief from a contract on account of a failure to read it before manifesting intent to be bound to it. This rule has been invoked on numerous occasions with respect to contracts of insurance. Many of these cases are older decisions,[20] but the rule has been invoked in many recent decisions as well.[21]

In some more recent cases, the principle that a party has a "duty" to read a contract before signing it is frequently disregarded. In the situation where one party misrepresents the content of a writing to another and the other person relies on the misrepresentation without bothering to read the writing, many courts have granted relief to the relying party.[22] This exception has been often applied in insurance cases. A number of courts have held that the insured who fails to read the policy and has no knowledge of a particular provision in a policy that is contrary to an oral representation of the agent is entitled to claim that the insurer is estopped to deny the agent's representation, despite the failure to read the policy. Similarly, courts have held that if a policy is issued upon an oral application and the insured fails to read the policy, the insured is nevertheless entitled to assume that the policy conforms with the application and covers the risk for which insurance was sought.[23] Not surprisingly, the insured's failure to read the policy is typically overlooked if the insured is illiterate or unable to read English.[24]

[20] See, e.g., Equitable Life Assur. Soc'y of U.S. v. Johnson, 81 F.2d 543 (6th Cir. 1936); Karp v. Metropolitan Life Ins. Co., 164 A. 219 (N.H. 1933); Minsker v. John Hancock Mutual Life Insurance Co., 173 N.E. 4 (N.Y. 1930); Drogula v. Federal Life Ins. Co., 227 N.W. 692 (Mich. 1929); Dowagiac Mfg. Co. v. Schroeder, 84 N.W. 14 (Wis. 1900).

[21] See, e.g., Western Cas. & Sur. Co. v. Sliter, 555 F. Supp. 369 (E.D. Mich. 1983); Feather v. State Farm Fire & Cas. Co., 872 P.2d 1177 (Wyo. 1994); Booska v. Hubbard Ins. Agency, Inc., 627 A.2d 333 (Vt. 1993); Twelve Knotts Ltd. Partnership v. Fireman's Fund Ins. Co., 589 A.2d 105 (Md. 1991); Vasquez v. Bankers Ins. Co., 502 So. 2d 894 (Fla. 1987); Soliva v. Shand, Morahan & Co., Inc., 345 S.E.2d 33 (W.Va. 1986); Maw v. McAlister, 166 S.E.2d 203 (S.C. 1969); Jim Anderson & Co. v. Partraining Corp., 454 S.E.2d 210 (Ga. Ct. App. 1995); Strother v. Capitol Bankers Life Ins. Co., 842 P.2d 504 (Wash.App. 1992); Schoonover v. American Fam. Ins. Co., 572 N.E.2d 1258 (Ill. App. Ct. 1991); Aetna Cas. & Sur. Co. v. Richmond, 143 Cal. Rptr. 75 (Cal. Ct. App. 1977).

[22] See, e.g., Estate of Blakely v. Federal Kemper Life Assur. Co., 640 N.E.2d 961 (Ill. Ct. App. 1994); Underwriters Ins. Co. v. Purdie, 193 Cal. Rptr. 248 (Cal. Ct. App. 1983); Saylor v. Handley Motor Co., 169 A.2d 683 (D.C. Ct. App. 1961); Providence Jewelry Co. v. Crowe, 129 N.W. 224 (Minn. 1911).

[23] See, e.g., Fli-Back Co. v. Philadelphia Mfrs. Mut. Ins. Co., 502 F.2d 214 (4th Cir. 1974); Kelly v. South Car. Farm Bur. Mut. Ins. Co., 450 S.E.2d 59 (S.C. 1994); King v. Brasington, 312 S.E.2d 111 (Ga. 1984); Rempel v. Nationwide Life Ins. Co., 370 A.2d 366 (Pa. 1977); Harr v. Allstate Ins. Co., 255 A.2d 208 (N.J. 1969); Mogil v. Maryland Cas. Co., 26 N.W.2d 126 (Neb. 1947). See also Schafer Distributing Co. v. Maryland Cas. Co., 123 F. Supp. 873 (E.D. S.C. 1954); Portella v. Sonnenberg, 181 A.2d 385 (N.J. Super. Ct. App. Div. 1962).

[24] E.g., Osendorf v. American Fam. Ins. Co., 318 N.W.2d 237 (Minn. 1982); Rider v. Lynch, 201 A.2d 561 (N.J. 1964).

The reduced adherence to the rigid rule that the insured is bound to the contract if he or she fails to read it is simply one manifestation of the increased willingness of courts to protect insureds and other consumers who would suffer forfeiture but for the relaxation of traditional contract rules. As one court has explained it, the "duty to read is insufficient to bind an insured to unusual or unfair language."[25] In settings where the contracts are long, complicated, and difficult to understand even if read, it may not be reasonable to expect people to take the time to read the contracts before manifesting intent to be bound to them. In forming a contract, an insured relies not upon the text of the policies but on the general descriptions of the coverage provided by the insurer and its agents during the time the insured was considering whether to submit an application. Absent a special request, an insured will not see the text of the policy until after the application has been submitted and the first premium paid. Under these circumstances, it is not surprising that the so-called "duty to read" has less significance in modern cases.

Yet the doctrine can still have force, and it must not be overlooked in contemporary litigation. In *Dahlke v. John F. Zimmer Ins. Agency*,[26] a 1994 Nebraska decision, the court approved a rule that the insured's failure to read the policy, absent a valid excuse for not doing so, would insulate the agent from liability for failing to explain the policy if the policy were otherwise clear and unambiguous. It has also been held that an insured's claim against the agent for failure to procure proper insurance would be defeated by the insured's failure to read the policy, assuming the policy was understandable and nothing excused the failure to read.[27] Other courts have held that the insured's failure to read a policy can be raised as contributory negligence.[28] These cases suggest that the insurer is not the only party which must act reasonably; the insured also has some responsibility to protect his or her own interests, and the failure to take reasonable steps to this end may result in rejection of the insured's claim that the policy covered the insured's loss.

To summarize, jurisdictions are divided on whether the insured has a duty to read the policy, and this disagreement has enormous implications for how particular cases are decided.

[c] The Insurer's Duty to Explain the Policy

Like the duty to read, courts have not reached a consensus on whether the insurer has a duty to explain coverage to the insured. In most jurisdictions, if the terms of an insurance policy are clear, unambiguous, and explicit, the insurer has no affirmative duty to explain the policy or its exclusions to the insured.[29] As stated

---

[25] Fields v. Blue Shield of Cal., 209 Cal. Rptr. 781, 785 (Cal. Ct. App. 1985).

[26] 515 N.W.2d 767 (Neb. 1994).

[27] See Underwriters Adjusting Co. v. Knight, 389 S.E.2d 24 (Ga. Ct. App. 1989); Heritage Manor of Blaylock v. Peterson, 677 S.W.2d 689 (Tex. Ct. App. 1984). See also Hadland v. NN Investors Life Ins. Co., Inc., 30 Cal. Rptr.2d 88 (Cal.App. 1994) (insurer cannot be held liable for fraud absent showing of justifiable reliance, which does not exist where insured does not read policy).

[28] See Martini v. Beaverton Ins. Agency, Inc., 838 P.2d 1061 (Or. 1992); Town & Country Mut. Ins. Co. v. Savage, 421 N.E.2d 704 (Ind. Ct. App. 1981).

[29] See, e.g., Mutual of Omaha Ins. Co. v. Russell, 402 F.2d 339 (10th Cir. 1968), *cert. denied*, 394 U.S. 973 (1969); Standard Venetian Blind Co. v. American Empire Ins. Co., 469

by one court, "[w]hen a court is reviewing claims under an insurance policy, it must hold the insured bound by clear and conspicuous provisions in the policy even if evidence suggests that the insured did not read or understand them."[30] This position, however, is subject to some important caveats, two of which can be explained briefly.

First, the doctrine of reasonable expectations can operate to impose *de facto* a duty on the insurer to explain the policy's coverage to the insured. If a court holds that an insured's reasonable expectations entitle the insured to coverage despite policy language to the contrary, the court has said, in effect, that the insurer must pay for the loss because the insurer failed to explain the limitations on coverage to the insured. In other words, if the insurer had provided an explanation of the coverage, the insured's expectations of different coverage would have been rendered unreasonable.[31]

Second, in the area of automobile insurance where legislatures have made certain kinds of coverage optional, usually uninsured or underinsured motorist insurance, courts have sometimes imposed a duty on the insurer to explain the options to the insured. Where insurers have failed to do so, they have been held liable for loss despite the fact that the policy as issued did not provide the coverage.[32] Not all courts, however, agree with this result.[33]

Beyond these two areas where what is tantamount to a duty to explain coverage is sometimes imposed on insurers, the law involving the activities of agents and brokers also has the effect in some circumstances of imposing a duty to explain on insurers. As discussed in a later section,[34] agents owe their customers a duty to exercise the skill and care that a reasonable agent would exercise in the circumstances. This duty encompasses in many situations an obligation to advise the consumer about the kinds of coverage available and to help the applicant select appropriate coverage.[35] To the extent agents and the insurers who retain them are held liable for the negligence of agents in performing their professional duties, a duty to explain coverage is effectively imposed upon the insurer.

A.2d 563 (Pa. 1983); Realin v. State Farm Fire and Cas. Co., 418 So. 2d 431 (Fla. Dist. Ct. App. 1982) (no duty to explain uninsured motorist protection unless asked; however, duty exists to inform applicant of availability of higher limits and to offer those limits).

[30] Sarchett v. Blue Shield of Cal., 729 P.2d 267 (Cal. 1987).

[31] See § 25D, *supra.*

[32] See, e.g., Cloninger v. National Gen. Ins. Co., 488 N.E.2d 548 (Ill. 1985); Hastings v. United Pacific Ins. Co., 318 N.W.2d 849 (Minn. 1982).

[33] See, e.g., Carlson v. Mutual Serv. Ins., 494 N.W.2d 885 (Minn. 1993); American Fam. Mut. Ins. Co. v. Dye, 634 N.E.2d 844 (Ind. Ct. App. 1994); Pabitzky v. Frager, 210 Cal. Rptr. 426 (Cal. Ct. App. 1985); Gibson v. Government Employees Ins. Co., 208 Cal. Rptr. 511 (Cal. Ct. App. 1984).

[34] See § 35[f], *infra.*

[35] See Dimeo v. Burns, Brooks & McNeil, Inc., 504 A.2d 557 (Conn.App.Ct. 1986); McNeill v. McDavid Ins. Agency, 594 S.W.2d 198 (Tex. Ct. App. 1980); but see Heritage Manor of Blaylock Properties, Inc. v. Peterson, 677 S.W.2d 689 (Tex. Ct. App. 1984). For more discussion of this issue, see § 35[f][2][ii], *infra.*

But there is potentially much more to the agent's duty, more than the obligations that arise in connection with the agent providing advice to applicants about prospective coverages. Although some courts have held that an agent has no duty to explain a policy's coverage to an insured,[36] other courts have taken a more tempered view of this issue and have held that a duty to explain exists in some circumstances. This issue was discussed in detail in *Dahlke v. John F. Zimmer Insurance Agency, Inc.,*[37] a 1994 Nebraska decision. Dahlke's business provided roofing, construction, and waterproofing services. One of the risks of his business was "overspray": when certain coatings were applied with sprayers, some of the coating could drift to other objects, causing damage. Since 1980 Dahlke had insurance for damage due to overspray, and in 1984 he was covered for an incident that damaged four to six cars. In 1984, Dahlke paid a single, "per-occurrence" deductible. In 1988, another overspray incident resulted in 25 claims, but in the meantime his coverage had changed to a "per-claim" deductible. Accordingly, the insurer informed Dahlke that he was obligated to pay a separate deductible for each claim. Earlier that year, Dahlke learned from his agent that the insurer underwriting the policies since 1980 would no longer cover roofing companies, but the agent searched for and did find another insurer to cover Dahlke. But this new insurance policy, which applied to the 1988 incident, had a per-claim deductible. Dahlke alleged that he was not informed of this change in coverage, and at the time of the incident he had not received a copy of the applicable policy.[38]

The court searched out a middle ground on the question of the agent's duty to explain:

> On the one hand, insurance agents should not carry the overwhelming responsibility of explaining to insureds every provision of every policy. On the other hand, insurance agents should not be able to avoid exercising a reasonable amount of care for their clients . . . . We therefore find most persuasive those cases which recognize that an agent has a legal duty to explain policy terms,

---

[36] See Ohio Cas. Ins. Co. v. Rynearson, 507 F.2d 573 (7th Cir. 1974); Scott-Huff Ins. Agency v. Sandusky, 887 S.W.2d 516 (Ark. 1994); Carolina Production Maintenance, inc. v. United States Fidelity and Guar. Co., 425 S.E.2d 39 (S.C. Ct. App. 1993); Banker v. Valley Forge Ins. Co., 526 A.2d 434 (Pa. Super. Ct. 1987); Greenway v. Insurance Co., 241 S.E.2d 339 (N.C. Ct. App. 1978); Bush v. Mayerstein-Burnell Financial Services, 499 N.E.2d 755 (Ind. Ct. App. 1986).

[37] 515 N.W.2d 767 (Neb. 1994).

[38] Actually, the pre-occurrence deductible had been changed to a per-claim deductible two years earlier under the old policy. Dahlke contended that this change had not been explained to him. On a related issue, the court held that absent an excuse for failing to read a policy, a failure to read clear and unambiguous policy provisions will insulate the agent from liability for failing to explain the provision in question. The fact that Dahlke did not have access to the 1988 policy excused his failure to read the clear and unambiguous provisions of that policy. 515 N.W.2d at 806. However, Dahlke admitted he had not read the 1986 and 1987 policies which also had per-claim deductibles and which had been in his possession. The court was unable to determine, since the 1986 and 1987 policies were not in the record, whether those polices were clear and unambiguous. Thus, the case was remanded, with instructions that if the 1986 and 1987 policies were clear and unambiguous, Dahlke's failure to read them would entitle the agency to judgment. 515 N.W.2d at 772-73.

but also require certain circumstances to trigger that duty. The triggering circumstances cannot be stated as an arbitrary list, but must, of necessity, be developed on a case-by-case basis.[39]

In *Dahlke* the court found those additional circumstances to be present: "When an agent knows that a provision of the insured's policy has been invoked, the agent has a duty to explain any changes to that provision appearing in a subsequent policy."[40] Other circumstances which might trigger the duty to explain include the agent representing that he or she has special expertise with respect to coverages and inviting the insured's reliance on that expertise or the insured paying the agent a special consideration for advice.[41]

If the agent has a duty to explain coverage and the agent is acting within the scope of his or her authority, it follows that the insurer will be responsible for the agent's failure to explain coverage. Thus, cases like *Dahlke* that impose on the agent a duty to explain coverage have the effect of imposing that same duty on insurers.

Finally, when the insured disputes a denial of coverage, the duty of good faith and fair dealing may impose an obligation on the insurer to alert the insured to his or her rights. In *Sarchett v. Blue Shield of California*,[42] a 1987 California Supreme Court decision, the insurer denied the insured's claim under a health policy without informing the insured of his contractual right to impartial review and arbitration. The Court stated:

> Once it becomes clear to the insurer that its insured disputes its denial of coverage, . . . the duty of good faith does not permit the insurer passively to assume that its insured is aware of his or her rights under the policy. The insurer must instead take affirmative steps to make sure that the insured is informed of remedial rights.[43]

In *Sarchett*, the arbitration clause was prominently displayed with a boldface heading. Nevertheless, the Court reasoned that the insurer had reason to know that the insured was unaware of his rights, because he repeatedly protested the denial of coverage without requesting review by an impartial panel of physicians. The insurer's failure to mention the availability of impartial review caused the court to conclude that the insurer's "course of conduct appears designed to mislead subscribers into forfeiting their contractual right to impartial review and arbitration of disputed claims."[44]

Sarchett stopped short of imposing a general duty on the insurer to explain to the insured all aspects of the coverage. Indeed, because the policy itself gave adequate notice of the arbitration provision, it is far from obvious that the insurer, having given adequate notice of a provision that was easy to understand, failed to explain the coverage to the insured who neglected to read the policy. However, the insurer

---

[39] 515 N.W.2d at 771.

[40] 515 N.W.2d at 771-72.

[41] For more discussion, see § 35[f][2][ii], *infra*.

[42] 729 P.2d 267 (Cal. 1987).

[43] 233 Cal. Rptr. at 85-86.

[44] 233 Cal. Rptr. at 86.

in *Sarchett* could easily have informed the insured of his right to impartial review in the letter responding to his objection to the denial of coverage. It is reasonable to impose such an obligation on all insurers if they are aware that the insured disputes the denial of coverage under circumstances where it is not clear that the insured understands his or her right to review of the denial. No additional cost or hardship is placed on the insurer who must add a sentence to some of its letters responding to insureds' objections to denials of coverage with words to this effect: "you are entitled under the policy to seek review of our denial of coverage and here is how you do it."

Pennsylvania courts have grappled with the extent of the insurer's duty to explain an insurance policy in a celebrated line of cases. In *Hionis v. Northern Mutual Insurance Co.,*[45] a 1974 Pennsylvania Superior Court case, the court articulated a rule which imposed such a duty on the insurer: "[W]here a policy is written in unambiguous terms, the burden of establishing the applicability of the exclusion or limitation involves proof that the insured was aware of the exclusion or limitation and that the effect thereof was explained to him."[46] *Hionis* was followed in subsequent Pennsylvania cases,[47] but the breadth of its ruling resulted in some exceptions to the rule. If the insured and insurer had equal bargaining power or if the facts showed the insured clearly understood the terms independently of any explanation by the insurer, the *Hionis* rule did not apply.[48]

In 1983, the Pennsylvania Supreme Court rejected the *Hionis* rule altogether in *Standard Venetian Blind Co. v. American Empire Insurance Co.:*[49]

> [T]he burden imposed by *Hionis* fails to accord proper significance to the written contract, which has historically been the true test of the parties' intentions. By focusing on what was said and was not said at the time of contract formation rather than on the parties' writing, *Hionis* makes the question of the scope of insurance coverage in any given case depend upon how a factfinder resolves questions of credibility. Such a process, apart from the obvious uncertainty of the results, unnecessarily delays the resolution of controversy, adding only unwanted costs to the cost of procuring insurance. Thus, *Hionis,* which would permit an insured to avoid the application of a clear and unambiguous limitation clause in an insurance contract, is not to be followed.[50]

No subsequent court has adopted a rule as broad as that stated in *Hionis,* but other doctrines, including the doctrine of reasonable expectations, can be applied in a manner that leads to results consistent with what the *Hionis* rule would demand.

---

[45] 327 A.2d 363 (Pa. Super. Ct. 1974).

[46] 327 A.2d at 365.

[47] See, e.g., Daburlos v. Commercial Ins. Co. of Newark, 521 F.2d 18 (3d Cir. 1975); Weiss v. CNA, 468 F. Supp. 1291 (W.D. Pa. 1979); Kelmo Enterprises, Inc. v. Commercial Union Ins. Co., 426 A.2d 680 (Pa. Super. Ct. 1981).

[48] See Selected Risks Ins. Co. v. Bruno, 718 F.2d 67 (3d Cir. 1983); Mattes v. National Fidelity Life Ins. Co., 506 F. Supp. 955 (M.D.Pa. 1980), *aff'd,* 659 F.2d 1069, *cert. denied,* 454 U.S. 966 (1981).

[49] 469 A.2d 563 (Pa. 1983).

[50] 469 A.2d at 567.

Moreover, as the remainder of this subsection illustrates, other rationales exist for imposing on the insurer an obligation which is tantamount to a duty to explain.

[d] The Role of Standardization and the Use of Forms

Standard form contracts pervade modern commerce. The loan from the bank, the rules governing a checking account, the service agreement for an appliance, the apartment lease, the ticket stub for parking one's car in a garage, and an insurance policy — all of these are examples of standardized contracts. Such contracts are advantageous in several respects: considerable time is saved that otherwise would be required to negotiate individual contracts; judicial interpretation of one contract can serve as a guide for the interpretation of all contracts of that class; and risks can be evaluated by the insurer on a more predictable basis.[51] However, standardization carries the risk that one party with superior knowledge and bargaining power may impose its will on a weaker, less informed party.

Except for a few rare transactions involving insureds with enormous financial interests, standardization is the rule with regard to insurance contracts. The contents of many insurance policies are prescribed by statutory law, either literally or in substance. The purpose of such regulation is ostensibly to prevent less scrupulous insurers from offering a lower quality product at a lower or perhaps equal price. This oversight is effected through statutes and administrative regulations that prescribe, if not the entire policy form verbatim, the content of certain mandatory provisions, or that prohibit certain kinds of provisions. Furthermore, the tradition of cooperative ratemaking in insurance law has resulted in cooperative drafting of forms: the benefits of cooperative ratemaking cannot be achieved fully without standardization of the product being marketed. Where competition exists, there is a tendency for insurers to gravitate toward policy language that works well, which standardizes forms even in the absence of overt cooperation.

The process of creating a contractual obligation on the terms of a standardized form does not resemble the classic model of offer and acceptance, which envisions parties with equal bargaining power and information negotiating about the terms of their relationship and ultimately reducing their agreement to writing. With a standardized form, the drafter is typically in a position of telling the other party to "take it or leave it." The potential for overreaching, unfairness, and deception in this process is greater than in the classic bargaining model. It is the judiciary's — and ultimately society's — concern about the potential harshness to consumers that has prompted heightened judicial scrutiny of insurance contracts. This theme appears throughout insurance law, but its genesis is in the peculiar process of offer and acceptance that typifies the insurer-insured relationship.[52]

[e] Vending Machine Marketing

The often impersonal nature of the insurance marketing process reaches its penultimate when insurance policies are sold through a vending machine. Those who

---

[51] See generally Friedrich Kessler, *Contracts of Adhesion—Some Thoughts About Freedom of Contract,* 43 Colum. L. Rev. 629, 631–32 (1943).

[52] See generally Gerhardt v. Continental Ins. Cos., 225 A.2d 328 (N.J. 1966); Maretti v. Midland Nat'l Ins. Co., 190 N.E.2d 597 (Ill. App. Ct. 1963).

(Matthew Bender & Co., Inc.)

travel by airplane are generally aware of the existence of vending machines through which a short-term trip insurance policy might be purchased. The applicant purchases a policy, the substance of which is described in general terms on the outside of the machine, by depositing a specified sum of money in the machine, which will cause a policy to be released. The insured then fills out the detachable application on the outside of the policy, which is returned to a slot in the machine.

A variation of this marketing process exists in busier airports. A selection of forms is made available on racks adjacent to a vending machine or perhaps in an air-travel insurance booth staffed by a representative of the insurer. The forms are folded to a size roughly one-third that of a sheet of letter-sized paper; the outside of the form is a detachable application. Ideally, the potential applicant should pick up a copy of the form, study it, fill out the application, and either deposit the application with the premium in the vending machine or give the application and premium to the person in the booth. In actuality, the applicant usually stops briefly at a machine or booth to fill out the form at a time the applicant is preoccupied with the imminent trip, and the application is submitted and the premium paid without taking the time to give much thought to the coverage.

Mutual of Omaha Insurance Co. v. Russell, [53] a 1968 Tenth Circuit decision, illustrates the difficulties to which such marketing procedures can lead. Plaintiff's wife decided to fly from Kansas City to Texas for the funeral of her brother. Reservations were made for a Friday flight to Texas, but the return flight was left open because the funeral was not yet scheduled. While walking through the Kansas City airport to the plane, the plaintiff decided that his wife should have flight insurance. He approached a machine which dispensed a "T-20" policy, which covered insureds for accidents incurred during a round-trip flight while aboard an airplane or in limousines going to or coming from the airport. Lacking the correct change to purchase the policy through the machine, the plaintiff and his wife visited a booth where the insurer's agent sold plaintiff's wife a more expensive "T-18" policy that covered all risks — whether air related or not — during the life of the policy. However, the policy term was stated in twenty-four hour periods up to thirty-one days. Plaintiff's wife purchased a policy for four days of coverage. Her return flight from Texas was delayed, and she was killed when her plane crashed attempting to land at the Kansas City airport twelve hours after the policy expired according to its terms.

Plaintiff argued that the insurer had a duty, which it breached in this case, to tell the insured that several insurance policies were available and to explain fully the provisions and limitations of those policies. However, the court was troubled about as to how much explanation would be required in any given case. In rejecting plaintiff's request that the T-18 policy be reformed to provide the coverage of the T-20 policy in this circumstance, the court stated:

> We think that imposing a duty to offer such explanations under circumstances of this kind — requiring as it does an effort by lay persons to interpret the legal

_____

[53] 402 F.2d 339 (10th Cir. 1968), *cert. denied,* 394 U.S. 973 (1969). See also Travelers Ins. Co. v. Morrow, 645 F.2d 41 (10th Cir. 1981); Annot., *Rights and Liabilities Under Airplane Passengers' Trip Insurance Policy,* 29 A.L.R.3d 766 (1970).

> meaning of the proposed contract as well as others available — would be fraught with great danger to the stability of contracts.[54]

This result was certainly difficult medicine for the plaintiff, who purchased a T-18 policy only because no one with him had the exact change at the time he attempted to use the machine. The insured's and the beneficiary's expectations were doubtless that she was covered while making the round-trip flight. Had the insurer's agent informed the insured or her husband of the implications of the purchasing decision they made, her expectations probably would have conformed to the language of the policy. Yet had the insurer's agent taken the time to explain the alternative policies (or the other nine that were also available for sale) the plaintiff's wife might have missed her flight or would have decided to forget about the insurance altogether.

The insurer fared less well in *Steven v. Fidelity & Casualty Co.*,[55] a 1962 California decision. The insured purchased a policy of life insurance from an airport vending machine. The top of the policy stated in capital letters: "Do not purchase more than a total of $62,500 principal sum — nor for travel on other than scheduled air carriers." The insured's return to Los Angeles from Dayton, Ohio included stops at Terre Haute, Indiana and Chicago. At Terre Haute, he discovered that the Lake Central airlines plane he planned to take to Chicago was grounded in Indianapolis and that some delay would ensue. When it became clear that neither Lake Central nor any railroad, bus company, or rental car company could get him to Chicago in time to make his connection with his Los Angeles flight, the insured with two other passengers chartered a Turner Aviation Corporation plane to Chicago. Turner was not a scheduled air carrier. The Turner flight crashed before reaching Chicago and the insured was killed.

The insurer denied recovery on the ground that the nonscheduled carrier flight was not within the terms of the policy, and the trial court agreed. However, the California Supreme Court reversed, noting:

> The purpose and intent of the insured in taking out the insurance was to obtain insurance protection for the trip. The insured could fairly believe that the policy would cover a reasonable emergency substitution necessitated by the exigencies of the situation. . . . A reasonable person . . . would normally expect that if a flight were interrupted by breakdown or other causes, his coverage would apply to substitute transportation for the same flight.[56]

Language in the policy pointing away from coverage was disregarded as being too inconspicuous:

> The company so arranged this transaction that [the insured] could not possibly read the policy before purchase and could not practically consult the policy after purchase. The language of the policy in itself was insufficient to afford the necessary notice of non-coverage. . . . While the insurer has every right to sell insurance policies by methods of mechanization, and present-day economic conditions may well justify such distribution, the insurer cannot then rely upon

---

[54] 402 F.2d at 246.

[55] 377 P.2d 284 (Cal. 1962).

[56] 377 P.2d at 288–89.

esoteric provisions to limit coverage. If it deals with the public upon a mass basis, the notice of non-coverage of the policy, in a situation in which the public may reasonably expect coverage, must be conspicuous, plain and clear.[57]

The court held that the language of the policy was not sufficiently conspicuous, plain, and clear, and the court entered a judgment for the insured's beneficiary.

Results in cases involving travel insurance sold through machines (or the not-dissimilar booths) turn predominantly on their facts.[58] The language of such policies is likely to be interpreted even more strictly against the insurer, but at the same time courts appear unwilling to impose burdens on insurers incompatible with the context in which the policies are sold.

§ 33   The Binder

[a]   Nature and Purposes

Because policies cannot be delivered immediately upon the insured's application, the insurer's representative is often authorized to make the insurance binding in favor of the insured by issuing a *binder*. Ordinarily, a binder is a document given to the insured which obligates the insurer to pay insurance if a loss occurs before the insurer acts upon the application. Since a binder is actually a temporary contract of insurance, it must meet all the requirements for forming a contract: mutual assent must exist, and the contract must be supported by a consideration and be sufficiently definite. As a practical matter, this requires the subject matter of the contract, the risks covered, the duration, the amount of coverage, and the premium to be specified in the binder. The binder is usually issued after the applicant pays the first premium, which typically occurs at the time the applicant submits the application for coverage.

The binder ordinarily includes the following provisions: a) identification of the insured; b) if a binder for property insurance, a description of the property, perhaps including its location; c) the limit of proceeds payable upon a loss; d) the risks insured against; e) the time at which the binder commences coverage; f) the maximum length of time that the binder can remain in effect;[1] g) a statement that the binder terminates either upon the issuance of the policy or the rejection of the application, whichever first occurs; and h) a statement that the terms and conditions of the policy to be issued are incorporated into the binder.[2] Since a binder is usually

---

[57] 377 P.2d at 294.

[58] See, e.g., Lacks v. Fidelity & Cas. Co., 118 N.E.2d 555 (N.Y. 1954) (placement of vending machine in front of charter airline's counter made otherwise clear exclusion for nonscheduled airlines ambiguous, where insured purchased policy and died on a charter flight).

[1] Sometimes statutes limit the length of time for which a binder can be issued. See, e.g., Wash. Rev. Code Ann. § 48.18.230 (ninety days maximum); Ariz. Rev. Stat. Ann. § 20-1120 (ninety days maximum); Okla. Stat. tit. 36, § 3622 (ninety days maximum).

[2] Where this statement is omitted, the terms and provisions of the policy are generally incorporated into the binder as a matter of law. See Maxton v. Garegnani, 627 N.E.2d 723 (Ill. App. Ct. 1994).

a short memorandum, it obviously cannot contain all of the provisions of the policy contemplated by the parties. Where the binder is ambiguous, courts often look to the policy for assistance in interpreting the binder.

Binders are advantageous both to the insurer and insured. Without a binder, the insured is subject to the risk that a loss may occur between the time that the application is submitted and the insurance is issued. In life insurance, the applicant is also subject to the risk that he or she might acquire some condition that makes the applicant uninsurable before the insurer completes its investigation. Through the binder, the insured obtains the obvious benefit of receiving immediate coverage before the insurer acts upon the application.

The insurer also benefits from the use of binders. The consumer's application is merely an offer that might be revoked prior to the insurer's acceptance of it through issuance of the policy. Investigating the risk entails costs; if the applicant revokes the offer, the insurer will be unable to recoup these expenses. Giving the applicant something of value at the very outset is sound marketing strategy; the applicant will be less likely to revoke the offer and apply to another company. Furthermore, the temporary binder enables the insurer to give something to the applicant without exposing the insurer to a long-term risk.

[b] Oral Binders

Usually the binder is a written document, but a binder can be oral.[3] The oral binder typically appears — and is often a subject of considerable dispute — in the situation where the applicant submits the application form, the agent takes the insured's premium, and the agent states orally, "you're now covered." If a loss occurs before the insurer acts upon the application and the insurer denies coverage on the ground that it would have rejected the application, difficult factual and legal questions can be presented by the conversation between the applicant and the agent at the time the application was submitted.

Of course, the oral binder is unlikely to be specific about its terms; the factors listed above as ordinarily being included in written binders are not likely to be spoken orally. However, under the same reasoning that incorporates into a written binder the terms and conditions of the policy for which application was made when the binder is silent on what terms are incorporated, the terms and conditions of the policy for which application was made are incorporated into an oral binder. This means that all ordinary, standard provisions and exclusions of the policy are read into and become a part of the temporary binder of insurance, unless there is an express agreement at the time the oral binder is issued that such exclusions will not apply.[4]

---

[3] See Lindsay Ins. Agency v. Mead, 508 N.W.2d 820, 825 (Neb. 1993); Dixie Ins. Co. v. Joe Works Chevrolet, Inc., 766 S.W.2d 4 (Ariz. 1989); Green Mountain Ins. Co. v. Bonney, 561 A.2d 1057 (N.H. 1989); McDuffie v. Criterion Cas. Co., 449 S.E.2d 133 (Ga. Ct. App. 1994)(to create binder, only need language or conduct showing meeting of minds).

[4] See Harmon v. American Interinsurance Exch. Co., 197 N.W.2d 307 (Mich. Ct. App. 1972).

[c] Types of Binders

Although the following terminology is not uniformly used, it is helpful to distinguish three different kinds of binders: an approval binder; a conditional binder; and an unconditional temporary binder.[5]

An *approval binder* provides that the coverage takes effect as of the date of the binder, except that the application must first be approved by the company. When one thinks about the "except" clause in the foregoing formulation, it becomes apparent that the exception very nearly swallows the whole. It is as if the binder says, "you have coverage, except you don't have coverage until we approve your application — which won't happen until shortly before we deliver the policy to you." Thus, this kind of binder is almost entirely illusory because it provides nothing to the applicant upon its issuance. What it does provide by its terms is coverage for a short period of time, the time after approval of the application but before the issuance of the policy.

To illustrate what this binder provides more concretely (and create an example for comparing the other two kinds of binders), consider this example: Applicant applies for insurance on day 1 on a form that says that the insurance being applied for becomes effective on the day the policy is delivered to Applicant; an approval binder is issued by the agent on day 1; Applicant suffers "loss 1" on day 5; the insurer approves the application on day 10; "loss 2" occurs on day 13; and the policy is delivered on day 16. "Loss 1" is not covered, because Applicant's application has not been approved. However, the binder's coverage becomes effective on day 10, and "loss 2" is covered under the approval binder. Had no binder been issued, "loss 2" would not have been covered because the policy had not been delivered to Applicant. Of course, if Applicant's application is never approved and no policy is ever issued, Applicant has no coverage for either loss.

The *conditional binder* creates an immediate contract of coverage conditional upon the applicant's insurability, meaning that the coverage does not exist until the insurer is satisfied that the risk is acceptable. In a life insurance transaction, for example, this satisfaction will ordinarily exist at the time the applicant passes a medical examination. Like the approval binder, the conditional binder gives the insurer the benefit of holding the first premium payment without having to provide coverage to the applicant. However, the conditional binder is broader than the approval binder because losses prior to the insurer's expression of satisfaction with the insurability of the risk (that is, the "approval") are covered if it turns out that the insurer was satisfied with the insurability of the risk. Thus, to continue with the life insurance example, if the applicant passes the medical exam but dies before the paperwork is processed, the beneficiaries would receive coverage under the conditional binder; but if the applicant died before the medical exam occurred, no proceeds would be paid. Thus, the conditional binder seeks to reserve to the insurer the right to deny coverage for a loss that occurs prior to the issuance of the formal policy on the ground that the risk was uninsurable.

---

[5] See generally Arnold P. Anderson, *Life Insurance Conditional Receipts and Judicial Intervention*, 63 Marq. L. Rev. 593 (1980); James T. Potter, Comment, *Conditional Receipts: New York Precedent and the Potential for Change*, 43 Alb. L. Rev. 645 (1979).

The potential difficulty with the conditional binder, from the applicant's perspective, is that the insurer might decide to reject an application simply because a loss occurred before the insurer communicated what would have been, but for the loss, an acceptance of the application. In fact, in numerous cases the conditional binder has been held to provide no coverage in circumstances where the insurer rejected the application after the loss occurred.[6] The assumption underlying these holdings is, of course, that the insurers exercised their discretion to accept or reject the application in good faith. The premise of the conditional binder is that the insurer will pay proceeds for a loss that occurs prior to the issuance of the policy if in the normal course the insurer would have issued the policy to the applicant. If, however, the insurer denies coverage in bad faith, the bad faith serves to excuse the nonsatisfaction of the condition to coverage (the condition being that the insurer be satisfied that the risk is acceptable), leaving the insurer with an unconditional duty to pay proceeds.[7] Thus, to illustrate the conditional binder using the example in the prior discussion, if the binder given Applicant were a conditional binder, both "loss 1" and "loss 2" would be covered because the insurer ultimately accepted the risk. However, if the insurer ultimately rejected the application in good faith, neither the first nor the second loss would be covered.

The *unconditional temporary binder* creates a contract under which the insurer provides immediate coverage, except that the insurer's duty to pay proceeds terminates if the company determines that it does not wish to undertake the risk.[8] In the interim, however, the applicant has effective, valid insurance.

The different legal effect of the conditional binder and the unconditional temporary insurance binder devolves from the different kinds of conditions that the binders contain. In the conditional binder, the condition to coverage functions as a condition precedent: the insurer need not perform its duty (that is, pay proceeds for a loss) unless and until the condition is satisfied. In the unconditional temporary binder, the condition to coverage functions as a condition subsequent: the insurer has a duty to pay proceeds upon a loss, a duty subject to being discharged if the condition is not satisfied. Thus, with the unconditional temporary binder, if the insurer ultimately determines that it does not wish to undertake the risk, the insurer nevertheless has an obligation to pay proceeds until that determination is made. To return to the example of Applicant and the two losses, if the binder issued Applicant were an unconditional temporary insurance binder, both of Applicant's losses would have been covered, regardless of whether the insurer would have ultimately accepted or rejected the application. In other words, coverage under this kind of binder ceases to exist only upon the insurer's communication to the applicant that the application is being rejected.

---

[6] See, e.g., Brown v. Equitable Life Ins. Co. of Iowa, 211 N.W.2d 431 (Wis. 1973); Hildebrand v. Franklin Life Ins. Co., 455 N.E.2d 553 (Ill. App. Ct. 1983); McLean v. Life of Virginia, 180 S.E.2d 431 (N.C. Ct. App. 1971).

[7] E.g., Rohde v. Massachusetts Mut. Life Ins. Co., 632 F.2d 667 (6th Cir. 1980).

[8] "Unconditional" in this usage does not mean incontestable. For example, misrepresentation by an applicant is a legitimate defense for an insurer under a binder. E.g., Haas v. Integrity Mut. Ins. Co., 90 N.W.2d 146 (Wis. 1958); Leibler v. Unionmutual Stock Life Ins. Co., 394 N.Y.S.2d 208 (N.Y. App. Div. 1977).

Over the years, insurers have used approval or conditional binders more often in life insurance than in property or liability insurance. The main reason for this disparity is that less expertise is needed to inspect property adequately than to evaluate a person's health. If, for example, the applicant seeks insurance for a building, it is relatively easy for the insurer's agent to visit the structure, determine whether the building is brick or wood and has a sprinkler system or a fireplace, calculate its size, etc. With life, health, or disability insurance, an expert assessment of the applicant's medical condition is needed. Thus, insurers are more willing to give their agents the authority to issue unconditional binders (and sometimes even to bind the permanent contract in the field) with respect to property and liability insurance.[9] Also, the policy limits — and hence the exposure to the insurer — is often less with property insurance than with life insurance. Furthermore, if a mistake is made and a property risk is ill-advisedly underwritten by the insurer, the mistake is relatively easy to correct: when the policy is up for renewal in six months or a year, the insurer can simply decline to renew the coverage. Life insurance involves a longer commitment; accordingly, insurers are usually more careful about undertaking such risks.

[d]   Judicial Regulation of Binders

Although many older decisions upheld the literal language of the binders, courts eventually rendered decisions that in effect rewrote the binders as providing something of greater value. One of the early leading cases taking this bold approach was *Gaunt v. John Hancock Mutual Life Insurance Co.*[10] The applicant was insurable, but the applicant died before his application was approved and the insurer denied coverage. Judge Learned Hand opined:

> [T]he application was not to be submitted to underwriters; it was to go persons utterly unacquainted with the niceties of life insurance, who would read it colloquially. It is the understanding of such persons that counts. . . . The ordinary applicant who has paid his first premium and has successfully passed his physical examination, would not by the remotest chance understand the clause as leaving him uncovered until the insurer at its leisure approved the risk; he would assume that he was getting immediate coverage for his money.[11]

Most recent cases have adopted Judge Hand's view of the binder and have tended to construe such receipts as providing unconditional coverage between the period

---

[9] Liability and property insurers are usually represented by "general" agents who have the authority to bind the company. Life insurers are usually represented by "soliciting" agents who lack the authority to bind the company absent the home office's approval. The binders issued by soliciting agents are typically conditional; the binders issued by general agents may be unconditional.

[10] 160 F.2d 599 (2d Cir.) *cert. denied,* 331 U.S. 849 (1947).

[11] 160 F.2d at 601. Judge Hand then continued with what has become a famous observation, often quoted in subsequent cases: "[I]nsurers who seek to impose upon words of common speech an esoteric significance intelligible only to their craft, must bear the burden of any resulting confusion. We can think of few situations where that canon is more appropriate than in such a case as this." 160 F.2d at 602.

that the application is submitted and the insurer acts upon the application.[12] Typical of these cases is *Dunford v. United of Omaha,*[13] a 1973 Idaho case, in which Hillman, a practicing attorney, applied for a life insurance policy and received a "conditional premium receipt" from the agents. The receipt provided that the insurance would be effective on the date of application or the date of any required medical examination, subject to requirements on the reverse side of the receipt. Two of these requirements were that the company find the applicant to be insurable under its rules for the policy being applied for and issuance of the policy exactly as applied for within sixty days from the date of the application.

About six weeks after Hillman applied for the policy, the Omaha office issued the policy and sent it to its agent. The issued policy had two changes: the premium was increased and a provision excluding any waiver of premiums upon disablement was added. These changes were made due to findings about a drinking problem Hillman had and the fact that Hillman had one more birthday since the application. Three days after the policy was issued, but before delivery to the applicant and ratification of the changes, Hillman was killed in a car accident. The policy was returned by the agent to the home office, and the policy was canceled.

The insurer refused to pay proceeds to the beneficiary, arguing that under the terms of the binder, the coverage never became effective because the policy was not issued on the terms applied for. The policy with different terms sent to Hillman was actually a counteroffer that was not accepted by the insured prior to his death. However, the court rejected this argument, observing that Hillman had not received notice of the rejection of his application prior to his death, which meant that the temporary contract of insurance was still in effect. The court in *Dunbar* refused to enforce the conditional binding receipt according to its terms. Instead, the court viewed the receipt as creating a binding temporary contract of insurance, a contract which would not terminate until the applicant received notice of the rejection of his application.

This approach, which recognizes an immediate, unconditional interim policy, has been followed in many recent cases,[14] and it makes much sense. Under the older view, if after the applicant's death the insurer could show that it would have rejected the application, no coverage would exist. Obviously, an insurer in such a situation had a strong temptation to conclude that it would have rejected the risk. Courts required that the decision to decline the risk be made in good faith, but the leverage

---

[12] E.g., Collister v. Nationwide Life Ins. Co., 388 A.2d 1346 (Pa. 1978), *cert. denied,* 439 U.S. 1089 (1979); Simses v. North Am. Co. for Life & Health Ins., 394 A.2d 710 (Conn. 1978); Smith v. Westland Life Ins. Co., 539 P.2d 433 (Cal. 1975); Prudential Ins. Co. v. Lamme, 425 P.2d 346 (Nev. 1967); Allen v. Metropolitan Life Ins Co., 208 A.2d 638 (N.J. 1965); but see Rohde v. Massachusetts Mut. Life Ins. Co., 632 F.2d 667 (6th Cir. 1980) (in absence of ambiguity in conditional receipt, receipt must be enforced as written); Cannon v. Southland Life Ins. Co., 283 A.2d 404 (Md. 1971) (applicant must meet insurer's objective test of insurability to have coverage under binder).

[13] 506 P.2d 1355 (Idaho 1973).

[14] See, e.g., Anderson v. Country Life Ins. Co., 886 P.2d 1381 (Ariz. Ct. App. 1994); Glarner v. Time Ins. Co., 465 N.W.2d 591 (Minn. Ct. App. 1991); Powell v. Republic Nat'l Life Ins. Co., 337 So. 2d 1291 (Ala. 1976).

that insurers possessed worked to the detriment of many applicants. The modern approach, by recognizing immediate, effective insurance, induces insurers to act quickly upon applications so as to minimize the time that the insurer underwrites the risk without having a full comprehension of its nature. Furthermore, in many and perhaps most instances, the applicant reasonably believes, upon receiving the binder, that full coverage is provided, at least temporarily. The applicant's payment of a premium buttresses this belief, for the applicant is not likely to think the payment purchased nothing at all. The contract formed in these circumstances should be interpreted in favor of the insured, and the conclusion follows that the binder was intended to create present, effective insurance.[15]

What if the binder in clear and unambiguous language reasonably understandable by the insured states that no coverage exists until approval of the insurance application by the home office (or similar limiting language)? A four-corners approach to interpretation, particularly if coupled with a requirement that a party has a duty to read any agreement into which the party enters, would conclude that coverage does not exist.[16] Yet one court that otherwise follows strict, formal rules of interpretation has held that the insurer has an "affirmative duty . . . to show either that the insured has read and understood a conditional receipt clause or that the clause was read and explained to the insured by the agent."[17] Under this test, an insurer that is unable to show, at a minimum, that its agent brought the clause to the applicant's attention and correctly explained its meaning to the applicant, extends coverage even if the clear language of the binder is to the contrary.

Because of the uncertainty inherent in knowing whether or not a binder provides coverage, some life insurers have decided to issue unconditional temporary binders as a matter of routine practice. In theory, such a binder should lead to some adverse selection as higher-risk individuals seek to secure unconditional coverage for at least a temporary time. Insurers, however, control the length of this period of enhanced risk; by acting on applications with expedition, this period of free, temporary coverage for the person who cannot meet the insurers's underwriting requirements is limited. Moreover, it is doubtful that uninsurable persons will exploit the coverage of the temporary binder in sufficient numbers to affect the insurer's risk pool. To the extent this occurs (which is unlikely given the relatively small number of applications that are rejected), the cost of providing temporary unconditional coverage can be spread across the insurer's entire risk pool, perhaps at no more cost than

---

[15] E.g., State Farm Mut. Auto. Ins. Co. v. Khoe, 884 F.2d 401 (9th Cir. 1989); Collister v. Nationwide Life Ins. Co., 479 Pa. 579, 388 A.2d 1346 (1978), *cert. denied,* 439 U.S. 1089 (1979); Anderson v. Country Life Ins. Co., 886 P.2d 1381 (Ariz. Ct. App. 1994); Wernle v. Country Life Ins. Co., 491 N.E.2d 449 (Ill. App. Ct. 1986).

[16] See, e.g., State Farm Mut. Auto. Ins. Co. v. Khoe, 884 F.2d 401, 407 (9th Cir. 1989) (insurer did "unambiguously and unequivocally condition coverage [in binder] on issuance of a policy and that the language of the clause would not give rise to a contract of temporary insurance"); Thomas v. Thomas, 824 P.2d 971 (Kan. 1992); Protective Life Ins. Co. v. Robinson, 387 S.E.2d 603 (Ga. Ct. App. 1989).

[17] State Farm Mut. Auto. Ins. Co. v. Khoe, 884 F.2d 401, 407 (9th Cir. 1989) (applying California law).

that involved in reserving for claims under conditional or approval binders in an environment where their enforcement is uncertain.[18]

Indeed, it is arguable that in order to achieve the advantages of a system where people are not misled about the coverage provided by the temporary receipt, it is essential that binders — regardless of their language — be treated as unconditional temporary binders. This, it could be argued, fairly balances the interests of insurer and applicant. Consumers, at the time they submit their applications, desire immediate, permanent coverage, but consumers do not receive this when the insurer uses the language of a conditional or approval binder to give itself the opportunity to investigate the risk before committing to permanent coverage. The insurer, on the other hand, desires the chance to investigate the risk. Because the insurer obtains what it wants, it seems only fair that the insurer should give up something of value in return — such as the right to back out of coverage in the interim between taking the consumer's application and payment for the first premium and the insurer's acting on the application. Indeed, if this approach is not followed, the insurer gains the advantage of receiving the premium payment by the insured without giving unconditional coverage in return (although this advantage has little, if any, value if the insurer does not use the applicant's money, as is the case if the insurer does not cash the applicant's check drawn to pay the first premium; in that instance, the insurer simply *returns* the applicant's check, as distinguished from *refunding* the applicant's premium payment). If the insurer does not wish to be bound on the risk, in fairness the insurer should not issue a binder and should forego receipt of the premium until the policy is delivered.[19]

Giving all recipients of binders immediate, effective insurance entails some disadvantages, but it is arguable that these disadvantages are outweighed by the advantages of abandoning a system where many people are misled about the coverage provided by the binder. Yet in the final analysis, the more important question may be the proper scope of judicial regulation. Should courts, based on the perception that unconditional temporary binders are better, construe all binders as unconditional temporary binders, thereby abolishing approval and conditional binders? Or should this matter of private contract be regulated, if at all, by the legislature, which is arguably the appropriate branch of government to decide whether public policy requires abolishing approval and conditional binders? Or should this issue be left to the market, with insurers weighing the costs and benefits

---

[18] This analysis is less persuasive in health insurance, where the applicant who receives an unconditional binder has some ability to control whether health services are received. In other words, the adverse selection consequences are different in life and health insurance: the higher-risk life insured is unlikely to seek his or her own death during the interim period (and the two-year suicide exclusion handles the worst cases of moral hazard); but the higher-risk health insured may postpone medical treatment until after the application is submitted. If, as discussed below, courts decided to treat all binders as unconditional temporary binders, health insurers might decline to issue any binders; but this answer, i.e., having no binders in health insurance, might be better than having some binders, particularly when those binders tend to mislead applicants about the scope of their coverage prior to issuance of the policy.

[19] See Collister v. Nationwide Life Ins. Co., 479 Pa. 579, 388 A.2d 1346 (1978), *cert. denied,* 439 U.S. 1089 (1979); Damm v. Nat'l Ins. Co., 200 N.W.2d 616 (N.D. 1972).

of different kinds of binders, with cognizance that an ambiguous binder or a binder not specifically called to the applicant's attention may be enforced by a court in the applicant's favor pursuant to rules of contract interpretation? How one answers these questions depends on considerations that transcend the field of insurance law.

§ 34 Delivery of the Policy

[a] The Event and Its Purpose

Delivery is the act of putting the insurance policy — the physical document — into the possession of the insured. The fact of delivery is important for several reasons. First, it has evidentiary value. Delivery does not conclusively indicate that the policy is in effect, but it is a strong indication of the policy's effectiveness. Second, delivery may be the means by which the insurer communicates to the applicant its acceptance of the applicant's offer. Finally, delivery may affect the term of the coverage. Some policies provide that the coverage terminates one year after delivery; delivery, therefore, becomes the important fact for determining when the policy ends. The widespread use of binding receipts has made delivery less important than it used to be in the process of forming a contract between insurer and insured, but delivery still has significance as the "decisive act that ordinarily marks the end of the insurer's opportunity to decline coverage."[1]

For purposes of determining when delivery has occurred, the overt acts of the insurer are not as important as the insurer's manifested intention. Indeed, the essence of delivery is intention. If the insurer by some word or act indicates that it is putting the policy outside its legal control, even if not outside its physical control, a delivery has ordinarily occurred. If the insurer regularly makes use of the mail to correspond with applicants, the depositing of a policy in the mail, as the first step in transmitting an approved policy to the applicant, constitutes delivery.[2] Similarly, the physical act of turning the policy over to the insured does not constitute delivery if the beneficiary fraudulently induced the delivery of the policy (such as by failing to inform the insurer that the insured is now deceased). In such a case, the delivery is ineffective because of the concealment of information from the insurer.[3]

[b] Constructive Delivery

Sometimes the insurer argues that no contract exists because a requirement that the policy be physically delivered to the applicant has not been met. Most cases dealing with the question of whether the policy has been properly delivered involve life insurance, where the application often states that the insurance does not become effective unless and until the policy is delivered to the applicant.

The typical fact pattern in which controversy arises is as follows: the insurer, after approving the application, sends the policy to its agent for delivery to the applicant,

---

[1] Robert E. Keeton, *Insurance Law* 61 (1971).

[2] For further discussion, see APPLEMAN § 7157 (1981).

[3] See, e.g., Glickman v. New York Life Ins. Co., 50 N.E.2d 538 (N.Y. 1942); Hahsen v. Continental Cas. Co., 287 P. 894 (Wash. 1930).

but the policy is not delivered until after the applicant dies. The insurer denies coverage on the ground that the coverage did not become effective because the policy was not delivered. Judicial responses to the insurers' argument vary. Some courts enforce the language of the policy as written and conclude that no coverage exists.[4] Most courts, however, attempt to find a "constructive delivery" in the facts that satisfies the language of the policy.[5] For example, the court might reason that for purposes of delivery the insurance agent functioned as the applicant's agent (in the legal sense), so that delivery of the policy to the insurance agent constituted delivery to the applicant, making the coverage effective. Generally, when an insurer mails a policy to an agent, if nothing remains to be done by the insurer or agent except for the actual delivery of the policy to the applicant, the mailing constitutes constructive delivery of the policy.[6]

[c] Good Health Clauses and Other Conditions on the Effectiveness of Delivery

In transactions where delivery is the moment that the insurer becomes obligated to the applicant, the legal effectiveness of the delivery is frequently subject to some conditions. For example, in a Delaware case,[7] the plaintiff applied for a policy of disability insurance. The application was approved, and the policy was sent to the agent for delivery to the applicant. On the day the agent received the policy and prior to the policy's delivery to the applicant, the applicant was disabled in an accident at work. Thereafter, the applicant attempted to pay the first premium, which had not been submitted with the application since the applicant desired to first see what the policy's coverage would be before paying for it. The plaintiff contended that the policy had been "constructively delivered" because the policy was in the agent's hands.[8] However, the court held that there was no coverage because the application stated that the insurer would be liable only "when the policy is issued and *full first policy premium paid* during the lifetime of and while the health of the person(s) proposed for insurance is as here described on the policy date."[9] The court held that the delivery of the policy was conditioned on specified events, the nonoccurrence of which prevented coverage from becoming effective upon delivery. Other courts have so held.[10]

---

[4] See, e.g., Trotter v. Prudential Ins. Co. of Am., 133 N.W.2d 182 (Mich. 1965); Reynolds v. Guarantee Reserve Life Ins. Co., 358 N.E.2d 940 (Ill. App. Ct. 1976).

[5] See, e.g., Jackson Nat'l Life Ins. Co. v. Rececconi, 827 P.2d 118, 124-25 (N.M. 1992); Kramer v. Metropolitan Life Ins. Co., 494 F. Supp. 1026 (D.N.J. 1980); Wanshura v. State Farm Life Ins. Co., 275 N.W.2d 559 (Minn. 1978).

[6] See Tarleton v. De Veuve, 113 F.2d 290 (9th Cir. 1940); Annot., *Transmission of Insurance Policy to Insurance Agent as Satisfying Provision Requiring Delivery to Insured,* 19 A.L.R.3d 953, 964-67 (1968).

[7] Megee v. United States Fidelity and Guaranty Co., 391 A.2d 189 (Del. 1978).

[8] Numerous courts have so held. See, e.g., Krause v. Washington Nat'l Ins. Co., 468 P.2d 513 (Or. 1970); Prudence Mut. Cas. Co. v. Switzer, 175 So. 2d 476 (Miss. 1965); Millner v. New Jersey Ins. Underwriting Ass'n, 475 A.2d 653 (N.J. Super. Ct. App. Div. 1984).

[9] 391 A.2d at 191.

[10] See, e.g., Jackson Nat'l Life Ins. Co. v. Rececconi, 827 P.2d 118 (N.M. 1992); G.P. Enterprises, Inc. v. Jackson Nat'l Life Ins. Co., 509 N.W.2d 780 (Mich. Ct. App. 1993).

Perhaps the most common condition to the legal effect of delivery is that the delivery occur (and perhaps, as in the foregoing case, the first premium be paid) while the insured is in good health. Usually the clause is contained both in the application and the policy. There are several alternative formulations of this condition: that no material change occur in the applicant's health between the time of the medical exam and the delivery of the policy; that the applicant remain continually insurable during this interim period; or that the applicant be in the same health on the date of delivery as on the date of the application for the insurance.

The insurer's good health clause defense is not the same thing as a defense based on fraud or misrepresentation. If the applicant is asked about his or her health and the applicant misrepresents that he or she is in good health, the insurer has a defense only if the misrepresentation is intentional. Intent is an element of fraud; although intent is not an element of misrepresentation, a misrepresentation of belief regarding the state of one's health cannot occur without intent. Many courts, however, do not require the insured to know of a deficient state of health at the time of the delivery of the policy for the insurer to possess a valid good health clause defense. For example, courts agree that the term "good health" should not be taken literally, but instead should be given a reasonable construction. Minor ailments at the time of delivery are irrelevant; only diseases so serious that they tend to shorten life are the kinds of diseases causing the good health clause to be unsatisfied.

Courts have devised a number of ways to protect applicants in situations where the applicant's health was not good at the time of the delivery of the policy. In a Ninth Circuit decision where Montana law was being applied,[11] the applicant at the time the life insurance policy was delivered did not know that he was suffering from terminal cancer. When he later died, the insurer denied coverage on the ground that the insured's good health at the time of delivery was a condition precedent to coverage and this condition was not satisfied, making the coverage void. The court reasoned that the good health clause in the application was ambiguous. The clause stated:

> I understand and agree that there shall be no insurance in force until the policy hereby applied for is issued and delivered to me during my lifetime and good health and the first premium is paid by me in which event the insurance shall be effective as of the date of issue stated in the policy.

The court observed that the clause might be construed to require good health at the time the policy was issued or merely to establish that no coverage was provided until the policy issued. In addition, the clause was not precise regarding which of two meanings of good health should be used: "objective good health," which the applicant did not possess, or "subjective good health," which the applicant did possess because he believed he was healthy. The court construed these ambiguities in favor of the insured and held that the good health clause did not bar recovery.

Numerous other decisions have held that a medical condition extant but undetected at the time of the medical examination could not be the basis for the insurer denying coverage on the ground that the applicant was not in good health at the time

---

[11] Friez v. National Old Line Ins. Co., 703 F.2d 1093 (9th Cir. 1983).

the policy was delivered.[12] The extent to which a court might be willing to take this principle is illustrated by a California decision, *Harte v. United Benefit Life Insurance Co.*[13] The applicant had a minor stomach condition that, unknown to him or to either his own doctor or the insurer's doctor who examined him, was actually terminal cancer. Prior to the delivery of the policy, surgery on the applicant revealed the cancer; the wife was informed about the illness, but the applicant was not. When the policy was delivered by the agent to the applicant's wife at their home, the wife did not reveal — and was not asked questions which if answered would have revealed — that the applicant was hospitalized and had been diagnosed as having terminal cancer. After the insured died, the insurer denied coverage on the ground that the insured was not in good health at the time the policy was delivered. However, the court applied a rule that "where the applicant believes in good faith that his health has not materially changed between the time of application for the policy and its delivery, . . . it is the insured's own knowledge of the state of his health which is decisive rather than the uncommunicated knowledge of a third person."[14] Accordingly, the court held that the jury could have found that the applicant believed in good faith that he was in good health, and a judgment for the insurer was reversed.

§ 35   The Intermediary's Role in Contract Formation

[a]   Overview

When a dispute arises between insurer and insured, the circumstances of the negotiation and formation of the contract are often extremely important. The insurer will have conducted the negotiations and entered into the contract through the auspices of some third party. The actual or apparent authority of this intermediary is often crucial to the resolution of the dispute between insurer and insured.

Insurers use the terms "agent" and "broker" to describe the people who sell insurance products to consumers — the intermediary between the insurer and the insured. An insurance agent is a person expressly or impliedly authorized by the insurer to represent it in dealings with third parties in insurance matters. An agent is typically a salaried employee. In contrast, the broker is for most purposes the agent of the insured: the broker arranges insurance coverage for the client, but receives a commission from the insurer. For some purposes, the broker is the insurer's agent; the broker has some actual authority from the insurer, but usually much less than an agent. Because the insurer deals with the applicant through its representatives and through brokers, agents and brokers play an important role in the process of forming insurance contracts (and often in implementing them as well).

Unfortunately, assessing and drawing conclusions about the legal status of an intermediary in insurance transactions is often quite difficult. This is a function of two problems. First, the facts of particular cases are often less than clear on the

---

[12] Ortega v. North Am. Co. for Life & Health Ins., 193 N.W.2d 254 (Neb. 1971).
[13] 424 P.2d 329 (Cal. 1967).
[14] 424 P.2d at 331.

question of how much authority a particular person actually had to act as the insurer's agent. Second, even when the facts seem clear, courts often apply agency rules loosely in order to reach the results thought appropriate in the circumstances. Therefore, one must proceed cautiously in the face of an assertion in an insurance dispute that a principle of agency law points to a particular result or conclusion. In addition, agency law concepts are obscured in insurance law by varied uses of the term "agent." In common parlance, the term "agent" describes anyone who sells insurance. Consumers frequently refer to their own "insurance agent," much like consumers identify their own lawyers or doctors. At the same time, those in the insurance trade often give the term "agent" a special, albeit nonlegal, meaning. Making sense out of these disparate uses of language is no easy feat.

The precise authority of someone who functions as the intermediary between an insured and the insurer cannot be calculated without examining the facts of a particular case. However, a few generalities can be stated if one is careful to note that the specific facts of cases can produce results at variance with these generalities.

[b] General Principles of Agency

Generally speaking, the principles of agency law apply to insurance companies and their agents. An agent's authority can be either *actual* or *apparent*. Actual authority is explicitly created by the principal or by statute, while apparent authority results from the principal's conduct which causes a third person reasonably to believe that a particular person — who may not even be the principal's agent — has authority to represent the principal.

Apparent authority can be created by the same kinds of manifestations through which actual authority is created; the difference is that with apparent authority the manifestation is made by the principal to third persons or is made by someone with the principal's acquiescence. One court explained the distinction in this way:

> There are two main kinds of agency, actual (express) and ostensible (apparent). If there is evidence that the principal has delegated authority by oral or written words which authorize the agent to do a certain act or series of acts, then the authority of the agent is express. . . . If there is no such express authority, or if intent to create such authority cannot be implied from the actions of the principal and agent, then the next question is whether there is apparent agency. . . . "The ostensible agent is one where the principal has intentionally or inadvertently induced third persons to believe that such a person was its agent although no actual or express authority was conferred on him as agent."[1]

Apparent authority does not exist simply because a person acts as if he or she is an agent. Rather, some sort of affirmative conduct or acquiescence on the part of the principal is necessary. As explained by one court:

> To establish that an agent ha[s] apparent authority to bind its principal it must be shown that the principal knowingly permitted the agent to exercise the authority in question, or in some manner manifested its consent that such authority be exercised.[2]

---

[1] Gulf Ins. Co. v. Grisham, 613 P.2d 283, 286 (Ariz. 1980).

[2] Travelers Ins. Co. v. Morrow, 645 F.2d 41, 44–45 (10th Cir. 1981).

Sometimes courts refer to establishing the liability of a principal through "agency by estoppel,"[3] but in reality this kind of liability is very similar to that created by apparent authority. The essence of agency by estoppel involves a principal being estopped to deny that a certain person is an agent or possesses the authority of an agent. As with apparent authority, this kind of liability arises when the principal causes or allows a person to act so as to justify a reasonable third person in concluding that the person is the principal's agent. But liability by estoppel involves an additional element, because the elements of an estoppel normally require the injured party to establish some kind of detrimental reliance. Although courts and writers sometimes use the terms interchangeably,[4] liability by estoppel is more likely to be alleged when the victim's injury arises out of the agent's tortious conduct and there is no contract formed between victim and agent (as would be the case if the principal's negligence permitted a person to imitate a principal's agent, and in this capacity the agent stole the victim's assets through deception). Apparent authority is more likely to be urged when the victim's injury is grounded in contract (as would be the case if the victim reasonably thought a contract was being formed with the principal due to acts or omissions by the principal that created this impression, notwithstanding the fact that the agent lacked actual authority to bind the principal).

[c]   General Agency Principles in the Context of Insurance

An "insurance agent," from the insurer's perspective, is anyone authorized, either expressly or implicitly, to represent the insurer when dealing with third parties regarding insurance-related matters. The insurer-agent relationship is created in the same way that any principal-agent relationship is created. One usually becomes an agent through *express authorization:* if A communicates to B a desire to make B an agent, B immediately possesses the powers of an agent, although B does not become A' s agent until B accepts those powers. Often the arrangement is an express contract, but any kind of oral or written statement suffices. Also, conduct of the principal communicated directly or indirectly to the agent can create the relationship. *Ratification* is another common way to create an agency relationship: if one person without authority does an act on another's behalf and no objection to the conduct is forthcoming, that failure to object is tantamount to authorizing the actor to continue whatever he or she is doing. *Statutory enactment* can also create an agency relationship. Most states have statutes providing that all persons who transact specified kinds of insurance business for a company are agents of the company.[5]

When the agent makes statements or acts within the scope of the agent's authority, the insurer is bound by those statements or acts. The insurer, like any principal, is free to limit the authority of its agents or to classify its agents into categories with varying degrees of authority. If an agent acts outside the agent's explicitly created or "actual" authority, the insurer will not be bound by the agent's acts, unless the agent had "apparent" authority to do the acts or the insurer ratifies the agent's unauthorized acts.

---

[3] See, e.g., Trefethen v. New Hampshire Ins. Group, 645 A.2d 72 (N.H. 1994); Whitlow v. Good Samaritan Hosp., 536 N.E.2d 659 (Ohio Ct.App. 1987).

[4] See, e.g., Buist M. Anderson, *Anderson on Life Insurance* 384-85 (1991) (referring to apparent authority as "Apparent Powers—Estoppel.")

[5] See Fryar v. Employers Ins. of Wausau, 607 P.2d 615 (N.M. 1980).

The fact that an agent had no actual authority to bind the insurer could be irrelevant if the agent had apparent authority to represent the insurer in a particular transaction. Just as actual authority results from what a principal communicates to an agent, apparent authority results from the principal's conduct which causes a third person reasonably to believe that a particular person — who may not even be the principal's agent — has authority to represent the principal. It is insufficient that the third person, perhaps induced by deception, reasonably believes that the person has authority. Instead, the person interacting with the agent must show that the principal created, permitted, or allowed the appearance of authority that led the person to believe that the agent possessed the authority the agent acted as if he or she had. Normally, this showing is made by demonstrating that the agent did certain things with the permission or acquiescence of the insurer. If the insured can make this showing, the insurer will be bound by the acts of its agent (or, for that matter, any other person) who has acted in excess of the person's actual authority, if any.

Thus, the insurance agent's apparent authority is essentially as broad as that which the insurer knowingly permits the agent to assume. However, if the agent acts on the insurer's behalf without actual authority, the insurer will be bound to third parties only if the third party can prove that the insurer was responsible in some way for the appearance of authority.[6] If the agent acting without actual authority succeeds in binding the insurer through acts within the scope of apparent authority, it does not follow that the insurer ultimately bears the loss caused by the agent's unauthorized acts. This is because an insurer who is bound to a third party by virtue of an agent's acts beyond the scope of actual authority has a claim against the agent for damages.[7] Indeed, the insurer will typically insist in its contracts with its own agents that the agents indemnify the insurer for losses caused the insurer by the agent's acts outside the scope of actual authority, and the agents will insure against this risk of liability by purchasing errors and omissions insurance.

Insurers also try to reduce the risk that unauthorized acts of their agents will produce liability. This is attempted primarily through two mechanisms: limitations on the agent's authority articulated in the application form submitted by a person seeking insurance; and limitations on the agent's authority to modify the policy or waive conditions articulated in the text of the policy itself. These devices fall short, however, of guaranteeing an insurer protection from obligations that arise out of the activities or omissions or their agents. These issues are discussed in more detail in a later subsection.[8]

[d] Types of Agents

If an agent has actual authority to do certain acts, it makes no difference whether the agent is labeled a "general agent," "special agent," "local agent," or "soliciting agent": the insurer is bound by acts within the scope of the agent's actual authority. However, because insurers sometimes attach special meanings to the labels and this might be relevant to the scope of the agent's actual authority, it is important to have

---

[6] See Inland USA, Inc. v. Reed Stenhouse, Inc., 660 S.W.2d 727 (Mo. Ct. App. 1983).

[7] See, e.g., Elmer Tallant Agency, Inc. v. Bailey Wood Products, Inc., 374 So. 2d 1312 (Ala. 1979); Corbitt v. Federal Kemper Ins. Co., 594 S.W.2d 728 (Tenn. Ct. App. 1979).

[8] See § 35[g], *infra*.

an understanding of the commonly used categories and definitions of insurance agents.

The normal understanding of the term "general agent" varies depending upon the kind of insurance involved. In all lines of insurance except life, the term general agent usually refers to a person authorized by the principal (i.e., the insurer) to make insurance contracts on behalf of the insurer. Also, in all lines but life, the general agent typically has authority to handle financial transactions and sometimes is allowed to adjust claims. In life insurance, a general agent almost always lacks the authority to bind the insurer; this power is retained in the insurer's home office. The only authority the general agent might have to bind the life insurer would concern contracts of temporary insurance under binders or conditional receipts. Ordinarily, in life insurance, the term general agent merely refers to the senior person or manager in a district or branch office. Thus, the general agent in life insurance is sometimes referred to as the "district agent."

Frequently a distinction is drawn between a general agent and a "special agent." The term special agent, which is generally synonymous with "solicitor" or "soliciting agent," in its broadest sense refers to any representative of the insurer given some authority to do some acts on the insurer's behalf. In this usage, the term includes adjusters, medical examiners, attorneys, appraisers, and numerous others. In its narrower and more usual sense, the term refers to agents with limited contractual powers, normally including the authority to seek applications, to receive them for transmission to the insurer, and to receive policies for delivery to approved insureds. Sometimes, the term "special agent" is used synonymously with the term "local agent." This is unfortunate, since the word "local" denotes nothing in particular, except that the agent has authority to operate in a limited place or territory, and is therefore not a "district" agent; indeed, the local agent might have "general" authority to act for the insurer within the narrow geographical area. In life insurance, the differences between general agents and special agents are less, but in most instances the terms denote relative degrees of status in the insurer's hierarchy.

Regardless of the terminology used to describe an intermediary in a particular transaction, it is always possible that the intermediary has more or less authority than his or her "label" apparently indicates. In short, the precise legal status and the authority of an intermediary depends on the facts of the particular case.[9]

[e]   Agents versus Brokers

A distinction is often made between agents and brokers. Agents are usually employees of the insurer. An agent usually receives a salary, although depending on the company some or perhaps most of an agent's income may consist of commissions earned through the placement of insurance. In contrast, brokers are not salaried employees of the insurer; they consequently have a different legal relationship with the insurer.

Using "agent" in the sense that word is used in the law of agency, a broker is a limited agent. The broker is the insurer's agent for some purposes, such as

---

[9] See § 35, *infra*.

collecting premiums and submitting applications, but not others. The broker may have limited actual authority from several companies at once; the so-called "independent agent" is really a broker with limited authority from several companies. This kind of broker may have the authority to bind each of several different insurers to contracts, but usually the broker has limited actual authority from most of the insurers he or she represents. However, if the broker has been permitted to act in certain ways on the insurer's behalf in the past although not actually authorized to do so, it is possible that the broker will be deemed to have apparent authority to perform those acts. Despite the foregoing, sometimes the term "broker" is used to refer generically to various kinds of agents for the insurer, including both special agents and general agents.

For many purposes, the broker is an agent for the insured. In fact, in its normal usage, the term broker refers to a person engaged in the business of procuring insurance for individuals. Thus, it can be said that the broker is the agent of the insured for some purposes and the agent of the insurer for others. This "dual agency" relationship which is commonly found in many insurance transactions is unusual, but not unique in the law.[10] As long as the agent's duties owed the insurer and insured are not incompatible, nothing precludes a dual agency where the agent acts as the insurer's agent for some purposes and the insured's agent for others. The principal's right to control the agent is an essential element of a principal-agent relationship, but it is possible that the insurer will have the right to control the agent for some purposes, while the insured will have the right to control the agent for other purposes. For example, if the broker is employed by a consumer to obtain insurance (as is often the case), the principal-agent relationship between consumer and broker terminates when the insurance is successfully obtained. For other purposes, such as receiving notice of cancellation of the policy or sending out renewal reminders, the broker is not the insured's agent. Because the dual agent's responsibilities to each principal are independent, the insured's release of the insurer will not function to release the agent from liability.[11]

In deciding cases involving agents or brokers, it is not so important what the intermediary is called. Rather, the key point is the extent of the intermediary's authority to act for the insurer. This is the fact upon which significant issues will turn, such as whether the company is bound by the intermediary's representation, whether notice of a loss to the intermediary is good against the insurer, or whether the insurer is liable for the intermediary's misstatement.[12]

---

[10] See Appleton Chinese Food Service, Inc. v. Murken Ins., Inc., 519 N.W.2d 674, 678 (Wis. Ct. App. 1994); Edwards-Warren Tire Co. v. Cole, Sanford & Whitmire, 373 S.E.2d 83 (Ga. Ct. App. 1988).

[11] See Appleton Chinese Food Service, Inc. v. Murken Ins., Inc., 519 N.W.2d 674, 679 (Wis. Ct. App. 1994).

[12] See generally Bertram Harnett, *Responsibilities of Insurance Agents and Brokers*, §§ 2.01–2.07 (1986).

[f] Liability of Agents or Brokers

[1] Liability of Agents to Insurer

Under general agency law, an agent owes the principal a duty to serve the principal with due care and to act only within the scope of the agent's authority.[13] The agent must obey all reasonable instructions given by the insurer with regard to the performance of the agent's undertakings. If these duties are violated and the agent's principal is damaged as a result, the agent is liable to the principal for the damage. The cases provide several examples of situations where insurance agents have been held liable to insurers,[14] including failing to cancel a policy when the agent has authority to do so and has been requested to do so;[15] orally binding coverage without forwarding the application to the insurer;[16] failing to notify the insurer of a material fact;[17] making unauthorized representations to the insured;[18] binding a risk the agent knows is poor,[19] accepting a first premium payment on a life insurance policy while failing to notify the insurer of the applicant's deteriorated health in circumstances where the policy is conditioned on the insured's good health at the time of delivery,[20] and otherwise failing to follow the insurer's instructions.[21] Of course, if the agent commits dishonest or fraudulent acts that injure the insurer, the agent may be held liable for resulting damage.

---

[13] For a general review of these principles, see Bertram Harnett, *Responsibility of Insurance Agents and Brokers* (1986); Tort & Insurance Practice Section of the American Bar Association, *Insurance Agent and Broker Liability: Current Litigation and Emerging Case Law* (1991); Annot., *Liability of Insurance Agent, For Exposure of Insurer to Liability, Because of Issuance of Policy Beyond Authority or Contrary to Instructions,* 35 A.L.R.3d 907 (1971).

[14] See generally Annot., *Liability of Insurance Agent, For Exposure of Insurer to Liability, Because of Failure to Cancel or Reduce Risk,* 35 A.L.R.3d 792 (1971).

[15] See Gulf Ins. Co. v. Kolob Corp., 404 F.2d 115 (10th Cir. 1968); Strickland General Agency v. Puritan Ins. Co., 361 S.E.2d 186 (Ga. Ct. App. 1987); Withers v. Worldwide Ins. Brokers, Inc., 500 So. 2d 914 (La. Ct. App. 1987); Cameron Mut. Ins. Co. v. Bouse, 635 S.W.2d 488 (Mo.App. 1982) (stating general rule); Annot., *Liability of Insurance Agent, For Exposure of Insurer to Liability, Because of Failure To Cancel or Reduce Risk,* 35 A.L.R.3d 792 (1971).

[16] See Milwaukee Mut. Ins. Co. v. Wessels, 449 N.E.2d 897 (Ill. App. Ct. 1983).

[17] See Utica Mut. Ins. Co. v. Coastal Marine, Inc., 578 F. Supp. 1376 (E.D. La. 1984) (failure to notify insurer of litigation progress); Alabama Farm Bureau Mut. Cas. Ins. Co. v. Moore, 435 So. 2d 712 (Ala. 1983) (facts material to underwriting decision); Reliance Ins. Co. v. Substation Products, 404 So. 2d 598 (Ala. 1981) (failure to list known owner-lessor of property as the named insured when asked to do so by insured-lessee); Annot., *Liability of Insurance Agent, For Exposure of Insurer to Liability, Because of Failure to Fully Disclose or Assess Risk or To Report Issuance of Policy,* 35 A.L.R.3d 821 (1971).

[18] See Elmer Tallant Agency v. Bailey Wood Products, Inc., 374 So. 2d 1312 (Ala. 1979); Dunn v. Commercial Union Ins. Co., 27 A.D.2d 240 (N.Y. Sup. Ct. 1967).

[19] See Hawkeye Cas. Co. v. Frisbee, 25 N.W.2d 521 (Mich. 1947); cf. Regino v. Aetna Cas. & Sur. Co., 490 A.2d 362 (N.J. Super.Ct.App. Div. 1985).

[20] Jackson Nat'l Life Ins. Co. v. Receconi, 827 P.2d 118 (N.M. 1992).

[21] See, e.g., Hays v. Farm Bureau Mut. Ins. Co., 589 P.2d 579 (Kan. 1979); Richard v. American Federation of Unions Local 102, 378 So. 2d 564 (La. Ct. App. 1979); Progressive Cas. Ins. Co. v. Blythe, 350 So. 2d 1062 (ALa. Ct. App. 1977).

There is, however, authority for the proposition that if the agent's or broker's negligent conduct within the zone of actual authority does not alter the risk that the insurer was willing to undertake, the intermediary's conduct is not the cause of the insurer's loss, and the intermediary is therefore not liable to the insurer for the loss.[22] For example, in *United Pacific Insurance Co. v. Price,*[23] a 1979 Oregon case, the agent incorrectly informed the insured that his coverage became effective on July 14, when in fact the coverage commenced on July 24. This representation caused the insured to cancel his prior coverage effective July 14, and the insured suffered a loss on July 17. The insurer settled the insured's claim, even though it was technically outside the coverage, and then sought indemnity from the agent. The court reasoned that the agent's negligence did not increase the insurer's risk or bind the insurer to a risk that it would not have undertaken, and therefore the agent was not liable to the insurer. The court distinguished those cases where agents had been held liable as follows:

> These cases [where the agent is held liable] stand for the proposition that the breach of duty by the agent caused the insurance company to be liable for a loss it would have rejected had the agent's actions not prevented it from making the decision. The risks were of a class the insurer was unwilling to accept but was held liable for because of the agent's actions in binding it to do so. The agent's breach of duty was in each case the cause of the insurance company's loss.

In contrast, courts have been unwilling to hold the agent responsible for the amount the insurer was obligated to pay where the agent, albeit negligently, was acting within its authority, and where the insurer was not drawn into accepting a risk it was unwilling to take.[24] The court further explained that if, because of the agent's error, the premium collected were lower than what the insurer ordinarily required for the risk in question, the agent should be held liable only for the difference in the premium amounts,[25] a conclusion with which other courts have agreed.[26]

[2] Liability of Agent or Broker to Insured or Applicant

An intermediary, whether a broker or an agent, who undertakes to perform services for either an applicant or an insured owes duties to that person. The theories that are asserted against intermediaries and the kinds of circumstances giving rise to claims against them are varied.

---

[22] See, e.g., Fireman's Fund Ins. Co. v. Jamieson, 531 F. Supp. 423 (W.D. Tenn. 1982); Country Mut. Ins. Co. v. Adams, 407 N.E.2d 103 (Ill. App. Ct. 1980). Compare Benner v. Farm Bureau Mut. Ins. Co., 528 P.2d 193 (Idaho 1974).

[23] 593 P.2d 1214 (Or. Ct. App. 1979).

[24] 593 P.2d at 1215.

[25] 593 P.2d at 1215-16.

[26] See, e.g., Millers Mut. Fire Ins. Co. v. Russell, 443 S.W.2d 536 (Ark. 1969); Lumbermen's Ins. Co. v. Heiner, 245 P.2d 415 (Ariz. 1952).

[i]   The Professional's Duty of Care

An agent or broker owes a professional duty to the insured or the applicant, and the agent can be held liable in tort for breaching this duty. An individual who holds himself out as having professional expertise in a given field is expected to conduct his or her affairs in the manner expected of similar professionals. Thus, a person who represents himself as having expertise in insurance is expected to be able to do more than simply fill out an application form.[27] For example, an insurance professional who holds himself or herself out as being able to offer tax counseling or financial planning will be expected to perform those duties with the same care as a tax counselor or financial planner. Likewise, an insurance professional who represents that he or she possesses the skill needed to arrange a complex package of coverages for a business will be expected to perform this task in a manner commensurate with the skills represented.

Generally speaking, the principle approved by most courts that have addressed the issue is that the agent, simply by undertaking to function as an agent, assumes a professional duty of care in all of the services he or she provides clients. But absent special circumstances, this duty does not include a duty to give advice about what particular coverages the insured should purchase, or to explain a policy's coverage, or to procure certain kinds of coverage. Special circumstances, however, may cause the agent to acquire additional, more substantial duties, such as a duty to advise the insured about coverages or a duty to procure insurance.

Cases in which insureds (or prospective insureds) allege the agent's breach of the professional duty of care involve a few common fact patterns. In the most common situation, the agent fails to advise the insured-client about the need for a particular coverage or policy, the insured fails to purchase the right kind of coverage, and a loss occurs that would have been covered if a different policy were purchased. The question raised in this kind of case, and several other closely related situations, is whether the agent breached a duty to advise. Another common fact pattern involves the agent undertaking to procure insurance for the insured, failing to do so, and a loss occurs that would have been covered if the requested insurance had been procured. The question in this kind of case is whether the agent breached a duty to procure insurance. Each situation will be discussed in turn, but these categories do tend to overlap in some situations, such as when the insured claims that the agent failed to give good advice about what kind of insurance should be procured and consequently failed to procure the coverages the insured desired.

[ii]   Liability of Agents or Brokers to Insured for Failure to Provide Proper Advice

The agent's or broker's general duty of care may, depending on the circumstances, impose upon the agent or broker a duty to advise the insured about particular coverages.[28] The most common fact pattern is as follows: the agent or broker fails

---

[27] See Bell v. O'Leary, 744 F.2d 1370 (8th Cir. 1984); Rawlings v. Fruhwirth, 455 N.W.2d 574 (N.D. 1990) (agent has duty to exercise "skill and care which a reasonably prudent person engaged in the insurance business would use under similar circumstances.")

[28] See generally Annot., *Liability of Insurer or Agent of Insurer for Failure to Advise Insured as to Coverage Needs,* 88 A.L.R.4th 249 (1991).

to give advice or gives the wrong advice; the insured fails to obtain insurance for a particular risk on account of the improper or insufficient advice; and the insured suffers a loss of the kind for which he or she would have obtained insurance if properly advised. Agents or brokers have been held liable for such losses in some situations, notwithstanding the widespread recognition that the mere creation of a principal-agent relationship between the insured and the intermediary does not create, in and of itself, a duty to advise.[29]

Hardt v. Brink[30] is illustrative. The insured's broker had held himself out to be an expert in commercial insurance, and the insured relied on the broker to recommend coverages. Before moving a portion of his business to another location, the insured advised the broker that he would be leasing a new building. An expert witness testified that when advising a client known to be occupying premises as a lessee, a prudent insurance agent would recommend an examination of the lease in order to determine if the client were assuming potential liabilities requiring additional coverage. The insured's broker did not do this, and the insured did not obtain coverage for a fire loss that subsequently occurred. The court observed that the creation of the agency relationship did not by itself create a duty on the broker to provide advice, but that an agent could assume additional duties, including a duty to advise, either by express agreement, in which case the duty would be contractually based, or by "a holding out" of himself as an expert, in which case the duty would be grounded in tort.[31] The court held that the agent in *Hardt* breached his tort duty to advise the insured about his insurance needs, that proper advice would have resulted in the insured purchasing appropriate coverages, and that the plaintiff's uninsured loss was therefore the responsibility of the agent.[32]

Under the reasoning of *Hardt* and similar cases,[33] no duty to give advice about coverages is created simply because the insurance intermediary becomes a person's agent. This applies both to advice about what policies should be purchased[34] as well as advice about what coverage is contained in an insured's existing policy.[35] It has

---

[29] The closely-related issue of the insurer's duty to explain the policy, a duty which must necessarily be performed by agents of the insurer, is discussed in an earlier section. See § 32[c], *supra.*

[30] 192 F. Supp. 879 (W.D. Wash. 1961).

[31] 192 F. Supp. at 881.

[32] 192 F. Supp. at 882.

[33] See cases infra notes 34 and 35.

[34] See, e.g., Brant v. GEICO Gen. Ins. Co., 3 F.3d 1172 (8th Cir. 1993) (applying Iowa law); Wang v. Allstate Ins. Co., 592 A.2d 527 (N.J. 1991); Szelenyi v. Morse, Payson & Noyes Ins., 594 A.2d 1092 (Me. 1991); Nelson v. Davidson, 456 N.W.2d 343 (Wis. 1990); Farmers Ins. Co., Inc. v. McCarthy, 871 S.W.2d 82 (Mo. Ct. App. 1994); Shults v. Griffin-Rahn Ins. Agency, Inc., 550 N.E.2d 232 (Ill. App. Ct. 1990).

[35] See, e.g., Ohio Cas. Ins. Co. v. Rynearson, 507 F.2d 573 (7th Cir. 1974); Lisa's Style Shop, Inc. v. Hagen Ins. Agency, Inc., 511 N.W.2d 849 (Wis. 1994); Booska v. Hubbard Ins. Agency, Inc., 627 A.2d 333 (Vt. 1993) (mere fact that agent provided services to insured for 12 years did not create fiduciary duties, and does not create special relationship giving rise to higher duties); Carolina Production Maintenance, Inc. v. United States Fidelity and Guar. Co., 425 S.E.2d 39 (S.C. Ct. App. 1992); Shows v. Pemberton, 868 P.2d 164 (Wash. Ct. App. 1994) Kilmore v. Erie Ins. Co., 595 A.2d 623 (Pa. Super. Ct. 1991); Greenway v. Insurance Co., 241 S.E.2d 339 (N.C. Ct. App. 1978).

been held that an agent does not generally have a duty to keep informed about changes in the insured's circumstances that would bring the insured within the scope of an exclusion.[36] But accepting the responsibilities of an insurance agent is, in and of itself, at least an implied representation that the agent or broker is capable of functioning with the skill and competence that a typical, reasonable insurance agent should possess, and this imposes a duty on the agent to function at least up to that standard. An agent who fails to do so could be held liable for the resulting damages, irrespective of the amount of counseling provided the applicant or the precise nature of the agent's undertaking.[37]

Thus, whether the insured-agent relationship gives rise to more substantial duties than those inherent in any agent's relationship with his or her client turns on whether the agent or broker assumes additional responsibilities beyond those which attach to an ordinary, reasonable agent possessing normal competencies and skills.[38] An Indiana court explained the situation in this way:

> The question becomes what components establish an agent "plus" relationship. At a minimum, the insured and insurer must be engaged in a long-term relationship for the purpose of securing insurance coverage. . . . [But] it is the *nature* of the relationship, and not merely the number of years associated therewith, that triggers the duty to advise. [citation omitted] Some of the factors relevant to developing entrustment between the insured and the insurer include: exercising broad discretion to service the insured's needs; counseling the insured concerning specialized insurance coverage; holding oneself out as a highly-skilled insurance expert, coupled with the insured's reliance upon the expertise; and receiving compensation, above the customary premium paid, for expert advice provided.[39]

----

[36] See Gabrielson v. Warnemunde, 443 N.W.2d 540 (Minn. 1989).

[37] See, e.g., Gulf Coast Bdlg. Systems, Inc. v. United American Surety Co., 614 So. 2d 1360, 1365 (La. Ct. App. 1993) ("insurance broker is not a mere 'order taker ' "); Westrick v. State Farm Ins., 187 Cal. Rptr. 214 (Cal. Ct. App. 1982); Eddy v. Republic Nat'l Life Ins. Co., 290 N.W.2d 174 (Minn. 1980); Johnson v. Smith, 293 S.E.2d 644 (N.C. Ct. App. 1982).

[38] See, e.g., Dahlke v. John F. Zimmer Ins. Agency, Inc., 515 N.W.2d 767, 772 (Neb. 1994) (where provision in insured's policy that has previously been invoked is changed in subsequent policy issued same insured, agent has duty to point out and explain the change); Mullins v. Commonwealth Life Ins. Co., 839 S.W.2d 245 (Ky. 1992) (implied assumption of duty to advise may be present when insured pays agent consideration beyond premium, course of dealing exists that puts agent on notice that advice is being sought, or insured requests advice); Rawlings v. Fruhwirth, 455 N.W.2d 574 (N.D. 1990); Melin v. Johnson, 387 N.W.2d 230 (Minn. Ct. App. 1986) (where agent knows insured expects coverage, agent has duty to inform insured of policy provisions inconsistent with insured's expectation); Precision Castparts Corp. v. Johnson & Higgins, 607 P.2d 763 (Or. Ct. App. 1980) (agent who presents insured with several policies for consideration has duty to explain differences among the policies); Craven v. State Farm Mut. Auto. Ins. Co., 588 N.E.2d 1294 (Ind. Ct. App. 1992) (agent has duty to advise "only upon a showing of an intimate long term relationship between the parties or some other special circumstance.") In Iowa, it is also a prerequisite to an "expanded agency relationship" that the agent or broker receive compensation for the advice apart from the premiums paid by the insured. Sandbulte v. Farm Bureau Mut. Ins. Co., 343 N.W.2d 457 (Iowa 1984).

[39] Parker v. State Farm Mut. Auto. Ins. Co., 630 N.E.2d 567, 569-70 (Ind. Ct. App. 1994).

If the agent fails to explain a limitation in a policy's coverage but the insured would have understood the limitation if he or she had read it, does the insured's failure to read the policy insulate the agent from liability? The issue is one of causation: if insureds have a duty to read their policies and fail to do so in circumstances where the policy is clear, the agent's failure to perform a duty to explain the coverage is not the proximate cause of the loss. In *Dahlke v. John F. Zimmer Insurance Agency, Inc.,*[40] the court found that in the circumstances presented, the agent had a duty to explain to the insured that the policy's deductible had been changed from per-occurrence (and the insured had familiarity with this provision because of an earlier loss which the insurer had paid) to per-claim. But the insured had not read the policy. The court reasoned that, absent an excuse for not reading the policy, the insured's failure to read the policy provision in question will insulate the agent from liability for failing to explain the provision if the provision is clear and unambiguous.[41] In the circumstances presented, the insured's failure to read the policy that applied at the time of the occurrence was excused because the insured had not yet received a copy of the policy. The case was remanded, however, because the record did not show whether the insured had read earlier versions of the policy containing the changed deductible provision, and whether these earlier provisions were clear and unambiguous.[42] The analysis of the court in *Dahlke* is, of course, predicated on an assumption that the insured has a duty to read the policy. Although in recent years courts have been more willing to overlook any such obligation,[43] *Dahlke* reminds us that the obligation still has considerable force in some jurisdictions and may carry weight in the right circumstances in any jurisdiction.[44]

To summarize, where the agent does not expressly assume additional responsibilities or represent that he or she has special skills, the agent does not assume a duty to advise. Thus, if an agent does not agree to provide advice to the insured and if the agent does not cause the insured to reasonably believe that the insured would receive advice, the agent has no duty to advise the insured of specific exclusions or gaps in coverage; if in such a situation a loss subsequently occurs within a gap in coverage, the agent is not liable to the insured.[45] But if the agent or broker explicitly assumes additional responsibilities to the client, or has such responsibilities imposed upon him or her by virtue of special circumstances, the agent or broker may be held liable for the consequences of poor or insufficient advice.

---

40 515 N.W.2d 767 (Neb. 1994).

41 515 N.W.2d at 772.

42 515 N.W.2d at 772-73.

43 See § 32[b], *supra.*

44 See Booska v. Hubbard Ins. Agency, Inc., 627 A.2d 333, 335-6 (Vt. 1993) ("As long as the agent does the job without negligence, as between the agent and the purchaser, the task of reading and understanding the policy text is that of the purchasers.")

45 See, e.g., Polski v. Powers, 377 N.W.2d 106 (Neb. 1985).

[iii] Liability of Agents or Brokers to Insured for Failure to Procure Insurance

It is well settled that an insurance agent or broker who undertakes to procure insurance for another and fails to do so may be held liable for damages resulting from the failure to procure insurance.[46] As noted above, the insurance agent, like any professional, has a duty to use the skill of a reasonably competent agent when performing the functions of an intermediary. Accordingly, many courts have ruled that if the agent undertakes to procure insurance for the applicant, the agent assumes a duty to exercise reasonable skill, care, and diligence in the endeavor, and the breach of this duty is a tort.[47] The logic of these cases is that if the agent undertakes to procure adequate insurance for the applicant and fails to secure enough coverage in circumstances where a reasonably competent agent would have obtained adequate coverage, the agent may be liable for the damages resulting from the shoddy performance.[48] The scope of the agent's duty may depend on the extent to which the applicant advised the agent about what coverage was desired; the insured's failure to provide sufficient information may prevent finding a duty on the agent to procure the coverage.[49]

In addition to assuming a tort duty, the agent may promise to obtain insurance for the applicant, thereby creating a contract to procure insurance. The contract might be either express or implied from the circumstances.[50] To illustrate, if the applicant specifically requests that the agent obtain burglary coverage, the agent agrees to do so, and the agent fails to perform as promised, the agent may be held to have breached a contract with the insured.[51]

---

[46] See Barker v. Sauls, 345 S.E.2d 244 (S.C. 1986); Chandler v. Jones, 532 So. 2d 402 (La. Ct. App. 1988); Steward v. City of Mt. Vernon, 497 N.E.2d 939 (Ind. Ct. App. 1986); Annot., *Liability of Insurance Broker or Agent to Insured for Failure to Procure Insurance*, 64 A.L.R.3d 398 (1975). Compare Kenney Mfg. Co. v. Starkweather & Shepley, Inc., 643 A.2d 203 (R.I. 1994) (holding that no contract to procure coverage was formed between insured and broker); Flamme v. Wolf Ins. Agency, 476 N.W.2d 802 (Neb. 1991) (in absence of request by insured to obtain insurance, agency and agent cannot be held liable for failing to obtain insurance).

[47] See, e.g., Lipitz v. Washington Nat'l Ins. Co., 513 F. Supp. 606 (E.D. Pa. 1981) (tort); Riddle-Duckworth, Inc. v. Sullivan, 171 S.E.2d 486 (S.C. 1969) (tort).

[48] See Reidman Agency, Inc. v. Meaott Constr. Corp., 90 A.D.2d 963 (N.Y. Sup. Ct. 1982); Annot., *Liability of Insurance Agent or Broker on Ground of Inadequacy of Liability Insurance Coverage Procured*, 72 A.L.R.3d 704 (1976); Annot., *Liability of Insurance Agent or Broker on Ground of Inadequacy of Life, Health, and Accident Insurance Coverage Procured*, 72 A.L.R.3d 735 (1976).

[49] See Dahlke v. John F. Zimmer Ins. Agency, Inc., 515 N.W.2d 767, 770 (Neb. 1994) (agent's duty is predicated on the insured fulfilling a duty to advise the agent about what insurance is desired); Sinex v. Wallis, 611 A.2d 31, 33 (Del.Super.Ct. 1991) (applicant has duty to request a specific amount of coverage).

[50] See, e.g., Southside, Inc. v. Clark, 460 So. 2d 113 (Miss. 1984) (contract and tort); Wheaton Nat'l Bank v. Dudek, 376 N.E.2d 633 (Ill. App. Ct. 1978) (contract and tort); Marshel Investments, Inc. v. Cohen, 634 P.2d 133 (Kan.Ct.App. 1981) (contract and tort).

[51] See, e.g., National Liberty Ins. Co. v. Jones, 183 S.E. 443 (Va. 1936); Hans Coiffures Int'l, Inc. v. Hejna, 469 S.W.2d 38 (Mo. Ct. App. 1971). Because the promise to procure the

Neither the tort nor the contract theory treats the agent as an "insurer." Rather, each theory views the agent as a professional who has breached a duty to *procure* insurance.[52] Tort law does not impose a general duty to insure; thus, the tort duty to procure insurance is not derived from an obligation to insure. Rather, the tort duty is derived from the obligation which exists whenever any person undertakes to act for the benefit of another. Although an agent who undertakes to procure insurance owes a duty to the applicant to perform the undertaking in a non-negligent manner, the agent does not undertake to be the applicant's insurer.

Similarly, the agent who promises to procure insurance is not promising to be the insurer for the applicant. This point can be understood by focusing upon the definiteness requirement, a prerequisite to the enforcement of any contract. To meet this requirement, the parties to a contract to insure must at least agree upon the coverage and premium. But a contract to procure insurance can be sufficiently definite without specifying the coverage and premium; if the applicant tells the agent "get me the coverage I need" and the agent agrees to do so but thereafter does nothing, the term "coverage I need" in the particular context may be definite enough to create a legally enforceable contract to procure insurance.

Although the agent's liability to the applicant derives from breaching either a tort-based or contract-based duty to procure insurance, a few cases exist where the agent has effectively become an insurer by virtue of the breach of duty. These decisions seem tenuous because it is hard to imagine any applicant for insurance reasonably believing that the agent manifested an intent to provide the insurance himself, and it is difficult to perceive the social policy served by making agents "insurers." But courts have occasionally suggested that agents can be liable for breach of a contract to insure in appropriate circumstances. In *Anderson v. Dudley L. Moore Insurance Co.*,[53] a 1982 Tennessee case, a mobile homeowner applied with an agency, that was acting as a broker, for fire insurance on his mobile home. A representative of the agency assured the applicant that he was covered upon submission of the application, which was on the insurer's form. The agency, however, failed to mail the application to the insurer. Three months later the mobile home burned, and the insurer denied coverage because it had received no application. The court held that the agency, by failing to comply with the insurer's instructions on effecting coverage, had become the insurer of the loss. Had the court held for the applicant on the ground that the agency had failed to procure insurance, the result should have been the same: the applicant's damages would have been the losses the applicant suffered that could have been avoided by procuring insurance, and that sum would be equivalent to the amount of insurance.[54]

insurance can be performed within a year, the one-year provision of the Statute of Frauds presents no problem, even if the insurance which is sought is a multi-year policy. See Cabrini Medical Ctr. v. KM Ins. Brokers, 142 A.D.2d 529 (N.Y. Sup. Ct. 1988).

[52] See, e.g., Sroga v. Lund, 106 N.W.2d 913 (Minn. 1961); Hamacher v. Tumy, 352 P.2d 493 (Or. 1960); Stockberger v. Meridian Mut. Ins. Co., 395 N.E.2d 1272 (Ind. Ct. App. 1979).

[53] 640 S.W.2d 556 (Tenn. Ct. App. 1982).

[54] See Appleton Chinese Food Service, Inc. v. Murken Ins., Inc., 519 N.W.2d 674, 679 (Wis. Ct. App. 1994) ("Damages arising out of a broker's failure to procure insurance are commonly determined by the terms of the policy the agent failed to procure.")

Whether the breach of the duty to procure insurance is viewed as a tort or a breach of contract will make little difference in most cases. Some courts have said that the action lies in both — the plaintiff can elect the theory.[55] In most cases, the contract theory will be sufficient to provide a full and complete remedy to the applicant. When an agent promises to procure insurance for the applicant and fails to do so, a breach of contract has occurred. The contract consists of the agent's promise to procure insurance for the applicant, which is exchanged for the applicant's promise to pay a premium for the policy ultimately obtained. If the contract is breached, no damages will result unless a loss that would have been covered occurs before the applicant obtains insurance elsewhere. The damages caused by the event, up to the policy limits that would have been in effect had insurance been procured, is a foreseeable, natural consequence of the breach of contract. Awarding these damages should be adequate to make the applicant whole — or at least as whole as the applicant would be if the insurance had been procured.[56]

To establish a breach of contract, it is necessary to show only the existence of a legally enforceable promise and its nonperformance. If the applicant's action against the agent is brought in tort, it is necessary to show that the agent was negligent in failing to act as a reasonable agent would have acted in the same circumstances. In tort, the applicant will have a wider array of potential consequential damages (such as emotional distress damages) because the limit on recovering consequential damages is not as strict in tort law as it is in contract law.[57] Yet it will be a rare case where the pecuniary damages are not enough to provide a complete remedy for the applicant.

There are two aspects of the choice of tort or contract theory that could be important in some cases. First, in most states, the statute of limitations differs for contract actions and tort actions.[58] An action may be time-barred under one theory but still permitted under the other. If the applicant is allowed to elect the theory, the applicant would be able to take advantage of the longer limitations period.

Second, tort law requires a causal relationship between the breach of duty and the resulting damages. If the agent or broker breaches a duty of care owed the insured in failing to take appropriate steps to procure insurance but the coverage sought was not available from any source, it can be argued that the agent's negligence does not cause the insured's loss because no insurance could have been obtained covering the loss in question. A number of courts have accepted this argument and denied

---

[55] See Southside, Inc. v. Clark, 460 So. 2d 113 (Miss. 1984); Hursh Agency, Inc. v. Wigwam Homes, Inc., 664 P.2d 27 (Wyo. 1983); Marshel Investments, Inc. v. Cohen, 634 P.2d 133 (Kan.Ct.App. 1981).

[56] If the premium is not paid by the applicant, this amount should be deducted from the recovery, since these are expenses saved as a result of the agent's breach of contract.

[57] See Topmiller v. Cain, 657 P.2d 638 (N.M.Ct.App. 1983) (in situation where agent failed to procure homeowner's coverage and applicant's home thereafter burned, applicant entitled to recover additional consequential damages representing the interest on new financing because the bank would not lend additional money under the old financing arrangement).

[58] The contract statute of limitations is usually longer than the tort statute of limitations. 3 Am. Jur. *Trials* § 21 (1965); 3 M. Belli, *Modern Trials* § 3.3 (1982).

a recovery for the insured.[59] Other courts, however, have held that causation need not be proved, the logic presumably being that the unavailability of coverage is something which the agent or broker should have known and conveyed to the applicant or insured.[60] If the agent or broker is sued in contract for failure to keep a promise to procure insurance, the unavailabity of the coverage should not matter, since the agent promised that coverage would be procured and this promise was not kept.

In most situations, the agent only undertakes to procure insurance for the client; when the policy is obtained, the agent's obligations end. However, in some situations, the agent agrees to keep the policy in force, usually by arranging for appropriate renewals or to otherwise service the policy. If the agent makes such an agreement, the agent can be liable for failing to keep it.[61]

Closely related to the action based on the intermediary's failure to procure insurance is the situation where the agent or broker, although not having undertaken a duty to procure insurance, is unable to procure insurance and fails to notify the consumer of the inability to place the risk. An agent who undertakes to place the risk assumes at least a duty to make reasonable and prompt efforts to locate an insurer. Having made these efforts, it may be that the agent will be unable to place the insurance. If this occurs, the agent should within a reasonable time notify the consumer of the inability to place insurance so that the consumer is not misled into thinking that coverage has been obtained. The risk to the consumer from the lack of notice is that he or she will be lulled into thinking that coverage has been obtained, and thus fail to take steps to secure the coverage elsewhere. Thus, failing to inform the consumer of the inability to secure the coverage may be enough, by itself, to impose liability on the agent.[62]

[iv]   Liability for Placing Insurance with Insolvent or Unauthorized Insurer

Whether brokers can be liable for placing insurance with insolvent or unauthorized insurers is an issue that arises in connection with intermediaries who have limited authority from several companies and are able to choose with which of the companies the coverage will be placed. Obviously, if the broker secures a policy

---

[59] See, e.g., Bayly, Martin & Fay, Inc. v. Pete's Satire, Inc., 739 P.2d 239 (Colo. 1987) (en banc); Pacific Dredging Co. v. Hurley, 397 P.2d 819 (Wash. 1964); Stinson v. Cravens, Dargan & Co., 579 S.W.2d 298 (Tex. Ct. App. 1979); MacDonald v. Carpenter & Pelton, Inc., 298 N.Y.S.2d 780 (N.Y. App. Div. 1969).

[60] See, e.g., Patterson Agency, Inc. v. Turner, 372 A.2d 258 (Md.Ct.Spec.App. 1977); Hans Coiffures Int'l, Inc. v. Hejna, 469 S.W.2d 38 (Mo. Ct. App. 1971).

[61] See American Cyanamid Co. v. U.S. Fidelity and Guar. Co., 459 So. 2d 851 (Ala. 1984); Glekas v. Boss & Phelps, Inc., 437 A.2d 584 (D.C.Cir. 1981); Wright Body Works v. Columbus Interstate Ins., 210 S.E.2d 801 (Ga. 1974); Ezell v. Associates Capital Corp., 518 S.W.2d 232 (Tenn. 1974); Nelson v. Glens Falls Ins. Co., 475 S.W.2d 690 (Ark. 1972); Woodham v. Moore, 428 So. 2d 280 (Fla. Dist. Ct. App. 1983); Erica Trading Corp. v. Nathan Butwin Co. Inc., 100 Misc.2d 830 (N.Y. Sup. Ct. 1979).

[62] See Nu-Air Mfg. Co. v. Frank B. Hall & Co. of New York, 822 F.2d 987 (11th Cir. 1987); Bell v. O'Leary, 744 F.2d 1370 (8th Cir. 1984).

for the applicant from a competent, solvent insurer, the broker has discharged the duty owed the applicant.[63] Also, if the broker purchases the policy from a company that the applicant specifically requested, the broker has discharged his or her duty. In the usual case, however, the applicant does not designate a specific company, leaving the choice to the broker who the applicant presumes will protect the applicant's best interests. If the broker places the insurance with an insolvent insurer or one not authorized to do business in the applicant's state, the applicant may later look to the broker for reimbursement of the loss that the insurer cannot or will not cover.

The weight of authority holds that a broker, while not a guarantor of the solvency of an insurer with which the broker does business on his or her clients' behalf, has an obligation to use reasonable care to understand the financial soundness of insurers with which the broker chooses to place insurance on his or her clients' behalf, and not to place coverage with a company that the broker knows or should know, in the exercise of reasonable diligence, to be insolvent.[64] Yet one can fairly read these cases as imposing a relatively low standard of care on brokers, in recognition of the fact that determining the solvency of an insurance company is an extremely complicated task, one which is generally left to the regulatory function performed by state insurance departments. This reality was influential to a California court in *Wilson v. All Service Insurance Corporation,*[65] which held that an insurance broker owes no duty to his clients to investigate the financial condition of a company licensed by the State Insurance Commissioner before placing insurance with that company.[66] The court observed that brokers should not duplicate the work of insurance departments and noted that brokers, unlike insurance departments, have no power to compel insurers to divulge financial information.

Clearly, the holding in *Wilson* has limits. A broker who has knowledge of the financial difficulties of a particular company and nevertheless places insurance with that company would probably be held in breach of the duty of care owed the client. At a minimum, the agent should have a duty to ascertain that he or she is in fact dealing with a licensed company, a relatively easy thing to do. Moreover, a broker who places the insurance with a company unauthorized to do business within the state may be held liable to the applicant for breach of a duty to inquire into the status of the company.[67] Yet it should not be improper in all circumstances for a broker

---

[63] See Mayo v. American Fire & Cas. Co., 192 S.E.2d 828 (N.C. 1972).

[64] See Carter Lincoln-Mercury, Inc., Leasing Div. v. Emar Group, Inc., 638 A.2d 1288 (N.J. 1994); Williams-Berryman Ins. Co. v. Morphis, 461 S.W.2d 577 (Ark. 1971); Sternoff Metals Corp. v. Vertecs Corp., 693 P.2d 175 (Wash. Ct. App. 1984); Nidiffer v. Clinchfield R.R., 600 S.W.2d 242 (Tenn. Ct. App. 1980) (employer who undertakes to procure insurance on behalf of employee must use reasonable care to select solvent insurer).

[65] 153 Cal. Rptr. 121 (Cal. Ct. App. 1979).

[66] See also Carter Lincoln-Mercury, Inc., Leasing Div. v. Emar Group, Inc., 638 A.2d 1288 (N.J. 1994) (O'Hern, J., dissenting) (urging court to consider whether "comprehensive system of regulations" is adequate to protect insureds "before imposing a separate and independent duty that is realistically beyond the capacity of an insurance department, much less the capacity of an insurance broker in a small town.")

[67] See Lowitt v. Pearsall Chemical Corp., 219 A.2d 67 (Md. 1966); Gerald v. Universal Agency, Inc., 153 A.2d 359 (N.J. Super. Ct. App. Div. 1959).

to place insurance with unlicensed companies, such as insurance companies that are established outside the United States. However, if an unusual extraterritorial company is considered, the applicant should be involved in the choice and the broker should contemplate the possibility of being subjected to a duty to inquire into the financial status of the company.

[v]   An Aside on the Duty to Procure: Obligations of Those Outside the Insurance Business to Procure Insurance

An issue that has arisen in some settings, although not technically an insurance law question, is whether one party has a duty to procure insurance for the benefit of another party simply because of his or her relationship to that party. For example, if one party promises in a contract to procure insurance for another, the first party has a contract duty, and whether that duty is performed will be measured by the usual rules of contract law. A more interesting question is whether in some situations the relationship of one party to another will create a tort duty pursuant to which one party must procure insurance for another. For example, it is common knowledge that a certain number of high school and collegiate football players will suffer serious injuries each year, and some of these injuries (particularly injuries to the neck and spinal cord), though few relative to the total number of high school and collegiate football players in the nation, will be serious and permanently disabling. Obviously, it would be negligence for a high school to send players onto the field for a contact scrimmage without providing the players with helmets. The question asked in at least a couple of cases is whether it is no less negligent for a high school to send players into contact scrimmages without providing them with first-party insurance for catastrophic, disabling injuries, under the reasoning that insurance for a football player is "equipment" no less important than a helmet.

In the football player example, two courts that have addressed the issue have held that the school does not owe a tort duty to its players to procure first-party insurance for the players' benefit.[68] In the Illinois decision, plaintiff conceded that the Board of Education "had no duty at all to furnish or arrange for the purchase of insurance for the plaintiff."[69] Instead, it was plaintiff's argument that the Board, by collecting a fee to help pay for the expense of medical treatment for injuries, had assumed a tort duty to provide adequate disability insurance. The court was concerned about what constitutes "adequate" insurance, indicating that the test for determining whether the Board had performed its duty would be "purely subjective."[70] Cases involving a broker's duty to procure insurance for a prospective insured were explicitly distinguished under the reasoning that those cases involve a professional care obligation.[71] The reasoning of the Kansas court was similar, except the defendant in the Kansas case was a private school. The Kansas Supreme Court cited "public policy considerations that forbid this court from imposing upon a private school a greater duty than that imposed by the legislature on the public schools."

---

[68] See Wicina v. Strecker, 747 P.2d 167 (Kan. 1987); Friederich v. Board of Educ. of Community Unit Sch. Dist. # 304, Carroll Cty., 375 N.E.2d 141 (Ill. App. Ct. 1978).

[69] 375 N.E.2d at 143.

[70] 375 N.E.2d at 144.

[71] 375 N.E.2d at 144.

because public schools had no duty to purchase disability insurance for football players, the private school had no such duty either.[72]

These two cases are reasonable decisions, even if the results are somewhat unsettling. If a tort duty to procure insurance is imposed on schools, where does the duty end? There is, as was mentioned in the Illinois decision, the question of how much insurance to purchase. In addition, with respect to what other sports does a school have a duty to procure insurance? Football is clearly the most injurious of all amateur sports that are common in high schools and colleges, but other sports also have a risk of serious injury, as anyone who has participated in lacrosse, hockey, gymnastics, diving, basketball, or even soccer can attest. Must insurance be purchased for participants in these sports, too? Moreover, who should purchase the insurance? One might reason that the obligation to insure against injury belongs to the athlete, i.e., that person's family, which if concerned about the risk should purchase ample first-party health and disability insurance. If the costs are borne by the participants rather than the school which sponsors the activity, the individual players can decide whether they wish to participate in the activity, given the risks and costs of insuring the risks. Putting the cost on the school may spread the cost across the school's entire budget (or all tuition-paying students in a private school), but if the insurance is too expensive for the school's budget, an inefficient outcome — no sport will be played even though there are some who would play it without insurance given their own assessment that the risk of injury is low — might occur.

In settings not involving insurance professionals where the duty to procure issue has been raised, courts have been very reluctant to impose a duty. Thus, absent a contract obligation to the contrary, a mortgagee is not obligated to purchase insurance for the benefit of the mortgagor and mortgagee,[73] and an employer need not maintain liability insurance for the benefit of its employees.[74]

If there is something unsettling about the result in the football example, it probably extends from the suggestion that began this discussion — that a school should no more send players onto the field without helmets than it should fail to take steps to alleviate the effects of devastating injuries, which everyone knows will occur every year. But if the judgment that one should take responsibility to protect oneself against harm rather than rely on the sponsoring organization to do so trumps this observation, it may be, then, that the duty which exists, if at all, is for the school to advise its participants about the risks of the activity and what kinds of things the participants may wish to do themselves (e.g., purchase insurance) to guard against these risks. At the bottom line, the heart of the issue is how our society will choose to deal with the economic effects of accidental injuries; if our society had better ways to compensate the group of people who suffer accidental injuries of all kinds, there would be less reason even to ask whether a party, like a school, has a duty to procure insurance for the benefit of students.

---

[72] 747 P.2d at 173.

[73] See, e.g., Valle De Oro Bank v. Gamboa, 23 Cal. Rptr.2d 329 (Cal. Ct. App. 1994); Brown v. C & S Real Estate Services, Inc., 445 S.E.2d 463 (S.C. Ct. App. 1994).

[74] See, e.g., Couillard v. Pick, 493 N.E.2d 865 (Mass. 1986).

[3] Liability of Agent or Broker to Third Party

In a few cases, courts have held an agent liable to third parties who would have benefitted had the agent performed the obligation to procure insurance for the insured. In a California case, a permissive user of an automobile incurred a liability while operating the owner's vehicle, but the owner lacked insurance. The permissive user recovered from the owner's agent on the theory that the agent was negligent in failing to renew the coverage.[75] A similar result was reached in a Georgia case, where the agent was held liable to an injured employee because the agent negligently failed to procure worker's compensation coverage or otherwise qualify the employer as a self-insurer.[76] In the foregoing cases, the theory of recovery sounds in tort: the agent undertakes a duty to an applicant; if this duty is negligently performed, it is a foreseeable consequence of the breach of the duty that third parties might be injured.

An alternative theory of recovery looks to contract law's scheme of third-party beneficiary rights. If two parties contract intending to benefit a third party, the third party may be able to enforce the contract even though that party is not in privity with either of the contracting parties. In a Wisconsin case, the court refused to dismiss a complaint brought by the owner of a building and some equipment that were destroyed by fire to recover under an insurance policy, even though the owner was not listed as an insured on the policy. The owner's theory was that he was a third-party beneficiary of an oral contract between the lessee of the premises and the insurance agency to procure fire insurance for the premises.[77]

There are additional considerations when the person claiming third party rights is the victim of an accident: can the third party recover against the tortfeasor's agent for failure to provide adequate liability coverage to the tortfeasor? On the one hand, it could be argued that liability insurance is purchased for the benefit of third parties.[78] However, most courts have concluded that a general liability insurance policy does not make the injured party a third-party beneficiary, in that there is no intent to benefit a particular third party at the time the insurance is purchased.[79] But many courts adhering to the majority view will recognize third-party rights if a statute mandates that liability insurance be purchased. Financial responsibility statutes are intended in large measure to assure that victims of torts will have a remedy; thus, liability insurance compelled by these statutes are arguably for the benefit of third parties, and an agent who fails to procure such insurance for an individual who later injures a third party may be liable to that third party.[80]

---

[75] See Mid-Century Ins. Co. v. Hutsel, 89 Cal. Rptr. 421 (Cal. Ct. App. 1970) (agent liable up to limits of the policy he agreed to procure).

[76] Crawford v. Holt, 323 S.E.2d 245 (Ga. Ct. App. 1984). To the same effect is Robinson v. John E. Hunt & Associates, Inc., 490 So. 2d 1291 (Fla. Dist. Ct. App. 1986).

[77] See Pappas v. Jack O.A. Nelson Agency, Inc., 260 N.W.2d 721 (Wis. 1978).

[78] See Eschle v. Eastern Freight Ways, Inc., 319 A.2d 786 (N.J. Super. Ct. App. Div. 1974); Gothberg v. Nemerovski, 208 N.E.2d 12 (Ill.App. 1965).

[79] See Mercado v. Mitchell, 264 N.W.2d 532 (Wis. 1978).

[80] See, e.g., Flattery v. Gregory, 489 N.E.2d 1257 (Mass. 1986) (plaintiff-victim of accident held entitled to recover from agent on third-party beneficiary theory for compulsory coverages, but not entitled to recovery under tort theory for negligent failure to obtain optional

[4] Liability of Insurer to Agent or Broker for Damages Caused by Insurer's Nonpayment of Proceeds

When an agent or broker is sued for failure to procure the correct coverage, failure to advise about coverage, or similar claims, it is possible that the precipitating event for the suit is an insurer's denial of coverage for a claim on the ground that the policy issued to the insured does not cover the loss in question. In some recent cases, the issue has arisen as to whether the insurer, which has refused to pay policy proceeds to an insured or has denied coverage, is liable to an agent or broker for the damages caused the agent or broker as a result of the nonpayment or denial.[81] For example, suppose an agent secures for the applicant a policy issued by an insurer. The insurer later unjustifiably denies a claim, and the insured sues both the insurer and the agent. In the suit, the insurer is held liable for the claim, but the agent is found to have breached no duty. Yet the insurer's breach caused the agent to incur expenses in the defense of a claim on which the agent was later vindicated (this defense would in the ordinary case be provided by the agent's errors and omissions liability insurer). In these circumstances, it is arguably appropriate for the insurer to indemnify the agent for its expenses, whether or not there is a specific indemnity contract between the insurer and the agent.[82]

A threshold question in such circumstances is identifying the source of the insurer's duty, owed to the agent or broker, to provide indemnity. If there is a contract between agent and insurer, the duty to indemnify might be expressly stated therein; if not, the duty might be considered an implied term of that contract.[83] In the absence of a contract, the duty to indemnify comes from the common law of agency. *Restatement (Second) of Agency* § 438(2) provides: "In the absence of terms to the contrary in the agreement of employment, the principal has a duty to indemnify the agent where the agent . . . (b) suffers a loss which, because of their relation, it is fair that the principal should bear." This concept receives elaboration in section 439: "Unless otherwise agreed, a principal is subject to a duty to exonerate an agent who is not barred by the illegality of his conduct to indemnify him for: . . . (d) expenses of defending actions by third persons brought because of the agent's unauthorized conduct, such actions being unfounded but not brought in bad faith . . . ."

Because it is foreseeable that an agent or broker could be damaged by the insurer's failure to perform its obligations to insureds, application of these common law principles to require the insurer's indemnification of the agent or broker in

---

coverages); Mercado v. Mitchell, 264 N.W.2d 532 (Wis. 1978); see generally Annot., *Liability of Tortfeasor's Insurance Agent or Broker to Injured Party for Failure to Procure or Maintain Liability Insurance,* 72 A.L.R.4th 1095 (1989).

[81] See generally Annot., *Insurer's Liability to Insurance Agent or Broker for Damages Suffered As Result of Insurer's Denial of Coverage Or Refusal To Pay Policy Proceeds to Insured,* 6 A.L.R.5th 611 (1992).

[82] See, e.g., Mutual Life Ins. Co. v. Estate of Wesson, 517 So. 2d 521 (Miss.), cert. denied, 486 U.S. 1043 (1987); Southern Farm Bur. Cas. Ins. Co. v. Gooding, 565 S.W.2d 421 (Ark. 1978).

[83] See *Restatement (Second) of Agency* § 438(1) ("A principal is under a duty to indemnify the agent in accordance with the terms of the agreement with him.")

appropriate circumstances is proper. An example of an inappropriate circumstance for requiring the insurer's indemnity of the agent or broker is where the agent's negligence or unauthorized conduct within the scope of apparent authority causes the insurer's liability.[84] This principle is part of the common law of agency, which relieves the principal from an indemnity obligation where the loss or harm arises from "the performance of unauthorized acts" or results "solely from the agent's negligence or other fault."[85]

[g]   Ability of Intermediary to Bind Insurer

Under general agency law principles, an insurer will not be liable for losses where the agent lacked authority, either actual or apparent, to bind the insurer. However, the insurer will be bound by agents acting within the scope of their authority.[86] For example, a soliciting agent is the insurer's agent, but a soliciting agent's authority is limited. Such an agent is usually only authorized to solicit insurance and submit applications; the agent has no authority to bind the insurer, and the insurer will not be bound by the agent's unauthorized acts.[87]

Two caveats are important, however. If conduct of the insurer led the person dealing with the agent to assume that the agent had authority to bind the insurer, the agent will be clothed with apparent authority and the insurer will be bound. Several cases have considered the question of whether an insurer, having sent a valid cancellation notice to the insured, is bound by the agent's representation to the insured that the cancellation is of no effect. Numerous courts have said that the insurer is not bound by the agent's representation on the ground that the agent lacked actual authority to alter the effect of the cancellation notice.[88] Those courts which have held for the insured have usually done so on the ground that the agent had apparent authority to revoke the cancellation.[89] Also, courts construe liberally the scope of the agent's actual authority; ambiguities are very likely to be construed against the insurer.

The following subsections discuss some of the common issues and fact patterns where it is claimed that the conduct of an intermediary has bound the insurer.

---

[84] See, e.g., Nelson v. Glens Falls Ins. Co., 475 S.W.2d 690 (Ark. 1972); INA Ins. Co. v. Valley Forge Ins. Co., 722 P.2d 975 (Ariz. Ct. App. 1986).

[85] *Restatement (Second) of Agency* § 440(a).

[86] See Pacific Mut. Life Ins. Co. v. Haslip, 111 S.Ct. 1032 (1991); Tynes v. Bankers Life Co., 730 P.2d 1115 (Mont. 1986); Coolman v. Trans World Life Ins. Co., 482 So. 2d 979 (La. Ct. App. 1986); Royal Ins. Co. v. Alliance Ins. Co., 690 S.W.2d 541 (Tenn. Ct. App. 1985).

[87] See, e.g., Meier v. New Jersey Life Ins. Co., 503 A.2d 862 (N.J. 1986); American Nat'l Ins. Co. v. Montgomery, 640 S.W.2d 346 (Tex. Ct. App. 1982).

[88] See, e.g., Mid-Century Ins. Co. v. Norgaard, 273 N.E.2d 191 (S.D. 1979); Hartford Acc. & Indem. Co. v. Estate of Ball, 387 N.Y.S.2d 462 (N.Y. App. Div. 1976).

[89] See, e.g., Hodge v. Allstate Ins. Co., 546 A.2d 1078 (N.H. 1988); Riverside Ins. Co. v. Parker, 375 S.W.2d 225 (Ark. 1964). See generally Annot., *Insurance Agent's Statement or Conduct Indicating That Insurer's Cancellation of Policy Shall Not Take Effect as Binding on Insurer*, 3 A.L.R.3d 1135 (1965).

[1] Power of Intermediary to Contract on Insurer's Behalf

An agent may be authorized to enter into contracts on the insurer's behalf. This kind of authority is, of course, broader than the authority to submit applications to the insurer, to issue and deliver policies regarding risks which the company has decided to underwrite, to collect premiums, or to cancel policies at the direction of the company. In property, liability, and marine insurance, it is more common for the insurer to cloak its agents with the authority to enter into binding contracts in the field.[90] If the agent has the authority to enter into a written contract on the company's behalf, the agent probably possesses the authority to enter into oral contracts binding the company. The agent who can enter into contracts for the company is also likely to have the authority to renew existing contracts.

General principles of agency law provide that an agent is not personally liable to a third party if, with authority to do so, the agent secures a binding contract between the agent's disclosed principal and the third party. The duty to perform the contract is owed by the principal to the third party, not by the agent. Therefore, an insurance agent acting on behalf of and within the authority granted by a disclosed insurer can have no liability to the third party, assuming the contract secured by the agent conforms with whatever coverage the agent may have promised to procure.[91] If the policy does not conform with what the agent and the insured agreed would be secured, or if the agent were negligent in trying to procure such policy, the agent might be held personally liable for the damages caused by the failure to secure the agreed-upon policy.[92]

Different rules exist where the agent is working on behalf of an undisclosed principal. The agent who makes a contract for an undisclosed principal will be personally liable on the contract. Under this rule, an agent who makes a contract with an insured without revealing the insurer's identity is personally liable on the contract.[93]

A number of cases have considered the question of what steps a broker, who has been granted limited authority from several companies to place insurance with each of those companies, must take in order to bind a company. The typical fact pattern involves a broker being directed by an applicant to obtain insurance (the applicant does not designate any particular carrier), the broker commences but never completes the process of placing the insurance with a particular carrier, a loss occurs, and the insurer (in this instance, the particular carrier that the broker identified for receipt of the application) denies coverage on the ground that no contract was ever

---

[90] See, e.g., Gulbrandson v. Empire Mut. Ins. Co., 87 N.W.2d 850 (Minn. 1958) (hail insurance).

[91] See, e.g., Ledoux v. Old Republic Life Ins. Co., 233 So. 2d 731 (La. Ct. App. 1970); Walker v. Home Indem. Co., 302 P.2d 361 (Cal. Ct. App. 1956).

[92] See, e.g., Crump v. Geer Bros., Inc. 336 So. 2d 1091 (Ala. 1976); Wright Body Works, Inc. v. Columbus Interstate Ins. Agency, 210 S.E.2d 801 (Ga. 1974) (subject of annotation beginning at 72 A.L.R.3d 743 (1976)).

[93] See, e.g., Keller Lorenz Co., Inc. v. Insurance Associates Corp., 570 P.2d 1366 (Idaho 1977); Norswing v. Lakeland Flying Service, Inc., 237 P.2d 586 (Or. 1951); Annes v. Carolan-Graham-Hoffman, Inc., 168 N.E. 637 (Ill. 1929).

formed. The broker may have an undisclosed intention to place the insurance with a particular company, but the general rule is that in the absence of some act indicating that the insurance is about to be placed with a particular company, no insurance contract exists.[94]

[2] Ability of Intermediary to Modify or Alter Coverage

If an agent has the actual or apparent power to enter into a contract of insurance, the agent, absent an express limitation on his or her authority, also has the power to modify or alter existing policies and to waive policy provisions. Such modifications, alterations, and waivers are binding on the insurer in the absence of fraud or collusion between the agent and the applicant.[95] Insurers, however, often seek to place express limitations on the authority of agents to modify or alter coverage. This occurs through limitations placed either in the application or the policy language. The issues raised by these limitations are discussed in a later subsection.[96]

Usually, an agent will have no actual authority to fix or change premium rates. However, an agent may have apparent authority to make binding representations as to the amount of premiums and the time for their payment, and the agent's exercise of this apparent authority can be binding on the insurer.

If the agent is acting within the scope of actual authority, an interpretation of the policy is binding on the insurer. A statement in the policy that an agent cannot alter the terms of the policy does not prevent the agent from making binding interpretations of doubtful language.[97] Moreover, courts that recognize an agent's ability to waive policy terms can label an agent's interpretation of doubtful language as a waiver, which has the effect of making a particular construction of a policy's language unavailable to the insurer.

If the agent acts outside the scope of actual authority and modifies or alters contract language without the insurer's approval, the insurer is not without recourse. An insurer is likely to secure an agreement from each of its agents promising to reimburse the insurer for loss the insurer suffers by virtue of the agent acting outside actual authority. These agreements are enforceable. The agent will in turn purchase errors and omission coverage (in essence, liability insurance that pays for loss caused third parties, including the insurer, as a result of the agent's errors or omissions) that protects the agent from being required to reimburse the insurer out of personal assets for any loss the agent negligently causes the insurer to suffer.

[3] Effect of Misstatements on Application Prepared by Agent

Most courts have held that an agent who procures an application for insurance and reduces it to writing acts as the insurer's agent. Thus, the errors or misstatements of the agent when filling out the application are usually treated as the company's,

---

[94] See Maryland Cas. Co. v. Foster, 414 P.2d 672 (N.M. 1966).

[95] See, e.g., Security Ins. Co. v. Greer, 437 P.2d 243 (Okla. 1968); Investors Heritage Life Ins. Co. v. Colson, 717 S.W.2d 840 (Ky. Ct. App. 1986); All American Assur. Co. v. Brown, 339 S.E.2d 611 (Ga. Ct. App. 1985).

[96] See § 35[g], *infra.*

[97] See, e.g., Bayer v. Lutheran Mut. Life Ins. Co., 172 N.W.2d 400 (Neb. 1969); Michigan Mut. Liab. Co. v. Hoover Bros., Inc., 237 N.E.2d 754 (Ill. App. Ct. 1968).

not the applicant's, errors. As stated by one court, "the insurer cannot rely on incorrectly recorded answers known to the insured where the incorrect answers are entered pursuant to the agent's advice, suggestion or interpretation."[98] Similarly, if the agent misrepresents a fact to the applicant, such representation binds the insurer. The applicant, however, is not bound by the agent's misrepresentation to the insurer unless the applicant has knowledge of the misrepresentation or has otherwise participated in making it.[99] This is subject to one caveat: the applicant cannot escape the effect of the incorrect statements if the jurisdiction imposes on the applicant a duty to read the application and binds the applicant to the literal language of the application if it is not read.[100] Similarly, if the insured is sent a copy of the policy with the application attached, it has been held that the insured has an opportunity and hence a duty to read the application and correct any misrepresentations on it. Uncorrected misrepresentations are deemed ratified by the insured, and hence available to the insurer seeking to invalidate the coverage.[101]

[4] Legal Effect of Limitations on Powers in Application or Policy

Under basic principles of agency law, if parties dealing with an agent know the extent of the agent's authority, those parties cannot later claim the benefit of acts or statements exceeding the agent's authority. Thus, if an insurance agent discloses the limitations of his or her authority to the person with whom the agent is dealing, that person cannot later claim that the agent bound the insurer by virtue of acts in excess of the disclosed authority. (By the same token, limitations on an agent's authority not disclosed to the applicant cannot be used to invalidate a contract that the agent had apparent authority to make.) Insurers seeking to take advantage of this general principle of agency law often insert statements in the application or the policy which purport to limit the authority of the insurer's agents. Many courts have held that such language, if sufficient to put a reasonable person on notice of limitations in the agent's authority, prevents the prospective insured from binding the insurer to commitments exceeding the agent's actual authority.[102] Some courts have applied an even stricter standard with regard to applications, holding that the insured is presumed to know the limitations upon the power of an agent that are

---

[98] Stewart v. Mutual of Omaha Ins. Co., 817 P.2d 44, 53 (Ariz. Ct. App. 1991).

[99] See, e.g., Bristol v. Commercial Union Life Ins. Co. of Am., 560 A.2d 460, 464 (Conn. 1989); Reserve Life Ins. Co. v. Meeks, 174 S.E.2d 585 (Ga. Ct. App. 1970); Saunders v. Allstate Ins. Co., 151 N.E.2d 1 (Ohio 1958); Atlas Life Ins. Co. v. Eastman, 320 P.2d 397 (Okla. 1957).

[100] See, e.g., Jones v. New York Life & Annuity Corp., 985 F.2d 503 (10th Cir. 1993), appeal after remand, 61 F.3d 799 (10th Cir. 1995); Manz v. Continental Am. Life Ins. co., 849 P.2d 549 (Or. Ct. App. 1993); Small v. Prudential Life Ins. Co., 617 N.E.2d 80 (Ill. App. Ct. 1993).

[101] See Strother v. Capitol Bankers Life Ins. Co., 842 P.2d 504 (Wash. Ct. App. 1992); Hidary v. Maccabees Life Ins. Co., 591 N.Y.S.2d 706 (N.Y. App. Div. 1992).

[102] See, e.g., Gannaway v. Standard Accident Ins. Co., 85 F.2d 144 (10th Cir. 1936); Broughton v. Dona, 475 N.Y.S.2d 595 (N.Y. App. Div. 1984); Van Dyne v. Fidelity-Phenix Ins. Co., 244 N.E.2d 752 (Ohio Ct.App. 1969); Bailey v. Life & Cas. Ins. Co. of Tenn., 250 S.W.2d 99 (Tenn. Ct. App. 1951); Prudential Ins. Co. of Am. v. Lampley, 180 S.W.2d 399 (Ky. 1944); Jones v. New York Life Ins. Co., 253 P. 200 (Utah 1926).

set forth in the application, even if the insured did not read the application.[103] These pro-insurer results are is premised on the notion that the insurance contract itself, whether or not read, is absolutely binding, and the insured has no right to claim that the agent bound the insurer through acts in excess of the agent's stated authority.

As one might expect, however, insurers do not always prevail in these cases, particularly where the circumstances suggest that the insured did not receive ample notice of limitations on the agent's authority. In such cases, insurers have been held bound by agents' representations.[104] Even in the older decisions, courts did not strictly adhere to the rule that limitations on the authority of agents set forth in the policy or the application are absolutely binding.[105] A distinction between statements of the agent affecting the scope of coverage and statements or acts of the agent occurring in the mechanics of claims processing was recognized; the logic was that a limitation in the policy could only affect the agent's authority with respect to coverage, not the agent's authority with respect to processing claims.

More recently, many courts have held that an agent with authority to write and issue policies and to make modifications in policies without the prior approval of the insurer has the ability to waive a provision in the policy orally, notwithstanding a provision in the policy that no modification shall be valid unless in writing.[106] The reasoning of these courts recognizes that if the agent has apparent authority to modify policy language, this authority should extend to the clause that purports to limit the ability of the agent to modify the policy. Obviously, much depends on the circumstances of the particular case.

Other recent decisions treat limitations in the policy on the authority of agents to bind the insurer as ineffective until the contract of insurance is formed and the policy delivered to the insured. According to these courts, it is unfair to presume that the insured had notice of the limitations before receiving the policy. Unless the insured actually knew of the limitations before the contract of insurance was formed and the policy delivered, the insured should not be bound to unread limitations stated in the policy.[107]

Still other courts refuse to enforce a limitation in the policy on the agent's authority if the insured lacks knowledge of the limitation and if the agent has apparent

---

[103] See, e.g., Braman v. Mutual Life Ins. Co., 73 F.2d 391 (8th Cir. 1934); Metropolitan Life Ins. Co. v. Tannenbaum, 240 S.W.2d 566 (Ky. 1951); Poeppelmeyer v. Shelter Life Ins. Co., 688 S.W.2d 48 (Mo. Ct. App. 1985); Anderson v. Continental Assur. Co., 666 P.2d 245 (OkLa. Ct. App. 1983).

[104] See, e.g., Broidy v. State Mut. Life Assur. Co., 186 F.2d 490 (2d Cir. 1951); Protective Life Ins. Co. v. Atkins, 389 So. 2d 117 (Ala. 1980).

[105] See, e.g., Home Ins. Co. v. Hightower, 22 F.2d 882 (5th Cir. 1927), cert. denied, 276 U.S. 634 (1928); Enfantino v. United States Fire Ins. Co., 3 P.2d 331 (Cal. Ct. App. 1931).

[106] See, e.g., Jackson Nat'l Life Ins. Co. v. Receconi, 827 P.2d 118, 128-29 (N.M. 1992); Van Dyne v. Fidelity-Phenix Ins. Co., 244 N.E.2d 752 (Ohio Ct.App. 1969); Martin v. Argonaut Ins. Co., 434 P.2d 103 (Idaho 1967); Thomas v. Union Fidelity Life Ins. Co., 308 S.E.2d 609 (Ga. Ct. App. 1983), aff'd, 312 S.E.2d 333 (Ga. 1984).

[107] See, e.g., McKinney v. Providence Washington Ins. Co., 109 S.E.2d 480 (W.Va. 1959); Reserve Life Ins. Co. v. Beardin, 101 S.E.2d 120 (Ga. Ct. App. 1957), aff'd, 102 S.E.2d 494 (Ga. 1958).

authority to do what the policy purports to preclude. If the agent has apparent authority exceeding the actual authority as set forth in the policy, the agent who acts within the scope of such apparent authority will bind the insurer, and the insurer will be estopped from relying on the policy's provisions.[108] The rationale for these decisions is that if the insurer has cloaked the agent with apparent authority, the insurer by contract stipulation cannot change agency law in a way that relieves itself from liability for the acts of its agents.

When the cases rejecting limitations set forth by the insurer in the application or policy are viewed cumulatively, it is apparent that insurers seeking to limit the authority of their agents through language in the application or policy have no guarantee that liability for the unauthorized acts of their agents will be avoided.

[5] Effect of Giving Notice to Intermediary

It is well settled that notice to an insurer's agent or knowledge obtained by the agent while acting within the scope of the agent's authority is considered notice to and knowledge of the insurer.[109] If at the time a policy is issued the insurer's agent has knowledge of a fact constituting a violation of the policy, the insurer will be estopped to assert such fact by way of claiming the policy's invalidity.[110]

Similarly, after a loss occurs, notice and proof of loss given to an authorized agent of the insurer discharges the insured's duties under the policy.[111] Just as an agent can waive certain policy provisions, an agent can waive defects in the manner by which the insured has attempted to satisfy the notice of loss and proof of loss provisions.

Since a broker is the insured's agent, notice to a broker does not constitute notice to the insurer, unless the insurer, either actually or apparently, has given the broker the authority to receive notices on the insurer's behalf.

§ 36 Conflict of Laws

Contract disputes do not raise conflict of law questions as frequently as other subjects, largely because contract law tends to be uniform throughout the country.[1] However, in insurance law, jurisdictions often differ in both statutory and decisional

---

[108] See, e.g., Pearce v. American Defender Life Ins. Co., 343 S.E.2d 174 (N.C. 1986); Blair v. National Reserve Ins. Co., 199 N.E. 337 (Mass. 1936); Mayfield v. North River Ins. Co., 239 N.W. 197 (Neb. 1931); Hood v. Millers' Mut. Ins. Ass'n, 578 S.W.2d 605 (Mo. Ct. App. 1979).

[109] See, e.g., Olszak v. Peerless Ins. Co., 406 A.2d 711 (N.H. 1979); Rocky Mountain Fire & Cas. Co. v. Rose, 385 P.2d 45 (Wash. 1963).

[110] See, e.g., Commercial Standard Ins. Co. v. Remer, 119 F.2d 66 (10th Cir. 1941); Gilcreast v. Providential Life Ins. Co., 683 S.W.2d 942 (Ark.Ct.App. 1985); All American Assur. Co. v. Brown, 339 S.E.2d 611 (Ga. Ct. App. 1985).

[111] See, e.g., Wendel v. Swanberg, 185 N.W.2d 348 (Mich. 1971); Century Indem. Co. v. United States Cas. Co., 306 F.2d 956 (5th Cir. 1962).

[1] William M. Richman & William L. Reynolds, *Understanding Conflict of Laws* § 85, at 253 (2d ed. 1993).

law, which sometimes makes it necessary to determine which state's law applies to an insurance transaction.[2]

Under the first *Restatement of Conflicts,* the place where the contract was made provided the governing law.[3] Under general contract rules, a contract is formed at the place the acceptance is dispatched. The *Restatement (Second) of Conflicts* specifically recognizes the authority of the parties to choose the applicable law; absent such a choice, the *Restatement (Second)* lists some presumptive rules for certain kinds of contracts. For life insurance contracts, the *Restatement (Second)* states that the controlling law is the "local law of the state where the insured was domiciled at the time the policy was applied for, unless, with respect to the particular issue, some other state has a more significant relationship" to the transaction and the parties.[4] For fire, surety, and casualty insurance, the *Restatement (Second)* states that the controlling law is the "local law of the state which the parties understood was to be the principal location of the insured risk during the term of the policy, unless with respect to the particular issue, some other state has a more significant relationship" to the transaction and the parties.[5] With respect to automobile liability policies, for example, the place where the vehicle is garaged is typically viewed as the place where the risk is located, making the law of that location applicable.[6] The "significant relationship" standard, which can override the presumptive rule, identifies several factors relevant to the choice of law determination, including the place of contracting, the place of negotiation of the contract, place of contract performance, and the domicile, residence, place of incorporation, and place of business of the parties.[7]

A number of courts have used the factors listed in the *Restatement (Second)* to resolve the conflict of law question, and have applied a "significant relationship" or "substantial relationship" test in lieu of a test that establishes as a presumptive choice the law the jurisdiction where the insured risk is located.[8] A prominent

---

[2] For further discussion, see Frederick J. Pomerantz & Sarah D. Strum, *Choice of Law Provisions in Reinsurance Agreements,* 29 Tort & Ins. L. J. 158 (1993); Annot., *Conflict of Laws in Determination of Coverage Under Automobile Liability Insurance Policy,* 20 A.L.R.4th 738 (1983).

[3] Richman & Reynolds, note 1, *supra,* § 65 at 177.

[4] *Restatement (Second) of Conflicts* § 192 (1980). The presumptive rule applies only to insurance issued to the applicant who seeks coverage on his or her own life. *Id.,* comment a. As for group life, the presumptive law is that which governs the master policy. Absent a choice of law, this will usually be the law of the place where the employer has its business. *Id.,* comment h.

[5] *Restatement (Second) of Conflicts* § 193 (1980).

[6] See, e.g., Jepson v. General Cas. Co. of Wisconsin, 513 N.W.2d 467 (Minn. 1994); Amica Mut. Ins. Co. v. Bourgault, 429 S.E.2d 908 (Ga. 1993); Nadler v. Liberty Mut. Fire Ins. Co., 424 S.E.2d 256 (W.Va. 1992); Ward v. Nationwide Mut. Auto. Ins. Co., 614 A.2d 85 (Md. 1992).

[7] *Restatement (Second) of Conflicts* § 188 (1980).

[8] See, e.g., Williams v. United Services Auto. Ass'n, 849 P.2d 265 (Nev. 1993); Van Vonno v. Hertz Corp., 841 P.2d 1244 (Wash. 1992); American Home Assur. Co. v. Safway Steel Products Co., Inc., 743 S.W.2d 693 (Tex. Ct. App. 1987); Walker v. State Farm Mut. Auto. Ins. Co., 973 F.2d 634 (8th Cir. 1992) (applying Iowa law).

example of a state's "significant relationship" trumping the presumptive choice-of-law rule are those cases where a pollutant comes to rest in the state which has been selected as the forum even though the pollutant was manufactured and the insurance contract was formed elsewhere. The reasoning of these cases is that the forum state has a substantial interest in how the coverage questions are decided when the pollutant is causing damage in that jurisdiction.[9]

The evolution of choice of law principles in the two *Restatements* has caused choice of law rules followed in the states to diverge.[10] If the insurance contract specifies the governing law, this designation is usually enforced.[11] In the absence of an effective designation, in most cases the law of the place where the contract was made is applied to construe and test the validity of the insurance policy.[12] To determine this location, some courts search for the "last essential act" needed to form the contract, which is typically the acceptance of the policy; the location of this act is deemed controlling.[13] Some courts favor the place of issuance of the policy,[14] while other courts favor the place of the policy's delivery.[15]

There is, however, authority in some jurisdictions for tests other than the place of contracting. In New York, for example, courts analyze the policies of the states that are promoted by the conflicting state rules and evaluate the "grouping of contacts" between the competing jurisdictions.[16] This approach favors the law of the jurisdiction most closely concerned with the outcome of the litigation, although recently this test has more closely resembled the "substantial relationship" test of

---

[9] See Gilbert Spruance Co. v. Pennsylvania Mfrs. Ass'n Ins. Co.,603 A.2d 61 (N.J. Super. Ct. App. Div. 1992); Joy Technologies, Inc. v. Liberty Mut. Ins. Co., 421 S.E.2d 493 (W.Va. 1992).

[10] See Diamond International Corp. v. Allstate Ins. Co., 712 F.2d 1498 (1st Cir. 1983).

[11] See, e.g., Ins. Co. of N. Am. v. English, 395 F.2d 854 (5th Cir. 1968); Prudential Ins. Co. v. O'Grady, 396 P.2d 246 (Ariz. 1964); Swanberg v. Mutual Benefit Life Ins. Co., 398 N.E.2d 299 (Ill. App. Ct. 1979).

[12] See, e.g., Jaramillo v. Mercury Ins. Co., 494 N.W.2d 335 (Neb. 1993); Fried v. North River Ins. Co., 710 F.2d 1022 (4th Cir. 1983); Melick v. Stanley, 416 A.2d 415 (N.J. Super. Ct. App. Div. 11980), *aff'd*, 436 A.2d 954 (N.J. Super. Ct. App. Div. 1981); Government Employees Ins. Co. v. Halfpenny, 103 Misc.2d 128 (N.Y. Sup.Ct. 1980).

[13] See, e.g., Supreme Lodge, Knights of Pythias v. Meyer, 198 U.S., 508 (1905); New York Life Ins. Co. v. Baum, 700 F.2d 928, *rhr'g granted on other grounds,* 707 F.2d 870 (5th Cir. 1983); Eastern Stainless Corp. v. American Protection Ins. Co., 829 F. Supp. 797 (D.Md. 1993); Briggs v. United Services Life Ins. Co., 117 N.W.2d 804 (S.D. 1962); State Farm Mut. Auto. Ins. Co. v. Baker, 797 P.2d 168 (Kan.App. 1990); Travelers Ins. Co. v. Eviston, 37 N.E.2d 310 (Ind.App. 1941); Fields v. Equitable Life Assur. Soc'y of the U.S., 118 S.W.2d 521 (Mo.App. 1938).

[14] See, e.g., Pound v. Insurance Co. of N. Am., 439 F.2d 1059 (10th Cir. 1971); Maryland Cas. Co. v. Coman, 212 A.2d 703 (N.H. 1965).

[15] See, e.g., Johnson v. Occidental Fire & Cas. Co. of N.C., 954 F.2d 1581 (11th Cir. 1992) (applying Georgia law); Woods v. National Life & Accident Ins. Co., 347 F.2d 760 (3rd Cir. 1965); Pink v. A.A.A. Highway Express, 13 S.E.2d 337, *aff'd,* 314 U.S. 201 (Ga. 1941).

[16] See Krauss v. Manhattan Life Ins. Co., 643 F.2d 98 (2d Cir. 1981); Colonial Penn. Ins. Co. v. Minkoff, 40 A.D.2d 819, *aff'd,* 33 301 N.E.2d 424 (N.Y.Sup. 1972).

(Matthew Bender & Co., Inc.)

the *Restatement (Second)*.[17] The law of the place of performance has been selected by some courts,[18] and other courts have approved still other tests.[19]

Group insurance policies, because of their tripartite nature,[20] sometimes present particularly complicated issues, and the outcomes in cases with similar facts often vary.[21] The main point of contention in group insurance is whether the choice of law should be determined by the law of the state where the master policy is located or by the law of the state where the group member's certificate was issued.[22]

Although most insurance cases involve contract claims, it is very possible that the insured's claim against the insurer could involve a tort claim of some sort, such as the tort of bad faith that has been recognized in many jurisdictions. In that event, the choice of law rule applied to resolve a conflict of law situation should be that which applies to tort claims, rather than contract claims.[23]

---

[17] See In re Allstate Ins. Co., 613 N.E.2d 936 (N.Y. 1993).

[18] See, e.g., Chemtec Midwest Services, Inc. v. Ins. Co. of N. Am. 279 F. Supp. 539 (D.Wis. 1968); Clinton v. Aetna Life and Sur. Co., 594 A.2d 1046 (Conn.Super.Ct. 1991); Blair v. New York Life Ins. Co., 104 P.2d 1075 (Cal. Ct. App. 1940).

[19] See Board of Regents of University of Minnesota v. Royal Ins. Co. of America, 503 N.W.2d 486 (Minn. Ct. App. 1993), *aff'd in part & rev'd in part,* 517 N.W.2d 888 (Minn. 1994) ("most significant contacts" test applied; five-factor test involves predictability of result, maintenance of interstate and/or international order, simplification of judicial task, advancing the forum's governmental interest, and application of the best rule of law); Peavy Co. v. M/V ANPA, 971 F.2d 1168 (5th Cir. 1992) (applying Louisiana law, which is a combination of interest analysis and the most significant relationship test).

[20] See § 121, *infra.*

[21] Compare Boseman v. Connecticut General Life Ins. Co., 301 U.S. 196 (1937) (individual insureds under group policy bound by choice-of-law designation in master policy), with Hofeld v. Nationwide Life Ins. Co., 287 N.E.2d 215 (Ill. App. Ct. 1972) (choice-of-law designation in master policy not enforced where certificate holder had no knowledge of it). See generally Annot., *Validity and Effect of Choice-of-Law Provision in Group Insurance Policy,* 53 A.L.R.3d 1095 (1973).

[22] See Simms v. Metropolitan Life Ins. Co.,685 P.2d 321 (Kan.Ct.App. 1984) (law of place where master policy issued controls); Erickson v. Sentry Life Ins. Co., 719 P.2d 160 (Wash. Ct. App. 1986) (law of place where master policy issued controls); Harrison v. Insurance Co. of N. Am., 318 So. 2d 253 (Ala. 1975) (law of place where certificate issued controls).

[23] See, e.g., Nationwide Ins. Co. v. Fryer, 577 N.E.2d 746 (Ohio Ct.App. 1990) (principles of tort law, not contract law, govern an action in tort, and different choice of law rule applies).

CHAPTER 4

THE INSURABLE INTEREST REQUIREMENT

§ 40 Origins and Purposes of the Insurable Interest Requirement

The insurable interest doctrine has its origins in the common practice of eighteenth century English marine insurers of not requiring the insured to demonstrate either ownership in or some other legal relationship to the ship or cargo being underwritten. This failure to require the insured to show an "interest" permitted the placing of wagers or bets on whether the insured vessel would successfully complete its voyage.[1] Also, the temptations to frustrate a voyage's success were substantial, and fraud was widespread. As Parliament explained in the preamble to an Act passed in 1746, experience showed that insurance was commonly written "interest or no interest, or without further proof of interest than the policy," which caused "many pernicious practices, whereby great numbers of ships with their cargoes, hath either been fraudulently lost or destroyed, or taken by the enemy in time of war. . . ." Parliament declared that this "introduc[ed] a mischievous kind of gaming or wagering, under the pretense of assuring the risque on shipping," and that this had "perverted" the "institution and laudable design of making assurances."

To deter these practices, Parliament enacted a statute requiring, as a prerequisite to the validity of a policy of marine insurance, the insured to possess an interest in the insured property:

> [N]o assurance or assurances shall be made by any person or persons, bodies corporate or politick, on any ship, or ships belonging to his Majesty, or any of his subjects, or on any goods, merchandizes, or effects, laden or to be laden on board of any such ship or ships, interest or no interest, or without further proof of interest than the policy, or by way of gaming or wagering, or without benefit of salvage to the assurer; and that every such assurance shall be null and void to all intents and purposes.[2]

---

[1] There are even earlier indications that insurance was widely used as a gambling device. An English commentary reports that "[s]o-called insurance offices which were little better than betting establishments came into being in the seventeenth century. The war with France provided ample scope for a certain class of 'war' risk that might or might not be related to the personal prosperity of the insured. [A 1697 essayist wrote that] '[w]agering . . . as now practised by [policies] and contracts, has become a branch of assurance; it was before, more properly, a part of gaming, and as it deserved had but a very low esteem. . . .' " F.J. MacLean, *The Human Side of Insurance* 36 (c. 1929).

[2] Act of 1746, St. 19 Geo. 2, c. 37 § 1 (Eng.).

The 1746 Act did not halt the practice of writing marine insurance without proof of an insurable interest, but not all such policies were illegitimate. Because the actual interests of some insureds were too difficult to substantiate, some policies were written with their enforcement depending solely on the "honor" of the underwriter. These policies, which became known as "honor policies," were not enforceable in court under the 1746 Act even if the insured possessed an insurable interest, but such policies served a legitimate economic purpose.

In life insurance, similar "gaming" practices developed in the eighteenth century. Popular accounts of the period describe the practice of purchasing insurance on the lives of those being tried for capital crimes. These policies constituted naked wagers on whether the accused would ultimately be convicted and executed for the alleged offense. A related practice was the purchase of insurance on the lives of famous, elderly persons; the premium would be a function of what was known about the person's health, including any recent illnesses. Insuring a life in which one has no interest creates a temptation to bring the insured's life to an early end, but the greater concern in eighteenth-century England was the practice of wagering.[3] Thus, when Parliament enacted an insurable interest statute for life insurance in 1774, the articulated concern in the statute was gaming, not the risk that the insured's life might be destroyed. The 1774 statute prohibited issuing insurance on "the life or lives of any person or persons, or any other event or events whatsoever, wherein the person or persons for whose use, benefit, or on whose account such policy or policies shall be made, shall have no interest, or by way of gaming or wagering."[4] Like the 1746 Act, the effect of the 1774 Act was to prohibit judicial enforcement of policies issued without satisfying the insurable interest requirement. Today, the policy of the 1746 Act is carried forward in the Marine Insurance Act of 1906,[5] which contains the prohibition first enacted in 1746: "Every contract of marine insurance by way of gaming or wagering is void."[6] The 1774 Act states the applicable insurable interest requirements for life insurance in England today.

In the United States, the insurable interest doctrine was first adopted by courts, although many state legislatures later enacted insurable interest statutes. These statutes are typically written in broad language, leaving considerable room for judicial interpretation. For example, in about thirty states, an insurable interest in property is defined by statute as "any lawful and substantial economic interest in the safety or preservation of property from loss, destruction or pecuniary damage."[7]

---

[3] Interestingly, the English law expressed no particular concern about the rights of remaindermen, even though the temptations created by the possibility of pecuniary gain after the life tenant's death exist in that setting as well. See Grigsby v. Russell, 222 U.S. 149, 156 (1911).

[4] The Life Assurance Act of 1774, 14 Geo. 3, c. 48 (Eng.). See generally Merkin, *Gambling by Insurance—A Study of the Life Assurance Act of 1774*, 9 Anglo-Am. L. Rev. 331 (1980).

[5] The Marine Insurance Act of 1906, 6 Edw. 7, c. 41 (Eng.).

[6] *Id.*, § 4. These policies are reiterated in the Marine Insurance (Gambling Policies) Act of 1909, 9 Edw. 7, c. 12 (Eng.).

[7] See, e.g., N.Y. Ins. Law § 3401; Wash. Rev. Code § 48.18.040(2); Okla. Stat. tit. 36, § 3605(B); Nev. Rev. Stat. § 687B.060(2).

In about the same number of states, an insurable interest in a life is defined as "in the case of persons closely related by blood or by law, a substantial interest engendered by love and affection," and "in the case of other persons, a lawful and substantial economic interest in the continued life, health or bodily safety of the person insured, as distinguished from an interest which would arise only by, or would be enhanced in value by, the death, disablement or injury of the insured."[8] With terms such as "lawful" and "substantial" left undefined, the American insurable interest doctrine is still viewed as a "decisional" doctrine, as opposed to a statutory requirement.

It is apparent that the insurable interest requirement was created to deal with what eighteenth-century England perceived to be problems of great social importance. Although gambling has always been a popular, widely practiced activity,[9] the problems it creates when practiced to excess have caused concern for hundreds of years. According to one account,

> It was in the early part of the eighteenth century that betting was made a part of professional gambling, as we read in Smollett's *Adventures of Ferdinand, Count Fathom.* On his return to England "he perceived that gaming was now managed in such a manner, as rendered skill and dexterity of no advantage; for the spirit of play having overspread the land, like a pestilence, raged to such a degree of madness and desperation, that the unhappy people who were infected, laid aside all thoughts of amusement, economy, or caution, and risqued their fortunes upon issues equally extravagant, childish and absurd."[10]

Although gambling remains controversial to some extent today, the criticisms of gambling currently carry less force, as evidenced by the encouragement of gambling by state governments which rely on state-administered lotteries, parimutuel betting, casinos, and other forms of gambling for revenue. But even if most people do not perceive gambling as a terrible evil, the predominant view remains that insurance, an economically valuable transaction,[11] should not be used as a subterfuge for gambling. A gambling transaction merely transfers wealth; to the extent anything is produced by a gambling transaction, it is merely the possibility of fortuitous gains. An insurance transaction is economically valuable in that it serves the socially useful function of protecting against fortuitous losses; it is not the purpose of insurance to provide the insured with opportunities for profit. Moreover, if insurance can be used as a vehicle to garner fortuitous gains, moral hazard is increased. The increased probability that the insured will destroy the insured property or life in order to "win the bet" has obvious public policy implications. Not surprisingly, then, the insurable

---

[8] N.Y. Ins. Code § 3205; Ariz. Rev. Stat. Ann. § 20-1104(c); 18 Del. Code Ann. tit. 18, § 2704; Maine Rev. Stat. Ann. tit. 24A, § 2404.

[9] See generally A. Steinmetz, *The Gaming Table* (1870).

[10] J. Ashton, *The History of Gambling in England* 155 (1898). See also J. Eddy & L. Loewe, *The New Law of Betting and Gaming* 10–11 (1961) (purpose of 1853 English Betting Act was to prevent youths from being led into life of crime through the evils of betting shops); but see *id.* at 10 (purpose of 1541 Unlawful Games Act was not to "safeguard the moral well-being of the nation" but was to enable the sport of archery to be maintained).

[11] See § 10, *supra*.

interest doctrine has survived to the end of the twentieth century as a means to reduce the possibility that insurance might be used for the sole purpose of turning a quick profit.

To summarize, the purposes of the insurable interest requirement remain those that prompted the doctrine's creation: (1) discouraging the practice of using insurance as a device for gambling or wagering; and (2) removing the incentive for the procurer of the insurance to destroy the subject matter of the insurance, whether it be a life or an item of property. Of these two purposes, the more important is the second: because gambling is not perceived, in and of itself, to be a terrible evil, the reason for disallowing insurance policies to serve as disguised wagers is the incentive such contracts create for destroying the insured property or life. Thus, increased moral hazard is the reason most often given to justify the insurable interest requirement, but it is not uncommon to find courts, when asked to decide whether an insurable interest exists in a particular insurance transaction, inquiring into whether the insurance contract in question functions as a wager.

Whether the insurable interest doctrine is needed to deter insurers from issuing policies that amount to wagering contracts or that are part of a scheme to destroy an insured property or life is debatable. There are few reasons to believe that insurers deliberately enter into insurance contracts with people who lack insurable interests. If the true owner of property or an heir of an insured could establish that an insurer deliberately sold a policy to a party lacking an insurable interest and that this contributed to the destruction of the property or the death of the insured, the insurer could face substantial liability. Moreover, it is difficult to imagine circumstances where an insurer could be misled by someone who has absolutely no relationship to an item of property or who is a stranger to the person on whose life the policy is sought and consequently induced to issue an insurance policy. Furthermore, where the person purchasing the insurance lacks an insurable interest, the risk underwritten by the insurer is greater; it is in insurers' self-interest to avoid this additional risk. Thus, in the overwhelming majority of insurance transactions, the insurable interest doctrine is inconsequential, because insurers are not likely to sell insurance to people who lack such an interest, and will not do so knowingly except in the most unusual circumstances.

The cases where the doctrine comes into play usually involve situations where the insurer did not know about the absence of the interest when issuing the insurance. This kind of situation may involve an insured who at one time had an insurable interest in the life or property in question, but whose interest has since been extinguished or transferred. In fact, in most reported cases, the insured has some relationship to the property or life in question, and the issue is whether this relationship is sufficient to create an insurable interest. Where the insurable interest doctrine is invoked to void coverage, the doctrine's effect is to limit the freedom of the parties to contract, but this freedom is limited because of the public policies furthered by the doctrine, public policies which trump the values inherent in freedom of contract.

§ 41   Relationship of the Insurable Interest Requirement to the Principle of Indemnity

The insurable interest requirement has a close nexus to the principle of indemnity. Indemnity refers to the compensation necessary to reimburse the insured's loss. One goal of an insurance transaction is to transfer the insured's risk of loss to the insurer. When the insured suffers a loss, the insurer pays proceeds, a benefit, to the insured in an amount that offsets the loss. This arrangement is based upon the assumption that the value of the benefit paid the insured will not exceed the amount of the loss (i.e., benefit $\leq$ loss). In other words, insurance aims to reimburse and to do nothing more. It is consistent with the principle of indemnity to pay the insured a benefit *less than* the loss, but the principle of indemnity is violated if the insured is paid a benefit greater than the loss.

Property insurance is fundamentally a contract of indemnity. Property values are relatively easy to measure, and property insurance is oriented toward reimbursing the impairment of a property's value. Life insurance has some elements of indemnity, although the indemnity principle clearly carries less weight in the life insurance setting. To illustrate, an insurer will not allow an insured to insure a $15,000 automobile for $50,000. If the vehicle is totally destroyed, the insured only needs $15,000 to be made whole, and nothing is served by insuring the vehicle for a larger sum, except perhaps to create an incentive in the insured to destroy the vehicle to gain a $35,000 windfall profit. However, an insured can ordinarily purchase as much insurance on the insured's own life as he or she chooses — be it $15,000 or $1,500,000. In the usual case, life insurance is purchased to provide security to the insured's beneficiaries in the event the insured suffers an early death. In a real sense, the insurance is designed to "indemnify" the beneficiaries for the loss they suffer as a result of being deprived of the earning power of the insured. However, it is unrealistic to attempt to place a precise value on a human life. Thus, life insurance is not pure indemnity insurance, and property insurance has more indemnity characteristics than life insurance.

Return to the example of property insurance, since its indemnity characteristics are stronger: because a contract of property insurance is essentially a contract of indemnity, and because the principle of indemnity holds that the value of the benefit cannot exceed the amount of the loss, in circumstances where the insured suffers no loss, the insured has no recovery. It is at this point that the relationship between indemnity and insurable interest is apparent: logically, if the insured has no interest in the destroyed property, the insured sustains no loss by its destruction. Therefore, in order to recover under a policy of insurance, one must have an interest — an *insurable* interest — in the subject matter of the insurance. If the insured suffers a loss to an insurable interest, the insured's loss will be indemnified.

To summarize, an insurable interest is that interest which the law requires the owner of an insurance policy to have in the thing or person insured. This definition links the interest required with the principle of indemnity, but this definition is inevitably tautological. The doctrine is simply a test that attempts to identify those situations where courts are concerned that the insurance contract might create incentives for wagering or the intentional destruction of property or life. If the court concludes that no insurable interest exists, the contract of insurance will be held void. Where the insurance policy is invalidated, the premium is ordinarily returned to the owner of the policy, assuming the party is not in "pari delicto" with the insurer.[1]

§ 42 Property Insurance and the Insurable Interest Requirement

The English statutes that created the requirement that the insured have an interest in the insured property or life did not define "interest" and did not explain what sorts of interests would satisfy the statutes' requirements. Thus, courts were left with the task of articulating tests for what sort of interest would satisfy the insurable interest requirement. The first cases arose in the property setting, and controversy over the proper test for an insurable interest developed almost immediately.

[a] Legal Interest versus Factual Expectancy: The Early English Cases

A debate started early on among jurists over whether the insurable interest doctrine requires the owner of the insurance to have a "legal expectancy" or a "factual expectancy" or something in-between.

The factual expectancy test was articulated by Lord Mansfield in *Le Cras v. Hughes,*[1] a 1782 English case. During the war with Spain, British naval forces captured the Spanish ship "St. Domingo" and its cargo in the harbor of St. Fernando de Omoa. Under an Act of Parliament called the "Prize Act," captors of ships taken from the Spanish were entitled to be vested through proclamation by the Crown with rights to the seized property. To protect their bounty, the captain and crew insured the "St. Domingo" for the voyage back to England, during which it was lost due to the perils of the sea. The insurer refused to pay the claim on the ground that the insureds lacked an interest, and the insureds sued on the policy.

Lord Mansfield stated that whether the Captain and crew had an insurable interest depended, first, on the Prize Act and proclamation, and, second, regardless of the effect of the statute and proclamation, "on the possession, and on the expectation, warranted by almost universal practice." Lord Mansfield described the first factor as "the strongest ground, because it gives an interest which will support an action." The fact that soldiers assisted in the capture of the ship did not eliminate the Navy's right to the property; that conclusion, Lord Mansfield stated, put "an end of [i.e., to] the question." Thus, the legal right to the ship and cargo afforded by the statute constituted a "legal interest" that satisfied the statutory insurable interest requirement.

However, as an alternative ground for the pro-insured result, Lord Mansfield found the existence of a "factual expectancy." It was clear that the British captain and crew anticipated being granted rights to the cargo; as Lord Mansfield explained,

---

[1] E.g., Commonwealth Life Ins. Co. v. George, 28 So. 2d 910 (Ala. 1947); Washington v. Atlanta Life Ins. Co., 136 S.W.2d 493 (Tenn. 1940); but see American Mut. Life Ins. Co. v. Mead, 79 N.E. 526 (Ind. Ct. App. 1906).

[1] 99 Eng. Rep. 549 (K.B. 1782).

"wherever a capture has been made, since the Revolution, by sea or land, the Crown has made a grant: there is no instance to the contrary." This expectation was enough, in Lord Mansfield's view, to support an insurable interest:

> An interest is necessary, but no particular kind of interest is required. Master Holford's insurance [in *Grant v. Parkinson,* 3 Dougl. 16, 99 K.B. 515 (1781)] was not a legal interest; but [in that case] the profits of a voyage, though not a vested interest, were held insurable. An agent of prizes may insure his profits though they are in contingency. Such an insurance prevents risks from neutral claims; it also guards against a loss arising from the disappointment of an expectation which hitherto has never been disappointed. On either ground [the legal interest or factual expectancy], I think the policy a good one.[2]

Thus, in *Le Cras v. Hughes,* both a legal interest and a factual expectancy supported the existence of an insurable interest. On the one hand, the legal rights given by the statute amounted to an insurable interest; alternatively, the factual expectancy of an advantage amounted to an insurable interest.

The second English case that was instrumental in the development of the insurable interest doctrine was *Lucena v. Craufurd.*[3] In this case, several Dutch vessels were captured at St. Helena. The Royal Commissioners were authorized in wartime to take possession of ships and cargoes of the then-neutral Dutch and to bring them into ports of England. The Royal Commissioners insured the ships; before reaching England, some of the vessels were lost or seriously damaged in a storm. In the meantime, hostilities were declared against the Dutch; one of the vessels was lost at sea before hostilities were declared, and the remainder were lost after the declaration. The underwriters denied the Commissioners' claim on the ground that the Commissioners had no right or interest in the vessels until the vessels arrived in an English port, and the Commissioners brought an action on the policy. The first count alleged that the Commissioners possessed an insurable interest; the second count alleged that the insurance was obtained for the benefit of the Crown, who had an insurable interest; and the third count alleged an interest in foreigners, on whose behalf the insurance was allegedly purchased.

In the Court of Exchequer Chamber, a verdict was entered for the Commissioners on the first count, but for the defendants on the second and third counts. The Commissioners initially prevailed on their argument that they possessed an insurable interest at the time they took out the policies. The House of Lords, however, ordered a new trial on the first count because the jury received an improper instruction on a different issue. Lord Eldon opposed the decision of the Exchequer Chamber; in explaining his view, he discussed at length the nature of the insurable interest requirement, even though those views were not essential to the disposition of the appeal. At the second trial, plaintiffs recovered on the second count as to all the vessels, and this verdict was sustained on appeal to the House of Lords.

The various opinions in *Lucena v. Craufurd,* a case fraught with procedural complexity, contain two — and perhaps three — different views of the insurable interest doctrine.

---

[2] 99 K.B. at 552.

[3] 127 Eng. Rep. 630 (H.L. 1805).

Judge Lawrence articulated a broad factual expectancy doctrine, more or less consistent with the factual expectancy doctrine set forth by Judge Mansfield in *Le Cras v. Hughes*. Judge Lawrence reasoned that it is the purpose of a contract of insurance to protect insureds from the risk of suffering a loss or losing a prospective advantage. He stated that the nature of an insurance contract is

> to protect men against uncertain events which may in any wise be of disadvantage to them; not only those persons to whom positive loss may arise by such events, occasioning the deprivation of that which they may possess, but those also who in consequence of such events may have intercepted from them the advantage or profit, which but for such events they would acquire according to the ordinary and probable course of things.[4]

This being the nature of an insurance contract, Judge Lawrence reasoned that the possibility of insurance being used as a wager exists only where the insured lacks an incentive to preserve the property. A full-fledged property right is not essential to create an incentive in the insured to preserve the property. If the continued existence of the property is essential to securing the advantage (or avoiding the loss), there is little chance that the insured will make a wager based on the property's continued existence. Judge Lawrence explained:

> That a man must somehow or other be interested in the preservation of the subject-matter exposed to perils, follows from the nature of this contract, when not used as a mode of wager, but as applicable to the purposes for which it was originally introduced; but to confine it to the protection of the interest which arises out of property, is adding a restriction to the contract which does not arise out of its nature.[5]

In essence, Judge Lawrence's view of insurable interest was based on a factual expectancy of continued advantage from the nonoccurrence of a peril, or, conversely, a factual expectancy of loss from the occurrence of the peril.

In contrast to Judge Lawrence's broad conception of insurable interest, Lord Eldon articulated a narrow conception that depended upon the existence of a legal right. He defined an insurable interest as requiring "a right in the property, or a right derivable out of some contract about the property, which in either case may be lost upon some contingency affecting the possession or enjoyment of the party."[6] He specifically stated his disagreement with Judge Mansfield's reasoning in *Le Cras v. Hughes*: "If the *Omoa* case was decided upon the expectation of a grant from the crown, I never can give my assent to such a doctrine. That expectation, though founded upon the highest probability, was not interest . . ., whatever might have been the chances in favour of the expectation."[7] As for the instant case, he opined that the Commissioners also lacked such a legal interest:

> [I]n the present case the commissioners do not insure in respect of any benefit to themselves, nor of any benefit to the crown, or to any other person or persons

---

[4] 127 Eng. Rep. at 642.
[5] 127 Eng. Rep. at 643.
[6] 127 Eng. Rep. at 650.
[7] 127 Eng. Rep. at 651.

stated on this record; they insure merely as commissioners, and if they have a right so to insure, it seems to me that any person who is directed to take goods into his warehouse may insure; and that there is nothing to prevent the West India Dock Company from insuring all the ships and goods which come to their docks. If moral certainty be a ground of insurable interest, there are hundreds, perhaps thousands, who would be entitled to insure. First the dock company, then the dock-master, then the warehouse-keeper, then the porter, then every other person who to a moral certainty would have anything to do with the property, and of course get something by it.[8]

For Lord Eldon, a technical legal interest created an insurable interest, even if it were virtually certain that the legal right would never have value. Conversely, even a virtual certainty of acquiring an economic interest would not supply an insurable interest if no technical legal interest existed. Lord Eldon gave these oft-quoted examples:

Suppose A. to be possessed of a ship limited to B. in case A. dies without issue; that A. has 20 children, the eldest of whom is 20 years of age; and B. 90 years of age; it is a moral certainty that B. will never come into possession, yet this is a clear interest. On the other hand, suppose the case of the heir at law of a man who has an estate worth 20,000 a year, who is 90 years of age; upon his death-bed intestate, and incapable from incurable lunacy of making a will, there is no man who will deny that such an heir at law has a moral certainty of succeeding to the estate; yet the law will not allow that he has any interest, or any thing more than a mere expectation.[9]

In short, Lord Eldon's view of insurable interest requires some sort of legally enforceable right. His view has influenced subsequent English cases, which appear to require a legal interest in order to satisfy the insurable interest requirement.[10]

A third opinion in *Lucena v. Craufurd* might be read as representing yet another view of the insurable interest doctrine. The opinion attributed to Baron Graham and six others could be read as requiring both an expectancy and a legal interest to satisfy the insurable interest doctrine. This opinion stated that "[w]here there is an expectancy coupled with a present existing title, there is an insurable interest . . . ."[11] However, another passage of the opinion seemed to endorse the factual expectation doctrine articulated by Lord Mansfield in *Le Cras v. Hughes*.[12] Thus, exactly where Baron Graham and his colleagues stood is difficult to know. This uncertainty might be conveniently ignored were it not for some more recent formulations of the insurable interest doctrine, such as that of Professor Vance in his 1951

---

[8] 127 Eng. Rep. at 651–52.

[9] 127 Eng. Rep. at 652.

[10] See generally 25 *Halsbury's Laws of England* ¶¶ 632–39, at 327–30 (1978).

[11] 127 Eng. Rep. at 639.

[12] 127 Eng. Rep. at 640 ("The doctrine there laid down [in *Le Cras v. Hughes*] . . . has been recognized as law in subsequent cases; and if it were now to be decided that the interest of these commissioners was not insurable, it would render unintelligible that doctrine upon which merchants and underwriters have acted for years, and paid and received many thousand pounds.")

treatise on insurance law, which have described the insurable interest requirement in terms consistent with the Baron Graham opinion. Professor Vance described Lord Eldon's opinion in *Lucena v. Craufurd* as standing for an insurable interest requirement consisting of "an expectation supported by a legal basis."[13] However, as Professor Keeton has noted, Lord Eldon's opinion did not require an expectation — and for that matter Judge Lawrence's opinion in *Lucena* did not require a legal basis either. Only the separate opinion attributed to Baron Graham and six other members of the court arguably supports Professor Vance's conception of the insurable interest doctrine.

It is unclear how this third formulation differs from either the legal interest theory or the factual expectations theory; indeed, it may be that Baron Graham — and perhaps Professor Vance — were searching for a middle ground between the two theories. Thus, the third approach is probably best viewed as a cumulative test. Where someone has a technical legal right that is certain never to have value, one would conclude that no insurable interest exists due to the lack of expectancy. To borrow Lord Eldon's example, *B* at age 90 may have a legal right to inherit *A's* property if *A* dies without issue; but if *A* has twenty children the eldest of whom is 20 years of age, it is a virtual certainty that *B's* technical legal right will never mature into one with value, and one should conclude that *B* has no insurable interest.

On the other hand, if one has an expectancy devoid of any identifiable legal right, that person, under the cumulative approach, would be said to lack an insurable interest. Thus, *A*, who commutes to San Francisco daily over the Golden Gate Bridge, will suffer a loss should the Bridge be closed and A is forced to commute the considerable extra distance to use another bridge for access to the city. Yet this factual expectancy, under the cumulative approach, is not enough to support A's insurable interest in the Bridge, since A lacks any legal interest in it.

The controversy over how *Lucena v. Craufurd* should be read reflects not only on the complexity of the case but also on the difficulty inherent in articulating a cogent theory of insurable interest.

[b] The Legal Interest Test

In applying the legal interest test, courts have recognized three kinds of interests that provide an insurable interest: property rights, contract rights, and legal liability.[14] In a jurisdiction adhering to the legal interest test, the insurance policy will ordinarily be declared invalid and unenforceable in the absence of one of these interests The classic case often cited for this proposition is *Farmers' Mutual Insurance Co. v. New Holland Turnpike Road Co.*,[15] an 1888 Pennsylvania case. In this case, the turnpike company had obtained insurance on a bridge on a county road that was a means of access to the turnpike. The bridge was accidentally destroyed, and the issue was whether the turnpike company had an insurable interest

---

[13] William R. Vance, *Vance on Insurance* 156–57 (3d ed. 1951).

[14] A four-part classification scheme for insurable interest in the property setting — involving legal and equitable property rights, contract rights, the possibility of legal liability, and factual expectancy — was first proposed in Bertram Harnett & John V. Thornton, *Insurable Interest in Property*, 48 Colum. L. Rev. 1162 (1948).

[15] 15 A. 563 (Pa. 1888).

in it. The company had voluntarily contributed one-third of the total cost of building the bridge, but the company had no obligation to contribute to the bridge's reconstruction. The court held that the company had no insurable interest under those circumstances. The court opined that "all the definitions of an 'insurable interest' import an interest in the property insured which can be enforced at law or in equity,"[16] and the company lacked such an interest. The circumstances in which the interest does exist are discussed in the following subections.

[1] Property Rights

Legal or equitable title of virtually any nature and quality will satisfy the insurable interest requirement.[17] A fee simple obviously suffices,[18] as does a remote, technical interest in a legal title, such as, to use Lord Eldon's example, when the insured is a remainderman in case A dies without issue and A has twenty children the eldest of whom is age twenty. The insured is virtually certain not to acquire the property in fee simple, but the insured's remainderman interest will supply the insurable interest necessary to validate the insurance.[19] Life tenants,[20] possess a legal interest in property, as do lessors, lessees, and sublessees.[21] Although not all courts agree, there is some authority for valuing the lessee's insurable interest at an amount greater than the leasehold interest if the lessee has an option to purchase the property.[22]

Most courts hold that the legal title can even be voidable or void and yet suffice as an insurable interest if the insured reasonably believes that the title is valid.[23] For example, in *Counihan v. Allstate Ins. Co.,*[24] the insured was held to have an

---

[16] 122 Pa. at 46, 15 A. at 565.

[17] See, e.g., Splish Splash Waterslides, Inc. v. Cherokee Ins. Co., 307 S.E.2d 107 (Ga. Ct. App. 1983); see also Anderson v. State Farm Fire and Cas. Co., 397 N.W.2d 416 (Minn. Ct. App. 1986) (no insurable interest where no legal or equitable title); Fischer, *The Rule of Insurable Interest and the Principle of Indemnity: Are They Measures of Damages in Property Insurance?* 56 Ind. L.J. 445 (1981).

[18] See Brewster v. Michigan Millers Mutual Ins. Co., 274 So. 2d 213 (La. Ct. App. 1993).

[19] See Hunter v. State Farm Fire & Cas. Co., 543 So. 2d 679 (Ala. 1979); Morris v. Morris, 544 P.2d 1034 (Or. 1976).

[20] See Schonwald v. Sun Ins. Office, Ltd., 276 F. Supp. 775 (D.C.Okla. 1967); Hunter v. State Farm Fire & Cas. Co., 543 So. 2d 679 (Ala. 1989).

[21] See Virginia Heart Institute, Ltd., v. Northwest Penn. Bank & Trust Co., 448 F. Supp. 215 (W.D. Pa. 1978); Alexander v. Ennia Ins. Co. (U.K.), Ltd., 771 S.W.2d 917 (Mo. Ct. App. 1989).

[22] See G.M. Battery & Boat Co. v. L.K.N. Corp., 747 S.W.2d 624 (Mo. 1988); contra, Beard v. American Agency Life Ins. Co., 550 A.2d 677 (Md. 1988); Travelers Indem. Co. v. Duffy's Little Tavern, Inc., 478 So. 2d 1095 (Fla. Dist. Ct. App. 1985); see generally Annot., *Insurable Interest In Property of Lessee with Option to Purchase Property,* 74 A.L.R.4th 883 (1989).

[23] See, e.g., Morgan v. Patrons Mut. Ins. Ass'n, 813 F. Supp. 1502 (D.Kan. 1993)(vendee under oral sales contract unenforceable under Statute of Frauds has insurable interest); Home Ins. Co. of New York v. Gilman, 13 N.E. 118 (Ind. 1887). This issue is usually encountered in cases involving possession of stolen goods. See § 46[a], *infra.*

[24] 25 F.3d 109 (2d Cir. 1994), *rev'g* 827 F. Supp. 132 (E.D. N.Y. 1993).

insurable interest in property at the time the fire loss occurred, despite the fact that the property's title was subject to forfeiture under federal law on the basis of an earlier use of the property for illegal drug activities, and the federal statute provided that the property owner (i.e., the insured) should forfeit "any right, title, and interest" as of the date of the act giving rise to forfeiture. This outcome increases moral hazard: after *Counihan,* drug traffickers whose property is subject to forfeiture have an incentive to destroy their property and collect the insurance proceeds. Of course, the drug traffickers' involvement in any intentional destruction of property will void the coverage, *if* detected. And while the government has other ways to access the insurance proceeds absent proof of arson,[25] in the meantime the public safety is implicated through the varied risks associated with fires, and insurers still pay for the destruction, even if the drug traffickers do not profit. Yet *Counihan* is consistent with cases in other settings that recognize the existence of an insurable interest as long as the insured has some vestige of legal (or equitable) title (or a factual expectancy).

Even a future interest in property will supply the insurable interest; remaindermen and reversioners possess an insurable interest.[26] Courts have found an insurable interest in property that the insured has not yet acquired or which is not even in existence at the time of contracting if it is understood that the insurance only applies in the future and to the extent that the insured acquires an actual interest in the property.[27] This serves a useful economic function by allowing shippers to contract in advance for cargo that they will take on the ship in the future, perhaps in a distant port.

Equitable title of virtually any form also provides an insurable interest. Thus, the purchaser of real estate under a contract for sale has an insurable interest in the property even though the closing has not yet occurred and the title has not yet been transferred.[28] A mortgagor holding the right to redeem property has an insurable interest in the property.[29] Individuals who have lost legal title to their property due to a tax sale foreclosure but who have a right to redeem their property have an insurable interest.[30] The mortgagor who has sold the property and who is still liable

---

[25] 25 F.3d at 113.

[26] See Allemannia Fire Ins. Co. v. Winding Gulf Collieries, 60 F. Supp. 65 (S.D. W.Va. 1945); Neubauer v. Hostetter, 485 N.W.2d 87 (Iowa 1992).

[27] See Musselman v. Mountain West Farm Bur. Mut. Ins. Co., 824 P.2d 271 (Mont. 1992); Thurston Nat'l Ins. Co. v. Hays, 544 S.W.2d 853 (Ark. 1977).

[28] See Morgan v. Patrons Mutual Ins. Ass'n, 813 F. Supp. 1502 (D.Kan. 1993); Filiatreau v. Allstate Insurance, 358 S.E.2d 829 (W.Va. 1987); Overton v. Progressive Ins. Co., 585 So. 2d 445 (Fla. Dist. Ct. App. 1991).

[29] See Reynolds v. Allstate Ins. Co., 629 F.2d 1111 (5th Cir. 1981); State Farm Fire & Cas. Co. v. Ramsey, 719 F. Supp. 1337 (S.D. Miss. 1989); Watts v. St. Katherin Ins. Co., 820 S.W.2d 259 (Tex. Ct. App. 1991).

[30] See Crowell v. Delafield Farmers Mut. Fire Ins. Co., 463 N.W.2d 737 (Minn. 1990); Miller v. New Jersey Ins. Underwriting Ass'n, 414 A.2d 1322 (N.J. 1980); Watts v. St. Katherine Ins. Co., 820 S.W.2d 259 (Tex. Ct. App. 1991). In *Miller* the parties also continued to occupy the premises after foreclosure, which supports an insurable interest under a factual expectancy theory.

for the mortgage debt has an insurable interest in the property, even if the grantee has assumed the mortgage.[31] The beneficiary of a trust has an insurable interest in the trust assets.[32] It has been held that a buyer of goods under a long-term contract has an equitable interest in the property being purchased sufficient to create an insurable interest in the entire property, and not just to the extent that the buyer has made payments under the contract.[33]

One of several holders of property possesses an insurable interest to the extent of that person's own interest. Thus, shareholders of corporations,[34] joint tenants,[35] tenants in common,[36] and spouses in community property states[37] all possess an insurable interest in the jointly-held property. Similarly, a mere possessory interest is ordinarily enough to supply an insurable interest to the extent of the value of the interest.[38] Thus, one who borrows property has an insurable interest in the property, even if he is not legally liable for the property's loss. The holder of property in a representative, trust, or bailment relationship has an insurable interest in the property.[39] In each of these situations, the holder of the property is ordinarily required to hold the proceeds from the loss of the property in trust for the property's owner.

[2] Contract Rights

As a general proposition, one whose contract rights depend directly on the continued existence of property has an insurable interest that will support a policy of insurance on that property. The archetypical example is that of a secured creditor, who has a contract right to foreclose against property in the event a debtor fails to make timely payments. The secured creditor has an insurable interest in the property that is subject to the security interest, whether the security interest arises by way of mortgage, mechanic's lien, or otherwise.[40] (An unsecured creditor, though having

---

[31] E.g., Reid v. Hardware Mut. Ins. Co. of Carolinas, 166 S.E.2d 317 (S.C. 1969); Farmers' & Merchants' Bank v. Hartford Fire Ins. Co., 253 P. 379 (Idaho 1926); Lumberman's Nat'l. Bank v. Corrigan, 166 N.W. 650 (Wis. 1918); Hanover Fire Ins. Co. v. Bohn, 67 N.W. 774 (Neb. 1896).

[32] See Goldin v. Federal Deposit Ins. Corp., 985 F.2d 261 (6th Cir. 1993); Lambert v. Federal Deposit Ins. Corp., 847 F.2d 604 (9th Cir. 1988); Queen v. Vermont Mut. Ins. Co., 589 N.E.2d 325 (Mass.App.Ct. 1992). But see Hymel v. Federal Deposit Ins. Corp., 925 F.2d 881 (5th Cir. 1991).

[33] Iehle v. Coleman, 584 A.2d 988, 990 (Pa. Super. Ct. 1991).

[34] See McKee v. Penick, 947 F.2d 1403 (9th Cir. 1991); Travelers Cos. v. Wolfe, 838 S.W.2d 708 (Tex. Ct. App. 1992).

[35] See Russell v. Williams, 374 P.2d 827 (Cal. 1962); Republic Ins. Co. v. Jernigan, 719 P.2d 331 (Colo.Ct.App. 1985), *judgment aff'd & remanded,* 753 P.2d 229 (Colo. 1988).

[36] See Collins v. Quincy Mut. Fire Ins. Co., 256 S.E.2d 718 (N.C. 1979); Cafey v. Caffey, 625 S.W.2d 444 (Ark. 1981).

[37] See Amason v. Franklin Life Ins. Co., 428 F.2d 1144 (5th Cir. 1970); McDivitt v. Pymatuning Mut. Fire Ins. Co., 449 A.2d 612 (Pa. Super. Ct. 1982).

[38] See Geller v. General Agents Ins. Co. of Am., Inc., 841 S.W.2d 205 (Mo. Ct. App. 1992).

[39] Hinkle v. Perry, 752 S.W.2d 267 (Ark. 1988) (bailees); Estate of Harry Block, Jr. v. Commissioner, 78 T.C. 850 (1982) (trustee).

[40] See Southwestern Graphite v. Fidelity & Guar. Ins. Corp., 201 F.2d 553 (5th Cir. 1953) (mortgagee's interest); Reid v. Hardware Mut. Ins. Co., 166 S.E.2d 317 (S.C. 1969); Hyman v. Sun Ins. Co., 175 A.2d 247 (N.J.Super.Ct. 1961).

an insurable interest in the life of the debtor, ordinarily lacks an insurable interest in the property of the debtor.) Other kinds of arrangements can give rise to a contract right that supports an insurable interest. In one case, an insured who entered into a long-term contract to operate a factory was held to possess an insurable interest in the factory's equipment.[41] In another, a shipper insured a cargo of sugar being shipped from the Philippines to the United States, even though the contract specified "no arrival, no sale." Although title never passed to the buyer, the court held that the buyer possessed an insurable interest in the sugar while it was in transit.[42] In these cases, the courts predicated the insurable interest not so much on the existence of a right to property as on the possibility of economic loss accompanying the non-satisfaction of a contract right. It is here that the overlap of the legal interest and factual expectancy tests is apparent. Even if a contract right is a "legal interest," the essence of the contract right is the expectation created by the right to the full performance of the other party's duty; where this expectation's fulfillment depends on the continued existence of property, the contracting party has an insurable interest in that property.

[3] Legal Liability

If a person would suffer legal liability in the event property is lost or damaged, that person has an insurable interest in the property. Thus, one can explain the insurable interest of a bailee as being based upon the legal liability the bailee would incur if the property that is the subject of the bailment were lost or damaged. This interest should be distinguished from the insurable interest that one has in one's own personal liability. A liability insurance policy does not pay for the destruction of the insured's own property; instead, it covers the liability one might incur as a result of causing injury or damage to some other person. And just as one has an unlimited insurable interest to support any amount of insurance on one's own life, one has an unlimited insurable interest to support insurance for prospective, possible, personal liabilities. The legal liability basis for the legal interest theory of insurable interest reaffirms the property right basis; after all, the bailee also has a property right which in and of itself gives rise to an insurable interest. But the legal liability test allows an individual to purchase a policy of first-party property insurance where the only link between the insured and the property is the insured's legal liability should the property be damaged or destroyed.

In *Clevenger v. Allstate Ins. Co.*,[43] the requirements of the Michigan law requiring the registrant of a vehicle to acquire liability insurance for the vehicle created the insured's insurable interest. The insured, upon selling her car and signing over the certificate of title to buyer, told the buyer that buyer could operate the vehicle with the insured's registration and license plates until Monday. Under the Michigan no-fault law, the insured remained responsible for acquiring liability insurance on the vehicle under threat of criminal sanctions. The court explained: "In this limited context, [the insured's] insurable interest was not contingent upon title or ownership

---

[41] Graham v. American Fire Ins. Co. of Philadelphia, 26 S.E. 323 (S.C. 1897).

[42] Harrison v. Fortlage, 161 U.S. 57 (1896).

[43] 505 N.W.2d 553 (Mich. 1993).

to the automobile, but, rather, upon personal pecuniary damage created by the no-fault statute itself."[44]

In *Clevenger,* a statute created the legal liability, but the same result follows if the liability is created by contract. If one person is contractually bound to obtain insurance on property, that person has a sufficient interest to insure the property because of the resulting liability for breach of contract should the insurance not be procured. This was the situation in *Village of Constantine v. Home Ins. Co.,*[45] a 1970 Sixth Circuit decision. Scott sold some generators to the Village of Constantine pursuant to title-retaining conditional sales contracts that required Scott to "insure the equipment for breakdown insurance." Thereafter, Scott sold the conditional sales contracts to a Nebraska bank, without making any effort to assign the insurance policy to the bank or to reissue it. When two generators broke down, the insurer refused to pay under the policy on the ground that Scott lacked an insurable interest in the generators at the time of the loss. The court reasoned that the insurance contract was not converted into a wagering contract simply because Scott had divested himself of his interest in the property. In this case, Scott was still liable on his promise to procure damage insurance, and if he failed to do so he would have become liable to the Village for its ensuing loss: "While Scott had neither ownership interest in the property insured nor anything to gain from it, he clearly did have something to lose."[46]

[c] The Factual Expectancy Test

This test, first articulated by Lord Mansfield in *Le Cras v. Hughes,* is broader than the legal interest test. A factual expectancy is the expectation of economic advantage if the insured property continues to exist, or, conversely, the expectation of economic loss accruing upon damage to the insured property. Such an expectancy can exist without a legal interest and, in the view of many courts and commentators, is enough to support an insurable interest.[47] The expectancy must be substantial, however; the insured must have a current relationship to the property which directly affects the insured's economic well-being. For example, an insurable interest is not created by a mere expectancy that sometime in the future the owner of property will bequeath it to the insured[48] or a mere hope that a future gift of the property will be made

---

[44] 505 N.W.2d at 560. See also Omaha Prop. and Cas. Co. v. Crosby, 756 F. Supp. 1380 (D.Mont. 1990), *aff'd,* 951 F.2d 361 (9th Cir. 1991).

[45] 427 F.2d 1338 (6th Cir. 1970).

[46] 427 F.2d at 1340.

[47] E.g., Suggs v. State Farm Fire & Cas. Co., 833 F.2d 883 (10th Cir. 1987); Heyden v. Safeco Title Ins. Co., 498 N.W.2d 905 (Wis. 1993); Fire Ass'n of Philadelphia v. Ward, 42 S.E.2d 713 (W.Va. 1947); Erie-Haven, Inc. v. Tippmann Refrigeration Constr., 486 N.E.2d 646 (Ind. Ct. App. 1985); Friscia v. Safeguard Ins. Co., 57 Misc.2d 759, (N.Y.Civ.Ct. 1968).

[48] See Brewton v. Alabama Farm Bureau Mut. Cas. Ins. Co., Inc., 474 So. 2d 1120, 1123 (Ala. 1985). The result may be different when the insured is actually a legatee. See Francois v. Automobile Ins. Co. of Hartford, Conn., 37 A.2d 525 (Pa. 1944); Home Ins. Co. of New York v. Mendenhall, 45 N.E. 1078 (Ill. 1897). See generally Annot., *Fire Insurance: Insurable Interest of One Expecting to Inherit Property or Take by Will,* 52 A.L.R.4th 1273 (1987).

to the insured. One court has held that tenants at sufferance, who are subject to immediate eviction at any time, have no insurable interest; the at-will nature of the tenancy means that, in addition to lacking a legal interest, the tenants have no pecuniary stake in the continued existence of the property.[49]

A typical formulation of the factual expectancy test is like that found in a 1992 New Jersey decision, *Lancellotti v. Maryland Casualty Co.*:[50] "The test of insurable interest in property is whether the insured has such a right, title or interest therein, or relation thereto, that he will be benefitted by its preservation and continued existence or suffer a direct pecuniary loss from its destruction or injury by the peril insured against."[51] The language "right, title or interest therein" is language of legal interest, but the legal interest must have the direct economic relevance to the insured described in the quoted passage for an insurable interest to exist. Furthermore, the language "or relation thereto" indicates that a legal interest is not necessary if the insured has a relationship of any kind to the property such that the property's continued existence will directly affect the insured's economic well-being. A case like *New Holland Turnpike*, discussed in the preceding subsection, would be decided differently under the factual expectancy test.

Unlike *New Holland Turnpike*, however, in many situations the factual expectancy test does not change the result that should be reached if the legal interest test were applied properly. In some cases, this can create difficulty in determining exactly what approach the court is following. This uncertainty is not surprising, because it dates to Lord Mansfield's opinion in *Le Cras v. Hughes,* where alternative bases for the result in that case were offered, one utilizing a legal interest theory and the other a factual expectation theory. In these early cases, one can only speculate whether an insurable interest would have been found had no legal interest existed. Consider, for example, *Harrison v. Fortlage,*[52] an 1896 United States Supreme Court decision, in which the Court held that a buyer of goods to be shipped via a specified vessel possessed an insurable interest in the goods even though the purchase contract provided "no arrival, no sale." Justice Gray wrote that "[i]t is well settled that any person has an insurable interest in property, by the existence of which he will gain an advantage, or by the destruction of which he will suffer a loss, whether he has or has not any title in, or lien upon, or possession of the property itself."[53] Yet in that case the plaintiffs had a contract in writing by which title of the goods sought to be insured would accrue to them upon arrival and delivery. Although they lacked title to the insured goods, they did have a contract right to the goods, which is enough to supply a legal interest.

Another leading case is *National Filtering Oil Co. v. Citizens' Insurance Co.,*[54] where the insured had a contract under which payment was based on a percentage of the monetary value of the total output of an oil refinery. The insured was held

---

[49] Jones v. Texas Pacific Indem. Co., 853 S.W.2d 791, 795 (Tex. Ct. App. 1993).

[50] 617 A.2d 296 (N.J. Super. 1992).

[51] 617 A.2d at 298.

[52] 161 U.S. 57 (1896).

[53] 161 U.S. at 65.

[54] 13 N.E. 337 (N.Y. 1887).

to possess an insurable interest in the oil refinery premises and was allowed to recover on a fire insurance policy that insured him against decreased royalties. The court appeared to base the insurable interest, not on the existence of the contract right, but on the factual expectancy. After citing three earlier New York cases, the court stated: "[These cases] decide that an interest legal or equitable in the property burned is not necessary to support an insurance upon it; that it is enough if the assured is so situated as to be liable to loss if it be destroyed by the peril insured against. . . ."[55] The court held that the insured had "brought its case within these principles";[56] yet the contract right, the value of which depended on the existence of the insured property, should have been sufficient by itself to create an insurable interest.

If the purpose of the insurable interest doctrine is to prevent inducements to the destruction of property or lives and to prevent wagering, the factual expectancy theory is more logical. It is the insured's factual expectations — not the presence of a technical legal interest — that provides the deterrent to wagering and to the destruction of property or lives. Given the statutory language, discussed above, which has been approved in at least thirty states[57] and the judicial decisions of some others, it is probably fair to assert that most American jurisdictions now adhere to the factual expectancy theory of insurable interest.

In some situations, insisting upon a legal interest can prevent a recovery where a factual expectancy exists. In *Faygal v. Shelter Insurance Co.,*[58] a father purchased a truck from his employer, an automobile manufacturer, under a program that gave the employee a discount on the condition that the employee keep the title of the vehicle for one year. The father intended the vehicle to be used by his son-in-law, and it was the understanding of the father and son-in-law that the truck "belonged" to the son-in-law. The son-in-law had exclusive possession of the truck and was responsible for maintenance, payment of taxes, and securing insurance. After one year, the father planned to transfer title to the son-in-law, who would then pay off the note. The insurer issued a policy of insurance on the truck to the son-in-law. The son-in-law alleged that he told the insurer he lacked title. The agent denied this, but the agent testified he did not inquire into who owned the truck. After the truck was stolen, the insurer denied coverage on the ground that the son-in-law lacked an insurable interest in the truck.

Missouri law prohibited any person from selling a vehicle to another without transferring a certificate of ownership and provided that any such sale was void. The court held that because the son-in-law did not comply with the Missouri statute, he lacked an insurable interest in the truck and therefore could recover nothing for its loss. As the court itself conceded, this result was a "painful" one. The plaintiff lacked title and he lacked an enforceable contract right due to the Missouri statute. But he definitely possessed a factual expectancy regarding the truck's preservation, due to his substantial economic interest in it. By this logic, a wife has no insurable interest

---

[55] 13 N.E. at 339.

[56] *Id.*

[57] See § 40, *supra.*

[58] 689 S.W.2d 724 (Mo. Ct. App. 1985).

in jointly-used property titled in her husband's name, an anomalous result which has been rejected in the decided cases.[59] Many parents purchase cars and trucks for their children, with the understanding that the vehicles "belong" to the children, but fortunately most of these vehicles are insured by the parents. Where little risk exists that the property will be intentionally destroyed, little reason exists to prevent a child (with capacity to contract) who happens to arrange for the insurance from recovering under the policy in the event of loss.

§ 43 Life Insurance and the Insurable Interest Requirement

Cases in which the issue is whether the owner of a life insurance policy had an insurable interest in the insured's life are not ordinarily decided by reference to the presence (or lack thereof) of a "legal interest" or "factual expectancy," the common parlance with which insurance interests in property are described. Yet the tests of insurable interest in life insurance are corollaries of the tests in property insurance. Instead of asking whether the owner of a life insurance policy has a "legal interest" in the life of the insured, one asks whether there is a sufficiently close relationship by blood or operation of law to establish the insurable interest. In the absence of the close familial relationship, one asks whether the owner of the policy has a pecuniary interest in the life of the insured such that he or she will derive an economic benefit from the insured's continued living (or a loss in the event of the insured's death). This economic interest resembles the "factual expectancy" test of insurable interest, which searches for a relationship between the policyholder and the insured property where the policyholder's well-being depends upon the continued existence of property. Beyond these observations, the insurable interest requirement in life insurance involves some different issues and some different rules.

What constitutes an "interest" in a life? Clearly, every person has an insurable interest in his or her own life.[1] This does not mean that one has a pecuniary interest in one's own life. No one expects to suffer pecuniary loss as a result of one's own death, since death means finality in all earthly pursuits. Nor can it be said that one's estate suffers pecuniary loss as a result of one's death, since the estate exists only because of the person's death and serves as a temporary substitute for one's administration of owned assets during life. It might be said that the "family relationship" of an individual with himself or herself is very close, but this observation obscures the fundamental point. When one takes out insurance on one's own life, society's concerns that the insured is wagering on the insured's own death or is inclined to self-destruct for the purpose of bestowing a financial benefit on others are minimal. The person who takes out insurance on his or her own life has the power to designate any beneficiary; it is presumed that the person will not designate a beneficiary likely to murder the insured. In virtually every state, it is

---

[59] See 4 APPLEMAN § 2149 (1969).

[1] See, e.g., Ellison v. Independent Life & Accident Ins. Co., 58 S.E.2d 890 (S.C. 1950); Pierce v. Metropolitan Life Ins. Co., 187 N.E. 77 (Ohio Ct.App. 1933).

not necessary that the named beneficiary have an insurable interest in the life of the insured.[2]

However, the rule that every person has an insurable interest in his or her own life is not applied rigidly. If a third person, named as beneficiary, encourages the insured to take out the policy on the insured's own life and pays the premiums, some courts may void the policy as a wager.[3] For the court to take this step, the beneficiary must lack an interest, either economic or familial, in the continued life of the insured.

Where an individual takes out insurance on the life of another, a greater risk exists that the evils to which the insurable interest doctrine is directed — destruction of the insured and wagering — will occur. However, if a strong familial or economic relationship exists, a court is likely to conclude that the person taking out the insurance possesses the requisite insurable interest.

The closer the familial relationship, the more likely it is that an insurable interest exists. It is not denied anywhere that one has an insurable interest in the life of his or her spouse.[4] This relationship is so close and the affection normally so great that it is presumed that the evils to which the doctrine is directed will not occur. A divorce ordinarily terminates the insurable interest of one spouse in the life of the other,[5] although a divorce decree, such as one that requires one spouse to pay alimony to the other, may create an economic relationship (akin to debtor-creditor) that gives rise to an insurable interest. For the same reasons that spouses have an insurable interest in their partner's lives, courts are in agreement that a parent and minor child have an insurable interest in the life of each other.[6] However, courts are not in agreement beyond the spousal and parental-minor child relationships on the degree of familial proximity that will support the existence of an insurable interest.

Some courts recognize an insurable interest in these other relationships, such as siblings and parent-adult child, solely on the strength of the familial relationship.[7]

---

[2] Texas is the only state where recent (i.e., post-World War II) precedent requires the beneficiary designated by an insured who has taken out a policy on the insured's own life to have an insurable interest in the insured's life, and this rule no longer applies to policies issued by legal reserve or mutual assessment life insurance companies. See Tex. Ins. Code § 3.49–1; Kennedy v. Laird, 503 S.W.2d 664 (Tex. Ct. App. 1973). The Couch treatise cites some older decisions from a few states other than Texas which required the beneficiary of a life insurance policy to have an interest in the life of the insured or be related to the insured in a designated degree of kinship. See 3 COUCH 2d §§ 24:116–24:117 (1984). The extent to which these older decisions state the current law is open to question.

[3] See, e.g., New England Mut. Life Ins. Co. v. Null, 605 F.2d 421 (8th Cir. 1979); Commercial Travelers' Ins. Co. v. Carlson, 137 P.2d 656 (Utah 1943).

[4] See Jenkins v. Lovelady, 273 So. 2d 189 (Ala. 1973); Shaw v. Board of Administration, 241 P.2d 635 (Cal. Ct. App. 1952).

[5] See Hopkins v. Hopkins, 614 A.2d 96, 99 (Md. 1992); Morgan v. American Sec. Ins. Co., 522 So. 2d 454 (Fla. Dist. Ct. App. 1988); Wren v. New York Life Ins. Co., 493 F.2d 839 (5th Cir. 1974); but see Meehan v. Transamerica Occidental Life Ins. Co., 499 N.E.2d 602 (Ill. Ct. App. 1986).

[6] See Bowman v. Zenith Life Ins. Co., 384 N.E.2d 949 (Ill. Ct. App. 1978); North River Ins. Co. v. Fisher, 481 S.W.2d 443 (Tex. Ct. App. 1972).

[7] See, e.g., Mutual Savings Life Ins. Co. v. Noah, 282 So. 2d 271 (Ala. 1973)(siblings); Penn v. Lighthouse Life Ins. Co., 392 So. 2d 181 (La. Ct. App. 1980)(siblings); United Ins.

Most courts have held that the relationships between an aunt/uncle and a nephew/ niece to be too remote to provide the insurable interest.[8] There is little law on the question, but it would not appear that the relationships between a mother-in-law/ father-in-law and a son-in-law/daughter-in-law, and between a brother-in-law and a sister-in-law are close enough to support an insurable interest.[9] As for the relationship between a stepfather/stepmother and stepchild, the courts are not uniform;[10] It would seem that whether the step-parent/step-child relationship, without more, creates an insurable interest should turn on whether the relationship is functionally equivalent to other kinds of familial relationships where the insurable interest is found. For example, one court has held that adopting parents have an insurable interest in a child after the child has been placed in the parents' home but before the adoption decree becomes final.[11] Although this decision can be explained based on the economic interest adopting parents have both in the adoptee and in the adoption process being brought to a successful conclusion, this result can also be founded on the fact that the adopting family during the post-placement, pre-final decree period resembles, for all practical purposes, other family units.

If an economic interest combines with a weak familial relationship, it is more likely that a court will find the insurable interest requirement satisfied.[12] Depending on the nature of the familial relationship, courts typically require the party taking out the insurance to have a pecuniary interest in the continued life of the insured, such as would be the case if a grandparent relied upon the earnings of a grandchild for support. The extent to which a pecuniary interest is required is, roughly speaking, inversely related to the strength of the familial relationship.[13] According to one court, the foster parent-foster child relationship does not create an insurable interest based solely on "blood" or "law," as those terms appear in many statutes; because the state pays the expenses of caring for the child, there is no pecuniary relationship that creates an insurable interest.[14]

Co. of Am. v. Hadden, 190 S.E.2d 638 (Ga. Ct. App. 1972); Golden State Mut. Life Ins. Co. v. White, 374 S.W.2d 901 (Tex. Ct. App. 1964)(parent-adult child); Annot., *Insurable Interest of Brother or Sister in Life of Sibling,* 60 A.L.R.3d 98 (1974).

[8] See Peoples First Nat'l Bank & Trust Co. v. Christ, 65 A.2d 393 (Pa. 1949); but see Brockton v. Southern Life and Health Ins. Co., 556 So. 2d 1138 (Fla. Dist. Ct. App. 1989)(aunt slightly younger than niece and had life-long familial relationship; insurable interest exists).

[9] See King v. Cram, 69 N.E. 1049 (Mass. 1904).

[10] Compare Young v. Hipple, 117 A. 185 (Pa. 1922) (insurable interest exists) with United Brethren Mut. Aid Soc'y v. McDonald, 15 A. 439 (Pa. 1888) (no insurable interest).

[11] Volunteer State Life Ins. Co. v. Pioneer Bank, 327 S.W.2d 59 (Tenn. Ct. App. 1959).

[12] See Young v. Hipple, 117 A. 185 (Pa. 1922) (step-parent/step-child relationship creates insurable interest based on familial relationship; but if not, pecuniary relationship establishes insurable interest); Holmes v. Nationwide Mut. Ins. Co., 40 Misc.2d 894, (N.Y. 1963) (brother-in-law relationship combining with pecuniary relationship created by loan).

[13] In Cronin v. Vermont Life Ins. Co., 40 A. 497 (R.I. 1898), an aunt and niece had lived together for many years, the probability that the niece would be disposed to help the aunt financially if the need arose was sufficient to give the aunt an insurable interest in the niece's life. See also Rubenstein v. Mutual Life Ins. Co. of New York, 584 F. Supp. 272 (E.D. La. 1984).

[14] Willingham v. United Ins. Co. of Am. 628 So. 2d 328, 331 (Ala. 1993).

Where there is no familial relationship to support the existence of an insurable interest, courts sometimes find the insurable interest requirement satisfied by a pecuniary interest alone. Thus, if one person is likely to suffer an economic loss because of the death of a business associate or someone with whom that person is in a contractual relationship, courts generally hold that the person has an insurable interest in the life of that other person. Under this reasoning, a partner has an insurable interest in the life of his or her partner,[15] and an employer and employee can have an insurable interest in the life of each other,[16] although as an organization becomes larger and the relationships between employers and employees more distant, the likelihood of finding an insurable interest diminish. A creditor — even an unsecured creditor (who lacks an insurable interest in the property of the debtor) — has an insurable interest in the life of the debtor.[17] One court explained the pecuniary relationship required to support an insurable interest in this way:

> [I]t is an interest determined by monetary considerations, viewed from the standpoint of the beneficiary — would the beneficiary regard himself as better off from the standpoint of money, would he enjoy more substantial economic returns should the insured continue to live [which cuts in favor of finding an insurable interest] or would he have more in the form of the proceeds of the policy should the insured die [which cuts against finding an insurable interest].[18]

Where the insurable interest is based on the familial relationship, no limit exists on the amount of insurance that might be purchased. However, where the insurable interest is based only on the economic interest, most courts have held that the value of the pecuniary involvement fixes a limit upon the amount of insurance that can be purchased.[19] The rationale for this result was explained by one court as follows:

> The amount of a creditor's insurable interest is the amount of the debt. If the amount of [the creditor's] insurable interest in [the debtor] . . . exceeded the cash surrender value of the policies, it would not offend public policy if [the creditor] retained the policies. If the proceeds realized from the policies on [the

---

[15] See Herman v. Provident Mut. Life Ins. Co. of Philadelphia, 886 F.2d 529 (2d Cir. 1989); Steiniger v. Marmis, 800 P.2d 975 (Ariz. 1990); Graves v. Norred, 510 So. 2d 816 (Ala. 1987) (insurable interest does not terminate on partnership's dissolution where partner dies before final accounting); Rich v. Class, 643 S.W.2d 872 (Mo.App.Ct. 1982).

[16] Chapman v. Lipscomb-Ellis Co., 22 S.E.2d 353 (Ga. 1942); Secor v. Pioneer Foundry Co., 173 N.E.2d 780 (Mich. Ct. App. 1969).

[17] See, e.g., Theatre Guild Productions, Inc. v. Insurance Corp. of Ireland, 25 A.D.2d 109, (N.Y. 1966), aff'd, 225 N.E.2d 216 (N.Y. 1967); American Cas. Co. v. Rose, 340 F.2d 469 (10th Cir. 1964).

[18] Drane v. Jefferson Standard Life Ins. Co., 161 S.W.2d 1057, 1059 (Tex.Comm.App. 1942).

[19] See Froiland v. Tritle, 484 N.W.2d 310 (S.D. 1992); Jimenez v. Protective Life Ins. Co., 10 Cal. Rptr.2d 326 (Cal. Ct. App. 1992) ("'bright line' test is more practicable than the amorphous 'proportionality' test"; creditor's insurable interest limited to amount of debt, plus refund of first (and only) premium, plus interest on those two amounts, where creditor purchased $160,000 of insurance to secure $5500 debt); Vulcan Life & Accident Ins. Co. v. United Banking Co., 162 S.E.2d 798 (Ga. Ct. App. 1968); Arrowood v. Duff, 152 S.W.2d 291 (Ky. 1941).

debtor's] death were less than the amount of the debt, [the creditor] would be allowed to keep the entire amount thereof. The rule, as so applied, permits the creditor to realize, to the extent that the proceeds from the policies may do so, the amount of the creditor's insurable interest, while at the same time it prevents the creditor from realizing more than the amount to which the creditor is equitably entitled.

If the amount received by the creditor is equal to the debt, there is no objection on the ground of a "gambling contract." If the amount received is greater than the debt, there is an "unjust enrichment" with liability [to the debtor's estate] for the amount exceeding the amount of the debt plus interest.[20]

A separate line of cases, consisting mostly of older authorities, holds that a creditor cannot purchase an amount of life insurance on the debtor's life greatly in excess of the amount of the debt. Under these authorities, the amount of insurance may exceed the amount of the debt if the excess is not grossly disproportionate.[21] If the excess is grossly disproportionate to the debt, a court might hold the insurance policy void in its entirety, rather than reduce the proceeds paid to the beneficiary to the amount of the debt.[22] The obvious problem created by a gross disproportion between the amount of coverage and the debt is increased moral hazard; the creditor may succumb to a temptation to hasten the debtor's death in order to get the proceeds. Rather, however, than void an entire policy to combat the moral hazard, courts will more often limit the creditor's recovery to the amount of the creditor's insurable interest, that is, the amount of the debt.

In support of the rule which allows the creditor to insure the debtor's life for more than the debt provided the insurance is not grossly disproportionate to the amount of the debt, it is argued that the creditor is not made whole if the debtor dies after the creditor has paid premiums for the policy and before the debt has been repaid. To protect against this possibility, the creditor should be allowed, the argument goes, to purchase more insurance on the debtor's life than the amount of the debt, and as long as the excess is not unreasonable, the creditor should be allowed to keep all proceeds. This argument assumes that insurance is like collateral; the creditor is entitled to be paid in full in the event of the debtor's default through death, and insurance is the means to that end. But unlike taking a security interest in the debtor's property, where the creditor must return to the debtor any proceeds upon foreclosure exceeding the amount of the debt, the insurance transaction creates the possibility that the creditor will profit from the debtor's death. This moral hazard, when coupled with the inherent imprecision in applying a rule of "proportionality" or "gross disproportion," makes the per se rule — a creditor cannot insure the debtor's life for more than the amount of the debt (plus premiums and interest) — more attractive.

---

[20] Albrent v. Spencer, 88 N.W.2d 333, 335 (Wis. 1958).

[21] See Rubenstein v. Mutual Life Ins. Co. of New York, 584 F. Supp. 272 (E.D. La. 1984); Mutual Aid Union v. White, 267 S.W. 137 (Ark. 1924); Ulrich v. Reinoehl, 22 A. 862 (Pa. 1891). Although lacking discussion of the issue, Kentucky Cent. Life Ins. Co. v. McNabb, 825 F. Supp. 269 (D.Kan. 1993), and Lowe v. Rennert, 869 S.W.2d 199, 208-09 (Mo. Ct. App. 1993), appear to approve this rule.

[22] See, e.g., Rubenstein v. Mutual Life Ins. Co. of New York, 584 F. Supp. 272 (E.D. La. 1984); but see Secor v. Pioneer Foundry Co., 173 N.W.2d 780 (Mich. Ct. App. 1969).

§ 44   Timing: When Must the Insurable Interest Exist?

[a]   Property Insurance

In property insurance, most courts adhere to the rule that the insurable interest must only exist at the time of loss, but there is some confusion concerning this rule. A dictum in *Sadlers Co. v. Badcock*,[1] an old English case, stated that insureds should have an interest in property at the time of insuring *and* at the time of loss. Many American cases have repeated this old dictum without realizing that the policies of the indemnity principle which underlies the insurable interest doctrine are satisfied if the interest exists only at the time of loss.[2]

Obviously, it is not enough to require an insurable interest only at the time of contracting. If the interest is terminated after the contract is formed, an incentive for the property's destruction would exist, which is precisely what the insurable interest doctrine seeks to avoid. Yet it follows from this observation that no purpose is served if a person having an insurable interest at the time of loss is denied a recovery due to lack of an insurable interest at the time of contracting. A person having an interest at the time of loss is not likely to destroy the property for a windfall gain. Refusing to enforce such contracts might deter the issuance of policies to people lacking an insurable interest; this, however, assumes that insurers with full knowledge of the facts enter into such contracts, and this assumption is doubtful.

For example, a substantial difference exists between a case where one party insures the house of that party's neighbor, simply as a wager on the probability of the neighbor's house being destroyed, and a case where one expects to buy the neighbor's house and purchases a policy of insurance which becomes effective upon acquisition of title to the neighbor's house. The fact that in the latter case no insurable interest existed at the time the insurance policy was purchased should not void the policy, there being no pernicious purpose to the contracting.

Fortunately, in most cases where the *Sadlers Co.* rule is applied, an insurable interest either exists both at the time of insuring and the time of loss, or at neither time. Thus, the confusion about the rule normally makes no practical difference in outcomes. In those cases where the rule matters, most courts have examined the rule carefully and decided only to require an insurable interest at the time of the loss.

With respect to insurance on goods subject to a sale, the Uniform Commercial Code in § 2-501 states that a buyer obtains an insurable interest in goods when the goods are identified to the contract. Identification can be made at any time and in any manner agreed to by the parties; in the absence of agreement, it occurs when the contract is made if the goods are already existing and when the goods are shipped if the contract is for the sale of future goods. The seller retains an insurable interest in goods so long as the seller has title to or a security interest in the goods. The code specifies that "[n]othing in this section impairs any insurable interest recognized under any other statute or rule of law." Thus, the UCC states specific

---

[1] Sadlers Co. v. Badcock, 2 Atk. 554, 1 Wils. 10, 26 Eng.Rpt. 733 (1743).

[2] See, e.g., Powell v. Insurance Co. of N. Am., 330 S.E.2d 550 (S.C. 1985); Kingston v. Great Southwest Fire Ins. Co., 578 P.2d 1278 (Utah 1978).

conditions under which an insurable interest exists; however, if other rules recognize an insurable interest in a situation where the UCC does not, an insurable interest exists.[3]

[b] Life Insurance

In life insurance, it is commonly said that the insurable interest must exist at the time that the contract is made, and the lack of the interest at the time of the insured's death is irrelevant.[1] To fulfill the purposes of the insurable interest doctrine, it is important that the interest exist at the time the contract is formed. Wagering and the incentive to murder appear in situations where a person obtains insurance on the life of another and designates himself or herself as beneficiary. If the owner-beneficiary has an insurable interest at the time of contracting, the risk that the policy was purchased as a wager or as part of a scheme to murder is reduced.

If the insurable interest doctrine required the presence of an interest at the time of loss (as distinct from the time of contracting), the rule would pick up some cases where a pecuniary interest disappeared after the contract was formed. These situations, however, will be rare. If the insurable interest at the time of contracting is based on a family relationship established by blood, such an interest will not disappear by the time of the insured's death. Family relationships based on legal adoption are rarely severed. It is possible that an insurable interest based on the family relationship of husband and wife may be terminated by the time of loss due to divorce, but this presents a possible problem only in the situation where one spouse has purchased a policy on the life of the other, since the owner of a policy on one's own life is free to name any beneficiary the owner desires. Even where a spouse has purchased a policy on the life of the other spouse and divorce has terminated the marital relationship, a pecuniary relationship usually survives the dissolution of the marriage, and this pecuniary relationship is enough to satisfy the insurable interest requirement. For this reason, the majority rule that divorce does not terminate the beneficiary's interest in a preexisting policy on the life of an ex-spouse is a sound one.[2] Similarly, when the insurable interest was initially based on a pecuniary interest which has disappeared in the interim (such as is the case where a partner takes out a policy on the other partner's life but the partnership is dissolved), the termination of the economic interest does not render the policy void.[3] This result is potentially at odds with the moral hazard underpinnings of the insurable interest doctrine, but the result can be harmonized with the doctrine if one assumes

---

[3] See generally John M. Stockton, Note, *Insurable Interest Under Article Two,* 17 Vand. L. Rev. 815 (1964).

[1] E.g., Herman v. Provident Mutual Life Ins. Co., 886 F.2d 529 (2d Cir. 1989); Lowe v. Rennert, 869 S.W.2d 199, 202 (Mo. Ct. App. 1993); Secor v. Pioneer Foundry Co., 173 N.W.2d 780 (Mich. Ct. App. 1969). See generally William T. Vukowich, *Insurable Interest: When It Must Exist in Property and Life Insurance,* 7 Williamette L.J. 1 (1971).

[2] See, e.g., Connecticut Mut. Life Ins. Co. v. Schaefer, 94 U.S. 457 (1876); Meerwarth v. Meerwarth, 319 A.2d 779 (N.J.Super.Ct. 1974), *aff'd,* 366 A.2d 979 (N.J. 1976).

[3] See, e.g., Trent v. Parker, 591 S.W.2d 769 (Tenn. Ct. App. 1979); Amalgamated Labor Life Ins. Co. v. Rowe, 421 S.W.2d 364 (Ky. 1967); Atkins v. Cotter, 224 S.W. 624 (Ark. 1920).

that one partner's economic interest in the other often survives the formal dissolution of the partnership, much like the situation when a marital relationship is dissolved.

[c]   Liability Insurance

In liability insurance, questions of insurable interest are not particularly important. Most courts hold that liability insurance, like other kinds of insurance, must be supported by an insurable interest.[4] However, the essence of liability insurance is to provide coverage for legal liability that one might incur to others, and an insured always has an interest in protecting against this liability. Therefore, liability insurance — assuming one qualifies as an insured — is always supported by an insurable interest.[5] Thus, even if one were to conclude that an insurable interest is not required for liability insurance, such a rule would have no significant adverse implications.

The notion that liability insurance is always supported by an insurable interest is related to the "legal liability" type of insurable interest under the legal interest theory.[6] The legal interest test for an insurable interest can be satisfied by entering into a contract under which one is liable for failing to obtain insurance on a given piece of property. It is the party's potential liability that provides the interest to support a policy of property insurance. Similarly, a person is potentially liable in tort to a broad range of individuals; thus, a person has an interest in securing liability insurance for protection against liability to others.

Many of the cases in the liability insurance setting where insurable interest has been at issue involve questions of title to property. For example, one who does not own a vehicle cannot obtain owner's liability insurance on the vehicle.[7] Obviously, a person who does not own a vehicle cannot be liable for negligence in the status of an owner. It could be said that the nonowner of a vehicle who has purchased liability insurance with regard to that vehicle's use lacks an insurable interest in the liability coverage, but the important fact is that the person has no legal interest in the vehicle or factual expectancy of being held liable for a loss arising out of the vehicle's use. However, if a person who does not own a vehicle has a relationship to it such that he or she might be held vicariously liable for injuries caused through the automobile's use, that person has an insurable interest in the vehicle sufficient to support a policy of liability insurance.[8]

---

[4] See, e.g., Nationwide Mut. Ins. Co. v. Edwards, 312 S.E.2d 656 (N.C. Ct. App. 1984); Special Jet Services, Inc. v. Federal Ins. Co., 643 F.2d 977 (3d Cir. 1981); Alabama Farm Bureau Mut. Ins. Co., v. Davis, 354 So. 2d 15 (Ala.Civ.App.Ct. 1978).

[5] See United Fire & Cas. Co. v. Reeder, 9 F.3d 15 (5th Cir. 1993); Industrial Indem. Co. v. Goettl, 674 P.2d 869 (Ariz.App. 1983); 6B APPLEMAN § 4253, at 18–19 (1979); see also Western Cas. & Sur. Co. v. Herman, 318 F.2d 50 (8th Cir. 1963); Ohio Farmers Ins. Co. v. Lantz, 246 F.2d 182 (7th Cir. 1957), cert. denied, 355 U.S. 883.

[6] See § 42[b], supra.

[7] See Johnson v. Aetna Life and Cas. Co., 472 So. 2d 859 (Fla. Dist. Ct. App. 1985); Nationwide Mut. Ins. Co. v. Edwards, 312 S.E.2d 656 (N.C. Ct. App. 1984).

[8] See James v. Pennsylvania Gen. Ins. Co., 306 S.E.2d 422 (Ga. Ct. App. 1983) (father transferred title of car to son; father, though not owner, had potential liability under family car doctrine; father had insurable interest to support policy of liability insurance); Auto-Owners Ins. Co. v. Smith, 343 S.E.2d 129 (Ga. Ct. App. 1986).

§ 45   Waiver and Estoppel: Preventing an Insurer from Denying the Existence of an Insurable Interest

Most courts that have considered the subject have held that the insurer cannot waive or be estopped to assert the insurable interest requirement.[1] The issue usually arises in this way: the insured or beneficiary claims the proceeds, the insurer refuses the claim on the ground that the insured or beneficiary lacks an insurable interest, and the insured or beneficiary responds to the refusal by asserting that the insurer has made some statement or done something that amounts to a waiver of the insurable interest defense or which estops the insurer to assert the defense. Courts that adhere to the rule that the insurable interest defense cannot be waived or that the insurer cannot be estopped to assert it give great weight to the public policies served by the rule. In the view of these courts, these policies would be ill-served by allowing the doctrine to be evaded on a case-by-case basis, even in the name of fairness.

Some courts temper the general rule by allowing waiver or estoppel to defeat the insurable interest defense in circumstances where the insurer is merely alleging that the value of the interest is less than the proceeds claimed under the policy.[2] This argument has particular appeal where the insurer issues a valued policy, collects a premium based upon the stipulated value, and then after a loss argues that the value of the insured's insurable interest in the property is less than the stipulated coverage.[3] Conceptually, estopping the insurer from claiming that the insured's interest was overvalued differs from estopping the insurer from alleging that there was no insurable interest at all. But granting that estopping the insurer from claiming the insurable interest had no value would be tantamount to estopping the insurer from asserting the absence of an interest, one might still contend that the public policies affected by allowing the assertion of a waiver or estoppel are not as great when the only question is what value to place on the interest. If the concern is with the risk of destruction of the property, allowing waiver and estoppel to bar the insurer from asserting facts going to the value of property once destroyed will not increase this risk. In the same vein, the insurer's act of filing an interpleader and depositing the proceeds of a life insurance policy in court waives the insurer's right to claim that

---

[1] E.g., Beard v. American Agency Life Ins. Co., 550 A.2d 677 (Md. 1988); Elmore v. Life Ins. Co. of Virginia, 198 S.E. 5 (S.C. 1938); Hack v. Metz, 176 S.E. 314 (S.C. 1934); Colver v. Central States Fire Ins. Co., 287 P. 266 (Kan. 1930); Farm Bureau Mut. Ins. Co. of Arkansas, Inc., v. Glover, 616 S.W.2d 755 (Ark.Ct.App. 1981); Bell v. National Life & Accident Ins. Co., 123 So. 2d 598 (ALa. Ct. App. 1960). But see Morgan v. Patrons Mut. Ins. Ass'n, 813 F. Supp. 1502, 1507 (D.Kan. 1993); National Sec. Fire & Cas. Co. v. Hester, 298 So. 2d 236 (Ala. 1974); Kelly v. Prudential Ins. Co. of Am., 6 A.2d 55 (Pa. 1939); Whitten v. Cincinnati Ins. Co., 544 N.E.2d 1169 (Ill. App. Ct. 1989); Ferrara v. Insurance Co. of N. Am., 135 A.D.2d 366, (N.Y. 1987). See generally Ingram, *Insurable Interest: Who Can Question It? Do Waiver and Estoppel Apply?* 52 Ins. Counsel J. 647 (1985); Annot., *Estoppel Of, or Waiver By, Issuer of Life Insurance Policy to Assert Defense of Lack of Insurable Interest,* 86 A.L.R.4th 828 (1991). For a discussion of waiver and estoppel generally, see § 25E, *supra.*

[2] E.g., Filiatreau v. Allstate Insurance, 358 S.E.2d 829 (W.Va. 1987); Liverpool & London & Globe Ins. Co., Ltd. v. Bolling, 10 S.E.2d 518 (Va. 1940).

[3] See G.M. Battery and Boat Co. v. L.K.N. Corp., 747 S.W.2d 624 (Mo. 1988) (en banc).

the policy is invalid due to lack of an insurable interest.[4] When an interpleader is filed, the risk of loss cannot be increased, since a loss has already occurred.

Courts have also declined to follow the general rule in circumstances where the agent writing the policy knew that the person obtaining the insurance lacked an interest in the insured person or property but wrote the policy anyway.[5] For example, in *Republic Insurance Co. v. Silverton Elevators, Inc.*, a Texas case,[6] an employer provided its employee with a house as part of the employee's compensation. The employer also provided insurance on the house and the employee's possessions. The agent selling the policy knew that the employer owned the house, did not own the employee's possessions, and intended to purchase coverage for both the house and the possessions. The court rejected the insurer's claim that no proceeds were payable on the household goods destroyed by a tornado due to the employer's lack of an insurable interest in those goods:

> [T]he knowledge of [the employee's] ownership of the household goods by Republic's local agent and his actions with respect thereto were imputed to and binding upon Republic. Issuance of the policy and collection of the premiums with such knowledge operates as a waiver of any requirement that the named insured own or possess a beneficial interest in the insured property.[7]

A similar case is *McGehee v. Farmers Insurance Co.*,[8] a recent Tenth Circuit decision. Plaintiffs, a married couple, were the named insureds on a homeowner's policy issued by the insurer for property owned by the husband's parents. The agent, apparently thinking that the parents intended to give the property to their son and daughter-in-law in the future, wrote the policy with the plaintiffs as the named insureds even though they had no title to the house at the time of contracting. The couple continued to live in the house for four years before it was destroyed by fire, and they never acquired the title. The district court sustained the insurer's claim that the plaintiffs lacked an insurable interest in the home. The Tenth Circuit reversed, reasoning that disclosures made to the soliciting agent were imputable to the insurer:

> We are impressed with the fact that the [plaintiff's father] made a complete disclosure to the agent [about who had title to the property] and the agent wrote the policy as he did with the son and his wife as the insureds and the [father] and his wife as mortgagees. It was the agent's choice which the [father] accepted. The company was estopped from taking a contrary position.[9]

Absent in the facts of *Silverton Elevators* and *McGehee* were indications that the named insureds would destroy the insured property to collect the insurance proceeds. Moreover, in each case, the named insureds' forfeiture would have been substantial had the policies been declared unenforceable. Both cases are good candidates for recognizing an exception to the general rule that the insurer cannot waive or be

---

[4] See Prudential Ins. Co. of Am. v. Tutalo, 178 A. 859 (R.I. 1935).

[5] See, e.g., McGehee v. Farmers Ins. Co., Inc., 734 F.2d 1422 (10th Cir. 1984); National Sec. Fire & Cas. Co. v. Hester, 298 So. 2d 236 (Ala. 1974).

[6] 493 S.W.2d 748 (Tex. 1973).

[7] 493 S.W.2d at 750.

[8] 734 F.2d 1422 (10th Cir. 1984).

[9] 734 F.2d at 1424–25.

estopped to assert the insurable interest doctrine; both cases stand as examples of courts bending an ordinarily rigid rule to work fairness in an extreme set of facts. Of course, not all courts are as willing to bend rigid rules. For example, in *Vance v. Wiley T. Booth, Inc.*,[10] a North Carolina court ruled that the insurer was not estopped from asserting the insured's lack of insurable interest and then held that no insurable interest existed in circumstances where the insured-plaintiff deeded the insured real estate to her mother, told the insurer's agent about the title transfer but did not change the coverage, and continued to pay premiums on the policy.[11] However, an Alabama court ruled in circumstances where no insurable interest existed that the insurer's acceptance of premium payments on the void policies was sufficient evidence of "damage" to support a claim of fraud against the insurer.[12]

§ 46   Property Insurance and the Insurable Interest Requirement: Some Troublespots

[a]   Stolen Property

Since automobiles are frequently stolen for the purpose of resale, automobile insurance policies are often purchased by people who are the unwitting owners of stolen vehicles. Thereafter, the car may be damaged or stolen once again. In a number of cases, the insurer discovered after the insured submitted a claim that the insured, as the possessor of stolen goods, lacked perfect title to the vehicle. Armed with this information, the insurer denied the insured's claim on the ground that the insured lacked an insurable interest in the vehicle. Although the cases addressing the question of insurable interest in stolen property typically involve automobiles, the logic of these cases should apply to all kinds of stolen property.

A number of the courts that first confronted the issue agreed with the insurers' contention that a good faith purchaser of a stolen automobile has no insurable interest in it.[1] These courts typically reasoned that the good faith purchaser has no legal or equitable title in the stolen vehicle; instead, such a purchaser only has a right of possession. This right is subject to being extinguished should the true owner reclaim the automobile. Since the right to possession is subject to total eradication, it does not follow that the possessor has a substantial economic interest in the property. Of course, the thief has no insurable interest in the automobile, because the thief lacks any kind of title and has no substantial economic interest in the property.

In the more recent cases, however, courts have held that a good faith purchaser of a stolen vehicle does have an insurable interest in the vehicle. This result is better

---

[10] 436 S.E.2d 256 (N.C. Ct. App. 1993). See also Liverpool & London & Globe Ins. Co., Ltd. v. Bolling, 10 S.E.2d 518 (Va. 1940).

[11] 436 S.E.2d at 257-58.

[12] Willingham v. United Ins. Co. of Am. 628 So. 2d 328, 332 (Ala. 1993).

[1] See Ernie Miller Pontiac, Inc. v. Home Ins. Co., 534 P.2d 1 (Okla. 1975); Insurance Co. of N. Am. v. Cliff Pettit Motors, Inc., 513 S.W.2d 785 (Tenn. 1974) (overruled by Duncan v. State Farm Fire & Cas. Co., 587 S.W.2d 375 (Tenn. 1979)); Herrington v. American Sec. Ins. Co., 184 S.E.2d 673 (Ga. Ct. App. 1971). See generally Annot., *Automobile Fire, Theft, and Collision Insurance: Insurable Interest in Stolen Motor Vehicle*, 38 A.L.R.4th 538 (1985).

reasoned; the owner of stolen property, assuming the owner neither knew nor had reason to know that the property was stolen, has good, lawful title against everyone except the true owner, and this is sufficient to constitute an insurable interest.[2] This result is also consistent with the factual expectancy theory of insurable interest: the insured has a substantial economic interest in the preservation of the property, since the insured probably paid a significant sum of money for the vehicle, which would be lost if the vehicle were destroyed in an accident.[3] It is essential that the insured be an innocent, bona fide purchaser. Whether a jurisdiction adheres to a legal interest or factual expectancy theory of insurable interest, the insured's interest in the property must be a lawful one, and this is not the case if the insured acquires the property illegally or knows or has reason to know that the property in question is stolen.[4]

In a few cases, courts have considered whether the innocent purchaser of a stolen vehicle can recover under the comprehensive coverage of the purchaser's automobile insurance policy when the vehicle is repossessed by the true owner. Those courts which have answered the question in the affirmative have involved policies where the language defining what losses are covered is broad (e.g., "direct loss of or damage to the automobile except loss caused by collision") and loss due to repossession of a stolen vehicle is not specifically excluded.[5]

Most automobile policies now enumerate the circumstances which will constitute "loss other than by collision," and repossession of a stolen vehicle by the true owner is not among them. One court has opined that the confiscation of a vehicle by the police while enforcing the true owner's rights is "not a risk within the expectation of a purchaser of automobile insurance."[6] The remedy of the insured in these circumstances is to pursue an action for breach of warranty of title against the person who sold the insured the vehicle; eventually, the assertion of this claim back through the chain of possessors of the property will leave the loss on the party that dealt with the thief, assuming the thief cannot be located, or the last person in the chain

---

[2] E.g., Shockley v. Harleysville Mut. Ins. Co., 553 A.2d 973, 974-75 (Pa. Super. Ct. 1988); Snethen v. Oklahoma State Union of Farmers Educational and Co-op. Union of America, 664 P.2d 377 (Okla. 1983) (overruling *Ernie Miller Pontiac, supra*); Castle Cars, Inc. v. United States Fire Ins. Co., 273 S.E.2d 793 (Va. 1981); Butler v. Farmers Ins. Co. of Ariz., 616 P.2d 46 (Ariz. 1980); Phillips v. Cincinnati Ins. Co., 398 N.E.2d 564 (Ohio 1979); Duncan v. State Farm Fire & Cas. Co., 587 S.W.2d 375 (Tenn. 1979) (overruling *Cliff Pettit Motors, supra*); Reznick v. Home Ins. Co., 4 Ill.Dec. 525, 360 N.E.2d 461 (Ill. App. Ct. 1977); Scarola v. Insurance Co. of North Am., 292 N.E.2d 776 (N.Y. 1972).

[3] See § 42[c], *supra*.

[4] See Howard v. State Farm Mut. Auto. Ins. Co., 496 N.W.2d 862 (Neb. 1993) (purchaser has no insurable interest in stolen vehicle in light of the "suspicious nature of the transaction they described and of the fire itself" which destroyed the vehicle); Richard Halegua Fantastic Things, Inc. v. Crum & Forster Commercial Ins., 623 N.E.2d 1334 (Ohio Ct.App. 1993) (knowledge that goods are stolen defeats insurable interest, even if the motive for acquiring the stolen property are well-intentioned, e.g., reacquiring the stolen property so that it can be returned to the true owner).

[5] See Butler v. Farmers Ins. Co. of Arizona, 616 P.2d 46 (Ariz. 1980); Reznick v. Home Ins. Co., 360 N.E.2d 461 (Ill. App. Ct. 1977).

[6] Cueto v. Allstate Ins. Co., 544 A.2d 906, 908 (N.J.Super.Ct. 1987).

of possession who can be found. Note that if one concludes that the automobile insurer does not insure title, the insurer which reimburses the innocent purchaser of stolen property for the loss of the property by fire, theft, or some other covered peril presumably would not have a subrogation right against the party that sold the insured the stolen vehicle; rather, the insurer's subrogation rights would run only to the party whose negligence or intent caused the vehicle's destruction or loss.[7] In the same vein, the innocent purchaser of a stolen vehicle who receives insurance proceeds for the destruction or loss of the vehicle due to a covered peril should, in logic, hold those proceeds in trust for the true owner as a substitution for the destroyed or lost vehicle,[8] inasmuch as the innocent purchaser, upon loss or destruction of the stolen property, would be liable in tort for conversion.[9] Under this reasoning, the innocent purchaser who, unable to return the vehicle, is required to surrender the proceeds of insurance to the true owner would still possess a means of redress through pursuit of a claim for breach of warranty of title.

[b] Property with a "Negative" Value

A particularly thorny problem is presented when property has a negative value, meaning that the property has no useful value and needs to be demolished, which is a cost to its owner. The risk in such a situation is that the owner will be encouraged to destroy the building (for example, by arson) in an effort to recover insurance proceeds on the structure. For the owner, an arrangement under which the building is destroyed and the insurer pays for it is the best economic result possible.

An illustrative case is *Tublitz v. Glen Falls Ins. Co.,*[10] a 1981 New Jersey decision. The owner of three buildings, which were insured by the defendant, entered into a contract to be performed within ten days to demolish the buildings. Four days later, one of the buildings was destroyed by fire. The owner submitted a claim under the insurance policy, but the insurer refused to pay any proceeds on the ground that the insured had suffered no loss since the insured intended to demolish the buildings. The court refused to accept the insurer's argument, noting that most courts have held the existence of an executory contract to demolish a building does not deprive the owner of an insurable interest in it.[11] The court reasoned that the existence of the contract does not mean that demolition will necessarily occur. Unless the contract is one which could be specifically enforced in an action in equity, the insured may decide to cancel the contract, even if it means paying damages for its breach. The court also referred to the reasonable expectations principle: "it is reasonable to infer from all the surrounding circumstances that plaintiff expected his fire insurance coverage to be in force until demolition was actually begun."[12]

---

[7] See Schockley v. Harleysville Mut. Ins. Co., 553 A.2d 973 (Pa. Super. 1988).

[8] See Duncan v. State Farm Fire & Cas. Co., 587 S.W.2d 375 (Tenn. 1979).

[9] See Beeck v. Aquaslide 'N' Dive Corp, 350 N.W.2d 149 (Iowa 1984); Coffman v. Faulkner, 591 S.W.2d 23 (Mo. Ct. App. 1979).

[10] 431 A.2d 201 (N.J.Super.Ct. 1981).

[11] 431 A.2d at 202. See also Garcy Corp. v. Home Ins. Co., 496 F.2d 479 (7th Cir. 1974), *cert. denied,* 419 U.S. 843 (1974); Gendron v. Pawtucket Mut. Ins. Co., 384 A.2d 694 (Me. 1978); Dubin Paper Co. v. Insurance Co. of N. Am., 63 A.2d 85 (Pa. 1949).

[12] 431 A.2d at 202.

Under the reasoning of the court in *Tublitz*, once demolition begins, the insured no longer has an insurable interest in the property.[13] Commencing demolition is tantamount to an irrevocable commitment to demolish the property, and the insured at that moment ceases to possess an insurable interest in the property. However, until the irrevocable commitment is made, the insured possesses an insurable interest. Thus, if the insured has entered into a contract of demolition that is specifically enforceable against the insured, it follows that the insured has made an irrevocable commitment to demolish the property and lacks an insurable interest in it.[14]

If the insured has an insurable interest in the property under a contract of demolition, it does not necessarily follow that the insured suffers any loss if the building is destroyed by fire prior to the planned demolition. The court in *Tublitz* specifically left open the question of the amount of the insured's recovery under the policy.[15] If the insured has an insurable interest, the insurance contract is not void, but the value of a building about to be demolished could be zero. Under the indemnity principle — which exists independently of the insurable interest doctrine — the insured cannot recover proceeds exceeding the loss, and thus such an insured, even though prevailing on the argument that the policy is valid, may nevertheless recover nothing.

This proposition can be illustrated by exploring *Chicago Title & Trust Co. v. United States Fidelity and Guaranty Co.,*[16] a 1973 case decided by an Illinois federal district court. Plaintiff owned title to a building that on May 1, 1972 was substantially damaged by fire and was thereafter demolished. A few weeks prior to the fire, a county court had ordered the building vacated, boarded, and secured due to numerous building code violations. Plaintiff sought to recover under the insurance policy for the building's destruction. The court thought it nonsensical to allow the plaintiff to recover any amount of proceeds:

> [W]hen the subject building was destroyed on May 1, 1972, it was an economically useless building. It was empty, secured and boarded. It had been gutted by a previous fire. It was not being used in any way . . . it would be ludicrous to allow the plaintiff to recover a substantial amount of money representing the replacement cost less depreciation of a building that was for all practical purposes nonexistent.[17]

Under the reasoning of *Tublitz*, one could conclude in *Chicago Title* as follows: on the date of the insured's loss (i.e., the date of the fire) the insured possessed an

---

[13] See Board of Educ. of Hancock Cty. v. Hartford Fire Ins. Co., 19 S.E.2d 448 (W.Va. 1942); cf. Aetna State Bank v. Maryland Cas. Co., 345 F. Supp. 903 (N.D. Ill. 1972) (no actual cash value in property irrevocably in process of demolition); but see Eagle Square Mfg. Co. v. Vermont Mut. Fire Ins. Co., 212 A.2d 636 (Vt. 1965).

[14] See Royal Ins. Co. v. Sisters of Presentation, 430 F.2d 759 (9th Cir. 1970) (even though title to convent had not been transferred to wrecking company, irrevocable contract to demolish eliminated insurable interest); Lieberman v. Hartford Fire Ins. Co., 287 N.E.2d 38 (Ill. App. Ct. 1972).

[15] 431 A.2d at 202 n.3.

[16] 376 F. Supp. 767 (N.D. Ill. 1973).

[17] 376 F. Supp. at 770.

insurable interest in the building; however, the insured suffered no loss upon destruction of the building. By this logic, the insured would recover nothing, which is the result that the court favored. The court in *Chicago Title,* however, concluded that no insurable interest existed: "In the instant case, the building was economically useless at the time of the fire . . . we conclude that under all the precedents, there was no insurable interest in the building at the time of the fire on May 1, 1972."[18] Plainly, the court's result is a good one, but its analysis is perplexing because the insured definitely had a property interest in the building, which supports an insurable interest under the legal interest theory. This interest has some value, since the property at least had value as scrap (although it is difficult to imagine a scenario where damage could be done to the value of the building as scrap). Furthermore, the court's analysis cannot be reconciled with the prevailing judicial doctrine that an owner of a building has an insurable interest in it as long as an irrevocable commitment to demolish the building has not been made.

In short, the public policies underlying the insurable interest doctrine are not disserved if the insured is deemed to possess an insurable interest in property subject to a contract of demolition, so long as that interest is properly valued. This is true even with respect to property that is definitely about to be demolished. An insured who owns legal title to a building that is subject to an irrevocable contract of demolition arguably has an insurable interest in the property; the value of the interest, however, is zero, since the building as a standing structure has no value and its accidental destruction prior to a planned demolition causes the insured no loss.[19]

§ 47 Life Insurance and the Insurable Interest Requirement: Some Troublespots

[a] Assigning a Life Insurance Policy to One Lacking an Insurable Interest

Whether the owner of a life insurance policy should be allowed to assign the policy to one who lacks an insurable interest in the life of the insured is a hotly disputed question. Most courts allow free assignability of insurance policies,[1] but a minority of courts will invalidate a policy assigned to someone without an insurable interest in the life of the insured.[2] When a policy is assigned, all of the

---

[18] 376 F. Supp. at 770–71.

[19] In California, insurable interest is defined as a "pecuniary interest." Thus, the court reasoned in Royal Ins. Co. v. Sisters of the Presentation, 430 F.2d 759 (9th Cir. 1970), that nuns who had made an irrevocable contract with a wrecking company to demolish a convent but retained title to the convent lacked a pecuniary interest — and therefore an insurable interest — in the property.

[1] See, e.g., Grigsby v. Russell, 222 U.S. 149 (1911); Hammers v. Prudential Life Ins. Co. of Am., 216 S.W.2d 703 (Tenn. 1948); Mutual Life Ins. Co. v. Allen, (Mass. 1884).

[2] E.g., Mutual Life Ins. Co v. Allen, 52 Am.Rep. 245 (Mass. 1884); Land v. West Coast Life Ins. Co., 270 P.2d 154 (Or. 1954); United Ins. Co. of Am. v. Hadden, 190 S.E.2d 638 (Ga. Ct. App. 1972).

ownership rights of the policy — including the right to change the beneficiary —
are transferred to someone else. One of the protections for a person who purchases
a policy of life insurance on that person's own life is the ability to designate a
different beneficiary should the relationship between the insured and the first
beneficiary deteriorate. If the policy is assigned to someone else, the insured loses
this protection. In fact, if a policy can be purchased by the owner and assigned to
a person lacking an insurable interest, the result is the same as if the person lacking
an insurable interest took out the policy on the life of the insured in the first place.

On the other hand, life insurance is often viewed as an investment. To maximize
its value as an investment, free assignability is necessary. Moreover, a person committed to assigning the policy to someone lacking an insurable interest in the
insured's life can do so through circuitous means. For example, a person could
purchase life insurance on his or her own life, designate his or her estate as
beneficiary, and enter into a contract with the "assignee" to bequeath the proceeds
of the insurance to the "assignee." Thus, some courts uphold the assignment of a
life insurance policy to an individual lacking an insurable interest in the assignor's
life.[3]

Even under the majority view, if a court finds that the assignment was part of
a plan from the beginning on the part of the assignee to obtain a wager, the
assignment will be held invalid. The occurrence of the assignment almost immediately after the policy is purchased may invite such an inquiry.[4]

[b]   Standing to Question Insurable Interest

Most courts adhere to the view that only the insurer has standing to raise the
absence of insurable interest.[5] Although this rule is stated broadly, it has little
relevance outside the area of life insurance. In property or liability insurance, a third
party has no reason to raise the issue of lack of insurable interest, since a third party
has nothing to gain by invalidating someone else's policy. The rule that only the
insurer can raise the absence of insurable interest is derived from the notion that
only a party to the contract should have standing to raise an issue that might void
the contract. This is somewhat perplexing, since the insurable interest doctrine
evolved to protect the public from wagering contracts and incentives to the
destruction of property or lives, not to protect the interests of insurers.

It is nonsensical to apply the rule so rigidly as to prevent a named insured from
canceling the contract upon discovery that someone without an insurable interest

---

[3] See Grigsby v. Russell, 222 U.S. 149 (1911) (distinguishing Warnock v. Davis, 104 U.S.
775 (1881)); Werenzinski v. Prudential Ins. Co. of Am., 14 A.2d 279 (Pa. 1940); Gray v.
Penn Mut. Life Ins. Co. of Philadelphia,126 N.E.2d 409 (Ill. App. Ct. 1955).

[4] See, e.g., Lakin v. Postal Life & Cas. Ins. Co., 316 S.W.2d 542 (Mo. 1958); Annot.,
*Validity of Assignment of Life Insurance Policy to One Who Has No Insurable Interest in
Insured,* 30 A.L.R.2d 1310, 1359 (1953).

[5] See, e.g., Lowe v. Rennert, 869 S.W.2d 199, 203 (Mo. Ct. App. 1993); Ryan v. Tickle,
316 N.W.2d 580 (Neb. 1982); Poland v. Fisher's Estate, 329 S.W.2d 768 (Mo. 1959); see
generally Ingram, *Insurable Interest: Who Can Question It? Do Waiver and Estoppel Apply?*
52 Ins. Counsel J. 647 (1985).

has taken out a policy on the insured's life without obtaining the insured's consent, since the insured is the person whose life may be at risk due to the arrangement. The named insured while alive, even if not the owner of the policy, should be able unilaterally to invalidate the insurance contract issued to someone lacking an insurable interest in the insured's life. If an insurer can be held liable in tort for failing to investigate when the named insured reveals the beneficiary's criminal motive in taking out the policy,[6] it would make little sense to say that a named insured who is surprised to discover that someone without an insurable interest has taken out a policy on the insured's life could not unilaterally declare the policy void. Indeed, it may be tortious for an insurer who receives a request to cancel the policy from the named insured to fail to carry out the request in this situation.

A more difficult case is presented where the named insured previously consented to the issuance of a policy to a person possessing an insurable interest in the individual's life, but that interest has since been extinguished and the named insured now wants the policy canceled. A typical fact pattern involves a firm that purchased a policy on a key employee who subsequently left the company, thereby extinguishing the insurable interest. Under the rule that a life insurance policy is valid if an insurable interest exists at the time of the policy's issuance, the insurance policy is still enforceable. Yet the insured may have a legitimate fear that he or she will suffer a premature "accidental" death if the company should later have financial difficulties and need a quick source of cash. The issue is whether the insured's prior consent to the issuance of the policy is sufficient to deny the insured the right to demand cancellation of the policies upon the extinguishment of the relationship supplying the insurable interest. One court has held that the insured had no right to demand cancellation of the policies in such a situation, but the court specifically noted that there "appears to be no imminent danger" to the insured.[7]

The practical significance of the standing limitation is to prevent one who claims the proceeds of life insurance once the named insured is dead from arguing that the designated beneficiary should not get the proceeds due to lack of an insurable interest.[8] This is not as illogical as it might seem at first glance. If the beneficiary takes out the policy on the life of another, the beneficiary should get the proceeds since, after all, it was the beneficiary who paid the premiums — assuming, of course, that the beneficiary did not bring about the insured's death. If the beneficiary did bring about the insured's death, there is no need to give a cause of action to an heir or contingent beneficiary to raise the lack of insurable interest, since the estate of the insured and contingent beneficiaries have standing to allege that the primary beneficiary is disqualified on account of causing the insured's death. Moreover, the absence of beneficiary standing is mitigated by statutes in at least twenty-five states which give the individual insured or the executor or administrator of the insured's estate a cause of action against any beneficiary, assignee, or other payee who

---

[6] See Life Ins. Co. of Georgia v. Lopez, 443 So. 2d 947 (Fla. 1983).

[7] See Trent v. Parker, 591 S.W.2d 769 (Tenn. Ct. App. 1979); see also Meehan v. Transamerica Occidental Life Ins. Co., 499 N.E.2d 602 (Ill. App. Ct. 1986).

[8] E.g., Ryan v. Tickle, 316 N.W.2d 580 (Neb. 1982); Secor v. Pioneer Foundry Co., 173 N.W.2d 780 (Mich.Ct.Ct.App. 1969).

receives the proceeds of insurance under a policy issued in violation of the insurable interest requirement.[9]

Despite widespread articulation of the rule, some courts have simply overlooked the rule limiting standing to insurers and have allowed third parties to raise the issue.[10] These cases usually involve the situation where the named insured has assigned the policy to someone lacking an insurable interest, a situation which raises special issues.[11]

[c] Incontestability Clauses

Life insurance contracts usually contain, and sometimes are required by state statute to contain, clauses providing that the policy shall be "incontestable" after a certain period, such as one or two years. The purposes of such clauses are to eliminate the use by insurers of stale defenses and to make the insurance contract reliable in the sense that beneficiaries, after the specified period of time expires, can rely upon the existence of the coverage.[12]

In some instances, the policies underlying incontestability clauses collide with the policies of the insurable interest doctrine. A choice must be made between these two principles, and most courts conclude that the insurable interest doctrine, which is intended to deter the evils of wagering and destruction of property and lives, should be enforced despite the unfairness to individuals who benefit from incontestability clauses.[13]

Public policy supports the conclusion that the lack of an insurable interest should not become incontestable after the contestability period expires, since the evils of

---

[9] See, e.g, 24 Hawaii Rev. Stat. 24 § 431:10- 204; Md. Code Ann., tit. 48A, § 366; Okla. Stat. Ann., tit. 36, § 3604.

[10] E.g., Butterworth v. Mississippi Valley Trust Co., 240 S.W.2d 676 (Mo. 1951); Allgood v. Wilmington Savings & Trust Co., 88 S.E.2d 825 (N.C. 1955); Smith v. Coleman, 183 Va. 601, 32 S.E.2d 704, *vacated on other grounds on reh'g,* 32 S.E.2d 704 (Va. 1945).

[11] See § 52B, *infra.*

[12] For further discussion of incontestability clauses, see § 104B, *infra.*

[13] See, e.g., Beard v. American Agency Life Ins. Co., 550 A.2d 677, 688-89 (Md. 1988); Wood v. New York Life Ins. Co., 336 S.E.2d 806 (Ga. 1985); Crump v. Northwestern Nat'l Life Ins. Co., 45 Cal. Rptr. 814, 819 (Cal. Ct. App. 1965); Obertuch v. Security Mut. Life Ins. Co., 114 F.2d 873 (7th Cir. 1940), *cert. denied,* 312 U.S. 696 (1941). But see Bogacki v. Great-West Life Assur. Co., 234 N.W. 865 (Mich. 1931) (statute requiring incontestability clause and listing exceptions to requirement does not include insurable interest doctrine; therefore, incontestability clause bars insurable interest defense). Examples of statutes in force today that would appear to fit the description of the statute at issue in *Bogacki* include Ala. Code § 27- 15-4 (policy shall be incontestable except for nonpayment of premiums); Alaska Stat. § 21.84.270(b)(9) (policy shall be incontestable except for nonpayment of premiums, violation of provisions relating to service in armed forces, and violation of provisions relating to suspension or expulsion); Cal. Ins. Code § 10244(2) (policy shall be incontestable except for suicide, nonpayment of premiums, or violation of policy conditions relating to military service during time of war); N.H. Stat. § 418:23 (policy shall be incontestable except for nonpayment of premiums, risks limited or not assumed, violation of provisions relating to military or naval service, and violation of provisions relating to religion, occupation, suspension or expulsion).

wagering and intentional destruction of property and lives do not become less deviant at that time. This conclusion is defensible from a theoretical standpoint as well. The incontestability clause bars claims going to the contract's validity; in other words, the clause presupposes that the policy has been "in force" for a period of time. If the contract *never* became valid in the first place because it offended public policy due to the lack of an insurable interest, it cannot be enforced by a court. The distinction is, in effect, one between a contract that is "void" and one that is "voidable." A void contract was never a contract at all; lack of an insurable interest makes the contract "void." In contrast, breach of warranty, fraud, and misrepresentation are defenses that make a contract voidable at the option of the insurer; the contract was in existence, but it is voidable. The incontestability clause bars defenses that might be asserted to invalidate an *existing* contract. Given this analysis, the view that the insurer should be precluded from asserting the lack of insurable interest as a defense after the incontestability period has expired has not gained widespread favor.

[d] Tort Liability for Issuing Policy to One Lacking an Interest in the Insured's Life and the Role of Consent

A few cases have considered whether an insurer can be held liable for selling a policy of life insurance to someone who lacks an insurable interest in the life of the insured in circumstances where the underwriting is alleged to have caused or contributed to the death of the insured.[14] Two of these cases have particular prominence.

In *Liberty National Life Insurance Co. v. Weldon*,[15] an Alabama decision, an aunt-in-law submitted applications to three insurance companies for insurance on the life of her infant niece, naming herself as beneficiary. The aunt-in-law did not live with the niece; on the application, she designated herself as the insured's "aunt." After the policies were issued (and two of them delivered), the aunt-in-law murdered her niece. Under Alabama law, the family relationship of aunt-niece is insufficient to create an insurable interest. Also, the conduct of the agents in *Weldon* left much to be desired. One agent knew the child's parents well but did not inform them of the aunt-in-law's application, did not seek the parents' consent to the issuance of the policy, and did not comply with his company's underwriting requirements. Another agent visited the child's parents without informing them of the reason for his visit. The third agent visited the child's home and was told by the child's father that he did not want anyone taking out life insurance on his daughter.

The child's father brought a wrongful death action against the companies, alleging that the aunt-in-law lacked an insurable interest, that the insurers knew or should have known this fact, and that the negligent issuance of the policies contributed to

---

14 See Ramey v. Carolina Life Ins. Co., 135 S.E.2d 362 (S.C. 1964); Liberty Nat'l. Life Ins. Co. v. Weldon, 100 So. 2d 696 (Ala. 1957); Life Ins. Co. of Georgia v. Lopez, 443 So. 2d 947 (Fla. 1983). See generally Kingree, *Life Insurers' Liability for Negligent Underwriting*, 53 Ins. Counsel J. 655 (1985); Annot., *Insurer's Tort Liability for Wrongful or Negligent Issuance of Life Policy*, 37 A.L.R.4th 972 (1985).

15 100 So. 2d 696 (Ala. 1957).

the aunt-in-law's murdering of the child. A jury trial resulted in a verdict against the insurers.[16]

The Alabama Supreme Court first observed the general rule that all persons have a duty to exercise reasonable care not to injure another. Insurers through careless underwriting can put insureds in serious danger; in the absence of an insurable interest, a greater risk exists that the owner of a policy will murder the insured. Accordingly, insurers have a duty to use reasonable care not to issue policies to persons lacking an interest in the life of the insured, lest they create a situation which may incite murder. The court held that sufficient evidence supported the jury's finding that the insurers were not concerned about the insurable interest requirement and that they failed to exercise reasonable care not to issue a policy to the aunt, who lacked an insurable interest.

The underlying problem in the *Weldon* case is that the insurer issued the policies on the life of the niece without obtaining her parents' consent. In many cases, the consent of the insured to the policy being issued provides sufficient protection against the threat that the beneficiary will murder the insured. The insured is unlikely to give consent in a situation where murder is the likely reason that the applicant is seeking the policy. Indeed, in nearly half the states, the consent of the insured is statutorily required prior to the policy's issuance except in cases where a spousal relationship is involved or a parent seeks insurance in the life of a minor child.[17]

The presence of consent is obvious in the situation in which one purchases insurance on one's own life. It is sometimes said that one always has an insurable interest in one's own life, but this does not hold up under close analysis, since an individual suffers no economic detriment as a result of one's own death. The principle is sound, however, because when one takes out insurance on one's own life, one gives consent to the purchase. Indeed, taking out insurance on one's own life is giving consent in its purest form.

That requiring the insured to consent to the issuance of insurance on the insured's life can protect against the incentive to murder is illustrated by *Ramey v. Carolina Life Insurance Co.,*[18] a South Carolina case. A wife obtained a policy, naming herself as beneficiary, on her husband's life without his consent by forging his signature on the application. She attempted to murder him with poison; her effort failed, but the husband suffered personal injuries as a result. He sued the insurer for damages, claiming that the insurer was negligent in issuing the policy when it knew that he neither was aware of nor had consented to the policy's issuance. He claimed that the insurer's negligence proximately caused his wife to attempt to kill him and collect the proceeds. Quoting extensively from *Weldon,* the court held that his complaint stated a cause of action; it ruled that the insurer had a duty to "use

---

[16] In a criminal proceeding brought by the state against the aunt-in-law, a judgment was entered for the state, and the aunt-in-law was executed.

[17] See, e.g., Ariz. Rev. Stat. Ann. § 20-1107; Ark. Code Ann. § 23-79-105; Ga. Code Ann. § 33-24-6; N.Y. Ins. Code § 3205. At common law, there is no consent requirement. See Connecticut Gen. Life Ins. Co. v. Wood, 631 F. Supp. 9 (N.D. Ga. 1984).

[18] 135 S.E.2d 362 (S.C. 1964).

reasonable care not to create a situation which may prove to be a stimulus for murder."[19]

Curiously, the court explicitly declined to rule that a wife "invariably" has an insurable interest in the life of her husband, despite the great weight of authority to the contrary. Apparently, the court desired to assist the husband's litigation: if the wife lacked an insurable interest in his life, an alternative ground would exist for holding the insurer liable to the husband. This analysis, however, does considerable damage to the insurable interest doctrine: if the court's allusion to the fact that a wife may not always have an insurable interest in the life of the husband is taken seriously, there are no relationships where the existence of an insurable interest is certain. Yet, if one starts with the premise that the wife possessed an insurable interest in her husband's life, the argument that the insurer was negligent for issuing a policy where no insurable interest existed is foreclosed. Rather, the negligence of the company, if it existed, must be found in the company's failure to get the husband's consent to the policy being taken out on his own life. The wife's insistence upon forging the signature of her husband on the application should have put the insurer on notice that something was amiss in the transaction and perhaps in the relationship of the wife and husband.

Consent, however, is not a talisman for all cases. In *Dixon v. Western Union Assurance Co.,*[20] the parents of a serviceman on duty in Vietnam received a proposal for insurance on their son's life from an insurer. The parents completed the application and returned it to the insurer with the first premium on February 14. On February 17, the insurers mailed a certificate to the parents confirming that the policy was in force as of the date of the postmarked application. On February 14, at 1:00 a.m. E.S.T., the parents' son was killed in action. The insurer, upon learning of the serviceman's death, denied liability and tendered return of the premium. The insurer alleged in the parents' suit that public policy precluded enforcement of the contract because it was issued without the knowledge or consent of the insured, but the court rejected this argument and held that the death benefit was recoverable.

This result was plainly the correct one. Given the manner by which the insurer marketed the policies, the insurer was estopped to claim that the policies were void for lack of the insured's consent. Yet this case shows that no single rule can serve all the relevant public interests. Consent can do much to diminish an incentive to destroy insured lives. In close familial relationships, it can be presumed that consent is given by the insured to the family member to purchase insurance on the insured's life. Unless other facts put the insurer on notice that the family member purchasing the insurance has an illegitimate purpose in mind, it is reasonable for the insurer to presume that consent was given. In distant familial relationships or nonfamily relationships, it may be appropriate to require evidence of actual consent for the purchase of the insurance. If the insured voluntarily and knowingly gives the consent, it is probably safe to assume that there is little risk that the owner of the policy is using the insurance as a wager and the chances are reduced that the beneficiary will intentionally bring about the death of the insured.

---

[19] 135 S.E.2d at 367.

[20] 164 S.E.2d 214 (S.C. 1968).

Even the consent rule, however, will not eliminate the risk that a person might be murdered by a beneficiary for the insurance money. One can take out insurance on one's own life; the consent rule does not help the unsuspecting insured who is duped into applying for insurance on the insured's own life and who names a beneficiary who then has or who may later develop a plan to kill the insured.[21]

[e] Insurable Interest in Industrial Life Insurance

Some courts have held that the normal insurable interest requirements do not exist in industrial life insurance.[22] Normally, such insurance is sold in small amounts, and there is presumably little danger that someone would purchase such a small policy with the intention of murdering the insured. Also, one of the advantages (and there are few) of such policies is the speed with which proceeds can be paid. Strict adherence to the insurable interest requirement would diminish this advantage.

---

[21] See New England Mut. Life Ins. Co. v. Null, 605 F.2d 421 (8th Cir. 1979); Lopez v. Life Ins. Co. of Am., 406 So. 2d 1155 (Fla. 1981); Burton v. John Hancock Mut. Life Ins. Co., 298 S.E.2d 575 (Ga. Ct. App. 1982).

[22] See Fulcher v. Parker, 194 S.E. 714 (Va. 1938); see also Dight v. Palladium Life Ins. Co., 276 N.W. 3 (Minn. 1937) (appears to require insurable interest, but neither notice to nor consent of insured is required).

CHAPTER 5

SCOPE OF OBLIGATIONS:
PERSONS AND INTERESTS PROTECTED

§ 50 The Meaning of "Insured"

In all lines of insurance, the "insured" is the person whose loss triggers the insurer's duty to pay proceeds. Except in life insurance where different relationships exist, the insured is almost always the person who enters into a contract with the insurer; in the event of a loss, the proceeds of the insurance are almost always paid to the insured. However, it is possible, as discussed below, for the insured to assign the proceeds of the insurance to someone else or to designate a loss payee who receives part or all of the proceeds along with the insured.

In life insurance, the insured is the person whose life is covered. This person need not be the person who contracted with the insurer; instead, an individual might contract to insure another person's life (assuming that individual has an insurable interest in the life of the proposed insured). The individual who contracts with the insurer is the owner of the policy, but this individual is not the insured. In life insurance, the proceeds are usually paid to one or more designated beneficiaries, although there are occasions where the proceeds are paid to the insured's estate.

§ 51 Identifying the Insured (or Payee)

Insurance policies use various techniques to identify the insured. Some of the common ways of identifying the insured are discussed in this section.

[a] Specific Designations

The most common technique of identifying the insured is to designate specifically the person whose life, property, or other interests are covered. A life insurance policy is likely to have a cover sheet with the space or line for the designation of the person insured. Later in the form, a definition is likely to appear, stating in so many words that "the person whose life is insured is the person identified on page x."

In property and liability insurance, the policy is likely to state that the insurer "does insure _____," and the insured's name is inserted in the blank. If there are multiple insureds, each will probably be listed by name. If no effort is made to describe the interests of each insured being protected, it is presumed that the named

(Matthew Bender & Co., Inc.)   (Pub.837)

insureds intend to share any proceeds equally. The designation of insureds may be followed by a phrase "as their interests may appear." This phrase means that each designated insured will share the proceeds in proportion to the damage to his or her specific interest in the insured property. Another approach to designation lists each insured by name; each name is followed by a specific description of each insured's interest, such as "mortgagor," "mortgagee," "lessor," "bailor," etc.

Many property and liability policy forms, particularly fire insurance forms, specify that the policy covers "_____ and legal representatives." The effect of this designation is that if the named insured should die, the coverage extends to the named insured's estate, who becomes the insured's legal representative. The right to recover the proceeds under such a designation will belong to the legal representative of the deceased insured. Some more recent policies are more explicit about what happens if the insured dies while the policy is in force, containing a specific provision that extends coverage to the named insured's estate. A designation that the policy covers "_____ and his heirs and assigns" means that the cause of action for the proceeds lies with the heir or assign having title to the property at the time of the loss, rather than the legal representative.

After a policy is issued, the insured might desire to designate additional persons as insureds under the policy. If the policy is already in force, the additional insureds can be added through an endorsement on the policy. For example, if the named insured wants to extend the policy's coverage to the vendee of property until the title to the property is actually delivered and the insurer agrees to this extension, this can be accomplished by adding an endorsement to the policy designating the vendee as an additional named insured.[1]

[b] The Omnibus Clause and Omnibus Coverage

Liability policies often designate at least one insured by name and other insureds by description, usually as classes of people who have some relationship to the named insured. In automobile insurance, this coverage is usually mandated by statute because of the strong public policy in broadening the class of insureds so as to minimize the risk that someone will be injured by a financially irresponsible individual. A typical statutory requirement is that an owner's policy of liability insurance on an automobile shall insure anyone using the vehicle "with the express or implied permission of the named insured."[2] If a policy does not include an "omnibus clause" providing the coverage, the statutory mandate of omnibus coverage will be read into the policy anyway.[3]

When an omnibus clause is included in a policy, it will usually read like the following example from an automobile insurance policy, which defined "insured" as

---

[1] See generally Mark Pomerantz, Note, *Recognizing the Unique Status of Additional Named Insureds,* 53 Fordham L. Rev. 117 (1984).

[2] E.g., Haw. Rev. Stat. § 287-25(2); Va. Code § 38.2-2204.

[3] See AIG Hawaii Ins. Co. v. Vicente, 891 P.2d 1041, 1043 (Haw. 1995) (language of statutes is "read into the policy in issue.")

(1) the named insured, and (2) if the named insured is a person or persons, . . . his or their spouse(s), if a resident of the same household, and (3) if residents of the same household, the relatives of the first person named in the declarations, or of his spouse, and (4) any other person while using the owned motor vehicle, provided the operation and the actual use of such vehicle are with the permission of the named insured or such spouse and are within the scope of such permission, and (5) under coverages A and B any other person or organization, but only with respect to his or its liability for the use of such owned motor vehicle by an insured as defined in the four subsections above.[4]

The foregoing clause defines "insured" in terms of four classes other than the named insured, each of which includes individuals who have a specified relationship to the named insured. Each person within each described class is an insured for purposes of the policy's coverage. Moreover, under the principle that an insurer cannot have subrogation against its own insured,[5] each person within one of the described classes is immune from subrogation by the insurer.

It has been less common to insert omnibus clauses in automobile policies in recent years, but the statutory mandates mean that such coverage is provided anyway, with interpretations of the scope of the coverage being provided by case law precedents involving omnibus clauses. A number of policies,[6] sometimes called "easy reading" policies,[7] address the omnibus coverage issue by defining "insured" as both "you or any 'family member' for the ownership, maintenance, or use of any auto" (which covers the named insured and family members for the use of any auto anywhere) and "any person using your covered auto." The coverage for any person using the insured's auto suggests that even a thief would be entitled to the benefits of the insured's liability coverage, but this unsound result is prevented by an exclusion from coverage for the use of a vehicle "without a reasonable belief that that person is entitled to do so." "Permission or consent" may not be coterminous with "reasonable belief," but a person who has been denied permission to use a vehicle would plainly lack a reasonable belief that he or she could use it,[8] and a person who receives permission from someone whom the recipient knows (or perhaps has reason to know) is not allowed to offer permission lacks a reasonable belief.[9] Whether an unlicensed driver can ever have a reasonable belief that he or she has permission to use a vehicle remains open to question.[10] It would seem clear that a thief lacks

---

[4] This clause was the subject of litigation in Curtis v. State Farm Mut. Auto. Ins. Co., 591 F.2d 572 (10th Cir. 1979). See generally Gary D. Stump, Comment, *Defining "Relative," "Member of the Household," "Member of the Family" or "Resident" within the Meaning of Homeowner's and Automobile Liability Policies,* 26 Drake L. Rev. 824 (1976–77).

[5] See § 96[f], *infra.*

[6] See *Policy Kit* at 1 (ISO Form PP 00 01 12 89).

[7] See Cincinnati Ins. Co. v. Plummer, 444 S.E.2d 378, 380 (Ga. Ct. App. 1994).

[8] See State Farm Fire & Cas. Co. v. Martin, 869 P.2d 79 (Wash. Ct. App. 1994); Nationwide Mut. Ins. Co. v. Baer, 439 S.E.2d 202 (N.C. Ct. App. 1994).

[9] See Omaha Prop. & Cas. Ins. Co. v. Peterson, 865 S.W.2d 789 (Mo. Ct. App. 1993).

[10] Compare Safeway Ins. Co. v. Jones, 415 S.E.2d 19 (Ga. Ct. App. 1992)(unlicensed driver could not have reasonably believed he was entitled to drive any vehicle) with Allied Group Ins. Co. v. Allstate Ins. Co., 852 P.2d 485 (Idaho 1993) (lack of express permission does not rule out possibility of implied permission; *citing with approval* Abbs v. Redmond, 132 P.2d 1044 (Idaho 1943), which involved 14-year-old driver).

permission and cannot have a reasonable belief about his or her permission to use a stolen vehicle,[11] although at least one court has held that a policy provided coverage where a car dealer gave permission to a person to test-drive a vehicle and the person proceeded to steal the vehicle.[12]

The "reasonable belief" clause has been construed by some courts to exclude coverage for a family member who is operating the vehicle without the permission of the named insured. The usual case involves a son or daughter (in many cases the minor is unlicensed or too young to drive legally) who without the permission of the named-insured parent or in defiance of a prior instruction operates the vehicle and causes an accident. Although the case law is not uniform,[13] most courts have concluded that the exclusion is clear and that no person, including the named insured or a family member, operating a vehicle without a reasonable belief that he or she has permission to do so is entitled to coverage.[14] Additional facts in some cases have made the issues even more difficult. In one case, a court held that a 15-year-old recently-licensed son could have a reasonable belief of permission to drive at night, even though state law made it illegal for a person of that age to drive at night, when

[11] See, e.g., United States Fid. & Guar. Co. v. McManus, 356 N.E.2d 78 (Ill. 1976). See also State Farm Mut. Auto. Ins. Co. v. Nissen, 851 P.2d 165 (Colo. 1993) (en banc) (injuries insured incurred when she attempted to stop thief from stealing her car were covered under insured's uninsured motorist coverage; when thief drove away with car thus triggering application of exclusion, insured's auto became uninsured).

[12] See Universal Underwriters Ins. Co. v. Taylor, 508 S.E.2d 358 (W.Va. 1991) (insurer obligated to provide coverage under the reasoning that the initial permission to test-drive was not affected by the subsequent theft or the fact that the person who stole the vehicle used a fictitious name and otherwise deceived the car dealer).

[13] See Paychex, Inc. v. Covenant Ins. Co., 549 N.Y.S.2d 237 (N.Y.Sup. 1989)(unlicensed son driving without permission was covered; policy is ambiguous); United Services Auto. Ass'n v. Dunn, 598 So. 2d 1169 (La. Ct. App. 1992)(to exclude coverage for family member driving vehicle without permission, insurer should have referred to "covered person" in exclusion; at the least the policy is ambiguous; held that policy provides coverage to son driving parents' car without permission). See generally Annot., *Application of Automobile Insurance "Entitlement" Exclusion to Family Member*, 25 A.L.R.5th 60 (1994).

[14] See, e.g., Newell v. Nationwide Mut. Ins. Co., 432 S.E.2d 284 (N.C. 1993)(son whose license had been revoked and who had been told by parents not to drive held not to have reasonable belief of permission to use vehicle); Harlan v. Valley Ins. Co., 875 P.2d 471 (Or. Ct. App. 1994) (en banc); Cincinnati Ins. Co. v. Plummer, 444 S.E.2d 378 (Ga.App. 1994)(unlicensed underage daughter lacked reasonable belief of permission to use vehicle); Omaha Prop. & Cas. Ins. Co. v. Johnson, 866 S.W.2d 539 (Tenn. Ct. App. 1993). See also Allied Group Ins. Co. v. Allstate Ins. Co., 852 P.2d 485 (Idaho 1993) (exclusion applies to family members; summary judgment vacated for determination on remand of whether son had implied permission to use vehicle). Note that if a minor child operating a vehicle without permission causes injury to someone, and if the automobile policy does not provide coverage because of the exclusion, and if the parents' homeowner's policy does not provide coverage for a claim that the parents negligently supervised the child because the loss is excluded from coverage because it arises out of the use of the automobile, the loss may be an uninsured event. One wonders whether insurers intended this reduction in coverage from that provided with the typical omnibus clause by virtue of the new, "easy reading" standard automobile liability form.

his father, a district judge, asked him to assume the wheel.[15] In another case, a court held that a husband who had been told by his wife not to drive her car while intoxicated had a reasonable belief that he had permission to do so for purposes of the exclusion.[16]

In cases involving the omnibus clauses, issues also arise concerning whether a particular person has permission from the named insured (or other covered person) to use the vehicle identified in the policy. The results turn largely on the facts of particular cases. Courts follow three different approaches when interpreting and applying omnibus clauses (or deciding what kind of use falls within the scope of a particular grant of permission to use a vehicle).

The first approach to omnibus clause interpretation is the "liberal" or "initial permission" approach. This approach maximizes the coverage afforded by the clause by broadening the class of insureds. Under the liberal approach, if (using the common example of automobile insurance) the subject vehicle were entrusted to a third person by one having authority to do so, the vehicle's resulting use will be treated as being within the scope of permission regardless of how substantially the scope of the permission may have been violated. This means that if the named insured gave initial permission to the user, this is enough to bring the subsequent use within coverage, even if the user violates express restrictions placed on the use.[17]

The second approach, the "conservative" approach, is basically the opposite of the liberal approach: the grant of permission to use a vehicle is construed strictly; any use outside the scope of permission is not covered. Thus, any use which violates geographical limitations, time limitations, or limitations on the nature of the use is outside the coverage. This approach is sometimes described as the "conversion" rule: if the bailee's use of the vehicle exceeds the scope of the permission to an extent that would make the bailee liable in an action brought by the bailor for conversion, the use is not covered.[18]

Most jurisdictions follow a third approach, a middle-of-the-road approach, called the "minor deviation" rule.[19] If the use made of the vehicle by the bailee is not a

---

[15] See Sledge v. Continental Cas. Co., 639 So. 2d 805 (La. Ct. App. 1994).

[16] See State Auto Prop. and Cas. Ins. Co. v. Gibbs, 444 S.E.2d 504 (S.C. 1994).

[17] See, e.g., Universal Underwriters Ins. Co. v. Taylor, 408 S.E.2d 358 (W.Va. 1991); Commercial Union Ins. Co. v. Johnson, 745 S.W.2d 589 (Ark. 1988); Spears v. Preble, 661 P.2d 1337 (Okla. 1983); Matits v. Nationwide Mut. Ins. Co., 166 A.2d 345 (N.J. 1960).

[18] See, e.g., Leegaard v. Universal Underwriters Ins. Co., 255 N.W.2d 819 (Minn. 1977); Eagle Fire Co. v. Mullins, 120 S.E.2d 1 (S.C. 1961).

[19] See, e.g., Rhiner v. State Farm Mut. Auto. Ins. Co., 158 S.E.2d 891 (N.C. 1968); State Farm Fire & Cas. Co. v. Martin, 869 P.2d 79 (Wash. Ct. App. 1994); Kobetitsch v. American Manufacturers' Mut. Ins. Co., 390 So. 2d 76 (Fla. Dist. Ct. App. 1980). Some courts have attempted to stake out a position thought to be somewhere between the liberal approach and the minor deviation approach, see Columbia Cas. Co. v. Hoohuli, 437 P.2d 99 (Haw. 1968); Ryan v. Western Pacific Ins. Co., 408 P.2d 84 (Or. 1965); American Fid. Co. v. North Brit. & Merc. Ins. Co., 204 A.2d 110 (Vt. 1964), but because the minor deviation approach is flexible, it is not easy to discern in what respect these decisions represent a fourth approach.

gross violation of the terms upon which permission to use the vehicle was granted, the use is covered, even though the use was a deviation from the permission given. In other words, some deviation from the scope of permission will not prevent coverage, but too much deviation will. This approach seeks to accommodate two competing values. On the one hand, it is desirable to provide compensation for as many accident victims as possible, and this requires viewing permission broadly to embrace a large number of uses. Yet it is undesirable to bring with the ambit of coverage uses that insureds, in the exercise of their own judgment, do not permit, often because the use is unduly risky or dangerous. Covering such uses under a broad view of permission requires all insureds, including those who successfully prevent unpermitted uses, to pay the costs of the extra coverage. But striving for an appropriate balance between competing goals has led to a standard that makes it difficult to predict the outcome of particular cases.

A few examples help illustrate the majority approach. In *Fisher v. Fireman's Fund Indem. Co.,* [20] the insurer issued a policy of insurance on a pickup truck to a partnership. On Christmas Eve, an employee of the partnership received permission to take the truck to his residence that evening and drive it to a city fifteen miles away on Christmas Day to have dinner with his parents. However, he drove the truck on a route not even close to the city in which his parents lived, and he was involved in an accident one hundred miles from the city in which the partnership did business. The court concluded that this deviation was a major one, and no coverage existed. A similar case is *Mid-Continent Casualty Co. v. Everett.* [21] A bus company employed a driver, whose route was between Wichita, Kansas and a city in Oklahoma. The driver would leave Wichita at 6:00 a.m. and return the bus in the evening. However, one day the driver drove the bus away late in the evening, and the next morning he had an accident about twenty-five blocks from the Wichita bus terminal, while driving the bus in the wrong direction on his route (although he was operating the bus at the proper time) while intoxicated. The court concluded that this use was a major deviation: the employee had deviated in time, purpose, and direction to such an extent that the actual use was not within the employer's contemplation.

A contrasting case is *Allied Mutual Casualty Co. v. Nelson,* [22] a Minnesota decision. A father gave his teenage daughter permission to drive the family car to a movie and then directly home. However, the daughter gave permission to her date to drive the car, and they decided not to go to the movie. An accident occurred while the young people were "driving around." The court concluded that this use was only a minor deviation, and coverage existed.

It is difficult to generalize about the permission cases, but a couple of observations are possible. First, courts tend to treat non-business permission as more comprehensive. The Minnesota case, for example, involved social permission; deviant uses are more likely to be tolerated in the non-business setting. Courts are not as willing to tolerate deviant uses when an employee is using the vehicle with permission.

---

[20] 244 F.2d 194 (10th Cir. 1957).
[21] 340 F.2d 65 (10th Cir. 1965).
[22] 143 N.W.2d 635 (Minn. 1966).

Second, if a limitation exists on the ability of the named insured to give permission, such as if the named insured has already transferred his title to the car to someone else, the user of the vehicle will not be covered by the named insured's policy, since the person purporting to give permission had no authority to do so.[23]

A recurring problem in applying omnibus clauses is the "permittee's permittee" situation. Take, for example, the following fact pattern: Named insured gives permission to one permittee, who gives permission to operate a vehicle to a second person:

$$NI \text{------} P_1 \text{------} P_2$$

Several questions are appropriate: 1) Did NI give permission to P_1 to operate the vehicle? 2) Was P_1 authorized to give permission to P_2? 3) Did P_1 give permission to P_2? 4) Was the nature of the use of the vehicle by P_2 within the scope of permission of P_1, and was the permission which P_1 gave within the scope of the permission given by NI?

The essence of the "permittee's permittee" problem is that the person driving the vehicle at the time of the accident is a person with whom the named insured had no communication. A minority of jurisdictions, building upon the "liberal" approach, take the position that the original permission extends to second permittees, despite efforts of the named insured to limit the scope of the permission.[24] In addressing a situation where a parent in giving permission to the son to drive the vehicle instructed him not to give permission to others, one court sought to explain the logic of this broad view of coverage with the observation that "it is as likely that a son or daughter will violate a parent's instruction not to let someone else drive as it is that the youngster will violate an instruction not to speed or not to deviate from a specific purpose or course of travel."[25] Under the conservative view, the original permission given by the named insured to the first permittee does not authorize the first permittee to give permission to a second permittee. This result is based on the assumption that while the insurer expects the insured to designate permittees and to exercise discretion in doing so, the insurer does not agree to bear the risk of a designated permittee giving permission, without the approval of the named insured, to third parties to operate the insured's vehicle.[26]

---

[23] See Keystone Ins. Co. v. Fidelity & Cas. Co., 260 A.2d 275 (Md. 1970).

[24] See, e.g., United Services Auto. Ass'n v. National Farmers Union Prop. & Cas., 891 P.2d 538 (N.M. 1995); Murphy v. Clancy, 404 N.E.2d 287 (Ill.App. 1980), aff'd in part & rev'd in part sub. nom, Murphy v. Urso, 430 N.E.2d 1079 (Ill. 1981); Subscribers v. McClanahan, 607 S.W.2d 718 (Mo. Ct. App. 1980); Indemnity Ins. Co. v. Metropolitan Cas. Co., 166 A.2d 355 (N.J. 1960); see generally Annot., Omnibus Clause as Extending Automobile Liability Coverage to Third Person Using Car with Consent of Permittee of Named Insured, 21 A.L.R.4th 1146, 1159–63 (1983); Annot., Validity and Operation of "Step-down" Provision of Automobile Liability Policy Reducing Coverage for Permissive Users, 29 A.L.R.5th 469 (1995).

[25] United Services Auto. Ass'n v. National Farmers Union Prop. & Cas., 891 P.2d 538, 541 (N.M. 1995).

[26] See, e.g., Odolecki v. Hartford Accident & Indem. Co., 264 A.2d 38 (N.J. 1970); Card v. Commercial Cas. Ins. Co., 95 S.W.2d 1281 (Tenn. Ct. App. 1936). The only exception recognized in this line of authority is the emergency situation, discussed above.

Most courts, however, follow a less categorical approach, and ask a number of fact-oriented questions to try to sort out such situations. Obviously, much depends on the scope of the permission granted by the named insured. If the original permittee was expressly authorized to give others permission to operate the vehicle, no particular difficulty is presented; the second permittee's use of the car is within the coverage.[27] In most situations, however, the named insured will not specify whether the permittee has authority to give permission to a third party. Consider what happens, for example, in the typical conversation among college roommates: one will ask the other, "May I use your car?" and the response is "Sure," not "Sure, but don't give permission to third parties."[28] The results in most of these cases will turn on the scope of implied permission. Most courts apply this kind of analysis: if granting permission to third parties is expressly prohibited by the named insured, the permittee's permittee will ordinarily not be covered unless it can be shown that the named insured impliedly gave permission for certain specific purposes despite a general prohibition. If implied permission is found, the permittee's permittee will be covered.[29] Most courts that have considered the issue have held that an emergency which disables the permittee from operating the vehicle is a case of "implied permission," and a permittee's permittee in that situation will be covered in the face of the named insured's instruction not to allow anyone else to operate the vehicle.[30]

An exemplar permittee's permittee case is *Curtis v. State Farm Mutual Automobile Insurance Co.*,[31] a Tenth Circuit decision. The Ahrens family had three cars — an Oldsmobile, a Volkswagen, and a pickup truck — and three daughters, Beth and Shawnna, who were licensed, and a fourteen-year-old, Deborah. The older daughters had permission to use the Oldsmobile and the Volkswagen "as they needed or liked." Deborah, with her friend Helen Curtis, who was spending the night of July 4, 1973, at the Ahrenses' home, made arrangements with two boys to meet at the local ballpark between 1:00 and 2:00 a.m. on July 5 to shoot fireworks. Deborah, without her parents' knowledge, took the Volkswagen keys and proceeded to drive the car to the ballpark. On the way out of the neighborhood, the two girls met Beth driving home in the Oldsmobile. They stopped and talked for a few minutes, but Deborah's use of the Volkswagen was not discussed. The other daughter, Shawnna, knew what the girls were doing, but she had neither consented to nor forbade the activity. Also, neither Beth nor Shawnna knew that Deborah planned to pick up the boys in the Volkswagen. Deborah and Helen picked up the

---

[27] See, e.g., Mercer Cas. Co. v. Kreamer, 11 N.E.2d 84 (Ind. Ct. App. 1937).

[28] Imagine this additional complicating factor: the roommate's car actually belongs to his father; the father has loaned the car to the son for the weekend, and has not specified whether the son has permission to let others use the car. To further complicate things, suppose the borrower of the car authorizes a friend to drive the borrower somewhere. These events commonly occur, and the legal questions they raise are difficult.

[29] See AIG Hawaii Ins. Co. v. Vicente, 891 P.2d 1041 (Haw. 1995); Perkins v. McDow, 615 So. 2d 312 (La. 1993); United States Auto. Ass'n v. Russom, 241 F.2d 296 (5th Cir. 1957); Boston Ins. Co. v. Pendarvis, 195 So. 2d 692 (La. Ct. App. 1967).

[30] See State Farm Mut. Auto. Ins. Co. v. Geico Indem. Co., 402 S.E.2d 21 (Va. 1991).

[31] 591 F.2d 572 (10th Cir. 1979).

two boys, and the four of them shot the fireworks. On the way home, one of the boys, Joe Wallace, asked to drive the car and Deborah agreed. About five minutes later, an accident occurred due to Joe's driving the car at an excessive speed, and Helen suffered serious injuries. Helen's father, the plaintiff, brought a suit against the Ahrenses' insurer, claiming that the insurer was obligated to defend and indemnify Joe.

Since Joe did not have express permission from the named insureds, Mr. and Mrs. Ahrens, the first question was whether he had implied permission to use the Volkswagen. Because Mrs. Ahrens was blind, plaintiff argued that the two older daughters had permission to operate the vehicles as if they were owners (for family-related trips, e.g., grocery shopping), and that the older daughters — through their awareness of Deborah's plans — gave permission to Deborah both to operate the car and to authorize third parties to operate it. Thus, Deborah's actual permission to Joe Wallace was, plaintiff argued, impliedly authorized by the named insureds, Mr. and Mrs. Ahrens. The court agreed that Deborah might have had permission to operate the vehicle, but it disagreed that Joe Wallace had permission as a third permittee. Neither Beth nor Shawnna — the first permittees — knew that Joe Wallace would be in the car, let alone allowed to drive it. Thus, no coverage existed under the Ahrenses' automobile policy for the injuries to Helen Curtis.

The *Curtis* case presented an even more complicated set of relationships than the simple three-party case (NI, P_1, and P_2) discussed above. *Curtis* involved the following relationships:

Mr. & Mrs. Ahrens (NI) — Beth & Shawnna (P_1) —

Deborah (P_2) — Joe Wallace (P_3)

Whatever Deborah might have been permitted to do with the Volkswagen, neither the parents nor the older daughters had given permission to Deborah to give permission to Joe. Since the scope of Deborah's authority was not unlimited, it could not be concluded that Deborah had authority to give permission to Joe. It is important to note that the loser in this case is Helen, who cannot be reimbursed for her injuries by the Ahrenses' insurer. However, it is improbable that Helen will be left without a remedy: she would be allowed to collect some expenses from her own (i.e., her parents') health insurance policy (if they had one), from her own automobile insurer (through her parents' coverage if either mandatory first-party medical protection existed or her parents purchased optional coverage), and from Joe Wallace's liability insurer (pursuant, probably, to the omnibus clause under his parents' liability coverage).[32]

---

[32] For a case similar to *Curtis,* see Grange Ins. Ass'n v. Ochoa, 691 P.2d 248 (Wash. Ct. App. 1984). It should be noted that Helen's ability to recover under any automobile policy may be precluded by the common policy exclusion for any person "using a vehicle without a reasonable belief [she] is entitled to do so." In Safeco Insurance Co. v. Davis, 721 P.2d 550 (Wash. Ct. App. 1986), the exclusion was deemed ambiguous, and the court held that the exclusion did not preclude coverage of the insureds' 14-year-old unlicensed daughter who was driving a car, owned by the parents of an 18-year-old friend, with the permission of the friend.

It is not even necessary, however, that a complicated string of permittees exist in order to create a highly confused picture. In *Fireman's Fund Insurance Co. v. Brandt,*[33] two Dartmouth college students, Summers and Straus, were attending a party at an inn outside Hanover, New Hampshire. Summers gave permission to a friend to drive his car back to Hanover. When the friend did not return as expected, Summers and Brandt went into the parking lot where they found Straus's car with the keys in it. Without asking permission from Straus to drive the car, Summers and Brandt took the car to Hanover to search for the friend, and an accident occurred en route. Straus testified that had Summers asked to use the car he probably would have agreed. It was a general custom at Dartmouth to lend cars to one another, but Summers had never driven Straus's car before; they were acquainted as classmates but were not close friends who frequently socialized together. The issue was whether permission could be implied from Straus to Summers to operate the vehicle; and the court's answer was no: "There is simply nothing in the prior conduct of the parties which could give rise to an implication of consent on the part of Straus to the possession or use of the car by Summers."[34]

Omnibus clauses are important to insureds, who want coverage for those who are in special relationships to them. Also, omnibus clauses are important to the public, which desires liability coverage, particularly with regard to automobiles, to be as broad as possible so that injured victims will not lack financial assistance. On the other hand, omnibus clauses invite litigation over subtle factual questions. No one, however, seriously suggests abandoning the use of omnibus clauses; the advantages far outweigh the disadvantages.

[c]   The "Loss Payable" Clause

Multiple parties who share an interest in property are often all designated as insureds. In the event of damage to the property, each person is entitled to some measure of reimbursement.[35] However, sometimes a party is designated to receive all or part of the proceeds without regard to whether he or she owns a portion of the property. This may occur where the insurance policy is intended as collateral for an unsecured debt or as protection for a party who possesses a security interest in the insured property. The named insured will be designated in the "does insure" clause, and a second person will be named as payee of the proceeds in a clause stating "loss, if any, payable to _____." Because of the language in the clause, the clause is often referred to as a "loss payable clause."

§ 52   The Interests in a Life Insurance Policy

The person who owns a life insurance policy is not necessarily the insured. It is possible for one person to purchase a policy on the life of another (assuming the insurable interest requirement is met); the person purchasing the policy is the owner

---

[33] 217 F. Supp. 893 (D.N.H. 1962).

[34] *Id.* at 894.

[35] This depends on how the insureds are designated. See § 51, *supra.*

of the policy, and the rights of ownership belong not to the insured, but to the policy's purchaser.

A life insurance policy confers valuable rights on its owner. In whole life insurance, the owner has the right to obtain a loan against the cash value, to surrender the policy to obtain the cash value, and to withdraw the dividends, if any. Two other important rights attach to life insurance policies, whether whole life or term: the right to receive proceeds at death and the right to designate a beneficiary. An individual may name oneself — meaning one's estate — as the beneficiary of the contract or the insured may name a third party, such as a relative, a friend, a corporation, or an association.

Typically a person purchases a policy of insurance on his or her own life; this person owns the policy and all of its attendant rights. The person who insures his or her own life usually keeps some of these rights and gives some of these rights to someone else. For example, the right to receive proceeds is usually given to someone else (the beneficiary), but the insured usually retains the right to name or change the beneficiary. The rights to the dividends and to borrow against the cash value are usually retained by the owner of the policy, but even these rights can be assigned to someone else.

The next section discusses the rules governing the rights of beneficiaries on life insurance policies, and the following section discusses the rights of assignees of life insurance policies.

§ 52A Beneficiaries Under Life Insurance Policies

A life insurance policy confers valuable rights on its owner, including the right to designate a beneficiary. The term "beneficiary" is usually used in insurance law to describe the person who, although not a party to the contract, is entitled to receive the proceeds of the insurance. An individual may name his or her estate as the beneficiary of the contract or may name a third party. This section discusses the rules governing the management of this right.

[a] When the Beneficiary's Rights Vest

In old life insurance policies, the beneficiary, once designated by the insured, could not be changed without the beneficiary's consent. In other words, the rights of a person unconditionally designated as the beneficiary vested immediately upon the designation.[1] Under this old approach, the ownership rights of the policy, in effect, belonged to the beneficiary, not the insured. However, these rights were conditional in a significant respect: if the insured committed an act which voided the coverage, the insured's act would deprive the beneficiary of his or her rights.

---

[1] In Central National Bank v. Hume, 128 U.S. 195 (1888), Chief Justice Fuller stated: "It is indeed the general rule that a policy, and the money to become due under it, belong, the moment it is issued, to the person or persons named in it as the beneficiary or beneficiaries, and that there is no power in the person procuring the insurance by any act of his, by deed or by will, to transfer to any other person the interest of the person named." 128 U.S. at 206.

This result followed from basic contract law principles; the beneficiary's rights, although vested, are subject to any defenses that the promisor (the insurer) has against the promisee (the insured).

Modern life insurance policies explicitly reserve to the insured the power to change the beneficiary without the designated beneficiary's consent. Similarly, the insured is reserved the power to receive the cash value of the policy, to take out loans against that cash value, to surrender the policy in exchange for the cash value, or to assign the policy, all without the designated beneficiary's consent. In the modern policy, the insured does not have a vested right, and only has an expectancy of receiving proceeds under the insurance.

Reserving the right to change beneficiaries to the policy's owner is plainly a better approach. The person who purchases the life insurance policy deserves to be able to allocate its benefits however he or she sees fit. The satisfaction of the owner of a product, whether it be a widget or a life insurance policy, can be maximized with certainty only if that person has control over the product; purchases of such products will be deterred if the owner cannot be sure that his or her satisfaction will be maximized. If the beneficiary desires a "vested right" in the policy's proceeds, the beneficiary should secure those rights by purchasing the policy (or giving consideration for an assignment), thereby entitling the beneficiary to the rights of ownership.

[b] Naming and Designating the Beneficiary

Most modern insurance policies give the policyholder the right both to name and to change the beneficiary. Policies typically provide for the designation of primary and contingent beneficiaries. The primary beneficiary is the person who will receive the death benefit assuming that person is alive at the time of the insured's death.[2] If no primary beneficiary is living at the time of the insured's death, the proceeds are paid to the contingent beneficiary. Multiple primary or contingent beneficiaries can be named. If there are multiple primary beneficiaries, upon the insured's death each primary beneficiary takes a pro rata share of the proceeds; the same pro rata division occurs if no primary beneficiaries survive the insured but a class of contingent beneficiaries exist. Most modern life insurance policies provide that in the absence of a qualified designated beneficiary the estate of the insured receives the proceeds. Thus, failure to designate a beneficiary, a rare occurrence, means only that the insured's estate receives the proceeds.

Generally, the person who takes out insurance on his or her own life can designate any beneficiary he or she chooses. Spouses and children are the frequent designees, but sometimes employers, partnerships, corporations, trustees, and charitable organizations are designated. In recent years, some charitable organizations (particularly educational and religious institutions) and some associations (such as fraternities and sororities), at the urging of insurance agents and brokers, have encouraged their members to purchase life insurance policies and name the organization as the beneficiary. This does not guarantee the organization that it will receive the proceeds, since the beneficiary designation is subject to change at the insured's option.

---

[2] The beneficiary must also be "qualified," i.e., must not have done things that disqualify the beneficiary from entitlement to the proceeds. This concept is discussed later.

But if the beneficiary designation is accompanied by an assignment of the policy to the organization, the organization acquires both the ownership rights and the entitlement to proceeds.

Occasionally, an heir of the deceased insured is surprised to discover that the insured's life insurance policies are payable to someone else. *American Casualty Co. v. Rose,*[3] a 1964 Tenth Circuit case, is illustrative. Rose, an automobile stunt performer, left his family in Utah early in 1961 and went to Illinois, where he was employed by John King in an "Auto Thrill Circus." Rose purchased a $50,000 thirty-day policy for accidental death, and he was accidentally killed while the policy was in effect. His employer was named as the beneficiary. The insurer denied liability, but then settled King's claim for $24,000. Thereafter, Rose's family brought an action claiming that King was designated as beneficiary on the policy as trustee for Rose's family and that the proceeds belonged to them. The trial court said that King's only interest in Rose's life was a small debt Rose owed him, and that the proceeds in excess of the amount of this debt belonged to Rose's family. The Tenth Circuit reversed, stating: "Rose had an insurable interest in his own life, and in the absence of statute, was free to take out insurance on it and to name anyone he saw fit as beneficiary, regardless of whether the beneficiary had an insurable interest in the insured."[4] Although some facts suggested that Rose intended by purchasing the insurance to provide for his family, the court found these facts insufficient to establish that King was designated the beneficiary as trustee for Rose's family.

The right to designate any beneficiary desired is subject to a few limitations in some situations. First, the rules change when an individual purchases a policy on someone else's life; the person purchasing the insurance on someone else's life must have an insurable interest in that person's life.[5] If an insurable interest exists, the policyowner can designate himself or herself as the beneficiary. If the policyholder chooses to designate a third party, that party must also have an insurable interest in the life of the insured. In a community property state, a situation discussed in more detail below,[6] the policyowner's power to designate a beneficiary is not absolute when the policy is purchased with community funds. With respect to group insurance, many state statutes prohibit the person insured from designating the policyholder as the beneficiary.[7] Also, if the beneficiary designation or change is made under undue influence or pursuant to some other kind of fraud, the designation can be invalidated.[8] A designation or change can also be invalidated if the

---

[3] 340 F.2d 469 (10th Cir. 1964).

[4] *Id.* at 471.

[5] See § 43, *supra.*

[6] See § 52A[f], *infra.*

[7] See, e.g., N.J. Stat. Ann. § 17B-24-6; 40 Pa. Cons. Stat. Ann. §§ 532.1–532.6. The logic of this prohibition is presumably that most group insurance is offered by employers as a benefit to employees; it would defeat the purposes for which such insurance is encouraged if the employer, through either direct or implicit coercion, could convert the employee benefit to an employer benefit.

[8] See, e.g., Leimbach v. Allen, 976 F.2d 912 (4th Cir. 1992), *cert. denied,* 113 S.Ct. 1322 (1993) (applying Maryland law); Metropolitan Life Ins. Co. v. Parker, 721 F. Supp. 227 (E.D. Mo. 1989); Goff v. Weeks, 517 N.W.2d 387 (Neb. 1994); Estate of Erickson v. Michigan Conf. Ass'n of Seventh-Day Adventists, 508 N.W.2d 181, 183 (Mich. Ct. App. 1993).

policyholder was incompetent or insane at the time of the designation or change.[9]

Usually, the insurer can pay the designated beneficiary of record without liability, assuming the insurer has no knowledge of a possible adverse claim or a reason that the designated beneficiary is disqualified. Therefore, it is important to the insured that the beneficiary designation be clear and current. Otherwise, the insured's intent may not be fulfilled. This is particularly important in the context of divorce: absent a settlement agreement or divorce decree to the contrary, a divorce between the policy's owner and the beneficiary does not affect the rights created by the policy. Frequently, a divorce decree will require one spouse to keep a policy in force for the benefit of the other spouse and any children. However, absent such a decree or a specific agreement, the policyowner might later name someone else as the beneficiary (perhaps a new spouse). This subsequent designation is enforceable. In some cases where a subsequent designation is made, the former spouse might be expected to argue that the subsequent designation violates the terms of a prior agreement or decree. If such a claim is made, the insurer may ultimately have to interplead the parties to resolve competing claims to the proceeds.[10]

It is common for beneficiary designations to contain descriptions of the individual, e.g., "John Jay, husband of the insured." Courts usually hold that the phrase "husband of the insured" is descriptive only; the name itself is what is controlling. This had a poignant effect in *Scherer v. Wahlstrom,*[11] a 1958 Texas case. The insured, a member of the military, designated "Mariam Amelia Tatum, Fiancee" as the beneficiary. About six months before his death in the service, he received a letter from his fiancee telling him she was going to marry another man. The insured neglected to change the beneficiary designation. The deceased's father claimed the proceeds, but the court, in an interpleader action, ruled that the former fiancee was entitled to the proceeds under the beneficiary designation.[12] Sometimes a class of people, such as "all my nieces and nephews," is designated as the beneficiary; this can be risky, however, because if the class is large, the payment of proceeds may be held up until each member of the class can be accounted for. On the other hand, a designation by description needs no amendment as new people are born into the class. Thus, "all my children" is a common beneficiary designation. A beneficiary designation which is vague (such as "to my family") and incapable of interpretation will be disregarded; contingent beneficiaries or the insured's estate would then receive the proceeds.[13]

---

[9] See Weed v. Equitable Life Assur. Soc'y of the U.S., 463 F.2d 463 (5th Cir.), cert. denied, 368 U.S. 821 (1961); Bigley v. Pacific Standard Life Ins. Co., 642 A.2d 4, 6 (Conn. 1994); Estate of Erickson v. Michigan Conf. Ass'n of Seventh-Day Adventists, 508 N.W.2d 181, 183 (Mich. Ct. App. 1993).

[10] For more discussion, see Mark Davis, Note, *Life Insurance Beneficiaries and Divorce,* 65 Tex. L. Rev. 635 (1987); Annot., *Divorce and Separation: Effect of Court Order Prohibiting Sale or Transfer of Property on Party's Right to Change Beneficiary of Insurance Policy,* 68 A.L.R.4th 929 (1989); Annot., *Property Settlement Agreement As Affecting Divorced Spouse's Right to Recover as Named Beneficiary Under Former Spouse's Life Insurance Policy,* 31 A.L.R.4th 59 (1984).

[11] 318 S.W.2d 456 (Tex. Ct. App. 1958).

[12] See also Belote v. Belote, 306 S.E.2d 340 (Ga. Ct. App. 1983).

[13] See Empire General Life Ins. Co. v. Silverman, 399 N.W.2d 910 (Wis. 1987).

Industrial life insurance policies usually contain a "facility of payment" clause which allows the insurer to pay anyone who reasonably appears to be equitably entitled to the proceeds of the insurance. These clauses enable the insurer to pay out the proceeds quickly, usually to the person who bore the expenses of the insured's final illness and burial.

[c] Changing the Beneficiary

As noted above, most modern policies allow the insured to change the beneficiary, but there are some limitations on this right. Community property rules sometimes limit the right to change the beneficiary; divorce decrees often limit the policy-owner's discretion to make future changes; and individuals who are incompetent entirely lack the power to make valid changes. Furthermore, with respect to life insurance issued under the Federal Employee Group Life Insurance program and the Serviceman's Group Life Insurance program, Congress has specified that beneficiaries can be changed only in accordance with the explicit statutory and regulatory requirements, and courts have been unwilling to depart from these mandates even though the rationale for them is unclear.[14]

The insurance policy typically prescribes the manner for making a change of beneficiary. Most policies require that the insured execute and deliver to the insurer a written request for a change and that the insurer endorse this change on the policy. Some policies also require that the insured send the request with the policy to the insurer, but this procedure is being used less frequently today. If the policyholder complies with these procedures, the change of beneficiary is effective, even though the change is made without the knowledge or consent of either the prior or the new beneficiary.

In most jurisdictions, the change will be deemed effective if the insured "substantially complies" with the procedures specified by the insurer.[15] Under this rule, if the policyowner has done virtually everything possible to comply with the specified procedures but has failed to comply in some immaterial respect, or if the policyowner has failed to comply with the procedures due to circumstances beyond the policyholder's control, the change is effective despite the noncompliance. The rule is grounded in equity; it is designed to work fairness by carrying out the intent of the insured. For example, if the insured seeks to change the beneficiary from his ex-wife to his mother, but his ex-wife intercepts the insured's mail, including the forms necessary to process the change, and the insured dies before discovering the ex-wife's successful interference, it would be highly unfair to conclude that the insured failed to make an effective change of beneficiary.[16]

The tension in the change of beneficiary cases is the classic one between form and substance: should the intent of the insured be paramount, or should the formal

[14] See Ward v. Stratton, 988 F.2d 65 (8th Cir. 1993) (FEGLI policy); Prudential Ins. Co. of Am. v. Parker, 840 F.2d 6 (7th Cir. 1988) (SGLI policy).

[15] See, e.g., Fidelity Bankers Life Ins. Co. v. Dortch, 348 S.E.2d 794 (N.C. 1986); Horne v. Gulf Life Ins. Co., 287 S.E.2d 144 (S.C. 1982); Capitol Life Ins. Co. v. Porter, 719 S.W.2d 908 (Mo.App. 1986); Klein v. Klein, 638 S.W.2d 94 (Tex. Ct. App. 1982); Travelers Ins. Co. v. Smith, 435 N.E.2d 1188 (Ill. App. Ct. 1982).

[16] See Standard Life & Accident Ins. Co. v. Pylant, 424 So. 2d 377 (La.App. 1982).

requirements of the policy control? The substantial compliance standard attempts to strike a balance between these two interests. A review of two cases will help understand this balance. First, in *Occidental Life Insurance Co. v. Row,* [17] Mrs. Allie owned a policy of insurance on the life of her husband, Mr. Allie; she designated herself as beneficiary. After Mrs. Allie died on May 19, 1966, Mr. Allie, who was the sole beneficiary under her will, advised the insurance agent of his desire to change the beneficiary of the policy to his daughter Margaret. The agent indicated that some guidance on procedures from the home office would be necessary; Mr. Allie filled out a change of beneficiary form so that the process might be expedited. The home office outlined the procedures for effecting the change, but before this procedure could be implemented, Mr. Allie died.

The issue in the litigation which followed concerned the right to the proceeds. If Mr. Allie successfully changed the beneficiary designation, Margaret was entitled to all of the proceeds. If he did not change the beneficiary, the proceeds would pass through Mrs. Allie's estate to Mr. Allie, and then through his estate to Margaret and two other children, who would share the proceeds equally. The court reasoned that Mr. Allie had done everything in his power to change the beneficiary; his attempt to change the beneficiary was unequivocal. Also, there was little doubt that he would have complied with the company's procedures, whatever they might have been, had he lived. The rule of substantial compliance is designed to implement, not thwart, the policyowner's intent, and here there was no doubt as to Mr. Allie's wishes. Therefore, the court held that Mr. Allie substantially complied with the change of beneficiary procedures, and Margaret was held entitled to the proceeds.[18]

The insured was held not to have substantially complied with the change of beneficiary procedures in *Manhattan Life Insurance Co. v. Barnes.* [19] Victor Barnes held a certificate in a group life insurance plan; in 1960, when the policy was issued, he designated Margaret Ann Barnes, his wife, as the beneficiary. Prior to his death, however, Victor and Margaret were divorced. Two of his three daughters contended that twenty-two months before his death he executed a change of beneficiary form

---

[17] 271 F. Supp. 920 (S.D. W.Va. 1967).

[18] For other examples of where the substantial compliance test was met, see Bell v. Parker, 563 So. 2d 594 (Miss. 1990); Bergen v. Travelers Ins. Co. of Ill., 776 P.2d 659 (Utah 1989); IDS Life Ins. Co. v. Estate of Groshong, 736 P.2d 1301 (Idaho 1987); Strauss v. Teachers Ins. and Annuity Ass'n of Am., 639 N.E.2d 1106 (N.Y. App. Div. 1994); Larsen v. Northwestern Nat'l Life Ins. Co., 463 N.W.2d 777 (Minn. Ct. App. 1991); Anglen v. Heimburger, 803 S.W.2d 109 (Mo. Ct. App. 1990). See also Messier v. Metropolitan Life Ins. Co., 578 A.2d 98 (Vt. 1990) (granting request of decedent's finance to vacate summary judgment for parents of deceased).

[19] 462 F.2d 629 (9th Cir. 1972). For other examples where the substantial compliance test was held not met, see Eschler v. Eschler, 849 P.2d 196, 202 (Mont. 1993); Shaw v. Loeffler, 796 P.2d 633 (Okla. 1990); Penn Mut. Life Ins. Co. v. Abramson, 530 A.2d 1202 (D.C.App. 1987); In re Group Life Ins. Proceeds of Mallory, 872 S.W.2d 800 (Tex. Ct. App. 1994); DeCeglia v. Estate of Colletti, 625 A.2d 590 (N.J.Super. 1993); Sun Life Assur. Co. of Canada v. Hicks, 844 S.W.2d 652 (Tenn. Ct. App. 1992); National Western Life Ins. Co. v. Schmeh, 749 P.2d 974 (Colo.Ct.App. 1987); In re Estate of Capone, 518 N.E.2d 619 (Ohio Prob. Ct. 1987).

in which he requested that his three daughters be named the new beneficiaries. One of the daughters allegedly found the change of beneficiary request card among some of her father's papers about a month after his death. A handwritten note also was in the file which read "Change Manhattan, beneficiary of Manhattan policies." The daughters testified that their father had indicated he believed he had changed the beneficiary, but Margaret contradicted this testimony.

The court noted that no evidence indicated that Mr. Barnes was incapacitated during the twenty-two months after he filled out the beneficiary change form or that anything prevented him from completing the change of beneficiary. In the court's view, he could have done more to satisfy the change of beneficiary requirements. Therefore, his ex-wife, Margaret, was held entitled to the proceeds because the beneficiary designation had not been changed.

Barnes can be explained as a case where the evidence was not sufficient to show that the insured definitely intended to change the beneficiary. Perhaps at one time he had such an intent; he probably took preliminary steps to effect a change. It is also conceivable that he had a change of heart, which caused him to postpone completing the change of beneficiary. Also, although there was no indication of fraud in the facts of *Barnes,* giving credence to subsequently discovered handwritten notes requesting that a beneficiary change be made could facilitate fraud in some cases. The two cases, when read together, show that the policyholder's mere statement of intent to change the beneficiary is not enough to accomplish the change. Something more is required: the insured must make a substantial effort to effect the change. If the change is never completed, it must not be on account of a reason that calls into question the insured's desire to make the change.

Having stated these general guidelines to assist in the determination of whether the insured has completed a change of beneficiary, it is inevitable that cases will arise that fall into the uncertain "grey" area. Such a case is *Connecticut General Life Insurance Co. v. Gulley,* [20] a 1982 Seventh Circuit decision. Julious Balsley was insured under a group life insurance policy issued by his employer; initially, he designated his wife as the beneficiary. On May 11, 1979, Julious, while competent and in the presence of a witness, executed a change of beneficiary form designating his daughter as the new beneficiary. He told his daughter that he wanted her to receive the proceeds, as he had otherwise provided for other family members. He left the form with his daughter, saying he would return to get it and deliver it to his employer. During the next week, he worked each day, but he did not see his daughter and he did not return to get the form. He spoke with her once on Sunday, March 18, but the insurance was not discussed. That evening he suffered a fatal heart attack. On March 20, the daughter mailed a copy of the change of beneficiary form to the employer; no evidence existed that the daughter was authorized to mail in the form or that Julious intended that she do so.

Julious did not strictly comply with the change of beneficiary procedures. Nothing unusual prevented Julious from picking up the form and delivering it to the employer the week before he died. However, there were a number of things that Julious did

---

[20] 668 F.2d 325 (7th Cir.), *cert. denied,* 456 U.S. 974 (1982).

in the presence of witnesses that indicated it was his intent to change the beneficiary, and only one thing remained for him to complete the process. The district court held that Julious did not substantially comply with the change of beneficiary procedure, but the Seventh Circuit reversed, holding that he did. It is inevitable that cases like *Gulley* will arise where applying the substantial compliance test is extremely difficult.

A number of courts have asserted that the procedures specified in policies for changing the beneficiary are for the insurer's benefit. This assertion is not entirely accurate because the original beneficiary has an interest in the insured's compliance with those procedures necessary to extinguish the original beneficiary's interest.[21] Furthermore, the policyholder has an interest in formalities which preclude the possibility of a fraudulent claim that the policyholder changed his or her mind. The policyholder, of course, will not live to rebut any such claim; the formalities for changing the beneficiary guard against such a claim succeeding, thereby vitiating the insured's intent.

However, from the observation that change of beneficiary procedures are for the insurer's benefit, courts have reasoned that the procedures can be waived by the insurer. Waiver is said to occur in two instances: first, where the insurer endorses the change of beneficiary in the absence of the insured's compliance with specified procedures; and second, where the insurer files an interpleader and deposits the proceeds in court. The first instance is hardly controversial; if the insurer endorses the change without compliance, the insurer is hardly in a position to claim later that the procedures were not satisfied. As for the second instance, in the equitable action of interpleader, the insurer seeks to be discharged from its contractual obligations; if the contract is discharged, the insurer no longer cares who receives the proceeds, and the insurer is obviously in no position to contest the change. The significance of the waiver argument, however, pertains to whether the procedures need to be satisfied at all. If the procedures are for the insurer's benefit and if the insurer waives compliance with these procedures, it logically follows that the procedures for changing the beneficiary have no relevance at all. The implications of this conclusion are that the court, when faced with competing claims to the proceeds, should decide who receives the proceeds in accordance with equitable principles, and should disregard whether the mechanics of the beneficiary change were satisfied.[22]

Lastly, divorce, in and of itself, does not change a beneficiary designation. However, the documents effecting the divorce will often determine what happens to the right to receive the proceeds of the insurance. If a divorce decree specifies what is to happen with regard to the beneficiary designation, that decree ordinarily controls, even if the change is not made or the designation is changed but is subsequently altered.[23] The divorce decree is tantamount to the insured contracting away

---

[21] See Rouse v. Crum, 313 S.E.2d 140 (Ga. Ct. App. 1984).

[22] See Zeigler v. Cardona, 830 F. Supp. 1395 (N.D. Ala. 1993); Metropolitan Life Ins. Co. v. Barnes, 770 F. Supp. 1393 (E.D. Mo. 1991); Bimestefer v. Bimestefer, 109 A.2d 768 (Md. 1954); Lopez v. Massachusetts Mut. Life Ins. Co., 566 N.Y.S.2d 359 (N.Y. Sup. Ct. 1991); Travelers Ins. Co. v. Smith, 435 N.E.2d 1188 (Ill. App. Ct. 1982).

[23] See Metropolitan Life Ins. co. v. Frawley, 712 F. Supp. 131 (S.D. Ohio 1989); Metropolitan Life Ins. Co. v. Beaty, 493 N.W.2d 627 (Neb. 1993); Aetna Life Ins. Co. v.

his or her right to change the beneficiary,[24] which is particularly evident when the decree incorporates a settlement agreement by reference. If the change in beneficiary mandated by a divorce decree is not actually made, or if a subsequent change in the beneficiary in violation of the divorce decree is made, the persons entitled to the proceeds under the divorce decree will have an equitable right to the proceeds.[25] However, if a decree is in general terms and does not specifically require a change of beneficiary, the beneficiary designation will be enforced as it appears.[26] All of this can create a problem for the insurer if it is not notified of a divorce decree that supersedes a beneficiary designation and the designation is not subsequently changed (or is changed in violation of the decree). A person who a divorce decree requires be named as beneficiary would be wise to forward a copy of the divorce decree to the insurer, but if this does not occur the insurer is at some risk of paying the wrong beneficiary. There is not much the insurer can do to protect itself in this situation, except to inquire into the marital status of the claimant when payment of proceeds is requested; if a divorce has occurred since the policy was issued, the insurer should request a copy of the decree to confirm that the beneficiary designation on file with the insurer is consistent with the decree.

[d] Claims to Proceeds

In a variety of situations, a dispute can arise between the beneficiary and someone else claiming the proceeds.

[1] Creditor versus Beneficiary

In some situations, creditors of the insured and the beneficiary make competing claims to the proceeds of the policy. For example, during the life of the insured, a creditor of the insured might attempt to attach the policy's cash value. Also, after the insured's death, creditors might claim a superior interest in the proceeds.

A creditor who lacks an interest in the insurance contract, either as owner of the policy, assignee, or beneficiary, cannot make a claim on the contract itself. Nothing prevents a creditor from owning a policy or being designated as the beneficiary or assignee, but in the absence of such ownership or designation, the creditor can only argue a right to the contract's *value,* as distinct from asserting a contract right. In other words, the insurer must treat the policy as if it were the debtor's property, much like the debtor's car or boat. However, laws in most states in varying degrees exempt insurance policies from the claims of creditors. In fact, the insurance exemption is one of the most important exemptions provided by state law.

Hussey, 590 N.E.2d 724 (Ohio 1992); Bowers v. Bowers, 637 S.W.2d 456 (Tenn. 1982); In re Estate of Lemer, 306 N.W.2d 244 (S.D. 1981); Gillespie v. Moore, 635 S.W.2d 927 (Tex. Ct. App. 1982); Posey v. Prudential Ins. Co., 383 So. 2d 849 (ALa. Ct. App. 1980).

[24] See Dubois v. Smith, 599 A.2d 493, 497 (N.H. 1991).

[25] See, e.g., Travelers Ins. Co. v. Lewis, 531 P.2d 484 (Utah 1975); Della Terza v. Estate of Della Terza, 647 A.2d 180 (N.J.Super.Ct. 1994); Pernick v. Brandt, 506 N.W.2d 243 (Mich. Ct. App. 1993).

[26] See, e.g., Eschler v. Eschler, 849 P.2d 196 (Mont. 1993); Dubois v. Smith, 599 A.2d 493, 499 (N.H. 1991); Christensen v. Sabad, 773 P.2d 538 (Colo. 1989)(en banc); Giard v. Pardun, 318 N.W.2d 137 (S.D. 1982).

State laws providing the insurance exemption vary widely in their content.[27] Generalization is extremely difficult; resort must be had to the particulars of the statutes and the judicial decisions interpreting those laws. Whenever a question of exemption arises, the requirements of state law may turn, depending on the particular state, on one or more factors: (1) whether the cash value or the proceeds are being claimed as exempt; (2) the kind of policy involved (e.g., life, annuity, disability, etc.); (3) the relationship of the debtor to the policy, meaning whether the debtor owns the policy or is the beneficiary (or both); (4) if the debtor is the owner, whether the debtor has the right to change beneficiaries; (5) the relationship of the beneficiary to the insured; (6) the amount of the annual premiums. The purpose of the state exemption statutes is basically to protect the debtor's family, who depend on the debtor's purchase of insurance for their financial needs in the event of the debtor's death.

At the risk of overgeneralizing, a few observations can nevertheless be made. In many states, if an individual takes out a policy of insurance on his or her own life and names immediate family members as beneficiaries, the proceeds are exempt from the claims of the insured's creditors. In these jurisdictions, cash values ordinarily cannot be seized during the life of the insured either, since that would defeat the statutory purpose of protecting the proceeds, but contrary results have been reached in states where the statutes only exempt proceeds. If the insured names oneself or one's own estate as beneficiary, the cash value or proceeds are less likely to be immune to creditor's claims. Such an insurance policy is, purely and simply, the insured's asset, much like a bank account; accordingly, the public policy shifts in favor of allowing creditors to attach such policies. If the insurance policy on which the insured is also named as the beneficiary is unmatured and does not have an identifiable money value, it is less likely that the creditor will be allowed to attach it.

The insured's creditors may also be allowed to attach cash values or the proceeds of a policy in circumstances where money was misappropriated from the creditor by the insured and the policy's premiums were paid with such funds. Similarly, creditors may be allowed to attach cash values or proceeds where the purchase of the insurance was part of a scheme to defraud creditors, which might be the case if the insured attempted to shield assets as the insured neared bankruptcy.[28]

Whether the *beneficiary's* creditors can attach proceeds received also depends on several things — the applicable state law, whether the proceeds are paid in a lump sum or in periodic payments, and the provisions of the particular policy. This question can arise in property insurance as well. A person may be designated to receive the proceeds of insurance on exempt property. The weight of authority is that if the property would have been exempt under state law, the proceeds of insurance on the property are also exempt.[29]

---

[27] State exemption statutes are collected in *Collier on Bankruptcy,* vol. 7 (15th ed. 1986).

[28] See In re Aldman, 541 F.2d 999 (2d Cir. 1976); see generally 5 COUCH 2d § 29:118 et seq. (1984); Janice Grieder, Muriel Crawford, and William Beadles, *Law and the Life Insurance Contract* 251–55 (6th ed. 1989).

[29] 3 *Collier on Bankruptcy* ¶ 522.24, at 522-74 (1986).

[2] Creditor As Beneficiary

In most cases, no problem is created by designating a creditor as the insured's beneficiary, assuming the proceeds do not exceed the amount of the debt. However, if the proceeds exceed the amount of the debt, another person (such as a family member) may assert a claim to the excess proceeds.[30] Most courts infer that the insured intended to designate the creditor as a beneficiary only to the extent of the debt. The excess proceeds are held in trust by the creditor for the benefit of the insured, meaning the estate. However, a minority of courts, particularly where the creditor procured the insurance and designated itself as beneficiary, allow the creditor to retain all of the proceeds.[31] Some courts that follow the minority rule recognize an exception where there is evidence other than the insured's designation of the beneficiary showing that the insured intended that the creditor would be entitled to proceeds only up to the amount of the debt.[32] Also, if the amount of the proceeds greatly exceeds the debt, the contract resembles a wagering contract, and it might be invalidated, or invalidated in part, for lack of an insurable interest.[33]

[3] Trustee in Bankruptcy versus Beneficiary

Under the Bankruptcy Reform Act of 1978,[34] a bankrupt debtor is allowed to choose between state exemptions and federal exemptions unless a state prohibits election of federal exemptions.[35] A substantial majority of the states have already enacted legislation prohibiting debtors from electing the federal exemptions. Under the federal exemptions, a debtor is allowed an exemption for any unmatured life insurance policies that the debtor owns, other than credit life insurance contracts. The loan value of an unmatured life insurance contract (meaning the cash value, any accrued dividends, and interest) are exempt to the extent of $8,000.[36] If the debtor chooses the state exemptions, the law varies widely from state to state.[37]

[4] Assignee versus Beneficiary

Most modern policies contain a provision setting forth both the procedures for effecting an assignment and its legal effect. One form in common use provides:

> You may assign this policy. We assume no responsibility for the validity of any assignment, and we will not be considered to have knowledge of it unless it is filed in writing at our Home Office. When it is filed, your rights and those of any Beneficiary will be subject to it.[38]

---

[30] See, e.g., Warnock v. Davis, 104 U.S. 775 (1881).

[31] See generally 5 COUCH 2d §§ 29:115–116 (1984).

[32] See In re Estate of Tanenblatt, 609 N.Y.S.2d 532 (N.Y.Surr. 1994) (separation agreement shows insured's intent that designation of former wife as beneficiary was intended only to secure balance of payments owed former wife on insured's death).

[33] See § 43, *supra.*

[34] 11 U.S.C. §§ 101–151326 (1983).

[35] *Id.* § 522(b).

[36] *Id.* § 522(d)(8).

[37] See note 27, *supra.* For a discussion of creditors' rights and debtors' privileges with regard to life insurance, see J. Grieder et al., note 28, *supra,* at 248–58 (1984).

[38] *Policy Kit* at 111 (AM-629 E 1-80). Usually, a certificate holder's interest in a group insurance policy is not assignable. See Bimestefer v. Bimestefer, 109 A.2d 768 (Md. 1954).

This language suggests that if the assignment is filed with the insurer, the assignee's rights are superior to those of the beneficiary. However, if the assignment is not filed with the insurer and the insurer pays the proceeds to a qualified beneficiary of record, the insurer will not be liable to the assignee.

Although the language in policies dealing with assignment varies, and some policies have provisions considerably more elaborate than the quoted passage above, most courts in construing such clauses have held that when the policyholder complies with the procedures specified by the insurer for assigning a policy, the assignee's rights are superior to the beneficiaries.[39] This approach gives preference to the rights of the owner of the policy. Indeed, the beneficiary's expectancy interest is subject to being extinguished at any time during the life of the insured. If the insured executes a valid assignment of the policy, the insured is simply exercising the powers the insured possesses. The beneficiary has no power or right that limits the discretion of the insured in this respect. However, concern for the beneficiary's expectation and the possibility of fraud may become a factor where an attempted assignment does not comply with the policy's procedures. It has been held that the beneficiary's rights are superior unless the assignment was made under a procedure conforming to that specified for changing the beneficiary.[40]

Beyond the foregoing generalizations, courts are divided on the implications of finding the assignee's rights to be superior to the beneficiaries. Often an assignment is made to secure a debt, and it has been held that the assignee's rights are superior only up to the amount of the debt. Any excess proceeds belong to the designated beneficiary.[41] Other courts have held that the creditor is entitled to all of the proceeds, under the reasoning that the assignment itself functions as a change of beneficiary.[42] Whether creditors are involved or not, courts are sharply divided on whether an assignment functions as a change of beneficiary.[43]

---

[39] See, e.g., Hebert v. Page, 351 So. 2d 529 (Miss. 1977); Rountree v. Frazee, 209 So. 2d 424 (Ala. 1968); Bourne v. Haynes, 235 N.Y.S.2d 332 (N.Y. Sup. Ct. 1962); Hackney v. Sharp, 157 S.W.2d 827 (Tenn. 1942); Baldwin v. Atlanta Jt. Stockland Bank, 7 S.E.2d 178 (Ga. 1940). See generally Annot., *Right of Life Insurance Beneficiary Against Estate of Insured Who Used Policy as Collateral,* 91 A.L.R.2d 496 (1963).

[40] See West v. Founders Life Assur. Co. of Florida, 547 So. 2d 870 (Ala. 1989); Goldman v. Moses, 191 N.E. 873 (Mass. 1934).

[41] See, e.g., Wages v. Wages, 42 S.E.2d 481 (Ga. 1947); Balcer v. Peters, 195 N.W.2d 83 (Mich. Ct. App. 1972).

[42] See, e.g., Esswein v. Rogers, 30 Cal. Rptr. 738 (Cal. Ct. App. 1963); Rattray v. Banks, 121 S.E. 516 (Ga. Ct. App. 1924).

[43] Compare Hebert v. Pace, 351 So. 2d 529 (Miss. 1977) (assignee is entitled to proceeds of policy to extent of assignee's interest, and beneficiary's interest is not vested) and Rountree v. Frazee, 209 So. 2d 424 (Ala. 1968) (assignment of life policy to mortgagee did not change beneficiary or divest named beneficiary of any interest in policy) with Hollaway v. Selvidge, 548 P.2d 835 (Kan. 1976)(right of beneficiary is subject to divestment by assignment) and Bell v. Garcia, 639 S.W.2d 185 (Mo. Ct. App. 1982) (beneficiary's rights are subject to divestment anytime during life of insured by assignment). See generally 2 APPLEMAN § 987 (1995).

For a recent case addressing these issues, see Little v. X-Pert Corp., 867 S.W.2d 15 (Tex. 1993). Four couples (each husband and wife) established a corporation, with each couple

Owners of life insurance policies often assign the right to receive insurance proceeds to their creditors, and absent some expression of intent to the contrary, the better rule appears to be that the assignee has superior rights only to the extent of the debt. Although it is commonly said that an assignee takes all of the ownership rights of a policy, where the language of a policy refers to change of ownership, assignment, and change of beneficiary, as do a number of modern forms,[44] it makes sense to distinguish ownership rights from the rights of an assignee.[45] Assigning a policy should be tantamount to assigning irrevocably the right to payment of proceeds, which would trump the beneficiary's rights. If the assignment's purpose is to secure a debt, the beneficiary's rights return to the extent the amount of proceeds payable exceeds the amount of the debt.[46] An interesting wrinkle is presented if the creditor's debt is barred by the statute of limitations. The assignee is likely to argue that the fact that the action to enforce the debt is barred does not mean that the debt does not exist, and thus the assignee's rights under the life insurance policy are not affected by the running of the statute of limitations on the debt. The beneficiary is likely to argue that the running of the statute of limitations extinguishes the debt, in effect terminating the relationship of creditor and debtor; this has the effect of voiding the assignment, since the assignment was implicitly conditioned on the existence of a creditor-debtor relationship. The issue will be resolved according to

owning 25 percent of the corporation's outstanding shares. The shareholders agreed in a buy-sell arrangement to purchase life insurance on the four men, with the corporation named as beneficiary. Upon the death of any insured shareholder, the surviving spouse could opt to take the insurance proceeds in exchange for her 25 percent stock ownership, or of remaining a 25 percent shareholder with the insurance proceeds becoming an asset of the corporation. In March 1991 shareholder James Little and his wife sold all of their stock to a fellow shareholder, and James Little died one month later. The corporation claimed the proceeds of the insurance. Mrs. Little argued that the buy-sell agreement gave her the right to the proceeds, and the court agreed with her: "The Buy-Sell Agreement was an ongoing contract creating rights in the insurance proceeds independent of who was named as the legal beneficiary under the policy. . . . It would be an anomaly to construe [the Agreement] as automatically transferring ownership of the insurance policy but not the proceeds." 867 S.W.2d at 18. The court did not state that the buy-sell agreement functioned as an assignment of the claim for proceeds, but instead apparently reasoned that the Littles had the right to elect to own the policy, and that the buy-sell agreement did not require them to take affirmative action to exercise that right (either by asking for an assignment or change of beneficiary), 867 S.W.2d at 17-18, and that when the ownership rights in the policy passed to the Littles pursuant to the buy-sell agreement the right to proceeds went along with those rights. 867 S.W.2d at 18. Unfortunately, the court's decision blurs the distinction between assignment of proceeds and assignment of a policy, a matter of considerable important to any insurer attempting to determine to whom it should pay proceeds. In this case, the insurer was not disadvantaged; it paid the proceeds to the corporation, the named beneficiary, but obtained a temporary restraining order prohibiting the corporation from spending or commingling the proceeds. 867 S.W.2d at 16.

[44] See *Policy Kit* at 111 (AM-629 E 1-80), 118 (AM-30DT 1/80).

[45] See Livingston v. Shelton, 526 P.2d 385 (Wash. Ct. App. 1974).

[46] See *In re Estate of Devine*, 628 N.E.2d 1227 (Ind. Ct. App. 1994).

what effect the jurisdiction gives the running of a statute of limitations; authority exists on both sides.[47]

[e] Disqualification of the Beneficiary

A principle that applies to all kinds of insurance is that no insured can recover proceeds for a loss the insured has intentionally caused. It follows from this principle that a beneficiary who intentionally and unlawfully causes the death of the insured, and any person claiming through such beneficiary, cannot receive the proceeds of the insurance.[48] The public policies are particularly strong with regard to life insurance: no person should be allowed to profit by deliberately taking another's life.

The general insurance rule requires that the beneficiary "intend" to kill the insured, but the intent required is not exactly the same as the intent required for culpability in criminal law or torts. In insurance law, ordinarily there must be intent to bring about death or to cause some other kind of injury from which death is a likely, foreseeable result. Negligent, grossly negligent, or even reckless conduct that causes the death of the insured does not disqualify the beneficiary.[49] One court recently held that a husband's guilty plea to a charge of vehicular homicide, arising out of an auto accident in which his wife was killed, did not cause the husband to forfeit is right to receive the proceeds of a policy on his wife's life since he did not intend to kill her.[50] The "unlawfulness" element in the insurance rule indicates that not all intentional killings of the insured by the beneficiary disqualify the beneficiary. For example, if the beneficiary intentionally kills the insured in self-defense, the beneficiary's rights are not extinguished.[51]

Some jurisdictions have statutes that disqualify beneficiaries, but many jurisdictions rely entirely on case law. Interestingly, a number of states have statutes that disqualify heirs in the descent and distribution context but no equivalent statute regarding the disqualification of life insurance beneficiaries. No good reason exists for treating the slaying heir differently than the slaying life insurance beneficiary.[52]

----

[47] Compare Hawkins v. Southern Pipe & Supply Co., 259 So. 2d 696 (Miss. 1972) (beneficiary wins) with Gallaher v. American-Amicable Life Ins. Co., 462 S.W.2d 626 (Tex. Ct. App. 1971) (assignee wins).

[48] See, e.g., Mutual Life Ins. Co. v. Armstrong, 117 U.S. 591 (1886); First Kentucky Trust Co. v. United States, 737 F.2d 557 (6th Cir. 1984); Rowland v. Faulkenbury, 883 S.W.2d 848 (Ark.Ct.App. 1994) (beneficiary who commits willful, unlawful, and felonious killing of insured forfeits all rights); Stephens v. Adkins, 448 S.E.2d 734 (Ga. Ct. App. 1994) (conviction for voluntary manslaughter disqualifies beneficiary); see generally Annot., *Killing of Insured by Beneficiary as Affecting Life Insurance or Its Proceeds,* 27 A.L.R.3d 794 (1969).

[49] See McClure v. McClure, 403 S.E.2d 197 (W.Va. 1991); State Mut. Life Assur. Co. v. Hampton, 696 P.2d 1027 (Okla. 1985); Rumbaut v. Labagnara, 791 S.W.2d 195 (Tex. Ct. App. 1990); Huff v. Union Fidelity Life Ins. Co., 470 N.E.2d 236 (Ohio Ct.App. 1984). See also Ford v. Ford, 512 A.2d 389 (Md. 1986) (insane killer not responsible and therefore not disqualified).

[50] See Moore v. State Farm Life Ins. Co., 878 S.W.2d 946 (Tenn. 1994).

[51] See Metropolitan Life Ins. Co. v. Fogle, 419 S.E.2d 825 (S.C. Ct. App. 1992).

[52] See John W. Wade, *Acquisition of Property by Willfully Killing Another — A Statutory Solution,* 49 Harv. L. Rev. 715 (1936).

If the beneficiary kills the insured and is thereby disqualified, this does not mean that the insurer need not pay proceeds to anyone. In the ordinary case where the murdering beneficiary is not the owner of the policy, the disqualified beneficiary is treated as having predeceased the insured, which means the proceeds go to any remaining primary beneficiaries or, if there are none, to designated contingent beneficiaries.[53] If there are no surviving qualified beneficiaries, most policies prescribe that the proceeds are paid to the estate of the insured. An alternative approach, followed by only a very few courts, is to have the murdering beneficiary hold the proceeds in trust for the insured's estate.[54] This approach is less desirable, since it is less likely to fulfill the insured's intent, as expressed in the beneficiary designations, with regard to how the proceeds should be distributed. If the slaying beneficiary is the only named beneficiary, it is correct to pay the proceeds to the insured's estate, and this may explain why the rule continues to be articulated from time to time.[55]

A different result might be reached if the murdering beneficiary has purchased the insurance on the life of the insured and paid the premiums. It is often said that a policy of insurance purchased on the life of another with the intent to murder the insured is *void ab initio*.[56] The theory of this principle is that the purchaser of the insurance has committed the most vicious kind of fraud and concealment, which prevents a valid contract from coming into existence.[57] Some courts have applied the rule in situations where the beneficiary, having formulated a plan to murder someone, induces the "planned decedent" to purchase insurance on his or her own life, and then murders the insured.[58]

Treating the policy as void is tantamount to rescinding the contract, which creates a problem regarding what to do with the premiums paid by the slaying beneficiary.

---

[53] See, e.g., Lee v. Aylward, 790 S.W.2d 462 (Mo. 1990) (en banc); Brooks v. Thompson, 521 S.W.2d 563 (Tenn. 1975); Neff v. Massachusetts Mut. Life Ins. Co., 107 N.E.2d 100 (Ohio 1952); National Home Life Assur. v. Patterson, 746 P.2d 696 (OkLa. Ct. App. 1987).

[54] See Cockrell v. Life Ins. Co. of Georgia, 692 F.2d 1164 (8th Cir. 1982); Horn v. Cole, 156 S.W.2d 787 (Ark. 1941); *Restatement of Restitution,* § 189(1) (1937).

[55] See Estate of Chesi v. First Citizens Bank, 613 N.E.2d 14 (Ind. 1993) (indicating that slaying beneficiary forfeits rights and holds proceeds in constructive trust for estate of insured; but in facts of case slaying beneficiary was only primary beneficiary and there were no contingent beneficiaries). In fact, in New York Life Ins. Co. v. Henriksen, 415 N.E.2d 146 (Ind. Ct. App. 1981), the court observed that the rule that the slaying beneficiary holds the proceeds in trust for the insured's estate applies only when there are no beneficiaries other than the slaying beneficiary.

[56] See, e.g., National Aid Life Ass'n v. May, 207 P.2d 292 (Okla. 1949); Chute v. Old Am. Ins. Co., 629 P.2d 734 (Kan.Ct.App. 1981); Lofton v. Lofton, 215 S.E.2d 861 (N.C. Ct. App. 1975).

[57] Although referring to the beneficiary's failure to reveal his intention to arrange for the insured's slaying a "misrepresentation," which is technically incorrect, see § 102, *infra,* the link between disqualification rules and concealment rules was noted by the court in Federal Kemper Life Assur. Co. v. Eichwedel, 639 N.E.2d 246, 251 (Ill. App. Ct. 1994).

[58] See Ellis v. John Hancock Mut. Life Ins. Co., 586 F. Supp. 649 (E.D. Ark. 1984); New England Mut. Life Ins. Co. v. Calvert, 459 F. Supp. 979 (E.D. Mo. 1978), *aff'd,* 605 F.2d 421 (8th Cir. 1979).

Although this sum of money is unlikely to be large, the insurer should not be allowed to keep the premiums, as this would constitute a windfall for the insurer. Although giving the premiums to the estate of the deceased is an attractive outcome, this result does not follow from contract law, although such a result might be possible in equity under the reasoning that the slaying beneficiary, to whom the premiums in theory should be returned if the contract is rescinded, holds the premiums in constructive trust for the benefit of the insured's estate. If this answer stretches the equitable doctrine of constructive trust too far, one would hope that these assets would eventually make their way into the estate of the deceased insured pursuant to the tort claim that the estate possesses against the slaying beneficiary.

Some decisions have refused to disqualify the beneficiary in circumstances where an applicable statute requires that the beneficiary be convicted of specific offenses before the beneficiary can be prohibited from receiving the insurance proceeds.[59] These statutes have difficulties: if a beneficiary is indicted for murdering the insured but dies prior to being convicted, or if the beneficiary is never convicted due to a technical criminal defense, the beneficiary would not be disqualified from taking the proceeds. This has led most courts to hold that the common law rule barring the beneficiary who intentionally and unlawfully kills the insured from taking the proceeds is not displaced by, and instead can coexist with, statutes requiring convictions.[60]

Thus, in most states a conviction is not required to bar the slaying beneficiary from taking the proceeds. If the beneficiary is convicted, the common law standard for disqualifying the beneficiary is, of course, met. An acquittal simply means that the state lacked enough evidence to convince a jury that the beneficiary was guilty beyond a reasonable doubt. The same jury might have been persuaded by a preponderance of the evidence that the beneficiary murdered the insured. The question of who is entitled to the proceeds of a life insurance policy is civil in nature; thus, if it is established by a preponderance of the evidence that the beneficiary killed the insured, the beneficiary is disqualified. Accordingly, a beneficiary who is acquitted of criminal charges that he or she murdered the insured may nevertheless have to defeat a claim in a civil action alleging disqualification for having slain the insured.[61]

When the insured perishes under circumstances where the beneficiary's involvement is suspected but no criminal prosecution has commenced or seems likely, and no other person is contesting the beneficiary's right to the proceeds, how should the

---

[59] See, e.g., Life Ins. Co. of N. Am. v. Wollett, 766 P.2d 893 (Nev. 1988) (beneficiary charged with murder pleaded guilty to involuntary manslaughter pursuant to plea bargain; held, statute requiring criminal conviction for murder to bar beneficiary from taking proceeds must be construed strictly and preempts common law); United Trust Co. v. Pyke, 427 P.2d 67 (Kan. 1967) (subsequently overruled; see note 60, *infra*).

[60] See, e.g., Peoples Sec. Life Ins. Co. v. Arrington, 412 S.E.2d 705 (Va. 1992); State Mut. Life Assur. Co. v. Hampton, 696 P.2d 1027 (Okla. 1985); Harper v. Prudential Ins. Co. of Am., 662 P.2d 1264 (Kan. 1983); Smith v. Todd, 152 S.E. 506 (S.C. 1930).

[61] See McClure v. McClure, 403 S.E.2d 197 (W.Va. 1991); Schrader v. Equitable Life Assur. Soc'y, 485 N.E.2d 1031 (Ohio 1985); Jones v. All Am. Life Ins. Co., 316 S.E.2d 122 (N.C. Ct. App. 1984).

insurer respond? It is reasonable for the insurer to analyze the situation independently and to confer with authorities responsible for investigating the insured's death, but the insurer cannot delay indefinitely paying proceeds to a person whose innocence is presumed under criminal law. If there is a reasonable basis for believing that the beneficiary was involved in unlawfully killing the insured, the insurer should initiate an interpleader action. But absent evidence implicating the primary beneficiary, the insurer should pay the proceeds in accordance with the provisions of the policy. If it later turns out that the beneficiary did intentionally bring about the insured's death, the insurer's good faith payment to the beneficiary of record should relieve it from liability to contingent beneficiaries or the insured's estate.[62]

A practical problem is presented to the insurer when the primary beneficiary is convicted of murdering the insured but states an intent to appeal the conviction. The conviction is, of course, conclusive on the question of whether the beneficiary is disqualified. If the insurer pays the proceeds to the contingent beneficiary and the conviction is subsequently vacated, the slaying beneficiary will probably make a claim for the proceeds, which creates the possibility that the insurer will be subjected to a double liability since the proceeds were already paid to the contingent beneficiary. This can be avoided if the contingent beneficiary returns the proceeds to the insurer, but the contingent beneficiary is unlikely to do so, instead preferring to initiate a civil proceeding in which the contingent beneficiary will attempt to show, by a preponderance of the evidence, that the primary beneficiary is disqualified. Yet it is not certain that the contingent beneficiary will prevail in this proceeding; the insurer will be under a contract liability to the slaying beneficiary, and if the proceeds have been depleted by the contingent beneficiary, recoupment will be impossible. In these situations, it is necessary to secure the court's assistance in fashioning appropriate orders to protect the insurer's interests, such as ordering the proceeds to be paid to the contingent beneficiary in one- or two-year certificates of deposits, which can be easily recouped in the event the primary beneficiary's conviction is ultimately vacated.

[f]   Community Property Laws

Approximately eight states in the south and west — including, notably, California and Texas — have community property laws.[63] These laws differ from state to state, but the essence of the statutory scheme is that a husband and wife each own an undivided one-half interest in community property. Community property is all property acquired by the spouses during marriage, except property acquired separately by one of the spouses through gift or inheritance. When one spouse dies, the other has a right to one-half of the community property, and the remainder

---

[62] See Lundsford v. Western States Life Ins., 872 P.2d 1308 (Colo.Ct.App. 1993) (insurer not liable to contingent beneficiaries, who had made no claim for proceeds, when primary beneficiary to whom proceeds had been paid subsequently admitted being involved in insured's murder); Doe v. American Gen. Life Ins. Co. of N.Y., 526 N.Y.S.2d 904 (N.Y. Sup. Ct. 1988) ("insurer cannot wait without paying on its policy unless [beneficiary's] complicity [in insured's death] is established.")

[63] W.S. McClanahan, *Community Property Laws in the United States* 2 (1982).

belongs to the estate of the deceased. Acquisition of life insurance with community funds affects rights to life insurance proceeds.[64]

Life insurance may or may not be community property, depending on when the policy was acquired and what funds were used to purchase it. When one spouse applies for and is issued a policy of life insurance during marriage, pays the premiums out of community funds, and designates someone other than the other spouse as the beneficiary, the policy constitutes community property. If the estate of the spouse who applied for the insurance is the designated beneficiary or the beneficiary by default, the proceeds are community property nonetheless. If, however, one of the spouses (for example, the husband) purchases a policy of insurance on his own life during the marriage with community funds and designates his wife as the beneficiary, the proceeds are usually considered the wife's separate property on the theory that the husband had made a gift of community proceeds to the other.

As the foregoing paragraph suggests, the named insured who purchases the policy with community funds has the right to designate and change the beneficiary, but the named insured's spouse still has an interest in the proceeds. Thus, the named insured's right to designate and change the beneficiary is not absolute. The policyowner in a community property state who names someone other than his or her spouse as beneficiary on a policy that is purchased with community funds has, in effect, made a gift to the third party. If the policyowner's spouse does not consent to the making of the gift, the spouse might claim that the spouse is entitled to one-half, or perhaps all, of the proceeds.[65] The named beneficiary's claim to the proceeds is stronger if the beneficiary gave some consideration for the designation.[66] Similarly, if the insured elects a settlement option contrary to the wishes of his or her spouse, the spouse can defeat the chosen option. A California case is illustrative: the insured husband changed the method of payment under the policy from lump-sum to payment for life with ten years guaranteed, with the three grown daughters being the contingent payees. The wife did not know of this choice, and she challenged it after his death. The court held that the wife could receive one-half of the lump sum, but the remaining one-half was paid according to the settlement option that the husband selected.[67]

Many of the difficulties in community property states regarding life insurance arise in connection with termination of the husband-wife relationship by divorce. Upon divorce, community property is divided between the parties, either by stipulation or by court order. The courts of several states have held that the cash value of a life insurance policy is community property if premiums were paid with community funds; under this logic, each of the spouses is entitled to one-half of the

---

[64] For an overview of the effect of community properly law on insurance, see O'Connell v. O'Connell, 10 Cal. Rptr.2d 334 (Cal. Ct. App. 1992).

[65] See, e.g., O'Connell v. O'Connell, 10 Cal. Rptr.2d 334 (Cal. Ct. App. 1992); Guerrero v. Guerrero, 502 P.2d 1077 (Ariz. Ct. App. 1972).

[66] See, e.g., Anderson v. Idaho Mut. Benefit Ass'n, 292 P.2d 760 (Idaho 1956); Aetna Life Ins. Co. v. Brock, 249 P.2d 383 (Wash. 1953).

[67] See Tyre v. Aetna Life Ins. Co., 353 P.2d 725, (Cal. 1960).

cash value upon termination of the marriage.[68] Under this same logic, if a life insurance policy on one spouse is purchased with community funds, and the insured spouse is murdered by the beneficiary-spouse, it has been held that the slaying spouse does not forfeit his or her one-half vested interest in the life insurance policy.[69]

In community property states, because the spouse of a named insured may claim that the insured designated a beneficiary without the spouse's consent and therefore the spouse is entitled to part of the proceeds, legislatures have provided insurers with a "safety net" for circumstances where insurers pay, in good faith and without knowledge of adverse claims, the proceeds to the designated beneficiary. So-called "exoneration statutes" excuse the insurer from liability if a spouse should make a claim for proceeds paid to a third party where the insurer had no notice of the adverse claim and otherwise acted reasonably.[70]

Because the community property laws vary widely from state to state, additional generalizations about the effect of these statutes are not particularly useful. The law of particular states must be consulted for answers to specific questions.[71]

[g]   The Common Disaster Problem

For many years, a perplexing problem was presented by the situation where the insured and the beneficiary died in the same accident and no proof existed regarding who died first. The question was whether the beneficiary predeceased the insured: if so (and if no other qualified beneficiaries existed), the proceeds passed to the insured's estate; if not, the proceeds passed to the beneficiary's estate.

In 1940, the National Conference of Commissioners on Uniform State Laws proposed a Uniform Simultaneous Death Act ("1940 model act.") This model statute, as amended in 1953, provided that when there was no sufficient evidence that two people died otherwise than simultaneously, each individual's property is distributed as if he or she survived the other. The advantages of this approach are that when, for example, a husband and wife perish in the same event, each spouse's property passes to that spouse's relatives rather than to the other's relatives, and double administrative costs are avoided when property does not pass from one estate to another estate. When insurance policies are involved, the 1940 model act provided that in the absence of sufficient evidence showing that the insured and beneficiary died other than simultaneously, the proceeds are distributed as if the insured survived the beneficiary.[72] In community property states, the 1940 model act recommended that if the policy is community property of the insured and his or her spouse, and no alternative beneficiary exists except the estate of the insured, one half of the proceeds are distributed as if the husband survived the wife and the other half are

---

[68] See Womack v. Womack, 172 S.W.2d 307 (Tex. 1943).

[69] See New York Life Ins. Co. v. Cawthorne, 121 Cal. Rptr. 808 (Cal. Ct. App. 1975).

[70] See, e.g., Wash. Rev. Code § 48.18.370; 1 Ariz. Rev. Stat. Ann. § 20-1128.

[71] For further discussion, see McClanahan, note 63, *supra*, at 362–65; Robert L. Mennell, *Community Property in a Nutshell* 185–92 (1982).

[72] 8B *Uniform Laws Annotated* 267, 289-90 (1993).

distributed as if the wife survived the husband. By 1991, all but a handful of states had adopted a statute based on the 1940 model act.[73]

The 1940 model act, as adopted in most of the states, operates only when there is no evidence sufficient to establish that one party survived the other. This leaves open the possibility that heirs or beneficiaries might in some cases attempt to prove, often with gruesome medical evidence, that one person survived the other by an instant. To expand the scope of the model act, in 1991 the Commissioners on Uniform State Laws promulgated a new Uniform Simultaneous Death Act. This act underwent technical amendments in 1993; as revised this new act ("1993 model act") provides that "an individual who is not established by clear and convincing evidence to have survived the event by 120 hours is deemed to have predeceased the event."[74] The logic of this change is that even if medical evidence shows indisputably that one of two deceased persons survived the other in a common disaster, the policy of the model act should nevertheless apply. The 120-hour provision eliminated the need for a specific provision on insurance, and the 1993 model act contains none. Thus, if an insured and beneficiary both die within 120 hours of a common disaster, the beneficiary will be treated as predeceasing the disaster, which means the proceeds of insurance will go to contingent beneficiaries or the insured's estate. As of 1994, seven states had adopted the 1993 model act, and the 1940 model act remained in force in other jurisdictions.[75] The 1993 model act will almost certainly replace the 1940 model act in most jurisdictions.

With respect to insurance, the 1940 model act creates a conclusive presumption that the insured survived the beneficiary in circumstances when sufficient evidence is unavailable to show otherwise. The 1993 model act leaves this presumption unchanged, except that the presumption will also apply in circumstances where sufficient evidence is available to establish that the beneficiary survived the insured but died within 120 hours of the event.

In most cases, the result contemplated by both the 1940 and 1993 model acts most closely approximates the probable intent of the insured. If this presumption does not represent the probable intent of the insured, the insured is free to provide otherwise in the insurance policy. For additional certainty in jurisdictions that still follow the 1940 model act's approach or to change the 120-hour provision of the 1993 model act,[76] it is possible to insert in a policy a provision to the following effect: if the beneficiary dies within x days or hours of the insured, it is conclusively presumed that the beneficiary predeceased the insured. Under such a provision, if the beneficiary survives for a period of time after an accident less than the designated period in the policy, the beneficiary is treated as having predeceased the insured.

Another significant provision in the 1993 model act provides that insurers and other payors who make a payment to a person named in a governing instrument (such as a designated beneficiary) are not liable if the payment is made in reliance on a

---

[73] *Id.* at 267-68 (1993).

[74] 8B U.L.A. 20, 21 (1995 supp.).

[75] *Id.* at 17.

[76] Section 6 of the 1993 model act provides that a clause in a governing instrument dealing with common disasters preempts the 120-hour requirement. *Id.* at 23.

survivor's apparent entitlement to succeed to property and before the payor receives written notice of a claimed lack of entitlement under the act.[77] Although it is unlikely that many insurers would receive a claim and be able to pay it within five days after a death occurs, and while the insurer is likely in most common disaster situations to have some reason to know whether the 120-hour provision is pertinent to the claimant, this provision provides a safe harbor for an insurer which does act promptly to pay proceeds in reasonable reliance on a beneficiary designation.

[h] Payment to Wrong Beneficiary

Occasionally, an insurer makes a payment to the wrong beneficiary. The general rule is that the obligation of a debtor who pays the wrong person is not discharged, and this means that an insurer's obligation to pay the proper beneficiary is not discharged by paying the wrong person.[78] This is why an insurer that is reasonably doubtful about who is the proper recipient of proceeds should file an interpleader to resolve the ambiguity.

When payment is made to the wrong person due to a good faith mistake of fact or law, courts typically hold that the insurer is entitled to restitution from the person who incorrectly received the proceeds.[79] Disallowing restitution would give the person who received the money a windfall that should not in good conscience be retained and would impose a forfeiture on the insurer, which otherwise must pay the proceeds twice. The insurer's request for restitution may be disallowed, however, if the person who received the money has spent the money or otherwise depleted the proceeds. In other words, reasonable reliance on the receipt of the proceeds has the effect of estopping the insurer from requesting restitution. Also, under principles of equity, the insurer may be required to incur the forfeiture if it should reasonably have conducted additional investigation to determine who was entitled to the proceeds.

§ 52B Assignees

[a] Overview: The Nature of an Assignment

Under general contract law, one who possesses a contract right is entitled to assign that right to another party. All that is necessary to assign the right is the manifestation of intent to make a present transfer of the right without further action by either the assignor or a person obligated to perform on the assignor's behalf. Thus, one may have a right to receive insurance proceeds from an insurer; one can transfer this right to anyone without the designation of a new insured and without transferring insured property. It is not necessary that the assignee have an insurable interest in the insured property or the insured life. A "loss payable clause" can be viewed as one kind of

---

[77] *Id.* at 25-26.

[78] See, e.g., Santiny v. Pitre, 591 So. 2d 1245 (La.App. 1991).

[79] See, e.g., Glover v. Metropolitan Life Ins. Co., 664 F.2d 1101 (8th Cir. 1981) (insurer misinterprets ambiguous property settlement agreement incidental to a divorce); American Western Life Ins. Co. v. Hooker, 622 P.2d 775 (Utah 1980); Aetna Life Ins. Co. v. Nix, 512 P.2d 1251 (N.M. 1973).

assignment: the insured in the text of the policy itself assigns the right to receive proceeds to a third party. It is not necessary, however, that the assignment be made in the text of the policy; an assignment can be made through a completely separate document.

[b]　Assignment of Right to Proceeds versus Assignment of Entire Policy

An assignment of the "right to receive proceeds" is often used when a debtor wishes to designate the creditor as the receiver of payments from the insurer in the event insured property is destroyed. In essence, an assignment of a right to receive proceeds is no different from the assignment of any right a person might have under a contract. If X is entitled to receive payments under a contract, X is entitled to assign to Y her right to receive those payments. Similarly, if X's right is to receive payments under an insurance contract, nothing prohibits X from assigning that right to Y.

The assignment of the right to receive proceeds is frequently used to provide protection for an unsecured creditor. A creditor lacking a lien or security interest in the debtor's property has no insurable interest in that property; thus, the creditor could not be named as an additional insured on the debtor's insurance policy for the property. However, identifying the creditor as the assignee of the proceeds has essentially the same effect as being designated as an insured.

An assignment of a "right to receive proceeds" is fundamentally different from the assignment of an insurance "policy." One court explained the difference in this way as it upheld the assignment of a right to proceeds in the face of the insurer's argument that the assignment was prohibited by the policy's no-assignment clause:

> The rationale for [upholding the assignment of the claim] is related to the purpose behind a no-assignment clause in a casualty or liability policy which is to protect the insurer from insuring a different risk than intended. Assignment of the right to collect or to enforce the right to proceed under a casualty or liability policy does not alter, in any meaningful way, the obligations the insurer accepted under the policy. The assignment only changes the identity of the entity enforcing the insurer's obligation to insure the same risk. Thus, the purpose behind the no-assignment clause is not inhibited by allowing claim, as opposed to policy, assignment.[1]

[c]　Assignment in Property and Liability Insurance

In property insurance, mere transfer of insured property does not automatically cause the insurance to be assigned. The explanation is relatively simple: the bundle of rights considered "property" do not include contracts which have as their subject the property itself. The one exception to this observation involves situations where the policy provides that the coverage runs "for the account of whom it may concern" or language to similar effect. This clause, which appears most often in marine insurance policies, means that any person who subsequently acquires an interest in the property is covered by the policy. This clause is enforced if it appears that the transferee of the property was one whom the insured intended to have the benefits

---

[1] Elat, Inç. v. Aetna Cas. & Sur. Co., 654 A.2d 503, 505-06 (N.J.Super. 1995).

of the coverage, either because of some specific manifestation by the insured or because at the time the insurance was issued the insurer and insured anticipated that a transferee would subsequently exist with an interest in the property.[2] Thus, assignment of a policy of property insurance usually requires that specific action be taken with respect to the policy itself.

In property insurance, one who seeks to assign a policy is attempting to transfer all of the assignor's interest in the policy to another person, who would then become the new insured. Suppose, for example, that X transfers insured property to Y; it is logical that X might desire to transfer the insurance coverage to Y as well. Through an assignment of the policy, X seeks to designate Y as the insured, in effect substituting Y for X. This is in lieu of designating Y as an additional insured.

To validly assign a property policy to another, two requirements must ordinarily be met. First, the assignee must have an insurable interest in the insured property. Otherwise, the purposes underlying the insurable interest doctrine could be completely frustrated. Second, the insurer must consent to the assignment. Property insurance policies typically contain a clause prohibiting assignment of the policy unless the insurer consents. This, too, is understandable. Insurers desire to make their own decisions about which risks they will underwrite. The risk of fire in a particular residence is a function not only of the home's characteristics but also of the person living in the residence. Thus, the insurer does not want any particular insured to have an unrestricted right to assign the policy to anyone he or she chooses, even if the purported assignee has an insurable interest in the property. As stated by one court with respect to a fire insurance policy, property insurance "is a *personal* contract of indemnity, and is on the insured's *interest* in the property, *not on the property itself.*"[3] With regard to the insurer, an assignment without the insurer's consent is void.[4] However, the assignment may be valid as between the assignor and assignee, meaning that the assignee becomes entitled to the proceeds.[5] If the insurer does consent to the assignment, a novation occurs, which terminates the contractual relationship between insurer and assignor and puts in its place the contractual relationship between insurer and assignee. Also, it is possible for an insurer to waive a no-assignment-without-consent clause through a prolonged course of conduct with the insured's assignee.[6]

The analysis is identical with respect to liability policies, which cover a particular person's or entity's exposure and thus are not transferable without an insurer's consent. Thus, if the owner of a car sells it to someone else, the owner's liability

---

[2] See 5A APPLEMAN § 3336 (1970).

[3] Christ Gospel Temple v. Liberty Mut. Ins. Co., 417 A.2d 660, 662–3 (Pa. Super. Ct. 1979), *cert. denied,* 449 U.S. 995 (1980) (emphasis in original).

[4] See, e.g., Porat v. Hanover Ins. Co., 583 F. Supp. 35 (E.D. Pa. 1983); Parrish Chiropractic Centers, P.C. v. Progressive Cas. Ins. Co., 874 P.2d 1049 (Colo. 1994); Carle Place Plaza Corp. v. Excelsior Ins. Co., 534 N.Y.S.2d 397 (N.Y. App. 1988); Smith v. R.B. Jones of St. Louis, Inc., 672 S.W.2d 185 (Mo. Ct. App. 1984).

[5] See Crossley v. Allstate Ins. Co., 362 N.W.2d 760 (Mich. Ct. App. 1984).

[6] See Canal Ins. Co. v. Savannah Bank & Trust Co., 352 S.E.2d 835 (Ga. Ct. App. 1987).

insurance purchased in connection with that vehicle is not assignable to the car's buyer.[7]

[d] Assignment in Life Insurance

In life insurance, assignment of the policy does not involve designating a new insured or a new beneficiary. Rather, an assignment of a life insurance policy is ordinarily viewed as a transfer of the ownership rights to the policy, such as the right to borrow against the cash value, the right to surrender the policy for cash, the right to designate a different beneficiary, and the right to select the settlement option. As discussed earlier, courts are divided on the effect of assignment on the beneficiary's rights, including the question of whether the assignment is tantamount to a change of beneficiary. Most courts treat the assignee's rights as superior to those of the beneficiary, assuming the policyowner complies with the policy's requirements for making a valid assignment, but there is no uniformity in the case law on these matters.[8]

Assignments of life insurance policies commonly occur when the owners of policies offer them as security for a debt. As with property insurance, it is important to distinguish assignment of the right to receive proceeds from the assignment of the policy itself. The beneficiary, unless also the owner, cannot assign the policy as such. However, the beneficiary might assign his or her right to receive proceeds; this commonly occurs after the insured's death, when the beneficiary assigns the right to receive proceeds to the funeral home as security for payment of the funeral and burial expenses.[9]

Most courts allow a person who has taken out insurance on one's own life to assign the policy to anyone, even a party lacking an insurable interest. This result, which differs from the rule in property insurance, is defended on the ground that if the insured can designate any beneficiary he or she desires, no reason exists to preclude the insured from designating any assignee he or she chooses. Under the same logic, if someone has a policy on someone else's life, that person should be allowed to assign the policy only to another person possessing an insurable interest. This is because one cannot take out a policy on someone else's life without an insurable interest in that life; allowing assignment of the policy to one lacking such an interest would frustrate the purposes of the insurable interest doctrine.[10]

The ability of the owner of a life insurance policy to assign it is important for the purpose of securing debts. When it is clear that this is the assignment's purpose, proceeds are ordinarily paid to the assignee only to the extent of the amount of the debt.

The procedures for assignment of life insurance policies are relatively straightforward. The policies themselves typically prescribe certain formalities for making a valid assignment. Compliance with them is tantamount to obtaining the insurer's

---

[7] See Touchet v. Guidry, 550 So. 2d 308 (La. Ct. App. 1989).

[8] See § 52A[d], *supra.*

[9] See Powell v. Reliable Life Ins. Co., 662 S.W.2d 294 (Mo. Ct. App. 1983).

[10] See § 47[a], *supra.*

consent to the assignment. Substantial compliance with these formalities is ordinarily all that is required to effect an assignment.[11]

§ 53   Special Problems in Property Insurance

In property insurance, difficulties sometimes arise because the total interest associated with a piece or article of property is frequently not in one bundle possessed by one person. "Partial interests in property" raise special problems, which are discussed in the sections that follow.

§ 53A   Mortgages and Conditional Sales

Whenever a purchaser of property borrows money from the bank or savings and loan to help finance the purchase, the purchaser, in exchange for receiving a loan of money from the financial institution, gives a mortgage to the institution. The debtor (the purchaser of the property) is the "mortgagor" and the creditor (the lender) is the "mortgagee." The mortgage provides that if the debtor fails to pay back the loan, the mortgagee is entitled to foreclose against the property to secure the loan's payment. As a secured party, the mortgagee has a definite interest in the preservation of the property; this interest supplies the mortgagee with an insurable interest in the property under both the legal interest and factual expectancy theories.[1]

Sales of homes and commercial real estate commonly result in the creation of a mortgage, but many other kinds of sale transactions involving land and goods result in the creation of mortgages and other similar security interests. The discussion which follows uses real estate transactions for most examples, but it should not be assumed that real estate is the only setting in which the principles discussed in this section are relevant.

[a]   The Standard Mortgage Clause

There are several ways to insure a mortgagee's interest in property. One way is to designate the mortgagee as a named insured on the policy; another is for the mortgagee to purchase a separate policy on its interest. The typical method, however, involves the insurer providing in the policy issued to the mortgagor that the proceeds will be paid to the mortgagee to the extent of the mortgagee's interest in the property. This is usually accomplished through the inclusion in the policy of a "does insure" clause, a loss payable clause, and what is called a "standard" or "union" mortgage clause.

In most insurance policies on mortgaged real estate, the mortgagor's name will appear in the "does insure" clause; this makes the mortgagor the named insured. The mortgagee's name will then appear in a provision stating that subject to the provisions of the mortgage clause, loss shall be payable to the "mortgagee." One

---

[11] This result should follow by analogy to the rules that require substantial compliance with the formalities for changing the beneficiary. See § 52A[c], *supra*.

[1] See § 42, *supra*.

might wonder why the "does insure clause" and the loss payable provision are not enough to protect the mortgagee's interest. After all, if the mortgagor purchases the insurance and assigns the right to the proceeds to the mortgagee, in the event of a loss the mortgagee's interest would appear to be protected. This is true, however, only as long as the insurer lacks defenses against the mortgagor. Under legal principles applicable to assignments generally, any defense good against the assignor (mortgagor) is also good against the assignee (mortgagee). Thus, if the mortgagor is disqualified from coverage through some act or neglect, the mortgagee under a simple assignment of proceeds is not protected.[2] This, ultimately, is the reason for the standard mortgage clause.

The third element of the typical insurance arrangement in the mortgagor-mortgagee situation is the standard mortgage clause. (The person who loans funds to another to purchase any kind of property, whether it be real estate, an automobile, or furniture, is likely to take a security interest in the property. Nothing prevents a standard mortgage clause from being inserted in a policy of automobile insurance, but most current automobile policies simply have a place for designating the loss payee and do not contain language like that commonly found in insurance policies on real estate.)[3]

The mortgage clause has three principal elements. First, the clause provides that loss shall be payable to the mortgagee "as interest may appear." This means that the mortgagee receives the proceeds of the insurance to the extent of its interest in the property. Second, the clause provides that the insurance on the mortgagee's interest "shall not be invalidated by any act or neglect of the mortgagor." Under this provision, if the mortgagor violates a warranty or condition of the policy, the mortgagor may lose coverage, but the mortgagor's act or neglect will not prevent the mortgagee from receiving proceeds to protect its interest.[4] Third, the clause states that whenever the insurer pays the mortgagee and establishes that no liability exists to the mortgagor because of the mortgagor's act or neglect, the insurer shall be subrogated to the mortgagee's rights against the mortgagor on the mortgage debt, subject to the mortgagee's right to be reimbursed in full for the amount of its claim against the mortgagor.[5]

---

[2] See Vargas v. Nautilus Ins. Co., 811 P.2d 868 (Kan. 1991).

[3] See generally James R. Dwyer & Carey S. Barney, *Analysis of Standard Mortgage Clause and Selected Provisions of the New York Standard Fire Policy,* 19 Forum 639 (1984); Ronald A. Lev, *Mortgagees and Insurers: The Legal Nuts and Bolts of Their Relationship,* 12 Forum 1012, 1013 (1977); *Policy Kit* at 1-12 (ISO Form PP 00 01 12 89).

[4] See, e.g., Foremost Ins. Co. v. Allstate Ins. Co., 486 N.W.2d 600 (Mich. 1992); Meade v. North Country Co-Operative Ins. Co., 487 N.Y.S.2d 983 (N.Y. Sup. Ct. 1985), *aff'd,* 501 N.Y.S.2d 94 (N.Y. App. Div. 1986).

[5] A typical clause reads as follows: "If a mortgagee is named in this policy, any loss payable under [coverages for dwelling and other structures] will be paid to the mortgagee and you, as interests appear. If more than one mortgagee is named, the order of payment will be the same as the order of precedence of the mortgages. . . . If we deny your claim, that denial will not apply to a valid claim of the mortgagee, if the mortgagee: a. Notifies us of any change in ownership, occupancy or substantial change in risk of which the mortgagee is aware; b. Pays any premium due under this policy on demand if you have neglected to

Under the standard mortgage clause, the mortgagor is the policy's named insured. However, the clause's effect is to convert the mortgagor into one who is not an "insured" if he or she violates the policy's terms by committing an act or neglecting to do something.[6] As discussed in a later section,[7] the general rule is that the insurer cannot have subrogation against its own insured. If the mortgagor through action or neglect becomes one who is not the insured, the insurer is entitled to subrogation against the mortgagor. Thus, the effect of the standard mortgage clause is to subrogate the insurer to the mortgagee's rights against the mortgagor if the mortgagor invalidates the mortgagor's own coverage.

Thus, the mortgagor is the named insured, but the mortgagee effectively has the status of an insured under the standard mortgage clause. The clause creates, in effect, a direct, independent contractual relationship between the insurer and the mortgagee.[8] This means that if the insurer is under an obligation to both the mortgagor and the mortgagee, the insurer is not entitled to subrogation,[9] even against the mortgagee.[10] It also means that the mortgagee, as a separate insured, has no obligation to prevent the mortgagor from rendering the mortgagor's coverage void through the mortgagor's own act or neglect (although the mortgagee is obligated to inform the insurer of any increase of hazard or risk of which the mortgagee is aware).[11] Similarly, because the mortgagee has the status of a separate insured, the mortgagor's failure to pay the premium does not necessarily void the mortgagee's coverage; only if the

pay the premium; and c. Submits a signed, sworn statement of loss within 60 days after receiving notice from us of your failure to do so. Policy conditions relating to Appraisal, Suit Against Us, and Loss Payment apply to the mortgagee. . . . If we decide to cancel or not to renew this policy, the mortgagee will be notified at least 10 days before the date cancellation or nonrenewal takes effect. . . . If we pay the mortgagee for any loss and deny payment to you: a. We are subrogated to all the rights of the mortgagee granted under the mortgage on the property; or b. At our option, we may pay to the mortgagee the whole principal on the mortgage plus any accrued interest. In this event, we will receive a full assignment and transfer of the mortgage and all securities held as collateral to the mortgage debt. . . . Subrogation will not impair the right of the mortgagee to recover the full amount of the mortgagee's claim." *Policy Kit* at 28 (ISO Form HO 00 03 04 91).

[6] See, e.g., McAlpine v. State Mut. Fire Ins. Co., 295 N.W. 224 (Mich. 1940); Dalangauskas v. State Farm Fire & Cas. Co., [1983-84] Fire & Cas. Cases (CCH), at 1022 (Tenn. Ct. App. 1983); Quincy Mut. Fire Ins. Co. v. Jones, 486 S.W.2d 126 (Tex. Ct. App. 1972).

[7] See § 96[f], *infra*.

[8] See, e.g., Burritt Mut. Sav. Bank of New Britain v. Transamerica Ins. Co., 428 A.2d 333 (Conn. 1980); 495 Corp. v. New Jersey Ins. Underwriting Ass'n, 430 A.2d 203 (N.J. 1981); Northwestern Nat'l Cas. Co. v. Khosa, Inc., 520 N.W.2d 771 (Minn. Ct. App. 1994); Heritage Fed. Sav. Bank v. Cincinnati Ins. Co., 448 N.W.2d 39 (Mich. Ct. App. 1989).

[9] See, e.g., United Stores of Am., Inc. v. Fireman's Fund Ins. Co., 420 F.2d 337 (8th Cir. 1970). But see Dalrymple v. Royal-Globe Ins. Co., 659 S.W.2d 938 (Ark. 1983) (holding that loss payee was not an "insured" in every sense; loss payee did not have immunity to named insured; insurer can assert named insured's right, as subrogee, against loss payee).

[10] See Miller v. Russell, 674 S.W.2d 290 (Tenn. Ct. App. 1983); but see Dalrymple v. Royal-Globe Ins. Co., 659 S.W.2d 938 (Ark. 1983).

[11] See, e.g., Nassar v. Utah Mortgage & Loan Corp., 671 P.2d 667 (N.M.Ct.App. 1983).

mortgagee fails to make the mortgagor's premium payment upon demand is the policy voided with respect to the mortgagee.[12]

The foregoing reveals yet another purpose of the standard mortgage clause. Imagine that the only two elements of a relationship between insurer, mortgagor, and mortgagee are a "does insure" clause and a loss payable clause. If the mortgagor suffers a loss due to some act or neglect by the mortgagee, the insurer after paying proceeds on behalf of its insured would be subrogated to the insured's rights against third parties that caused the loss — in this instance, the mortgagee. The mortgagee who is merely an assignee does not benefit from the rule that an insurer has no subrogation against its own insured. One purpose, then, of the standard mortgage clause is to protect the mortgagee from a subrogation action brought by the insurer.

To illustrate the operation and effects of the standard mortgage clause, suppose Morrow (MOR) borrows $60,000 from the Mee Bank (MEE) to purchase a house; MOR contributed $20,000 of MOR's own funds. To secure the loan, MOR gave MEE a mortgage; MOR is the mortgagor, and MEE is the mortgagee. MOR purchases a policy of homeowner's insurance from Insurer (IR), which contains a standard mortgage clause, names MEE as the loss payee, and which contains MOR's warranty that MOR will not commit an act which increases the risk of the house's destruction. Before MOR makes any payments to MEE, MOR sets up a fireworks shop in the basement; thereafter, a fireworks explosion destroys the entire house. IR correctly refuses to pay MOR anything for the loss on the ground that MOR has breached a warranty. However, IR is obligated to reimburse MEE for its loss, which is $60,000, despite the invalidity of the coverage as to MOR. Furthermore, IR is subrogated to MEE's rights against MOR, which is the contract right to be repaid $60,000, and IR will recover $60,000 from MOR. When all rights are asserted and enforced, MOR will have, in effect, purchased the house for $80,000, even though it has been destroyed by the explosion. It is as if MOR had paid $80,000 cash for the house instead of borrowing money from the bank, had purchased insurance on MOR's house, and then had disqualified himself or herself from coverage due to MOR's breach of warranty.[13]

Since the mortgagee is essentially an additional insured, the mortgagee has some duties which must be fulfilled as a prerequisite to coverage. Once a loss occurs, the mortgagee must file a proof of loss if the mortgagor does not do so. The mortgagee must cooperate with the insurer during the investigation of the claim. The mortgagee is subject to the ordinary limitations for filing a suit against the insurer on the policy.

---

[12] See, e.g., American Nat'l Bank and Trust Co. v. Young, 329 N.W.2d 805 (Minn. 1983); Progressive Am. Ins. Co. v. Florida Bank at Daytona, 452 So. 2d 42 (Fla. Dist. Ct. App. 1984); Fort Hill Fed. Sav. & Loan Ass'n v. South Carolina Farm Bur. Ins. Co., 316 S.E.2d 684 (S.C. Ct. App. 1984).

[13] See, e.g., Wholesale Sports Warehouse Co. v. Pekin Ins. Co., 587 F. Supp. 916 (S.D. Iowa 1984); White v. Stratton, [1983–84] Fire & Cas. Cases (CCH), at 1478 (Tenn. Ct. App. 1984). Mortgagors have argued in such situations that the payment to the mortgagee discharges the mortgagor's debt, thereby frustrating any effort at subrogation, but this argument has been rejected in the cases considering it. See Wholesale Sports Warehouse Co. v. Pekin Ins. Co., 587 F. Supp. 916 (S.D. Iowa 1984); Savings Bank of Ansonia v. Schancupp, 144 A. 36 (Conn. 1928).

Another significant obligation of the mortgagee is to notify the insurer of any increase of hazard or change of occupancy of which it has knowledge. It is not clear that the mortgagee must have actual knowledge of a changed circumstance in order to have a duty to notify the insurer; in some circumstances, apparently, it is sufficient that the mortgagee only have "constructive knowledge," meaning that the mortgagee should know of the changed circumstance.[14]

The standard mortgage clause was developed because the open mortgage clause provided inadequate protection for most mortgagees. The open mortgage clause is discussed in the next subsection.

[b]   The Open Mortgage Clause

The standard mortgage clause is typically the type of mortgage clause that appears in a policy of property insurance. Another kind of coverage is so-called "open mortgage" coverage. The standard mortgage clause covers the mortgagee as a separate insured; it is as if the mortgagee has its own policy of coverage. In the "open mortgage" arrangement, no standard clause exists; the mortgagee is simply identified as the loss payee, with no further rights. In the "open" arrangement, the mortgagee's coverage is barred by any act or neglect of the mortgagor which would void the policy as to the mortgagor. The mortgagee's rights are therefore derivative of the rights of the mortgagor; if the mortgagor has no rights under the policy, neither does the mortgagee.[15] Because most mortgagees are currently insured under standard mortgage clauses, the distinction between the standard mortgage clause and the open mortgage clause is of declining importance.[16]

The distinction between the two kinds of mortgage clauses is illustrated by *Whitney National Bank of New Orleans v. State Farm Fire and Casualty Co.,*[17] a 1981 Louisiana decision. A fire deliberately set by the mortgagor destroyed an auto parts store. Whitney was the mortgagee on movable property inside the store, which was also destroyed in the blaze. The mortgage clause began with the phrase "applicable to buildings only." The insurer argued that the arson of the mortgagor barred Whitney from recovering for its loss of its security interest in the *contents* of the store, as distinct from the structure itself. The court concluded that Whitney was not protected by a standard mortgage clause with regard to the contents, and thus Whitney's rights under the policy were extinguished by the mortgagor's arson: "Louisiana law is in accord with the law in almost all jurisdictions to the effect that where there are loss payees in a policy of insurance pursuant to an open mortgage clause, i.e. without inclusion of a standard or union mortgage clause, their right to

---

[14] Compare New York Underwriters Ins. Co. v. Central Union Bank, 65 F.2d 738 (4th Cir. 1933), *cert. denied,* 290 U.S. 679 (1933) with Weekly v. Missouri Property Ins. Placement Facility, 538 S.W.2d 375 (Mo. Ct. App. 1976).

[15] See, e.g., Business Dev. Corp. of Ga., Inc. v. Hartford Fire Ins. Co., 747 F.2d 628 (11th Cir. 1984); Northwestern Nat'l Cas. Co. v. Khosa, Inc., 520 N.W.2d 771 (Minn. Ct. App. 1994); DeMay v. Dependable Ins. Co., 638 So. 2d 96 (Fla. Dist. Ct. App. 1994); Pittsburgh Nat'l Bank v. Motorists Mut. Ins. Co., 621 N.E.2d 875 (Ohio Ct.App. 1993).

[16] See Lev, note 3, *supra,* at 1013.

[17] 518 F. Supp. 359 (E.D. La. 1981).

recover is contingent upon, and purely derivative of the right of the mortgagor to recover from the insurer."[18]

[c]   Special Problems in Applying the Standard Mortgage Clause

[1]   Mortgagee's Right to Satisfaction of Debt

Although the standard mortgage clause is relatively straightforward, there are a number of situations where the relative rights of mortgagees and mortgagors are not apparent. When property securing a debt owed by a mortgagor to a mortgagee is destroyed, the interests of both parties are damaged. The mortgagee, by virtue of the loss payable clause, is entitled to have its interests protected; thus, proceeds are payable to the mortgagee up to the amount of the mortgage debt (and, of course, subject to the limits of the policy).

The limitation on the mortgagee's recovery to the amount of the debt implies what is a fundamental premise of the relative rights of mortgagor and mortgagee: the mortgagee is entitled to one satisfaction of its interest.[19] This is because the mortgagee's interest is a debt, for which the insured property is security. If the debt is satisfied, the mortgagee no longer has an insurable interest; by the same token, if the debt is satisfied, it can be said with certainty that a mortgagee has not and cannot suffer a loss, because the mortgagee has been made whole. If after the mortgagee's debt has been satisfied the insured property is destroyed, the mortgagee has suffered no damage because its interest has already been fully satisfied by the payment of the debt, and it follows in that situation that the mortgagee (actually, former mortgagee once the formality of the release of the mortgage is recorded) cannot recover under the insurance policy. Indeed, giving the mortgagee such a right would be nothing more than a windfall.

The foregoing discussion also reveals another fundamental premise of the rights of mortgagor and mortgagee: the interests of parties with respect to property insurance are fixed at the time of loss. Consider first the mortgagor- insured's situation. This person owns property, and when the property is damaged the owner suffers a loss. The amount of the loss is fixed at the time of loss; normally, this calculation is the difference between the property's value in an undamaged state and the property's value after the covered occurrence, and the owner is entitled to recover this amount. What if the owner sells the damaged property to a third party after the loss? Naturally this extinguishes the owner's interest because a third-party takes title to the property. But the mortgagor-insured presumably could not sell the damaged property for as high a price as he or she could sell undamaged property (unless the mortgagor-insured also assigns the right to receive proceeds under the policy to the purchaser). To be made whole, the mortgagor-insured will need to receive insurance proceeds covering the damage plus the amount paid by the purchaser for the damaged property. But the insurance policy will do this, because the parties' interests are fixed at the time of loss, and even if the owner-mortgagor subsequent

---

[18] *Id.* at 362.

[19] See Hellman v. Capurro, 549 P.2d 750 (Nev. 1976).

to the loss conveys the property to someone else, the owner-mortgagor (absent an assignment of the right to proceeds) is entitled to proceeds.[20]

Similarly, the mortgagee's interests in property are also fixed at the time of loss, subject to some caveats to be discussed shortly. When the security for the mortgage loan is damaged, the mortgagee suffers injury; when the loss occurs, the mortgagee can make a claim under the owner-mortgagee policy and receive payment up to the amount of the mortgage debt and subject to the limits of the policy. But what if the mortgagee's interest is eliminated after loss and prior to reimbursement? Recall that the owner-mortgagor who sells the property after a loss, which eliminates the owner-mortgagor's interest in the property, still collects proceeds. The mortgagee's situation is handled differently: the mortgagee cannot collect the proceeds when the mortgagee's interest is eliminated after loss and prior to reimbursement. This is because the mortgagee's interest is different from an owner-mortgagor's interest. The mortgagee's interest is a debt, for which the property is security. If the mortgagee's interest is satisfied, as noted above, then we can say with certainty that there has been no loss, and there is nothing left to reimburse. This is tantamount to saying that the mortgagee is entitled to one reimbursement of its interest, which can come either from the mortgagor (i.e., from the debt itself) or from the insurer. This observation has implications for the situation where the mortgagee forecloses on insured property, which is discussed in one of the next subsections.[21]

When property subject to a mortgage is destroyed, an issue sometimes arises regarding the order in which proceeds should be applied. In other words, the issue is whether the mortgagee is entitled to have the balance of the mortgage debt paid out of the insurance proceeds, or alternatively whether the mortgagors have the right to use the insurance proceeds to rebuild or repair buildings that were damaged or destroyed. Property insurance policies themselves typically do not answer this question.

In many (and probably most) situations, the mortgagee will not object to the proceeds being used to rebuild the property. Consider, for example, a mortgagor whose home is valued at $150,000, with $40,000 of that sum being attributable to the lot on which the home sits. The amount of the mortgage debt is $65,000. The house is damaged by fire to the extent of $100,000; the mortgagor-homeowner desires to use all of the $100,000 in insurance proceeds to rebuild. The mortgagee probably will not oppose the mortgagor's plans. Rebuilding maintains the security; when the construction is finished, the mortgagee will still have ample security — a structure worth at least $110,000 plus $40,000 worth of land — for the outstanding

---

[20] See Alabama Farm Bur. Mut. Ins. Co. v. Meyers, 516 So. 2d 661 (Ala.Civ.App. 1987). Suppose the owner-mortgagor sells the damaged property to a third party for as much as he or she had paid for the property before the loss. Allowing the owner-mortgagor to collect the insurance proceeds in the event of a conveyance of the property after loss does not mean the owner-mortgagor receives a windfall; indeed, one would presume that if the damage to the property had not occurred the owner-mortgagor would have been able to sell the property to the third party for even more. In short, the damage to the property decreases the owner-mortgagor's assets, and the property insurance policy reimburses this loss.

[21] See § 53[c][3], infra.

loan balance of $65,000. Moreover, the mortgagee, if a bank or other lending institution, will probably have an interest in maintaining its customers' goodwill, and the mortgagee may for this reason alone conclude that it is in the mortgagee's self-interest to assist the mortgagor in rebuilding the property, particularly if the property is the mortgagor's home.

In other situations, however, the mortgagee will desire to use the proceeds to reduce the mortgagor's debt. In the preceding example, a different case might be presented if interest rates had risen since the date of the original loan; the mortgagee might wish to apply the proceeds to the outstanding debt and issue the mortgagor a new construction loan at a higher interest rate. If commercial property is involved, the mortgagee may be unenthusiastic about rebuilding. For example, suppose commercial rental property which cost its owner $150,000 is subject to a $50,000 mortgage; the land is valued at $15,000. A fire causes damage to the structure in the amount of $125,000. Prior to the fire, the mortgagee had $150,000 worth of security for a $50,000 loan. If after the fire the structure is replaced by the mortgagor with a $60,000 building intended for a different commercial use, the mortgagee now has only $75,000 worth of security for a $50,000 loan. Instead of participating in the reconstruction of a less elaborate building that may be less profitable, the mortgagee may prefer to have its share of the proceeds applied to discharging the mortgage.

In the absence of a statute specifying how the problem should be resolved[22] or a provision in the mortgage agreement specifying that the mortgagee can apply the proceeds to the mortgage debt,[23] courts have reached different results. The majority view is that the mortgagee has an absolute right to the proceeds, which are applied to the mortgage debt.[24] The leading case for this view is *Savarese v. Ohio Farmers' Insurance Co.,*[25] a 1932 New York case. A building insured for $7,500 was damaged by fire to the extent of $4,230. Plaintiffs held a mortgage on the property securing a loan with a balance due of $6,500. The owner rebuilt the structure,

---

[22] Sometimes state statutes deal with this problem. In New York, for example, a statute provides that if the mortgagor repairs or rebuilds damaged property within three years after its destruction, the mortgagee must pay over to the mortgagor a defined sum from the insurance proceeds received by the mortgagee, unless the mortgagee rejects the mortgagor's proof of the cost of repairs. *N.Y. Real Prop. Law* § 254(4).

[23] See First Fed. Sav. and Loan Ass'n of Gary v. Stone, 467 N.E.2d 1226 (Ind. Ct. App. 1984).

[24] See, e.g., Walter v. Marine Office of Am., 537 F.2d 89 (5th Cir. 1976); Necaise v. Oak Tree Sav. Bank, 645 So. 2d 1311 (Miss. 1994) (where debt exceeded amount of insurance proceeds, mortgagee was entitled to entire proceeds payable in connection with destruction of mobile home); General G.M.C. Sales, Inc. v. Passarella, 481 A.2d 307 (N.J. Super. Ct. App. Div. 1984), *aff'd,* 499 A.2d 1017 (N.J. 1985); English v. Fischer, 660 S.W.2d 521 (Tex. 1983); Montgomery v. First Nat'l Bank, 508 P.2d 428 (Or. 1973); Kintzel v. Wheatland Mut. Ins. Co., 203 N.W.2d 799 (Iowa 1973); Arkansas Teacher Retirement Sys. v. Coronado Properties, Ltd., 801 S.W.2d 50 (Ark.Ct.App. 1990); Rollins v. Bravos, 565 A.2d 382 (Md.Ct.App. 1989); First Fed. Sav. and Loan Ass'n v. Stone, 467 N.E.2d 1226 (Ind. Ct. App. 1985).

[25] 182 N.E. 665 (N.Y. App. Div. 1932).

assigning his interest in the proceeds to the contractors who made the repairs. The mortgagees sued for $4,230, the full amount of the loss. The court held that the standard mortgage clause gave independent insurance coverage to the mortgagee; at the time of the loss, the mortgagee's right to the insurance proceeds vested absolutely.

A minority of courts have followed a different path, instead giving mortgagors the right to use the proceeds of insurance to rebuild or replace the damaged property.[26] In most cases, it is the mortgagor, not the mortgagee, who pays for the insurance to cover both interests; in fairness, when the interests collide, the mortgagor's interest in rebuilding should prevail.[27] It is true that when the mortgagee applies the proceeds to reduce the debt, the mortgagor benefits, and the mortgagor and mortgagee remain in the same relative position they occupied prior to the loss. However, one incident of a loan is the right to pay it back over a long term; requiring proceeds to be committed to loan repayment is inconsistent with part of what the debtor bargained for.

Moreover, the majority approach may not leave the insured-mortgagor with sufficient financial resources to rebuild the property. In theory the insured should be able to obtain a construction loan, but changed economic conditions may foreclose this option, and the end result may be the insured's default on the remaining loan balance and loss of the property. This occurred in *Schoolcraft v. Ross*,[28] a 1978 California case, where the court embraced the minority approach. The plaintiffs, in purchasing a home from defendant Ross, executed a promissory note secured by a deed of trust naming Ross as beneficiary. Under the terms of the deed, Ross had the right to retain insurance proceeds in the event of the property's destruction. The insurance policy which plaintiffs purchased on the property gave them two options in the event of loss: to collect the cash value of the house ($8250), or alternatively, to rebuild and receive reimbursement from the insurer up to $14,100.

The house was destroyed by fire, and the insurer issued a check payable to the mortgagors and the mortgagee in the amount of the house's cash value. The mortgagee, claiming that she was old and sick and needed the money for medical expenses, refused to allow the proceeds to be used to rebuild the house. The mortgagors, unable to afford to pay on the note and rent an apartment simultaneously, eventually defaulted on the loan and the property was repossessed. The mortgagee bought the property at a private foreclosure sale for $600, and later resold the property for $6,000. The court held that the mortgagee breached her implied obligation of good faith and fair dealing and could not "unilaterally cut off the borrower's right to use the loaned funds" — meaning, presumably, that the creditor could not accelerate the loan's due date by applying insurance proceeds to the loan

---

[26] See, e.g., Cottman Co. v. Continental Trust Co., 182 A. 551 (Md. 1936); Madero v. Henness, 607 N.Y.S.2d 153 (N.Y. App. Div. 1994); Starkman v. Sigmond, 446 A.2d 1249 (N.J.Super.Ch. 1982).

[27] George E. Osbourne, Grant S. Nelson & Dale A. Whitman, *Real Estate Finance Law* § 4.15 at 159 (3d stud. ed. 1994).

[28] 146 Cal. Rptr. 57 (Cal. Ct. App. 1978).

— unless the security was impaired. The court said the security was not impaired, since the security would have been restored if the house had been rebuilt. Accordingly, the mortgagor was entitled to use the insurance proceeds to rebuild.

The minority approach is criticized on the ground that in some cases the mortgagee will be placed at risk by having its mortgage on an existing structure converted into a construction mortgage for a new building. Also, disputes might arise regarding the value of the security after the damage to it, the value of the repaired or replaced structure, the amount and frequency of progress payments, the kind of structure that will replace the damaged structure, and other matters. For most courts, these disadvantages are too high a price to pay for a rule allowing the mortgagor to insist that the proceeds be directed to rebuilding. Yet for other courts, the fairness that exists in protecting the mortgagor who has paid for the insurance in the first place and may not have the resources to rebuild is more important.

[2] Right of Mortgagee to Assign Interest in Policy to Successor Mortgagee

Because the mortgagor must obtain the consent of the insurer before assigning the mortgagor's interest in the policy, and because the standard mortgage clause in effect treats the mortgagee as an insured, a question sometimes arises regarding whether the mortgagee must obtain the consent of the insurer before assigning the mortgage and the mortgagee's interest in the insurance to someone else. It would seem that the mortgagee should be able to assign its interest in the policy without the insurer's consent.[29] The assignment by the lending institution of its right to receive payment from the mortgagor usually has no effect upon the risk of the property's destruction. It might be argued that a substituted mortgagee is more likely to be further removed from the property in question and thus less likely to discover and notify the insurer of uses of the property which increase the risk of loss. However, a strong public policy exists favoring the free assignability of rights to payment under debt instruments in order to facilitate commercial activity, and this policy outweighs whatever increased risk may develop by virtue of the substitution of a new, more remote mortgagee.

[3] Effect of Mortgagee's Foreclosure on Insured Property

When a mortgagor falls behind in repaying the debt, the mortgagee ordinarily acquires a right to foreclose on the insured property to satisfy the mortgage debt. Although foreclosure is ordinarily something the mortgagee does to protect its own interests, in recent years many mortgagees have suffered loss when they foreclosed on insured property after it was damaged and purchased the property themselves at the foreclosure sale.[30] The surprise has generally been caused by mortgagees'

---

[29] See, e.g., Central Union Bank v. New York Underwriters' Ins. Co., 52 F.2d 823 (4th Cir. 1931); Kintzel v. Wheatland Mut. Ins. Ass'n, 203 N.W.2d 799 (Iowa 1973); Sprouse v. North River Ins. Co., 344 S.E.2d 555 (N.C.App. 1986); see generally 5A APPLEMAN § 3452 (1970).

[30] In one case, the mortgagee claimed that the insurer owed a duty to explain to the mortgagee prior to the foreclosure the consequences upon the coverage of the mortgagee's foreseeable acts. In Altus Bank v. State Farm Fire & Cas. Co., 758 F. Supp. 567, 571-72 (C.D.Cal. 1991), aff'd, 979 F.2d 854 (9th Cir. 1992), the court held that the insurer, through

failure to recognize that the general rule that interests in property insurance are fixed at the time of loss is subject to the observation, discussed above, that the mortgagee is entitled to one satisfaction of its interest. Once the mortgagee is made whole, the mortgagee is not entitled to a claim against the insurance.

In the absence of a loss to the insured property, foreclosure functions essentially as follows: at a foreclosure sale, the property which secures the owner-mortgagor's debt is sold. If the proceeds of the sale are less than the amount of the debt, the mortgagee keeps all of the proceeds and can pursue the mortgagor for a deficiency judgment, i.e., the amount of the debt less the proceeds obtained. If the proceeds of the sale equal the amount of the debt, the mortgagee is made whole and the mortgagor's debt is discharged. If the proceeds exceed the amount of the debt, the mortgagee is made whole, the mortgagor's debt is discharged, and whatever is left over (after certain costs are paid) goes to the mortgagor.

Suppose now that prior to foreclosure the property is damaged in some amount less than the debt. At a foreclosure sale, one would expect, all else being equal, for the property to sell for some lesser amount due to the damage. The amount of insurance proceeds plus the proceeds from the foreclosure sale should equal the property's total value. Thus, if the mortgagee collects the insurance proceeds and the proceeds of the sale, the mortgagee will probably be made whole, and there may be some funds left over for the mortgagor.

It has been a common practice for some mortgagees to automatically bid at a foreclosure sale the amount of the debt, without regard to the actual value of the property. If the mortgagee is the high bidder, this discharges the mortgagor, and enables the mortgagee to take the loan off its books. Then the mortgagee focuses on reselling the property which it now, pursuant to the foreclosure, owns. But if the mortgagee without considering the circumstances bids in the amount of the debt on property that prior to the sale has been damaged, the mortgagee has, in effect, just declared by its bid that the mortgagee believes the property in its damaged condition to be equal in value to the amount of the debt. This discharges the mortgagor, eliminates the mortgagee's interest as a mortgagee, and for all apparent purposes makes the mortgagee whole. Because the mortgagee's interest has been satisfied and the mortgagee is entitled to only one satisfaction, the insurer need not reimburse the mortgagee for the previously incurred damage to the property.

This was the situation in the leading case on this subject, *Whitestone Savings & Loan Association v. Allstate Insurance Co.,*[31] a 1971 New York case. The insured property had a value of $18,000, was insured for $14,000, and was subject to a mortgage in favor of the savings and loan in the amount of $11,500. At the foreclosure sale, the mortgagee bid the full amount of the mortgage debt and obtained a deed to the property. If the proceeds from the sale had exceeded the outstanding debt, the excess would have belonged to the mortgagor, as the mortgagee was entitled only to recover the full amount of the mortgagor's

----

its attorneys, did not have a duty to explain to the mortgagee's attorneys that if the mortgagee bid in the full amount of the debt at a foreclosure sale the mortgagee's insurable interest would be eliminated and the mortgagee would be unable to recover under the insurance policy.

[31] 270 N.E.2d 694 (N.Y. 1971).

indebtedness. However, by purchasing the property at the sale for the full amount of the indebtedness, the mortgage debt was extinguished, the mortgagee had no insurable interest, and thus the mortgagee had no right to recover anything from the insurer. The dissent argued that the mortgagee should be allowed to show that the value of the property exceeded the amount of the mortgage debt, and thus the mortgagee should be allowed to show that it suffered a greater loss. The majority, however, rejected this analysis, reasoning that the mortgagee is only entitled to one satisfaction of the debt and that the mortgagee should not be allowed to recover more than this amount.

Most cases have followed the reasoning of *Whitestone Savings & Loan*.[32] Cases in which courts have held that the mortgagee's rights are fixed at the time of loss are not inconsistent if no foreclosure occurs or if the loss occurs after the foreclosure and the mortgagee's interest has changed, in effect, into an owner's interest. Where the loss occurs after foreclosure, the payment of proceeds serves to restore the property to its condition at the time of the foreclosure.[33] Also, one court has recognized an exception for the situation where the mortgagee who purchased property at the foreclosure sale was unaware, notwithstanding its exercise of due care and diligence, of a loss to the property prior to foreclosure.[34] The cases are not uniform, however. A small number of cases have held that the mortgagee who bids the full amount of the debt at a foreclosure for property worth less has suffered a pecuniary loss that the insurer must reimburse.[35]

To summarize, if the mortgagee forecloses on the property after the loss and the property is resold for an amount at least equivalent to the unpaid balance of the mortgage debt, the mortgage debt is extinguished, and the mortgagee simultaneously loses its insurable interest. This prevents the mortgagee from recovering under the insurance policy. The same result follows if the mortgagee takes a deed in lieu of foreclosure, for this also extinguishes the mortgage debt, and hence the mortgagee's insurable interest. If the property is resold for less than the mortgage debt, the

---

[32] See, e.g., Altus Bank v. State Farm Fire & Cas. Co., 758 F. Supp. 567 (C.D.Cal. 1991), *aff'd*, 979 F.2d 854 (9th Cir. 1992); In re Chrysler First Fin. Serv. Corp., 608 So. 2d 734 (Ala. 1992); Farmers & Merchants Savings Bank v. Farm Bureau Mut. Ins. Co., 405 N.W.2d 834 (Iowa 1987); Burritt Mut. Savings Bank of New Britain v. Transamerica Ins. Co., 428 A.2d 333 (Conn. 1980); Smith v. General Mort. Corp., 261 N.W.2d 710 (Mich. 1978); Margaretten & Co. v. Illinois Farmers Ins. Co., 526 N.W.2d 389 (Minn. Ct. App. 1995); Singletary v. Aetna Cas. & Sur. Co., 447 S.E.2d 869 (S.C. Ct. App. 1994); First Inv. Co. v. Allstate Ins. Co., 1994 WL 421429 (Tenn. Ct. App. 1994). See also Mann v. Glens Falls Ins. Co., 541 F.2d 819, 823 (9th Cir. 1976) ("destruction of the mortgage by the mortgagee defeats the mortgagee's right to recover from the insurance company"); Pantano v. Maryland Plaza Partnership, 507 N.W.2d 484 (Neb. 1993) (trust deed beneficiary is substantial equivalent of mortgagee).

[33] See City of Chicago v. Maynur, 329 N.E.2d 312 (Ill. App. Ct. 1975).

[34] In re Chrysler First Fin. Serv. Corp., 608 So. 2d 734 (Ala. 1992).

[35] See Georgia Farm Bur. Mut. Ins. Co. v. Brewer, 413 S.E.2d 770 (Ga. Ct. App. 1991). Also, at least one court has recognized a distinction between strict foreclosure and foreclosure by sale, with the mortgagee being allowed to establish a difference between the amount of the debt and the value of the property if strict foreclosure is involved. See Burritt Mut. Sav. Bank of New Britain v. Transamerica Ins. Co., 428 A.2d 333, 338-39 (Conn. 1980).

mortgagee would have a deficiency judgment for the balance owed, and the mortgagee should be able to file a claim against the insurer for this amount. The insurer, after paying, would be subrogated to the mortgagee's right to enforce the judgment. The moral of the story is that a mortgagee on insured property that is damaged before foreclosure should not automatically bid in the full amount of the debt at the foreclosure sale; stated otherwise, the mortgagee should never bid at such a sale more than the property is actually worth.

If the damage to the property occurs *after* foreclosure, the mortgagee is actually the owner of the property and is entitled to be reimbursed in full for the loss. Interestingly, courts allow recovery even though the "mortgagee" no longer enjoys the precise status of a mortgagee, having been transformed into the owner.[36] This result actually has its foundation in the language of the standard mortgage clause because the clause protects owner and mortgagee "as interests appears." This clause refers to the mortgagee's "interest" in the property itself, which is a debt initially, but the mortgagee's interest does not cease with the foreclosure sale or other method of acquiring title, even though the debt is satisfied thereby. In effect, when the mortgagee's interest is transformed into an owner's interest, the insurer's promise to protect that interest "as it appears" means that the insurer promises to protect that interest when its transforms into an owner's interest. Because the mortgagee-turned-into-owner has a full interest in the property, the mortgagee-turned-into-owner's recovery is not restricted to the amount of the mortgage debt, which was formerly the limit of the mortgagee's insurable interest.[37]

[4] Reimbursing a Partial Loss When the Mortgagor Is Disqualified from Coverage

As noted above, if the insured property is destroyed under circumstances where the mortgagor is disqualified from collecting the proceeds, the standard mortgage clause requires the insurer to pay the mortgagee for its loss, and the insurer is subrogated to the mortgagee's rights against the mortgagor. If the loss is partial, the insurer's payment of the loss will not discharge the mortgage debt. To the extent of the insurer's payment, the insurer will be assigned a portion of the mortgagee's right against the mortgagor, but the insurer's right will be subordinate to the mortgagee's right to have the debt paid in full. This means that the insurer must wait to be reimbursed until the mortgagee has been paid in full by the mortgagor. If the mortgagee commences foreclosure proceedings, the insurer will also need to participate in those proceedings to protect its secondary interest.

One commentator suggests that the insurer in the foregoing situation obtains more flexibility and is better able to protect its interests if it pays enough money to purchase the mortgagee's entire interest when a partial loss occurs, taking in return an assignment of the note evidencing the debt as well as the security interest. One disadvantage of this approach is that the insurer will need to pay more than the

---

[36] See City of Chicago v. Maynur, 329 N.E.2d 312 (Ill. App. Ct. 1975).

[37] See 495 Corp. v. New Jersey Ins. Underwriting Ass'n, 430 A.2d 203 (N.J. 1981); Murray Cty. State Bank v. Milwaukee Mut. Ins. Co., 513 N.W.2d 1 (Minn. Ct. App. 1994); Hoffpauir v. State Farm Fire & Cas. Ins. Co., 615 So. 2d 520 (La. Ct. App. 1993); Lev, note 3, *supra,* at 1016–17; Dwyer & Barney, note 3, *supra,* at 643.

amount of the loss to purchase the mortgagee's interest. However, this is counterbalanced by the elimination of the need to wait for the debtor to satisfy the mortgagee's interest before the insurer is reimbursed. Moreover, if the mortgagor should default, the insurer can proceed immediately to sell the property and reduce its loss.[38]

[5] The Unnamed Mortgagee

If the mortgagor promises to obtain insurance for the benefit of the mortgagee but fails to designate the mortgagee as the loss payee, the question of who is entitled to the proceeds is likely to be raised. The general rule is that the unnamed mortgagee has an equitable lien on the proceeds due the named insured.[39] Since the mortgagee's rights are only equitable, the mortgagee's entitlement to proceeds depends entirely on the rights of the mortgagor. Thus, if the insurer possesses a defense against the mortgagor, this defense is also good against the mortgagee. In other words, the mortgagee with only an equitable interest does not possess the legal interest that the separate contract of insurance under the standard mortgage clause would have provided.[40]

§ 53B   Vendor-Purchaser Transactions

Another situation where the interest of an insured in particular property may only be a "partial" one is the vendor-purchaser transaction. The archetypal fact pattern is the following: the vendor and purchaser enter into a contract of sale, which provides that the title shall be transferred at a later specified date, and the property is destroyed before the title is transferred.[1]

The starting point in analyzing the situation is to determine who bears the risk of loss of the property between the time of contracting and the time title is transferred.[2] The party owning the property obviously bears the risk until a particular time, at which time the buyer of the property assumes the risk; thus, the question is when the risk of loss shifts to the buyer. In many contracts, the parties will specify the time at which the risk of loss is assumed by the buyer, and the law will uphold this choice.[3] Indeed, carefully drafted contracts will almost always allocate the risk. However, when the parties fail to specify the time when this transfer occurs, courts

---

[38] See Tom Connally, *Mortgagor-mortgagee Problems and the Standard Mortgage Clause,* 13 Forum 786 (1978).

[39] See, e.g., McGory v. Allstate Ins. Co., 527 So. 2d 632 (Miss. 1988); Leon A. Minsky, Inc. v. Providence Fashions, Inc., 404 So. 2d 1275 (La. Ct. App. 1981).

[40] See Nor-Shire Associates, Inc. v. Commercial Union Ins. Co., 270 N.Y.S.2d 38 (N.Y. App. Div. 1966).

[1] See generally Roger A. Bixby, *The Vendor-Vendee Problem: How Do We Slice the Insurance Pie?,* 19 Forum 112 (1983).

[2] See generally Allen P. Fineberg, Comment, *Risk of Loss in Executory Contracts for the Sale of Real Property,* 14 Colum. J. L. & Soc. Probs. 453 (1979); Annot., *Risk of Loss By Casualty Pending Contract for Conveyance of Real Property — Modern Cases,* 85 A.L.R.4th 233 (1991).

[3] See, e.g., Holscher v. James, 860 P.2d 646 (Idaho 1993); Caulfield v. Improved Risk Mutuals, Inc., 488 N.E.2d 833 (N.Y. 1985).

may be forced to fill the gap in the contract with an implied term regarding the time of transfer.

There are four choices as to the time at which the risk of loss shifts to the buyer: the time of contracting; the time title is transferred; the time upon which the parties agree to transfer title, whether or not the title actually transfers; and the time the buyer takes possession of the property. Most states follow the rule that the risk of loss shifts to the purchaser at the time the contract of sale is formed,[4] but there is support for other rules. An important deviation from the majority rule is found in the twelve states, including California, New York, and Texas, that as of the end of 1994 had adopted the Uniform Vendor and Purchaser Risk Act.[5] This statute provides that when neither legal title nor possession has been transferred and the property is destroyed, the purchaser is entitled to recover any portion of the price paid; but if either legal title or possession has been transferred and the property is destroyed, the purchaser is not relieved of the duty to pay the price. Thus, under this statute, risk of loss transfers upon the passing of title or possession, whichever occurs first.

If in a given case the vendor bears the risk of loss or the purchaser bears the risk of loss, and the vendor or purchaser, as the case may be, has insurance for his or her own loss, the insurer reimburses that party for the loss and that is the end of the matter. Consider the following two illustrations:

> *Case 1.* Vendor contracts to sell house to purchaser, with closing to be at a date in the future. Assume that prior to closing, vendor bears risk of loss. House is destroyed prior to closing. Vendor purchased policy covering the house from Insurer.

> *Case 2.* Vendor contracts to sell house to purchaser, with closing to be at a date in the future. Assume that prior to closing, purchaser bears risk of loss. House is destroyed prior to closing. Purchaser bought policy covering the house from Insurer.

Although problems of valuing an interest can always exist,[6] these two cases are relatively straightforward. In *Case 1,* the Insurer pays vendor for vendor's loss. In *Case 2,* the Insurer pays purchaser for vendor's loss.[7]

---

[4] See, e.g., Bryant v. Willison Real Estate Co., 350 S.E.2d 748 (W.Va. 1986); Mutual Ben. Ins. Co. v. Goschenhoppen Mut. Ins. Co., 572 A.2d 1275 (Pa. Super. Ct. 1990); Unger v. Nunda Tp. Rural Fire Protection Dist., 482 N.E.2d 123 (Ill.App. 1985); In re Foreclosure of a Deed of Trust Given by Taylor, 298 S.E.2d 163 (N.C. Ct. App. 1982).

[5] Uniform Vendor and Purchaser Risk Act, 14 U.L.A. 469 (1990 & 1995 supp.).

[6] For an example of a struggle over the value of the purchaser's interest where the purchaser sought reimbursement from its own insurer for a loss after contracting but prior to closing, see Whitten v. Cincinnati Ins. Co., 544 N.E.2d 1169 (Ill. App. Ct. 1989) (held insureds' recovery would be based upon policy amount less amount which vendor recovered from its insurer). Normally, the value of the purchaser's interest should be the purchaser's cash investment in the property (e.g., down payment, any partial payments, improvements) prior to the event causing loss.

[7] See Brown v. Harris, 466 F. Supp. 210 (E.D. Mich. 1979).

More complex problems are presented when one of parties, who does not bear the risk of loss under the applicable rules, has insurance, and the party who bears the risk of loss does not. Consider the following case:

> *Case 3.* Vendor contracts to sell house to purchaser, with closing to be at a date in the future. Assume that prior to closing, purchaser bears risk of loss. House is destroyed prior to closing. Vendor has insurance with Insurer, which vendor carries forward throughout the interim period prior to closing. Purchaser has no insurance.

Case 3 is the kind of troublesome case that can arise in a jurisdiction following the majority rule on allocating the risk of loss. The purchaser frequently is unaware that he or she assumed the risk of loss at the time of contracting, so purchasers frequently fail to purchase insurance. The vendor, unaware that he or she no longer has the risk of loss, takes no steps to cancel the vendor's own insurance. If a real estate broker is involved, chances are that a form will be used that specifies who bears the risk of loss. But if the parties attempt to do the transaction themselves without legal advice of any kind or if the forms used in the transaction are poorly constructed, the scenario in *Case 3* is, unfortunately, distinctly possible.

One can imagine a variety of fair outcomes in *Case 3*. The vendor could rescind the contract and collect the insurance proceeds covering vendor's loss. With these proceeds, the vendor might rebuild the house and attempt to resell it, although nothing, of course, requires the vendor to do so. Another fair outcome is for the vendor to hold the purchaser to the contract, collect the proceeds of the insurance, and make a gift of the proceeds to the purchaser. The vendor is compensated for vendor's house, and the purchaser has proceeds with which the destroyed house can be rebuilt. One can also imagine an unfair outcome: the vendor might claim, as some vendors have done in such situations, that the vendor is entitled not only to the insurance proceeds but also to the payment of the purchase price by the purchaser. A question raised in such a situation is whether the vendor should be entitled to both remedies.

Closely related to *Case 3* is *Case 3A:*

> *Case 3A.* Vendor contracts to sell house to purchaser, with closing to be at a date in the future. Assume that prior to closing, purchaser bears risk of loss. House is destroyed prior to closing. Vendor has insurance with Insurer X. Purchaser has also purchased insurance on the house from Insurer Y.

In *Case 3A*, as in *Case 3*, vendor can enforce the contract against purchaser. Purchaser plainly has an insurable interest in the property, and purchaser's insurer is obligated to pay purchaser for the loss, as in *Case 2*. Yet vendor also has an insurable interest in the property since the vendor still holds title. Can vendor also collect on vendor's insurance policy, even though the vendor did not bear the risk of loss after the contract for sale of the property was formed?

In *Cases 3* and *3A*, the courts are widely split on how the situations should be resolved. One answer is that each insurer is liable for the loss to the respective insurable interests.[8] Under this approach, if vendor has insurance, vendor is

---

[8] See Whitley v. Irwin, 465 S.W.2d 906 (Ark. 1971); Aetna Cas. & Sur. Co. v. Cameron Clay Products, Inc., 151 S.E.2d 305 (W.Va. 1966); Brownell v. Board of Educ., 146 N.E.

protected; if purchaser has insurance, purchaser is protected. However, if purchaser bears the risk of loss and has no insurance, purchaser recovers nothing. At first glance, this seems fair: the approach "what is mine is mine and what is yours is yours" requires parties to be informed about their potential risks and to bear the consequences if they are not. The contract of insurance is a personal one, and the court will not look beyond the face of the contract to prevent a double recovery or to protect the equitable rights of nonparties to the insurance contract.

Upon further scrutiny, however, this answer is a poor one.[9] In *Case 3,* vendor, who has an insurable interest, collects vendor's insurance proceeds. Also, vendor is entitled to enforce the contract against purchaser. This results in a windfall to the vendor: vendor collects, in effect, twice for the house, and purchaser pays for a house that has been destroyed.[10] In *Case 3A,* purchaser does not lose, because purchaser is reimbursed by purchaser's own insurer. Yet vendor still recovers twice, because vendor collects vendor's own insurance plus the contract price from purchaser. The purchaser's payment of the contract price is, in effect, reimbursed by the insurer, but the vendor receives a windfall. Viewed in another way, the "total interest" of the vendor and purchaser can only add up to one house, since that is the only property that exists. Yet the sum of the proceeds received from the insurers by the vendor and purchaser will, under this answer, exceed the value of the property. This violates the principle of indemnity.[11] Indeed, if a vendor perceives the opportunity for such a windfall, the vendor may well ask a purchaser to enter into a sham transaction where both parties get insurance, the property is intentionally destroyed, and the parties share in the windfall generated through the payments of multiple insurers.

The problem with the foregoing answer leads some courts to provide a second one: each insurer is liable for the loss to the respective insurable interests (like the first answer), but each insurer is subrogated to the rights of its insured against the other party.[12] Thus, in *Case 3,* when the vendor's insurer pays proceeds to vendor, the vendor's insurer is subrogated to the vendor's rights against the purchaser, namely, the right to receive payment of the purchase price. This prevents vendor

---

630 (N.Y. 1925); Hendricks v. M.C.I., Inc., 448 N.W.2d 289 (Wis. Ct. App. 1989) (holding, apparently, where vendee owed $60,000 on land sale contract and building insured for $200,000 on land burned, first $60,000 of insurance paid vendee's remaining debt and remainder of proceeds belonged to vendor).

[9] See Risken v. Clayman, 398 N.W.2d 833 (Iowa 1987) (if mortgagor receives proceeds after foreclosure, vendee must receive proceeds after vendee is forfeited out, "or else forfeiture, which is not favored by the courts, will be more advantageous to the creditor than foreclosure.")

[10] The vendor received a windfall under the logic criticized here in Musselman v. Mountain West Farm Bur. Mut. Ins. Co., 824 P.2d 271 (Mont. 1992), but a major distinguishing factor was that the vendor's insurance was a valued policy, and the house was totally destroyed by fire. For discussion of how valued policies are inconsistent with the principle of indemnity, see § 93[c], *infra.*

[11] See Vogel v. Northern Assurance Co., 219 F.2d 409 (3d Cir. 1955) (loss stipulated at $12,000 but purchaser collects $15,000: $6000 from his own policy and $9000 under vendor's policy pursuant to an assignment of vendor's claim against vendor's insurer).

[12] See Twin City Fire Ins. Co. v. Walter B. Hannah, Inc., 444 S.W.2d 131 (Ky. 1969).

from obtaining a double recovery; the loss ultimately falls on the purchaser. Similarly in *Case 3A,* the vendor's insurer is subrogated to the vendor's rights against the purchaser; vendor will not obtain a double recovery, and purchaser — actually, in this case, the purchaser's insurer — will bear the loss. In fact, in *Case 3A,* both insurers are entitled to assert subrogation rights. Perhaps purchaser has a claim against vendor that the house was delivered in a defective condition, and this defect resulted in the loss. If purchaser's insurer pays purchaser for the loss, purchaser's insurer is subrogated to whatever claims purchaser has against vendor.

The second answer — each insurer indemnifies its insured's interests, which is followed by each insurer asserting subrogation rights — is disadvantageous in that subrogation entails transaction costs. Yet its advantages seem to outweigh these costs. First, the chances of a double recovery are eliminated. More importantly, the loss ultimately falls on the party who bears the risk of loss under the rules of the particular jurisdiction. To illustrate, consider the following case:

> *Case 4.* Vendor contracts to sell house to purchaser, with closing to be at a date in the future. Assume that prior to purchaser taking possession, vendor bears risk of loss. House is destroyed prior to purchaser taking possession. Vendor has insurance with Insurer X. Purchaser has insurance with Insurer Y.

Vendor is obligated to deliver a house in good condition to purchaser. The destruction of the house is vendor's loss, for which Insurer X must provide indemnification. If vendor uses the proceeds to rebuild the house and transfers this house to purchaser, purchaser suffers no loss and, of course, cannot recover from purchasers's insurer. There is no windfall, and the loss falls on vendor's insurer, the insurer of the party who bears the risk of loss.[13]

Consider another illustration:

> *Case 5.* Vendor contracts to sell house to purchaser, with closing to be at a date sometime in the future. Assume that prior to purchaser taking possession, vendor bears the risk of loss. Purchaser takes possession prior to closing. The house is destroyed after purchaser takes possession. Vendor has insurance with Insurer X, and purchaser has insurance with Insurer Y. Purchaser refuses to close (i.e., accept the title and pay the price) because the house is destroyed.

In *Case 5,* the first part of our analysis is that each insurer must pay each insured for the loss to the respective insurable interests. At this point, vendor has proceeds, and purchaser has proceeds. Yet at this point purchaser has a windfall, since purchaser did not purchase the premises (yet) and purchaser has the insurance proceeds. The subrogation portion of the rule says that Insurer X is subrogated to vendor's rights against purchaser. Thus, Insurer X will recover the purchase price from purchaser, which means vendor is whole (having been reimbursed by Insurer X) and vendor's insurer is whole (having paid proceeds to vendor but having been reimbursed for this through the recovery from purchaser). Purchaser is stuck with

---

[13] See Munshower v. Martin, 641 So. 2d 909 (Fla. Dist. Ct. App. 1994), *aff'd,* 1995 WL 553028 (Fla. Dist. Ct. App. 1995)(where vendor has assumed risk of loss, proceeds for damages suffered between contract and closing are property of vendor, but vendor must indemnify vendee for loss caused by casualty).

a burned-down house — for which purchaser has paid the purchase price but for which purchaser has received proceeds from its insurer. Purchaser is made whole, and purchaser's insurer is out-of-pocket the amount of the proceeds. However, this is as it should be: if purchaser had no insurance, purchaser would bear the loss. Purchaser had a risk of loss, and purchaser transferred this risk to an insurer for a price. Thus, purchaser's insurer bears the loss, since it was, after all, purchaser who had the risk of loss.

Yet a third approach exists to resolving how proceeds are distributed in the vendor-purchaser situation. This approach is usually referred to as the "constructive trust" approach; it is usually applied in situations like *Case 3,* where the purchaser bore the risk of loss, the purchaser lacked insurance, and the vendor carried forward its insurance throughout the interim period prior to closing. Under this approach, each insurer pays proceeds to its respective insureds, except that the vendor holds any excess proceeds in constructive trust for the purchaser. The vendor gets to keep the proceeds of the insurance that are necessary to make the vendor whole. If the purchaser has paid only a part of the purchase price, for example, the vendor is not made whole by virtue of the payments, and the vendor gets to keep proceeds to make up the amount the purchaser has not paid. Any excess proceeds over that amount are held in trust for the purchaser's benefit. The effect of this approach is to apply the vendor's insurance proceeds to the unpaid portion of the purchaser's debt.[14] Of course, if the vendor receives proceeds equal to the vendee's unpaid debt on a land sale contract, the land should then be conveyed to the vendee, as keeping the both proceeds and the land would be a windfall to the vendor.[15]

This approach prevents the vendor from profiting from the loss. The logic of the approach is that the vendor holds legal title, but the purchaser is the true beneficial owner of the property. The vendor should be allowed to recover the insurance proceeds, but the vendor holds them in trust for the owner of the equitable title, the purchaser. Since the proceeds are held for the purchaser's benefit, the purchaser should be required to reimburse the vendor for any costs incurred in maintaining the insurance during the time of the purchaser's possession of the property.

The constructive trust approach seems to work properly in a situation like *Case 3,* but what about a situation like *Case 3A,* where both the vendor and purchaser have insurance? This fact pattern was presented in *Paramount Fire Insurance Co. v. Aetna Casualty & Surety Co.,*[16] a 1962 Texas decision. Before the closing, the property was destroyed by fire, at a time when the purchaser bore the risk of loss. Buyers proceeded to close anyway; at the closing, sellers assigned their rights against sellers' insurer to buyers. The insurers settled with the buyers, reserving their rights to litigate against each other the question of who was really liable to the buyer.

---

[14] See, e.g., Acree v. Hanover Ins. Co., 561 F.2d 216 (10th Cir. 1977); Wilson v. Fireman's Ins. Co. of Newark, 269 N.W.2d 170 (Mich. 1978); Gilles v. Sprout, 196 N.W.2d 612 (Minn. 1972); Mutual Ben. Ins. Co. v. Goschenhoppen Mut. Ins. Co., 572 A.2d 1275 (Pa. Super. Ct. 1990); Alabama Farm Bur. Mut. Ins. Co. v. Meyers, 516 So. 2d 661 (Ala.Civ.App. 1987).

[15] See Hendricks v. M.C.I., Inc., 448 N.W.2d 289 (Wis. Ct. App. 1989).

[16] 353 S.W.2d 841 (Tex. 1962).

The court began by noting the general rule that the vendor holds the proceeds of its insurance policy in such a situation in trust for the purchaser. Such a rule, the court noted, is eminently equitable: "The rationale is that a purchaser pays the full contract price for property which has been damaged or destroyed by fire, it is only equitable to allow him the benefit of any insurance proceeds rather than to give the vendor both the insurance proceeds and the proceeds of sale."[17] The court, however, decided not to follow the general rule in situations, like the one in *Paramount,* where the purchaser had its own insurance. The court reasoned that the vendor suffered "no legal loss" if it had a right of specific performance against the purchaser and thereby could collect the full purchase price despite the fire damage. Although this logic would seem to foreclose the constructive trust theory in a situation where the purchaser lacked insurance, because the vendor would have a specific performance remedy and no "legal loss" in that situation as well, the court specifically declined to decide how proceeds would be allocated if the vendee lacked insurance.[18]

It would seem that the fairest answer and the one most consistent with the principle of indemnity would involve, as the dissent urged in *Paramount,* prorating the insurers' coverage obligations in proportion to the value of the insurable interests of the vendor and vendee at the time of the fire, with each insurer paying proceeds to its own insured.[19] Taking the time to make these calculations and coordinate the coverage of two insurance plans, when a per se rule of easy application and some rationality (i.e., let the insurer whose insured bears the risk cover the entire loss) is available, is wasteful. Thus, it seems reasonable to support the result in *Paramount* for situations where both vendor and vendee have coverage, while supporting a constructive trust approach for situations where the vendee bears the risk and lacks insurance.

§ 53C   Mortgages and Real Estate Sales: An Observation

When *X* sells real estate to *Y*, there are two principal ways that *Y* might finance the purchase. *Y* might go to the bank and get a loan, and use the proceeds of this loan plus *Y*'s cash on hand to pay *X* in full for the real estate. As security for the loan, the bank will obtain a mortgage on the property from *Y*, and thus will become the mortgagee. Alternatively, *X* might finance *Y*'s purchase of the house under a

---

[17] 353 S.W.2d at 845.

[18] This issue received attention in Texas in Indiana Lumbermens Mut. Ins. Co. v. Metro Material Mrktg., Inc., 646 S.W.2d 547 (Tex. Ct. App. 1982), where a mortgagee named as beneficiary of a builder's risk policy bought a building at a foreclosure sale and immediately agreed to resell it, and the building was destroyed before the closing and the contract with vendee was renegotiated to provide that vendee pay full the contract price and the mortgagee would pay vendee the insurance proceeds, the insurance proceeds were payable to mortgagee, who in turn, held proceeds in trust for vendee. This recognition of a constructive trust avoided the possibility of a double recovery for the mortgagee.

[19] See North Carolina Farm Bur. Mut. Ins. Co., 429 S.E.2d 759 (N.C. Ct. App. 1993) (trial court did not err in awarding vendor $46,000 in proceeds and vendee $4,000 in proceeds, where vendee had accumulated $4,000 in equity in house at time of fire); Mutual Ben. Ins. Co. v. Goschenhoppen Mut. Ins. Co., 572 A.2d 1275, 1278 (Pa. Super. Ct. 1990).

variety of mechanisms; in other words, *X* might assume the role of the financing seller.

As discussed earlier,[1] if the bank is the mortgagee, the bank will be treated, in effect, as a separate insured; this is true whether the mortgagor purchases insurance that also benefits the mortgagee or whether the mortgagee purchases a policy of mortgagee-only insurance. Most courts hold that the mortgagor is not entitled to the benefits of the mortgagee's insurance. Moreover, the mortgagee's insurer is entitled to assert, as a subrogee, any rights the mortgagee has against the mortgagor. However, if a financing seller, such as *X*, purchases insurance, courts often hold that the insurance is held by the vendor in trust for the benefit of the vendee; this means that the insurer is not entitled to be subrogated to the seller's suit against the buyer for the price of the real estate which has been damaged or destroyed.

As Professors White and Summers have observed, "[t]he financing seller on the one hand and the financing mortgagee on the other are often in identical economic positions; risk of the insurer may be identical in both cases. Why the courts distinguish the two cases is a mystery."[2] Part of the answer may be found in the fact that vendor-vendee law has been created usually in the context of a loss between the date of contracting and the date of closing; the vendor holds legal title, but the vendee holds equitable title during this period. Treating the vendor as a constructive trustee in this situation is consistent with how the law otherwise views the relationship of these parties. That courts would extend this analysis to any situation where the vendor retains some interest in the property, such as where the seller finances buyer's purchasers, is not particularly surprising. On the other hand, the mortgagee has no legal title and does not expect to acquire it. The mortgagee is a secured party only, holding no title for the mortgagor's benefit, and so the fact that courts treat mortgagors and mortgagees under owner-mortgagee insurance as having independent coverages is not terribly surprising either.

Another difference is that in jurisdictions where the vendee bears the risk of loss after contracting to purchase but prior to closing, the vendee unfamiliar with the law's allocation of risks is vulnerable to surprise should the property be destroyed prior to closing. The mortgagee, however, is not similarly vulnerable,[3] and in circumstances where mortgagees require the mortgagor to acquire insurance, the mortgagee is in a position to insist upon particular coverage (e.g., a standard mortgage clause) and confirm whether the mortgagor followed through. Accordingly, it is understandable that courts have extended more protection to vendees than to mortgagees.

---

[1] See § 53A, *supra*.

[2] James J. White & Robert S. Summers, 1 *Uniform Commercial Code* 256 (3d prac. ed. 1988).

[3] A mortgagee who is unaware of the implications of the rule that eliminates the insurable interest upon satisfaction of the debt is vulnerable in a different way. A vendee does not expect to suffer a loss during the period between contracting and closing, and the event creating the vendee's loss is an unexpected event. The mortgagee's act of foreclosing is deliberate, and it is reasonable to expect the mortgagee, more than the vendee, to become familiar with the consequences of planned acts.

Though the foregoing distinctions can be made between the financing seller and the mortgagee, the fact remains that the two cases have more in common than not. This observation underscores why the subject of partial interests in property is today a most perplexing area of insurance law.

§ 53D   Life Tenant-Remainderman

Problems sometimes arise when an owner of insured property dies and the owner's successors in interest are a life tenant and a remainderman. How should the proceeds be divided? Most courts conclude that the life tenant only has a life estate interest in the proceeds; the value of this interest can be calculated by reference to life expectancy tables and the probable return on the property if it were invested or otherwise put to productive use. Dividing the proceeds between life tenant and remainderman may result in giving the life tenant something of relatively slight value when compared to the value of the life estate property itself. For example, suppose the life estate is a house, which is destroyed by fire. Giving the life tenant a "life estate interest in the proceeds" is likely to be inadequate to replace the loss without supplementation from other funds. If the remainderman is unwilling to contribute the proceeds to reconstructing the house, the life tenant might suffer a net disadvantage.

The same problem is confronted when the following question is asked: whether a person holding a life estate can insure the property to the full extent of its value. As explained above, the value of the property may well exceed the value of the life estate: does the insured have an insurable interest in the property's full value? Most jurisdictions allow the holder of a life estate to insure the full value of the property. If the property is destroyed, most courts allow the life tenant who insures the property to keep all of the proceeds, without giving any portion of the proceeds to the remainderman.[1] If, however, the life tenant agrees to procure the insurance for the benefit of both the life tenant and the remainderman, or if the life tenant has some sort of fiduciary responsibility apart from the tenancy to procure insurance for the remainderman, the remainderman might have a right to a portion of the proceeds.[2] Similarly, if the life tenant intended to insure the interest of the remainderman, the remainderman may be found entitled to part of the proceeds. To further the principle of indemnity, it is fair to assume, at least in some cases, that the life tenant did in fact intend to benefit the remainderman. In this event, the proceeds would be paid in their entirety to the life tenant, with the life tenant holding the proceeds in excess of the value of the life estate in trust for the remainderman.

---

[1] See, e.g., Estate of Murrell v. Quin, 454 So. 2d 437 (Miss. 1984); Morris v. Morris, 544 P.2d 1034 (Or. 1976); Home Ins. Co. v. Adler, 309 A.2d 751 (Md. 1973); Lynch v. Johnson, 84 S.E.2d 419 (Va. 1954); Carlton v. Wilson, 665 S.W.2d 356 (Mo. Ct. App. 1984).

[2] See Barner v. Barner, 407 S.W.2d 747 (Ark. 1966). See also Converse v. Boston Safe Deposit & Trust Co., 53 N.E.2d 841 (Mass. 1944). Consistent with this principle, it has been held that where a life tenant had an obligation to repair damage to a house that occurred before the life tenant's death, the remaindermen, rather than the life tenant's estate, were entitled to insurance proceeds stemming from the hail damage. See Alabama Farm Bur. Mut. Ins. Co. v. Meyers, 516 So. 2d 661 (ALa. Ct. App. 1987).

§ 53E   Lessor-Lessee

The partial interest problem also surfaces in the situation where property, particularly residential property, is leased. The lessor or the lessee, or both, will probably have insurance on the property, and the question which often arises in such situations is who is entitled to claim the proceeds. As a general rule, in the absence of an agreement to the contrary, the proceeds of insurance obtained by either lessor or lessee cannot be claimed by the other. This is true even though the policy covers the value of the interests of both in the property.[1] Therefore, if a tenant insures his or her interest in a leasehold against fire damage, the tenant is entitled to collect the proceeds, not the landlord. Similarly, the tenant has no claim on the proceeds of the landlord's insurance.

If, however, either the lessor or the lessee agreed to purchase a policy of insurance for the benefit of the other party or both parties, the general rule stated above is usually not followed. Instead, the party for whose benefit the insurance was purchased ordinarily receives the proceeds.[2] This result has nothing in particular to do with the relationship between insurer and insured in this situation; rather, it is due to the contractual relationship between the lessor and lessee. For example, in one case involving the lease of a mobile home with an option to buy, an obligation placed on the lessee to purchase insurance was interpreted as an obligation to secure insurance for the benefit of both lessor and lessee, payable as their respective interests might appear.[3] Many courts have construed language in leases mentioning the possibility of the premises' destruction as placing the burden of insuring the premises on the lessor, assuming there is no clear language or extrinsic evidence showing an agreement to the contrary.[4]

In some situations, both lessor and lessee purchase insurance on leased property. If the property is destroyed and the lessee uses the proceeds of the insurance to repair the leased property, it is inconsistent with the indemnity principle to allow the lessor to recover for the damage from its insurer as well.[5] If the lessee repairs the property, the lessor obviously suffers no loss. To allow the lessor to recover constitutes a windfall, much like the result many courts seek to avoid in the vendor-vendee setting.

If only the lessee takes out insurance on the property, insurable interest rules may come into play. The lessee's insurable interest in property is the value of the right

---

[1] See, e.g., Transportation Equipment Rentals, Inc. v. Oregon Auto. Ins. Co., 478 P.2d 620 (Or. 1970). Cf. Russell v. Williams, 374 P.2d 827 (Cal. 1962).

[2] See, e.g., Resta Corp. v. Childers, 403 So. 2d 904 (Ala. 1981); Maryland Cas. Co. v. Delzer, 283 N.W.2d 244 (S.D. 1979); Wunschel v. Transcontinental Ins. Co., 839 P.2d 64 (Kan.Ct.App. 1992).

[3] See Graves v. Stanton, 621 S.W.2d 524 (Mo. Ct. App. 1981).

[4] See Safeco Ins. Co. v. Capri, 705 P.2d 659 (Nev. 1985); Parsons Mfg. Corp. v. Superior Court, 203 Cal. Rptr. 419 (Cal. Ct. App. 1984). See also Continental Cas. Co. v. Polk Bros., Inc., 457 N.E.2d 1271 (Ill. App. Ct. 1983).

[5] See Ransdell v. Insurance Co. of N. Am., 221 N.W. 654 (Wis. 1928). But see Citizens Ins. Co. v. Foxbilt, Inc., 226 F.2d 641 (8th Cir. 1955) (subject of annotation at 53 A.L.R.2d 1376 (1957)).

to use the property, not the value of the property itself. Thus, if leased property is destroyed, the recovery should be not the property's value, but the value of the right to use the property for the remainder of the leased term — presumably the amount of the lease for the remainder of the term.[6]

The insurer's right to subrogation often becomes an issue in the lessor-lessee situation. Of course, if a lessor insures property rented to lessee, and a third party with no contractual or legal relationship to the lessor destroys the property, the insurer's right to subrogation against that third party is not in doubt. If the lessee damages the property, the insurer, after paying proceeds to the lessor, may seek subrogation against the lessee. The question is whether the contractual relationship between lessor and lessee alters the typical application of the subrogation principles, and most courts hold that it does: if the lessor contracts in a lease to maintain insurance on the property, and the lease does not clearly state that the lessee is liable for loss caused by the lessee's negligence, the lessee is treated as an implied coinsured, thereby defeating the insurer's subrogation claim.[7] One court explained the rationale for this rule in the fire insurance context as follows:

> First, it would be an undue hardship to require a tenant to insure against the tenant's own negligence when the tenant is paying, through the rent, for the fire insurance which covers the premises in favor of the lessor. . . . Second, insurance companies expect to pay their insureds for negligently caused fire, and they adjust their rates accordingly. In this context, an insurer should not be allowed to treat a tenant, who is in privity with the insured landlord, as a negligent third party when it could not collect against its own insured had the insured negligently caused the fire. In effect, the tenant stands in the shoes of the insured landlord for the limited purpose of defeating a subrogation claim.[8]

Not all decided cases are in accord with the no-subrogation rule.[9] As one court explained, "on a case-by-case basis, the trier of fact must focus on the terms of the lease agreement itself to determine what the reasonable expectations of the parties were as to who should bear the risk of loss for fire damage to the leased premises," meaning that it is not presumed that the landlord obtains insurance for the joint benefit of landlord and tenant, rendering them co-insureds which in turn gives rise to the no-subrogation rule.[10]

---

[6] See, e.g., Eighty-Niner Inn, Ltd. v. American Employers Ins. Co., 412 F.2d 104 (10th Cir. 1969); Third Establishment, Inc. v. 1931 N. Park Apartments, 417 N.E.2d 167 (Ill. App. Ct. 1981).

[7] See, e.g., Community Credit Union of New Rockford, N.D. v. Homelvig, 487 N.W.2d 602 (N.D. 1992); Alaska Ins. Co. v. R.C.A. Alaska Communications, Inc., 623 P.2d 1216 (Alaska 1981); Agra-By-Products, Inc. v. Agway, Inc., 347 N.W.2d 142 (N.D. 1984); Parsons Mfg. Corp., Inc. v. Superior Court, 203 Cal. Rptr. 419 (Cal. Ct. App. 1984); Sutton v. Jondahl, 532 P.2d 478 (OkLa. Ct. App. 1975).

[8] Rizzuto v. Morris, 592 P.2d 688, 690 (Wash. Ct. App. 1979).

[9] See, e.g., Regent Ins. Co. v. Economy Preferred Ins. Co., 749 F. Supp. 191 (C.D.Ill. 1990); Neubauer v. Hostetter, 485 N.W.2d 87 (Iowa 1992); Britton v. Wooten, 817 S.W.2d 443 (Ky. 1991); Page v. Scott, 567 S.W.2d 101 (Ark. 1978).

[10] Bannock Bldg. Co. v. Sahlberg, 887 P.2d 1052, 1055 (Idaho 1994).

§ 53F   Transactions in Goods

Another area where partial interests may exist for insurance purposes are goods transactions. As with the vendor-vendee real estate transaction, the starting point in a goods transaction is to determine how the law allocates the risk of loss.

As with real estate, the parties are free to allocate the risk of loss however they see fit.[1] If the parties do not specify how the risk of loss should be allocated, the Uniform Commercial Code will do so, in effect filling in the gap in the parties' agreement. One of the basic policies of the Code is to allocate the risk of loss to the party most likely to have insurance:

> The underlying theory of this rule (that generally the risk of loss passes to the buyer on is receipt of the goods if the seller is a merchant, and otherwise the risk passes on tender of delivery) is that a merchant who is to make physical delivery at merchant's place continues meanwhile to control the goods and can be expected to insure the merchant's interest in them. The buyer, on the other hand, has no control of the goods, and it is extremely unlikely that the buyer will carry insurance on goods not yet in buyer's possession.[2]

The Uniform Commercial Code separates risk of loss allocations in goods transactions into three categories: shipper or carrier transactions; bailments; and all other transactions. Shipper or carrier transactions are governed by U.C.C. § 2-509(1), which provides that if the contract requires or authorizes the seller to ship goods by carrier and if it does not require the seller to deliver the goods at a particular destination, the risk of loss passes to the buyer when the goods are delivered. However, if the contract requires the seller to ship goods to a particular destination, and the goods are tendered there while in the carrier's possession, the risk of loss passes to the buyer when the goods are tendered. Section 2-509(1) must be read in conjunction with other sections stating the legal effect of trade terms such as "F.O.B." and "C.I.F." terms; these provisions complete the picture, informing the seller whether risk of loss passes when the goods are put in the possession of the carrier or when the goods reach the buyer.[3]

Bailments are governed by U.C.C. § 2-509(2), which provides that where goods are held by a bailee to be delivered without being moved, the risk of loss passes to the buyer (a) on receipt of a negotiable document of title; (b) on acknowledgment by the bailee of the buyer's right to possession of the goods; or (c) after receipt of a nonnegotiable document of title unless the bailee refuses to recognize it, in which case risk of loss remains on the seller until the buyer has had a reasonable time to present the document. This section applies to the situation where goods are in the possession of a warehouseman and the seller passes a document of title covering the goods to the buyer. In the ordinary case, the risk of loss passes to the buyer upon the receipt of the document of title.[4]

---

[1] U.C.C. § 2-509(4).

[2] U.C.C. § 2-509 comment 3.

[3] For a detailed discussion of these provisions and their interaction with U.C.C. § 2-509, see James J. White & Robert S. Summers, *Uniform Commercial Code* (3d student ed. 1988), § 5-2.

[4] See generally *id.* § 5-3.

The rule for all other cases not falling into the shipper-carrier or the bailment categories is set forth in U.C.C. § 2-509(3), which reads:

> In any case not within subsection (1) or (2), the risk of loss passes to the buyer on receipt of the goods if the seller is a merchant; otherwise the risk passes to the buyer on tender of delivery.

Receipt means the taking possession of the goods; tender of delivery has its own definition in § 2-503, the essence of which is that the tender occurs when the seller puts conforming goods at the buyer's disposition and gives the buyer any notice necessary to enable the buyer to take delivery.[5]

Breach has the effect of altering the foregoing rules in some situations.[6] If the seller breaches by tendering nonconforming goods, the risk of loss remains on the seller until cure or acceptance of the goods by the buyer.[7] If the buyer rightfully revokes acceptance, the buyer may treat the risk of loss as having rested on the seller from the beginning "to the extent of any deficiency in his effective insurance coverage."[8] If the buyer breaches before risk of loss passes to buyer, the seller "may to the extent of any deficiency in his effective insurance coverage" treat the risk of loss as resting on the buyer for a commercially reasonable time.[9]

Sections 2-510(2) and 2-510(3) show the Code's tendency to place the loss on insurers to the maximum extent possible. These provisions are essentially "anti-subrogation" clauses which serve to place the loss on an insurer if one is in the picture. In other words, the risk is transferred to the breaching party only to the extent of a deficiency in the aggrieved party's insurance coverage. The aggrieved but fully insured party cannot shift the risk of loss to the other party; thus, since the aggrieved, fully insured party has no claim against the breaching party for the loss of the goods, there is no right to which the insurer can be subrogated. Suppose the seller has a contract to sell goods to the buyer; the goods are in the seller's possession and are covered by the seller's insurance. The buyer repudiates the contract; then the goods are accidentally destroyed in a fire. Under § 2-510(3), the seller could treat the risk of loss as being on the buyer if the seller were uninsured; however, because seller is fully insured, this section has no effect. Seller's insurer pays seller for seller's loss; seller cannot treat the risk as being on the buyer; seller's insurer has no subrogation right against the buyer.[10]

The provisions in § 2-510 that place the loss on insurers of aggrieved parties by not shifting the risk of loss to the breaching party interact with §§ 2-509(1) and 2-509(2), which pertain to risk of loss in the shipper-carrier and bailment situations. For example, when goods are held in a warehouse to be delivered to the buyer

---

[5] See generally *id.* § 5-4.

[6] U.C.C. § 2-510; see generally White & Summers stud. ed., at note 3 *supra*, § 5-5.

[7] U.C.C. § 2-510(1).

[8] *Id.* at § 2-510(2). See Design Data Corp. v. Maryland Cas. Co., 503 N.W.2d 552 (Neb. 1993)(buyer's revocation of acceptance of computer equipment was timely, so that risk of loss remained with seller and seller had insurable interest in equipment at time damage was discovered).

[9] *Id.* at § 2-510(3).

[10] See White & Summers prac. ed., *supra* note 2, § 5-7.

without being moved, the risk of loss passes to the buyer when the buyer receives a negotiable document of title. However, if the goods are nonconforming and the buyer rightfully revokes acceptance, the risk of loss may be transferred back to the seller unless the buyer has effective insurance coverage.

In the bailment context, the loss may also fall ultimately on the insurer — that is, the insurer may have no subrogation rights — due to broad constructions of the so-called "in trust or on commission" clause commonly found in bailment and warehousemen's insurance policies. This clause extends coverage to damage or loss of property held but not owned by the insured. Generally, courts have construed these clauses to provide greater coverage than their literal terms would otherwise suggest. For example, in *United States Fidelity & Guaranty Co. v. Slifkin,*[11] a diamond merchant held goods of others on consignment for resale. His insurance policy contained an "in trust or on commission" clause and coverage for goods "held by him in any capacity whether or not the insured is liable for the loss thereof." The court held that the merchant's policy provided coverage to the consignors of stolen diamonds. Under the rule that an insurer has no subrogation against its own insured, the insurer could not assert the merchant's rights against the consignors, because those persons enjoyed the status of insureds under the merchant's policy.

Another effort to limit the insurer's subrogation right appears in bills of lading commonly used by railroads and other common carriers. The shipper's insurer typically provides in its policy that it is subrogated to all claims possessed by the insured, which by inference includes claims that the shipper has against the carrier. The bill of lading typically provides that the carrier shall have the benefit of all insurance purchased by anyone with whom the carrier deals. The issue, then, is which language prevails — that of the insurer which says it may recover from the carrier, or that of the carrier which says it is entitled to the benefit of the shipper's insurance. Unlike the bailee's insurer in the battle over how to interpret the "in trust or on commission" clause, the shipper's insurer has generally prevailed in this episode of the battle of the forms:

> Contradictory provisions and stipulations in contracts of insurance and carriage must be resolved in spite of logical difficulties. "The apparent circularity of expression may be resolved by interpreting the provision in the bill of lading as entitling the carrier to the insurance if there is no opposing *stipulation* in the policy or contract of insurance, that is no warranty or provision for avoidance; and not, if there is. Consequently, the insured may recover from the insurer; the insurer is effectively subrogated to his cause of action against the carrier; and the carrier is not entitled to the insurance."[12]

The risk of loss provisions of the Uniform Commercial Code are complicated enough without layering insurance issues, particularly subrogation and coordination of coverage issues, on top of them. But this subject is very important to those who trade in goods. More detailed discussion is available in treatises on the sale of goods.[13]

---

[11] 200 F. Supp. 563 (N.D. Ala. 1961).

[12] Richard D. Brew & Co. v. Auclair Transp., Inc., 211 A.2d 897, 899 (N.H. 1965), *quoting* Morton C. Campbell, *Non-Consensual Suretyship,* 45 Yale L.J. 69, 85 (1935).

[13] See White & Summers, prac. ed., *supra* note 2, §§ 5-6 to 5-10.

§ 53G Bailments

A bailment can exist, of course, without an accompanying sale of goods transaction. One who arranges for a fur coat to be stored with a furrier over the summer creates a bailment; no sale is involved. When a bailor delivers property to a bailee, the bailee is obligated to exercise reasonable care with respect to the property while it is in the bailee's possession and to return the property to the bailor when the purpose of the bailment is completed. Bailees often attempt to limit their liability in documents incidental to the creation of the bailment, such as receipts or an agreement of bailment itself. Although less common, bailees sometimes expand their common law liability by agreeing to be absolutely liable for any loss to the bailed property. Also, some bailees agree to procure insurance on the bailed property, and if the bailee breaches this duty, the bailee will be liable to the extent the insurance would have paid proceeds.[1]

Professional bailees typically carry liability insurance and insurance coverage for the property of others held in their custody. Although such bailees are not obligated to purchase insurance for the property of others absent an agreement so requiring, many bailees do so for the benefit of their customers and their own goodwill with them. The scope of the "in trust or on commission" clause has been the subject of some controversy; most courts treat it as coverage on property and do not require that the insured-bailee be legally liable for the loss.[2] Exemplar of the majority rule is *Folger Coffee Co. v. Great American Insurance Co.*,[3] a 1971 federal district court decision. A warehouseman had a policy of insurance purporting to cover "property of others held by the insured for which the insured is liable." The plaintiff's property was destroyed while warehoused with the insured, and the plaintiff sought to recover under the bailee's policy. The defendant insurer argued that the word "liable" in the policy required the plaintiff to show the bailee was negligent before it could recover under the policy. The court stated that "the true meaning of the contract, properly construed in light of the admitted facts, is that it covers *property* rather than *liability*. Under the law of Missouri, . . . this has the effect of including property of others possessed by the insured."[4] In the court's view, the word "liable" "does not refer to any fixed legal liability of the insured to respond in damages, but should be construed more broadly to mean 'responsible.' "[5]

Some courts, however, have construed the "in trust or on commission" clause to require the insured's liability for a loss as a prerequisite for coverage.[6] Under this

---

[1] See, e.g., Siegel v. Spear & Co., 138 N.E. 414 (N.Y. 1923); Farney v. Hauser, 198 P. 178 (Kan. 1921).

[2] See Paktank Louisiana, Inc. v. Marsh & McLennan, Inc., 688 F. Supp. 1087 (E.D. La. 1988); United States v. Globe and Rutgers Fire Ins. Co., 104 F. Supp. 632 (N.D. Tex. 1952), *aff'd*, 202 F.2d 696 (5th Cir. 1953); Penn v. Commercial Union Fire Ins. Co. of N.Y., 101 So. 2d 535 (Miss. 1958).

[3] 333 F. Supp. 1272 (W.D. Mo. 1971).

[4] *Id.* at 1280.

[5] *Id.* at 1274.

[6] See Clarence R. Conklin, *Insurance of Warehousing and Other Bailment Risks*, 1957 U. Ill. L. F. 560, 573-83 (favoring majority rule); Robert E. Keeton & Alan I. Widiss, *Insurance Law* § 4.5 (2d ed. 1988) (favoring minority rule).

narrower interpretation, bailees who want to provide insurance for their customers' property must secure additional insurance for losses for which the bailees are not "legally liable." Under the broader interpretation, this coverage is provided, but this assumes that all bailees want this coverage (for the benefit of their bailors) and desire to pay for it. This assumption may not be true, as some bailees may prefer that bailors insurer their own property for losses that do not result from acts of omissions that render the bailee legally liable. Yet bailees are usually in the best position to control risks to property in their possession, and it arguably makes more sense for bailees' insurers, who are no doubt more familiar with the business of particularly bailees and therefore in a better position to assess risk than bailors' insurers, to provide this coverage.

If both the bailor and bailee have insurance on the destroyed property, an overlapping coverage problem is created, which will need to be resolved by resort to the "other insurance" rules discussed in a later section.[7]

---

[7] See § 97, *infra*.

CHAPTER 6

SCOPE OF OBLIGATIONS: THE RISKS COVERED

§ 60   The Scope of Coverage

One of the first things someone contemplating the purchase of insurance is likely to want to know is what the policy covers. In the sections that follow, various aspects of the manner in which coverage is affirmatively granted will be discussed. This discussion will set the stage for an analysis of how coverage, once granted, is limited, both explicitly and implicitly.

§ 60A   All-risk versus Specified-risk Coverage

The distinction between all-risk and specified-risk coverage is an important one. All-risk insurance covers the insured for damage to the subject matter of the policy from all causes except those specifically excepted in the policy. In contrast, specified risk insurance covers damage to the subject matter of the policy only if it results from specifically identified causes listed in the policy.[1]

The language of the policy is helpful but not necessarily determinative on whether a policy is all-risk or specified-risk. Language such as "this vessel is insured for physical loss or damage from any external cause" except for certain explicit exclusions is all-risk coverage. In contrast, a homeowner's policy which lists several insured events is ordinarily treated as a specified-risk policy. The historical development of the policy can be important in determining whether the policy covers all risks. Marine insurance, for example, has traditionally been treated as all-risk insurance; the so-called "jeweler's block insurance" was developed to provide jewelers with coverage regardless of the cause, and thus traditionally has been treated as all-risk insurance. On the other hand, homeowner's insurance, normally treated as specified-risk insurance, evolved by joining several distinct coverages — fire, liability, theft, etc. — in one policy.

Three of the four major categories of insurance are essentially all-risk coverages. Marine insurance, the earliest form of insurance, has always been all-risk coverage. (As one would expect, inland marine insurance, a branch of property insurance which grew out of marine insurance, was predominantly all-risk coverage.) In the typical life insurance policy, proceeds are payable upon the insured's death

---

[1] For discussion of a variety of issues that surface in all-risk insurance coverages, see generally Paul B. Butler, ed., *The All Risk Policy: Its Problems, Perils and Practical Applications* (1986); Annot., *Coverage Under All-Risk Insurance,* 30 A.L.R.5th 170 (1995).

regardless of cause, subject to specific exclusions in the policy (such as death by suicide within two years of the policy's issuance).[2] Liability insurance is typically all-risk, in that it covers any liability the insured incurs to a third-party, except for liability caused by specified acts or neglect of the insured.

The distinction between all-risk and specified-risk coverage is most important, however, in property insurance. Some property insurance policies are specified-risk, while others are all-risk. The typical homeowner's property coverage is specified-risk; it indemnifies the insured against loss caused by a number of specifically identified perils. Other kinds of policies purport to cover loss to the designated property regardless of cause.

All-risk insurance is thought to be advantageous in several respects: the coverage is presumably simpler to understand; duplication of coverages and premiums from separate, specified-risk policies is avoided; pressures toward adverse selection are minimized;[3] and the policies are easier and less expensive for the insurer to administer.[4] However, the most widely perceived advantage is the avoidance of gaps in coverage: losses that would otherwise fall within the gaps of specified-risk coverage will be indemnified if a policy is deemed to be all-risk.

The observation that "all-risk insurance fills in all the gaps" needs to be substantially qualified, however. Coverage under all-risk policies is hardly absolute. For example, it is a fundamental prerequisite to any policy's coverage that the loss be "fortuitous." As explained by one court, "the 'all-risk' event so covered would not include an undisclosed event that existed prior to coverage, or an event caused by the consummation during the period of coverage of an indwelling fault in the goods that had existed prior to that coverage."[5] If a loss is certain to occur, such as loss due to normal wear and tear, the loss is not fortuitous and therefore is not insurable.[6] Furthermore, exclusions can take away much of what the all-risk policy gives. These exclusions are often very difficult to understand and apply; the expectations of the insured who thinks "all-risk" coverage means the insurer will reimburse any loss are often disappointed. Also, all-risk coverage does not alter basic insurance law principles that can operate to limit coverage, such as the insurable

---

[2] The accidental death "double indemnity" rider is properly viewed as specified-risk coverage: the proceeds are payable only if the insured dies as a result of a specified risk, an accident.

[3] For a discussion of adverse selection, see § 10[c], *supra*.

[4] 2 *Richards on Insurance* § 212 (5th ed. 1952).

[5] Greene v. Cheetham, 293 F.2d 933, 936–37 (2d Cir. 1961). Numerous other cases agree. See, e.g., Leafland Group-II Montgomery Towers Ltd. Partnership v. Insurance Co. of N. Am., 881 P.2d 26 (N.M. 1994); Avis v. Hartford Fire Ins. Co., 195 S.E.2d 545 (N.C. 1973). See generally Andrew C. Hecker, Jr. & M. Jane Goode, *Wear and Tear, Inherent Vice, Deterioration, Etc.: The Multi-faceted All-Risk Exclusions*, 21 Tort & Ins. L.J. 634 (1986).

[6] See Compagnie des Bauxites de Guinee v. Insurance Co. of N. Am., 566 F. Supp. 258 (W.D. Pa. 1983), *rev'd without op.*, 735 F.2d 1348 (3d Cir. 1984). One might say that death is certain to occur and therefore death is not fortuitous. However, the time at which death will occur is not certain. It is on this basis that death is a fortuitous event.

interest requirement, causation rules, the requirement that the loss not be intentionally caused by the insured, and implied exceptions (such as the friendly fire rule).[7]

All-risk insurance may not broaden coverage as much as commonly perceived, but in another respect all-risk insurance offers the consumer a significant comparative advantage over specified risk coverage. This advantage is derived from the impact of all-risk coverage on how the burden of proof is allocated between insurer and insured. The insured under a specified-risk policy must establish not only that a loss occurred but also that the loss was caused by one of the specified, covered perils. Once this showing is made, the burden shifts to the insurer to show an applicable exclusion, if any. In contrast, the all-risk insured needs to establish only that a loss occurred; the burden then shifts to the insurer to show that the loss was caused by an exception.[8] Thus, where the cause of a loss is difficult to identify and prove, an all-risk policy can be highly beneficial to the insured.

Two cases involving notorious facts illustrate well the potential advantage to an insured from having all-risk coverage. In *Northwest Airlines, Inc. v. Globe Indemnity Co.*,[9] a hijacker — the infamous D.B. Cooper — extorted a large sum of money from the airline and then parachuted from the jet over the northwest. The airline's policy had five categories of coverage, two of which were "loss inside the premises" and "loss outside the premises." The insurer argued that the loss did not fall within the technical limits of any of these coverages, but the court reasoned that the policy read as a whole would be interpreted as all-risk coverage, meaning that the loss was covered unless the insurer could show that the specific risk was excluded. Since no explicit exclusion pertained to the hijacking risk, the insured's loss was covered. The same point is illustrated by *Pan American World Airways, Inc. v. Aetna Casualty & Surety Co.*,[10] a 1974 Second Circuit case. A Pan American Boeing 747 was hijacked and ultimately destroyed by members of the Popular Front for the Liberation of Palestine. The insurers argued that three specific exclusions barred Pan Am's recovery for the loss of the aircraft: capture or seizure of property by governmental authority or agent; war, invasion, or civil war; and strikes, riots, or civil commotion. The Court of Appeals, however, treating the policy as all-risk coverage, held that Pan Am was entitled to indemnity for its loss. The Court ruled that the insurers had failed to prove that the cause of the loss was within the scope of the policy's exclusions. Consistently with well-established rules of interpretation,[11] the exclusions were construed in a manner most beneficial to the insured. Also, it did not help the insurers' cause that they knew at the time the policies were issued that their exclusions were ambiguous as applied to a political hijacking. Despite this knowledge, the insurers took no steps to clarify their exclusions, such as by using the terms "hijacking" or "act for political or terrorist purposes."

---

[7] See generally Lauren E. Roberts, *All-Risk Property Insurance: Problems in Determining the Scope of Coverage,* 53 Ins. Couns. J. 88 (1986).

[8] All states, with the possible exception of Texas, appear to follow this rule. Roberts, note 7, *supra,* at 93.

[9] 225 N.W.2d 831 (Minn. 1975).

[10] 505 F.2d 989 (2d Cir. 1974).

[11] See § 25A[b], *supra.*

If the policies in *Northwest Airlines* or *Pan American World Airways* had been specified-risk, the insurers might have prevailed. The insurers' difficulty in showing that the cause of the loss fell within an exclusion would have instead been the insured's problem of showing that a covered peril caused the loss. If the coverage-granting provisions in a specified-risk policy did not identify "hijacking" or "act for political or terrorist purposes" as covered perils, it is improbable that the insured would have succeeded in carrying its burden of bringing the loss within the terms of the policy's coverage. As in many other settings, the allocation of the burden of proof can be determinative of the outcome of a case. The all-risk policy diminishes the burden placed on the insured, and thus makes pro-insured outcomes more likely.

§ 60B   The Nature of Coverage Provisions

[a]   The Personal Nature of Insurance

It is convenient to divide insurance into four broad groupings: personal, property, liability, and marine. But regardless of how it is categorized, all insurance shares a common trait of "personalness." The category of personal insurance, which includes life, health, accident, and disability insurance, is plainly "personal": the insurance only applies to a particular individual, and it is not possible for the insured to transfer his interest in insuring his own life or health to someone else.[1] The problems and unfairness of one person unilaterally declaring that his health insurance policy shall now be deemed to cover the health of someone else are obvious. Liability insurance is also personal in the same sense: each person purchases coverage for his own (or a group of related persons') potential liability to others. The insurer prices the coverage depending on the characteristics and traits of the particular insured.

Property insurance is likewise "personal" in this limited sense. With good reason, the typical person thinks that when he or she purchases insurance on a house that the *house itself* is insured, but this understanding is technically incorrect. The insurance is on the *insured's interest* in the property, not on the property itself. It is the damage to the *personal interest,* not the house, that is being reimbursed under a policy of property insurance.[2] If the insurance were on the property, the insurance would automatically follow the property in the event the property were sold or transferred to someone else. This, however, is not what happens. It is necessary for an insured to take affirmative steps to assign the policy, which usually includes obtaining the insurer's approval of the assignment. Insurers typically insist upon approving assignments so that they can investigate how the use of the property might change and what risks might be added by virtue of the changed ownership of the property.

---

[1] In life insurance, an insured might be able to assign his ownership rights in the policy to someone else. However, the insured could not substitute someone else's life as the insured risk.

[2] See Christ Gospel Temple v. Liberty Mut. Ins. Co., 417 A.2d 660 (Pa. Super. Ct. 1979), *cert. denied,* 449 U.S. 955 (1980).

[b] An Overview of the Various Kinds of Common Coverages

A comprehensive review of the various kinds of insurance coverages available is, obviously, impossible within the scope of this text. In this subsection only a few highlights of the various coverages are presented. For more detailed information, one of the several available insurance texts (commonly used in business school insurance courses) might be consulted.[3] For even more detailed information, one should consult the policy forms themselves; these are compiled annually in a book published by the Alliance of American Insurers.[4] With respect to personal property, the two items of greatest value that are commonly owned by individuals are real estate improvements and vehicles. These assets can be insured by a homeowners policy and a personal auto policy, respectively. Prior to the late 1950s, a homeowner needed to purchase several different kinds of policies, such as fire insurance, theft insurance, and other coverages to get complete coverage. In the late 1950s, insurers developed the homeowners' policy — known in the trade as the HO policy — which incorporated into one policy several kinds of property coverages, additional living expenses in the event of the dwelling's damage or destruction, comprehensive personal liability coverage, and replacement-cost coverage on the dwelling and sometimes the contents. Today, there are six standard HO policies, designated as HO-1 through HO-6. HO-1 provides limited coverage, HO-2 expands the HO-1 to seventeen specifically named perils, HO-3 is broader still in that it purports to cover all risks, HO-4 is designed for apartment dwellers seeking to cover their personal property, HO-5 is all-risk coverage for buildings and contents, and HO-6 is specially designed for condominium owners. The specific contents of the HO policies are best explored by simply reviewing such a policy.[5]

Many consumers purchase personal property floaters to supplement the coverage of the HO policy. The HO policy will usually cover such things as jewelry, valuable paintings, cameras, silverware, and antiques, but only to a limited extent. Also, the HO policy typically has a deductible in the property coverage, ranging anywhere from $100 to $1000, which would apply to the loss of any particular piece of property. Thus, many consumers choose to purchase the floater; this covers specifically designated pieces of property only, usually without a deductible.[6] Many other kinds of commonly-requested coverages are added to the HO policy as an endorsement. For example, if an individual has more than one personal computer at home or one particularly powerful computer with many peripherals, the individual may add a special computer endorsement. Many people purchase replacement cost coverage, and may acquire an endorsement that automatically increases the coverage to account for inflation. Many people desire more liability coverage than provided

---

[3] See, e.g., M. Dorfman, *Introduction to Insurance* (2d ed. 1982); Albert H. Mowbray, Ralph H. Blanchard, C. Arthur Williams, Jr., *Insurance: Its Theory and Practice in the United States* (6th ed. 1969); Curtis M. Elliot & Emmett J. Vaughan, *Fundamentals of Risk and Insurance* (1972).

[4] Alliance of American Insurers, *1995 Policy Kit For Students of Insurance*. The *Kit* is published annually.

[5] See *id.* at 17-77.

[6] *Id.* at 47.

by the standard HO (or automobile) policy, and personal umbrella policies, which provide another layer of liability protection beyond the basic HO (or automobile) policy are often purchased to provide this additional coverage.

The typical automobile policy, like the HO policy, is a package of property and liability coverages. The policy protects the owner both from physical damage to the automobile and the liability to others for damage to their persons or property. The model form used today by most insurers is the Personal Auto Policy form (called the PAP in the trade). After the declarations, the PAP has six parts: Part A states the liability coverages; Part B provides the medical payments coverage (meaning the payments for medical expenses sustained by a covered person in an accident); Part C provides coverage for damages the insured is entitled to recover from an uninsured motorist; Part D provides property damage coverage for the automobile; Part E states the insured's duties after an accident or loss; and Part F contains general provisions, such as the subrogation clause, the other insurance clause, termination provisions, and other provisions.[7]

With respect to commercial entities, the basic property insurance policy is the standard fire insurance policy. This policy may be issued as a single form, may be expanded by endorsements of one kind or another, or may be incorporated into a "package" policy such as a homeowner's policy. The same fire insurance policy form is used by almost all insurers; it is technically known as the 1943 New York Standard Fire Insurance Policy. The coverage in this form is for "direct loss by fire, lightning and other perils insured against in this policy including removal from premises endangered by the perils insured against in this policy, except as hereinafter provided."[8]

The fire policy is limited in the perils covered; thus, it is common to add endorsements to this policy which adapt it to particular classes of property or types of coverage. Some endorsements specify that, for example, the building and permanently attached machinery of the insured are covered, or personal property kept on the premises is covered. Businesses that have property in more than one location may have the "multiple-location reporting form" added to their policy. Also, endorsements might be added to cover other specific causes of loss, such as windstorm and hail, smoke, explosion, riot, and damage by aircraft and-autos. A wide range of coverages are available for commercial crime, such as employee dishonesty, forgery, theft, robbery and safe burglary, and computer crime. Special endorsements are also available for hotels, theaters, schools, and other enterprises.[9]

As discussed in Chapter 1, liability insurance is designed to indemnify the insured against liability owing to others. Liability coverages are thus "general," but many forms exist that are tailored to serve the needs of individuals, businesses, and organizations.[10] For the insured seeking coverage for personal liability, liability coverage is provided, as noted above, in the homeowner's and the automobile policies. To supplement this coverage, many consumers purchase an "umbrella" policy, which

---

[7] *Id.* at 1.

[8] Alliance of American Insurers, *1987 Policy Kit* at 1.

[9] For examples of many of these coverages, see *Policy Kit* at 141–245.

[10] See *id.* at 258–97.

provides a layer of liability insurance in excess of that provided by the homeowner's and automobile policies.[11] Commercial liability coverage is handled differently. The first commercial liability policies, which emerged in the late nineteenth century, were designed to protect employers from liability claims of their employees. Products liability coverage soon followed, and when workers compensation systems were established early in this century, policies were created to cover the employer's obligations under these systems.[12] Until the 1940s, most business firm liability insurance was sold for bodily injury and property damage caused by specific activities, such as landlord's liability, contractor's liability, etc. In 1941, the first "Comprehensive General Liability" policy, or "CGL," was marketed. The purpose of the CGL was to provide general coverage to an insured regardless of the nature of the insured's business, although for many years it was the practice to supplement the CGL form with provisions drafted for particular kinds of businesses.[13] The policy was amended periodically, and the 1986 revision changed the name of the policy to "Commercial General Liability" policy, although the acronym "CGL" remained the same.

In addition to the CGL, specific coverages are available for commercial automobile uses (including commercial carriers and garages), professional liability, agricultural businesses, and directors and officers in corporations.[14]

The major category of personal insurance seeks to guard against four different risks: the risk of a premature death due to accident or natural causes, which might cause financial hardship to those who depend on the well-being of a person; the risk of a long life, where the individual's expenses after his or her working years might outstrip a lifetime's savings; the risk of an illness and the concomitant medical expenses that deplete savings; and the risk of disability caused by illness or accident that prevents one from working and thereby providing support both to oneself and his or her dependents.

Life insurance is the product that protects against the risk of a premature death. Life insurance policies have many labels, but they are basically of two types — term and whole life. Proceeds are payable upon the insured's death. The nature of these coverages is more fully discussed in Chapter 1.[15] Annuities are essentially the opposite of life insurance; annuities provide protection against the risk of a long life.[16] Health insurance addresses the concern of medical expenses, although most health insurance plans do much more than address the major illnesses that are the greatest risk to savings and sometimes have the potential to cause bankruptcy. Thus, health insurance products resemble welfare or benefit plans (where income is often irrelevant, or only marginally relevant, to coverage or premium) more than other

[11] *Id.* at 282–89.

[12] See Solomon S. Huebner et al, *Property and Liability Insurance* 353 (3d ed. 1982).

[13] See Kenneth S. Abraham, *Environmental Liability Insurance Law* 24-25 (1991) (discussing the history of the CGL).

[14] For examples, see *Policy Kit* at 337-506.

[15] See § 13A[b], *supra*.

[16] The prospect of long-term care expenses at the end of one's life can be insured through annuities or policies specially tailored for this particular risk. For more discussion of annuities, see § 13A[b] *supra*.

insurance products. Disability insurance reimburses income lost due to illness or accident. Disability is thus a logical adjunct to life insurance; the predominant purpose of both is to guard against lost income, either for the disabled person or his beneficiaries (or both).[17]

§ 61 Expanding Coverage Beyond the Policy's Literal Language

[a] Creating Coverage Through Estoppel

It is commonly stated that insurance contracts cannot be created by estoppel and that estoppel cannot be used to create coverage that does not exist according to the terms of the policy.[1] *Hunter v. Insurance Co.,*[2] a 1955 North Carolina case, states the general rule:

> [T]he doctrines of waiver or estoppel can have a field of operation only when the subject matter is within the terms of the contract, and they cannot operate radically to change the terms of the policy so as to cover additional subject matter. Accordingly, it has been held by the weight of authority that waiver or estoppel cannot create a contract of insurance or so apply as to bring within the coverage of the policy property, or a loss or risk, which by the terms of the policy is expressly excepted or otherwise excluded. . . .[3]

A number of recent decisions have considered the rule articulated in *Hunter* to be excessively broad, and it has been rejected in a growing number of jurisdictions.[4]

---

[17] For more discussion of health insurance and disability insurance, see §§ 64[b], 64[c], *supra.*

[1] See 16B APPLEMAN, § 9090, at 576 (1981); Continental Graphics Services, Inc. v. Continental Cas. Co., 681 F.2d 743 (11th Cir. 1982); C. Douglas Wilson & Co v. Insurance Co. of N. Am., 590 F.2d 1275 (4th Cir.), *cert. denied,* 441 U.S. 831 (1979); Design Data Corp. v. Maryland Cas. Co., 503 N.W.2d 552 (Neb. 1993); DeJonge v. Mutual of Enumclaw, 843 P.2d 914 (Or. 1992) (en banc); Shannon v. Shannon, 442 N.W.2d 25 (Wis. 1989); St. Paul Fire & Marine Ins. Co. v. Albany Cty. Sch. Dist. No. 1, 763 F.2d 1255 (Wyo. 1988); McGee v. Guardian Life Ins. Co., 472 So. 2d 993 (Ala. 1985); State Compensation Fund v. Industrial Comm'n of Ariz., 666 P.2d 542 (Ariz. Ct. App. 1983); Hunter v. Jefferson Standard Life Ins. Co., 86 S.E.2d 78 (N.C. 1955); American States Ins. Co. v. Zippro Constr. Co., 455 S.E.2d 133 (Ga. Ct. App. 1995); Wausau Ins. Cos. v. Feldman, 623 N.Y.S.2d 242 (N.Y. App. Div. 1995); Von Hillman v. Colonial Penn Ins. Co., 869 P.2d 248 (Kan.Ct.App. 1994); Community Title Co. v. Safeco Ins. Co. of Am., 795 S.W.2d 453 (Mo. Ct. App. 1990); Twin City Hide v. Transamerica Ins. Co., 358 N.W.2d 90 (Minn. Ct. App. 1984); Annot., *Doctrine of Estoppel or Waiver as Available to Bring Within Coverage of Insurance Policy Risks Not Covered By Its Terms Or Expressly Excluded Therefrom,* 1 A.L.R.3d 1139 (1965).

[2] 86 S.E.2d 78 (N.C. 1955).

[3] 86 S.E.2d at 80 (quoting 45 *C.J.S. Insurance* § 674, p. 616 (1946)).

[4] E.g., Schifalacqua v. CNA Ins., 567 F.2d 1255 (3d Cir. 1977); United States Steel Corp. v. Hartford Accident & Indem. Co., 511 F.2d 96 (7th Cir. 1975); Bill Brown Constr. Co., Inc. v. Glens Falls Ins. Co., 818 S.W.2d 1 (Tenn. 1991); Hunter v. Farmers Ins. Group, 554 P.2d 1239 (Wyo. 1976); King v. Travelers Ins. Co., 505 P.2d 1226 (N.M. 1973); Harr v. Allstate Ins. Co., 255 A.2d 208 (N.J. 1969); Crown Life Ins. Co. v. McBride, 517 So. 2d 660 (Fla.App. 1987); Time Ins. Co. v. Graves, 734 S.W.2d 213 (Ark.App. 1987)(en banc).

The doctrines of waiver and estoppel have been used to deprive insurers of defenses in virtually every context in which the insurer might deny liability. Given this fact, it is somewhat surprising that courts in most jurisdictions hold that the doctrines are not available to "broaden" coverage.[5] But these courts should not be understood as holding that an insurer is incapable of intentionally abandoning a right or inducing another party to rely detrimentally on a statement simply because a question of the policy's coverage is involved. Indeed, waiver and estoppel, doctrines with which courts are comfortable, have always had a relationship to "coverage," because the doctrines help determine whether the insurer owes an obligation to the insured.

Moreover, the position that insurance coverage cannot be created by estoppel ignores the well-developed body of contract law where obligations are created through the doctrine of promissory estoppel. Under that doctrine, which is enshrined in section 90 of the *Restatement (Second) of Contracts,* a promise is enforceable if the promisor should reasonably expect the promise to induce action or forbearance on the part of the promisee, the promise does induce such action or forbearance, and injustice can be avoided only by enforcing the promise. In some jurisdictions, the promisee's reliance can even substitute for the writing requirement of the statute of frauds.[6] Moreover, where one party has misrepresented an existing fact which led the other party to assume that a contractual relationship existed, it has long been held that the party who committed the misrepresentation will be estopped to deny the existence of a contract under the doctrine of equitable estoppel.[7] For example, if the insured asks whether the renewal premium has been paid and the insurer incorrectly answers "yes," the insurer will later be estopped from claiming that the policy lapsed for nonpayment of the premium.

In short, the general rule is that contractual obligations *can* be created through estoppel, and the rationale for excepting insurance transactions from the general rule is hardly self-evident. *Harr v. Allstate Insurance Co.,*[8] a 1969 New Jersey decision, is the leading case in opposition to the majority rule. In *Harr,* the insured, who owned both a homeowners' policy and a fire policy issued by the insurer, kept business merchandise in the basement of his residence. The homeowners' policy, which he had obtained first and which covered damage resulting from bursting pipes, excluded coverage for the business merchandise. The insured understood this

---

[5] For a discussion of the incongruities in this area and a detailed history of the related doctrines in one state, see Bill Brown Constr. Co. v. Glens Falls Ins. Co., 818 S.W.2d 1 (Tenn. 1991).

[6] See, e.g., Brookside Farms v. Mama Rizzo's, Inc., 873 F. Supp. 1029 (S.D. Tex. 1995); Cardone v. Empire Blue Cross & Blue Shield, 884 F. Supp. 838 (S.D. N.Y. 1995); Siam Numhong Products Co. v. Eastimpex, 866 F. Supp. 445 (N.D. Cal. 1994); Warder & Lee Elevator, Inc. v. Britten, 274 N.W.2d 339 (Iowa 1979); Sanders v. Dantzler, 375 So. 2d 774 (Miss. 1979). But see Architectural Metal Systems, Inc. v. Consolidated Systems, Inc., 58 F.3d 1227 (7th Cir. 1995) (applying Illinois law); Greaves v. Medical Imaging Systems, Inc., 879 P.2d 276 (Wash. 1994).

[7] See, e.g., Loeb v. Gendel, 179 N.E.2d 7 (Ill. 1961); Seymour v. Oelrichs, 106 P. 88 (Cal. 1909).

[8] 255 A.2d 208 (N.J. 1969).

limitation on coverage in the homeowners' policy, and this led him to telephone his agent to obtain additional insurance for the merchandise. According to the insured's testimony, the agent stated "we can cover you for $7,500 and you are fully covered." The nature of the coverage was neither discussed nor explained; the insured testified that he trusted the agent to take care of his needs. The insurance which the agent arranged was a fire insurance policy; the insured paid the premium for the fire policy which, unlike the homeowners' policy, excluded from coverage damage resulting from "ruptured or bursting water pipes." Shortly thereafter, a water pipe burst in the insured's home, damaging the merchandise plus some of the insured's other property. The insured filed a claim for the entire loss. The insurer paid for damage to the nonbusiness property under the homeowner's policy but denied liability under either policy for damage to the business merchandise.

The insured sued on the theory that, even though neither policy covered the loss, the insurer was estopped to deny coverage under the fire insurance policy. The estoppel allegedly arose out of the insured's reliance on the agent's statement that he was "fully covered" and his reasonable assumption that the new policy would cover the same perils as did the homeowners' policy. The insurer contended that the doctrine of equitable estoppel could not be used to enlarge coverage and that any oral representations made by the agent were merged in the policy by the parol evidence rule. The trial court granted the insurer an involuntary dismissal, holding that the parol evidence rule excluded statements made at the time of contract formation, thereby preventing their being considered to broaden coverage. The New Jersey Supreme Court reversed, holding that equitable estoppel is available under proper circumstances to broaden the coverage of an insurance policy:

> [W]here an insurer or its agent misrepresents, even though innocently, the coverage of an insurance contract, or the exclusions therefrom, to an insured before or at the inception of the contract, and the insured reasonably relies thereupon to his ultimate detriment, the insurer is estopped to deny coverage after a loss on a risk or from a peril actually not covered by the terms of the policy.[9]

The court was unpersuaded by the arguments usually offered to support the proposition that estoppel should not be used to broaden coverage. It is sometimes argued that extending coverage by estoppel is tantamount to the court making a contract for the parties. In a sense, the argument is correct; however, it is difficult to understand the unfairness in binding the insurer to a promise it made which induced the insured's detrimental reliance. Another argument offered against extending coverage by estoppel is that an insurer should not be required to pay for a loss for which it charged no premium. Yet courts have long used estoppel to prevent insurers from asserting forfeiture provisions in situations where the insured

---

[9] 255 A.2d at 219; see also Preferred Risk Mut. Ins. Co. v. Thomas, 372 F.2d 227 (4th Cir. 1967). For a detailed discussion of *Harr*, see Note, *Insurance Law Extension of Coverage by Estoppel*, 1970 Wis. L. Rev. 1234.

has breached,[10] and this is tantamount to insisting that an insurer reimburse a loss it did not plan to cover and for which it presumably collected no premium.

Furthermore, in many cases, what constitutes a "forfeiture provision" has been defined so broadly as to encompass virtually any condition in the policy that, if enforced, would cause the insured to suffer a forfeiture. Under this broad definition, the ability of estoppel to broaden coverage is virtually unbounded. For example, in *Durham v. Cox,*[11] a 1984 North Carolina decision, a garage which the insured used for business purposes was destroyed. The policy excluded coverage for structures used for business purposes and provided that a waiver of a policy provision would not be valid unless in writing. The court concluded, however, that the "business use" provision was a "condition working a forfeiture, which may be impliedly waived by the acts and conduct of the insurer."[12] The court reasoned that the structure was already within the policy's "coverage," and therefore coverage was not being expanded. This reasoning disregarded the fact that the structure was covered only if used for nonbusiness purposes; allowing the forfeiture provision to be waived would actually have the effect of broadening the coverage from nonbusiness uses to all uses, including business uses. In short, in vacating the summary judgment for the insurer and remanding the case for a trial where evidence that the insurer's agent expressly agreed to assume the enhanced risk would be received and considered, the court allowed waiver and estoppel to be used as coverage-broadening devices, despite the court's attempt to characterize the business-use exclusion as a forfeiture provision.

Separate from the issue of whether estoppel can be used to create coverage is a distinct but related question: whether post-contract conduct by an insurer or its agents can give rise to an estoppel. Some courts have held that it cannot;[13] in a jurisdiction otherwise favorably disposed to estoppel, limiting estoppels to post-contract conduct significantly constrains the reach of the minority rule. *Roseth v. St. Paul Property and Liability Insurance Co.*[14] is illustrative. The South Dakota Supreme Court had approved the minority rule in a two-decade old decision,[15] but the court limited the rule's application to representations made by the agent or the insurer "before or at the inception of the contract."[16] This had unfortunate consequences for the insured under a cargo insurance policy who followed the advice of the insurer's agent to sell promptly on the market calves injured while being transported. The insured told the agent that he believed the policy would cover

---

[10] E.g., Ahnapee & W. Ry. Co. v. Challoner, 148 N.W.2d 646 (Wis. 1967); State Farm Mut. Auto. Ins. Co. v. Hinestrosa, 614 So. 2d 633 (Fla. Dist. Ct. App. 1993) (estoppel can be sued to prevent forfeiture, but not to expand coverage); Durham v. Cox, 310 S.E.2d 371 (N.C. Ct. App. 1984) (business use exclusion was a forfeiture provision subject to being waived by the insurer).

[11] 310 S.E.2d 371 (N.C. Ct. App. 1984).

[12] 310 S.E.2d at 376.

[13] See Roseth v. St. Paul Prop. & Liab. Ins. Co., 374 N.W.2d 105 (S.D. 1985); Writers, Inc. v. West Bend Mut. Ins. Co., 465 N.W.2d 419 (Minn. Ct. App. 1991).

[14] 374 N.W.2d 105 (S.D. 1985).

[15] Farmers Mut. Auto. Ins. Co. v. Bechard, 122 N.W.2d 86 (S.D. 1963).

[16] 374 N.W.2d at 107. This language was used in *Harr.* See note 8, *supra*.

the decrease in value of his injured livestock; the agent did not disabuse the insured of this understanding, even though the agent knew that the policy would not cover this loss. The insured testified that if his understanding of the policy's coverage had been corrected, he would have nurtured the injured calves back to health and sold them later at a better price. The court, however, held that since the misrepresentation of coverage did not occur before or at the inception of the contract, estoppel would not lie to prevent the insurer from asserting the exclusion to coverage.[17] Notwithstanding decisions like *Roseth*, other courts have been less concerned with drawing a pre-contract versus post-contract distinction, and have granted the insured relief when the conduct giving rise to the estoppel occurred after contracting.[18]

It is difficult to make much sense out of the limitations on the scope of estoppel in insurance coverage cases. Proponents of the parol evidence rule would argue that cases like *Roseth* have the law backwards; pre-contract representations are more problematic than post-contract modifications, and it makes little sense to allow coverage to be created by the former but not the latter. Because reliance is an element of any kind of estoppel, it is arguable that no distinction should be made between pre- contract and post-contract estoppels; in either case, the plaintiff's burden is a heavy one.[19] To the extent promissory estoppel is a positive development in contract law, it is difficult to explain its tepid reception in insurance law. Yet in the final analysis, the lack of enthusiasm for estoppel may matter little given the availability of other doctrines that can be used to expand insurer liability, such as the doctrine of reasonable expectations, aggressive use of contra proferentum, and recognizing broad authority in agents to bind insurers.

The rule that estoppel cannot be used to expand the coverage of insurance policies is still the majority rule, but the minority rule seems destined to displace the majority rule someday. Historically, the doctrines of waiver and estoppel have been used to protect consumers, and notwithstanding the open-ended nature of these doctrines, for the most part courts have acted with reasonable restraint. As Professor Morris observed some years ago in his important article on waiver and estoppel:

> Of course this process of favoring consumers can be carried too far. Insurance companies need and are entitled to reasonable limits on their responsibilities; the public is prejudiced when company liabilities are by generous caprice stretched over risks that cannot be profitably underwritten at a just premium. By and large, however, the courts have not been overgenerous to the public.

---

[17] The court's holding was met with a strong dissenting opinion. 374 N.W.2d at 108–111 (Henderson, J. dissenting).

[18] See, e.g., Tomerlin v. Canadian Indem. Co., 394 P.2d 571 (Cal. 1964). Anytime an insurer undertakes to defend an insured under a liability policy without a reservation of rights, the estoppel that prevents the insurer from later denying coverage arises from insurer conduct after the time of contracting. See Turner Liquidating Co. v. St. Paul Surplus Lines Ins. Co., 638 N.E.2d 174 (Ohio Ct.App. 1994).

[19] See, e.g., Brown v. Woodmen Accident and Life Co., 616 N.E.2d 278 (Ohio Ct.App. 1992)(party who is chargeable with knowledge of facts, as where party either knows them or is in position to know them, has not been misled and cannot claim estoppel).

> Judges have limited their use of the doctrines of waiver and estoppel because of their awareness of important underwriting realities.[20]

Professor Morris' observation that judges have acted with restraint when asked to invoke the doctrine of estoppel is not shared by all commentators,[21] but the limitations on estoppel which many courts impose may well stand as examples, albeit somewhat illogical ones, of the judicial restraint about which Professor Morris wrote.

[b]   Other Doctrines

Creating coverage through estoppel where the underlying theory is promissory (as opposed to equitable) estoppel amounts to the creation of a contract because of the justifiable detrimental reliance of an insured on a promise by the insurer or its agent that the promisor should understand would lead to the reliance. Beyond promissory estoppel, it is worth noting that any number of doctrines — equitable estoppel when used to take away an insurer's defense to coverage; the doctrine of reasonable expectations; waiver; estoppel; rules of interpretation; implied warranty; the duty of good faith and fair dealing; and reformation — can function to create coverage that would not otherwise exist.[22] These other doctrines differ from promissory estoppel in this respect: these other doctrines do not "create" a contract as such, but instead operate upon an existing contract to determine the parties' rights and obligations. For the insured who successfully asserts any of these doctrines, however, the result is the same: the insured recovers for his or her loss notwithstanding the insurer's argument that the policy creates no obligation to the insured.

[c]   The Parol Evidence Rule

Whenever one speaks of broadening the language of a contract beyond its literal terms, one must take account of the parol evidence rule. The rule is essentially this: when the parties to a contract put their agreement in writing, intending the writing to be the final expression of their agreement, the terms of the writing may not be contradicted — or perhaps even supplemented — by evidence of any prior or contemporaneous agreement or negotiations.[23] If an insurance contract is intended as the final and perhaps complete agreement of the parties, the insurer might argue that the parol evidence rule prevents the insured from offering evidence that the insurer or its agent orally represented the existence of coverage inconsistent with

---

[20] Clarence Morris, *Waiver and Estoppel in Insurance Policy Litigation,* 105 U. Pa. L. Rev. 925, 926 (1957).

[21] See Allen D. Windt, 1 *Insurance Claims and Disputes* § 6.34, at 464–67 (3d ed. 1995) (arguing that at least six situations exist where some courts have been too willing to find an estoppel creating coverage).

[22] For further discussion, see §§ 25-25H *supra.*

[23] For additional discussion of the parol evidence rule, see E. Allen Farnsworth, *Contracts* 470–80, 485–92 (2d ed. 1990); John D. Calamari and Joseph M. Perillo, *A Plea for a Uniform Parol Evidence Rule and Principles of Contract Interpretation,* 42 Ind. L.J. 333 (1967); John E. Murray, Jr. *The Parol Evidence Rule: A Clarification,* 4 Duq. L. Rev. 337 (1966); Arthur L. Corbin, *The Interpretation of Words and the Parol Evidence Rule,* 50 Cornell L.Q. 161 (1965).

the policy's literal language. If the parol evidence rule surfaces in a coverage dispute, it is the insurer who will raise it. An insured, in attempting to meet the rule, is likely to argue that the insurer, under the doctrines of waiver or estoppel, is not entitled to rely on the rule.

Considerable controversy exists over the circumstances under which parol evidence should be admitted to supplement a writing. Under the strict view,[24] if the contract is clear on its face, as indicated by evaluation of the "four corners" of the document, parol evidence is inadmissible to contradict the writing. This approach has been applied to assertedly "unambiguous" insurance policies; parol testimony seeking to alter the coverage terms has been held inadmissible.[25] Under the broader, more modern view, evidence concerning the circumstances surrounding the contract's formation, including negotiation and prior dealings and conduct, are all admissible to determine whether the contract is "integrated," a finding preliminary to applying the parol evidence rule.[26]

The potentially harsh results that can occur if the parol evidence rule is strictly applied are illustrated by *Union Mutual Life Insurance Co. v. Mowry,*[27] an 1877 United States Supreme Court decision. The agent, in an effort to persuade an individual to apply for insurance, promised the applicant that he would receive notice when each premium was due. This promise was not contained in the policy subsequently issued, and the insured failed to pay the premium when it became due, relying on the promise that notice would be given. The company, having given no notice, declared the policy forfeited. The Supreme Court held the evidence of the prior agreement inadmissible under the parol evidence rule. This strict approach appeared with such sufficient frequency that in 1951 Professor Vance could write that the courts of several states and the federal courts "refuse to receive proof of estoppels arising before or at the inception of the contract on the assumption that the rule of policy known as the parol evidence rule would be thereby violated; and sometimes referring to the parol evidence rule, many other courts refuse to apply the doctrine of equitable estoppel to cases where the insured retained, without reading, his policy which contained the false statements inserted by the insurer's agent."[28]

Recent courts, however, tend to adhere to a more liberal view. In *Harr v. Allstate Insurance Co.,*[29] the New Jersey Supreme Court ruled that "speaking broadly, equitable estoppel is available to bar a defense in an action on a policy even where the estopping conduct arose before or at the inception of the contract, and that the

---

[24] Professor Williston subscribed to the strict view as a general matter, but he did observe that "relaxation of the parol evidence rule is discernible . . . in insurance contracts." 7 *Williston on Contracts* § 900, at 33 (3d ed. Jaeger 1963).

[25] See Rolling v. Miller, 233 So. 2d 723 (La. Ct. App. 1970); Light v. Ohio Cas. Ins. Co., 161 N.W.2d 764 (Mich. Ct. App. 1968).

[26] The more modern view is favored by the *Restatement (Second) of Contracts.* It has received slight attention, however, in insurance cases. An important exception is Darner Motor Sales, Inc. v. Universal Underwriters Ins. Co., 682 P.2d 388 (Ariz. 1984).

[27] 96 U.S. 544, 24 L.Ed. 674 (1877).

[28] William R. Vance, *Handbook on the Law of Insurance* 513–14 (3d ed. Anderson 1951).

[29] 255 A.2d 208 (N.J. 1969).

parol evidence rule does not apply in such situations."[30] In *Darner Motor Sales, Inc. v. Universal Underwriters Insurance Co.,*[31] the Arizona Supreme Court adopted the *Restatement (Second) of Contracts'* definition of integration for standardized contracts, which are used in most insurance transactions: with standardized agreements, the writing is "an integrated agreement with respect to the terms included in the writing."[32] This means that collateral terms which do not contradict the writing are *always* admissible to supplement the writing. Also, as understood by that court, the rule it adopted "will relieve the insured from certain clauses of an agreement" in proper circumstances.[33] The rule contemplates that the insurer might be estopped to assert that it or its agent did not enter into an oral agreement — even one prior to the formation of the written contract and inconsistent with the terms of the writing.[34]

Harr and *Darner Motor Sales* indicate the path of the law's probable evolution. In most cases, the parol evidence rule will not present a serious barrier to showing coverage inconsistent with the literal language of the policy. As is evident from the foregoing discussion, one reason for this is that the role of the parol evidence rule in determining the terms of standardized agreements is changing, largely under the influence of the *Restatement (Second) of Contracts.* Also, it is well settled that the parol evidence rule does not proscribe the admission of evidence to interpret a writing. Thus, if a writing is ambiguous — and insurance policies often are — parol evidence is admissible to explain what the terms mean.[35] Nor does the parol evidence rule prevent the admission of evidence for the purpose of showing fraud, duress, mistake, or any other cause that might invalidate a contract.[36] Finally, the parol evidence rule does not apply to subsequent modifications of a contract, even oral ones. It only precludes the introduction of communications occurring in the period prior to or contemporaneous with the contract's formation. If after an insurance policy is issued the parties make an oral or written contract to modify it, the parol evidence rule will not prevent enforcement of the modification.[37] When these principles are viewed in their totality, it is apparent that in only a few instances will the parol evidence rule be used successfully to confine the coverage of insurance contracts to the literal terms of the policy.

---

[30] 255 A.2d at 218.

[31] 682 P.2d 388 (Ariz. 1984).

[32] *Restatement (Second) of Contracts* § 211(1).

[33] 682 P.2d at 399.

[34] 682 P.2d at 400–01.

[35] See, e.g., Blount v. McCurdy, 593 S.W.2d 468 (Ark.Ct.App. 1980); Carter v. Hochman, 74 Cal. Rptr. 667 (Cal. Ct. App. 1969); Michigan Mut. Liab. Co. v. Hoover Bros., Inc., 237 N.E.2d 754 (Ill. App. Ct. 1968).

[36] *Restatement (Second) of Contracts* § 214(d) (1981).

[37] See Clarke v. Progressive Am. Ins. Co., 469 So. 2d 319 (La. Ct. App. 1985). In the same term that the United States Supreme Court decided *Mowry,* discussed above, the court also decided *Knickerbocker Life Ins. Co. v. Norton,* 96 U.S. 234 (1877). In that case, the court held that the company's agents could, after the contract was formed, waive a condition in the contract requiring payment of premiums or notes at the policy's maturity to prevent the policy from becoming void. Whether the waiver occurred could be proved, the court held, with parol evidence.

§ 62   Limitations on Coverage: Generally

The subject of limitations on coverage is of great concern to insurers and insureds alike. Through explicit language, insurers seek to constrain the scope of coverage to particular risks. As discussed in Chapter 5, the policy will explicitly state who is covered and what interests are protected. Such a statement, by negative inference, denies coverage to certain persons and interests; this can be viewed, then, as an explicit limitation on coverage.

Explicit limitations can appear either in the affirmative grants of coverage or in specific limitations on those affirmative grants. The preceding sections discussed the affirmative grants of coverage in insurance policies. These coverage provisions, however, sometimes set forth explicit limitations on the coverage. For example, an insurance policy may state that it covers liability "arising out of the ownership, maintenance, or use of a motor vehicle."[1] This phrase serves to state affirmatively what the policy covers; at the same time, however, it expressly limits the coverage. The line between coverage and noncoverage is drawn at the point where the "use" of the motor vehicle ceases. Also, the requirement that the loss "arise out of" the use imposes a significant limitation on coverage.

Even more significant in the typical insurance policy is the set of "exclusions" or "exceptions" to coverage, which carve out areas in the affirmative grant of coverage where no coverage will be provided. A policy may cover all damage to property, but except damage caused by a nuclear accident or by war. The source of these limitations, which are construed strictly against the insurer, is the insurance contract itself.

Another explicit limitation on coverage which should not be overlooked is the pecuniary limitation. A life insurance policy will state a specified amount of coverage; this is an express limitation on coverage. A home will be insured for damages not in excess of a specified amount; this explicit limitation will be enforced, even if the house is totally destroyed and its actual market value is more than the designated limit. Liability insurance will contain a pecuniary limitation; if a judgment against the insured exceeds this amount, the insured is personally responsible for the excess.[2]

Finally, public policy often gives rise to implicit limitations on coverage. These judicially-recognized limitations have no clear referent in the express language of the policy, but they are just as binding on the parties.

§ 62A   Explicit Limitation: Duration of Coverage

[a]   Commencement of Coverage

An insurance policy is a contract. Therefore, as a general rule, the coverage under an insurance policy commences when the contract is formed or at such other time

---

[1] See § 136A, *infra*.

[2] This limitation ordinarily does not apply to the costs of defense. See § 95, *infra*.

specifically designated in the contract. It is well settled that the parties can contract for insurance to begin on a particular date.[1]

Because insurance is designed to cover fortuitous loss only,[2] it is often said that one cannot insure against the consequences of an event which has already occurred or already begun. The logic of this statement is that once something has or is occurring, it is a certain event, and once risk is eliminated, no contract of insurance can exist.[3] This general statement is subject to two caveats. First, it is common in liability insurance for an insured to purchase coverage for claims made against the insured during the current year arising out of past events.[4] The assumption, however, is that although the event has occurred the loss, from the perspective of the liability insured, is unknown at the time of contracting and that the claim will be filed during the coverage period is uncertain. Second, while extremely unusual, some contracts styled as insurance contracts have been sold for past losses. A prominent recent example is the sale of an insurance policy in 1981 by a consortium of insurers to MGM Grand Hotels, Inc. for claims arising out of a 1980 fire in Las Vegas that killed 85 people and injured approximately 1,000 more.[5] Whether such a contract is properly considered insurance is doubtful, although it can be argued that the insurance in the MGM example was provided against an uncertain *amount* of liability in circumstances where some liability was certain.

The contract often specifies that the insurer will pay for losses accruing after the date of the policy's issuance, although it is also common for insurers to issue binders providing temporary coverage from the time of the application until the policy is issued or the application rejected.[6] In life insurance, the commencement of coverage is sometimes linked to the date of the policy's delivery or other conditions (such as delivery while the applicant is in good health). Coverage does not become effective until all of the conditions are met.[7] It is also common for the policy to state

---

[1] See Watts v. Life Ins. Co. of Ark., 782 S.W.2d 47 (Ark.App. 1990) (provision of group accidental death policy stating that it was effective on the first day of the month following approval of application did not violate public policy and was unambiguous); Hartford Ins. Co. v. Surrency, 537 So. 2d 208 (Fla. Dist. Ct. App. 1989).

[2] For discussion of the fortuity requirement, see § 63, *infra*.

[3] See, e.g., SCA Services, Inc. v. Transportation Ins. Co., 646 N.E.2d 394 (Mass. 1995); Leafland Group-II, Montgomery Towers Ltd. Partnership v. Insurance Co. of N. Am., 881 P.2d 26 (N.M. 1994).

[4] See § 62A[e], *infra*.

[5] The hotel paid $39 million for $170 million in coverage; the insurers expected to get huge returns on investments during what they believed would be a lengthy litigation process. MGM settled the lawsuit sooner than the insurers expected, and MGM eventually had to sue the insurers to collect. The insurers ultimately paid $87.5 million of MGM's total obligation. *New York Times*, June 9, 1986, p. 23, c. 5–6. See National Can Corp. v. Industrial Comm'n, 500 N.E.2d 437 (Ill. App. Ct. 1986) (parties can designate date on which coverage begins, including antecedent date).

[6] See Klopp v. Keystone Ins. Cos., 595 A.2d 1 (Pa. 1991) (absent defect in application process, policy is deemed effective from date binder is issued); Watts v. Life Ins. Co. of Ark., 782 S.W.2d 47 (Ark.Ct.App. 1990). For more discussion of binders, see § 33, *supra*.

[7] See G.P. Enterprises, Inc. v. Jackson Nat'l Life Ins. Co., 509 N.W.2d 780 (Mich. Ct. App. 1993).

that coverage is provided as of the date of the application. This designation entails some unfairness, in that the insurer was free to reject the application and thus deny coverage during the period between the submission of the application and its rejection. If the application is approved, the insurance is, in effect, "back-dated." This gives the insurer the benefit of the insured's premium during this interval without providing any coverage. An essentially identical problem exists with respect to binders; the problem and its solution are discussed in a previous section.[8]

Occasionally the date that the coverage commences is not the same as the date on the face of the policy. For example, if the policy is one that becomes effective on delivery and the delivery did not occur on the date stated on the face of the policy, a discrepancy exists, and the question is whether coverage expires on the anniversary of the date of delivery or the date on the policy's face. Most decisions treat the date stated in the policy as the controlling date.[9] This rule is one of convenience: the delivery date will not be recorded on the policy, and the date on the policy's face is easy to ascertain. The objection to this approach is that the insured's first premium buys less than a full term's coverage; if the policy's stated anniversary date is January 1 and the policy becomes effective upon delivery on January 5, the insured obtains only 360 days of coverage for the first year's premium payment. This means that some discrimination occurs since insureds receive different amounts of coverage for the same premium. For this reason, a few courts have held that the anniversary of the policy is the date on which the policy became effective, such as the delivery date, despite the existence of an earlier date stated in the policy.[10]

Determining the date the policy commences is important to a number of questions, such as the running of the incontestability period, the deadline for the exercise of options under the policy, and the policy's termination date.

[b] Termination of Coverage

Insurance coverage can terminate for any number of reasons, including nonpayment of premiums and the insured's misrepresentation, concealment, or breach of warranty. With respect to termination on account of the insured's misrepresentation, concealment, or breach of warranty, some courts hold that the insurer need not do anything to invalidate the coverage. Other courts hold that the insurer only acquires the option to invalidate the policy and must exercise its election to cancel the policy to terminate the coverage.[11] Whatever the analysis, the policy terminates on the date of the breach of warranty, the misrepresentation, or the concealment. If the misrepresentation or concealment occurred in the application, the insurer is entitled to rescind the policy, which is tantamount to saying that the policy "terminated" before coverage even began.

---

[8] See § 33, *supra.*

[9] See, e.g., D&P Terminal, Inc. v. Western Life Ins. Co., 368 F.2d 743 (8th Cir. 1966); Olsen v. Federal Kemper Life Assur. Co., 700 P.2d 231 (Or. 1985); Juster v. John Hancock Mut. Life Ins. Co., 260 N.W. 493 (Minn. 1935); Carpenter v. Besco Corp., 482 So. 2d 42 (La. Ct. App. 1986).

[10] See, e.g., Lentin v. Continental Assur. Co., 105 N.E.2d 735 (Ill. 1952); Dougherty v. Mutual Life Ins. Co. of N.Y., 44 S.W.2d 206 (Mo. Ct. App. 1931).

[11] See generally 6A APPLEMAN § 4149 (1972).

Of course, if the insured fails to pay a premium when due, the coverage terminates on the last day of the period for which a premium was paid. Grace periods might lengthen the time allowed to pay an overdue premium, but grace periods do not lengthen the period of coverage. In personal insurance, grace periods might have the effect of extending the duration of the policy's coverage if a loss occurs during the grace period while a premium remains unpaid. The insured pays for this coverage, however, because the premium is deducted from the proceeds payable. If the premium is not paid within the grace period, the coverage terminates on the last day of the period for which the premium was paid.[12]

When an insurance contract has been fully performed, the parties' duties are discharged and the contract terminates. For example, if the insurer agrees to extend coverage to the house of the insured for any loss occurring during the 1988 calendar year, the policy is fully performed — whether or not a loss occurs — at the end of the calendar year, and the coverage terminates by its own terms. The parties might mutually agree to renew the policy by extending it for another year, but neither party is obligated to do so. The renewal agreement is a new contract entered into by insurer and insured, and its validity will be tested against all of the normal requirements for forming a contract (i.e., offer and acceptance, consideration, statute of frauds, capacity, definiteness).

Generally speaking, an insurer is not obligated either to notify the insured that the coverage has expired by its own terms or to renew the coverage automatically.[13] However, statutes in some states for some kinds of insurance require the insurer to notify the insured that the policy term has expired and the policy needs to be renewed. Moreover, the parties can agree that the insurer will notify the insured when the coverage expires. Also, a course of dealing with a particular insured may create an expectation that notice will be given, and some courts will protect the insured who fails to renew the policy when the insurer should have provided such notice but did not do so. Finally, agents acting within the scope of their authority might bind the company to give notice otherwise not required. Since agents often handle policy renewals, this is a fertile area for allegations that the agent has bound the company in ways that the company did not expect or intend.

[c] Cancellation of Coverage

[1] General Principles

One of the defenses an insurer might assert in resisting a claim for payment of proceeds is that the policy has been canceled, which causes the coverage to terminate. Coverage can be canceled in four ways. First, an insurance contract, like any contract, can be rescinded by mutual agreement of the parties. Second, an insured has an implicit right to cancel a policy unilaterally at the end of a premium period by simply refusing to pay the next premium. Third, an insured may also have an

---

[12] See § 72, *infra*.

[13] See, e.g., Mardirosian v. Lincoln Nat'l Life Ins. Co., 739 F.2d 474 (9th Cir. 1984); Kapahua v. Hawaiian Ins. and Guar. Co., 447 P.2d 669 (Haw. 1968). See also Annot., *Insured's Right of Action for Arbitrary Nonrenewal of Policy, Where Insurer Has Option Not To Renew,* 37 A.L.R.4th 862 (1985).

explicit right under the contract to terminate the insurance policy unilaterally. Fourth, an insurer often has the right to terminate the policy unilaterally, although such a right is sometimes restricted by statute.

[2] Unilateral Cancellation

Any number of circumstances might justify the insurer in canceling an insurance policy. The insurer always has the right to terminate a policy because of the insured's misrepresentation or concealment at the time of contract formation. This right has long been recognized as a part of the common law of contracts. Similarly, if the insured breaches a warranty, the insurer has not only a defense to coverage but also a reason to cancel the coverage unilaterally. Also, even if the insurance contract does not say so explicitly (as it usually will), the insurer has the right to terminate the coverage if the insured does not pay the premium. Absent the existence of one of the foregoing justifications for canceling a policy, the explicit reservation in the policy of the right to cancel, or the grant of such a right by statute, the insurer has no authority to unilaterally cancel it during its term.

Unlike the insurer, the insured usually can unilaterally cancel the policy at any time. No consideration is required to effect the cancellation; as explained by one court, "[t]he insurance contract . . . is a continuing obligation by the insurance company to pay benefits, subject to the unilateral power of termination by the insured."[14] The insured always has an option not to renew a policy upon its termination date. In a policy where the premiums are paid periodically, the insured has the ability to terminate the coverage unilaterally by refusing to pay the premium when due. This does not mean, of course, that the insured can recoup the premium for the period that the insurer has been on the risk. However, the insured typically can withdraw from unperformed portions of the contract. Furthermore, statutes or administrative regulations in most states allow the applicant for insurance ten days after the delivery of the policy to cancel the coverage without any obligation to the insurer. This regulation is designed to protect the consumer who has second thoughts after applying for insurance and to allow the consumer an opportunity to read the coverage before being finally bound. This regulation essentially permits rescission at the insured's option if the insured makes a choice to rescind within the first ten days of the policy's life.

All of the foregoing methods of cancellation exist even if no explicit reference to them exists in the insurance contract itself. However, policies often specify cancellation rights as well. Most property and liability policies contain a clause allowing either the insured or the insurer to cancel the policy by giving written notice to the other party. These provisions typically state conditions to an effective cancellation, such as giving the proper notice or refunding the premiums. When the contract gives a party the right to cancel the policy, the consent of the other is not necessary to effect the cancellation.

In life insurance, policies usually do not have cancellation provisions. Because of the substantial reliance of insureds and their beneficiaries on the security afforded by life insurance, insurers have no right to cancel such policies, except for the

---

[14] Coe v. Farmers New World Life Ins. Co., 257 Cal. Rptr. 411, 415 (Cal. Ct. App. 1989).

reasons recognized at common law (such as fraud and misrepresentation) and for nonpayment of premiums. The insured needs no explicit cancellation right in life insurance, since coverage can be terminated by the insured's refusal to pay the next premium. In whole life insurance, the policies typically contain provisions authorizing the insured to "surrender" the policy and receive the policy's cash value and a refund of the unearned premium.

Policies that explicitly authorize the insured's termination of the policy typically require the insured to give written notice of the cancellation to the insurer. Unless a time is specified for the effective date of the coverage's termination, the cancellation is effective upon receipt by the insurer. Upon cancellation, the insured is ordinarily entitled to receive a refund of the unearned premium (meaning that portion of the premium which has not yet been "allocated" to the risk; this will be less than an amount proportionate to the period of coverage canceled). If the insured has second thoughts after canceling the policy, the insured might seek the insurer's agreement to ignore the notice of cancellation. If the insurer's agreement is forthcoming, the cancellation is negated.

If the insurer after receiving a cancellation accepts premiums from the insured, the insurer will be estopped to claim that the policy was canceled. If the insurer cancels the policy and returns only the unearned portion of the premium, the insurer will be liable for losses occurring prior to the date of the cancellation. If the insurer wishes to cancel the policy from its inception for a reason that voids the entire policy (such as fraud, misrepresentation, or breach of warranty), it is necessary for the insurer to return the entire premium. In other words, a cancellation might be prospective only, in which case the unearned premium must be returned, or a cancellation might be in the nature of a rescission, in which event the parties — including the insured — are entitled to be put in the place they were in before the contract was formed.

The operation of the rules requiring a refund of the unearned premium in the event of prospective cancellation and of the entire premium in the event of rescission is illustrated by *Dairyland Insurance Co. v. Kammerer,*[15] a 1982 Nebraska case. On March 5, 1980, the insurer, through one of its agents, issued a binder to the insured on an automobile. On March 27, the car, while being operated by a third person with the insured's permission, was involved in an accident causing injuries to a third party. On April 10, the insurer sent the insured a notice of cancellation, effective April 27, and refunded the unearned portion of the premium. The insurer contended that the policy was void ab initio because the insured had failed to disclose that the driver of the vehicle at the time of the accident resided in the insured's home and was therefore a member of the household. The court stated that the insurer, when it learned of the fraud, had two options: either to cancel the policy from its inception and return the entire premium or to waive the alleged fraud, cancel the policy prospectively, and keep the premium earned until the date of the cancellation. Under the second option, the insurer would be liable for the damages caused by the accident prior to the cancellation. By failing to return the entire premium, the court held that

---

[15] 327 N.W.2d 618 (Neb. 1982).

the insurer waived its right to rescind the policy and was liable to its insured under the policy.

In *Kammerer,* the court did not discuss the maximum time that the insurer had to exercise its right to rescind. The insurer had knowledge of the fraud at least by the time it filed an answer in the case, but it stood by its decision to retain a portion of the premium. If the insurer intends to cancel a policy, it must return the premium within a reasonable time, which depends on all of the circumstances. For example, in *General Insurance Co. of America v. Killen,*[16] the Alabama Supreme Court held that tender of the return of premium over eighteen months after it was collected and almost a year after the insured filed a suit on the policy was too late.

If the insurer wrongfully cancels the insurance, the insured has essentially three options: (1) considering the policy to be terminated and recovering such damages as the court may allow; (2) instituting an action to obtain specific performance of the contract; (3) waiting until the policy becomes payable and then testing the cancellation in an action on the policy.[17]

[3] Statutory Cancellation Procedures

In the 1960s, general public concern about the availability and affordability of automobile insurance[18] was accompanied by specific criticism of the cancellation procedures utilized by some insurers. This led to statutory regulation in many states limiting insurers' rights to cancel automobile insurance policies. In the 1980s, problems of availability of property and liability insurance prompted a similar legislative response in many states. A typical statute is one that was enacted in Kansas in 1985:

> No policy of property or casualty insurance, other than accident or sickness, used primarily for business or professional needs that has been in effect for 90 days or more may be canceled except for one of the following reasons: (a) nonpayment of premium; (b) the policy was issued because of a material misrepresentation; (c) any insured violated any of the material terms and conditions of the policy; (d) unfavorable underwriting factors, specific to the insured, exist that were not present at the inception of the policy; (e) a determination by the commissioner that continuation of coverage could place the insurer in a hazardous financial condition or in violation of the laws of this state; or (f) a determination by the commissioner that the insurer no longer has adequate reinsurance to meet the insurer's needs.[19]

Whether these statutes preempt an insurer's common law rights to terminate coverage has received different answers in different cases.[20]

---

[16] 120 So. 2d 887 (Ala. 1960).

[17] See generally Annot., *Remedies and Measure of Damages for Wrongful Cancellation of Life, Health, and Accident Insurance,* 34 A.L.R.3d 245 (1970).

[18] See generally § 131, *infra.*

[19] Kan. Stat. Ann. § 40-2,120. Other states have similar statutes. See, e.g., Ariz. Rev. Stat. Ann. § 20-1652; S.C.Code Ann. § 38-75-730; Tenn. Code Ann. § 56-7-1803; Wis. Stat. Ann. § 631.36(2); Wyo. Stat. § 26-35-202.

[20] See, e.g., Klopp v. Keystone Ins. Cos., 595 A.2d 1 (Pa. 1991)(statute does not preempt common law right to rescind auto policy for 60 days after policy is written); Ferrell v.

Most statutes require the insurer to give notice to the insured to effect a cancellation. The purpose of this requirement is to give the insured both the opportunity and sufficient time to procure other insurance to replace the policy being canceled.[21] If the policy terminates according to its own terms (such as for nonpayment of premiums), statutes ordinarily do not require that the insurer give notice of cancellation. The statutory requirements are normally concerned with the situation where the insurer chooses unilaterally to terminate the coverage; this concern is not present where the insured, through an act within the insured's own control, allows the policy to terminate.[22]

The rules often differ when statutorily-mandated insurance is involved. Statutes requiring insureds to have insurance, such as compulsory automobile liability insurance statutes, are based largely on the concern for the interests of third parties injured by drivers lacking adequate assets to pay the damages of the victim. Because obtaining automobile insurance is a condition to operating a vehicle on public highways in many states, state laws often provide that cancellation of an auto policy by the insurer must be accompanied by notice both to the insured and to the state agency in charge of motor vehicle registration. If the notice is not given in the statutorily-prescribed manner, the coverage is not canceled, perhaps even if the insured has failed to pay the premium.[23] The purpose of requiring notice to the insured is to give the insured an opportunity to oppose the cancellation or procure a replacement policy. The requirement that notice be given to the motor vehicles department is designed to give the state the chance to take measures that would prevent the insured from driving the vehicle without adequate coverage.

State statutes ordinarily require that the policy's cancellation not become effective until a given number of days elapse. Where the insurer has given such notice and a loss occurs prior to the expiration of the period, coverage exists.[24]

The results in cases where the propriety of the cancellation procedures have been challenged are diverse. Some courts have held that the insurer had no obligation to follow statutory cancellation procedures in circumstances where the insured initiated

---

Columbia Mut. Cas. Ins. Co., 816 S.W.2d 593 (Ark. 1991) (statute does not preempt insurer's common law right to rescind when policy has been in effect less than 60 days and noncompulsory provision of policy is involved); Wisconsin Housing & Economic Development Authority v. Verex Assur., Inc., 480 N.W.2d 490 (Wis. 1992) (statute prohibited mortgage insurer from exercising its common-law right of rescission); Glockel v. State Farm Mut. Auto. Ins. Co., 400 N.W.2d 250 (Neb. 1987) (statute limits but does not eliminate insurer's common-law rights to cancel policy).

[21] See, e.g., Merrimack Mut. Fire Ins. Co. v. Scott, 240 S.W.2d 666 (Ark. 1951).

[22] See, e.g., King v. Guardian Life Ins. Co. of Am., 686 F.2d 894 (11th Cir. 1982); but see Miller v. Reis, 460 A.2d 210 (N.J. Super. Ct. App. Div. 1983).

[23] See Hales v. North Carolina Ins. Guar. Ass'n, 445 S.E.2d 590 (N.C. 1994); Moore v. Scottsdale Ins. Co., 450 S.E.2d 198 (Ga. 1994); Automobile Club Ins. Co. v. Jackson, 865 P.2d 965 (Idaho 1993).

[24] E.g., Maryland Cas. Co. v. Baker, 200 S.W.2d 757 (Ky. 1947); Pennsylvania Nat'l Mut. Cas. Ins. Co. v. Person, 297 S.E.2d 337 (Ga. Ct. App. 1982); La Salle Cas. Ins. Co. v. American Underwriters, Inc., 269 N.E.2d 563 (Ind. Ct. App. 1971).

the policy's cancellation.[25] On the other hand, some cases, giving weight to the public policy underlying the requirement for giving notice to state officials, have held a cancellation requested by the insured ineffective where state officials were not notified.[26] Courts do agree that if the cancellation is initiated by the insurer, failure to send notice to the insured or to state government officials will render the cancellation void.[27] In a California case, the failure of the insurer to follow statutory cancellation procedures constituted an automatic renewal of the policy, even though the insured failed to pay the renewal premium in a timely fashion.[28] Statutory specifications of procedures that insurers must follow to cancel a policy are ordinarily applied strictly against the insurer.[29]

In most cancellation cases, no dispute exists over the legitimacy of the cancellation; usually the insurer has a valid reason for terminating coverage. Typically, the dispute is over the procedures followed by the insurer in canceling the policy. The most common targets of the insured's claim that the policy was not properly canceled are the nature and the sufficiency of the notice. Sometimes the insurer and insured dispute whether notice was actually received. In some jurisdictions, it is enough that the insurer establish that under its ordinary business practices the cancellation notice was deposited in the mail.[30] Other jurisdictions, however, require proof of actual delivery to the insured.[31] In these states, the expense of registered or certified mailings and the evidentiary burden of establishing actual notice present additional impediments to insurers seeking to terminate a policy's coverage.[32]

---

[25] E.g., Country-Wide Ins. Co. v. Wagoner, 395 N.Y.S.2d 300 (N.Y. App. Div. 1977), *rev'd on other grounds,* 384 N.E.2d 653 (N.Y. 1978); Hanover Ins. Co v. Eggelton, 453 N.Y.S.2d 898 (N.Y. App. Div. 1982), *aff'd,* 443 N.E.2d 954 (N.Y. 1982); Faizan v. Grain Dealers Mut. Ins. Co., 118 S.E.2d 303 (N.C. 1961); Nationwide Mut. Ins. Co. v. Cotten, 185 S.E.2d 182 (N.C. 1971).

[26] See Midstate Hauling Co. v. Reliable Ins. Co., 437 F.2d 616 (5th Cir. 1971); Nassau Ins. Co. v. Samuels, 436 N.Y.S.2d 762 (N.Y. App. Div. 1981).

[27] E.g., Wausau Ins. Cos. v. Harpaul, 455 N.Y.S.2d 635 (N.Y. App. Div. 1982); Royal Indem. Co. v. Adams, 455 A.2d 135 (Pa. Super. Ct. 1983); Government Employees Ins. Co. v. Concord Gen. Mut. Ins. Co. 458 A.2d 1205 (Me. 1983)

[28] See National Auto. & Cas. Ins. Co. v. California Cas. Ins. Co., 188 Cal. Rptr. 670 (Cal. Ct. App. 1983).

[29] See, e.g., Osborne v. Unigard Indem. Co., 719 S.W.2d 737 (Ky. Ct. App. 1986); Aetna Cas. & Sur. Co. v. Garrett, 296 N.Y.S.2d 12 (N.Y. App. Div. 1968), *aff'd,* 257 N.E.2d 284 (N.Y. 1970); Koehn v. Central Nat'l Ins. Co., 354 P.2d 352 (Kan. 1960); accord, Donarski v. Lardy, 88 N.W.2d 7 (Minn. 1958); but see Westmoreland v. General Accident, Fire & Life Assur. Corp., 129 A.2d 623 (Conn. 1957).

[30] E.g., Feldt v. Union Ins. Co., 726 P.2d 1341 (Kan. 1986) (insurer need only mail notice by certified or registered mail and need not prove actual receipt); Hill v. Allstate Ins. Co., 260 S.E.2d 370 (Ga. Ct. App. 1979); Kyer v. General Cas. Co., 218 N.Y.S.2d 185 (N.Y. App. Div. 1961).

[31] E.g., Citizens Ins. Co. of Am. v. Lemaster, 298 N.W.2d 19 (Mich. Ct. App. 1980) (certified mail receipts signed by relatives of insured in household did not bring about cancellation).

[32] Numerous other issues arise in this area exist, such as the contents of the notice, disputes when the notice was allegedly sent to the wrong address, the type size of the notice, whether the insured has waived a required notice of cancellation, and other matters. See generally

[4] Public Policy Restrictions on Cancellation by the Insurer

Even though the insurance policy may give the insurer the right to cancel the policy, some recent cases have held that for reasons of public policy it may constitute a breach of contract for a liability insurer to exercise the cancellation provision. In *L'Orange v. Medical Protective Co.,*[33] a medical malpractice liability insurer which had continuously insured a practicing dentist for nearly thirty years canceled the dentist's policy immediately after he had testified under subpoena in a malpractice suit resulting in a $25,000 verdict against another dentist, who was covered by a policy of medical malpractice insurance issued by the same company. The insurer complied with the notice requirements and refunded the unearned premium. The insured alleged that the policy was canceled to injure the insured and to intimidate him against testifying in future lawsuits. The court held that the need for expert testimony in medical malpractice cases plus the reluctance of medical professionals to testify against their peers rendered the public policy against intimidating a witness compelling. If insurers were allowed to terminate coverage for such a reason, it would be unlikely that witnesses could be found for plaintiffs in medical malpractice actions. Therefore, the court reversed the trial court's dismissal of the complaint for failure to state a claim.

The difficulties that cancellation can cause for insureds are substantial. Imagine a business that has a policy of liability insurance with an insurer. The policy covers claims filed against the insured during the policy period, and the policy gives the insurer the right to cancel the policy on ten days notice. After taking out the insurance, the insured sells two thousand widgets, and within a few weeks, the insured learns that it is being sued for ten accidents caused by defects in the widgets. The insured ceases further sales of the widgets. After receiving notice of the claims, the insurer, although agreeing to provide coverage for the claims already filed, cancels the policy, leaving the insured without coverage for other claims virtually certain to follow. Moreover, with the knowledge of the hazard in the widgets, it will be impossible for the business to obtain insurance from another company. Despite the hardship, most courts have held that the insurer may cancel the policy.[34] However, as discussed earlier, statutes recently enacted in some states may limit the insurer's right to cancel in such circumstances.[35]

Annot., *Cancellation of Compulsory or "Financial Responsibility" Automobile Insurance,* 44 A.L.R.4th 13 (1986); Annot., *What Constitutes Waiver by Insured or Insured's Agent of Required Notice of Cancellation of Insurance Policy,* 86 A.L.R.4th 886 (1994); Annot., *Actual Receipt of Cancellation Notice Mailed by Insurer as Prerequisite to Cancellation of Insurance,* 40 A.L.R.4th 867 (1985); Annot., *Construction, Application, and Effect of Clause That Liability Insurance Policy May Be Canceled By Insured By Mailing To Insurer Written Notice Stating When Thereafter Such Cancellation Shall be Effective,* 11 A.L.R.4th 456 (1982).

[33] 394 F.2d 57 (6th Cir. 1968).

[34] See Scott v. Keever, 512 P.2d 346 (Kan. 1973); Silver Eagle Co. v. National Union Fire Ins. Co., 423 P.2d 944 (Or. 1967); see Annot., *Liability Insurer's Unconditional Right to Cancel Policy as Affected by Considerations of Public Policy,* 40 A.L.R.3d 1439 (1971).

[35] See § 62A[c][3], *supra.* These statutes specify the grounds on which insurers can cancel policies. One of the grounds sometimes listed is that the insurer's risk has substantially increased; arguably, substantial "losses" do not necessarily equate with increased risk.

In a case like *L'Orange*, would it have made a difference to the outcome if the insurer, instead of canceling the coverage immediately after his testimony, had waited until the policy was up for renewal and had chosen not to renew it at that time? In *Gahres v. Phico Insurance Co.*[36] a 1987 Virginia case, a medical malpractice insurer failed to win approval from the insurance department for a rate increase. When existing policies were ready for renewal, the insurer refused to renew its policies. The insureds argued that the insurer owed a good faith duty to renew the policies, but the court disagreed:

> Murphy[37] and other cases plaintiffs cite are inapposite. Murphy concerned an insurer's exercise of a cancellation clause. Here, however, PHICO has exercised its rights under a non-renewal clause. This difference is significant. When an insurance company exercises its rights under a cancellation clause, there is, then existing, a contractual relationship between the parties. By contrast, when an insurance company chooses not to renew a policy, it has already fully performed the contract; there is no obligation that remains or persists beyond the term of the contract.[38]

The court contrasted other kinds of coverage where the state legislature had imposed a duty on insurers to renew coverage; in the absence of such a legislative mandate in the medical malpractice area, the court was unwilling to impose a good-faith duty to renew on the insurer.[39]

The distinction between cancellation and non-renewal is a subtle one, but the court's appeal in *Gahres* to the legislature to resolve the issue was not so subtle. At the heart of cases like *Gahres* and *L'Orange* is a fundamental public policy question best answered by a legislature or an administrator with delegated authority: the extent to which an insurer that does business in a state must offer certain kinds of coverage and the bases on which the insurer, having chosen to do business, can cancel, terminate, or decide not to renew the coverage. Although courts have and will continue to use "public policy" as a test to decide such questions in tough cases, insurers will no doubt prefer more predictable standards. In the final analysis, courts cannot compel insurers to do business in a state, even if courts can enforce judgments arising out of already-issued policies. If insurers decide, for example, that providing certain kinds of coverage (such as medical malpractice liability or earthquake or hurricane property coverage) is too expensive or that their ability to terminate some insureds or some kinds of coverage is too unpredictable, insurers may opt not to do some kinds of business in some states, and the ramifications to consumers and regional economies more generally will be substantial.

---

[36] 672 F. Supp. 249 (E.D. Va. 1987).

[37] Murphy v. Seed-Roberts Agency, Inc., 261 N.W.2d 198 (Mich. Ct. App. 1977).

[38] 672 F. Supp. at 253.

[39] 672 F. Supp. at 253-54. Other cases are in accord with this result. See, e.g, Gautreau v. Southern Farm Bur., 429 So. 2d 866 (La. 1983); Egnatz v. Medical Protective Co., 581 N.E.2d 438 (Ind. Ct. App. 1991); Coira v. Florida Medical Ass'n, 429 So. 2d 23 (Fla. Dist. Ct. App. 1983).

[d] Reinstatement

Personal insurance policies, such as life, health, and disability, commonly contain provisions allowing the insured to reinstate the policy, in the event it lapses for nonpayment of premiums, by complying with specified conditions. In some states, reinstatement provisions are required by statute. In property and liability insurance, insurers are often willing to reinstate a policy upon the payment of a late premium, and will issue a "reinstatement endorsement" for that purpose. Where the insured has a right under the policy to reinstate it for a given period of time after lapse, this right can be very valuable to the insured, particularly if premiums for new insurance have increased or if equally favorable settlement options (the terms on which the beneficiary can choose to have the proceeds paid) are no longer available.

Reinstatement provisions are not entirely for the insured's benefit, however. Insurers prefer that insureds keep their policies in force; reinstatement is much preferred to letting the policy lapse altogether. In the long run, the insurer earns less profit if it must incur the costs of restoring the business by writing coverage to another person.

Reinstatement procedures are typically less complicated than the procedures for securing new insurance. An insurer may even reinstate the policy without further proof of insurability, although insurers ordinarily reserve the right to require such proof as they deem necessary. A common condition of reinstatement is that the insured pay any premiums past due.

When a policy is reinstated, a question can arise as to whether the reinstated policy is a new contract or a continuation of the old one. For example, if the incontestability period has expired under the policy which lapsed and the reinstated policy is merely a continuation of the old contract, no new incontestability period would run. Yet if the reinstated policy is a new contract, a new incontestability period would exist, and the insured would again be vulnerable to defenses based on fraud, misrepresentation, and breach of warranty that were not available to the insurer before the policy lapsed.

The policy may, of course, answer the question directly by specifying what rights exist upon reinstatement. In property or liability insurance, a reinstatement endorsement may specify whether, for example, the reinstatement occurs without a lapse, the reinstatement occurs with a lapse between the cancellation date and the reinstatement date, or the reinstatement occurs with no lapse subject to the insured's warranty that there have been no claims during the lapse.[40] Absent a specification in the policy, most courts treat the reinstated policy as merely a continuation of the old.[41] This is the most sensible approach. In the usual case, the reinstated policy has the same terms, the same premiums, and the same coverage as the lapsed policy.

----

[40] See Vargas v. Nautilus Ins. Co., 811 P.2d 868 (Kan. 1991).

[41] See, e.g., Bruegger v. National Old Line Ins. Co., 387 F. Supp. 1177 (D.Wyo. 1975), *remanded on other grounds,* 529 F.2d 869 (10th Cir. 1976); American Bankers Ins. Co. v. Farley, 403 S.W.2d 545 (Tex. Ct. App. 1966). But see Hammond v. Missouri Prop. Ins. Placement Facility, 731 S.W.2d 360 (Mo. Ct. App. 1987) (reinstatement of lapsed policy constitutes new contract).

If, however, the insured needs to make new representations to obtain the reinstate-ment, it is fair to treat the policy as a new one with regard to those new representa-tions, and a contestability period would exist for those representations which were not a part of the lapsed policy. Thus, where the reinstatement is procured through fraud or misrepresentation, the reinstated policy should be voidable by the insurer. Under the majority rule, reinstatement "cures" the lapse, except that losses suffered between the time of the lapse and the reinstatement are not covered.

[e] Defining the Time During Which Loss Must Be Suffered

In most situations, determining the time when a loss occurs is easy. In life insur-ance, a loss is suffered when the insured dies. In property insurance, a loss is suffered when some catastrophe befalls the covered property. In other settings, however, the determination is not as simple. In health insurance, one could say that the loss is suffered at the time the illness is contracted or the injury-producing accident occurs; alternatively, one could say that the loss is suffered at the time the medical services are received and charges incurred. In liability insurance, one could say that the loss occurs at the time of the event which created the insured's liability (and even this may be a subject of considerable dispute, as in the case where a long-term exposure to a toxic substance results in the appearance and diagnosis of a disease years later).[42] Alternatively, one could say that the loss occurs at the time the claim is filed against the insured. In each of these examples, if coverage is provided for a limited term, how one defines when the loss occurs can be determinative of the coverage.

In liability insurance, liability insurers have traditionally provided coverage on an "occurrence" basis, but for a period in the 1980s "claims-made" coverage became more prevalent. Also, claims-made coverage is the norm in most professional malpractice insurance.[43]

In essence, occurrence policies protect insureds against liability imposed upon them as damages because of bodily injury or property damage if the insured's policy was in effect when the bodily injury or property damage occurred. Coverage does not depend on when the act or neglect causing the damage took place, the time that the act or neglect was discovered,[44] the time that a claim was filed with the insurer, or the time that liability is actually imposed. Under occurrence-based liability policies, the time of occurrence is when the bodily injury or property damage occurs.[45] In most losses, the damage occurs at the same time as the event; so it is sometimes said that occurrence policies provide coverage if the event insured against takes place during the policy period, regardless of when the claim is presented.[46] In some cases, the time of the damage may be far removed from the time of the event (or

---

[42] This question is discussed in § 65[e], *infra.*

[43] See generally Susan M. Popik, *Introduction to the CGL Policy Form: Occurrence ver-sus Claims-Made Policy Forms,* 658 PLI/Comm 37 (May-June 1993).

[44] Chas. T. Main, Inc. v. Fireman's Fund Ins. Co., 551 N.E.2d 28 (Mass. 1990).

[45] See Tacker v. American Family Mut. Ins. Co., 530 N.W.2d 674 (Iowa 1995).

[46] See Sentinel Ins. Co., Ltd. v. First Ins. Co. of Haw., Ltd., 875 P.2d 894 (Haw. 1994); Hasbrouck v. St. Paul Fire and Marine Ins. Co., 511 N.W.2d 364 (Iowa 1993).

exposure or accident), and this raises difficult problems discussed in a later section.[47] But the essential issue for occurrence-based coverage is identifying when the property damage or bodily injury occurred. Thus, when a stone contractor negligently installed a fireplace during the policy period but the actual fire damage did not occur until after the policy expired, the "occurrence" took place on the date of the fire, rather than the date of the wrongful or negligent act.[48]

In contrast, claims-made policies provide coverage if the act or neglect is discovered and brought to the insurer's attention during the policy's term, regardless of when the act occurred.[49] Unlike an occurrence policy where the insured event is keyed to the time of the damage, which emphasizes the time of the act or neglect, in the claims-made policy the insured event is the filing of the claim itself. Also, the "direction" of coverage differs. Unlike an occurrence policy where no retroactive coverage is provided but potentially unlimited (subject only to the relevant statute of limitations) prospective coverage exists, in a claims-made policy no prospective coverage is provided but potentially unlimited retroactive coverage exists.

In many kinds of ordinary accidents, such as a typical automobile accident, whether the liability coverage is occurrence or claims-made will not matter. If the accident occurs and the claim is filed within the coverage period, it does not matter whether the coverage is occurrence- or claims-based. In other situations, however, the distinction is very significant, often translating into relative disadvantages for occurrence-based coverage when viewed from the insurer's perspective.

First, when writing insurance on an occurrence basis, insurers rely in part on state statutes of limitations to restrict their exposure. For example, if the insurer issues policies in a state that has a three-year statute of limitations for torts, the insurer reasonably expects that for a 1992 policy all claims will be made under the policy by 1995; subsequent claims against the insured will fail due to the barring effect of the statute of limitations. However, in recent years, state statutes of limitations have become a less reliable tool for limiting insurer liability. Expansion of the bases on which the statutes are tolled and the doctrines under which the running of the statutes are delayed have with respect to some kinds of claims forced insurers to pay proceeds many years after the periods for which the premiums were collected. In this respect, the claims-made policy is advantageous to the insurer because it obviates the insurer's need to rely on the state statutes of limitations for an outer limit on the insurer's exposure.

---

[47] See § 65[e], *infra*.

[48] See Friendship Homes, Inc. v. American States Ins. Cos., 450 N.W.2d 778 (N.D. 1990).

[49] See, e.g., National Union Fire Ins. Co. v. Talcott, 931 F.2d 166 (1st Cir. 1991); Textron, Inc. v. Liberty Mut. Ins. Co., 639 A.2d 1358 (R.I. 1994); Concord Hosp. v. New Hampshire Medical Malpractice Joint Underwriting Ass'n, 633 A.2d 1384 (N.H. 1993); Chas. T. Main, Inc. v. Fireman's Fund Ins. Co., 551 N.E.2d 28 (Mass. 1990). In Employers Ins. of Wausau v. Bodi-Wachs Aviation Ins. Agency, Inc., 39 F.3d 138 (7th Cir. 1994), the court held that under a professional liability policy the claim was not made until the insured was actually sued for damages. The claim was not made when the agent was named in a declaratory judgment action seeking a determination of coverage, or when the claimant informed the liability insurer of a possible negligence claim against the insured.

Another disadvantage of the occurrence policy is the problem of the long "tail," the lapse of time between the date of the act or neglect and the time the claim is made. For example, a professional may commit an act of malpractice in one year, but the consequences may not be apparent until several years later. Similarly, in progressive disease cases, it is often difficult to determine exactly when the essential causal event in the progression of the disease occurred. The uncertainty in knowing when the loss occurred and the lapse of time between an identifiable event and the loss prevents the insurer from accurately matching premiums against proceeds paid, and this puts the insurer at risk that inflation or the emergence of new theories of liability in tort law may make the premiums collected inadequate to pay the future claims. Writing insurance on a claims-made basis helps the insurer accurately calculate the premiums: if for a certain risk x number of claims were filed last year and the year before, the insurer can be reasonably confident that the same number of claims will be filed this year, and the insurance can be priced accordingly, without worry that inflation or new theories of liability will render the premium inadequate.[50] Stated otherwise, if an occurrence-based liability policy is priced accurately, converting the basis of liability to claims-made should enable the premium to be reduced because the maximum tail exposure is limited to one year, unlike an occurrence policy which has theoretically unlimited tail exposure.

The claims-made policy is not without disadvantages of its own. One disadvantage is that claims-made policies provide no prospective coverage for the professional who wishes to go out of business and yet have coverage in the future for events occurring during the last years of practice. This problem, however, can be remedied through the purchase of "tail" coverage, which protects the insured who has purchased a claims-made policy against claims made after the policy terminates. In effect, tail coverage converts a claims-made policy into occurrence-based coverage.

Another disadvantage of the claims-made policy is that it provides unlimited retroactive coverage. As a result, insurers typically insert a requirement that the act or neglect resulting in the claim must have occurred after a specified date. This limits the retroactivity of a policy, but it creates the possibility of a gap in coverage when insureds change from one claims-made policy to another: if subsequent policies use a later retroactive date (for example, if Policy A covering calendar year 1996 with a "retro date" of January 1, 1994 is replaced with Policy B covering calendar year 1997 with a retro date of January 1, 1995), an occurrence during calendar year 1994 giving rise to a claim in 1997 would not be covered under either Policy A or Policy B. This was the essence of the problem in *Sparks v. St. Paul Ins. Co.*,[51] a 1985 New Jersey decision, where the court held retroactive limitations in a claims-made policy invalid. Between June and August 1980, the insurer received notice of the insured's legal malpractice, which had been committed in 1979 and led to the entry of default judgments against the insured's clients in 1980 and 1981. The insured had claims-made coverage in effect for three successive one-year periods from November 6, 1976 to November 6, 1979, with retro dates in each of November 6, 1976. The court

---

[50] For a discussion of the history of the evolution of claims-made policies, see Zuckerman v. National Union Fire Ins. Co., 495 A.2d 395 (N.J. 1985).

[51] 495 A.2d 406 (N.J. 1985).

held that the first-year policy's retro date, which was the same as the policy's effective date, was "unrealistically narrow"[52] and that as a result the policy should be viewed as "one analogous to an 'occurrence' policy."[53]. In these circumstances, the 1980 notice of the claim was held sufficiently timely to invoke the coverage.[54] The logic of the decision in *Sparks* is not easy to discern, given that an earlier retroactive date in the insured's policy would not have altered the fact that the claim was made after the policy's expiration.

What *Sparks* does evidence is continuing skepticism about the fairness of claims-made coverage. This skepticism is somewhat surprising; except for the situation noted above when an insured wishes to switch policies and in doing so must accept a later retro date, claims-made coverage does not necessitate coverage gaps. An insured who wishes to go out of business can acquire coverage for "tails." An insured who is just beginning his or her business is fully protected by claims-made coverage and does not need a retro date before the policy's effective date. An insured who switches from occurrence coverage to claims-made coverage suffers no gap, assuming the retro date under the claims-made coverage immediately follows the last day of the occurrence coverage. What probably drives the reluctance to embrace claims-made coverage is the realization that the cost-savings made possible by eliminating tail coverage are gained at the detriment of insureds who ordinarily desire (and arguably reasonable expect) coverage for future liabilities arising out of present events. From this perspective, claims-made coverage seems at odds with competition and freedom of contract, given that insureds who desire coverage against future liabilities are "locked" into future purchases of insurance, perhaps even from the same insurer if the insured cannot locate a substitute insurer willing to maintain the insured's first retro date.

These difficulties, plus the fact that consumers often simply do not understand claims-made coverage,[55] have engendered some resistance to the claims-made policy.[56] In *Jones v. Continental Casualty Co.,*[57] the court refused on public policy grounds to enforce a claims-made policy with very limited retroactive coverage. The insurance policy in *Jones* only covered the insured retroactively if the error, omission, or negligent act was covered by a prior policy issued by that insurer.[58] But other courts have upheld claims-made policies with limited retroactive coverage,[59] sometimes noting that the limited retroactive coverage was presumably

---

[52] 495 A.2d at 415.

[53] 495 A.2d at 416.

[54] 495 A.2d at 416.

[55] See Concord Hospital v New Hampshire Medical Malpractice Joint Underwriting Ass'n, 633 A.2d 1384 (N.H. 1993) ("the layperson of average intelligence does not know what 'claims made' refers to.")

[56] See, e.g., St. Paul Fire & Mar. Ins. Co. v. Parzen, 569 F. Supp. 753 (E.D. Mich. 1983) (provision of claims-made policy requiring notice to be given within policiy period is ineffective because it was not reasonably possible for insured to give notice within policiy period).

[57] 303 A.2d 91 (N.J.Super. 1973).

[58] 303 A.2d at 93.

[59] James & Hackworth v. Continental Cas. Co., 522 F. Supp. 785 (N.D. Ala. 1980); Gulf Ins. Co. v. Dolan, Fertig & Curtis, 433 So. 2d 512 (Fla. 1983); Troy & Stalder Co. v. Continental Cas. Co., 290 N.W.2d 809 (Neb. 1980).

accompanied by a premium reduction.[60] In other cases where the policies were said to have ambiguous policy language, courts have refused to enforce the limitations of claims-made coverage, sometimes on the ground that the reasonable expectations of the insured would be disappointed.[61]

Another reason claims-made policies have not become commonplace is that they have been met with regulatory opposition in some states. For example, in 1985 the New York Insurance Department rejected a filing by the Insurance Services Office that proposed modifying the commercial general liability (CGL) form to, among other things, substitute a claims-made approach for an occurrence approach as the trigger of coverage. In its opinion, the Department stated that claims-made coverage "should only be utilized on risks involving long-tail or latent injury exposures where there is a determined availability problem." Also, the Department stated that claims-made coverage "is generally inferior to occurrence coverage and . . . the widespread use of claims-made policy is inappropriate and unnecessary on most exposures."[62]

Despite the criticism of claims-made forms in some circles, most courts have upheld the validity of claims-made policies when challenged on public policy grounds.[63] The importance of matching premiums with risks has been highly influential to courts considering the validity of such forms. One court noted that it is not against the public interest for the insurer to limit coverage when otherwise premiums would be unaffordable.[64] As long as consumers have access to a clear explanation of the limitations inherent in claims-made coverage and alternative occurrence coverage is available, no good reason exists for not having claims-made coverage available to consumers.[65]

---

[60] See Stine v. Continental Cas. Co., 349 N.W.2d 127 (Mich. 1984); Gereboff v. Home Indem. Co., 383 A.2d 1024 (R.I. 1978); Livingston Parish Sch. Bd. v. Fireman's Fund Am. Ins. Co., 282 So. 2d 478 (La. 1973).

[61] See J.G. Link & Co. v. Continental Cas. Co., 470 F.2d 1133 (9th Cir. 1972), *cert. denied,* 414 U.S. 829 (1973); Sparks v. St. Paul Ins. Co., 495 A.2d 406 (N.J. 1985); Gyler v. Mission Ins. Co., 514 P.2d 1219 (Cal. 1973).

[62] See Op. of N.Y. State Ins. Dept., 4 J. of Ins. Reg. 39 (1986).

[63] See, e.g., Scarborough v. Travelers Ins. Co., 718 F.2d 702 (5th Cir. 1983); Brander v. Nabors, 443 F. Supp. 764 (N.D. Miss.), *aff'd,* 579 F.2d 888 (5th Cir. 1978); Soliva v. Shand, Morahan & Co., Inc., 345 S.E.2d 33 (W.Va. 1986); Zuckerman v. National Union Fire Ins. Co., 495 A.2d 395 (N.J. 1985); Stine v. Continental Cas. Co., 349 N.W.2d 127 (Mich. 1984); Gulf Ins. Co. v. Dolan, Fertig and Curtis, 433 So. 2d 512 (Fla. 1983); Gereboff v. Home Indem. Co., 383 A.2d 1024 (R.I. 1978); Mission Ins. Co. v. Nethers, 581 P.2d 250 (Ariz. Ct. App. 1978).

[64] See Brander v. Nabors, 443 F. Supp. 764 (N.D. Miss.), *aff'd,* 579 F.2d 888 (5th Cir. 1978).

[65] It appears that occurrence policies will continue to dominate the liability insurance market for the foreseeable future. But insurers will probably continue to have a strong interest in claims-made coverage for insureds with high-risk or long-tail exposures (such as lawyers, doctors, and other professionals). For additional discussion of claims made coverage, see Solomon S. Kroll, *The Professional Liability Policy "Claims Made"* 13 Forum 842 (1978); John K. Parker, *The Untimely Demise of the "Claims Made" Insurance Form? A Critique of Stine v. Continental Casualty Company,* 1983 Det. C. L. Rev. 25; Gerald Kroll, Comment, *The "Claims Made" Dilemma in Professional Liability Insurance,* 22 UCLA L. Rev. 925 (1975).

Although claims-made coverage has no judicial or regulatory impediments in most jurisdictions, one point with respect to claims-made policies remains contentious. Because most claims-made policies require not only that a claim be made during the policy period but also that it be reported to the insurer during that period, the issue is whether the reporting of the claim must actually occur during the policy period or whether some reasonable period of extension must be granted after the termination (either by cancellation or non-renewal) of the claims-made coverage. With respect to policies that are not claims-made, courts have been relatively tolerant of insureds' late notice of loss to insurers.[66] Generally, courts are less tolerant of late notice in claims-made coverage because the reporting of the claim during the policy period is an essential element of the coverage, and many courts have upheld unambiguous reporting requirements.[67] However, some courts have implied that requiring the insured to report the claim within the policy period is void as against public policy,[68] and some states require a thirty- or sixty-day reporting extension after the policy's termination pursuant to administrative regulation[69] or statute.[70]

Finally, although not usually denominated as such, the claims-made characteristics of health insurance gives rise to a substantial coverage issue under most health care plans. If an insured has coverage under a group policy provided by the employer as a part of the employee's compensation, the policy will probably provide that the coverage terminates when the employee's employment terminates. If the employee has developed an illness requiring ongoing medical care, the employee who changes jobs may not be able to qualify for coverage under the eligibility requirements of the new employer's group health insurer. If the former policy pays for charges incurred while the employee is covered (i.e., a claims-made format), the employee may end up with no insurance for a lifetime of medical bills. In addition to this serious coverage gap, the possibility of lost coverage when a person changes employment is now a serious impediment to mobility in labor markets. These problems, of course, do not exist if an employee has the financial means to convert the group policy into a much more expensive individual policy upon the termination of employment, but most cases are less easily resolved. A variant on these problems is that the typical group policy covers employees and their dependents for as long as the dependency continues; if a dependent spouse suffers a disabling injury requiring ongoing medical care and if the injured spouse is later divorced from the

---

[66] See § 81, *infra*.

[67] See, e.g., DiLuglio v. New England Ins. Co., 959 F.2d 355 (1st Cir. 1992); Esmailzadeh v. Johnson & Speakman, 869 F.2d 422 (8th Cir. 1989); Calocerinos & Spina Consulting Engineers, P.C. v. Prudential Reins. Co., 856 F. Supp. 775 (W.D. N.Y. 1994); Textron, Inc. v. Liberty Mut. Ins. Co., 639 A.2d 1358 (R.I. 1994); Zuckerman v. National Union Fire Ins. Co., 495 A.2d 395 (N.J. 1985); Gulf v. Dolan, Fertig & Curtis, 433 So. 2d 512 (Fla. 1983).

[68] See Doctors' Co. v. Insurance Corp. of Am., 864 P.2d 1018 (Wyo. 1993); Burns v. International Ins. Co., 709 F. Supp. 187 (N.D. Cal. 1989), *aff'd,* 929 F.2d 1422 (9th Cir. 1991).

[69] See, e.g., Conn. Agencies Regs. §§ 38a-327- 1(g); N.Y. Comp. Codes R. & Regs., tit. 11 § 73.3(d).

[70] See Pa.Stat.Ann. 40-3405. For a survey of the law of all states on this question, see Barry R. Ostrager & Thomas R. Newman, *Handbook on Insurance Coverage Disputes* 95-100 (7th ed. 1994).

covered spouse, the insurer's payment for medical bills for continuing charges will cease. This problem could be avoided if the injured spouse had his or her own primary coverage, but this may not be feasible if the injured spouse is unemployed and is unable to afford an expensive individual policy.

Courts can deal to some extent with such cases by resorting to interpretation techniques and the doctrine of reasonable expectations,[71] but these solutions tend to depend on the existence of ambiguous policy language which insurers strive mightily to avoid. Furthermore, healthy insureds have a strong incentive to support insurers' effort to keep ill and otherwise high-risk insureds out of their pools, because this increases the cost of insurance to healthy insureds. If all health insurance policies lacked pre-existing condition clauses,[72] the coverage gap discussed here would disappear; such a development would, in effect, make the claims-made aspect of health insurance irrelevant. In eliminating the coverage gap, system-wide costs would go up to some extent, but these costs would be spread across all insureds, which is arguably preferable to requiring only insureds who lose or change jobs or whose dependency relationships change to bear these costs. It is unlikely that the coverage gap will be eliminated without regulatory intervention, and this is one kind of legislative reform which is likely to be adopted sometime in the near future.[73]

§ 62B   Conditions as Explicit Limitations on Coverage

[a]   An Overview

In contract law, a condition is an event uncertain to occur which must occur, unless excused, before performance of a duty becomes due.[1] In traditional parlance, conditions have been divided into two categories — conditions precedent and conditions subsequent. A condition precedent is a condition that must occur *before* a duty is due and owing; a condition subsequent is a condition that must be satisfied in order to avoid the discharge or termination of a duty that is already due and owing. The drafters of the *Restatement (Second) of Contracts* declined to use this traditional distinction. Instead, in the *Restatement (Second)*, conditions are defined as only including condition precedents, and conditions subsequent are dealt with under events that can lead to the discharge of a duty.

In insurance law, the terms warranty and condition precedent are often used interchangeably. As explained by one court:

> [T]he term "warranty" in an insurance contract ordinarily imports an assurance on the part of the policy holder that a certain situation exists or will continue, which diminishes the likelihood that the event insured against will occur; and

---

[71] See §§ 25A, 25D, *supra*.

[72] See § 64[c][2], *infra*.

[73] In 1986, Congress enacted legislation (commonly called "COBRA") which provides some relief for the problem discussed in the text. Severe coverage gaps remain, however. For further details, see § 126, *infra*.

[1] *Restatement (Second) of Contracts* § 224 (1981).

hence "warranty" and "condition precedent" are often used interchangeably to create a condition of the insured's promise.[2]

Conditions precedent purport to state limitations on coverage; therefore, conditions precedent, like all express conditions, must be strictly satisfied. As discussed in a later section, the common law rule on warranties is that warranties must also be strictly satisfied.[3] If one's analysis proceeds no further, one might conclude that no difference exists in the legal ramifications of conditions and warranties. However, warranties are subject to certain mitigating doctrines which do not apply to conditions. Therefore, it is helpful to one's understanding of the coverage of insurance policies to distinguish conditions and warranties, even if all courts and commentators do not make the distinction; this subject is discussed in a later section.[4]

[b] Evidentiary Conditions

Occasionally a condition designed to limit coverage operates in a manner that causes hardship to the insured. The insured's expectations are likely to be disappointed, and an effort will be made to apply or devise a theory that provides coverage to the insured despite failure to satisfy a condition to the insurer's duty to pay. One such theory is found in the evidentiary condition doctrine: if a condition is an "evidentiary condition," it imposes a rule of evidence upon the insured to establish that a loss was caused by a risk that the policy was intended to cover, and failure to satisfy the literal language of the condition will not prevent coverage so long as the insured carries the evidentiary burden.

The evidentiary condition doctrine figures most prominently in disputes over the effect of "visible marks" clauses in theft policies. One example of a burglary endorsement on a businessowner's policy covers loss by burglary defined as "the abstraction of insured property from within the premises by a person making felonious entry or exit therein or therefrom by actual force and violence, evidenced by visible marks made by tools, explosives, electricity, chemicals, or physical damage to the exterior or interior of the premises at the place of such entry or exit."[5] Another example of the definition of "burglary" in a 'Premises Burglary Coverage Form' reads "the taking of Property from inside the 'premises' by a person unlawfully entering or leaving the 'premises' as evidenced by marks of forcible entry or exit."[6]

The purpose of such a clause is to limit coverage to the forcible taking of property by "outsiders," meaning persons other than the insured or those who work for the insured.[7] It is the insured's responsibility to take reasonable steps to secure the

---

[2] Fidelity-Phenix Fire Ins. Co. v. Pilot Freight Carriers, Inc., 193 F.2d 812, 816 (4th Cir. 1952).

[3] See § 101, *infra*.

[4] See § 101[f], *infra*.

[5] *1987 Policy Kit* at 177 (Ed. 05 76).

[6] *Policy Kit* (1995) at 235 (ISO Form CR 00 06 10 90).

[7] Note that in the computer age it is possible for some to commit property crimes by modem, which obviously leave no "visible marks." The computer age, obviously, creates new perils that require new kinds of coverage. See, e.g., Computer Fraud Coverage Form, *Policy Kit* at 236 (ISO Form CR 00 07 10 90).

insured's own property; the insurer does not want to be liable if the insured fails to take such steps, such as locking a door. Moreover, the insurer does not intend to provide coverage for "inside jobs" — thefts by the insured or the insured's employees. It is the responsibility of the insured to maintain safeguards against theft by persons with regular access to areas where property is stored. In the absence of visible marks of forcible entry, it is more likely that property has simply been mislaid or that the insured or an employee appropriated the property.

Although the "visible marks requirement" most commonly appears in theft insurance, it also appears in some accident policies. Some policies contain a provision that the insurer shall not be liable for the insured's death or injury unless there is proof that the death or injury resulted from "external, violent and accidental means" evidenced by a contusion or external and visible sign on the body of the insured, except in cases of drowning or internal injuries revealed by an autopsy. Through such a clause, the insurer seeks to avoid liability for injuries or deaths due to natural causes and for feigned injuries. An insured's claim that an injury was due to an accident is difficult to disprove, but the visible marks requirement gives the insurer some protection against paying proceeds for nonaccidental deaths or injuries.[8]

Although the clauses are drafted with good intentions, sometimes an insured will be burglarized and no visible marks will be left by the burglar, and sometimes insureds will be injured in accidents and no visible marks will be present on their bodies. It is in these cases that courts have sometimes interpreted the visible marks condition as an evidentiary requirement not determinative of coverage. Other courts have enforced the conditions according to their literal terms. Two cases from the property area illustrate the disparate treatment of such clauses.

In *Cochran v. MFA Mutual Insurance Co.*,[9] a 1976 Nebraska case, tools were allegedly stolen from the insured's locked vehicle. The policy excluded coverage for loss of property while unattended in a motor vehicle, "unless the loss is the result of forcible entry into such vehicle" while the doors and windows were closed and locked "provided there are visible signs of forcible entry upon the exterior of such vehicle." No visible marks appeared on the exterior of the vehicle. The insured testified that the vehicle was moved from the location where he had parked it, that all windows and doors had been closed and locked, and that when the vehicle was found, tools were missing and a "jiggle" key was found in the ignition switch. The insured, a locksmith and hardwareman by occupation, testified that the theft had resulted by use of the jiggle key. The insured argued that the loss by use of a jiggle key constitutes a forcible entry within the policy's coverage. The court, however, rejected the argument and opted for a literal application of the policy's language. The visible marks requirement, according to the court, "was intended to be and is a limitation on liability and not an attempt to determine the character of evidence to show liability."[10] Instead of treating the condition as an "evidentiary condition,"

---

[8] See, e.g., Regan v. National Postal Transport Ass'n, 280 N.Y.S.2d 319 (N.Y.Sup. 1967).

[9] 271 N.W.2d 331 (Neb. 1978).

[10] 271 N.W.2d at 333. See Prince Check Cashing Corp. v. Federal Ins. Co., 582 N.Y.S.2d 751 (N.Y. App. Div. 1992)("it is well established that an insurer may require signs of visible force in a policy of insurance for burglary.")

the court treats the condition as "substantive," which is conclusive on the question of coverage.

In contrast to *Cochran* is *Ferguson v. Phoenix Assurance Co.,*[11] a 1962 Kansas case. The insured, who operated a drug store, was insured under a "Storekeepers Burglary and Robbery Policy." The policy purported to cover "loss by safe burglary of money, securities and merchandise," but it excluded loss due to "any fraudulent, dishonest or criminal act by any insured, a partner therein, or an officer, employee, [etc.]" The purpose of the exclusion was to preclude coverage for inside jobs. The exclusion was amended by an attached rider that defined safe burglary as

> the felonious abstraction of insured property from within a vault or safe, the door of which is equipped with a combination lock, located within the premises by a person making felonious entry into such vault or such safe and any vault containing the safe, when all doors thereof are duly closed and locked by all combination locks thereon, provided such entry shall be made by actual force and violence, of which force and violence there are visible marks made by tools, explosives, electricity or chemicals upon the exterior of (a) all of said doors of such vault or such safe and any vault containing the safe, if entry is made through such doors. . . .[12]

The safe in the drug store had two doors, the outer one having a combination lock and the inner door having a key lock. One evening, the insured's store was broken into by forcing the front door open, as evidenced by tool marks. Both doors of the safe were locked. Access was gained to the safe by manipulating the combination lock on the outer door, leaving no visible marks; the inner door was opened by punching out the lock, and the marks of this entry were obvious. Money was removed from the safe, but the insurer denied coverage for this loss on the ground that the visible marks condition of the policy had not been satisfied.

The court rejected the insurer's argument. It reasoned that the condition that there be visible marks upon all the doors of the safe, an unambiguous provision, was "merely evidentiary to show an entry into the safe by actual force and violence."[13] No one denied that a forcible entry had occurred and there was no reason to believe that this burglary was an inside job. In these circumstances, the court ruled that "the 'visible marks' clause imposes a rule of evidence upon the assured to establish that entry was made into the safe by actual force and violence."[14] The court concluded that it would violate the public policy of the state of Kansas to enforce such a condition "beyond the reasonable requirements necessary to prevent fraudulent claims."[15]

Cochran and *Ferguson* are two diametrically opposed approaches to applying the visible marks condition. *Cochran* opts for a rule that enforces plain and clear policy language according to its terms. The advantage of the *Cochran* rule is the certainty

---

[11] 370 P.2d 379 (Kan. 1962).
[12] 370 P.2d at 381.
[13] 370 P.2d at 384.
[14] 370 P.2d at 386.
[15] 370 P.2d at 387.

inherent in a rule that is easy to apply. *Ferguson* opts for a rule that looks to the underlying purpose of the provision and asks whether that purpose is fulfilled in the facts of a given case. If it is apparent that the risks the policy excludes or does not cover have not occurred, such as an inside job or the failure of the owner to secure the premises, this rule refuses to enforce the condition.

The disadvantage of the *Ferguson* approach is that it invites a dispute between insurer and insured in circumstances where the cause of the loss is suspicious. For example, suppose that an employee of the insured burglarizes the insured's warehouse by using a key, leaving behind no visible marks; the employee successfully escapes detection. The insurer, not suspecting the employee, submits a claim to the insurer. The insurer, naturally wary of the claim in the absence of the visible marks, suspects an inside job. If the insurer pays the claim to avoid the dispute, the insurance has essentially been converted to coverage for inside jobs as well, which works to the detriment of all who pay premiums for the same coverage.

Yet the *Cochran* approach has disadvantages as well. It is not true that literal application of the terms of the policy results in less litigation. If visible marks are required, insurer and insured will dispute whether a scratch[16] or a moved bolt or lock[17] constitutes evidence of a forcible entry or a visible mark within the meaning of the policy. Moreover, it is questionable whether treating such clauses as substantive conditions can prevent inside jobs. If an insured similarly situated to the insured in *Cochran* desired to recover upon a feigned claim, the easiest way to ensure a recovery would be to smash a hole in the car's window, thus creating the visible mark.[18] It seems plain that the visible marks requirement cannot deter inside jobs by knowledgeable insureds. It may prevent recovery when the insured fails to secure the premises, but it also prevents recovery when the burglary is accomplished by an extremely effective, efficient thief. If applied rigidly, the *Cochran* approach can lead to entirely displeasing results. In one case, an insured was denied a recovery under a theft policy because of lack of visible marks in circumstances where the thief extorted the safe's combination by holding a pistol to the head of a security guard.[19] In another case, the thief hid in the ceiling of a drugstore during business hours and burglarized the store at night, leaving no visible marks at the place of entry or exit from the store as required by the policy; although visible marks existed where the thief hid in the ceiling, the court denied recovery.[20] In such cases, it is

---

16 Compare McCarty v. Great Cent. Mut. Ins. Co., 78 N.E.2d 176 (Ohio Ct.App. 1947) (screwdriver marks sufficient) with Sydor v. Harris, 480 F. Supp. 804 (E.D. N.Y. 1979) (slight scratches around keyhole of lock cylinder did not constitute visible marks).

17 Compare Abrams v. National Fire Ins. Co., 186 A.2d 232 (D.C. 1962) (turned handle of lock to new position not a mark or sign of forcible entry) with National Sur. Co. v. Silberberg Bros., 176 S.W. 97 (Tex. Ct. App. 1915) (slipping of bolt lock held mark of forcible entry).

18 Once when negotiating with the agent of a mover of household goods, the author was advised that if he packed his own belongings in boxes and the contents were later damaged, the insurance he could purchase would not cover the loss in the absence of visible marks on the exterior of the boxes. The agent volunteered the following advice: if such damage occurs, be sure to kick a hole in the box that contained the damaged goods.

19 See Komroff v. Maryland Casualty Co., 135 A. 388 (Conn. 1926).

20 See Western Cas. & Sur. Co. v. Smith-Caldwell Drug Store, Inc., 506 S.W.2d 116 (Ark. 1974).

clear that the underlying purpose of the requirement is not frustrated and it seems unfair to disappoint the insured's reasonable expectations. Indeed, the doctrine of reasonable expectations [21] was the rationale for the court's decision in *Atwater Creamery Co. v. Western National Mutual Insurance Co.,* [22] where the court agreed with *Cochran* that the clear definition could not be viewed as a rule of evidence, but was uncomfortable with the result in *Cochran* in circumstances where, as in *Ferguson*, it was clear that finding coverage would be consistent with the undisputed underwriting purposes of the visible marks requirement. In *Atwater Creamery*, the court held that the "technical definition of burglary," i.e., the visible marks requirement, would not be interpreted so as to defeat the insured's reasonable expectations, and that the insured did have a reasonable expectation that the policy would cover the loss in question despite the absence of visible marks. [23]

With regard to accident insurance policies that require external and visible marks of injury as a condition to coverage, courts tend to interpret the policies liberally in favor of the insured or the beneficiary. Unusual color of skin, unusual odors, testimony of a physician that by touch the presence of an internal injury could be determined, a nosebleed, water running from the mouth of a person who has just drowned, and other such evidence have been held to constitute external signs of an injury by accident. Also, the marks need not be visible immediately and need not endure. [24]

[c] Some Common Conditions and Their Legal Effects

Insurance policies contain many different kinds of conditions, and a book of this scope cannot begin to cover them all. In this subsection, a few of the common, most frequently litigated conditions are examined. The manner in which courts resolve disputes involving these common conditions illustrates how other kinds of conditions are interpreted and applied in an insurance policy.

[1] Increase of Hazard Clauses

The standard fire insurance policy and many other kinds of property insurance policies state that the insurer shall not be liable for loss occurring "while the hazard is increased by any means within the control or knowledge of the insured." [25] This clause can be viewed as a modern-day warranty. Instead of including a laundry-list of situations in which insureds would forfeit coverage if they failed to take certain risk-reducing measures, insurers now state that insureds lose coverage in the event the hazard is increased. Such a condition is eminently reasonable; even if this provision were not set forth in an insurance policy in express terms, it would be an implied term in the policy that the insured could not do anything to materially increase the risk during the policy's term without forfeiting the coverage. But in articulating an all-encompassing standard, insurers have inevitably interjected a lack of certainty into the scope of coverage, an uncertainty that would not exist if insurers

---

[21] See § 25D, *supra.*

[22] 366 N.W.2d 271 (Minn. 1985).

[23] 366 N.W.2d at 278–79.

[24] See 1A APPLEMAN §§ 364–65 (1981).

[25] *Policy Kit* at 2 (ISO Form PP 00 01 12 89).

drafted coverage by using warranty provisions to identify the situations where coverage would be lost. Moreover, literal application of the clause would result in the elimination of coverage for trivial increases in risk. Thus, courts regulate the impact of the clause, and two rules followed by courts are particularly significant.

If the typical increase of hazard clause were applied according to its terms, "control" and "knowledge" would be viewed as alternative requirements because the two words are separated by "or," not "and." Yet most cases that have considered the force of the clause have held that the insured's knowledge or constructive knowledge is required, and that the insured's mere control is not, by itself, sufficient to eliminate coverage.[26] Thus, a landlord-insured who did not know that the tenant was operating an illegal methamphetamine lab on the leased premises did not lose coverage by virtue of the increase of hazard clause, where there was no evidence that the landlord knew or by exercising ordinary care should have known of the tenant's activity.[27] In another case, the named insureds were held not to have increased the hazard in circumstances where an employee of the insureds turned off a building's water sprinkler system and the insureds did not know this despite the exercise of due diligence in periodically inspecting the system. Even though the insureds were given a reduced rate for having an operable sprinkler system, the court reasoned that the insureds could not have "control" without "knowledge."[28]

Another significant gloss on the increase of hazard clause is the courts' requirement that the increase of hazard constitute a substantial change of circumstances materially increasing the risk. A negligent act that only temporarily increases the risk will not cause the insured to forfeit his coverage.[29] To illustrate, smoking in bed, a relatively common practice, increases the hazard and the risk of a fire loss, but such a loss is covered by a fire insurance policy. Apparently, the increase in hazard is not significant enough. Using kerosene to start a fire in a woodburning stove may be negligent and certainly increases the hazard, but an excessive fire which results will probably be covered by the policy.[30] Storing a small amount of gasoline in one's garage to operate a lawnmower increases the risk that a serious fire will occur in the garage, but this common practice does not suspend the policy's coverage; such a use of a garage is expected and part of the risk that the insurer undertakes. However, filling several forty-gallon garbage cans with gasoline and storing them in the garage during a fuel shortage is not a normal use of a residential

---

[26] See, e.g., Patriotic Ins. Co. of Am. v. Franciscus, 55 F.2d 844 (8th Cir. 1932); Commercial Union Ins. Co. v. Taylor, 312 S.E.2d 177 (Ga. Ct. App. 1983) ("'control' presupposes knowledge and . . . it would be unreasonable to hold that a person had control of a thing of which he had no knowledge.") Compare Industrial Dev. Associates v. Commercial Union Surplus Lines Ins. Co., 536 A.2d 787 (N.J. Super. Ct. App. Div. 1988) (prior fires in pipes known by insured's representative constituted sufficient knowledge of chemical residue in pipes; negligence is not prerequisite to application of increase of hazard clause).

[27] See Farmers Ins. Co. of Oregon v. Trutanich, 858 P.2d 1332 (Or. Ct. App. 1993).

[28] See Commercial Union Ins. Co. v. Taylor, 312 S.E.2d 177 (Ga. Ct. App. 1983).

[29] See, e.g., Smith v. Peninsular Ins. Co., 181 So. 2d 212 (Fla. Dist. Ct. App. 1965); Central Mfrs. Mut. Ins. Co. v. Elliott, 177 F.2d 1011 (10th Cir. 1949).

[30] See Angier v. Western Assur. Co., 71 N.W. 761 (S.D. 1897).

garage; such a storage would very likely suspend the coverage.[31] Putting warning signs on the boundary of insured premises that the house thereon is protected by a spring-loaded gun increases the risk of loss; firefighters will be highly reluctant to enter the premises to save it in the event of a fire.[32] Cutting off the fuel supplies to a house in the winter in Michigan increases the risk of a loss due to freezing in a house insured against such a peril.[33] By the same token, the circumstances that give rise to an increase of hazard must not be known by the insurer at the time of contracting; otherwise, the increase in hazard is contemplated by the insurer at the time it underwrites the risk.[34]

As the foregoing examples indicate, what constitutes an increase in hazard requires a common-sense judgment about what constitutes a normal, expected use of property, the character of and necessity for the risk-increasing conduct, and the extent to which the likelihood of a loss is enhanced.

The increase of hazard can be either an increase in a physical hazard, as in the foregoing cases, or an increase in a moral hazard. A moral hazard is the probability that the insured will destroy, or permit to be destroyed, the insured property for the purpose of collecting the insurance. Anything within the control of the insured that increases this risk is potentially an increase in the moral hazard. This can be either an act that increases the temptation to destroy the property, an act that reduces the value of the property in relation to the amount of insurance, or the act of procuring insurance in excess of the property's value.[35] For example, in *Future Realty, Inc. v. Fireman's Fund Insurance Co.*,[36] a case which is discussed in more detail in the next section, the court found the moral hazard increased and the policy's coverage suspended in circumstances where the plaintiff had learned that a high-rise apartment could not be built on land it had purchased, the structure present on the purchased land was a dilapidated tavern, the plaintiff had lost money when leasing the tavern during the previous year, and at the time of the intentionally-set fire which destroyed the tavern the insured was unable to lease the premises.

Although *Future Realty* suggests that what constitutes an increase in moral hazard can be viewed broadly, not all changes in circumstances which marginally contribute to the possibility of loss amount to an increase of hazard. Some circumstances outside the insured's control, such as the deteriorating profitability of a business,

---

[31] Compare Smith v. German Ins. Co., 65 N.W. 236 (Mich. 1895) and Springfield Fire & Marine Ins. Co. v. Wade, 68 S.W. 977 (Tex. 1902), with Sperry v. Springfield Fire & Marine Ins. Co., 26 F. 234 (C.C.Colo. 1886); Lutz v. Royal Ins. Co., 54 A. 721 (Pa. 1903); Steinbach v. Relief Fire Ins. Co., 80 U.S. 183 (1871).

[32] See Boyd v. Aetna Ins. Co., 192 F. Supp. 435 (S.D. Fla. 1960), *aff'd,* 288 F.2d 471 (5th Cir. 1961).

[33] See Smith v. Lumberman's Mut. Ins. Co., 300 N.W.2d 457 (Mich. Ct. App. 1980).

[34] See Eselin-Bullock & Associates Ins. Agency, Inc. v. National Gen. Ins. Co., 604 So. 2d 236 (Miss. 1992) (hurricane could not increase the hazard because possibility of hurricane was known at the beginning of the contract).

[35] See, e.g., Nemojeski v. Bubolz Mut. Town Fire Ins. Co., 74 N.W.2d 196 (Wis. 1956). An important purpose of "other insurance" clauses, discussed in § 97, *infra,* is to reduce moral hazard.

[36] 315 F. Supp. 1109 (S.D. Miss. 1970).

increase the temptation to destroy the business' property. However, changing business fortunes are foreseeable developments, and such changes do not necessarily amount to an increase in moral hazard. As one court explained, "the act or change that avoids insurance coverage contemplates that the alteration is material and substantial as would be viewed by a person of ordinary intelligence, care, and diligence."[37]

[2]   Reporting Conditions

Businesses whose inventory fluctuates widely and frequently may prefer to purchase value-reporting insurance (or, as it is sometimes called, monthly-reporting insurance, reporting-form insurance, or provisional insurance). Under this kind of coverage, the amount of the insurance varies with the value of the changing stock or merchandise of a going concern. The fluctuation in coverage eliminates the need to maintain insurance in excess of the value of the property, which is necessary to avoid being insufficiently covered at other points in the cycle of inventory. The amount of the premium to be paid varies in direct proportion to the value of the goods on hand. The insured reports the value of its merchandise to the insurer each month, and the insurer uses these reports to determine the value of the property to be covered under the policy and the premium to be paid.

The insured ordinarily pays an initial provisional premium based upon its best estimate of the maximum amount of reportable property it will have. At the end of the term, the provisional premium is adjusted on the basis of the average total values reported by the insured. An adjusted premium bill is then sent to the insured which shows either an additional premium due or a refund from the premium paid at the beginning of the policy period. The arrangement is beneficial not only to the insured but also the insurer: the insurer avoids undertaking too great a risk for the premium charged.

In a number of cases, insureds have been late in filing their monthly inventory reports. Such policies typically condition the insurer's obligations on compliance with the reporting provisions. Sometimes, this situation leads to litigation, as in *Watchung Pool Supplies, Inc. v. Aetna Casualty & Surety Co.*[38] The policy in *Watchung* required the insured to report to the insurer in writing the location and cash value of property "not later than 30 days after the last day of each calendar month." The policy stated the consequences for late filing: "At the time of any loss, if the insured has failed to file with the Company reports of values as above required, this policy . . . shall cover only . . . the amounts included in the last report of values filed prior to the loss." The insured suffered a loss by fire on July 7, 1977, and the value reports for the months of May and June, 1977, were filed on July 13, 1977, six days after the fire. The April, 1977 report, which had been filed on May 12, 1977 (the only report during the nine-month period prior to the loss that was filed on time), listed the inventory as a sum nearly a third less in value than the June, 1977 inventory. The insurer argued that it was liable only for the loss measured by the inventory reported in the April report; the insured argued that it was entitled to

---

[37] Wallace v. Employers Mut. Cas. Co., 443 So. 2d 843, 849 (Miss. 1983).

[38] 404 A.2d 1281 (N.J.Super.Ct.Law Div. 1979).

recover for the full loss because of the thirty-day grace period for filing inventory reports.

The court interpreted and applied the language of the policy literally, as have all courts that have confronted the issue, and the insurer's liability was limited to the last value report filed prior to the loss. The court emphasized the purpose of the provision; it noted that any other interpretation would allow the insured to consistently understate the amount of property on hand, thereby enjoying a low premium, and then defraud the insurer by submitting an inflated report at a time when verifying earlier values would be difficult and perhaps impossible.[39] Thus, the condition in *Wachtung* was applied literally, but this was an easier result for the court because the insured's forfeiture on account of failing to satisfy the condition was not total. The insured was reimbursed for part of the loss; in effect, the insured was a coinsurer for property acquired after the filing of the last report.

[3] Vacancy and Occupancy Clauses

Policies of property insurance commonly include a provision that no coverage exists in the event the premises become vacant or unoccupied. The standard fire insurance form under the heading "Conditions suspending or restricting insurance" states that the insurer shall not be liable for a loss occurring while a building "is vacant or unoccupied beyond a period of sixty consecutive days."[40] These clauses are enforced by courts, but decisions on how these clauses should be interpreted have been diverse. Much depends on the character of the particular premises and the uses to which the premises are being put or for which they are available.

Most courts say that the terms "vacancy" and "occupancy" are not synonymous. Vacancy usually refers to the absence of inanimate objects.[41] Thus, if *X* leaves *X*'s

---

[39] 404 A.2d at 1287; see also Camilla Feed Mills, Inc. v. St. Paul Fire & Marine Ins. Co., 177 F.2d 746 (5th Cir. 1949); Wallace v. World Fire & Marine Ins. Co., 70 F. Supp. 193 (S.D. Cal. 1947), *aff'd per curiam,* 166 F.2d 571 (9th Cir. 1948); compare Sack v. Glens Falls Ins. Co., 52 A.2d 173 (Pa. 1947) (report filed after loss but within 30-day grace period could be used to determine insurer's liability for loss, but policy did not include a limitation of coverage to last reported value filed prior to the loss).

[40] The Standard Fire Policy states as one of the "Conditions suspending or restricting insurance" that no coverage exists for "loss occurring . . . (b) while a described building . . . is vacant or unoccupied beyond a period of sixty consecutive days." *Policy Kit* (1985) at 2 (Standard Fire Policy). Another common formulation is in the standard homeowners policy, which excludes from the peril "freezing" loss on the premises while the dwelling is "unoccupied" unless reasonable care has been used to maintain heat in the building or shut off the water and drain the water supply system. A variation on the language of the Standard Fire Policy appears in more recent forms. See *Policy Kit* at 151 (ISO Form CP 00 10 10 91) ("If the building where loss or damage occurs has been vacant for more than 60 consecutive days before that loss or damage, we will: (a) Not pay . . . .") The significance of the difference in the language is discussed below.

[41] See Shaffner v. Farmers Mut. Fire Ins. Co., 859 S.W.2d 902 (Mo. Ct. App. 1993); Jerry v. Kentucky Central Ins. Co., 836 S.W.2d 812 (Tex. Ct. App. 1992) ("vacant" means "entire abandonment, deprived of contents, empty, that is, without contents of substantial utility"; case otherwise unremarkable except for fact that plaintiff has unusual last name of author of this text).

house for an extended vacation, the house is not vacant because personal belongings remain there. Occupancy usually refers to the presence or absence of people.[42] Thus, in the foregoing example, it might be said that X's house is unoccupied. If X anticipates such an absence, it would be prudent for X to obtain an endorsement from the insurer extending the coverage during the period of absence.

Occupancy is a particularly difficult term to apply, and courts have had great difficulty with it. If X leaves his or her house for a one-week vacation, X is only temporarily absent from the house. Thus, courts typically say that the house is "occupied": X has an intent to return and that is enough to meet the test for the purposes of the policy. The longer the period of absence, however, the more likely it is that a court would say the house is not occupied. Thus, if X took a one-year leave of absence from X's job and left X's house for that period, a court is likely, though not certain, to say that, notwithstanding X's intent to return to the house, the house was unoccupied. If X leaves for the summer, predicting how a court would treat the situation is difficult.

If X asks a relative or neighbor to watch after the house during the period of absence, a court will be less likely to conclude that the house is unoccupied. Nevertheless, depending on the circumstances, some courts have said that having someone else watch or monitor the house is not the same as occupancy.

Schools, barns, and churches are, of course, used in different ways than a home. Thus, the character of the use necessary to establish occupancy or nonvacancy differs. When such a structure is used in its customary manner, a court considers the structure to be occupied and not vacant. A barn that is no longer being used on a daily basis might be considered unoccupied; but a school that is closed down for several weeks due to an epidemic would not be considered unoccupied. Consistent with the common-sense approach to these clauses, where a building is rental property, gaps in occupancy between tenants is normal and within the contemplation of the parties to the contract. Thus, courts do not treat those periods as times of vacancy and unoccupancy.

The difficulty in these cases is that a continuum of possible uses of buildings exists. At one extreme, the residents of the building are physically present in the premises at the time of loss. This is clearly not a vacant or unoccupied building. At the other extreme, at the time of loss the building is devoid of all signs of human habitation and no evidence of recent use exists. Such a building is clearly vacant and unoccupied. In between these two extremes, there are an infinite number of possibilities. When cases are closer on the continuum, subtle distinctions must be made.

To take two examples, consider first *Future Realty, Inc. v. Fireman's Fund Insurance Co.*,[43] a 1970 decision. On March 25, 1969, a fire destroyed a building that had been used as a "beverage parlor." After October, 1968, the building was

---

[42] See, e.g., Coutu v. Exchange Ins. Co., 579 N.Y.S.2d 751 (N.Y. App. Div. 1992); Alcock v. Farmers Mut. Fire Ins. Co., 591 S.W.2d 126 (Mo. Ct. App. 1979); Independent Fire Ins. Co. v. Butler, 362 So. 2d 980 (Fla. Dist. Ct. App. 1978).

[43] 315 F. Supp. 1109 (S.D. Miss. 1970).

not used as a business, had no one living in it, and had no electric or gas service. A few days before the fire, the building was leased by the corporation that owned it to two individuals, one of whom was a convicted felon. A part-time fireman was hired to clean up the premises; the day before the fire, the fireman, his wife, and a third person spent a few hours cleaning up the premises, which at the time they entered it contained a great deal of debris, a bar, some old chairs, an old bandstand, and a vagrant sleeping on the upper floor. Expert testimony indicated that the fire was deliberately set in three separate locations. The insurer denied coverage, claiming that the building was vacant. The plaintiff corporation argued that the building was not vacant because of the presence of some items in the building and the effort the day before to clean the premises. The court concluded that the plaintiff failed to show by a preponderance of the evidence that the building "was occupied and thus not vacant during sixty consecutive days prior to the fire."

By way of contrast, in *Knight v. United States Fidelity & Guaranty Co.*,[44] the plaintiff closed her service station-restaurant in 1964, leaving all of her equipment — fixtures, booths, stools, coffee urn, and stove — in the building. She decided to reopen in 1966. She installed a new refrigerator, painted the premises, installed a music box, reconnected the electrical service, and did other work over a period of several weeks prior to the fire. Summary judgment was entered for the insurer, who denied coverage on the ground that the premises were unoccupied. On appeal, the court said that issues of material fact existed for jury resolution: "[A]s we construe the evidence, it does not conclusively show that the property was unoccupied for more than 60 days prior to the fire. Her . . . activities [are] consistent with making the premises ready for use for the very purpose for which it was insured. These activities are also all reasonably consistent with occupancy within the meaning of the policies."[45]

In *Future Realty* and *Knight*, the uses are distinguishable. Valuable equipment was left in the building in *Knight*, but not in *Future Realty*. The quality and intensity of the preparation work was greater in *Knight*, and the premises were kept more secure during the period they were not in use. Also, the fact that the fires were intentionally set in *Future Realty* was influential; the opinion has strong hints that the court believed the plaintiffs were involved in the arson. These two cases fit close together on a continuum of possible uses, and the results seem sensible. Nevertheless, reconciling all of the cases involving hazard and occupancy clauses is impossible. One thing is clear, however: once the vacancy or unoccupancy threshold is crossed, a condition to coverage has not been satisfied.[46] The insured has no coverage, and it is not necessary for the insurer to establish that the vacancy or lack of occupancy contributed to the loss or increased the risk of loss.

How is the sixty-day period which triggers application of the vacancy or lack of occupancy exclusion measured when the period of vacancy or unoccupany begins

---

[44] 182 S.E.2d 693 (Ga. Ct. App. 1971).

[45] 182 S.E.2d at 669. See also Limbaugh v. Columbia Ins. Co., 368 S.W.2d 921 (Mo. Ct. App. 1963).

[46] See e.g., Will Realty Corp. v. Transportation Ins. Co. 492 N.E.2d 372 (Mass.App.Ct. 1986); Fields v. Barton Cty. Mut. Ins. Co., 708 S.W.2d 204 (Mo. Ct. App. 1986); Hawkins v. State Capital Ins. Co., 328 S.E.2d 793 (N.C. Ct. App. 1985).

(Matthew Bender & Co., Inc.)

before the policy's inception date? If the policy excludes coverage when the premises are "vacant or unoccupied beyond a period of sixty consecutive days,"[47] the scope of the clause is arguably ambiguous in situations like the following: on day 1, a period of vacancy begins; on day 30, the insurer issues a policy of insurance on the building; on day 62, the building is destroyed by fire. The insurer will argue that the building has been vacant for a period exceeding sixty days and therefore no coverage exists. The insured will argue that the sixty-day period is prospective, meaning that the period runs from the inception of the policy, not a date before the policy was issued. Moreover, the insured will argue that the insurer could have inquired into the occupancy and vacancy status of the building at the time the application was received. All else being equal, insureds should be expected to prevail in such situations, and some courts have so held.[48]

Mindful of this possibility, drafters of more recent versions of the exclusion have added a retrospective orientation to the clause. These exclusions provide that no coverage exists when the premises have been "vacant or unoccupied for more than 60 days before that loss or damage."[49] By its plain terms, such a clause changes the analysis, allowing the sixty-day period to be computed from dates prior to a policy's inception date. The clause reduces the importance of the insurer's inquiry or investigation at the time a policy is issued with respect to the occupancy or vacancy status of an insured property. More importantly, the clause helps combat moral hazard by providing another basis for denying coverage when an insured purchases insurance on property with a concealed intention to encourage or arrange the its destruction. Under the former version, an insured who has property that has been vacant or unoccupied for months or even years could insure it and recover for its destruction if the loss occurs during the first sixty days after the policy's issuance (and if the insured's intentional destruction of the property is not detected). The newer version of the clause eliminates this possibility.[50]

§ 63 Intentional Conduct: An Overview

It is a fundamental requirement in insurance law that the insurer will not pay for a loss unless the loss is "fortuitous," meaning that the loss must be accidental in some sense.[1] The public policy underlying the fortuity requirement is so strong that

---

[47] See note 40, *supra*.

[48] See, e.g., Old Colony Ins. Co. v. Garvey, 253 F.2d 299 (4th Cir. 1958); Thomas v. Industrial Fire & Cas. Co., 255 So. 2d 486 (La. Ct. App. 1971).

[49] See note 40, *supra*.

[50] See Gas Kwick, Inc. v. United Pac. Ins. Co., 58 F.3d 1536 (11th Cir. 1995) (coverage denied for fire loss to building where loss occurred thirteen days after the binder's issuance and the building had been vacant for more than sixty days.

[1] See Waller v. Truck Ins. Exch., 1995 WL 516406 (Cal. 1995), slip op. at 6 ("This concept of fortuity is basic to insurance law.")

                                                    (Pub.837)

if the insurance policy itself does not expressly require that the loss be accidental courts will imply such a requirement.[2]

Whether a given loss is fortuitous depends on the point of view one takes toward the loss. For example, suppose X has a life insurance policy with an accidental death benefit rider on his or her own life, and X is murdered by Y, a stranger. X's loss was intentionally caused; however, from X's viewpoint and the viewpoint of his or her beneficiaries, X's death, assuming neither X nor one of the beneficiaries helped bring it about, was fortuitous — in effect, an accident. Unless there is a specific exclusion in the policy for death intentionally caused by a third party,[3] X's death will be covered under both the life insurance policy and the accidental death rider. No reason exists for viewing the death from the viewpoint of the aggressor, but doing so would obviously change the analysis and the outcome.

Liability insurance, where policies typically exclude injuries or damage intentionally caused by the insured, presents a similar question. If the victim's viewpoint is used, coverage will almost always exist; the insured may have intentionally caused the injury, but from the victim's viewpoint the injury is fortuitous. However, if the insured's viewpoint is used, the exclusion for intentional conduct will apply. A slightly different situation is presented if an insured employer is held vicariously liable for the intentional assault of a third party by an employees. In the absence of an express exclusion, the employer-insured will not be denied reimbursement under an implied exception, since from the insured's viewpoint the loss was fortuitous. The question of "viewpoint" for determining fortuity is given more attention below.

It is usually unnecessary to apply an implied exception for intentional conduct for the simple reason that virtually all modern insurance policies contain explicit language imposing some sort of fortuity requirement. Sometimes this language appears in the primary definition of coverage which affirmatively grants coverage. An accidental death rider on a life insurance policy is the most obvious example of such a provision. By stating affirmatively that the policy covers accidental death, death due to illness or suicide is inferentially excluded (and may be expressly excluded as well).

At other times, the requirement that the loss be accidental is stated as a limitation on the primary grant of coverage. For example, many insurance policies have language of one sort or another explicitly limiting coverage for intentionally caused

---

[2] Although uncommon, a product called "retroactive insurance" at first glance appears to violate the principle of fortuity. The most prominent example of retroactive insurance is the $170 million in liability insurance purchased by MGM after a 1981 hotel fire killed 84 people at its Las Vegas hotel/casino. See § 13A[b][3], note 17, *supra*. The insurance for MGM's liability covered losses that were known but which were uncertain in amount and as to the time they would be paid. Retroactive insurance is also sometimes purchased for suspected losses. These uncertainties arguably amount to "fortuity," although one could argue that these arrangements do not fit the definition of insurance. For more discussion, see Michael L. Smith & Robert C. Witt, *An Economic Analysis of Retroactive Liability Insurance*, 52 J. Risk & Ins. 379 (1985).

[3] See, e.g., Drew v. Life Ins. Co. of Ga., 316 S.E.2d 512 (Ga. Ct. App. 1984).

losses. Life insurance policies commonly contain a clause providing that if the insured commits suicide within two years from the date of the policy's issuance, the insurer's only obligation is to refund the premiums. Under this provision, which is discussed in a later section,[4] if the insured intentionally takes his or her own life within the first two years of the policy, no coverage exists. Accidental death riders usually have more exclusions; for example, such a policy might provide that no coverage exists if the death occurs from suicide at any time (i.e., more than two years after the policy is issued) or as a result of the discharge of a firearm (which has the effect of taking hunting accidents as well as criminal assaults on the victim involving guns outside of the coverage).[5] The standard homeowners' form for property loss excludes "any loss arising out of any act committed: (1) by or at the direction of an insured; and (2) with the intent to cause a loss." The personal liability and medical payments coverages of the same form exclude coverage for "bodily injury or property damage: a. which is expected or intended by the insured."[6] Similar provisions appear in automobile insurance policies.[7]

The question of when an exclusion of coverage for intentional conduct is operative has different implications in different lines of insurance. The sections which follow explore these implications.

§ 63A   Intentional Conduct and Property Insurance

In first-party property insurance, the intentional loss exclusion is not particularly troublesome. If the insured intentionally causes damage to his or her own property, the loss is not covered.[1] The public policy supporting this exclusion is identical to that which supports the insurable interest requirement. Insureds should not receive coverage for destroying their own property. Otherwise, insureds would have an incentive in many instances to destroy their property and collect the proceeds. In the same vein, when the insured intentionally fails to take steps to preserve property after it is damaged, the insured cannot recover from the insurer for the additional loss caused by this failure.[2] This duty to mitigate the effects of the loss, if not express, should be implied in the policy, as it furthers the public policy of avoiding economic waste. Regardless, property insurance policies typically impose a duty on the insured to protect the property from further damage and to make reasonable and necessary repairs to protect the property (the expenses for which are usually covered by the insurance policy).

---

[4] See § 91, *infra*.

[5] Accidental death riders are also likely to exclude fortuitous death while the insured is involved in activities that involve more risk, such as flying an airplane, hang-gliding, or auto racing.

[6] *Policy Kit* at 26, 29 (ISO Form HO 00 03 04 91).

[7] *Id.* at 124.

[1] See, e.g., Neises v. Solomon State Bank, 696 P.2d 372 (Kan. 1985); St. Paul Fire & Marine Ins. Co. v. Cumiskey, 665 P.2d 223 (Mont. 1983). See also Allstate Ins. Co. v. Malec, 514 A.2d 832 (N.J. 1986) (intentional act exclusion does not violate policy of no-fault law).

[2] See, e.g., Slay Warehousing Co. v. Reliance Ins. Co., 471 F.2d 1364 (8th Cir. 1973); Downing v. Rockford Dist. Mut. Tornado Ins. Co., 250 N.E.2d 827 (Ill. App. Ct. 1969).

Problems have arisen, however, when jointly owned insured property is intentionally destroyed by one of the co-owners.[3] The question is whether the innocent owner of the property should be allowed to recover under the policy of insurance purchased jointly to cover the joint interest. A recurring fact pattern involves property owned in the marital relationship: one of the spouses becomes enraged and destroys the jointly owned property; the innocent spouse attempts to secure indemnity for the loss, but the insurer refuses since the property was intentionally destroyed by one of the insureds.[4]

For many years in most jurisdictions, the rule was that the innocent coinsured was unable to recover under the insurance contract when another coinsured intentionally destroyed the insured property.[5] The logic of this approach was that coinsureds own the property jointly and thus have a joint interest in the insurance policy. The joint interest in the policy means that the insureds have joint obligations, such as joint duties to use all reasonable means to save and preserve the property, and a joint duty not to defraud the insurer. Because the duties are joint, a breach of the duty by one coinsured is chargeable to the other.[6] It was also been suggested that when property is owned in the entirety, it is impossible to determine or separate out the interest of the innocent coinsured, which requires that no recovery whatever be allowed.[7] Finally, there were concerns that the public policies underlying the rule that proceeds are not payable for intentionally caused loss will be subverted if innocent coinsureds were allowed to recover. It was feared that in many cases the proceeds awarded to the innocent coinsured would ultimately benefit the guilty insured. Moreover, collusion among coinsureds to defraud the insurer would be encouraged if recovery were allowed.

In recent years, a number of courts moved away from the rule barring recovery to a rule that permits recovery by an innocent coinsured of a loss intentionally caused by the another coinsured.[8] These cases rejected the assumptions underlying the rule

---

[3] See § 104C, *infra*.

[4] See generally Annot., *Theft and Vandalism Insurance: Coinsured's Misconduct as Barring Innocent Coinsured's Right to Recover on Policy*, 64 A.L.R.4th 714 (1988); Annot., *Right of Innocent Insured to Recover Under Fire Policy Covering Property Intentionally Burned by Another Insured*, 11 A.L.R.4th 1228 (1982).

[5] See, e.g., Western Fire Ins. Co. v. Sanchez, 671 S.W.2d 666 (Tex. Ct. App. 1984); Rockingham Mut. Ins. Co. v. Hummel, 250 S.E.2d 774 (Va. 1979); Short v. Oklahoma Farmers Union Ins. Co., 619 P.2d 588 (Okla. 1980).

[6] See Rockingham Mut. Ins. Co. v. Hummel, 250 S.E.2d 774 (Va. 1979).

[7] See, e.g., Short v. Oklahoma Farmers Union Ins. Co., 619 P.2d 588 (Okla. 1980); Cooperative Fire Ins. Ass'n of Vt. v. Domina, 399 A.2d 502 (Vt. 1979); Rockingham Mut. Ins. Co. v. Hummel, 250 S.E.2d 774 (Va. 1979).

[8] See, e.g., Jensen v. Jefferson County Mut. Ins. Ass'n, 510 N.W.2d 870 (Iowa 1994); Woodhouse v. Farmers Union Mut. Ins. Co., 785 P.2d 192 (Mont. 1990); Hedtcke v. Sentry Ins. Co., 326 N.W.2d 727 (Wis. 1982); Lovell v. Rowan Mut. Fire Ins. Co., 274 S.E.2d 170 (N.C. 1981); Hosey v. Seibels Bruce Group, S.C. Ins. Co., 363 So. 2d 751 (Ala. 1978); Hildebrand v. Holyoke Mut. Fire Ins. Co., 386 A.2d 329 (Me. 1978); Steigler v. Insurance. Co. of N. Am., 384 A.2d 398 (Del. 1978); Travelers Cos. v. Wolfe, 838 S.W.2d 708 (Tex. Ct. App. 1992); Maravich v. Aetna Life and Cas. Co., 504 A.2d 896 (Pa. Super. Ct. 1986); American Economy Ins. Co. v. Liggett, 426 N.E.2d 136 (Ind. Ct. App. 1981); Howell v. Ohio Cas. Ins. Co., 327 A.2d 240 (N.J. Super. Ct. App. Div. 1974).

disallowing recovery. First, although the interest in property may be joint, it does not follow that the interest in the policy insuring the property is joint. Instead, the insurance policy is a contract between insurer and insured, and the interests of coinsureds are severable. The unilateral acts of one coinsured cannot divest the other coinsured of her separate contract rights under the insurance policy.[9] In the marital setting, the rule that the intentional act of one spouse destroys the contract rights of the other is based on the "fictional oneness" of the marriage relationship, an out-of-date understanding of the legal significance of marriage.[10] Furthermore, it is one individual who is responsible for the wrongdoing, not all the coinsureds. The reasonable expectations of the insured probably are not that the intentional act of a coinsured can destroy all the insureds' rights to proceeds. If one has an undivided interest in property and insures one's own interest only, such a person would probably not understand that the intentional act of another owner could void the coverage.[11]

Not all courts approving the rule allowing innocent coinsureds to recover were comfortable doing so. To deal with the obvious possibility that the new rule could encourage some additional intentional destruction of property, some courts suggested an individual analysis of the facts of each case to determine whether the guilty party would benefit from the proceeds; where such a benefit was likely, steps should be taken to prevent it.[12] Other courts have adopted a rule that inquires on a case-by-case basis into whether the coinsureds have a joint or severable interest in the policy. Where the interest is joint, an innocent coinsured cannot recover; the outcome is different if the interests are found to be severable.[13]

In response to the extension of coverage worked by courts in the decided cases, in the 1980s insurers began to insert language in policies that denied coverage if "any insured" was found to have caused the loss to the covered property. This language sought to limit the insurer's extension of coverage along the lines of the former judicial rule. As long as the language is clear, and in most situations it is, courts generally uphold the restriction barring an innocent coinsured from recovering whenever any insured destroys the property.[14]

---

[9] See Howell v. Ohio Cas. Ins. Co., 327 A.2d 240 (N.J.Super. 1974).

[10] See American Economy Ins. Co. v. Liggett, 426 N.E.2d 136 (Ind. Ct. App. 1981).

[11] See Hedtcke v. Sentry Ins. Co., 326 N.W.2d 727 (Wis. 1982).

[12] See American Economy Ins. Co. v. Liggett, 426 N.E.2d 136 (Ind. Ct. App. 1981); Hedtcke v. Sentry Ins. Co., 326 N.W.2d 727 (Wis. 1982).

[13] See McAllister v. Millville Mut. Ins. Co., 640 A.2d 1283 (Pa.Super. 1994); Iemma v. Adventure RV Rentals, Inc., 632 N.E.2d 1178 (Ind. Ct. App. 1994).

[14] See, e.g., Amick v. State Farm Fire & Cas. Co., 862 F.2d 704 (8th Cir. 1988); Saless v. State Farm Fire & Cas. Co., 849 F.2d 1383 (11th Cir. 1988); Spezialetti v. Pacific Employers Ins. Co., 759 F.2d 1139 (3d Cir. 1985); Bryant v. Allstate Ins. Co., 592 F. Supp. 39 (E.D. Ky. 1984); Noland v. Farmers Ins. Co., 892 S.W.2d 271 (Ark. 1995); Dolcy v. Rhode Island Joint Reins. Ass'n, 589 A.2d 313 (R.I. 1991); Reitzner v. State Farm Fire & Cas. Co., 510 N.W.2d 20 (Minn. Ct. App. 1993); Fernandez v. Cigna Prop. & Cas. Ins. Co., 590 N.Y.S.2d 925 (N.Y. App. Div. 1992); State Farm Fire & Cas. Ins. Co. v. Walker, 459 N.W.2d 605 (Wis. Ct. App. 1990). Compare Spence v. Allstate Ins. Co., 883 S.W.2d 586 (Tenn. 1994) (holding policy ambiguous in circumstances where special Tennessee endorsement stated that

A recent Michigan case, however, struck down the coverage restriction. In *Borman v. State Farm Fire & Casualty Co.,*[15] A strong dissent argued that the limitation on innocent coinsureds' recovery was not inconsistent[16] with the statutory fire insurance policy.[17]

The *Borman* decision is a source of considerable frustration to property insurers. The decision, however, is limited because the court's logic depends on statutorily mandated policy language; the court explicitly declined to premise its decision on the ground that public policy prohibits the exclusion in all circumstances.[18] To what extent other jurisdictions will embrace *Borman* is uncertain. Because arson remains a serious national problem, one would expect some, and perhaps many, courts to support exclusions in insurance policies that reduce moral hazard, and this suggests *Borman* will not be followed in all jurisdictions. Yet the reluctance to penalize innocent insureds along with those who commit the wrongful acts suggests that courts will favor the claims of innocent coinsureds.[19]

An issue that has received some attention is the amount of the innocent coinsured's recovery in circumstances where this recovery is allowed. The proper approach is to reimburse the innocent coinsured for the amount of the damage to his or her interest; having said that, there are different views on how that interest should be valued. Some courts have held that the innocent coinsured spouse can recover one-half of the amount of property damage up to the policy limits.[20] Other courts have held that the innocent coinsured spouse could recover one-half of the amount of the damage up to one-half of the policy limits.[21] This approach makes sense only if one views the insurance policy as being shared equally between the coinsureds; the better view, it would seem, is to treat the entire policy limits as being available for the entire amount of the damage to an insured's interests. One court has held that the interest of the innocent spouse is equal to one-half of the equity

---

intentional act exclusion only applied to persons who commit, conspire, etc. in such acts); Atlas Assur. Co. of Am. v. Mistic, 822 P.2d 897 (Alaska 1991) (approving rule, but finding language of particular policy ambiguous).

[15] 521 N.W.2d 266 (Mich. 1994), the Michigan Supreme Court invalidated the provisions of the standard homeowner's policy insofar as they denied fire coverage to an innocent coinsured. The court reasoned that the statute mandating the text of the standard fire insurance policy did not allow a provision denying an innocent coinsured recovery. The statute's reference to concealment fraud voids coverage if "the insured" wilfully conceals or misrepresents a material fact, and this was construed in a prior case not to mean that coverage would be voided as to all insureds if one (i.e., "the") insured committed fraud.

[16] See Morgan v. Cincinnati Ins. Co., 307 N.W.2d 53 (Mich. 1981).

[17] 521 N.W.2d at 274.

[18] 521 N.W.2d at 270.

[19] See Osbon v. National Union Fire Ins. Co., 632 So. 2d 1158 (La. 1994)(holding that state statute supersedes policy provision excluding coverage for innocent coinsured when property is intentionally destroyed by another insured).

[20] See, e.g., Republic Ins. Co. v. Jernigan, 753 P.2d 229 (Colo. 1988)(en banc); Steigler v. Insurance Co. of N. Am., 384 A.2d 398 (Del. 1978); Lewis v. Homeowners Ins. Co., 432 N.W.2d 334 (Mich. Ct. App. 1988).

[21] See, e.g., Delph v. Potomac Ins. Co., 620 P.2d 1282 (N.M. 1980).

interest in the property,[22] which under that court's logic may have been overly generous since the equity interest was not apportioned between the structure (which suffered the fire damage) and the land (which suffered no damage). Of course, where property is jointly owned, proceeds equal to one-half of the damage does not make the innocent coinsured whole; but the difficulty is apparent when one realizes that paying the innocent coinsured 100 percent of the damage increases the likelihood that the wrongdoer benefits from his or her intentional destruction of the property. In short, the valuation issue has no single answer that works well in all cases. In any event, the modern rule concludes that absolutely barring recovery by the innocent coinsured is too harsh a result, particularly in cases where the intentional destruction was intended by the destroying coinsured as retribution against the innocent one.

§ 63B   Intentional Conduct and Personal Insurance: Life and Accidental Death

[a]   Suicide

Most life insurance policies exclude from coverage death due to suicide that occurs within two years after the policy is issued. The obvious purpose of this exclusion is to prevent an individual from purchasing insurance while having the intent to kill oneself for the enrichment of beneficiaries. Assuming the exclusion is clear, no court questions its enforceability.[1] The two-year period is the same as the incontestability period in most policies; if the insured commits suicide after this period, the proceeds are payable to the beneficiaries.[2]

In the absence of a specific exclusion, almost all American courts allow the beneficiary to recover life insurance benefits when the insured takes his or her own life. From the beneficiary's point of view, the death is fortuitous.[3] Although the practice is controversial, the suicide of an individual facing a painful, incurable terminal illness, where the decision was made after careful and considerable analysis, has a different quality than that of the individual who takes his or her own life to enrich beneficiaries. Only a few American courts have spoken approvingly of the "English rule" that holds it against public policy for a beneficiary to recover under

---

[22] See Jonax v. Allstate Ins. Co., 582 A.2d 1050 (N.J. Super. Ct. App. Div. 1990).

[1] See, e.g., Malcom v. Farmers New World Life Ins. Co., 5 Cal. Rptr.2d 584 (Cal. Ct. App. 1992); Mirza v. Maccabees Life & Annnuity Co., 466 N.W.2d 340 (Mich. Ct. App. 1991); Brindis v. Mutual Life Ins. Co. of N.Y., 560 N.E.2d 722 (Mass.App.Ct. 1990).

[2] In some policies, the time periods differ. The insurer might exclude coverage for suicide, regardless of when it occurs, and have a two-year incontestability provision as well. Some courts have held that the defense of suicide is barred after the incontestability period expires, but the better reasoning is to view the clauses as completely distinct. See 1B APPLEMAN § 499 (1981).

[3] See, e.g., Turkett v. Gulf Life Ins. Co., 306 S.E.2d 602 (S.C. 1983); Prudential Ins. Co. v. Rice, 52 N.E.2d 624 (Ind. 1944); Domico v. Metropolitan Life Ins. Co., 253 N.W. 538 (Minn. 1934).

a policy where the insured, while sane, committed suicide.[4] These cases are old and of dubious authority today.

With respect to accidental death benefits, as opposed to the life insurance benefits, suicide has different implications. Since suicide is an intentional act by the insured, the insured's beneficiaries are not entitled to recover the proceeds of an accidental death benefit. Accidental self-destruction, whether through negligence or inadvertence, is not the same thing as suicide. Thus, suicide is inherently nonaccidental, and specific exclusions usually make this clear. Since the policy covers accidents, the burden is on the beneficiary to show that the insured died in an accident; thus the beneficiary bears the burden to show that the death was not by suicide.[5]

Because suicide is by definition an intentional act of self-destruction, some of the same problems present in other areas of insurance law are confronted in this area: was the insured's death an intentional act or was it an accident? For example, if the insured was insane at the time of the suicide, the intent to cause one's own death might be negated and the death might be deemed accidental.[6] However, most life insurance policies now exclude coverage for death due to suicide, whether the insured is sane or insane, and these clauses are enforceable.[7] These clauses obviously assist the insurer in meeting the argument beneficiaries would be inclined

----

[4] See, e.g., Davis v. Supreme Council Royal Arcanum, 81 N.E. 294 (Mass. 1907); Courtemanche v. Supreme Court I.O.F., 98 N.W. 749 (Mich. 1904). The English rule's origins appear to be in the criminalization of suicide. "Although suicide is no longer a criminal offense [in England] if the insured kills himself whilst not mentally disordered, the insurer can avoid liability on the groudn that he cannot take advantage of his own intentional act." 25 *Halsbury's Laws of England* § 530, at 302 (4th ed. reissue 1994). This is analogous to the beneficiary killing the insured for his or her own benefit. See § 52A[e], *supra*. It does not follow from such a holding that a beneficiary who is not the estate of the insured should not recover when the insured, while sane, commits suicide.

[5] See Pollard v. Metropolitan Life Ins. Co., 598 F.2d 1284 (3d Cir.), *cert. denied,* 444 U.S. 917 (1979).

[6] See, e.g., Cole v. Combined Ins. Co. of Am., 480 A.2d 178 (N.H. 1984); Aetna Life Ins. Co. v. McLaughlin, 380 S.W.2d 101 (Tex. 1964); Skaggs v. Aetna Life Ins. Co., 884 S.W.2d 45 (Mo.App. 1994)("the taking of one's life while sane is not an accident; however, committing suicide while insane is considered an accident.") For a case raising the same issue in the health insurance area, see Casey v. Uddeholm Corp., 32 F.3d 1094 (7th Cir. 1994), (insured, who threw himself in front of elevated train in unsuccessful suicide attempt, raised material disputed issues with regard to his claimed entitlement to health insurance coverage for injuries suffered, which required vacating summary judgment for insurer).

[7] Approximately 20 states have statutes explicitly authorizing the use of the exception. See, e.g., Tenn. Code Ann. § 56-7-2308(5)(A); Ga. Code Ann. § 33-25-5(a)(5); Md. Code Ann. § 410(a)(5). Judicial decisions in other states support the exception. See, e.g., Johnson v. Metropolitan Life Ins. Co., 404 F.2d 1202 (3d Cir. 1968); Searle v. Allstate Ins. Co., 696 P.2d 1308 (Cal. 1985); Atkinson v. Life Ins. Co. of Va., 228 S.E.2d 117 (Va. 1976). In Charney v. Illinois Mut. Life Cas. Co., 764 F.2d 1441 (11th Cir. 1985), the exclusion was declared unambiguous and enforceable in a situation where the insured took his own life when under the influence of a prescription drug, a known side-effect of which is depression. For more information, see Gary Schuman, *Suicide and the Life Insurance Contract: Was the Insured Sane or Insane? That is the Question—Or Is It?,* 28 Tort & Ins. L. J. 745 (1993).

to raise absent the exclusion: that the insured was insane as evidenced by the act of self-destruction. If the insured engages in an act that is likely, but not certain, to lead to his or her own death, is the act suicide? Normally this issue arises in context of whether the beneficiaries are entitled to the accidental death benefit, a subject which is discussed in a later subsection.[8] But if the death occurs during the two-year period after the policy's issuance, the same issue can arise with respect to the basic life insurance benefit. In a Florida case, the court held that an insured who, while despondent over the breakup of his marriage, had placed one round in a revolver and played Russian Roulette with fatal consequences, had committed suicide; because the death was within two years of the policy's issuance, the beneficiaries were not entitled to the proceeds.[9]

[b] Death While Intentionally Involved in Unlawful Conduct

A few life insurance and some accidental death benefit policies contain explicit provisions prohibiting the payment of proceeds when the insured's death results from or occurs during a criminal act.[10] Sometimes accidental death benefit policies go further to exclude the insured's death if caused by a gunshot or pistol wound unless unintentionally inflicted by someone other than the insured, or if death results from bodily injury intentionally inflicted by a third person, or if death results from bodily injury intentionally inflicted by a third person if the insured was the aggressor.[11] These exclusions are not controversial in and of themselves; in any given case interpretation questions might arise, but this is not unusual whenever a general policy provision embraces a wide variety of factual situations.

In the absence of an express exclusion, the question is whether the policy should be enforced where the insured dies while intentionally involved in criminal conduct. With respect to basic life insurance (as distinct from an accidental death rider), most courts reason that the death is fortuitous from the point of view of the beneficiary and allow recovery.[12] As explained by one court, "[i]t is not to be presumed that policyholders as a class, or any appreciable number of them, will go out and seek death in unlawful pursuits in order to mature their policies."[13] Moreover, unlike accidental death benefits, life insurance policies typically involve significant savings and investments features. As one court stated, "[f]orfeiture of savings and investment to the insurer may deter crime, but it seems out of harmony with related policies in modern times."[14] The few courts that adhere to the opposite view and deny recovery are dwindling in number.[15]

---

[8] See § 63B[d], *infra.*

[9] See C.M. Life Ins. Co. v. Ortega, 562 So. 2d 702 (Fla. Dist. Ct. App. 1990).

[10] See, e.g., Richardson v. Colonial Life & Accident Ins. Co., 723 S.W.2d 912 (Mo.App. 1987) (enforcing exclusions for death occurring while insured was committing a crime).

[11] See Drew v. Life Ins. Co. of Ga., 316 S.E.2d 512 (Ga. Ct. App. 1984); Evans v. National Life Acc. Ins. Co., 467 N.E.2d 1216 (Ind. Ct. App. 1984).

[12] See Home State Life Ins. Co. v. Russell, 53 P.2d 562, 563 (Okla. 1936); Davis v. Boston Mut. Life Ins. Co., 351 N.E.2d 207 (Mass. 1976).

[13] Home State Life Ins. Co. v. Russell, 53 P.2d 562, 563 (Okla. 1936).

[14] Davis v. Boston Mut. Life Ins. Co., 351 N.E.2d 207, 209 (Mass. 1976).

[15] See, e.g., Molloy v. John Hancock Mut. Life Ins. Co., 97 N.E.2d 422 (Mass. 1951), *overruled by* Davis v. Boston Mut. Life Ins. Co., 351 N.E.2d 207 (Mass. 1976).

The question is more complicated when accidental death benefits are at issue. If the insured dies while engaged intentionally in criminal conduct or some sort of wrongful aggression upon another, it is less clear that the insured's death is an "accident" for which benefits must be paid to the beneficiary. This issue was confronted in *Wetzel v. Westinghouse Electric Corp.,*[16] a 1978 Pennsylvania decision, in which the insured, enraged over his income taxes, engaged his son in hand-to-hand combat, which resulted in the father being killed by his son. The son was found not guilty of murder and voluntary manslaughter. The widow, the decedent's beneficiary, hoped to recover the double indemnity benefits, but the insurer refused to pay. The question was whether the insured's death occurred through "accidental means" as the insurance policy required.

In cases like *Wetzel,* in the absence of a provision explicitly excluding coverage for losses resulting from the insured's criminal acts, courts generally follow one of two different approaches. One approach, followed by a minority of courts, is to imply a clause in the policy, based on public policy, that if a loss occurs resulting from the insured's violation of law, no coverage results. The rationale is that permitting coverage is actually encouraging crime, because the criminal is protected from the adverse consequences of his act. Most courts reject this approach, reasoning that if an innocent beneficiary is suing for a recovery under the policy, the loss is fortuitous from the point of view of the beneficiary and the implied exception should not prevent the beneficiary from recovering.

A second approach involves asking whether the occurrence was a foreseeable consequence of the acts of the insured from the insured's viewpoint. One court expressed the rule as follows:

> Generally, in regard to accidental death benefit policies where the insured is innocent of aggression or wrongdoing and is killed in an encounter with another, the insured's death is considered accidental within the meaning of the usual accident policy, but if the insured is the aggressor in an assault and knew, or should have anticipated, that the other might kill the insured in the encounter, the death is not to be considered accidental.[17]

The lower court in *Wetzel* followed this approach. It reasoned that the decedent could reasonably foresee that when he engaged his son in hand-to-hand combat he could be killed. Therefore, his death was not an accident and no coverage resulted. Although this result was reversed on appeal,[18] if one accepts the factual conclusion

---

[16] 393 A.2d 470 (Pa. Super. Ct. 1978).

[17] Drew v. Life Ins. Co. of Ga., 316 S.E.2d 512 (Ga. Ct. App. 1984); see also Young v. J.C. Penney Life Ins. Co., 701 F.2d 709 (7th Cir. 1983). If the insured while insane engages in aggressive conduct that results in his or her own death, and if the insured lacked the capacity to appreciate that the conduct might result in death, the death might be labeled accidental. See Hoffman v. Life Ins. Co. of North America, 669 P.2d 410 (Utah 1983).

[18] On appeal in *Wetzel, supra,* the court criticized the result below, noting that there was no link between the crime and the securing of insurance; whether insurance exists will have no effect on whether these kinds of events occur. The court concluded that if there is no link between the procuring of the insurance and the crime, the event will be called an accident. The difficulty with this approach is that there is rarely a link between procuring the insurance

that the insured should have reasonably foreseen his death from engaging in this activity, the result is sound.

Similar facts which led to a different conclusion are found in *Tucker v. Fireman's Fund American Life Insurance Co.,*[19] a 1984 Tennessee case. The teenage son of the insured, while trying to persuade his father to stop beating his mother, shot and killed his father with a shotgun he believed to be unloaded. The son asked his father to stop the beating (his father had heeded these requests on previous occasions); on this occasion, the father stopped and then approached the son who, while aiming the gun in his father's direction, continued to back away until he bumped against a wall, which caused the gun to discharge and inflict the fatal wound. The insurer argued that the father's death was not an accident because he should have foreseen that he could be killed or injured when he began to advance toward his son who was holding a shotgun at the time. The court said that the outcome must depend on the facts of each case, but it is distinctly possible that a parent would not expect a child to use deadly force to restrain a parent in a family quarrel situation. In the facts of *Tucker,* the court concluded that the trial court did not err in finding the father's death to be accidental.[20]

Most cases do not present fact patterns quite as difficult to analyze as *Wetzel* and *Tucker.* The more typical case involves the insured through an aggressive act placing another person in fear of physical injury, with the foreseeable consequence being the infliction of deadly force in response.[21] As stated by one court, "a person is a victim of an accident when, from the victim's point of view, the occurrence causing the injury or death is not a natural and probable result of the victim's own acts."[22] Illustrative is *Roque v. Nationwide Mutual Insurance Co.,*[23] a Pennsylvania Supreme Court decision. The insured, trapped in a home by police while he was burglarizing it, called out a warning to a policeman to get out or he would kill him. The insured emerged from a bedroom carrying a gun; he was promptly shot and fatally wounded by a police officer. The trial court entered a summary judgment for the insurer, and this was affirmed:

> In *Mohn,* [[24]] the insured was shot and killed by police as he fled from a record shop which he had attempted to burglarize. As there was nothing on the record to indicate that the insured had threatened or otherwise provoked the officer

---

and the event which causes the death. The result might be justified on the ground that is very favorable toward beneficiaries, but it can be fairly said that insurers do not intend to pay double recovery for death that occurs when the insured undertakes an activity where death is a likely, foreseeable consequence.

[19] [1983–85] Life, Health & Accident Cases (CCH), at 1243 (Tenn.App. 1984).

[20] See also Floyd v. Equitable Life Assur. Soc'y, 264 S.E.2d 648 (W.Va. 1980) (foreseeability of spouse's death in marital violence situation is jury question); Pfeifer v. World Service Life Ins., 360 N.W.2d 65 (Wis. Ct. App. 1984).

[21] See, e.g., O'Bar v. Southern Life & Health Ins. Co., 168 So. 580 (Ala. 1936); Sanders v. Prudential Ins. Co. of Am., 697 S.W.2d 80 (Tex. Ct. App. 1985).

[22] Hoffman v. Life Ins. Co. of North Am., 669 P.2d 410, 416 (Utah 1983) (emphasis deleted).

[23] 467 A.2d 1128 (Pa. 1983).

[24] Mohn v. American Casualty Co., 326 A.2d 346 (Pa. 1974).

who fired the fatal shot, this court permitted recovery under a medical insurance policy that limited coverage to accidental injuries. In this case, unlike *Mohn,* the insured not only repeatedly told police officers that he had a gun and intended to shoot to kill, but also pointed the gun at the police officers and cocked it. In these circumstances, it must be concluded that the insured's conduct provoked the shooting and the insured's death was thus not accidental.[25]

As a general rule, if one advances on another while the other is armed and the person dies in the encounter, the death is not accidental.[26] Nevertheless, it is not possible to reconcile all cases with this general rule, as *Howard v. Southern Life & Health Insurance Co.,*[27] a 1985 Alabama case, illustrates. While the insured and the plaintiff-beneficiary were separated, the insured attacked the plaintiff three times, twice with a knife and once by chasing her around her yard on a motorcycle. During the second knife attack, the plaintiff shot the insured in the leg with a pistol in self-defense. The day after the second knife attack, insured and plaintiff argued, and plaintiff fired several unaimed warning shots with the pistol. Insured approached plaintiff with a knife, and this time the plaintiff shot and killed the insured. The trial court granted the insurer's summary judgment motion, finding as a matter of law that the insured's death was not accidental. The Alabama Supreme Court reversed, however, and remanded the case for a new trial. Despite the fact that the plaintiff had shot and wounded the insured the preceding day, the court reasoned that plaintiff's past conduct did not give the insured reason to believe that she would shoot and kill him if he approached her with a knife. In addition, the court observed that the fact that the insured approached the insured armed "only" with a knife supported the inference that he did not expect the plaintiff to fire a fatal shot.[28]

Notwithstanding the general rule that the death of one who advances on an armed person is not accidental, if it appears that the insured was insane or otherwise mentally incapacitated when the actions were taken that resulted in the insured's death, the death might be deemed accidental.[29] However, courts are reluctant to treat

---

[25] Rogue v. Nationwide Mut. Ins. Co., 467 A.2d 1128, 1129 (Pa. 1983).

[26] See, e.g., Valley Dental Ass'n, P.C. v. Great-West Life Assur. Co., 842 P.2d 1340 (Ariz. Ct. App. 1992) (insured who was stabbed to death by hitchhiker he had just raped did not die by "accidental means" as required by policy; held, beneficiaries of insured could not recover accidental death benefit); Moss v. Protective Life Ins. Co., 417 S.E.2d 340 (Ga. Ct. App. 1992) (spouse failed to raise material issue of disputed fact regarding whether insured's death was accidental where insured was shot and killed by police after he fired at them, wounding one); Krulls v. Hartford Acc. & Indem. Co., 535 N.Y.S.2d 157 (N.Y. App. Div. 1988) (one who while armed with deadly weapon attacks police must expect deadly resistance, and death in such circumstances is not accidental); Funchess v. Metropolitan Life Ins. Co., 419 N.E.2d 706 (Ill. App. Ct. 1981).

[27] 474 So. 2d 1109 (Ala. 1985).

[28] See generally William F. Thomson, *Domestic or Family Altercations and Accidental Death Benefits Under the Life Insurance Contract: Is It an Accident?* 53 Ins. Counsel J. 351 (1986) (arguing that the husband who repeatedly batters a wife foresees that the wife may one day kill him, and thus the husband's death in such altercations is not an accident).

[29] See, e.g., Hoffman v. Life Ins. Co. of N. Am., 669 P.2d 410 (Utah 1983); Continental Cas. Co. v. Maguire, 471 P.2d 636 (Colo.Ct.App. 1970).

the insured's death as accidental where the acts were precipitated by a voluntary act that caused the incapacity. For example, if the insured in a drunken state beats his or her spouse, causing the spouse to defend with deadly force, the test is not likely to be what the insured expected in an intoxicated condition, but what a reasonable person in the same circumstances would assume would result from such aggression.[30]

[c]   Execution of Insured

Related to the question discussed in the preceding subsection of whether beneficiaries can recover proceeds when the insured dies while engaged in unlawful conduct is the question of whether the beneficiaries of an individual executed for a crime can recover the proceeds. The long hiatus in implementing the death penalty in the 1960s and 1970s mooted the question of whether proceeds are payable for the death of an insured executed for a crime. Now that the death penalty is being used more frequently for serious crimes, it is inevitable that this question will soon arise again.

Most of the cases are older ones, and their results are diverse.[31] One commentator opined in 1925 that the majority of cases have refused to allow the beneficiary of a policy of insurance on the life of an individual executed for wrongful conduct to recover the proceeds.[32] One more recent federal district court apparently thought this to be the prevailing rule,[33] but a contrary rule was followed in a still more recent decision. In *Tarrance v. John Hancock Mutual Life Insurance Co.*,[34] a 1956 federal court decision later affirmed by the Sixth Circuit, the court held that the beneficiary of insurance on an individual executed for murder was entitled to the proceeds of the insurance. Following the reasoning of a New York case,[35] the court observed that the deceased criminal receives no benefit if the beneficiary recovers. Moreover, it is highly unlikely that an insured would be more likely to commit a crime punishable by death simply because beneficiaries could collect the insurance proceeds; since the likelihood of being executed did not deter the crime, it is absurd to think that the denial of insurance proceeds to the criminal's beneficiaries would deter the wrongful act.[36] This view is found in a number of older cases, including those that justify allowing the beneficiary to recover on the ground that the execution occurred after the policy's incontestability period had expired.[37]

Unfortunately, the reported decisions shed little light on how today's courts will deal with the situation where the insured is executed for unlawful conduct. In the

---

[30] See Herbst v. J.C. Penney Ins. Co., 679 S.W.2d 381 (Mo. Ct. App. 1984).

[31] See generally Annot., *Liability Under Policy of Life Insurnace Where Insured is Executed for Crime*, 36 A.L.R. 1255 (1925).

[32] *Id.* at 1258. See Smith v. Metropolitan Life Ins. Co., 211 N.Y.S. 755 (N.Y. Sup. Ct 1925).

[33] Simmons v. United States, 120 F. Supp. 641 (M.D.Pa. 1954).

[34] 139 F. Supp. 769 (W.D. Ky. 1956), *aff'd*, 244 F.2d 86 (6th Cir. 1957).

[35] Prudential Ins. Co. v. Goldstein, 43 F. Supp. 765 (E.D. N.Y. 1942).

[36] See also Payne v. Louisiana Indus. Life Ins. Co., 33 So. 2d 444 (La. Ct. App. 1948); Austin Fire Ins. v. Adams-Childers Co., 246 S.W. 365 (Tex.Comm.App. 1923).

[37] See, e.g., Modern Woodmen of Am. v. Kehoe, 25 So. 2d 463 (Miss. 1946).

absence of an explicit exclusion in a policy clarifying the matter, and absent proof that the insured took out life insurance with the intent to commit an unlawful act for which the insured would be executed, there seems little reason to disallow a beneficiary from recovering the basic life insurance benefit when the insured loses his or her life through judicial process. With respect to the accidental death benefit, the analysis is more troublesome. If one reasons from the unlawful conduct cases, one might ask whether death was a foreseeable consequence of the conduct in which the insured engaged. If one concludes that an insured should foresee being executed for a heinous crime, it would follow that accidental death proceeds should not be paid to the beneficiaries. This result seems harsh, however, since most criminals no doubt commit their acts without taking into account such possibilities.

[d]   Accidental Death Benefit: Distinguishing Intentional Acts and Accidents

The difficulty of evaluating "intent" is pervasive in determining the coverage of accidental death benefit riders. In the foregoing sections, this problem was addressed in two settings: whether an insured's death is accidental when it results from intentional unlawful acts or aggression upon another, and whether an insured is capable of acting intentionally when suffering from diminished mental capacity. The issue, however, surfaces in numerous other settings as well, and the question is essentially the same: when an insured places himself or herself in a situation where death is a natural, probable, foreseeable consequence, but the insured does not necessarily intend to die, can it be said that the insured's death was an accident for purposes of the accidental death benefit? If a specific exclusion proscribes coverage for death resulting from the exact kind of intentional conduct in which the insured engaged, no particular difficulty exists. However, policy language is incapable of anticipating all the kinds of situations in which insureds perish.

Take, for example, the simple situation where the insured uses an illegal drug, such as heroin, and dies as a result.[38] On the one hand, it might be argued that the insured's act of injecting the drug was intentional, and therefore the death was not an accident. In *Patch v. Metropolitan Life Insurance Co.,*[39] the Fourth Circuit observed that the dangers of heroin usage are "well known and require no lengthy elaboration." The court held that the insured's death after injecting himself with heroin was a natural and probable consequence of the insured's knowing actions and therefore his death did not result from accidental means.[40] Yet the insured certainly did not "intend" his death; probably the insured had used heroin safely

---

[38] See Guest v. Horace Mann Ins. Co., 310 S.E.2d 241 (Ga. Ct. App. 1983).

[39] 733 F.2d 302 (4th Cir. 1984); see also Hargreaves v. Metropolitan Life Ins. Co., 163 Cal. Rptr. 857 (Cal. Ct. App. 1980).

[40] See also Winters v. Reliance Standard Life Ins. Co., 433 S.E.2d 363 (Ga. Ct. App. 1993) (decedent's voluntary and intentional intake of lethal amount of ethyl alcohol rendered decedent's death non-accidental and outside coverage of group accident and life insurance policy). See also Lloyd v. First Farwest Life Ins. Co., 773 P.2d 426 (Wash.App. 1989) (medical care expenses due to ruptured cerebral aneurysm caused by deliberate, nonmedical inhalation of cocaine was not a bodily injury caused by accident and no coverage allowed under health policy; also, public policy prohibited insured's recovery).

before, and had no expectation that the next use would be fatal. Following this analysis, the Fifth Circuit in *O'Toole v. New York Life Insurance Co.*[41] affirmed the trial court's finding that the insured's death following a self-administered injection of cocaine was "accidental." The policy excluded death by suicide, but death from self-administered drugs was not explicitly excepted. The court said that the insured intentionally injected himself with cocaine, but he neither intended nor anticipated that this would cause his death.[42]

Varying results can be found in other contexts as well. In two Fourth Circuit decisions, the court held that death caused by "autoerotic hanging" is not accidental. In *Runge v. Metropolitan Life Insurance Co.,*[43] the deceased insured sought to heighten the masturbation experience by partially asphyxiating himself; he placed his head in a noose at the end of a cord so that his feet barely touched the ground. In this instance, however, the results were tragic; he lost consciousness and strangled to death. The court found that death, although unintended, was a natural and probable consequence of the insured's conduct, and coverage was denied under the "accidental means" policy. *International Underwriters, Inc. v. Home Insurance Co.*[44] involved similar facts, except that a pulley system designed by the insured to protect him if he lost consciousness jammed and failed. The court held that no coverage existed under the "accidental results" policy, because the insured "was bound to have foreseen that death or serious bodily injury could have resulted when he voluntarily induced unconsciousness with a noose around his neck."[45] However, other courts[46] have held that an insured's death under similar circumstances was an accident because the insured did not intend to cause his own death. A Wisconsin court summarized its rationale as follows:

> We recognize . . . that there are occasions when an insured participates in some act where serious injury or death is highly probable or an inevitable result. Under no circumstances can or should that conduct be termed accidental. It would defeat the very purpose or underlying function of accidental life insurance. However, the intentional or unnecessary exposure to risks, as well as the negligent creation of risks to one's own safety, does not prevent the result from being accidental. The customary expectation of a policyholder is that the injury or death is accidental if there is some reasonable basis for the belief that his conduct does not make the injury or death an expected result.
>
> More is required than a simple showing that injury or death might result. It is only when the consequences of the act are so natural and probable that it can be said the insured, in effect, intended the result and it was therefore not

---

[41] 671 F.2d 913 (5th Cir. 1982).

[42] See also Hardy v. Beneficial Life Ins. Co., 787 P.2d 1 (Utah App. 1990) (death of insured from narcotic intoxification was accidental in absence of any evidence that insured intended to commit suicide or expected to die from consuming drugs).

[43] 537 F.2d 1157 (4th Cir. 1976).

[44] 662 F.2d 1084 (4th Cir. 1981).

[45] 662 F.2d at 1087.

[46] See, e.g., Kennedy v. Washington Nat'l Ins. Co., 401 N.W.2d 842 (Wis. Ct. App. 1987); Connecticut Gen. Life Ins. Co. v. Tommie, 619 S.W.2d 199 (Tex. Ct. App. 1981).

accidental. It must be demonstrated in some way that he knew or should have known that his actions would probably result in his death.[47]

Some insurers have sought to narrow the scope of coverage by requiring that the insured's death be caused by "accidental means."[48] This language draws a distinction between accidental means and accidental results. Sometimes an intentional act has unintended results, and it is common to refer to the loss as an accident in such circumstances. However, the requirement that the loss be a result of accidental means insists that the mechanism through which the loss was produced be accidental. The effect of this requirement is to make the insurer liable for a range of losses somewhat narrower than the set of all fortuitous losses.

Numerous courts continue to adhere to a distinction between accidents and losses produced through accidental means.[49] Illustrative is *Linder v. Prudential Insurance Company of America,*[50] a 1979 North Carolina case. The insured and his wife, the beneficiary, had a disagreement over the wife's preference not to attend a movie one evening. The insured then retrieved a handgun from the kitchen, and while tossing it asked, "We are still not going to a movie tonight?" whereupon the wife answered "No." The insured then raised the gun toward his head and said in a joking tone, "Do you want me to do this?" The wife said "No" while looking away, and at that time the gun discharged and the insured fell, mortally wounded, to the floor.

The court referred to an earlier decision which explained the accidental means concept as follows:

> "Accidental means" refers to the occurrence or happening which produces the result and not to the result. That is, "accidental" is descriptive of the term "means." The motivating, operative and causal factor must be accidental in the sense that it is unusual, unforeseen and unexpected. Under the majority view the emphasis is upon the accidental character of the causation — not upon the accidental nature of the ultimate sequence of the chain of causation.[51]

This test required the court to identify the causal factor in the chain of events leading to the insured's death. The court said that the insured's pulling of the trigger was the cause, but here the court was unwilling to conclude as a matter of law that the insured's act was intentional: "even when an insured exposes himself or herself to reasonably foreseeable danger, if the ultimate causal factor is a 'mischance, slip or mishap occurring in doing the act,' the resulting injury is caused by 'accidental means.'. . ."[52]

---

[47] Kennedy v. Washington Nat'l Ins. Co., 401 N.W.2d 842, 846 (Wis.App. 1987.) See generally Annot., *Accident Or Life Insurance: Death by Autoerotic Asphyxiation as Accidental,* 62 A.L.R.4th 823 (1988).

[48] See generally Barry Rothman, *The Meaning of the "Accidental Means" Clause in Accident Insurance Policies,* 48 Ins. Counsel J. 231 (1981).

[49] See, e.g., Laney v. Continental Ins. Co., 757 F.2d 1190 (11th Cir. 1985); Thomason v. United States Fidelity & Guar. Co., 248 F.2d 417 (5th Cir. 1957); Winters v. Reliance Standard Life Ins. Co., 433 S.E.2d 363 (Ga. Ct. App. 1993); Hargreaves v. Metropolitan Life Ins. Co., 163 Cal. Rptr. 857 (Cal. Ct. App. 1980).

[50] 250 S.E.2d 662 (N.C. Ct. App. 1979).

[51] 250 S.E.2d at 665, quoting Fletcher v. Trust Co., 16 S.E.2d 687, 688 (N.C. 1941).

[52] 250 S.E.2d at 665.

If literally enforced, such clauses have the potential to narrow coverage. For this reason, a number of courts have rejected the accidental means versus accidental results distinction. One of the leading cases so holding is the 1946 New York Court of Appeals decision in *Burr v. Commercial Travelers Mutual Accident Association,*[53] where the court ruled that no distinction would be made in New York between "accidental death and death by accidental means, nor between accidental means and accidental results." Most courts since the *Burr* decision have followed that case's reasoning.[54]

Exemplar is *Knight v. Metropolitan Life Insurance Co.,*[55] a 1968 Arizona decision. At the time of his death, the insured had a policy which provided for coverage if the insured died "solely through violent, external and accidental means." The insured, at the age of 22, died after making a voluntary dive from the top of the Coolidge Dam. Knight, an experienced diver, had successfully dived from the top of the Dam before, but he apparently misjudged his final dive. The issue was whether the insured's death was accidental. From the insurer's perspective, the death did not result from accidental means, since the insured intentionally dove off the top of the dam, and death was a natural, probable consequence of this act. It was clear that the insured believed he could perform the daring feat and that he did not intend to kill himself. The court said that "an accident is an accident whether it be in the 'means' or the 'result.' " As a result, the insured was covered; he intended to insure, and no doubt believed that he possessed coverage, against "the fortuitous, the unintentional, and the unexpected, that which happens through mishap, mischance or misjudgment."[56]

To summarize, the decisions in which courts attempt to distinguish an intentionally caused death which is not covered and an accidental death which is prompt more questions than they answer. With regard to the cases holding that one can reasonably foresee that death will result from injecting heroin and therefore the death is not accidental, is death due to the taking of less obviously dangerous drugs also nonaccidental? Cardiac arrest due to cocaine intoxication was not widely perceived

---

[53] 67 N.E.2d 248 (N.Y. 1946).

[54] See, e.g., Carroll v. CUNA Mut. Ins. Soc'y, 894 P.2d 746 (Colo. 1995)(en banc); Vallejos v. Colonial Life & Acc. Ins. Co., 571 P.2d 404 (N.M. 1977); Republic Nat'l Life Ins. Co. v. Heyward, 536 S.W.2d 549 (Tex. 1976); Beckham v. Travelers Ins. Co., 225 A.2d 532 (Pa. 1967); Taylor v. John Hancock Mut. Life Ins. Co., 142 N.E.2d 5 (Ill. 1957); Murphy v. Travelers Ins. Co., 2 N.W.2d 576 (Neb. 1942); Allstate Ins. Co. v. Sparks, 493 A.2d 1110 (Md.Ct.Spec.App. 1985).

[55] 437 P.2d 416 (Ariz. 1968).

[56] The analysis in *Knight* suggests that an intentional act with the unintended result of death is covered by the policy as a fortuitous loss. In the twilight area of plausibility, one might ask the following: does it follow that an unintentional act which leads to an intended result is also covered? Suppose X develops a plan to kill Y by sabotaging the brakes on Y's car before Y is about to drive down a steep hill. Before X implements his plan, X negligently operates his car and hits a car operated by a third party; coincidentally, Y is a passenger in the car and is killed. Is X's negligence covered by X's liability insurer? The answer should be yes; an accident has occurred whether it be in the "means" or the "result" and X's insurer is liable.

as a potential risk until some prominent athletes lost their lives to the drug in the mid-1980s. What about death from taking too many doses of an over-the-counter medication contrary to the drug's label warnings? Mountain climbing and white-water rafting entail certain risks, particularly on some mountains and streams. Is death in such an activity accidental? Even if perishing in an attempted climb of Mt. Everest is foreseeable (much like the ever-present chance of death when one drives a racing car), can the same be said of a climb of Mt. Hood?[57] It is well known that excessive alcohol consumption can cause death; are such deaths accidents, or the natural and probable consequences of knowing actions?[58] Is a death in an automobile accident while driving under the influence of alcohol an "accident" for purposes of the double indemnity provision, or is it a natural, probable consequence of the knowing action?[59] Or, in these cases, does it depend on how risky the mountain is, or on how alcohol one has consumed before driving?[60] In effect, this

---

[57] Only highly skilled climbers attempt Mt. Everest; and the mountain has claimed many lives nevertheless. Mt. Hood is a 14,000 foot peak in Oregon, which is climbed each year by hundreds of hiking enthusiasts, but, like many things in the wilderness, Mt. Hood can be dangerous, and it has claimed several lives in recent years in avalanches and storm-related incidents.

[58] See Laney v. Continental Ins. Co., 757 F.2d 1190 (11th Cir. 1985); Consumers Life Ins. Co. v. Smith, 587 A.2d 1119 (Md.Ct.Spec.App. 1991) (public policy did not preclude insured's estate from receiving accidental death benefits even though evidence showed insured was intoxicated at time he drove vehicle into tree with fatal results); Collins v. Nationwide Life Ins. Co., 294 N.W.2d 194 (Mich. 1980) (holding that voluntary alcohol intoxication that results in death is accidental where insured did not intend or expect death). Of course, a clear exclusion in an accidental death policy for death caused by or resulting from operation of a motor vehicle while intoxicated should be enforced. See Ober v. Cuna Mut. Soc'y, 645 So. 2d 231 (La. Ct. App. 1994); Jefferson Pilot Life Ins. Co. v. Clark, 414 S.E.2d 521 (Ga. Ct. App. 1991).

[59] In Hearn v. Southern Life and Health Ins. Co., 454 So. 2d 932 (Ala. 1984), the insured, while fleeing the police at high speeds and intoxicated, was killed when his truck left the road and crashed. The policy did not explicitly exclude coverage for accidents while speeding or violating the law. The court held that even though the insured voluntarily exposed himself to unnecessary danger the trial court erred in directing a verdict for the insurer, since the evidence supported an inference that the insured's death was an accident. See also Harbeintner v. Crown Life Ins. Co., 612 P.2d 334 (Or. Ct. App. 1980); Metropolitan Life Ins. Co. v. Henkel, 234 F.2d 69 (4th Cir. 1956); Dooley v. Metropolitan Life Ins. Co., 250 A.2d 168 (N.J.Super.Ct.Law Div. 1969); Rodgers v. Reserve Life Ins. Co., 132 N.E.2d 692 (Ill. App. Ct. 1956).

It should be noted that a death which results while driving with a blood alcohol level exceeding the legal limit might constitute a "crime" within the meaning of a life insurance policy exclusion for loss resulting from commission of a crime. See United Commercial Travelers of Am. v. Tripp, 63 F.2d 37 (10th Cir. 1933); Sasloe v. Home Life Ins. Co., 416 So. 2d 867 (Fla. Dist. Ct. App. 1982); Geddes & Moss Undertaking & Embalming Co. v. First Nat'l Life Ins. Co., 167 So. 881 (La. Ct. App. 1936); but see Adkins v. Home Life Ins. Co., 372 N.W.2d 671 (Mich. Ct. App. 1985) (holding that death while driving drunk is not a crime within meaning of exclusion); see discussion in § 63B[b], *supra,* on death while committing a crime.

[60] In Hobbs v. Provident Life and Acc. Co., 535 S.W.2d 864 (Tenn. Ct. App. 1975), the court ruled that "the danger of injury or death as result of operating a motor vehicle while

is the same issue in the *Knight* case: when the insured dove off the Coolidge dam and perished, was his death accidental or was it the natural and probable consequence of a highly dangerous stunt? There is no mechanical rule that provides answers to these questions, although the rules of particular cases give guidance on likely outcomes.

§ 63C   Intentional Conduct and Liability Insurance

That liability insurers have a legitimate interest in excluding coverage for injury or damage intentionally caused by the insured is not seriously questioned. The insurer bases its rates on the probabilities of fortuitous losses; if the insured is in control of the insured risk, which is the case if the policy covers intentional acts, the ability of the insurer to calculate fair rates is frustrated.[1] Moreover, public policy forbids contracts indemnifying a person against loss resulting from his or her own willful wrongdoing. An insured should not be able to act wrongfully, all the time knowing that the insurer will pick up the tab for any damages or injury he or she causes.[2]

Despite the straightforward policy underlying the intentional act exclusion in liability insurance, the exclusion has not been an easy one to apply in many situations. Prior to the mid-1960s, liability policies typically contained an exclusion which provided that "bodily injury or property damage caused intentionally by or at the direction of the insured" would not be covered. The phrase "caused intentionally" was problematic because it was not clear whose viewpoint was to be used to determine whether a loss was "caused intentionally." Some courts, desiring to further the public policy of providing financial relief for the victims of torts, held that the point of view was that of the victim. This approach gave broad coverage: in many cases of intentionally-caused loss, the victim neither expects nor foresees the injury; from the victim's point of view, the loss is fortuitous. This liberal approach to coverage was criticized on the ground that it was the will of the perpetrator that should control; insureds should not be allowed to shift to their insurers the punishment they receive for having committed intentional torts. Thus, after the mid-1960s it became common to find liability policies stating that coverage would not exist for "bodily injury or property damage which is either expected or intended from the standpoint of the insured."[3]

---

intoxicated is a foreseeable one and . . . death is not caused by accidental means, within the meaning of an insurance policy, if it is a foreseeable result of a voluntary and unnecessary act or course of conduct of the insured." However, in Miller v. American Cas. Co., 377 F.2d 479 (6th Cir. 1967), the court, purporting to apply Tennessee law, disagreed, stating "[w]e see no mandate in law or public policy for this court to imply such an exclusion [for injuries due to driving when intoxicated] when none such was agreed on by the parties when the insurance contract was signed."

[1] 7A APPLEMAN § 4492.01 at 21 (1979).

[2] See Transamerica Ins. Group v. Meere, 694 P.2d 181 (Ariz. 1984).

[3] See generally Sam P. Rynearson, *Exclusion of Expected or Intended Personal Injury or Property Damage Under the Occurrence Definition of the Standard Comprehensive General Liability Policy,* 19 Forum 513 (1984).

Despite this clarification, courts continued to have difficulty applying the exclusion, and some of these problems persist today. Although the analysis is similar in both personal and commercial insurance, commercial liability coverage has some additional complexities, and these are discussed in subsequent sections.[4]

[a] "Intended" and "Expected"

The reference to both intent and expectations in the post- 1960s formulation of the exclusion raised the question whether "intended" had some different meaning than "expected." This suggested the argument that someone could expect to cause injury in a situation where none was intended. Some courts have concluded that the terms are essentially synonymous.[5] Other courts have concluded that the terms have different meanings.[6] One court has explained it as follows:

> [A] purely subjective standard governs the determination of whether the insured . . . either expected or intended to inflict bodily injury upon his brother. . . . Under this subjective test, an injury is "intended from the standpoint of the insured" if the insured possessed the specific intent to cause bodily injury to another, whereas an injury is "expected from the standpoint of the insured" if the insured subjectively possessed a high degree of certainty that bodily injury to another would result from his or her act.[7]

If the terms do not have different meanings, no purpose is served in having both terms in the clause.[8] Thus, a "plain-meaning" analysis begins with the observation that the provision has two separate prongs, notwithstanding that both prongs refer to the insured's state of mind. What the court in the above-quoted passage was attempting to express was this: when bodily injury or property damage is "intended," the insured has a *desire* that the injury or damage occur. However, bodily injury or property damage is "expected" when the insured *anticipates* that injury or damage will occur but has no desire that it occur. Thus, an insured can intend and expect harm to occur, intend but not expect harm to occur, or expect but not intend harm to occur. What the "expected" prong adds to the "intended" prong is an exclusion from coverage in circumstances where the insured's subjective state of mind with respect to desire is not clear, but the circumstances are such that the insured, even if not clearly desiring to cause harm, should surely have anticipated that harm would result. The difficulty with the foregoing analysis is that giving the "expected" prong this broader-range of operation creates the possibility that an insurer might refuse coverage for any injury or damage — even one from an unintentional tort — if the insured should have expected the injury or damage in the natural course of things. Some courts have contended that such a broad exclusion from coverage was never contemplated, and that the exclusion, insofar as it is ambiguous, should be construed

---

[4] See § 65, *infra.*

[5] See, e.g., State Farm Fire & Cas. Co. v. Muth, 207 N.W.2d 364 (Neb. 1973); Grange Mut. Cas. Co. v. Thomas, 301 So. 2d 158 (Fla. Dist. Ct. App. 1974).

[6] See, e.g., Patrons-Oxford Mut. Ins. Co. v. Dodge, 426 A.2d 888 (Me. 1981); Northwestern Nat'l Cas. Co. v. Phalen, 597 P.2d 720 (Mont. 1979); State Farm Fire & Cas. Co. v. Jenkins, 382 N.W.2d 796 (Mich. Ct. App. 1985).

[7] See Alabama Farm Bur. Mut. Cas. Ins. Co. v. Dyer, 454 So. 2d 921 (Ala. 1984).

[8] See Badger Mut. Ins. Co. v. Murry, 370 N.E.2d 295 (Ill. App. Ct. 1977).

against the insurer.[9] The challenge, then, is how one gives the "expected" prong some kind of content which does not convert all foreseeable consequences of an act into non-covered liability. Professor Abraham has observed that efforts to make the "expected" prong operational involve three separate issues: probability of harm; awareness of the probability; and specificity of the expectation of harm.[10]

An insured who "expects" injury or damage must be aware that the injury or damage has a high probability of occurring as a consequence of the insured's act or neglect. Explaining this probability component was the essence of the court's decision in *Honeycomb Systems, Inc. v. Admiral Insurance Co.,*[11] Honeycomb manufactured a large dryer for Scott Paper Company; the dryer was to be used in Scott's toilet paper manufacturing business. After two years of operation (and some intermittent problems), the dryer's hub developed a large crack, and Honeycomb sought coverage under its liability policy with Admiral for Honeycomb's liability to Scott. Admiral did not dispute that the hub crack was an unintended accident that resulted in property damage, but Admiral argued that the crack was "expected" from the insured's standpoint and therefore excluded from coverage. Admiral initially argued that any "reasonably foreseeable" event must be considered expected, but the court observed that such a test would allow coverage only when the insured is not negligent and hence not in need of any coverage at all.[12] Instead, the court used a test approved by the Maine Supreme Court in an earlier case:[13] "expected" injury or damage is that which the insured "in fact subjectively foresaw as practically certain."[14] The "practically certain" test indicates that a high degree of probability is required before it can be said that the insured "expects" injury or damage. Other courts have used tests like "substantial probability,"[15] and "substantial certainty."[16]

In addition to the harm or injury being highly probable in some sense, the insured must be aware of this probability. Clearly, when the insured knows that harm is probable, the awareness element is present. When the insured's knowledge cannot be proved, however, the question becomes whether a subjective or objective test of awareness should be used. Some courts ask whether a reasonable person in the shoes of the insured should have expected the harm or injury.[17] If, however, the drafters

---

[9] See, e.g., Grange Mut. Cas. Co. v. Thomas, 301 So. 2d 158 (Fla. Dist. Ct. App. 1974).

[10] Kenneth S. Abraham, *Environmental Liability Insurance Law* 132 (1991). Although Professor Abraham's discussion is in the context of commercial liability coverages, the analysis is pertinent to the exclusion in all settings.

[11] 567 F. Supp. 1400 (D.Me. 1983).

[12] This was the test approved in Gassaway v. Travelers Ins. Co., 439 S.W.2d 605 (Tenn. 1969).

[13] See Patrons-Oxford Mut. Ins. Co. v. Dodge, 426 A.2d 888 (Me. 1981).

[14] 567 F. Supp. at 1404.

[15] See City of Carter Lake v. Aetna Cas. & Sur. Co., 604 F.2d 1052 (8th Cir. 1979).

[16] See, e.g., Quincy Mut. Fire Ins. Co. v. Abernathy, 469 N.E.2d 797, 800 (Mass. 1984); United Serv. Auto. Ass'n v. Elitzky, 517 A.2d 982 (Pa. Super. Ct. 1986). See also Brown Foundation v. St. Paul Fire & Marine Ins. Co., 814 S.W.2d 273, 278 (Ky. 1991) ("practically certain or expected-to-be"); Shell Oil Co. v. Winterthur Swiss Ins. Co., 15 Cal. Rptr.2d 815 (Cal. Ct. App. 1993) ("anticipation with a high degree of probability"); Indiana Farmers Mut. Ins. Co. v. Graham, 537 N.E.2d 510, 512 (Ind. Ct. App. 1989) ("practically certain.")

[17] See, e.g., Calvert Ins. Co. v. Western Ins. Co., 874 F.2d 396 (7th Cir. 1989).

of the policy language intended an objective test, the language could have been clearer; for example, harm or injury "reasonably expected from the standpoint of the insured" would have better communicated this idea.[18] Thus, other courts hold that awareness must be measured subjectively,[19] even if this prove must be constructed from circumstantial evidence out of which the inference of subjective intent is made. Whatever the test, the upshot is that the insured must be "highly aware" in some sense that injury or damage is probable.

The third component of the "expected" prong is the specificity of the insured's awareness. As discussed more fully with respect to the "intended" prong in the next subsection, it is possible that the harm which results may differ in character and magnitude from what the insured anticipated. If one insists that the resulting harm be precisely what the insured anticipated, the "expected" prong will have a narrow scope, which expands coverage. If it does not matter at all what kind of harm results, the "expected" prong will have a broader scope, which constricts coverage. A mid-range position, which Professor Abraham urges,[20] would hold that an insured "expects" injury or damage when the resulting harm is of the same general type that the insured expected. Liability policies in use today do not settle this issue by their own terms, and the choice of test is left to the discretion of courts.

[b] "Intended" Construed

The confusion over the language "intended or expected" sets the stage for additional disarray over construction of the word "intended." The question is essentially whether the injury or damage caused by the insured was "caused intentionally" so as to deprive the insured — and the victim — of insurance coverage.

Three different constructions of "intended" have developed. Under the minority view, the view which provides the narrowest coverage and the most pro-insurer results, the classic tort doctrine of looking to the natural and probable consequences of the insured's act determines intent. In other words, if the intentional act by the insured results in injuries or damage that are a natural and probable result of the act, the loss is intentional for purposes of the exclusion and no coverage exists.[21]

Under the majority view, which sits in the midrange of the three views insofar as coverage is concerned, the insured must have intended both the act *and* to cause some kind of injury or damage.[22] Intent to cause the injury or damage can be

---

[18] Abraham, *supra* note 10, at 134.

[19] See City of Johnstown v. Bankers Standard Ins. Co., 877 F.2d 1146 (2d Cir. 1989); Patrons-Oxford Mut. Ins. Co. v. Dodge, 426 A.2d 888 (Me. 1981).

[20] Abraham, *supra* note 10, at 136-37.

[21] See St. Paul Ins. Cos. v. Talladega Nursing Home, Inc., 606 F.2d 631 (5th Cir. 1979)(applying Alabama law).

[22] See, e.g., Allstate Ins. Co. v. Dillard, 859 F. Supp. 1501 (M.D.Ga. 1994); Green Mountain Ins. Co. v. Foreman, 641 A.2d 230 (N.H. 1994); Amco Ins. Co. v. Haht, 490 N.W.2d 843 (Iowa 1992); Tennessee Farmers Mut. Ins. Co. v. Evans, 814 S.W.2d 49 (Tenn. 1991); American Family Mut. Ins. Co. v. Johnson, 816 P.2d 952 (Colo. 1991) (en banc); Farmer in the Dell Enter., Inc. v. Farmers Mut. Ins. Co., 514 A.2d 1097 (Del. 1986); Mutual Service Cas. Ins. Co. v. McGehee, 711 P.2d 826 (Mont. 1986); Pachucki v. Republic Ins. Co., 278 N.W.2d 898 (Wis. 1979).

inferred from the nature of the act and the foreseeability that harm would result.[23] It is not essential, however, that the harm be of the same character and magnitude as that intended.

The third approach, which provides the broadest coverage and the fewest pro-insurer results, is that for the exclusion to apply the insured must have had the specific intent not only to injure but also to cause the particular type of injury suffered.[24]

At one extreme on the continuum of possible fact situations, each of the three tests would result in excluding coverage for the insured. Suppose, for example, that the insured, without provocation, privilege, or excuse, hits the victim in the face with a closed fist with power; the insured intends to break the victim's nose and succeeds in doing so.[25] Under any test — the insured must intend to cause the type of injury suffered; the insured must intend to act and cause some kind of injury; the act must be intentional and result in injuries that are natural and probable outcomes of the act — the victim's injury was "caused intentionally" and no coverage exists. As fact situations move away from this continuum, however, the different tests can lead to different outcomes.

Consider, for example, the situation where the insured intends the act but it is less clear that the insured intends the resulting injury. This situation is illustrated by *Farmers Insurance Group v. Hastings,*[26] a 1984 Minnesota case. At a party, Kenyon, the insured, became involved in an altercation with a guest who was accused of spreading an offensive rumor about Kenyon. Hastings, Kenyon's good friend, attempted to intercede, and a scuffle broke out between Hastings and Kenyon. Hastings gained the advantage; conciliatory words were exchanged, and the scuffle ceased. A few seconds later, as the two began walking toward the street, Kenyon grabbed Hastings and struck him in the left eye with his right hand. Hastings suffered severe, permanent injury to both eyes.

It would seem that Kenyon intended his act; it would also seem that a natural, foreseeable (though not inevitable) result of striking someone in the face with a fist is serious, permanent injury. Under the minority view, the insurer would not be bound to pay proceeds for Hastings' injury. However, it is less clear that Kenyon intended to cause injury to Hastings — let alone serious injury. As the Court of Appeals indicated, the insured and the victim were good friends, there was no evidence of a prior conflict between them, Kenyon's anger was triggered not by

---

[23] See Mottolo v. Fireman's Fund Ins. Co., 830 F. Supp. 658 (D.N.H. 1993) (in environmental damage case, proof of subjective intent to injure can be inferred where insured's acts are inherently injurious).

[24] See, e.g., Providence Mut. Fire Ins. Co. v. Scanlon, 638 A.2d 1246 (N.H. 1994); Physicians Ins. Co. of Ohio v. Swanson, 569 N.E.2d 906 (Ohio 1991); see generally Annot., *Construction and Application of Provision of Liability Insurance Policy Expressly Excluding Injuries Intended or Expected by Insured,* 31 A.L.R.4th 957 (1984).

[25] These are essentially the facts of Shelter Ins. Cos. v. Smith, 479 N.E.2d 365 (Ill. App. Ct. 1985). The court concluded that the insured acted with intent and that the "injuries were of such a nature that they should reasonably have been anticipated by [the insured]."

[26] 358 N.W.2d 473 (Minn. Ct. App. 1984), *rev'd,* 366 N.W.2d 293 (Minn. 1985).

Hastings but by a third party, and only a short time existed between the scuffle and the act causing the injury — suggesting that Kenyon's action was reflexive in nature. Based on these considerations, the Court of Appeals reversed the trial court's determination that Kenyon intended to injure Hastings.[27]

To illustrate the difference between the majority approach (which requires a showing that the insured intended to cause some injury) and the approach which requires a showing that the specific injury was intended,[28] consider the situation where the insured shoots at X intending to injure X but misses and injures Y, a stranger, instead.[29] In this circumstance, the insured intended the act and to cause some kind of injury; under the majority approach, the insured's act would be excluded. However, if intent to cause the specific injury is required to exclude the insured's act, the insured's liability would be covered in this situation. The insured did not intend to cause the specific injury which resulted, and the victim would recover under the insured's liability policy. *Unigard Mutual Insurance Co. v. Argonaut Insurance Co.,*[30] a 1978 Washington decision, illustrates the majority view. The insured's son broke into a school building and set a fire in a trash can. After watching it burn for a time, he tried without success to extinguish it. He became frightened, ran away, and notified no one of the blaze. The fire spread and ultimately caused $250,000 worth of damage to the building. The court ruled that the damage was excluded under the insured's liability policy. His son intended to start the fire, but did not intend to cause such extensive damage to the school. However, since some damage was expected and since the insured knew the fire could spread, the court held that the entire loss was within the exclusion.

The minority view,[31] which draws on the tests of tort and criminal law and presumes that persons intend the natural and foreseeable consequences of their

---

[27] The Supreme Court later reversed the Court of Appeals and reinstated the trial court's judgment, holding that the appeals court lacked the authority to reverse the trial court's finding of fact given the record before it. Farmers Ins. Group v. Hastings, 366 N.W.2d 293 (Minn. 1985). For other illustrations, see American Family Mut. Ins. Co. v. Pacchetti, 808 S.W.2d 369 (Mo. 1991) (en banc) (finding that death of visitor at insured's residence, which resulted from insured injecting or assisting visitor in injecting cocaine, was not "expected or intended" and would not be disturbed on appeal); Alabama Farm Bur. Mut. Cas. Ins. Co. v. Dyer, 454 So. 2d 921 (Ala. 1984) (insured, while drinking, shoots and kills brother; insured goes into shock and within moments kills himself; affirms finding that insured neither expected nor intended that the gun would discharge and kill brother)

[28] See, e.g., Talley v. MFA Mut. Ins. Co., 620 S.W.2d 260 (Ark. 1981); Lumbermens Mut. Ins. Co. v. Blackburn, 477 P.2d 62 (Okla. 1970).

[29] These are essentially the facts of Earl Mutual Ins. Co. v. Burkholder Estate, [1984–85] Fire & Cas. Cases (CCH), at 1386 (Pa.Commw.Ct. 1984). The insured shot at his wife, not intending to injure the daughter, but missed and killed his daughter instead. The court held that the exclusionary clause for intentionally caused injury did not apply. For a similar case which deeply divided the Michigan Supreme Court (insured fired at unoccupied vehicle and ricochet injured nearby person), see Buczkowski v. Allstate Ins. Co., 526 N.W.2d 589 (Mich. 1994).

[30] 579 P.2d 1015 (Wash. Ct. App. 1978).

[31] See, e.g., Hins v. Heer, 259 N.W.2d 38 (N.D. 1977); Casualty Reciprocal Exch. v. Thomas, 647 P.2d 1361 (Kan.Ct.App. 1982).

actions, has been specifically repudiated in a number of jurisdictions.[32] The difficulty with this approach is that its breadth has the effect of eliminating financial resources for innocent victims in a great many situations. A case which, in rejecting the minority view, illustrates its weaknesses is *Farmers Insurance Co. v. Vagnozzi,*[33] a 1983 Arizona case. The policy specifically excluded from coverage damage "arising as a result of intentional acts of the insured." The insured injured the victim in a roughly-played three-on-three recreational league basketball game. The injury in question occurred during the game when the insured was knocked down by the victim. While the ball was still in play, the insured angrily sprang up and swung his elbow toward the victim's chest while lunging toward the player with the ball. At that instant, the victim bent over and the insured's elbow struck him the face. The victim was knocked backwards and rendered unconscious when he hit his head on the concrete court surface.

The trial court, following the minority view, held that the result of the blow, though different in character and magnitude than that intended, was nevertheless the natural and probable result of an intentional act. The Supreme Court reversed, specifically rejecting the trial court's use of the tort standard of foreseeability: "The presumption that a person intends the ordinary consequences of his voluntary actions, used in determining responsibility for the voluntary act, has no application to the interpretation of terms used in insurance contracts." Accordingly, the court said the intentional act exclusion would apply "if the insured *acts with the intent or expectation* that bodily injury will result even though the result is different in character from the injury that was intended."

In *Vagnozzi,* it was not clear from the record on appeal that the insured acted with subjective intent to cause an injury. In some circumstances, the act may be so certain to cause injury that intent can be inferred.[34] For example, as stated by the Kansas Supreme Court in *Bell v. Tilton,*[35] "the act of shooting another in the face with a BB pellet is one which is recognized as an act so certain to cause a particular kind of harm it can be said an actor who performed the act intended the resulting harm, and his statement to the contrary does nothing to refute that rule of law."[36] However, the throwing of an elbow in a basketball game, even in anger and frustration, is not necessarily an act which the actor intends as injurious. A deliberate punch in the face, on the one hand, is so certain to result in injury that the insured will not be heard to argue that the insured had no subjective intent to cause injury.[37] However,

---

[32] See, e.g., Rajspic v. Nationwide Mut. Ins. Co., 718 P.2d 1167 (Idaho 1986); Continental W. Ins. Co. v. Toal, 244 N.W.2d 121 (Minn. 1976); Poston v. United States Fidelity & Guar. Co., 320 N.W.2d 9 (Wis. Ct. App. 1982).

[33] 675 P.2d 703 (Ariz. 1983).

[34] See, e.g., Smith v. Senst, 313 N.W.2d 202 (Minn. 1981); Patrons-Oxford Mut. Ins. Co. v. Dodge, 426 A.2d 888 (Me. 1981).

[35] 674 P.2d 468 (Kan. 1983).

[36] 674 P.2d at 476. See also Harris v. Richards, 867 P.2d 325 (Kan. 1994) (when insured fired two shotgun blasts into occupied cab of pickup truck when he knew it was occupied, injuries were a natural and probable consequence of insured's act and fall within intentional act exclusion).

[37] See Smith v. State Farm Ins. Cos., 870 P.2d 74 (Mont. 1994) (insured's act of hitting his daughter's babysitter in face with his fist was within intentional act exclusion even though

an elbow thrown in a basketball game is not as certain to cause injury, and the inference of subjective intent to injure does not definitely follow. Therefore, the Court in *Vagnozzi* ruled that a trial was required to determine the nature of the insured's intent.

It is not always easy to determine which of the three approaches a court is following. Part of the difficulty is that some cases are easy, falling within the exclusion regardless of the approach prevailing in a jurisdiction. The obviousness of a result may cause a court to be less than precise with the language offering the rationale for the result; this can lead to difficulty in subsequent cases that present closer questions. Indeed, in some states, decisions exist that purport to adhere to an approach distinct from that followed in earlier cases, and no effort is made in these decisions to distinguish or overrule the earlier decisions.[38] Furthermore, the distinctions between the three tests are subtle and not easy to comprehend.

In two areas, the determination of "intent" for purposes of applying the intentional act exclusion has presented particular difficulties. In the "prank" cases, someone typically plays a practical joke on another that goes awry and causes injury or damage. The joker usually exercises bad judgment and lacks intent to injure the victim of the prank. However, injury is often a natural and a foreseeable result of the prank. In one case,[39] a teenager threw a pumpkin from an overpass which shattered a car's windshield and caused the driver serious injuries. The teenager maintained that he attempted to throw the pumpkin in front of or alongside the vehicle in an effort to scare the driver. The act was intentional, but the court concluded that the trial court's finding that there was intent to injure was clearly erroneous. In another case,[40] one employee, as a joke, squirted smoke in a colleague's respirator causing him serious injury. The court said that the injury was not excluded from coverage, since although the act was intended, the injury was not. A different result might have been appropriate if the employee, although intending a joke, had reason to know that the smoke was dangerous.

The second area of difficulty is that presented by the several cases of the past few years involving sexual conduct.[41] To use the example of a recent Minnesota Supreme Court case,[42] if an insured intentionally engages in unprotected sex and

---

insured claimed he was momentarily unconscious after babysitter had hit him on head and he hit her in reflex action).

[38] See Annot., *Construction and Application of Provision of Liability Insurance Policy Expressly Excluding Injuries Intended or Expected by Insured*, 31 A.L.R.4th 957, 994–99 (1984); see generally Annot., *Criminal Conviction as Rendering Conduct for Which Insured Convicted Within Provision of Liability Insurance Policy Expressly Excluding Coverage for Damage or Injury Intended or Expected by Insured*, 35 A.L.R.4th 1063 (1985).

[39] Vermont Mut. Ins. Co. v. Dalzell, 218 N.W.2d 52 (Mich. Ct. App. 1974).

[40] Millers Mut. Ins. Co. v. Strainer, 663 P.2d 338 (Mont. 1983). See also Quincy Mut. Fire Ins. Co. v. Abernathy, 469 N.E.2d 797 (Mass. 1984) (summary judgment for insurer inappropriate where minor throws asphalt through window of moving car).

[41] See generally Noel Mckibbin, Note, *Defending Sexual Molestation Claims Under a Comprehensive General Liability Policy: Issues of Scope, Occurrence, and Expert Witness Testimony*, 39 Drake L. Rev. 477 (1989/90).

[42] R.W. v. T.P., 528 N.W.2d 869 (Minn. 1995).

negligently (i.e., unintentionally) transmits genital herpes to his or her partner, is the resulting damage caused intentionally? The Minnesota court held that the insured's intent could be inferred as a matter of law, even though the insured's acts were not malicious; the insured knew or should have known that he had herpes and could transmit it through unprotected sex; his awareness of a substantial probability of harm was enough to render the resulting injury "intentional." The Texas Supreme Court reached the opposite conclusion, holding that whether the insured intended harm or injury to result from the intentional act presented a question of fact, and that the insured's intent to injure would not be inferred as a matter of law for purposes of applying the intentional injury exclusion of a homeowner's policy.[43] In recent years, a number of insurance coverage cases have been litigated where the underlying facts involve the molestation of children by adults. The difficulty in these cases is that the insured who assaults a child, although intending the act, may not subjectively intend to injure the child. Indeed, it is not uncommon for the adult to believe — as unreasonable and repugnant as this belief is — that the child is benefiting in some way. The courts have almost uniformly held, however, that the injury resulting from sexual molestation by the insured is not covered by the insured's liability policy.[44] Some courts in jurisdictions adhering to the subjective test of intent have ruled that the subjective test simply does not apply when the injury results from an adult's sexual abuse of a minor; in such cases, intent to cause injury is inferred as a matter of law.[45] Another court explained the result in this way: "The test is what a plain ordinary person would expect and intend to result from a mature man's deliberately debauching his six-year-old stepdaughter and continuing to do so for years."[46] Such a person would expect injury to result; therefore, the insured's liability policy provides no coverage. It would seem that the same logic should apply to any case of intentional sexual assault[47] (with the possible exception of the situation where a child who lacks an understanding of the nature of his or her acts sexually abuses another child),[48] but at least one court has refused to apply the

---

[43] See State Farm Fire & Cas. Co. v. S.S. & G.W., 858 S.W.2d 374 (Tex. 1993). Note that some recent policy forms address this issue directly by excluding coverage for liability "[w]hich arises out of the transmission of a communicable disease by an 'insured'." See *Policy Kit* at 31 (ISO Form HO 00 03 04 91).

[44] See, e.g., American Family Mut. Ins. Co. v. Purdy, 483 N.W.2d 197 (S.D. 1992), cert. denied sub. nom, D.L. v. American Family Mut. Ins. Co., 113 S.Ct. 202 (1992); Allstate Ins. Co. v. Mugavero, 589 N.E.2d 365 (N.Y. 1992); MacKinnon v. Hanover Ins. Co., 471 A.2d 1166 (N.H. 1984); State Farm Fire & Cas. Co. v. Williams, 355 N.W.2d 421 (Minn. 1984); Linebaugh v. Berdish, 376 N.W.2d 400 (Mich. Ct. App. 1985); Allstate Ins. Co. v. Kim W., 206 Cal. Rptr. 609 (Cal. Ct. App. 1984).

[45] Wiley v. State Farm Fire & Cas. Co., 995 F.2d 457 (3d Cir. 1993); State Farm Fire & Cas. Co. v. Davis, 612 So. 2d 458 (Ala. 1993).

[46] CNA Insurance Co. v. McGinnis, 666 S.W.2d 689, 691 (Ark. 1984).

[47] See Allstate Ins. Co. v. S.F., 518 N.W.2d 37 (Minn. 1994) (intentional sexual assaults alleged in complaint against insured could not be characterized as "accidents"; exclusion applies). Compare State Farm Fire & Cas. Co. v. Nycum, 943 F.2d 1100 (9th Cir. 1991) (allegation that insured had sexually molested child did not preclude coverage under homeowner's policy absent showing that insured's act was intentional molestation).

[48] See Fire Ins. Exch. v. Diehl, 520 N.W.2d 675 (Mich. Ct. App. 1994) (under "reasonable child" standard, boy, who was between 7 and 9 years of age at times he sexually abused girl 3 years younger, intent to injure would not be inferred).

"inferred intent" rule in a civil action arising out of an adult's alleged rape of another adult.[49] This issue will be litigated less in the future because recent policies often contain an exclusion for liability arising out of sexual assault and other kinds of abusive conduct.[50]

The foregoing analysis has been applied in sexual harassment cases also. Alleged intentional acts of sexual harassment have been held not to arise from an "occurrence" within the meaning of a liability policy which excludes coverage for bodily injury expected or intended from the standpoint of the insured.[51]

[c] Self-Defense

Another difficulty concerning the intentional act exclusion is whether acts in self-defense that cause injury to another are excluded from coverage. Interestingly, the courts are split on this question.[52] In a number of cases, courts have held that injury inflicted in self-defense is expected or intended under the intentional injury exclusion clause.[53] As explained by one court,[54] "although a claim of self-defense may raise the criminal defense of justification for an intentionally caused injury, it does not vitiate the actual intent to cause the injury."[55] These courts give great weight to the literal language of the policy; allowing coverage of acts committed in self-defense appears to some courts as naked rewriting of the policy.[56] Other courts have taken a different approach. In the view of these courts, the purpose of self-defense is not to injure, but is instead to prevent injury to oneself. Therefore,

---

[49] See Aetna Life & Cas. Co. v. Barthelemy, 33 F.3d 189 (3d Cir. 1994).

[50] See *Policy Kit* at 31 (ISO form HO 00 03 04 91) (exclusion for liability "[a]rising out of sexual molestation, corporal punishment or physical or mental abuse.") There is disagreement over the utility of spanking as a means for the discipline of children, but the cited policy language, by its terms, appears to exclude coverage for injury inflicted as a result of spanking for disciplinary purposes.

[51] See, e.g., Commercial Union Ins. Cos. v. Sky, Inc., 810 F. Supp. 249 (W.D. Ark. 1992); Old Republic Ins. Co. v. Comprehensive Health Care, 786 F. Supp. 629 (N.D. Tex. 1992); Sena v. Travelers Ins. Co., 801 F. Supp. 471 (D.N.M. 1992); State Farm Fire & Cas. Co. v. Compupay, Inc., 654 So. 2d 944 (Fla. Dist. Ct. App. 1995); Board of Educ. of East Syracuse-Minoa Cent. Sch. Dist. v. Continental Ins. Co., 604 N.Y.S.2d 399 (N.Y.Sup. 1993); Pylant v. Lofton, 626 So. 2d 83 (La. Ct. App. 1993); McLeod v. Tecorp Int'l, Ltd., 844 P.2d 925 (Or.App. 1992); Continental Ins. Co. v. McDaniel, 772 P.2d 6 (Ariz.App. 1988); Greenman v. Michigan Mut. Ins. Co., 433 N.W.2d 346 (Mich.App. 1988).

[52] See generally Annot., *Acts in Self-Defense as Within Provision of Liability Insurance Policy Expressly Excluding Coverage for Damage or Injury Intended or Expected by Insured,* 34 A.L.R.4th 761 (1984).

[53] See, e.g., Espinet v. Horvath, 597 A.2d 307 (Vt. 1991); Grange Ins. Co. v. Brosseau, 776 P.2d 123 (Wash. 1989); McAndrews v. Farm Bur. Mut. Ins. Co., 349 N.W.2d 117 (Iowa 1984); Allstate Ins. Co. v. Grayes, 454 S.E.2d 616 (Ga. Ct. App. 1995); State Farm Fire & Cas. Co. v. Caldwell, 630 So. 2d 668 (Fla. Dist. Ct. App. 1994); Home Ins. Co. v. Neilsen, 332 N.E.2d 240 (Ind. Ct. App. 1975).

[54] Stein v. Massachusetts Bay Ins. Co., 324 S.E.2d 510 (Ga. Ct. App. 1984).

[55] 324 S.E.2d at 511.

[56] See, e.g., Home Ins. Co. v. Neilsen, 332 N.E.2d 240 (Ind. Ct. App. 1975).

an injury inflicted on another in self-defense is neither expected nor intended from the standpoint of the insured, and thus is not excluded from the coverage.[57]

With regard to the proceeds of insurance, in many cases the controversy over whether intentional acts committed in self-defense are covered has no practical significance. If the insured acts within the zone of legitimate self-defense, the insured will not be liable to the victim, and no proceeds will be owed the victim whether or not the policy provides coverage. If the insured did not act in self-defense, there was no privilege to act intentionally so as to injure the plaintiff, and no coverage would be provided and hence no proceeds paid. This analysis is subject to two important caveats, however. The insurer has a duty to defend any claim within coverage; if intentional acts of self-defense are within coverage, the insurer has a duty to defend the insured whenever the insured claims he or she acted in self-defense and the plaintiff was injured thereby.[58] Conversely, if intentional acts in self-defense are not covered, the insurer has no duty to defend the insured. Secondly, it is possible that a person acting in self-defense, though having a privilege to so act, might have used more force than necessary. A party can be held liable in damages for using excessive force; therefore, whether intentional acts committed in self-defense are covered by the liability policy will determine whether an insured will be covered for having used excessive force.

Allowing coverage of intentional acts committed in self-defense is not clearly violative of public policy. In the non-self-defense situation where the insured acts with intent, the insured is in control of the risk. This is not the case when the insured acts in self-defense; instead, the insured is attempting to avoid a calamity that has fallen upon him or her. Extending coverage would force insurers to defend many claims — a substantial expense — for insureds who without good cause claim that their intentional acts were in self-defense. Such a claim is plausible in almost any assault situation; providing coverage would require insurers to defend almost all of these claims. Yet this is arguably what the insured purchases: coverage for liability to others arising out of fortuitous circumstances, and being assaulted by a third party and attempting to defend oneself is certainly a fortuitous circumstance.

[d] Diminished Mental Capacity

Another difficulty presented by the intentional act exclusion is whether the insured's diminished mental capacity will render otherwise intentional conduct unintentional for the purposes of the exclusion.[59] Most courts have accepted the

---

[57] See, e.g., Aetna Cas. & Sur. Co. v. Cochran, 651 A.2d 859 (Md. 1995); Vermont Mut. Ins. Co. v. Singleton, 446 S.E.2d 417 (S.C. 1994); Transamerica Ins. Group v. Meere, 694 P.2d 181 (Ariz. 1984); Allstate Ins. Co. v. Novak, 313 N.W.2d 636 (Neb. 1981); Western Fire Ins. Co. v. Persons, 393 N.W.2d 234 (Minn. Ct. App. 1986); Mullen v. Glens Falls Ins. Co., 140 Cal. Rptr. 605 (Cal. Ct. App. 1977).

[58] See § 111[c], *infra*.

[59] See generally Catherine A. Salton, *Mental Incapacity and Liability Insurance Exclusionary Clauses: The Effect of Insanity Upon Intent*, 78 Cal.L.Rev. 1027 (1990); Annot., *Liability Insurance: Intoxication or Other Mental Incapacity Avoiding Application of Clause in Liability Policy Specifically Exempting Coverage of Injury or Damage Caused Intentionally By or At Direction of Insured*, 33 A.L.R.4th 983 (1984).

view that if an insured suffered from a lack of mental capacity when he or she acted with apparent intent to injure another, the insured's act cannot be treated as "intentional" within the meaning of the exclusion and coverage exists.[60] *Globe American Casualty Co. v. Lyons,*[61] a 1981 Arizona case, is illustrative. The insured drove her automobile directly into a pickup truck occupied by the victims, causing personal injuries. The insurer sought a declaratory judgment that it was not liable under the policy. The victims argued that the insured did not act intentionally because she suffered from a mental illness that rendered her incapable of distinguishing right from wrong, and that she was actually attempting to commit suicide in an uncontrollable response to auditory hallucinations. The insurer argued that the insured's mental capacity was irrelevant for purposes of the policy's exclusion. The court rejected the insurer's argument and agreed with the victims. First, the court noted that exclusionary clauses are strictly construed against the insurer. Furthermore, the purpose of the exclusion is to prevent individuals from receiving economic protection when they act intentionally, and this purpose cannot be served when the insured lacks the mental capacity necessary to conform her conduct to reasonable standards.[62]

An alternative approach is followed by many courts, including many that have addressed the issue in recent years.[63] Under this opposing view, "an injury inflicted by an insane person is intentional if the actor understands the physical nature and consequences of the act."[64] This approach is premised on the belief that a person who is considered insane may nevertheless be capable of forming the intent to do certain acts, even if the intent results from the mental deficiency. Such a person can intend to act, and thus fall within the exclusion to coverage, "even if the person did not fully understand what he or she was doing at the time of the crime" or otherwise wrongful act.[65]

---

[60] See, e.g., Nationwide Ins. Co. v. Estate of Kollstedt, 646 N.E.2d 816 (Ohio 1995) (exclusion in policy for expected and intended injuries did not apply where insured, due to Alzheimer's dementia, lacked mental capacity to commit murder); Cooperative Fire Ins. Ass'n v. Combs, 648 A.2d 857 (Vt. 1994); State Farm Fire & Cas. Co. v. Wicks, 474 N.W.2d 324 (Minn. 1991); Ruvolo v. American Cas. Co., 189 A.2d 204 (N.J. 1963); Globe Am. Cas. Co. v. Lyons, 641 P.2d 251 (Ariz. Ct. App. 1981); Mangus v. Western Cas. & Surety Co., 585 P.2d 304 (Colo.Ct.App. 1978).

[61] 641 P.2d 251 (Ariz. Ct. App. 1981).

[62] See Johnson v. Insurance Co. of N. Am., 350 S.E.2d 616 (Va. 1986) (an individual who lacks mental capacity to conform conduct to acceptable standards will not be deterred by the existence or nonexistence of insurance coverage).

[63] See, e.g., Municipal Mut. Ins. Co. of W. Va. v. Mangus, 443 S.E.2d 455 (W.Va. 1994) (insured, although mentally ill and under delusions, fully understood what he was doing when he shot neighbor; held, intentional act exclusion applies); Economy Preferred Ins. Co. v. Mass, 497 N.W.2d 6 (Neb. 1993); Auto-Owners Ins. Co. v. Churchman, 489 N.W.2d 431 (Mich. 1992) (insured, who was mentally ill or insane, was not covered for murder committed "purposely"); Mallin v. Farmers Ins. Exch., 839 P.2d 105 (Nev. 1992); Shelter Mut. Ins. Co. v. Williams, 804 P.2d 1374 (Kan. 1991); Johnson v. Insurance Co. of N. Am., 350 S.E.2d 616 (Va. 1986); Rajspic v. Nationwide Mut. Ins. Co., 662 P.2d 534 (Idaho 1983), *later proceeding,* 718 P.2d 1167 (Idaho 1986).

[64] See Prasad v. Allstate Ins. Co., 644 So. 2d 992 (Fla. 1994).

[65] 644 So. 2d at 995.

Most courts reject the view that the criminal standard for determining insanity is the appropriate test for determining lack of mental capacity.[66] These courts note that exclusionary clauses are for the benefit of, and therefore should be construed strictly against, the insurer. Thus, mental incapacity that would excuse a defendant's conduct under the criminal law is sufficient to take the insured outside the exclusion, but, in the words of one court, "coverage should not be limited to cases which satisfy that definition."[67] This analysis is crucial to those courts which adhere to the rule that an insane person's acts can be intentional for purposes of the intentional act exclusion but unintentional for purposes of criminal law. As one court has observed, there is no inconsistency in this analysis because there are many situations where someone can act intentionally but not be subject to criminal punishment.[68]

Whether intoxication vitiates the capacity to form the intent necessary to trigger the intentional act exclusion is unsettled.[69] Most courts that have considered the issue have held that intoxication can vitiate capacity, but the burden is on the insurer to bring the facts of a case within the exclusion.[70] On the other hand, it has been held that the insured's intoxication is completely irrelevant to the question of coverage, and that voluntary intoxication could not turn otherwise intentional acts into unintentional ones.[71] In *Allstate Insurance Co. v. Sherrill*,[72] the insured sexually assaulted his victim while allegedly under the influence of alcohol and hallucinogenic drugs. The insurer argued that coverage under the liability policy of his homeowner's policy was excluded due to the intentional nature of his acts, and the court agreed; the insured voluntarily ingested the drugs and alcohol, and "public policy demands that a voluntary departure of one's good judgment and rational decision-making abilities should not permit the insured to abrogate his financial

---

[66] See, e.g., Municipal Mut. Ins. Co. of W. Va. v. Mangus, 443 S.E.2d 455 (W.Va. 1994); Ruvolo v. American Cas. Co., 189 A.2d 204 (N.J. 1963); Burd v. Sussex Mut. Ins. Co., 267 A.2d 7 (N.J. 1970); Globe American Cas. Co. v. Lyons, 641 P.2d 251 (Ariz. Ct. App. 1981).

[67] Ruvolo v. American Cas. Co., 189 A.2d 204, 209 (N.J. 1963).

[68] See Johnson v. Insurance Co. of N. Am., 350 S.E.2d 616, 620-21 (Va. 1986).

[69] See generally Tracy E. Silverman, Note, *Voluntary Intoxication: A Defense to Intentional Injury Exclusion Clauses in Homeowner's Policies?*, 90 Mich. L. Rev. 2113 (1992).

[70] See, e.g., Hanover Ins. Co. v. Talhouni, 604 N.E.2d 689 (Mass. 1992); State Farm Fire & Cas. Co. v. Morgan, 368 S.E.2d 509 (Ga. 1988); Burd v. Sussex Mut. Ins. Co., 267 A.2d 7 (N.J. 1970); Beneshunas v. Independence Life & Acc. Ins. Co., 512 A.2d 6 (Pa. Super. Ct. 1986); MacKinnon v. Hanover Ins. Co., 471 A.2d 1166 (N.H. 1984); Republic Ins. Co. v. Feidler, 875 P.2d 187 (Ariz. Ct. App. 1993); Long v. Coates, 806 P.2d 1256 (Wash. Ct. App. 1990). This burden was carried by the insurer in Mutual Fire Ins. Co. v. Hancock, 634 A.2d 1312 (Me. 1993), where the court held as a matter of a law that a systematic, hours-long brutal beating was not reckless and can only be intentional, notwithstanding the insured's claim of intoxication. For the same result in a situation where insured's son while intoxicated resisted arrest for more than an hour, see Group Ins. Co. of Mich. v. Czopek, 489 N.W.2d 444 (Mich. 1992).

[71] See, e.g., American Fam. Mut. Ins. Co. v. Peterson, 405 N.W.2d 418 (Minn. 1987); Prudential Prop. & Cas. Ins. Co. v. Kerwin, 576 N.E.2d 94 (Ill. App. Ct. 1991); Allstate Ins. Co. v. Hampton, 433 N.W.2d 334 (Mich. Ct. App. 1988); Hanover Ins. Co. v. Newcomer, 585 S.W.2d 285 (Mo. Ct. App. 1979).

[72] [1983–84] Fire & Cas. Cases (CCH), at 852 (E.D. Mich. 1983).

responsibility to those he brutally injures." The opposing point of view doubts that allowing intoxication to negate the intentional act exclusion will encourage people "to seek sufficient intoxicants to negate capacity and preclude personal liability for otherwise intentional acts."[73] But if an insured intentionally and voluntarily became intoxicated in order to fortify a resolve to cause injury to persons or property, courts following the majority rule would probably embrace an exception to the rule.[74]

In the diminished capacity cases, several values compete with each other for dominance. It is in the public interest for coverage to be construed broadly so that the victims of torts can be compensated for their injuries. This interest commends a narrow construction of the exclusion; where insureds act without full appreciation of their behavior, even if they voluntarily put themselves in the diminished state, the policy of protecting victims suggests that the conduct should be deemed nonintentional. However, the public's interest is that tortious conduct be deterred, and this includes deterring behavior (such as the ingestion of drugs) that could lead to such behavior. Moreover, the literal language of the policy states that the insured's intentional acts are excluded, without a caveat for acts committed while the insured is not in full control of his or her conduct. The underlying policy, however, is that insurance is purchased for fortuitous losses; where the insured has some control over the risk no coverage should exist, but in other cases no good reason exists to deny the victim access to the resources necessary to reimburse the victim's loss.

§ 64 Particular Coverage Issues in Personal Insurance

[a] Life Insurance

[1] Accidental Death: Defining "Accident"

When the insured's death is a prerequisite to receiving insurance proceeds, usually little dispute surrounds whether death has occurred.[1] Recent medical advances make it possible to prolong the body's functions after the brain has died, and this has confused the determination of when death occurs to some extent. Sometimes disputes arise over whether a disappeared person whose body has not been found is dead, but in this situation the question is whether a nonphysical test of death is met; in most jurisdictions, a person is legally presumed to be dead after being absent and unheard of for a period of time in circumstances where communication is expected. In most cases, the question of whether the insured has died has an obvious answer.

When a dispute does arise concerning the event of death, it usually relates to the manner in which the death occurred. Such disputes are rare with respect to the basic

----

[73] Hanover Ins. Co. v. Talhouni, 604 N.E.2d 689, 692 (Mass. 1992).

[74] *Id.*, 604 N.E.2d at 692; James A. Fischer, *The Exclusion From Insurance Coverage of Losses Caused by the Intentional Acts of the Insured: A Policy in Search of a Justification,* 30 Santa Clara L. Rev. 95, 147 (1990).

[1] One exception to this generalization involves the fraudulent practice of documenting a phony death overseas, with the assistance of lax or corrupt foreign officials, for the purpose of collecting insurance proceeds. Disproving the deaths is difficult and expensive for insurers. See *Wall St. J.,* July 1, 1986, p. 1, c. 1.

(Matthew Bender & Co., Inc.)   (Pub.837)

life insurance coverage, which is usually paid irrespective of the manner of the insured's death (the notable exception being when the insured commits suicide during the first two years after the policy is issued). However, many life insurance policies contain an endorsement for additional proceeds when death is accidental, and it is here that considerable difficulties sometimes surface.

The accidental death benefit is usually provided in an amount equal to the amount of insurance provided by the life policy. Thus, if the policy provides $50,000 of insurance, the accidental death benefit means that the insurer will pay $100,000 if the insured dies in an accident. This indicates the origin of the phrase "double-indemnity": the policy pays double if the insured's death is accidental. The accidental death benefit endorsement typically has its own set of exclusions, including some exclusions that do not exist with the regular life insurance coverage, such as suicide, war or acts incidental to war (declared or undeclared), physical or mental disease or ailment, and death by poison, chemical, gas or fumes (whether taken, administered, absorbed, or inhaled). If an exclusion applies, the accidental death benefit will not be paid, although the beneficiaries could still recover under the basic life insurance coverage (assuming an exclusion in the life insurance policy does not pertain to the death as well).

In common parlance, an accident is an unusual event that the insured does not foresee. The event happens suddenly, unexpectedly, and without the insured's intent. Often an element of force or violence is present in the death. However, determining whether an event was foreseeable, intended, sudden, expected, or violent can be difficult in many circumstances. As discussed in a preceding section,[2] the issue of whether an accident has occurred often arises in a situation where some intentional act of the insured contributes to the insured's death. In such circumstances, the insurer might argue that the insured's death was intentional, while the insured's beneficiaries might argue that the insured's death was accidental because the insured did not intend to bring about his or her own death.

Determining whether a death was accidental involves inquiring not only into whether the event was fortuitous but also into the question of causation. It is essential that the accident *cause* the death. Unfortunately, additional complexities are added when multiple causes, some of which are not accidental in any ordinary sense and some of which are truly unforeseen and unexpected, combine to produce the death. Most policies have some kind of exclusionary language relevant to causation. For example, the policy at issue in one case provided accidental death benefits if the insured died as a result of accidental bodily injury "directly and independently of all other causes" but provided that the benefit is not payable if death were "contributed to by: (1) disease or bodily or mental infirmity . . . ."[3] The reason for excluding diseases and physical or mental infirmities from the coverage is to limit the coverage to accidents. Death from disease is not an accident; indeed, every person who does not die in an accident will ultimately die as a result of some sort of physical or mental ailment. The language also purports to exclude death "contributed to" by disease, indicating that if multiple causes played a role in the

---

[2] See § 63B, *supra*.

[3] Arata v. California-Western States Life Ins. Co., 123 Cal. Rptr. 631 (Cal. Ct. App. 1975).

death, the accidental death benefits are not available. As one court explained it, an ordinary person when purchasing accidental death and dismemberment insurance would expect that the policy would not cover death by "natural" causes or perhaps suicide, but would cover death physically caused by events and conditions that are "external to the body."[4]

As a general rule, whether the insured's death is accidental is determined from the point of view of the insured.[5] For example, if the insured is assaulted and fatally stabbed without provocation, the insured would describe his or her own death as an accident; the insured would say that death was fortuitous, unforeseen, and unintended by him or her. The same would be true if the insured is killed by a bolt of lightning: the insured would say that death was an accident.

Beyond these observations, generalities are difficult to make. The fact situations are so diverse, the causation patterns so varied, and the judicial decisions so divergent that guideposts for predicting results in particular cases are virtually non-existent. Consider, for example, deaths caused by falls. When an insured dies from a fall without the interaction of some other cause, whether it be slipping off a cliff while hiking or a stumble down the stairs, the death is an accident.[6] However, when a disease combines with a fall to produce a death, a difficult question is presented. Some courts state that if a disease causes the fall which results in death, the death is not an accident.[7] Thus, to these courts, a brain tumor which causes the hiker to lose consciousness and fall off the cliff is a death caused by disease, not by accident. However, some courts reason that falls caused by diseases are covered if it appears that the fall is the dominant cause of the death. Thus, in one case, the insured's death from a concussion when he fell and hit his head on a table was an accident, although the fall resulted from dizziness attributable to arteriosclerosis, hypertension, and diabetes.[8] On the other hand, if the fall directly produces a disease which results in death, the death is accidental.[9] If, however, the fall results in hospitalization, which results in the insured getting an infection which causes death, the death may not be accidental.[10]

---

[4] Buck v. Gulf Life Ins. Co., 548 So. 2d 715 (Fla. Dist. Ct. App. 1989).

[5] See, e.g., Estate of Wade v. Continental Ins. Co., 514 F.2d 304 (8th Cir. 1975); Miller v. Continental Ins. Co., 358 N.E.2d 258 (N.Y. 1976).

[6] See, e.g., Lindemann v. General Am. Life Ins. Co., 485 S.W.2d 477 (Mo. Ct. App. 1977); Home Ins. Co. v. Denning, 177 So. 2d 348 (Fla. Dist. Ct. App. 1965).

[7] See, e.g., Chesson v. Pilot Life Ins. Co., 150 S.E.2d 40 (N.C. 1966); Reserve Life Ins. Co. v. Whittemore, 442 S.W.2d 266 (Tenn. Ct. App. 1969).

[8] See Wells v. Prudential Ins. Co. of Am., 142 N.W.2d 57 (Mich. Ct. App. 1966) (if death caused by hitting head on table during fall, death is an accident, even if fall caused by dizziness due to disease; direction of fall is fortuitous); but see Sekel v. Aetna Life Ins. Co., 704 F.2d 1335 (5th Cir. 1983) (held no accident on similar facts; death caused by illness).

[9] See, e.g., Prudential Ins. Co. of Am. v. Van Wey, 59 N.E.2d 721 (Ind. 1945); Provident Life & Accident Ins. Co. v. Watkins, 76 S.W.2d 889 (Ky. 1934).

[10] See Richardson v. Pilot Life Ins. Co., 115 S.E.2d 500 (S.C. 1960) (student's leg in cast from prior fracture; crutch slips causing injury to same leg presents jury question on whether accident occurred).

In the foregoing cases, a factual determination was made about whether the disease or the fall was the dominant contributor to the insured's death. The outcome in many of these cases was no doubt ordained by how the facts were developed and presented to the factfinder. Occasionally, however, it is virtually impossible to separate the disease and the fall in the chain of causation. One such case is *Arata v. California-Western States Life Insurance Co.*,[11] where the insured, who suffered from hemophilia, slipped and fell to the floor. The bodily injuries from the fall, which would not have been enough to injure fatally a person not suffering from hemophilia, resulted in internal bleeding that caused the insured's death several days later. Plainly, an accident occurred in *Arata:* an unexpected fall, which was neither anticipated nor foreseen and which occurred without intentional causation on the insured's part. However, death would not have occurred due to the accident but for the existence of the insured's disease. The same could be said of the disease: death would not have occurred due to the disease but for the occurrence of the accident. The court, construing the exclusionary clause narrowly, held that the evidence did support the conclusion of law that the insured died as a result of an accidental bodily injury and, consequently, his beneficiaries were entitled to the double indemnity benefits.

The opposite result was reached in *Carroll v. CUNA Mutual Insurance Society*,[12] a 1995 Colorado case. The insured died of a massive hemorrhage caused in turn by the rupture of a preexisting cerebral aneurysm during intercourse with her husband. The court first concluded that the insured's death was an "accident" within the meaning of the policy; "accident" was not defined, but the court indicated that an "unanticipated or unusual result flowing from a commonplace cause" may be an accident.[13] While conceding the definition to be a broad one, the court observed that insurers were free to provide a narrower definition in their policies if they desired to do so. In the circumstances, the court said that her death was "certainly not an expected, intended, or foreseeable result."[14] However, the policy at issue required that the injury must not only be caused by accident but also must result directly and independently of all other causes of loss covered by the policy. The court reasoned that the mere presence of a bodily infirmity should not automatically preclude recovery,[15] but that the clause required the "accident" to be the "predominant cause of injury."[16] In the facts of the case, viewing the evidence in a light most favorable to the plaintiff, the court held that the record was clear that the preexisting aneurysm was the predominant cause of the insured's death, and that the accidental death benefits were therefore not available to her beneficiary.[17] Clearly, what the court in *Carroll* sought was a common-sense understanding of what caused the insured's death — an accident or something else. If the insured's death had occurred during a different kind of activity — for example, if the insured had been involved

---

[11] 123 Cal. Rptr. 631 (Cal. Ct. App. 1975).
[12] 894 P.2d 746 (Colo. 1995)(en banc).
[13] 894 P.2d at 753.
[14] 894 P.2d at 753.
[15] 894 P.2d at 753.
[16] 894 P.2d at 755.
[17] 894 P.2d at 756.

in a minor auto accident moments before the fatal rupture of the aneurysm —
perhaps the result would have been different.

There are, obviously, many kinds of fact situations where the question of whether
an accident occurred often arises. Overexertion which results in death has been
highly perplexing for courts, such as the common situation where the insured
engages in vigorous exercise which is followed by a fatal heart attack. Some courts
reason that, unless some mishap or fall occurred during the exercise, the heart attack
was not an accident.[18] Other courts deny recovery on the ground that a pre-existing
health condition — a weak heart — caused the death, which is not an accident.[19]
Still other courts have concluded that the insured's death after exertion or exercise
is an accident, since the heart attack was an unexpected result of the exercise.[20] Yet
some courts view the rupture of a blood vessel during unusual exercise as an
accident, notwithstanding that a weakened blood vessel is fairly described as a
diseased condition that accident policies are not meant to cover.[21] A closely related
fact pattern involves death due to sunstroke or heatstroke. Most courts appear to hold
that death from sunstroke or heatstroke is an accident, but some courts seem to insist
that some unexpected or unusual fact must have contributed to the death.[22] In short,
the cases are impossible to reconcile.[23]

Yet another problem area involves death caused by choking or suffocating on
regurgitated food or drink. Courts are split on whether such deaths are accidental;
some courts find coverage,[24] while others do not.[25] Courts are also split on whether
death caused by the voluntary consumption of alcoholic beverages is accidental.[26]

---

[18] See, e.g., Duvall v. Massachusetts Indem. and Life Ins. Co., 748 S.W.2d 650 (Ark. 1988)
(death of pulpwood cutter, who died from Marfan's syndrome while engaged in regular
employment, was not an accident, in circumstances where strenuous work culminated in
rupture of aorta); Bristol v. Metropolitan Life Ins. Co., 265 P.2d 552 (Cal. Ct. App. 1954).

[19] See, e.g., Kluge v. Benefit Ass'n of Ry. Employees, 149 N.W.2d 681 (Minn. 1967);
Dunn v. Maryland Cas. Co., 488 A.2d 313 (Pa. Super. Ct. 1985).

[20] See, e.g, Carrothers v. Knights of Columbus, 295 N.E.2d 307 (Ill. App. Ct. 1973) (heart
attack after stress from altercation); Rankin v. United Commercial Travelers of Am., 392 P.2d
894 (Kan. 1964) (heart attack after fighting pasture fire); Brown v. Metropolitan Life Ins.
Co., 327 S.W.2d 252 (Mo. 1959) (emotional stress after verbal assault).

[21] Compare Goldstein v. Paul Revere Life Ins. Co., 164 So. 2d 576 (Fla. Dist. Ct. App.
1964) (heart attack while lifting planks is not accident) with Continental Cas. Co. v. King,
423 S.W.2d 395 (Tex. Ct. App. 1967) (occlusion of blood vessel while driving truck was
bodily injury by accident).

[22] See 1B APPLEMAN § 377 (1981); Landress v. Phoenix Mut. Life Ins. Co., 291 U.S.
491 (1934) (death by sunstroke when golfing on a hot day held not an accident).

[23] See generally Annot., *Heart Attack Following Exertion or Exercise as Within Terms
of Accident Provision of Insurance Policy,* 1 A.L.R.4th 1319 (1980).

[24] See, e.g., Ike v. Jefferson Nat'l Life Ins. co., 884 P.2d 471 (Mont. 1994); Cobb v. Aetna
Life Ins. Co., 274 N.W.2d 911 (Minn. 1979); Life Ins. Co. of Ga. v. Thomas, 210 S.E.2d
250 (Ga. Ct. App. 1974).

[25] See, e.g., Liberty Nat'l Life Ins. Co. v. Windham, 529 So. 2d 967 (Ala. 1988); Christensen v. Prudential Ins. Co. of Am., 384 P.2d 142 (Or. 1963); Weaver v. Home Sec. Life Ins.
Co., 201 S.E.2d 63 (N.C. Ct. App. 1973).

[26] Compare Fryman v. Pilot Life Ins. Co., 704 S.W.2d 205 (Ky. 1986) (death in motorcycle
accident occurring while insured was drunk and driving motorcycle at excessive speeds was

Where death results directly from partaking tainted food or drink, most courts have concluded that the death is accidental; but if the partaking results in a disease that causes death, the courts reach divergent results.[27] Another highly controversial area is death occurring during or after surgery. In some cases, courts hold that such a death is not accidental because the surgery is voluntarily undertaken. Other courts, often emphasizing the particular facts of a case, find a cause in the preexisting disease and deny coverage. Other courts, however, treat the death as accidental when unexpected events during surgery cause the death.[28]

The possible fact patterns raising the question of whether an accident caused the death are virtually infinite.[29] Indeed, new technologies will give rise to new cases: for example, at least two courts have held that the failure of an artificial heart valve is not an accidental death within the meaning of double indemnity provisions of life insurance policies.[30] In a Maryland case, the court held that the insured's death due to AIDS contracted after receiving a blood transfusion to treat his hemophilia did not fall within the scope of the accidental death policy.[31] The court reasoned that the death was due to disease and the medical treatment for it, not the "accident" of receiving tainted blood.[32]

In the accidental death cases, whether coverage exists depends on the particular facts of the case, the equities of the situation as perceived by the court, and the public

---

"accidental"); Adkins v. Home Life Ins. Co., 372 N.W.2d 671 (Mich. Ct. App. 1985) (holding that death while driving drunk is not a crime within meaning of exclusion), with Laney v. Continental Ins. Co., 757 F.2d 1190 (11th Cir. 1985) (drinking oneself to death is not death by "accident"); Order of United Commercial Travelers of America v. Tripp, 63 F.2d 37 (10th Cir. 1933) (death while driving intoxicated was a crime that precludes coverage); Sasloe v. Home Life Ins. Co., 416 So. 2d 867 (Fla. Dist. Ct. App. 1982) (to same effect).

[27] See generally Annot., *Accident Insurance: Death or Disability Incident to Partaking of Food or Drink as Within Provision as to External, Violent, and Accidental Means*, 29 A.L.R.4th 1230 (1984).

[28] See Annot., *Death During Or Allegedly Resulting From Surgery As Accidental Or From Accidental Means Within Coverage Of Health Or Accident Insurance Policy*, 91 A.L.R.3d 1042 (1979); Fagan v. J.C. Penney Ins. Co., 692 P.2d 887 (Wash. Ct. App. 1984) (angulation of arteries during surgery, which caused death, not foreseen; death is accidental).

[29] As a representative sample, consider the following cases: Gay v. American Motorists Ins. Co., 714 F.2d 13 (4th Cir. 1983) (death due to infection from scrape on arm where insured's immune system severely weakened by chemotherapy treatment for cancer held not an accident); Bradshaw v. Fireman's Fund American Life Ins. Co., 1983–85 Life, Health & Accident Cases (CCH), at 905 (Tenn. Ct. App. 1984) (fall results in broken leg, requiring immobilization, which leads to blood clot, which migrates to heart and causes fatal heart attack; held accidental death); Papa v. The Travelers Ins. Co., 460 N.Y.S.2d 328 (N.Y. App. Div. 1983) (whether death due to bee sting was death by disease or accident presents question of fact); Huff v. Aetna Life Ins. Co., 587 P.2d 267 (Ariz. Ct. App. 1978) (no recovery where heart attack causes auto accident, and force of accident causes broken rib to perforate heart and cause death).

[30] See Century Cos. of Am. v. Krahling, 484 N.W.2d 197 (Iowa 1992); Cassidy v. Occidental Life Ins. Co., 601 P.2d 325 (Ariz. Ct. App. 1979).

[31] See Cheney v. Bell Nat'l Life Ins. Co., 556 A.2d 1135 (Md. 1989).

[32] 556 A.2d at 1140.

policies as perceived by the court. The simple fact is that health policies, which cover losses associated with disease, and accident policies are rated on different criteria; health policies are more expensive than accident policies. There is a bona fide public policy that accident policies should not be converted to health policies by broad constructions of what constitutes an accident. Such a course would eventually inflate premiums to a point that one desiring coverage for accidents in the traditional sense would find the insurance product greatly overpriced. At the same time, there is the important public policy of protecting the insured's reasonable expectations. These competing interests combine to produce results in the cases that are impossible to reconcile and virtually impossible to explain in any cogent way.

The most that can be accomplished is the articulation of a framework for deciding such cases. First, it is necessary to determine whether the death-producing event was an accident. Here the inquiry should examine whether the event is unforeseen and unexpected from the viewpoint of the insured. Second, if the event is "accidental," it is necessary to determine that the accident caused the death. Where there are multiple causes, the "net" of causation must be analyzed in two ways — first, it must be determined that the accident was not too remote to be labeled the cause, and second, it must be determined that the accident was the dominant cause among all the other causes. Thus, if disease and an accident combine to produce death, it must be determined that the accident was not too remote and was the dominant cause of the loss. If these conditions exist, the presence of disease as a contributing factor should not prevent coverage. This approach is probably most consistent with the expectations of the insured, even if it is not completely consistent with the language of some policies that attempt to impose additional restrictions on coverage.

[2]   Accidental Death: Limits on the Time Between the Accident and the Death

Most accidental death benefit endorsements to life insurance policies (so-called double indemnity provisions) require that the accidental death result within a specified number of days, often 90 or 120, after the injury that causes the death. (Similar provisions are found in dismemberment policies, which provide compensation when the insured loses a limb or use of a bodily function due to some kind of accident; the issues discussed here are virtually identical in this setting as well.) The purpose of these clauses is to provide a contractual limitations period beyond which the insurer is certain that the insured will not claim that the death was accidental. Also, these provisions minimize the uncertainty over what conditions or circumstances caused the insured's death. In recent years, however, medical advances have made it possible to prolong life for extended periods of time. This has created the possibility that an individual will suffer an injury in an accident and live for an extended period of time, longer than the limitations period, before succumbing to the injury. This situation has led to the argument in a few cases that these limitation clauses are void as being against public policy.[33]

---

[33] See generally Samuel J. Arena, Jr., Comment, *The Validity of Time Limitations in Accidental Multiple Indemnity Death Provisions of Life Insurance Policies,* 28 Vill. L. Rev. 378 (1983).

Prior to the early 1970s, it was correct to state that "[c]lauses limiting payments for accidental death or loss of a member to cases in which the death or loss occurred within a specified time after the accident have been uniformly upheld when attacked on the ground that they are unreasonable, unconscionable, or against public policy."[34] In 1973, however, a Pennsylvania case, *Burne v. Franklin Life Insurance Co.*,[35] invalidated such a provision on public policy grounds. In *Burne*, the insured was kept alive through sophisticated medical techniques for four and one-half years after the accident. The insurer conceded that the sole cause of the death was the accident, but argued that the insured's death was outside the double indemnity coverage by virtue of the 90-day requirement. The Pennsylvania Supreme Court held the requirement invalid. The court observed that the cases holding that such requirements were valid were decided long before recent advances in medical science had made it much more likely to prolong life. These advances, in the court's view, had made the 90-day provision obsolete. Furthermore, the court felt that matters such as whether insurance proceeds would be received should not be a factor in the decision on whether or how to prolong life. Finally, the court considered it fundamentally unjust to allow a beneficiary who has endured little or no prolonged expense and anxiety to receive a full recovery of the accidental death benefits while disallowing any recovery to those who suffer the longest and endure the greatest expenses. Other cases have followed the logic and holding of *Burne*.[36]

Other decisions have declined to follow the reasoning of *Burne*.[37] The Illinois Supreme Court's decision in *Kirk v. Financial Security Life Insurance Co.*,[38] is illustrative. The court in *Kirk* made several points. First, the court expressed concern over the increased litigation that would result if no limitations existed: "Without the finality of a time limitation, the accompanying uncertainty as to the cause of death as the time between the event and the injury increases will spawn a substantial amount of litigation as beneficiaries attempt to establish some injury-connected cause of their insured decedent's death."[39] Moreover, the court noted, as had several other courts, that the limitations provision reflects the insurer's underwriting decision: the 90-day limitation clearly affects risk and is thus reflected in the rates charged. To enforce the provision is to give the insured precisely what the insured paid for. The court was unpersuaded by the argument that medical advances had made the limitations period obsolete; regardless of the period chosen, there will always be those who succumb in the day before the period expires, and those who

---

[34] See Annot., *Validity and Construction of Provision in Accident Insurance Policy Limiting Coverage for Death or Loss of Member to Death or Loss Occurring Within Specified Period After Accident*, 39 A.L.R.3d 1311, 1313 (1971).

[35] 301 A.2d 799 (Pa. 1973).

[36] See Strickland v. Gulf Life Ins. Co., 242 S.E.2d 148 (Ga. 1978); Karl v. New York Life Ins. Co., 381 A.2d 62 (N.J. Super. Ct. App. Div. 1977).

[37] See, e.g., Smith v. Independent Life and Acc. Ins. Co., 346 S.E.2d 22 (S.C. 1986); Hawes v. Kansas Farm Bureau, 710 P.2d 1312 (Kan. 1985); Major v. Lincoln Nat'l Life Ins. Co., 616 N.E.2d 598 (Ohio Ct.App. 1992); Brendle v. Shenandoah Life Ins. Co., 332 S.E.2d 515 (N.C. Ct. App. 1985).

[38] 389 N.E.2d 144 (Ill. 1978).

[39] 389 N.E.2d at 148.

succumb the day after, regardless of the state of the art on prolonging life. As for the possibility that the existence of such a provision might encourage some people to "pull the plug" on insureds, the court noted that this problem is not unique — it exists in life insurance generally, and the problem is dealt with effectively there.

In short, the provisions in accidental death endorsements requiring that the insured's death be within a specified number of days of the death-inducing injury are controversial, and will become more so as the medical profession's ability to prolong life improves.

[b] Disability Insurance

Disability insurance was first offered in the form of a waiver of premium payments under life insurance policies: if an insured under a life policy became disabled, the obligation to make periodic premium payments was waived. Shortly thereafter, life insurers added a periodic income benefit. Eventually, insurers separated the income benefit from the life policy, so that it became possible to purchase a policy of disability insurance. Disability insurance is intended to compensate a person who, due to an accident or illness, is unable to earn all or part of his or her former income. In other words, the insurance payments are a substitute for part or all of the income lost due to an accident or illness.

Disability insurance is much less prevalent than either life or health insurance. No doubt part of the reason is that social insurance programs (such as Social Security and Veteran's Benefits) provide minimum, subsistence benefits when a person becomes disabled. Another factor is that the coverage seems expensive to most insureds, particularly in circumstances where many people underestimate the likelihood that one day they will be disabled due to illness or accident. Death and illness, in contrast, seem much more probable, and insureds are more likely to purchase coverage against these risks. The coverage is, in fact, not inexpensive, and this no doubt has something to do with the particularly acute moral hazard and adverse selection pressures in disability insurance. First, it is not easy for insurers to determine whether a person is able to return to work once disabled; denying or terminating benefits is often a high-risk and certainly litigation-inviting strategy for an insurer, and this probably results in some doubtful claims being fully paid. Second, some insureds no doubt seek an early retirement funded by disability insurance; the possibility of feigned claims is significant, and the transaction costs involved with addressing them increase costs for all insureds.

It is a prerequisite to eligibility for benefits that the insured be "disabled," and this raises one of the fundamental difficulties in disability insurance. An insured is either disabled or not; there is no in-between status. It may be helpful to contrast disability insurance with state workers compensation systems: workers compensation systems recognize a range of partial disabilities, which eliminates the harsh either-or choice in disability insurance. On the other hand, workers compensation systems struggle with the assessments in individual cases of degrees of disability, something which a rigid either-or system avoids. A cost, however, of the rigid either-or choice in disability insurance is that insureds who are partially disabled face "all-or-nothing" alternatives.

To amplify this problem further, whether an individual is totally disabled ultimately depends on whether he or she is rendered physically immobile or incompetent, but "total disability" fails to capture the more complex situation confronted by most individuals who suffer a disabling illness or injury. A professional football player who suffers a career-ending knee injury cannot play on the field, but there is much that he can do either in football (perhaps as a coach) or in other endeavors, although probably at an income far below what he earned as an athlete. A concert pianist who loses one hand would be unable to perform recitals, although the artist would presumably be able to teach music or do other worthwhile work. Neither the football player nor the concert pianist is *completely* disabled, but each person has suffered serious, disabling injuries rendering that person unable to perform the work in which he or she was engaged prior to the injury. These cases illustrate the difficulty in determining at what point a person becomes "disabled" within the meaning of a disability insurance policy.[40]

In response to these difficulties, disability insurance's coverage provisions are defined in terms of the loss of one's capacity to work, not one's loss of income, and there are two basic kinds of disability coverage relating to capacity to work. Most disability policies are "occupational disability" policies, which provide coverage if the insured is disabled from transacting duties of the particular occupation in which the insured is then engaged.[41] This is to be contrasted with the "general" disability policy, which provides that the insured must be unable to pursue any occupation for profit for which he or she is reasonably suited by education, training, or experience.[42] Obviously, total helplessness is not required to demonstrate that the insured is entitled to coverage under an occupational disability policy, because the test is whether the insured can perform the material and substantial duties of the job. If the insured after suffering an injury or illness is unable to perform the material duties of his or her actual occupation in substantially the same manner as before, the insured may recover under the policy. Conversely, if the only activities the insured can no longer do are not material aspects of the business, the insured cannot recover.[43] Thus, a college professor who suffers dermatitis is not totally disabled, but a surgeon who must terminate a medical practice due to dermatitis may well be totally disabled.[44]

With respect to general disability coverage, most courts have also concluded that total helplessness is not required to establish total disability under a general disability

---

[40] See generally Annot., *What Constitutes Total Disability Within Coverage of Disability Insurance Policy Issued to a Lawyer,* 6 A.L.R.4th 422 (1981).

[41] See, e.g., Beneficial Standard Life Ins. Co. v. Hamby, 236 S.E.2d 116 (Ga. Ct. App. 1977); Coker v. Pilot Life Ins. Co., 217 S.E.2d 784 (S.C. 1975).

[42] See, e.g., CUNA Mut. Ins. Soc'y v. Matzke, 532 N.W.2d 759 (Iowa 1995); Centennial Life Ins. Co. v. Scherrer, 594 N.Y.S.2d 768 (N.Y. App. Div. 1993); Moots v. Bankers Life Co., 707 P.2d 1083 (Kan.Ct.App. 1985).

[43] See, e.g., Ryan v. ITT Life Ins. Corp., 450 N.W.2d 126 (Minn. 1990); Brown v. Continental Cas. Co., 498 P.2d 26 (Kan. 1972); Woods v. Central States Life Ins. Co., 271 N.W. 850 (Neb. 1937).

[44] See Dixon v. Pacific Mut. Life Ins. Co., 268 F.2d 812 (2d Cir. 1959), *cert. denied,* 361 U.S. 948 (1960).

policy, and thus the fact that the insured continues to do some work in order to subsist does not, by itself, bar the insured's recovery.[45] The focus is on whether the insured can or cannot perform the material and substantial acts necessary for any occupation.[46] Courts look at all the circumstances, including the insured's occupation, education, training, and the nature of the injury.[47]

A common configuration of coverage in disability policies is to combine occupational disability coverage for, say, the first twelve or twenty-four months of the policy, with general disability coverage coming into existence thereafter.[48] This kind of policy switches the more generous occupational coverage to a more strict general coverage. The idea, of course, is during the first twelve- or twenty-four-month period the insured will have enough time to find employment for which he or she is reasonably suited, despite the disability from his or her prior employment.

Some policies, particularly older ones, require that the disability be "total and permanent." Although not as prevalent today, where a permanency requirement exists, most courts have interpreted the test to require that the disability be one that will persist for a long, indefinite period of time.[49] A few decisions have insisted that the disability be one that is likely to continue for the remainder of the insured's life.[50]

If the insured through medical treatment or care can have the disability cured, is an insured obligated to accept the treatment? In *Heller v. The Equitable Life Assurance Society of the U.S.,*[51] the Seventh Circuit held that a board-certified cardiovascular surgeon who had developed carpal tunnel syndrome could not be compelled to undergo surgery on his hand as a condition to continued payment of disability benefits. The policy's requirement that the insured be under the regular care and attendance of a physician, a common clause in disability policies, did not require the insured to undergo what the court viewed as an invasive and somewhat risky procedure. It was also important to the court that the policy did not by its terms

---

[45] Mutual Life Ins. Co. v. Clark, 502 S.W.2d 110 (Ark. 1973); Moots v. Bankers Life Co., 707 P.2d 1083 (Kan.Ct.App. 1985).

[46] See Lamar Life Ins. Co. v. Shaw, 502 So. 2d 323 (Miss. 1987).

[47] See, e.g., Mason v. Connecticut Gen. Life Ins. Co., 367 So. 2d 1374 (Ala. 1979); Colaluca v. Monarch Life Ins. Co., 226 A.2d 405 (R.I. 1967); Kooker v. Benefit Ass'n of Ry. Employees, 246 N.W.2d 743 (N.D. 1976); Erreca v. Western States Life Ins. Co., 121 P.2d 689 (Cal. 1942); Moore v. American United Life Ins. Co., 197 Cal. Rptr. 878 (Cal. Ct. App. 1984); Matza v. Empire State Mut. Life Ins. Co., 375 N.Y.S.2d 578 (N.Y. App. Div. 1975).

[48] See, e.g., Ryan v. ITT Life Ins. Corp., 450 N.W.2d 126 (Minn. 1990)(occupational for 5 years followed by general); Thomas v. First Assur. Life of Am., 606 So. 2d 957 (La. Ct. App. 1992)(occupational for 12 months followed by general); Moots v. Bankers Life Co., 707 P.2d 1083 (Kan.Ct.App. 1985) (occupational for 24 months followed by general).

[49] See, e.g., Bowler v. Fidelity & Cas. Co., 250 A.2d 580 (N.J. 1969); Moore v. Pilot Life Ins. Co., 32 S.E.2d 757 (S.C. 1945); Madison v. Prudential Ins. Co. of Am., 181 So. 871 (La. 1937).

[50] See, e.g., Prudential Ins. Co. of America v. Bond, 88 S.W.2d 988 (Ky. 1935); Culver v. Prudential Ins. Co., 179 A. 400 (Del.Super.Ct. 1935).

[51] 833 F.2d 1253 (7th Cir. 1987).

specifically require the insured to submit to treatment in order to receive benefits. *Heller* did not address the question of the extent to which an insurer can require, as a condition to the payment of proceeds, medical treatment. It seems reasonable to allow an insurer to condition benefits on the insured submitting to routine, low-risk medical care.[52] Whether an insurer could insist on the insured submitting to more risky, invasive procedures is more troublesome. On the one hand, public policy considerations suggest that the insured's contract rights should not be so conditioned, but it is not unreasonable to argue that insurers who commit to pay large sums of money should be allowed to condition benefits on substantial efforts by insureds to mitigate losses.[53]

[c] Health Insurance

Needless to say, health care reform is and will continue to be one of the most prominent issues on national and state political agendas. Most people depend on health insurance in one form or another for access to the health care system, so it is not surprising that a variety of legal issues involving health insurance have become important in recent years. Because health care and health insurance are such large, complex industries, this discussion can only sketch the contours of some of these issues.

Another preliminary observation is appropriate. Although public policy considerations are deeply intertwined with most insurance law issues, the relationship between public policy and the legal issues in health insurance is both strong and stark. It is not possible even to understand many of the legal issues in this area without having some sense of the larger public policy questions affecting the delivery of health care more generally. The heart of the public policy debate is how to assure adequate access to health care at an affordable cost. Some of the issues which connect to the public policy question are discussed in other sections of this text,[54] but more are discussed in this section. Before considering some of these

---

[52] See, e.g., Goomar v. Centennial Life Ins. Co., 855 F. Supp. 319 (S.D. Cal. 1994)(insured who did not receive any care or treatment until two years after he canceled disability policy did not meet requirement that insured be receiving regular care and attendance of physician for the disability); Rahman v. Paul Revere Life Ins. Co., 684 F. Supp. 192 (N.D. Ill. 1988)("regular and personal attendance" of physician did not require insured to go to doctor every month but that insured periodically consult and be examined by treating physician at intervals to be determined by physician); Occidental Life Ins. Co. v. Vervack, 429 S.W.2d 116 (Ark. 1968)(condition in policy that insured be regularly visited and attended by qualified physician or surgeon is met if insured is under regular treatment).

[53] See, e.g., Reliable Life Ins. Co. v. Steptoe, 471 S.W.2d 430 (Tex. Ct. App. 1971)(insured did not suffer "complete loss of sight" in eye in circumstances where cataract operation had very high chance of restoring sight to eye and "there is no evidence as to why an ordinary prudent man in the same or similar circumstances could not or would not undergo a cataract operation . . . to recover his sight"); Papas v. Equitable Life Assur. Soc'y of U.S., 44 N.Y.S.2d 389 (N.Y. App. Div. 1943) (insured failed to establish permanent disability where he refused to submit to insulin treatment for diabetes).

[54] For example, coordination of benefits clauses, which seek to dovetail overlapping coverages and thereby reduce costs, are discussed in § 97, *infra*, and subrogation issues are discussed in § 96, *infra*.

questions, this discussion begins with an overview of the broader social and economic environment in which health insurance operates.

[1] Health Insurance and Health Care Reform

Few would disagree that the American health care system is currently in considerable disarray.[55] Although the quality of care is generally high and the technological advances of recent years in treating illness and accidental injuries are truly remarkable, and while many people (particularly those at the upper-ends of the wealth and income ladders) receive as much superb medical care as they want, there is a consensus among most observers that the health care system suffers from two problems (even if there is less consensus about the problems' severity): many people lack access to care, and the cost of health care is increasing to dangerously high levels. These problems are, of course, interrelated. To the extent the cost of care increases, more people find health care unaffordable, which further reduces access. To the extent access to health care is increased for those who cannot afford it, system-wide expenditures for health care increase, and these expenses must be assumed by somebody. When access to health care is increased, it is necessary (assuming the care is not given free of charge, as some health care is) to charge those who pay for health care higher prices (resulting in higher insurance premiums) or increase government subsidies through publicly-provided health care, which adds to government's tax burdens at a time the prevailing mood is that the governmental role (and the concomitant tax burden) should be decreased.

Even if there is some measure of consensus on the twin problems facing the health care system, there is no consensus on the solutions. Health care is such a vast industry that there are many different health care constituencies with widely divergent interests. Some constituencies have an enormous financial stake in the solutions; this is certainly true of, for example, hospitals, drug manufacturers, physicians, and the corporations which are organized throughout the health care sector, and it is also true of large segments of the population, such as the elderly, who consume a large portion of health care services and have well-organized and well-funded lobbying efforts. There is even disagreement on the fundamental values which underlie the health care system. Is health care a right, something to be distributed as a social good? Or is health care more like an ordinary commodity produced in a market, something that those with means can purchase and that those who lack means must do without?[56] The social-good answer suggests a national

---

[55] There are numerous places where one can find discussions of the issues underlying health care reform initiatives. See, e.g., Paul J. Feldstein, *Health Policy Issues: An Economic Perspective on Health Reform (1994);* Clark C. Havighurst, *Health Care Choices: Private Contracts as Instruments of Health Reform* 89-109 (1995); Barry R. Furrow, et al., *Health Law* 851-64 (1995) (and sources cited in notes); Robert J. Blendon, et al., *Making the Critical Choices,* 267 JAMA 2509 (1992). Voluminous data can be found in the various reports, studies, and media reports surrounding the preparation, announcement, debate, and ultimate rejection of the Clinton health care proposal in 1994.

[56] The essence of this dichotomy is described in a thoughtful, accessible way in Deborah A. Stone, *The Struggle for the Soul of Health Insurance,* 18 J. Health Pol., Pol'y & L. 287 (1993).

health care system, where all people are promised minimum benefits and the cost is funded through tax mechanisms, presumably mechanisms with broad applicability. The market-good answer suggests a system where insurers pool insureds into risk classifications, and the economic efficiencies will result in higher-risk people paying more and lower-risk people paying less. The current system mixes the two answers together, but, as Professor Deborah Stone has argued, the two answers are fundamentally incompatible. Each answer, of course, has its own proponents, thus evidencing the fundamental disagreement about what is expected of the nation's health care system.

It is probably easier to understand the struggle over the future of health care by focusing on the two problems facing the health care delivery system today. The access issue is usually described with reference to the number of people in the country who lack health insurance of any kind. Because health care is expensive, insurance essentially equals access. It is estimated that approximately 37 million Americans lack health insurance at any particular time, but a closer look shows this group to be both diverse and fluid. Not surprisingly, the poor are disproportionately represented among the uninsureds, as are minorities. Because most health insurance is provided by employers as a fringe benefit in employee compensation packages, those who are chronically unemployed as well as those who are between jobs make up a significant portion of the uninsured population. Many uninsured people are employed, but in low-wage positions where the employer does not offer health insurance. Many uninsureds are young adults who have recently departed their parents' households, where they were covered as dependents on one or both parents' policies. In other words, the uninsured population is much more diverse than most people realize.

But lack of insurance is only one part of the access issue. Many people who have insurance find that their coverage has significant exclusions or limitations. For example, as discussed in one of the next subsections, most health insurance policies have pre-existing condition clauses, which provide that insureds have no coverage, usually for a specific period of time after a policy is issued, for illnesses or conditions that pre-dated the policy's effective date. Thus, a person who changes jobs and obtains new insurance through a new employer may find that his or her (or his or her dependent's) existing condition is not covered by the new policy. Most policies have deductibles or co-insurance clauses. As discussed earlier in this text,[57] the presence of these loss-sharing clauses helps reduce the premium charged for insurance, and this may be good to the extent it makes insurance more available. But the deductibles and co-insurance requirements themselves may make it difficult for insureds to obtain health care if the insured cannot afford the out-of-pocket payments. Some policies have lifetime limits, which place a cap on the insurer's total payments under the policy; this leaves some insureds without coverage for catastrophic illnesses or injuries once the policy limits are exhausted.

And the access issue is even more involved than this. Just because an individual lacks insurance, it does not follow that the person receives no medical care. Without insurance, a person may be more likely to forego preventive care; but when a person

---

[57] See § 10[c], *supra.*

suffers a very serious medical condition, that person is likely to go a health care provider — most probably the emergency room of the nearest hospital — where that person will receive treatment. If a person is too poor to have insurance, the person will be too poor to pay the hospital's bill; and even if the person is not indigent, the expenses of even a short hospital stay are likely to be beyond that person's ability to pay. Hospitals and physicians write-off some of these bills as uncompensated professional services (and, of course, many health care professionals provide some free care for those who cannot afford it, just as many lawyers give some pro bono service). But many of these unpaid bills must be shifted to other paying patients, which increases the cost of care, and hence the cost of insurance, for the insured population. As these costs rise, some insureds lose their ability to afford coverage, and these people become part of the uninsured population whose health care expenses will, in turn, be shouldered by the remaining insureds.

Furthermore, the uninsured person who receives care at, say, an emergency room only after a condition has become acute receives one of the most expensive forms of medical care. The care is also "inefficient" in the economic sense in at least two respects. First, it would have been better to treat the person's condition earlier when it would have been less expensive to do so, rather than delay to a point when more expensive treatments are needed. Second, it is inefficient to use trauma centers to treat ear or sinus infections that have suddenly become quite painful. To add to the problem, an uninsured who is a rationale economic actor is unwilling to invest his or her first discretionary dollars in health insurance when he or she knows that free care is available at the emergency room or from other health care providers. This is particularly true of young adults who tend to be healthy, and therefore do not perceive a need for health insurance; for many such persons, making a monthly car payment seems to have more utility than paying a health insurance premium. To the extent young, healthy people do not purchase insurance, the remaining portion of the population tends to be older, and therefore more prone to use health care services. This makes health insurance relatively more expensive, which makes it even less likely that a young, healthy adult will perceive health insurance to be a sensible investment.

The access issue is an extremely difficult and complicated one, but it becomes more intransigent when viewed along with the cost issue. The statistics quickly become dated, but the trends are unmistakable and widely documented: per-family spending for health care as a percentage of total family income has increased significantly; as a percentage of gross domestic product, total spending on health care has increased significantly; health care costs are growing at about twice the general rate of inflation. To some extent, this may reflect the desire of a more affluent society to spend more on health care than on other goods and services; in other words, spending a lot on something is not necessarily bad if this reflects a conscious, voluntary allocation of resources, in the same sense that if people like to play golf a lot, people will spend more of their wealth on golf.[58] Also, it is undeniable that

_____

[58] To take another example, it is not uncommon to hear commentators bemoan the large amount of money spent in our nation each year on pets, dog food, hamsters, etc., and to compare that sum with the amounts spent on school lunch programs, immunizations for

health care is a peculiar kind of consumable; when a parent's child is ill, a parent is likely to insist on the very best care possible, regardless of cost. When faced with a life-or-death illness or injury, few people make medical care decisions motivated primarily, or even significantly, by price sensitivity. Indeed, most people prefer extensive medical care when faced with life-threatening illnesses, even if much of the care only extends life briefly with no chance of altering an inevitable outcome.[59] All of this is understandable, but it means that the incentives and motivations to consume medical care differ from the reasons one has to purchase cars, movie tickets, and other consumer goods and services.

But even if some portion of the increased expenditure for health care is explainable as a voluntary, "willing" choice, cost containment is a problem in health care. Few would question that large segments of the current system have excessively high administrative costs. The new technologies most people praise are expensive, but these increase the cost of medical care. Although the magnitude of the effect is vigorously debated, it is believed by many that the legal system encourages enough unnecessary medical care to affect the cost of health care paid by everyone. Unnecessary duplication of expensive medical technologies also increases costs. To illustrate, it seems doubtful that two hospitals within ten blocks of each other in most urban centers each need an open-heart surgery capability. It is arguable that every county in rural parts of the central, plains states does not need a hospital, but the controversy over this issue is easy to imagine. The resident of a county where the hospital has much excess capacity and needs to be closed would observe that he or she does not want the ambulance to have to drive an extra fifty miles to get to the hospital in the next county after the person's heart attack. But if an under-utilized hospital is kept open and consolidation is spurned, this means the cost of each service must go up to pay for the unutilized overhead. The extent to which the health care industry is sufficiently competitive is much discussed; some believe that certain parts of the industry, such as drug companies, are earning excess profits, while others view high drug prices as necessary to cover the high costs of bringing new drugs to the market. Each of these cost factors is complex, and the extent to which it contributes to higher health care prices is very much debated.

Perhaps the most important factor increasing the cost of medical care is one that is the most deeply entrenched. The federal tax code allows employers to deduct health insurance provided as a fringe benefit to its employees, and the benefit is excluded from the employee's income.[60] This has greatly increased the amount of

---

children, drug education, aid for the homeless, etc., the implication being that our society's priorities are flawed. The counterpoint asserts that we march with our feet and have selected the priorities we desire, even if our choices are not beneficent. This discussion is essentially a simple exposition of the differences between those who favor market-based resource allocation and those who believe the market fails to make good choices and that more, not less, governmental regulation is appropriate.

[59] The point still holds even when one acknowledges the increasing number of people who through "living wills" or other arrangements are rejecting extraordinarily invasive, futile treatment at the last moments of life.

[60] For more detail on this, see § 13A[d], *supra.*

health insurance in force, which has greatly increased the demand for health care: an insured who has 75 percent of his or her health care bill covered by insurance will continue to consume health care until an additional $1 of health care services is worth less than 25 cents to the insured. This translates to an enormous increase in demand for health care services; to the extent demand rises faster than supply, prices must increase. When to this increased demand for services is added the increased demand generated by government-funded health care programs (i.e., Medicare and Medicaid, or Medicaid-substitutes in some states), a simple supply-demand curve chart predicts significant increases in price. As price increases, access declines. To the extent programs are initiated to increase access, demand goes up, and prices increase. One of the great challenges facing our society today is figuring out a way, one which enjoys widespread support among constituencies with vastly different interests, to break the reduced access-higher cost spiral.

[2] Pre-Existing Conditions

A pre-existing condition clause is a provision that excludes coverage for sickness or illness commencing before the effective date of coverage. A typical clause defines a pre-existing condition as follows:

> any condition that was diagnosed or treated by a physician within 24 months prior to the effective date of the coverage or produced symptoms within 12 months prior to the effective date of coverage that would have caused an ordinary prudent person to seek medical diagnosis or treatment.[61]

Insurers insert such clauses in policies to help control adverse selection. If an insured could obtain coverage for a current illness or condition by purchasing insurance, insureds would wait until the illness or condition occurred to obtain insurance. Thus, insureds would pay nothing (and insurers would collect nothing) for the periods during which insureds are healthy.[62] The presence of the clause, if it is known and understood, encourages consumers to purchase insurance when they are healthy. More importantly, it eliminates coverage for illnesses or conditions that motivate the first acquisition of insurance. Thus, the pre-existing condition clause plays a role in containing health care costs.

The foregoing analysis makes sense when applied to a person's first purchase of health insurance. However, the clause is problematic when applied to a person who, already having health insurance, switches employers (and hence insurers) and then confronts once again a pre-existing condition clause. At a minimum, this creates a gap in coverage, a problem of access to health care. At worst, the clause constrains the movement of employees in labor markets; employees with health conditions (or who have dependents with health conditions) may not be able to afford to improve

---

[61] This was the coverage provision at issue in Holub v. Holy Family Soc'y, 518 N.E.2d 419 (Ill.App. 1987).

[62] To the extent a policy were drafted to deny coverage to illnesses the insured had on the first day of coverage, the policy would create an incentive for insureds to conceal their illnesses and claim they arose subsequent to the policy's effective date. In this sense, the pre-existing condition clause can be viewed as combatting the fraud and concealment that would occur in the absence of the clause. See Mogil v. California Physicians Corp., 267 Cal. Rptr. 487 (Cal. Ct. App. 1990).

(Matthew Bender & Co., Inc.)

their employment status if they must forfeit coverage for pre-existing medical conditions.

No single insurer can be expected to incur voluntarily the adverse selection costs generated by eliminating the pre-existing condition clause; indeed, such an insurer would attract a disproportionate number of bad risks and would have to raise premiums above the level of its competitors, who would then have a competitive advantage in the market. Since the pre-existing condition clause is unlikely to be abolished in the private market, this may be an area where governmental regulation is needed — specifically, regulation that would prohibit such clauses in health insurance policies, except for persons who are acquiring health insurance for the first time.

In a number of cases, insureds have sought to avoid the coverage-limiting effect of pre-existing clauses. Many of these decisions turn on issues of interpretation. Where the language of the clause prohibits coverage for conditions for which "treatment" was received in the past, some courts have decided that the physician made a "diagnosis," but did not "treat" the patient, thus taking the insured's condition outside the clause.[63] Other courts have interpreted the clauses to apply only to conditions about which the insured was aware at or before the policy's effective date. Thus, an illness which the insured did not recognize as such, or which had not manifested symptoms that would inform the insured about the presence of the illness, has been held not to fall within the clause.[64] The logic of this approach protects insureds from losing benefits on account of unknown pre-existing conditions. At the same time, it acknowledges the purpose of the pre-existing condition clause in protecting insurers from adverse selection; an insured who is unaware of an illness cannot be motivated by adverse selection considerations to acquire insurance. The risk, of course, is that insureds will obtain the insurance and understate the significance of their symptoms about which at the time they purchased the insurance they actually had great concern. Thus, a condition thought to be minor but found to be more significant after the policy's issuance may trigger the pre-existing condition clause.[65]

---

[63] See, e.g., Franceschi v. American Motorists, Ins. Co., 852 F.2d 1217 (9th Cir. 1988) (prior colonoscopy and biopsies were diagnostic procedures, not treatment, and therefore outside clause); Mannino v. Agway, Inc. Group Trust, 600 N.Y.S.2d 723 (N.Y. App. Div. 1993) ("treatment" excludes diagnostic testing). See also Hughes v. Boston Mut. Life Ins. Co., 26 F.3d 264 (1st Cir. 1994) (fact question, which could not be resolved on summary judgment motion, existed as to whether insured received treatment "for" multiple sclerosis before policy's effective date).

[64] See, e.g., State v. Carper, 545 So. 2d 1 (Miss. 1989) (policy excludes only conditions that manifested themselves prior to date of coverage); Holub v. Holy Family Soc'y, 518 N.E.2d 419 (Ill. App. Ct. 1987) (insured who had minor bowel symptoms and who was told by doctor she had "nothing to worry about," but who in fact had rectal cancer, had coverage despite pre-existing condition clause).

[65] See, e.g., Golden Rule Ins. Co. v. Atallah, 45 F.3d 512 (1st Cir. 1995) (pre-existing condition clause does not require insured to suspect a particular diagnosis; if insured experiences symptoms, whatever illness is ultimately determined to have caused those symptoms is a pre-existing condition and is excluded from coverage; no exception exists for

Courts have taken different positions on who bears the burden of proof on the question of the pre-existing condition. Some courts have treated the clause as an exclusion and have applied the general rule that insurers have the burden to prove the applicability of exclusions from coverage.[66] Other courts have treated the clause a coverage position under the reasoning that the insured must prove that the illness or injury for which the insured seeks coverage arose during the term that the policy was in effect.[67]

[3]   Experimental Treatments

Most health insurance policies have some kind of language which eliminates coverage for experimental treatments.[68] The rationale for the exclusion is cost-containment: there are few serious, life-threatening illnesses for which there are not some treatments that are experimental; being experimental, the value of the treatments is unknown, and perhaps even dubious.[69] If an insurer promised to reimburse any possible treatment for any illness, the costs to the insurer (and ultimately to insureds) would be enormous. On the other hand, insureds who have perhaps only one hope — an experimental, expensive treatment — for survival (or perhaps only one hope of postponing imminent death)[70] often bring considerable pressure to bear upon insurers in an effort to obtain a commitment to pay for the procedure.

---

insured who in good faith obtained an incomplete or incorrect diagnosis and therefore failed to disclose the full extent of the illness before purchasing insurance); Hardester v. Lincoln Nat'l Life Ins. Co., 33 F.3d 330 (4th Cir. 1994) (pre-existing condition clause applied to medical treatment for breast mass thought to be benign but discovered to be cancerous after the effective date of coverage); Mogil v. California Physicians Corp., 267 Cal. Rptr. 487 (Cal. Ct. App. 1990) (cancerous mole was pre-existing condition, in circumstances where insured's prior moles had been benign but insured knew that moles needed continued monitoring).

[66] See, e.g., Beggs v. Pacific Mut. Life Ins. Co., 318 S.E.2d 836 (Ga. Ct. App. 1984).

[67] See, e.g., Klar v. Associated Hosp. Serv., 211 N.Y.S.2d 538 (N.Y. App. Div. 1959).

[68] John Gresham, a famous author of popular fiction read by many lawyers and law students in particular, made an insurer's refusal under, inter alia, the experimental treatment exclusion to pay for an insured's treatment for leukemia the predicate for a insurance bad faith claim, the trial of which was the main plot of the story, in the 1995 bestseller *The Rainmaker.*

[69] If of unknown or dubious value, the treatment may also be considered not to be "medically necessary" because of the lack of an apparent benefit. The closely-related medical necessity issue is discussed in the next subsection. Although the subjects are treated separately here, it may make sense to view them as raising a common question of "medical appropriateness." For a thoughtful treatment of the entire area, see Mark A. Hall & Gerald F. Anderson, *Health Insurers' Assessment of Medical Necessity,* 140 U. Pa. L. Rev. 1637 (1992).

[70] One court described one insured's stake in a particular treatment this way: "[T]wenty to thirty percent of Stage IV breast cancer patients receiving HDC-ABMT have a long-term survival rate of at least two or three years free of cancer with no need for additional treatment. On the other hand, the Stage IV breast cancer patients who receive conventional chemotherapy have a cancer-free outlook of zero percent." Taylor v. Blue Cross/Blue Shield of Mich., 517 N.W.2d 864, 869 (Mich. Ct. App. 1994).

Policies have variously defined 'experimental or investigative" treatment, and sometimes have not defined the policy terms at all.[71] Common formulations have included criteria such as local or national professional standards, scientific standards, or standards created by independent organizations or entities.[72] In some cases, courts have refused to enforce the exclusion on the grounds that the definition was inadequate or lacking in sufficient detail, and therefore ambiguous.[73] Not surprisingly, when insurers have found a treatment to be experimental and therefore outside coverage by applying standards not found in the insurance policy, courts have refused to apply the exclusion.[74] In one recent case, the court, noting the absence of guidelines or criteria in the coverage at issue, articulated its own non-exclusive list of factors to determine whether a procedure is experimental.[75]

A troublesome aspect of the case law on the experimental treatment exclusion is that, not surprisingly, different courts have reached different outcomes on identical facts. A particularly prominent example of this conflict among courts involves the refusal of some insurers to provide coverage for bone marrow transplants[76] to treat certain kinds of cancers.[77] Insureds have prevailed in most cases,[78] but have lost

---

[71] See generally Barbara Fisfis, Comment, *Who Should Rightfully Decide Whether a Medical Treatment Necessarily Incurred Should be Excluded From Coverage Under a Health Insurance Policy Provision Which Excludes From Coverage "Experimental" Medical Treatments?*, 31 Duq. L. Rev. 777 (1993); Jennifer Belk, Comment, *Undefined Experimental Treatment Exclusions in Health Insurance Contracts: A Proposal for Judicial Response*, 66 Wash. L. Rev. 809 (1991).

[72] See, e.g., Fuja v. Benefit Trust Life Ins. Co., 18 F.3d 1405 (7th Cir. 1994); Lubeznik v. Healthchicago, Inc., 644 N.E.2d 777 (Ill. App. Ct. 1994) ("appropriate technology assessment bodies.")

[73] See, e.g, Dahl-Eimers v. Mutual of Omaha Life Ins. Co., 986 F.2d 1379 (11th Cir. 1993)("considered experimental" held ambiguous because policy did not specify who would make determination); Pirozzi v. Blue Cross/Blue Shield, 741 F. Supp. 586 (E.D. Va. 1990) (policy failed to define "experimental" or "clinical investigative" and failed to indicate what evidence was required to classify a treatment as experimental); Tepe v. Rocky Mountain Hosp. and Medical Serv., 893 P.2d 1323 (Colo.App. 1994) (history of plan changes culminating in exclusion was unclear and misleading to insured, who had reasonable expectations of coverage); Taylor v. Blue Cross/Blue Shield of Mich., 517 N.W.2d 864 (Mich. Ct. App. 1994) ("experimental" and "research in nature" are ambiguous).

[74] See, e.g., Kekis v. Blue Cross & Blue Shield, 815 F. Supp. 571 (N.D. N.Y. 1993)(insurer used wrong definition of "experimental"); Pirozzi v. Blue Cross/Blue Shield, 741 F. Supp. 586 (E.D. Va. 1990) (use of technical evaluation was unacceptable because such criteria were not specified in policy).

[75] See Heasley v. Belden & Blake Corp., 2 F.3d 1249 (3d Cir. 1993) (judgment of other insurers and medical bodies; amount of experience with the procedure; demonstrated effectiveness of the procedure).

[76] More specifically, the procedure is high dose chemotherapy with autologous bone marrow transplant, or "HDCT-ABMT." The treatment involves removing part of a patient's bone marrow, giving the patient extremely high doses of chemotherapy, and then replacing the bone marrow.

[77] There is evidence that insurers, let alone courts, do not make consistent decisions on this particular coverage issue. A 1994 study of the process through which insurers approve breast cancer treatment with HDCT-ABMT in grant-sponsored clinical trials noted "substan-

in some.[79] This means that a potentially life-or-death coverage determination — because absent insurance coverage, few insureds have the personal resources to pay for the expenses of the treatment — will turn on the jurisdiction in which the insured resides. Moreover, the cases are difficult at another level: "how experimental" does a treatment need to be before it is appropriate to deny coverage? Many medical experts believe the transplant treatment is not experimental; so should not the benefit of the doubt on these issues cut in favor of coverage? But "who" decides? How many experts must share the view that the treatment has progressed from experimental to conventional? And when experts disagree, how does a court select the "correct" expert opinion?

Some insurers have attempted to make the experimental exclusion more precise by actually listing the particular procedures that are declared experimental. Thus, if a bone marrow transplant is listed as an excluded procedure, there is no room to interpret the policy otherwise, and some courts have enforced these specific exclusions.[80]

[4]   Medically Necessary Services

It is common for health insurance policies to limit coverage to "medically necessary" services. The term "medically necessary" is defined in different ways in various policies. For example, in one case the term was defined as services that are:

> required and appropriate for care of the Sickness or the Injury; and that are given in accordance with generally accepted principles of medical practice in the U.S at the time furnished; and that are approved for reimbursement by the Health Care Financing Administration; and that are not deemed to be experimental, educational or investigational in nature by any appropriate

---

tial inconsistency in the frequency of approval of coverage both among insurers and between decisions made by some individual insurers, even for patients in the same study protocol." William P. Peters & Mark C. Rogers, *Variation in Approval by Insurance Companies of Coverage for Autologous Bone Marrow Transplantation for Breast Cancer,* 330 N. Eng. J. Med. 473 (Feb. 17, 1994).

[78] See, e.g., Kekis v. Blue Cross & Blue Shield, 815 F. Supp. 571 (N.D. N.Y. 1993); Adams v. Blue Cross/Blue Shield, 757 F. Supp. 661 (D.Md. 1991); Kulakowski v. Rochester Hosp. Serv. Corp., 779 F. Supp. 710 (W.D. N.Y. 1991); White v. Caterpillar, Inc., 765 F. Supp. 1418 (W.D. Mo.), aff'd, 985 F.2d 564 (8th Cir. 1991); Pirozzi v. Blue Cross-Blue Shield, 741 F. Supp. 586 (E.D. Va. 1990); Tepe v. Rocky Mountain Hosp. and Medical Serv., 893 P.2d 1323 (Colo.Ct.App. 1994); Lubeznik v. Healthchicago, Inc., 644 N.E.2d 777 (Ill. App. Ct. 1994); Taylor v. Blue Cross/Blue Shield of Mich., 517 N.W.2d 864 (Mich. Ct. App. 1994).

[79] See, e.g., Harris v. Mutual of Omaha Cos., 992 F.2d 706 (7th Cir. 1993); Nesseim v. Mail Handlers Benefit Plan, 995 F.2d 804 (8th Cir. 1993); Holder v. Prudential Ins. Co. of Am., 951 F.2d 89 (5th Cir. 1992). For more discussion, see Paul E. Pongrace, *Comment, HDC/ABMT: Experimental Treatment or Cure All? (Ask the Insurance Companies),* 2 J. Pharm. & L. 329 (1994).

[80] See, e.g., Caudill v. Blue Cross & Blue Shield, 999 F.2d 74 (4th Cir. 1993); Nesseim v. Mail Handlers Benefit Plan, 995 F.2d 804 (8th Cir. 1993).

technological assessment body established by any state or federal government; and that are not furnished in connection with medical or other research.[81]

The foregoing definition demonstrates the linkage between experimental treatments and medical necessity; the notion is that a treatment which does not comport with accepted medical care protocols is not "medically necessary." Under this clause, an insurer would not be required to pay for the care for an insured who, facing certain death, agrees to undergo a rarely or never attempted treatment in the hope that the effort might lead to knowledge that would assist the medical profession in fashioning cures for a dreaded ailment. By the same token, treatment has been held not "medically necessary" when the treatment is far outside the mainstream of the usual, customary practice of medicine.[82]

This linkage between experimentation and medical necessity was apparent in *Free v. Travelers Insurance Co.,*[83] a 1982 Maryland federal decision, where the court held that laetrile treatments were not an expense necessarily incurred as a treatment for cancer and were therefore not within the policy's coverage. The court reasoned that laetrile treatment was "not wise in light of the facts known at the time [treatment] was rendered," nor was it "appropriate" or "reasonably calculated to shorten and relieve an ordeal of agonizing pain and thereby effectuate the most rapid recovery possible."[84] The fact that the insured had relied on his doctor's advise was inconsequential: "it is simply not enough to show that some people, even experts, have a belief in [the] safety and effectiveness [of a particular drug]. A reasonable number of Americans will sincerely attest to the worth of almost any product of even idea."[85] The court apparently felt that disapproval by most experts was enough to

---

[81] Fuja v. Benefit Trust Life Ins. Co., 18 F.3d 1405, 1408 (7th Cir. 1994).

[82] See, e.g., Trustees of the Northwest Laundry and Dry Cleaners Health & Welfare Trust Fund v. Burzynski, 27 F.3d 153 (5th Cir. 1994), *cert. denied,* 115 S.Ct. 1110 (1995) (physician's "antineoplastons cancer treatments" were not "medically necessary" and physician was not entitled to reimbursement); Farley v. Benefit Trust Life Ins. Co., 979 F.2d 653 (8th Cir. 1992) (insured's high-dose chemotherapy treatment accompanied by autologous bone marrow transplant was not given in accordance with generally accepted principles of medical practice and was not "medically necessary.") Compare Grethe v. Trustmark Ins. Co., 881 F. Supp. 1160 (N.D. Ill. 1995) (50-year-old person suffering from inoperable, terminal breast cancer is not entitled to preliminary injunction requiring insurer to pay for HDCT/ABMT or peripheral stem cell rescue (PSCR); such treatment is not "medically necessary" because it is not reimbursable by Medicare and is administered in connection with medical research). For a different twist on the medical necessity question, see Wachtel v. Metropolitan Life Ins. Co., 559 N.Y.S.2d 85 (N.Y. Sup. Ct. 1990) (manual wheelchair to be used by insured on days she could not use due to religious beliefs motorized wheelchair, was not medically necessary; insurer had met "medical necessity" requirement by providing motorized wheelchair). See generally Annot., *What Services, Equipment, or Supplies Are "Medically Necessary" for Purposes of Coverage Under Medical Insurance,* 75 A.L.R.4th 763 (1990).

[83] 551 F. Supp. 554(D.Md. 1982).

[84] 551 F. Supp. at 560 (quoting Abernathy v. Prudential Ins. Co. of Am., 264 S.E.2d 836, 838 (S.C. 1980); Victum v. Martin, 326 N.E.2d 12, 16 (Mass. 1975), and Group Hospitalization, Inc. v. Levin, 305 A.2d 248, 250 (D.C.App. 1973).

[85] 551 F. Supp. at 560 (quoting United States v. Articles of Food and Drug Coli-Trol, 372 F. Supp. 915, 920 (N.D. Ga. 1974), *judgment aff'd,* 518 F.2d 743 (5th Cir. 1975).

take the treatment outside the coverage: "the plaintiff, by his own admission, was well aware that laetrile and nutritional therapy are disapproved of by the majority of cancer specialists."[86] Even though laetrile treatment is of dubious value in the opinion of most medical experts, this result required the court, which lacked any medical expertise of its own, to second-guess the judgment of a medical care professional who had prescribed the treatment and choose among the differing opinions of medical experts. Other courts have been less willing to question the professional opinions of physicians, particularly where the exercise of professional expertise is not inordinately far from conventional medical practice.[87]

The above-quoted policy language also excludes another category of medical care — care which, under generally accepted protocols of medical practice, is simply not needed. A leading case exploring this aspect of "medical necessity" is *Sarchett v. Blue Shield of California*,[88] a 1987 California Supreme Court decision. At the time of his employment Sarchett was offered two different health plans by his employer. One was a Blue Shield plan that allowed Sarchett to choose any physician he wanted, but which allowed for retrospective review by the insurer of whether the care received by the insured was "medically necessary"; if determined not to be "medically necessary," the claim would not be paid. The other plan was an HMO which required the insured to use only the HMO's physicians in order to receive coverage, but which did not impose any kind of retrospective review. Sarchett chose the Blue Shield plan. Thereafter, Sarchett's physician ordered Sarchett hospitalized for diagnosis of a variety of symptoms; the physician feared a life-threatening bleeding ulcer or leukemia. Blue Shield paid for the medical and diagnostic testing bills, but denied coverage for the hospital stay under the reasoning that the hospital admission was not necessary to the treatment or diagnosis.

Sarchett argued that the policy was ambiguous because it did not clearly indicate who would decide whether hospitalization was medically necessary, and that his treating physician's determination of medical necessity should be dispositive. The court, however, disagreed, noting that the policy's arbitration procedures made it clear enough how questions of medical necessity would ultimately be decided.[89] Moreover, the court rejected Sarchett's argument that public policy should bar insurers from refusing coverage for hospitalization ordered by treating physicians. Sarchett argued that he had a limited choice: declining to follow his treating doctor's recommendations about the hospital stay is not something Sarchett could reasonably be expected to do, as that would be knowingly increasing a risk to his own health; but if he follows the doctor's advice, the insurer might later deny coverage, leaving the patient with the bill for all of the services rendered.[90] The court, however, noted

---

[86] 551 F. Supp. at 560.

[87] See, e.g., Tudor v. Metropolitan Life Ins. Co., 539 N.Y.S.2d 690 (N.Y.Civ.Ct. 1989) (questions of necessity of treatment must be decided in first instance by treating physician); Carmouche v. CNA Ins. Cos., 535 So. 2d 1279 (La. Ct. App. 1988) (chiropractic treatment ordered by treating physician held medically necessary).

[88] 729 P.2d 267 (Cal. 1987).

[89] 729 P.2d at 271-72.

[90] 729 P.2d at 274.

the problem with Sarchett's argument: few doctors would prescribe medical procedures they thought unnecessary; thus, under Sarchett's argument, all treatment prescribed by any physician would be medically necessary. This outcome would eviscerate the cost-containment objectives of retrospective review.[91] Moreover, the court noted that Sarchett did have a choice: if he did not want to endure retrospective review, he could have avoided it by joining the HMO.[92] In essence, HMOs screen for "medical necessity" by limiting the selection of doctors to whom the insured could go for medical treatment. In the final analysis, Sarchett asked both to choose his own doctor and to be free from retrospective review, but the court refused to let him have both; for cost containment reasons, the coverage provided through the employer put Sarchett to a choice of one or the other. Having made his choice, Sarchett was bound by the consequences of his decision.

Sarchett is an interesting decision for one reason in particular. Insurance law has many doctrines which protect an insured when a coverage limitation is not clear or not brought home to the insured in a way that enables the insured to understand it.[93] Indeed, it is not much of a stretch to conclude that Sarchett did not reasonably expect that if he followed the advice of a licensed, competent physician he would later be forced to pay for a hospital stay out of his own pocket. In this setting, however, the cost-containment imperative inherent in the retrospective review authorized by the Blue Shield plan (and inherent in the HMO plan's constraint on physician choice) was so important that it trumped doctrines which in another setting could have easily justified a pro-insured result. In other words, any other result in this case would have wrecked this insurer's effort to attempt to brake the escalation in health care costs, and would otherwise have fueled further increases in health care costs.

Finally, it should be observed that when a court (or legislature or administrative agency) decides what is "necessary" medical treatment, some fundamental, and sometimes difficult, value judgments are being made. Some cases are easy; clearly, the cast needed to repair the broken bone and the antibiotic needed to cure the pneumonia are necessary treatments. Also, "necessary" means more than just curing an existing ailment or injury; a great deal of preventive care, such as immunizations, is necessary. A child is not certain to get measles or mumps if not immunized, but the odds are so high and the cost of the preventive measure is so low that it would be clearly wrong if health insurance did not cover this kind of care. Indeed, insurers have an economic incentive to cover such care, given the high costs of treating illnesses and their complications which can be prevented at low cost. If someone suffers from fatigue, is a medication or treatment than enhances that person's energy to make the person fully functional "necessary"? Most people would answer with an unequivocal yes. Is treatment for infertility "necessary"? Under one point of view, infertility does not impair health, shorten one's lifespan, or affect one's ability to

---

[91] For a decision more sympathetic to Sarchett's position, see Strassberg v. Connecticut Gen. Life Ins Co., 583 N.Y.S.2d 48 (N.Y. App. Div. 1992) (ambiguous language construed in favor of insured, and insured was entitled to coverage solely upon the good-faith recommendation of a physician who had determined such care was medically necessary).

[92] 729 P.2d at 274.

[93] See §§ 25-25H, *supra*.

work.[94] From another point of view, an infertile person is not fully functional, and treatment to restore one's full physical capability is "necessary."[95] Is cosmetic surgery necessary? If the surgery is designed to alleviate the consequences of a disfiguring accident, arguably it is; but if the disfigurement does not impair bodily functions or shorten lifespan, should it be considered necessary? Presumably a decision to have a more attractive nose does not make cosmetic surgery necessary; but if the decision is based on a mixed motive, such as improving nasal breathing and improving appearance, is the case different? The issue can arise in a variety of ways, and in many cases the answers are difficult because so much is at stake.

[5] Mandated Coverages

In recent years while many insurers and federal regulators were attempting to contain rising health care costs, some state legislatures enacted so-called "mandated coverage" statutes. These statutes, the content of which varies greatly, require that health or disability insurance policies sold in the state contain certain minimum coverages, such as, to take a few examples, in-patient and out-patient kidney disease treatment,[96] in-patient treatment of mental disorders, alcoholism, and drug abuse,[97] hospitalization for childbirth,[98] payment for blood products,[99] infertility treatments,[100] payment in full (i.e., without co-payment or deductible) for "routine and necessary immunizations for all newly born children."[101] expenses from the moment of birth of newly-born children of insureds,[102] expenses from the moment of birth of newly-born children adopted by insureds,[103] and hair prostheses worn for hair loss suffered as a result of alopecia areata.[104] This list is by no means

---

[94] See Kinzie v. Physician's Liab. Ins. Co., 750 P.2d 1140 (OkLa. Ct. App. 1987) (in vitro fertilization procedure was not "medically necessary"); Annot., *Coverage of Artificial Insemination Procedures or Other Infertility Treatments by Health, Sickness, or Hospitalization Insurance,* 80 A.L.R.4th 1059 (1990).

[95] See Ralston v. Connecticut Gen. Life Ins. Co., 617 So. 2d 1379 (La. Ct. App. 1993), vacated, 625 So. 2d 156 (La. 1993) (in vitro fertilization procedures to induce pregnancy was treatment for a "sickness," and was therefore covered by health policy).

[96] See Wis. Stat. Ann. § 632.895(4).

[97] See Wis. Stat. § 632.89(2)(a); 48A Md. Ann. Code § 490F.

[98] See 48A Md. Ann. Code § 2354F.

[99] See 48A Md. Ann. Code § 354E.

[100] See, e.g., Cal. Ins. Code § 10119.6 (infertility treatment except in vitro fertilization); Haw. Rev. Stat. § 431:10A-116.5 (infertility treatment, including one-time-only in vitro fertilization, provided policy provides pregnancy benefits); Ill. Ann. Stat. ch. 215, par. 5/356m (infertility treatment, including in vitro fertilization, uterine embryo lavage, embryo transfer, gamete intrafallopian tube transfer, zygote intrafallopian tube transfer, and low tubal ovum transfer).

[101] See Kan. Stat. Ann. § 40-2,102(a).

[102] See, e.g., Alaska Stat. § 21.42.345.

[103] See, e.g., 48A Md. Ann. Code § 438A; Kan Stat. Ann. § 40-2,102(b). The Kansas statute also requires all health insurance policies to offer an optional coverage that would reimburse the delivery expenses at birth of the birth mother of a child adopted within ninety days of the birth. Kan. Stat. Ann. § 40-2,102(b).

[104] See Minn. Stat. Ann. § 62A.28(2), 62E.06.

exhaustive. Every item on the list is defensible as good social policy. For example, the statutes mandating coverage for the expenses from the moment of birth of newly-born children who are subsequently adopted help reduce the out-of-pocket costs to adopting parents of adopting a child in private placements, which thereby encourages adoption, which plays an important role in encouraging the formation of families and, arguably, addressing some of the consequences of various policies that currently make abortion more difficult to obtain. Only covering expenses from the moment of adoption would make adoption less affordable for many people because birthmothers in private placements would undoubtedly require as a condition of a placement that the child's post-birth and pre-adoption expenses be paid by the adopting parents (assuming the birth mother does not have insurance for these expenses herself).[105]

The Minnesota statute requiring coverage for hair prostheses to remedy the disfiguration of alopecia areata is perhaps the most interesting mandated benefit on this list. In one section of the Minnesota statute, the mandated benefit requirement reads "prostheses other than dental but including scalp hair prostheses worn for hair loss suffered as a result of alopecia areata."[106] The rationale for covering a prosthetic device for a loss of limb is obvious; the device allows a significant, though usually not total, recovery of a bodily function. The scalp hair prosthesis is a cosmetic device, one that is unnecessary to any physical, bodily function. Interestingly, dental prostheses, which have a much closer connection to physical health and the bodily function of eating, are not mandated by the Minnesota statute. No one would dispute that loss of hair due to alopecia areata can be an extremely traumatic experience, one that may compromise a person's mental health and well-being. (Query: Is the trauma greater for a woman than a man given cultural norms that tolerate baldness in men more than women? Can such a distinction even be validly made?) Yet the cosmetic effects of loss of teeth are substantial and traumatic. Are dentists less favored than other health care providers? Do dentists have less political power in Minnesota? Did a legislator or legislative staffer in Minnesota have the unfortunate experience of contracting alopecia areata? There are potentially many reasons why particular coverages are mandated; some are good, and no doubt some are weak. It is obvious that both suppliers (e.g., podiatrists, chiropractors, dentists, fertility clinics, mental health specialists, etc.) and consumers (who may form interest groups based on particular health care needs) have a strong stake in what is included in any package of mandated, minimum coverage.[107] This has

---

[105] The Kansas statute stops short of encouraging adoption by mandating that the medical expenses of the birthmother, as distinguished from the medical expenses of the child, be covered. Depending on the difficulty of the birth, the birthmother's expenses can be thousands of dollars. This expense makes adoption unaffordable for many people. Of course, requiring that health insurers offer the coverage as an option is a step in the direction of encouraging adoption, but the effect of this requirement is questionable, since many adopting parents may not know at the time they purchase their health insurance coverage that they will in the future need coverage for expenses relating to adoption.

[106] Minn. Stat. Ann. § 62E.06(9).

[107] The politicized nature of some aspects of the debate is apparent in recent controversy over shortened maternity hospital stays. Bipartisan legislation introduced in the Congress in

considerable importance for any effort to create a program of national health insurance that defines a minimum benefit package; interest groups will lobby for the inclusion of particular benefits, and the inability of legislators or administrators to resist these efforts would ultimately be fatal to the cost-containment goals of any national health care plan.

In other words, each mandated-benefit provision increases the cost of health care insurance, thereby making insurance less accessible to some people. In addition, to the extent the insurance increases utilization of health care, this extra demand must further increase prices, which accumulates more access problems.[108]

The debate over coverage of experimental treatment is now spilling over into the mandated benefits area. Recently, legislation introduced in some states would require health plans and insurers to provide coverage for experimental treatments.[109] Some of the treatments are very expensive; the most-litigated of the treatments, high-dose chemotherapy with bone marrow transplants for the purpose of battling cancer, costs, in some cases, up to $150,000.[110] The ramifications of these proposals for cost-containment efforts are extremely significant.

To summarize, the experience with existing mandated-coverage statutes raises a fundamental question. If health care reform does not occur at the federal level through a national, uniform plan, will fifty individual states be able to enact a cogent, cost-effective health care policy? Or will individual states be inclined to yield to the requests of particular legislators or interest groups to add favorite coverages to health care plans, thereby fueling the cost-containment problem which already has national proportions? At its root, this raises the issue of the appropriate relationship between federal and state regulatory authority, an issue that surfaces in other settings as well.[111]

June 1995 would require all health care plans, including self-funded plans, to provide a minimum of 48 hours in-patient care for mother and infant after a vaginal delivery and a minimum of 96 hours of inpatient care following a Caesarean section. See *Maternity Stay Backlash Grows,* Bus. Ins., July 10, 1995, at 1.

[108] Similar problems are created, arguably, by mandated provider laws (which provide that if an insurer pays a physician for a given service, it must also pay all non-physicians who are licensed to render the same service, such as, e.g., chiropractors) and willing-provider statutes (which provide that any health care provider willing to meet the contractual provisions offered by preferred-provider organization must be allowed to contract with the organization, which arguably undercuts managed care organizations seeking to limit utilization through careful selection of physicians). For more discussion, see Alice C. Gosfield et al., eds., *Nat'l Health Lawyers Ass'n, Health Law Practice Guide* § 14.02[3] (1995).

[109] See *Coverage for Experimental Treatments Proposed in Numerous Bills This Year,"* BNA Health Care Daily, April 8, 1994 (referring to California); *Paying for Experimental Treatment,* Newsday, Sept. 14, 1994 (referring to New York).

[110] *"Experimental" Debate is Intensifying,* National Underwriter, April 24, 1995, at 5 (quoting John Cova, health insurance industry consultant).

[111] See § 21, *supra.*

§ 65 Particular Coverage Issues in Liability Insurance

[a] The Scope of the CGL

The Commercial General Liability ("CGL") Policy is the successor to the Comprehensive General Liability Policy that had been used since the 1940s.[1] The CGL policy provides general liability coverage for businesses, and individuals receive their liability coverage through other policies, such as homeowner's or renter's policies, automobile policies, and umbrella policies.

The basic insuring agreement of the CGL provides:

> The Company will pay on behalf of the insured all sums which the insured shall become legally obligated to pay as damages because of
>
> A. bodily injury, or
>
> B. property damage
>
> to which this insurance applies caused by an occurrence during the policy period.

Several phrases in this basic agreement have been extensively litigated in a variety of circumstances.

The phrase "to which this insurance applies" recognizes that there are specified perils covered by the CGL as well as specific exclusions to the affirmative grants of coverage. The company's obligation only extends to liability to which the insurance applies, not all liabilities imaginable. There are three main kinds of specified perils, and these perils are quite broad in scope. The "premises/operations hazard" provision typically extends coverage for the insured's liability to third parties for bodily injury and property damage "arising out of the ownership, maintenance, or use of the insured premises and all operations necessary or incidental thereto." The "completed operations" provision generally provides coverage for an insurer's liability for bodily injury or property damage in connection with losses that occur away from the insured's premises and arise from the insured's operations after those operations have been completed. The "products hazard" generally provides liability coverage for bodily injury or property damage arising out of the insured's products, or reliance on a representation or warranty made with respect to the products, provided the injury or damage occurs away from premises owned by or rented to the insured and after physical possession of the products has been relinquished to others.[2] When one combines the scope of these three coverages, it is fair to say that the CGL provides "general" liability coverage for insured businesses.

The phrase "bodily injury" is an important one, for it specifies one of the two kinds of loss for which the CGL will provide protection. Most CGL policies define bodily injury as "bodily injury, sickness or disease sustained by any person which occurs during the policy period, including death at any time resulting therefrom."

---

[1] See § 60B[b], *supra*.

[2] For detailed discussion of these provisions, see Barry R. Ostrager & Thomas R. Newman, *Handbook on Insurance Coverage Disputes* 221-32 (7th ed. 1994).

What this definition makes clear is that to be "bodily injury" within the scope of the insuring agreement, the injury must "occur" during the policy period, but as discussed in a subsequent subsection, this only begins the inquiry.[3] Courts are divided on whether emotional injury constitutes "bodily injury." Most courts hold that "bodily injury" refers to physical injuries only and not to purely nonphysical or emotional harm.[4] If, however, emotional distress itself causes physical manifestations, most courts hold that the bodily injury definition is met.[5] A few courts have held that pure emotional distress unaccompanied by physical injury constitutes "bodily injury."[6] Both the Ninth Circuit and California Supreme Court held in recent cases that emotional or physical distress induced by noncovered economic loss was not within the scope of "bodily injury" covered by the CGL in circumstances where all of the alleged injuries suffered arose from economic loss, and economic loss does not constitute damage or injury to tangible property covered by the CGL.[7]

The phrase "property damage," which is typically paired with "bodily injury," is an equally important phrase in the CGL insuring agreement.[8] This component of the CGL underwent revision in both 1966, 1973, and 1986. As defined in the 1986 revision,[9] "property damage" means:

     a.   Physical injury to tangible property, including all resulting loss of use of that property. All such loss of use shall be deemed to occur at the time of the physical injury that caused it; or

     b.   Loss of use of tangible property that is not physically injured. All such loss of use shall be deemed to occur at the time of the "occurrence" that caused it.

---

[3] See § 65[e], *infra.*

[4] See, e.g., National Cas. Co. v. Great Southwest Fire Ins. Co., 833 P.2d 741 (Colo. 1992); SL Industries, Inc. v. American Motorists Ins. Co., 607 A.2d 1266 (N.J. 1992); Aetna Cas. & Sur. Co. v. First Sec. Bank, 662 F. Supp. 1126 (D.Mont. 1987).

[5] See, e.g., Equal Employment Opportunity Comm'n v. Southern Publishing Co., 894 F.2d 785 (5th Cir. 1990); Garvis v. Employers Mut. Cas. Co., 497 N.W.2d 254 (Minn. 1993); Voorhees v. Preferred Mut. Ins. Co., 607 A.2d 1255 (N.J. 1992).

[6] See, e.g., Lavanant v. General Acc. Ins. Co. of Am., 584 N.E.2d 744 (N.Y. 1992); State Farm Mut. Auto. Ins. Co. v. Ramsey, 368 S.E.2d 477 (S.C. Ct. App.), *aff'd,* 374 S.E.2d 896 (S.C. 1988). For discussion of this issue as it arises with respect to the homeowner's liability form, see Annot., *Homeowner's Liability Insurnace Coverage of Emotional Distress Allegedly Inflicted on Third Party by Insured,* 8 A.L.R.5th 254 (1992). It is possible to argue that every "pure" emotional distress injury is in fact a physical injury. As stated by the court in Pekin Ins. Co. v. Hugh, 501 N.W.2d 508 (Iowa 1993), "[a]ny attempt to distinguish between 'physical' and 'psychological' injuries just clouds the issue. This is because the medical community now knows that 'every emotional disturbance has a physical aspect and every physical disturbance has an emotional aspect.' Comment, *Negligently Inflicted Mental Distress: The Case For An Independent Tort,* 59 Geo. L.J. 1237, 1241, n 24 (1971)." 501 N.W.2d at 512.

[7] See Keating v. National Union Fire Ins. Co., 995 F.2d 154 (9th Cir. 1993); Waller v. Truck Ins. Exch., 1995 WL 516406 (Cal. 1995).

[8] For more discussion of this phrase, see John P. Arness & Randall D. Eliason, *Insurance Coverage for "Property Damage" in Asbestos and Other Toxic Tort Cases,* 72 Va. L. Rev. 943 (1986).

[9] *Policy Kit* at 309 (ISO Form CG 00 01 10 93).

Beginning with the 1966 revisions, the standard CGL form has sought to limit the property damage to "tangible property," which generally has been interpreted to mean property that is capable of being physically handled or touched. Damage to intangible property, such as investments, lost profits, copyrights, goodwill etc., has almost uniformly been held not to constitute property damage.[10] As stated by one court, "[t]he focus of coverage for property damage is . . . the property itself, and does not include intangible economic losses, violation of antitrust laws or non-performance of contractual obligations."[11] It is also apparent from the definition that both physical injury to tangible property and loss of its use are covered. Moreover, because the insuring agreement refers to liability imposed "because of . . . property damage," an economic loss that causally follows from a direct physical injury to tangible property or a loss of use of tangible property is within the coverage of the CGL.[12]

How the property damage definition applies to situations in which the insured's defective component is involved in a larger product or system has presented difficulties.[13]

The "as damages" phrase has been the subject of vigorous litigation; this issue is discussed in a subsequent subsection.[14] Also, the CGL insuring agreement requires an "occurrence" that occurs "during the policy period." These issues are also discussed in subsequent sections.[15]

Like any policy, the basic insuring agreement is subject to a package of conditions and exclusions.[16] Some of the important exclusions are discussed in other parts of this text.[17]

---

[10] See, e.g., Travelers Ins. Cos. v. Penda Corp., 974 F.2d 823 (7th Cir. 1992)(economic loss is not property damage); Giddings v. Industrial Indem. Co., 169 Cal. Rptr. 278 (Cal. Ct. App. 1980)(economic losses are not recoverable as tangible property); General Ins. Co. of Am. v. Chopot, 623 P.2d 7309 (Wash. Ct. App. 1981) (copyrights are not tangible property). See also Annot., *Liability Policy Coverage for Insured's Injury to Third Party's Investments, Anticipated Profits, Goodwill, or the Like, Unaccompanied by Physical Property Damage,* 18 A.L.R.5th 187 (1994).

[11] Waller v. Truck Ins. Exch., 1995 WL 516406 (Cal. 1995), slip op. at 6. In another part of the opinion, the court stated: "the occurrence or act leading to coverage must be an injury to tangible property, not to one's economic interest." *Id.*, slip op. at 14.

[12] See, e.g., Aetna Cas. & Sur. Co. v. General Time Corp., 704 F.2d 80 (2d Cir. 1983); Federated Mut. Ins. Co. v. Concrete Units, Inc., 363 N.W.2d 751 (Minn. 1985).

[13] See Hamilton Die Cast, Inc. v. United States Fid. & Guar. Co., 508 F.2d 417 (7th Cir. 1975) (if defective tire causes auto crash, the component-tire caused the damage to the auto; if tires are defective and manufacturer withdraws car from market, component-tire has not caused damage to auto); Goodyear Rubber & Supply Co. v. Great Am. Ins. Co., 471 F.2d 1343 (9th Cir. 1973) (ship's defective hatch gaskets constitute property damage); Elco Indus., Inc. v. Liberty Mut. Ins. Co., 414 N.E.2d 41 (Ill. App. Ct. 1980) (damage to gaskets in third party's engines from replacing defective pins constitutes property damage). See generally Ostrager & Newman, *supra* note 2, at 247-249.

[14] See § 65[f][2], *infra.*

[15] See § 65[e], *infra.*

[16] See generally Irene A. Sullivan & Peri Erlanger, *Introduction to the Comprehensive General Liability (CGL) Policy,* 658 PLI/Comm 7 (May-June 1993).

[17] See, e.g., § 63C, *supra;* §§ 65[f][6], 65[f][7], *infra.*

[b] The Meaning of Occurrence

Liability insurance provides coverage for legal liability imposed upon the insured as a result of unintentional and unexpected personal injury or property damage. Until 1966, the coverage was keyed to the word "accident," which was defined as "a sudden and unforeseeable event." One of the difficulties with this definition was that the insured had no coverage if the event was not "sudden." For example, if toxic chemicals leaked from a storage site over a long period of time, the insured's liability would not be covered.

In 1966, the standard comprehensive liability form was revised to key the coverage to the word "occurrence." In 1973, further revisions were made in the definition of occurrence in the Comprehensive General Liability ("CGL") policy used for commercial entities. Under these revisions, liability policies defined "occurrence" as "an accident, including continuous or repeated exposure to conditions, which results in bodily injury or property damage neither expected nor intended from the standpoint of the insured." The word "accident" was retained in the definition, but it was clarified to embrace events that are not sudden. Thus, the word "occurrence" denoted wider coverage than the word "accident." Yet under the plain language of the clause, a repeated exposure to conditions was *one* accident, meaning that the policy limits apply once, regardless of the number of losses. In 1986, further revisions in the CGL moved the "neither expected nor intended from the standpoint of the insured" language from the definition of occurrence to the exclusions, and this shift is found in some personal liability policies as well. The "expected nor intended" phrase pours much content into the meaning of "occurrence," and this phrase is discussed in detail in a prior section.[18]

[c] Problems with the Word "Accident"

The term accident has always been difficult for courts.[1] In common parlance, an accident is something that is sudden, usually accompanied by some kind of violent force. Courts have defined accident in different ways, but the common theme in these definitions, whether it arises in property, personal, or liability insurance, is that an accident is an unforeseen, unexpected, and unintended event that results from some cause, either known or unknown.[2] The concept of accident embraces the fortuity requirement that is inherent in all aspects of insurance law.[3]

Consistent with this understanding of the nature of the term "accident," it follows that there can be no liability insurance coverage for losses intentionally caused by the insured or which the insured expects will occur.[4] Moreover, there can be no liability insurance coverage for a loss that the insured knows about at the time the policy is issued.[5] Closely related to known losses are what are termed "losses in

---

[18] See § 63C[a], *supra*.

[1] Prior to 1966 the word "accident" was usually left undefined in insurance policies.

[2] See, e.g., Diana v. Western Nat'l Assur. Co., 785 P.2d 479 (Wash. Ct. App. 1990).

[3] See § 63, *supra*.

[4] See § 63C, *supra*.

[5] See, e.g., Summers v. Harris, 573 F.2d 869 (5th Cir. 1978); MAPCO Alaska Petroleum, Inc. v. Central Nat'l Ins. Co., 795 F. Supp. 941 (D.Alaska 1991). For more discussion of this issue, see § 63, *supra*.

progress," which have given rise to the so-called "loss in progress rule" under which some courts have held there is no coverage under policies for continuous losses when the policy is issued after initial manifestation of the loss.[6] As explained by the California Supreme Court in a 1990 decision, "insurers whose policy terms commence after initial manifestation of the loss are not responsible for any potential claim relating to the previously discovered and manifested loss."[7] This understanding of the fortuity requirement is buttressed by the intentional act exclusion in the CGL, because the property damage resulting from a loss-in-progress is certainly "expected" from the insured's standpoint. But where liability is uncertain or contingent, the loss-in-progress rule should not be applied. As explained by the California Supreme Court in a 1995 decision, "the loss-in-progress rule will not defeat coverage for a claimed loss where it had yet to be established, at the time the insurer entered into the contract of insurance with the policyholder, that the insured had a legal obligation to pay damages to a third party in connection with a loss."[8] Also, losses-in-progress should be distinguished from "known risks,"[9] since the whole point of liability insurance is to protect the insured from risks and it would be anomalous to take away coverage simply because the insured was aware of a risk, as distinguished from a loss.[10]

Definitions that stress the absence of foreseeability as an element of an accident raise the question of whether negligent activity on the party of the insured is excluded from coverage. In tort law, "accidents" are often distinguished from "negligent acts," and foreseeability is an element of establishing negligence. However, excluding negligent acts from a liability policy's coverage vitiates much of the coverage.[11] For this reason some courts have rejected tort law's foreseeability test in determining whether an accident has occurred.[12] Some courts have gone to

---

[6] See, e.g., Inland Waters Pollution Control, Inc. v. National Union Fire Ins. Co., 997 F.2d 172 (6th Cir. 1993); Continental Ins. Co. v. Beechum, Inc., 836 F. Supp. 1027 (D.N.J. 1993).

[7] Prudential-LMI Commercial Ins. Co. v. Superior Court, 798 P.2d 1230, 1246-47 (Cal. 1990).

[8] Montrose Chem. Corp. v. Admiral Ins. Co., 42 Cal. Rptr.2d 324 (Cal. 1995).

[9] This distinction is made in Montrose Chem. Corp. of Cal. v. Admiral Ins. Co., 42 Cal. Rptr.2d 324 (Cal. 1995) (mere fact that EPA considered insured a potentially responsible party and that suit was likely did not make insured's liability inevitable; held, insurer had duty to defend and indemnify).

[10] For more discussion of these points, see Kenneth S. Abraham, *Environmental Liability Insurance Law* 141-145 (1991).

[11] See, e.g., Kuckenberg v. Hartford Acc. & Indem. Co., 226 F.2d 225 (9th Cir. 1955) (blasting resulted in unexpectedly heavy slides, but since damage in some degree was foreseen no accident resulted); Millard Warehouse, Inc. v. Hartford Fire Ins. Co., 283 N.W.2d 56 (Neb. 1979) (increase in the flood level as a consequence of warehouse destruction, about which insured had been warned, held not an accident); Town of Tieton v. General Ins. Co. of Am., 380 P.2d 127 (Wash. 1963) (city is informed that lagoon construction project might contaminate well; on advice of engineers, city proceeds with project anyway; resulting contamination of well is not an accident, and no coverage exists).

[12] See, e.g., Cross v. Zurich Gen. Acc. & Liab. Ins. Co., 184 F.2d 609 (7th Cir. 1950); Pachucki v. Republic Ins. Co., 278 N.W.2d 898 (Wis. 1979); Iowa Mut. Ins. Co. v. Fred M. Simmons, Inc., 138 S.E.2d 512 (N.C. 1964).

the other extreme and have required the insurer to show that the insured intended to cause the specific kind of harm that resulted before denying coverage.[13]

Prior to 1966, a split in authority existed as to whether an accident must be determined from the standpoint of the insured or the victim. Viewing the incident from the viewpoint of the victim would almost always lead to a conclusion that the loss in question was an accident and therefore covered, since victims rarely foresee, intend, or expect the loss caused by the insured. However, the 1966 revision specifically required that whether an accident occurred be determined from the insured's viewpoint.[14] This revision constricted coverage and mooted the conflict in the older cases, at least in situations where the applicable policy contained the revision. Under the new language, an insured who is vicariously liable for the intentional act of an another is covered so long as the loss was not intended or expected from the insured's viewpoint.[15] Although no dramatic shift resulted from the 1966 revisions in the policy forms, it does appear that a higher degree of certainty that damage will result from a particular act is required to bar coverage under the definition of occurrence. It is not necessary that the insured literally intend the results from his or her acts, but a high degree of certainty that damages will occur must exist to bar coverage.[16]

In policies where the limiting language "expected or intended from the standpoint of the insured" appears in the exclusions and not in the definition of "occurrence" or "accident," the threshold question of whether an "occurrence" happened, which is distinct from the question of whether the intentional act exclusion applies, can result in difficulty. This is evident in a 1994 Michigan Supreme Court decision, *Auto Club Group Insurance Co. v. Marzonie,*[17] where a deeply-divided court struggled with the coverage questions arising out a fairly simple set of facts. An obscene gesture made by someone in one vehicle to someone in another, where both vehicles were occupied by a number of people, led to taunting, a high-speed chase, and thrown beer bottles. This led to one party, the insured, retrieving from his home a

---

[13] E.g., Moffat v. Metropolitan Cas. Ins. Co., 238 F. Supp. 165 (M.D.Pa. 1964) (insured intended to burn refuse, but did not intend that the fumes would damage adjacent property; held an accident); Geurin Contractors, Inc. v. Bituminous Cas. Corp., 636 S.W.2d 638 (Ark.Ct.App. 1982) (insured road contractor who undercut a highway to correct unstable soil condition, thereby causing a store to lose access when heavy rain filled the undercut, did not expect or intend the loss, and thus an accident had occurred). For further discussion, see § 63C[b], *supra.*

[14] See Continental Cas. Co. v. Parker, 288 S.E.2d 776 (Ga. Ct. App. 1982) (the requirement is "clear and unambiguous and capable of only one reasonable interpretation.")

[15] E.g., McBride v. Lyles, 303 So. 2d 795 (La. Ct. App. 1974) (father who was vicariously liable for son's intentional assault is covered under homeowner's policy); Edwards v. Akion, 279 S.E.2d 894 (N.C. Ct. App.), *aff'd,* 284 S.E.2d 518 (N.C. 1981) (city, vicariously liable for assault of employee, was covered).

[16] Sam P. Rynearson, "Exclusion of Expected or Intended Personal Injury or Property Damage Under the Occurrence Definition of the Standard Comprehensive General Liability Policy," in Aretha J. Liederman, ed., *The Comprehensive General Liability Policy: A Critique of Selected Provisions* 3–21 (1985). For a more detailed discussion of the issues raised in this subsection, see § 63C[b], *supra.*

[17] 527 N.W.2d 760 (Mich. 1994).

shotgun he had never fired, and using it initially to try to scare off the other vehicle's occupants. When this failed, the insured aimed at the other car's grill and fired, but his aim was poor and the shot hit an occupant in the vehicle, causing injury. The insured testified that he did not intend to hit the victim, noting that he had the opportunity to do so easily at one stage in the fracas but instead shot at the grill. The insurer denied coverage.

The insured's policy defined "occurrence" as an "accident . . . which results . . . in bodily injury or property damage," but did not define accident and did not state whose perspective is controlling on whether an accident occurs. Because the coverage-granting definition of occurrence did not contain the limitation found in the exclusions referring to the insured's viewpoint, the majority, while acknowledging a split of authority in the decided cases, held that "where the policy is silent with respect to perspective, . . . the accidental nature of the event must be evaluated from the injured party's standpoint."[18] In these circumstances, the majority was unable to determine whether the victim's injury was an "accident" as a matter of law because of the authorities recognizing that someone who provokes an incident and who has reason to foresee the outcome may not, from that perspective, consider the injury an accident.[19] Nevertheless, the majority found that the intentional act exclusion eliminated any possibility of coverage because anyone firing a shotgun at an occupied vehicle "should have known" that bodily injury, rather than just property damage, was likely to result.[20]

Although agreeing with the result, Justice Griffin in a separate opinion joined by two justices took issue with the majority's conclusion that an "occurrence" could exist in these facts. He argued that the insured's viewpoint should control on the question of whether an accident occurred, and in these circumstances there was no accident and therefore no occurrence, despite the lack of a subjective intent by the insured to cause damage or injury. He thought that the "direct risk of harm intentionally created by the insured's actions" eliminated any possibility of coverage.[21] Justice Levin in dissent agreed that the insured's viewpoint should be used to determine whether an accident occurred, but reasoned that because the trier of fact concluded that the bodily injury was neither intended nor expected by the insured, an "occurrence" had happened in these facts.[22]

The differing, lengthy opinions in *Marzonie* demonstrate that after a half-century of experience with the terms "accident" and "occurrence" there is still much uncertainty in common fact patterns about how the terms should be applied.[23]

---

[18] 527 N.W.2d at 764.

[19] 527 N.W.2d at 766-67.

[20] 527 N.W.2d at 768.

[21] 527 N.W.2d at 770.

[22] 527 N.W.2d at 772.

[23] For further insights into the different views of the Michigan Supreme Court, see Buczkowski v. Allstate Ins. Co., 526 N.W.2d 589 (Mich. 1994), decided one day after *Marzonie*, where a majority agreed that shooting a shotgun in a residential neighborhood in the middle of the night at an unoccupied car does not necessarily lead, as a matter of law, to a reasonable expectation of bodily injury. 526 N.W.2d at 590. Thus, it was a question for the trier of fact whether an intentional discharge of a shotgun at an unoccupied vehicle, where the ricochet

[d] Problems of Multiple Losses from a Single Cause

When multiple losses attributable to the same covered cause occur, a problem exists in determining the scope of a liability policy's coverage. In such a situation, it is sometimes difficult to determine whether there has been one occurrence or multiple occurrences. Suppose a driver loses control of an automobile, strikes one car, bounces off this car and strikes another car, and then spins away and hits a building: has there been one occurrence or three separate occurrences? Suppose a drug manufacturer releases defective drugs into the marketplace and twenty people are injured: has there been one occurrence or twenty separate occurrences?

The majority rule follows "cause analysis": the number of occurrences depends on the number of causes. If there is one cause (such as one loss of control of a vehicle or one release of drugs into the market), there is one occurrence.[24] Under this rule, there is only one cause if there "was but one proximate, uninterrupted, and continuing cause which resulted in all of the injuries and damage."[25] Under the cause theory, if a time interval separates the two events, a court might conclude that multiple causes existed, meaning that multiple occurrences resulted.[26] The minority

---

of the fired slug hit the victim who was sitting at a nearby picnic table. In a separate opinion supporting that result, Justice Brickley wrote that "simply because a person's actions are foolhardy, potentially dangerous, or even criminal, does not mean that personal injuries are necessarily an expected result of those actions." 526 N.W.2d at 591. Three dissenting justices signed an opinion written by Justice Boyle, believed that the insured's acts "were of such a nature as to forewarn a reasonably prudent person that personal injury was highly likely to occur" and that the intentional act exclusion should apply as a matter of law. 526 N.W.2d at 598-99.

[24] E.g., Appalachian Ins. Co. v. Liberty Mut. Ins. Co., 676 F.2d 56 (3d Cir. 1982); Champion Int'l Corp. v. Continental Cas. Co., 546 F.2d 502 (2d Cir. 1976), cert. denied, 434 U.S. 819 (1977); St. Paul-Mercury Indem. Co. v. Rutland, 225 F.2d 689 (5th Cir. 1955) (truck hit train causing derailment of 16 railroad cars belonging to 14 different owners held one occurrence); Bush v. Guaranty Nat'l Ins. Co., 848 P.2d 1057 (Nev. 1993) (held one occurrence where insured twice ran over daughter, once by backing over her and then, after hearing neighbor's scream and realizing what she had done, stopped, put car in forward gear, and ran over child again); Olsen v. Moore, 202 N.W.2d 236 (Wis. 1972) (auto crossing interstate median and hitting two different vehicles in two separate lanes held one occurrence); Truck Ins. Exch. v. Rohde, 303 P.2d 659 (Wash. 1956) (auto hits three motorcyclists in a continuous, uninterrupted motion; held one occurrence). See generally Annot., *What Constitutes Single Accident or Occurrence Within Liability Policy Limiting Insurer's Liability to a Specified Amount Per Accident or Occurrence,* 64 A.L.R.4th 668 (1988).

[25] Michigan Chem. Corp. v. American Home Assur. Co., 728 F.2d 374 (6th Cir. 1984). In *Michigan Chemical,* the underlying lawsuit involved hundreds of claims brought by farmers who had sustained property damage resulting from the distribution of livestock feed contaminated with polybrominated biphenyl (PBB). Damage from the exposure occurred during a two-year period. The cause of the damage was a single shipment of PBB by Michigan Chemical. The Sixth Circuit reversed the trial court's decision that the number of occurrences equaled the number of claims and held that the shipment was the sole occurrence. See also Bartholomew v. Insurance Co. of N. Am., 502 F. Supp. 246, 251 (D. R.I. 1980), *aff'd,* 655 F.2d 27 (1st Cir. 1981).

[26] See, e.g., Honeycomb Sys., Inc. v. Admiral Ins. Co., 567 F. Supp. 1400 (D. Me. 1983) (breakdown in weld and crack were completely separate causes; held two occurrences); Voigt

rule, found mostly in older cases, follows "effect analysis": the situation is viewed from the perspective of the injured party, so that multiple results constitute multiple occurrences.[27]

The arguments of the parties in *Home Indemnity Co. v. City of Mobile,*[28] a 1984 Eleventh Circuit case, illustrate the two theories. Major rains on April 13, 1980, May 16–17, 1980, and May 5–6, 1981, caused overflows at various points in the surface water drainage system maintained by the City of Mobile. Over two hundred lawsuits were filed against the city alleging flood damage due to the City's negligence in the planning, construction, operation, and maintenance of the system. The City's liability insurance policy indemnified the City against property damage liability up to $100,000 for each occurrence. The insurer argued in favor of the cause theory: there were three separate rainfalls and therefore only three occurrences. The City and numerous flood victims argued in favor of the effect theory: the coverage should be defined in terms of the resulting damage, meaning that each incident of flooding to the property of an individual property owner was an occurrence. The court noted that Alabama law adheres to cause theory,[29] but the court said that the insurer's view of the cause was too narrow. The insurance policy covered the City's liability, and this was the key to the decision:

> The rainfall and flooding itself were not the "occurrences," since those were Acts of God for which the City is not liable; it is the intervening negligence of the City in maintaining its water drainage system which creates the City's liability. . . . We hold that each discrete act or omission, or series or acts or omissions, on the part of the City of Mobile which caused water to flood and damage properties instead of draining properly is a single "occurrence" within the terms of the insurance policy.[30]

Under this reasoning, each drain blocked due to the City's negligence, or each storm sewer broken due to the City's negligence constituted a separate occurrence.

This problem of determining what constitutes the "occurrence" is particularly acute in the products liability setting where the insured might send a product onto the market that causes many different injuries. For example, in one case, the insured sold contaminated bird seed to eight dealers who in turn sold the feed to one hundred

---

v. Riesterer, 523 N.W.2d 133 (Wis. Ct. App. 1994) (first impact and second impact of automobiles were separate occurrences where 3-5 minutes separated the two impacts); American Indem. Co. v. McQuaig, 435 So. 2d 414 (Fla. Dist. Ct. App. 1983) (insured fired shotgun twice with two-minute interval between shots; cause theory applied; held two occurrences).

[27] E.g., Liberty Mut. Ins. Co. v. Rawls, 404 F.2d 880 (5th Cir. 1968) (where insured auto hit two autos and insured never lost control after first impact, held two occurrences; but note that same result might have been reached under cause analysis); Anchor Cas. Co. v. McCaleb, 178 F.2d 322 (5th Cir. 1949) (oil well explosion caused eruptions intermittently over two days, each of which deposited oil, mud, etc. on property of surrounding land owners; each claim was a separate occurrence); Elston- Richards Storage Co. v. Indemnity Ins. Co. of N. Am., 194 F. Supp. 673 (W.D. Mich. 1960), *aff'd*, 291 F.2d 627 (6th Cir. 1961).

[28] 749 F.2d 659 (11th Cir. 1984).

[29] See United States Fire Ins. Co. v. Safeco Ins. Co., 444 So. 2d 844 (Ala. 1983).

[30] 749 F.2d at 663.

bird owners, each of whom filed a claim for damages. The court concluded that on these facts there had been eight occurrences.[31] In another case, a court ruled that 1,400 individual, defective installations of vinyl-covered panels by the insured constituted one occurrence.[32] One court held that twenty-eight separate property damage claims were subject to a single "per occurrence" policy limit where the cause of the claims was the insured's failure to warn users of its product about how to use the product properly.[33] Another court held that when a blood bank allegedly distributed HIV-contaminated blood, each act of distribution constituted an occurrence for purposes of the policy's per occurrence limit.[34]

The problem is also difficult where a pattern of conduct results in injury to one or more persons. Consider, for example, the situation where a pattern of company decision-making results in injury to multiple parties. In one case, one insurer (the plaintiff) sought indemnity from another for sums that it paid to settle a case arising out of alleged sex discrimination in employment practices. The court denied the indemnity claim on the ground that all of the injuries resulted from one common occurrence — the plaintiff-insurer's decision to adopt discriminatory employment practices — that predated the defendant-insurer's coverage.[35] In a similar case, a court found that a company-wide policy of racial discrimination constituted a single occurrence.[36] Other cases have considered whether a pattern of sexual misconduct causing injury to another person over a period of time constitutes one occurrence or multiple occurrences, and courts have divided on this issue. It has been held that multiple acts of sexual abuse or harassment constitute one occurrence,[37] but recent decisions in the Fifth and Ninth Circuits held that a victim's exposure to, and sexual molestation by, negligently supervised priests in different policy periods constituted a separate occurrence in each of the policy periods.[38]

When the dispute between insurer and insured concerns the limits of the coverage, the insurer benefits from a finding that the facts involved only one occurrence.

---

[31] Maurice Pincoffs Co. v. St. Paul Fire & Marine Ins. Co., 447 F.2d 204 (5th Cir. 1971).

[32] Champion Int'l Corp. v. Continental Cas. Co., 546 F.2d 502 (2d Cir. 1976). The panels were the kind used by manufacturers of houseboats, campers, motor homes, etc. The panels "delaminated" — meaning, split apart — after installation. See also Industrial Steel Container Co. v. Fireman's Fund Ins. Co., 399 N.W.2d 156 (Minn. Ct. App. 1987) (pollution by toxic substances at landfill involved more than one occurrence).

[33] See Chemstar, Inc. v. Liberty Mut. Ins. Co., 797 F. Supp. 1541 (C.D.Cal. 1992), aff'd, 41 F.3d 429 (9th Cir. 1994).

[34] See American Red Cross v. Travelers Indem. Co. of R.I., 816 F. Supp. 755 (D.C.D.C. 1993).

[35] Appalachian Ins. Co. v. Liberty Mut. Ins. Co., 676 F.2d 56 (3d Cir. 1982).

[36] Transport Ins. Co. v. Lee Way Motor Freight, 487 F. Supp. 1325 (N.D. Tex. 1980).

[37] See, e.g., Lee v. Interstate Fire & Cas. Co., 826 F. Supp. 1156 (N.D. Ill. 1993) (applying Rhode Island law, court holds that continuous acts of priest in sexually abusing child and negligent supervision of priest by diocese officials constituted one occurrence within meaning of liabilty policies, even though abuse spanned two policy periods and priest abused child in two different locations).

[38] See Interstate Fire & Cas. Co. v. Archdiocese of Portland, 35 F.3d 1325 (9th Cir. 1994) (rev'g 747 F. Supp. 618 (D.Or. 1990)); Society of the Roman Catholic Church of the Diocese of Lafayette and Lake Charles, Inc. v. Interstate Fire & Cas. Co., 26 F.3d 1359 (5th Cir. 1994).

Insurance policies limit an insurer's liability to a certain sum per "occurrence"; if more than one occurrence exists in the facts, the insurer's potential liability (assuming there is no aggregate limit) is multiplied.[39] However, sometimes the question of number of occurrences is important not for determining policy limits but for determining the effect of the deductible. The deductible typically applies per occurrence. If the insured has suffered a series of small losses each below the deductible, the insured benefits if the multiple losses are treated as one occurrence.[40] All of this becomes more complicated, however, if an aggregate limit is also involved. If the liability for each loss equals or exceeds the aggregate limit, it does not matter how many occurrences are involved. Moreover, there may come a point where an insured confronting a series of large losses with small deductibles may urge whichever approach reduced the number of occurrences. For example, if an insured has a policy with limits of $1 million per occurrence (with a deductible of $50,000 per occurrence) and there is no aggregate limit, the insured gains $950,000 in coverage for each additional occurrence. If, however, the insured's policy has an aggregate limit of $20 million, the insured will benefit from each additional occurrence up to and including 20 occurrences; every additional occurrence beyond 20 will reduce the insured's coverage by $50,000, the amount of the per-occurrence deductible. In short, the insured's (or the insurer's) preference for cause analysis or effect analysis in any particular case will depend on the per-occurrence limit of liability, the aggregate limit of liability, the amount of the deductible, and the amount of potential total liability.

To what extent can an insurer draft the policy to deal with the multiple-cause issue more precisely? The CGLs of 1966, 1973, and 1986 all contain some kind of language that purports to make, to quote the 1973 CGL, "repeated exposure to substantially the same general conditions" to be "considered as arising out of one occurrence." This language, which has come to be known as the "unifying directive," is incorporated directly into the definition of occurrence in the 1986 CGL form; an "occurrence" is defined as "an accident, including continuous or repeated exposure to substantially the same harmful conditions." Exactly what constitutes "the same general conditions" is not explained in any of the policies, but this directive at least suggests the possibility that some multiple-cause or multiple-effect cases should be viewed as one-occurrence cases. The unifying directive is unlikely to be dispositive in most cases, and it is questionable whether the directive should operate to define the coverage provided by other policies that were in force during different years for the same continuous occurrence.[41] It does provide, however, a basis for arguing in some situations that the number of occurrences is fewer rather than more.

---

[39] See Michigan Chem. Corp. v. American Home Assur. Co., 728 F.2d 374 (6th Cir. 1984) (contaminated feed shipped by manufacturer to distributor, who sold to various dairy farmers; cattle were contaminated and destroyed; a finding of one occurrence would limit the insurers' maximum liability).

[40] See Champion Int'l Corp. v. Continental Cas. Co., 546 F.2d 502 (2d Cir. 1976) (a series of small claims, each below the deductible, cause insured to argue that there was one occurrence; held one occurrence).

[41] See Lori J. Khan, Comment, *Untangling the Insurance Fibers in Asbestos Litigation: Toward a National Solution to the Asbestos Injury Crisis*, 68 Tul. L. Rev. 195, 218 (1993).

[e]　Problems of What Triggers Coverage

Under the 1986 CGL policy, the insurer is obligated to pay on behalf of the insured sums which the insured "shall become legally obligated to pay as damages *because of A. bodily injury, or B. property damage* to which this insurance applies caused by an occurrence during the policy period." As discussed in an earlier section,[42] the meaning of "occurrence" is crucial. It includes accidents in the normal sense — an unforeseen, sudden event, usually involving some kind of force or violence, that causes an unanticipated loss. "Occurrence" also includes events that last over a longer period of time. For example, if a company repeatedly but unintentionally discharges small portions of a toxic substance into a community's water supply, and if the cumulative effect of many months of discharges renders the water unsafe, the pattern of discharges, although not sudden in the usual sense of an accident, is an "occurrence" under the CGL policy.

Under the plain language of the CGL policy, the "occurrence" must result during the policy period in "bodily injury or property damage." Thus, the date of the occurrence is very important. The event need not happen during the policy period, but the *result* of the event must happen during the policy period.[43] Thus, long-term exposures to a toxic substance need not happen during the policy's term, but the drafters of the CGL made clear that the result of the exposures — the bodily injury or property damage — must occur during the policy's term. The drafters, however, did not define how one determines when the injury or damage occurs in circumstances where the injury or damage involves long exposures.[44] They provided no guidance on when bodily injury is deemed to occur, and the 1986 revision falls short of defining that time when property damage is involved.[45]

---

[42] See § 65[g], *supra.*

[43] See, e.g., Smith v. Hughes Aircraft Co., 22 F.3d 1432 (9th Cir. 1993); Montrose Chem. Corp. of Cal. v. Admiral Ins. Co., 42 Cal. Rptr.2d 324 (Cal. 1995); Sting Sec., Inc. v. First Mercury Syndicate, Inc., 791 F. Supp. 555 (D.Md. 1992). See generally Annot., *Event Triggering Liability Insurance Coverage as Occurring Within Period of Time Covered by Liability Insurance Policy Where Injury or Damage is Delayed—Modern Cases,* 14 A.L.R.5th 695 (1993); Julian J. Hubbard, *The Occurrence Controversies Revisited: Further Updates on Property Damage Claims and Coverage Triggers with Analytical Models,* 14 Ins. Litig. Rptr. 100 (1992).

[44] The drafting history on this issue has received much attention, and it appears that the drafters addressed the issue and explicitly declined to adopt a restrictive or limited trigger. That is, the drafters apparently contemplated that more than one policy might provide coverage in cases involving progressive diseases. See John G. Buchanan et al., *The Trigger of Coverage Under CGL Policies,* 477 PLI/Lit 145 (Sept. 1993).

[45] As quoted above, see § 65[a], *supra,* the definition of property damage indicates that damage to tangible property occurs at the time of the "physical injury," but this time is left undefined, and loss of use damage is deemed to occur at the time of the "occurrence." Three different times could be used to determine when the injury or damage occurs: the date of the injurious contact (the exposure trigger), the date of manifestation of symptoms (the manifestation trigger), and the date of measurable injury (the diagnosis trigger). A fourth approach would combine the coverage of the other three triggers (triple- or continuous-trigger).

At the outset, it should be noted that a progressive disease — such as asbestosis or silicosis — plainly constitutes a bodily injury and is therefore covered under the CGL policy. However, that is where the clarity ends. The CGL's definition of "bodily injury" refers to both "bodily injury" and "disease" and casts them in the alternative, indicating that a bodily injury can be something distinct from a disease. At one level, this seems obvious: a bodily injury occurs when some force or violence strikes a person, whereas a disease occurs when someone becomes ill. Yet diseases are often preceded by bodily injuries, and in one sense all diseases are preceded by bodily injuries, that is, a "localized abnormal condition of the living body."[46] Under this definition, a bodily injury might exist before a disease exists, because the effect of the occurrence might exist in the body — an abnormal condition might have been created — before anyone is aware of it. For example, a virus invades the body and attacks an organ or body system, resulting in a "bodily injury," and only some time after the injury occurs will the abnormality be noticed by the individual and understood as a disease. Similarly difficult questions can be asked of property damage, because a long period of time can pass from the time a damage-causing event occurs (e.g., the installation of asbestos insulation), its breakdown and/or contamination of surrounding areas, the time at which the contamination and/or damage to surrounding areas is noticed, and the time at which expenses are incurred in removing or treating the damage-causing product.

Since a bodily injury is not necessarily simultaneous with a disease, and since property damage can be said to result at any number of times, this raises a more difficult question: when does bodily injury or property damage occur? In other words, what triggers coverage? Thus far, courts have provided four different answers to it: the manifestation rule; the exposure rule; the actual injury rule; and the multiple- or continuous-trigger rule.

The "manifestation trigger" limits coverage solely to liability for injuries that manifest themselves during the policy period. This approach was adopted by the First Circuit in *Eagle-Picher Industries, Inc. v. Liberty Mut. Ins. Co.*[47] The insured manufactured and sold asbestos products until 1971 or 1972 but had no insurance until 1968 and no excess coverage until 1973. Numerous plaintiffs alleged personal injury or wrongful death resulting from the inhalation of asbestos from Eagle-Picher's products. The court reasoned that asbestosis, which is commonly understood as a disease, consists of two things: an accident, which includes exposure to conditions, and a bodily injury resulting from the accident. The medical evidence before the district court was that "insults" to the lung tissue do not occur simultaneously with exposure to asbestos, and that not all exposures lead to the disease. Thus, the evidence showed that exposure is logically distinct from the resulting injury or disease. The policy required that the resulting injury, not the exposure, occur during the policy period. Since the inception of asbestosis, the inhalation of the fibers, is not an injury discernible by the claimant, the court decided that the

---

[46] Ins. Co. of N. Am. v. Forty-Eight Insulations, Inc., 633 F.2d 1212, 1222 (6th Cir. 1980) (quoting 1A APPLEMAN § 355 (1965)), *aff'd on reh'g,* 657 F.2d 814 (6th Cir.), *cert. denied,* 454 U.S. 1109 (1981).

[47] 682 F.2d 12 (1st Cir. 1982), *cert. denied,* 460 U.S. 1028 (1983).

appropriate time for concluding that the injury occurred is when the claimant first experienced symptoms of the disease that impaired the claimant's "sense of well-being," or the time when a doctor could detect sufficient scarring of lung tissue "to make a prognosis that the onset of manifested disease was inevitable."[48] The Fourth Circuit adopted the manifestation rule in an environmental property damage case,[49] but that court's prediction of Maryland law was later rejected by the Maryland Court of Appeals.[50] Although fewer courts have applied the manifestation trigger alone, it does have some support in the cases.[51]

The manifestation trigger provides narrow coverage, particularly compared to the other triggers. Liability tends to fall on the small group of insurers that provided coverage when the existence of a disease becomes obvious, which is likely to be the same time the disease is diagnosed on a widespread basis. This tends to allocate losses to the more recent policy years. Furthermore, once diagnosis of a disease becomes widespread, policy cancellations are likely. This leaves policyholders unprotected against future claims for injury, which often means that the liability falls upon the insured. If this scenario develops, insureds' reasonable expectations of coverage are likely to be completely destroyed.[52]

Under the "exposure rule," exposure to the injury- or damage-causing substance triggers coverage. All insurers who provided coverage while exposure occurred, whether it be the first exposure or a continuing exposure, must contribute to reimbursing the insured's tort liability. With environmental property damage, the period of exposure is either the period of waste disposal or the period of release of pollutants from a site, up to and until the date of discovery. In the bodily injury context, the period is the time during which the victim is exposed to the injurious substances. This approach was adopted by the Sixth Circuit in *Insurance Co. of North America v. Forty-Eight Insulations, Inc.*,[53] the first federal appellate court decision to address insurance coverage issues in the asbestos context. INA sought a declaratory judgment that coverage for injury under its CGL policies should be

---

[48] 682 F.2d at 17, 19, 24.

[49] See Mraz v. Canadian Universal Ins. Co., 804 F.2d 1325 (4th Cir. 1986).

[50] See Harford Cty. v. Harford Mut. Ins. Co., 610 A.2d 286 (Md. 1992).

[51] E.g., General Dynamics Corp. v. Benefits Review Bd., 565 F.2d 208 (2d Cir. 1977) (workers' compensation asbestos claim); Hartford Acc. & Indem. Co., 483 A.2d 402 (N.J. 1984); Cohen v. North Am. Life & Cas. Co., 185 N.W. 939 (Minn. 1921) (coverage under health insurance policy under manifestation rule even though claimant's medical disability was partially attributable to disease already present but unmanifested when policy was purchased); American Motorists Ins. Co. v. E.R. Squibb & Sons, Inc., 406 N.Y.S.2d 658 (N.Y. Sup. Ct. 1978) (effective date of coverage for DES-related injuries is the date of discovery). See also Jackson v. State Farm Fire & Cas. Co., 835 P.2d 786 (Nev. 1992) (approving manifestation trigger in first-party context).

[52] This was noted by the court in *Keene*. See 667 F.2d at 1044. See generally Pamela J. Layton, Comment, *Manifestation: The Least Defensible Insurance Coverage Theory for Asbestos-Related Disease Suits,* 7 U. Puget Sound L. Rev. 167 (1983); Kevin C. Logue, Note, *The Insurance Problem in Asbestosis Litigation: A Case for the Manifestation Theory,* 57 St. John's L. Rev. 485 (1983).

[53] 633 F.2d 1212 (6th Cir. 1980), *aff'd on reh'g,* 657 F.2d 814 (6th Cir. 1981), *cert. denied,* 454 U.S. 1109 (1981).

determined according to the manifestation rule. The policyholders urged the exposure rule instead, and the court approved this test. At one point, the court seemed to understand the time of inhalation as the time of exposure, but at a later point in the opinion the court referred to the period of inhalation combining with continuing injury thereafter.[54] Despite this ambiguity in *Forty-Eight Insulations,* the exposure rule has been approved by other courts,[55] most notably by the Fifth Circuit in *Porter v. American Optical Corp.*[56]

The differences between the manifestation rule and the exposure rule are apparent. Unlike the manifestation rule, the exposure rule does not enable insurers to escape their obligations once a disease is diagnosed on a widespread basis. If the claimant was exposed to the injury-producing substance while the policy was in force, the claimant is entitled to coverage. Moreover, if exposure continued over a long period of time while several different policies were in effect, each policy provides coverage.

The exposure rule takes a broader approach to coverage, but it does not necessarily follow that the rule coincides with the reasonable expectations of insureds. Many insureds no doubt believe that when they purchase coverage, protection has been secured from all liability for damage occurring during the policy period, including not-yet-known injuries resulting from exposure to products during the period prior to coverage. Until the statute of limitations runs, insureds are potentially liable in tort for injuries resulting from pre-coverage exposures. Insureds who desire and expect their liability coverage to be coextensive with the entirety of their liability for unintentional torts are not covered if the damage results from exposures that occurred before the effective date of the coverage.

The "injury-in-fact" approach is not a simple one to understand. Under one formulation in the bodily injury context, an injury-in-fact occurs and coverage is triggered when the body's defenses are "overwhelmed" and disability or premature death becomes inevitable.[57] Under this formulation, the injury-in-fact definitely comes later than the exposure, and often comes later than the manifestation. Yet if the injury-in-fact is treated as an abnormality which need not be understood by the claimant or diagnosed, the injury-in-fact may even precede the manifestation. Whenever the injury-in-fact occurs, insurers on the risk after the date of actual injury are bound to provide coverage. Thus, if the insured has switched insurers from time to time, this approach tends to diffuse the coverage among various insurers, functioning more like a continuous trigger. The Second Circuit, according to its decision

---

[54] See 633 F.2d at 1217–18, 1233, 1238, 1240.

[55] E.g., Hancock Laboratories, Inc. v. Admiral Ins. Co., 777 F.2d 520 (9th Cir. 1985); Commercial Union Ins. Co. v. Sepco Corp., 765 F.2d 1543 (11th Cir. 1990); Commercial Union Ins. Co. v. Pittsburgh Corning Corp., 553 F. Supp. 425 (E.D. Pa. 1981); Allstate Ins. Co. v. Colonial Realty Co., 468 N.Y.S.2d 800 (N.Y. Sup. Ct. 1983).

[56] 641 F.2d 1128 (5th Cir.), *cert. denied,* 454 U.S. 1109 (1981). *Porter* was deemed controlling in Commercial Union Ins. Co. v. Sepco Corp., 765 F.2d 1543 (11th Cir. 1985). In addition to the asbestos situation, the Fifth Circuit has applied this approach in a silica dust/sandblasting case. See Ducre v. The Executive Officers of Halter Marine, Inc., 752 F.2d 976 (5th Cir. 1985).

[57] See Insurance Co. of N. Am. v. Forty-Eight Insulations, 633 F.2d 1212 (6th Cir. 1980), *clarified,* 657 F.2d 814 (6th Cir.), *cert. denied,* 454 U.S. 1109 (1981).

in *American Home Products Corp. v. Liberty Mut. Ins. Co.,*[58] purports to adhere to the injury-in-fact rule. *American Home* arose out of claims based on the use of six different pharmaceutical products, including DES, oral contraceptives, and Anacin. The district court rejected both the exposure and manifestation theories of coverage and ruled that

> an occurrence of "personal injury, sickness or disease" is read to mean any point in time at which a finder of fact determines that the effects of exposure to a drug actually resulted in a diagnosable and compensable injury. Depending upon the facts of each case, the drug involved, the period and intensity of exposure, and the person affected, an injury may occur in this sense upon exposure, at some point in time after exposure but before manifestation of the injury, and at manifestation.[59]

On appeal, the Second Circuit disapproved of the district court's use of the terms "diagnosable" and "compensable," and deleted those terms from the judgment,[60] but it otherwise affirmed the district court's decision:

> First, no clause in the policy uses either of those terms or any equivalents. Second, compensability is a legal concept that is not material to the determination of whether an injury has in fact occurred. . . . [D]iagnosability need not coincide with the actual occurrence of injury; to add the requirement that an injury be diagnosable limits the scope of the "injury-in-fact" trigger-of-coverage clause in a way that is not justified by the policies' language. . . . To paraphrase the district court's analysis rejecting the manifestation theory, "a real but undiscovered injury, proved in retrospect to have existed at the relevant time, would establish coverage, irrespective of the time the injury became [diagnosable]."[61]

The injury-in-fact approach has been approved by other courts as well,[62] and has also been followed in the property damage context.[63]

---

[58] 565 F. Supp. 1485 (S.D.N.Y. 1983), *aff'd with modifications,* 748 F.2d 760 (2d Cir. 1984). See generally David J. Dykhouse & Joseph L. Falik, *Trigger of Coverage: The Business Context, the Plain Language, and American Home Products,* 16 Conn. L. Rev. 497 (1984).

[59] 565 F. Supp. at 1489.

[60] 748 F.2d at 766.

[61] 748 F.2d at 765–66.

[62] E.g., Sandoz, Inc. v. Employer's Liab. Assur. Corp., 554 F. Supp. 257, 265 (D.N.J. 1983) ("liability is triggered when bodily injury, in the form of tissue damage, results during the policy period.")

[63] See, e.g., Detrex Chem. Indus. Inc. v. Employers Ins. of Wausau, 746 F. Supp. 1310 (N.D. Ohio 1990); Dow Chem. Co. v. Associated Indem. Corp., 724 F. Supp. 474 (E.D. Mich. 1989); Kief Farmers Co-op. Elevator Co. v. Farmland Mut. Ins. Co., 543 N.W.2d 28 (N.D. 1995) ("real but undiscovered loss" triggers coverage, and manifestation theory is rejected); Sentinel Ins. Co. v. First Ins. Co. of Hawaii, Ltd., 875 P.2d 894 (Haw. 1994) (event that triggers coverage under occurrence policy is sustaining of actual damage by complaining party); Northern States Power Co. v. Fidelity & Cas. Co. of N.Y., 523 N.W.2d 657 (Minn. 1994).

The disadvantage of the injury-in-fact approach in the bodily injury context is that determining when the body's defenses were overwhelmed or when a "real injury" first arose requires expert testimony. With respect to many diseases, including asbestosis, it is difficult for a doctor to state accurately when the disease developed to a point that it became an "injury-in-fact." In practice, however, the rule probably serves merely to provide the opportunity to the insured (or claimant) to establish that the bodily injury occurred prior to the manifestation. When a disease is diagnosed or becomes manifest, it may be possible to infer that the harm must have begun sometime before. If the insured can show that the prior exposure caused a medical injury (not necessarily a diagnosable injury), the insured would be entitled to coverage under policies in force before the date of manifestation.

The fourth approach is the "multiple-trigger approach," which combines the coverage of the various individual approaches.[64] This approach views progressive diseases as cases of continuous injury; any insurer that was on the risk during the progression is liable. This is the broadest of the various approaches; it makes virtually all insurers that ever provided coverage potentially liable for indemnification.

The leading case espousing this approach is *Keene Corporation v. Insurance Co. of North America,*[65] in which the United States Court of Appeals for the District of Columbia Circuit considered when an injury due to asbestos exposure and inhalation occurred. The court said the policy did not clearly point to either manifestation or exposure as the triggers of coverage. Therefore, the court interpreted bodily injury to mean "any part of the single injurious process that asbestos-related diseases entail," including inhalation, development of the disease after inhalation, and manifestation of the disease.[66] This analysis made all policies covering periods from first exposure through manifestation jointly and severally liable for the claim. A number of courts have followed the *Keene* approach,[67] including the Third Circuit.[68]

Cases such as *Keene* reveal that the relief-granting powers of the courts are limited. The question actually confronted in *Keene* was a basic one: in circumstances

---

[64] One court approved both the exposure and manifestation triggers in the same case, thus giving rise to what has been labeled the "double-trigger" approach. See Zurich Ins. Co. v. Raymark Industries, 514 N.E.2d 150 (Ill. 1987).

[65] 667 F.2d 1034 (D.C.Cir. 1981), *cert. denied,* 455 U.S. 1007 (1982).

[66] 667 F.2d at 1041, 1043, 1047.

[67] E.g., Lac D'Amiante Du Quebec v. American Home Assurance Co., 613 F. Supp. 1549 (D.N.J. 1985); Montrose Chemical Corp. v. Admiral Ins. Co., 42 Cal. Rptr.2d 324 (Cal. 1995) (also discussing past case law on this issue in detail); Owens-Illinois, Inc. v. United Ins. Co., 650 A.2d 974 (N.J. 1994); J.H.France Refractories Co. v. Allstate Ins. Co., 626 A.2d 502 (Pa. 1993); Eli Lilly & Co. v. Home Ins. Co., 482 N.E.2d 467 (Ind. 1985); California Union Ins. Co. v. Landmark Ins. Co., 193 Cal. Rptr. 461 (Cal. Ct. App. 1983). In two cases, the District of Columbia Circuit declined to apply *Keene* in situations where the law of other jurisdictions controlled. See Abex Corp. v. Maryland Cas. Co., 790 F.2d 119 (D.C. Cir. 1986) (applying injury-in-fact approach in case where New York law controlled); Eli Lilly and Co. v. Home Ins. Co., 764 F.2d 876 (D.C. Cir. 1985) (where Indiana law controls and is unclear, court certifies question of appropriate trigger to Indiana Supreme Court).

[68] See ACS, Inc. v. Aetna Cas. and Sur. Co., 764 F.2d 968 (3d Cir. 1985).

where the assets of an industry are inadequate to remedy all of the injuries it has caused, to what extent should the risk be transferred to insurers? The court decided to transfer the maximum amount of risk to insurers by applying a multiple-trigger approach, thus making available to victims the deepest-possible pocket of financial relief, subject only to the limitation that one policy's limits apply to each injury, which prevents the insured from obtaining more coverage than that purchased. Despite the far-reaching potential of such a remedy, the available funds, consisting of both manufacturer and insurer assets, are, according to some analysts, insufficient to provide compensation for all present and future asbestosis claims.[69]

Unfortunately, once one wades through the morass of the conflicting trigger of coverage issue, another significant problem must be confronted: how to allocate the defense and indemnity obligations of the various insurers that have coverage obligations under whatever trigger theory was used. In *Keene,* where a continuous trigger approach was followed, the court held that once an insurer's policy is triggered, the insurer is required to defend and indemnify a policyholder to the extent of the entire policy limits, without proration, even though part of the injury occurred when the policyholder was self-insured.[70] However, only one policy's limits apply to each injury, and the policyholder may select the policy under which it desires to be indemnified. If more than one policy applies to the loss, the "other insurance" clauses of the policies provide the method for apportioning the insurers' liability among the various insurers.[71]

The joint-and-several liability approach of *Keene* was explicitly rejected in *Forty-Eight Insulations.*[72] The court reasoned that the basis for the liability of the insurers is contractual, not tort, and that joint-and-several concepts should not be used. Instead, each insurer's liability should be "individual and proportionate."[73] The court held that the indemnity and defense costs should be allocated among the policies according to the years in which workers were exposed to asbestos, and the court followed Judge Wald's suggestion that the manufacturer should be treated as self-insured for those years of exposure in which it did not have insurance.[74]

---

[69] See Rebecca C. Earnest, Note, *Insurance Law and Asbestosis—When Is Coverage of a Progressive Disease Triggered?* 58 Wash. L. Rev. 63 (1982); see also John P. Arness & Randall D. Eliason, *Insurance Coverage for "Property Damage" in Asbestos and Other Toxic Tort Cases,* 72 Va. L. Rev. 943 (1986).

[70] 667 F.2d at 1047. In a concurring opinion, Judge Wald indicated that she favored requiring the manufacturer to share in the liability for those periods when it had no insurance. Unless the manufacturer shares pro rata for periods when it was uninsured, it acquires certainty of coverage without paying for the coverage, or at least part of it. See 667 F.2d at 1058.

[71] 667 F.2d at 1049–50. Almost all courts agree with the "anti-stacking" holding of *Keene.* See Ostrager and Newman, *supra* note 2, at 375-78. Compare Northern States Power Co. v. Fidelity & Cas. Co. of N.Y., 523 N.W.2d 657 (Minn. 1994) (favoring allocation to several sequential liability policies under injury-in-fact trigger theory in proportion to period of time each was on risk).

[72] See 633 F.2d at 1225.

[73] 633 F.2d at 1225.

[74] 633 F.2d at 1224-25.

To what extent can an insurer resolve the trigger of coverage issue through more precise drafting? Under a so-called "deemer clause," in circumstances where an occurrence spans multiple years, the occurrence is "deemed" to occur during the policy term that is the latest of all of the potentially applicable coverages. Inserting such a clause into the CGL was considered but rejected in the 1960s.[75] Such a clause has been inserted in some non-standard forms, but it has not been widely used, perhaps because insurers have felt comfortable using "other insurance" clauses to apportion coverage when more than one policy provides coverage. Also, the clause has received very little judicial attention.[76] Whether courts would allow the definition of "occurrence" in one policy to influence the coverage provided by *other* policies is questionable, particularly if insureds were not fully informed about the presence and effect of the deemer clause.

In short, the trigger issue as well as the allocation and proration issues are complex. Beyond these complexities lurk broader questions of public policy. The American legal system presumes that persons injured by defective products should be compensated for their injury, and that the producers of such products should provide the compensation. The assumption is that liability will deter manufacturers from producing harmful products and distributing them in the marketplace. The American system also contemplates that manufacturers can transfer their liability for damages, whether based on a finding of negligence or imposed under a strict liability doctrine, to an insurer. If the insurance is priced according to the underlying risk, manufacturers who tend to send dangerous products into the marketplace end up paying more for insurance. For most kinds of liabilities, this system, although far from ideal, is at least functional; injured parties are compensated for their losses to some extent. However, some kinds of injuries — asbestosis, for example — are so widespread and so expensive that the total potential liability is too great for either the insurers or the industry to manage. If the total cost of asbestosis claims exceeds the combined assets of both the manufacturers and their insurers, it is inevitable that some victims will never be compensated, unless the federal government is prepared to help pay some of the claims by in effect spreading the risk across the entire nation through the taxing power. This bottom line may be a disappointing one, but the problem of how to compensate victims of occupational illnesses, toxic torts, and other similar hazards is a profound one, and workable solutions are elusive.[77]

---

[75] See Ronald R. Robinson, *"Sudden Impact": The History of the Drafting of the 1973 CGL Policy's Pollution Exclusion, in Environmental Insurance Coverage Claims and Litigation* 719 PLI/Comm 403 (April-May 1995).

[76] In Abex Corp. v. Maryland Cas. Co., 790 F.2d 119 (D.C. Cir. 1986), the court noted the presence of a deemer clause in some policies in question, observed that the clauses could limit the insurer's obligations in the circumstances, and asked the trial court to consider the applicability of the clauses on remand. 790 F.2d at 122, 128. Similar language in a policy in another case — "[t]he policy does not apply to such injury, death, or destruction caused by such continuous or repeated exposure any part of which occurs after the termination of the policy" — was not given an expansive reading (which would have constrained coverage) in American Home Products Corp. v. Liberty Mut. Ins. Co., 748 F.2d 760 (2d Cir. 1984).

[77] For more discussion of this issue in the environmental damage context, see Frona M. Powell, *Insuring Environmental Cleanup: Triggering Coverage for Environmental Property Damage Under the Terms of a Comprehensive General Liability Insurance Policy,* 71 Neb. L. Rev. 1194 (1992).

[f]   Problems of Environmental Liability

In recent years, claims for property damage, personal injury, and cleanup expenses arising out of hazardous waste disposal have multiplied. These environmental liability claims involve a recurring fact pattern: the insured intentionally stored or handled the waste, but the insured did not intend the resulting harm. Sometimes, the harm itself is not discovered until much later. The coverage issues presented by such claims are extraordinarily difficult; moreover, it is possible that there is no issue in all of business law more vigorously contested today.[78]

[1]   The Regulatory Context

The insurance coverage issues in environmental liability situations cannot be understood without a basic grasp of the regulatory environment for hazardous wastes. Two federal statutes constitute the bulk of governmental regulation of hazardous wastes. The Resource Conservation and Recovery Act of 1976 ("RCRA")[79] regulates the handling, treatment, storage, and disposal of hazardous waste currently being generated. The Comprehensive Environmental Response, Compensation, and Liability Act of 1980 ("CERCLA," but commonly known as the "Superfund Act")[80] has as its purpose the removal and cleanup of hazardous waste sites created in the past. CERCLA creates a fund to assist in the cleanup of these sites, but more importantly, CERCLA creates some novel (indeed, unprecedented) forms of liability that have great significance for liability insurers and their insureds.

First, section 107 of CERCLA imposes strict liability for the costs of cleaning up hazardous waste sites (called "response costs" in the Act) on three kinds of parties: the past and present owners and operators of hazardous waste sites; some parties that transported wastes to these sites; and any party that generated material for disposal of the sites. Any of these parties — owners and operators; transporters; generators — may be a "potentially responsible party," or "PRP." Actions seeking to impose section 107 liability on any PRP may be brought by the United States, by a state, or by a private party that has incurred the cost of cleanup. In addition to being strict, the liability that section 107 can impose is also retroactive; in other

---

[78] This section, by necessity, can only briefly sketch the issues raised by environmental liability claims. Writing on the subject is voluminous. For thorough discussions of these issues, see Kenneth S. Abraham, *Environmental Liability Insurance Law* (1991); Tod I. Zuckerman & Mark C. Raskoff, *Environmental Insurance Litigation: Law and Practice* (1992). For briefer presentations, see Craig R. Brown & Julie B. Pollack, *Overview of Environmental Coverage Litigation for Comprehensive General Liability Policies, in Environmental Insurance Coverage Claims and Litigation,* 718 PLI/Comm 7 (1995); Kenneth S. Abraham, Monsanto Lecture: *Cleaning Up the Environmental Liability Insurance Mess,* 27 Val. U. L. Rev. 601 (1993); Kirk A. Pasich, *The Breadth of Insurance Coverage for Environmental Claims,* 52 Ohio St. L. J. 1131 (1991). Although the issue has received less attention in recent years, similar coverage issues can arise under first-party property coverages. For more discussion, see Dale L. Kingman, *First Party Property Policies and Pollution Coverage,* 28 Gonz. L. Rev. 449 (1992/93).

[79] 42 U.S.C. §§ 6901-6992k.

[80] 42 U.S.C. §§ 9601-9674. This Act was amended by the Superfund Amendments and Reauthorization Act of 1986 ("SARA.")

words, section 107 liability can be imposed on a PRP for actions taken before CERCLA was enacted and before it was possible for a PRP to know that its actions in connection with a hazardous waste site might lead to environmental injury. In addition, section 107's liability is joint and several when it is not possible to determine which PRP was responsible for the particular dangers posed at a site. CERCLA also creates rights of contribution among various PRPs. Thus, if the government cleans up a particular site, it might bring a section 107 action against the PRPs — or only one of the PRPs, since the liability is several. There are some defenses under section 107 available to PRPs, but the defenses are very limited.

Second, section 106 of CERCLA allows the federal government to issue administrative orders or seek injunctions to secure such relief as may be necessary to prevent an actual or threatened release of a hazardous substance that threatens "imminent and substantial" danger. Under the Act, the EPA has considerable authority to induce PRPs to undertake cleanup of hazardous waste sites themselves, and the mere threat that the EPA can make of prospective action often results in "voluntary" cleanup of sites by PRPs, or agreements among PRPs to cleanup sites that are set forth in consent decrees that are filed in court as section 106 orders.

Third, section 107 imposes on PRPs, in addition to the cost of cleanup, liability for damages for the injury, destruction, or loss of natural resources (provided the damage did not result from a release of hazardous substances that occurred entirely before CERCLA was enacted in 1980).

In addition to the foregoing, some states have adopted their own statutory framework, and there is also the prospect of common law liability for pollution damage. When PRPs take action in anticipation or as a result of the various kinds of liabilities that are possible under CERCLA, or if PRPs are otherwise held liability for environmental damage, these parties will turn to their liability insurers for reimbursement of their expenses and for a defense of the existing or prospective EPA action, and this will raise a variety of issues.

[2] The "As Damages" Issue

Under the CGL's insuring agreement, the insurer promises to pay for liability imposed on the insured "as damages." Because most CGL policies do not define "damages," this issue has been litigated in probably all environmental liability insurance coverage cases.[81] At first, the courts confronting this issue sharply divided, but most courts have now concluded that "damages" includes government-mandated response costs under CERCLA.[82] This result has much to commend it,[83]

---

[81] For more detailed discussion, see Kenneth S. Abraham, *Environmental Liability Insurance Law* 50-71 (1991); David W. Miller, *Whether Governmentally Compelled Cleanup Costs Constitute "Damages" Under CGL Policies: The Nationwide Environmental Liability Dilemma and a California Model for its Resolution*, 16 Colum. J. Envtl. L. 73 (1991); Jordan S. Stanzler & Charles A. Yuen, *Coverage for Environmental Cleanup Costs: History of the Word "Damages" in the Standard Form Comprehensive General Liability Policy*, 1990 Colum. Bus. L. Rev. 449; Laurence T. Vetter, Note, *Law, Equity and the Comprehensive General Liability Policy: The Scope of Coverage for CERCLA Cleanup Costs*, 11 Va. Envtl. L.J. 157 (1991).

[82] See, e.g., Avondale Indus. Inc. v. Travelers Indem. Co., 887 F.2d 1200 (2d Cir. 1989), reh'g denied, 894 F.2d 498 (1990), cert. denied, 496 U.S. 906 (1990); Vermont Gas Sys. v.

particularly since it would make little public policy sense to provide coverage for insureds who failed to clean up their sites and were sued for damages by others who did, but deny coverage to insureds who took steps to clean up the sites under government order. But this outcome was hardly inevitable, given the common-sense holdings in other contexts that insurers have no duty to defend suits against insureds seeking injunctive relief when the policy clearly states that it provides coverage for suits seeking damages.[84] The better-reasoned view, however, is that the fact that an insured incurs costs of cleanup pursuant to a government order should be irrelevant to the issue of coverage under the liability policy.

[3]   The Voluntary Cleanup Issue

Related to the "as damage" issue is another question: If the insured in anticipation of governmental or private action against it undertakes to voluntarily cleanup a toxic waste site, is the liability insurer responsible for these cleanup costs? If the insured had not cleaned up the site and someone else did, with that other party then suing the insured for the expenses of the cleanup, the liability insurer would be required to defend and indemnify the insured. Thus, it makes sense that if the insured voluntarily incurs expenses, particularly if the voluntary action mitigates future damage, the liability insurer should provide coverage. Although courts are split on this issue, the weight of authority holds that voluntary cleanup expenses are covered by the CGL policy.[85] Some courts oppose this view, reasoning that the CGL's requirement that the insured be "legally obligated to pay" the sums in question is not met when the insured voluntarily cleans up a site in the absence of any order or requirement that it do so.[86] Clearly, it would make little sense for an insured who voluntarily fixes the brakes on his or her car before they fail and cause an accident to be able to obtain reimbursement from the insurer for the fix-up costs under the reasoning that the repair prevented an accident that would have been covered under the liability policy. That an accident imposing liability on the insured will occur in the future due to brake failure is far from certain. In contrast, Congress has imposed a regime of strict, retroactive liability on PRPs; although there is no certainty that the government or a private party will force a future cleanup, those parties' right to

United States Fid. & Guar. Co., 805 F. Supp. 227 (D.Vt. 1992); Morton Int'l, Inc. v. General Acc. Ins. Co. of Am., 629 A.2d 831 (N.J. 1993), *cert. denied,* 114 S.Ct. 2764 (1994); Bausch & Lomb, Inc. v. Utica Mut. Ins. Co., 625 A.2d 1021 (Md. 1993); A.Y. McDonald Indus., Inc. v. Insurance Co. of N.Am., 475 N.W.2d 607 (Iowa 1991).

[83] See Jordan S. Stanzier & Charles A. Yuen, *Coverage for Environmental Cleanup Costs: History of the Word "Damages" in the Standard Form Comprehensive General Liability Policy,* 1990 Colum. Bus. L. Rev. 449.

[84] See § 65[f][2], *infra.* Probably the leading case adopting the view that government-mandated response costs under CERCLA are not "damages" is Continental Ins. Co. v. Northeastern Pharmaceutical & Chem. Co., 842 F.2d 977 (8th Cir.), cert. denied, 488 U.S. 821 (1988).

[85] See, e.g., Port of Portland v. Water Quality Ins. Syndicate, 549 F. Supp. 233 (D.Or. 1982), *aff'd in part, rev'd in part, and remanded,* 796 F.2d 1188 (9th Cir. 1988); Weyerhauser Co. v. Aetna Cas. & Sur. Co., 874 P.2d 142 (Wash. 1994); Compass Ins. Co. v. Cravens, Daggin & Co., 748 P.2d 724 (Wyo. 1988).

[86] See, e.g., Ohio Cas. Ins. Co. v. Ross, 222 F. Supp. 292 (D.Md. 1963); City of Edgerton v. General Cas. Co. of Wis., 517 N.W.2d 463 (Wis. 1994).

require such a cleanup is a present, existing right, which distinguishes this case from a voluntary brake repair.

[4] PRP Letters and the Duty to Defend

The typical CGL policy states that the insurer shall have the duty to defend "any suit" with the coverage of the policy "seeking damages" against the insured. This raises the damages issue discussed above, but another issue arises of even greater difficulty: If an insured receives a letter from the EPA (the so-called "PRP letter") advising the insured of its potential liability for cleaning up a toxic waste site, does the liability insurer have a duty to defend the insured in the administrative proceedings which follow such a letter? Courts have given different answers to this question. A number of courts have held that the PRP letter is the first step of an adverse administrative process that is functionally equivalent to a lawsuit, and that the threatened use of legal process by the government to coerce payment or conduct by an insured is sufficient to trigger the duty to defend.[87] Some courts have focused on the language of the letter itself, asking whether it is sufficiently coercive to rise to the level of the suit[88] or whether the letter is merely an invitation for voluntary action without a threat of adverse legal consequences.[89] Still other courts have held that a PRP letter is not a "suit" and therefore does not trigger the duty to defend.[90] Given the peculiar regulatory scheme of CERCLA and the new kinds of liabilities created by the statute, those cases which recognize a duty to defend when a PRP letter is sent are on strong ground, but the issue is a close one.

[5] The Existence of an Occurrence

The CGL policy covers "occurrences," and the incident giving rise to the potential liability must be an "occurrence" for coverage to exist at all. As discussed in an earlier section,[91] prior to 1966 liability policies defined coverage in terms of "accidents." In pollution cases, the term "accident" was problematical. Consider the case where a firm intentionally stores hazardous wastes, but the wastes leach out of the storage area and contaminate a nearby drinking water supply. On the one hand, it could be argued that no accident occurred since the storage was part of the firm's regular business and nothing had happened in a "sudden" fashion, which is one of the characteristics of an accident. By the same token, it could be argued in similar cases (such as where a pollutant was dumped in a water supply) that the act was intentional, and therefore the non-accidental character of the incident took the

---

[87] See, e.g, Aetna Cas. & Sur. Co. v. Pintlar Corp., 948 F.2d 1507 (9th Cir. 1991); Fireman's Fund Ins. Cos. v. Ex-Cell-O Corp., 662 F. Supp. 71 (E.D. Mich. 1987); Michigan Millers Mut. Ins. Co. v. Bronson Plating Co., 519 N.W.2d 864 (Mich. 1994); United States Fid. & Guar. Co. v. Specialty Coatings Co., 535 N.E.2d 1071 (Ill. App. Ct.), *app. denied*, 545 N.E.2d 133 (Ill. 1989).

[88] See Hazan Paper v. United States Fid. & Guar. Co., 555 N.E.2d 576 (Mass. 1990).

[89] See Avondale Indus. Inc. v. Travelers Indem. Co., 887 F.2d 1200 (2d Cir. 1989), reh'g denied, 894 F.2d 498 (1990), *cert. denied*, 496 U.S. 906 (1990).

[90] See, e.g., Ray Indus. v. Liberty Mut. Ins. Co., 974 F.2d 754 (6th Cir. 1992); Detrex Chem. Indus. Inc. v. Employers Ins. of Wausau, 681 F. Supp. 438 (N.D. Ohio 1987); City of Edgerton v. General Cas. Co. of Wis., 517 N.W.2d 463 (Wis. 1994).

[91] See § 65[a], *supra*.

insured outside the coverage. On the other hand, neither the leaching of the wastes nor the resulting damage may have been foreseen or expected, and thus it could be argued that an accident occurred. If one focuses upon the moment of invasion of the area of the storage site, one could conclude that the damage occurred "suddenly" and then continued over time. Given the ambiguity, courts tended to construe "accident" broadly; in many cases, claims based on long-term exposures to injurious substances were deemed covered by the liability policy.[92]

In 1966, CGL policies were modified to cover "occurrences," and occurrence was defined as "an accident, including continuous or repeated exposure to conditions." This change made clear that the liability policy was intended to provide coverage not only for sudden, unexpected events but also for long-term exposures to harmful conditions or substances which resulted in damage during the policy period. This language, however, had the effect of broadening coverage for pollution-related loss beyond that which insurers were willing to underwrite. Therefore, a pollution exclusion was inserted in the policies under the 1973 CGL revision, and this exclusion is discussed in a subsequent subsection.[93] The key point, however, is that the CGL will provide no coverage for a pollution-related liability unless there is an "occurrence," and this in many cases is a subject of substantial dispute.

In addition and closely related to the foregoing, the issue of the appropriate trigger of coverage has often been a substantial issue in environmental liability coverage cases. Hazardous wastes are very often involved in progressive-injury situations, and the complex issues discussed in a preceding section[94] are deeply intertwined in the environmental cases.

[6]   The Pollution Exclusions

As noted above, the expansion of the definition of "occurrence" in the 1966 CGL revision led directly to the insertion in the 1973 CGL of a pollution exclusion. The exclusion stated that coverage would not apply to bodily injury or property damage

> (1) arising out of pollution or contamination caused by oil or (2) arising out of the discharge, dispersal, release or escape of smoke, vapors, soot, fumes, acids, alkalis, toxic chemicals, liquids or gases, waste materials or other irritants, contaminants or pollutants into or upon the land, the atmosphere or any water course of body of water; but this exclusion does not apply if such discharge, dispersal, release or escape is sudden and accidental.

When viewed along with the insuring agreement, the CGL, as it existed from 1973 to 1986, had a three-step process for determining whether an environmental liability was covered by the CGL: (1) did an "occurrence" occur? If not, there is no coverage (i.e., there is no covered loss). If so, (2) does the pollution exclusion apply, i.e., was the injury or damage caused by one of the named materials in connection with one of the four events ("discharge," etc.) in the exclusion? If not, there is coverage (i.e., there is a covered, non-excluded loss). If so, (3) does the exception to the exclusion

---

[92] E.g., Beryllium Corp. v. American Mut. Liab. Ins. Co., 223 F.2d 71 (3d Cir. 1955); Canadian Radium & Uranium Corp. v. Indem. Ins. Co. of N. Am., 104 N.E.2d 250 (Ill. 1952).

[93] See § 65[f][6], *infra*.

[94] See § 65[e], *supra*.

apply, i.e., was the event "sudden and accidental?" If so, there is coverage (i.e, there
is a covered loss, and the exclusion does not apply by virtue of the exception to the
exclusion).[95] If not, there is no coverage (i.e., there is a covered loss, but the
exclusion takes away the coverage). This three-step process was complicated, but
by no means beyond comprehension. Unfortunately, the three-step process disguised
some exceedingly difficult questions, and the bottom line is that the pollution
exclusion did little to clarify the coverage of liability insurance for pollution-causing
incidents.[96]

In most cases, the contentious portion of the exclusion was the "sudden and
accidental" phrase. In the context of the clause, the plain language of the provision
suggests that the actual movement of the pollutant (the four events — "discharge,
dispersal, release or escape") must be "sudden and accidental," without regard to
how sudden or accidental the harm or damage actually is. The term "accidental"
is often difficult to apply in particular fact situations, as explained in an earlier
section discussing intentional acts versus accidents, even if the term has a long
history which helps pour meaning into it.[97] The term "sudden" was more problematic. From one point of view, because "accidental" means "unexpected," "sudden"
must mean something different from unexpected. Therefore, "sudden" must have
a temporal meaning in the sense that a sudden event occurs at a point or moment
in time. Thus, a "sudden" event might be viewed as an event short in duration,
although this construction would create an inconsistency with the word "dispersal"
that "sudden and accidental" purports to modify, because a dispersal implies
something that occurs over a long duration. Moreover, this construction may be
entirely wrong because something can be sudden in the sense that it begins abruptly
and then has a longer duration, like a "sudden storm." From another view, however,
the phrase "sudden and accidental" was used for years in boiler and machinery

---

[95] The general rule is that insureds bear the burden of proof on establishing coverage, but
insurers bear the burden of establishing any exclusion to the coverage. See § 60A, *supra*. As
for who should bear the burden of proof on the exception to the exclusion, most courts have
held that the insured has the burden on the exception because the exception creates coverage
that would not otherwise exist because of the exclusion. See, e.g., Aeroquip Corp. v. Aetna
Cas. & Sur. Co., 26 F.3d 893 (9th Cir. 1994); St. Paul Fire & Marine Ins. Co. v. Warwick
Dyeing Corp., 26 F.3d 1195 (1st cir. 1994).

[96] Writing on the pollution exclusion is voluminous. See, e.g., Kenneth S. Abraham, *Environmental Liability Insurance Law* 145-62 (1991); Scott D. Marrs, *Pollution Exclusion
Clauses: Validity and Applicability*, 26 Tort & Ins. L. J. 662 (1991); John S. Vishneski et
al., *The Insurance Industry's 1970 Pollution Exclusion: An Exercise in Ambiguity*, 23 Loy.
U. Chi. L.J. 67 (1991); Nancer Ballard & Peter Manus, *Clearing Muddy Waters: Anatomy
of the Comprehensive General Liability Pollution Exclusion*, 75 Cornell L. Rev. 610 (1990);
Sharon M. Murphy, Note, *The "Sudden and Accidental" Exception to the Pollution Exclusion
Clause in Comprehensive General Liability Insurance Policies: The Gordian Knot of
Environmental Liability*, 45 Vand. L. Rev. 161 (1992); Annot., Liability Insurance Coverage
for Violations of Antipollution Laws, 87 A.L.R.4th 444 (1991); Annot., *Property Damage:
What Constitutes "Contamination" Within Policy Clause Excluding Coverage*, 72 A.L.R.4th
633 (1989).

[97] See § 65[c], *supra*.

insurance, and had been interpreted in that context to mean "unexpected and unintended,"[98] which takes any temporal aspect out of the phrase.

Faced with this morass, some courts held the term "sudden" is ambiguous and interpreted the exception to the pollution exclusion in a light most favorable to insureds and in favor of coverage. Exemplar of this approach is *Jackson Township Municipal Utilities Authority v. Hartford Acc. and Indemnity Co.,*[99] a 1982 New Jersey case. The insured township was sued in two actions in which plaintiffs claimed that the township negligently selected, designed, and maintained a landfill, which resulted in the seepage of pollutants into the residents' groundwater. The court held that the plaintiffs' claims were within coverage:

> [T]he clause [the pollution exclusion] can be interpreted as simply a restatement of the definition of "occurrence" — that is, that the policy will cover claims where the injury was "neither expected nor intended." It is a reaffirmation of the principle that coverage will not be provided for intended results of intentional acts but will be provided for the unintended results of an intentional act.[100]

While many courts have been consistent with the pro-insured approach in *Jackson Township,*[101] other courts have taken a very different view, finding the language in the policy defining "occurrence" and setting forth the pollution exclusion to be clear and straightforward. A leading example of this approach is *Waste Management of Carolinas, Inc. v. Peerless Insurance Co.,*[102] a 1986 North Carolina decision. The insured sought coverage under its liability policies for any liability it might incur for the alleged depositing of toxic waste material in a landfill which had leached into and contaminated groundwater beneath it, rendering the well water for several surrounding households unsafe for human consumption. The insurer denied coverage. The court stated:

> We do not perceive these provisions to be either ambiguous or, except for the repeated appearance of "accident," redundant. In our view, this is an instance where nontechnical words (except for "occurrence," which is defined in the policy) can be given the same meaning they usually receive in ordinary speech.

---

[98] See New Castle Cty. v. Hartford Acc. & Indem. Co., 933 F.2d 1162 (3d Cir. 1991).

[99] 451 A.2d 990 (N.J.Super.Ct.Law Div. 1982).

[100] 451 A.2d at 994. This reading of the clause was influenced by 3 Long, *Law of Liability Insurance,* App. 98, 99, which stated that the exclusion was intended to eliminate "coverage for damages arising out of pollution or contamination, where such damages appear to be expected or intended on the part of the insured and hence are excluded by definition of 'occurrence.' " See 451 A.3d at 993.

[101] See, e.g., Queen City Farms, Inc. v. Central Nat'l Ins. Co., 882 P.2d 703 (Wash. 1994)(en banc); Outboard Marine Corp. v. Liberty Mut. Ins. Co., 607 N.E.2d 1204 (Ill. 1992); Hecla Mining Co. v. New Hampshire Ins. Co., 811 P.2d 1083 (Colo. 1991); Claussen v. Aetna Cas. & Sur. Co., 380 S.E.2d 686 (Ga. 1989); Molton, Allen and Williams, Inc. v. St. Paul Fire and Marine Ins. Co., 347 So. 2d 95 (Ala. 1977); Shapiro v. Public Service Mut. Ins. Co., 477 N.E.2d 146 (Mass.App. 1985); United Pac. Ins. Co. v. Van's Westlake Union, Inc., 664 P.2d 1262 (Wash. Ct. App. 1983); Buckeye Union Ins. Co. v. Liberty Solvents and Chemicals Co., 477 N.E.2d 1227 (Ohio Ct.App. 1984).

[102] 340 S.E.2d 374 (N.C. 1986).

> Nor does their context require us to do otherwise. . . . A common sense reading of that language reveals that the exclusion narrows a virtually limitless class of events termed "occurrences," which can occur suddenly or over the course of time, to non-polluting events or to polluting events that occur "suddenly and accidentally."[103]

The court reasoned that the acts of depositing waste materials at the landfill over the years were not occurrences because such acts were not sudden and accidental. The court acknowledged, nevertheless, that the leaching that resulted in the contamination was arguably "accidental" because it was arguably unexpected and unintended. In the final step of the its analysis, however, the court treated the loss as falling within the exclusion — and therefore outside the coverage — because the release or escape was not "sudden."[104] The weight of authority in the recent cases is more sympathetic to the *Waste Management* analysis, and a growing number of cases have held that in cases of gradual pollution the pollution exclusion is applicable and no coverage is provided.[105]

Where does all of this leave us? At one extreme, the 1973 CGL was obviously intended to provide coverage for loss arising out of a train accident where a tank car derails, ruptures, and spills a toxic cargo into a river. Such an incident is "sudden and accidental," outside the scope of the exclusion, and within the policy's coverage. At the other extreme, a company that deliberately deposits toxic wastes into a river commits an intentional act for which no coverage is provided. The act is intentional, not accidental. Also, the resulting damage from the act is probably known in advance and is certainly foreseeable; thus, it follows that the result is intended as well.[106]

It is the gray area between these two extremes that is problematic. Consider the example of an underground fuel storage tank. Such tanks have a finite life, and this is known at the time the tank is buried in the ground. Eventually and inevitably, the tank will deteriorate and begin leaking. Thus, it can be said that the leaching of fuel into surrounding soil and the resulting damage is both expectable and foreseeable. Since the burying of the tank is not an accident and the eventual consequences are known, the resulting damage is arguably outside the scope of the

---

103 340 S.E.2d at 379.

104 340 S.E.2d at 383. See also Techalloy Co. v. Reliance Ins. Co., 487 A.2d 820 (Pa. Super. Ct. 1984); Great Lakes Container Corp. v. National Union Fire Ins. Co., 727 F.2d 30 (1st Cir. 1984); American States Ins. Co. v. Maryland Cas. Co., 587 F. Supp. 1549 (E.D. Mich. 1984).

105 See, e.g., Aetna Cas. & Sur. Co. v. General Dynamics Corp., 968 F.2d 707 (8th Cir. 1992); Ray Indus. Inc. v. Liberty Mut. Ins. Co., 974 F.2d 754 (6th Cir. 1992); Ogden Corp. v. Travelers Indem. Co., 924 F.2d 39 (2d Cir. 1991); Grant-Southern Iron & Metal Co. v. CNA Ins. Co., 905 F.2d 954 (6th Cir. 1990); In re Texas Eastern Transmission Corp. PCB contamination Ins. Coverage Litigation, 15 F.3d 1230 (3d Cir. 1994), *opinion reinstated in part,* 15 F.3d 1249 (3d Cir. 1994), *cert. denied,* 115 S.Ct. 291 (1994); Dimmitt Chevrolet, Inc. v. Southeastern Fid. Ins. Corp., 636 So. 2d 700 (Fla. 1993); Lumbermens Mut. Cas. Co. v. Belleville Indus., Inc., 555 N.E.2d 568 (Mass. 1990); Shell Oil Co. v. Winterthur Swiss Ins. Co., 15 Cal. Rptr.2d 815 (Cal. Ct. App. 1993).

106 See American States Ins. Co. v. Maryland Cas. Co., 587 F. Supp. 1549 (E.D. Mich. 1984).

coverage; results of acts that have expectable, foreseeable — indeed, certain — consequences are not accidental, and one could argue that such damage is not an "occurrence." Yet from the insured's perspective, no intent exists to cause the leak or the resulting damage. There is a known risk, but the transformation of risk into actual harm is truly accidental. Also, when the tank first suffers a leak, the "rupture" is sudden, not expected or foreseen at the precise moment it occurs. Thus, it is arguable that the resulting liability is within the coverage.

The 1973 pollution exclusion, in combination with the occurrence language of the insuring agreement, is the policy language to be used to decide these cases. Unfortunately, the language of the CGL fell short — far short — of solving the problem easily. What did the industry intend to accomplish through the 1973 CGL? Although this question is the subject of much controversy,[107] it is difficult to believe that the industry did not intend to narrow the scope of coverage for environmental liability from the pre-1973 CGL. Thus, the 1973 pollution exclusion was not meant as mere restatement of the language of "occurrence" in the insuring agreement.

Interestingly, however, insurance industry representatives said something very different when they sought approval from regulatory authorities for the 1973 pollution exclusion. In a series of filings and statements at hearings on the exclusion, the industry represented that the exclusion merely "clarified" the meaning of "occurrence" in the insuring agreement and that coverage for unintended pollution would not be excluded.[108] Exactly what these representations meant is subject to interpretation as well,[109] but it is distinctly possible that the industry agreed (even if it did not intend) that the pollution exclusion does not preclude coverage for liability for the unintended and unexpected results of intentional pollution. It is also possible that the industry at the time did not understand its own language very well; if the industry understood the language, it is possible that industry officials were saying what they thought regulators needed to hear before approving the exclusion, which the industry officials assumed would later be enforced more strictly against insureds. This led one court to ignore what might otherwise have yielded a pro-insurer result on the coverage issue: "Had full disclosure been made, we would not hesitate to enforce the pollution-exclusion clause as written, resolving nuances inherent in the meaning of 'sudden' on a case-by-case basis. . . . Having profited from that nondisclosure by maintaining pre-existing rates for substantially-reduced coverage, the industry justly should be required to bear the burden of its omission by providing coverage at a level consistent with its representations to regulatory authorities."[110]

---

[107] See generally Ronald R. Robinson, *"Sudden Impact": The History of the Drafting of the 1973 CGL Policy's Pollution Exclusion, in Environmental Insurance Coverage Claims and Litigation* 719 PLI/Comm 403 (April-May 1995).

[108] See Morton Int'l, Inc. v. General Acc. Ins. Co. of Am., 629 A.2d 831 (N.J. 1993), cert. denied, 114 S.Ct. 2764 (1994); Just v. Land Reclamation, Ltd, 456 Nw.2d 570 (Wis. 1990); Claussen v. Aetna Cas. & Sur. Co., 380 S.E.2d 686 (Ga. 1989).

[109] See Abraham, *supra* note 96, at 159-60; Finley Harckham, *The Regulatory History Debate — A Tale of Two Regulators,* PLI Order No. A4-4477 (Apr.-May 1995), at 129.

[110] Morton International, Inc. v. General Acc. Ins. Co. of Am., 629 A.2d 831, 876 (N.J. 1993), *cert. denied,* 114 S.Ct. 2764 (1994). But in Federated Mut. Ins. Co. v. Botkin Grain

It may be that only one thing is clear from this rather remarkable history. Given the enormous perplexities in the 1973 pollution exclusion, the drafters of the 1986 CGL, apparently desiring to eliminate coverage for all environmental pollution incidents and perhaps simply tired of all of the turmoil, included in the CGL revision what became known as the "absolute pollution exclusion." The exclusion, which is set forth in full in the footnotes,[111] is a detailed provision dealing with virtually every contentious issue under the CGL that was in effect from 1973 to 1986. Not all commercial liability forms have used the same language as the pollution · exclusion in the 1986 CGL, but the common thread among the exclusions is an intention to eliminate coverage for environmental liability. A number of cases have

---

Co., 64 F.3d 537 (10th Cir. 1995), the court held that the proceedings before the Kansas Insurance Department, which allegedly involved misrepresentations by insurers about the scope of the exclusion, would not affect the exclusion's application in the instant case to deny coverage to the insured.

111

This insurance does not apply to: . . . (f) Pollution.

(1) "Bodily injury" or "property damage" arising out of the actual, alleged, or threatened discharge, dispersal, seepage, migration, release or escape of pollutants:

(a) At or from any premises, site or location which is or was at any time owned or occupied by, or rented or loaned to, any insured;

(b) At or from any premises, site or location which is or was at any time used by or for any insured or others for the handling, storage, disposal, processing or treatment of waste;

(c) Which are or were at any time transported, handled, stored, treated, disposed of, or processed as waste by or for any insured or any person or organization for whom you may be legally responsible; or

(d) At or from any premises, site or location on which any insured or any contractors or subcontractors working directly or indirectly on any insured's behalf are performing operations: (i) if the pollutants are brought on or to the premises, site or location in connection with such operations by such insured, contractor or subcontractor; or (ii) if the operations are to test for, monitor, clean up, remove, contain, treat, detoxify or neutralize, or in any way respond to, or assess the effects of pollutants.

Subparagraphs (a) and (d)(i) do not apply to "bodily injury" or "property damage" arising out of heat, smoke or fumes from a hostile fire.

As used in this exclusion, a hostile fire means one which becomes uncontrollable or breaks out from where it was intended to be.

(2) Any loss, cost or expense arising out of any:

(a) request, demand or order that any insured or others test for, monitor, clean up, remove, contain, treat, detoxify or neutralize, or in any way respond to, or assess the effects of pollutants; or

(b) Claim or suit by or on behalf of a governmental authority for damages because of testing for, monitoring, cleaning up, removing, containing, treating, detoxifying or neutralizing or in any way responding to, or assessing the effects of pollutants.

Pollutants means any solid, liquid, gaseous or thermal irritant or contaminant, including smoke, vapor, soot, fumes, acids, alkalis, chemicals and waste. Waste includes materials to be recycled, reconditioned or reclaimed. [*Policy Kit* at 310 (ISO Form CG 00 01 10 93).]

considered the absolute pollution exclusion, and the results are uniform in the environmental damage setting: it has been interpreted to bar coverage for all property damage caused by pollution, including the costs incurred in cleaning up toxic waste sites.[112]

The absolute pollution exclusion has engendered controversy in other settings. however. In some settings outside the environmental damage context, the exclusion has been applied according to its clear terms. For example, a few courts have held that absolute exclusions (specifically, ones lacking the CGL's clarification for smoke or soot damage in hostile fire situations) operated to eliminate coverage for the insureds' liabilities for smoke or soot damage.[113] One court has held that the exclusion applied to the insured's use of PVC in a bagging operation,[114] and another has held that the exclusion precludes coverage for claims that the insured negligently allowed lead paint chips to contaminate surrounding property while painting the outside of a building.[115]

It has also been held that the exclusion bars coverage for liability resulting from carbon monoxide poisoning.[116] This last result is very troublesome. Death or injury by carbon monoxide poisoning (due, for example, to a faulty heater or furnace) is not the kind of pollution (even if it is pollution, which is arguable given its natural existence in air) with which the pollution exclusion has been concerned through the years.[117] Other courts have reached the opposite result, holding that carbon

---

[112] See, e.g, Park-Ohio Indus. Inc. v. Home Indem. Co., 975 F.2d 1215 (6th Cir. 1992); Pipefitters Welfare Educ. Fund v. Westchester Fire Ins. Co., 976 F.2d 1037 (7th Cir. 1992); Western World Ins. Co. v. Stack Oil, Inc., 922 F.2d 118 (2d Cir. 1990); Alcolac Inc. v. California Union Ins. Co., 716 F. Supp. 1541 (D.Md. 1989); Guilford Indus., Inc. v. Liberty Mut. Ins. Co., 688 F. Supp. 792 (D.Me. 1988), aff'd, 879 F.2d 853 (1st Cir. 1989). But see Red Panther Chem. Co. v. Insurance Co. of State of Pa., 43 F.3d 514 (10th Cir. 1994) (absolute pollution exclusion does not, as a matter of law, bar coverage for injuries resulting when a container of toxic material falls from a truck).

[113] See Park-Ohio Indus., Inc. v. Home Indem Co., 785 F. Supp. 670 (N.D. Ohio 1991), aff'd, 975 F.2d 1215 (6th Cir. 1992) (plaintiffs alleged smoke and soot damage leading to respiratory problems; held, no coverage); Demakos v. Travelers Ins. Co., 613 N.Y.S.2d 709 (N.Y. App. Div. 1994) (smoke damage outside coverage due to pollution exclusion). A more difficult question is presented if a hostile fire breaks out at a waste site, and the smoke from the waste site fire causes damage or injury. Is the liability excluded by the pollution exclusion, or is the liability covered by virtue of the hostile fire exception to the exclusion? One court in that situation held the exclusion ambiguous and found coverage for the insured. See American Star Ins. Co. v. Grice, 854 P.2d 622 (Wash. 1993) (en banc).

[114] See Crabtree v. Hayes-Dockside, Inc., 612 So. 2d 249 (La. Ct. App. 1992).

[115] See United States Liab. Ins. Co. v. Bourbeau, 49 F.3d 786 (1st Cir. 1995).

[116] See, e.g., Essex Ins. Co. v. Tri-Town Corp., 863 F. Supp. 38 (D.Mass. 1994); Bernhardt v. Hartford Fire Ins. Co., 648 A.2d 1047 (Md.Ct.App. 1994), cert. granted, (1995).

[117] Tennis fans, of which the author is one, will recall the tragic death of Vitas Gerulaitis in 1994, who succumbed to accidental carbon monoxide poisoning when visiting a friend's cottage. If an heir later claims that the host is legally responsible for the death and the host has liability insurance, the question could arise regarding whether the absolute pollution exclusion, or some variation of it, eliminates the host's liability coverage. The argument that this type of loss is precisely the kind of fortuitous, catastrophic loss for which one purchases liability insurance is a compelling one.

monoxide-related loss is not the type of environmental damage contemplated by the absolute pollution exclusion.[118] Other courts have been reluctant to apply the pollution exclusion outside the environmental pollution area.[119]

Although the 1986 revision of the pollution exclusion dramatically changed the coverage of the CGL, the prior exclusion, which was in widespread use from 1973 to 1986, will continue to be a source of litigation for many years to come. Environmental damage that occurred during the years the older version of the exclusion was used will continue to be discovered, and many future cases will be decided with reference to policy language that was in place ten to twenty years ago (or longer). In addition, the lessons of the pollution exclusion experience are not likely to be lost on drafters of future standard liability forms, and one fallout of this history is that future forms for significant commercial risks are likely to be drafted with more precision, even if this requires "per se" language that significantly constricts coverage.

[7] The Owned-Property Exclusion

For many years, CGL policies have contained exclusions for damage to property either "owned or occupied by the insured" and for damage to property under the "care, custody or control" of the insured. The most basic purpose of the exclusions is to make clear that the CGL policy does not provide first-party coverage and is instead intended, as the name of the policy indicates, to provide coverage for liabilities to others.[120] In the environmental damage context, the exclusion has been held by some courts to eliminate coverage for the costs of cleaning up the insured's own property.[121] The difficulty with this result is that it increases moral hazard; it

---

[118] See, e.g., Stoney Run Co. v. Prudential-LMI Commercial Ins. Co., 47 F.3d 34 (2d Cir. 1995); Regional Bank of Colo. v. St. Paul Fire & Marine Ins. Co., 35 F.3d 494 (10th Cir. 1994); Gamble Farm Inn, Inc. v. Selective Ins. Co., 656 A.2d 142 (Pa.Super. 1995); Kenyon v. Security Ins. Co. of Hartford (DPIC Cos.), 626 N.Y.S.2d 347 (N.Y.Sup. 1993); Thompson v. Temple, 580 So. 2d 1133 (La. Ct. App. 1991). Although supporters of this result may take comfort in the weight of authority favoring coverage, it should not be lost on any reader that in each of the cases cited an insurer initially took and subsequently asserted in litigation the position that the policy provided no coverage for the loss in question.

[119] See Westchester Fire Ins. Co. v. City of Pittsburg, Kan., 768 F. Supp. 1463 (D.Kan. 1991), aff'd sub nom. Pennsylvania Nat'l Mut. Cas. Ins. Co. v. City of Pittsburg, Kansas, 987 F.2d 1516 (10th Cir. 1993) (personal injury claims asserted against municipality arising out of inhalation of insecticide not barred by absolute pollution exclusion); Karroll v. Atomergic Chemetals Corp., 600 N.Y.S.2d 101 (N.Y. App. Div. 1993), app. dismissed, 632 N.E.2d 465 (N.Y. 1994) (personal injury claim arising from ruptured sulfuric acid bottle not barred by absolute pollution exclusion); Minerva Enterprises, Inc. v. Bituminous Cas. Corp., 851 S.W.2d 403 (Ark. 1993) (damage caused by backup of septic system and flooding of mobile home with solid and liquid sewage).

[120] For more discussion of the exclusion, see Kenneth S. Abraham, Environmental Liability Insurance Law 160-73 (1991); Eugene I. Annis, The Owned Property and Care Custody and Control Exclusions of the Comprehensive General Liability Policy, 28 Gonz. L. Rev. 439 (1992/93).

[121] See, e.g, State Dep't of Env. Protection v. Signo Trading Int'l, Inc., 612 A.2d 932 (N.J. 1992); Compass Ins. Co. v. Cravens, Dargan & Co., 748 P.2d 724 (Wyo. 1988); United States Fid. & Guar. Co. v. Johnson Shoes, Inc., 461 A.2d 85 (N.H. 1983); Shell Oil Co. v. Winterthur Swiss Ins. Co., 15 Cal. Rptr. 2d 815 (Cal. Ct. App. 1993).

gives insureds an incentive not to clean up hazardous waste sites that cause damage to others and instead wait for the third-party to seek to impose liability on the insured, which then may be covered. As a result, some courts have taken a more expansive view of coverage and have limited the impact of the owned-property exclusion.[122] Under the prevailing view, if pollution on owned premises has not caused damage to the property of third-parties, the exclusion bars coverage for the cost of cleaning up the owned premises,[123] although a few courts have held to the contrary when the threat of damage to other property is imminent.[124]

When there is damage to non-owned, off-site property, extremely difficult problems of allocation of coverage must be confronted. If damage to off-site property is not excluded and damage to owned-property is excluded, how does one measure the damage and allocate coverage in circumstances where waste on owned property has migrated through groundwater to cause damage to the off-site property? Does the fact that the clean-up of the groundwater benefits the owned property make any difference? Recall that the purpose of the owned-property exclusion is to prevent the insured from improving his or her own property at the insurer's expense. This suggests that the relative benefits to owned and non-owned property should be considered, but how does one actually measure "benefits" in circumstances where many uses have intangible values (such as recreation areas)? These questions defy answers that work for all situations.[125]

[g] Coverage of Punitive Damages Assessed Against the Insured

Punitive damages are sums awarded to a plaintiff over and above the plaintiff's actual loss for the purposes of punishing a defendant for outrageous conduct and deterring the defendant and others from engaging in similar conduct in the future.[126]

---

[122] See Shell Oil Co. v. Winterhur Swiss Ins. Co., 15 Cal. Rptr.2d 815 (Cal. Ct. App, 1993) (expenses solely for cleanup of insured's property were not covered unless necessary to prevent imminent damage to third-party's property); Diamond Shamrock Chemicals Co. v. Aetna Cas. & Sur. Co., 554 A.2d 1342 (N.J. Super. Ct. App. Div. 1989).

[123] See, e.g., State v. Signo Trading Int'l, Inc., 612 A.2d 932 (N.J. 1992); Compass Ins. Co. v. Cravens, Dargan & Co., 748 P.2d 724 (Wyo. 1988); United States Fid. & Guar. Co. v. Johnson Shoes, Inc. 461 A.2d 85 (N.H. 1983).

[124] See, e.g., Intel Corp. v. Hartford Acc. & Indem. Co., 952 F.2d 1551 (9th Cir. 1991); Patz v. St. Paul Fire & Marine Ins. Co., 817 F. Supp. 781 (E.D. Wis. 1993), aff'd, 15 F.3d 699 (7th Cir. 1994); Summit Assoc., Inc. v. Liberty Mut. Fire Ins. Co., 550 A.2d 1235 (N.J. Super. Ct. App. Div. 1988).

[125] For more discussion, see Kirby Griffis, *Apportionment of Environmental Cleanup Costs under the Owned-Property Exclusion in CGL Insurance Policies*, 80 Va.L.Rev. 1351 (1994).

[126] *Restatement (Second) of Torts* § 908 (1979). The subject of punitive damages is vast, with entire treatises devoted to the subject. See, e.g., James D. Ghiardi & John J. Kircher, *Punitive Damages Law and Practice* (1985); Linda L. Schlueter & Kenneth R. Redden, *Punitive Damages (2d ed. 1989)*; Dan B. Dobbs, *Dobbs Law of Remedies* § 3.11 (2d ed. 1993). In recent years, the availability of punitive damages has been constricted in many states, and it has been reported that "more than half the states prohibit or cap punitive damages, or raise evidence standards to award them." *Chart, "The State of Punitive Damages,"* 79 ABA Journal 75 (April 1995) (using information supplied by American Tort Reform Association, chart shows that 5 states prohibit punitive damages; 10 states cap the amount of punitive damages

If an insured covered by a policy of liability insurance is held liable to a third party for punitive damages, a substantial question might arise: is the award of punitive damages covered by the insurance policy?[127]

Courts are uniform in holding that it is against public policy to permit insurance coverage for an intentional tort.[128] Therefore, punitive damages for an intentional tort are not within the scope of any liability policy's coverage. The only exception to this rule applies where liability coverage is compulsory by statute for the benefit of third parties; in that instance, the policy favoring compensating victims of torts sometimes outweighs the policies involved in not allowing a tortfeasor to shift liability to the insurer.[129] Therefore, the real dispute is whether public policy should prevent coverage for punitive damages awarded for gross, wanton, or reckless conduct.

Whether insurance coverage is available to cover the insured's punitive damages liability to a third party is determined first by referring to the language of the insurance policy. If coverage of punitive damages is specifically excluded, the analysis is simple: no coverage exists.[130] However, insurance policies are rarely this specific. Often the policy will simply state that the insurer provides coverage "for all sums which the insured shall become legally obligated to pay." If the policy covers the insured's liability for damages generally and does not specifically mention punitive damages, courts usually conclude that the language of the policy is broad enough to cover punitive damages.[131] Once this conclusion is reached, a

---

awardable; 19 states, including 5 of the 10 states with caps, require clear and convincing evidence to award such damages; 7 states, including one state with caps and three others which require the clear and convincing evidence standard to be met, require that a portion of the award be paid to the state).

[127] See generally Alan I. Widiss, *Liability Insurance Coverage for Punitive Damages?*, 39 Vill. L. Rev. 455 (1994); Grace M. Giesel, *The Knowledge of Insurers and the Posture of the Parties in the Determination of the Insurability of Punitive Damages*, 39 Kan. L. Rev. 355 (1991); Alyssa Walden, *The Publicly Held Corporation and the Insurability of Punitive Damages*, 53 Fordham L. Rev. 1383 (1985); Harriet M. King, *The Insurability of Punitive Damages: A New Solution to an Old Dilemma*, 16 Wake Forest L. Rev. 345 (1980); Joseph C. Hagner, *Punitive Damages—Insurance and Reinsurance*, 47 Ins. Counsel J. 72 (1980).

[128] See, e.g., Hensley v. Erie Ins. Co., 283 S.E.2d 227 (W.Va. 1981); Harrell v. Travelers Indem. Co., 567 P.2d 1013 (Or. 1977); Continental Ins. Cos. v. Hancock, 507 S.W.2d 146 (Ky. 1973); Southern Farm Bur. Cas. Ins. Co. v. Daniel, 440 S.W.2d 582 (Ark. 1969). See § 63, *supra*.

[129] See §§ 110[e], 133, *infra*.

[130] Policy language excluding coverage for intentional torts is normally not applied to preclude punitive damage recovery. See Caspersen v. Webber, 213 N.W.2d 327 (Minn. 1973). See generally Charles M. Louderback, Comment, *The Exclusion Clause: A Simple and Genuine Solution to the Insurance for Punitive Damages Controversy*, 12 U.S.F. L. Rev. 743 (1978).

[131] See Ridgeway v. Gulf Life Ins. Co., 578 F.2d 1026 (5th Cir. 1978); South Carolina State Budget & Control Bd. v. Prince, 403 S.E.2d 643 (S.C. 1991); Hensley v. Erie Ins. Co., 283 S.E.2d 227 (W.Va. 1981); Southern Farm Bur. Cas. Ins. Co. v. Daniel, 440 S.W.2d 582 (Ark. 1969); Carroway v. Johnson, 139 S.E.2d 908 (S.C. 1965); Lazenby v. Universal Underwriters Ins. Co., 383 S.W.2d 1 (Tenn. 1964). But see Burley v. Berkshire Mut. Ins. Co., 440 A.2d 359 (Me. 1982); Cavin's Inc., v. Atlantic Mut. Ins. Co., 220 S.E.2d 403 (N.C. Ct. App. 1975).

second question must be considered: whether the public policy of the state permits the insured to shift punitive damages liability to an insurer.[132]

Some liability insurance forms state that coverage is not available for punitive damages if state law would be violated. These provisions are problematical because they can raise troublesome choice of law issues. At the outset, it is necessary to determine what law applies, and this may depend both upon where the plaintiff's claim arose and where the contract between insurer and insured was formed. Once the choice of law questions are resolved, however, this kind of liability form raises directly the question of whether state public policy prohibits the insurability of punitive damages.

The debate over whether the public policy of a state permits coverage of punitive damages liability occurs on several fronts, and the arguments can be broken down into several categories. The first argument concerns *freedom of contract*. In support of coverage of punitive damages, it is argued that allowing the parties to contract for the coverage of punitive damages is consistent with notions of the sanctity of private contract. The parties agreed, either explicitly or implicitly, that the insurer would provide such coverage, and the insurer elected to receive a premium for providing it. No reason exists, it is argued, for disturbing the private agreement of the parties. Those opposing insurability respond, however, that the deference afforded the private agreement of parties must yield when the agreement is inconsistent with public policy.

The major battleground in the debate over the insurability of punitive damages concerns the question of *deterrence*. Opponents of insurability argue that allowing punitive damages to be insured frustrates the very purpose of the award and therefore contravenes public policy. Punitive damages are designed to deter parties from engaging in certain kinds of conduct, but this purpose will not be achieved if a party can insure against the consequences of that conduct and someone other than the tortfeasor pays the judgment.

Proponents of insurability reject the proposition that a causal link exists between punitive damages and deterrence; in the absence of such a link, it is claimed that no reason exists to disallow insurability of the damages. In this regard, the proponents of insurability note that it is important to distinguish between intentional conduct and reckless conduct. An intentional act is more culpable than a reckless act; deterrence might occur to some extent with intentional acts, but there is no link between deterrence and reckless conduct. Indeed, damages awarded for negligent acts are insurable, but there is no evidence that the existence of insurance has caused more negligence. There is equally little likelihood that the existence of insurance

---

[132] Given the difficulties that are about to be discussed, it is curious that insurers do not clarify their forms so as to disallow coverage of punitive damage liability. In 1977, the ISO introduced a policy endorsement indicating that coverage for punitive damages is excluded from property and liability insurance contracts, and within a few months the exclusion was approved in 33 jurisdictions and disapproved in only eight. But in the face of concern voiced in some quarters about the differing bases for the imposition of punitive damages among the states, the ISO withdrew the proposal in March 1978. No effort has since been mounted to draft an exclusion of general applicability. Ghiardi & Kircher, *supra* note 126, § 7.10.

for reckless or wanton acts would encourage more reckless or wanton behavior. Moreover, juries occasionally award punitive damages for conduct not considered or known to be wrongful prior to the imposition of the award. In this circumstance, forbidding coverage after the conduct has occurred will not — nor could it — deter such conduct and may impose an injustice on unsuspecting defendants.[133]

Related to the debate over deterrence is the issue of *fair allocation of the burden of the remedy*. Opponents of insurability argue that the burden should be borne solely by the tortfeasor personally. Punitive damages constitute "punishment," and punishment does not occur if the tortfeasor does not bear the burden of the remedy. Allowing coverage not only enables the tortfeasor to escape punishment but also shifts the burden of the wrong to the insurer, which in turn shifts the burden to the premium-paying public. When the risk-shifting ends, the public pays for the tortfeasor's egregious conduct, not the tortfeasor. No one would contemplate allowing an individual to insure against a fine imposed by the criminal law; punitive damages are simply fines imposed by the civil law. The illogic of making the public bear the burden of a criminal fine is no less in the situation where a civil fine is involved.

Proponents of insurability argue that the opponents' fairness analysis simply does not square with reality. Juries are liberal in awarding punitive damages, and it is unfair to make individuals bear the burden of jury liberality by paying such judgments out of their own pockets. Whatever the law says, juries in fact view punitive damages as another way to compensate the victim, and damages designed to compensate are fairly allocable to the insurer.

Another argument in the dispute over the insurability of punitive damages concerns *collectibility*. Proponents of insurability argue that if punitive damages are not covered, a distinct possibility exists in many cases that the injured victim will not collect on the judgment. One of the purposes of liability insurance is protection of the victim against the possibility that the insured tortfeasor will lack sufficient personal resources to pay the resulting judgment. Indeed, if punitive damages are not covered, a danger exists that an insured who is not allowed to pass punitive damages through to the insurer will become bankrupt, and encouraging bankruptcy is not a favored policy of the law.

Opponents of insurability reject the premise that collectibility with regard to a punitive damages judgment is even a relevant consideration. Compensatory damages are designed to make the victim whole; punitive damages are literally a windfall to the injured party, and the fact that a tortfeasor may lack the resources to pay the judgment is irrelevant. If punitive damages should be paid to anyone, it is suggested that the state should receive these damages, not the victim. One rebuttal to the opponent's attack asserts that the purposes of punitive damages are to deter and to punish, not to compensate. Yet, it is argued, no good reason exists for failing to recognize that the injured party does benefit from an award of punitive damages and that for this reason alone collectibility is a relevant consideration.

---

[133] See First Bank (N.A.)—Billings v. Transamerica Ins. Co., 679 P.2d 1217 (Mont. 1984).

The debate is a vigorous one. Not surprisingly, courts are split on the question of whether punitive damages liability for reckless, wanton, or grossly negligent conduct is insurable. Roughly two-thirds of the states that have considered the question have held that punitive damages are insurable,[134] and the remaining states have held that punitive damages are not insurable.[135] Where punitive damages are insurable, however, all states that have considered the matter recognize an exception when the insured's conduct is intentional.[136]

Legislatures rarely speak to the matter. In a few states, legislatures have declared that it is not against the state's public policy to allow insurability of punitive damages vicariously imposed.[137] A South Carolina statute requires that liability insurance cover punitive damages.[138] Where the legislature speaks, the legislative pronouncement is, of course, controlling. Where the legislature has not spoken, courts inclined to allow insurability of punitive damages have concluded that punitive damages are insurable because (1) the state statutes authorize the issuance of liability insurance and (2) punitive damages constitute a legal liability.[139]

---

[134] See, e.g., Collins & Aikman Corp. v. Hartford Acc. & Indem. Co., 436 S.E.2d 243 (N.C. 1993); Whalen v. On-Deck, Inc., 514 A.2d 1072 (Del. 1986); Hensley v. Erie Ins. Co., 283 S.E.2d 227 (W.Va. 1981); Harrell v. Travelers Indem. Co., 567 P.2d 1013 (Or. 1977); Price v. Hartford Acc. & Indem. Co., 502 P.2d 522 (Ariz. 1972); Lazenby v. Universal Underwriters Ins. Co., 383 S.W.2d 1 (Tenn. 1964). One survey reports that of the 37 states and territories that have confronted the question, 21 states have allowed punitive damage liability to be insured and 16 have disallowed the coverage. Of the 16 not allowing insurability, nine have considered whether punitive damages vicariously imposed are insurable, and all have concluded that they are. See "Jurisdiction Survey on the Insurability of Punitive Damages," in Barry R. Ostrager & Thomas R. Newman, co-eds. *Insurance, Excess and Reinsurance Coverage Disputes 1994* , § 14.06, at 630-39. See also *"Excessive" Punitive Awards a Matter of Debate*, Bus. Ins., Feb. 6, 1995, at 1 (chart indicating that 15 states do not allow punitive damages to be insured; but in 9 of the those 15 states, insurance is allowed for liability vicariously imposed; 24 states and the District of Columbia allow punitive damages to be insured; but in two states among those 25 jurisdictions insurance is prohibited for intentional conduct; 11 states have unclear precedent or none at all).

[135] See, e.g., American Sur. Co. v. Gold, 375 F.2d 523 (10th Cir. 1966); Northwestern Nat'l Cas. Co. v. McNulty, 307 F.2d 432 (5th Cir. 1962); Rosenbloom v. Flygare, 501 N.W.2d 597 (Minn. 1993); City of Fort Pierre v. United Fire & Cas. Co., 463 N.W.2d 845 (S.D. 1990); U.S. Concrete Pipe Co. v. Bould, 437 So. 2d 1061 (Fla. 1983); Dayton Hudson Corp. v. American Mut. Liab. Ins. Co., 621 P.2d 1155 (Okla. 1980); Hartford Acc. & Indem. Co. v. Village of Hempstead, 397 N.E.2d 737 (N.Y. 1979). Compare Continental Cas. Co. v. Kinsey, 499 N.W.2d 574 (N.D. 1993) (insurer obligated under policy, which had special endorsement covering punitive damages, to pay punitive damages award to plaintiff-victim up to policy limits; however, because of statute prohibiting person from being indemnified for their own intentional conduct, insurer was entitled to seek indemnity from its insured for payment to third-party injured by insured).

[136] See § 63, *supra*.

[137] See, e.g., Kan. Stat. Ann. § 40-2,115; Va. Code Ann. § 38.2-227.

[138] See S.C. Code Ann. § 38-77-30(4).

[139] See, e.g., Mazza v. Medical Mut. Ins. Co., 319 S.E.2d 217 (N.C. 1984); Greenwood Cemetery, Inc. v. Travelers Indem. Co., 232 S.E.2d 910 (Ga. 1977).

Where punitive damages are vicariously imposed, the public policies against coverage of punitive damages are much less compelling. For example, consider the situation where a business purchases insurance. An employee of the business, while in the course of employment, becomes intoxicated and runs over a pedestrian with a delivery truck. After a trial, the business is held vicariously liable for the injured victim's loss and punitive damages are awarded against the business. The employer had no meaningful ability to prevent the conduct of an employee bent on acting in such a destructive way. At best, the employer was simply negligent — not reckless or grossly negligent — in failing to supervise the employee. In such a situation, it does not seem fair to require the employer to bear the costs of the employee's misconduct. Such an employer should instead be allowed to shift its liability for punitive damages to an insurer.

It is important in the foregoing example that the employer is presumed to have no real blame for the injurious incident. If the employer had some measure of complicity in the incident, such as would be the case if the employer knew the employee was intoxicated when the employee left with the truck, the policy of deterrence associated with requiring a party to bear personally the punitive damage liability is more relevant. Agency law has two competing theories for imposition of vicarious liability, which reflect the concerns outlined above. One doctrine, the complicity doctrine, requires some sort of blameworthiness on the employer's part before liability is vicariously imposed. The other doctrine, the respondeat superior doctrine, basically holds the employer strictly liable for punitive damages assessed against the employee. Under this approach, to recover punitive damages from an employer, all that the plaintiff must show is that the employee committed willful, wanton, or malicious acts within the scope of employment. No separate acts of the employer contributing to, participating in, or ratifying the employee's conduct are necessary. Most states follow the respondeat superior doctrine, but the complicity doctrine is accepted by the *Restatement (Second) of Torts* and the *Restatement (Second) of Agency,* and a minority of courts follow it.[140]

If the employer is held strictly liable for the acts of its employee, it seems unfair not to allow the employer to purchase insurance for the liability vicariously imposed. If the employer's involvement in the tortious conduct is only negligent, as opposed to reckless or wanton, it seems reasonable to allow the employer to purchase insurance for the loss, just as any person can insure against the consequences of his or her negligent conduct. Yet if some element of blameworthiness (probably exceeding mere negligence) is a prerequisite to the employer's vicarious liability, the case is stronger for not allowing the employer to purchase insurance for vicariously imposed punitive damages.

Most states adhere to the respondeat superior doctrine; thus, it follows that — at least for liability vicariously imposed — in these states punitive damages should be insurable. In all states that have addressed the issue either by judicial decision or statute, insurability of punitive damages vicariously imposed is permitted, regardless of whether the state adheres to the respondeat superior doctrine or the complicity

---

140 See, e.g., Plains Resources, Inc. v. Gable, 682 P.2d 653 (Kan. 1984); Mercury Motors Express, Inc. v. Smith, 393 So. 2d 545 (Fla. 1981).

doctrine.[141] In those states refusing to permit punitive damages to be insured, the vicarious liability rule constitutes an exception to the general rule prohibiting insurability of punitive damages.

§ 66   Particular Coverage Issues in Property Insurance: The Friendly Fire Rule

Fire insurance policies do not by their terms explicitly limit the coverage depending on the kind of fire that causes the loss. However, courts have long recognized an implied exception under which losses caused by "friendly" as opposed to "hostile" fires are not covered by fire insurance policies. A friendly fire is one that burns in an ordinary place where a fire is expected to be found, such as in a stove, a furnace, or in a fireplace. Hostile fires are those that occur in a place where they are not supposed to be. The hostile fire category includes both fires that begin in a place where they are unexpected and fires that begin as a friendly fire but escape their ordinary confines.[1]

The terminology seems odd when it is first encountered, but the "hostile" versus "friendly" phraseology is easier to understand if one reflects on the differing character of fires. Fireplace fires, campfires, and candlelight are often associated with images of relaxation, protection, romance, and warmth; these fires are "friendly." Yet anyone who has seen a trash bag full of holiday wrapping paper blazing in the middle of a home's living room because a lighted match inadvertently fell into the bag or a grease fire spreading from a stove top across a kitchen counter understands that some fires have a completely different character, one that is accurately described as "hostile." For most fires, if one is asked how to determine whether the fire is friendly or hostile, it is fair to answer "I know it when I see it." Unfortunately, the line is not always easy to draw.

The friendly fire-hostile fire distinction is thought to date to an 1815 English case titled *Austin v. Drew*.[2] In that case, the insured premises, a seven- or eight-story building, were used to manufacture sugar. On the ground floor were a stove and pans for boiling sugar; a chimney or flue went from the stove to the top of the building, passing through each floor. At each floor, a register in the chimney could be opened or closed so that the amount of heat introduced into the room could be adjusted. One morning when the fire was lit on the ground floor as was the typical practice, the servant on the top floor forgot to open the register. As a result, smoke, sparks, and heat were forced into a room on a lower floor where the sugars were drying. Fortunately, the register was opened before the entire building burned to the ground (although two men suffocated during the efforts to open the register); at no time throughout the incident did flame get beyond the chimney and there was never

---

[141] See, e.g., U.S. Concrete Pipe Co. v. Bould, 437 So. 2d 1061 (Fla. 1983); Dayton Hudson Corp. v. American Mut. Liab. Ins. Co., 621 P.2d 1155 (Okla. 1980). In at least one state, this rule is statutory. Kan. Stat. Ann. § 40-2,115.

[1] For more discussion, see John D. Ingram, *The Friendly Fire Doctrine: Judicial Misconstruction Run Amok,* 22 Tort & Ins. L. J. 312 (1987).

[2] 4 Camp. 360, 171 Eng.Rep. 115 (1815).

more fire than what was needed to manufacture the sugar. However, considerable damage was done to the building and its contents by the smoke and heat.

The report of the proceedings state:

GIBBS, C.J.—I am of opinion that this action is not maintainable. There was no more fire than always exists when the manufacture is going on. Nothing was consumed by fire. The plaintiff's loss arose from the negligent management of their machinery. The sugars were chiefly damaged by the heat; and what produced that heat? Not any fire against which the company insures, but the fire for heating the pans, which continued all the time to burn without any excess. The servant forgot to open the register by which the smoke ought to have escaped, and the heat to have been tempered.

Juryman. If my servant by negligence sets my house on fire, and it is burnt down, I expect, my Lord, to be paid by the insurance office.

GIBBS, C.J.—And so you would, Sir: but then there would be a fire, whereas here there has been none . . . in this case there was no fire except in the stove and the flue, as there ought to have been, and the loss was occasioned by the confinement of heat. Had the fire been brought out of the flue, and anything had been burnt, the company would have been liable. But can this be said, where the fire never was at all excessive, and was always confined within its proper limits? This is not a fire within the meaning of the policy, nor a loss for which the company undertake. They might as well be sued for the damage done to drawing-room furniture by a smoky chimney.

The jury, with great reluctance, found a verdict for the defendant.[3]

The plaintiff moved for a new trial, claiming that it was not essential for recovery under an insurance policy that the fire actually touch the damaged objects. In the instant case, counsel for plaintiff argued, the heat became excessively strong, and this caused the damage. Counsel argued that if excessive heat from a chimney ignited neighboring buildings, the loss should be covered even though the fire in the chimney was confined to its usual place. If a chimney caught fire, it would be the result of soot in the chimney because the usual amount of fire would remain below, but the loss would still be covered. Chief Justice Gibbs, however, thought it unnecessary "to determine any of those extreme questions." He explained: "In the present case, I think no loss was sustained by any of the risks in the policy. The loss was occasioned by the extreme mismanagement by the Plaintiffs of their register."[4]

The rule of *Austin v. Drew*, then, is that damage caused by a fire which remains within its normal place and does not become excessive is not a loss for which an insurer can be held liable under a fire insurance policy. For many common situations, this rule will be easy to apply. If a fire develops in the chimney, such a fire is not in the fireplace where it is supposed to be, and thus such a fire is hostile.[5] A fire

---

[3] 4 Camp. at 361–62, 171 Eng.Rep. at 115–16.

[4] 6 Taunt. 436, 439, 128 Eng.Rep. 1104, 1105 (1816).

[5] See, e.g., Washington Tp. Mut. Fire & Lightning Ins. Ass'n v. Sherrer, 168 N.E. 234 (Ohio Ct.App. 1927); Way v. Abington Mut. Fire Ins. Co., 43 N.E. 1032 (Mass. 1896). Obviously, if the fire spreads from the chimney to the roof, the fire on the roof is hostile.

in a sofa is plainly a hostile fire. A fire in a rug caused by a lighted cigarette is hostile.[6] A lighted cigarette or match held in the hand is a friendly fire, since the fire is where it is supposed to be. However, if the lighted cigarette or match is dropped, the fire becomes hostile, because it is not where it is supposed to be.[7] Similarly, if a lighted tip of the cigarette falls to the floor, the fire is hostile. A match in the hand is friendly, but if a spark (a fire) flies off the match while it is being struck, the spark is hostile. A normal fire in the fireplace which damages the fireplace brick is friendly, but a spark from the fireplace that escapes the fireplace is hostile. Under the logic of the rule, a number of courts have held that the damage to or destruction of objects inadvertently thrown into a friendly fire is not covered under a fire insurance policy because the fire is friendly, not hostile.[8]

However, in numerous other situations, the *Austin* rule provides insufficient guidance or actually leads to an undesirable result. Smoke and soot damage presents a common problem. If the smoke and soot damage comes from a hostile fire, the damage is covered.[9] *Austin* apparently holds that such damage from a friendly fire is not covered, and some courts have adhered to this reasoning. However, a number of courts have rejected this logic and have held that where heat and smoke escape from a fire in a furnace or stove and cause damage, the loss is covered.[10] According to these courts, when soot or smoke damage occurs, it is because the fire did not behave in a manner expected by the insured. Indemnity against loss from the fire's fortuitous behavior is presumably what the insured thought was being purchased when the fire insurance policy was secured, and thus a strong case can be made for coverage.

The difficulty can be illustrated with this example. Suppose a fire in the fireplace is extinguished, apparently, when the insured-homeowner retires for the night, and the insured closes the damper; but during the night, coals cause a few remaining pieces of wood in the hearth to ignite spontaneously, and the closed damper results in smoke pouring throughout the house instead of going up the chimney, causing

---

   [6] See Swerling v. Connecticut Fire Ins. Co., 180 A. 343 (R.I. 1935).

   [7] See Heuer v. Northwestern Nat'l Ins Co., 33 N.E. 411 (Ill. 1893) (lighted match in hand which caused gas explosion is friendly fire).

   [8] See, e.g., Youse v. Employers Fire Ins. Co., 238 P.2d 472 (Kan. 1951); Reliance Ins. Co. v. Naman, 6 S.W.2d 743 (Tex. 1928); compare Watson v. American Colony Ins. Co., 183 S.E. 692 (S.C. 1936) (tissue holding jewelry on mantle catches fire, a hostile fire; insured throws burning mass into stove, a normal place for a fire; whether loss is covered presents a jury question); but see Salmon v. Concordia Fire Ins. Co., 161 So. 340 (La. Ct. App. 1935). The results in these cases indicate that an insured should purchase property insurance — a floater — that covers the specific property from loss due to any cause, including hostile and friendly fires.

   [9] See, e.g., Fire Ass'n of Philadelphia v. Nelson, 10 P.2d 943 (Colo. 1932); City of New York Ins. Co. v. Gugenheim, 7 S.W.2d 588 (Tex. Ct. App. 1928). Compare Washington State Hop Producers, Inc. v. Harbor Ins. Co., 660 P.2d 768 (Wash. Ct. App. 1983) (damage to hops stored in warehouse by browning where there is no evidence of flame is not covered by fire insurance policy).

   [10] See, e.g., Bowes v. North Carolina Farm Bur. Mut. Ins. Co., 215 S.E.2d 855 (N.C. Ct. App. 1975); O'Connor v. Queen Ins. Co. of Am., 122 N.W. 1038 (Wis. 1909).

considerable smoke damage. Is the fire friendly because it is maintained in a place where such fires are ordinarily intended? Or is the fire hostile because it is occurring at a time when no fire is intended, albeit in a normal place? Failure to extinguish the fire thoroughly is much like the negligence of the servant in *Austin,* but the reasonable expectations of the insured could be disappointed if recovery under the policy is not allowed.

Another difficult problem is presented by the cases where a fire burns at a normal, non-excessive rate in its usual place but for too long a time, leading to damage. *Engel v. Redwood Cty. Farmers Mut. Ins. Co.,*[11] a 1979 Minnesota case, is illustrative. The insured maintained a hog barn which was heated by a furnace controlled by a thermostat that could be adjusted to shut off the fan and furnace at a pre-set temperature. The insured set the thermostat at 75°, but a short in the thermostat allowed the furnace to continue to blow hot air into the barn until the temperature reached 120° and a high-limit control shut down the furnace. Almost all of the insured's hogs died due to inadequate oxygen caused by the excessive heat. At all times, the fire in the furnace burned at its usual rate in its usual place; no damage was caused to the barn, either by heat, smoke, or soot.

The insurer denied recovery on the ground that the fire was friendly. On its facts, the case strongly resembled *Austin,* except that the loss to the hog farmer was not caused by his negligence. The court in *Engel,* however, noted that the fire in *Austin* had been labeled as "not excessive." A fire that does not shut itself off as planned, in the court's view, constituted an excessive, uncontrolled fire and thus fell within the category of a hostile fire. Therefore, the insured was allowed to recover for his loss.

The result in *Engel* seems fair in the circumstances. The fire damage was a fortuitous, unexpected loss that the insured would reasonably expect (although perhaps this, too, is arguable) to be covered by his fire insurance. This approach has also been followed in two cases where thermostats in bakery ovens failed, causing the flames to burn too long and resulting in excessive heat and damage to the ovens.[12] Would the courts in these cases have allowed a recovery if the farmer or the bakers had accidentally set the thermostats too high, resulting in the losses? With those facts, these cases would be more like *Austin,* suggesting that coverage is less appropriate. Yet if someone negligently drops a lighted match, the resulting loss is covered by the fire insurance policy; why should a different result follow if the thermostat is negligently set, causing the fire to burn too long? If one concludes that a loss caused by negligently setting a thermostat should be covered, should a distinction be made between the baker who sets the thermostat too high and burns pies and the baker who makes the same error but destroys a $150,000 oven? The family cook who burns the evening meal because of setting the thermostat too high

---

[11] 281 N.W.2d 331 (Minn. 1979).

[12] See Schulze and Burch Biscuit Co. v. American Protection Ins. Co., 421 N.E.2d 331 (Ill. App. Ct. 1981); L.L. Freeburg Pie Co. v. St. Paul Mut. Ins. Co., 100 N.W.2d 753 (Minn. 1960). Other cases are consistent with these decisions. See, e.g., Bowes v. North Carolina Farm Bur. Mut. Ins. Co., 215 S.E.2d 855 (N.C. Ct. App. 1975); Barcalo Mfg. Co. v. Firemen's Mut. Ins. Co., 263 N.Y.S.2d 807 (N.Y. App. Div. 1965).

does not expect coverage under a fire insurance policy, but is the case different if the family's stove is ruined?

The hostile fire-friendly fire distinction is simply not a satisfactory doctrine with which to resolve such questions. Like many rules, its virtue is its apparent simplicity and seeming ability to obtain answers through mechanistic application, but upon further probing the rule's limitations become apparent. What the rule seeks to accomplish is to limit coverage to fortuitous, accidental losses not within the zone of the kind of losses that someone might reasonably expect from a course of doing business or day-to-day living. The burned pies are an expectable cost of doing business, and the ruined evening meal is a relatively common occurrence; for neither event is insurance coverage either sought or intended. If the hog farmer's only loss in *Engel* had been the cost of the extra gas needed to operate the furnace, one would probably be inclined to provide no coverage under the logic that such expenses are expectable costs of business. On the other hand, it is not expectable that hogs will be killed or ovens will be ruined from fires that burn too hot or too long. These kinds of losses, like the loss of the living room sofa due to a dropped cigarette or the loss of the roof due to a chimney fire, are the kinds for which insurance is sought and coverage is expected. The efforts of courts to escape the mechanistic answers suggested by the hostile fire-friendly fire distinction are best viewed as judicial efforts to serve the underlying purposes of the implied exception, without jettisoning the distinction altogether.

However, it is not inconceivable that future decisions might repudiate the distinction in favor of an approach more consistent with the evolving reasonable expectations doctrine. A notable case that might indicate the course of future decisions is *Sadlowski v. Liberty Mut. Ins. Co.,*[13] a 1984 Delaware case, where the court rejected the hostile fire-friendly fire distinction and opted for a reasonable expectations approach instead. In *Sadlowski,* the insureds' programmable thermostat allegedly malfunctioned, causing excessive fire and heat to be generated, which damaged the insured's home. The insurer moved for summary judgment on the ground that the damage was caused by a friendly fire, not a hostile fire, and thus the loss was not covered. The insureds urged the court to reject the friendly fire-hostile fire doctrine and to adopt a reasonable expectations approach, and the court agreed: "Because the insurance policy is ambiguous, it should be interpreted in accordance with the reasonable expectations of the purchaser, in this instance, plaintiffs."[14] Because no evidence of the insureds' expectations was set forth in the record, the insurer's motion for summary judgment was denied.[15]

---

[13] 487 A.2d 1146 (Del.Super.Ct. 1984).

[14] 487 A.2d at 1149.

[15] See generally John D. Ingram, *The Friendly Fire Doctrine: Judicial Construction Run Amok,* 22 Tort & Ins. L.J. 312 (1987) (favoring reasonable expectations approach).

§ 67   Coverage of Remote or Distant Causes of Loss

[a]   The Basic Problem

The concept of causation, at first glance, appears simple: if one event leads to another, it is said that the first event causes the later one. Unfortunately, life does not proceed in such a simple manner. As an English jurist explained, "[c]ausation is not a chain, but a net. At each point influences, forces, events, precedent and simultaneous, meet; and the radiation from each point extends infinitely."[1] How one views the "net of causation" depends upon one's vantage point. As explained by one scholar over a century ago:

> For each different purpose with which we investigate we shall find a different circumstance, which we shall then intelligibly and properly call the cause. The man may have committed suicide; we say he himself was the cause of his death. He may have been pushed into the water by another; we say that other person was the cause. The drowned man may have been blind, and have fallen in while his attendant was wrongfully absent; we say the negligence of his attendant was the cause. Suppose him to have been drowned at a ford which was unexpectedly swollen by rain; we may properly say that the height of the water was the cause of his death. A medical man may say that the cause of his death was suffocation by water entering his lungs. A comparative anatomist may say that the cause of his death was the fact that he had lungs instead of gills like a fish. The illustration might be carried to an indefinite extent. From every point of view from which we look at the facts, a new cause appears.[2]

The elusiveness of the concept of causation is highly relevant to insurance. Most insurance policies utilize somewhere in their text language of causation. A typical property insurance policy states that "the policy insures against all direct loss caused by" specified perils. Exclusions in the policy state that losses caused by other perils are not covered. A liability policy may state that coverage exists if the liability is caused by certain acts, or that no coverage exists if the loss is caused by other designated acts. In the double indemnity provision of a life insurance policy, the question of coverage may turn upon whether death was caused by an accident or by some nonaccidental cause. Language of causation is simple, but it disguises extremely complex and difficult legal questions.

This difficulty has led to a profusion of inconsistent cases on remarkably similar facts. To take one example, in *Abady v. Hanover Fire Insurance Co.*,[3] the insured's policy covered direct loss by windstorm, but excluded losses caused directly by frost or cold weather. The insured claimed that during a windstorm a hatch cover was blown off the roof of his building, allowing cold air to enter. As a result, the water

---

[1] Leyland Shipping Co. v. Norwich Union Fire Ins. Soc'y, Ltd., 32 T.L.R. 569 (1916), *aff'd*, 1 K.B. 873 (C.A. 1917), *aff'd*, A.C. 35, 369 (1918) (concurring opinion of Lord Shaw of Dunfermline).

[2] Green, *Proximate and Remote Cause,* 4 Am. L. Rev. 201, 212 (1870), *quoted in* William C. Brewer, *Concurrent Causation in Insurance Contracts,* 59 Mich. L. Rev. 1141, 1166 (1961).

[3] 266 F.2d 362 (4th Cir. 1959) (applying Virginia law).

pipes froze and burst, and his property was damaged. The court thought that the insured's evidence only showed a possibility that the wind had blown the hatch cover off the building; the court was influenced by the fact that the storm occurred eleven days prior to the discovery of the frozen pipes. But the court thought that even if the wind had dislodged the hatch cover, that event was too remote from the actual damage to fall within the policy's coverage. Thus, the court treated the cold weather, not the wind, as the cause of the loss, and denied coverage.

The facts of *Abady* are similar to those in *Mork v. Eureka-Security Fire and Marine Insurance Co.,* a 1950 Minnesota case.[4] An oil-burning furnace ceased to function because of an explosion in its combustion chamber. (The explosion was preceded by a leak in the hot water coil in the chamber; when the leaking water came in contact with the hot firebricks, it immediately created enough steam to cause the explosion.) The explosion, which did not damage any property outside the combustion chamber, led to a loss of heat, which in turn resulted in frozen pipes which burst and caused a loss. The question was whether the loss caused by the frozen pipes, a noncovered peril, was "direct loss or damage by explosion" under a fire policy. The court reasoned that the type of explosion was reasonably foreseeable, and that the freezing was a foreseeable, immediate, and direct result of the explosion even though the explosion did not damage anything outside the furnace. Accordingly, the court concluded that the frozen pipe damage was covered under the fire insurance policy.

One can, of course, construct explanations that seem to reconcile these results. In *Abady*, the reasonable factfinder might be less certain that the insured took adequate precautions to protect his property. Perhaps the hatch was left open by the insured when he was repairing the roof; even if the windstorm removed the hatch, he knew that a serious windstorm had occurred but arguably did not use due diligence to inspect his property, even though he should have known that wind damage can precipitate a more serious problem in the cold weather. A hot water coil inside a furnace is more difficult to inspect, and in *Mork* there is no apparent factual predicate for suggesting that the insured failed to correct a known hazard. But from the perspective of causation, one simple fact remains: one court (*Mork*) was willing to look farther back in the chain of causation than the other court (*Abady*) and this made all of the difference in the outcomes.

Because causation as a theory or doctrine is so elusive, inconsistent outcomes in the cases must be expected, and these differing outcomes will often turn on subtle factual distinctions. The attempted reconciliation of the cases above is, therefore, important, for it provides a basis for explaining why one court was willing to go farther back in the chain than the other. Perhaps the most useful exercise, then, to help garner an understanding of causation issues in insurance law is to construct a framework for discussing causation issues, a framework on which fact patterns will be hung and analyzed during the process of determining whether a loss was caused by a covered risk or some other risk outside the coverage.

---

[4] 42 N.W.2d 33 (Minn. 1950).

[b]   The Doctrine of the Efficient or Predominant Cause

Through the years numerous scholars have articulated frameworks for the analysis of causation issues in insurance law.[5] None of these frameworks, however, has had any apparent sustained influence on the development of the law of causation, and the terminology offered in each has not become a part of the legal vocabulary. This discussion begins with an explanation of the most common approach to resolving causation issues, and from this starting point additional observations will be made.

The prevailing approach to multiple causation is, in some respects, disappointing in its apparent simplicity: under the approach to causation followed by most courts, if multiple concurrent causes exist and if the dominant, most significant, or most important cause is a covered peril, coverage exists for the entire loss; otherwise, the loss is not covered.[6] This is, one would hope, the common-sense answer most people would give if asked what circumstances produced a particular loss. In some cases, the issue and the analysis are probably no more difficult than that. Three cases are selected here to illustrate the prevailing approach.

Consider first *Shinrone, Inc. v. Insurance Co. of North America.*[7] The insureds' calves were killed during a storm that produced high winds, damp snow, and muddy field conditions. The policy insured the livestock against death by windstorm, but did not cover for loss caused by "dampness of the atmosphere or extremes of temperature." Expert testimony indicated that the calves died due to a combination of causes — wind, cold temperature, snow, the size and age of the cattle, the muddy conditions, and the lack of adequate wind protection. The trial court gave an instruction that asked the jury to determine whether the windstorm was the "efficient

---

[5] The most widely known is that articulated by Professor Patterson in the first edition of his historic insurance law treatise. See Edwin W. Patterson, *Essentials of Insurance Law* 199-235 (1935). In the second edition, he expanded and elaborated upon his framework. See Edwin W. Patterson, *Essentials of Insurance Law* 226-71 (2d ed. 1957). A modified version of this framework was offered in the first edition of Professor Robert Keeton's insurance law treatise. See Robert E. Keeton, *Insurance Law: Basic Text* 306-19 (1971). A thoughtful but not widely discussed framework appeared in William C. Brewer, Jr., *Concurrent Causation In Insurance Contracts,* 59 Mich. L. Rev. 1141 (1961). The same can be said of R. Dennis Withers, *Proximate Cause and Multiple Causation in First-Party Insurance Cases,* 20 Forum 256 (1985). The first edition of this text articulated yet another framework which was more closely related to Brewer's analysis than the others. See Robert H. Jerry, II, *Understanding Insurance Law* 361-64 (1987).

[6] See, e.g., Ovbey v. Continental Ins. Co., 613 F. Supp. 726 (N.D. Ga. 1985), *aff'd without opinion,* 782 F.2d 178 (11th Cir. 1986); Essex House v. St. Paul Fire & Marine Ins. Co., 404 F. Supp. 978 (S.D. Ohio 1975); Vanguard Ins. Co. v. Clarke, 475 N.W.2d 48 (Mich. 1991); Grace v. Lititz Mutual Ins. Co., 257 So. 2d 217 (Miss. 1972); Frontis v. Milwaukee Ins. Co., 242 A.2d 749 (Conn. 1968); La Bris v. Western Nat'l Ins. Co., 59 S.E.2d 236 (W.Va. 1950); Pennsylvania Fire Ins. Co. v. Sikes, 168 P.2d 1016 (Okla. 1946); Holcomb v. United States Fire Ins. Co., 279 S.E.2d 50 (N.C. Ct. App. 1981); Stephens v. Cotton States Mut. Ins. Co., 121 S.E.2d 838 (Ga. Ct. App. 1961).

[7] 570 F.2d 715 (8th Cir. 1978). *Shinrone* is the subject of B. Joan White, *Reformation of Policy May Be Obtained on Ground of Mutual Mistake Even Where Agent's Representations Exceed Principal's Scope of Business,* 27 Drake L. Rev. 749 (1978).

or proximate cause of loss, notwithstanding the contribution of other factors to the loss."[8] The jury returned a verdict for the insured. The insurer's challenge to the trial court's instruction as an incorrect statement of the law was rejected on appeal, and the jury's verdict was affirmed. The insurer argued that if the wind had blown a barn down, thereby killing the cattle, the loss would be covered; but this is not what happened here; the wind alone did not kill the cattle; it was only because the wind blew the cold air and snow, in combination with the other factors, that the cattle died. The excluded cause of "extreme temperature" being a but-for cause of the cattle's death, it does not follow that the windstorm "caused" the loss of the cattle. But the jury agreed with the insured: among all of the causes, the wind was the most important; the wind enhanced the effect of all other causes; the temperature without wind may have been tolerable to the cattle, but the wind is what dropped the "effective temperature" to extreme levels; the wind was the dominant, the most important, the efficient cause of the loss.

A very similar analytic approach was followed by the court in *Graham v. Public Employees Mutual Insurance Co.,*[9] which arose out of events following the May 18, 1980 eruption of Mt. St. Helens. After the eruption, the first volcanic flows, accompanied by hot ash and debris, began melting the snow and ice around the mountain and glacial ice blocks in the Toutle River valley. This water combined with torrential rains from the eruption cloud, existing ground water, water displaced from Spirit Lake, and ash and debris, all of which created mudflows that began moving down the River valley after the eruption began. About ten hours after the eruption, the insureds' homes, twenty to twenty-five miles from the mountain, were destroyed by a mudflow after having been damaged by the flooding which preceded it. The homeowner's policies possessed by insureds excluded "loss resulting directly or indirectly from . . . 2. Earth Movement. Direct loss by fire, explosion, theft, . . . resulting from earth movement is covered. 3. Water damage, meaning: a. flood, ..." The insurers denied the insureds' claims on the ground that the damage was excludable as "earth movement" in the form of mudflows or a combination of earth movement and water damage. The trial court entered a summary judgment for the insurers.

The Washington Supreme Court vacated the summary judgment and remanded the case for a trial. The court said that whether the movement of Mt. St. Helens constituted an "explosion" within the terms of the insurance policies was a question of fact appropriate for jury determination. Also, the court said that "[b]ecause direct loss from an explosion resulting from earth movement is not excluded from coverage, the jury must also determine the factual issue of whether the earth movements were caused by the earthquakes and harmonic tremors which preceded the eruption."[10] If the jury were to determine that the eruption was an explosion resulting from earth movement, "it will then be necessary to reach the issue of whether the loss was a direct result of the eruption."[11]

---

[8] 570 F.2d at 718.

[9] 656 P.2d 1077 (Wash. 1983) (en banc).

[10] 656 P.2d at 1080.

[11] 656 P.2d at 1080.

To determine whether the loss was caused by the eruption (i.e. explosion), the court posited the following test:

> Where a peril specifically insured against sets other causes in motion which, in an unbroken sequence and connection between the act and final loss, produce the result for which recovery is sought, the insured peril is regarded as the "proximate cause" of the entire loss . . . .
>
> It is the efficient or predominant cause which sets into motion the chain of events producing the loss which is regarded as the proximate cause, not necessarily the last act in a chain of events.[12]

The court said that at trial the jury might find that the eruption was the dominant cause of the loss. The court observed that the mudflows would not have occurred without the eruption of the mountain, and a jury might find that the mudflows and other effects of the eruption were "mere manifestations of the eruption,"[13] potentially a covered cause.

Graham explicitly overruled *Bruener v. Twin City Fire Insurance Co.,*[14] which had adopted "immediate physical cause analysis," an approach that declared the last physical cause before the result would determine whether the loss was covered or not. As subsequently described by the court, the efficient proximate cause rule in Washington shifted the focus away from the last cause:

> By its own terms, the efficient proximate cause rule operates when an "insured risk" or covered peril sets into motion a chain of causation which leads to an uncovered loss. . . . If the efficient proximate cause of the final loss is a covered peril, then the loss is covered under the policy. In chain of causation cases, the efficient proximate cause rule is properly applied after (1) a determination of which single act or event is the efficient proximate cause of the loss and (2) a determination that the efficient proximate cause of the loss is a covered peril.[15]

The court in *Graham* had in mind that the jury might find the eruption to be an explosion and that the eruption was the efficient proximate cause in the sequence of events, i.e., the cause that set a chain of events in motion. Yet there is something ephemeral about viewing the eruption as the first cause, because the eruption itself was a product of earlier causes: the eruption was preceded by earthquakes and other earth movements that allowed magma to move toward the surface of the earth where the eruption would occur, and the earthquakes themselves could be said to be a product of shifting plates that are part and parcel of the process of continental drift. At the same time one recognizes that the event of the eruption itself has prior causes, it is apparent that choosing the efficient proximate, or dominant, cause involves exploring a web or chain of interconnected events and choosing the one that is the most important.

The third illustrative case has figured prominently in the evolution of causation rules in California. *Garvey v. State Farm Fire and Cas. Co.,*[16] involved the

---

[12] 656 P.2d at 1081.

[13] 656 P.2d at 1081.

[14] 222 P.2d 833 (Wash. 1950).

[15] McDonald v. State Farm Fire & Cas. Co., 837 P.2d 1000, 1004 (Wash. 1992).

[16] 770 P.2d 704 (Cal. 1989).

following facts: the insureds purchased their house in the mid-1970s; they soon noticed that an addition constructed in the early 1960s had begun to pull away from the main structure. The insureds' homeowner's policy excluded coverage for damage caused by earth movement but covered damage caused by negligence. The insureds argued that their loss was caused by negligent construction and was therefore covered; the insurer argued that the loss was caused by earth movement and was therefore not covered. The trial court instructed the jury, consistently with *Partridge,* that if one of the covered causes contributed to the loss, the insurer was liable for all of the damage. The jury found the insurer liable for $47,000 in policy benefits and $1 million in punitive damages. The insurer appealed.

In a split decision, the court of appeals reversed the entire judgment and sent the case back for a new trial.[17] This result was affirmed by a divided state supreme court, but the reasoning the court of appeals used to support the affirmance was rejected by the Supreme Court.[18] The court began its analysis by referring to its 1963 decision in *Sabella v. Wisler.*[19] In that case, inadequate fill (an excluded cause) led to the rupture of an improperly installed sewer pipe (a covered cause) which in turn caused water to leak from the pipe, which accelerated settling of the fill (an excluded cause), which severely damaged the foundation of the insured's dwelling. The *Sabella* court searched for the "moving" (or "efficient," "prime," or "proximate") cause, and concluded that because the broken sewer pipe was the moving cause, the loss was covered. As the court explained in *Sabella*:

> [I]n determining whether a loss is within an exception in a policy, where there is a concurrence of different causes, the efficient cause — the one that sets others in motion — is the cause to which the loss is to be attributed, though the other causes may follow it, and operate more immediately in producing the disaster.[20]

The court in *Garvey* elaborated:

> [W]e impliedly recognized that coverage would not exist if the covered risk was simply a remote cause of the loss, or if an excluded risk was the efficient proximate (meaning predominant) cause of the loss. On the other hand, the fact that na excluded risk contributed to the loss would not preclude coverage if such a risk was a remote cause of the loss.[21]

The court further explained that the analysis in *Sabella* "set forth a workable rule of coverage that provides a fair result within the reasonable expectations of both the insured and the insurer whenever there exists a causal or dependent relationship between covered and excluded perils."[22]

---

[17] 227 Cal. Rptr. 209 (Cal. Ct. App. 1986).

[18] The superseded reasoning of the court of appeals need not be pursued in depth here. The court of appeals' reasoning is explained and critiqued in the first edition of this text. See Robert H. Jerry, II, *Understanding Insurance Law* 371-73 (1987).

[19] 377 P.2d 889 (Cal. 1963).

[20] 377 P.2d at 895, quoting *Couch on Insurance* (1930) § 1466; passage quoted in *Garvey,* 770 P.2d at 707.

[21] 770 P.2d at 704.

[22] 770 P.2d at 708.

Having decided this much, the court was faced with the need to explain the meaning of its 1973 holding in *State Farm Mutual Automobile Insurance Co. v. Partridge,* [23] which has been described as the "leading case" on concurrent causation in other decisions.[24] In *Partridge,* the insured was covered under a homeowner's policy and an automobile policy, both issued by State Farm. The homeowner's policy contained an exclusion for injuries "arising out of the use" of an automobile. While negligently operating his vehicle, the insured caused the discharge of a .357 Magnum pistol, on which he had negligently filed down the gun trigger so as to have a sensitive "hair trigger." The discharge injured the insured's passenger. The issue was whether coverage existed for the insured's negligent acts under the homeowner's policy, despite the language of the exclusion clause. The court held the loss covered:

> Although there may be some question whether either of the two causes in the instant case can be properly characterized as the "prime," "moving" or "efficient" cause of the accident, we believe that coverage under a liability insurance policy is equally available to an insured whenever an insured risk constitutes simply *a* concurrent proximate cause of the injuries.[25]

Cases in California subsequent to *Partridge* followed the rule that where the loss occurs through a concurrence of covered and uncovered risks, the insurer is liable as long as one of the covered risks is a proximate cause,[26] and the *Partridge* analysis was not limited to the third-party setting. In addition, the reasoning of *Partridge* was followed in decisions outside California as well.[27]

---

[23] 514 P.2d 123 (Cal. 1973).

[24] See, e.g., Vanguard Ins. Co. v. Clarke, 475 N.W.2d 48 (Mich. 1991); Warrilow v. Norrell, 791 S.W.2d 515 (Tex. Ct. App. 1989); Mission Nat'l Ins. Co. v. Coachella Valley Water Dist., 258 Cal. Rptr. 639 (Cal. Ct. App. 1989).

[25] 514 P.2d at 130 (emphasis original). Partridge was followed in a first-party setting by the Ninth Circuit in Safeco Ins. Co. of Am. v. Guyton, 692 F.2d 551 (9th Cir. 1982). The insureds were covered under an all-risk policy which excluded loss "caused by, resulting from, contributed to or aggravated by . . . flood, surface water, waves, overflow of streams or other bodies of water, or spray from any of the foregoing, all whether driven by wind or not . . . ." A record rain accompanying a hurricane resulted in a flood that destroyed the insureds' property. The homeowners claimed that one of the proximate causes of the loss was the negligence of third persons in erecting and maintaining flood control facilities, a cause that was covered under the policy. The insurance companies sought a declaratory judgment that the policy did not cover the loss suffered, even though one proximate cause of the loss, third-party negligence, was covered. The district court agreed with the insurers and held that because the exclusionary clause barred recovery for flood, the policyholders were not entitled to damages: the flood control structures would not have collapsed but for the flood, which was an excluded cause. The Ninth Circuit reversed, holding that the insureds were entitled to recover because one of the proximate causes, third-party negligence, was a covered cause. In Garvey, as discussed in the text which follows, the court disavowed Guyton as an impermissible application of concurrent cause theory in a first-party setting.

[26] E.g., Premier Ins. Co. v. Welch, 189 Cal. Rptr. 657 (Cal. Ct. App. 1983); Farmers Ins. Exch. v. Adams, 216 Cal. Rptr. 287 (Cal. Ct. App. 1985).

[27] E.g., General Am. Transp. Corp. v. Sun Ins. Office, Ltd., 239 F. Supp. 844 (E.D. Tenn. 1965), aff'd, 369 F.2d 906 (6th Cir. 1966) (negligent welding by insured's workmen of flange

In *Garvey*, the court said it was inappropriate to use *Partridge*-type analysis in first-party insurance. After describing the obvious differences between first-party and third-party insurance,[28] the court explained that allowing any concurrent proximate cause to bring a loss within coverage in the property setting would "require[] ordinary insureds to bear the expense of increased premiums necessitated by the erroneous expansion of their insurers' potential liabilities"[29] because "[i]n most instances, the insured can point to some arguably covered contributing factor."[30]

Applying these rules to the facts of *Garvey*, the court concluded:

> "This case presents a classic *Sabella* situation. Coverage should be determined by a jury under an efficient proximate cause analysis. Accordingly, bearing in mind the facts here, we conclude the question of causation is for the jury to decide. If the earth movement was the efficient proximate cause of the loss, then coverage would be denied under *Sabella*. the other hand, if negligence was the efficient proximate cause of the loss, then coverage exists under *Sabella*.[31]

Thus, although it appeared for a time that California might lead the way in approving a more liberal approach to causation analysis, *Garvey* rejected the more liberal approach for first-party insurance, and one member of the Supreme Court would have abandoned it for third-party insurance as well. The more liberal approach to causation is discussed in the next subsection.

[c] The Liberal View of Causation

Partridge, discussed above, represents a different approach to causation than that found in cases adhering to the efficient proximate cause rule, and the difference is significant. *Partridge* reasons that where two causes both arise and operate independently of each other to produce a loss, the loss is covered if one of the causes is a covered peril. Presumably one assumption of this reasoning is that in a case where it is appropriate to apply *Partridge* it will be difficult or even impossible to segregate the independent causes and determine which one is the dominant one. An example of such a situation might involve the named insured negligently operating

---

at insert at a truss, a covered peril, which caused an entire structure to collapse, justifies coverage, even though other noncovered causes may have proximately contributed to the loss); Essex House v. St. Paul Fire & Marine Ins. Co., 404 F. Supp. 978 (S.D. Ohio 1975) (approving *General Am. Transp.*); Mattis v. State Farm Fire and Cas. Co., 454 N.E.2d 1156 (Ill. App. Ct. 1983) (improper design and construction, a covered peril, combines with settling of soil, excluded, to produce loss; court holds that coverage exists, without discussion of which cause was dominant); Benke v. Mukwonago-Vernon Mutual Ins. Co., 329 N.W.2d 243 (Wis. Ct. App. 1982) (snow on roof, excluded, combines with wind, covered, to blow down stable; court holds coverage exists, without discussion of which cause was dominant).

[28] 770 P.2d at 709-10.

[29] 770 P.2d at 711.

[30] 770 P.2d at 711.

[31] 770 P.2d at 715. But see Key Tronic Corp., Inc. v. Aetna (CIGNA) Fire Underwriters Ins. Co., 881 P.2d 201 (Wash. 1994) (en banc) (efficient, proximate cause rule means that efficient, covered cause which sets in motion a chain leading to loss will result in coverage; but it does not follow that efficient, excluded cause which sets in motion a chain leading to loss will result in no coverage).

a vehicle and running over the victim (an excluded cause in a homeowner's policy) at the same time the named insured's spouse negligently fells a tree in a direction that causes it to injure the victim (a covered cause). Concluding, as *Partridge* directs, that the presence and operation of an excluded cause at the time of the loss does not take away coverage makes much sense in this setting.

Unfortunately, it was not clear in *Partridge* that the facts were truly independent, even though the court described them as such. It is correct, as the court explained, that the filing of the trigger did not cause the negligent operation of the vehicle, and the negligent operation of the vehicle did not cause the filing of the trigger. It is also correct that these two causes combined to produce the loss, where neither by itself would have led to the loss.[32] In other words, as the court explained, the two causes *arose* independently, but how the clauses *operated* was a different question which the court failed to analyze separately. As Justice Kaufman pointed out in his concurrence in *Garvey*,[33] the hair-triggered weapon was an accident waiting to happen, but this cause was activated by and was dependent upon the other cause — the bouncing of the vehicle as it was operated negligently while the gun was pointed at the passenger. The causes arose independently, but they operated dependently. Under *Sabella*-type analysis, the efficient proximate cause was the negligent operation of the vehicle, which put in motion a chain of events that led to the discharge of the weapon.

Because most fact patterns lend themselves to some kind of sequential ordering (that is, it is a rare case where "the concurrent causes of [an] injury were wholly independent of each other and related to the injury in such a way that neither could fairly be said to be the 'efficient' or 'predominant' cause of the injury"[34], what *Partridge* invites by approving the liberal approach in the fact pattern involved in that case is a conclusion, even in cases where one cause in a multiple-cause situation results from another, that the causes are independent, even when they might not be, and therefore the loss is covered as long as any one of the causes involved is a covered cause.

Thus, *Partridge* is a much more liberal approach to coverage: as long as the insured can point to one covered cause in a multiple-cause situation where the causes are arguably independent, the insured has a good chance of establishing coverage. What *Garvey* did was to confine the liberal approach to coverage to liability insurance cases, and to reserve the *Sabella*-type analysis for first-party insurance cases. What would the court do if it were faced with a first-party insurance case where the two causes arose and operated independently to produce the loss? The court recognized this possibility in a footnote and even offered an example of such a situation: suppose an aircraft crashes into a house during an earthquake.[35] The court said it would leave that question for another day, but such a case would seem to be a very appropriate one for the outcome *Partridge* has always suggested: as

---

[32] 514 P.2d at 130.

[33] 770 P.2d at 715.

[34] 770 P.2d at 716, (Kaufman, J., concurring).

[35] 770 P.2d at 713 n.9.

long as one of the causes is covered, the entire loss is covered, notwithstanding the presence of excluded or noncovered causes.

Whether *Garvey* should have abandoned the liberal approach for all cases, as Justice Kaufman suggested should occur,[36] is a fair question. Instead, it may make more sense to have a system where one searches for the dominant, efficient, proximate cause in all cases, and in those cases where it is impossible to pick one such cause where covered and excluded causes combine to produce a loss, one finds coverage under the reasoning that ties go to the insured, which may be what *Partridge* has stood for all along. Yet it is understandable why the court in *Garvey* felt obligated to repudiate the liberal approach for first-party coverage. The prospects for a devastating earthquake in California in the foreseeable future are high, and in that event (as has been apparent in the smaller, but serious earthquakes of recent years) covered losses (e.g., fire) will combine with excluded losses (e.g., earthquake) to produce losses. From the perspective of an industry which has inadequate reserves at present to handle the major earthquake catastrophe, the notion that any covered cause existing in a net of causes results automatically in coverage is unacceptable. Some have argued that the industry never intended to provide such broad coverage.[37] The liberal approach, however, remains the law of California in liability insurance and, as noted above, has some scattered support in other jurisdictions.

[d] The Conservative View of Causation

At the opposite end of the spectrum is an alternative view of causation followed by a few courts and, more importantly, favored in many recently drafted standardized forms. Under this approach, if a covered cause combines with an excluded cause to produce the loss, the insured may not recover.

The use of the phrase "excluded cause" in the formulation of this approach is important. The conservative approach distinguishes between "excluded causes" and "noncovered causes": an excluded clause is explicitly excluded from coverage, but a noncovered cause is one not covered but not explicitly excluded. If a covered cause combines with a noncovered, but not excluded, cause to produce a loss, no court appears to deny coverage simply because the noncovered cause contributes to the loss; rather, if the covered cause is the dominant, efficient cause of the loss, coverage exists notwithstanding the contribution of an uncovered cause.[38] The conservative approach denies coverage when a covered cause combines with an excluded cause to produce the loss.

---

[36] 770 P.2d at 715 (Kaufman, J., concurring) ("I am doubtful that those differences [between first- and third-party insurance] compel or warrant two separate and entirely different rules for ascertaining the coverage provided by the two kinds of policies.")

[37] See Stuart M. Gordon & Diane R. Crowley, *Earth Movement and Water Damage Exposure: A Landslide in Coverage,* 50 Ins. Counsel J. 418, 425 (1983); Michael E. Bragg, *Concurrent Causation and the Art of Policy Drafting: New Perils for Property Insurers,* 20 Forum 385 (1985).

[38] E.g., Goodman v. Fireman's Fund Ins. Co., 600 F.2d 1040 (4th Cir. 1979); Beattie Bonded Warehouse Co. v. General Acci. Fire & Life Assur. Corp., 315 F. Supp. 996 (D.S.C. 1970); Graff v. Farmer's Mut. Home Ins. Co., 317 N.W.2d 741 (Neb. 1982); Federal Ins. Co v. Bock, 382 S.W.2d 305 (Tex. Ct. App. 1964).

The logic of the conservative approach is that the insurer should not be held responsible for any damage caused by an excluded peril. However, if part of a loss can be segregated and attributed to an excluded peril, the insured is entitled to recover for that portion of the loss attributed to the covered peril. When the segregation is difficult or impossible, the loss is not covered (i.e., ties go to the insurer).

A decision which purports to apply this approach is *Lydick v. Insurance Co. of North America*,[39] a 1971 Nebraska case. The insured had a policy covering his cattle for damage caused as the direct result of windstorm, but the policy excluded damage caused directly or indirectly by cold weather or ice. The insured claimed that his cattle descended into a sheltered area around a pond covered with ice and snow to seek protection against wind and cold. The cattle went upon the frozen pond, but the ice broke and the cattle drowned. The Nebraska Supreme Court affirmed a summary judgment for the insurer, holding that the immediate and direct cause of the loss was the collapse of the ice on which the cattle stood, an excluded cause. The court described its rule as follows: "The general rule that if a windstorm combines with a hazard expressly excluded from the policy coverage to produce the loss, the insured may not recover."[40]

Upon closer scrutiny, however, *Lydick* — notwithstanding the court's statement of a rule at odds with the majority approach — could have been decided the same way under the efficient proximate cause approach applied in most jurisdictions. Under the facts of that case, falling through the ice was arguably the dominant, efficient cause of the loss, not the windstorm. The undisputed testimony was that the loss would not have occurred but for the wind, but the same could be said of numerous other causes, all of which were excluded: the loss would not have occurred but for the cold weather, but for the fact that the most convenient shelter was a depression in which an ice-covered pond was located, but for the frozen ice, but for the three or four inches of snow on the ice that made the cattle willing to venture onto the ice, but for the thinness of the ice, and but for the fact over one hundred cattle gathered on the ice at the same time. Under these circumstances, a holding that the ice was the dominant cause of the loss would have been quite defensible.

In short, a number of courts are less willing to find coverage in concurrent causation cases, and these courts purport to follow the rule that whenever an excluded cause combines with a covered cause to produce a loss, no coverage exists.[41] Although it may be possible to explain these results under the efficient proximate cause approach, the conservative rule these courts purport to follow cannot be reconciled with the prevailing rule.

---

[39] 187 N.W.2d 602 (Neb. 1971).

[40] 187 N.W.2d at 605.

[41] E.g., Abady v. Hanover Fire Ins. Co., 266 F.2d 362 (4th Cir. 1959); Niagara Fire Ins. Co. v. Muhle, 208 F.2d 191 (8th Cir. 1953); Grain Dealers Mut. Ins. Co. v. Belk, 269 So. 2d 637 (Miss. 1972); Miller v. Farmers' Mut. Fire Ins. Ass'n, 152 S.E. 684 (N.C. 1930); National Fire Ins. Co. v. Crutchfield, 170 S.W. 187 (Ky. 1914); but see Wood v. Michigan Millers Mut. Fire Ins. Co., 96 S.E.2d 28 (N.C. 1957), which appears to adopt the prevailing view; Coyle v. Palatine Ins Co., 222 S.W. 973 (Tex. Ct. App. 1920).

During the last decade, insurers have revised their standardized forms in an apparent effort to make the conservative approach the controlling theory for sorting out causation issues in insurance. The court in *Garvey* alluded to this major change in policy language in a footnote, and expressly limited the scope of its opinion to policies that did not contain the new language.[42] For example, in the 1990 version of the homeowner's property form drafted by the ISO, the language introducing the policy's exclusions states: "We do not insure for loss caused directly or indirectly by any of the following. Such loss is excluded regardless of any other cause or event contributing concurrently or in any sequence to the loss."[43] By its terms, this language seems to say that if an excluded cause is part of any sequence that results in a loss, the loss is not covered, even if a covered cause contributes concurrently or sequentially to the loss. So construed, this language greatly narrows coverage. An earthquake (which is excluded) which results in a fire loss would be outside coverage. A windstorm (covered) which produces a large wave (excluded) that destroys a building would be outside the coverage, even if the wind produces the wave. Because "neglect" (defined as "neglect of the 'insured' to use all reasonable means to save and preserve property at and after the time of loss") is excluded, the insured's neglect at any point in the sequence of events, no matter how insignificant relative to the other causes contributing to the loss, would take the entire loss out of coverage. It remains to be seen whether this language, which is potentially very restrictive on coverage in some circumstances where reasonable expectations would be defeated, will be enforced as strictly as insurers no doubt intended it.

Although the "arising out of" language has been used for a long time to define and limit coverage, this language has the potential to affect causation issues in substantial ways. This phrase, pursuant to interpretations urged by insurers, functions to place outside the coverage any event that is related directly or indirectly to whatever the phrase "arising out of" modifies. For example, in one recent case, a patron at a tavern was injured in an altercation with a member of the tavern's security staff. The insurer alleged that it was not liable for injuries "arising out of assault and battery or out of any act or omission" resulting in assault and battery, and that this precluded coverage, even though the patron alleged a concurrent cause of the tavern's negligent hiring and supervision of its employees. The court held that the fact that the concurrent cause in negligence may have contributed to the patron's injuries did not change the fact that his injury "arose out of" an assault and battery, and hence that the policy exclusion precluded coverage.[44] Similarly, one court has held that an exclusion in a CGL policy for injuries "arising out of" the ownership, maintenance, operation, and use of any automobile owned by the insured precluded coverage under the policy for injuries suffered by a passenger in a logging truck, regardless of whether the injuries were caused by improper loading of the vehicle or failure to maintain functioning brakes.[45] The upshot of the argument is that if a loss is connected in some way, *i.e.* arises out of the operation of the excluded

---

[42] 770 P.2d at 710 n.6.

[43] *Policy Kit* at 25 (ISO Form HO 00 03 04 91).

[44] See Sphere Drake Ins. Co. v. Ross, 609 N.E.2d 1284 (Ohio Ct.App. 1992).

[45] First Fin. Ins. Co. v. National Indem. Co., 898 S.W.2d 63 (Ark.Ct.App. 1995).

cause, no coverage exists.[46] Other courts have insisted upon a "but for" causal relationship, but if the "arising out of" event fits anywhere in the sequence of causation, the "but for" test will have the effect of taking the loss out of coverage.[47] This has the effect of drawing all concurrent causes, no matter how substantial, proximate, or efficient, into the umbrella of the "arising out of" exclusion. This greatly constrains coverage, and as a result, some courts have refused to give "arising out of" a broad range of operation, particularly "where a nonexcluded cause is a substantial factor in producing the damage or injury."[48]

[e] Other Causation Frameworks

[1] The Patterson Framework

Probably the most detailed system of terminology in the area of causation was articulated by Professor Patterson. In his first insurance treatise, he sketched a distinction between exceptions and exclusions.[49] Twenty-two years later in the second edition of his treatise, he offered a more elaborate system for explaining the results in these cases.[50]

In detailing the specific kinds of coverage clauses,[51] Patterson thought it possible to distinguish three concepts — cause, event, and result. A lighted match (the cause) might cause the fire (the event) which results in the destruction of the house (the loss).[52] Two initial difficulties are apparent. Why not view the fire as a cause of

---

[46] See, e.g., Holy Trinity Church of God in Christ v. Aetna Cas. & Sur. Co., 571 A.2d 107 (Conn. 1990) (exclusion in church's comprehensive liability policy for injury and damage "arising out of" demolition operations performed by or on behalf of insured unambiguously signified that causal relationship between injury and excluded activity removed injury from ambit of policy's coverage); New Hampshire Ins. Co. v. Jefferson Ins. Co. of N.Y., 624 N.Y.S.2d 392 (N.Y. App. Div. 1995); Krempl v. Unigard Sec. Ins. Co., 850 P.2d 533 (Wash. Ct. App. 1993) (it is not necessary to analyze causation issues when policy contains "arising out of" language; held, no coverage where injury flowed from use of auto, even if covered causes followed in chain of events). For more discussion of "use" in this context, see § 136A, *infra*.

[47] For decisions approving the "but for" analysis of "arising out of," see Northern Ins. Co. of N.Y. v. Ekstrom, 784 P.2d 320 (Colo. 1989) (en banc); Shell Oil Co. v. AC&S, Inc., 649 N.E.2d 946 (Ill. App. Ct. 1995).

[48] See Allstate Ins. Co. v. Watts, 811 S.W.2d 883, 887 (Tenn. 1991).

[49] See Edwin W. Patterson, *Essentials of Insurance Law* 199–235 (1935).

[50] See Edwin W. Patterson, *Essentials of Insurance Law* 226–71 (2d ed. 1957).

[51] At the outset, Patterson distinguished between "coverage provisions" and "warranties." A coverage provision has one or more characteristics: (1) it deals with actual causes of loss, as distinguished from potential causes of loss; (2) it deals with the existence of facts that determine whether an insured event has occurred, as distinguished from facts that affect the risk that an insured event will occur; (3) it identifies the risk, as opposed to ameliorates the risk; (4) it determines the scope of coverage according to the cause of loss, as opposed to suspending coverage irrespective of the cause of loss. *Id.* at 230–31, 249. Warranty provisions, in contrast, deal with potential causes of loss, facts that affect the risk that an insured event will occur, amelioration of risk, and suspending coverage without regard to cause. *Id.* at 254, 282–83.

[52] *Id.* at 230–35, 249, 257.

the loss? And what is to be done when the chain of causes and events is longer? Is the cause immediately prior to the loss an event, or can something farther "upstream" be an event? Patterson understood this difficulty; he wrote that "[t]he insured event is a cause of its subsequent consequences and is itself a consequence of antecedent causes." [53]

Yet taking the three concepts — cause, event, and result — as givens, Patterson based three definitions of kinds of coverage clauses on them. An "exception" concerns a cause of the insured event, an upstream link in the chain of causation; an "exclusion" concerns the event itself, the central link; and a "consequence clause" deals with the result, what ensues from the loss, which is the last link in the chain.[54]

A consequence clause might read as follows: "This policy does not cover loss of profits due to destruction of the insured property." This clause limits the coverage to certain kinds of results. Such a clause is similar to an exception in this sense: it does not limit what events are covered, but pares away at coverage by cutting back on end-results, in the same way that an exception does not limit what events are covered, but pares away at coverage by cutting back on the causes of the event that will be covered.

Identifying and distinguishing between exceptions and exclusions is the major difficulty in the Patterson framework. According to the framework, whether the policy uses the term "except" or "exclude" in focusing on the cause is not determinative. Rather, the label "exception" or "exclusion" is designed to describe the legal effect of the clause. For example, imagine a marine insurance policy that covers "all loss from perils of the sea . . . except for loss caused by . . . capture. . . ." If this clause is treated as an exclusion, no coverage exists in the event "capture" occurs. It is irrelevant if some peril of the sea contributed to the loss by making possible a capture that would not have occurred. The clause operates to exclude all loss connected with the event of capture. Alternatively, if the clause is treated as an exception, coverage would exist if a covered incident, such as a windstorm, occurs and the capture follows as a consequence of the windstorm. If the clause is an exception, the clause does not negate liability altogether, as does an exclusion, but merely states what pattern of facts are insufficient to fall within the policy's coverage.

The Patterson framework does not allow one to examine a policy and tell whether a particular provision limiting coverage is an exclusion or exception. Indeed, it is a disadvantage of the framework that neither drafters of policies nor courts use the Patterson terminology to describe the legal effect of clauses limiting coverage. However, the framework is a way to describe a judicial decision. To illustrate, consider this language from the comprehensive coverage of an automobile insurance policy: all risks are covered, except that no liability exists for "loss caused by collision or upset."

First, consider the outcomes if the clause is treated as an exclusion. A collision occurs, which results in a fire in the interior of the vehicle. Since the event of

---

[53] *Id.* at 248.
[54] *Id.* at 230–34, 249.

collision is conclusive against coverage, none of the loss is covered under the comprehensive policy. If the sequence is reversed, and a fire in the dashboard of the automobile, a covered cause, distracts the driver and results in a collision, the loss that can be segregated and tied to the fire is covered by the insurance policy, but the additional loss attributable to the collision is not covered. If it is not possible to segregate the fire loss and the collision loss, none of the loss is covered.

Now, consider the outcomes if the clause is treated as an exception. A collision occurs, which results in a fire in the interior of the vehicle. No coverage exists for the loss attributable to the collision, but the loss to which the fire was a contributing cause, if it is possible to segregate that loss, is recoverable. If the sequence is reversed, and a fire in the dashboard of the automobile distracts the driver and results in a collision, coverage exists for the entire loss on the theory that fire caused the entire loss.

A pair of contrasting cases can be used to illustrate how the Patterson framework can categorize cases. In *Bruener v. Twin City Fire Insurance Co.,*[55] the insured's vehicle skidded on icy pavement and collided with an embankment. The comprehensive coverage purported to cover "[a]ny direct and accidental loss of or damage to the automobile except loss caused by collision of the automobile with another object or by upset of the automobile. . . ."[56] The issue was whether the loss was caused by collision and thus not covered. The court concluded that the loss was caused by collision: "we find no difficulty in attributing the injury to [the collision with the embankment], rather than the skidding because had there been only a skidding there would have been no damage. The collision itself is the direct, violent and efficient cause of the damage."[57] In *Bruener,* the court treated the collision and upset provision as an exclusion. Even though a covered peril, skidding, contributed to the loss, the collision was treated as an event to which no coverage would attach for loss resulting therefrom.[58]

In contrast to *Bruener* is *Standard Accident Insurance Co. v. Christy.*[59] The insured carried comprehensive automobile coverage which excluded loss due to

---

[55] 222 P.2d 833 (Wash. 1950). *Bruener* was subsequently overruled in Graham v. Public Employees Mut. Ins. Co., 656 P.2d 1077 (Wash. 1983) (en banc).

[56] 222 P.2d at 834.

[57] 222 P.2d at 835.

[58] It is arguable that skidding is not a covered peril under comprehensive coverage, since comprehensive coverage is not intended for risks attendant to operating a vehicle. However, the policy in *Bruener* was apparently all risk coverage, in that the policy purported to cover "any direct and accidental loss of or damage to the automobile except loss caused by collision."

A similar case is Fogarty v. Fidelity & Cas. Co., 188 A. 481 (Conn. 1936), where the loss occurred when a fire broke out in the truck operated by the insured's employee, resulting in the driver veering the truck off the road, where a collision occurred and a fire entirely consumed the truck. The insured sought to bring the loss within its collision coverage which excluded damage by fire. Even though a collision contributed to the loss, the court concluded that the chain of causation commenced with the fire and that a fire insurance policy would have covered the whole loss. Therefore, the loss was damage by fire and the entire loss was not covered.

[59] 360 S.W.2d 195 (Ark. 1962).

mechanical failure. A fire of unexplained origin burned the radiator and air conditioner hoses of the insured's car while it was being operated. Water from the radiator extinguished the fire, but the loss of water in the cooling system caused severe damage to the motor before the insured became aware of the fire and was able to stop the car. The insured argued that the entire loss was caused by fire, a covered risk, and the court agreed. The court treated the mechanical failure provision as an exception, which was not conclusive as to coverage.

The Patterson framework can assist in categorizing cases, but the framework provides no help in predicting what results might emerge from facts like those in *Bruener* or *Christy*. Although Patterson's scheme is the most elaborate ever developed, drafters seem to pay no attention to his scheme when attaching labels to limits on coverage, and courts make little use of his framework either. Indeed, the framework is so complicated that some commentators who have tried to explain his framework have misunderstood it and misstated it.[60]

[2] The Brewer Framework

An analytical framework articulated by William Brewer in a 1961 article in the *Michigan Law Review*[61] provides additional insights into causation analysis. Brewer's scheme for analysis of causation assumes three kinds of cause.[62] An "actual cause" is a cause in fact. This term simply describes the relationship between an event and a result flowing from it, the so-called "chain" or "net" that ties events together. A "substantial cause" is an actual cause that has passed the test of remoteness. If a cause is too remote from the event in question, the cause will have no legal significance. A "responsible cause" is a substantial cause to which legal consequences should attach, meaning the cause to which the loss should be attributed. In essence, determining the responsible cause is tantamount to determining the proximate, efficient cause.

In Brewer's framework, a problem of "concurrent causation" can be described as a situation where two substantial causes combine with each other to cause a loss; the process of determining the rights of the parties in such a situation is essentially the process of labeling one of the substantial causes as the responsible (i.e., proximate, efficient) cause. To determine the responsible cause applying Brewer's framework, one would ask three questions: First, is the event in question an actual cause? Second, if so, does it constitute a substantial cause, or is it too remote? Third, if more than one substantial cause exists, which cause is responsible, that is, to which cause shall legal consequences be attached?[63] The first question involves essentially searching the world and finding an array of all potentially relevant causes. The second question asks which causes in this potentially huge array of causes should be disregarded under the reasoning that the causes are so remote as to lack any legal significance at all. The third question calls for an evaluation of the remaining causes

---

[60] See Brewer, note 2, *supra,* at 1162–63 (incorrectly describing legal effects of exceptions and exclusions); Robert E. Keeton, *Insurance Law* 309 n. 13 (1971) (noting two sources that appear to understand Patterson incorrectly).

[61] Brewer, note 2, *supra.*

[62] 59 Mich. L. Rev. at 1144.

[63] *Id.* at 1154.

to determine which is the most important, and therefore shall be determinative on the question of coverage.

The insights of Brewer, Patterson, and others, along with the analysis found in the many cases that have had explored this issue in the past, suggest a "dual-filter" framework for causation, which is discussed in the next subsection.

[3]   A Dual-Filter Approach To Causation

To restate the basic issue, whenever an insured cause joins with an excluded cause or an uncovered cause to create a loss, a problem of multiple causation exists. Multiple causation can give rise to a dispute between insurer and insured as to whether the loss was caused by a peril within coverage or by one outside the coverage.

Analyzing multiple causation is essential a process of applying two filters to a set of causes that produces a loss. At the outset, one determines the universe of causes that precedes, either directly or indirectly, a loss. Having done this, one then applies a *remoteness* filter. For example, in a chain or succession of causes (i.e., if A causes B, which in turn causes C, which in turn causes D, which in turn causes a loss), the application of the remoteness filter requires asking where in the chain one draws a line and declares all preceding events to be too remote to have legal significance. Thus, in a case like *Graham*, the application of the remoteness filter may rule out all causes of the loss preceding the eruption of Mt. St. Helens.

When the insurer and insured dispute coverage in connection with the remoteness filter, the issue is essentially how far back in the chain or succession of causation one should go in looking for a proximate, efficient cause. If a remote cause is excluded from coverage but a recent cause is covered, the insured will argue in favor of looking only to the most recent causes, while the insurer will argue that the search for the cause be extended to more remote causes. If the situation is reversed (so that the remote cause is covered and the recent cause excluded), the parties will argue the converse.

A pair of cases illustrate the application of the first filter.[64] Consider first leading case in the causation area, is *Bird v. St. Paul Fire & Marine Insurance Co.,*[65] a 1918 New York decision written by Justice Cardozo. In *Bird,* the insured purchased a policy of insurance on the hull and contents of his canal boat. The policy covered the perils "of the sounds, harbors, bays, rivers, canals, and fires, that shall come to the damage of the said boat, or any part thereof."[66] The policy contained no exclusion for damage caused by explosion. On the night in question, a fire of unknown origin broke out beneath some freight cars loaded with war munitions in a railroad company's freight yard in New York harbor, where the insured's boat was anchored. After the fire burned for at least thirty minutes, the contents of the cars exploded.

---

[64] At the risk of confusing — or even dismantling — this framework, the answers would not change if all of the causes under consideration in these cases passed the screen of the first filter but were then declared, instead of being too remote under the first screen, not dominant under the second filter.

[65] 120 N.E. 86 (N.Y. 1918).

[66] 120 N.E. at 86.

This explosion caused another fire in the freight yard, which in turn caused an explosion of a large quantity of dynamite and other explosives stored in the yard. This second explosion caused a concussion of the air which damaged the insured's boat, located about one thousand feet away, to the extent of $675. No fire reached the boat; the damages resulted only from the concussion caused by the second explosion. The question was whether the loss was covered by the insured's insurance policy.

The lower court had ruled that the fire was the proximate or efficient cause of the loss and that coverage therefore existed. Justice Cardozo, however, disagreed. He felt that the spacial relationship of the boat and the fire was a relevant consideration: "There is no use in arguing that distance ought not to count, if life and experience tells us that it does." In other words, Justice Cardozo chose to give great weight to the reasonable expectations of businessmen in making contracts:

> Our guide is the reasonable expectation and purpose of the ordinary business man when making an ordinary business contract. It is his intention, expressed or fairly to be inferred, that counts. There are times when the law permits us to go far back in tracing events to causes. The inquiry for us is how far the parties to this contract *intended* us to go. The causes within their contemplation are the only causes that concern us.[67]

Justice Cardozo proceeded to find that the concussion damage to the boat caused by the second fire was not a loss by fire within the meaning of the policy. The damage was instead caused by concussion; the concussion was caused, not by the fire, but by the explosion: "Fire must reach the thing insured, or come within such proximity to it that damage, direct or indirect is within the compass of reasonable probability. Then only is it the proximate cause, because then only may we suppose that it was within the contemplation of the contract."[68]

A more recent case following Justice Cardozo's reasoning is *Pan American World Airlines v. Aetna Casualty & Surety Co.*[69] This case involved the hijacking of a regularly scheduled Pan American airplane flight from Brussels to New York over London by two men acting for the Popular Front for the Liberation of Palestine (the "PFLP.") The aircraft, a Boeing 747, was flown to Egypt while under PFLP control. In Cairo, after the passengers were evacuated, the terrorists destroyed the aircraft. Pan American had insured its aircraft under various policies, each of which purported to cover all physical loss of or damage to the aircraft, except for certain enumerated exclusions including damage by military or usurped power, war, warlike operations, insurrection, strikes, civil commotion, or riot. No specific exclusion existed for "hijacking."

One issue in the case was whether a hijacking amounted to "war, insurrection, [or] riot" excluded from the coverage. The court noted that various causes of the loss could be identified: "Of course, in some attenuated 'cause of causes' sense, the loss may have resulted from the Fedayeen or PFLP pattern of military operations

---

[67] 120 N.E. at 86 (emphasis original).

[68] 120 N.E. at 88.

[69] 505 F.2d 989 (2d Cir. 1974).

against Israel, from the domestic unrest in Jordan, or from the most recent of the three wars which prior to 1970 had convulsed the Middle East." The difficulty for the court was choosing which cause, from among all of the causes, should be credited as the relevant cause of insurance purposes. The court opted for a test that looked to the most recent causes:

> Remote causes of causes are not relevant to the characterization of an insurance loss. In the context of this commercial litigation, the causation inquiry stops at the efficient physical cause of the loss; it does not trace events back to their metaphysical beginnings. The words "due to or resulting from" limit the inquiry to the facts immediately surrounding the loss.[70]

When applying this test, the court concluded that the cause of the loss was the hijacking, a peril not excluded from the coverage.

In neither *Bird* nor *Pan American* was the court willing to look far back in the chain of causation to identify the cause determining coverage. Rather, each court limited itself to the most recent causes in determining what caused the loss for the purpose of coverage. However, other decisions exist where courts have been willing to go farther back in the chain of causation. In these cases, the common thread seems to be that the insured is benefitted (usually, not always) by going farther back in the chain of causation.[71] Conversely, where insurers argue that a loss was caused by an excluded peril in circumstances where the more remote cause was excluded and the more recent cause supports coverage, courts have a tendency to find legal significance in only the more recent causes.[72]

Once the remoteness filter is applied to remove from consideration all excessively remote causes from further analysis, a second filter is applied to the remaining causes. But just as people with different eyesight have different prescriptions for

---

[70] 505 F.2d at 1006.

[71] See, e.g., Fred Meyer, Inc. v. Central Mut. Ins. Co., 235 F. Supp. 540 (D.Or. 1964) (insured had coverage for loss due to wind; policy did not cover loss due to failure of refrigeration equipment; windstorm destroyed electric power lines, which caused the insured's refrigerator not to work, which resulted in the spoilage of food; insured argued that the food spoilage was covered by the insurance, notwithstanding that the immediate cause of the loss was the failure of the refrigerator to function; held, food spoilage was a direct loss by windstorm that fell within the coverage); Providence Washington Ins. Co. v. Weaver, 133 So. 2d 635 (Miss. 1961) (insured owned a policy on his truck and its contents; he did not have insurance for his cattle which he hauled in the truck; while transporting the cattle in the truck, the truck upset on a highway, and the cattle were freed, and proceeded to wander off and disappear in quicksand along a river; insured argued that the loss of the cattle was covered under the insurance on the vehicle; held, coverage exists, because the legally significant cause of the loss was the vehicle's upset, even though had the cattle not wandered into the quicksand no loss would have occurred). See also Blaine Richards & Co. v. Marine Indem. Ins. Co. of Am., 635 F.2d 1051 (2d Cir. 1980); Henri's Food Products Co. v. Home Ins. Co., 474 F. Supp. 889 (E.D. Wis. 1979).

[72] See, e.g., Sabella v. Wisler, 377 P.2d 889 (Cal. 1963); Henning Nelson Constr. Co. v. Fireman's Fund Am. Life Ins. Co., 361 N.W.2d 446 (Minn. Ct. App. 1985), *aff'd with modifications,* 383 N.W.2d 645 (Minn. 1986); Broome v. Allstate Ins. Co., 241 S.E.2d 34 (Ga. Ct. App. 1977); Vormelker v. Oleksinski, 199 N.W.2d 287 (Mich. Ct. App. 1972).

their glasses, the precise nature of this second filter varies depending on what "vision" a court has for how multiple cause cases should be decided. In most jurisdictions, courts follow the efficient, proximate cause rule, and this filter requires a sorting of remaining causes to find the predominant, most important cause. If this cause is covered, the loss is covered; if this cause is excluded, the loss is excluded.[73] In jurisdictions or cases where the liberal approach is followed, the second filter simply asks whether any of the causes is covered; if so, the loss is covered, regardless of the relative dominance of the cause. (Presumably, to use the terminology of *Garvey*, the remoteness inquiry would have screened out any cause that is not "proximate," so that the remaining set of causes would all be "proximate causes," and any covered cause in that set of causes would be enough to support a finding of coverage.) Conversely, under the conservative approach, the application of the second filter will simply inquire as to whether any of the causes is excluded; if so, the loss is not covered, regardless of the relative dominance of the cause.

If the second filter involves a search for the proximate, efficient cause, and if it is impossible to declare any one cause the dominant one in a set of covered and excluded causes, the prior discussion suggests that the loss should be covered. This is tantamount to saying ties go to the insured; it is also tantamount to saying that if the proximate, efficient cause approach does not produce an answer, the liberal approach is then substituted for the proximate, efficient cause approach.

[4]   Problems with the Term "Proximate"

By this point, it should be apparent that sorting out causation in insurance has been a struggle through the years. Part of the problem has been that courts and scholars have sometimes used the same words while meaning different things. For example, some have used "concurrent causation" to refer to any problem of multiple causation, while others have used "concurrent causation" to refer only to the narrow situation where two causes both arise and operate independently to produce a loss. The overworked phrase "proximate cause" has been part of the problem in insurance law.

Sometimes proximate cause, as used in insurance law causation, describes the process of applying the first filter, but at other times it is used to apply the second filter, where the coverage issue is finally decided. That proximate cause would carry with it this confusion is not surprising; in the field of torts where the proximate cause test does most of its work, distinguished scholars have described the test as "unfortunate" and have used the term "fruitless" to describe the "quest for a universal

---

[73] Interestingly, a recent decision of the Washington Supreme Court, the same court that decided *Graham*, calls into question part of this analysis when it declined to rule that an excluded risk which sets in motion a chain of events would disqualify coverage under the proximate, efficient cause rule. See Key Tronic Corp., Inc. v. Aetna (CIGNA) Fire Underwriters Ins. Co., 881 P.2d 201 (Wash. 1994)(en banc.) On the other hand, a recent California case illustrates (although the case history shows that *Garvey* did not resolve all confusion in California) the second filter's effective functioning. In State Farm Fire & Cas. Co. v. Von Der Lieth, 820 P.2d 285 (Cal. 1991)(en banc), the court held that the efficient proximate cause of the insureds' property loss was the negligence of third parties in failing to take proper measure to preserve the mesa, a covered cause, rather than earth movement caused by naturally rising groundwater levels, which was an excluded cause.

formula" of proximate cause.[74] In insurance cases, the most frequently quoted definition of proximate cause appears in an 1893 Massachusetts case, *Lynn Gas & Electric Co. v. Meriden Fire Insurance Co.*:[75] "The active efficient cause that sets in motion a train of events which brings about a result without the intervention of any force started and working actively from a new and independent source is the direct and proximate cause referred to in the cases."[76] This test looks very much like the standard for proximate, efficient cause used in *Graham*, discussed above.

Lynn Gas & Electric suggested that the proximate cause test is the same in tort and insurance law, but the absence of a clear statement of what proximate cause means in tort law gives the proximate cause test little value in insurance law unless the term is accompanied by some external referents such as those supplied in the more elaborate frameworks sketched out in the prior discussion. Indeed, perhaps influenced to some extent by the vagueness of proximate cause in tort law, many courts have explicitly stated that the proximate cause test is not the same in tort law and insurance law.[77] Thus, in *Bird v. St. Paul Fire & Marine Insurance Co.*,[78] Justice Cardozo observed that the insurance relationship depends on the existence of a contract, and this distinguishes insurance law from the field of tort law: "[I]n the law of torts, . . . there is a tendency to go farther back in the search for causes than there is in the law of contracts. . . . Especially in the law of insurance, the rule is that, 'you are not to trouble yourself with distant causes.' "[79] In Justice Cardozo's view, insurance law is better served by a test of "proximateness" that emphasizes the reasonable expectations and purposes of the parties to the contract, a standard which is derived from contract law, not tort law.

That insurance law and tort law should use different tests to determine what causes have legal significance is illustrated well by Brewer's discussion of *Metallic Compression Casting Co. v. Fitchburg R. Co.*,[80] an 1872 Massachusetts case. Plaintiff's mill was adjacent to the defendant's railroad track. A fire broke out in plaintiff's mill; to fight the fire, the firemen were required to lay a hose across the track from the water supply to the burning mill. The firemen's efforts to contain the fire would have succeeded if employees of the railroad had not knowingly run a train across the hose line, thereby cutting off the water supply. Plaintiff was permitted to recover in tort against the railroad on the ground that the railroad's employees' act was the proximate cause of the loss. Yet, at the same time, plaintiff was entitled to recover its entire loss under its fire insurance policy on the ground

---

[74] W. Page Keeton, et al., *Prosser and Keeton on the Law of Torts* 273, 279 (5th ed. 1984).
[75] 33 N.E. 690 (Mass. 1893).
[76] 33 N.E. at 691.
[77] E.g., New York, New Haven & Hartford R. Co. v. Gray, 240 F.2d 460, 465 (2d Cir.), *cert. denied*, 353 U.S. 966 (1957) ("the horrendous niceties of the doctrine of so-called 'proximate cause,' employed in negligence suits, apply in a limited manner only to insurance policies.")
[78] 120 N.E. 86 (N.Y. 1918).
[79] 120 N.E. at 88, *quoting* Ionides v. Universal Marine Ins. Co., 14 C.B.N.S. 289, 143 Eng.Rep. 445, 457 (1863). This same idea was espoused by Justice Kaufman in his concurring opinion in *Garvey,* discussed above.
[80] 109 Mass. 277 (1872).

that the fire caused the loss.[81] In the facts, no single cause of the loss existed. Both tort and insurance law favored a recovery in this case, but each legal theory was willing to credit a different cause.

[f] Summary

Because causation is such a murky subject, the rules in this area will undoubtedly continue to evolve in future cases. This evolution will be affected, most obviously, by changes in policy language in future forms, and less obviously by changes in the composition of courts that decide these cases.[82] Probably the most one can hope for is defining a framework that makes it possible to categorize cases, which in turn gives one a fighting chance of predicting future outcomes.

---

[81] Of course, the insurer, if it paid the insured's claim, would have subrogation rights against the railroad. See § 96, *infra*.

[82] The California Supreme Court is one example, where a change in composition of that court over the past decade has created a much more friendly environment for insurers, at least relative to prior years.

Part C

PERFORMING THE CONTRACTUAL OBLIGATIONS

CHAPTER **7**

_____

THE INSURED'S DUTY TO PAY PREMIUMS

§ 70   Nature of the Obligation to Pay Premiums

[a]   The Nature of a "Premium"

An insurance premium is what the insured pays the insurer to assume the risk. The premium is the consideration the insured provides in return for the insurer's promise to indemnify the insured for a loss or to pay proceeds upon the occurrence of some specified event. Premiums are paid periodically; the frequency of payment varies depending upon the agreement of the insurer and insured at the time the policy is issued.

The amount of the premium charged insureds is based upon a prediction of total losses that will occur during the policy term. The estimate of total losses is added to an estimate of the costs of administering the insurance program (which includes a reasonable allowance for profit if the insurer is a for-profit company) in determining what premium must be charged for each unit of insurance coverage. The term "net premium" refers to the portion of the premium that is chargeable directly to the risk that the insurer assumes. "Gross premium" refers to the total charge to the consumer, which necessarily includes the net premium plus charges for administrative expenses (such as the agent's commission, office expenses, management and employee salaries, lost interest through installment payments, advertising costs, and a surplus fund to cover unanticipated additional losses) and profits. The process of factoring these administrative expenses into the premium is referred to as "loading." Because premiums are collected at the beginning of each policy term, the insurer typically expects to earn some interest on the monies collected; this is also factored into the calculation of what the insurer needs to collect in order to cover future losses, expenses, and the profit margin.

Out of each premium collected, the insurer is expected to "reserve" a certain amount to meet liabilities anticipated during the year. Because it is statistically impossible for the insurer to incur liability on every policy that it issues in a given year, it is not necessary for the insurer to maintain reserves equal to the face values of all policies written. Instead, the insurer's anticipated liability is based on a prediction of losses that should occur during the year, and the insurer is required to maintain reserves for these expected losses. The prediction of losses is made liberally to avoid the risk of erring on the side of having inadequate reserves. In addition to maintaining reserves, the insurer allocates a portion of each premium to "surplus," which is in the nature of a contingency fund to enable the insurer to withstand unusual, unexpected losses in any given period.

507

[b]   The "Duty" to Pay Premiums

Paying the premium is the insured's duty, but only in a special sense of the word "duty." For most breaches of a contract duty, the promisor is liable in damages and in proper circumstances is subject to an order requiring specific performance of the duty. However, if the insured fails to perform the duty to pay premiums, the insurer is ordinarily not entitled to force the insured to make the payments or to collect damages for the insured's nonperformance. For example, the standard homeowner's insurance policy states that the parties' "agreement" is as follows: "We [the insurer] will provide the insurance described in this policy in return for the premium and compliance with all applicable provisions of this policy."[1] In effect, the insurer states "if you pay the premium, we will provide the coverage." The insured may promise, explicitly or implicitly, to pay the premium, but if the insured fails to keep this promise, the insurer's only recourse is to suspend its own performance; the insurer does not have the remedy of suing the insured for the unpaid premium. In this sense, paying the premium is more a condition to the insurer's duty to pay proceeds than it is a duty that the insured must perform.

[c]   Installment Premium Financing

The insured may assume what is, in effect, a duty to pay premiums if the insurer loans the insured the money to pay all of the policy's premiums in advance. This sort of arrangement, found almost exclusively in whole life insurance, is called "installment premium financing." Instead of collecting periodic premiums from the insured, the insurer loans the insured enough money to pay all of the policy's premiums in advance. The insured has a fully paid-up policy, but the insured assumes a contractual obligation to repay the loaned funds. Thus, the insured continues to make periodic payments to the insurer, but the payments are made on the outstanding loan balance, not for the premium. In effect, what the insurer does is to substitute the insured's promissory note for the insured's duty to pay premiums. Usually, the life insurance policy serves as security for the loan; if the insured prematurely dies before paying off the loan, the proceeds of the policy can be used to pay the loan, with any excess funds going to the insured's beneficiaries.

The financing arrangement is actually a separate contract between the insurer and insured. As a result, in situations where the financing arrangement has become a subject of litigation, most courts have held that the premium financing plans are separate from the business of insurance.[2] This means that federal laws regulating the creditor-debtor relationship, such as the federal Truth-in-Lending Act,[3] apply to the plans. These decisions are sound. The "business of insurance" that Congress intended to leave to state regulation is the risk-transferring relationship between the

---

[1] *Policy Kit* at 51 (ISO Form DP 00 02 07 88).

[2] See, e.g., Cochran v. Paco, Inc, 606 F.2d 460 (5th Cir. 1979); Perry v Fidelity Union Life Ins Co., 606 F.2d 468, *reh'g denied,* 608 F.2d 1373 (5th Cir. 1979), *cert. denied,* 446 U.S. 987 (1980); Cody v. Community Loan Corp., 606 F.2d 499, *reh'g denied,* 608 F.2d 1373 (5th Cir. 1979), *cert. denied,* 446 U.S. 988 (1980); Gerlach v. Allstate Ins. Co., 338 F. Supp. 642 (S.D. Fla. 1972).

[3] 15 U.S.C. §§ 1601–1693 (1982).

insurer and insured.[4] The reliability of insurance policies, the details of coverage, and the enforcement of obligations under the insurance contract are not affected in any meaningful way by premium financing. Insofar as the insurance contract is concerned, it makes little difference whether the insurer or a bank provides the financing of the premiums. In its capacity as the loaner of funds to pay the premium, the insurer acts as a creditor, not as an insurer; the premium financing arrangement is ancillary to the transfer of risk. In its capacity as a creditor, the insurer should be subject to the same rules and regulations as any creditor.

The phaseout of the tax deduction for personal interest under the Tax Reform Act of 1986[5] eliminated one of the most significant advantages of the arrangement for insureds. It is likely, therefore, that installment premium financing will be less common in the future.

§ 71   The Necessity of Paying the Premium

[a]   Generally

If the insured neither pays nor promises to pay the first premium, it is probable that no consideration exists to support the insurer's promise to pay proceeds in the event of a loss. Therefore, it is important that the insured either pay the first premium (a performance) or promise to pay that premium (a promise of a performance) so that the insurer will be bound, if not to pay proceeds, at least to act upon the insured's application.[1] The foregoing proposition should surprise few people: a consumer must pay, or agree to pay, for a good or service in order to be entitled to receive it, and insurance is no different.

Moreover, the insured's payment of subsequent premiums when due is a condition to the insurer's obligation to pay proceeds in the event of loss. Therefore, it is important that the insured stay current in meeting the obligation to pay the premium. One court put it succinctly: "Continued payment of premiums by an insured on or before their due date is necessary to continue the policy in force, and the duty of the insurance company to pay benefits under the policy depends upon whether the premiums were paid when due."[2] Only in rare circumstances will the insured be excused from the duty to pay the premiums. Some of these situations are explored in the subsections which follow.

[b]   Conclusiveness of Representation in Policy that First Premium Has Been Paid

Insurance policies sometimes contain a statement to the effect "receipt of the insured's premium is hereby acknowledged." Some states have statutes providing that the recitation is conclusive for some purposes, usually to make the policy temporarily binding.[3] A few courts have construed such statutes as having effects

---

[4] See § 21, *supra*.

[5] See I.R.C. § 163(d).

[1] See Lamarque v. Massachusetts Indem. & Life Ins. Co., 794 F.2d 194 (5th Cir. 1986).

[2] Hyten v. Cape Mut. Ins. Co., 663 S.W.2d 430, 431 (Mo. Ct. App. 1983).

[3] See, e.g., Cal. Ins. Code § 484; N.D. Cent. Code § 26.1-24-02.

broader than those clearly indicated on the face of the statutes. In the absence of a statute, courts have reached diverse conclusions on the effect of the recitation; this is true regardless of the purpose for which the recitation is offered. In situations where insurers have claimed that the policy never became binding, have attempted to cancel the policy for nonpayment of the first premium, or have sought to recover the first premium payment, some courts have given the recitation conclusive effect, sometimes without the presence of the elements of estoppel.[4] Other courts, however, have held that the recitation only creates a rebuttable presumption or constitutes mere evidence of payment.[5]

[c] Necessity of Paying Premium Before Loss

Ordinarily, failure to pay the premium before the loss, absent some other circumstance under which the insurer led the insured to believe that the policy was in force, will prevent the insured from recovering under the policy.[6] This is hardly controversial. However, in some cases, a dispute has arisen over whether the premium must "actually" be paid or whether it is sufficient merely to "tender" the payment.

For example, in *Wanshura v. State Farm Life Insurance Co.,*[7] a 1978 Minnesota case, Wanshura's application for life insurance disclosed a prior history of cancer but the insurer's medical examination failed to discover a renewed cancerous condition. The insurer's agent telephoned the applicant's wife, indicating that the premium was higher and that he wanted to deliver the policy the following day. In the conversation, the wife, the authorized agent of her husband, agreed to the increased premium and to the delivery. Also, in this conversation, the wife asked whether the policy was effective at delivery or issuance, and the agent said issuance. The wife then stated her reason for asking was that her husband had just been released from the hospital and had developed problems. On the following day, the agent canceled the appointment; the policy was never delivered, and no premium was collected prior to the applicant's death from cancer about six months later. The court affirmed the trial court's finding that the premium was "tendered" in the telephone conversation between the wife and the insurance agent, and that the "tender of the premium" satisfied the requirement in the policy that the initial premium be paid prior to coverage.

Wanshura is indicative of the general theme in insurance law that it is unnecessary for the insured to comply with each and every technical requirement of the policy.

---

[4] See, e.g., St. Julian v. Financial Indem. Co., 77 Cal. Rptr. 843 (Cal. Ct. App. 1969); Bates v. Equitable Life Assur. Soc'y, 177 S.W.2d 360 (Tenn. Ct. App. 1943); see generally Annot., *Conclusiveness of Recitation, In Delivered Insurance Policy, That Initial Premium Has Been Paid,* 44 A.L.R.3d 1361 (1972).

[5] See, e.g., Martin v. Business Men's Assur. Co., 246 N.W. 882 (Minn. 1933); Bankers' Credit Life Ins. Co. v. Lee, 140 So. 609 (Ala. 1932).

[6] See, e.g., Life Ins. Co. v. Overstreet, 603 S.W.2d 780 (Tex. 1980); Zemler v. New York Life Ins. Co., 225 N.W. 81 (Minn. 1929); Martin v. Prudential Ins. Co. of Am., 263 P. 1055 (Kan. 1928).

[7] 275 N.W.2d 559 (Minn. 1978). See also New York Life Ins. Co. v. Greenlee, 84 N.E. 1101 (Ind. Ct. App. 1908); Going v. Mutual Benefit Life Ins. Co., 36 S.E. 556 (S.C. 1900).

In filling out a proof of loss or a change of beneficiary, most courts require only "substantial compliance." Notice of losses need be filed with a "reasonable" time. "Constructive delivery" is usually enough to satisfy a policy's delivery requirement; actual delivery is usually not required. In the same vein, if it appears that the insured has done all that was reasonably required with regard to the payment of premium and if it appears that injustice would result from insisting upon literal compliance with the policy's technical requirements, the insured will not be denied coverage simply because the final step in the process of payment never occurred, particularly if the insurer's action prevented this final step from occurring.

Because the requirement that the premium be paid prior to a loss is for the insurer's benefit, this requirement can be waived by the insurer.[8] For example, in *Kramer v. Metropolitan Life Insurance Co.,*[9] the insurer refused to pay benefits to the plaintiff under an accidental death benefits policy because the first premium was not paid in accordance with the policy's terms. The court found that the applicant offered to pay the first premium, but the insurer's agent refused it because he did not know whether the applicant would be insured and how much the premium would be. The policy was eventually issued. Although the insurer's documents purported to require that the first premium be paid in cash, the insurer inserted the policy into the insurer's "Check-O-Matic system," a system of making premium payments under which the insured's checking account would be automatically debited. The insurer did not intend for this to occur, but the fact that it did was enough, in the court's view, to constitute waiver of the insurer's requirement that the first premium be paid in cash in advance.

In *Kramer,* it was important that the insured had offered to pay the first premium, an offer which the agent declined, and that the insurer had unilaterally instituted an alternative payment mechanism. These acts could be fairly described as the insurer's knowing relinquishment of its rights. The knowing relinquishment of a right, the essence of a waiver, was not present in *Tighe v. Security National Life Insurance Co.*[10] In that case, the insurer sent overdue notices to the insured for three months after the last payment, and the insurer carried the insured's policy as an account receivable on its computer records during this time. The court applied the "general rule" that "a mere demand for overdue premiums by an insurer having knowledge of a cause for forfeiture does not amount to a waiver if the insured does not comply with the demand."[11] Simply carrying the amounts due for premiums as an account receivable did not indicate that the insurer had waived its right to declare the policy lapsed. Moreover, no possibility existed in the facts of the case that the insured had relied on the insurer's accounting system; thus, no basis existed for a finding that the insurer was estopped to deny that the policy was in force. In contrast to *Tighe* is *Martinez v. Great American Insurance Co. of New York,*[12] where the court held

---

[8] See Lawrimore v. American Health & Life Ins. Co., 276 S.E.2d 296 (S.C. 1981). See also § 25E, *supra.*

[9] 494 F. Supp. 1026 (D.N.J. 1980).

[10] 214 N.W.2d 622 (Neb. 1974).

[11] 214 N.W.2d at 625.

[12] 286 F. Supp. 141 (W.D. Tex. 1968)

that the insurer's carrying of a premium due as an account receivable did estop the insurer from denying the existence of coverage. However, other facts in *Martinez* easily distinguish the case from *Tighe*: the insurer sent a renewal certificate to the insured, the insured relied on the certificate, and the insured had paid a portion of the premium in cash.

[d]   Mode of Paying Premiums

If a premium is paid in cash, no particular problem is presented. Difficulties arise if a payment is by check and the check is dishonored. Most courts hold that if the check is dishonored, the premium is not paid; in other words, the check is merely a conditional payment.[13] Other courts, however, hold that if the insurer issues a receipt for the check, the insurer has elected to treat the check as the premium payment; the insurer's recourse is not to cancel the policy but to seek a recovery from the drawer of the check.[14] A 1995 Utah case[15] illustrates these rules. The insured applied for an auto insurance policy; the check which accompanied the application was returned for insufficient funds. On the same day the insurer received notice of the returned check, it issued the written insurance policy for the coverage for which the insured had applied. Eight days later, the insurer mailed a notice to the insured canceling the coverage retroactive to the date of the application on the ground that the check had been dishonored. Four days after the notice was mailed, the insured was killed in an auto accident. The insured's heirs sought benefits under the policy, but the insurer claimed that no coverage was in force.

The court viewed the transaction as two contracts. The first was a temporary binder that became effective at the time of the application. This temporary coverage, however, was conditioned by a specific term on the application: "if my premium payment is not honored by the bank, no coverage will be considered bound." The court viewed the word "bound" as referring to the binder of temporary coverage, not to the formal contract memorialized in the policy. Because the condition was not satisfied, no temporary binder was effective.[16]

The written policy was a different matter. The court cited the general rule that coverage is conditioned on the initial premium being paid by check, but that this rule can be altered: "under certain circumstances, a check may be considered proper consideration for an insurance contract even though subsequently dishonored by the payee bank."[17] The court found the circumstances that altered the general rule: the insurer issued the policy on the same day it received notice of the dishonored check; three days later an agent of the insurer countersigned the policy, indicating final validation of the policy's effectiveness; the cancellation notice served to cancel an existing policy rather than reject the application; and the policy lacked specific

---

[13] See, e.g., McDuffie v. Criterion Cas. Co., 449 S.E.2d 133 (Ga. Ct. App. 1994); Bolz v. Security Mut. Life Ins. Co., 721 P.2d 1216 (Colo.Ct.App. 1986); Snowden v. United of Omaha Life Ins. Co., 450 So. 2d 731 (La. Ct. App. 1984).

[14] See Statewide Ins. Corp. v. Dewar, 694 P.2d 1167 (Ariz. 1984); Culotta v. Kemper Corp., 397 N.E.2d 1372 (Ill. 1979).

[15] Phoenix Indem. Ins. Co. v. Bell, 896 P.2d 32 (Utah 1995).

[16] 896 P.2d at 36.

[17] 896 P.2d at 36.

language making actual payment a condition precedent to the effectiveness of coverage. In these circumstances, the court held that the cancellation could not be effective, as provided by statute, until ten days after delivery of the notice; because the insured's death occurred during the ten-day period, the insurer was obligated to provide coverage.[18]

In life insurance, if a premium is not paid and the insurer has in its possession dividends belonging to the insured sufficient to pay the premium, the insurer cannot declare the policy lapsed. Instead, most courts impose a duty on the insurer to apply the dividends to the premium. Cases not applying this rule typically involve a situation where the policy provides that the dividends be applied in a certain way or the insured has given other directions on how the dividends should be applied. The rationale for this rule is the judicial abhorrence for a forfeiture: the insurer should be required to take a simple step to protect the insured's interests, instead of declaring the policy invalid.[19]

[e]   Time for Payment

Usually, the time at which the premium payment is due is determined by examining the insurance policy.[20] Unless the policy provides otherwise, after a policy lapses the insurer is under no obligation to accept a late premium payment.[21] However, some cases involve ambiguous policy provisions, and in these cases the ambiguities tend to be decided in favor of the insured and coverage.[22] For example, in *State Security Life Insurance Co. v. Kintner,*[23] the Indiana Supreme Court considered whether the due date for premium payment should be calculated from the date of the application, in which case the policy lapsed for nonpayment of the premium, or the date of delivery of the policy, in which case the insured's death would have been within the policy's coverage. The court observed that the insurer would have denied coverage had the insured died between the date of application and the date of the policy's delivery. Therefore, the court reasoned that the due date for the premium should be calculated from the date of delivery.

Sometimes the insurer's conduct can have the effect of altering the premium's due date from the date specified in the policy.[24] For example, in *Northeast Insurance*

---

[18] 896 P.2d at 36-37.

[19] See, e.g., Crum v. Prudential Ins. Co. of Am., 356 F. Supp. 1054 (N.D. Miss. 1973); Gaunt v. Prudential Ins. Co. of Am., 62 Cal. Rptr. 624 (Cal. Ct. App. 1967); see generally Annot., Dividends As Preventing Lapse Of Policy For Nonpayment Of Premiums, 8 A.L.R.3d 862 (1966).

[20] See, e.g., D&P Terminal, Inc. v. Western Life Ins. Co., 368 F.2d 743 (8th Cir. 1966); Life Ins. Co. of the Southwest v. Overstreet, 603 S.W.2d 780 (Tex. 1980).

[21] See, e.g., In re First Capital Life Ins. Co., 40 Cal. Rptr.2d 816 (Cal. Ct. App. 1995).

[22] See generally Annot., *Effective Date of Life, Health, Or Accident Insurance Policy, As Between Premium Date Stated In Policy And Later Date Either Of Approval, Acceptance, Or Delivery Of Policy, Or Of Payment Of Premium,* 44 A.L.R.2d 472 (1955).

[23] 185 N.E.2d 527 (Ind. 1962).

[24] See, e.g., Mardirosian v. Lincoln Nat'l Life Ins. Co., 739 F.2d 474 (9th Cir. 1984); Sereno v. Lumbermens Mut. Cas. Co., 647 P.2d 1144 (Ariz. 1982) (late installment payments on *existing* contract might estop insurer to deny coverage, but does not estop insurer from

Co. v. Concord General Mutual Insurance Co.,[25] a 1983 Maine case, the insured's son was injured in an automobile accident on November 29, 1976. The insured had been in default for a premium covering the period from August 27 to December 1, and had received a notice in early November that he should pay by November 18 or the policy would be canceled. The insurer's agent accepted his payment on November 19; sometime after the accident, the insurer returned the premium to the agent for return to the insured, and denied coverage. The court noted that "[b]y accepting late payment of premiums without question, an insurer waives any right to consider the policy terminated or canceled for lack of timely payment."[26] As a result, the insurer was bound to the risk at the time of the accident.

Other circumstances can excuse an insured's late payment. An insurer can offer to reinstate a policy after it has lapsed (or to extend a life insurance policy's grace period), and the insured's payment during this period will reinstate (or continue, in the case of an extension of a grace period) the coverage,[27] provided the insured has complied with the terms of the offer.[28] Absent such an offer, if an insurer accepts a premium payment for a month subsequent to a month where the premium was unpaid, the insurer may be held to have waived the prior delinquency.[29] Also, the insurer's repeated acceptance of late premium payments may give rise to a course of dealing under which the due date for premium payments is altered;[30] one acceptance of one late premium payment is, barring other circumstances, insufficient to establish a course of dealing that alters to premium's due date.[31]

If a loss occurs while a premium payment is overdue and the insurer accepts a premium payment after the loss, the insurer might later attempt to refund the premium and declare the policy lapsed. If the insurer accepted the premium payment with full knowledge of the occurrence of the loss, a court is likely to conclude that the insurer waived its right to declare the policy lapsed for nonpayment of a

---

refusing late payment to *renew* the policy). But see Williams v. Prudential Ins. Co. of Am., 447 So. 2d 685 (Ala. 1984) (accepting premiums during the grace period does not establish a custom or habit that waives the policy's forfeiture provision).

[25] 461 A.2d 1056 (Me. 1983).

[26] 461 A.2d at 1058.

[27] See, e.g., Flood v. Midland Nat'l Life Ins. Co., 643 N.E.2d 439 (Mass. 1994) (life insurer's unilateral offer to extend grace period in which to pay past due premiums could be and was accepted by beneficiary by meeting all express conditions of offer).

[28] See Glass v. Harvest Life Ins. Co., 425 N.W.2d 107 (Mich. Ct. App. 1988).

[29] See, e.g., Greene v. Durham Life Ins. Co., 336 S.E.2d 478 (S.C. 1985); Northeast Ins. Co. v. Concord General Mut. Ins. Co., 461 A.2d 1056 (Me. 1983); Grassham v. Farm Bureau Town and Country Ins. Co., 684 S.W.2d 892 (Mo. Ct. App. 1984); Brand v. International Investors Ins. Co., 521 P.2d 423 (OkLa. Ct. App. 1974).

[30] See, e.g., Cormier v. Lone Star Life Ins. Co., 500 So. 2d 431 (La. Ct. App. 1986); General Am. Life Ins. Co. v. Samples, 307 S.E.2d 51 (Ga. Ct. App. 1983); but see Gurley v. State Farm Mut. Auto. Ins. Co., 428 N.E.2d 916 (Ill. App. Ct. 1981).

[31] Goble v. Emerson Electric Co., [1983-85] Life, Health & Accident Cases (CCH), at 1489 (Tenn. Ct. App. 1984) (insurer's acceptance of one late premium payment in the course of a year of weekly payments under a sickness and accident policy was insufficient to establish a custom or course of dealing whereby the insurer waived the premium deadline).

premium.[32] The logic of this result is that the insurer cannot accept the benefit of the contract (the premiums) without also assuming the burdens of the contract (the duty to pay proceeds). The waiver analysis also applies if the insurer accepts the premium payment with knowledge of a circumstance (such as a breach of warranty) that invalidates the coverage.

However, in circumstances where the insurer lacked knowledge of the loss after the policy's lapse but prior to the tender of the late premium, some courts have allowed the insurer to refund the premium without liability. In some of these cases, the policy provided that payment of the late premium revives coverage which was suspended when the premium became overdue, and no facts support the conclusion that the insurer knowingly waived the suspension of the coverage.[33] Other courts have reasoned in circumstances where the policy has expired and no grace period is applicable that no coverage exists because merely cashing a check (and later attempting to refund the money) cannot be a basis for imposing contractual liability where none otherwise exists.[34] One court held that the insured's willful concealment of a loss after the policy's expiration date prevented the insured from invoking the doctrine of waiver or estoppel against the insurer, which prevented the insured's post-loss late payment from continuing the coverage in circumstances where the insurer had a prior practice of accepting the insured's late payments. Absent the insured's deliberate concealment, the court observed that the insurer would have been precluded from denying coverage for a loss during the lapsed period.[35] Another court held that an insurer's practice of accepting late premium payments for a life insurance policy in circumstances where the insurer's agents inquired before accepting the late payments about whether the insured was still alive did not estop the insurer from denying coverage when the insured later died while premium payments were unpaid after the grace period had expired.[36]

Other courts, however, have held the insurer liable for the loss, despite the insurer's lack of knowledge of the loss when it accepted the late premium. The reasoning in most of these cases is that the prior conduct of the insurer in accepting late premium payments for earlier periods of coverage now estops the insurer from denying the effect of the late payment where a loss has already occurred.[37] Waiver is not appropriate in these circumstances because the insurer lacks knowledge of the relevant facts prior to accepting payment, and therefore cannot be said to have knowingly relinquished a right. But it may be appropriate to say in many situations

---

[32] See, e.g., Van Hulle v. State Farm Mut. Auto. Ins. Co., 254 N.E.2d 457 (Ill. 1969); Eichten v. Klein, 160 N.W.2d 33 (Minn. 1968); Glass v. Harvest Life Ins. Co., 425 N.W.2d 107 (Mich. Ct. App. 1988).

[33] See, e.g., Crum v. Prudential Ins. Co. of Am., 356 F. Supp. 1054 (N.D. Miss. 1973); Fidelity Phoenix Fire Ins. Co. v. Watkins, 140 S.W.2d 152 (Tenn. 1940).

[34] See, e.g., Couch v. Farmers Ins. Group, 374 F. Supp. 306 (W.D. Ark. 1974); Troutman v. Nationwide Mut. Ins. Co., 400 S.W.2d 215 (Ky. 1966).

[35] Farley v. St. Charles Ins. Agency, Inc., 807 S.W.2d 168, 169-170 (Mo. Ct. App. 1991).

[36] See Brand v. Monumental Life Ins. Co., 417 N.E.2d 297 (Ind. 1981).

[37] See, e.g., Farley v. St. Charles Ins. Agency, Inc., 807 S.W.2d 168 (Mo. Ct. App. 1991)(dictum); Horace Mann Life Ins. Co. v. Lunsford, 324 S.E.2d 808 (Ga. Ct. App. 1984); Starcher v. Reserve Ins. Co., 428 N.E.2d 461 (Ohio Ct.App. 1980).

that an insured relies on an insurer's pattern of accepting late premium payments and disregarding what would otherwise be lapses in coverage. Thus, in several cases, courts have reasoned that the prior conduct of the insurer in accepting late premium payments for earlier periods of coverage estops the insurer from denying the effect of the late payment when a loss has already occurred.[38]

In short, when the insurer accepts a late premium payment after a loss has occurred, whether the loss is covered depends on the language of the insurance policy, the insurer's knowledge about the situation, the authority of the agent for the insured, and the court's perception of what fairness requires in the circumstances.[39]

[f] Timeliness of Payment

Separate from the question of when payment is due is whether the insured has made a timely payment. Many courts adhere to what is called the "deposit-payment" rule, which holds that where an insurer requests or acquiesces in the sending of premiums by mail, the payment is deemed to be made at the time the payment is deposited in the mail.[40] This rule, however, can be superseded by the agreement of the parties. Thus, if the policy provides that the payment is effective upon receipt, the policy term controls.[41]

The timeliness of payment question should not be confused with the "mailbox rule" that determines when an acceptance of an offer is effective, thereby forming a contractual relationship. The issue of timeliness of payment involves the performance of an obligation under an on-going, already formed contract. Because contract performance is different issue from contract formation, mailbox-rule precedents are irrelevant to determining whether a premium payment under an existing insurance policy is timely. However, mailbox-rule precedents may be relevant to determine whether an offer to reinstate a lapsed policy has been accepted.[42]

---

[38] See, e.g., Farley v. St. Charles Ins. Agency, Inc., 807 S.W.2d 168 (Mo. Ct. App. 1991)(dictum); Horace Mann Life Ins. Co. v. Lunsford, 324 S.E.2d 808 (Ga. Ct. App. 1984); Starcher v. Reserve Ins. Co., 428 N.E.2d 461 (Ohio Ct.App. 1980).

[39] For additional discussion and case citations, see generally Annot., *Insurer's Acceptance Of Defaulted Premium Payment Or Defaulted Payment On Premium Note, As Affecting Liability For Loss Which Occurred During Period Of Default,* 7 A.L.R.3d 414 (1966); Annot., *Insurer's Denial Of Renewal Of Policy: Waiver And Estoppel,* 85 A.L.R.2d 1410 (1962).

[40] See, e.g., Tayloe v. Merchants' Fire Ins. Co., 50 U.S. 390 (1850); Hartford Life & Ann. Ins. Co. v. Eastman, 74 N.W. 394 (Neb. 1898); Government Employees Ins. Co. v. Solaman, 597 N.Y.S.2d 990 (N.Y. Sup. Ct. 1993); Clarke v. American Concept Ins. Co., 758 P.2d 470 (Utah 1988).

[41] See, e.g., Dalton Buick, Oldsmobile, Pontiac, Cadillac, Inc. v. Universal Underwriters Ins. Co., 512 N.W.2d 633 (Neb. 1994); Clarke v. American Concept Ins. Co., 758 P.2d 470 (Utah 1988). Compare Cox v. Gulf Ins. Co., 858 S.W.2d 615 (Tex. Ct. App. 1993) (insurer's subsequent written offer to reinstatement policy upon insured's making late premium payment by mail by specified date invoked rule that payment is effective upon deposit in mail, and superseded policy provision that payment is effective on receipt).

[42] See, e.g., Cox v. Gulf Ins. Co., 858 S.W.2d 615 (Tex. Ct. App. 1993) (mailbox rule applies, even though insurer's notice states that reinstatement of policy is conditional upon receipt of payment by definite time, where remittance is made by mail as authorized prior to due date and not received until after due date).

§ 72   Grace Periods

Every modern individual life insurance policy and many other kinds of personal insurance policies have a thirty or thirty-one-day grace period for the payment of an overdue premium.[1] If the insured is late in paying a premium, the grace period allows the insured a specified period of time to pay the premium without suffering a gap in coverage. In effect, the insurer gives up its right to cancel the policy if the premium is paid before the grace period expires. Paying within the grace period has the same effect as if the premium payment were made on time. Paying within the grace period can be likened to reinstating the policy without requiring the insured to go through the insurer's procedures for reinstatement (which may include requiring the insured to pass another medical examination). If the late premium is not paid within the grace period, the coverage lapses.[2]

Another way to explain the grace period is as follows: the grace period in an insurance policy is not paid by the previous premium. Instead, during the grace period the insured is temporarily indebted to the insurer for the new premium.[3] If the new premium is not paid during the grace period, the policy terminates as of the date that the premium was due, i.e., the date the grace period began. If the premium is paid during the grace period, the policy is renewed on the same terms as if the premium had been paid on time. If the insured dies during the grace period without having paid the premium, the indebtedness for the new premium is paid out of the proceeds distributed to the beneficiary.

It is also common in property and liability insurance for the policy to set forth a short period during which the insured can pay an overdue premium. However, these provisions do not always function in the same way as grace periods in life insurance. For example, the insurer may condition "revival" of the policy upon "acceptance" of the late premium by the insurer. If a loss occurs while the premium is overdue, the insurer will probably decline to accept the late payment, meaning that the insured lacked coverage. In personal insurance, the contract typically obligates the insurer to accept any payment made within the grace period.

Grace periods are similar to so-called "anti-forfeiture" provisions in whole life insurance. A whole life policy that has been in force for a few years will have accumulated a cash value. Most whole life policies provide that if the insured defaults on a premium payment, the insurance converts into term insurance, with the cash value being used to pay the premium on the term insurance until the cash

---

[1] In group life insurance, the provisions of policies and judicial enforcement of the provisions differ in many respects. See generally §§ 120–126, *infra;* Annot., *Termination of Employee's Individual Coverage Under Group Policy For Nonpayment of Premiums,* 22 A.L.R.4th 321 (1983).

[2] See, e.g., Loyd v. Federal Kemper Life Assur. Co., 518 N.W.2d 374 (Iowa 1994) (life policy which provided 31-day grace period after the first of the month was unambiguous in not extending coverage to the 32nd day when the grace period ended on a Sunday); Grimes v. Liberty Nat'l Life Ins. Co., 551 So. 2d 329 (Ala. 1989) (life policy lapsed for nonpayment of premiums where policy provided it would lapse if premium were not paid by end of grace period and last premium was paid approximately 15 months before death of insured).

[3] See, e.g., Royal Ins. Co. v. Western Cas. Ins. Co., 444 N.W.2d 846 (Minn. Ct. App. 1989).

value is exhausted. The insured, of course, who chooses voluntarily to let a whole life policy lapse is not bound to convert the policy to term insurance. The insured can withdraw the cash value or designate some other settlement authorized by the policy. However, if the insured defaults and fails to tell the insurer what to do with the cash value, the insurer ordinarily gives the insured the extended term option.

The grace period, unlike an anti-forfeiture provision, is not an automatic extension of coverage. Instead, it is simply a contractual right the insured possesses to reinstate the policy within a set period after the policy terminates for nonpayment of premiums. If the contract is terminated, it follows that the right to reinstate the policy, a right provided by the contract, no longer exists. For example, suppose the premiums on a policy are due on July 1 of each year, but on June 25 the insured calls the insurer and says, "I don't want this insurance, and I want to cancel this policy effective July 1," and the insurer sends the insured a notice on July 1 stating that the policy is canceled. (Assume that the policy is either term or whole-life without a cash value, so that the anti-forfeiture provision will have no effect.) In such a circumstance, the contract has been rescinded by mutual consent of the parties. If the insured dies on July 20, the insured's beneficiary cannot claim coverage by virtue of the grace period. The contract which contemplated a grace period was rescinded before the grace period was allowed to run.[4]

Ironically, it would be better if the insured in the foregoing example chose to let the policy lapse on July 1 by simply not paying the premium. In that event, the insured would have the "protection" of the grace period: if the insured died during the grace period, the coverage would be effective and the proceeds paid to the beneficiary, subject to an offset for the premium not paid. One would expect courts, consistent with the general philosophy of favoring insureds, to find in close cases a unilateral decision on the part of the insured to let the policy lapse as opposed to a mutual agreement of rescission. In a Texas case, the insured during the grace period wrote to her insurer, "I wish to drop my life insurance." The company later replied that her policy "was permitted to lapse." Subsequently but during the grace period, the insured died in an accident; the court allowed the beneficiary to recover, rejecting the argument that the insured had agreed to rescind the contract.[5]

That the grace period is not equivalent to an automatic extension of coverage is illustrated by *Furtado v. Metropolitan Life Insurance Co.*[6] Plaintiff was the beneficiary under a policy of whole life insurance on his son. Payments were due on the twelfth day of each month; the payment due August 12, 1973 was not paid.

---

4 See Davis v. Metropolitan Life Ins. Co., 32 S.W.2d 1034 (Tenn. 1930); Coe v. Farmers New World Life Ins. Co., 257 Cal. Rptr. 411 (Cal. Ct. App. 1989); Bennett v. Colonial Life & Acc. Ins. Co., 643 P.2d 1133 (Kan.Ct.App. 1982). Compare Gillespie v. Safeco Life Ins. Co., 565 So. 2d 150 (Ala. 1990) (insurer disregarded insured's cancellation letter; insurer sent letter to insured indicating policy had lapsed and asking for premium payment; insured did not pay but died within grace period; held, insured was covered by virtue of insurer's disregard of cancellation letter).

5 See Satery v. Great Am. Reserve Ins. Co., 278 S.W.2d 377 (Tex. Ct. App. 1955).

6 131 Cal. Rptr. 250 (Cal. Ct. App. 1976).

Plaintiff's son died seventy-five days later on October 26, 1973. The policy had a thirty-one day grace period as well as an anti-forfeiture provision that provided a period of extended term insurance of sixty days "measured from the due date of the premium in default." The insurer denied the coverage on the theory that the policy had lapsed. The plaintiff argued that the grace period of thirty-one days and the sixty-day period of extended term insurance should run consecutively, not concurrently. He argued that a premium is not in default until the grace period expires.

The plaintiff's argument was flawed and was rejected by the court on the ground that the policy clearly provided that the period of term insurance ran from the *due date* of the premium in default, which was August 12 — which meant the term insurance expired before his son's death. However, the plaintiff's argument was flawed for other reasons as well. Plaintiff's theory incorrectly presupposed that a grace period provides a period of free insurance. It is true that if an insured fails to pay a premium when due and dies within the grace period, the beneficiary receives the proceeds, but the amount of the unpaid premium is deducted from the proceeds — so the insured, if death occurs during the grace period, actually pays for the insurance provided during the grace period. If the insured pays the premium during the grace period before dying, the same result occurs: the beneficiary receives the proceeds, and the insured pays for the insurance. In *Furtado,* the insured lived through the grace period, but he was not "covered" during this period under the whole life policy because he never paid the premium. He was covered during this period under the term insurance which his cash value bought. It is true that the insurer did not know to apply the cash value to the term insurance until the grace period expired, for only then was it clear that the insured had survived the grace period and had not reinstated the whole life policy. However, to have allowed the grace period and the term insurance coverage to run consecutively would have given the insured something he did not pay for.

§ 73   Automatic Premium Payments Through Financial Institutions: Special Problems

One of the major changes in America during the last quarter-century is the effort of entrepreneurs to make business convenient for consumers. This trend manifests itself in many ways, but one of the more obvious is the automation of the banking business. Banks and other depositories for savings and checking accounts have implemented automatic account debiting procedures whereby a bank customer can arrange for payments either to the bank or some third party to be automatically withdrawn from the customer's account when due. Insurance companies have taken advantage of this convenient way of paying bills; with the cooperation of banks and other similar institutions, insurers often make it possible for the insured's premium payments to be deducted automatically from the insured's checking or savings account and forwarded to the insurer.[1] As convenient as these systems are, the

---

[1] For an explanation of this system, see H. Scott, *New Payment Systems: A Report to the 3-4-8 Committee of the Permanent Editorial Board for the Uniform Commercial Code* 13–17 (1978), *reprinted in* Lionel H. Frankel, Julian B. McDonnell, & Raymond T. Nimmer, *Commercial Transactions: Payment Systems* 284–86 (1982).

computers which manage the transactions are only as perfect as their programs and operators. Some lawsuits have already been caused by the failure of automatic check debiting procedures to function efficiently and more are likely in the future.[2]

Consider, for example, *Horace Mann Life Insurance Co. v. Lunsford*,[3] a 1984 Georgia case. The insured's premiums on a life insurance were paid for September, October, and November, 1981, under a "check-o-matic" plan. The December draft was dishonored for insufficient funds, and the January draft was returned to the insurer marked "account closed." Prior to the return of the second draft, the insurer advised the insured it would present another draft on February 15 for the overdue December premium. However, after the second draft was returned unpaid, the insurer wrote to the insured and advised him that the policy was being switched from the check-o-matic plan to direct billing, and that he needed to pay a monthly premium within three weeks to prevent a lapse. Eleven days later, the insured was killed in an auto accident. What followed was a complicated series of contradictory communications: on one occasion, the insurer refused one of the widow's tender of past premiums but on another occasion a separate, identical tender was accepted; on one occasion, the insurer acknowledged the insured's death in a letter to the widow, but later the insurer sent the deceased a receipt acknowledging his payment of premiums (actually made by the widow) and indicating that his payments were current. In this complicated fact pattern, the court concluded that summary judgment for the widow was appropriate:

> If an insurance company receives, accepts, and retains past-due premiums which are paid subsequent to the due date and expiration of the grace period, it renews the contract and waives the forfeiture for nonpayments provided the acceptance is unconditional and the facts are known.[4]

Kramer v. Metropolitan Life Insurance Co.,[5] a New Jersey federal district court case, presents an equally confused fact pattern. The insurer secured an "Authorization to Honor Checks" from its applicant, which was one of the documents necessary to establish an automatic account-debiting program. The Authorization stated that upon delivery of the policy (which never occurred), the initial premium was to be paid in cash, with the remaining premiums to be deducted from the insured's account automatically. The insurer issued the policy in question on June 5, sending it to the agent for delivery to the applicant. The agent finally telephoned on June 13 to arrange an appointment for delivery of the policy, only to learn that the applicant had died just a few hours previously. On June 3, prior to the June 5 issue date, the insurer mailed to the applicant's bank the authorization to debit the account. For four months after the applicant's death, the applicant's account, jointly held with his wife, was debited for the premiums, due to an unartfully designed check debiting system. Under these circumstances, the court held that the placing of the policy in

---

[2] In addition to the cases discussed in this section, see First Alabama Bank v. Prudential Life Ins. Co. of Am., 619 So. 2d 1313 (Ala. 1993); Haupt v. Midland Nat'l Life Ins. Co., 567 So. 2d 1319 (Ala. 1990).

[3] 324 S.E.2d 808 (Ga. Ct. App. 1984).

[4] 324 S.E.2d at 811.

[5] 494 F. Supp. 1026 (D.N.J. 1980).

the automatic debiting system constituted a waiver of the insurer's requirement that the first premium be paid in cash, and a judgment was ultimately entered for the insured's beneficiary.

The possible mishaps in this sort of payment system are virtually limitless. In such situations, the insurer's liability to the insured will ordinarily be determined both by the contract and by the application of principles such as waiver and estoppel.[6]

---

[6] For further discussion of this subject, see generally Annot., *Construction and Effect of Arrangement Under Which Insurance Premiums Are Paid Automatically Via Insurer's Draft On Insured's Bank Account,* 45 A.L.R.3d 1349 (1972).

CHAPTER 8

THE MECHANICS OF CLAIM PRESENTATION

§ 80 Overview

To receive proceeds in the event of a loss, the insured must file a claim with the insurer. Insurance policies typically contain standard provisions prescribing the manner of presenting claims to the insurer.

In property insurance, the policy ordinarily specifies how and when the insured should give notice of the loss. Procedures for filing a proof of loss are also set forth. The policy is also likely to contain a provision stating that if the parties cannot agree on the value of damaged property or the amount of a loss, appraisers shall be appointed for the purpose of determining the amount of proceeds due. Also, most property insurance policies contain a provision placing restrictions on the time the insured has to bring a lawsuit against the insurer to compel payment of proceeds.

Other kinds of insurance policies have similar requirements. In liability insurance, there is no counterpart to appraisal or the proof of loss, but the insured is required to give notice to the insurer promptly after an accident or occurrence that might give rise to a liability within the coverage. Life insurance policies require the beneficiary to show proof of the insured's death; other kinds of personal insurance also require the insured to document the circumstances giving rise to the claim.

The insured has no affirmative duty to comply with claims processing requirements, meaning that failure to comply with the requirements will not give the insurer a cause of action against the insured for breach of contract. Instead, compliance is a condition to the insurer's duties to pay proceeds and perform other obligations. In other words, the insured's noncompliance with claims processing requirements provides the insurer with an excuse for not performing the duties it has undertaken.

§ 81 Notice of Loss Provisions

[a] Purpose of the Notice of Loss Provision

Property and liability insurance policies[1] usually require the insured to give the insurer notice of a loss shortly after the loss occurs or a claim is made against the

---

[1] Life insurance policies generally do not require that notice of loss be given at a particular time in order for the coverage to be valid. Rather, life insurance policies typically state that

insured. The primary purpose of the notice of loss provision is to enable the insurer to investigate the circumstances of the loss or claim before information becomes stale or disappears.[2]

There are, however, other advantages of requiring prompt notice of loss. Early discovery of information might assist the insurer in dealing with fraudulent claims, a benefit to all policyholders. In some situations, the insurer's investigation shortly after a loss may help avoid additional losses. For example, the insurer's investigation of a minor fire may discover defects in a sprinkler system which, if not repaired, could lead to additional, greater losses. Notice requirements probably deter the filing of some claims, which helps reduce the costs of coverage. Also, notice requirements play a role in the rate-setting process: to the extent notice requirements are enforced, insurers can assume that old events will not result in the payment of proceeds, and this tends to reduce the level of reserves that the insurer must maintain to meet future claims.[3]

[b] Manner of Giving Notice

Some policies require that the insured's notice of loss be in writing,[4] while other policies simply require that the insured give notice without specifying how that is to be done.[5] If notice is not required to be in writing, an oral notice is sufficient. While it might seem that such a provision is an incitement to disputes over whether notice was actually given, in most situations the insured will be required to submit a written proof of loss, to provide the insurer with copies of any written notices received, or to perform some other act which serves as evidence that the insurer was actually notified of the loss within a reasonable time. While courts sometimes say that oral notice is insufficient to satisfy a requirement that the notice be in writing,[6] an insurer will have extreme difficulty showing that it was prejudiced by the lack of written notice (where such judicially-imposed requirements exist)[7] or that the oral notice should not be deemed substantial compliance with the policy. Indeed, an insurer that receives oral notice and fails to inform the insured that written notice is required should be estopped to assert the insured's noncompliance with the notice

---

the insurer will pay the proceeds when it obtains "due proof" of the insured's death. Life insurance notice requirements are therefore discussed in the next section on proofs of loss.

[2] See, e.g., Vermont Mut. Ins. Co. v. Singleton, 446 S.E.2d 417 (S.C. 1994); Chas. T. Main, Inc. v. Fireman's Fund Ins. Co., 551 N.E.2d 28 (Mass. 1990); Aetna Cas. & Sur. Co. v. Murphy, 538 A.2d 219 (Conn. 1988); Kolbeck v. Rural Mut. Ins. Co., 235 N.W.2d 466 (Wis. 1975); Iowa Mut. Ins. Co. v. Meckna, 144 N.W.2d 73 (Neb. 1966).

[3] See, e.g., Olin Corp. v. Insurance Co. of N. Am., 966 F.2d 718 (2d Cir. 1992).

[4] See, e.g., *Policy Kit* at 74 (Federal Emergency Management Agency, Standard Flood Insurance Policy); 92 (personal umbrella policy, AK2191-1 4-81 25M); at 444 (aircraft policy).

[5] See, e.g., *Policy Kit* at 26 (homeowner's property coverage, ISO Form HO 00 03 04 91); at 10 (personal auto policy, ISO Form PP 00 01 12 89). See also *Policy Kit* at 85 (boatowner's form, Am. Assoc. of Ins. Services Form BT-100 Ed 1.0, providing "we may request written notice"); at 264 (contractors' equipment coverage form, Am. Assoc. of Ins. Services Form IM-7000 Ed 1.0).

[6] See Putney School, Inc. v. Schaaf, 599 A.2d 322 (Vt. 1991).

[7] See § 81[e], *infra.*

provision. Generally, the notice need only contain enough information to enable the insured to commence an investigation; thus, the notice will be deemed to have been sufficient if it had enough detail to inform the insurer that a loss occurred or that a claim is likely to be asserted against the insured.[8]

Normally, it is the insured's obligation to give notice of loss,[9] and some courts have held that this obligation is not met when the insurer acquires knowledge about a loss or claim from other sources.[10] However, since the notice provision is for the insurer's benefit in conducting a speedy investigation, it should make no difference who gives notice of the loss or the claim to the insurer, so long as the notice is timely.[11] Where courts have concluded that the receipt by an insurer of independent information about a loss or occurrence is insufficient to satisfy the notice requirement in circumstances where the insured has failed to provide notice, the cases seem to depend more on the quality of the information; for example, "general neighborhood gossip" should not satisfy the notice requirement[12] but information from someone else involved in an accident for which the insured may have coverage probably should.[13] Under the approaches which require either the insured or insurer to show prejudice or the lack thereof, which are discussed later in this section, the insurer who receives notice of the loss or claim from someone other than the insured cannot assert prejudice, which means coverage should not terminate. If the insured is under a duty to provide notice, fairness suggests that the insured's breach by failing to give the notice should be treated as an immaterial breach, which would not discharge the insurer's duty to perform, assuming that the insurer learns of the loss or claim through some other means.

There is one situation that can be greatly affected by the analysis that the notice of loss requirement is met when someone other than the insured gives notice to the insurer. In liability insurance, the insured's failure to give the insurer notice of a potential liability may deprive the injured third party of an important source of compensation. Thus, an injured third party who knows the identity of the tortfeasor's insurer should take steps to notify the insurer of the incident causing injury, rather than assume that the insured-tortfeasor will do so. This simple step could have the effect of eliminating one defense the insurer might assert to coverage.

Finally, it is essential that the insured give notice to the proper party, meaning that the notice must reach the insurer or the insurer's authorized agent. If the insured

---

[8] See, e.g., Hopkins v. Lawyers Title Ins. Corp., 514 So. 2d 786 (Ala. 1986); Mousa v. State Auto Ins. Cos., 460 N.W.2d 310 (Mich. Ct. App. 1990).

[9] In life insurance, obviously, this notice will be given by a beneficiary.

[10] See, e.g., American Home Assur. Co. v. Republic Ins. Co., 984 F.2d 76 (2d Cir.), cert. denied, 113 S.Ct. 2964 (1993); Insurance Co. of N. Am. v. Waldroup, 462 F. Supp. 161 (M.D.Ga. 1978).

[11] See, e.g., Goodwin v. Nationwide Ins. Co., 656 P.2d 135 (Idaho Ct.App. 1982); Employers Cas. Co. v. Glen Falls Ins. Co., 484 S.W.2d 570 (Tex. 1972); Mahone v. State Farm Mut. Auto. Ins. Co., 373 S.E.2d 809 (Ga. Ct. App. 1988); Philadelphia Elec. Co. v. Aetna Cas. & Sur. Co., 484 A.2d 768 (Pa.Super. 1984); Wilson v. United States Fidelity & Guar. Co., 633 P.2d 493 (Colo.Ct.App. 1981).

[12] See Allstate Ins. Co. v. Kepchar, 592 N.E.2d 694 (Ind. Ct. App. 1992).

[13] See Bantz v. Bongard, 864 P.2d 618 (Idaho 1993).

gives the notice to the wrong person — such as, for example, the insured's own broker who is not functioning as the insurer's agent — the notice requirement is not met.[14]

[c] When Notice Is Due

The initial problem in determining when notice of loss is due is determining what events or circumstances trigger the obligation to give notice. Most policies provide that the insured is obligated to give notice as soon as the insured has information from which one could reasonably conclude that an occurrence or loss that might invoke the coverage has taken place. This usually presents little difficulty. When property is damaged or destroyed, the obligation to give notice exists as soon as the damage is discovered. When an event has occurred which results in damage for which the insured might be liable, the test is what a reasonable insured would do in the same circumstances; if the circumstances would suggest to a reasonable person that there is a possibility of a claim, the insured has at that point an obligation to give notice.[15]

Most policies purport to require the insured to give the notice "immediately," "forthwith," or "as soon as possible," but courts have interpreted this language as requiring notice to be given within a reasonable time in light of all the circumstances.[16] This interpretation of the time limits gives the factfinder considerable flexibility, enabling it to reach a pro-insured result in a situation where the insured inadvertently delays in giving notice. If the factfinder concludes that the notice was given within a reasonable time under all the circumstances, the notice of loss provision is satisfied, and the analysis is over. No need exists to consider secondary issues, such as whether the insurer was prejudiced by the delay.

Not surprisingly, results in the cases vary widely. Notice has been held timely when the delay between the loss and the giving of notice was rather lengthy,[17] while

---

[14] See, e.g., Security Mut. Ins. Co. of N.Y. v. Acker Fitzsimons Corp., 293 N.E.2d 76 (N.Y. 1972) (notice to insured's own broker was not notice to insurer).

[15] See, e.g., Commercial Union Ins. Co. v. International Flavors & Fragrances, Inc., 822 F.2d 267 (2d Cir. 1987); State Farm Fire & Cas. Co. v. Walton, 423 S.E.2d 188 (Va. 1992); Great Am. Ins. Co. v. C.G. Tate Constr. Co., 340 S.E.2d 743 (N.C. 1986); Oregon Auto. Ins. Co. v. Fitzwater, 531 P.2d 894 (Or. 1975).

[16] See, e.g., Olin Corp. v. Insurance Co. of N. Am., 966 F.2d 718 (2d Cir. 1992); Yale v. Nat'l Indem. Co., 664 F.2d 406 (4th Cir. 1981); Vermont Mut. Ins. Co. v. Singleton, 446 S.E.2d 417 (S.C. 1994); Putney School, Inc. v. Schaaf, 599 A.2d 322 (Vt. 1991); State Auto. Mut. Ins. Co. v. Youler, 396 S.E.2d 737 (W.Va. 1990); State Farm Fire & Cas. Co. v. Scott, 372 S.E.2d 383 (Va. 1988); Jostens, Inc. v. CNA Ins./Continental Cas. Co., 403 N.W.2d 625 (Minn. 1987); State Farm Mut. Auto. Ins. Co. v. Burgess, 474 So. 2d 634 (Ala. 1985); Bates v. Holyoke Mut. Ins. Co., 324 S.E.2d 474 (Ga. 1985); Mighty Midgets, Inc. v. Centennial Ins. Co., 389 N.E.2d 1080 (N.Y. 1979).

[17] E.g., Fagan v. Bankers Multiple Line Ins. Co., 669 F.2d 293 (5th Cir. 1982) (notice nearly 180 days after accident was timely even though policy required notice within 20 days); Hague v. Liberty Mut. Ins. Co., 571 F.2d 262 (5th Cir. 1978) (two-year delay reasonable under all the circumstances); Sanderson v. Postal Life Ins. Co., 87 F.2d 58 (10th Cir. 1936) (16-year delay excused due to party's ignorance as to existence of coverage); Middlesex Mut. Ins. Co. v. Wells, 453 F. Supp. 808 (N.D. Ala. 1978) (one and one-half-year delay excused where

in other cases the notice has been held untimely when the interval between the loss and the giving of notice was shorter.[18] Much depends on the particular circumstances and the reasonableness of the insured's conduct in those circumstances. *Lord v. State Farm Mut. Auto. Ins. Co.,* [19] a 1982 Virginia case, is illustrative. The insured, a student and library employee at the University of Virginia, had just been admitted to law school. On August 26, 1978, while moving from one apartment to another in Charlottesville, the insured carried a stack of books to his automobile, which was parked on the street near the premises he was vacating. As he rested his books on the side of the vehicle and reached into his pocket for his car keys, he was attacked by an unknown assailant. In the ensuing scuffle, the insured was stabbed in the abdomen, which caused him to be hospitalized for about nine days and to incur over $4,000 in medical expenses.

The insured was not aware that his automobile insurance policy might cover his medical expenses, so he did not give notice of the occurrence to the insurer. He consulted an attorney in February, 1979, who furnished the insurer with its first and only notice of loss, which was received 173 days after the incident. The insured argued that he had a claim which one unskilled in insurance matters would not expect to be covered under an automobile policy, and as such he should be excused for tardily filing the notice of loss. But the court disagreed:

> [The insured] was a well-educated person, and a prospective law student. He was hospitalized for only nine days. He was not prevented by his injury, or any other circumstance, from personally notifying [the insurer] seasonably, or from having someone notify the insurer on his behalf. He simply was ignorant of the policy provisions which, arguably, may have covered his medical expenses. Under these circumstances, the delayed notice, without sufficient justification, constitutes a breach of the notice conditions of the policy in question . . .[20]

Two members of the seven-justice court dissented, asserting that the insured's delay was neither unreasonable nor prejudicial to the insurer.

---

plaintiff did not know that father's auto insurance covered son's motorcycle accident); Western Auto. Cas. Co. v. Lee, 55 S.W.2d 1 (Ky. 1932) (64 days); Simon v. Mechanics' Ins. Co., 121 S.E. 342 (Ga. Ct. App. 1923) (60 days). See also Lawler v. Government Employees Ins. Co., 569 So. 2d 1151 (Miss. 1990) (7-year delay in giving notice was not late as a matter of law). As one would expect, long delays usually do not satisfy the notice requirement. See, e.g., Met-Coil Sys. Corp. v. Columbia Cas. Co., 524 N.W.2d 650 (Iowa 1994) (5-year delay unreasonable); Busch Corp. v. State Farm Fire & Cas. Co., 743 P.2d 1217 (Utah 1987) (5-year delay constituted unreasonable delay); Protective Ins. Co. v. Johnson, 352 S.E.2d 760 (Ga. 1987); Marez v. Dairyland Ins. Co., 638 P.2d 286 (Colo. 1981) (30-month delay unreasonable); Structure Tone, Inc. v. Zurich Ins. Co., 597 N.Y.S.2d 702 (N.Y. App. Div. 1993) (3-year delay unreasonable); West Am. Ins. Co. v. Hardin, 571 N.E.2d 449 (Ohio Ct.App. 1989) (8-year delay unreasonable).

[18] E.g., Hannuniemi v. Carruth, 179 N.E. 597 (Mass. 1932) (40 days); Wilcox v. Massachusetts Protective Ass'n, 165 N.E. 429 (Mass. 1929) (5 days).

[19] 295 S.E.2d 796 (Va. 1982).

[20] 295 S.E.2d at 799–800.

The majority in *Lord* gave particular significance to the subtle, close factual questions that the insurer, had it received earlier notice, would have been better able to investigate. Coverage hinged on whether the insured was "entering into" the vehicle, and this determination depended on facts showing the insured's proximity to the vehicle before the attack, his intention, and his location at the time of the injury. There were eyewitnesses to the incident, but the insured's tardiness in submitting his notice of loss prevented the insurer from interviewing these witnesses until long after the events. Despite the intuitive appeal of some aspects of the majority's reasoning, the result is nonetheless unsettling. Despite the court's assertions to the contrary, it is likely that many, and perhaps most, people, including prospective and present law students, would not expect their automobile medical payments coverage to insure them for medical expenses incurred as a result of injuries suffered when assaulted while trying to enter their automobiles.

In contrast to *Lord* is *Weaver Brothers, Inc. v. Chappel*,[21] a 1984 Alaska case. The insured and two of his family members were killed on September 4, 1974, when their Volkswagon van was hit head-on by a tractor-trailer driven by an employee of Weaver Brothers, Inc. (WBI). In 1975, the estates of the two family members filed a wrongful death suit against WBI. The case went to trial in 1979, and a jury verdict for the estates was entered. Pending appeal, WBI settled with the estates. On October 27, 1980, WBI filed a claim for contribution against the insured's estate and notified the insured's insurer of this claim on November 11, 1980. This notice, over six years after the accident, was the insurer's first notice of the accident. Summary judgment for the insurer was granted on the contribution claim on the ground that notice was untimely and the delay was unreasonable, unjustifiable, and prejudicial.

The Alaska Supreme Court reversed the summary judgment and remanded for further proceedings. The court refused to rule that the six-year delay was unreasonable as a matter of law. Regardless of the reasons for the late notice — and apparently regardless of the period of the delay, the court said the insurer would not be excused unless the insurer could demonstrate that it was prejudiced by the delay. The court cited the strong public interest in protecting accident victims, even though this interest could have been served in the instant case by holding WBI alone responsible for the wrongful deaths.

In short, a notice of loss must be filed within a reasonable time, but what is a reasonable time varies with the circumstances, the court, and the parties. The flexible rule gives little certainty, but its virtue is its capability of being used to achieve fairness.

[d] Excuses for Noncompliance

Under extenuating circumstances, the insured will be excused from complying with the notice of loss requirement. Compliance has been excused where the insured was an additional, unnamed insured who lacked notice of the existence of the policy and had not acted unreasonably in not knowing of the policy's existence;[22] where

---

[21] 684 P.2d 123 (Alaska 1984).

[22] E.g., Finstad v. Steiger Tractor, Inc. 301 N.W.2d 392 (N.D. 1981); American Liberty Ins. Co. v. Soules, 258 So. 2d 872 (Ala. 1972). But see Olin Corp. v. Insurance Co. of N.

the insured lacked knowledge of the coverage;[23] where the insured, despite acting reasonably, lacked knowledge of the loss;[24] where the insured reasonably believed that the event was so insignificant a loss had not occurred or that a claim against the insured would not result[25] (although where a reasonable person can envision possible liability, that person has a duty to make some inquiry into the circumstances);[26] where the insured reasonably believed that no claim could be asserted within the policy's coverage;[27] and where the insured, through sickness or disability, was incapable of giving notice of the loss.[28] By the same token, noncompliance has been excused in circumstances where the insurer had already denied the existence of coverage, which then arguably renders the giving of notice futile,[29] and in circumstances where the insurer is otherwise found to have waived the notice requirement.[30] In each of these situations and others similar to them, substantial mitigating circumstances existed that justified excusing the insured from the notice requirement.

[e] Effect of Noncompliance

Because failure to give notice within a reasonable time may provide the insurer with a defense to coverage, insureds should give notice under any policy that might provide coverage whenever the insured knows or suspects that a loss has been suffered or a claim might be asserted against the insured. The consequences to an insured of failing to give notice in a timely manner can be catastrophic for an insured. In many jurisdictions, if no mitigating circumstance justifies the insured's failure to give timely notice, the insured is not entitled to benefits.[31]

Am., 966 F.2d 718 (2d Cir. 1992) (lack of knowledge of insurance policy does not excuse delay in notification of an occurrence).

[23] See, e.g., Insurance Co. of N. Am. v. Waldroup, 462 F. Supp. 161 (M.D.Ga. 1978); Reid v. Monticello, 40 So. 2d 814 (La. 1949).

[24] E.g., Renuart-Bailey-Cheely Lumber & Supply Co. v. Phoenix of Hartford Ins. Co., 474 F.2d 555 (5th Cir. 1972); West Am. Ins. Co. v. Bank of Isle of Wight, 673 F. Supp. 760 (E.D. Va. 1987); Insurance Co. of N. Am. v. Asarco, Inc., 562 S.W.2d 557 (Tex. Ct. App. 1978).

[25] E.g., United States Fid. & Guar. Co v. Giroux, 274 A.2d 487 (Vt. 1971); Henschel v. Hawkeye-Security Ins. Co., 178 N.W.2d 409, 415 (Iowa 1970).

[26] See Met-Coil Sys. Corp. v. Columbia Cas. Co., 524 N.W.2d 650 (Iowa 1994); White v. City of New York, 615 N.E.2d 216 (N.Y. 1993).

[27] See, e.g., Insurance Co. of N. Am. v. Waldroup, 462 F. Supp. 161 (M.D.Ga. 1978); Farmers Auto. Ins. Ass'n v. Hamilton, 355 N.E.2d 1 (Ill. 1976).

[28] See Royal-Globe Ins. Co. v. Craven, 585 N.E.2d 315 (Mass. 1992) (insured was excused from 24-hour notice requirement during time insured was in intensive care in hospital; but delay for three months after release from hospital was not excused); Lusk v. Doe, 338 S.E.2d 375 (W.Va. 1985); Seabra v. Puritan Life Ins. Co., 369 A.2d 652 (R.I. 1977).

[29] See Hartford Fire Ins. Co. v. Daniels, 201 F.2d 787 (9th Cir. 1953); Comunale v. Traders & Gen. Ins. Co., 253 P.2d 495 (Cal. Ct. App. 1953).

[30] See, e.g., New York v. AMRO Realty Corp., 936 F.2d 1420 (2d Cir. 1991); Ara v. Erie Ins. Co., 387 S.E.2d 320 (W.Va. 1989) (estoppel); Allstate Ins. Co. v. First of Ga. Ins. Co., 753 S.W.2d 672 (Tenn. 1988); Aguirre v. City of New York, 625 N.Y.S.2d 597 (N.Y. App. Div. 1995).

[31] For a state-by-state summary of the consequences of late notice, see Bart Tesoriero, Finley Harckham & David Roland, *The Draconian Late Notice Forfeiture Rule: "Off With the Policyholders' Heads,"* 13 Ins. Litig. Rptr. 113, 124-27 (1993).

The traditional rule, and one that is still followed in some jurisdictions, is that timely notice is a condition precedent to coverage, and unexcused delay in giving notice will relieve the insurer of its obligations to the insured, whether or not the delay prejudiced the insurer.[32] New York is the most prominent jurisdiction still adhering to the strict notice rule; illustrative of the traditional approach is *Gardner-Denver Co. v. Dic-Underhill Construction Co.*[33] The plaintiff sued the owner of a construction site and the contractor for the value of an air compressor it had leased to defendants and which was presumably stolen from the site. At the time the compressor was stolen, defendants notified American Home Assurance Company, which had issued a policy of builder's risk insurance to the contractor and the siteowner. Defendants assumed that American Home would cover the claim, but nearly two years later American Home notified the defendants that the claim was outside the policy's coverage. Within a month after the denial, the contractor filed a claim under its bailees' policy with St. Paul. A few months later, St. Paul denied coverage, and when defendants sued, St. Paul moved for summary judgment on the ground that the defendants failed to comply with the provision of their insurance contract that required notice of any loss "as soon as practicable." Under New York law, compliance with a notice provision is a condition to coverage; absent a valid excuse for the failure to give notice, no coverage exists. The court held that the good faith belief that the loss would be covered by American Home did not excuse the contractor's failure to notify St. Paul of the loss in a timely manner. Accordingly, the twenty-month delay after the date of loss in giving notice was held unreasonable as a matter of law.

When viewed along with the many insurance law rules that are sympathetic to insureds and which excuse technical, literal compliance with policy requirements, that the traditional view treating timely notice as a condition precedent to coverage has any following at all may seem aberrational. Yet the strict view may not be as harsh as first appearances suggest. If a court adhering to the traditional view takes a particularly lenient view of what constitutes a reasonable time, there may be as many pro-insured results in that court as in a court which takes a shorter view of what constitutes a reasonable time but excuses the late notice when there is no demonstrated prejudice to the insurer.[34] Moreover, if a court adhering to the

---

[32] See, e.g, Canadyne-Georgia Corp. v. Continental Ins. Co., 999 F.2d 1547 (11th Cir. 1993)(applying Georgia law); American Home Assur. Co. v. Republic Ins. Co., 984 F.2d 76 (2d Cir.), *cert. denied,* 113 S.Ct. 2964 (1993) (applying New York law); American Employers Ins. Co. v. Metro Regional Transit Authority, 12 F.3d 591 (6th Cir. 1993) (applying Ohio law); Bolivar Cty. Bd. of Supervisors v. Forum Ins. Co., 779 F.2d 1081 (5th Cir. 1986) (under Mississippi law, if notice is not given "as soon as practicable," insured cannot recover, irrespective of prejudice to insurer).

[33] 416 F. Supp. 934 (S.D. N.Y. 1976).

[34] A good example is Mighty Midgets, Inc. v. Centennial Ins. Co., 389 N.E.2d 1080 (N.Y. 1979). A 9-year-old boy, a member of a boys' football team, was injured when a scalding pot of water being used to boil hot dogs fell on him. The 21-year-old volunteer president of the non-profit corporation which ran the league informed his broker of the accident, and relying on this advice immediately notified the accident and health insurer of the incident but not the liability insurer. Notice to the liability insurer did not occur until over seven months later. In the circumstances the court held the failure to give notice "was not unreasonable."

traditional view considers the question of prejudice to the insurer when determining whether notice is reasonable, the traditional view may differ little from approaches followed in other jurisdictions.[35]

In most jurisdictions, the traditional view yields to another approach which does not treat the failure to give prompt notice, standing alone, as enough to eliminate coverage. Under the modern view, late notice does not discharge the insurer's duties unless the insurer is prejudiced as a result of the late notice. These courts fall into two groups: one group, which represents the majority position under the modern view, holds that an unexcused failure to give notice will not result in a loss of benefits unless the insurer can show that it was prejudiced by the delay,[36] while a smaller group holds that late notice will terminate the coverage unless the insured can demonstrate that the insurer was not prejudiced by the late notice.[37]

The rationale underlying the prejudice requirement is straightforward. Notice is what is necessary to inform the insurer that an event has occurred, and delayed notice usually frustrates the insurer's investigation, which in turn can prejudice the company's ability to prepare an adequate defense. But if no prejudice exists from the late notice, no harm has been caused, and it is therefore considered unreasonable to require the insured to forfeit coverage when the failure to fulfill the condition was inconsequential. To borrow a concept from sports, the prejudice requirement is much like a "no harm, no foul" rule.[38]

---

[35] See, e.g., Karson v. City of New York, 373 N.Y.S.2d 456 (N.Y. Sup. Ct. 1975) (whether insurer suffered prejudice by delayed notice is issue to be considered by jury in deciding whether notice is reasonable).

[36] E.g., Bough Constr. Co. v. Mission Ins. Co., 836 F.2d 1164 (9th Cir. 1988) (applying Washington law); Travelers Ins. Co. v. Feld Car & Truck Leasing Corp., 517 F. Supp. 1132 (D.Kan. 1981); Greycoat Hanover F Street Ltd. Partnership v. Liberty Mut. Ins. Co., 657 A.2d 764 (D.C.App. 1995); Dairyland Ins. Co. v. Voshel, 428 S.E.2d 542 (W.Va. 1993); Jones v. Bituminous Cas. Corp., 821 S.W.2d 798 (Ky. 1991); Darcy v. Hartford Ins. Co., 554 N.E.2d 28 (Mass. 1990); Ouellette v. Maine Bonding & Cas. Co., 495 A.2d 1232 (Me. 1985); Weaver Bros. Inc. v. Chappel, 684 P.2d 123 (Alaska 1984); Cooley v. John M. Anderson Co., 443 A.2d 435 (R.I. 1982); Independent School Dist. No. 1 v. Jackson, 608 P.2d 1153 (Okla. 1980); Brakeman v. Potomac Ins. Co., 371 A.2d 193 (Pa. 1977); Wendel v. Swanberg, 185 N.W.2d 348 (Mich. 1971); Campbell v. Allstate Ins. Co., 384 P.2d 155 (Cal. 1963).

[37] E.g., Montgomery v. Professional Mut. Ins. Co., 611 F.2d 818 (10th Cir. 1980) (New Mexico law); Aetna Cas. & Sur. Co. v. Samson, 471 F. Supp. 1041 (D.Colo. 1979); Met-Coil Sys. Corp. v. Columbia Cas. Co., 524 N.W.2d 650 (Iowa 1994); Aetna Cas. & Sur. Co. v. Murphy, 538 A.2d 219 (Conn. 1988); Miller v. Dilts, 463 N.E.2d 257 (Ind. 1984); National Gypsum Co. v. Travelers Indem. Co., 417 So. 2d 254 (Fla. 1982); Henschel v. Hawkeye-Security Ins. Co., 178 N.W.2d 409 (Iowa 1970). For a survey of the law in the various states, see Barry R. Ostrager & Thomas R. Newman, *Handbook on Insurance Coverage Disputes* 119-27 (7th ed. 1994). See generally Annot., *Modern Status of Rules Requiring Liability Insurer to Show Prejudice to Escape Liability Because of Insured's Failure or Delay in Giving Notice of Accident or Claim, or in Forwarding Suit Papers,* 32 A.L.R.4th 141 (1984).

[38] For readers who could care less about basketball, an explanation is in order: fouls, at least as defined by the rules, occur much more frequently in basketball than referees call them; pursuant to a custom that has developed, when contact of one player upon another which technically constitutes a foul (not to be confused with a "technical foul") causes no impairment of the fouled players movement, no foul is called; the logic is if there is no harm, there is no foul.

Where courts disagree is on the issue of which party should bear the burden of proof on the question of prejudice. The minority view, which requires the insured to demonstrate that the insurer was not prejudiced by the late notice, is closer conceptually to the traditional view. The minority view essentially proceeds from the assumption that prejudice to the insurer is presumed to exist anytime there is late notice, and it is the responsibility of the insured to rebut this assumption and demonstrate that the insurer was not prejudiced. Casting the insured in the position of proving a negative obviously creates a difficult hurdle for the insured. However, this is arguably a reasonable burden to place on the insured who, after all, was the party which created the situation in the first place by failing to give timely notice.

The majority view, which places the burden on the insurer to show that it was prejudiced by the lack of timely notice, rejects the presumption of prejudice and refuses to cause a forfeiture of coverage unless the insurer can demonstrate why this is fair. Just as an insurer carries the burden to establish that a loss is within an exclusion and therefore outside coverage, this approach requires the insurer to carry the burden of establishing that the notice condition should be invoked to eliminate coverage. Whichever side must show prejudice has a heavy burden, and it is very difficult for insurers to prove prejudice, which means that under this rule late notice rarely provides a basis for terminating coverage. Nevertheless, the insurer, with its expertise in investigating accidents and claims, is in a better position to prove prejudice than the insured is in to prove lack of prejudice. Moreover, placing the burden on the insurer is likely to cause the insurer to make a prompt preliminary investigation of the claim to protect its interests, regardless of when the notice is given. In a situation where the notice appears to be excessively late, the insurer will investigate anyway, and the worst that can happen is that the insurer will decide it has been prejudiced, refuse to pay the claim, and wait for the insured to bring a suit upon the policy. In many instances, however, the insurer's investigation will reveal that the insurer has not been prejudiced and that the claim is valid. In these instances, the insured will be paid and the controversy will never reach a court.

The North Carolina Supreme Court has added a third step to the process of determining whether an insured has satisfied the notice of loss requirements. When the insurer claims that it did not receive notice of a loss in a timely fashion, the trier of fact must determine, first, whether the notice was given as soon as practicable, and, second, whether the insured has demonstrated that he or she acted in good faith. Only if notice is timely and in good faith is it necessary to proceed to the third test, where the insurer is required to show that it was prejudiced by the insured's delay.[39] The Court explained its "good faith" requirement as follows:

> This test of lack of good faith involves a two-part inquiry: 1) Was the insured aware of his or her possible fault, and 2) Did the insured purposefully and knowingly fail to notify the insurer? Both of these are, in the legal sense of the term, "subjective" inquiries—they ask not what a reasonable person in the position of the insured would have known, but what the insured *actually did know*. . . .

---

[39] See Great Am. Ins. Co. v. C.G. Tate Constr. Co., 279 S.E.2d 769 (N.C. 1981), *later proceeding*, 340 S.E.2d 743 (N.C. 1986).

The good faith test is phrased in the conjunctive: both knowledge *and* the deliberate decision not to notify must be met for lack of good faith to be shown.[40]

In first-party insurance, the good faith requirement is unnecessary. Rarely does an insured serve his or her own interests by intentionally withholding notice of a claim. If the insured delays for some other reason, the "excuse" doctrines are adequate to protect the interests of both insureds and insurers. In third-party insurance, the context in which the North Carolina Supreme Court articulated the doctrine, the good faith requirement plays a role, since an insured's cooperation with the insurer in this setting is not always forthcoming. Nevertheless, the good faith requirement is implicitly present in the two-part test followed by most courts, and it therefore seems superfluous — though certainly not harmful — to recognize it as a separate requirement. For example, if the insured knows that he or she is liable for someone else's loss or that others claim the insured is liable, and if, despite this knowledge, the insured fails to give notice to the insurer, the insured is not acting in good faith — and presumably has not given notice as soon as practicable. If an insured is unaware of the loss or the incident giving rise to potential liability, the insured has not intentionally (meaning, in bad faith) failed to notify the insurer, but under the excuse doctrines the insured has a good reason for the late notice. Thus far, other courts have not felt it necessary to add the good faith requirement in the liability insurance setting.

What constitutes prejudice is not a simple question. Obviously, prejudice will necessarily have something to do with the purpose of the notice of loss condition, meaning that courts will inquire into whether the late notice impaired or frustrated the insurer's ability to investigate or defend the claim. In *Morales v. National Grange Mutual Insurance Co.,*[41] a New Jersey court opined that establishing prejudice involves two inquiries: first, whether "substantial rights pertaining to a defense against the claim have been irretrievably lost," and second, whether the possibility or likelihood of the insurer's successfully defending the claim had been diminished.[42] Implicit in *Morales* is the notion that the prejudice must be material in some sense; a minor inconvenience to the insurer is not sufficient to constitute prejudice. It is not essential that the insurer establish a tangible loss, but the insurer must establish that it was somehow worse off as a result of the late notice. In extreme cases, the prejudice is obvious. For example, the failure of an insured to give notice of a suit against it until after a default judgment has been entered against the insured and the judgment has become final and nonappealable is prejudicial, almost certainly as a matter of law.[43] Prejudice may also be found in other less-extreme circumstances. Thus, prejudice may be found where the late notice prevented the insurer from settling a claim prior to judgment,[44] from determining whether affirmative

---

[40] Great Am. Ins. Co. v. C.G. Tate Constr. Co., 340 S.E.2d 743, 747 (N.C. 1986).

[41] 423 A.2d 325 (N.J.Super.Ct.Law Div. 1980).

[42] 423 A.2d at 329 (emphasis deleted).

[43] See Harwell v. State Farm Mut. Auto. Ins. Co., 896 S.W.2d 170 (Tex. 1995).

[44] See Allstate Ins. Co. v. Kepchar, 592 N.E.2d 694 (Ind. Ct. App. 1992); Select Ins. Co. v. Superior Court, 276 Cal. Rptr. 598 (Cal. Ct. App. 1990).

defenses are available,[45] from appointing defense counsel to take control of the case,[46] from adequately investigating the loss or claim,[47] or from making suggestions to the insured that could reduce the insurer's liability.[48] At the bottom line, whether prejudice occurred is a question of fact, and the answer will depend on all the circumstances.

§ 82   Proof of Loss

[a]   Overview

Contracts of property insurance usually require the insured to produce some information to support the claim that proceeds should be paid. This information is typically presented to the insurer in a written document called a "proof of loss," which the policy usually specifies must be filed within a specified number of days after the insurer requests it.[1] The proof of loss must describe in detail and otherwise document the circumstances and nature of the insured's loss. Life insurance has an analogous requirement, and the form itself is sometimes called a proof of loss. In liability insurance if damaged property that is the subject of a liability claim is within the insured's control, the insured will probably be required to issue a sworn statement regarding the loss, which is very similar to a proof of loss.

The purposes of the proof of loss requirement are similar to those of the notice of loss requirement: to give the insurer an adequate opportunity to investigate the loss, and to prevent fraud against the insurer, all before the evidence about the loss becomes stale or unavailable. More so than the notice of loss, however, the proof of loss provides details about the loss and requires the insured, in a sworn statement, to commit to a specific claim upon the policy.

[b]   Substantive Requirements

The insurance policy itself usually specifies what information shall be contained in a proof of loss. A typical homeowner's policy, for example, requires the insured to submit a "sworn proof of loss" setting forth the time and cause of loss, identification of all who have an interest in the property, of all insurance that might cover the loss, changes in title or occupancy during the policy's term, specifications of damaged buildings and detailed repair estimates, an inventory of damaged personal property, and receipts for expenses incurred as a result of the loss.

The requirements for the proof of loss in life insurance are ordinarily less specific and rarely present difficulties. A typical policy usually states only that the proceeds

---

[45] See Kermans v. Pendleton, 233 N.W.2d 658 (Mich. Ct. App. 1975).

[46] See Allstate Ins. Co. v. Kepchar, 592 N.E.2d 694 (Ind.App. 1992).

[47] See Henderson v. Biron, 360 N.W.2d 230 (Mich. Ct. App. 1984).

[48] See West Bay Exploration Co. v. AIG Speciality Agencier of Tex., Inc., 915 F.2d 1030 (6th Cir. 1990).

[1] See Ball v. Allstate Ins. Co., 611 N.E.2d 750 (N.Y. 1993) (requirement that insurer "furnish" proof of loss requires that insureds place proof of loss in the mail within 60 days of receiving demand for it, not that insurer receive proof within that time).

will be paid upon receiving "proof" or "due proof" of the death of the insured. Proving a death is typically a fairly simple matter, and a valid death certificate is conclusive on the question. Depending on the circumstances, a certificate of an attending physician or a newspaper obituary notice, though somewhat less reliable, may be all that a particular insurer requires to prove a death.

In life insurance, the proof of loss is essentially what provides notice to the insurer that the death has occurred. If the beneficiary calls the insurer to inform the insurer that the insured has died, the insurer will instruct the beneficiary to submit a proof of death. As discussed in the preceding section, time limits exist for giving notice of the loss and filing the proof of loss in property insurance. In life insurance, as a practical matter, the only time limits for filing a life insurance policy claim are those imposed by the statute of limitations for contract claims. It is necessary, however, for the beneficiary to show that the death occurred while the policy was in force. For example, if the insured allowed the policy to lapse prior to the insured's death, the beneficiary will not be entitled to proceeds.

Occasionally, beneficiaries have no knowledge that they are entitled to proceeds upon the death of the insured. If the insurer learns of the insured's death, a question might arise as to whether the insurer has an obligation to bring this fact to the beneficiary's attention, to inform the beneficiary that he or she is entitled to proceeds, and to take other steps to facilitate the payment to the beneficiary. Apparently no cases have considered this specific point,[2] but the fair result is to impose a duty on the insurer, in circumstances where the insurer is aware of a beneficiary's entitlement to proceeds, to bring such information to the beneficiary's attention.[3]

The proof of loss requirements in life insurance are potentially more important in two situations. When the beneficiary seeks to establish that the insured's death was caused by accident in order to recover double indemnity benefits, the proofs must be sufficient to establish the accidental cause of death. An automobile accident report, a coroner's statement, or a sworn eyewitness account of the death are ordinarily sufficient to meet this requirement. Also more difficult is the situation where the insured disappears and no body is found. The absence of an insured for a period of seven years from the insured's usual abode is presumptive evidence of death. The presumption does not arise if the insured asserts that the insured is leaving his or her abode and intends never to return again. However, proof of the insured's absence and the fact that the insured has not been heard from by people who had

---

[2] In Merten v. Nathan, 321 N.W.2d 173 (Wis. 1982), Justice Callow in a dissenting opinion indicated that he was aware of no cases imposing a duty on the insurer to disclose the existence of a policy to the beneficiary, 321 N.W.2d at 180 n.1, but the issue in the case was whether a contract for horse-riding lessons containing a false statement to the effect that the riding school had no insurance was enforceable. Obviously, a beneficiary who is unaware of a policy's existence will never have the knowledge necessary even to assert the claim that the insurer should have taken affirmative steps to bring the coverage to the insured's attention; if, upon discovering a policy, the beneficiary files a claim and the insurer pays proceeds, there is no issue worth litigating.

[3] See Andrea G. Podolsky, Note, *Insurer's Duty to Disclose the Existence of a Policy*, 76 Colum. L. Rev. 825 (1976).

reason to expect communications with the insured is ordinarily sufficient to establish both the insured's death and a valid claim to the proceeds of a policy in force. If the premiums for the policy have not been paid, which is likely to be the case if the insured takes out a policy on the insured's own life and disappears, the probabilities are high that the policy will have lapsed prior to the running of the seven-year period.[4]

[c]   Effect of Noncompliance

An insurer will rarely escape liability because of the insured's failure to comply with the policy's provisions on proof of loss. Unless the policy provides otherwise, it is not necessary to submit the proof of loss in any particular form. In fact, the standard of compliance is a flexible one: courts only insist upon "substantial compliance" with proof of loss requirements.[5] As stated by one court, "[j]ustice mandates that an insurer should not escape a liability it has expressly undertaken on overly technical grounds."[6] All that is necessary is the submission of a form reasonably suggesting that the insured's claim may be valid.[7] If the insured fails to make the submission, courts usually allow someone else to submit the form on the insured's behalf.[8] Moreover, if the insurer admits liability, offers to settle the claim, or has independent knowledge of the loss, some courts have held that the

---

[4] See Security Bank v. Equitable Life Assur. Soc'y, 71 S.E. 647 (Va. 1911) (insured who disappeared did not "die" prior to lapse of policy 13 months after disappearance). For a brief discussion of the common law presumption of death, see Jeanne L. Carriere, *The Rights of the Living Dead: Absent Persons in the Civil Law,* 50 La. L. Rev. 901 (1990). The Uniform Absence as Evidence of Death and Absentees' Property Act, 8A U.L.A. 1 (1993), abolishes the common law presumption of death, and the issue of whether an absent person is dead is decided by a jury. However, only two states have adopted the Uniform Act, and one of these (Wisconsin) omitted the section abolishing the common law presumption, leaving Tennessee and Louisiana (see Carriere, *supra*) as the only states without the common law presumption. This led to an interesting result in White v. White, 876 S.W.2d 837 (Tenn. 1994), where the court held that the six-year statute of limitations for insurance actions began to run on the date the insurer was notified of the insured's absence. Because the seven-years absence rule had no relevance in Tennessee, a beneficiary's suit to obtain proceeds under the policy brought six years and nine months after the alleged disappearance and asserting the insured's absence for seven years as a basis for relief was held barred by the statute of limitations.

[5] See, e.g., Walker v. American Bankers Ins. Group, 836 P.2d 59 (Nev. 1992); Canyon Country Store v. Bracey, 781 P.2d 414 (Utah 1989); Brinkman v. Aid Ins. Co., 766 P.2d 1227 (Idaho 1988); General Elec. Capital Corp. v. Royal Ins. Co. of Am., 613 N.Y.S.2d 392 (N.Y. App. Div. 1994). See also Green v. General Acc. Ins. Co. of Am., 746 P.2d 152 (N.M. 1987) (failure of insurer's representative to furnish insured with a proof of loss form until eight months after being notified of loss was inconsistent with intention to demand exact compliance from proof of loss and time to sue provisions in policy).

[6] Zieba v. Middlesex Mut. Assur. Co., 549 F. Supp. 1318, 1320 (D.Conn. 1982).

[7] See, e.g., Rogers v. Aetna Cas & Sur Co., 601 F.2d 840 (5th Cir. 1979); Raymond v. Allstate Ins. Co., 464 N.Y.S.2d 155 (N.Y. App. Div. 1983); Henry v. Aetna Cas. & Sur. Co., 633 S.W.2d 583 (Tex. Ct. App. 1982).

[8] See Second New Haven Bank v. Kobrite, Inc., 408 N.E.2d 369 (Ill.App. 1980).

insured's need to comply with the proof of loss filing requirement is excused or that the insurer is estopped to assert the proof of loss filing requirement.[9]

As with the notice of loss, courts will not excuse the insurer from its duties on account of the insured's failure to file a proof of loss if it were impossible for the insured to do so.[10] Even though many policies state a specific time limit for filing the proof of loss, these provisions are not enforced strictly if forfeiture would result or if the intent of the parties would not be served.[11] Similarly, if a proof of loss is deficient in some way, courts usually insist that the insurer give the insured an opportunity to correct the deficiency before refusing to pay the proceeds.[12] In fact, the insurer, if unconvinced that a loss occurred or that the circumstances were as the insured described them, can always demand additional documentation of the loss, but the insurer cannot insist on more than what the law would require as reasonably sufficient evidence to establish a fact as true.[13]

Finally, most courts allow an insurer to deny coverage based on the insured's failure to file a timely proof of loss only if the insurer can prove that it was prejudiced by the delay.[14] In the situation with the prejudice requirement where the insured fails to give notice of loss in a timely fashion, establishing prejudice due to the delay in filing a proof of loss is difficult. This prevents most insurers from refusing to pay benefits on account of the insured's failure to comply with proof of loss requirements.

The insured may lose coverage, however, if he or she engages in false swearing on the proof of loss.

[d] False Swearing

Many insurance policies provide that the policy is void if the insured wilfully conceals or misrepresents a material fact concerning a loss. This issue often arises in connection with the insurer's defense to coverage based on a claim that the insured wilfully misrepresented the facts of the loss in a proof of loss statement. The insurer, to have a valid defense based on false swearing, must usually show that the insured intentionally concealed or misrepresented a material fact. Absent a statute to the contrary, no separate requirement exists that the insurer show it was prejudiced by

[9] See, e.g., Llerena v. Lumbermen's Mut. Cas Co., 379 So. 2d 166 (Fla. Dist. Ct. App. 1980); Deville v. Louisiana Farm Bureau Mut. Ins Co., 378 So. 2d 457 (La. Ct. App. 1979); Petrice v. Federal Kemper Ins. Co., 260 S.E.2d 276 (W.Va. 1979).

[10] See, e.g., Proctor v. Southland Life Ins. Co., 522 S.W.2d 261 (Tex. Ct. App. 1975); Hayes v. Equitable Life Assur. Soc'y, 150 S.W.2d 1113 (Mo. Ct. App. 1941).

[11] See, e.g., Siravo v. Great Am. Ins. Co., 410 A.2d 116 (R.I. 1980); Smith v. Nationwide Mut. Ins. Co., 306 So. 2d 385 (La. Ct. App. 1975).

[12] See Tennessee Farmers Mut. Ins. Co. v. Wheeler, 341 S.E.2d 898 (Ga. Ct. App. 1986).

[13] See, e.g., John Hancock Mut. Life Ins. Co. v. Highley, 445 P.2d 241 (Okla. 1968); Equitable Life Assur. Soc'y v. Dorriety, 157 So. 59 (Ala. 1934).

[14] See, e.g., Canyon Country Store v. Bracey, 781 P.2d 414 (Utah 1989); Foundation Reserve Ins. Co. v. Esquibel, 607 P.2d 1150 (N.M. 1980); Maryland Cas. Co. v. Clements, 487 P.2d 437 (Ariz. Ct. App. 1971).

the false swearing.[15] In essence, this defense is an extension of the misrepresentation defense for inaccurate statements made on an application for insurance. One court explained it in this way:

> When an insurer clearly warns in a "concealment of fraud" clause that it does not provide coverage if the insured makes a material misrepresentation about any material fact or circumstances relating to the insurance, the warning should apply not only to the insured's misrepresentations made when applying for insurance, but also to those made when the insurer is investigating a loss. Such misrepresentations strike at the heart of the insurer's ability to acquire the information necessary to determine its obligations and to protect itself from false claims. Thus, an insured's commitment not to misrepresent material facts extends beyond the inception of the policy to a post-loss investigation.[16]

In circumstances where the insured makes mistakes or exaggerates the amount of the loss, courts do not presume that false swearing has occurred. However, intentional overstatements of a loss, which sometimes occur as the insured tries to acquire leverage in negotiating a settlement with the insurer, are tantamount to false swearing. Sometimes the distinction between exaggeration and intentional misrepresentation is difficult to draw.

Such a difficulty was present in *Nagel-Taylor Automotive Supplies, Inc. v. Aetna Cas. & Sur. Co.*[17] Plaintiffs were covered for actual business interruption losses on a building which they owned and operated as a nightclub. The relevant provision provided that the insureds would be reimbursed for the amount by which their profits decreased (or losses increased) during the interruption "but not exceeding the reduction in gross earning less charges and expenses which do not necessarily continue during the interruption of business." The limit of liability under the policy was $50,000, and in a sworn proof of loss the insureds estimated their loss to be in excess of $100,000. The actual financial records showed a deficit exceeding $17,000 for eight months of operation on total receipts of about $95,000. The insurer's accountant, after reviewing the poorly maintained records, concluded that no business interruption loss was suffered. The jury agreed, awarding the plaintiff $125,000 for damage to the building and $50,000 for damage to its contents, but nothing for business interruption. The trial court granted a judgment notwithstanding the verdict to the insurer, ruling that the insurer had proved as a matter of law that the insureds had committed fraud and false swearing in the proof of loss forms, and the coverage was therefore voided.

The Court of Appeals reinstated the jury's verdict. It noted that, although the insureds' estimate of business interruption losses was unreasonably high, the jury could have concluded that the estimate was merely an overstated, good faith estimate of future earnings. *Nagel-Taylor* demonstrates that inherently speculative estimates are difficult to make the basis of a false swearing defense, particularly when the

---

[15] See, e.g., Woods v. Independent Fire Ins. Co., 749 F.2d 1493 (11th Cir. 1985); Mamco, Inc. v. American Employers Ins. Co., 736 F.2d 187 (5th Cir. 1984); Carlin v. Crum & Forster Ins. Co., 595 N.Y.S.2d 420 (N.Y.Sup.App. Div. 1993).

[16] Longobardi v. Chubb Ins. Co., 582 A.2d 1257, 1261 (N.J. 1990).

[17] 402 N.E.2d 302 (Ill. App. Ct. 1980).

estimate is made by a nonexpert. However, obvious, deliberate misstatements on the proof of loss submission will cause problems for the insured. Thus, in *Lykos v. American Home Ins. Co.,*[18] the insureds submitted a modest claim for business interruption losses, but submitted obviously inflated claims for damage to the building, equipment, and inventory. The court concluded that the deliberate and obvious inflated statement of loss for some items defeated the insureds' claim to proceeds for all of their claims. This was, the court said, a plan to gain a position of advantage in settling the loss, and as such the insureds' coverage was voided.

Some states, to avoid the problem of distinguishing between intentional false statements on proofs of loss and innocent misstatements, have passed so-called "antitechnicality statutes," which provide that misrepresentations or false statements made in a proof of loss have no effect unless it is shown at trial that the false statements were fraudulently made and the insurer was misled thereby.[19] An example of such a statute is provided by the Texas Insurance Code:

> Any provision in any contract or policy of insurance issued or contracted for in this State which provides that the same shall be void or voidable, if any misrepresentations or false statements be made in proofs of loss or of death, as the case may be, shall be of no effect, and shall not constitute any defense to any suit brought upon such contract or policy, unless it be shown upon the trial of such suit that the false statement made in such proofs of loss or death was fraudulently made and misrepresented a fact material to the question of the liability of the insurance company upon the contract of insurance sued on, and that the insurance company was thereby misled and caused to waive or lose some valid defense to the policy.[20]

Although the false swearing defense usually arises in connection with proofs of loss, the defense can be relevant to other aspects of claims processing. For example, in *Fine v. Bellefonte Underwriters Ins. Co.,*[21] the insured's coverage was voided because the insured made false statements under oath when responding to the insurer's questions during the investigation of the claim. The insured obtained a policy of fire insurance on three buildings rented for commercial uses in New York City. The buildings had a single heating system that employed a single boiler. The insured desired to convert the buildings to residential use; as part of his plan to encourage tenants to leave the premises, he told a building superintendent to set the heat timer so that the boiler would not operate until a subfreezing temperature was reached. During the winter a fire occurred which destroyed the three buildings. The buildings' sprinkler system did not operate due to blockage that the trial court found was caused by ice in the pipes; the trial court found that had the sprinklers functioned normally, the fire could have been controlled.

The trial court entered a judgment for the insured. It found that the insured had testified falsely in sworn examinations conducted by the insurer when investigating

---

[18] 609 F.2d 314 (7th Cir. 1979), *cert. denied,* 444 U.S. 1079 (1980).

[19] See, e.g., Ala. Code § 27-14-7; Ga. Code Ann. § 33-24-7.

[20] Tex. Ins. Code Ann. art. 21.19. For a case applying this statute, see Aetna Cas. and Sur. Co. v. Guynes, 713 F.2d 1187 (5th Cir. 1983).

[21] 725 F.2d 179 (2d Cir.), *cert. denied,* 469 U.S. 874 (1984).

the claim. The insured claimed he had told the building superintendent to set the heat timer at 40 degrees; in truth, he had told the superintendent to set the timer at a subfreezing temperature. However, the trial court concluded that the insured's false statements were not material to the loss. The appeals court reversed on the ground that the insured had violated the false swearing provision of the policy, thereby voiding the coverage. The appeals court concluded that the trial court had taken too narrow a view of materiality. The court explained:

> The law is clear that the materiality of false statements during an insurance company investigation is not to be judged by what the facts later turn out to have been. The purpose of a provision requiring an insured to submit to an examination under oath is to enable the insurance company to acquire knowledge or information that may aid it in its further investigation or that may otherwise be significant to the company in determining its liability under the policy and the position it should take with respect to a claim. Thus the materiality requirement is satisfied if the false statement concerns a subject relevant and germane to the insurer's investigation as it was then proceeding.[22]

Under the appeals court's analysis, it was enough to void the coverage that the insured's deliberate misrepresentations were made when the insurer was investigating a plausible theory based on available facts and the insurer's questions were material to the investigation.

Most courts have held that misrepresentations made during litigation do not provide an insurer with a basis for voiding the coverage.[23] This view is based on the fact that once litigation begins between the insurer and insured, the parties are adversaries and they "no longer deal on the nonadversarial level required" by the policy's provisions prohibiting fraud and false swearing.[24] Also, the insurer should not be permitted to use the litigation process to develop reasons for denying coverage; whatever reasons exist for denying coverage should be ones that exist before litigation begins.[25] There are contrary decisions; under the minority rule, material misrepresentations made by the insured during coverage litigation can provide the insurer with an independent basis for denying coverage.[26]

Finally, in circumstances where there are multiple insureds and only one insured has committed the false swearing, an issue is raised virtually identical to that which arises when one insured intentionally destroys property and there are innocent co-insureds. The question is whether the false swearing of one insured should invalidate the coverage in its entirety, or only with respect to the culpable insured, thereby

---

[22] 725 F.2d at 183.

[23] See, e.g., Mercantile Trust Co. v. New York Underwriters Ins. Co., 376 F.2d 502 (7th Cir. 1967); American Paint Serv., Inc. v. Home Ins. Co., 246 F.2d 91 (3d Cir. 1957); Rego v. Connecticut Ins. Placement Facility, 593 A.2d 491 (Conn. 1991); Ocean-Clear, Inc. v. Continental Cas. Co., 462 N.Y.S.2d 251 (N.Y. App. Div. 1983).

[24] American Paint Serv., Inc. v. Home Ins Co., 246 F.2d 91, 94 (3d Cir. 1957).

[25] See id.

[26] See, e.g., Lomartira v. American Auto. Ins. Co., 371 F.2d 550 (2d Cir. 1967); Thomas v. New Jersey Ins. Underwriting Ass'n, 649 A.2d 1383 (N.J.Super.Ct. 1994).

leaving the coverage in force for innocent co- insureds.[27] The competing considerations and different answers to this question are discussed in a prior section.[28]

§ 83   Disposition of Claims: Alternatives to Litigation

[a]   Appraisal (Property Insurance)

Most property insurance policies provide that if the insurer and insured fail to agree on the value of the destroyed property or the amount of a loss, either party may demand an appraisal. The appraisal is normally conducted by two appraisers, one appointed by each party. Also, the two appraisers normally designate an umpire, who remains available to resolve any disagreements between the appraisers.

The appraisal proceeding is meant to resolve only questions of property valuation and questions of fact concerning the loss, not other disputed issues. For example, in one case, the question of the value of a set of miniature paintings was submitted to appraisers. The appraisers, however, based their award on a conclusion — that the insured did not own the paintings he claimed to own — that was outside the scope of the appraisers' authority. As a result, the appraisal award was vacated.[1] Appraisal can be fairly viewed as a kind of limited arbitration; the work of appraisers is analogous to that of masters, who reach findings on particular submitted fact questions for the benefit of the court that must decide the entire case.

[b]   Arbitration

Arbitration is a method of alternative dispute resolution: the contending parties submit the disputed matter to one or more persons designated for the purpose of resolving the claim outside an official judicial proceeding.[2] At common law, contracts to arbitrate disputes, whether existing or prospective, were not enforceable. Thus, if a party to an arbitration agreement later decided that trial by court or jury were preferable, the party would not be bound to arbitrate. The common law is today modified by statutes in every state that in varying degrees modify the common law's unwillingness to enforce arbitration agreements.[3] Most of these statutes are modeled on the Uniform Arbitration Act,[4] approved in 1955 by the National Conference of

---

[27] See, e.g., Hogs Unlimited v. Farm Bur. Mut. Ins. Co., 401 N.W.2d 381 (Minn. 1987).

[28] See § 63A, *supra*.

[1] Safeco Ins. Co. of Am. v. Sharma, 207 Cal. Rptr. 104 (Cal. Ct. App. 1984). See also Elberon Bathing Co., Inc. v. Ambassador Ins. Co., 389 A.2d 439 (N.J. 1978); Jefferson Ins. Co. v. Superior Court, 475 P.2d 880 (Cal. 1970).

[2] For an extensive summary of arbitration in the insurance context, see American Arbitration Association, *Insurance ADR Manual* (1993). This volume is a collection of chapters on negotiation, mediation, arbitration, private judging, court-annexed ADR programs, special masters, and ADR in particular lines of insurance. For a more general treatment of alternative dispute resolution, including arbitration, see Edward A. Dauer, *Manual of Dispute Resolution* (1994).

[3] See Alan I. Widiss, "Uninsured and Underinsured Motorist Insurance Claims Disputes," in *Insurance ADR Manual, supra* note 2, at 207.

[4] 7 U.L.A. 1 (1985).

commissioners on Uniform State Laws. The Federal Arbitration Act[5] also validates agreements to arbitrate, and this statute affects contracts "evidencing a transaction involving commerce"[6] and which are the subject of disputes in federal courts. These statutes have shifted the prevailing climate to one that favors the enforcement of agreements to arbitrate. An important element of this shift has been the willingness of courts to uphold state statutes against constitutional attack, which usually has been predicated on state constitutional guarantees of the right to trial by jury.[7]

State arbitration statutes, viewed collectively, are more ambivalent on the desirability of arbitration in the insurance setting. On the one hand, statutes have been enacted in some states requiring property insurance policies to provide for binding arbitration of the amount of a loss when insurer and insured are unable to agree about it.[8] But some state arbitration acts of general application explicitly except contracts of insurance from their scope.[9] In these states insureds (and insurers) are free to seek resolution of disputes between insurer and insured in court despite the presence of an arbitration clause in the insurance policy.

Although disputes over whether agreements to arbitrate are enforceable are less common, the extent to which arbitration *should* be used as a substitute for judicial proceedings remains a controversial topic. The asserted advantages of arbitration over judicial proceedings are its speed, lower cost, and informality. The asserted disadvantages of arbitration are the lack of evidentiary rules and protections, the lack of judicial review (sometimes), and the other benefits associated with trial by a jury of one's peers. Arbitration is sometimes promoted as a means of reducing the litigation burden on courts. However one assesses these questions, the trend toward alternative dispute resolution mechanisms is unmistakable,[10] and arbitration figures prominently among the various options for reducing the costs of dispute resolution.

If two parties voluntarily agree to submit a present or prospective dispute to arbitration, the prevailing wisdom is that the agreement should be enforced, assuming the agreement is otherwise valid under general principles of contract law. An obvious problem exists if one party desiring arbitration imposes its will on the other, thereby forcing the other party to relinquish its right to have a dispute resolved in an official judicial proceeding. Thus, at least in situations where the arbitration clause is not mandated by statute, courts will inquire into the fairness of the

---

[5] 9 U.S.C. §§ 1 et seq.

[6] This phrase, found in section 2 of the Act, defines the scope of the statute.

[7] See Eden Corp. v. Utica Mut. Ins. Co., 350 F. Supp. 637 (W.D. Va. 1972); Molodyh v. Truck Ins. Exch., 744 P.2d 992 (Or. 1987); Madden v. Kaiser Found. Hosp., 552 P.2d 1178 (Cal. 1976); Prudential Prop. and Cas. Ins. Co. v. Muir, 513 A.2d 1129 (Pa.Commw.Ct. 1986); Appalachian Ins. Co. v. Rivcom Corp., 182 Cal. Rptr. 11 (Cal. Ct. App. 1982).

[8] See, e.g., Cal. Ins. Code § 2071; Va. Code Ann. § 38.2-2105.

[9] See, e.g., Kan. Stat. Ann. § 5-401; Ky. Rev. Stat. § 417.050; Okla. Stat. Ann. tit. 15, § 802; Neb. Rev. Stat. § 25-2602 (partial exception).

[10] Every state has at least one kind of court- annexed ADR program, and one writer reports as many as 12,000 different court-annexed ADR programs in the nation. See Harry N. Mazadoorian, "State Court-Annexed ADR Programs," in *Insurance ADR Manual, supra* note 2, at 145-46.

underlying agreement to arbitrate.[11] Moreover, the widespread use of standardized forms in the insurance setting, and the accompanying notion that such contracts are adhesive,[12] raises the question of whether arbitration clauses in insurance contracts should be enforced. In the view of Professor Widiss, "[a] compelling case can be made for the proposition that the arbitration provision in an uninsured or underinsured motorist coverage does not constitute the type of voluntary written agreement contemplated by the arbitration statutes and, therefore, an insurance company should not be allowed to compel claimants to arbitrate these disputes."[13] This logic would presumably apply to any standardized insurance policy purchased in the traditional process by which personal insurance policies are marketed.[14] To the extent insurers wish to arbitrate but are uncertain about the extent to which insureds are willing to arbitrate and awards entered in such processes are enforceable, arbitration's potential savings cannot be realized and cannot be reflected in premium reductions.

Another difficulty is the extent to which courts will review an arbitration award. If the parties agree to have their dispute settled in a private proceeding, courts should not lightly upset the results of such proceedings. This is tantamount to rewriting a contract — letting one party out of what is, in hindsight, a bad bargain. Generally speaking, courts give arbitration awards a high degree of finality, and judicial review of such awards is limited.[15] Yet some courts are jealous of other forums exercising judicial power and are otherwise suspicious of arbitration generally; these courts are more inclined to review the decisions of arbitrators, particularly when arbitration is not voluntary.[16] Thus, the extent to which arbitration of insurance disputes enjoys favorable treatment by courts varies considerably.[17]

§ 84   Disposition of Claims: Litigation

[a]   Timeliness of the Suit Against the Insurer

If the insurer does not process the insured's claims in a manner satisfactory to the insured, the insured may assert its claim against the insurer in court. As with any claim a party might have, the insured must assert the claim in a timely manner. Limitations on the time that the insured has to file its claim come from two sources: the relevant state statute of limitations, and the contract between insurer and insured.

---

[11] See Nationwide Mut. Ins. Co. v. Marsh, 472 N.E.2d 1061 (Ohio 1984); Ramirez v. Superior Court, 163 Cal. Rptr. 223 (Cal. Ct. App. 1980).

[12] See § 25C, *supra*.

[13] Alan I. Widiss, *supra* note 2, at 219.

[14] See § 30, *supra*.

[15] Widiss, *supra* note 2, at 234.

[16] See *id.*, at 235-41.

[17] See, e.g., Brethren Mut. Ins. Co. v. Filsinger, 458 A.2d 880 (Md.Ct.Spec.App. 1983); Schreiber v. Pacific Coast Fire Ins. Co., 75 A.2d 108 (Md. 1950). See generally James R. Cumbee, Comment, *Example for Reform: the Insurance Industry Arbitration Process,* 47 UMKC L. Rev. 444 (1979); Annot., *Uninsured and Underinsured Motorist Coverage: Enforceability of Policy Provision Limiting Appeals from Arbitration,* 23 A.L.R.5th 801 (1994).

The insured who seeks to sue the insurer for nonperformance of its obligations must bring the suit within the applicable statute of limitations. Often the greatest difficulty in determining whether the insured's suit is timely is ascertaining whether the insured's claim sounds in tort or contract. In most jurisdictions, a different limitations period will apply depending on how the cause of action is styled. Ironically, it is conceivable that an insurer might be found arguing that the insured's cause of action sounds in tort — where more damages might be recovered if the insured's claim is substantiated — so that the claim is time-barred under the ordinarily shorter tort statute of limitations.

However, the more important limitation on the typical insured's suit against the insurer, however, is that imposed by the contract itself. Many first-party insurance contracts contain provisions that require any suit against the insurer under the policy to be brought within a specified period of time after the loss occurs. Sometimes the provisions are required by state statute,[1] but this authority is not required.[2] Through such provisions, insurers attempt to cut off stale claims and achieve certainty, which is what a statute of limitations also seeks to accomplish. Contractual limitations periods are more important than statutes of limitations because the contractual periods are usually shorter.

Contractual limitations are enforced as long as they neither seek to lengthen the statutory limitations period nor attempt to shorten unreasonably the period for bringing a claim. Almost uniformly, courts have held contractual limitations periods as short as one year to be reasonable in length.[3] In most states, no requirement exists that the insurer show prejudice from the insured's delay in bringing the suit. Although there are cases to the contrary,[4] waiting too long to commence the suit

---

[1] E.g., Pa Stat. Ann. tit. 40, § 636(2); Mo. Ann. Stat. § 376.777(11). Some of these statutes have as their purpose extending the standard one-year limitations period to a longer time. See, e.g., N.Y. Ins. Law § 3404 (24 months); Mass.Ann.Laws ch. 175, § 99 (2 years); Me. Rev. Stat. Ann. tit. 24A § 2433 (2 years from time cause of action accrues).

[2] See Douglass v. American Fam. Mut. Ins. Co., 508 N.W.2d 665 (Iowa 1993) (authority to limit time to bring suit springs from general contract principles').

[3] See, e.g., Lane v. Grange Mut. Cos., 543 N.E.2d 488 (Ohio 1989); L&A United Grocers, Inc. v. Safeguard Ins. Co., 460 A.2d 587 (Me. 1983); Schreiber v. Pennsylvania Lumberman's Mut. Ins. Co., 444 A.2d 647 (Pa. 1982); Martin v. Liberty Mut. Fire Ins. Co., 293 N.W.2d 168 (Wis. 1980); Monteiro v. American Home Assur. Co., 416 A.2d 1189 (Conn. 1979); Doherty v. Hartford, 574 P.2d 132 (Haw. 1978); Minnesota Mut. Fire & Cas. Co. v. North Lakes Constr. Inc., 400 N.W.2d 367 (Minn. Ct. App. 1987); Ashburn v. SAFECO Ins. Co., 713 P.2d 742 (Wash. Ct. App. 1986); Closser v. Penn Mut. Fire Ins. Co., 457 A.2d 1081 (Del.Super.Ct. 1983); but see Miller v. Progressive Cas. Ins. Co., 635 N.E.2d 317 (Ohio 1994) (provision of uninsured motorist coverage limiting insured to one-year period to demand arbitration or file suit was contrary to purpose of statute requiring that such coverage be offered); Henning Nelson Constr. Co. v. Fireman's Fund Am. Life Ins. Co., 383 N.W.2d 645 (Minn. 1986) (one-year provision in business risk policy unreasonably short and unenforceable); Signal Ins. Co. v. Walden, 517 P.2d 611 (Wash. Ct. App. 1973) (one-year limitation in uninsured motorist policy conflicted with legislative purpose of giving insured same rights against uninsured motorist as he would have against financially responsible third party).

[4] See, e.g., Estes v. Alaska Ins. Guar. Ass'n, 774 P.2d 1315 (Alaska 1989) (suit brought seven days after one-year limitation period expired not barred; insurer must show prejudice

results in an automatic loss of benefits.[5] *Schreiber v. Pennsylvania Lumberman's Mutual Insurance Co.*[6] is typical; the court held that the legislature's mandating that every policy of fire insurance issued in the state contain a contractual limitations clause prevented courts, absent extenuating circumstances not present in that case, from refusing to enforce the provision.

However, in extenuating circumstances, courts have refused to enforce a contractual limitations provision. Virtually all courts refuse to enforce the provision if the insurer led the insured to believe that the provision would not be enforced. Thus, under circumstances where the insurer promised to pay the claim, led the insured to believe that the insurer had lengthened the limitations period, or misled the insured about the possibility of settlement, courts have held either that the insurer was estopped to enforce the provision or that the insurer had waived it.[7] In another case, the one-year limitations period was not enforced in circumstances where the insured had not received copies of the policies and the insurance broker from whom the insured purchased the policies was the insurer's, and not the insured's, agent.[8]

A representative case is *Closser v. Penn Mutual Fire Insurance Co.*[9] The insured and his wife owned a policy of fire insurance covering their home, which was destroyed by a fire of suspicious origin. While efforts to settle the claim proceeded, the insured was indicted for arson, but the charges were dismissed a few months later. When the insured attempted to reopen settlement negotiations with the insured, the insurer rejected the claim and denied liability. In the meantime, the insurer paid the insured's wife's claim. The insured tried yet again to renew negotiations, but this effort also failed. When the insured sued the insurer, the insurer obtained a summary judgment on the ground that the insured's suit was time-barred.

On appeal, the court rejected the insured's contention that the contractual limitations provision was unreasonable and unfair. However, the court concluded that the record contained evidence that a factfinder could credit supporting the conclusions that the insured invoked the appraisal procedures of the policy, that the

---

from delay); Green v. General Acc. Ins. Co. of Am., 746 P.2d 152 (N.M. 1987) (failure of insurer's representative to furnish insured with a proof of loss form until eight months after being notified of loss was inconsistent with intention to demand exact compliance from proof of loss and time to sue provisions in policy).

[5] See, e.g., Little v. Allstate Ins. Co., 369 S.E.2d 248 (Ga. 1988); Sachritz v. Pennsylvania Nat'l Mut. Cas. Ins. Co., 455 A.2d 101 (Pa. 1982); Rawlins v. Aetna Cas. & Sur. Co., 284 N.W.2d 782 (Mich. Ct. App. 1979).

[6] 444 A.2d 647 (Pa. 1982).

[7] E.g., Aceves v. Allstate Ins. Co., 827 F. Supp. 1473 (S.D. Cal. 1993); Pini v. Allstate Ins. Co., 499 F. Supp. 1003 (E.D. Pa. 1980), *aff'd mem.*, 659 F.2d 1070 (3d Cir. 1981); Asher v. Reliance Ins. Co., 308 F. Supp. 847 (N.D. Cal. 1970); Walker v. American Bankers Ins. Group, 836 P.2d 59 (Nev. 1992); General State Auth. v. Planet Ins. Co., 346 A.2d 265 (Pa. 1975). But see Edmondson v. Pennsylvania Nat'l Mut. Cas. Ins. Co., 781 S.W.2d 753 (Ky. 1989) (fire insurer did not waive contractual one-year limitations period for bring suit by sending letters extending offers for settlement, when letters specified that insurer reserved all rights and defenses and waived nothing).

[8] See Canyon Country Store v. Bracey, 781 P.2d 414 (Utah 1989).

[9] 457 A.2d 1081 (Del.Super.Ct. 1983).

insurer did not deal fairly with the insured in responding to his requests for an appraisal, and that this misled the insured to assume that there was no need to file suit within the policy's time limitations. Accordingly, the court ruled that the grant of summary judgment to the insurer had been erroneous.

If contractual limitations provisions were enforced strictly, one might expect some insurers to delay informing the insured whether a claim would be paid until shortly before the limitations period expires, hoping to trap the insured into not bringing a suit on the policy until the limitations period has elapsed. In such a situation, the fair analysis is that the insurer led the insured to believe that the claim would be paid, and that the contractual limitations provision is tolled during the period of the insured's delay.

Although the analysis is questionable, one court has used the dependency inherent in reciprocal duties to excuse the insured's failure to comply with a contractual limitations period.[10] The starting point in the analysis is that if the insurer unjustifiably denies coverage, the insurer has breached one of its material duties — the duty to pay proceeds. Under general contract law principles, one party's material breach of a duty excuses the other party from performing its duties under a contract. If bringing any suit against the insurer before the expiration of the contractual limitations period is viewed as one of the insured's duties, it follows that the insurer's material breach of a duty should excuse the insured from its duty to bring suit on the policy within the specified period of time. The difficulty with this analysis is that bringing a suit within a certain period of time is not a duty that the insured owes; instead, the contractual limitations period is a condition to the insurer's contract duties. To be more specific, the contractual limitations period is essentially a condition subsequent to the insurer's duties: in the event the insured fails to bring suit on a claim within a year (or whatever time is specified), the insurer's duties under the contract (with respect to the claim in question) are discharged.

One of the difficulties in applying contractual limitations provisions is determining when the loss occurs that begins the "running" of the period during which the suit must be commenced, if at all. The typical fire insurance policy requires that an action on a policy be commenced within twelve months of the "inception of the loss." The traditional interpretation, approved by most courts that have considered the issue, is that this language refers to the time of the event which causes the insured's loss, such as the fire or other casualty.[11] In some situations, particularly those involving progressive injuries,[12] it may not be clear when the event occurs.

---

[10] Warren v. Employers' Fire Ins. Co., 250 A.2d 578 (N.J. 1969).

[11] See, e.g., Troutman v. State Farm Fire & Cas. Co., 570 F.2d 658 (6th Cir. 1978); Lardas v. Underwriters Ins. Co., 231 A.2d 740 (Pa. 1967); Proc v. Home Ins. Co., 217 N.E.2d 136 (N.Y. 1966); Ramsey v. Home Ins. Co., 125 S.E.2d 201 (Va. 1962); Borgen v. Economy Preferred Ins. Co., 500 N.W.2d 419 (Wis. Ct. App. 1993); Brunner v. Economy Preferred Ins. Co., 597 N.E.2d 1317 (Ind. Ct. App. 1992); Williams Studio v. Nationwide Mut. Fire Ins. Co., 550 A.2d 1333 (Pa. Super. Ct. 1988); Marshburn v. Associated Indem. Corp., 353 S.E.2d 123 (N.C. Ct. App. 1987); Simms v. Allstate Ins. Co., 621 P.2d 155 (Wash. Ct. App. 1980); Florsheim v. Travelers Indem. Co., 393 N.E.2d 1223 (Ill. App. Ct. 1979).

[12] For discussion of some of the complexities raised by progressive injuries, see § 65[e], *supra*.

In addition, in cases where the loss or damage is difficult to discover, measuring the limitations period from the time of the event can be unfair to insureds. Concerned about these problems, the California Supreme Court recently adopted the so-called "delayed discovery rule," under which the "inception of the loss" is defined as "that point in time when appreciable damage occurs and is or should be known to the insured, such that a reasonable insured would be aware that his notification duty under the policy has been triggered."[13] To receive the benefits of this rule, the insured must be "diligent in the face of discovered facts," and the more apparent the nature of the damage discovered ("the greater its deviation from what a reasonable person would consider normal wear and tear"), the more prompt must be the insured's notice.[14] What the delayed-discovery rule does is to substitute a flexible rule that is less certain in its application, and thus more likely to lead to disputes about whether a suit is timely, for a mechanical, per se rule that is easy to apply in most cases.[15]

Other courts have held that the period does not begin to run until the insurer denies the insured's claim, thereby creating the cause of action against the insurer.[16] Part of the logic commending this last approach, which has been called "equitable tolling,"[17] is that the policy typically gives the insured a specified amount of time to file a proof of loss and allows the insurer a period of time to consider the proof. The insured's time to commence the suit, it is argued, should be tolled for the period of time that these policy-mandated procedures are being followed. Otherwise, it is possible that an insured might need to bring suit on the policy before the insurer has denied the claim, an outcome that makes no sense in circumstances where the insurer legitimately needs that much time to complete the investigation. Moreover, this approach avoids the problem discussed above: the insurer waiting until shortly before the limitations period expires to deny the claim so as to force the insured to accept a settlement or commence litigation.

Whether the contractual limitations period applies to an insured's claims sounding in tort has divided courts. Some courts, under the reasoning that the contractual limitation period cannot bar a claim that does not depend on the contract for its existence, have held that the contractual limitations period does not apply to actions

---

[13] Prudential-LMI Commercial Ins. v. Superior Court, 798 P.2d 1230 (Cal. 1990). Other cases approving a discovery rule include Phoenix Ins. Co. v. Brown, 381 S.W.2d 573 (Tenn. Ct. App. 1964). A Louisiana decision approved this rule, Finkelstein v. American Ins. Co., 62 So. 2d 820 (La. 1952), but this decision was subsequently overruled. See Gremillion v. Travelers Indem. Co., 240 So. 2d 727 (La. 1970).

[14] 798 P.2d at 1230.

[15] With respect to a policy using the word "date" in place of "inception," one court has held that the delayed discovery rule applies in cases involving latent or progressive property damage. See O'Reilly v. Allstate Ins. Co., 474 N.W.2d 221 (Minn. Ct. App. 1991).

[16] See, e.g., Prudential-LMI Commercial Ins. v. Superior Court, 798 P.2d 1230 (Cal. 1990); Ford Motor Co. v. Lumbermens Mut. Cas. Co., 319 N.W.2d 320 (Mich. 1982); Clark v. Truck Ins. Exch., 598 P.2d 628 (Nev. 1979); Firemen's Fund Ins. Co. v. Sand Lake Lounge, Inc., 514 P.2d 223 (Alaska 1973); Peloso v. Hartford Fire Ins. co., 267 A.2d 498 (N.J. 1970); Phoenix Ins. Co. v. Brown, 381 S.W.2d 573 (Tenn.App. 1964).

[17] Prudential-LMI Commercial Ins. v. Superior Court, 798 P.2d 1230 (Cal. 1990).

sounding in tort.[18] Other courts, however, have held that the contractual limitations period applies to all claims the insured has against the insured, under the reasoning that the insured would not have any claims but for the existence of the contract and the contractual limitations period should therefore control.[19] If the insurer's duty is one imposed by law instead of by contract, it would seem that the contractual limitations period should be irrelevant to when the claim for breach of the law-imposed duty must be asserted. Private contracts shortening legislatively-imposed statutes of limitations for tort claims would appear to contravene public policy.

[b]   No-Action Clauses and Direct Action Statutes

The question of who gets to sue the insurer when the insurer does not perform is not problematic in most situations. The insured, of course, has a claim against the insurer in both first-party and third-party insurance. The insured's pursuit of this claim is adequate in most instances to secure relief for the insurer's nonperformance. However, in third-party insurance, the victim of the tort also has an interest in whether the insurer performs its duties. This raises the question of whether and under what circumstances the third party who is injured by the insured can sue the insurer directly.

Apart from a few exceptional situations, the victim of the insured's tort does not possess a direct action against the insurer. Liability policies typically contain a "no action clause" which provides that no action lies against the insurer until the underlying liability of the insured to the third party is established.[20] The following language is typical:

> No one will have the right to join us as a party to any action against an insured. Also, no action . . . can be brought against us until the obligation of the "insured" has been determined by final judgment or agreement signed by us.[21]

Thus, if a third party sued the insurer as a beneficiary of the contract between insurer and insured, the third party would lose because the contract specifies that the insurer has no contract obligations to the insured — and concomitantly to any third party — until the insured's liability to the claimant is established. The purposes of no-action clauses are to protect the insurer from having to defend nonmeritorious claims and to keep the insurer from having to appear before the jury.

---

[18] See, e.g., Davis v. State Farm Fire & Cas. Co., 545 F. Supp. 370 (D.Nev. 1982); Asher v. Reliance Ins. Co., 308 F. Supp. 847 (N.D. Cal. 1970) (applying Alaska law); Hearn v. Rickenbacker, 400 N.W.2d 90 (Mich. 1987) (where fraud and negligence claims are pleaded as cause of action separate from alleged breach of contract, they are governed by applicable statute of limitations rather than limitations provisions contained in policy); Florsheim v. Travelers Indem. Co., 393 N.E.2d 1223 (Ill. App. Ct. 1979).

[19] See, e.g., Martin v. Liberty Mut. Fire Ins. Co., 293 N.W.2d 168 (Wis. 1980); Modern Carpet Indus., Inc. v. Factory Ins. Ass'n, 186 S.E.2d 586 (Ga. Ct. App. 1971). See generally Annot., *Policy Provision Limiting Time Within Which Action May Be Brought on the Policy As Applicable to Tort Action by Insured Against Insurer,* 66 A.L.R.4th 859 (1988).

[20] See, e.g., Dvorak v. American Family Mut. Ins. Co., 508 N.W.2d 329 (N.D. 1993); Outboard Marine Corp. v. Liberty Mut. Ins. Co., 607 N.E.2d 1204 (Ill. 1992).

[21] *Policy Kit* at 34 (ISO Form HO 00 03 04 91).

No-action clauses can create an interesting problem if the insured under a liability policy is bankrupt. If the injured third party has no judgment against the bankrupt-insured, that party cannot sue the insurer. Similarly, if the injured third party has not established the insured's liability, the bankrupt-insured has no basis for contending that the insurer has breached its duties.[22] The problem is that the Bankruptcy Code stays all suits against the debtor, effectively preventing the injured third-party from securing a judgment against the insured.[23] The interaction of these rules would seem to have the effect of preventing the injured third party from ever being compensated for his or her injuries. This de facto immunity for insurers, which results from the victim's inability to commence a lawsuit against a bankrupt insured is not what liability insurance policies contemplate; all modern liability policies provide that the bankruptcy or insolvency of the insured will not relieve the insurer of its obligations under the policy.[24] However, the Bankruptcy Code, at first glance, sets up a procedural barrier that ultimately prevents enforcement of the insurer's obligation. The solution is for the bankruptcy court to lift the stay and allow a judgment to be obtained against the debtor, subject to the condition that the plaintiffs, if successful, will not attempt to execute the judgment against the insured's assets and will instead look only to the insurer for reimbursement.[25]

The exceptional situations in which direct actions are allowed against the insurer fall into four categories. First, direct actions by the third-party victim against the insurer are appropriate once the third party has a judgment against the insured. This is almost self-evident: the no-action clause, by its terms, does not prevent an action subsequent to the judgment or settlement agreement. Second, with respect to uninsured motorist automobile insurance coverage,[26] most courts have recognized a limited form of direct action: it is not necessary for the insured to secure a judgment against the uninsured motorist before suing the insurer.[27] If the insurer providing the insured with uninsured motorist coverage is viewed as the insurer for the uninsured motorist, it is easier to see why this line of cases is sometimes described as a limited direct action exception. In actuality, this is not a direct action exception,

---

[22] See Cissell v. American Home Assur. Co., 521 F.2d 790 (6th Cir. 1975), *cert. denied,* 423 U.S. 1074 (1976).

[23] See 11 U.S.C. § 362.

[24] For judicial discussion, see Jarboe v. Shelter Ins. Co., 877 S.W.2d 930 (Ark. 1994); but cf. Black v. First City Bank, 642 So. 2d 151 (La. 1994) (Louisiana allows direct actions; "No action clauses shield insurers from paying damage judgments against insolvent insureds.")

[25] See, e.g., Sullivan v. American Cas. Co., 605 N.E.2d 134 (Ind. 1992); Lane v. State Farm Mut. Auto. Ins. Co., 308 N.W.2d 503 (Neb. 1981); Wood v. Millers Nat'l Ins. Co., 632 P.2d 1163 (N.M. 1981); Gonzales v. Callison, 683 P.2d 454 (Kan.Ct.App. 1984). In the jurisdictions where courts adhere to this rule, the state uninsured motorist statute does not provide specific procedures for suits against uninsured motorists. Where procedures for suing uninsured motorists exist, parties injured by such motorists are required to follow the procedures before suing the insurer. See, e.g., Midwest Mut. Ins. Co. v. Aetna Cas. & Sur. Co., 223 S.E.2d 901 (Va. 1976).

[26] See § 134, *infra.*

[27] See, e.g., Lane v. State Farm Mut. Auto. Ins. Co., 308 N.W.2d 503 (Neb. 1981); Guess v. Gulf Ins. Co., 627 P.2d 869 (N.M. 1981); Annot., *Insured's Right To Bring Direct Action Against Insurer For Uninsured Motorist Benefits,* 73 A.L.R.3d 632 (1976).

since the insurer basically provides the insured with first-party coverage against loss suffered at the hands of uninsured motorists.

Third, a few states and territories — Wisconsin, Louisiana, Rhode Island, Puerto Rico, and Guam — have "direct action statutes." [28] The specific provisions of these statutes vary considerably, but their common characteristics are making the insurer directly liable to the injured party and permitting liability to be established in a single action against the insured and insurer jointly, or in an action against the insurer alone. Florida flirted briefly with a judicially-created direct action. In a 1969 decision, the Florida Supreme Court held that no-action clauses violated a provision in the state constitution providing for judicial remedies and that the clause interfered with the constitutional authority of the judicial branch.[29] The Florida legislature sought to overturn the decision by enacting a statute specifically authorizing insurers to insert no-action clauses in liability policies and purporting to declare them valid.[30] Despite the seeming impermissibility of the legislature's effort to authorize a provision in a contract that violated the state constitution, the Florida Supreme Court upheld the statute.[31]

Finally, in some situations insurers have been found to have waived the no-action clause or have been held estopped to assert it.[32] These cases generally fall into one of three categories: the injured unjustifiably denies liability on a claim before the insured is sued on the claim[33] (but some courts have held to the contrary);[34] the insurer unjustifiably delayed settlement of the insured's claim;[35] or the insurer conducts, or fails to conduct, the defense in some manner that is adverse to the interests of the insured.[36]

The effect of direct action statutes is to give the injured third party an independent cause of action against the insurer. According to one source, this broad right to sue has made courts in these states "magnets for suits" against insurers.[37] Direct action statutes are significant for other reasons, however. First, they allow the insurer to

---

[28] Guam Govt. Code § 43354; La. Rev. Stat. Ann. 22:655, 22:983; R.I. Gen. Laws 27-7-1, 27-7-2; Wis. Stat. Ann. 632.24, 632.34, 803.04; P.R. Laws Ann., tit. 26, §§ 2001, 2003. The constitutionality of the Louisiana statute was settled in Watson v. Employers Liab. Assur. Corp., 348 U.S. 66 (1954).

[29] Shingleton v. Bussey, 223 So. 2d 713 (Fla. 1969).

[30] Fla. Stat. Ann. § 627.4136.

[31] VanBibber v. Hartford Acc. & Indem. Ins. Co., 439 So. 2d 880 (Fla. 1983).

[32] See generally Annot., Liability Insurer's Postloss Conduct As Waiver Of, Or Estoppel To Assert, "No-Action" Clause, 68 A.L.R.4th 389 (1989).

[33] See Thomas W. Hooley & Sons v. Zurich Gen. Acc. & Liab. Ins. Co., 103 So. 2d 449 (La. 1958).

[34] See Marvel Heat Corp. v. Travelers Indem. Co. 92 N.E.2d 233 (Mass. 1950); Piper v. State Farm Mut. Auto. Ins. Co., 116 N.E.2d 86 (Ill. App. Ct. 1953).

[35] See Emile M. Babst Co. v. Nichols Constr. Corp., 488 So. 2d 699 (La. Ct. App. 1986).

[36] See, e.g., Milbank Mut. Ins. Co. v. Wentz, 352 F.2d 592 (8th Cir. 1965) (withdrawal from defense of suit against insured); Idaho v. Bunker Hill Co., 647 F.Supp. 1064 (D.Idaho 1986) (refusal to defend insured).

[37] William E. Young & Eric M. Holmes, *Cases and Materials on the Law of Insurance* 112 (2d ed. 1985).

be sued immediately, before the insured's liability is established. Second, they require the insurer to appear as a party before the jury. Insurers have long loathed being a named party in a jury trial, fearing that juries will be more likely to award large damages when the presence of insurance is known. Third, in the direct action, defenses that the insurer might have against the insured, such as failure to give notice or lack of cooperation, cannot be asserted against the third party.[38]

Although the direct action statutes have uniformly been interpreted as creating substantive instead of procedural rights, a number of courts have refused to give direct action statutes extraterritorial effect.[39] In many states, disclosure of liability insurance at a trial in which the insured's negligence is at issue constitutes prejudicial error. If this rule indicates the public policy of the forum, the direct action statute would seem to contravene that public policy.

§ 85   The Insured's Duty to Cooperate With the Insurer

The duty to cooperate is sometimes expressly included in the contract; at other times, the duty is implied. In either case, the insured's performance of this duty is a condition to the insurer's obligation to perform its duties. The duty to cooperate is extremely important in liability insurance because the insurer's ability to perform its duty to defend claims brought against the insured depends upon the insured's cooperation. The insured's duty to cooperate in the preparation of a defense will be explored in a later section.[1] This section examines the more general obligation, similar to that owed by any party to any contract, to cooperate with the insurer. Before exploring the nature of the duty to cooperate in more detail, it is useful both to review the relationship of conditions and duties and to examine the distinction between express and implied terms.

[a]   Duties, Conditions, Express and Implied Terms

[1]   Generally

As a general matter, duties need not be expressly stated in contracts; sometimes duties are implied from the circumstances. In the famous case of *Wood v. Lucy, Lady Duff Gordon,*[2] the defendant's agent was held to have an implied duty to use reasonable efforts in effecting sales of goods carrying the defendant's endorsement. The agent made no such promise expressly, but the promise was "fairly to be implied" in the circumstances of the case.[3] In effect, the agent was held to have a duty to cooperate with the defendant in the promotion of the joint enterprise; this duty, based on an implied promise, was inherent in the nature of the contractual relationship.

---

[38] See, e.g., Snell v. Stein, 259 So. 2d 876 (La. 1972); Stippich v. Morrison, 107 N.W.2d 125 (Wis. 1961); Bourque v. Duplechin, 331 So. 2d 40 (La. Ct. App. 1976).

[39] See, e.g., Marchlik v. Coronet Ins. Co., 239 N.E.2d 799 (Ill. 1968); Cook v. State Farm Mut. Ins. Co., 128 So. 2d 363 (Miss.), *cert. denied,* 368 U.S. 898 (1961).

[1] See § 110, *infra.*

[2] 118 N.E. 214 (N.Y. 1917).

[3] 118 N.E. at 214.

A party's duties, whether express or implied, are usually conditioned on certain events of one kind or another. Some of these conditions are express, as is the case when the insurer promises to pay proceeds on the condition that, *inter alia,* it receives notice of the loss within a reasonable time. In this example, the insured's performance of an act — giving notice reasonably promptly — is a prerequisite to the insurer's duty to perform becoming due. At other times, conditions to one's duties are implied. For example, the "constructive condition of exchange" is an implied condition in contracts. At the core of the theory that contracts are exchange relationships is the notion that each side's promised performance is conditioned on the tender of performance from the other side. If one party does not tender its performance, the duty of the other party is at least suspended and may later be discharged. This condition is not expressly included in the contract, but instead is implied from the nature of the relationship. In general contract law, it is also possible to have implied duties, which in turn serve as constructive conditions to the other party's performance.

Professor Corbin effectively summed up the essence of the obligation to cooperate:

> If the performance promised by one party is such that it cannot be performed until the promisee has first laid the foundation on which it is to be built or otherwise done, the laying of that foundation is a constructive condition of the duty of the promisor. In addition to this, the court has sometimes found an implied promise to lay that foundation, for breach of which a suit for damages can be maintained.[4]

Under basic contract principles, a party may not suspend his or her own performance in response to an insignificant or immaterial breach by the other party. Refusing to allow the nonbreaching party to suspend performance in response to an immaterial breach serves the purpose of avoiding a forfeiture for the breaching party. In other words, a nonbreaching party is not entitled to suspend performance upon the other party's breach absent some substantial impairment of the nonbreaching party's reasonable expectations under the contract. If a party fails to fulfill its duty to cooperate, that party is in breach; the other party's duty to perform will be suspended, and ultimately discharged, only if the breach of the duty to cooperate is material.

[2]   As Applied to Insurance

The insured's duty to cooperate, like any other contract duty, can be either express or implied. In liability insurance, the policies typically impose an express duty on the insured to cooperate with the insurer in the investigation, defense, and settlement of a claim against the insured. If the duty were not express, some sort of duty to cooperate would certainly be implied, since it makes little sense for an insurer to promise to defend the insured against lawsuits filed against the insured if the insurer could not count on the insured's cooperation in this effort. Regardless of the liability policy's provisions, general contract law makes the insured's performance of the duty to cooperate a constructive condition to the insurer's duty to pay proceeds.

---

[4] Joseph M. Perillo & Helen H. Bender, 3 *Corbin on Contracts* § 5.27, at 134 (Rev.ed. 1995).

In first-party insurance, the duty to cooperate is rarely set forth in explicit words "the insured shall cooperate," but such policies almost always impose specific obligations on insureds that necessarily require the insured's cooperation. The standard fire insurance policy, for example, requires that the insured cooperate with the insurer in investigating the fire, showing the damaged property, submitting to examination under oath, and producing books and records. Whatever the scope of the expressly articulated duty to cooperate in a first-party insurance relationship, a duty to cooperate is also implicit in the nature of the relationship. The reason for including cooperation clauses in a first-party contract is, in the words of one court, "obvious enough. The company is entitled to obtain, promptly and while the information is still fresh, 'all knowledge, and all information as to other sources and means of knowledge, in regard to the facts, material to their rights to enable them to decide upon their obligations, and to protect them against false claims.' "[5]

[b]　What Constitutes Noncooperation

In extreme cases, determining whether an insured has breached the duty to cooperate is easy. In most cases, the analysis is more difficult and depends on the facts and circumstances of each case.[6] To take a more obvious example, the insured who makes false statements to the insurer in the proof of loss or during the insurer's investigation of the claim is not cooperating with the insurer.[7] Similarly, if the insured refuses to assist the insurer in investigating the claim, or makes himself or herself unavailable for questioning, or otherwise attempts to frustrate the insurer's investigation, it is fair to say that the insured is in breach of the duty to cooperate.[8] When the insured claims damages for a loss of property due to fire and arson is suspected, the failure of the insured to furnish his or her income tax records to the insurer constitutes non cooperation.[9]

At the other end of the spectrum, it is fairly easy to determine that the insured is cooperating. For example, a mistaken false statement, if subsequently corrected, is not a basis for voiding the policy for breach of the cooperation clause.[10] The single

---

[5] Dyno-Bite, Inc. v. The Travelers Cos., 439 N.Y.S.2d 558 (N.Y. App. Div. 1981), *quoting* Claflin v. Commonwealth Ins. Co., 110 U.S. 81, 94-95 (1884). See generally Annot., *Insured's Nondisclosure of Information Regarding Value of Property as Ground for Avoiding Liability Under Property Insurance Policy,* 15 A.L.R.4th 1109 (1982).

[6] See, e.g., Gabor v. State Farm Mut. Auto. Ins. Co., 583 N.E.2d 1041 (Ohio Ct.App. 1990) (whether insured violated cooperation clause is question to be determined in view of facts and circumstances of each case).

[7] See, e.g., Fine v. Bellefonte Underwriters Ins. Co., 725 F.2d 179 (2d Cir. 1984), *on remand,* 589 F. Supp. 438 (S.D. N.Y. 1984), *aff'd,* 758 F.2d 50 (2d Cir. 1985), *cert. denied,* 474 U.S. 826 (1985) (discussed in § 82, *supra*); Quintin v. Miller, 417 A.2d 941 (Vt. 1980).

[8] See Halcome v. Cincinnati Ins. Co., 334 S.E.2d 155 (Ga. 1985); State Farm Mut. Auto. Ins. Co. v. Davies, 310 S.E.2d 167 (Va. 1983); Williams v. Alabama Farm Bureau Mut. Cas. Ins. Co., 416 So. 2d 744 (Ala. 1982).

[9] See Gabor v. State Farm Mut. Auto. Ins. Co., 583 N.E.2d 1041 (Ohio Ct.App. 1990). The self-incrimination ramifications of this answer are discussed later in this subsection.

[10] See, e.g., Wheeler v. Lumbermen's Mut. Cas. Co., 5 F. Supp. 193 (D.Me. 1933); Hayes v. City of Alexandria, 495 So. 2d 384 (La. Ct. App. 1986). *Cf.* Wojna v. Merchants Ins. Group, 464 N.Y.S.2d 664 (N.Y. Sup. Ct. 1983).

postponement of an oral examination of the insured, in circumstances where the insurer made no further effort to reschedule the examination, does not rise to the level of non cooperation by the insured.[11] In the same vein, an isolated act of intransigence by the insured, even if showing a lack of cooperation, should not rise to the level of a breach of the duty to cooperate which causes the insured to lose coverage, assuming the insured otherwise cooperates with the insurer.

In short, some acts of noncooperation are trivial, and others are more significant. Whether a particular act of noncooperation invalidates the coverage is determined by reference to well-known contract law principles: material breaches by one party discharge the other side's duty to perform, but immaterial breaches by one party do not relieve the other party of its obligation to give the return performance. As it turns out, the instances in which the insured's noncooperation invalidates the coverage are relatively few.

[c]   When Noncooperation Gives the Insurer a Valid Defense

The general principles of contract law discussed above indicate that the party who commits the first material breach gives the other party the right to suspend performance. Thus, if the insurer commits the first material breach, subsequent noncooperation by the insured has no legal consequence. For example, the insurer that repudiates its duty to pay proceeds cannot later attempt to justify its breach on the ground that the insured failed to cooperate. In most cases, however, the issue presented is whether the insured has committed the first material breach through some act of noncooperation.

In most jurisdictions, the principle that only material breaches excuse a party's duty to perform its contractual undertakings is reflected in the following rule of insurance law: the insured's noncooperation must be substantial and material to invalidate the coverage.[12] Most of the cases come from liability insurance, but the lessons of these cases also apply to first-party policies. For example, in *Auto-Owners Insurance Co. v. Rodgers,*[13] the insured's failure to meet with the liability insurer's investigators after repeated requests by telephone and by letter that he do so was held inconsequential. The insurer contended that it was unable to locate witnesses because of the insured's noncooperation, but the court observed that the insurer had access to the police report which listed some witnesses and had ways to learn the identity of some others. Under those circumstances, the insured's noncooperation was neither material nor substantial. The insurer was not entitled to suspend its own performance because of the insured's slight transgressions.

Furthermore, an insurer cannot suspend its own performance on account of the insured's failure to cooperate unless it has made some efforts to secure that cooperation. As one court has explained, the insurer has no defense "if the insurer was not

---

[11] See McCullough v. Travelers Cos., 424 N.W.2d 542 (Minn. 1988).

[12] See, e.g., Home Indem. Co. v. Reed Equip. Co., 381 So. 2d 45 (Ala. 1980); State Farm Mut. Auto. Ins. Co. v. Porter, 272 S.E.2d 196 (Va. 1980); O'Leary v. Lumbermen's Mut. Cas. Co., 420 A.2d 888 (Conn. 1979); Garcia v. Abrams, 471 N.Y.S.2d 161 (N.Y. App. Div. 1983).

[13] 360 So. 2d 716 (Ala. 1978).

sufficiently diligent in its attempts to secure" the cooperation of the insured or if the insured's lack of cooperation "is found to have occurred through lack of timely effort and diligence on the part of the insurer."[14]

Many factors are relevant to determining whether the insurer has done enough to secure the insured's cooperation. In one case, the court held that the insured's failure to respond to the insurer's letters was not a substantial and material lack of cooperation because the letters did not offer to pay the insured's expenses to attend a meeting, contained no offer to make up the insured's lost wages, and did not attempt to set up a meeting at a time convenient to the insured.[15] In another case, the insurer's failure to do anything other than send letters to the insured advising her of court dates was deemed an insufficient effort to secure the insured's cooperation. The court also noted that the insurer had reason to believe the insured might be illiterate, a fact that may have explained the insured's failure to respond to the letters.[16] The insurer's obligation may go so far as to require advising the insured of the consequences of failing to cooperate. In one case, the insurer was held to have waived the defense of noncooperation because of its failure to inform the insured of the consequences of not cooperating,[17] which is analogous to the requirement that the insurer give the insured an opportunity to correct a deficient proof of loss before relying upon the deficiency to deny coverage.

Some courts appear to require willful or intentional noncooperation as an element of the insurer's noncooperation defense.[18] It is fair to wonder whether this adds much; if the insured is found to have breached the duty to cooperate, it is highly likely that the insured's breach was deliberate.

Before an insurer can void a policy on account of the insured's noncooperation, most jurisdictions require the insurer to demonstrate that it was prejudiced as a result of the lack of cooperation.[19] This additional requirement has significant implications

---

[14] Watson v. Jones, 610 P.2d 619, 623 (Kan. 1980). See also Grant v. Transit Cas. Co., 693 P.2d 1328 (Or. Ct. App. 1985); Garcia v. Abrams, 471 N.Y.S.2d 161 (N.Y. App. Div. 1983).

[15] See Auto-Owners Ins. Co. v. Rodgers, 360 So. 2d 716 (Ala. 1978).

[16] See Lappo v. Thompson, 409 N.E.2d 26 (Ill. App. Ct. 1980).

[17] See Johnson v. Wade, 365 N.E.2d 11 (Ill. App. Ct. 1977).

[18] See, e.g., C-Suzanne Beauty Salon, Ltd, v. General Ins Co. of Am., 574 F.2d 106 (2d Cir. 1978); American Policyholder's Ins. Co. v. Baker, 409 A.2d 1346 (N.H. 1979); General Acc. Ins. Group v. Cirucci, 387 N.E.2d 223, (N.Y. 1979); Garcia v. Abrams, 471 N.Y.S.2d 161 (N.Y. App. Div. 1983).

[19] See, e.g., Martin v. Travelers Indem. Co., 450 F.2d 542 (5th Cir. 1971); Hodges v. State Farm Mut. Auto. Ins. Co., 488 F. Supp. 1057 (D.S.C. 1980); State Farm Mut. Auto. Ins. Co. v. Commercial Union Ins. Co., 394 So. 2d 890 (Miss. 1981); Home Indem. Co v. Reed Equip. Co., 381 So. 2d 45 (Ala. 1980); Foundation Reserve Ins. Co. v. Esquibel, 607 P.2d 1150 (N.M. 1980) (requires "substantial prejudice"); Clemmer v. Hartford Ins. Co., 587 P.2d 1098 (Cal. 1978); Gabor v. State Farm Mut. Auto. Ins. Co., 583 N.E.2d 1041 (Ohio Ct.App. 1990); but see State Farm Mut. Auto. Ins. Co. v. Porter, 272 S.E.2d 196 (Va. 1980) (insurer need not show prejudice, but prejudice is to be considered on question of materiality of information insured failed to give).

Some courts, however, presume the existence of prejudice arising from the breach of the cooperation clause and place the burden on the insured to establish lack of prejudice. See, e.g., Western Mut. Ins. Co. v. Baldwin, 137 N.W.2d 918 (Iowa 1965).

for the noncooperation defense. As a threshold matter, "prejudice" must be defined. In most cases arising in liability insurance, the insurer is deemed to have been prejudiced by the insured's noncooperation under circumstances where if the cooperation or notice clause had not been breached, it is substantially likely that the insurer would not have been held liable.[20] In first-party insurance, the insurer is prejudiced if the noncooperation altered the amount of proceeds the insurer paid.

In extreme cases, demonstrating prejudice does not present difficult problems. If the insurer can show that it would have been able to negate liability if the insured had cooperated, prejudice is demonstrated. For example, subsequently locating a significant piece of evidence or a material witness who was unavailable due to the insured's noncooperation may be enough to establish that a different outcome would have resulted had the insured cooperated. In most cases (in liability insurance), it would seem that wilful failure to testify would prejudice the insurer substantially, thereby voiding the policy for breach of the cooperation clause.[21] First-party insurance contracts typically require that the insured provide the insurer access to his or her books and records and submit to examination under oath by the insurer. The insured's outright refusal to make books and records available and to submit to examination under oath generally invalidates the coverage.[22] These cases do not always discuss whether prejudice has occurred, but prejudice is so probable that it is fair to presume prejudice in these kinds of cases.

Short of the foregoing situations, it will be difficult for the insurer to establish prejudice in most cases. Rarely in liability insurance will the insurer be able to demonstrate that a verdict would have been different had the insured cooperated. For example, the insurer may be able to establish that the insured failed to reveal certain evidence to the insurer, but if the passage of time does not make the evidence any less useful, the insurer will not prevail in having its duties discharged. In *Home Indemnity Co. v. Reed Equipment Co., Inc.,*[23] a 1980 Alabama case, the insurer was not advised for eleven months after an accident of the existence of a wheel that allegedly came off the insured's vehicle and caused the accident, which in the absence of the wheel and the concomitant explanation was attributed to another cause. After the accident, the wheel was recovered and placed under lock and key on the insured's premises. The insurer argued that it was prejudiced by not being allowed to examine the wheel while the evidence was "fresh." It was undisputed that the insured made the wheel available to the insurer once actions against the insured commenced. Under these circumstances, the court reasoned that to the extent the wheel was evidence adverse to the insurer's defense of its insured, the evidence

---

[20] See, e.g., State Farm Mut. Auto. Ins. Co. v. Davies, 310 S.E.2d 167 (Va. 1983); Harleysville Ins. Co. v. Rosenbaum, 351 A.2d 197 (Md.Ct.Spec.App. 1976).

[21] See State Farm Mut. Auto. Ins. Co. v. Davies, 310 S.E.2d 167 (Va. 1983); but see Boone v. Lowry, 657 P.2d 64 (Kan.Ct.App. 1983).

[22] See, e.g., Do-Re Knit, Inc. v. National Union Fire Ins. Co., 491 F. Supp. 1334 (E.D. N.Y. 1980); Lentini Bros. Moving & Storage Co. v. New York Prop. Ins. Underwriting Ass'n, 422 N.E.2d 819 (N.Y. 1981); Home Ins. Co. v. Olmstead, 355 So. 2d 310 (Miss. 1978). See generally Annot., *Requirement Under Property Insurance Policy That Insured Submit to Examination Under Oath as to Loss,* 16 A.L.R.5th 412 (1993).

[23] 381 So. 2d 45 (Ala. 1980).

was neither more nor less damaging later than it was immediately after the accident. Therefore, the insurer failed to show prejudice from the insured's lack of cooperation.

Thus, one might conclude that the prejudice requirement created by courts frustrates the purpose of the duty to cooperate. As the Appleman treatise states, the substantial prejudice test is "probably salutary where it is evident that the insured's infraction did not seriously impair the insurer's investigation or defense of the action. But if the rule is carried to the point of imposing an almost insurmountable burden of proving that the verdict was the result of lack of cooperation, it would amount to a perversion of such contractual provision."[24] On the other hand, one might conclude that requiring the noncooperation to prejudice the insurer is as sensible as the requirement that the insurer be prejudiced when the insured fails to give timely notice of a loss or fails to comply with the proof of loss requirements. In these situations, it is fair to view the insured's obligations as particular facets of the duty to cooperate, and most jurisdictions do not excuse the insurer from its obligations without a showing of prejudice from untimely notice or filing of a proof of loss.

Occasionally an insured refuses to provide information requested by the insurer on the ground that to do so would require the insured to forfeit the right against self-incrimination guaranteed by the Fifth Amendment to the United States Constitution. This frequently arises in cases of fire loss, where the insured has filed a claim and the insured is under suspicion of having committed arson. At first glance, one might think that the insurer seeking the information is attempting to persuade the insured to relinquish a constitutional right; if the insured does not waive the right and reveal all information, some of which might be incriminating, the insured forfeits the coverage. However, upon closer scrutiny, it is apparent that the insurer's right to information is contractually grounded in a private agreement. No action of the state is involved in the giving of the information. No *public* compulsion exists. Thus, the giving of the information is voluntary in the constitutional sense: the insured is free to choose not to give the information, even though this may mean forfeiting contract rights.[25]

In liability insurance, several specific duties exist that are merely derivations of the broader duty to cooperate, such as the obligation to forward demand letters and litigation documents to the insurer, and the duty not to settle claims against tortfeasors without the insurer's consent. These subjects are covered in later sections.[26]

---

[24] 8 APPLEMAN § 4773, at 228 (1981).

[25] See, e.g., Hudson Tire Mart, Inc. v. Aetna Cas. & Sur. Co., 518 F.2d 671 (2d Cir. 1975); United States v. Moeller, 402 F. Supp. 49 (D.Conn. 1975); Hickman v. London Assur. Corp., 195 P. 45 (Cal. 1920); Warrilow v. Superior Court, 689 P.2d 193 (Ariz. Ct. App. 1984); Standard Mut. Ins. Co. v. Boyd, 452 N.E.2d 1074 (Ind. Ct. App. 1983); Gross v. United States Fire Ins. Co., 337 N.Y.S.2d 221 (N.Y. Sup. Ct. 1972); but cf. Gibson v. Group Ins. Co., 369 N.W.2d 484 (Mich. Ct. App. 1985) (insured refused to supply information on Fifth Amendment grounds, but insured nevertheless substantially performed his obligation to cooperate with the insurer's investigation of the fire).

[26] See §§ 96[h], 110, *infra*.

THE INSURER'S DUTY TO PAY PROCEEDS

§ 90   Source of the Duty

The insurer's duty to pay proceeds in the event of the insured's loss is, from the insured's perspective, undoubtedly the most important duty the insurer undertakes. In first-party insurance, this duty is obviously the most basic of the insurer's obligations. In third-party insurance, the insurer promises to indemnify the insured for sums the insured becomes legally obligated to pay to others, and this duty probably figures more prominently in the insured's expectations than the duty to defend. The source of the duty is firmly grounded in the contract itself: the insurer expressly promises to pay proceeds if a loss within coverage occurs.

§ 91   Failure of the Insured to Mitigate the Amount of Loss

The insurer's duty to pay proceeds may be discharged in its entirety by any number of events or circumstances, many of which are discussed elsewhere in this book.[1] One that might cause the insurer's obligation to pay proceeds to be reduced, either in full or in part, involves the insured's failure to take reasonable steps to avoid the consequences of a loss.

It is important to recognize that most insurance policies condition the insurer's obligations on the insured exercising reasonable care to minimize the extent of damage after a loss. For example, the typical homeowner's policy provides:

> In case of a loss to covered property, you must see that the following are done:
> . . . d. (1) Protect the property from further damage. If repairs to the property are required, you must: (1) Make reasonable and necessary repairs to protect the property; and (2) Keep an accurate record of repair expenses; . . . .[2]

---

[1] Any of the defenses to coverage based upon the insured's conduct or lack thereof — breach of warranty; nonsatisfaction of a condition; failure to give notice; false swearing, etc. — may operate to suspend and ultimately discharge the insurer's duty to pay proceeds.

[2] *Policy Kit* at 26 (ISO Form HO 00 03 04 91) Compare ABCD... Vision, Inc. v. Fireman's Fund Ins. Cos., 734 P.2d 1376 (Or. Ct. App.), *aff'd in part, rev'd in part and remanded,* 744 P.2d 998 (Or. 1987) (requirement that insured safeguard property after loss requires only that insured safeguard damaged property and not that insured safeguard all of insured's property).

(Matthew Bender & Co., Inc.)   (Pub.837)

But it is clear that an insured would be expected to minimize damage even in the absence of explicit contract language conditioning the insurer's duty to pay proceeds on the insured's mitigation of the loss.

The common law of contract remedies has long recognized that a party aggrieved by the other side's breach cannot recover damages that he or she could have reasonably avoided.[3]

Thus, in the face of the other side's breach, an aggrieved party cannot deliberately increase the damages by continuing his or her reliance and continuing to render the contracted-for performance; instead, the aggrieved party should stop performing.[4] Also, when confronted with the other side's breach, this principle expects in appropriate circumstances that the aggrieved party will take *affirmative* steps to minimize the consequences of the other side's breach.[5]

In circumstances where an insurer declines to pay a claim, the contract law principle that limits the aggrieved party's recovery to consequences that could not be reasonably avoided speaks directly to an insured's responsibilities: the insured, knowing that the insurer has refused to pay a claim, cannot then, either by action or inaction, take steps that maximize the amount of the claim. Moreover, under the contract law principle, the insured in such circumstances must take reasonable steps to limit the amount of the loss. In such a case, the insurer is the breaching party; and the insured, as the aggrieved party, cannot recover for losses that could have reasonably been avoided.

This analysis is buttressed by another important insurance law principle: the insured can recover only for fortuitous loss.[6] A premise of the contract law limitation is that the insured has awareness that his or her acts or neglect might increase the amount of loss. If loss is subject to being increased through action or neglect within the insured's knowledge and control, it cannot be said that the additional loss is fortuitous.

In the vast majority of situations, however, the insured will suffer a loss through some occurrence before the insured learns whether the insurer will pay the loss. Normally, the time at which the insured can take action to prevent additional loss is immediately after the event. The contract law principle concerning non-recovery of avoidable consequences does not speak directly to the usual situation in insurance law, because at the time of the loss there has been no breach by the insurer — the breach does not occur until the insurer denies a claim within coverage. Although

---

[3] See generally E. Allen Farnsworth, Contracts § 12.12 (2d ed. 1990). This principle is commonly described as a "duty to mitigate damages," but this description is a misnomer because an aggrieved party has no "duty" to do anything after the other side breaches. Rather, the notion of the principle is that the breaching party's obligation to pay damages will be reduced (that is, the aggrieved party cannot recover) to the extent the aggrieved party fails to take reasonable steps to mitigate damages.

[4] See, e.g., Rockingham Cty. v. Luten Bridge Co., 35 F.2d 301 (4th Cir. 1929) (when county notified plaintiff that it would not proceed with project, "plaintiff . . . had no right thus to pile up damages by proceeding with the erection of a useless bridge.")

[5] See Farnsworth, *supra* note 3, at 897-902.

[6] See § 63, *supra*.

courts often disregard the distinction and refer generically to the insured's implied-in-law duty to mitigate,[7] the policies which underlie the avoidable consequences limitation in contract law are equally applicable to insureds who have the opportunity to mitigate their loss.

The economic ramifications of failing to reduce loss are obvious; such losses are wasteful, whether they follow the breach of a contracting party or an accident suffered by an insured.[8] With respect to a contract breach, the waste caused by an aggrieved party's failure to mitigate is reflected (absent a limitation on the aggrieved party's damage recovery) in an increase in the breaching party's cost of performing the contract; in other words, an aggrieved party's failure to take reasonable steps to reduce loss increases the cost to the breaching party of what is required to put the aggrieved party in the same position he or she would have occupied if the contract had been fully performed.[9] When the insured suffers a covered loss, the insured's failure to mitigate the consequences of that loss increases the insurer's cost of performance, namely, the amount of proceeds that the insurer must pay. Thus, it makes good sense to limit an insured's recovery under the policy to losses the insured could not have avoided through reasonable affirmative acts. Of course, as is the case in contract law, determining what is a "reasonable" response to a loss depends on the circumstances, and is likely to be a point of contention in many situations.

In most insurance policies, the insured's taking reasonable steps to limit the consequences of loss is contained in a section of the policy called "conditions," and may also be labeled a "duty."[10] Technically, the insured's taking reasonable steps is a condition to coverage, in the same sense that the insured's failure to give timely notice of loss or file a timely proof of loss is a condition. When the insurer seeks to invoke the condition, the insurer must carry the burden of proving that the insured failed to mitigate.[11] If the insured fails to take reasonable steps to prevent further loss, does the insured lose all coverage? The answer should be no. The non-satisfaction of notice of loss conditions[12] has sometimes been held to invalidate coverage in its entirety, but most courts require that the insurer be prejudiced before coverage is forfeited, and other courts use a variety of techniques to soften the effect of the notice requirement. In other words, the notice condition is applied flexibly

---

[7] See, e.g., City of Edgerton v. General Cas. Co., 493 N.W.2d 768, 780 (Wis. Ct. App. 1992), aff'd in part, rev'd in part and remanded, 517 N.W.2d 463 (Wis. 1994); Beach v. Middlesex Mut. Assur. Co., 532 A.2d 1297, 1301 n.2 (Conn. 1987); Johnson v. General Mut. Ins. Co., 246 N.E.2d 713, 717 (N.Y. 1969).

[8] See Beach v. Middlesex Mut. Assur. Co., 532 A.2d 1297 (Conn. 1987) (requiring insured to await actual collapse of building would be economically wasteful and would conflict with insured's contractual and common law duty to mitigate damages; held, "collapse" within meaning of policy included substantial impairment of structural integrity of building).

[9] See Charles J. Goetz & Robert E. Scott, The Mitigation Principle: Toward a General Theory of Contractual Obligation, 69 Va. L. Rev. 967, 969 (1983) (each party must act "so as to minimize the joint costs of providing performance or its equivalent.")

[10] See, e.g., Policy Kit at 26 (ISO Form HO 00 03 04 91).

[11] See Lawrence v. Will Darrah & Assocs., Inc. 516 N.W.2d 43 (Mich. 1994).

[12] See § 81, supra.

to achieve its underlying purpose, and forfeiture of coverage is avoided whenever possible. By the same token, forfeiture of coverage is not necessary to serve the underlying purposes of the requirement that the insured mitigate the consequences of loss; rather, all that is necessary is that the insured lose the right to recover for any loss that could have been avoided by reasonable affirmative steps. *Travelers Indemnity Co. v. Rawson,* **13** a 1969 Mississippi case, is illustrative. The roof and interior of the insureds' house were allegedly damaged by windstorm, but no repairs were made for two years. This allowed rain to enter holes in the damaged roof, causing additional damage to the interior and exterior of the house. The court held that the insureds had failed to comply with their duty to remedy the situation within a reasonable time and thereby prevent subsequent damage. Accordingly, the court approved a jury instruction stating that the insureds would not be allowed to recover for the additional damages caused by their own failure to remedy the damage promptly.

Lumpkin v. Alabama Farm Bureau Mutual Casualty Insurance Co., **14** a 1977 Alabama case, takes an even stronger position on mitigation: the insured was denied recovery because he failed to correct a situation that threatened to cause a loss but had not yet done so. During a hurricane, a limb fell out of a tree which overhung the insured's house; the broken limb remained suspended in the tree for over six months, until it finally fell out of the tree during a light wind and crashed into the house. During the sixth months of imminent and obvious danger, the insured sought free removal of the limb by City, Power Company, and National Guard authorities, none of whom had any legal obligation to assist in removing the branch. The court referred to the provisions of the policy which excused the insurer from liability if the insured neglected to use all reasonable means to protect his property "at and after a loss" and which suspended coverage while the hazard was increased by any means within the insured's knowledge or control. The court upheld a directed verdict for the insurer, reasoning that the insured's neglect in removing the limb from the tree voided the coverage.

There are circumstances where the insured's failure to mitigate is excused. For example, an insured who declines an insurer's offer to repair damage for free when the offer is tied to the insured surrendering other rights under the contract does not lose coverage on account of a failure to mitigate.**15** In circumstances where the insured, while intoxicated, drove her vehicle into a tree with such force that the vehicle was valueless, her continued operation of the vehicle immediately after the accident, with further damage resulting, was not a failure to mitigate damage because

---

13 222 So. 2d 131 (Miss. 1969). See also Stockdale v. Jamison, 330 N.W.2d 389 (Mich. 1982) (insured had duty to mitigate damages by hiring substitute counsel to present his defense when insurer declined to do so); Steel Products Co. v. Millers Nat'l Ins. Co., 209 N.W.2d 32 (Iowa 1973) (insured has duty to mitigate his earnings loss by resuming operations during period of business interruption). The *Stockdale* opinion in footnote 15 suggested that the remedy approved in that case, recovery of the policy limits, would also serve as the measure of damages when the insurer breached the duty to settle. This dictum was specifically repudiated in Frankenmuth Mut. Ins. Co. v. Keeley, 447 N.W.2d 691 (Mich. 1989).

14 343 So. 2d 1238 (Ala.Civ.App. 1977).

15 See Bailey v. Farmers Union Co-Op. Ins. Co., 498 N.W.2d 591 (Neb. 1992).

the vehicle was already a total loss.[16] As is the case in contract law generally, the insured need not do unreasonable or impracticable acts in order to mitigate loss.[17]

If the insured takes reasonable steps to prevent additional loss, must the insurer reimburse the insured for the expenses of mitigating that loss? Some policies explicitly provide coverage for the expenses of avoiding additional loss.[18] In the absence of explicit coverage, the correct answer would seem to be that the insurer should reimburse mitigation expenses incurred by the insured, since the mitigation is for the insurer's benefit and the insurer mandates that the insured undertake those expenses by imposing the duty to mitigate.[19] Moreover, it is the covered peril which causes the insured to incur the expenses of mitigation. If the policy requires the insured to keep records of expenses incurred in mitigating loss, one might infer that the insurer expects to reimburse these expenses, under the reasoning that the record-keeping requirement has as its purpose making that reimbursement possible.[20] Although an insurer may have some concern that insureds will spend unreasonably large sums to mitigate loss, if notice of loss is given timely, the insurer is given an opportunity to direct what actions should be taken to avoid further loss; lack of timely notice itself in such circumstances may well constitute exactly the kind of prejudice that gives the insurer a defense to coverage for part or all of a claim. Most courts, however, have held that where the policy has no provision specifying who bears the expense of mitigation of loss, the insured is responsible for mitigation expenditures.[21]

When the insured's liability for property damage to third parties is the potential loss that the insured seeks to avoid by incurring certain expenses, some confusion in the cases is encountered. Some courts have refused to force the insurer to reimburse the insured for expenses incurred in avoiding damage to the property of others on the ground that such expenditures are not specifically covered by the policy

---

[16] See Georgia Farm Bur. Mut. Ins. Co. v. Murphy, 411 S.E.2d 791 (Ga. Ct. App. 1991) (after car hit tree, its frame was bent and vehicle was total loss; insured continued to drive car, and 11 miles later right rear tire assembly fell off, and 20 more miles later the car caught on fire; rear tire and fire damage was irrelevant, since vehicle was already total loss).

[17] See Bohna v. Hughes, Thorsness, Gantz, Powell & Brundin, 828 P.2d 745 (Alaska 1992) (insured client had no duty to take bankruptcy to mitigate damages for which his lawyer or insurer might be liable); Valle De Oro Bank v. Gamboa, 32 Cal. Rptr.2d 329 (Cal. Ct. App. 1994).

[18] See Policy Kit at 21 (ISO Form HO 00 03 04 91; "we will pay the reasonable cost incurred by you for necessary measures taken solely to protect against further damage.")

[19] See Metalmasters of Minneapolis, Inc. v. Liberty Mut. Ins. Co., 461 N.W.2d 496 (Minn.App. 1990) ("mitigation cost is recoverable so long as it is reasonable and less than the damages would have been without it.")

[20] See Curtis O. Griess & Sons, Inc. v. Farm Bur. Ins. Co. of Neb., 528 N.W.2d 329 (Neb. 1995).

[21] See, e.g., Henri's Food Products Co. v. Home Ins. Co., 474 F. Supp. 889 (E.D. Wis. 1979); Winkler v. Great Am. Ins. Co., 447 F. Supp. 135 (E.D. N.Y. 1978); Gowans v. Northwestern Pac. Indem. Co., 489 P.2d 947 (Or. 1971). See generally Annot., *Recoverability, Under Property Insurance Against Liability for Property Damage, Of Insured's Expenses To Prevent or Mitigate Damages*, 33 A.L.R.3d 1262 (1970).

and the legal liability of the insured has not been established.[22] Other courts have allowed reimbursement on the ground that the insured's action benefited the insurer by relieving it of possible damage claims.[23]

The mitigation issue with respect to property damage to third parties has become particularly contentious in environmental pollution cases. One issue is whether the cost to clean up toxic waste sites, thereby preventing further harm to third parties, is recoverable "as damages" under the Comprehensive General Liability Form even though the insured has not suffered any liability for the payment of damages. The answer usually given is yes; this issue is discussed in detail in another section.[24] Another issue is whether the "owned-property" exclusion in liability policies precludes coverage for the remediation of on-site damage undertaken for the purpose of preventing injury to off-site property. This issue is also discussed in another section.[25] Both of these issues involve questions of an insured's duty to mitigate and whether mitigation expenses are covered.[26]

§ 92   Measuring the Amount of Loss: Marine Insurance

Marine insurance is the oldest form of insurance. In many respects, it has evolved into a unique, seemingly completely separate body of insurance, with rules that often have little overlap with or resemblance to the rules in the other principal kinds of insurance. Yet many rules in other kinds of insurance — particularly the rules regarding payment of proceeds in property insurance — have a close nexus to the rules of marine insurance.

In this discussion, only the essentials of marine insurance will be briefly sketched.[1] The most understandable aspects of marine insurance involve damage

---

[22] See Prime Drilling Co. v. Standard Acc. Ins. Co., 304 F.2d 221 (10th Cir. 1962); Young's Market Co. v. American Home Assur. Co., 481 P.2d 817 (Cal. 1971); Farr v. Traders & Gen. Ins. Co., 357 S.W.2d 544 (Ark. 1962); J.L. Simmons Co. v. Lumbermens Mut. Ins. Co., 228 N.E.2d 227 (Ill. App. Ct. 1967).

[23] See Teeples v. Tolson, 207 F. Supp. 212 (D.Or. 1962); Aetna Cas. & Sur. Co. v. Summar, 545 S.W.2d 730 (Tenn. 1977); Leebov v. United States Fid. & Guar. Co., 165 A.2d 82 (Pa. 1960); Grand Pelican Furniture Co. v. Cambridge Mut. Fire Ins. Co., 263 So. 2d 91 (La. Ct. App. 1972).

[24] See § 65[f][2], *supra.*

[25] See § 65[f][7], *supra.*

[26] See, e.g., City of Edgerton v. General Cas. Co., 493 N.W.2d 768, 780 (Wis. Ct. App. 1992), *aff'd in part, rev'd in part and remanded,* 517 N.W.2d 463 (Wis. 1994) (mitigation cost in clean-up of toxic site held recoverable as long as performed for insurer's benefit); Rhone-Poulenc Basic Chemicals Co. v. American Motorists Ins. Co., 616 A.2d 1192 (Del. 1992) (mitigation provisions of policy precluded coverage for cost of measures taken or to be taken to prevent additional release of pollutants from landfill); Monsanto Co. v. Aetna Cas. & Sur. Co., No. 88C -JA-118, 1993 WL 563248 (Del.Super. 1993) (applying Missouri law; insured's expenses of mitigating environmental harm held precluded from coverage).

[1] For more information about maritime losses and marine insurance, see Leslie J. Buglass, *Marine Insurance and the General Average in the United States,* (2d ed. 1981); William H. Rodda, *Marine Insurance: Ocean and Inland* (3d ed. 1970); William D. Winter, *Marine Insurance: Its Principles and Practice* (2d ed. 1929); Richard E. Burke, *An Introduction to Marine Insurance,* 15 Forum 729 (1981).

to or loss of vessels and cargo; paying proceeds for these kinds of losses will be emphasized in the discussion in this section. Yet many things can happen whenever a vessel puts out to sea, and these events are all capable of being insured. If, for example, a vessel sinks, the shipper's payment might never be received, and anticipated profits or commissions to be derived from the sale of goods might be lost; these potential losses are insurable, just like the vessel or cargo.

[a]   Total Loss, Partial Loss, and "Average"

The maritime industry utilizes special terminology to describe losses. A total loss can be one of two kinds: "actual" or "constructive." An "actual total loss" (sometimes called an "absolute total loss") occurs when a casualty within coverage so extensively damages the property that no value remains. Generally speaking, if the property is taken out of the possession or control of the insured or is so extensively damaged that it is impossible for the property to reach its destination without complete destruction, an actual total loss has occurred. This test is met if, for example, the vessel and cargo sink, or the vessel and cargo are captured or stolen. A partial loss constitutes an actual total loss if no reasonable possibility exists that the partially damaged hull or cargo can be transported to its destination without complete destruction.

A "constructive total loss" occurs (under the English maritime rule) when it is possible for the damaged vessel or cargo to reach the final destination without complete destruction, but the cost of the remaining portion of the voyage exceeds the remaining value of the cargo or vessel. In such circumstances, the partial loss is for all practical purposes total. The cargo might continue to exist, but the cargo has no measurable value if the cost of shipping exceeds the value of the cargo in its damaged state. If the insured elects to treat a loss as a constructive total loss, the insured must notify the underwriter of this election and the insured must surrender or "abandon" to the underwriter all of the insured's rights in the subject matter of the insurance.

One of the few clear differences between English and American maritime law concerns the time at which the insured can elect to take a constructive total loss. Under American law, the insured may claim a constructive total loss when the cost of repair, reconditioning, refloating, or other efforts would exceed half of the value of the vessel or cargo. Under English law, unless the cost of salvage and repair equals or exceeds the value of the shipment, no claim can be made for a constructive total loss. This difference between the two legal systems has led to special clauses in marine insurance policies. Most policies on vessels or "hulls" — which are called "hull policies" — contain a clause which provides that the American rule shall not apply to vessels. The American rule, which requires less damage for a constructive total loss, is more likely to encourage abandonment of a vessel or cargo; whether that is good or bad is debatable. Nevertheless, marine insurance forms remove, at least with respect to vessels, whatever benefits the insured gets under the American version of constructive total loss.

A loss which is not total is a partial loss. In maritime law, a partial loss is called an "average." The concept of average has ancient historical roots. As early as 900

B.C. in Greece, the common practice was for merchants to travel with their goods in order to sell them at the destination and to buy other goods at the distant port for shipment to their home market. Most vessels transported several merchants and their goods at one time. In bad weather, to prevent a ship from sinking, some of the goods, usually the most accessible, would be thrown overboard, i.e., "jettisoned." In an emergency, no time would exist to debate whose goods should be cast aside. To prevent such delays, a system was devised (and which appears in the maritime law code promulgated by the Rhodians in 916 B.C.) to assess the value of the jettisoned goods pro rata over the entire value of the ship and cargo prior to the jettison. The term "average" developed to refer to this system of distribution of loss, and that term is still used today.

The concept of average, technically speaking, has nothing to do with marine insurance. An average is a potential risk facing every shipper and shipowner, whether the shipment or vessel is insured or not. However, owners of hulls and cargo typically secure insurance to indemnify them for any damage to the vessel or cargo; in other words, insurance is purchased to protect against the risk of an average. Thus, calculating the average is essentially the process of calculating the proceeds payable by the insurer for each shipper and the shipowner. The calculation of the proceeds payable under the insurance policy involves two steps: first, calculating the amount of the damage (or the average), and second, calculating the portion of that damage for which the insurer is liable.

[b] General Average

A "general average" is a loss which occurs when, under fortuitous circumstances, a sacrifice of part of a ship or cargo is voluntarily made or an expense is incurred for the sole purpose of preserving a common interest, such as saving the whole ship or the remainder of the cargo. Such a loss is charged to all interests at risk in a venture; each of the owners of property bears a proportionate share of the loss. Consider the following example. A shipment of goods occurs on the *Ruby,* a ship worth $200,000. There are four cargoes on the *Ruby:* cargo A is worth $400,000; cargo B is worth $250,000; cargo C is worth $100,000; and cargo D is worth $50,000. In a storm, some of the cargo ($100,000 of cargo A, and $100,000 of cargo B) is thrown overboard to save the remaining hull and cargo. The total value of the shipment, including the hull, is $1,000,000. As a percentage of the total value, the hull accounts for 20 percent; cargo A accounts for 40 percent; cargo B accounts for 25 percent; cargo C accounts for 10 percent; and cargo D accounts for 5 percent. The amount of loss is $200,000; each party must share in this loss based on the value of its property relative to the total shipment. Thus, the following contributions must be made to a "common fund": the owner of the *Ruby* must chip in $40,000, and the owners of the cargoes, A, B, C, and D, must chip in, respectively, $80,000, $50,000, $20,000, and $10,000. However, the owner of cargo A has already contributed $100,000 by virtue of the jettison, so this owner can withdraw $20,000 from the common fund; similarly, the owner of cargo B has contributed $100,000, so this owner can withdraw $50,000. When the process is completed, what happens is that the hull owner and the owners of cargoes C and D share in reimbursing the owners of cargoes A and B for part of their loss.

In our hypothetical, neither the owner of the *Ruby* nor the owners of the cargoes have to pay for these losses out of pocket, because each of these persons had purchased insurance prior to the voyage. The marine insurers indemnify the various parties for their loss, but each insurer's payment may not be 100 hundred percent of its insured's contribution to the common fund. This depends on whether each insured purchased coverage for the full market value of its property (either the hull or a portion of the cargo). If a shipper insures the cargo for less than its value, the shipper must share with the insurer any loss assessed that cargo.

For example, the actual (or "contributory") value of cargo C was $100,000, but suppose its owner and the insured stipulated that the cargo was worth $80,000 and the owner decided to insure the cargo for only $60,000. Nothing prevents the parties from stipulating a different value and from insuring the cargo for some amount less than the stipulated value. The loss assessed the owner of cargo C for the jettison of part of cargoes A and B was $20,000. To determine what portion of this $20,000 the owner of cargo C must pay and for what portion the insurer is responsible, the following calculation is made. First, the value of the cargo was stipulated at 80 percent of its "contributory" or actual value. Therefore, 20 percent of the $20,000 loss ($4,000) is the responsibility of the cargo owner. Second, the remaining $16,000 must be allocated. The value of the cargo was stipulated at $80,000, and the owner insured it for only 75 percent of its stipulated value. Therefore, the owner must bear 25 percent of the remaining $16,000 loss, or an additional $4,000. Therefore, of the $20,000 loss which cargo C is assessed, the owner must pay $8,000 and the insurer $12,000.[2]

[c]   A General Formula

Another way to state the insurer's liability in the foregoing example is as follows: the measure of the cargo owner's recovery against the insurer is calculated by determining the fraction of loss and multiplying that number by the smaller of (a) the underwritten amount or (b) the value of the cargo, either prime or stipulated.

What is the "fraction of loss"? Fraction of loss is a proportion of damage to be applied to the policy's value. Fraction of loss is calculated by comparing the "sound value" of the goods, which is the value the goods would have had at the port of destination if they had arrived without damage, to the value of the goods in their damaged condition at the port of destination. In the foregoing example, we assume that cargo C would have been worth $100,000 at the port of destination. However, under the law of general average, cargo C was assessed $20,000 of the total loss, meaning, in effect, that cargo C arrived in the port of destination with a value of $80,000. If

S = sound value at port of destination, and
D = damaged value at port of destination,
then the loss $(L) = S–D$.

L will be measured in monetary units at the port of adjustment, i.e., the port of destination. The fraction of loss is calculated as follows:

---

[2] The manner in which the responsibility for the $16,000 is allocated is an example of pure, or 100 percent, coinsurance. See § 93[b], *infra*.

Let %L = fraction of loss.

$$\%L = \frac{L}{S}, \text{ or } \frac{S - D}{S}$$

Fraction of loss is not an amount of money payable, but a fraction which expresses the proportion of damage to the value of the goods in an undamaged state. In our hypothetical, the fraction of loss equals 20 percent.

The fraction of loss must be multiplied by the smaller of the underwritten amount (here $60,000) or the value, either stipulated or prime. Value may be "stipulated" in a policy by the parties; this simply means that the parties agree upon the value of the hull or cargo. If value is stipulated, the policy is called a "valued policy."[3] The "stipulated value" is not the same thing as the "sum insured"; indeed, the parties might choose to insure the property for less than its stipulated value. Stipulating the value has many consequences. In the event of total loss, if the valuation and insured sum are the same, that amount is payable, regardless of the actual value at the time of loss or at any other time. If the insured sum is less than the stipulated value and a total loss occurs, the insurer pays only the stipulated value; the insured bears the remainder of the loss. If the value is stipulated at an amount greater than the actual value, the insured would get a windfall in the event of total loss. This may be disadvantageous in that it encourages abandonment or destruction of property. However, stipulating the values eliminates the need to determine after a loss has occurred what the pre-loss value of the property had been, a determination that may be both difficult and controversial.

If value is not stipulated, the policy is called an "open policy." In that event, the value of the vessel or cargo is referred to as the "prime value," which is the market value of the property at the port and time of departure. If prime value is used to calculate the proceeds payable, it can be said that the purpose of marine insurance is to restore the insured to the position occupied at the commencement of the voyage, as opposed to the position occupied just before the loss or that would have been occupied if the voyage had been completed (i.e., the port of destination reached) without a casualty.

Now, the following observation can be made:

If X = the proceeds the insurer is obligated to pay, and
if P = prime value, and
if ST = stipulated value, and
if U = underwritten amount,
X = %L multiplied by the smaller of U or either P or ST (either P or ST will be compared to U, depending on whether the policy is open or valued).

In our hypothetical, there is a stipulated value, $80,000. But the underwritten amount is smaller: $60,000. The fraction of loss, 20 percent, times the underwritten amount yields $12,000, which is the amount the insurer is obligated to contribute to the loss.

Several additional observations are possible:

---

[3] Note that this is the same terminology used in other lines of insurance where the value of the insured property is stipulated. See § 93[c], *infra*.

If S = the sound value at the port of destination, and
if D = the damaged value at the port of destination,

$$L = S - D, \text{ and } \%L = \frac{L}{S}, \text{ or } \frac{S - D}{S}$$

If it is also assumed that U is less than ST, it follows that

$$X = \%L(U) = \left(\frac{L}{S}\right) U = \left(\frac{S-D}{S}\right) U = L\left(\frac{U}{S}\right)$$

As will be developed in the next section, the foregoing formula for determining the proceeds payable in marine insurance is the ancestor of the standard coinsurance clause used in property insurance in the United States.

[d]   Particular Average

A partial loss, if not a general average, is a "particular average." A particular average is a partial loss that falls entirely on one interest because the law of general average does not apply.

If a particular average occurs, the amount of the insurer's contribution to the loss is calculated under the formula developed above. Under this formula, the insurer is liable for the entire loss only if the cargo is fully insured. If the owner of the cargo does not insure the cargo for all of its stipulated or prime value, the owner must bear part of a total or partial loss.

Unlike general average, where the rules are usually the same for hull losses and cargo losses, the rules of particular average treat hull losses and cargo losses differently. In general average, if the loss of a hull or cargo is total, the insured recovers the underwritten amount (unless no value is stipulated and the underwritten amount exceeds the prime value, in which case the insured recovers the prime value). However, hulls, unlike cargoes, are not designed to be sold at the end of a voyage. Using the sound or damaged value at the port of destination to calculate the proceeds payable for particular average to a hull may be difficult because there is not necessarily a market for the hull at the port of destination. Therefore, cost of repairs, sometimes offset by depreciation, is the usual measure of payment on claims for particular average to a hull.

[e]   The "Memorandum"

Because marine insurers did not want to cover certain kinds of losses, such as damage to commodities due to spoilage, breakage, or other types of normally expectable deterioration, insurers developed a provision in marine insurance forms that excludes particular average coverage for some types of goods. This provision is called a "memorandum." The effect of the memorandum is to provide insurance for general average only. The terminology is not always easy to understand. For example, a provision might cover "wheat in bags warranted by the assured free from average, unless general": this means that the insured pays for particular average, but if the wheat is jettisoned to save a common interest, the loss is covered. This is called an "FPA clause," meaning "free from particular average" clause. There are two kinds of FPA clauses — the American version and the English version. The English clause excepts particular average unless the vessel is stranded, burnt, sunk, or damaged by collision; there is no requirement that the stranding, burning, sinking, or damage *cause* the loss. The American version requires causation: the insurer is liable only if the particular average is *caused* by stranding, sinking, burning, or collision with another vessel.

Another memorandum provision might cover "wheat in bags warranted by the assured free from average under ten percent, unless general." This means that a particular average under ten percent is not covered, but particular averages of ten percent or more and general average are covered. The percentage term in such a clause is called the "franchise." Sometimes the franchise has a deductible — "free from average under ten percent which is deductible"— which means that the first ten percent of a particular average is always borne by the insured, to be contrasted with the no-deductible situation where if the loss exceeds ten percent the insurer pays for the entire particular average.

§ 93   Measuring the Amount of Loss: Property Insurance

[a]   The Principle of Indemnity

The calculation of the proceeds to which the insured is entitled for a covered loss under a policy of property insurance is controlled by the following principle: property insurance is a contract of indemnity. The goal of indemnity is to reimburse the insured for the loss sustained — and no more. The objective is to put the insured in the position the insured would have occupied had no loss occurred. The insured is not entitled to recover more than the damaged property is worth or more than its decline in value as a result of the damage.

Property insurance policies establish alternative limitations on what the insurer will pay the insured in the event of loss. The insurer must pay, and the insured can claim no more than, whichever alternative results in the smallest liability for the insurer: (1) the applicable limit of liability, or the policy limits; (2) the amount of the insured's interest in the property at the time of the loss; (3) the value of the property at the time of loss; (4) the cost to repair or replace the property with property of like kind and quality. Specific language in a particular policy may add coinsurance requirements (discussed below) or other limitations on the proceeds payable. Also, the "value" limitation may be stated with different words, such as "actual cash value" or "actual value," but these terms are not likely to be defined further in the policy. In some policies, a replacement endorsement supersedes the "value" limitation, so that if the property is totally destroyed, depreciation will not be taken into account in determining the amount of the insured's loss.

A few simple examples illustrate how the limitations operate in practice. Consider first the policy limits. Suppose the insured owns a house and lot for which the insured paid $25,000 fifteen years ago. The property has now appreciated, and the insured's best estimate is that the house and lot are now worth $80,000. The insured concludes that the house would cost about $60,000 to replace if it were totally destroyed; the insured purchases a policy of replacement cost coverage in which the insurer promises to pay $60,000 to replace the premises in the event of total loss. In fact, after a total loss, the cost to replace the premises is $64,000. The insured's loss will not be fully indemnified. The policy limits are $60,000, and this is the extent of the insured's recovery. Absent extraordinary circumstances,[1] an insurer will not reimburse an insured for an amount exceeding the limits of the policy's coverage. The policy limits specify the bounds of the insurer's contractual undertaking. If the insured's loss were partial, the insured still would not have been allowed to recover an amount exceeding the policy limits, even if the insured's actual loss were greater.

Whatever the limits of the policy, the insured will not be allowed to recover more than the insured's interest in the property. This is a particular application of the insurable interest doctrine: one cannot insure an interest one does not possess, and one cannot insure an interest for more than its value. Suppose the residence the insured owns in the foregoing example is one-half of a duplex; the entire structure's replacement cost is $120,000. The insured purchases a policy to cover one-half of the duplex with limits of $70,000. If the entire structure were destroyed, the insured could not recover $70,000, since the insured's interest in the premises is only $60,000, and this sum is the insured's maximum recovery.

The third restriction is the following: in no event can an insured recover more than the value of the property. Suppose the insured owns a ten-year old automobile that has been driven 125,000 miles. The body is rusted, the engine leaks oil, and cold weather often disables it. The car has no trade-in value toward the purchase of a new car; in books that still list cars of this age, an average vehicle of this vintage has a market value of $500. A tree falls on the car causing damage to the body that would cost $1500 to repair. The cost of repairs exceeds the actual value of the car; the insured is only entitled to recover the actual value, the lesser of the two sums. In effect, the car is a "total loss," even though the car is operable with the damage to the body caused by the tree.

When an insurer reimburses the insured for a total loss, the insurer essentially purchases the property from the insured. The insurer is entitled to receive title to the property, and the insurer may be able to dispose of the property for its salvage value. To allow the insured to recover the total value of the property and to keep the salvage value of the good would be to give the insured a windfall.[2] If the total

---

[1] In some situations where the insurer is thought to have breached a duty that justifies an award of extracontractual damages, proceeds exceeding the policy limits might be paid to the insured. See §§ 99, 111[g] and 112[e], *infra*. Otherwise, the policy limits operate independently of the other limitations in the policy. See Bingham v. St. Paul Ins. Co., 503 So. 2d 1043 (La. Ct. App. 1987).

[2] If the policy has a deductible, the insured gives up title to the property while having borne a portion of the loss. Insurers typically are willing to sell the property back to the insured for its salvage value, which means the insured, in the final analysis, receives in proceeds the amount of the total loss, less the deductible and less the salvage value.

An interesting 1989 Louisiana case, Peoples Bank and Trust Co. v. Insured Lloyds of New York, 537 So. 2d 1307 (La. Ct. App. 1989), provides an example of a court allowing the insured to receive a windfall. The insured, Louisiana Cottonseed, Inc., was in the business of buying and selling cottonseed for cattle feed. Some of LCI's cottonseed in one of its storage

loss were caused by theft and the goods are recovered, the insurer usually reserves the option to return the goods to the insured and recoup proceeds previously paid to the insured.

If property is not totally destroyed and is capable of being repaired, the "repair or replace" limitation may restrict an insured's recovery even further. Suppose the insured owns a new car, for which the insured had purchased coverage for loss by windstorm. A windstorm causes a tree to fall on the car, resulting in substantial, but repairable body damage. The insured is not entitled to a new car, but is only entitled to have the car repaired; that is, the insured is only entitled to have the car put in as good a position as it was in before the occurrence. The insured argues that a once wrecked and now repaired car is not worth as much as the car before the tree fell on it, and the insured may be correct: after body work, vehicles tend to rust sooner, the paint sometimes weathers differently, and the finish is often a notch below the former gloss. These factors may affect, later if not now, the car's resale value, which is a loss to the insured. If the insured can show that the car cannot by repair be placed in as good a condition as it had before the incident, some courts will allow the insured to recover, in addition to the cost of repairs, the difference between the reasonable value of the car before the incident and the reasonable market value after repair.[3] However, this will be a difficult burden to carry, and the costs of bringing such an action will often preclude the insured from seeking reimbursement for this relatively slight — but irritating — loss.

---

tanks was damaged by fire, and particularly the water used to put out the fire. The insurer, Lloyds, helped LCI find a buyer for the damaged cottonseed, who entered into a contract directly with LCI to purchase the damaged seed. Lloyds paid LCI for the difference between the value of the seed in an undamaged condition and the seed's salvage value (as measured by the contract price between LCI and the buyer for the damaged seed). Thereafter, the buyer of the damaged seed defaulted on the contract to purchase, and the assignee of LCI's claims sued Lloyds, alleging that the insurer was responsible for the value of the damaged cottonseed, not just the difference between the cottonseed in undamaged condition and the salvage value of the seed. The trial court agreed, and the appellate court affirmed: "The damaged cottonseed remaining after the fire was of no utility to LCI and could not be sold by it in its retail business and its total loss was proximately caused by fire. Lloyds was obligated to pay LCI for the value of the entire loss of the cottonseed. Whether or not Lloyds could mitigate its loss did not affect Lloyds' obligation to pay LCI for the total loss." 537 So. 2d at 1309. According to the majority opinion, the fact that LCI was not in the business of selling damaged, salvage-value seed meant that LCI had suffered a total loss. To compound this odd reasoning, the court found that Lloyds acted arbitrarily and capriciously, and awarded attorneys fees to the insured. 537 So. 2d at 1310. The dissenting judge had the better view: "There can be no question but that what LCI suffered was a partial loss, not a total loss. There can be no question, according to the terms of this contract, that it was Lloyd's option to pay LCI the value of any damaged goods and take them for itself. Therefore, if the option should not be exercised, the basis of payment would be, in the case of a partial loss, the difference in value before the loss and after the loss . . . The fire caused damage to some 1800 tons of cottonseed resulting in a diminished value of the seed, not total destruction of the seed." 537 So. 2d at 1312.

[3] See State v. Urbanek, 177 N.W.2d 14 (Iowa 1970); United States Fire Ins. Co. v. Welch, 294 S.E.2d 713 (Ga. Ct. App. 1982).

When electing to pay for the cost of repair or replacement, the insurer promises to pay the cost of repair or replacement "with property of like kind and quality." For example, if parts of an automobile are being replaced, the policy allows the insurer to cause parts of similar quality and suitability for the purposes contemplated to be used; either new or used parts may be used. Of course, the "like kind and quality" test is a potential point of disagreement. The insured may insist that only "genuine parts" made by the car's manufacturer be used, while the insurer might contend that cheaper parts of another manufacturer are equal in quality.[4] The policies do not provide specific guidance for such a dispute, which are typically resolved on a case-by-case basis.

When the measure of the insured's recovery is the cost of repair or replacement, the insurer typically has the option either to pay the amount of loss or to make arrangements to repair and rebuild the property.[5] The insurer must make this election reasonably promptly; in many instances, prompt action may be necessary to prevent further loss or damage. It is neither efficient nor fair to the insured for the insurer to delay its decision whether to repair or rebuild or to pay monetary damages. While the insurer delays, the insured is in a quandary. If the insured takes action to repair the property, the insurer might later claim that the expenses incurred were not reasonable and thus are not recoverable.[6] Yet if the insured does not take action, additional loss might occur that could be avoided.

The fact that the insurer has the option to pay the loss or repair the property means, by negative implication, that the insured does not have a right to collect the proceeds and not make the repair. Suppose the insured's car had a market value of $1500 and it suffered $500 worth of damage. The insured might desire to drive the car with additional dents and keep the $500. The typical automobile insurance policy states: "We [the insurer] may pay for loss in money or repair or replace the damaged or stolen property."[7] Thus, it is the insurer's option, not the insured's, as to the manner in which the loss will be indemnified. Insurers do not like insureds to pocket the costs of repairs and leave the property unrepaired. This provides an incentive for an insured to put some dents in his or her car in order to obtain some extra cash, a fraudulent practice that drives up the cost of insurance for everyone. A common way the insurer secures its objective of paying proceeds only for repairs that are performed is to make the check for reimbursement of the body work payable jointly to the insured and the repair shop doing the work; the check cannot be cashed unless

---

[4] Manufacturers of auto parts have a big stake in this issue, as reflected in recent public advertising campaigns. One large auto manufacturer recommends that consumers insist on "genuine GM parts," while advertisements for auto parts companies urge that they can provide high quality and service at low cost.

[5] See, e.g., Walker v. Republic Underwriters Ins. Co., 574 F. Supp. 686 (D.Minn. 1983); Venable v. Import Volkswagen, Inc., 519 P.2d 667 (Kan. 1974); Home Indem. Co. v. Bush, 513 P.2d 145 (Ariz. Ct. App. 1973). In Melancon v. USAA Cas. Ins. Co., 849 P.2d 1374 (Ariz. Ct. App. 1992), the court held that the insurer breached the contract when it deducted depreciation from what the insurer spent after it undertook to repair or replace the property.

[6] See Home Mut. Ins. Co. v. Stewart, 100 P.2d 159 (Colo. 1940); Howard v. Reserve Ins. Co., 254 N.E.2d 631 (Ill. App. Ct. 1969).

[7] *Policy Kit* at 9 (ISO Form PP 00 01 12 89).

the work is actually done.[8] Where moral hazard concerns are less, such as where a major hailstorm sweeps through a city damaging tens of thousands of automobiles, the insurer may expedite claims processing by writing checks directly to insureds. However, if an insured thereafter submits a claim for damage to the same vehicle arising out of a subsequent occurrence, the insured will have to prove that the repairs were made in order to collect proceeds for the second occurrence.[9] Another approach is found in the current version of the standard homeowner's policy: except for small losses (less than 5 percent of the amount of insurance and less than $2500), the insurer, with respect to losses for which the insurer is obligated to repair or replace, pays "no more than the actual cash value of the damage until actual repair or replacement is complete."[10]

When the insured is given proceeds to replace damaged property, sometimes a dispute arises regarding whether a particular purchase after a loss constitutes a replacement of the damaged property. Suppose, for example, the insured's house at 403 Campus Drive is destroyed by fire. The insured, instead of using the proceeds to rebuild the house, purchases a house at 111 Sunset Lane as a "replacement." Replacement is usually used in the sense of "substitute" or "successor," and since the new house was not built on the site of the destroyed house, a replacement probably has not occurred.[11] This problem should rarely surface if insurers consult with insureds regarding how the insured plans to spend the proceeds of the insurance.

[b]   Coinsurance Requirements

"Coinsurance" describes a kind of loss-sharing between insurer and insured. Generally speaking, under a coinsurance arrangement, the insured bears a portion of the loss that is a function of the percentage of the property's total value not covered by insurance. The "co-" signifies the relationship: the insured is also an insurer, along with the underwriter. If the underwritten amount is less than the value of the property, the insured is a coinsurer in the sense that the owner bears a portion of the risk. For example, if the owner insures property for 60 percent of its value, in a system of pure (or 100 percent) coinsurance (like marine insurance), the insured

---

[8] In liability insurance, see § 95, *infra,* the insurer is liable for whatever property damage the insured causes the third party. Often this will be the third party's cost of repairs, but it may be diminution in value, particularly if the third party chooses not to have the repairs performed. The liability insurer has no automatic right to insist that the injured third party repair the damaged property.

[9] To illustrate, suppose a 1995 hailstorm damages a car, and the hood is declared a total loss — not because the hood is not usable, but because the cost of hammering out the dents and refinishing the hood exceeds the cost of purchasing and installing a new hood. The insured writes a check to the insured equal to the cost of a new hood. The insured, who is not troubled by driving a car with a dented hood, cashes the check and does not make the repair. Thereafter, a tree falls on the car in 1996, making the hood completely unusable. The insurer will not reimburse the second loss unless the insured can prove that the hail damage was repaired. The insurer, in effect, tells the insured: "Take the money we gave you in 1995 to replace the hood, which you haven't spent on the hood yet, and use it now, in 1996, to replace the hood."

[10] *Policy Kit* at 27 (ISO Form HO 00 03 04 91).

[11] See Huggins v. Hanover Ins. Co., 423 So. 2d 147 (Ala. 1982); Edmund v. Fireman's Fund Ins. Co., 256 S.E.2d 268 (N.C. Ct. App. 1979).

bears 40 percent of the risk of loss and will recover from the underwriter only 60 percent of any loss, partial or total. (As explained below, the coinsurance system need not be pure or "100 percent"; the extent of the coinsurance system will determine what portion of the loss the insured ultimately bears.)

Like a coinsurance clause, a "deductible" provision causes the insurer and insured to share the loss. When coverage is subject to a deductible, the insured bears that portion of the loss up to the amount of the deductible; in other words, the insured bears 100 percent of the loss up to the amount of the deductible. However, the amount of the deductible bears no relationship to the extent of coverage of a property's total value. The portion of the loss the insured bears depends on the percentage of the total value of the property that is covered.

Coinsurance is advantageous to the insurer because it reduces moral hazard. If the insured must bear a portion of a loss, the insured will be more likely to take precautions to prevent a loss from occurring (and also less likely to destroy property intentionally). To this extent, a deductible and coinsurance have identical effects. However, coinsurance, unlike a deductible, also gives the insured who desires to avoid having to pay part of a loss an incentive to purchase more insurance. In a pure coinsurance system, the insured will pay part of any loss unless the property is insured for 100 percent of its value; this means that the insured will have to purchase more insurance — and pay more premium — to avoid having to pay part of a loss. For example, if the value of property is $1000 and the insured purchases $600 worth of coverage, in the event of a $100 loss the insurer will pay only $60. Increasing the coverage to $800 would have increased the insurer's payment to $80; only if the property were fully insured would the insurer pay all of a loss.

This beneficial effect for the insurer can be better understood by contrasting a "no-coinsurance" system. This kind of system involves no loss-sharing between insurer and insured. The insurer pays the entire amount of any loss, regardless of its size, until the policy limits are reached. In "zero coinsurance," if the insured has property valued at $1000 and insures it for $600, a $100 loss will be paid in full by the insurer — and the same with a $200 loss, a $400 loss, or a $600 loss. If the loss is $700, the insurer pays the first $600 — which exhausts the policy limits — and the insured pays the remaining $100. In the event of a total loss, the insurer pays $600 and the insured bears the rest of the loss. A no-coinsurance system gives the insured little incentive to attempt to prevent small losses. Indeed, an educated insured, realizing that most losses are partial ones, may choose to insure the property for less than its full value and self-insure for the upper layers of total losses, which are much less likely to occur.

The insurer, of course, will not favor a no-coinsurance system. Most claims will come to the insurer in small amounts, where the insured's coverage is total. Thus, the insurer makes less profit on the lower layers of coverage than on the upper layers of coverage.[12] The insurer, then, has an incentive to encourage people to purchase

---

[12] In other words, if a $50,000 house is insured for $50,000, most claims will be less than $10,000. If premiums are charged in "x dollars" for each $10,000 worth of insurance, the insurer will pay out more of the first layer of coverage than the fifth layer of coverage, where fewer claims will be made.

more insurance — that is, to purchase amounts of coverage closer to the full value of the property. To provide this incentive, insurers have borrowed the concept of coinsurance from marine insurance: if the insured does not carry coverage up to a specified percentage of the full value of the property insured, as computed at the time of loss, the insured becomes a coinsurer on any loss, regardless of the size of the loss.[13]

A coinsurance system can be established anywhere from 100 percent coinsurance to zero percent coinsurance, or no coinsurance. One hundred percent coinsurance provides the maximum incentive to the insured to purchase additional layers of insurance. No-coinsurance gives the insured no particular incentive to increase coverage beyond the levels where the insured believes most losses will occur. In the United States, most property policies are sold on an 80 percent coinsurance basis. A typical clause reads as follows:

> If, at the time of loss, the amount of insurance in this policy on the damaged building is less than 80% of the full replacement cost of the building immediately before the loss, we will pay the greater of the following amounts, but not more than the limit of liability under this policy that applies to the building:
>
> (a) The actual cash value of that part of the building damaged; or
>
> (b) That proportion of the cost to repair or replace, after application of the deductible and without deduction for depreciation, that part of the building damaged, which the total amount of insurance in this policy on the damaged building bears to 80% of the replacement cost of the building.

This clause can be best understood by breaking it down into its component parts. The (a) clause limits the insured to recovering actual cash value[14] unless the (b) clause provides a greater recovery. To calculate the amount under the (b) clause, let X equal the limit of the insurer's liability; it is the value of X that the (b) clause defines. The term "proportion" in the provision indicates that a percentage or ratio is being multiplied by something, and the clause expressly indicates that the "something" is the amount of the loss, i.e. the cost to repair or replace. Thus, we know that

X = (a ratio) times L (i.e., the loss).

What is the ratio? The clause says than the "total amount of insurance . . . bears to" something. The "total amount of insurance" is the underwritten amount, or U. Thus, we know that the amount of insurance is the numerator of the ratio, and we can now state the following:

X = (U divided by [something]) times L.

What is the denominator in the ratio? The clause states that the underwritten amount (the numerator) is divided by "80% of the replacement cost of the building." Thus, the denominator is the replacement cost times the coinsurance percentage. The

---

[13] For an argument that coinsurance clauses also promote rate equity, see Uriel Procaccia & Robert M. Shafton, *Coinsurance Clauses and Rate Equity,* 1978 Ins. L. J. 69.

[14] For discussion of the meaning of actual cash value, see § 93[d], *infra.*

coinsurance percentage is 80 percent, so this coinsurance clause means the following (assuming RC equals replacement cost):

$$X = \left(\frac{U}{.80 \text{ RC}}\right) L$$

The New York Standard Coinsurance Clause reads as follows:

This Company shall not be liable for a greater proportion of any loss to the property covered than the amount of insurance under this policy for such property bears to the amount produced by multiplying the actual cash value of such property at the time of the loss by the coinsurance percentage applicable (specified on the first page of this policy, or by endorsement). [*Policy Kit* (1987) at 4 (Form CF 00 11 (Ed. 01 83).

The analysis of this clause would track the analysis of the homeowner's clause set forth in the text, with these differences: The phrase "This Company shall be not be liable for a greater proportion" expresses a limit on the amount of coverage. Therefore, one should let X equal the limit of the insurer's liability. Thus,

X = (a ratio) times L (i.e., the loss).

Because the amount of insurance is the numerator of the ratio,

X = (U divided by [something]) times L.

As for the denominator, the clause states that the underwritten amount (the numerator) is divided by the "amount produced by multiplying the actual cash value . . . at the time of the loss by the coinsurance percentage applicable." Thus, the denominator is the actual cash value (ACV) times the coinsurance percentage. If the coinsurance percentage is 80 percent,

$$X = \left(\frac{U}{.80 \text{ ACV}}\right) L$$

In the New York Standard Clause, ACV serves the same functions as RC.

This formula should be compared to one of the marine insurance formulas:

$$X = \left(\frac{U}{S}\right) L$$

In the marine insurance formula, S, the sound value, is the value of the ship or cargo in good condition at the port of destination. Calculating S is essentially the same thing as calculating the actual cash value of the property (note that the homeowner's policy uses replacement cost, but this will not change the point being made in this discussion). One difference is that the replacement cost is multiplied by .80 in the coinsurance formula and there appears to be no multiplier for sound value in the marine insurance formula, but actually one (also, it is literally a "one," as will be explained shortly) is there. Marine insurance is pure, or 100 percent coinsurance; therefore, the multiplier in the denominator of the marine insurance formula is 1. Thus, the standard coinsurance clause is identical in form to the marine insurance formula, except for the change of the coinsurance percentage. It was observed that a coinsurance system can be anywhere from zero percent to 100 percent; to make calculations in a different system, all that need be done is to substitute a different percentage in the denominator of the general formula. Also, if actual cash value is used instead of replacement cost, one would substitute "ACV" into the denominator, rather than "RC."[15]

Another way to express what the coinsurance clause means is the following: an insured who fails to insure his or her property for at least 80 percent (or whatever the coinsurance percentage is) of its actual cash value (or replacement cost — depending on what the policy provides) will not recover in full for the loss. This concept is embraced in the following formula: if R equals the amount of insurance required for the insured to be reimbursed in full for any partial loss, then

R = RC times the coinsurance percentage (e.g., .80).

Thus, in the typical homeowner's policy, the insured has an incentive to cover property for at least 80 percent of its replacement cost. The following example illustrates this. Suppose the insured has a house with a replacement cost of $125,000. The insured secures $75,000 in coverage under a policy that utilizes an 80 percent coinsurance clause. In a windstorm, the house suffers damage of $20,000. The insured has purchased coverage for only 67 percent of its value; thus, the insured is not going to be indemnified in full by the company. What will the insured recover? Using the above formula, the insured will recover [$75,000 divided by (.80 times $125,000)] times the loss, which is 75/100, or 3/4, times $20,000. The insured only recovers $15,000. If the house had been insured for $100,000, which is 80 percent of its replacement cost, the insured would have recovered [$100,000 divided by (.80 times $125,000)] times the loss, which is 100/100, or 1, times $20,000, meaning the insured would recover the full amount of the partial loss.

Approaching the insured's problem in a different way aids one's understanding of the coinsurance requirement. Recalling that R equals the amount of insurance required (replacement cost times the coinsurance percentage, which is usually .80), it follows from a substitution into the formula derived above (R for .80 RC) that

$$X = \left(\frac{U}{R}\right) L$$

The ratio U divided by R indicates the extent to which the insured is a coinsurer. For the insured, U divided by R is $75,000 divided by (.80 times $125,000), or 3/4. This means that for any partial loss, the insurer pays 3/4 of it; the insured, in effect, is a 1/4 coinsurer of the loss. Because the loss is $20,000, the insurer pays $15,000 in proceeds and the insured bears the remaining $5,000 of the loss. Had the insured covered her house for at least 80 percent of its value, the ratio U divided by R would have been "1" (U divided by R can never be greater than one, or else the insured

---

[15] Of course, in a no-coinsurance system, putting a zero in the denominator destroys the formula, in that it makes the insurer's liability infinite. However, in a no-coinsurance system, calculations can be made easily without the formula if two principles are kept in mind: the insurer's liability can never exceed the policy limits, and the insured's recovery can never exceed the amount of the loss.

would be able to recover more than the loss) and multiplying the loss by "1" means that the insured's loss in such a situation is reimbursed in full.

Note that if the insured's policy were issued in a no-coinsurance system, the insured would have recovered the $20,000 loss in full. If the policy were issued in a pure, or 100 percent, coinsurance system, the house was covered for 60 percent of its value, meaning the insured would recover from the insurer only 60 percent of the $20,000 loss, or $12,000.

Finally, it should be emphasized that regardless of the results given by the coinsurance computations, in no event can the insured recover more than the policy limits. The policy limits always impose an upper limit on the insurer's obligation to indemnify. Thus, if a $125,000 house is insured for $100,000 (80 percent of its value), and the house is totally destroyed by a covered risk, the coinsurance formula would seem to indicate that the insured recovers $100,000/$100,000 times the loss ($125,000), or $125,000. However, the insurer's limit of liability must not be forgotten. The insured is only entitled to recover 100 percent of the loss *up to the policy limits,* which in this hypothetical is $100,000.

The coinsurance clause encourages insureds to purchase insurance in amounts closer to the actual value of their property. It should be noted, however, that in an inflationary economy where some assets (such as homes) are appreciating in value, the insured must periodically increase the amount of coverage on the property, lest appreciation outstrip the amount of coverage and cause a coinsurance penalty to be assessed in the event of a loss.

[c] Valued Policies

Occasionally, the parties to an insurance contract stipulate in the policy the value of property to be insured. This is very common in marine insurance, where the insurer and insured are likely to stipulate the "sound value" of the ship or cargo, meaning the value of the ship or cargo in its undamaged condition. In most nonmarine insurance, the parties do not stipulate the value of the property; the notable exceptions include policies covering valuable works of art or antiques. When the value of insured property is stipulated and a total loss occurs, this stipulation is conclusive; assuming the absence of fraud, collusion, or misrepresentation,[16] or a "gross overvaluation" of the property,[17] the insurer is bound to pay proceeds to the insured equal to the stipulated amount.[18] If a partial loss occurs, the policy (or

---

[16] See Filiatreau v. Allstate Ins. Co., 358 S.E.2d 829 (W.Va. 1987); DeWitt v. American Family Mut. Ins. Co., 667 S.W.2d 700, 708 (Mo. 1984)(en banc).

[17] See Casablanca Concerts, Inc. v. American Nat'l Gen. Agencies, Inc., 407 N.W.2d 440 (Minn. Ct. App. 1987); 3 Couch, *Cyclopedia of Insurance Law 2d,* § 24.2, at 14 (1984). If the amount of coverage is grossly disproportionate to the value of the insurable interest, the valued policy should be void as a wager. A mismatch between the value of the property and the amount of coverage should not lead to evaluation of the policy's validity, assuming the disparity between value and coverage is not extreme. Of course, once any degree of judicial regulation of the valued policy is permitted, some of the benefits of the per se stipulation in a valued policy are lost.

[18] It has been held that the valued policy statute is also for the benefit of the mortgagee in a policy of owner-mortgagee insurance. Sphere Drake Ins. Co. v. Bank of Wilson, 851 S.W.2d 430 (Ark. 1993).

a governing statute) might specify that the proceeds be calculated as a percentage of the valuation based on the percentage of the property destroyed. Usually, however, in cases of partial loss, the proceeds are calculated without regard to the fact that the policy is valued.

Valued policies should be contrasted with "open" policies. With open policies, the agreed sum written on the face of the policy designates, not the value of the property insured, but the maximum limit of recovery if the property is destroyed. With an open policy, the insurer is free to attempt to prove after the loss that the value of the property was less than the stated limits of coverage.

In a number of states, statutes require that the value of the insured property be fixed in the policy. These statutes, which are called "valued policy statutes," make the stated value conclusive with regard to the proceeds payable in the event of total loss. The insurer is denied the right to claim that the value of the destroyed property was less than the fixed value, and generally cannot assert that the amount of the insured's insurable interest in the property is less than the stipulated value.[19] However, depending on the statute, the insurer may be allowed to offset depreciation of the property after the date of the policy's issuance.[20] Such statutes usually apply to fire insurance, but they vary considerably in scope; each statute must be consulted to determine its precise effect. The statutes usually do not apply if the loss is partial.[21]

When the insured has more than one valued policy covering the same loss and the total coverage greatly exceeds the property's value, courts have generally found ways to limit the insured's recovery to an amount less than the total of the policies' coverages. For example, in *Underwriters at Lloyd's, London v. Pike*,[22] the insured had policies of $60,000 and $102,000 on the same property which according to one appraisal was worth $76,500. The court held that the insured was entitled to the

---

[19] See Musselman v. Mountain West Farm Bur. Mut. Ins. Co., 824 P.2d 271 (Mont. 1992).

[20] See West v. Shelter Mut. Ins. Co., 864 S.W.2d 458, 462 (Mo. Ct. App. 1993) (insured, having pleaded that policy was issued in 1985, could not now claim that policy was re-issued annually). It has also been held that public policy does not allow an insured under a builder's risk policy to collect the full stipulated value in the circumstances where the amount insured is adjusted according to the percentage of the building completed. Jones v. State Farm Fire and Cas. Co., 740 S.W.2d 708 (Mo.App. 1987).

[21] See, e.g., La. Rev. Stat. 22:695; Neb. Rev. Stat. § 501.02. A typical valued policy statute appears at Kan. Stat. Ann. § 40-905:

> Whenever any policy of insurance shall be written to insure any improvements upon real property in this state against loss by fire, tornado or lightning, and the property insured shall be wholly destroyed, without criminal fault on the part of the insured or his assigns, the amount of the insurance written in such policy shall be taken conclusively to be the true value of the property insured, and the true amount of loss and measure of damages, and the payment of money as a premium for insurance shall be prima facie evidence that the party paying such insurance is the owner of the property insured: *Provided,* That any insurance company may set up fraud in obtaining the policy as a defense to a suit thereon.

> Compare Cal. Ins. Code 2054, which requires that in the case of partial loss, the insurer shall pay the full amount of the partial loss.

[22] 812 F. Supp. 146 (W.D. Ark. 1993).

benefit of the largest of the two valued policies, but not both, and ordered that the two insurers prorate their share of the $102,000 based on their percentage share of the total insurance in force on the property.[23]

An obvious effect of valued policy statutes, and an advantage from the insured's perspective, is that the insured is relieved of the obligation to prove the value of destroyed property.[24] Another supposed advantage of valued policy statutes is that if the insurer is stripped of its right to contest the valuation when the claim is made, the insurer will investigate the risk more carefully before agreeing to underwrite it. Also, it is thought that valued policy laws deter insurance agents from selling policies with large face values on low-value premises in order to secure larger premiums (which means larger commissions).[25]

Whether valued policy statutes are, on balance, advantageous is an open question. For most insurers, more thoroughly investigating risks before deciding to assume them is more expensive than paying the losses associated with the few applicants who overstate their values to such an extent that the probability of loss is increased. Even if insurers were able to investigate fully and accurately the value of property before undertaking the risk, numerous factors can cause the value of the property to change while the coverage is in effect. Competition in the marketplace undercuts the tendency for agents to overprice their products. Moreover, it is equally likely that valued policies increase moral hazard; insureds have an incentive to fraudulently overvalue their property, which increases the possibility that the property will be deliberately destroyed.

For the foregoing reasons, valued policy statutes have been severely criticized.[26] Given public concern over the widespread incidence of arson, it is very possible that the public would be better served if valued policy statutes were repealed. Whatever one's view on the issue, the increasing use of replacement cost coverage serves to diminish the importance of the controversy over valued policies.

[d] "Actual Cash Value"

A limitation on the proceeds payable frequently found in property insurance policies is that the insured may not recover more than the "actual cash value" of the property. Sometimes the policy will express the actual cash value limitation along with a reference to depreciation, but in most policies marketed today the term actual cash value stands alone.[27] Except for a possible reference to depreciation,

---

[23] 812 F. Supp. at 151.

[24] See Musselman v. Mountain West Farm Bur. Mut. Ins. Co., 824 P.2d 271 (Mont. 1992).

[25] See LaHaye v. Allstate Ins. Co., 570 So. 2d 460 (La. Ct. App. 1990); Calnon v. Fidelity-Phenix Fire Ins. Co., 206 N.W. 765 (Neb. 1925).

[26] See, e.g., Robert E. Keeton, *Insurance Law: Basic Text* 140–142 (1971).

[27] Compare Tri-State Ins. Co. v. McCraw, 483 S.W.2d 212 (Ark. 1972) ("loss or damage shall be ascertained or estimated according to such actual cash value, with proper deduction for depreciation") with Thomas v. American Family Mut. Ins. Co., 666 P.2d 676 (Kan. 1983) (coverage provided "to the extent of the actual cash value of the property at the time of loss, but not exceeding the amount which it would cost to repair or replace the property with material of like kind and quality within a reasonable time after such loss"); Titus v. West Am. Ins. Co., 362 A.2d 1236 (N.J.Super.Ct. Law.Div. 1976).

policies typically do not define actual cash value, leaving it instead to courts to determine what the phrase means. The judicial answer varies.[28]

[1] Replacement Cost Less Depreciation

Most courts have defined actual cash value as replacement cost less depreciation.[29] For example, a machine which could be replaced for $100,000 at current market prices and which has been used for two-fifths of its useful life has an actual cash value of $60,000. Replacement cost, the first component of the standard, is usually determined by reference to what it would cost at the time of loss or a reasonable period after the loss to replace the destroyed goods with goods of like kind and quality. As a result, replacement cost fluctuates with changing market conditions. Depreciation, the second component of the standard, takes into account the age of the property at the time of loss, the extent of its use, its obsolescence, and other factors affecting its value. In tax law, depreciation is calculated by reference to schedules that may have little to do with a property's useful life. The calculation in insurance does not occur by reference to rigid schedules.

The most common criticism of the replacement-cost-less-depreciation measure is that it overstates the recovery in circumstances where property, without depreciating in any significant way, has become obsolete. If obsolescence is not included in the depreciation calculation in a situation where obsolescence is a material factor affecting a property's value, the insured has the potential to recover a windfall. The test works better in such cases, however, if an obsolete building is viewed as fully depreciated, thereby reducing the loss calculation to near zero. Introducing this kind of flexibility to the depreciation calculation, however, makes this test resemble the broad evidence rule, discussed below.

Although replacement-cost-less-depreciation is the most common definition of actual cash value, many courts have approved other definitions.

[2] Market Value

Some courts have defined actual cash value as market value in situations where the market value is easy to determine.[30] Thus, if the property is totally destroyed

---

[28] See generally Harold H. Reader, *Modern Day Actual Cash Value: Is It What the Insurers Intend?*, 22 Tort & Ins. L.J. 282 (1987); Charles E. Schalliol, *The Broad Evidence Rule and Fire Insurance and Tort Recoveries for Household Goods*, 1973 Ins. L.J. *365; James R. Detamore, Functional Value vs. Actual Cash Value in Partial Loss Settlements,* 50 Ins. Counsel J. 332 (1983).

[29] See, e.g., C.L. Maddox, Inc. v. Royal Ins. Co. of Am., 567 N.E.2d 749 (Ill. App. Ct. 1991); Snellen v. State Farm Fire and Cas. Co., 675 F. Supp. 1064, 1067 (W.D. Ky. 1987); Clemon v. Occidental Fire & Cas. Co., 264 N.W.2d 192 (Neb. 1978); First Preferred Ins. Co. v. Bell, 587 S.W.2d 798 (Tex. Ct. App. 1979). See generally Annot., *Depreciation as Factor in Determining Actual Cash Value for Partial Loss Under Insurance Policy,* 8 A.L.R.4th 533 (1981).

[30] See, e.g., Erin Rancho Motels, Inc. v. United States Fid. & Guar. Co., 352 N.W.2d 561 (Neb. 1984) (motel damaged by fire); Aetna Cas. & Sur. Co. v. Insurance Dep't of Iowa, 299 N.W.2d 484 (Iowa 1980); Forer v. Quincy Mut. Fire Ins. Co., 295 A.2d 247 (Me. 1972) (home damaged by freezing of plumbing and heating systems); Cassel v. Newark Ins. Co., 79 N.W.2d 101 (Wis. 1956) (stock merchandise); Titus v. West Am. Ins. Co., 362 A.2d 1236

and it is the kind of property that is bought and sold in a recognizable market, market value is the best estimate of what reimbursement the insured requires in order to be placed in the position the insured would have occupied had no loss occurred. The logic is that if the proceeds provide the insured with sufficient funds to purchase a replacement good, the insured is fully indemnified.

Market value as a measure of actual cash value has some limitations. For example, the market value of a house will not necessarily equate to the price at which the house and lot last sold, adjusted for recent inflation or deflation. Real estate markets have tended to be more volatile in recent times, and this makes mechanical formulae ineffective for calculating current market values for individual properties. Moreover, most buildings or homes are usually sold with the land on which they rest. Therefore, the structures have no market value independent of the land on which they rest; professional appraisers will put separate values on land and improvements, but in fully developed areas, placing a separate value on land, which is never traded without an improvement on it, involves a good deal of guesswork.

Another difficulty is that the market value of a good may understate its true value to the insured. For example, a suit of clothes that has been worn once could not be sold for very much in a used clothing store; that there is no buyer or market for a good should not mean that the good has no value.[31] In such circumstances, market value does not give an accurate measure of the value of the property to its owner. One court resolved the problem in this way: "The phrase 'actual cash value' . . . may mean 'market value,' or the more elastic standard of 'value to the owner.' If the goods are readily replaceable in a current market, 'market value' is the measure; but if there is no market, or if the market value is inadequate, the proper measure is the 'value to the owner,' or the loss he suffers in being deprived of the goods."[32] "Value to the owner," as used by this court, could mean replacement-cost-less-depreciation, or perhaps replacement cost without an offset for depreciation.

As an alternative to market value, replacement-cost-less-depreciation is not always to be preferred as a measure. Consider a large, old house located in a once-prestigious, but now deteriorated section of a city. It may be that the only buyers interested in the property are buyers interested in the land for commercial development; the house itself has a "negative value," in that potential buyers would have to bear the expense of leveling the house. In this circumstance, the destruction of the house would actually be a benefit, not a loss. The fair market value of such a house is small; yet the replacement cost of such a house, even when depreciation is taken into account, might be very large, as large as that for any house in the city. In the same vein, an old farmhouse in a remote, rural area may have no prospective purchasers if it were put up for sale; but this does not mean the farmhouse has no value to its current occupants as a residence. The fairest measure of value in such situations must depend on the uses to which the property is likely to be put.

(N.J.Super.Ct.Law Div. 1976) (automobile); Hanover Fire Ins. Co., v. Bock Jewelry Co., 435 S.W.2d 909 (Tex. Ct. App. 1968) (diamonds); Motors Ins. Corp. v. Smith, 67 So. 2d 294 (Miss. 1953) (automobile).

31 See C.L. Maddox, Inc. v. Royal Ins. Co. of Am., 567 N.E.2d 749 (Ill. App. Ct. 1991) (quoting Smith v. Allemania Fire Ins. Co., 219 Ill. App. Ct. 506 (1920)).

32 Clift v. Fulton Fire Ins. Co., 315 S.W.2d 9, 11 (Tenn. Ct. App. 1958).

[3] Replacement Cost

Other courts have opted for replacement or reproduction cost *without* offsetting depreciation.[33] The cases in which this approach is applied typically involve policies that utilize "actual cash value" as a limitation on recovery without referring to depreciation as an offset. Courts sometimes explain that they are enforcing the clauses according to their "plain meaning," in that the terms of the contract do not permit depreciation to be offset.[34] These decisions might also be explained as a specific application of the reasonable expectations doctrine. The Kansas Supreme Court, in holding that an insured was entitled to recover the full cost to repair a damaged roof without deducting depreciation, an amount that exceeded the actual cash value of the damaged portion of the roof, stated that "a reasonable person in the same predicament as appellee would not expect depreciation to be considered to reduce and impair his ability to repair his partially damaged dwelling."[35] In most cases, if a depreciation deduction is taken against the replacement cost, the insured will receive a sum insufficient to pay for repairing the property.

Whatever the explanation, the replacement cost approach can be highly beneficial to an insured. Imagine a roof which cost $4000 to install in 1986. In 1996, the roof, with one-half of its useful life remaining, costs $6000 to replace. If in 1996 the roof is totally destroyed and the insurer's liability is limited to the replacement cost less depreciation, the insurer will only pay $4000 in proceeds to the insured ($6000 replacement cost less $2000 depreciation), essentially leaving the insured with one-third of the risk of loss. Ignoring depreciation and concentrating on replacement cost avoids the out-of-pocket loss to the insured, but it also gives the insured a "free" roof for ten years. It is upon this basis that defining actual cash value as replacement cost without considering depreciation is criticized: failure to take depreciation into account in determining the loss puts the insured in a better financial position than the insured would have occupied had no loss occurred, and this violates the principle of indemnity. Particularly in situations where the damage is to a substantial portion of the structure or good, the repair of the building or good has the potential to increase, not just maintain, the useful life of the item. Also, replacement cost may exceed the true commercial value of a structure or a good, as measured by profits generated by the item, its usefulness to the owner, or its location and age. To the extent replacement cost exceeds the "real" value, the moral hazard is increased, since the potential insurance recovery exceeds the property's worth. The insured might have an incentive to destroy an old good in order to have its useful life extended by a repair paid for by the insurer.

---

[33] See, e.g., Thomas v. American Fam. Mut. Ins. Co., 666 P.2d 676 (Kan. 1983); Reese v. Northern Ins. Co., 215 A.2d 266 (Pa. Super. Ct. 1965). See generally Annot., *Construction and Effect of Property Insurance Provision Permitting Recovery of Replacement Cost of Property,* 1 A.L.R.5th 817 (1991).

[34] E.g., Thomas v. American Family Mut. Ins. Co., 666 P.2d 676 (Kan. 1983); Sperling v. Liberty Mut. Ins. Co., 281 So. 2d 297 (Fla. 1973).

[35] 666 P.2d at 679.

[4] Broad Evidence Rule

An increasing number of courts permit the admission of any evidence so long as it tends to support a fair, accurate estimate of value. This approach, described as the "broad evidence rule," allows the trier of facts to consider any evidence logically tending to establish the correct estimate of the value of the property at the time of the loss.[36]

The leading case supporting the broad evidence rule is *McAnarney v. Newark Fire Insurance Co.,*[37] a 1928 New York decision. In *McAnarney,* the insured's premises, which included several buildings, were designed for the manufacture of malt. The business conducted there was prosperous until Prohibition put an end to it in 1918. In January, 1920, policies insuring the buildings against loss by fire in the aggregate sum of $42,750 were purchased. In April, 1920, the buildings were destroyed by fire, and the insured submitted proofs of loss valuing the buildings at $60,000 and seeking recovery of the full proceeds of the policies. The case was tried before a jury, to which the following question was submitted: "What was the intrinsic or depreciated structural value of the buildings burned?" The jury was instructed to calculate "what it cost to build the structures, less depreciation proven in the case." The jury returned a verdict setting the value at $55,000.

The insurer appealed, claiming error in the trial court's refusal to admit evidence showing that the insured had been unable to sell the property, that the property had been offered for sale for $12,000 in 1919, and that no purchaser had offered more than $6,000 for the property. The appeals court, in reversing the trial court's judgment, rejected the insured's argument that the measure of damage was reproduction cost less depreciation. Rather, to determine the actual cash value of the buildings, the court said that all relevant evidence should be considered:

> Where insured buildings have been destroyed, the trier of fact may, and should, call to its aid, in order to effectuate complete indemnity, every fact and circumstance which would logically tend to the formation of a correct estimate of loss. It may consider original cost and cost of reproduction; the opinions upon value given by qualified witnesses; the declarations against interest which may have been made by the assured; the gainful uses to which the buildings might have been put; as well as any other fact reasonably tending to throw light upon the subject.[38]

Subsequent New York cases have held that the broad evidence rule and the "replacement cost less depreciation" formulation are mutually exclusive, and that if the policy defines actual cash value as "replacement cost less depreciation," this formulation controls, and the broad evidence rule cannot be applied.[39] The

---

36 See, e.g., Sullivan v. Liberty Mut. Fire Ins. Co., 384 A.2d 384 (Conn. 1978); Worcester Mut. Fire Ins. Co. v. Eisenberg, 147 So. 2d 575 (Fla. Dist. Ct. App. 1962). See generally John D. Ingram, *Reducing the Incentive for Arson: The "Broad Evidence Rule,"* 29 Drake L. Rev. 761 (1979–80).

37 159 N.E. 902 (N.Y. 1928).

38 159 N.E. at 905.

39 See Dickler v. CIGNA Property and Cas. Co., 957 F.2d 1088 (3d Cir. 1992)(applying New York law); Lazaroff v. Northwestern Nat'l Ins. Co., 121 N.Y.S.2d 122 (N.Y. Sup. Ct.), *aff'd,* 117 N.Y.S.2d 690 (N.Y. App. Div. 1952).

reasoning of these cases is that the language of the insurance contract controls, and any definition of actual cash value in the policy takes priority.

In recent years, numerous courts have approved the broad evidence rule.[40] When a market value is available, admitting all relevant evidence does little to improve the accuracy of the calculation and could needlessly prolong the valuation process. However, in many cases, the broad evidence approach seems best suited to determining the amount needed to effectuate complete indemnity. Where no market exists for the property at the time of loss and where replacement cost less depreciation is unrealistic, as it was in *McAnarney,* no good alternative to the broad evidence rule exists. For example, with growing crops or immature livestock, evidence of the ultimate market price less the costs of growing the crops or raising the animals is a good measure of actual cash value; the broad evidence rule's recognition that considerable relevant evidence might exist on value is highly appropriate in such a setting.[41] Furthermore, the term "actual cash value" is slippery, and a rule that allows the character of the insured property and the nature of the loss to be taken into account is best able to reach fair results in diverse factual settings.

[5]   Choosing a Measure: Some Problems

The broad evidence rule has the flexibility to reach fair results in a wide range of circumstances. Yet this approach, in a sense, only begs the question: of the various methods of valuation, which is the best in a particular situation?

[i]   Used Goods

Contrast two situations. First, consider a spare tire which is stolen out of the trunk of the insured's car. The tire has a useful life of 40,000 miles, but the tire has been used for 30,000 miles. A new tire costs $100. Should the insured recover $25, taking into account the tire's depreciation, or $100, the cost to replace the tire? Compare the situation where a three-year-old car has its hood damaged in a hailstorm (to the point that removing the dents will cost more than replacing the hood). Replacing the hood will cost $600, but the car will have a new hood. Should the old hood be depreciated in determining the insurer's liability? If a three-year-old car of similar make and model has depreciated sixty percent, should the insurer's liability be limited to $240?

Although each of the two situations involves used goods, the situations seem to call for different measurements. In four more years, the insured will own a seven-year old car with a four-year-old hood. The insured will never realize the value of the newer hood; the insured will not be able to take the newer hood off the car and

---

[40] See, e.g., Eagle Fire Co. v. Snyder, 392 F.2d 570 (10th Cir. 1968); Travelers Indem. Co. v. Armstrong, 442 N.E.2d 349 (Ind. 1982); Elberon Bathing Co. v. Ambassador Ins. Co., 389 A.2d 439 (N.J. 1978); Sullivan v. Liberty Mut. Fire Ins. Co., 384 A.2d 384 (Conn. 1978); Pinet v. New Hampshire Fire Ins. Co., 126 A.2d 262 (N.H. 1956); Surratt v. Grain Dealers Mut. Ins. Co., 328 S.E.2d 16 (N.C. Ct. App. 1985); Ohio Cas. Ins. Co. v. Ramsey, 439 N.E.2d 1162 (Ind. Ct. App. 1982).

[41] See Strauss Bros. Packing Co. v. American Ins. Co., 298 N.W.2d 108 (Wis. Ct. App. 1980).

sell it separately for a higher price, relative to its cost, than the rest of the car. Thus, to put the insured in the position he or she occupied before the damage, replacement cost is arguably the fairest measure of actual cash value. If the stolen spare tire is replaced with a new, unused tire, in a few years when the insured chooses to sell the car, the insured might remove the spare tire, sell it separately as an unused tire, and purchase a used tire as a substitute for the spare. Or, the insured might put the new tire into use immediately. If the insured had put the used tire into use, the insured would have had to replace it in 10,000 miles, but if the insured gets a new tire now and puts the new tire into use, the insured will not have to purchase another tire for 40,000 more miles, 30,000 miles later than the insured had planned to replace the tire. Thus, it can be said that the insured is likely to realize the gain from substituting a new tire for the stolen old tire; the fairest measure of value in this circumstance, arguably, is replacement cost less depreciation.

Returning to the example of the damaged car hood: If the insured receives a cash payment from the insurer equal to the replacement cost in circumstances where the hood is functional in its damaged condition and the insured does not replace the hood, the insured arguably receives a windfall: the insured receives replacement cost for item that has already started to depreciate, so the insured is, in a sense, better off. When the rest of the car is fully depreciated (i.e., when the rest of the car's depreciation schedule "catches up" to the accelerated depreciation for the hood that was damaged in the hailstorm), the insured will have had both the benefit of the full use of the car plus an insurance payment that more than compensated the insured for the accelerated depreciation that occurred when the hood was damaged. The insurance policy can be drafted to provide an answer to this problem: if the policy pays the insured replacement cost less depreciation in the event of loss, but upon replacement of the property pays the insured the full replacement cost, the insured will not get the windfall.[42] (Some mechanism should exist to commit the insurer to pay full replacement cost in advance of the replacement or rebuilding to deal with the situation where the insured cannot afford the cost of repair or replacement; this is likely to be the case, for example, if the property involved is a residential or commercial building.)

[ii] Appreciated Property

Home ownership is an important "institution" in this country, and how the asset is valued is extremely important for a variety of purposes. When depreciation is taken into account, the insured may suffer a hardship if the proceeds recovered from the insurance are inadequate to replace the property. Imagine an insured who has lived in a house for over twenty years; the house, for which the insured paid $15,000 in 1965, would cost $80,000 to reconstruct today. If the house is twenty-five years old, it may be that one-half of the house's useful life has passed. The value of the house, then, when depreciation is taken into account is only $40,000. Recovering $40,000 if the house is totally destroyed will not come close to putting the insured

---

[42] See Dickler v. CIGNA Prop. and Cas. Co., 957 F.2d 1088 (3d Cir. 1992); Snellen v. State Farm Fire and Cas. Co., 675 F. Supp. 1064, 1067 (W.D. Ky. 1987); Hess v. North Pac. Ins. Co., 859 P.2d 586 (Wash. 1993).

in the position the insured would have occupied but for the loss, since the home could not be rebuilt for less than $80,000.

To protect homeowners from this predicament, most homeowners' policies sold today include what is called "replacement cost coverage." Under these clauses, if at the time of loss the limit of liability for a dwelling is at least eighty percent or more of the replacement cost of the dwelling, the insurer will cover the full cost of repairing or replacing the dwelling without deduction for depreciation. Under replacement cost coverage, no proceeds will be paid unless the insured actually repairs or replaces the damaged property. Replacement cost coverage is important not only to homeowners but also to the owners of business buildings, equipment, and machinery. Yet, recalling the contrasting examples of the hood and the spare tire, it might be observed that taking depreciation into account in a commercial building is fairer than with a residential structure, in that the commercial operator may have, depending on the circumstances, a better chance of realizing the gain of replacing damaged property.[43]

Replacement cost coverage has the potential problem of giving an insured the incentive to arrange for the intentional destruction of old property in order to have it replaced with new. Yet the benefits of replacement cost coverage seem to outweigh this disadvantage. Realizing that some insureds may have an incentive to destroy property to collect the enhanced replacement proceeds, the requirement that the insured replace the property to get the proceeds will at least prevent an insured from destroying old property to make a quick cash profit.

[iii]   Obsolescent Property

An interesting question is presented by those cases where the insured seeks to recover for loss to property that is obsolescent or about to be destroyed. In the *McAnarney* case, the court said that obsolescence should be a factor in determining actual cash value, since obsolescence is relevant, as are other factors, to the true value of the property. The mere fact that property is obsolete does not necessarily

---

[43] An interesting question which has become more important recently is whether a "replacement cost" property insurer is obligated to pay for building code upgrades despite a policy's exclusion of such costs. A recent Alaska decision held that the insurer was so obligated because of the insured's reasonable expectations of coverage. See Bering Strait Sch. Dist. v. RLI Ins. Co., 873 P.2d 1292 (Alaska 1994). This issue has become particularly important in the aftermath of Hurricane Andrew, which struck the south Florida area in August 1992 with devastating consequences. The "Ordinance or Law" exclusion found in most homeowner's policies excludes from coverage any loss resulting from the "enforcement of any ordinance or law regulating the construction, repair, or demolition of a building or other structure, unless specifically provided under this policy." *Policy Kit* at 25 (ISO Form HO 00 03 04 91). The changes in building codes since many of the destroyed or damaged properties were constructed are significant, and insurers are balking at paying the costs of any repairs made solely to bring damaged properties "up to code." For more discussion, see Hugh L. Wood, Jr., Comment, *The Insurance Fallout Following Hurricane Andrew: Whether Insurance Companies are Legally Obligated to Pay for Building Code Upgrades Despite the "Ordinance or Law" Exclusion Contained in Most Homeowner's Policies,* 48 U. Miami L. Rev. 949 (1994).

(Matthew Bender & Co., Inc.)   (Pub.837)

reduce its value to zero. Yet if property is about to be condemned or demolished, one might argue that the property is absolutely valueless. Some courts have held that so long as a condemnation order is not final, a risk of loss from destruction of property subject to the order remains with its owner (or whomever holds title as a result of the condemnation proceeding). In theory, the condemnation proceeding might be abandoned, and in that event the owner has a legitimate interest in insuring the property. Yet if the insured recovers insurance proceeds and then demolishes the building, the insured obtains a windfall. This is a difficult problem to resolve. Most courts have opted for a rule that places the actual cash value of a building at zero if the insured has made an irrevocable commitment to have it demolished.[44]

[iv] Coinsurance Calculations

The choice of the measure for actual cash value can have important implications on the question of whether the insured is subject to a coinsurance penalty. This was the issue in *Jefferson Insurance Co. v. Superior Court*,[45] a 1970 California case. The insured owned a hotel building which, excluding the value of the land, had a fair market value of $65,000. Prior to the fire which damaged the hotel, the insured obtained insurance policies on the hotel in the total amount of $45,000; the policies contained 70 percent coinsurance clauses. The parties agreed that the amount of the loss was approximately $24,100, calculated as follows: $25,700, the cost of repairs, less $1,600 improvement in the property by virtue of the repairs. The insurers refused to pay that amount, however, claiming that the property was substantially underinsured. The insurers argued that the actual cash value was the replacement cost less depreciation, a figure that was in the vicinity of $170,000. The insured argued that fair market value constituted the property's actual cash value.

Appraisers were appointed upon the insurers' demand, according to the statutory appraisal clause in the policy, for the purpose of determining the building's actual cash value. The appraisers agreed with the insurers' view of both the meaning of actual cash value and the $170,000 assessment of the hotel's value. Based on this appraisal of the hotel's total value the insurer offered to pay approximately $10,000 of the insured's $24,100 loss. The insured rejected this offer and brought an action seeking to vacate the appraisal award.

The trial court rejected the appraisers' and the insurers' view of actual cash value, and the California Supreme Court affirmed the trial court. The Court referred to two prior cases in which actual cash value had been held synonymous with fair market value. It also discussed the provision of the California Insurance Code: the legislature's prescribed standard policy form insures "to the extent of the actual cash value of the property at the time of loss, but not exceeding the . . . cost to repair or replace the property." The court reasoned that because replacement cost less depreciation can never exceed the replacement cost, the court concluded that "actual cash value" as used in the policy must have meant something other than replacement cost less depreciation. Accordingly, fair market value was deemed the proper meaning of "actual cash value."

---

[44] See § 46[b], *supra*.
[45] 475 P.2d 880 (Cal. 1970).

This reasoning was very helpful to the insured in *Jefferson Insurance*. Concluding that actual cash value was equivalent to fair market value, the smaller figure, meant that the insured's coinsurance penalty was very small. By this analysis, the insured had insured the property for nearly seventy percent of its value. Had the facts been different, however, the insured might have been disadvantaged by this logic. If the insured's loss had been total, the most the insured could have recovered (absent a replacement cost endorsement) would be the fair market value of the building, the smaller figure. Similarly, if the issue in the case had been the amount of the loss instead of the value of the property in an undamaged condition, this approach could have worked a hardship on the insured. The parties stipulated in *Jefferson Insurance* that the amount of loss was a function of the cost to repair the building (less betterment). The cost of remedying the injury was not offset, apparently, by the depreciation of the damaged part of the structure.[46] If the parties had disputed the amount of the loss, the insurer might have prevailed on the argument that the loss equaled the fair market value of the unusable portion of the building, an amount presumably lower than the cost to repair the building.

However, in *Jefferson Insurance,* the insured received the best of both worlds: when determining the amount of loss, the largest measure available — repair or replacement cost — was used, but in determining the value of the building for purposes of the coinsurance penalty, the smallest measure available — fair market value — was used, so that the insured needed only a small amount of insurance in force to avoid incurring a coinsurance penalty. In a future case involving the same facts, one should expect the insurer to argue that if fair market value is used to value the property ($45,000 is about one-fourth the $170,000 replacement cost), fair market value should also be used to calculate the loss (the cost of repairs, $25,000, should be reduced by three-fourths to about $6,000) in determining the proceeds payable to the insured.[47]

[e] Interest

Interest is recoverable for the breach of a promise to pay money.[48] Thus, when the insurer promises to pay proceeds to the insured and the insurer fails to perform this promise, "prejudgment interest" is generally recoverable.[49] Also, consistently with the general rules applying to all judgments, "judgment interest" is recoverable; thus, if a judgment is recovered against the insurer, interest running from the date of the judgment until the judgment is paid is charged to the insurer.

---

[46] The court did not explain what the "betterment" offset from costs of repair constituted, but it probably referred to an absolute improvement in the premises in connection with the repair or replacement — such as would be the case if rewiring was not necessary to repair the premises to their prior state, but the insured decided to have this additional work done in connection with the repair work.

[47] See Schnitzer v. South Carolina Ins. Co., 661 P.2d 550 (Or. Ct. App. 1983) (buildings insured at replacement cost must be valued at replacement cost for purposes of the coinsurance calculation).

[48] See generally Dan D. Dobbs, 1 *Law of Remedies* § 3.6 (1993).

[49] See Annot., *Liability of Insurer for Prejudgment Interest in Excess of Policy Limits for Covered Loss,* 23 A.L.R.5th 75 (1994).

In the law of remedies, the most significant restriction on the recovery of prejudgment interest is the general rule that prejudgment interest may not be recovered on claims that are neither liquidated in a dollar amount or otherwise ascertainable according to some fixed standard.[50] Exactly what constitutes a liquidated claim is a subject of some disagreement. If neither the existence of a valid claim nor its amount is in dispute, the claim is fairly described as "liquidated." Sometimes the claim is deemed liquidated if the amount of loss can be definitively determined. In most cases, if the insurer refuses to pay a claim that is ascertainable, and if the insurer is subsequently determined to be in breach of contract, prejudgment interest will be awarded to the insured.[51] Under the converse of the foregoing rule, if the claim is "unliquidated," courts sometimes refuse to award prejudgment interest.[52] A growing number of courts, however, have awarded the insured prejudgment interest in cases where the debt is unliquidated for the avowed purpose of giving the insured full and fair compensation.[53] These rules can, of course, be regulated by statute, as is the situation in many states, and the statutory requirements are controlling.[54]

Considerable differences exist in the cases regarding the time from which prejudgment interest is calculated. As a general rule, interest on a debt is recoverable from the time when the debt becomes due. However, determining when an insurer's "debt" under an insurance policy becomes due is sometimes difficult. The time at which the insurer is obligated to pay proceeds is not necessarily the date of the loss.[55] If payment is due at the time of loss under the policy's terms, interest is usually calculated from that date.[56] There are cases where interest has been allowed from the date of the insurer's wrongful denial of coverage.[57] Still other courts have

---

[50] Dobbs, *supra* note 48, at 336. For decisional authority, see, e.g., Hansen v. Rothaus, 730 P.2d 662 (Wash. 1986); Outdoor Outfitters, Inc. v. Fireman's Fund Ins. Co., 649 N.E.2d 871 (Ohio Ct.App. 1994); Edens v. South Carolina Farm Bur. Mut. Ins. Co., 343 S.E.2d 49 (S.C. Ct. App. 1986). See generally Annot., *Insured's Right To Recover From Insurer Prejudgment Interest On Amount of Fire Loss,* 5 A.L.R.4th 126 (1981).

[51] See, e.g., St. Joseph Light & Power Co. v. Zurich Ins. Co., 698 F.2d 1351 (8th Cir. 1983); Polito v. Continental Cas. Co., 689 F.2d 457 (3d Cir. 1982); Otis v. Cambridge Mut. Fire Ins. Co., 850 S.W.2d 439 (Tenn. 1992); Huffstutter v. Michigan Mut. Ins. Co., 778 S.W.2d 391 (Mo. Ct. App. 1989).

[52] See, e.g., Thorp v. American Aviation & General Ins. Co., 212 F.2d 821 (3rd Cir. 1954); cases cited in note 50, *supra.*

[53] See, e.g, Casey Enterprises, Inc. v. American Hardware Mut. Ins. Co., 655 F.2d 598 (5th Cir. 1981); Braner v. Southern Trust Ins. Co., 335 S.E.2d 547 (Ga. 1985). State Farm Mut. Auto. Ins. Co. v. Bishop, 329 So. 2d 670 (Miss. 1976); Ellmex Constr. Co. v. Republic Ins. Co., 494 A.2d 339 (N.J. Super. Ct. App. Div. 1985).

[54] See, e.g., Outdoor Outfitters, Inc. v. Fireman's Fund Ins. Co., 649 N.E.2d 871 (Ohio Ct.App. 1994).

[55] See, e.g., St. Paul Fire & Mar. Ins. Co. v. Smith, 194 So. 2d 830 (Ala. 1967); Boston-Old Colony Ins. Co. v. Warr, 193 S.E.2d 624 (Ga. Ct. App. 1972).

[56] See, e.g., Rogers v. Aetna Cas. & Sur. Co., 601 F.2d 840 (5th Cir. 1979); Conestoga Chem. Corp. v. F.H. Simonton, Inc., 269 A.2d 237 (Del. 1970); Charles Dowd Box Co. v. Fireman's Fund Ins. Co., 218 N.E.2d 64 (Mass. 1966).

[57] See, e.g., Schulze & Burch Biscuit Co. v. American Protection Ins. Co., 421 N.E.2d 331 (Ill. App. Ct. 1981); Adams v. Northwest Farm Bur. Ins. Co., 594 P.2d 1256 (Or. Ct.

held that the time for computing interest runs from the date of the filing of the proof of loss, a certain number of days after the proof of loss is filed, the date the insured files suit against the insurer, or the date of the verdict in a third-party's suit against the insured. Sometimes, the different results can be explained by reference to the policy language at issue, but many decisions are impossible to reconcile.[58]

Because a recovery of interest by the insured is intended to compensate the insured for the loss of the use of his or her money, the insurer's tender of a sum of money to settle the insured's claim will suspend the accumulation of interest. The tender, however, must be made properly. If the tender is conditioned on the insured giving up some rights, the tender may not be sufficient to suspend the running of interest.[59]

§ 94   Measuring the Amount of Loss: Personal Insurance

[a]   Generally

Calculating the proceeds payable in personal insurance is usually far simpler than in property insurance; this is true whether one is speaking of life, health, disability, or some other form of personal insurance.

In life insurance, the proceeds payable at death are specified in the policy. Indeed, it is impossible to imagine life insurance be handled on any other basis. Placing a monetary value on human life is, obviously, quite difficult. Although this occurs in tort law when someone is held financially responsible for another's death, one cannot know with certainty what a person's future earning power would have been had that person lived, what inflation rates will exist in the future, or what will happen to interest rates (which affects the present value of money). Rather than attempt to make such judgments or impose limits on the amount of life insurance that a person might purchase, each person is allowed to purchase as much insurance on his or her own life as he or she desires (up to whatever limits the insurer is willing to provide). This concept is expressed in various ways: life insurance is not indemnity insurance; each individual has an unlimited insurable interest in his or her own life; life insurance policies are "valued policies" because the insurer pays whatever proceeds are stated on the face of the policy.

Although a substantial question of whether an insured is disabled may arise when coverage is sought under a disability policy,[1] once the finding of disability is made the calculation of benefits is relatively straightforward. The amount of the proceeds will ordinarily be determined by a formula that references a stated percentage of the person's income at the time of the disability or by resort to a schedule of benefits based on the nature of the disability.

App. 1979); I.H. Lawrence & Son v. Merchants' & Mechanics' Mut. Aid Soc'y, 277 S.W. 588 (Mo. Ct. App. 1925).

[58] See generally Annot., *Insured's Right To Recover From Insurer Prejudgment Interest On Amount of Fire Loss,* 5 A.L.R.4th 126 (1981).

[59] See *id.*

[1] See § 64[b], *supra.*

In health insurance and accident insurance, the proceeds payable are sometimes set by schedules that are a part of a policy or are incorporated into the policy. Whenever a described loss or a described kind of medical service is received, the policy pays a set sum to the insured or to the person or entity who provided the medical service. The proceeds may be subject to deductibles or coinsurance requirements, but these calculations present no special problems. The accidental death benefit often added to life insurance policies simply states that if the insured's death is accidental the insurer will pay total proceeds in an amount twice the policy's face value.

[b] Accelerated Benefits in Life Insurance

The AIDS epidemic[2] prompted an alternative approach to distributing life insurance proceeds in the late 1980s. Because terminally ill individuals had significantly higher expenses at the ends of their lives, the possibility of accessing life insurance benefits before death in order to pay these expenses and ease the financial burdens on family members and friends received serious attention. A number of insurance companies added a rider to their policies that allowed, under certain conditions, a terminally ill insured to receive a percentage of the policy's benefits earlier than his or her death. In 1990, the NAIC promulgated, first as a guideline, and then as a regulation in 1991, what is now the "Accelerated Benefits Model Regulation." The model regulation mandates certain disclosures to individuals obtain-ing accelerated benefits and imposes financial requirements on the provision of such benefits. As a general proposition, the life insurance benefit paid under such plans is discounted to present value, with appropriate deductions for certain expenses and an interest charge to account for the insurer's early payment of proceeds. Eligibility for accelerated benefits is typically triggered by a medical condition that limits the insured's expected life span to two more years or less, a condition requiring extraordinary medical intervention (e.g., through an organ transplant or continuous life support), a condition requiring the insured's residence in an institution for the rest of his or her life, and specified illnesses or conditions which have one or more of those characteristics (e.g., AIDS, end-stage renal failure, severe brain injury, etc.).

A more controversial practice of "viatical[3] settlement" arose during the same decade.[4] Recognizing that the owners of policies have the right to assign policies to third parties,[5] firms developed that offered to provide immediate cash payments

---

[2] See § 24[b], *supra.*

[3] The word "viatical" has its origin in the word "viaticum," which refers to traveling money, or a provision for a journey. The word also has an ecclesiastical meaning: the Eucharist administered to one who is dying, and thus about to set forth on a final voyage. See XIX *Oxford English Dictionary* 589 (2d ed. 1989).

[4] The creation of the option to receive death benefits during one's life has been attributed to a California insurer, Farmers New World Life Insurance Company, which is reported to have offered such an option in 1965. See Howard J. Saks, *Are Living Benefits an Emerging Trend?*, 16 Est. Plan. 58, 58 (1989). Whenever this option was first developed, it did not receive widespread attention until the 1980s.

[5] The viatical firm will lack an insurable interest in the life of the insured. Thus, the viatical arrangement is permissible only if the insured is permitted by law to assign a policy on his

to insureds with terminal conditions in an amount less than the expected death benefit in exchange for an assignment of the right to the policy's proceeds.[6] Depending on the insured's life expectancy, the cash payment might range anywhere from fifty to eighty percent of the expected death benefit.

On the plus side, viatical settlement arrangements, like accelerated benefits, provide insureds with terminal conditions a means to acquire assets that are needed immediately. The interests of designated beneficiaries are eliminated, which in many situations could be a burden for the dependents of insureds. But beneficiaries have no right to proceeds until the insured's death in any event, and until that time are vulnerable to being replaced by the insured with some other beneficiary. Moreover, the person who owns the policy should be the one to decide how his or her assets can best be deployed for the benefit of those who depend on the insured. In effect, from the beneficiary's perspective, a viatical settlement is little different in form than what would occur if the insured opted to change the beneficiary to his or her own estate. In addition, the existence of the viatical settlement option gives insureds additional options; if a viatical settlement firm will provide a more generous benefit than the insurer would provide through accelerated benefits, the insured is better off by having the viatical settlement option.

On the negative side, many have expressed concern that viatical settlement firms might exploit the terminally ill by paying low benefits at a time the insureds are in great need. For this reason, some have wanted to ban the viatical settlement industry altogether. Under administrative regulations applicable in most states, an insured can cancel a life insurance or annuity policy, without any detriment, within ten days of its issuance.[7] The right to cancel the transaction within ten days is normally not offered by viatical settlement firms, and is not a part of the standards of good practice that has been written by an association of viatical companies.[8]

In 1993, the NAIC proposed the "Viatical Settlements Model Act," which calls for the licensing of viatical settlement providers, approval by the insurance commissioner of viatical settlement contracts to be used within the commissioner's state, examination of the financial resources of the provider, disclosure to the insured by the provider of alternatives to viatical settlement and other information, and other

---

or her own life to someone lacking an insurable interest in his or her life. The rule allowing such assignments is widely followed, despite some old authority in a few jurisdictions to the contrary. See section 52B[b], *supra*.

[6] Some firms purchase the policies for their own account, while other firms function as brokers that, for a commission, match the insured with one or more persons willing to purchase the policy. Normally, the acquiring purchaser is designated as beneficiary and assignee, and the viatical company may obtain releases from previously named beneficiaries. See Thomas Hammack, *Regulating Viatical Transactions,* 45 Fed. of Ins. & Corp. Couns. Quar. 85, 90-91 (1994).

[7] See, e.g., 10 Cal. Admin. Code § 2522.8 (individual investment annuity policies); Conn. Agencies Regs. § 38a-433-4 (variable life insurance policies); *Id.,* § 38a-433-26 (modified guaranteed life insurance).

[8] See Hammack, *supra* note 6, at 110.

regulation.[9] It would seem that appropriate regulation of viatical settlement arrangements is preferable to prohibiting the option altogether.

One might, however, question whether viatical settlements should be regulated under the auspices of insurance at all. The sale of a pre-existing policy is not the "business of insurance" as that term is normally understood; there is no risk-spreading, and there need be no involvement whatever of an insurer in the transaction.[10] In a 1995 decision, a federal district judge in the District of Columbia granted a request by the Securities and Exchange Commission to preliminarily enjoin a viatical settlement firm's facilitation of the sale of life insurance policies from AIDS victims to investors at a discount on the ground that the firm's program constituted a sale of unregistered securities by an unregistered broker or dealer.[11] The court reasoned that viatical settlements "do not transfer or distribute risk," but that the purchaser of the policy "does undertake an investment risk that the seller will live longer than expected, thereby reducing the buyer's return on investment," and that "this does not serve the central purpose of insurance."[12]

Nevertheless, virtually all regulation that has occurred through the early 1990s has been under the rubric of insurance regulation.[13] This is presumably because assignment of insurance policies is something with which insurance law is interested, and the lack of regulation of the activities of viatical firms would create a situation where insurers offering accelerated benefits are regulated by insurance departments, but third-parties offering the same benefit, albeit through a different kind of transaction, are not.[14]

If one concludes that viatical settlements should be an option available to insureds, one of the next questions is whether the insurance industry's viatical settlement programs should be favored over the programs of viatical settlement firms. Life insurers should be able to provide accelerated benefits to their own insureds at lower costs than viatical settlement firms can arrange assignments in exchange for cash payments, which means that the presence of the viatical settlement industry should encourage more life insurers to offer the accelerated benefit option. Viatical settlement firms seek to maximize their own profits; with a lower-cost advantage,

---

[9] NAIC, "Viatical Settlements Model Act," *NAIC Model Laws, Regulations & Guidelines* 697-1 (1994).

[10] See Hammack, *supra* note 6, at 95.

[11] See Securities and Exchange Comm'n v. Life Partners, Inc., 1995 U.S. Dist. LEXIS 12657 (D.D.C. Aug. 30, 1995). The court's memorandum opinion described Life Partners as "the largest viatical settlement organizer in the country, accounting for approximately one half of the total settlement volume in 1994." Mem. Op. at 2.

[12] Mem. Op. at 8-9.

[13] As of 1995, approximately twenty states, either by statute or administrative regulation, had taken some steps to regulate accelerated benefit options.

[14] About half of the country's viatical firms have formed the "National Viatical Association," which has as one of its purposes the promulgation of standards of conduct and the promotion of self-regulation of the industry. The NVA opposes state regulation of the activities of association members, and argues that the NAIC's regulatory proposals are sponsored and promoted by insurance industry representatives that do not support the viatical settlement industry. Hammack, *supra* note 6, at 108.

life insurers should be able to market a more generous accelerated benefit directly, while at the same time increasing profits.[15] Whether life insurer's viatical settlement programs should be encouraged to the detriment of the programs of viatical settlement firms, or whether this issue should be left for a decision in the marketplace is an issue of considerable controversy.

§ 95   Measuring the Amount of Loss: Liability Insurance

[a]   Generally

The insurer's promise in liability insurance is to pay proceeds on behalf of the insured to the party to whom the insured is liable. Liability is generally measured by the judgment entered against the insured. The insurer typically limits its liability to a given amount, so that the insurer's liability eventually terminates if multiple judgments are entered against the insured.[1]

[b]   Interest, Expenses, and Costs

In addition to obligating the insurer to pay the insured's financial obligations to third parties arising out of covered occurrences, liability insurance policies typically obligate insurers to pay those expenses incurred and costs taxed against the insured in any suit the insurer defends, premiums on bonds required in a suit it defends, and reasonable expenses incurred by an insured on the insurer's behalf (such as loss of earnings for assisting in the investigation or defense of a claim). Both interest on the judgment which accrues after a judgment is entered against the insured and prejudgment interest awarded against the insured on that portion of the judgment which the insurer pays is ordinarily recoverable.[2] It is well settled that the insurer is obligated to pay costs relating to, and interest on, a judgment recovered against the insured, even though these sums, when added to the judgment recovered, bring the total amount beyond the limits set in the policy.[3]

Whether the insurer is obligated for interest and costs on that portion of a judgment recovered by a third party exceeding the policy limits is more problematical. The language of the insurance policy usually determines the scope of the insurer's obligation, but identical phrases have been interpreted differently by various

---

[15] For a comment supporting viatical settlement, see Lee Ann Dean, Note, *Acquired Immune Deficiency Syndrome, Viatical Settlement, and the Health Care Crisis: AIDS Patients Reach into the Future to Make Ends Meet,* 25 Rutgers L.J. 117 (1993).

[1] For further discussion, see § 111[e][2], *infra.*

[2] See State Farm Mut. Auto. Ins. Co. v. Agrippe, 445 S.E.2d 171 (W.Va. 1994)(absent bad faith claim against insurer, prejudgment interest exceeding policy limits cannot be assessed against insurer absent policy provision allowing such assessment); Metropolitan Prop. &Liab. Ins. Co. v. Ralph, 640 A.2d 763 (N.H. 1994); Wittmer v. Jones, 864 S.W.2d 885 (Ky. 1993); but see Monarch Cortland, Inc., v. Columbia Cas. Co., 626 N.Y.S.2d 426 (N.Y. Sup. Ct. 1995) (CGL insurer held not liable for prejudgment interest).

[3] See e.g., Hellmers v. Department of Transp. and Dev., 503 So. 2d 174 (La. Ct. App. 1987); Germer v. Public Serv. Mut. Ins. Co., 238 A.2d 713 (N.J.Super.Ct.Law Div. 1967); Annot., *Liability Insurer's Liability For Interest And Costs On Excess of Judgment Over Policy Limit,* 76 A.L.R.2d 983 (1961).

courts. One point of view emphasizes the insurer's ability to stop the running of interest and the accumulation of costs by tendering the amount for which it is liable. Because the insured has surrendered the right to control these expenses, the insurer must have impliedly agreed to pay all interest on and costs relating to the entire judgment. The alternative view emphasizes that interest is simply compensation for the use of money. Thus, the insurer is only liable to pay interest on the money due on that part of the judgment for which the insurer is liable; the insured has the use of the insured's own money which he or she will use for paying the remaining portion of the judgment.[4]

[c]   Insolvency Clauses and Statutes

The first liability insurance policies were designed, not to pay proceeds for the insured's liability to a third person, but to pay for the insured's *loss* arising out of its liability to a third person. Thus, if the insured suffered no loss because the judgment against the insured was uncollectible, the insurer had no obligation to pay proceeds. Under this logic, the insured's insolvency prevented the victim of the insured's tort from recovering anything from the insurer.

This unfairness caused legislatures in many states to enact statutes requiring liability policies to contain a provision that insolvency or bankruptcy of the insured shall not release the insurer from any of its obligations.[5] Now, all liability insurance policies contain a "bankruptcy provision," which provides that the insured's insolvency or bankruptcy does not relieve the insurer of its obligations.

More recent legislation in some states deprives the insurer from asserting other defenses against a claim by a third-party victim for proceeds. For example, if the insured gave the insurer late notice of the claim or failed to cooperate with the insurer, the insurer might assert a defense to coverage, thereby depriving the person injured by the insured's tortious conduct from recovering proceeds if the insured lacked enough assets to pay for the victim's judgment. Statutes in some states prevent liability insurers from asserting defenses good against insureds against third parties, but these statutes are often very limited in scope.[6]

[d]   Immunity of Insureds

Generally speaking, the recent history of immunities is one of abandonment. Almost all the states by statute have abrogated the doctrine of sovereign immunity to some extent. The Federal Tort Claims Act[7] allows the federal government to be sued in tort, although this right is subject to several restrictions. The judicially created charitable immunity doctrine has been repudiated either totally or partially

---

[4] See United States Fid. & Guar. Co. v. Safeco Ins. Co. of Am., 555 S.W.2d 848 (Mo. Ct. App. 1977); Marvin E. Verbeck, *A Reexamination of an Insurer's Obligation to Pay Interest on a Judgment,* 46 Ins. Counsel J. 93 (1979); Annot., 76 A.L.R.2d 983 (1961).

[5] See, e.g., Neb. Rev. Stat. 44-508; Ark. Code Ann. § 23-96-112.

[6] See, e.g., R.I. Gen. Laws 27-7-2.1; La. Rev. Stat. Ann. 22:655; Wis. Stat. Ann. 632.24.

[7] 60 Stat. 843, 28 U.S.C.A. §§ 1346, 1402, 1504, 2401, 2402, 2411, 2412, 2671, 2672, 2674-80.

by statute or court decision in most states.[8] However, where an organization or governmental body with some measure of immunity from tort liability obtains a liability insurance policy, the question sometimes arises as to whether the insurer is obligated to make payments to the victim injured by the insured's tort equal in amount to those that would have been made in the absence of the immunity. There are two lines of authority on this question. One answer is that the procuring of insurance by an organization or entity has no effect on the entity's immunity from tort liability.[9] The other answer, given by a roughly equal number of courts,[10] is that the purchase of liability insurance removes the immunity to the extent of the insurance policy's coverage.[11]

As a matter of public policy, nothing should prohibit an immune entity or organization from voluntarily compensating those who are injured by the organization's torts. If charitable organizations, for example, are willing to incur these expenses despite their immunities, the public interest is benefited because injured persons will not be left uncompensated. By the same analysis, public policy should not prohibit insurers from agreeing with immune insureds to pay proceeds to the victims of the insureds' torts. In other words, if an organization chooses to renounce its immunity, and if the organization enters into an agreement with an insurer that the insurer will pay the losses of third parties at the hands of the insured as if no immunity existed, the agreement between the insurer and the insured organization should be enforced. Also, if the insurer, through an endorsement on the insured's policy, agrees not to assert the insured's immunity in defending a claim by a third-party victim without the insured's written consent, this agreement — which is for the benefit of injured third parties — should be enforced.

In the absence of a knowing relinquishment of immunity, the argument that the mere purchase of liability insurance abrogates an immunity is less persuasive. Liability insurance is designed to pay for liability imposed by law. When the law declares a certain institution or entity immune from liability, the law imposes no liability. It may be good public policy to encourage further abrogation of immunities, but this choice, it can be argued, should be made explicitly by either courts or

---

[8] For more information on immunities generally, see W. Page Keeton, et al., *Prosser and Keeton on the Law of Torts* 1032–75 (5th ed. 1984); Annot., *Tort Immunity of Nongovernmental Charities — Modern Status,* 25 A.L.R.4th 517 (1983).

[9] See, e.g., Johnson v. Wesson Women's Hosp., 328 N.E.2d 490 (Mass. 1975); McGrath Bldg. Co. v. City of Bettendorf, 85 N.W.2d 616 (Iowa 1957); Mann v. County Bd., 98 S.E.2d 515 (Va. 1957); see also Snowten v. United States Fid. & Guar. Co., 475 So. 2d 1211 (Fla. 1985) (doctrine of interspousal immunity is not waived to extent of insurance coverage).

[10] According to one judge who counted the cases, as of 1991 the states were fairly evenly divided on the question of whether the purchase of liability insurance by an immune organization constituted a waiver of the immunity. See Alabama State Docks v. Saxon, 631 So. 2d 943, 949 (Ala. 1994) (Shores, J., dissenting).

[11] See, e.g., Morehouse College v. Russell, 135 S.E.2d 432 (Ga. 1964); Vendrell v. School Dist. No. 26C Malheur Cty., 360 P.2d 282 (Or. 1961), *modified in part by statute, as discussed in* Espinosa v. Southern Pac. Transp. Co., 635 P.2d 638 (Or. 1981). For additional discussion, see generally Annot., *Liability Or Indemnity Insurance Carried By Governmental Unit As Affecting Immunity From Tort Liability,* 68 A.L.R.2d 1437 (1959).

legislatures through modification of the immunity rules themselves, instead of by manipulating the rules of insurance law.

Even if one agrees that an organization can be immune from tort while simultaneously owning a policy of liability insurance, the more difficult question is whether the purchase of liability insurance means the organization has made a voluntary, willing choice to waive its immunity. This question may be answered conclusively by a state statute providing that the purchase of liability insurance constitutes a waiver of the immunity.[12] In the absence of a dispositive statute or a state constitutional provision constraining relinquishment of immunities,[13] it is possible to argue that the purchase of insurance itself constitutes the knowing relinquishment of immunity: if an insured organization is immune, it does not need liability insurance; therefore, the purchase of insurance itself must constitute an expression of an intent to waive immunity. If, however, a government agency obtains liability insurance for the organization and its employees in circumstances where the employees only enjoy a very limited form of immunity, it is arguable that the purchase of insurance is designed to fill in gaps where state law has not created broad immunities.[14] If a legislature authorizes a public entity to purchase insurance, it might be inferred that the legislature authorized that entity not only to purchase liability insurance but also to waive its immunity.[15] Indeed, given the many instances of legislative abolition of tort immunities and the underlying public policies furthered by such abrogations, the argument that an otherwise immune organization renounces its immunity by purchasing liability insurance has considerable appeal.

It is interesting nevertheless to speculate whether the trend favoring the abolition of immunities might one day reverse itself, at least with respect to governmental, public, and quasi-public organizations. In the mid-1980s when liability insurance was less available and many municipalities and charitable organizations encountered difficulties in obtaining coverage, there were calls in some quarters for the expansion of tort immunities for some organizations.[16] To the extent most current political

---

[12] See, e.g., N.C. Gen. Stat. § 115C-42 (board of education waives governmental immunity by purchasing liability insurance); Ga. Code Ann. § 33-24-51 (municipal corporations, counties, and political subdivisions); Ill. Ann. Stat. ch. 745 ¶ 10/9-103 (local public entities); Minn. Stat. Ann. § 466.06 (governing body of municipality); Miss. Code Ann. § 41-61-63(4) (state medical examiner).

[13] If an immunity is created by a state constitution, it may be that neither the legislature nor a state official has the legal authority to waive the immunity, which means that the purchase of insurance does not affect the immunity. See Alabama State Docks v. Saxon, 631 So. 2d 943 (Ala. 1994). See also Holland v. Western Airlines, Inc., 154 F. Supp. 457 (D.Mont. 1957) (it is beyond power of court to abrogate governmental immunity on ground that municipality purchased insurance; issue can be decided only by legislature).

[14] See Alabama State Docks v. Saxon, 631 So. 2d 943, 947 (Ala. 1994); see also Descant v. Administrators of Tulane Educ. Fund, 627 So. 2d 214 (La. Ct. App. 1993), aff'd, 639 So. 2d 246 (La. 1994) (liability insurance fills in gaps where immunity from liability does not exist).

[15] See Vendrell v. School Dist. No. 26C Malheur Cty., 360 P.2d 282 (Or. 1961).

[16] See generally National Conference of State Legislatures, *Resolving the Liability Insurance Crisis: State Legislative Activities in 1986* (1986).

opinion seems to be concerned about the frequency and cost of litigation generally, it seems likely that expansion, rather than contraction, of immunities may eventually be viewed more favorably. Thus, if the pendulum should swing the other direction and we find ourselves in an era where immunities expand, it seems inevitable that the related insurance law rules would be affected. The weight of authority would probably gravitate in favor of those decisions holding that the purchase of liability insurance does not affect the scope of immunities.

§ 96 The Insurer's Right of Subrogation

[a] Overview

Subrogation is an equitable right that enables one who is secondarily liable for a debt and who pays it to succeed to the rights, if any, that the creditors hold against the debtor. By asserting these rights, the party that pays the debt is made whole. At the same time, the loss is placed on the person who ultimately has the primary legal responsibility for the loss. Consider the following situation:

$$D1 \text{ (debtor)} \text{——————} C \text{ (creditor)}$$

$$D2 \text{ (surety)}$$

If *D2* pays *D1*'s debt to *C, D2* is subrogated to any rights *C* has against *D1*. In other words, *D2* is a surety for *D1;* if *D2* pays the debt, *D2* is placed in *C*'s shoes for the purpose of enforcing *D1*'s obligation. Since subrogation is an equitable right, it does not exist automatically in every case; rather, the particular facts and circumstances will determine whether *D2* is entitled to assert subrogation rights.

Insurance is, in a sense, merely an expansion of general principles of suretyship. As a consequence, subrogation plays an important role in insurance law. Subrogation enables the insurer to "stand in the shoes" of the insured and assert the insured's rights against a legally responsible third party. When subrogation runs its course, the legally responsible third party reimburses the insurer for having paid the debt which that party owed the insured. To take an easy case, consider the situation where the insured's house is destroyed by a fire negligently set by a tortfeasor:

$$ID \text{——————} TF$$

$$IR$$

The insurer, pursuant to the contract obligation it owes the insured, indemnifies the insured for the loss. The insurer, having paid the tortfeasor's "debt" to the insured, is now entitled to assert the insured's rights against the tortfeasor. In other words, the insurer (subrogee) is subrogated to the rights of the insured (subrogor) against the tortfeasor. If the insurer successfully asserts these rights, the insurer will be made whole, and the loss will ultimately rest on the person whose negligent actions caused the destruction of the property.

The operation of subrogation where the third party's debt arises out of a tort is perhaps the easiest to understand. However, subrogation is not limited to such situations. Another common situation where subrogation figures importantly is the mortgagor-mortgagee situation, where the debt is created by contract. Consider the situation where the mortgagee ("MEE") secures insurance to protect the mortgagee's security interest:

MEE (e.g., bank) ——————— MOR (owner)

IR

The mortgage secures a loan made by the mortgagee to the mortgagor ("MOR.") Thus, the mortgagor is required to make periodic payments to the mortgagee until the loan is paid in full. The insurer ("IR") assumes the mortgagee's risk that the property securing the loan might be destroyed; yet the mortgagee, in effect, has already transferred this risk to the mortgagor through loan documents that require the mortgagor to make periodic payments to the mortgagee whether or not the property continues to exist. Should the property be destroyed, the payments received by the mortgagee from the mortgagor would offset any loss suffered by the mortgagee due to the destruction of the property which secures the loan. Thus, if the property is destroyed and the insurer (under a policy of mortgagee-only insurance[1] reimburses the mortgagee for the loss of the property securing the loan, the insurer is subrogated to the mortgagee's rights to receive payments from the mortgagor.[2] This is true whether or not the mortgagor caused the loss. If some third party negligently destroyed the property, the mortgagor would have a claim against that third party (as would the mortgagee — to whose right the insurer would be subrogated as well). After all rights have been asserted, the loss will ultimately fall upon the legally responsible third party; both the insured and the insurer will be made whole.[3]

Because subrogation exists in equity, the right of subrogation for the insurer is not automatic. Moreover, the equitable nature of the doctrine means that its precise limits are not clear. As stated by one court, "[i]t is the universal rule that an insurer who has indemnified his assured for a property loss is subrogated to the assured's rights against any person wrongfully causing the loss. . . . But, there is no such general agreement in decisional law as to the right of the insurer to be subrogated to collateral rights which the assured may have against persons who did not cause the loss."[4] For example, if an insurer pays for the insured's fire loss caused by

---

[1] See § 53A[b], *supra* .

[2] See Garrison v. Great Southwest Ins. Co., 809 F.2d 500 (8th Cir. 1987); Pantano v. Maryland Plaza Partnership, 507 N.W.2d 484 (Neb. 1993).

[3] The effect of subrogation, at least in this respect, might be likened to that of "other insurance" clauses. See § 97, *infra*. When one party injures another and both are insured, the victim's insurer's subrogation action "coordinates" the coverage, in that responsibility is shifted to the "primary" policy, meaning the tortfeasor's policy. See Kenneth S. Abraham, *Distributing Risk: Insurance, Legal Theory, and Public Policy* 153–55 (1986).

[4] In re Future Mfg. Coop., Inc., 165 F. Supp. 111, 113 (N.D. Cal. 1958).

neighbor *X*, one would not assume that the insurer is therefore subrogated to the insured's right to collect proceeds for laundry services rendered by neighbor *Y* eighteen months earlier. In other words, the insurer does not succeed to *all* of the insured's rights against *all* third parties. If neighbor *X* and neighbor *Y* were the same person, the case would arguably be closer, but it still would not seem that equity or fairness requires the insured to turn over monies earned under a separate contract to the insurer. With a superficial glance, it may appear that the mortgagee's right to mortgage payments from the mortgagor is no less separate from the insurance contract between mortgagee and insurer. However, the mortgagee's insurance protects the mortgagee's interest in property, and here that interest constitutes security for a debt; if the mortgagee is reimbursed by the insurer for loss to the security, the mortgagee's right to payment on the debt should belong to the insurer. In one sense, this is no different from the insurer paying the insured for the total loss of the insured's vehicle under a property insurance policy; after payment is made, the vehicle then belongs to the insurer.[5] At the bottom line, what equity accomplishes by recognizing subrogation in appropriate cases is securing fairness.

The notion of "securing fairness" itself has two elements in this context, and these constitute the twin purposes of subrogation. As is evident from the foregoing discussion, one reason for recognizing the right of subrogation is to enable the loss to fall on the person who is legally responsible for causing it, instead of the party who pays the debt (such as the insurer). Subrogation is intended to work justice, and a just result is having the loss fall ultimately on the party legally responsible for it.

A second purpose of subrogation is to prevent the party to whom the debt is owed (such as the insured) from receiving a windfall. In either of the examples set forth above, if the insured were allowed to recover from the tortfeasor or mortgagor *and* the insurer, the insured would receive a double recovery. By allowing the insurer after paying the insured for a loss to assert the insured's rights against a third party, the insured only recovers once, which furthers the principle of indemnity.

Whatever the scope of the equitable right of subrogation, most policies of property and liability insurance, and some other policies as well, expressly create a *contractual* right of subrogation, which allows the insurer who pays proceeds to assert the insured's rights against third parties.[6] This is discussed more fully in the next subsection.

[b] Equitable versus Conventional Subrogation

As the foregoing overview indicates, two different kinds of subrogation exist. "Equitable subrogation" (sometimes called, curiously enough, "legal subrogation") is a principle of equity; it is effected by operation of law and arises out of a relationship that need not be contractually based. "Conventional subrogation" arises out of the contractual relationship of the parties. The distinction can be important.

---

[5] See § 93[a], *supra*.

[6] For an early but still useful discussion of subrogation, including the differences between equitable and conventional subrogation, see Spencer L. Kimball & Don A. Davis, *The Extension of Insurance Subrogation*, 60 Mich. L. Rev. 841 (1962).

If the requirements for equitable subrogation are not met in the facts of a particular case, subrogation can still occur if the right is given by contract. For example, equitable subrogation may be unavailable in a given case because of laches, unclean hands, or some other principle that bars equitable relief. These doctrines, however, have no necessary connection to conventional subrogation.[7] Although the two different kinds of subrogation are well recognized, some courts have ignored the distinction for the purpose of determining whether subrogation is available.[8] Moreover, whether the parties can by contract create conventional subrogation rights for an insurer that are greater than what equitable subrogation would allow is controversial.[9]

An appropriate starting point for acquiring an understanding of subrogation is to identify the elements of equitable subrogation. There are basically four: (1) the party claiming subrogation must have first paid the debt; (2) the party claiming subrogation must not have voluntarily paid the debt, but must have done so under some kind of legal compulsion; (3) the party claiming subrogation must be secondarily liable for the debt; (4) no injustice will be done by allowing subrogation.[10] These elements yield the following definition: subrogation is an equitable right whereby a nonvolunteer who has made a payment to another of a debt for which he or she is only secondarily liable succeeds to that party's rights against the third party who is primarily responsible for the debt.

---

[7] See J & B Schoenfeld, Fur Merchants, Inc. v. Albany Ins. Co., 492 N.Y.S.2d 38 (N.Y. App. Div. 1985) ("where the right of an insurer to subrogation is expressly provided for in the policy, its rights must be governed by the terms of the policy.")

Subrogation can also be created by statute. Workers' compensation insurers in most jurisdictions are entitled to subrogation as a result of explicit statutory provisions in the workers' compensation acts. In the absence of statutory authorization, courts are split on whether equitable subrogation is available. Some courts reason (incorrectly) that workers' compensation is analogous to personal, non-indemnity insurance; other courts reach the opposite conclusion. See Ronald C. Horn, *Subrogation In Insurance Theory and Practice* 248–52 (1964).

[8] See, e.g., American Ins. Co. v. City of Milwaukee, 187 N.W.2d 142 (Wis. 1971); Lyon v. Hartford Accident and Indem. Co., 480 P.2d 739 (Utah 1971); Maryland Cas. v. Cincinnati C. C. & St. L. Ry. Co., 124 N.E. 774 (Ind. Ct. App. 1919). Because, as discussed below, the insured must ordinarily be reimbursed in full for the loss before the insurer has an equitable right to subrogation, recognizing the distinction between equitable and conventional subrogation has been the basis for finding that the insurer has priority in the recovery from the responsible third party when the right to subrogation is created by contract. See, e.g., Peterson v. Ohio Farmers Ins. Co., 191 N.E.2d 157 (Ohio 1963); Shifrin v. McGuire and Hester Constr. Co., 48 Cal. Rptr. 799 (Cal. Ct. App. 1966). This result is controversial, as demonstrated by the cases in the next footnote.

[9] See Powell v. Blue Cross & Blue Shield of Ala., 581 So. 2d 772 (Ala. 1990); Culver v. Ins. Co., 535 A.2d 15 (N.J. Super. Ct. App. Div. 1987) (holding that an agreement giving the insurer a right of subrogation before the insured was made whole violated public policy), *rev'd*, 559 A.2d 400 (N.J. 1989) (approving general principle that parties may vary the rule that the insured is made whole first); Allum v. MedCenter Health Care, Inc., 371 N.W.2d 557 (Minn. Ct. App. 1985).

[10] See Hampton Loan and Exch. Bank v. Lightsey, 152 S.E. 425 (S.C. 1930).

Conventional subrogation is virtually identical to equitable subrogation, except that the conventional subrogation right is given by contract, the "volunteer" requirement is irrelevant, and equitable considerations are not necessarily pertinent to the determination of whether subrogation should be granted.

[c] Existence or Nonexistence of Subrogation by Line of Insurance

Historically, courts have decided whether subrogation is available in a particular setting according to the kind of insurance contract involved. Courts have tended to inquire into whether the insurance contract is one of "indemnity"; only if it is a contract of indemnity have many courts allowed subrogation.[11] In property insurance, for example, the principle of indemnity is strong. Thus, courts rarely disallow subrogation in property insurance. Liability insurance is usually treated as indemnity insurance because the insurer indemnifies the insured's liability for a judgment. Thus, subrogation is usually allowed in liability insurance. In contrast to property and liability insurance, the principle of indemnity is weak in life insurance, and subrogation is rarely, if ever, allowed in life insurance.

Between these extremes, courts reach different results on whether subrogation is available, and this often depends on whether or not the court identifies the insurance policy as one of indemnity. For example, accident insurance which fixes the recovery according to the kind of injury suffered without making any effort to assess the economic value of the loss is "weak indemnity." This kind of accident insurance resembles life insurance more than property insurance, and courts typically do not recognize subrogation rights.

The logic of the distinction between indemnity and non- indemnity contracts for purposes of the subrogation rule is not self-evident. After all, why not allow a life insurer to recoup the benefits it paid the deceased insured's beneficiary from the person who caused the insured's death? Note that allowing the life insurer subrogation in this setting would mean that the wrongful death action owned by the heirs of the insured would belong to the insurer, not the heirs.[12] This observation underlies each of the several answers to the question posed. Several explanations

---

[11] See, e.g., Cunningham v. Metropolitan Life Ins. Co., 360 N.W.2d 33 (Wis. 1985) (medical expense portion of health policy is indemnity and therefore subrogation is allowed; hospitalization and physicians' services portion is investment and therefore subrogation not allowed).

[12] At common law, the decedent has no cause of action for wrongful death. Thus, unless given by statute to the representatives of the deceased, no claim exists for wrongful death; any personal cause of action expires with the deceased. When a statute creates such a right, the right is created in the deceased's representative, not in the deceased. As a result, no right ever vests in the deceased to which the insurer of the decedent's life can succeed. In property insurance, by contrast, the right to which the insurer succeeds is owned by the insured. This technical explanation helps highlight the ramifications of giving a life insurer subrogation: it is tantamount to taking the deceased's representative's wrongful death action, created by statute and given explicitly to them — when legislatures must have understood that many decedents would have life insurance, and turning that cause of action over to the insurer. For a contrary point of view, see George S. Swan, *Subrogation in Life Insurance: Now is the Time*, 48 Ins. Counsel J. 634 (1981).

are possible. First, the beneficiary of the deceased — most often a widow, according to actuarial tables — should be allowed to collect from both the insurer and the party causing the death. Because insurance is not a dollar-for-dollar substitute for the decedent's continued life, it cannot be said that the insurance makes the survivor whole. As such, the beneficiary should have "first rights" to any damages recovery from a third party. Indeed, since no sum of money can make the beneficiary whole, the beneficiary is entitled to all of any supplemental damages recovery; this means that subrogation has no role to play in life insurance.[13] Second, whole life insurance has many of the incidents of an investment device, as opposed to a device for the transfer of risk, which is the essence of indemnity. The purposes for allowing subrogation seem to carry less force when the insurer's obligation is in the nature of a promise to pay back money with interest. Third, a life is more difficult to value than property, and thus the principle of indemnity, which subrogation seeks to further, carries less force in life insurance.

A troublesome situation between the extremes of indemnity and non-indemnity insurance is presented by health insurance. On the one hand, health insurance resembles indemnity insurance: the insured has out-of-pocket costs that the insurer indemnifies. Yet the personal nature of health insurance gives it a close nexus to life insurance. Regardless, insurers now routinely include subrogation clauses in health insurance contracts.[14] When these clauses first appeared, some courts enforced them, but other courts invalidated them on the ground that one cannot assign a cause of action for personal injury to someone else. Today, however, conventional subrogation is usually allowed in health insurance.[15]

[d]   The Requirement that the Insurer Must Have Paid the Debt

Insurance proceeds are sometimes inadequate to provide an insured with full reimbursement for his or her loss. In circumstances where the insured has not been fully compensated, the insured remains entitled to seek full compensation for his or her loss at the same time an insurer has a subrogation right. This raises a question about how a recovery from the responsible third party (e.g., the tortfeasor) should be allocated between the insured and insurer. Policy language rarely speaks to the issue. It is common, and usually helpful, for an insurer and insured to agree upon

---

[13] See, e.g., In re Estate of Schmidt, 398 N.E.2d 589 (Ill. App. Ct. 1989).

[14] But see Schultz v. Gotlund, 561 N.E.2d 652 (Ill. 1990) (group health insurer had no common-law or equitable right to subrogation in personal injury settlement between insured and tort-feasor because of absence of express subrogation clause in policy).

[15] See, e.g., Blue Cross & Blue Shield Mut. of Ohio v. Hrenko, 647 N.E.2d 1358 (Ohio 1995); Roy v. Ducnuigeen, 532 A.2d 1388 (N.H. 1987); International Underwriters, Inc. v. Blue Cross and Blue Shield, Inc., 449 A.2d 197 (Del. 1982); Palmer v. Blue Cross/Blue Shield, 460 So. 2d 199 (ALa. Ct. App. 1984); Associated Hosp. Serv. v. Pustilnik, 396 A.2d 1332 (Pa. Super. Ct. 1979), *vacated and remanded on other grounds,* 439 A.2d 1149 (Pa. 1981). See generally Capwell & Greenwald, *Legal and Practical Problems Arising from Subrogation Clauses in Health and Accident Policies,* 54 Marq. L. Rev. 255 (1971).

how a recovery should be apportioned.[16] If, for whatever reason, such an advance agreement is not formed, courts must decide how the apportionment is to be made.

Most courts try to effect two goals simultaneously. One of the purposes of subrogation is to prevent the insured from receiving a windfall at the expense of the insurer, but the insured is entitled nonetheless to a *full* recovery. This means that the insurer, as a general rule, must have reimbursed the insured's loss in full before the insurer is entitled to pursue subrogation.[17]

Referring to the law of suretyship helps explain the full reimbursement requirement. In an ordinary suretyship relationship, if the debt is only paid in part, the surety remains liable for the remainder of the debt. To give the surety (the counterpart of the insurer) a subrogation right before the creditor (the counterpart of the insured) receives full payment would make the surety a competitor with the creditor for the remainder of the debtor's payment. Since the surety is still liable for the remainder of the debt, the surety lacks the equitable standing to assert the equitable right to subrogation. This argument carries less weight in the insurance setting where the insurer has performed in full (that is, where the insurer has paid out the policy limits) even though the insured has not been reimbursed in full; because the insurer cannot be liable for the remainder of the debt, the incentive to compete for reimbursement from the debtor would seem to be reduced. Nevertheless, some potential for competition exists. As a result, most courts insist that the insured be reimbursed in full before the insurer can assert a right to subrogation. The rationale for this rule must be that until the insured is paid in full the insurer is competing with the insured for the recovery, which is an undesirable situation.

Although most courts adhere to the rule that indemnity must be complete before the insurer asserts a subrogation right, determining when the insured has obtained a full recovery presents difficulties. Whether the insured has been paid in "full" really has two aspects. First, the insurer might pay only a portion of the amount that it is required to pay under the policy; in this event, the insured obviously has not been indemnified in full for the loss and the insurer is not entitled to be subrogated

---

[16] See Elaine M. Rinaldi, *Apportionment of Recovery Between Insured and Insurer in a Subrogation Case,* 29 Tort & Ins. L. J. 803, 817 (1994) ("it is in the best interests of both the insured and the insurer to enter into a litigation agreement prior to commencing any action against a third-party tortfeasor.")

[17] See, e.g., Midland Bank & Trust Co. v. Fidelity & Deposit Co., 442 F. Supp. 960 (D.N.J. 1977); McCarter v. Alaska Nat'l Ins. Co., 883 P.2d 986 (Alaska 1994); DeTienne Associates Ltd. Partnership v. Farmers Union Mut. Ins. Co., 879 P.2d 704 (Mont. 1994); Shelter Ins. Cos. v. Frohlich, 498 N.W.2d 74 (Neb. 1993); Southern Farm Bur. Cas. Ins. Co. v. Sonnier, 406 So. 2d 178 (La. 1981); Pfeffer v. State Auto. and Cas. Underwriters Ins. Co., 292 N.W.2d 743 (Minn. 1980); Wimberly v. American Cas. Co., 584 S.W.2d 200 (Tenn. 1979); Garrity v. Rural Mut. Ins. Co., 253 N.W.2d 512 (Wis. 1977); Blaylock v. Georgia Mut. Ins. Co., 238 S.E.2d 105 (Ga. 1977); Skauge v. Mountain States Telephone & Telegraph Co., 565 P.2d 628 (Mont. 1977); Florida Farm Bur. Ins. Co. v. Martin, 377 So. 2d 827 (Fla. Dist. Ct. App. 1979); Associates Hosp. Serv. v. Pustilnik, 396 A.2d 1332 (Pa. Super. Ct. 1979), vacated and remanded on other grounds, 439 A.2d 1149 (Pa. 1981); St. Paul Fire & Marine Ins. Co. v. W.P. Rose Supply Co., 198 S.E.2d 482 (N.C. Ct. App. 1973). See generally Rinaldi, *supra* note 16, at 807 (list of jurisdictions following what is described as majority rule).

to the insured's rights.[18] Second, even though the insurer pays the insured the full amount due under the policy, this sum may be insufficient to indemnify the insured for the loss. In this circumstance, some courts have held that the insurer has no right of subrogation.[19] This means essentially that the claim against the responsible third party belongs to the insured; if the insured sues the tortfeasor and recovers, only if the recovery exceeds what is necessary to make the insured whole must the insured account for the excess to the insurer.[20]

A useful way to organize one's thinking about this issue involves recognizing that when a subrogee asserts a subrogation right, the subrogee owns the claim and has the right to bring and control the action, essentially stepping into the shoes of the subrogor.[21] If the insured has not been reimbursed in full for his or her loss, it is not possible for the insurer to own the insured's entire claim; some of the claim, necessarily, continues to be owned by the insured. Stated otherwise, the insurer does not own the entire claim unless the insured has been reimbursed in full for his or her loss; in the absence of full reimbursement, the insurer does not succeed to the status of a subrogee, does not own the claim, and does not have the right to bring and control the action. The insured who is not fully compensated by the insurance proceeds may well choose to sue the responsible third party and seek a full recovery (and the insurer may encourage the insured to do so, even to the extent of offering to underwrite and control the litigation if the insured is reluctant to go forward). In this circumstance, the insurer's right, prior to the insured's full recovery, is to be *reimbursed* out of any recovery the insured garners from the responsible third party to the extent the recovery exceeds what is needed to make the insured whole. In this latter case, then, it can be said that the insurer has a right of reimbursement, to be distinguished from a subrogation right.

Anyone familiar with insurance transactions knows, however, that insurers routinely assert subrogation rights in situations where the insured has not been reimbursed in full. For example, the insured's coverage will commonly be subject to a deductible; until the insured is reimbursed for the amount of the deductible, the insured has not been paid in full. In practice, insureds commonly agree to give the insurer a right of conventional subrogation to the extent the insurer makes payment to the insured. For example, the typical homeowner's policy states that "we [the insurer] may require an assignment of rights of recovery for a loss to the extent that payment is made by us."[22] It is common, then, that the insurer will assert, in the insured's name, a right of subrogation against a third party even though the insured has not been paid in full. In other words, the cases are clear that where the insurer only pays part of the insured's loss, the insurer has no right to equitable subrogation.

---

[18] E.g., Borserine v. Maryland Cas. Co., 112 F.2d 409 (8th Cir. 1940); Baillio v. Western Cas. & Sur. Co., 189 So. 2d 605 (La. Ct. App. 1966).

[19] E.g., Motors Ins. Corp. v. Home Indem. Co., 284 A.2d 58 (D.C. 1971); Capps v. Klebs, 382 N.E.2d 947 (Ind. Ct. App. 1978).

[20] E.g., Schweitz v. Robatham, 234 N.W.2d 834 (Neb. 1975); Florida Farm Bur. Ins. Co. v. Martin, 377 So. 2d 827 (Fla. Dist. Ct. App. 1979).

[21] As discussed below, this means the subrogee is the real party in interest and must sue in its own name. See § 96[h], *infra.*

[22] *Policy Kit* at 35 (ISO Form HO 00 03 04 91).

However, the insurer and insured often agree in the contract that the insurer has a right to subrogation before the insured is reimbursed in full, and it is under this authority that subrogation rights are asserted against third parties before the insured is fully indemnified.[23]

When a sum is recovered from the third party pursuant to the insurer's assertion, with or without the insured's participation, of the subrogation right, the question then arises as to how the sum should be apportioned. Several answers are possible; although, as noted above, most court require the insured to be reimbursed in whole first, this answer was not inevitable. One other answer is to treat the insurer as the owner of the insured's claim, and to allow the insurer the full amount recovered from the tortfeasor, regardless of whether it exceeds the amount paid by the insurer to the insured. This answer has basically nothing to commend it. It ignores the fact that the insurer's right is derivative of the insured's claim against the third party, that the insurer should not be allowed to recover more than the insured could recover from the third party, and that the insurer should not be allowed to retain a recovery exceeding what it paid to the insured. Moreover, allowing the insurer to be made whole or even to profit before the insured is indemnified is inconsistent with the equitable origins of subrogation.[24]

Another possible answer, which has been followed in a number of states and should therefore be labeled the minority rule, is to allow the insurer to be reimbursed first out of any recovery against the tortfeasor, with the insured receiving the balance. In other words, instead of requiring that the insured be made whole first, this approach makes the insurer whole first.[25] This approach does not allow the insurer

---

[23] Most courts are simply not clear about what they are doing when the apportionment issue arises. One commentator explained it this way: "By ignoring the contractual underpinnings of conventional subrogation in favor of the equitable principles of legal subrogation, most jurisdictions . . . adhere to the proposition that the insured is entitled to be made whole before the insurer may share in any recovery from a tortfeasor. The rationales used to reach this conclusion are varied and untenable at times. Perhaps most untenable is the apparent willingness of the courts to disregard the provisions of the insurance policy and the standard subrogation receipt. Thus, while the insured-whole rule clearly represents the majority position, it is a position without cohesiveness." Rinaldi, *supra* note 16, at 811. One court that was clear about what it was doing was the Minnesota Court of Appeals in Hershey v. Physicians Health Plan of Minn., Inc., 498 N.W.2d 519 (Minn.App. 1993). The court held that express contractual language in a health insurance policy providing for subrogation when the insured has not been fully compensated would be enforced, notwithstanding the "general rule" that subrogation is not allowed when the insured's total compensation is less than the insured's actual loss.

[24] See National Biscuit Co. v. Employers Mut. Liab. Ins. Co., 231 S.W.2d 52 (Ky. 1950) (subrogation under workers' compensation statute). See generally Jay S. Bybee, Comment, *Profits in Subrogation: An Insurer's Claim to Be More than Indemnified,* 1979 B.Y.U. L. Rev. 145 (1979).

[25] See, e.g., Higginbotham v. Arkansas Blue Cross & Blue Shield, 849 S.W.2d 464 (Ark. 1993); Peterson v. Ohio Farmers Ins. Co., 191 N.E.2d 157 (Ohio 1963); Pontiac Mut. Cty. Fire & Lightning Ins. Co. v. Sheibley, 116 N.E. 644 (Ill. 1917); Winkelmann v. Excelsior Ins. Co., 650 N.E.2d 841 (N.Y. App. Div. 1995); Travelers Indem. Co. v. Ingebretsen, 113 Cal. Rptr. 679 (Cal. Ct. App. 1974); Morgan v. General Ins. Co. of Am., 181 So. 2d 175 (Fla. Dist. Ct. App. 1965).

to profit before the insured is made whole, but it gives priority to providing full relief for the insured instead of for the insured. This approach also gives priority to conventional subrogation, in that the insurance contract's specifications that the insurer be reimbursed before the insured is made whole trumps any equitable notion that the insured is entitled to a full recovery before the insurer receives any reimbursement.

Another approach involves the insurer and insured prorating the recovery from the tortfeasor in accordance with the percentage of the insured's loss that the insurer paid, or according to some other equitable formula.[26] This calculation only coincidentally may make the insured whole. Its attractiveness, however, is that it favors neither party's interests over the other; neither the insurer nor the insured is made whole prior to the other.

The most widely favored approach requires that the insured to be reimbursed first for loss not covered by the insurance; once the insured is reimbursed in full, the insurer receives any excess funds.[27] Of the alternative approaches, this approach comes closest to the principle that the insured's indemnity must be complete before the insurer has a right to benefit from the recovery from a third party.[28] Ironically, this approach is sometimes justified on the ground that conventional subrogation — which is what enables a subrogation right to be asserted prior to the insured being reimbursed in full — should be treated no differently than equitable subrogation, meaning that the insured should be allowed to use the fund recovered from the tortfeasor to be made whole before the insurer is allowed to tap those proceeds.[29]

Another complexity involves how costs of investigation and litigation should be taken into account. Suppose the insured suffers a loss of $10,000. The insurer pays the insured $5,000, and a judgment of $10,000 is obtained from the party causing the loss, but expenses and costs of $2,000 are incurred in securing the judgment. Various approaches exist in the precedents. The prevailing approach requires reimbursing the party who expended money to recover the judgment to the extent of that party's costs, and then allocating the net proceeds according to the allocation formula followed in that jurisdiction.[30]

Yet another difficulty in allocating the proceeds recovered from a third party exists when the insured's claim against the third party is settled. A settlement is a

---

[26] See Aetna Life Ins. Co. v. Martinez, 454 N.E.2d 1338 (Ohio Ct.App. 1982). Compare Pontiac Mut. Cty. Fire & Lighting Ins. Co. v. Sheibley, 116 N.E. 644 (Ill. 1917) (enforcement of proration agreement between insurer and insured).

[27] See cases cited at note 17, *supra*.

[28] Robert E. Keeton, *Insurance Law* 160–61 (1971).

[29] See Garrity v. Rural Mut. Ins. Co., 253 N.W.2d 512 (Wis. 1977).

[30] E.g., Skauge v. Mountain States Tel. & Tel. Co., 565 P.2d 628 (Mont. 1977) (where insured sustains loss exceeding proceeds paid by insurer, insured is entitled to be made whole for its entire loss and any costs of recovery, including attorney fees, before insurer can assert a right of subrogation); Williams v. Gateway Ins. Co., 331 So. 2d 301 (Fla. 1976). In *Skauge* the insured incurred the expenses in obtaining the judgment; the rule of the case was applied to a situation where the insurer assisted the insured in obtaining the judgment in DeTienne Associates Ltd. Partnership v. Farmers Union Mut. Ins. Co., 879 P.2d 704 (Mont. 1994).

negotiated end to a lawsuit; to avoid the risks of litigation, the plaintiff normally accepts a sum less than the total amount of his or her claims, some of which may be for pain and suffering, mental anguish, and other items not readily reducible to a specific sum. The problem is determining at what point the insured has been reimbursed in full so that the insurer can collect proceeds to reimburse its outlays on the insured's behalf.

Associated Hospital Service v. Pustilnik,[31] a 1979 Pennsylvania case, illustrates both of the foregoing problems — allocating the costs of obtaining the judgment against the tortfeasor, and the effect of settlement on determining whether the insured is reimbursed in full. The insured suffered serious injuries when struck by a subway car; during his hospitalization, he accumulated medical bills exceeding $30,000. Under his subscription with Associated Hospital Service of Philadelphia (Blue Cross), he was given a credit of nearly $19,000 against these bills. After the accident, the insured brought a lawsuit against the subway. Blue Cross notified him of its subrogation interest in any recovery ultimately obtained from the subway. Blue Cross invited the insured's attorney to represent Blue Cross's interest in the suit in exchange for one-fourth of any recovery as an attorney's fee and one-third if the case went to trial, but the attorney rejected this offer, demanding one-half of any recovery.

The insured's suit was settled after the fifth day of trial for $235,000 in exchange for a release relieving the subway from further liability. Blue Cross demanded $30,000 of the settlement pursuant to its right of subrogation. A trial was held on Blue Cross's subrogation claim, and the trial court held that Blue Cross was entitled to subrogation for the amounts it spent on the insured's behalf. However, this sum was reduced by forty percent to account for a fee for the insured's attorney and an additional fifty percent on the ground that the insured's settlement was less than the full value of his personal injury claim. Blue Cross appealed.[32]

The appellate court reversed the reduction of Blue Cross's subrogation interest by fifty percent. The court held that when a subrogor (e.g., the insured) settles, he waives his right to determine his losses judicially; the settlement conclusively establishes the settlement amount as full compensation for his damages. Any other result would encourage the insured to take inconsistent positions in litigation; he would argue in the proceeding against the tortfeasor that the tortfeasor's liability was substantial, while he would argue in the subrogation action that the liability claims were weak, which justified settling a large damage claim for a small amount. The court sustained, however, the reduction of forty percent for the attorney's fees. In short, then, the insurer had a subrogation claim of $30,000, of which $12,000 was paid to the attorney for the insured, meaning that the insurer was entitled to $18,000 of the insured's recovery.

---

[31] 396 A.2d 1332 (Pa. Super. Ct. 1979), *vacated and remanded on other grounds,* 439 A.2d 1149 (Pa. 1981).

[32] Pustilnik also appealed on the ground that Blue Cross had an adequate remedy at law. As such, Blue Cross erred in bringing the action in equity, and the action should be dismissed entirely. The court rejected this argument, holding that subrogation is an equitable remedy, even when a contract provision exists giving a right to sue in equity. See 396 A.2d at 1336.

Although the court's conclusion in *Pustilnik* that the settlement constituted full compensation of the insured's loss has been criticized,[33] the court's analysis is sound. Most courts hold that a settlement (or a judgment) establishes conclusively the full amount of the insured's damages.[34] As a practical matter, no tortfeasor with knowledge of the existence of insurance should consent to a settlement with the insured unless the insurer agrees that its subrogation rights are also included in the settlement. Also, if the insured settles without the insurer's consent, the insured voids the coverage.[35] Thus, in most cases the best result is for the insurer and insured to agree on a proration of the settlement proceeds before the settlement occurs.[36] If an insured, however, for some reason (as in *Pustilnik*) proceeds with litigation against the tortfeasor and settles the claim, the insured should not be at liberty to claim, for example, that it was not reimbursed in full because all of the settlement was for pain and suffering and none of it for accrued medical expenses. If allowed to take such positions, insureds could routinely frustrate the insurer's subrogation interest and insurers would have no recourse. Treating the settlement as conclusive on the amount of the insured's loss still leaves the insured with sufficient flexibility. If the insured believes the settlement offer is too small, the insured can try the case. If the insured does not want the insurer's subrogation right to be reimbursed out of the settlement, the insured is free to pursue an agreement with the insurer for a reduction in the amount to be paid the insurer in settlement of its subrogation rights.

One final problem in determining whether the insured has been paid in full is encountered when the insurer uses a loan receipt as the vehicle of payment.[37] Sometimes the insurer advances money to the insured under a loan receipt that requires the insured to refund the loan in proportion to the amount recovered from the wrongdoer. In this situation, some courts have held that no "payment" was made and that the insurer had no subrogation rights.[38] However, in virtually identical circumstances, other courts have held that the advance of money to the insured under a loan receipt created a right of subrogation.[39] Loan receipts are discussed in more detail in a later section.[40]

[e] The Requirement that the Insurer Not Be a Volunteer

In equity, subrogation will not be enforced in favor of a party who merely "volunteers" to pay another's obligation. Ordinarily, the insurer pays the third party's

---

[33] See Alan D. Windt, 2 *Insurance Claims and Disputes,* § 10.06, at 135–38 (3d ed. 1995).

[34] See, e.g., Rimes v. State Farm Mut. Auto. Ins. Co., 316 N.W.2d 348 (Wis. 1982); United Pac. Ins. Co. v. Boyd, 661 P.2d 987 (Wash. Ct. App. 1983); Florida Farm Bur. Ins. Co. v. Martin, 377 So. 2d 827 (Fla.App. 1979).

[35] See § 96[g], *infra.*

[36] For a discussion of proration agreements and their enforceability, see Rinaldi, *supra* note 16, at 815-17.

[37] Loan receipts are discussed in § 96[i], *infra.*

[38] E.g., First Nat'l Bank of Ottawa v. Lloyd's of London, 116 F.2d 221 (7th Cir. 1940); Furrer v. Yew Creek Logging Co., 292 P.2d 499 (Or. 1956); Green v. Johns, 72 S.E.2d 78 (Ga. Ct. App. 1952).

[39] E.g., City Stores Co. v. Lerner Shops, Inc., 410 F.2d 1010 (D.C. Cir. 1969); McKenzie v. North River Ins. Co., 257 Ala. 265, 58 So. 2d 581 (1951).

[40] See § 96[i], *infra.*

"debt" under the legal compulsion of a contract of indemnity with an insured. However, if the insured's claim against the insurer is outside the coverage but the insurer pays the claim anyway, the insurer will not be entitled to subrogation against the party who caused the insured's loss: in that situation, the insurer was a mere volunteer and is not entitled to subrogation.[41]

The volunteer defense does not exist with respect to conventional subrogation. Equitable subrogation requires that there be compulsion or a reasonable belief on the part of the subrogee that there is an interest to protect. However, to effect conventional subrogation, it is only necessary that there be an assignment to the subrogee of the right to pursue the subrogor's claims. Whatever restrictions exist upon the assertion by the subrogee of the subrogor's rights are those set forth in the assignment's terms, which are controlled by the language of the policy.

However, most policies give the insurer a subrogation right for claims paid "under the policy," or to the extent "payments are made by us for a loss," or words of similar effect. Thus, if the insurer pays a claim that is not required "under the policy," or if the insured pays for a loss outside the coverage, it is arguable that the insurer has no subrogation right according to the terms of the assignment.[42] Thus, although the subrogee under conventional subrogation is not vulnerable to the volunteer defense, a similar defense might be asserted if the insurer's payment is for a debt not within the scope of the subrogor's assignment. The potential difficulty with this defense to subrogation is that, if successful, it enables the wrongdoer to escape liability for acts or neglect for which the wrongdoer is legally responsible. The insured after receiving proceeds is unlikely to pursue the wrongdoer; and if the insurer, due to the wrongdoer's successful argument that proceeds should not have been paid under the policy, loses its subrogation right, the third party pays nothing for the wrong. Consistently with the public policy that wrongdoers should not escape liability simply because the victim carried insurance, the wrongdoer's volunteer or "under the policy" defense should be given a narrow construction.

[f]   Subrogation Against Insured Not Allowed

The general rule is that no right of subrogation exists in favor of an insurer against its own insured. Subrogation rights exist only against third parties to whom the insurer owes no duties. The rationale for this rule is that allowing the insurer subrogation against its own insured would allow the insurer to pass the loss from itself to its own insured, thereby avoiding the coverage which the insured purchased.[43]

---

[41] See, e.g., Commercial Union Ins. Co. v. Postin, 610 P.2d 984 (Wyo. 1980); Nationwide Mut. Ins. Co. v. Weeks-Allen Motor Co., Inc., 198 S.E.2d 88 (N.C. Ct. App. 1973); compare Allstate Ins. Co. v. Auto Driveaway Co., 529 P.2d 303 (N.M.Ct.App. 1974).

[42] See, e.g., Commercial Union Ins. Co. v. Postin, 610 P.2d 984 (Wyo. 1980).

[43] See, e.g., Keystone Paper Converters, Inc. v. Neemar, Inc., 562 F. Supp. 1046 (E.D. Pa. 1983); Jindra v. Clayton, 529 N.W.2d 523 (Neb. 1995); Richards v. Allstate Ins. Co., 455 S.E.2d 803 (W.Va. 1995); North Star Reins. Corp. v. Continental Ins. Co., 624 N.E.2d 647 (N.Y. 1993); Dix Mut. Ins. Co. v. LaFramboise, 597 N.E.2d 622 (Ill. 1992); Travelers Ins. Cos. v. Dickey, 799 P.2d 625 (Okla. 1990); Rokeby-Johnson v. Aquatronics Int'l, Inc., 206 Cal. Rptr. 232 (Cal. Ct. App. 1984); Miller v. Russell, 674 S.W.2d 290 (Tenn. Ct. App. 1983).

Reeder v. Reeder,[44] a 1984 Nebraska case, is illustrative. Theodore Reeder and his wife owned a residence in Omaha which they were attempting to sell because they had moved to another city. Theodore's brother Bernard, who lived in Omaha, was constructing a new home for his family. Theodore gave Bernard and his family permission to live in Theodore's house while awaiting the completion of the construction of their new home. While Bernard's family occupied the house, one of his daughters lit a gas fireplace but failed to open the damper; the result was a fire which substantially destroyed the house. Theodore's insurer paid for the loss, but then sought subrogation against Bernard and his family. The court reasoned that Bernard and his family were Theodore's "guests" in the house, not licensees or tenants, and that allowing the insurer to assert subrogation rights against Bernard and his family was tantamount to allowing the insurer to sue the insured directly.

Similar results have been reached in the situation where the insured's tenant causes a fire that destroys the insured's premises. In the absence of an express provision in the lease establishing the tenant's liability for a negligently caused fire, the tenant "stands in the shoes" of the insured landlord for the limited purpose of defeating a subrogation claim.[45]

[g]   Defenses to Subrogation and the Effect of Releases on Coverage

[1]   The General Rule Regarding Defenses

The insurer is subrogated only to such rights that the insured has against other parties at the time of loss.[46] Therefore, any defense that the third party has which is good against the subrogor, such as laches, the statute of limitations, immunity, unclean hands, or illegality, is good against the subrogee.[47] The general rule is illustrated by a case where the insured's particularly poor judgment led to the predictable, dramatic result. The insured's newly-constructed home was totally destroyed in an explosion and fire caused in part by the negligence of defendants (a general contractor, the plumbing subcontractor, and the city which inspected the site), whose collective neglect created and allowed a gas leak to exist. The insured, however, was contributorily negligent in using a lighted match to determine the gas leak's location. The insured's insurer paid for the loss, and then sought to assert

---

See generally Comment, *Conflicts Regarding the "No Subrogation Against Insured" Rule,* 29 Drake L. Rev. 811 (1979–80).

[44] 348 N.W.2d 832 (Neb. 1984).

[45] See, e.g., Safeco Ins. Co. v. Capri, 429, 705 P.2d 659 (Nev. 1985); Monterey Corp. v. Hart, 224 S.E.2d 142 (Va. 1976); Rizzuto v. Morris, 592 P.2d 688 (Wash. Ct. App. 1979).

[46] See, e.g., Allstate Ins. Co. v. Amerisure Ins. Cos., 603 So. 2d 961 (Ala. 1992); Touchet Valley Grain Growers, Inc. v. Opp & Seibold Gen. Constr., Inc., 831 P.2d 724 (Wash. 1992); Fireman's Fund Ins. Co. v. Maryland Cas. Co., 26 Cal. Rptr.2d 762 (Cal. Ct. App. 1994); Northern Ins. Co. v. B. Elliot, Ltd., 323 N.W.2d 683 (Mich. Ct. App. 1982).

[47] See, e.g., Lexington Ins. Co. v. All Regions Chem. Labs, Inc., 647 N.E.2d 399 (Mass. 1995); St. Paul Fire & Marine Ins. Co. v. Glassing, 887 P.2d 218 (Mont. 1994); Patrons Mut. Ins. Ass'n v. Union Gas System, Inc., 830 P.2d 35 (Kan. 1992); Hanover Ins. Co. v. Fireman's Fund Ins. Co., 586 A.2d 567 (Conn. 1991); USAA Cas. Ins. Co. v. Brown, 614 N.Y.S.2d 571 (N.Y. App. Div. 1994). See generally Andrew C. Hecker, Jr., *Subrogation—Potential Defenses,* 18 Forum 615 (1983).

subrogation rights against the defendants. The court held that the insurer could not assert subrogation rights against the defendants due to its insured's contributory negligence; the insured's negligence provided a complete defense for the defendants to any claim that might be asserted by the subrogor.[48]

In the foregoing example, it was the insured's contributory negligence that created the defense to the insurer's subrogation right. The defense in that instance was not deliberately created by the insured, and there could have been no doubt that the loss caused in part by the insured's negligence was covered by the loss.[49] If the defense offered by the three defendants had been that the insured had given them a release from liability (presumably, one would hope, in exchange for some kind of compensation), the defendants' defense to the insurer's assertion of a subrogation right would have been just as effective. However, the insured's act of deliberately, knowingly, and intentionally giving the defendants a defense to the insurer's subrogation claim would have had ramifications for the insured's coverage. These questions are explored in the remaining subsections.

[2] Release of Tortfeasor Prior to Loss

If the insured prior to a loss (or even prior to becoming an insured) releases a third party from prospective liability, that release is good against the insurer under the rule that defenses good against the subrogor are also good against the subrogee. However, such a release does not constitute interference with the insurer's subrogation rights, and the insured does not lose coverage on that account.[50]

The tortfeasor's defense to the subrogation right flows from the general rule, and there is nothing particularly remarkable about that result. However, the fact that the insured's coverage is unaffected by giving the release is not as obvious a result, given that it is the insured's deliberate act which interferes with the insurer's subrogation right. The logic underlying this latter result essentially treats the insurer's subrogation right as something which vests at the time of the loss. (It is not correct to say that the subrogation right comes into existence at the time of the loss if the subrogation right is created by contract when the insured and insurer contract, which is probably the case. The idea is that the subrogation right is *perfected* or *accrues*[51]

---

[48] See Allstate Ins. Co. v. Town of Ville Platte, 269 So. 2d 298 (La. Ct. App. 1972).

[49] If the loss had been caused by the insured's negligence without any other contributing factor, the loss would still have been covered by the policy.

[50] See, e.g., Atlas Assur. Co. v. Harper, Robinson Shipping Co., 508 F.2d 1381 (9th Cir. 1975); Insurance Co. of N. Am. v. Universal Mort. Corp., 262 N.W.2d 92 (Wis. 1978).

[51] In Blume v. Evans Fur Company, 466 N.E.2d 1366 (Ill. App. Ct. 1984). See also Continental Cas. Co. v. Polk Brothers, 457 N.E.2d 1271 (Ill. App. Ct. 1983), the court used the term "accrues" to illustrate this concept. The insured stored her mink coat with a fur company, which proceeded to lose it. The receipt which the insured received at the time she put the coat in storage limited the company's liability to $100, and the court held that this release limited the insurer's subrogation rights against the negligent company. The court observed that "the subrogor's loss is a prerequisite to the accrual of subrogation rights," and "the subrogor's rights do not accrue until the subrogee has paid the debt." 466 N.E.2d at 1367. Compare Nimmick v. State Farm Mut. Auto. Ins. Co., 891 P.2d 1154 (Mont. 1995) (insurer's subrogation right "vests" upon its payment of claim).

at the time of the loss.) The insurer has no subrogation right at the time of the release because no loss has occurred; therefore, no interference has occurred.

Moreover, in situations where the release is given before the party becomes an insured, the insurer, if it had thought the matter important enough, could have inquired into whether the prospective insured had released any prospective tortfeasors. Because insurers do not do so, one can fairly assume that insurers are willing to provide coverage with a right to subrogation for prospective losses for which the insured gives a prior release. This is a good business practice, because insureds and prospective insureds routinely give releases to third parties prior to loss in their daily affairs. The person who agrees to lease an apartment may well exculpate the landlord from future acts of negligence. The person who parks his or her car in a downtown parking garage may see a sign upon entering the garage, which is reinforced by language on the back of the parking ticket, that the garage is not responsible for damage to or theft of vehicles or their contents. The person who attends a sporting event or a concert probably gives some kind of release to the organizer or sponsor of the event in connection with the purchase and sale of the ticket to it. In all of these situations and more, the insured gives a prospective release; insurance would be worth much less if each of these acts eliminated the insured's coverage.

As it turns out, most policies specifically state that a release given by the insured before the loss does not impair a subrogation right, and the vast weight of authority holds that pre-loss releases by the insured, while providing a defense to the insurer's subrogation action, does not eliminate the insured's coverage.[52]

A leading case on the effect of pre-loss releases on subrogation rights and coverage is *Great Northern Oil Co. v. St. Paul Fire and Marine Insurance Co.*,[53] a 1971 Minnesota case. Plaintiff Great Northern procured from St. Paul an all-risk insurance policy covering business interruption losses. The policy had a clause giving a right of subrogation to the insurer; it also stated that "[t]he Insured shall do nothing after loss to prejudice such rights." While the policy was in force, plaintiff contracted with Litwin Corporation to construct some facilities on Great Northern's site, and this contract contained a clause exculpating Litwin from liability for loss of use, loss of profits, or business interruption from the work. During construction, a crane accident caused damage to the partially completed work, and this led to a business interruption for which Great Northern sought reimbursement from St. Paul. St. Paul defended, inter alia, on the ground that Great Northern's release of Litwin had interfered with St. Paul's subrogation rights, and therefore Great Northern was not entitled to coverage. The court held that absent a prohibition in the policy between St. Paul and Great Northern on the insured entering into exculpatory

_____

[52] See, e.g., Great Northern Oil Co. v. St. Paul Fire and Marine Ins. Co., 189 N.W.2d 404 (Minn. 1971); Continental Cas. Co. v. Homontowski, 510 N.W.2d 743 (Wis. Ct. App. 1993). But see Liberty Mut. Ins. Co. v. Altfillisch Constr. Co., 139 Cal. Rptr. 91 (Cal.App. 1977) (policy did not contain referenced clause; court held that the insured's pre-loss release of the tortfeasor impaired the insurer's expectation of subrogation and constituted a breach of the insured's implied duty of good faith and fair dealing; insured was ordered to refund all the proceeds it had earlier received).

[53] 189 N.W.2d 404 (Minn. 1971).

arrangements with third parties, Great Northern would not be precluded from coverage for having done so.[54]

The court noted that exculpatory provisions in construction agreements are common and do not contravene public policy.[55] The court also acknowledged that the exculpatory provision eliminated the insurer's subrogation right.[56] St. Paul argued that the exculpatory clause allowed Great Northern to get its new facility at lower cost by relinquishing prospective claims against Litwin, and now Great Northern sought to impose the risk of loss due to Litwin's acts or neglect upon the insurer.[57] Stated otherwise, it was as if St. Paul, a first-party insurer for Great Northern, had become, without the payment of any additional premium, a liability insurer for Litwin, with whom it was not in privity and from whom it had received no premium payment for the assumption of the risk. The court, while acknowledging that St. Paul's argument was "not without merit," rejected the argument nonetheless.[58]

Clearly, St. Paul's argument did have merit. In the absence of an exculpatory clause, Litwin would have charged St. Paul more for the construction project — presumably whatever amount Litwin would have had to pay to secure liability insurance. In holding that the exculpatory clause did not eliminate Great Northern's coverage under the St. Paul policy, the court allowed an additional party, Litwin, to benefit from the coverage by virtue of its relationship to the named insured, a contracting party, and *only* by virtue of that relationship, since Litwin had no relationship to St. Paul. Although the court was not explicit on this point, what the court did was to find that other considerations trumped the inequity of having St. Paul extend free liability insurance to Litwin. As discussed above, insureds routinely enter into exculpatory agreements, and sometimes do not even realize when this has occurred. Eliminating insureds' coverage in all such instances creates unfair surprise and forfeiture. Moreover, property insurers are in a better position, arguably, to assess the risks involved with construction projects on an insured's own site; a liability insurer for a contractor would have more difficulty, arguably, in assessing the nature of the risks at a variety of different sites. Yet if St. Paul (and other insurers) must now cover the risks of construction projects at insureds' sites, the cost of coverage must go up, and all insureds will pay this cost whether the insureds are planning construction projects or not.

In the final analysis, the issue in cases like *Great Northern* turns on the insurer's ability to control the form. St. Paul's subrogation clause provided that the insured should do nothing "after loss" to prejudice St. Paul's subrogation rights. If St. Paul had wanted the coverage for a particular claim to cease in the event of a prospective release of a prospective tortfeasor, St. Paul could have drafted a subrogation clause to that effect and included it in the policy.[59] Having failed to take any of these steps

---

[54] 189 N.W.2d at 406.

[55] 189 N.W.2d at 407.

[56] 189 N.W.2d at 407-08.

[57] 189 N.W.2d at 408.

[58] 189 N.W.2d at 408-09.

[59] The court suggested that St. Paul could have inserted a clause that required the insured to give prior notice before entering into a contract with an exculpatory clause, after which notice the insurer could charge the insured an additional premium to assume the additional risk. See 189 N.W.2d at 409.

in circumstances where there are good reasons for preserving the insured's coverage, St. Paul could not prevail on its claim that the exculpatory clause interfered with its subrogation rights, thereby wiping out Great Northern's coverage.

The same analysis used for releases also applies in circumstances where the insured prior to the loss (or prior to becoming an insured) enter into an agreement with a third party that stipulates the amount of a future, possible loss. In this situation, the insurer, when asserting subrogation rights, is bound by the insured's stipulation pursuant to the general rule that defenses good against the insured are also good against the insurer asserting subrogation rights. The insured, however, does not lose coverage under the reasoning that the insured has interfered with the insurer's subrogation right by entering into the stipulation. For example, in *Blume v. Evans Fur Co.,*[60] Blume stored her mink coat with a fur company, which proceeded to lose the coat. Blume's insurer paid her over $3000 for the loss of her coat, and the insurer then asserted subrogation rights against the fur company. The company defended on the ground that the receipt issued to Blume stated the value of the coat to be $300 and limited Evans' liability to $100. The court, reasoning from the proposition that the subrogee can have no greater rights than the subrogor, held that the limitation on the fur company's liability to Blume also limited the insurer's subrogation rights.

[3]   Release of Tortfeasor After Loss

If the insured *after* a loss releases a third party without the insurer's assent, the insured has interfered with the insurer's right of subrogation. Except in the situation discussed below, the release will be effective against the insurer.[61] Also, the insured's act of releasing the third party will discharge the insurer's obligations to the insured under the policy and will entitle the insurer to return of any payments that may have already made to the insured.[62] The logic of these outcomes is straight-forward. Under the general rule, the release constitutes a defense to the insurer's subrogation claim. However, the insured has also violated the terms of the contract with the insurer by settling the claim against the third party without the insurer's consent. In almost every policy, the insured promises not to interfere with the insurer's subrogation rights, and absent such a clause is certainly breaching an express or implied duty to cooperate with the insurer. There are no special considerations like those which accompany prospective releases of prospective tortfeasors which point toward a different result.

---

[60] 466 N.E.2d 1366 (Ill. App. Ct. 1984).

[61] See, e.g., Insurance Co. of N. Am. v. Abiouness, 313 S.E.2d 663 (Va. 1984); Prudential Lines, Inc. v. Firemen's Ins. Co., 457 N.Y.S.2d 272 (N.Y. App. Div. 1982).

[62] E.g., Audubon Ins. Co. v. Farr, 453 So. 2d 232 (La. 1984); Motto v. State Farm Mut. Auto. Ins. Co., 462 P.2d 620 (N.M. 1969); Geertz v. State Farm Fire & Cas., 451 P.2d 860 (Or. 1969); Aetna Cas. & Sur. Co. v. Tennessee Farmers Mut. Ins. Co., 867 S.W.2d 321 (Tenn. Ct. App. 1993). Compare Ankney v. Franch, 652 A.2d 1138, 1145 (Md.Ct.App. 1995), cert. granted by 660 A.2d 431 (Md. June 27, 1995) (when insured without authority settles with tortfeasor after claim is paid, insurer's action against tortfeasor is not barred; however, when insured without authority settles claim before proceeds are paid, insurer's subrogation right is destroyed).

There is one major exception to this rule in most jurisdictions: if the tortfeasor secures the insured's release after acquiring knowledge that an insurer has an interest in the insured's claim as a potential (before payment is made from insurer to insured) or actual (after payment has been made by insurer to insured) subrogee, the insurer will still be allowed to assert subrogation rights. In other words, the release is ineffective as a defense against the insurer's subrogation claim if at the time the tortfeasor obtained the release the tortfeasor knew of the insured's coverage.[63] Where the insurer is the actual subrogee (i.e., has already paid proceeds to the insured) and the tortfeasor knows this, the result makes considerable sense. By paying proceeds to the insured, the insurer acquired and now owns the insured's claim; thus, the insured was neither entitled nor authorized to release the claim, and the tortfeasor knew this. Because the insured could not release a claim it did not own, the insurer is still free to assert it.[64]

It is a short but reasonable step beyond this analysis to reach the same result when the insurer's interest is as a potential subrogee. The tortfeasor who knows of the insurance should understand that the potential subrogee is likely to become an actual subrogee; a tortfeasor who tries to secure a release from the insured for a modest payment to the insured is, in effect, trying to effect a fraud on the insurer (as subrogee) and maybe on the insured as well. Even so, it would not seem unfair to decline to apply the knowledge-of-insurance exception in the situation where the insured has not yet received proceeds and nevertheless gives a release to the tortfeasor in exchange for a consideration. In the absence of overreaching by the tortfeasor, which may deserve its own remedy, the insured has impaired the insurer's subrogation right, and it seems reasonable to discharge the insurer from its obligation to pay the claim and to require the insured to be satisfied with whatever payment the insured obtained from the tortfeasor in exchange for the release.

When the knowledge-of-insurance exception is applied, the insurer has a valid subrogation claim; thus, it is not necessary for the insurer's protection to permit the insurer to retrieve the proceeds paid to the insured.[65] Thus, when the knowledge-of-insurance exception is applied, it is possible that the tortfeasor may end up paying twice for the same loss — once to the insured as consideration for the release, and

---

[63] See, e.g., Imperial Cas. & Indem. Co. v. General Cas. Co. of Wis., 458 N.W.2d 335 (N.D. 1990); Milbank Ins. Co. v. Henry, 441 N.W.2d 143 (Neb. 1989); Leader Nat'l Ins. Co. v. Torres, 779 P.2d 722 (Wash. 1989); Transamerica Ins. Co. v. Barnes, 505 P.2d 783 (Utah 1972); Hospital Service Corp. v. Pennsylvania Ins. Co., 227 A.2d 105 (R.I. 1967); Davenport v. State Farm Mut. Auto. Ins. Co., 404 P.2d 10 (Nev. 1965); Time Ins. Co. v. Opus Corp., 519 N.W.2d 470 (Minn. Ct. App. 1994); Ortega v. Motors Ins. Corp., 552 So. 2d 1127 (Fla. Dist. Ct. App. 1989); Gattorna v. American States Ins. Co., 461 N.E.2d 675 (Ill. App. Ct. 1984); but see Federal Ins. Co. v. Plaza Drugs, Inc., 333 F. Supp. 1305 (D.C.D.C. 1971) (settling wrongdoer can enforce release against insurer, even though wrongdoer knew of insurer's "interest," because insurer, not having paid the loss, had no "right" of which wrongdoer should have been aware).

[64] See Aetna Cas. & Sur. Co. v. Westinghouse Elec. Co., 327 S.E.2d 3990 (Ga. Ct. App. 1985).

[65] E.g., Sentry Ins. Co. v. Stuart, 439 S.W.2d 797 (Ark. 1969); Farm Bur. Mut. Ins. Co. v. Anderson, 360 S.W.2d 314 (Mo. Ct. App. 1962).

once to the insurer pursuant to the exercise of the subrogation right.[66] This is not unreasonable if one assumes that the tortfeasor, by attempting to secure a release with knowledge of the existence of insurance, is attempting to work a fraud upon the insurer. Also, although this possibility is remote, the insured may end up with a windfall if the insurer for some reason chooses not to pursue subrogation by virtue of receipt of proceeds from the insurer and consideration for the release paid by the tortfeasor (assuming, which may not be the case, that the sum total of proceeds exceeds the amount of the insured's loss).

Determining whether the third party knew of the insured's insurance when settling with the insured can present a difficult question. If the third party receives a letter or some other communication from the insurer, it is clear that the third party received sufficient notice of the existence of insurance.[67] Also, if litigation to enforce the insurer's subrogation claim is pending at the time of the settlement, it is fair to say that the tortfeasor had notice of the insurer's interest.[68] In a situation in which after an automobile accident the tortfeasor failed to inquire into the existence of the insured's collision insurance and the collision insurer failed to notify the tortfeasor of its interest, one court held that the insurer could not assert a subrogation right.[69]

[4] Summary

The sum total of the foregoing rules indicates that insureds should not release tortfeasors or other third parties with a relationship to the loss (e.g., mortgagors) without the insurer's express consent. Moreover, insureds should be cautious about giving any sort of release to a third party who might be expected to cause the insured a loss sometime in the future.

Although this does not justify an insured in proceeding without appropriate caution when giving releases, the insured's release of the tortfeasor will not terminate the insured's coverage if the insurer would not have had a subrogation right anyway. This situation may arise if the tortfeasor is also the insurer's insured, against whom the insurer would have no subrogation right in any event. In these circumstances, the insured cannot interfere with a subrogation right if the insurer never had such a right. Under similar reasoning, if the insured can show that the third party is judgment proof or that the insurer is estopped from denying coverage for some reason, the insured's release of the third party will not invalidate the coverage.[70]

In the same vein, an insured may be protected from the coverage-ending consequences of a release if under ordinary contract principles the release can be

---

[66] See Home Ins. Co. v. Hertz Corp., 375 N.E.2d 115 (Ill. 1978).

[67] See, e.g., Neuss, Hesslein & Co., Inc. v. 380 Canal St. Realty Corp., 168 N.Y.S.2d 579 (N.Y. Sup. Ct. 1957), *appeal dismissed,* 217 N.Y.S.2d 1017 (N.Y. App. 1961).

[68] See Miller v. Auto-Owners Ins. Co., 392 So. 2d 1201 (ALa. Ct. App. 1981).

[69] See Aetna Cas. & Sur. Co. v. Norwalk Foods, Inc., 480 N.Y.S.2d 851 (N.Y. App. Div. 1984).

[70] See, e.g., Courson v. Maryland Cas. Co., 475 F.2d 1030 (8th Cir. 1973) (insured asked for insurer's participation in releasing tortfeasor, insurer ignored insured, and insured was led to believe insurer had no objection to the release); Thiringer v. American Motors Ins. Co., 588 P.2d 191 (Wash. 1978) (third party judgment proof); Southeastern Fid. Ins. Co. v. Earnest, 395 So. 2d 230 (Fla. Dist. Ct. App. 1981) (third party judgment proof).

interpreted narrowly so as not to constitute an interference with subrogation rights.[71] Where the release contains an explicit reservation of the insurer's right to assert claims against the third party to the extent of payments made to the insured, no interference with a subrogation right has occurred.[72] This latter device is useful if the insured receives payment from the third party for a portion of the loss for which the insured will not be reimbursed by the insurer. The insured may wish to release the third party for that portion of the loss, but not the portion that the insurer will reimburse. Nothing proscribes such an arrangement; the insurer's subrogation rights are not impaired, and the insured's coverage should not be forfeited.

[h]   Parties in Interest

In all jurisdictions, the proper plaintiff in a lawsuit must be the "real party in interest."[73] If the real party in interest is not the plaintiff, the defendant can obtain a stay of the proceedings until the real party in interest is substituted as the party plaintiff. As a general rule, the real party in interest on a claim is the party who owns the claim, meaning the party who has the right to bring and control the action to enforce it.[74] If the claim is assigned to another party, that other party becomes the real party in interest. When an insurer reimburses the insured in full or in part for a loss and the insurer is subrogated to some or all of the insured's rights, a question sometimes arises regarding who is the real party in interest for the purpose of asserting the claims against a third party.[75]

Generally, when an insurer fully compensates the insured for the loss and the insurer obtains the insured's claim against a third party either by contract or pursuant to equitable subrogation, the insurer is the real party in interest and must prosecute the claim in its own name. In some states, this result is mandated by a rule of civil procedure,[76] and in some jurisdictions the rule is articulated by judicial decision.[77]

---

[71] See Record v. Royal Globe Ins. Co., 443 N.Y.S.2d 755 (N.Y. App. Div. 1981).

[72] See Holbert v. Safe Ins. Co., 171 S.E. 422 (W.Va. 1933); Connecticut Fire Ins. Co. v. Erie R.R. Co., 73 N.Y. 399 (1878).

[73] In the federal courts and in most states, a formally-stated real-party-in-interest rule exists. See Fed. R. Civ .P. 17(a) ("Every action shall be prosecuted in the name of the real party in interest.") Many states follow the quoted language of the federal rule verbatim. See, e.g., Ala. R. Civ. P. 17(a); Miss. R. Civ. P. 17(a); Mass. R. Civ. P. 17(a); Tenn. R. Civ. P. 17.01. In the absence of a formal real-party-in-interest rule, the same effect results from the requirements that a plaintiff must be able to state a claim for relief and that the plaintiff may not prosecute the suit under a fictitious name. See June F. Entman, *More Reasons for Abolishing Federal Rule of Civil Procedure 17(a): The Problem of the Proper Plaintiff and Insurance Subrogation,* 68 N. Car. L. Rev. 893, 894 n.4, 950-51 (1990) (hereafter "Entman I.")

[74] See Entman I, *supra* note 73, at 900.

[75] For a detailed analysis of the procedural rules relevant to this issue, see generally Entman I, *supra* note 73. See also Annot., *Proper Party Plaintiff, Under Real Party In Interest Statute, To Action Against Tortfeasor For Damage To Insured Property Where Insured Has Paid Part of Loss,* 13 A.L.R.3d 140 (1967).

[76] See, e.g., Ala. R. Civ. P. 17(a) ("In subrogation cases, regardless of whether subrogation has occurred by operation of law, assignment, loan receipt, or otherwise, if the subrogor no longer has a pecuniary interest in the claim, the action shall be brought in the name of the

A few courts, however, have ruled that the action must be brought in the insured's name, under the reasoning that the insured's tort action could not be assigned or the real-party-in-interest rule did not change the common law rule that the insurer's subrogation rights must be enforced in the insured's name.[78] Moreover, some states have enacted procedural rules that allow the insurer to bring an action in the insured's name even when the insurer has paid all of the insured's loss.[79] Similarly, some workers' compensation statutes permit the insurer to bring suit in the insured's name even though the insurer controls the lawsuit.[80]

When the insurer pays a portion of the insured's loss and thereby succeeds to a portion of the claim, the issue is much more complicated.[81] In this situation, the insured still has a claim and thus is a real party in interest. The insurer has no right to control the action against the responsible third-party, unless this right is given the insurer by the insurance policy or a subsequent agreement between insurer and insured. Thus, the insurer should be viewed as having a beneficial interest in the insured's claim; the insurer does not have a subrogation right because the insured's loss has not been paid in full, but the insurer has a right to reimbursement should the insured recover a sum which, when combined with the prior payment of insurance proceeds, exceeds the loss. As the holder of a beneficial interest only, the insurer should not be considered, by this reasoning, the real party in interest. A widespread view, however, is that the insured and insurer are both real parties in interest,[82] although this view has been substantially criticized.[83] Under the

---

subrogee. If the subrogor still has a pecuniary interest in the claim, the action shall be brought in the names of the subrogor and the subrogee."); Ill. St. ch 735, § 5/2-403(c) ("Any action hereafter brought by virtue of the subrogation provision of any contract or by virtue of subrogation by operation of law shall be brought either in the name or for the use of the subrogee."); Miss. R. Civ. P. 17(b) (language identical to Alabama rule).

[77] See, e.g., United States v. Aetna Cas. & Sur. Co., 338 U.S. 366, 380-81 (1949); Dondlinger & Sons' Constr. Co., Inc. v. Emcco, Inc., 606 P.2d 1026 (Kan. 1980); Connor v. Thompson Constr. & Dev. Co., 166 N.W.2d 109 (Iowa 1969); Newby v. Johnston's Fuel Liners, Inc., 122 N.W.2d 156 (N.D. 1963); Louisville & N.R. Co. v. Mack Mfg. Corp., 269 S.W.2d 707 (Ky. 1954); Muskogee Title Co. v. First Nat'l Bank & Trust Co. of Muskogee, 894 P.2d 1148 (Okla. Ct. App. 1995). See generally Charles A. Wright, Arthur R. Miller, & Mary Kay Kane, 6A *Federal Practice and Procedure* § 1546 (1990).

[78] For further discussion, see generally Annot., *Proper Party Plaintiff, Under Real Party In Interest Statute, To Action Against Tortfeasor For Damage To Insured Property Where Loss Is Entirely Covered By Insurance*, 13 A.L.R.3d 229 (1967).

[79] See, e.g., Mass. R. Civ. P. 17(a) ("An insurer who has paid all or part of a loss may sue in the name of the assured to whose rights it is subrogated."); Ind. R. Civ. P. 19(e)(3); Tenn. R. Civ. P. 17.01 (committee comment states that rule "authorizes suit by a party in his own name even though another has been subrogated to the right which the party seeks to enforce"); See Entman I at 912 n. 111.

[80] *Id.*

[81] See Entman I at 912.

[82] United States v. Aetna Cas. & Sur. Co., 338 U.S. 366, 380-81 (1949) ("If [the insurer] has paid only part of the loss, both the insured and insurer (and other insurers, if any, who have also paid portions of the loss) have substantive rights against the tortfeasor which qualify them as real parties in interest."); Liberty Mut. Ins. Co. v. National Consol. Warehouses, Inc., 609 N.E.2d 1243 (Mass.App.Ct. 1993) (in partial reimbursement situation, both insured and

prevailing view, at a minimum the insured can prosecute an action in his or her own name against the tortfeasor.[84] Whether the tortfeasor can compel joinder of the insurer depends on the particular jurisdiction, and the results are diverse.[85]

Finally, the impact of the real party in interest rules has been reduced by the 'loan receipt.'' This arrangement is discussed in detail in the next section.[86] Sometimes, however, courts do not give effect to such devices, and the real party in interest rules remain important.

To summarize, if an insurer has paid the insured's loss in full, in most jurisdictions the insurer is the only real party in interest and as a subrogee must pursue the responsible third-party in its own name. However, in some states, the insurer who has paid the insured's loss in full may nevertheless bring the action in the insured's name. If the insured's loss is not paid in full, the claim is split between insurer and insured; each state's law specifies (or should specify) who is the real party in interest in that situation. The prevailing view is that both parties have the status as real parties in interest, but some jurisdictions vest only one party, either the insurer or insured, with the right to sue.

Declaring (either by procedural rule or judicial decision) that an action against the responsible third party shall be brought in the insured's name when the insured has been reimbursed in full makes little sense. Such an insured no longer has even a beneficial interest in the claim, and the insurer, after paying the loss, owns the claim and has a right to control the action in its status as a subrogee. But that such an approach is favored in some jurisdictions is not particularly surprising; insurers are very reluctant to appear as named plaintiffs in litigation, and the rules in some jurisdictions are sympathetic to their concerns.[87]

[i] Loan Receipts

A loan receipt is an arrangement under which the insurer advances or "loans" to the insured the amount of loss up to the limits of the policy. The loan is repayable only if and to the extent the insured recovers a judgment from the party who caused the loss in excess of the amount necessary to indemnify the insured. As part of the

---

insurer are real parties in interest, with insurer as subrogee to extent of its payment); Balboa Ins. Co. v. Pixler Elec. of Spencer, Iowa, Inc., 484 N.W.2d 396 (Iowa Ct.App. 1992); 3A J. Moore & J. Lucas, *Moore's Federal Practice* ¶ 17.12 (2d ed. 1994).

[83] See Entman I at 912-31. See also Fashion Tanning Co., Inc. v. Fulton Cty. Elec. Contractors, Inc., 536 N.Y.S.2d 866 (N.Y. App. Div. 1989) (fire insurer was not real party in interest because insured received only partial recovery).

[84] See, e.g., Farm Bur. Ins. Co. v. Case Corp., 878 S.W.2d 741 (Ark. 1994) ("The general rule is that where an insurance company has only partially reimbursed an insured for his loss, the insured is the real party in interest and can maintain the action in his own name for the complete amount of his loss."); Western Motor Co., Inc. v. Koehn, 738 P.2d 466 (Kan.Ct.App. 1987), *aff'd,* 748 P.2d 851 (Kan. 1988).

[85] For a detailed discussion of this question, see June F. Entman, *Compulsory Joinder of Compensating Insurers: Federal Rule of Civil Procedure 19 and the Role of Substantive Law,* 45 Case W. L. Rev. 1 (1994) (hereafter "Entman II.")

[86] See § 96[i], *infra.*

[87] See generally Entman I, *supra* note 73; Entman II, *supra* note 85.

agreement, the insured promises to sue the third party, so that a fund might be recovered out of which the insurer is repaid. If the insured fails to sue the third party, the insured commits a breach of its loan receipt contract with the insurer. As contract damages, the insurer would recover the sum loaned the insured.[88]

Loan receipts emerged in the shipper-carrier commercial setting. If the shipper's goods were damaged due to the carrier's act or neglect, the shipper's insurer would loan the shipper a sum of money equal to the amount of property loss suffered, subject to being repaid out of any sum that the shipper recovered from the carrier. The United States Supreme Court approved the practice in an early case, calling it a means of obtaining "prompt settlement for loss (which is essential to actual indemnity and demanded in the interest of commerce)."[89]

As the Supreme Court's observation indicates, one of the purposes of a loan receipt is facilitating prompt payment of proceeds to the insured. However, the insurer also gets a substantial benefit: avoiding jury prejudice in its action against the tortfeasor as subrogee on the insured's claim. The insurer avoids the need to seek subrogation against the third-party tortfeasor, an action which the insurer is usually required to bring in its own name. The tort action is brought by the insured in its own name, and it is the insured who appears before the jury, not the insurer.[90]

Only brief reflection is necessary to understand that the loan receipt is a legal fiction. The insurer's objective is to avoid appearing before the jury, and this is accomplished through an arrangement which purports not to constitute "payment" to the insured, although that is what the loan really is. The reasoning underlying this fiction is that if the insurer has not "paid" the insured's loss and has instead merely loaned the insured money, the insurer has no subrogation right. If the insurer has no subrogation right, it cannot in the status of a subrogee sue the wrongdoer.

---

[88] See generally John W. Thornton & William A. Wick, *Loan Receipt Agreements: Are They Loans, Settlements, Wagering Contracts, or Unholy Alliances?*, 43 Ins. Counsel J. 226 (1976); Entman I, *supra* note 73, at 925-31.

[89] Luckenbach v. McCahan Sugar Ref. Co., 248 U.S. 139, 146 (1918). The loan receipt was originally developed to address the prompt payment issue noted above and not as a mechanism by which the insurer could avoid bringing a suit in its own name. In the late 19th century, carriers began to insert clauses in their contracts with shippers which released the carrier from liability upon the shipper's insurer paying the shipper for its loss. This release quashed any subrogation right that the insurer might wish to assert against the carrier after paying the claim. Insurers responded by inserting clauses in their policies providing that an insurer would have no obligation until the shipper's liability was decided in court. This arrangement delayed compensation to the insured-shipper, which was not the result insurers desired; insurers simply wanted to be able to compensate shippers without losing subrogation rights. The loan receipt developed to accommodate prompt payment while preserving the possibility of subrogation. See E. Michael Johnson, Note, *The Real Party Under Rule 17(A): The Loan Receipt and Insurers' Subrogation Revisited*, 74 Minn. L. Rev. 1107, 1113-18 (1990).

[90] See C & C Tile Co. v. Independent School Dist., 503 P.2d 554 (Okla. 1972); but see Executive Jet Aviation, Inc. v. United States, 507 F.2d 508 (6th Cir. 1974) (loan receipt arrangement constituted payment; insurers were subrogated to insured's claims and were real parties in interest under Fed. R. Civ. P. 17(a)).

Yet as a condition to the loan the insurer requires the insured to sue the tortfeasor. Indeed, the insurer will typically pay the costs of the insured's action against the wrongdoer. If the insured prevails in the action against the tortfeasor, the "loan" must be repaid; but if the insured recovers nothing against the tortfeasor, the loan need not be repaid. When stripped of the fiction, a loan receipt involves the insured asserting the rights that otherwise would belong to the insurer pursuant to the subrogation doctrine.

In many jurisdictions, loan receipts are honored.[91] According to these courts, the fact that the full amount of the claim is paid under a loan receipt does not mean that the insurer is making "payment" to the insured for the insured's loss.[92] Some jurisdictions, however, refuse to give effect to a loan receipt agreement according to its terms. These courts have held that the transaction constitutes a payment under which the insurer is subrogated to the claim of the insured. This means that the real party in interest is the insurer, not the insured, and if the insured brings the suit against the wrongdoer, the wrongdoer might secure the action's dismissal on the ground that the wrong party in interest has brought the suit.[93]

In jurisdictions where courts are not disposed to enforce loan receipt agreements, two situations exist where the loan receipt might be enforced. First, if the insurer's liability to the insured is uncertain, such as is the case if coverage is in doubt or the insurer's liability is not absolute, some courts hold that the insured — even if fully compensated for the loss — is the real party in interest, not the insurer. The rationale is that money advanced by the insurer in that instance is actually a loan, since the insurer's obligation to pay proceeds is not definite. However, if the insurer's obligation is absolute, the loan receipt would be deemed a subterfuge for the payment.[94] Second, if the insurer only partially compensates the insured via the loan receipt, the insured still has an interest in the claim. This makes the insured the real party in interest, suing on his or her own behalf and the insurer's behalf as well.[95]

Both sides in the debate over the validity of loan receipts are presented in *City Stores Co. v. Lerner Stores,*[96] a 1969 decision of the District of Columbia Circuit.

---

[91] See, e.g., Frank Briscoe Co. v. Georgia Sprinkler Co., 713 F.2d 1500 (11th Cir. 1983); Blasser Bros, Inc. v. Northern Pan-Am Line, 628 F.2d 376 (5th Cir. 1980); Bohna v. Hughes, Thorsness, Gantz, Powell & Brundin, 828 P.2d 745 (Alaska 1992); Hammond v. Nebraska Nat'l Gas Co., 309 N.W.2d 75 (Neb. 1981); Todd v. Ratcliffe, 603 S.W.2d 925 (Ky. 1980).

[92] See Central Nat'l Ins Co. v. Dixon, 559 P.2d 1187 (Nev. 1977); Hanover Ins. Co. v. State Farm Ins. Co., 235 S.E.2d 639 (Ga. Ct. App. 1977).

[93] See, e.g., City Stores Co. v. Lerner Shops, Inc., 410 F.2d 1010 (D.C. Cir. 1969); McNeil Constr. Co. v. Livingston State Bank, 185 F. Supp. 197 (D. Mont. 1960), aff'd, 300 F.2d 88 (9th Cir. 1962); Kopperud v. Chick, 135 N.W.2d 335 (Wis. 1965). See generally E. Michael Johnson, Note, *The Real Party Under Rule 17(A): The Loan Receipt and Insurers' Subrogation Revisited,* 74 Minn. L. Rev. 1107 (1990) (arguing that loan receipts should in most cases be deemed invalid as devices to avoid joinder under F.R.C.P. 17(a)).

[94] See City Stores Co. v. Lerner Shops, Inc., 410 F.2d 1010 (D.C. Cir. 1969); Duboise v. State Farm Mut. Auto Ins. Co., 619 P.2d 1223 (Nev. 1980); Lusk v. State Farm Mut. Auto Ins. Co., 569 P.2d 985 (Okla. 1977).

[95] See § 96[h], *supra.*

[96] 410 F.2d 1010 (D.C. Cir. 1969).

Defendant at the trial level lost its motion to join the insurers as real parties in interest under Rule 17(a) of the Federal Rules of Civil Procedure; the trial court did not agree with defendant that the loan receipts given by the insurers to the plaintiffs-insureds had the legal effect of subrogating the insurers to the rights of the plaintiffs, thereby requiring the insurer to join the proceeding as a party-plaintiff. The Court of Appeals, however, agreed with the defendant and reversed the trial court:

> [T]he loan agreement . . . is not an unconditional promise to pay at a time certain, and does not provide for interest. It can be more accurately described as a complete surrender to the insurer of the insured's right of action against third parties. By executing such a document, the insured simply sells to the insurance company the right to use the insured's name as party plaintiff in a suit brought against a third party which is to be exclusively directed and controlled by the insurer at its expense and for its benefit. The only consideration to the insured for such a sale is that perhaps the settlement will be received a bit earlier than if the insured had not executed the loan agreement.
>
> . . . . [W]hen an insurer whose liability is absolute settles a claim by the loan agreement method, it is subrogated to the rights of the insured and so is the real party in interest in a suit against a third party.[97]

Then-Circuit Judge Burger dissented to the majority's holding:

> The defendant in this action for damages would prefer to have the jurors know that the contest was between an insurance company and the defendant store rather than between two private litigants. And of course this is why the insurer for its interests wants to keep "out of sight." I can see no compelling reason of public policy or of common sense for failing to give effect to the agreements of the parties. It seems to me that there may well be some public policy served in having the triers decide the issues uninfluenced by the circumstance that "a large insurance company" will pay the bill.
>
> . . . [the defendant's motive in being] sued by an insurance company so that a jury verdict might be moderated by the realization that the injured plaintiff has coverage for his losses . . . seems hardly more worthy than the insurer's motive in suing in the insured's name so that its recovery will not be improperly minimized when the jury takes cognizance of the fact that an insurance company is suing to recover the losses in question.[98]

The judges' discussion of the parties' motives in *City Stores* is particularly interesting. The defendant desired to have the fact that an insurer was asserting a subrogation claim known by the jury; that would tend to minimize the jury verdict, since jurors are presumably less likely to award damages if they know the plaintiff's loss is covered by first-party insurance. Yet the defendant, whose liability was probably insured under a policy of third-party coverage, did not wish the fact that it possessed insurance coverage to be known by the jury, which then might be inclined, based on the knowledge that the insurer would pay the judgment instead of the defendant, to award a large judgment to the plaintiff. The plaintiff might ask:

[97] 410 F.2d at 1015.

[98] *Id.*

why should my insurer have to go public, but the defendant's insurer not? This raises the more general question of whether public policy is served by keeping the fact of insurance secret from the jury, a highly controversial topic.

Loan receipt agreements are even more controversial in the joint tortfeasor setting.[99] Consider, for example, the situation where a guest at a swimming pool party at someone's home is injured when the diving board attached to the pool breaks. The guest's lawsuit would probably name at least five defendants: the home owner, the manufacturer of the swimming pool, the manufacturer of the diving board component, the installer of the board and pool, and the seller of the swimming pool (including the board). Suppose that the seller of the pool (and its insurer) gives the injured guest an interest-free loan in exchange for the injured guest's covenant not to sue, the guest's promise to repay the loan out of the proceeds of any judgment or settlement obtained from the other defendants, and the guest's promise to release the seller at the end of the litigation.

The obvious difficulty is that the seller of the pool (and its insurer) now has interests that overlap with those of the injured guest. If the guest prevails in the suit against the other defendants, the seller of the pool (and its insurer) will recoup its loan to the guest. Thus, testimony extremely helpful to the guest's lawsuit should be expected from the seller of the pool. The potential unfairness is magnified if one imagines all the defendants except one entering into such an agreement with the guest; all of the defendants with such an agreement would, along with the plaintiff, try to pin the liability on the other remaining defendant. In essence, the fairness of the litigation process is compromised if a defendant remains in the suit (and, perhaps, participates as a witness) without the jury knowing the defendant's true interests. Thus, many courts have held that a loan receipt agreement between a plaintiff and a joint tortfeasor in exchange for a forbearance to sue is an absolute payment and not a loan. Thus, sums received from the defendants entering into the loan receipts constitute payments contributing toward any judgment obtained against the remaining defendants, which the loan receipt defendants may not recoup.[100]

The refusal of some courts to enforce loan receipts in the joint tortfeasor context is sensible. First, the joint tortfeasor situation differs substantially from the use of loan receipts in the first-party situation, where the first-party insurer seeks to reimburse the insured in a prompt fashion and to avoid bringing a subrogation suit in its own name. The contractual relationship between the insurer and the other party to the loan receipt existed prior to the tort which damaged the insured's property. In the joint tortfeasor situation, there is no prior contractual relationship between the parties to the loan receipt agreement. Instead, what happens is that the defendants

[99] A loan receipt issued in the liability insurance situation for the purposes discussed below is a particular kind of "Mary Carter agreement." For additional discussion, see June F. Entman, *Mary Carter Agreements: An Assessment of Attempted Solutions*, 38 U. Fla. L. Rev. 521 (1986); Alan D. Windt, 2 *Insurance Claims and Disputes*, §§ 10.17-10.20, at 164–71 (3d ed. 1995).

[100] See e.g., Dosdourian v. Carsten, 624 So. 2d 241 (Fla. 1993); Elbaor v. Smith, 845 S.W.2d 240 (Tex. 1992); American Chain & Cable Co., Inc. v. Brunson, 278 S.E.2d 719 (Ga. Ct. App. 1981).

who issue the loan receipt acquire, without any preexisting contractual relationship, an interest in the plaintiff's claim against the other insureds. This is essentially an assignment of the injured party's personal injury claim to other parties, which the law does not permit. Moreover, in the joint tortfeasor situation, one wrongdoer may receive reimbursement from another wrongdoer even though the substantive law would not allow that reimbursement. This may encourage multiple litigation, since the paying insurer may then seek indemnification or contribution from the lending insurer,[101] and if contribution is not allowed, the law's interest in an equitable distribution of the liability may be frustrated. Despite these problems, some courts nevertheless uphold loan receipts in the joint tortfeasor situation. These courts believe that private settlement of lawsuits should be favored and that insurers should be encouraged to voluntarily pay proceeds to injured victims, and they view loan receipts as a way to help further these objectives.[102]

Another potentially problematic use of the loan receipt is in the situation where the insured has two or more policies, but not all the insurers agree to pay. One insurer may enter into a loan receipt agreement with the insured, under which the insurer advances all or part of the money necessary to reimburse the insured. The money advanced is a loan, repayable out of proceeds obtained in a suit by the insured against the nonpaying insurer. This arrangement eliminates the need for the lender-insurer to bring a suit against the nonpaying insurer to obtain the proceeds; instead, the lender-insurer can rely on the insured to press the claim. If the result is to force the defendant insurer to contribute to part of the loss, the procedure is a reasonable one. If, however, the result is to force the nonpaying insurer to pay the entire loss and to allow the lending insurer to escape liability, the result is not fair.[103]

§ 97   Other Insurance Clauses

[a]   Overview

Because so many different kinds of insurance coverage exist and because so many different parties to a particular transaction or event are likely to have insurance, overlapping coverage is fairly common. To reduce or eliminate the liability of the insurer where the insured possesses other coverage of the same risk, almost all property, liability, and health policies, and many accident policies have "other insurance" clauses.[1] These clauses attempt to prioritize or coordinate the coverage of two or more applicable policies.

---

[101] See Transport Indem. Co. v. BB&S, Inc., 664 P.2d 1115 (Or. Ct. App. 1983).

[102] See, e.g., Bahna v. Hughes, Thorsness, Gantz, Powell & Brundin, 828 P.2d 745 (Alaska 1992); Reese v. Chicago, Burlington & Quincy Ry. Co., 303 N.E.2d 382 (Ill. 1973).

[103] Compare Sanders v. Liberty Mut. Ins. Co., 354 F.2d 777 (5th Cir. 1965) (allowing lender-insurer to sue another insurer through lawsuit brought in name of insured); O'Howell v. Continental Ins. Co., 654 S.W.2d 308 (Mo. Ct. App. 1983), with American Dredging Co. v. Federal Ins. Co., 309 F. Supp. 425 (S.D. N.Y. 1970) (disallowing loan receipt device in this setting).

[1] For a more detailed discussion of the economic and risk-distributional functions of other insurance clauses, see Kenneth S. Abraham, *Distributing Risk: Insurance, Legal Theory, and*

One of the primary purposes of other insurance clauses is to address the risk of moral hazard that accompanies multiple coverages which, in combination, exceed the value of interest insured. Nothing commends giving windfalls for losses, and other insurance clauses seek to reduce this possibility. In property insurance in particular, a moral hazard is created if there is a chance of recovery exceeding the value of the property, and limiting the insured to one recovery in the event of loss reduces this hazard. In all kinds of insurance, insurers should be able to offer premium reductions if a policy's coverage is coordinated with the coverage of other policies.

As for liability insurance, an insured whose negligence has exposed himself or herself to a massive judgment may desire to "stack" all possible liability coverages so as to minimize the insured's personal responsibility for a portion of the judgment. Other insurance clauses may well prevent this, although this is arguably not unfair to the insured who could have obtained additional protection by purchasing a policy with a higher limit. One should not, however, overlook the interests of the third-party who was injured by the insured's negligence; to the extent other insurance clauses operate to prevent the insured from stacking multiple liability coverages, the third-party victim has fewer sources of recovery. But even this may not be unfair; if the victim had been concerned about being injured by uninsured or underinsured tortfeasors, the victim should have purchased more first-party insurance to cover the kinds of losses in question.

[b] Other Insurance Clauses in Personal Insurance

Life insurance policies, unlike the kinds of policies noted above, do not contain other insurance clauses. This is because life insurance is not indemnity insurance. Property insurance, for example, is designed to indemnify the insured for the loss of specified property. Under the principle of indemnity, the insured's recovery should not exceed the loss; if an insured profits from a loss, an incentive to destruction of the property exists, and other insureds will pay the costs associated with allowing a few insureds to profit. Life insurance, although it has some indemnity aspects (such as reimbursing the beneficiaries for the loss of income caused by the insured's death), is not indemnity insurance in the strictest sense. In most cases, no effort is made to place a value on the insured's life; an individual can purchase an unlimited amount of insurance on his or her own life. No public policy reason exists to limit the beneficiaries' recovery simply because other insurance exists.

In health insurance, unlike life insurance, other insurance clauses are widely used. Other insurance clauses in health policies are usually called "coordination-of-benefits" clauses. These clauses have sometimes been attacked on public policy grounds, but the clauses have usually been enforced. One argument against such

---

Public Policy 136–47 (1986). For more general discussion of the other insurance problem, see Douglas R. Richmond, *Issues and Problems in "Other Insurance," Multiple Insurance, and Self-Insurance,* 22 Pepperdine L. Rev. 1373 (1995); Barry R. Ostrager & Thomas R. Newman, *Handbook on Insurance Coverage Disputes* § 11.01 et seq. (7th ed. 1994); Thomas B. Alleman, *Resolving the "Other Insurance" Dilemma: Ordering Disputes Among Primary and Excess Policies,* 30 Kan. L. Rev. 75 (1981).

clauses is that because they relieve the insurer from liability if other insurance exists, they discourage insureds from purchasing specialized additional coverage, since the amount of benefits of the additional policies would be credited against the amount paid under the primary policy. Insurers specializing in coverage for specific diseases, for example, have charged insurers issuing comprehensive policies containing coordination of benefits clauses with restraint of trade, but the Fifth Circuit specifically rejected such a challenge, noting that the coordination of benefits clause reduces the cost of broad-risk coverage and otherwise constitutes lawful competition.[2]

In other situations, insureds have argued that coordination of benefits clauses in health insurance policies should not be enforced due to their impact on the coverage purportedly provided by the policy. In *Cody v. Connecticut General Life Insurance Co.,*[3] the insured purchased a policy of disability insurance and was surprised to discover, upon becoming disabled, that his payments under the policy were reduced to nothing due to amounts he received from Social Security and workers' compensation. The trial court's judgment for the insurer was affirmed:

> [A] court should find that an insurance contract like that at issue in this case has substantial economic value as long as the premiums reflect the anticipated effect of any coordination-of-benefits clause. . . . we note that coordination-of-benefits clauses serve the public purpose of avoiding duplicate recoveries for the same injuries. . . . These clauses enable insurance companies to charge lower premiums. . . . We therefore conclude that unless the company engaged in misleading marketing practices, or the insurance contract as a whole is without substantial economic value, coordination-of-benefits clauses do not violate the public policy of this Commonwealth.[4]

This was no doubt of little comfort to the insured, who throughout the life of the policy had apparently been paying premiums for nothing. The contract may have had value to the group of insureds covered by it, but the contract had no value to this particular insured. The court left open the possibility — for future cases only — that insureds like the plaintiff in *Cody* might be able to invalidate the coordination of benefits clauses due to defects in the process of contract formation. *Cody* illustrates the lengths to which some courts go to achieve the cost-reducing benefits of other insurance clauses.

[c]   Types of Other Insurance Clauses

There are many kinds of other insurance clauses, but they divide into three basic categories: pro rata, excess, and escape.

The *pro rata* clause is the most common kind of clause in use today. Pro rata clauses declare that the insurer's liability shall be limited to a proportion of the loss not exceeding its proportion of the total insurance coverage. A common formulation states as follows: "If a loss covered by this policy is also covered by other insurance,

---

[2] See American Family Life Assur. Co. v. Blue Cross of Fla., Inc., 486 F.2d 225 (5th Cir. 1973), *cert. denied,* 416 U.S. 905 (1974).

[3] 439 N.E.2d 234 (Mass. 1982).

[4] 439 N.E.2d at 239; see also Milldrum v. Travelers Indem. Co., 688 S.W.2d 271 (Ark. 1985).

we will pay only the proportion of the loss that the limit of liability that applies under this policy bears to the total amount of insurance covering the loss."[5]

To illustrate the effect of a pro rata clause, suppose the insured has a hobby workshop in a garage detached from the insured's house. The workshop is insured against fire loss under the insured's homeowner's policy issued by Insurer X with limits of $20,000 for detached buildings, a special fire insurance policy with limits of $30,000 issued by Insurer Y, and a hobby workshop property policy with limits of $50,000 sold by Insurer Z through an association of woodcrafters. Each policy has a pro rata clause; assume that the policies have no deductibles or coinsurance clauses. If the workshop is damaged by fire to the extent of $40,000, the homeowner's policy (Insurer X) pays 20% of the loss (since the policy is 20% of the combined limits of $100,000), or $8,000; the fire insurance policy (Insurer Y) pays 30% of the loss, or $12,000; and the hobby workshop policy (Insurer Z) pays 50% of the loss, or $20,000.

The foregoing example illustrates how other insurance clauses reduce moral hazard. Perhaps the insured thought that by purchasing three policies a triple recovery would result in the event of loss. However, the other insurance clauses operate to limit the insured to one recovery for the loss, even though three premiums have been paid for overlapping coverage. The example also illustrates how other insurance clauses work to spread loss among insurers. When multiple coverages exist, no one insurer — at least in this example involving pro rata clauses — bears all of the risk. Other insurance clauses have the effect of diffusing to some extent risk over a broader range of insurers.

Another kind of other insurance clause is the *excess* other insurance clause. Such clauses provide that the insurer shall reimburse only the loss exceeding the coverage of other valid and collectible insurance. A common formulation states as follows: "The Company shall not be liable for loss if at the time of loss, there is any other insurance which would attach if this insurance had not been effected, except that this insurance shall apply only as excess and in no event as contributing insurance, and then only after all other insurance has been exhausted."[6]

To illustrate, suppose in the foregoing example, the insured's homeowner's and fire insurance policies had pro rata clauses but the hobby workshop policy contained an excess clause. Since the homeowner's and fire insurance policies are valid, collectible coverages, the hobby workshop policy would be triggered only after the coverages of the first two policies are exhausted. Thus, for the $40,000 loss, the homeowner's policy would pay 40 percent of the loss ($20,000 is 40 percent of the $50,000 total policy limits available), or $16,000, and the fire insurance policy would pay 60 percent of the loss, or $24,000 ($30,000 is 60 percent of the $50,000 total policy limits). Since the limits of neither policy were exhausted, the hobby workshop policy would not be used to provide any coverage.

If, however, the damage to the hobbyshop had been $60,000, the $20,000 policy limits under the homeowner's and the $30,000 policy limits under the fire insurance

---

[5] *Policy Kit* at 28 (ISO Form HO 00 03 04 91).

[6] *Id.* at 28.

policy if paid in full would not be enough to indemnify the insured for the loss. At that point, the hobby workshop policy would be triggered, and the remaining $10,000 would be paid by Insurer Z. (Note that if all three policies contained a pro rata clause and the loss were $60,000, the hobby workshop policy would pay one-half the loss, or $30,000. In this hypothetical as well as the $40,000 loss hypothetical, the presence of an excess clause in the hobby workshop policy in a situation where the other policies were pro rata reduced Insurer Z's liability considerably.)

A third type of other insurance clause is the *escape* (or as it is sometimes called *void coverage*) clause. This kind of clause provides that the insurer shall have no liability if there is other valid and collectible insurance. This kind of clause is the least common of the three, but where it exists it might read as follows: "It is hereby agreed that if other insurance is written on the insured interest . . ., this Company will be notified of the amounts of such other insurance. . . . It is further agreed that unless or until so notified of such other insurance the coverage under this policy shall be suspended."[7]

To illustrate, suppose in any of the foregoing examples that the hobby workshop insurance policy contained an escape clause. The coverage under the policy would be void, whether or not the other policies were sufficient to indemnify the insured. Interestingly, if all of the policies contained escape clauses, the insured would have no coverage whatever. The potential for hardship for the insured who is unaware that purchasing a second policy will void the first policy is substantial. However, this rule is defended on the ground that the fact of additional insurance in many instances increases the risk of loss and the insurer should not be held accountable in such a situation. Of course, if the risk involved is one outside the insured's control, such as the risk of weather damage to crops, this argument in favor of the escape clause has no force. As one might expect, where escape clauses are used, the question of whether a second policy of insurance constitutes "other insurance" has been vigorously disputed.[8]

The precise wording of other insurance clauses vary considerably, but the legal effect is usually the same within each of the three broad categories. Also, it is not uncommon to find other insurance clauses that embrace elements of two or more categories. For example, the other insurance clause might state that the coverage is pro rata with respect to other insurance for a defined set of situations, but with respect to other situations, the insurance is excess.[9] The current version of the CGL

---

[7] See N.C. Grange Mut. Ins. Co. v. Johnson, 276 S.E.2d 469 (N.C. Ct. App.), *review granted,* 281 S.E.2d 652 (N.C. 1981), *review vacated,* 285 S.E.2d 812 (N.C. 1982). See generally Annot., *Validity and Construction of Automobile Insurance Provision or Statute Automatically Terminating Coverage When Insured Obtains Another Policy Providing Similar Coverage,* 61 A.L.R.4th 1130 (1987).

[8] See generally Annot., *What Constitutes "Other Insurance" Within Meaning Of Insurance Policy Provisions Prohibiting Insured From Obtaining Other Insurance On Same Property,* 7 A.L.R.4th 494 (1981).

[9] *See, e.g., Policy Kit* at 348 (ISO Form CA 00 01 12 93, Business Auto Form; coverage is primary for any covered auto insured owns, but coverage is excess for any covered auto insured does not own).

form has a "combination" other insurance clause. The CGL is excess with respect to specified kinds of other insurance; with regard to other kinds of insurance, the CGL "permits contribution by equal shares" if the other insurance policies use equal shares; if the other policies do not use equal shares, the CGL is a pro rata policy, with the pro rata contribution being calculated according to each policy's limits as a ratio of the sum of all policy limits of all applicable coverages.[10] Another formulation, which is common in uninsured motorist coverages, combines features of an excess clause with an escape clause: under this formulation, the insurer is liable for the amount of loss in excess of other available coverage, but the insurer is not liable when other available insurance has limits equal to or greater than its own.[11]

[d] Conflicts Among Other Insurance Clauses and Other Problems of Enforcement

Because the public policies favoring the use of other insurance clauses are important ones, other insurance clauses are enforceable. However, there are some situations where the clauses will not be enforced. Suppose that the insured has two policies, A and B, providing coverage at the same level, and Policy A purports to be excess over other "valid and collectible" insurance. If Policy B is not valid due to the insured's misrepresentation or because of the insurer's insolvency, the insured's recovery under Policy A should not be reduced. In other words, the insurer under Policy A must pay for the insured's entire loss up to the policy limits. Sometimes the clauses contain language making clear that invalidity or uncollectibility of other insurance will not reduce the coverage available under the policy in which the clause appears; for example, the policy might say that this coverage is excess over other "valid and collectible" insurance, which indicates that the policy is triggered if other policies on the risk are unenforceable.[12]

Most difficulties in enforcing other insurance clauses involve the problem of conflicting language in the clauses. When multiple insurance policies have conflicting other insurance clauses, substantial problems are created. If both policies have excess clauses, which coverage is primary and which is the excess? If one policy has a pro rata clause and the other an excess clause, is it proper to hold the policy with the pro rata clause responsible for the entire loss up to its policy limits? Or should the excess policy be required to contribute pro rata with the other policy?

---

[10] *Policy Kit* at 316-17 (ISO Form CG 00 01 10 93).

[11] Richmond, *supra* note 1, calls this an "excess escape" clause. In theory, this clause should function as an ordinary excess clause, but in circumstances where an excess clause squares off against an excess clause in another policy, most courts prorate the coverages, and the excess escape clause would give the court a basis to put the entire loss on the policy with the excess clause, and none of the policy with the excess escape clause. See Liberty Mut. Ins. Co. v. Harbor Ins. Co., 603 A.2d 300, 301 n.2 (R.I. 1992).

[12] See Reserve Ins. Co. v. Pisciotta, 640 P.2d 764 (Cal. 1982); Gilbert v. Travelers Indem. Co., 379 So. 2d 371 (Fla. Dist. Ct. App. 1979). If, however, the excess insurer is providing a secondary level of coverage, the excess insurer — absent an ambiguity in the policy — should not be obligated to drop to a primary level and provide coverage if the primary insurance is invalid or uncollectible. See Guaranty Nat'l Ins. Co. v. Bayside Resort, Inc., 635 F. Supp. 1456 (D.V.I. 1986); Radar v. Duke Transp. Inc., 492 So. 2d 532 (La. Ct. App. 1986). This argument was made by the excess insurer in *Pisciotta* and was rejected.

Legislatures sometimes sort out these problems by declaring a particular policy to be primary in a particular context. For example, a California statute [13] provides that where two or more policies provide valid, collectible liability insurance to the same motor vehicle, the insurance in which the vehicle is described or rated as an owned automobile is primary and other policies are excess. Moreover, it is not uncommon for statutes or administrative regulations to specify coordination-of-coverage provisions for health insurance.[14] Despite the legislative clarification, there are many areas where no statute speaks and the insurers continue to employ other insurance clauses without clarifying the relationship of conflicting clauses. If a statute or administrative regulation is not controlling, and if the other insurance clauses by their terms do not coordinate the coverage, and if the parties cannot otherwise settle their differences, the court must then reconcile the clauses in some manner. In one court's view, the judiciary is forced "into a game that ought not, and need not, be played."[15]

Generally speaking, several approaches to reconciling conflicts appear in the cases. One approach evaluates the age of the policies and declares that the older policy is primary.[16] This approach is of dubious merit; the more recent policy may have been purchased for a different reason or with a different risk in mind. The age of a policy may only coincidentally equate with the intentions of the parties regarding the nature of the coverage. Yet age may be informative on how policies are layered: a policy purchased first in time may have been intended as the policy to provide the primary coverage, with a subsequently-purchased policy providing a layer that is excess, above and beyond the first policy.

Another approach has been used in circumstances where the insured is a named insured under one policy but an additional insured under the other. This approach treats the policy on which the insured is the named insured as the primary policy, and treats policies where the insured is an additional insured as secondary.[17] The problem with this approach is its arbitrary nature: a policy which covers an insured as an additional insured (e.g., pursuant to an omnibus clause) intends to provide as full protection to the insured as if the insured were named. Yet this approach may make sense in health insurance; if the insured is covered as a named insured on her own policy but is covered as a dependent on her husband's policy, it arguably makes sense to make her own policy primary for her own health care needs, letting her husband's policy fill in the gaps.

---

[13] Cal. Ins. Code § 11580.9.

[14] See, e.g., Conn. Stat. § 38a-554 (directing insurance commissioner to promulgate regulations specifying coordination of coverage); Ky. Stat. § 304.18-085 (directing insurance commissioner to prescribe coordination of benefit guidelines for group health plans); Ariz. Admin. Code R20-6-217 (specifying order of benefit determination); Kan. Adm. Reg. 40-4-34 (mandated content of non-duplication of benefits provision).

[15] Schoenecker v. Haines, 277 N.W.2d 782, 786 (Wis. 1979).

[16] See Automobile Ins. Co. v. Springfield Dyeing Co., 109 F.2d 533 (3d Cir. 1940).

[17] See, e.g., Hartford Acc. & Indem. Co. v. Kellman, 375 So. 2d 26 (Fla. Dist. Ct. App. 1979); Employers Mut. Liab. Ins. Co. v. Pacific Indem. Co., 334 P.2d 658 (Cal. Ct. App. 1959).

Two approaches have particular prominence. One looks for semantic differences in the clauses and attempts to determine which policy provides primary coverage. Under this approach, the most "specific" policy will be primary, or the policy most clearly intended to provide coverage for the particular kind of risk will be primary.[18] This approach is often problematic due to the hair-splitting required when distinguishing among clauses, but in some situations the approach works effectively.

The other important approach declares the conflicting clauses mutually repugnant and unenforceable. This "knockout" approach leaves the general coverage of all the policies in force, requiring only that a formula to prorate the loss among the insurers be chosen. These two approaches are discussed in more detail in the discussions of specific conflicts which follow.

[1] Pro Rata Clause versus Excess (or Escape) Clause

The situation where two policies apply to a loss, and one contains a pro rata clause while the other contains an excess clause, is one of the most controversial conflicts in this area. The pro rata insurer argues that the loss should be prorated between the two valid, collectible policies. The excess insurer argues, however, that the pro rata insurer should bear the entire loss up to its policy limits because the excess coverage is not collectible until the policy limits of the pro rata insurer are exhausted. Most courts agree with the excess insurer, under the reasoning that the clauses can be interpreted and reconciled according to their terms. But a strong minority agrees with the pro rata insurer under the reasoning, which applies in other conflict situations as well, that inconsistent other insurance clauses are mutually repugnant and knock each other out, leaving some kind of pro rata approach as a "gap filler" for the missing policy term.

The debate is neatly summarized in the majority and dissenting opinions in *Jones v. Medox, Inc.*[19] a 1981 decision of the District of Columbia Court of Appeals sitting en banc. Plaintiff brought a lawsuit claiming injuries from medical malpractice in connection with an injection administered by a nurse. Defendants were the nurse, the hospital, and the nurse's employer, a corporation providing temporary medical personnel to local doctors and hospitals. The case was settled, with the insurers, as the representatives of all defendants, reserving their rights to litigate responsibility. The central dispute in the subsequent litigation was between the nurse's insurer and her employer's insurer. The nurse's policy contained a pro rata clause, while the employer's policy contained an excess clause.

The majority opinion in *Jones* held, in accord with the view of most courts,[20] that the policy with the pro rata clause provided primary coverage and the policy

---

[18] See, e.g., Caribou Four Corners, Inc. v. Truck Ins. Exch., 443 F.2d 796 (10th Cir. 1971); Auto Owners Ins. Co. v. Northstar Mut. Ins. Co., 281 N.W.2d 700 (Minn. 1979).

[19] 430 A.2d 488 (D.C. 1981) (en banc).

[20] See, e.g., P.L. Kanter Agency, Inc. v. Continental Cas. Co., 541 F.2d 519 (6th Cir. 1976); State Farm Mut. Auto. Ins. Co. v. American Cas. Co., 433 F.2d 1007 (8th Cir. 1970); St. Paul Fire & Marine Ins. co. v. American Home Assur. Co., 514 N.W.2d 113 (Mich. 1994); Royal Globe Ins. Co. v. Hartford Acc. & Indem. Co., 485 A.2d 242 (Me. 1984); Jones v. Medox, Inc., 430 A.2d 488 (D.C. 1981); Demshar v. AAACon Auto Transp., Inc., 337 So. 2d 963 (Fla. 1976); Safeco Ins. Co. v. Ins. Co. of N. Am., 522 S.W.2d 867 (Tenn. 1975);

with the excess clause provided secondary coverage. The majority reasoned that where an insurer places an excess clause in the policy, it is the intent of the insurer not to provide coverage if other valid insurance exists. In contrast, where an insurer inserts a pro rata clause in a policy, the insurer intends to prorate the coverage with other valid *primary* insurance, as opposed to excess insurance.[21]

The dissenting opinion urged adoption of an approach followed by a minority of all courts,[22] the articulation of which is usually credited to the Oregon Supreme Court's decision in *Lamb-Weston, Inc. v. Oregon Automobile Insurance Co.*[23] In *Lamb-Weston*, an employee of plaintiff, while driving a truck plaintiff had leased, lost control of the vehicle due to a mechanical failure and crashed into a warehouse. The warehouse's owner settled with plaintiff's insurer (St. Paul Fire and Marine Insurance Company, which was also a plaintiff in the litigation) under a loan receipt arrangement; the St. Paul policy contained an excess clause. The lessor of the truck also had a policy of insurance protecting him from liability for property damage resulting from the operation of the leased truck; this policy (issued by the Oregon Automobile Insurance Company) contained a pro rata clause. The trial court held that Oregon provided the primary coverage and was liable for the entire loss. On appeal, Oregon argued that it was liable for only one-half of the loss by virtue of the pro rata clause and that St. Paul was liable for the other half.

The court reviewed other earlier cases, noting that some courts treat a pro rata policy as primary and the excess policy as secondary, some courts treat the earlier policy as primary, other courts attempt to decide which policy is more specific and declare it primary, and still other courts state that the insurance of the party primarily liable is primary.[24] The court concluded:

> From an examination of the above-cited cases and others of similar import we believe none can be logically acceptable and it is our view that any attempt to give effect to the "other insurance" provision of one policy while rejecting it in another is like pursuing a will o' the wisp.[25]

The court continued:

Putnam v. New Amsterdam Cas. Co., 269 N.E.2d 97 (Ill. 1970); State Farm Mut. Auto. Ins. Co. v. General Mut. Ins. Co., 210 So. 2d 688 (Ala. 1968); see generally Annot., *Resolution of Conflicts, In Non-Automobile Liability Insurance Policies, Between Excess or Pro-Rata "Other Insurance' Clauses,* 12 A.L.R.4th 993 (1982).

[21] 430 A.2d at 491–92.

[22] See, e.g., State Farm Mut. Auto. Ins. Co. v. U.S. Fid. & Guar. Co., 490 F.2d 407 (4th Cir. 1974); Sloviaczek v. Estate of Puckett, 565 P.2d 564 (Idaho 1977); Werley v. United Serv. Auto. Ass'n, 498 P.2d 112 (Alaska 1972); State Farm Mut. Auto. Ins. Co. v. General Mut. Ins. Co., 210 So. 2d 688 (Ala. 1968); Crown Center Redev. Corp. v. Occidental Fire & Cas. Co., 716 S.W.2d 348 (Mo. Ct. App. 1986); Farm Bur. Mut. Ins. Co. v. Horace Mann Ins. Co., 343 N.W.2d 655 (Mich. Ct. App. 1983); Indiana Ins. Co. v. Federated Mut. Ins. Co., 415 N.E.2d 80 (Ind. Ct. App. 1981).

[23] 341 P.2d 110 (Or.), *modified and reh'g denied,* 346 P.2d 643 (Or. 1959).

[24] 341 P.2d at 116, *quoting* Oregon Auto. Ins. Co. v. United States Fid. & Guar. Co., 195 F.2d 958, 959 (9th Cir. 1952).

[25] 341 P.2d at 115–116.

The "other insurance" clauses of all policies are but methods used by insurers to limit their liability. . . . In our opinion, whether one policy uses one clause or another [an escape, and excess or a pro rata clause], when any come in conflict with the "other insurance" clause of another insurer, regardless of the nature of the clause, they are in fact repugnant and each should be rejected in toto.[26]

The minority in *Jones* thought that the *Lamb-Weston* rule made the most sense:

[The *Lamb-Weston* rule] does not arbitrarily pick one of the conflicting clauses and give effect to it; it does not deprive the insured of any coverage; it is not prejudicial in giving a windfall to one insurer at the expense of another; it does not encourage litigation between insurers. It does not delay settlements. On the other hand, it does enable underwriters to predict the losses of the insurers more accurately; it does preclude the use of illogical rules developed by courts (e.g., first in time, specific v. general and primary tortfeasor doctrines); and it does give a basis for uniformity of result. In addition, prorating the loss among all insurers is a rule that can be applied regardless of the number of insurers involved and regardless of the type of conflicts that are created by the "other insurance" clauses. Finally, the rule is simpler, more convenient, and easier to apply than the majority rule.[27]

As explained by another court and quoted by the minority,

it is good public policy not to put an injured plaintiff, or a defendant who is fortunate enough to have duplicate coverages, in a position where there is any possibility one insurer can say, "After you, my dear Alphonse!" while the other says, "Oh, no, after you my dear Gaston." They must walk arm in arm through the door of responsibility.[28]

Most of the same considerations apply when the conflict is between a pro rata clause and an escape clause. The policy which contains the pro rata clause, under the majority view, is the primary policy, whereas the escape clause means that the second policy does not come into effect and that the second policy is not valid and collectible insurance from the perspective of the first policy.[29]

[2] Excess versus Excess (and Escape versus Escape)

In *Jones,* it was possible for the court to reconcile the other insurance clauses through the process of interpretation. The minority view would simply declare the clauses repugnant and prorate the liability whenever the clauses do not agree. In some situations, however, it is impossible to reconcile other insurance clauses through interpretation. For example, suppose each policy has an excess clause.

---

[26] 341 P.2d at 119.

[27] 430 A.2d at 496, *quoting* James L. Welch, Note, *Conflicts Between "Other Insurance" Clauses in Automobile Liability Policies,* 20 Hastings L.J. 1292, 1304 (1969).

[28] 430 A.2d at 495, *quoting* Firemen's Ins. Co. v. St. Paul Fire & Marine Ins. Co., 411 P.2d 271, 274 (Or. 1966).

[29] See, e.g., McFarland v. Chicago Express, Inc., 200 F.2d 5 (7th Cir. 1952); Preferred Risk Mut. Ins. Co. v. Mission Ins. Co., 495 P.2d 727 (Or. 1972); Miller v. Allstate Ins. Co., 405 P.2d 712 (Wash. 1965).

Literal application of excess clauses in such situation could yield no coverage at all for the insured, as each policy demands that the other policy pay first; in a case of double coverage, each insurer would escape liability and the insured might suffer a forfeiture.

In this situation, most courts hold that the excess clauses are mutually repugnant and knock each other out. The loss is then prorated between or among the insurers in accordance with whatever proration formula the jurisdiction favors.[30] One court explained the rationale for this answer as follows:

> We perceive no methodology which is neither arbitrary nor utterly mechanical by which we could rationally resolve the enigma of which policy should be given effect over the other. Both clauses attempt to occupy the same legal status. Any construction this Court renders should attempt to maintain this status quo. This goal can be achieved only by abandoning the search for the mythical "primary" insurer and insisting instead that both insurers share in the loss. Such an approach best carries out the intent of the insurers which was to reduce or limit their liability.[31]

What the court was suggesting in *Carriers* was that literal application of the clauses means neither insurer pays first, which means neither is primary; but if only one but not both policies was in force, the sole policy would be primary. It makes no sense that an insured could have two policies, either one of which alone would provide primary coverage, but have no primary coverage when two excess clauses sit side-by-side. Thus, both policies must be primary, and this result is accomplished only by cancelling out both excess clauses under the reasoning that they are mutually repugnant.

It would seem that this analysis should also be applied when an escape clause squares off against another escape clause. Although this issue has arisen rarely, it has been held that the escape clauses in this situation are mutually repugnant,[32] and other cases have intimated that this would be the result if the issue were to arise.[33]

A few isolated decisions have found one policy primary and the other secondary when two excess clauses have collided. These cases have interpreted the clauses in light of the perils insured and the nature of the loss in order to find one policy's coverage more directly implicated than the other's.[34] Indeed, one could impose an interpretive approach upon the excess-versus-excess or escape-versus-escape situation. For example, if policy A (having an escape clause) is followed by the purchase of policy B (also having an escape clause), one court reasoned that policy

---

[30] See, e.g., Atlantic Mut. Ins. Co. v. Truck Ins. Exch., 797 F.2d 1288 (5th Cir. 1986) (applying New York law); Werley v. United Servs. Auto. Ass'n, 498 P.2d 112 (Alaska 1972); Federal Ins. Co. v. Atlantic Nat'l Ins. Co., 250 N.E.2d 193 (N.Y. 1969); State Farm Mut. Auto. Ins. Co. v. Union Ins. Co., 147 N.W.2d 760 (Neb. 1967); Cosmopolitan Mut. Ins. Co. v. Continental Cas. Co., 147 A.2d 529 (N.J. 1959).

[31] Carriers Ins. Co. v. American Policyholders Ins. Co., 404 A.2d 216, 220 (Me. 1979).

[32] See Travelers Indem. Co. v. Chappell, 246 So. 2d 498 (Miss. 1971).

[33] See, e.g., Davis Yarn Co. v. Brooklyn Yarn Dye, Co., 56 N.E.2d 564 (N.Y. 1944).

[34] See Olson v. Hertz Corp., 133 N.W.2d 519 (Minn. 1965); Hartford Acc. & Indem. Co. v. Transport Indem. Co., 51 Cal. Rptr. 168 (Cal. Ct. App. 1966).

A became effective, but policy B never became effective because of the escape clause declaring it void if there was other valid and collectible insurance (and there was, Policy A). Thus, Policy B could never become effective, and Policy A was and is effective. The same kind of reasoning could make the first-in-time policy with an excess clause primary over the second-in-time policy with an excess clause. But this kind of analysis — essentially, the oldest policy is primary — credits an arbitrary rule even though both insurers intended to provide coverage and took a premium for the coverage. The result that seems most consistent with the expectations of all the parties is the one favored by most courts, which requires each of the policies to provide coverage to some extent.

This prevailing analysis works when both insurers intended to provide coverage at the same level. However, if the insured purchases Policy A to cover the first $300,000, and the insured purchases Policy B to cover the next $700,000, the fact that both policies have excess clauses does not mean that Policy B should participate in reimbursing a portion of the first $300,000 of loss.[35] Here, as before, it is important to distinguish primary coverage from true excess or umbrella-like coverage.[36]

[3]   Excess versus Escape

Where one policy contains an excess clause and the other an escape clause, three different approaches are evident in the decisions. One approach, which appears to be favored by most courts,[37] imposes primary liability on the insurer whose policy contains the escape clause, and treats the policy with the excess clause as excess insurance. This approach evolves from a preference for interpreting the language of the clauses to some kind of result where it is possible to do so. In this type of conflict, one reasons that the policy with the excess clause does not provide any valid and collectible coverage; as a result, there is no insurance which triggers the escape clause. Thus, the policy with the escape clause provides coverage to the extent other insurance is unavailable, and that is, arguably, precisely the other policy has an excess clause — there is no other available insurance.

---

[35] See State Farm Mut. Auto. Ins. Co. v. Home Indem. Ins. Co., 261 N.E.2d 128 (Ohio 1970) (two policies in question each contained excess clauses; one of the excess clauses (the Home clause) purported to make its coverage secondary to other primary and excess insurance, in effect subordinating the coverage to yet another level; the court described the Home clause as an escape clause and held that it created coverage secondary to that of the State Farm policy).

[36] See Annot., *Automobile Insurance: Umbrella or Catastrophe Policy Automobile Liability Coverage as Affected by Primary Policy "Other Insurance" Clause,* 67 A.L.R.4th 14 (1988).

[37] See, e.g., Insurance Co. of N. Am. v. Continental Cas. Co., 575 F.2d 1070 (3d Cir. 1978); Maryland Cas. Co. v. Horace Mann Ins. Co., 551 F. Supp. 907 (W.D. Pa. 1982), *aff'd without opinion,* 720 F.2d 664 (3d Cir. 1983); American Home Assur. Co. v. Fish, 451 A.2d 358 (N.H. 1982); Protective Nat'l Ins. Co. v. Bell, 361 So. 2d 1058 (Ala. 1978); Putnam v. New Amsterdam Cas. Co., 269 N.E.2d 78 (Ill. 1970); Allstate Ins. Co. v. Shelby Mut. Ins. Co., 152 S.E.2d 436 (N.C. 1967). But see Richmond, *supra* note 1, at 1394 ("It is presently impossible to state a majority rule.")

Other courts enforce the escape clause and hold the insurer with the excess clause primarily liable.[38] The logic favoring this approach is that the policy with the escape clause provides no coverage if other insurance exists, and the policy with the excess clause is other insurance. This means the policy with the escape clause never comes into existence, and the policy with the excess clause provides the primary coverage.

Still other courts hold the two clauses mutually repugnant and prorate the loss between the insurers.[39] This is simply one more context in which the knockout rule may operate: whenever other insurance clauses are in conflict, the clauses are held mutually repugnant and of no effect, and the loss is allocated among all the coverages in accordance with some kind of proration formula.

[4] The Problem of Secondary or "True Excess" Coverage

Part of the conceptual difficulty with other insurance issues comes from the fact that in some circumstances a package of insurance coverage involving multiple policies is deliberately arranged to provide layers of coverage. Thus, the insured and insurer contract with the understanding that Policy B is excess over the coverage provided by Policy A. Hopefully, if Policy A has limits of $300,000 and Policy B has limits of $1 million, Policy B will be clear that it has, in effect, a $300,000 deductible, which means that Policy B provides coverage only after Policy A is exhausted. Unfortunately, the issues are sometimes not so simple, particularly if the insured has assembled the insurance package piecemeal without informing all of the insurers what the insured is trying to accomplish. The language of the various policies in such a situation may not coordinate well, and when a loss occurs that "shoots through the layers" of coverage, the insurers may contest their relative priorities and obligations.

Consider, for example, the situation where the insured has Policy A with $20,000 of coverage and an excess clause, Policy B with $2 million of coverage and which was specifically written and intended to be excess over Policy A, Policy C with $500,000 of coverage and which was specifically written and intended to be excess over Policies A and B, Policy D with $1 million of coverage and an excess clause, and Policy E with $1 million of coverage excess over $2.5 million of underlying insurance.[40] It is tempting to throw one's hands in the air and simply conclude, "all policies apply and the coverage should be prorated," perhaps citing *Lamb-Weston*.

---

[38] See, e.g., Indiana Lumbermens Mut. Ins. Co. v. Mitchell, 409 F.2d 392 (7th Cir. 1969); Calder Race Course, Inc. v. Hialeah Race Course, Inc., 389 So. 2d 215 (Fla. Dist. Ct. App. 1980).

[39] See, e.g., State Farm Mut. Auto Ins. Co. v. United States Fid. & Guar. Co., 490 F.2d 407 (4th Cir. 1974); CC Housing Corp. v. Ryder Truck Rental, Inc., 746 P.2d 1109 (N.M. 1987); State Farm Mut. Auto. Ins. Co. v. Bogart, 717 P.2d 449 (Ariz. 1986); Royal-Globe Ins. Cos. v. Safeco Ins. Co., 560 S.W.2d 22 (Ky. 1977); Union Ins. Co. v. Iowa Hardware Mut. Ins. Co., 175 N.W.2d 413 (Iowa 1970). The *CC Housing* case is interesting because it represents a court that follows the majority view and seeks to reconcile other insurance clauses by resort to interpretation, but it found that reconciliation was impossible when an excess clause confronted an escape clause. See 746 P.2d at 1112.

[40] These are the facts of Olympic Ins. Co. v. Employers Surplus Lines Ins. Co., 178 Cal. Rptr. 908 (Cal. Ct. App. 1981).

But it makes sense that Policy E, which requires as a condition to its effectiveness that underlying insurance in an amount of $2.5 million be in existence, was intended only to provide an additional layer of coverage beyond other policies, and thus should not participate at the first layer of coverage, even if all other policies prorate.[41] Having reached that judgment, it is a small step toward concluding that Policy C, which is specifically intended as excess coverage, should not participate at the same level as Policies A and D, which under the majority approach would be left to prorate the loss as primary insurers.[42]

What if two policies are specifically written as secondary coverage (i.e., as policies that provide coverage in a second layer above the primary policy), and both policies contain excess clauses? This is simply an "excess versus excess" dispute, to be handled in accordance with the principles discussed above,[43] except that the battle is fought and the issue resolved within the confines of the second layer of coverage. In most situations, this means that the secondary policies prorate their coverage obligations after the first layer is exhausted.[44]

What if the primary policy has a hybrid other insurance clause, which provides that the primary policy is pro rata at that level but becomes excess in the event the loss occurs in some specified way?[45] Must two other policies specifically written as excess over the primary policy prorate with the primary policy when that policy converts into an excess policy? One could argue that the insurers on the secondary policies never intended to participate on the same level as the primary policy, and that the primary policy cannot "vault" into an upper level where it then creates a conflict among other insurance clauses and forces all of the secondary insurers to drop down to the primary level. But this analysis has been rejected under the reasoning that a primary policy which says it becomes excess in certain circumstances never intends to operate at the primary level in the event those circumstances arise, which means the primary policy simply becomes one of the excess policies, all of which provide coverage under the reasoning followed by most courts when excess-versus-excess conflicts arise.[46]

What if the secondary coverages include both policies written specifically as excess coverages over particular primary policies and umbrella policies with excess clauses? One alternative is to declare all of the secondary policies' other insurance clauses mutually repugnant, and require all policies to participate at a secondary level according to some kind of proration formula. Another alternative, one which was suggested above, is to treat the umbrella policies as the last layer of coverage,

---

[41] The trial court agreed with this proposition, but also felt that Policy C should be treated as secondary. This left Policies A, B, and D as the primary policies, which the trial court required be prorated. See 178 Cal. Rptr. at 910.

[42] This was the answer of the appellate court. See 178 Cal. Rptr. at 910. See also Merritt v. Jefferson Ins. Co., 445 N.Y.S.2d 972 (N.Y. Sup. Ct. 1982).

[43] See § 97[d][2], *supra*.

[44] See American Home Assur. Co. v. Hartford Ins. Co., 427 N.Y.S.2d 26 (N.Y.Sup. 1980).

[45] For example, an auto policy may be pro rata if the insured has a loss while driving a car he owns, but becomes excess if the insured has a loss while driving a non-owned vehicle.

[46] See Kansas City Fire & Marine Ins. Co. v. Hartford Ins. Group, 442 N.E.2d 1271 (N.Y. 1982).

i.e. excess over other specific excess policies. This last alternative has some support in the cases,[47] although it is not difficult to find cases which generically refer to umbrella policies as excess policies,[48] thereby inviting application of other rules.

[5] Impact of Insolvency of Primary Insurer

The issues discussed in this section become even more complicated if one or more insurers at the primary level is insolvent. The question is whether the insurer whose coverage is written as excess over underlying insurance can rely on the existence of that insurance, or whether the insolvency of the insurer on the underlying coverage requires the excess insurer to "drop down" and provide coverage. If the answer is that the excess insurer can rely on the existence of underlying insurance, the insured is effectively uninsured for the first layer of coverage (unless a guaranty association fills in this layer). If the answer is that the excess insurer must drop down, the excess insurer effectively bears the risk of the primary carrier's insolvency.

Courts are deeply divided on this issue, as a fifty-state survey by Ostrager and Newman shows.[49] Most courts have held that the excess insurer need not drop down and participate at the primary level.[50] This result seems incontrovertible in situations where the excess policy unambiguously places a duty on the insured to maintain valid and collectible underlying insurance. The assumption of this obligation (assuming there is not some other basis for excusing the insured's compliance with this provision) means that the insured agrees to bear the risk of the primary insurer's insolvency, and that the excess insurer's premium will presumably be adjusted in the insured's favor to reflect this fact. On the other hand, where the excess policy is unclear on the insured's duty to maintain valid and collectible insurance or has language to the effect that the secondary policy is excess over "the amount recoverable" under the primary policy, the situation is necessarily more opaque, and some courts have held that the excess insurer must drop down and provide coverage at the primary level if the primary insurer becomes insolvent.[51]

---

[47] See, e.g., Allstate Ins. Co. v. Employers Liab. Assur. Corp., 445 F.2d 1278 (5th Cir. 1971); Lumbermens Mut. Cas. Co. v. Allstate Ins. Co., 417 N.E.2d 66 (N.Y. 1980).

[48] See, e.g., Heyman Assoc. No. 1 v. Insurance Co. of St. of Pa., 653 A.2d 122 (Conn. 1995) ("excess liability policy" is also known as "umbrella policy"); Grant v. New Hampshire Ins. Co., 613 So. 2d 466 (Fla. 1993) (lessee has "true excess" liability coverage, like that provided in "certain umbrella" policies); Independent School Dist. No. 197 v. Accident & Cas. Ins., 525 N.W.2d 600 (Minn. Ct. App. 1995) (referring to "umbrella excess policies"); Maynor v. Vosburg, 648 So. 2d 411 (La. Ct. App. 1994) ("personal umbrella" policy was "excess policy.")

[49] See Ostrager & Newman, *supra* note 1, at § 13.12.

[50] See, e.g., Hartford Acc. & Indem. Co. v. Chicago Hous. Auth., 12 F.3d 92 (7th Cir. 1993) (applying Illinois law); Federal Ins. Co. v. Srivastava, 2 F.3d 98 (5th Cir. 1993); Continental Marble & Granite v. Canal Ins. Co., 785 F.2d 1258 (5th Cir. 1986); Molina v. United States Fire Ins. Co., 574 F.2d 1176 (4th Cir. 1978); Revco D.S., Inc. v. Government Employees Ins. Co., 791 F. Supp. 1254 (N.D. Ohio 1991), aff'd, 984 F.2d 154 (6th Cir. 1992); Louisiana Ins. Guar. Ass'n v. Interstate Fire & Cas. Co., 630 So. 2d 759 (La. 1994).

[51] See, e.g., Gulezian v. Lincoln Ins. Co., 506 N.E.2d 123 (Mass. 1987); Reserve Ins. Co. v. Pisciotta, 180 Cal. Rptr. 628 (Cal. 1982); Coca Cola Bottling Co. of San Diego v. Columbia Cas. Co., 14 Cal. Rptr.2d 643 (Cal. Ct. App. 1992); Donald B. MacNeal, Inc. v. Interstate Fire & Cas. Co., 477 N.E.2d 1322 (Ill.App. 1985).

[6]   Toward a Solution

The questions addressed above are extremely difficult, but they arise routinely because of the frequency of overlapping or layered coverage. With regard to most kinds of conflict among other insurance clauses, there is a split of authority in the cases. This invites efforts to identify common themes, or threads that can tie the disparate rulings together.

Minnesota courts, for example, have attempted to blend a variety of considerations into a more functional approach to the other insurance clause conundrum. In a 1976 decision, the Minnesota Supreme Court explained that, rather than look at the specific kinds of other insurance clauses involved, the preferred approach is to "allocate respective policy coverages in light of the total policy insuring intent, as determined by the primary risks upon which each policy's premiums were based and as determined by the primary function of each policy."[52]

Three years later, the Minnesota Supreme Court approved a "closest-to-the-risk" analysis, under which three factors need to be considered to determine which policy is primary: "(1) Which policy specifically described the accident-causing instrumentality? (2) Which premium is reflective of the greater contemplated exposure? (3) Does one policy contemplate the risk and use of the accident-causing instrumentality with greater specificity than the other policy — that is, is the coverage of the risk primary in one policy and incidental in the other?"[53] Although the Minnesota Supreme Court currently views these tests as alternatives,[54] it is not obvious how the tests are different and for what reasons one would choose one test but not the other in a particular case.[55] Yet it seems clear that the Minnesota Supreme Court is groping for some kind of approach where the results turn less on words and semantic distinctions and more on what seems reasonable and appropriate in all of the circumstances. Critics of this more functional approach can be expected to argue that if contracting parties cannot count on the objectively reasonable meaning of words used in insurance policies, there is little on which one can rely; it is better to be able to assume that the words chosen by parties have both meaning and purpose, and that if the parties want a particular result, they should choose the particular words that will obtain that result.

Of the prevailing approaches discussed in the preceding subsections, the knockout approach, which declares inconsistent other insurance clauses mutually repugnant and requires proration according to whatever formulae is favored in a particularly jurisdiction, provides an easy answer. But if a court ruthlessly applies this doctrine

---

[52] Integrity Mut. Ins. Co. v. State Auto. & Cas. Underwriters Ins. Co., 239 N.W.2d 445, 447 (Minn. 1976).

[53] Auto Owners Ins. Co. v. Northstar Mut. Ins. Co., 281 N.W.2d 700, 704 (Minn. 1979).

[54] See Interstate Fire & Cas. Co. v. Auto-Owners Ins. Co., 433 N.W.2d 82, 86 (Minn. 1988) ("in this case, rather than applying the three-part 'closest-to-the-risk' test, it is more helpful to use the broader approach . . . of allocating respective policy coverages in light of the total policy insuring intent.")

[55] For an example of a lower Minnesota court attempting to rationalize the prior precedents of the Minnesota Supreme Court, see Illinois Farmers Ins. Co. v. Depositors Ins. Co., 480 N.W.2d 657 (Minn. Ct. App. 1992).

and ignores evidence which shows the parties clearly intended one or more policies to be primary and the others secondary, the knockout approach may give the wrong answer. For example, if a policy's effectiveness is conditioned on the existence of underlying insurance, this is strong evidence that the policy was intended to provide secondary, excess coverage. Although evaluating the amount of premiums charged to form a judgment about the scope of coverage can be dangerous territory given the myriad factors that affect the price of insurance, the cost of coverage can be an important factor in determining whether a policy is intended as primary or secondary coverage. Secondary levels of coverage should be much less expensive than primary levels, given the reality that most losses are of a smaller nature. By the same token, an insured who pays a hefty premium for a policy with an excess clause (e.g., a premium similar in amount to that charged for similar policies with pro rata clauses) might reasonably expect that the excess clause would participate at the primary level of coverage, even if the policy was excess over other primary policies with pro rata clauses. Thus, the price of insurance can help determine at what level the coverage was intended to operate.

Absent evidence which justifies a preference for ordering the priority of overlapping coverages, whether semantic distinctions in other insurance clauses should be enough to justify prioritizing overlapping coverages presents a difficult question. On the one hand, one can give weight to the words used, and make one or more policies primary, and the others secondary. Yet it is fair to question whether the parties — particularly the insured — had any intention in mind when overlapping coverages were purchased, and thus the search for a semantic distinction becomes a simple puzzle-solving process without any relation to the manifested intentions of the contracting parties. Rather than engage in such an exercise when it has no anchor in the parties' intent, it may make more sense to choose an answer commonly favored when terms in conflicting standardized commercial forms are irreconcilable: knock out the different terms and substitute reasonable ones.[56] For the time being, however, there will be much disagreement about the right answers, and courts will continue to reach divergent results.

[e] Proration Formulas

If a court declares other insurance clauses in two or more policies mutually repugnant, one more problem remains: prorating the loss among the various insurers. Three different approaches are available.

Most courts adhere to the so-called *Lamb-Weston* proration rule,[57] which is the rule that was applied in the landmark Oregon case.[58] Under this rule, the insurers pay shares of the loss proportional to their limits of coverage. Suppose that two insurers, *X* and *Y,* have policies providing coverage for the insured's loss of

---

56 See UCC § 2-207.

57 See, e.g., Continental Cas. Co. v. Aetna Cas. & Sur. Co., 823 F.2d 708 (2d Cir. 1987); Georgia Cas. & Sur. Co. v. Universal Underwriters Ins. Co., 534 F.2d 1108, *reh'g denied,* 539 F.2d 710 (5th Cir. 1976); Sloviaczek v. Estate of Puckett, 565 P.2d 564 (Idaho 1977); Buckeye Union Ins. Co. v. State Auto. Mut. Ins. Co., 361 N.E.2d 1052 (Ohio 1977).

58 341 P.2d 110 (Or.), *modified,* 346 P.2d 643 (Or. 1959), see text at note 23, *supra.*

$120,000. Policy X has limits of $50,000 and Policy Y has limits of $150,000. This means that Insurer X will pay 25 percent of the insured's loss (because Insurer X underwrote $50,000 — 25 percent — of the $200,000 combined coverage), or $30,000; Insurer Y will pay 75 percent of the insured's loss (because Insurer Y underwrote $150,000 — 75 percent — of the $200,000 combined coverage), or $90,000. In support of the majority rule, it is argued that the burden should be shared by the insurers either on the basis of the risk they have undertaken or the benefits they have received. It is assumed that the risk undertaken by each insurer is generally proportional to the size of the premiums received; thus, assessing each insurer a portion of the loss equal to its portion of the total limits of all insurers is presumed to be fair.[59]

A minority of courts reject the *Lamb-Weston* proration formula and follow the so-called "equal shares" approach, under which each insurer shares the loss equally up to the limits of the lower policy.[60] In the foregoing example, each insurer contributes equally until the limits of the policy with the lowest limits is reached. This means that Insurer X and Insurer Y each contribute $50,000, a total of $100,000. This leaves $20,000 unreimbursed, and Insurer Y pays this remaining $20,000 (a total contribution by Insurer Y of $70,000). The minority approach requires Insurer X to make a larger (and Insurer Y a smaller) contribution than under the majority approach. If the insured's loss had only been $80,000, each insurer would have contributed $40,000 under the minority approach, while under the majority approach, Insurer X would have contributed $20,000 and Insurer Y $60,000.

The courts adhering to the minority rule reject the premise that each insurer's burden is proportional to the amount of insurance issued. This is because the cost of insurance does not increase proportionately with increases in policy limits. Most losses are small and few are total; thus, the lowest "layers" of coverage are the most costly to the insurer. In fact, the price to the consumer of the lower layers is more than the upper layers; once minimum coverage is purchased, substantial supplemental coverage can be purchased at a lower marginal cost.[61] Therefore, unless the policy limits of two or more policies are equal, apportioning a loss according to the policy limits does not equally apportion the risk the insurers have assumed.

A third approach, not followed in any modern decision but having support in some older cases,[62] apportions the loss according to premiums: each insurer's contribution is based on the percentage of premiums it received compared to the total premiums paid to all the insurers. Actually, this approach is perhaps the most sound one as a matter of pure theory; the amount of premiums collected should most accurately

59 See 346 P.2d at 647.

60 See, e.g., Reliance Ins. Co. v. St. Paul Surplus Lines Ins. Co., 753 F.2d 1288 (4th Cir. 1985); Liberty Mut. Ins. Co. v. Home Ins. Co., 583 F. Supp. 849 (W.D. Pa. 1984); Ruan Transp. Corp. v. Truck Rental, Inc., 278 F. Supp. 692 (D.Colo. 1968); Western Cas. and Sur. Co. v. Universal Underwriters Ins. Co., 657 P.2d 576 (Kan. 1983); Carriers Ins. Co. v. American Policyholders' Ins. Co., 404 A.2d 216 (Me. 1979).

61 See Cosmopolitan Mut. Ins. Co. v. Continental Cas. Co., 147 A.2d 529 (N.J. 1959).

62 See Insurance Co. of Tex. v. Employers Liab. Assur. Corp., 163 F. Supp. 143 (S.D. Cal. 1958); Cosmopolitan Mut. Ins. Co. v. Continental Cas. Co., 147 A.2d 529 (N.J. 1959).

reflect the amount of risk assumed by the insurer and therefore should most fairly allocate the loss. However, calculating premiums paid over the life of a policy would be a nightmarish, costly undertaking for several reasons, including the fact that most policies cover multiple risks and allocating the premium to the risk at issue would be extremely difficult and probably impossible. In short, the administrative expenses of such an approach make it unfeasible in practice, even if it is sound theory.[63]

Therefore, the next best solution, which like the *Lamb-Weston* rule is easy to administer, is to make each insurer pay equal shares (up to policy limits). Each insurer has undertaken equally to insure against low-level losses; therefore, at these levels, the insurers should share equally. This solution, which is followed by a minority of courts, is arguably inequitable in that it gives a windfall to the insurer with the higher limit. In the example above where the insured's loss ($80,000) was less than two times the limit of the policy with the lowest limit (Policy X had limits of $50,000), the insured's loss was shared equally between the insurers even though the policy limit of one of the insurers (Policy X had limits of $150,000) was three times greater than the other policy's limits. The response to this argument, however, is that each insurer received the same premium dollars for the coverage up to the limit of the lowest policy, and the insurers should therefore share the loss up to that limit equally.

One of these proration approaches is sometimes specified in a policy's pro rata other insurance clause. Most common is policy language that requires the insurers to contribute to the insured's loss in proportion to the policy limits (essentially the *Lamb-Weston* approach). Another common approach calls for proration in equal shares until a policy limit is exhausted (the minority approach). If multiple policies are involved with each specifying a different method of proration, a problem of conflict exists, and the court must either interpret the clauses or "knockout" the repugnant clauses and apply one of the "judicial" proration doctrines.

[f]   Some Additional Troublespots

The other insurance clause problems are almost intractable, and it seems unfair that even further difficulties should remain. Sadly, there are some.

[1]   Sharing Defense Costs

In liability insurance, the insurer has two primary duties: to pay proceeds and to pay defense costs. If there are multiple insurers, how should defense costs be apportioned? Most courts hold simply that the defense costs should be apportioned according to the same formula that is used to apportion the costs of indemnifying the insured.[64]

---

[63] See Nationwide Mut. Ins. Co. v. State Farm Mut. Auto. Ins. Co., 209 F. Supp. 83 (N.D. W.Va. 1962).

[64] See, e.g., P.L. Kanter Agency, Inc. v. Continental Cas. Co., 541 F.2d 519 (6th Cir. 1976) (since one insurer bears coverage responsibility, that insurer has sole duty to defend); General Acc. Fire & Life Ins. Co. v. Piazza, 152 N.E.2d 236 (N.Y. 1958) (insurer with duty to pay proceeds has duty to defend); Interstate Fire & Cas. Co. v. Hartford Fire Ins. Co., 548 F. Supp. 1185 (E.D. Mich. 1982) (both policies have equal shares clause; thus, defense costs should be shared equally); Burnett v. Western Pacific Ins. Co., 469 P.2d 602 (Or. 1970) (defense

Other courts, however, distinguish the duty to pay proceeds from the duty to defend. Because the duty to defend exists independently of the duty to pay proceeds and is not limited by the policy limits,[65] fairness requires, it is argued, that each insurer share the defense costs equally, and some courts have so held.[66]

[2]   Invalidity of Otherwise Collectible "Other Insurance" Due to Act or Neglect of Insured

If the insured has multiple coverages for a loss that is small relative to the policy's coverages, each insurer benefits because one or more other insurers will contribute to the indemnification of the insured according to one of the various proration formulas. However, if the insured, through some act or neglect, has invalidated one of the policies, the other insurers will be asked to bear a greater percentage of the loss. In this circumstance, the insurers liable under binding policies are likely to argue that the insured should bear a percentage of the loss on account of the insured's failure to maintain the validity of otherwise collectible insurance.

American Star Insurance Co. v. Allstate Insurance Co.,[67] is illustrative. American Star issued a million-dollar-per-person policy of liability insurance to the Oregon State Highway Commission. American Star was notified of two accidents occurring on the Commission's right-of-way property, and it settled the claims for modest amounts. The Commission, however, did not notify its other carrier, Allstate, of the accidents, and Allstate did not contribute to the settlements. Allstate eventually received notice of the accidents over two and one-half years after they occurred when American Star, having recently learned that Allstate was on the risk as well, sent letters to Allstate requesting contribution. Allstate denied coverage to the Commission — and hence denied its obligation to contribute to the loss — on the ground that notice of the losses was not timely and coverage was barred.

American Star argued that since the Commission had failed to give timely notice to Allstate, the Commission should contribute one-half of the settlements of the two accidents. The court rejected American Star's argument and held that where the insurer makes no inquiry of its insured seeking to discover other insurance and the insured was lax in notifying all potential insurers, the insurer may not demand contribution from its insured. The insured had not cooperated with the insurer by disclosing the other insurance, but this was not a basis for American Star avoiding its liability since it had not sought cooperation from its insured. In effect, the court

---

costs should be prorated in accordance with proportion that each insurer's coverage bears to total coverage); Liberty Mut. Ins. Co. v. Standard Acc. Ins. Co., 164 F. Supp. 261 (S.D. N.Y. 1958), *aff'd,* 264 F.2d 671 (2d Cir. 1959) (both policies have pro rata clauses, and defense costs must be shared on pro rata basis); General Acc. Fire & Life Assur. Corp. v. Piazza, 152 N.E.2d 236 (N.Y. 1958) (where one policy is primary and other excess, primary insurer has duty to defend).

[65] See § 111[a], *infra.*

[66] See, e.g., Emons Indus., Inc., v. Liberty Mut. Fire Ins. Co., 481 F. Supp. 1022 (S.D. N.Y. 1979); State Farm Mut. Auto. Ins. Co. v. General Mut. Ins. Co., 210 So. 2d 688 (Ala. 1968). See also St. Paul Mercury Ins. Co. v. Huitt, 336 F.2d 37 (6th Cir. 1964) (insured may demand defense from primary insurer, excess insurer, or both).

[67] 508 P.2d 244 (Or. Ct. App. 1973).

placed a duty on the insurer to inquire as to the existence of other applicable insurance, and since the insurer did not fulfill its duty it could not demand contribution.

American Star is properly reasoned. The rates charged by American Star were presumably based on there being no other insurance. Thus, it is not unfair to make American Star bear the entire loss. If the insurer's rates were based on the assumption that other insurance existed, the insurer should have inserted a coinsurance clause in the policy, requiring the insured to keep a specific amount of other insurance in force. Of course, if the insured had failed to reveal the existence of the other insurance upon American Star's inquiry, it would not have been unfair to require the insured to contribute to the loss.

[3] Self-Insurance as "Other Insurance"

The question has sometimes arisen as to whether a self- insurer must be treated as an "insurer" for purposes of other insurance clause issues.[68] Most courts that have considered this question have answered it in the negative.[69] This result makes sense. As one court has explained it, a party that has a self-insured retention is "essentially uninsured for that amount," and "cannot be viewed as having 'insurance,' as that term is plainly and ordinarily used, since it had no insurance fot valid claims made which were under' the amount of the retention.[70] As discussed in an earlier section,[71] a different rule may be appropriate when compulsory automobile insurance is involved. Businesses that have the means to self-insure fleets of automobiles should not, arguably, be excused the obligation to contribute to the reimbursement of an insured, where there are other applicable insurance policies, under the reasoning that the self-insurance program is not "valid and collectible" insurance.

[4] Deductibles and Coinsurance Requirements

Another problem concerns the effect of deductibles and coinsurance requirements. In property and liability insurance, the overlapping policies often provide coverage but have different deductibles. Fairness would seem to require that the insured only be subject to one deductible — the smaller one. Yet because most losses are small rather than large, the insurer with the larger deductible took on less risk (and presumably received a smaller premium) and therefore should not be bound to adhere to the smaller deductible. The few courts to struggle with this issue have offered less than satisfying explanations for their results.

---

[68] See § 12[c], *supra*.

[69] See, e.g., St. John's Regional Health Ctr. v. American Cas. Co., 980 F.2d 1222 (8th Cir. 1992); Wake Cty. Hosp. Sys., Inc. v. National Cas. Co., 804 F.Supp. 768 (E.D. N.C. 1992), *aff'd*, 996 F.2d 1213 (4th Cir. 1993); Hillsborough Cty. Hosp. & Welfare Bd. v. Taylor, 546 So. 2d 1055 (Fla. 1989); American Nurses Ass'n v. Passaic Gen. Hosp., 484 A.2d 670 (N.J. 1984); Physicians Ins. Co. v. Grandview Hosp. & Med. Ctr., 542 N.E.2d 706 (Ohio Ct.App. 1988). But see Southern Home Ins. Co. v. Burdette's Leasing Serv., Inc., 234 S.E.2d 870 (S.C. 1977). See generally Annot., *Self-Insurance as Other Insurance Within Meaning of Liability Insurance Policy*, 46 A.L.R.4th 707 (1986).

[70] Wake Cty. Hosp. Sys., Inc. v. National Cas. Co., 804 F. Supp. 768, 775 (E.D. N.C. 1992), *aff'd*, 996 F.2d 1213 (4th Cir. 1993).

[71] See § 12[c], *supra*.

One of the first courts to acknowledge the problem of different deductibles in overlapping coverage was the Ninth Circuit in a 1972 decision, *Pacific Power & Light Co. v. Transport Indemnity Co.*[72] The insured settled a claim against it for $25,000; Transport had issued the insured a liability policy with an excess clause and no deductible, and Home Insurance Company had issued the insured a policy with an excess clause and a $25,000 deductible. The court, applying *Lamb-Weston,*[73] held that the other insurance clauses were mutually repugnant and ordered the trial court on remand to calculate the appropriate pro rata contributions of the insurers.[74] In a footnote, the court suggested that proration should occur before the deductible is applied to Home's portion of the reimbursement.[75] The meant that whatever share of the loss Home would be required to reimburse would be wiped out by the deductible; because Transport's pro rata contribution would be less than $25,000, the insured would end up bearing a portion of the loss itself, even though it had purchased one policy that, if it alone were applicable, would cover the entire loss with no deductible. Such an outcome, plainly, makes little sense.

This flaw in *Pacific Power & Light* was recognized and avoided by the Eighth Circuit in *Cargill, Inc. v. Commercial Union Insurance Co.,*[76] a 1989 decision. A barge accident resulted in a $194,158.07 loss of grain. Cargill submitted the claim to Huffman, which was towing the barge at the time of the loss, and had agreed to procure insurance to protect Cargill's interest in the cargo. Huffman's insurer, Commercial Union ("CU"), initially denied coverage, although it later agreed that its policy with $600,000 in limits provided coverage, subject to a $10,000 deductible. By this time, St. Paul had paid Cargill $94,158.07, the amount of the loss less the $100,000 deductible under St. Paul's $2 million policy.[77] CU then paid $90,000 to Cargill, the unpaid balance of the claim less the $10,000 deductible. CU took the position that its responsibility should be prorated with St. Paul according to policy limits, without reference to the deductibles. This would have made CU responsible for 23.1 percent of the loss ($600,000 divided by total policy limits of $2.6 million), or $44,850.51, with St. Paul liable for the remainder ($149,307.56). St. Paul argued that after proration, the entire amount of St. Paul's deductible should be shifted to

[72] 460 F.2d 959 (9th Cir. 1972).

[73] See § 97[e], *supra.*

[74] 460 F.2d at 963.

[75] 460 F.2d at 962 n.5. The footnote is somewhat cryptic, but a subsequent court also interpreted the footnote as the text suggests. See Cargill, Inc. v. Commercial Union Ins. Co., 889 F.2d 174, 180 (8th Cir. 1989).

[76] 889 F.2d 174 (8th Cir. 1989).

[77] A close reader of the decision will find what must be errors in some of the figures used by the court. The more significant is the court's reference, 889 F.2d at 177, to policy limits of $2.6 million under the St. Paul policy. Yet when the court prorated the insurers' policies, it referred to $2.6 million as being the sum of the limits of the two policies, 889 F.2d at 180. The St. Paul policy probably provided $2.0 million in coverage; regardless, that assumption will be made here so that the computations used by the court can be discussed without further confusion. Also, when the court referred to St. Paul's payment of $94,157.07 representing the amount of the loss minus the $100,000 deductible, 889 F.2d at 176, the court probably meant $94,158.07; obviously, this $1 error is insignificant, unlike the possible error in describing policy limits, which significantly affects the application of the proration formulae.

CU, which would increase CU's liability to $144,850.51, and reduce St. Paul's liability to $49,307.56.

A federal magistrate put 100 percent of the loss on CU, but this answer was repudiated by the Eighth Circuit on appeal. Instead, the court concluded that the St. Paul and CU policies contained mutually repugnant other insurance clauses, and ordered proration according to the policy limits. As for the deductibles, the court concluded that they should be taken into account in determining the insurer's respective obligations, particularly since the large size of the St. Paul deductible reflected that St. Paul had assumed less risk of loss. The court calculated the insurer's respective obligations as follows: Under the proration formula, CU bore 23.1 percent of the risk, and St. Paul bore 76.9 percent of the risk. But before prorating the loss, the court shifted St. Paul's deductible to CU in this manner: the court multiplied the amount of the loss after applying St. Paul's deductible ($94,158.07) times 23.1 percent (the amount of CU's pro rata share) and added this amount ($21,750.51) to St. Paul's deductible ($100,000) to define CU's total liability at $121,750.51, subject to CU's deductible of $10,000, which when subtracted out left CU's liability at $111,750.51. (Huffman paid Cargill $10,000, the amount of the deductible.) This left St. Paul with an obligation to contribute the rest of the total loss, or $72,407.56.[78]

The court rejected the approach urged by St. Paul, which would have shifted the deductible to CU *after* prorating the loss. Under this approach, as described above, CU would have paid a larger proportion of the loss, and St. Paul would have paid less. But St. Paul's approach did not account for CU's deductible of $10,000, which neither insurer should have been obligated to pay.

An alternative approach,[79] which the court did not discuss, would have involved post-proration shifting of the deductible while accounting for the presence of both deductibles. In effect, this approach would (a) prorate the loss among the insurers according to one of the approaches; (b) subtract each insurer's deductible from its liability; (c) add to the liability of the insurer with the smaller deductible the amount of the larger deductible. Under the Windt approach, one gets these results: CU's pro rata share of the total loss ($44,850.51), after a setoff for the CU deductible ($10,000), plus an addition of the amount of the larger deductible of the St. Paul policy ($100,000) would produce a liability for CU of $134,850.51. St. Paul's pro rata share ($149,307.50), after subtraction of the St. Paul deductible ($100,000),

---

[78] The same answer could have been reached through the following four steps: (a) determining the amount of the insured's loss and subtracting the smaller deductible; (b) charging the insurer with the smaller deductible with liability for the difference between the two deductibles; (c) subtracting the amount in (b) from the amount in (a); and (d) prorating the amount computed in (c) according to the appropriate proration formula, and charging each insurer with that sum. The approach in this footnote is favored by Windt in subsequent editions of his treatise. See Allan D. Windt, 1 *Insurance Claims and Disputes: Representation of Insurance Companies and Insureds,* § 7.07, at 546 (3d ed. 1995).

[79] This approach was offered by Allen Windt in the first edition of his treatise. See Allen D. Windt, *Insurance Claims and Disputes* § 7.07, at 315 (1982). In the second edition of his treatise, Windt said that the approach he favored in his first edition "can prove to be extremely unfair to the carrier with the smaller deductible," and he endorsed an approach identical to that followed in *Cargill. Id.,* 2d ed., § 7.07 at 409 (1988).

would produce a liability for St. Paul of $49,307.50. The two insurers, together, would pay $184,158.01, leaving the insured responsible for $10,000 of the loss, the amount of the smaller deductible. Compared to the court's approach, the Windt approach would require CU to contribute more (and St. Paul less), but not as much more (and St. Paul less) as the approach urged by St. Paul.

Why did the court shift St. Paul's deductible to CU before prorating, instead of after? The court said that "[u]nder this method the insurers only share the loss to the extent that their 'other insurance' clauses are mutually repugnant."[80] This explanation misses the question; the problem is that the overlapping coverages had inconsistent policy limits and deductibles, meaning one insurer took more risk than the other; but how much more? The different approaches give different answers. The problem is similar to that faced when one must choose among competing proration formulas;[81] when two insurers with different policy limits must contribute to a loss, a equal shares approach causes the insurer with lower policy limits to bear more of the risk than a policy limits approach. The Windt approach requires an insurer with a lower deductible to bear more of the risk than the *Cargill* approach, presumably under the reasoning (like that embraced by the equal shares approach) that insurers with smaller deductibles take more economic risk and therefore should pay a greater proportion of the loss. On the other side of the ledger, the *Cargill* approach finds companionship with those who prefer to prorate coverage according to what one insurer's coverage bears as a percentage of total available policy limits.

Reasonable people could probably argue endlessly about the relative merits of these approaches, but a few points seem beyond reasonable dispute. First, if all of the contributing policies have a deductible of some size, the insured should be expected to contribute to or bear a portion of the loss equal to the smallest deductible. Second, after calculating the contributions of the various insurers, the insured should not receive less coverage than he or she would have received if any one of the policies had been in force alone. Third, the calculation of the contributions of various insurers should reflect the fact that different deductibles in different policies equates to the insurers assuming varying proportions of the risk, which in turn must translate into the insurers contributing different amounts to reimburse any given loss.

Whatever approach one chooses, it will work well only if the facts are relatively simple. Substantial difficulties are presented, however, in other cases, such as the following: (a) one policy uses the New York standard coinsurance clause and the other does not; (b) both policies use a New York standard coinsurance clause, but one policy uses 80 percent and the other 70 percent, and the 70 percent clause is met but the 80 percent clause is not; (c) either of the foregoing two situations coupled with different deductibles; (d) one policy has a pure coinsurance requirement and the other does not; (e) one policy has a pure coinsurance requirement and the other has a deductible.[82] Again, given the amount of overlapping coverage in force today, it is surprising that such substantial uncertainties remain.

---

80 889 F.2d at 181.

81 See § 97[e], *supra.*

82 See § 93[b], *supra,* for a discussion of coinsurance.

In health insurance, the issues are the same, but particular cases can be even more difficult.[83] The proration approach has the disadvantage of involving some duplication of claims investigation, claims processing, and settlement costs, for the simple reason that multiple insurers are paying proceeds instead of one primary insurer. In property and liability insurance, these costs are probably affordable. In health insurance, where the general issue of cost containment is extremely acute, they may not be. Health insurance involves larger numbers of claims, usually of smaller amounts, with a greater variety of deductible and coinsurance requirements. The additional cost and confusion in sorting out health insurance problems may demand that a completely different set of rules apply. This has been the judgment of the Kansas Supreme Court, which in an earlier decision not involving health insurance had opted for the *Lamb-Weston* rule of repugnancy and the minority rule on proration.[84] In a subsequent case,[85] the Kansas Supreme Court rejected this analysis in a case where an employee was covered under both her employer's health care plan (Riverside) and her husband's employer's health care plan (Blue Cross-Blue Shield). The Riverside plan contained an excess clause; the Blue Cross-Blue Shield plan contained a lengthy "nonduplication of benefits clause" that purported to make the Blue Cross-Blue Shield plan secondary to the Riverside plan. In commenting on the duplication of benefits, the court observed:

> Duplication of benefits accomplishes none of the goals of such plans, serving only to run up the cost of the plans. Hassles, such as the one before us, increase the costs of administration of the plans and can delay payment of the medical bills. . . . Obviously, litigation of the dispute between plans as to coverage should be avoided wherever possible.[86]

The court concluded that "the logical approach" was to treat the employee's own health plan provided by her own employer as primary coverage, and to treat the coverage she possessed as an additional insured under her husband's plan as secondary coverage. This eliminated the potential for duplication of benefits. However, it also repudiated in the health care setting the proration approach followed in property and liability insurance and substituted an approach that makes coverage primary or secondary depend on whether the insured is the named insured or an additional insured.

§ 98   Resolving Disputes on Who Gets the Proceeds: The Interpleader Remedy

Interpleader, a creature of equity, enables a person subjected to rival claims to bring the rival claimants into one action where the question of to whom the

---

[83] For a general discussion of other insurance clause conflicts in health insurance, see Annot., *Priority And Apportionment Of Liability Between Medical And Hospital Expense Insurers,* 25 A.L.R.4th 1022 (1983).

[84] See Western Cas. and Sur. Co. v. Universal Underwriters Ins. Co., 657 P.2d 576 (Kan. 1983).

[85] See Blue Cross and Blue Shield, Inc. v. Riverside Hospital, 703 P.2d 1384 (Kan. 1985).

[86] 703 P.2d at 1389.

obligation is owed can be resolved. Today, the rules of civil procedure in the federal and state courts specifically authorize interpleader, but interpleader would be available in equity even if statutes or court rules did not provide for the action. Insurers probably utilize interpleader more than any other kind of institution or private party.

In a situation where multiple claimants seek the proceeds of an insurance policy, the insurer, rather than run the risk of paying proceeds to the wrong person and being unable to recoup the proceeds later, often files an interpleader action.[1] The insurer deposits the proceeds (the "stake") with the clerk of the court, and the court is asked to determine who is entitled to the policy proceeds. The court's judgment settles the claims of the persons asserting rights to the proceeds and discharges the insurer from liability. The interpleader action also avoids the possibility that separate suits will be brought against the insurer. Multiplicity of litigation alone is a disadvantage to the insurer and to the judicial system; moreover, when multiple litigation occurs, a possibility exists that each claimant might win a judgment against the insurer, subjecting the insurer to multiple liability. Interpleader enables the insurer to protect itself against this possibility.

In the insurance setting specifically, interpleader is most often used by life insurers. Sometimes the life insurer concedes liability but is unsure to whom the proceeds should be paid. For example, two people may claim to be the rightful beneficiary, or a contingent beneficiary may claim that the primary beneficiary, who is also asserting a right to the proceeds, is disqualified from receiving benefits. Disputes can also arise between beneficiaries and assignees, and between beneficiaries and persons claiming community property rights. The insurer must proceed with care, lest it pay the proceeds to one person and learn later that the proceeds should have paid to someone else. If the insurer pays the proceeds to the wrong person, the insurer's contract obligation to the proper beneficiary is not discharged; the insurer would have to pay proceeds a second time and attempt to recoup the proceeds from the individual who wrongfully received them.[2]

Interpleader is sometimes used in the liability insurance setting. A liability insurer owes its insured not only the duty to pay proceeds but also the duty to defend. A liability insurer usually cannot discharge the duty to defend by tendering the policy limits.[3] Thus, the liability insurer cannot interplead all the competing third parties asserting tort claims against the insured and discharge its own obligation. However, when the issue is simply how several claims exceeding the policy limits should be prorated, the insurer need not participate in the settling of this claim; the insurer can interplead the competing claimants and force them to resolve the issue in the interpleading proceeding.

Interpleader also has a role in property insurance. A bailee may purchase insurance for all property stored with the bailee. If the property is destroyed and if the policy limits are less than the total loss, interpleader is available to prorate

---

[1] See generally John E. Morris, *The Use of an Interpleader Action to Resolve Multiple Claims from One Accident,* 51 Ins. Counsel J. 99 (1984).

[2] See § 99[e], *infra.*

[3] See § 111[e], *infra.*

the coverage among the bailors' competing claims. If a tenant purchases insurance on the leasehold and the landlord later claims an interest in the policy, interpleader would be available to settle the competing claims of landlord and tenant. If a vendor and vendee make competing claims to proceeds to be paid after the destruction of property that is subject to a contract for sale, an interpleader may be appropriate. Anytime competing claims exceeding the amount of the available proceeds exist, the insurer should consider filing an interpleader.

For the insurer's counsel, interpleader should be a routine pleading that can be prepared with a minimum of expense. Yet whatever expenses are incurred are generally reimbursed out of the proceeds.[4] This reduces the proceeds ultimately paid to the proper beneficiary, a disadvantage of interpleader. Moreover, interpleader takes time. The beneficiary entitled to the proceeds may not receive payment for a considerable period after the proceeds would normally have been paid. This disadvantage can, of course, be avoided if the conflicting claimants settle their claims among themselves. In the absence of such a settlement, the delay in paying the claim can only be viewed as part of the price of resolving conflicting claims to the proceeds.

Although there are many situations where interpleader is appropriate, it does not follow that an interpleader should always be filed when conflicting claims are asserted. In *Usable Life v. Fow,*[5] a 1991 Arkansas decision, the court upheld an award to plaintiffs of prejudgment interest, a statutory penalty, and attorney's fees because the insurer should have paid proceeds to the plaintiffs-beneficiaries instead of filing an interpleader. Plaintiffs, daughters of the insured, were the designated beneficiaries on a $2,500 life insurance policy pursuant to a change of beneficiary made by the insured almost a year before his death. After the insured's death, his widow telephoned the insurer, claimed to be the policy beneficiary, and threatened to file a lawsuit if she did not receive payment. The insurer requested that the widow provide written documentation to support her claim, but she did not do so. The insurer, over the objection of plaintiffs, commenced an interpleader action, and in this action was held responsible to the plaintiffs for the policy's proceeds, prejudgment interest, a twelve percent statutory penalty, and $1,070 in attorney's fees. On appeal, the court cited an Arkansas statute[6] that an insurer is discharged from liability on a policy when it pays a designated beneficiary in circumstances where the insurer has not received written notice by or on behalf of someone else claiming entitlement to the proceeds. Instead of availing itself of this option, and without making an investigation of the proper party for payment, the insurer filed an interpleader, which imposed litigation costs on the plaintiffs to obtain the monies that were properly theirs as the designated beneficiaries.[7] The court reasoned that this was inappropriate in circumstances where the competing claim was merely an

---

[4] See, e.g., Massachusetts Mut. Life Ins. Co. v. Morris, 61 F.2d 104 (9th Cir. 1932); General Am. Life Ins. Co. v. Rodriguez, 641 S.W.2d 264 (Tex. Ct. App. 1982); but see Raack v. Bohinc, 477 N.E.2d 1155 (Ohio Ct.App. 1983).

[5] 820 S.W.2d 453 (Ark. 1991).

[6] Ark. Code. Ann. § 23-79-125.

[7] 820 S.W.2d at 454.

oral assertion in a telephone contact, and after which the competing claimant made, apparently, no effort to pursue further.

The dissent in *Usable Life* believed that the insurer acted properly in filing an interpleader, reasoning that there were any number of arguments the widow might have made — such as the insured's lack of capacity — which would have made her the rightful payee.[8] Notwithstanding the dissent's assertion that no "prudent attorney for an insurance carrier would advise payment to the daughters knowing that the widow had put the carrier on notice of her claim,"[9] the majority's decision was correct given the circumstances of the case. A designated beneficiary should not be subjected to litigation costs and depletion of the stake (although the insurer apparently did not collect its expenses in *Usable Life*, if it had been reimbursed the $2500 in proceeds would have been significantly depleted) in the face of a mere oral assertion, without any further documentation or explanation or follow-up investigation by the insurer, — that someone else claims the proceeds. Recognizing that there are some situations where an interpleader should not be filed necessarily imposes a responsibility on insurers to exercise some judgment. It seems reasonable, however, to expect insurers to be able to exercise discretion in sorting competing claims that have a bona fide possibility of success from claims that after reasonable scrutiny and investigation have no apparent merit.

§ 99   Remedies for the Insurer's Breach of the Duty to Pay Proceeds

[a]   General Contract Remedies

[1]   Loss of the Bargain

Because the insurer's duty to pay proceeds is created by an express promise set forth in the language of the policy, an action for breach of the duty to pay proceeds sounds in contract. Contract remedies are designed to put the aggrieved party in the position that would have been occupied had the promise of the breaching party been performed. This is accomplished by giving the aggrieved party two things: damages for loss of the bargain and damages for other loss.[1]

Loss of bargain damages can be defined as the difference between the value of what the breaching party promised to do and what the breaching party did, less expenses saved as a result of the breach. In the insurance setting, the insurer promises to pay proceeds equal to the amount of the loss, as defined in the policy and as subject to the policy limits, the amount of any deductible, and any coinsurance requirements. Rarely will the insured save money as a result of the insurer's breach, since insurance coverage is purchased by paying premiums in advance; the insured fully performs, and thus saves nothing because of the breach. Thus, if the insurer fails to pay proceeds, the insured's loss of bargain is usually the amount of the proceeds the insurer failed to pay.

---

[8] 820 S.W.2d at 456 (Brown, J., dissenting).

[9] *Id.*

[1] See *Restatement (Second) of Contracts* § 347 (1981).

[2]   Other Loss

Also, under general contract law principles, incidental and consequential damages may be awarded for breach of contract. Incidental damages include additional costs incurred after the breach, such as interest on the amount owed by the breaching party and any costs incurred in a reasonable attempt to avoid further loss. Thus, under the rules set forth in a preceding section,[2] the insured may be entitled to prejudgment interest. Also, if the insurer's failure to pay proceeds for loss of business property led the insured to borrow money in order to replace the property so as to avoid further damage to the business, the interest on the borrowed money would be an incidental cost. Similarly, if the insurer is late making an owed payment, the insurer should be responsible for the foreseeable damage caused by the delay. If the insurer's delay is willful, the insurer might be liable for bad faith conduct or statutory penalties.[3]

Consequential damages include all injuries to person or property arising out of the breach of contract, and can include, depending on the circumstances, such items as lost profits, loss of use of property, loss of business opportunity, damage to a business, and mental anguish.[4] Consequential damages are potentially the most significant kind of contract damage because they have the potential to exceed greatly the loss of bargain damages. To avoid the dampening effect on commerce if unlimited consequential damages might be awarded for breaching a contract, contract law limits the potential range of consequential damages to those which arise naturally from the breach, were foreseeable at the time of contracting, and which can be calculated with reasonable certainty. Most courts take a fairly rigid view of these limitations in the insurance setting and decline to allow recovery for many kinds of consequential damages arising from breach of the insurance contract, including damages for emotional distress,[5] loss of employment and impaired health,[6] and loss of credit and property.[7] The underlying principle is that such damages are too remote from the insurer's breach of contract to be considered reasonably foreseeable at the time the contract was formed.

The prevailing approach, which restricts the consequential damages that are recoverable for breach of an insurance contract, arguably fails to take into account the realities of many insurance transactions. Consumers often purchase insurance because they cannot bear the financial losses associated with certain kinds of casualties, such as the loss of a home, the death or disability of the principal wage earner, or the costs of major medical care. Insurers know this when they sell insurance to consumers; indeed, warnings of such calamities figure prominently in

---

[2] See § 93[e], *supra.*

[3] See Annot., *Liability Insurance: Third Party's Right of Action for Insurer's Bad-Faith Tactics Designed to Delay Payment of Claim,* 62 A.L.R.4th 1113 (1987).

[4] See Lawton v. Great Southwest Fire Ins. Co., 392 A.2d 576 (N.H. 1978).

[5] See, e.g., Commercial Union Assur. Co. v. Pucci, 523 F. Supp. 1310 (D.Pa. 1981); Dawkins v. National Liberty Life Ins. Co., 252 F. Supp. 800 (D.S.C. 1966); National Security Fire & Cas. Co. v. Vintson, 414 So. 2d 49 (Ala. 1982); Spencer v. Aetna Life & Cas. Co., 611 P.2d 149 (Kan. 1980).

[6] See, e.g., Butler v. Gateway Ins. Co., 295 So. 2d 651 (Fla. Dist. Ct. App. 1974); Meridian Mut. Ins. Co. v. McMullen, 282 N.E.2d 558 (Ind. Ct. App. 1972).

[7] See Gross v. Connecticut Gen. Life Ins. Co., 390 S.W.2d 388 (Tex.App. 1965).

insurer advertising. Thus, it is may be incorrect to claim that the emotional distress that often accompanies an insurer's breach of the duty to pay proceeds is not foreseeable by the insurer at the time the insurer enters into the contact.

Of course, in arms-length bargains between commercial enterprises of equal size, these consequential losses are neither foreseeable nor likely. Contract law, however, makes the effort to distinguish cases where consequential losses are foreseeable and those where they are not. It is presumed that mental anguish damages are not recoverable in a contract action, and this is usually correct because such damages are not a normal, foreseeable consequence of a breach of a contract (such as a contract for the sale of a bushel of beans). Yet in situations where mental anguish is foreseeable (as in the case where the contract involves certain services associated with the funeral for and burial of a deceased relative[8]), contract law has not hesitated to award damages for mental distress.[9]

The problem with taking a broader view of the kinds of damages that are appropriate in contract actions is that these remedies are more open-ended than damages calculated with reference to liquidated sums. The risk of a huge judgment that is present whenever a case goes to a jury may over-deter insurers from denying coverage in cases where they should.[10] To the extent the common law of remedies, whether it be a tort-based or contractual remedy, is thought inadequate to give parties (particularly insurers) certainty about their potential liabilities, it may be that statutorily defining the limits of consequential damages for breach of contract may be appropriate. This is what many states have done with respect to the "other loss" component of contract remedies.

[b] Attorney's Fees and Penalties

At common law, a party who obtains a favorable judgment in a civil proceeding is not ordinarily entitled to have attorney's fees paid by the losing party.[11] The only exceptions are where the losing party acts in bad faith, acts vexatiously or wantonly, or has asserted frivolous claims or defenses. This general rule is as applicable in the insurance setting as anywhere else: normally, the insured who succeeds in prosecuting a claim against the insurer for payment of the proceeds under the policy is not entitled to reimbursement of attorney's fees.[12] However, in a few cases, courts have held that the insurer acted unreasonably in denying benefits, thereby entitling the insured to attorney's fees under the well-settled exception to the general rule.[13] Also, in one case, the insured's attorney's fees incurred in recovering the proceeds from an insurer that withheld them in bad faith were held recoverable as a consequential damage.[14]

---

[8] See Alderman v. Ford, 72 P.2d 981 (Kan. 1937).

[9] See Robert H. Jerry, II, *Remedying Insurers' Bad Faith Contract Performance: A Reassessment,* 18 Conn. L. Rev. 271, 298–99 (1986).

[10] For more discussion, see § 25G, *supra.*

[11] See Alyeska Pipeline Serv. Co. v. Wilderness Soc'y, 421 U.S. 240 (1975).

[12] See, e.g., Jefferson-Pilot Fire & Cas Co. v. Boothe, Prichard & Dudley, 638 F.2d 670 (4th Cir. 1980); Bibeault v. Hanover Ins. Co., 417 A.2d 313 (R.I. 1980).

[13] See, e.g., Aetna Cas. & Sur Co. v. Steele, 373 So. 2d 797 (Miss. 1979); Sukup v. State, 227 N.E.2d 842 (N.Y. 1967).

[14] See Mustachio v. Ohio Farmers Ins. Co., 118 Cal. Rptr. 581 (Cal. Ct. App. 1981).

In many states, statutes have been enacted that authorize the award of attorney's fees to the insured who successfully prosecutes a claim against the insurer for proceeds.[15] Under most of these statutes, the insured is required to establish that the insurer acted vexatiously or in bad faith, and this is sometimes a formidable hurdle. If the insurer has a reasonable argument or a reasonable interpretation of the policy's provisions, albeit an incorrect one, attorney's fees are ordinarily disallowed.[16] Some of the attorney's fees statutes also allow the successful insured to recover a "penalty" because of the insurer's unreasonable refusal to pay the proceeds owed under the policy. The penalty is often calculated as a percentage of the contract benefit due.[17]

[c]　Punitive Damages

Punitive damages are usually not awarded for an ordinary breach of contract. However, in most jurisdictions, an insurer could be liable for punitive damages because of its wrongful refusal to indemnify the insured for a loss. The insurer must do more than simply refuse to pay the claim, but exactly what else the insurer must do is difficult to describe. If the insurer commits an independent tort, punitive damages are a distinct possibility. The independent tort could be fraud, outrageous conduct, or bad faith.[18] In some jurisdictions, conduct that is tortious in nature, although falling somewhat short of constituting an independent tort, seems to be enough to justify an award of punitive damages.[19] As with the penalties provided by statute, which can be viewed as a statutorily mandated punitive damages award, punitive damages will not be awarded if the insurer had an arguable basis for refusing to pay proceeds.[20]

[d]　Tort Remedies

As suggested in the previous discussion, if the insurer's refusal to pay proceeds constitutes a tort, damages broader than those normally awarded in contract may

---

[15] See, e.g., Ark. Stat. Ann. § 66-3238; Ga. Code Ann. § 33-4-6; Okla. Stat., tit. 36, § 3629(B).

[16] See, e.g., Cartwright v. CUNA Mut. Ins. Soc'y, 476 So. 2d 915 (La. Ct. App. 1985); Colonial Life & Acc. Ins. Co. v. Donaldson, 322 S.E.2d 510 (Ga. Ct. App. 1984).

[17] See Ark. Stat. Ann. § 66-3238 (attorney's fees plus 12% damages on the amount recovered from the insurer); Ga. Code Ann. § 33-4-6 (attorney's fees plus 25% penalty in event of loss that insurer does not pay within 60 days); Ill. Rev. Stat., ch. 73, § 767 (attorney's fees plus penalty of $5,000, 25% of judgment, or difference between amount of judgment and amount company offered to pay prior to action in event insurer is guilty of unreasonable and vexatious denial of coverage); Me. Rev. Stat. Ann. tit. 24-A, § 2436 (attorney's fees plus interest of 1 1/2% per month after the due date).

[18] See, e.g., Craft v. Economy Fire & Cas Co., 572 F.2d 565 (7th Cir. 1978); Smith v. Canal Ins. Co., 269 S.E.2d 348 (S.C. 1980); Halpin v. Prudential Ins. Co. of Am., 401 N.E.2d 171 (N.Y. 1979).

[19] See, e.g., Corwin Chrysler-Plymouth, Inc. v. Westchester Fire Ins. Co., 279 N.W.2d 638, 645 (N.D. 1979); McIntosh v. Aetna Life Ins. Co., 268 A.2d 518 (D.C. 1970).

[20] See, e.g., Henderson v. U.S. Fid. & Guar. Co., 620 F.2d 530 (5th Cir.), *cert. denied*, 449 U.S. 1034 (1980); American Interstate Ins. Co. v. Revis, 274 S.E.2d 586 (Ga. Ct. App. 1980).

be available. In tort law, the range of consequential damages recoverable is broader than what is available in contract, due to the absence in tort law of contract law's foreseeability limitation. In tort law, the aggrieved party can recover damages proximately caused by the tortfeasor, and mental distress and a broad range of economic loss are often within the zone of proximate causation.[21]

The purported advantage of providing the insured with a remedy in tort is that the broader range of remedies is necessary to deter insurers from taking advantage of their insureds. In first-party insurance, the insurer has relatively little to lose by refusing to pay the insured's claim and forcing the insured to sue. The most that the insured can recover in the contract action is the amount of the claim plus interest; in many cases, consequential damages are likely to be small. If commercial rates of interest exceed legal rates, the insurer may actually profit by delaying payment of proceeds until a later time. Third-party insurance involves different consider-ations, which are discussed in later sections,[22] but for many of the same reasons the contract remedy is thought inadequate to deter insurers from simply refusing to perform and challenging the insured to sue. Cognizant of these criticisms of tort-based remedies, many states have enacted statutes authorizing the award of attorney's fees or a penalty to the insured if the insurer unreasonably refuses to perform.

The tort remedy also has some disadvantages. Where the tort remedy has been allowed, the incidence of large jury awards is alleged to have increased, although this is subject to some dispute. To the extent large awards have increased, the cost of these awards are ultimately borne by the premium-paying public. What is more likely is that the prospect of large damages has probably encouraged the filing of some marginal lawsuits, and has certainly prompted the inclusion of a bad faith count almost every time an insurer is alleged to have breached its duties. It seems inevitable that some insurers, fearful of excessive jury verdicts, settle some insureds' claims at sums exceeding their real value, and this cost is also borne by the premium-paying public.

The disagreement between those favoring contract remedies and those favoring the tort remedy is not an easy one to assess. Much of the debate revolves around the duty of good faith and fair dealing. Although the verdict is not even close to coming in, in the 1990s it is fair to assert that more attention is being given to the contractual underpinnings of bad faith, and it may be that courts will revisit in future cases some of the assumptions underlying the current prevailing jurisprudence which makes tort remedies available in many situations.[23]

[e] Effect of Mistaken Payment by the Insurer

If an insurer mistakenly pays proceeds to the wrong person, the insurer does not discharge its contractual obligation to the person who was supposed to receive the

---

[21] See, e.g., Kewin v. Massachusetts Mut. Life Ins. Co., 295 N.W.2d 50 (Mich. 1980); Robertson v. State Farm Mut. Auto Ins. Co., 464 F. Supp. 876 (D.S.C. 1979); Silberg v. California Life Ins. Co., 521 P.2d 1103 (Cal. 1974).

[22] See §§ 111[g], 112[e], *infra.*

[23] See generally *Symposium on the Law of Bad Faith in Contract and Insurance,* 72 Tex. L. Rev. 1203-1702 (1994); for more discussion, see § 25G, *supra.*

payment.[24] This is unremarkable; it is no different from the situation where a party contracts to have goods delivered to his or her residence, but the seller delivers the goods to the wrong residence. Assuming that the contracting party did not contribute to the mistake, the delivery of goods to the wrong person does not discharge the seller's obligation to the contracting buyer. Thus, it is important that the insurer pay proceeds to the right person to avoid the risk of having to pay proceeds twice.

If the insurer pays proceeds to the wrong person, is the insurer entitled to get the proceeds back? Under ordinary principles of restitution, the answer is usually yes. The insurer has conferred an unjust enrichment on a party that does not deserve it, and in fairness the recipient of the benefit is obligated to return it to the party who bestowed it. As explained by one court:

> It is a firmly established general rule that an insurer who has made a payment under an erroneous belief induced by a mistake of fact that the terms of the insurance contract required such payment is entitled to restitution from the payee, provided the payment has not caused such a change in the position of the payee that it would be unjust to require a refund. The rule is bottomed on the equitable doctrine that an action will lie for the recovery of money received by one to whom it does not in good conscience belong, the law presuming a promise to pay.[25]

Many courts have held that if the insurer makes payments to an insured under a mistake of fact or as a result of fraud or misrepresentation, the insurer is ordinarily held entitled to restitution.[26]

An exception to the general rule that the insurer is entitled to restitution applies in circumstances where the insurer mistakenly pays proceeds to someone claiming the right to proceeds after failing to take reasonable steps to inquire into the merit of the claim. The logic of this exception is that the insurer must state its reasons for refusing to pay proceeds before purporting to settle a claim; the risk of unfairness to a claimant is high if the insurer pays proceeds intending to investigate and perhaps declare the claim invalid at a later time.[27] This logic is not very compelling; it is doubtful that insurers deliberately follow a business practice of "paying now and

---

[24] See, e.g., Santiny v. Pitre, 591 So. 2d 1245 (La. Ct. App. 1991)(auto insurer which paid death benefits to mother of deceased 16-year-old, in circumstances where "everyone knew" that deceased had child out of wedlock, held obligated to pay benefits to mother of decedent's child, in circumstances where decedent's mother had already spent proceeds). See generally Annot., *Right of Insurer Under Automobile Insurance Policy to Restitution of Payments Made Under Mistake*, 37 A.L.R.4th 1048 (1985).

[25] U.S. Fid. and Guar. Co. v. Reagan, 122 S.E.2d 774, 780 (N.C. 1961).

[26] See, e.g., Massachusetts Cas. Ins. Co. v. Forman, 516 F.2d 425 (5th Cir. 1975), *cert. denied*, 424 U.S. 914 (1976); Perovich v. Glens Falls Ins. Co., 401 F.2d 145 (9th Cir. 1968); Home for Crippled Children v. Prudential Ins. Co. of Am., 590 F. Supp. 1490 (W.D. Pa. 1984); Community Mut. Ins. Co. v. Owen, 804 S.W.2d 602 (Tex. Ct. App. 1991) (insurer which mistakenly paid for medical care for spouse of insured twice, once by check to hospital and once by check to insured, held entitled to obtain restitution from insured); Martin v. Blue Cross & Blue Shield of Cent. N.Y., Inc., 561 N.Y.S.2d 997 (N.Y. App. Div. 1990).

[27] See Security Life Ins. Co. v. Blitch, 270 S.E.2d 349 (Ga. Ct. App. 1980).

investigating later" because of the obvious difficulty in getting the proceeds returned at a later time.[28]

Occasionally, a life insurer makes a payment to the wrong beneficiary. This situation illustrates well the competing interests involved in the issue of mistaken payment. Disallowing restitution gives the person who received the money a windfall that should not in good conscience be retained and imposes an extreme forfeiture on the insurer, who otherwise must pay the proceeds twice. On the other hand, the person who mistakenly receives the payment might have both expected it and reasonably relied upon it, perhaps by spending the money, and these circumstances might defeat the insurer's entitlement to restitution. These interests were examined in *Glover v. Metropolitan Life Insurance Co.,*[29] a 1981 Eighth Circuit decision. Mr. Woods was the insured under a policy of group life insurance provided through his employer. He originally designated his wife, Jeanne B. Woods (now Mrs. Glover) as the beneficiary. Mr. Woods and his wife Jeanne were subsequently divorced; under the terms of the property settlement, Jeanne was to remain the designated beneficiary. Mr. Woods's employer, the agent of the insurer for this purpose, had notice of the terms of the settlement agreement. After Mr. Woods's divorce, he married again, and, in violation of the settlement agreement, he designated the new Mrs. Woods as the sole beneficiary on the policy. When Mr. Woods died, the insurer paid the proceeds to his second wife. Mrs. Glover then brought a suit claiming that she was entitled to the proceeds under the property settlement agreement entered into at the time of the divorce.

The court held that Mrs. Woods was required to make restitution to the insurer. She had not spent the money (it appeared),[30] she had not relied on the payment, and the money "in equity and good conscience" did not belong to her. Making the insurer pay twice would be "intolerably unfair," particularly since the difficulty was created in the first place by Mr. Woods's attempt to break the settlement agreement with Mrs. Glover. The equities cut strongly in favor of restitution, despite the fact that the insurer's mistake was one of law — presumably misinterpreting the ambiguous property settlement agreement — for which relief by restitution was not allowed in Missouri.

The insurer's right to restitution was defeated by a third party's reasonable reliance in *Time Insurance Co. v. Fulton-DeKalb Hospital Authority,*[31] a 1993 Georgia decision. Taylor, who was the certificate holder under a group health insurance policy issued to his employer, was treated at a hospital for injuries sustained

---

[28] But see *Blitch,* note 27, *supra,* where the insurer paid the life insurance portion of the proceeds upon the insured's death but did not pay the accidental death proceeds. When the estate sued for the accidental death benefits, the insurer counterclaimed for return of the life insurance proceeds. The court held that the insurer was not entitled to return of the proceeds in the absence of a good reason for failing to ascertain, prior to making the payment, the allegedly "true" circumstances surrounding the insured's death. 270 S.E.2d at 354.

[29] 664 F.2d 1101 (8th Cir. 1981).

[30] In the petition for rehearing, Mrs. Woods asserted for the first time that the fund was not intact. The court therefore ordered the district court to inquire into the possibility of reducing the judgment against Mrs. Woods. See 664 F.2d at 1105.

[31] 438 S.E.2d 149 (Ga. Ct. App. 1993).

in a fire. The insurer paid the hospital approximately $184,000 as reimbursement for the health services it rendered Taylor. Thereafter, the insurer learned that Taylor's injuries were received in a fire he intentionally set and for which he had been convicted of arson. The insurer, under the reasoning that Taylor was not entitled to coverage under the exclusions for self-inflicted injury and injury resulting from the commission of a felony, sought restitution of the $184,000 from the hospital. The court held, however, that the hospital, as a third-party creditor of Taylor, was not unjustly enriched and could not be required to make restitution to the insurer. In these circumstances, the hospital was entitled "in good conscience" to keep the proceeds paid.[32]

To summarize, when an insurer makes payment to the wrong person due to a good faith mistake of fact or law, courts typically allow the insurer restitution from the person who without entitlement received the proceeds. However, if the insurer fails to investigate a claim adequately and makes a mistaken payment, the insurer may be denied restitution. Also, as *Glover* suggests, restitution may be disallowed if the person who received the money has reasonably relied by spending the money or otherwise depleting the proceeds.

---

[32] 438 S.E.2d at 151-52. Other courts have reached the same result on similar facts. See, e.g., National Ben. Administrators v. MMHRC, 748 F. Supp. 459 (S.D. Miss. 1990); Federated Mut. Ins. Co. v. Good Samaritan Hosp., 214 N.W.2d 493 (Neb. 1974); City of Hope Nat'l Med. Ctr. v. Superior Court, 10 Cal. Rptr.2d 465 (Cal. Ct. App. 1992); Lincoln Nat'l Life Ins. Co. v. Brown Schools, Inc., 757 S.W.2d 411 (Tex. Ct. App. 1988). Compare Lincoln Nat'l Life Ins. Co. v. Rittman, 790 S.W.2d 791 (Tex. Ct. App. 1990) (insurer mistakenly paid health care provider for too much of insured's bill for services rendered to insured's daughter; insurer sued insured for restitution; held, restitution would be inequitable in circumstances presented, where insured said he could not have afforded to keep child in hospital if mistaken payments had not been made and would have withdrawn child from hospital); Prudential Ins. Co. of Am. v. Couch, 376 S.E.2d 104 (W.Va. 1988) (insurer not entitled to summary judgment under restitution theory where insurer sued father and son to recover benefits mistakenly paid to several health care providers under a group health insurance plan).

CHAPTER 10

EXCUSES FOR THE INSURER'S NONPERFORMANCE

§ 100 Generally

In a contract, the substantial failure of one party to perform the duties it owes the other party will give the other party justification to suspend its own performance. In other words, each party's duties are constructively conditioned on the other party being ready and able to perform its duties when due. In an insurance contract, the insured promises to pay premiums when due. If the insured breaches this duty, the insurer is entitled to suspend its own performance. Thus, if a loss occurs when a premium remains unpaid, the insurer need not indemnify the insured for the loss.

The insurance contract also contains certain conditions to the insurer's obligations. In contract law generally, if a duty is subject to a condition and the condition is not satisfied, the duty need not be performed. Thus, if a condition to the insurer's duty is not satisfied, the insurer need not perform. The insurance contract requires the insured, as part of claims processing, to do certain things as prerequisites to the insurer's duty to pay proceeds. Giving notice of the loss within a reasonable time and filing a proof of loss are two examples of actions the insured must take in order to make the insurer's obligation to pay proceeds due and owing. If the insured fails to comply with these requirements of the policy, the insurer need not pay proceeds for the loss. The explanation for this result is that a condition to the insurer's duty to pay proceeds is not satisfied, and this excuses the insurer's nonperformance of its duty.

In this chapter, three other significant excuses for the insurer's nonperformance of its contract obligations are considered: breach of warranty; misrepresentation; and concealment.

§ 101 Insured's Breach of Warranty

[a] Definition

The term "warranty" refers to a statement or promise by the insured, set forth or incorporated in the policy, which if untrue or unfulfilled provides the insurer with a defense to a claim for coverage. In effect, the insured agrees that certain acts have been or shall be done, and the validity of the insurance contract depends upon the

(Matthew Bender & Co., Inc.) (Pub.837)

fulfillment of these acts.[1] As discussed in more detail in this section, perhaps the most salient feature of warranties in insurance policies during recent decades is that the potentially harsh effects of them on insureds have been substantially mitigated by statutes and judicial decisions.

[b] Creation of a Warranty

No particular formula exists for creating a warranty. Whether a warranty exists is primarily a question of intention, which is determined by the language of the policy and its subject matter. However, it is possible to generalize to this extent: A representation will be treated as a warranty if two requirements are met. First, the representation or promise must be included — either expressly or by express reference — in the insurance contract document.[2] Sometimes insurers meet this requirement by attaching the insured's application (with its questions and answers) to the policy, thereby making it a part of the contract. Second, the contract must show that the parties intended the rights of the insured to depend on the truth or fulfillment of the representation or promise.[3] Merely referring to the representation as a "warranty" is not enough to meet this requirement. Instead, there must be some clear indication, such as a statement in the policy that the insured promises the existence of certain facts as a prerequisite to having valid coverage, that the parties' intentions are predicated on the truth or existence of the warranted facts.[4] The theoretical underpinning of a warranty is that the parties agreed that all rights under the policy depended on the truth or fulfillment of the statement or promise. There is no separate requirement that a breach of warranty cause the loss for which the insured seeks a recovery. Just as an insurer is released by a breach of warranty regardless of whether the breach increased the risk or was committed for a good reason, the effect of a breach is not diminished by the fact that the breach did not cause the loss (unless a state statute overrides this rule).[5]

Because a breach of warranty can lead to the insured's loss of coverage, courts typically apply the foregoing requirements strictly. For example, in *Sanford v.*

---

[1] For example, Cal. Ins. Code § 445 defines a warranty in this way: "A statement in a policy, which imports that there is an intention to do or not to do a thing which materiallyaffects the risk, is a warranty that such act or omission will take place."

[2] See, e.g., Allied Bankers Life Ins. Co. v. De La Cerda, 584 S.W.2d 529 (Tex. Ct. App. 1979); Allstate Ins. Co. v. Boggs, 271 N.E.2d 855 (Ohio 1971); Brynildsen v. Ambassador Ins. Co., 274 A.2d 327 (N.J. Super. Ct. App. Div. 1971).

[3] See, e.g., Old Southern Life Ins. Co., Inc. v. Spann, 472 So. 2d 987 (Ala. 1985); Lane v. Travelers Indem. Co., 391 S.W.2d 399 (Tex. 1965); Brotherhood of R.R. Trainmen v. Wood, 79 S.W.2d 665 (Tex. Ct. App. 1935).

[4] See, e.g., Van Riper v. Equitable Life Assur. Soc'y, 561 F. Supp. 26 (E.D. Pa. 1982), *aff'd*, 707 F.2d 1397 (3d Cir. 1983); Allstate Ins. Co. v. Boggs, 271 N.E.2d 855 (Ohio 1971); Cartusciello v. Allied Life Ins. Co., 661 S.W.2d 285 (Tex. Ct. App. 1983); Morris v. Sovereign Camp, W.O.W., 9 So. 2d 835 (La. Ct. App. 1942); Spence v. Central Acc. Ins. Co., 86 N.E. 104 (Ill. 1908).

[5] See, e.g., Vlastos v. Sumitomo Marine and Fire Ins. Co. (Europe) Ltd., 707 F.2d 775 (3d Cir. 1983); Coffey v. Indiana Lumberman's Mut. Ins. Co., 372 F.2d 646 (6th Cir. 1967); Home Ins. Co. v. Ciconett, 179 F.2d 892 (6th Cir. 1950); Coleman Furniture Corp. v. Home Ins. Co., 67 F.2d 347 (4th Cir. 1933), *cert. denied,* 291 U.S. 669 (1934).

Federated Guaranty Insurance Co.,[6] language in the application that purported to make the insured's statements warranties. But the provision in the policy which incorporated the application into the policy contained language referring to the insured's "representations" in the policy's declarations. This was enough, in the court's view, to create an ambiguity as to whether the insured's statements were representations or warranties, and any ambiguity required that the statements be considered representations.[7] Under the same reasoning, if the insurer fails to physically attach an application to the policy or expressly incorporate the application into the policy, the insured's statements in the application will be treated as representations, and not warranties.[8]

[c]   Effect of Noncompliance with a Warranty

Lord Mansfield deserves most of the credit for developing the concept of a warranty.[9] According to Professor Vance, by the time Lord Mansfield retired, a distinction was being made between two kinds of descriptions of the risk on which the underwriter might rely: descriptions within the policy and descriptions outside the policy. If within the policy, the descriptions needed to be literally true, regardless of their materiality. If outside the policy, the insurance was valid unless the incorrect description was "substantial and material," meaning that the incorrect description injured the underwriter. At an early time, then, Lord Mansfield was describing the essence of the distinction between warranties and representations.

The reason for the strict rule that warranties needed to be literally satisfied for the insured to recover on the policy can be found in the economics of the marine industry in eighteenth century England. The recurrent wars of that century made it highly desirable that merchant vessels sail in a convoy; thus, insurers required shipowners to warrant that their ships would not sail alone, and if no warranty were given a much higher premium would be charged. Also, whether a ship constituted neutral property had much to do with the likelihood of the ship being seized by an enemy as a prize of war; a warranty that a ship was neutral was rewarded with a lower rate, and the warranty was strictly enforced. Sailing at certain times of the year was more dangerous; insurers might secure a warranty that a ship would sail at a particular time. Strict enforcement of warranties was thought important to protect the marine insurance industry, which was extremely important to the British economy.[10]

The strict, harsh rule was transposed to life insurance and fire insurance, and the English warranty rules were eventually adopted in the United States.[11] The

---

[6] 522 So. 2d 214 (Miss. 1988).

[7] 522 So. 2d at 216-17.

[8] Allstate Ins. Co. v. Boggs, 271 N.E.2d 855 (Ohio 1971).

[9] William R. Vance, *The History of the Development of the Warranty in Insurance Law,* 20 Yale L.J. 523 (1911).

[10] Edwin W. Patterson, *Essentials of Insurance Law* 274 (2d ed. 1957). See generally Steven E. Goldman, *Breach of Warranty in American Marine Insurance,* 52 Ins. Counsel J. 60 (1985); James R. Sutterfield, *Express Warranties and the Wilburn Boat Case,* 48 Ins. Counsel J. 76 (1981).

[11] See Home Ins. Co. v. Ciconett, 179 F.2d 892 (6th Cir. 1950).

arguments favoring strict application of the common law rules were several. Strict enforcement protects insurers by limiting indemnity to cases where the insured has answered all application questions honestly; strict enforcement deters applicants from making false representations; integrity in insurance contracts is promoted, and fraud and perjury are deterred; and a strict rule is simple to enforce.[12] However, the manner in which the warranty rule was applied neither furthered nor promoted these objectives. Instead, insurance forms became filled with technical, trivial warranties, whereby the insurer hoped to trap the insured and deny coverage.[13] The rules of warranty law had by this time become so deeply entrenched that it was not possible to turn back the clock and follow a principle that breach of an immaterial warranty has no consequence, just as an immaterial misrepresentation has no consequence. Courts did respond, however, by insisting that no statement or promise in a policy be construed as a warranty unless it was clearly and unmistakably intended as such by the parties, as evidenced by the language of the policy.

Today, the harshness of the strict warranty rule is substantially diminished by case law and statutory developments. Nevertheless, there are situations, particularly in marine insurance, where warranties still have bite.[14] For example, in *American Home Assurance Co. v. Harvey's Wagon Wheel, Inc.*[15] the insured lost its coverage by virtue of a breach of warranty. The fire insurance policy issued to a Las Vegas casino contained a provision titled "Automatic Sprinkler Warranty," the text of which was set forth in boldface capital letters:

> This policy being written at a reduced rate based on the protection of the premises by an automatic sprinkler system, it is a condition of this policy that so far as the sprinkler system and the water supply therefor are under the control of the insured, due diligence shall be used by the insured to maintain them in complete working order and that no change shall be made in said system or in the water supply therefore without the consent in writing of this company.[16]

Harvey's began a reconstruction project in the casino and adjacent restaurant areas, and the casino's sprinkler system was disconnected. While the project was under-way, a fire occurred which caused damage to the casino, but not the restaurant.

The insured contended that the warranty should be construed in a manner that would make it relevant only to the premium charged for the policy; in other words, the insurer's obligation to offer a reduced premium — as opposed to the coverage itself — was what depended on the truth of the warranty. The court was not

---

[12] See Cooper, *Misrepresentations and False Warranties in Insurance Applications,* 58 Ill. B.J. 962 (1970).

[13] See generally Vance, *supra* note 9.

[14] See, e.g., Steptore v. Masco Constr. Co., Inc., 619 So. 2d 1183 (La. Ct. App. 1993), *judgment aff'd in part and rev'd in part,* 643 So. 2d 1213 (La. 1994) (marine insurance); Aetna Ins. Co. v. Dudney, 595 So. 2d 238 (Fla. Dist. Ct. App. 1992) (marine insurance); Physicians Ins. Co. of Ohio v. Morehead, 623 N.E.2d 154 (Ohio Ct.App. 1993) (alleged misrepresentations in application for medical malpractice policy were warranties and not mere representations).

[15] 398 F. Supp. 379 (D.Nev. 1975), *aff'd without opinion,* 554 F.2d 1067 (1977).

[16] 398 F. Supp. at 381.

sympathetic to the insured's argument. The court described the warranty as unequivocal and invalidated the coverage on account of its breach:

> The automatic sprinkler endorsement was of the essence of the policy. It resulted in a premium rate approximately one-eighth the rate for non-sprinklered business premises. It was specifically bargained for by the insured and was discussed at about the time the policy was delivered. It was again called to the insured's attention when construction was underway. The unsprinklered areas were damaged by fire while the sprinklered areas were not. Law and equity require that the insurers be permitted the protection of the unambiguous policy warranty under these circumstances.[17]

In situations where parties with equal bargaining power expressly agree that certain circumstances are absolute prerequisites to the insurer's obligation to perform, the fairest result in most cases is to enforce the agreement of the parties. But outcomes like that in *Harvey's Wagon Wheel* are quite exceptional. If one proceeds from the reasonable assumptions that most insureds lack any meaningful bargaining power and the contract between insurer and insured is one of adhesion, it follows that the warranty doctrine has the potential to work severe unfairness on the insured. As a result, both courts and legislatures have seen fit to police the warranty doctrine in most situations, which has had the effect of conflating the law of warranty and misrepresentation in insurance generally.

[d]　Warranties versus Representations

A representation will only become a warranty if it is included in the contract of insurance. This means that the warranty must either be contained in the policy itself or be explicitly incorporated in the policy by reference. A representation, however, is collateral to the contract; it need not be contained in the contract and can be contained in a document completely separate from the insurance contract. It can even be oral.[18]

The legal effects of a warranty differ from those of a representation. The essence of a warranty is that it is intended as an absolute condition to coverage. Normally a warranty will be made regarding a fact material to the risk; unless the insurer seeks to trap the unwary insured, the insurer will only insist upon the insured's warranties for those factors important to its decision to underwrite the risk. Yet the theory of a warranty is that the parties agree to create it, and the parties are free to specify what facts are material. If the parties desire, they can agree that the truth of an inconsequential statement is an absolute condition to coverage (unless a statute prohibits such an agreement).

Thus, when a statement or representation is a warranty, the insured cannot avoid the effect of its breach by claiming that the matter warranted was not material to

---

[17] 398 F. Supp. at 384.

[18] See, e.g., Vlavtov v. Sumitomo Marine & Fire Ins. Co., Ltd., 707 F.2d 775 (3d Cir. 1983); Lane v. Travelers Indem. Co., 391 S.W.2d 399 (Tex. 1965); Whitehead v. Fleet Towing Co., 442 N.E.2d 1362 (Ill. App. Ct. 1982).

the risk.[19] A warranty is binding on the insured regardless of whether it is material; another way to express this idea is that the materiality of a warranty is conclusively presumed. The insured can recover under the policy only if the statement was exactly true or the promise was completely fulfilled. For example, if the insured warrants that a building will be used in a certain way, the fact that the noncomplying use does not increase the risk of loss — or even reduces the risk of loss — is irrelevant. This contrasts starkly with the rules applicable to representations. The insurer has the burden of proving the materiality of a representation to the risk before the insurer is entitled to avoid the contract for misrepresentation.[20] (It should be noted that statutes in some states, discussed below, have abrogated the rule that the materiality of a warranty is conclusively presumed.)

The rule that a warranty's materiality is conclusively presumed relates to a second legal effect of a warranty. A warranty must be *strictly* satisfied if the insured is to have coverage.[21] In contrast, a misrepresentation does not give the insurer grounds for voiding the contract as long as the representation is *substantially* true.[22] This difference is illustrated by the fact that courts only require, in many instances, the insured to believe the truth of the representation; only if the insured intentionally misrepresents a fact is the insurer given a defense to coverage.[23] However, whether warranties have been satisfied is ordinarily determined objectively, without regard to the insured's subjective intentions. It is ordinarily irrelevant if a warranty is broken that the insured did not intend to deceive or defraud the insurer, or, conversely, that the insured possessed a good faith, honest belief in the warranty's truth.[24] For example, if the applicant's statement that he or she is in good health is a representation, it is only a statement of opinion that will not invalidate the contract unless fraudulently made. If the statement is a warranty, however, its

---

[19] See, e.g., Allstate Ins. Co. v. Boggs, 271 N.E.2d 855 (Ohio 1971); Van Riper v. Equitable Life Assur. Soc'y of U.S., 561 F. Supp. 26 (E.D. Pa.), *aff'd without opinion,* 707 F.2d 161 (3d Cir. 1983).

[20] See, e.g., Proprietors Ins. Co. v. Northwestern Nat'l Bank of Minneapolis, 374 N.W.2d 772 (Minn. Ct. App. 1985); Willis v. Colonial Life & Acc. Ins. Co., 353 So. 2d 480 (La. Ct. App. 1977).

[21] See, e.g., Wilburn Boat Co. v. Fireman's Fund Ins. Co., 348 U.S. 310 (1955); Campbell v. Hartford Fire Ins. Co., 533 F.2d 496 (9th Cir. 1976); Violin v. Fireman's Fund Ins. Co., 406 P.2d 287 (Nev. 1965); Brynildsen v. Ambassador Ins. Co., 274 A.2d 327 (N.J. Super. Ct. App. Div. 1971).

[22] See, e.g., Sanford v. Federated Guar. Ins. Co., 522 So. 2d 214 (Miss. 1988); Whitehead v. Fleet Towing Co., 442 N.E.2d 1362 (Ill. App. Ct. 1982); Forbes v. Auerbach, 67 So. 2d 685 (Fla. 1953); Schuetzel v. Grand Aerie Fraternal Order of Eagles, 164 S.W.2d 135 (Mo. Ct. App. 1942).

[23] See, e.g., Henning Nelson Constr. Co. v. Fireman's Fund Am. Life Ins. Co., 383 N.W.2d 645 (Minn. 1986) (en banc); White v. Medico Life Ins. Co., 327 N.W.2d 606 (Neb. 1982); Mayes v. Massachusetts Mut. Life Ins. Co., 608 S.W.2d 612 (Tex. 1980); Ragan v. Pilgrim Life Ins. Co., 461 So. 2d 618 (La. Ct. App. 1984).

[24] See, e.g., Van Riper v. Equitable Life Assur. Soc'y, 561 F. Supp. 26 (E.D. Pa. 1982), *aff'd,* 707 F.2d 1397 (3d Cir. 1983); Fidelity & Cas. Co. v. Phelps, 64 F.2d 233 (4th Cir. 1933); Bankers' Reserve Life Co. v. Matthews, 39 F.2d 528 (8th Cir. 1930); Liguori v. Supreme Forest Woodmen Circle, 188 A. 169 (Pa. 1936).

incorrectness will wholly void the policy, according to most decisions, even if the insured acted in good faith.[25]

Notwithstanding the general rule, courts do tend to relax the strict rule that warranties must be literally fulfilled. One way to do this is to construe the warranty as a representation; this is frequently done with good health provisions.[26] There are some old decisions that adopt a rule of "substantial compliance" with respect to warranties; these cases hold that a promissory warranty need only be substantially true or substantially fulfilled.[27] A number of courts have held that "iron safe" clauses, under which the insured promises to keep an inventory of the insured property locked in a fireproof safe or some other place secure from fire damage, need only be substantially satisfied: "[T]he insured is not required to keep 'such books as would be kept by an expert bookkeeper or accountant,' and the safe is not required to be 'perfect in all respects and capable of withstanding any fire however intensive and fierce;' rather, the standard to be applied is that of sufficient compliance 'in the judgment of prudent men in the locality.' "[28] Also, as discussed below, statutes in some states have altered the common law rule that a warranty must be strictly satisfied.[29]

[e] Mitigating Doctrines

Because a warranty if breached has the potential to work a severe hardship on the insured, numerous devices that mitigate the strict effects of warranties have been recognized by courts and legislatures.

[1] Affirmative versus Promissory Warranties

In numerous cases, courts have drawn a distinction between affirmative warranties and promissory warranties.[30] An affirmative warranty is a statement concerning the accuracy of a fact as of the time the contract is formed. A promissory warranty is a statement concerning the future, in the nature of a promise that a certain state of facts will continue to exist or to be true. Unless a warranty is clearly shown to be

---

[25] See, e.g., Fidelity & Cas. Co. v. Phelps, 64 F.2d 233 (4th Cir. 1933); Lincoln Income Life Ins. Co. v. Mayberry, 347 S.W.2d 598 (Tex. 1961); Audubon Life Ins. Co. v. Lauzervich, 242 So. 2d 589 (La. Ct. App. 1970).

[26] See, e.g., Morris v. Sovereign Camp, W.O.W., 9 So. 2d 835, aff'd, 203 La. 507, 14 So. 2d 428 (1942); United Ins. Co. v. Dixon, 237 S.E.2d 661 (Ga. Ct. App. 1977); City Bank & Trust Co. v. Commercial Cas. Co., 176 So. 27 (La. Ct. App. 1937).

[27] See Phoenix Ins. Co. v. Benton, 87 Ind. 132 (1882); National Live Stock Ins. Co. v. Owens, 113 N.E. 1024 (Ind. Ct. App. 1916); Hanover Fire Ins. Co. v. Gustin, 59 N.W. 375 (Neb. 1894); SFI, Inc. v. U.S. Fire Ins. Co., 453 F. Supp. 502 (M.D.La. 1978), aff'd, 634 F.2d 879 (5th Cir. 1981).

[28] Liverpool & London & Globe Ins. Co. v. Kearney, 180 U.S. 132, 137, 21 S.Ct. 326, 45 L.Ed. 460 (1901). See also Dickerson v. Franklin Nat'l Ins. Co., 130 F.2d 35 (4th Cir. 1942); Georgian House of Interiors v. Glens Falls Ins. Co., 151 P.2d 598 (Wash. 1944).

[29] See § 101[f], infra.

[30] See, e.g., Benton Casing Service, Inc. v. Avemco Ins. Co., 379 So. 2d 225 (La. 1979); Automobile Ins. Co. v. Barnes-Manley Wet Wash Laundry Co., 168 F.2d 381 (10th Cir.), cert. denied, 335 U.S. 859 (1948); Orient Ins. Co. v. Van Zandt-Bruce Drug Co., 151 P. 323 (Okla. 1915).

promissory, courts usually presume that the warranty is affirmative.[31] Under this approach, if an insurance policy describes property as "a building used for making dolls," no warranty is made that the building will continue to be used for that purpose. The United States Supreme Court followed this approach in *Hosford v. Germania Fire Insurance Co.,*[32] when it held that a warranty in a contract of fire insurance that smoking not be allowed on the premises was not breached by the fact that the insured and others smoked there afterwards. It was enough to satisfy the warranty that smoking was forbidden on the premises at the time the contract was formed.

A more recent case utilizing the same approach is *Vlastos v. Sumitomo Marine & Fire Insurance Co. (Europe), Ltd.,*[33] a 1983 Third Circuit decision. The insured was the owner of a commercial building. She operated a luncheonette and bar on the first floor, and she leased the second floor and part of the third to a massage parlor. Her handyman-janitor also occupied part of the third floor. After the building was destroyed by fire, the insurer denied coverage on the ground that the insured had warranted that the third floor of the building was occupied exclusively as a janitor's residence. The policy contained a provision which stated "Warranted that the 3rd floor is occupied as Janitor's residence." The court ruled that this provision was not a promise that a janitor would occupy the third floor of the building in the future. Rather, this warranty was only a promise that the third floor was so occupied at the time of contracting. If the janitor occupied the floor on the date the policy was issued, the warranty was satisfied, even if the situation had changed by the time the fire occurred several months later. In other words, the court viewed the warranty as an affirmative warranty, not a promissory warranty.

If a warranty is promissory, its legal effect is essentially equivalent to that of a condition subsequent. If the warranted fact ceases to exist or to be true, the insurer's existing obligation to pay proceeds in the event of a loss is discharged. If the warranty, whether promissory or affirmative, is not satisfied on the date the policy is issued, the policy is rendered invalid from its inception.

[2] Judicial Interpretation

The rule that warranties needed to be strictly satisfied lest the insured lose coverage induced insurers to insert large numbers of technical, complex warranties into their policies. Because these warranties often lay a trap for the uninformed insured, courts responded to the insurers' efforts by interpreting warranties in specific cases so that the particular act or neglect of an insured would not void the coverage. Not surprisingly, the case law that resulted was a jumble of varied, inconsistent, and sometimes vague rules and precedents. A few observations can be made, however, about these cases.

In the absence of clear language to the contrary, courts are inclined to interpret a warranty as affirmative rather than promissory. As discussed above, an affirmative

---

[31] See Smith v. Mechanics' & Traders' Fire Ins. Co., 32 N.Y. 399 (1865); National Union Fire Ins. Co. v. Falciani, 208 A.2d 422 (N.J. Super. Ct. App. Div. 1965).

[32] 127 U.S. 399, 8 S.Ct. 1199, 32 L.Ed. 196 (1888).

[33] 707 F.2d 775 (3d Cir. 1983).

warranty amounts to a promise that a particular condition exists at the time of contracting, not an assurance that the condition will continue to exist indefinitely. Affirmative warranties are less likely to be breached than promissory warranties.

If possible, courts are inclined to interpret language of warranty as something else entirely. For example, courts sometimes try to interpret a purported warranty as a representation, which, unlike a warranty, need not be strictly satisfied. If the facts of the particular case permit, a court might reason that because the relevant language was not included in the text of the contract or because the insured was not informed in certain terms that the insured's rights depended upon the accuracy of the representation, the language is not a warranty at all.[34] Courts have also interpreted warranties as identifying clauses. If the clause of the policy states that the property is located at a certain address, the court might say that the clause is not a promise but is simply a means of identifying where the insured property is located.[35]

The *Vlastos* case, discussed above, is a good example of a court interpreting a warranty. The policy was endorsed so that the insured "[w]arranted that the 3rd floor is occupied as Janitor's residence." The insurer argued that this was a promise by the insured that the janitor was the exclusive occupant of the third floor, a promise which was not kept at the time of the fire that destroyed the insured's building. The court stated that "a reasonable person could have understood Vlastos to have warranted merely that her janitor lived on the third floor."[36] If asked whether a janitor occupied the third floor, the answer would probably not be "no, he occupies only part of it," but would be "yes, although he shares the space with a massage parlor." Because the policy did not involve warranties as to what uses the other floors were put, it seemed logical that the insurer wanted a promise that a resident janitor would live somewhere in the building, rather than exclusively occupy one of its floors. The insurer argued that exclusive occupancy of one floor by a janitor would reduce the risk, since a higher-risk tenant could not occupy the remainder of the floor, but the insured had no reason to understand this was the insurer's objective, particularly since the insurer did not insist that particular uses be made of the other floors. Under these circumstances, the court viewed the ambiguous clause in a light most favorable to the insured, and held that the insured warranted only that a janitor occupy some part of the third floor, not the entire floor. This warranty was not breached.[37]

A court might also try to interpret a warranty so as to minimize its effect. Thus, in *Wood v. Hartford Fire Insurance Co.,*[38] the court held that the descriptive warranty "paper-mill" did not mean that the building was required to be used as a paper mill but only that it be ready for use as a paper mill. The building was available

---

[34] See, e.g., Allied Bankers Life Ins. Co. v. De La Cerda, 584 S.W.2d 529 (Tex. Ct. App. 1979); Schuetzel v. Grand Aerie Fraternal Order of Eagles, 164 S.W.2d 135 (Mo. App. 1942); Spence v. Central Acc. Ins. Co., 86 N.E. 104 (Ill. 1908).

[35] See, e.g., Lane v. Travelers Indem. Co., 391 S.W.2d 399 (Tex. 1965); Wood v. Hartford Fire Ins. Co., 13 Conn. 533, 35 Am.Dec. 92 (1840).

[36] 707 F.2d at 778.

[37] 707 F.2d at 779.

[38] 13 Conn. 533, 35 Am.Dec. 92 (1840).

for this use at all relevant times, even though the building was used as a grist mill during part of this time. In the same vein, a court might "interpret the act" of the insured in a way that complies with the warranty. Illustrative is *Fidelity & Deposit Co. of Maryland v. Friedlander,*[39] where the insured's policy contained clauses requiring a custodian and "at least one other employee of the Assured" to be on the premises for the coverage to be effective. The insured had contracted with a local cleaning company for daily maintenance and janitorial services. A person was regularly sent to the insured's jewelry store to do this work and other tasks that the insured might request, but this person was paid by the cleaning company and was under its direction and control. The insured's store was robbed while the insured and the cleaning person were on the premises. The insurer denied coverage on the ground that the cleaning person was not an "employee." The court noted that the purpose of the policy provision was to deter in-house theft: such theft is less likely if two employees are on the premises at any given time. Although the cleaning person was not an employee, this person basically fulfilled the purpose of the clause; in the "sense of the controverted provisions of the policies," this person was an employee of the insured's and "this interpretation will satisfy the evident purpose of the provisions."[40]

Third, a court might interpret the warranty as only extending to a particular risk or a severable part of the policy. If this technique is used, the breach of warranty under one kind of risk will not avoid the policy with respect to other parts of the coverage.[41]

Fourth, a court might construe the breach of warranty as a mere "temporary breach" that does not terminate the policy's coverage. Under the doctrine of temporary breach, the insurer that does not take action to void the policy before the breach is cured has no defense. The curing of the breach is basically treated as reviving coverage that was only temporarily suspended.[42] This technique is usually used in circumstances where the risk is not substantially increased during the period of the breach. If the breach of warranty materially increases the risk, a revival of coverage may not be permitted.[43]

The particular circumstances have much to do with whether the temporary breach approach is available. For example, in *Vander Laan v. Educators Mutual Insurance Co.,*[44] the policy covered the insured while traveling as an airplane passenger but

---

[39] 101 F.2d 106 (6th Cir. 1939).

[40] 101 F.2d at 108.

[41] See, e.g., Pugh v. Commonwealth Mut. Fire Ins. Co., 195 F.2d 83 (3d Cir. 1952); Diesinger v. American & Foreign Ins. Co., 138 F.2d 91 (3d Cir. 1943); Adams v. Northern Ins. Co., 493 P.2d 504 (Ariz. Ct. App. 1972).

[42] See, e.g., Ranger Ins. Co. v. Macy, 227 N.W.2d 426 (S.D. 1975); Dale v. Mutual Fire Ins. Co., 103 A.2d 414 (Pa. 1954); Globe & Rutgers Fire Ins. Co. v. Pruitt, 64 S.W.2d 91 (Ark. 1933); Eastern Ins. Co. v. Austin, 396 So. 2d 823 (Fla. Dist. Ct. App. 1981).

[43] See, e.g., Powell Valley Electric Cooperative, Inc. v. U.S. Aviation Underwriters, Inc., 179 F. Supp. 616 (W.D. Va. 1959); Fidelity-Phenix Fire Ins. Co. v. Pilot Freight Carriers, Inc., 193 F.2d 812 (4th Cir. 1952); Henjes v. Aetna Ins. Co., 132 F.2d 715 (2d Cir. 1943).

[44] 97 N.W.2d 6 (Mich. 1959).

excluded from coverage loss resulting "while operating . . . or serving as a member of the crew of any aircraft." The insured, a licensed pilot, went on a fishing trip with another pilot and two other passengers. The two pilots alternated flying, but the other pilot was flying the airplane at the time of the crash. No evidence existed that the insured was assisting with navigation or other matters when the crash occurred. The court held that if the insured were not at the controls or performing crew duties when the crash occurred, he was a passenger within the terms of the policy and was therefore covered.[45]

A contrasting case is *Beckwith v. American Home Assurance Co.*[46] The insured was flying a private aircraft when a fuel problem developed. His copilot first noticed the problem and tried to correct it, but when these measures failed the copilot took control of the plane, commenced unsuccessful emergency procedures, and crash-landed the plane. The insured, who died later of his injuries, was not in control of the plane at the time of the crash, although he had been in control of it immediately before the problems developed. The court concluded that the insured's activities in the plane constituted a breach of the warranty, and his turning over the airplane's controls to someone else did not restore the coverage.

Vander Laan and *Beckwith* are difficult cases to reconcile. It would seem that if the insurer would not have canceled the policy upon learning of the temporary breach of warranty, it is unfair to allow the insurer after the loss to declare the policy invalid.[47] Yet determining in hindsight what an insurer would have done had it known of a temporary breach is a highly uncertain endeavor.

[3] Statutory Mitigation

Most states have enacted statutes that mitigate the harsh effects of warranties. The general approach of these statutes is the same: to change the legal effect of warranties to that of ordinary representations. But because the statutes differ widely in their specific language, there are diverse results on similar facts in different jurisdictions. This subsection examines some of the common statutory formulations that regulate warranties in insurance policies.

One common kind of statute provides that no misrepresentation or breach of warranty will constitute a defense for the insurer unless the risk of loss was materially increased by the misrepresentation or the breach.[48] What constitutes "materiality" is often left undefined, but the apparent purpose of this kind of statute is to equate the legal effects of warranties to misrepresentations: only if materiality of the breach is actually proved does the insurer have a defense. In *Los Angeles Mutual Insurance Co. v. Cawog,*[49] the court applied such a provision. Los Angeles

---

[45] To the same effect is Alliance Life Ins. Co. v. Ulysses Volunteer Fireman's Relief Ass'n, 529 P.2d 171 (Kan. 1974).

[46] 565 F. Supp. 458 (W.D. N.C. 1983).

[47] See Sumter Tobacco Warehouse Co. v. Phoenix Ins. Co., 56 S.E. 654 (S.C. 1907), *discussed in* Patterson, note 10, *supra*, at 318–19.

[48] See, e.g., Mich. Comp. Laws Ann. § 500.2218; N.M. Stat. Ann. § 59A–18–11(C); N.Y. Ins. Code § 3106; Tex. Stat. Ann. art. 21.16, 21.18.

[49] 106 Cal. Rptr. 307 (Cal. Ct. App. 1973).

Mutual ("LAM") issued its policy on the insured's hotel; on the date of issuance, the insured also maintained a policy with another company on the same hotel having an equal face value. LAM's policy contained the following provision: "It is understood and agreed that this policy being written in the amount of $10,000 is 50% of all contributing insurance. It is hereby warranted that all contributing insurance shall be maintained to the extent that this policy's participation will not exceed said 50%." The insured failed to renew the other policy, and the hotel was subsequently damaged by fire in an amount exceeding $20,000. LAM argued that it had no liability to the insured because he had failed to maintain the other policy. Under the relevant California statutes, an insurer has no right to avoid a policy on the ground that the insured has breached a warranty unless the breach materially affects the risk or the policy specifically states that the breach will avoid the policy. In *Cawog*, the insurer's failure to carry other insurance, as he promised, did not materially affect the risk and therefore the insurer's failure to maintain the coverage did not invalidate the LAM policy:

> It is only reasonable to conclude that the purpose of the coinsurance clause in the instant contract was to limit [LAM's] liability to 50 percent of the loss. So long as that limit was maintained it appears immaterial, whether the other 50 percent was covered by a policy of insurance or by Cawog as a self-insurer. More importantly, Cawog could have reasonably understood that it was of no consequence whether the remaining 50 percent came from insurance coverage or from his own resources as self-insurer.[50]

A distinction must be drawn between a breach which materially increases the risk of loss and a breach of a "material warranty." In theory, the parties could insert an immaterial warranty in a policy, but in reality this does not occur. Legislative and administrative regulations preclude such warranties and even if such regulations did not exist modern courts would not enforce them. Thus, virtually all warranties that appear in modern insurance policies are material to the risk in some sense. However, under a "material increase in risk" statute, only material breaches invalidate the coverage. Thus, a warranty that the insured is suffering from no illness at the time of applying for a health insurance policy is material; but if at the time the insured is suffering a minor sore throat, it would not be said that a material breach of the warranty had occurred.

The "material increase in risk" provision is sometimes coupled with statutory language requiring that the misrepresentation or breach of warranty be accompanied by either the intent to deceive or a resulting increase in risk.[51] Under this type of statute, an innocent misrepresentation or breach of warranty that increases the risk will provide a defense for the insurer. Moreover, a fraudulent misrepresentation that does not increase the risk would nevertheless provide a defense for the insurer. Courts have often stated that when the misrepresentation is intentional and fraudulent, it is unnecessary for the insurer to show materiality.[52] However, in those

---

[50] 106 Cal. Rptr. at 308.

[51] See, e.g., Mass. Gen. Laws Ann. ch. 175, § 186; Minn. Stat. Ann. § 60A.08 subd. 9; Or. Rev. Stat. § 743.042.

[52] See, e.g., Upton v. Western Life Ins. Co., 492 F.2d 148 (6th Cir. 1974); Northwestern Mut. Life Ins. Co. v. Yoe's Ex'r, 154 S.W.2d 559 (Ky. 1941); Fitzgerald v. Metropolitan Life Ins. Co., 98 A. 498 (Vt. 1916).

cases where a fraudulent misrepresentation has been held to void the coverage, it appears that the misrepresented fact was indeed a material one. Because of the courts' stated desire to avoid forfeitures, one should not expect to find many courts, if any, actually allowing an insurer a defense for a deliberately deceitful misrepresentation or breach that did not materially increase the risk, even though courts sometimes say they are applying a different rule.

How do courts determine whether or not the breach or misrepresentation has increased the risk? At least three different tests have been used by courts. One test is whether the breach or misrepresentation, if known by the insurer, would have affected this particular insurer's decision to insure this risk at the given premium.[53] A second test is whether the breach or misrepresentation, if known, would have affected a reasonable insurer's decision to insure this risk at the given premium.[54] A third test is whether, as an objective fact, the risk actually and materially increased the risk.[55] The application of any of these tests is normally treated as a question for the factfinder, usually the jury.[56]

A second kind of statute provides that all statements by the insured will be considered representations and not warranties, provided the statements were not made fraudulently.[57] By converting warranties into representations, the insurer is required to show more in order to avoid providing coverage; that is, the insurer must ordinarily show the statement's materiality and its own reliance, and if the statement is found to be substantially, as opposed to strictly, true, the insurer will have no defense. By the terms of these statutes, only if the statement is made by the insured with intent to defraud will the warranty not be converted into a representation. Under these statutes, it is impossible for an immaterial breach of a warranty to invalidate coverage in the absence of the insured's fraud.

A third type of statute provides that a breach of warranty will constitute a defense for the insurer only if it actually contributed to causing the loss, as distinct from merely increasing the risk of loss.[58] This kind of statute is most destructive of warranties, since in many cases it will be very hard for the insurer to establish (if

---

[53] See, e.g., Martin v. Security Industry Ins. Co., 367 So. 2d 420 (La. Ct. App. 1979); Santilli v. State Farm Life Ins. Co., 562 P.2d 965 (Or. 1977); Countryside Cas. Co. v. Orr, 523 F.2d 870 (8th Cir. 1975).

[54] See, e.g., Sentry Indem. Co. v. Brady, 264 S.E.2d 702 (Ga. Ct. App. 1980); Lincoln Income Life Ins. Co. v. Burchfield, 394 S.W.2d 468 (Ky. 1965); Central Nat'l Life Ins. Co. v. Peterson, 529 P.2d 1213 (Ariz. Ct. App. 1975).

[55] See, e.g., Unger v. Metropolitan Life Ins. Co., 242 N.E.2d 907 (Ill. App. Ct. 1968); Hofmann v. John Hancock Mut. Life Ins. Co., 400 F. Supp. 827 (D.C.Md. 1975); Weekly v. Missouri Property Ins. Placement Facility, 538 S.W.2d 375 (Mo.App. 1976); Billington v. Prudential Ins. Co., 254 F.2d 428 (7th Cir. 1958).

[56] See, e.g., American Family Mut. Ins. Co. v. Kivela, 408 N.E.2d 805 (Ind. Ct. App. 1980); National Life & Acc. Ins. Co. v. Gordon, 411 A.2d 1087 (Md.Ct.App. 1980); Bailey v. Interstate Life and Acc. Ins. Co., 270 S.E.2d 287 (Ga. Ct. App. 1980).

[57] See, e.g., Ala. Code § 27-14-7; Mo. Stat. § 379.178; Mont. Code Ann. § 33-20-106; Neb. Rev. Stat. § 44-502(4); S.D. Codified Laws Ann. § 58-15-8; Tenn. Code § 56-7-103.

[58] See, e.g., Kan. Stat. Ann. § 40-418; Mo. Rev. Stat. § 376-580; R.I. Gen. Laws § 27-4-10.

the burden of proving causation is placed on the insurer)[59] that the breach of warranty actually caused the loss. When such a statute is applicable, courts will be tempted to interpret the statute and apply it in a manner that works a fair result in the circumstances.

Whether the "actual contribution to loss" statute is desirable is very controversial. These statutes are defended on the ground that they classify loss experience in a way not taken into account by the insurer's rating criteria. As Professor Patterson has explained, if a building is used as a dwelling, such a building will have a lower risk of fire damage than if the same kind of building were used as a dry-cleaning business. Owners of the dry-cleaning business should pay a higher premium. If the owner of such a business pays the lower premium, and a fire from an adjacent building destroys the building, the owner should not lose the coverage, since the owner paid the proper premium — the premium based on use of a dwelling — to protect the premises from the kind of loss that occurred. Only if the business use contributed to the loss should the insured lose coverage. To counter this argument, it is claimed that often the causes of loss will not be apparent, and — unless the burden of proof is placed on the insured — the insurer in many cases will be unable to establish that a breach of warranty caused the loss, and the result will be that some losses will be paid by insurers for which the insured paid too small a premium.[60]

A fourth kind of statute that limits the effect of warranties in the life insurance setting is the incontestability statute. These statutes are discussed in a later section,[61] but it should be noted here that the statute will not allow an insurer after the period of incontestability (typically two years) has expired to avoid the policy on the grounds of misrepresentation or breach of warranty. Under these statutes, the rule of strict compliance with a warranty — if not already displaced by a statute requiring that warranties be deemed representations — could apply only during the first two years after the policy became effective. Thus, in life insurance, the rule that a warranty must be strictly satisfied has little practical significance.

Frequently state statutes by their terms apply to statements made by the insured in the application or in the process of negotiation of the contract.[62] By negative implication, it would seem that these statutes do not apply to warranties, which are set forth in the insurance contract itself. However, if a jurisdiction with such a statute adheres to a separate rule that an application for insurance is not a part of the contract unless it is attached to the policy, as is the case in West Virginia,[63] then these statutes can be viewed as turning all statements in applications into representations, and not warranties. For example, the West Virginia statute[64] provides that "all statements and descriptions in any application for an insurance policy or in negotiations

---

[59] This is likely to be the case, since the burden of establishing the defense is on the insurer. See Szalpa v. National Travelers Life Ins. Co., 231 N.W.2d 270 (Mich. Ct. App. 1975).

[60] See Patterson, note 10, *supra,* at 356–57.

[61] See § 104B, *infra.*

[62] See, e.g., Wis. Stat. Ann. § 209.06; Va. Code § 38.2-309. But see N.Y. Ins. Law § 3106.

[63] See W.Va. Code, 33-6-6(a).

[64] See W.Va. Code, 33-6-7.

therefor" are representations and not warranties. Moreover, the statute provides that "misrepresentations, omissions, concealments of facts, and incorrect statements" do no prevent recovery under a policy unless fraudulent, material to the risk, or the insurer in good faith would not have provided coverage if it had known the true facts. The West Virginia Supreme Court held in a 1989 case that this statute "abolished the common law concept of warranties with regard to statements by an insured in an application for insurance."[65]

[4] Is Mitigation Appropriate?

The legal significance of warranties has been substantially eroded by judicial and statutory mitigation of their effects, and this seems desirable in situations where the warranty is immaterial to the risk of loss or where the insured's bargaining position is decidedly unequal with that of the insurer. But it is important to observe that the erosion of the strict satisfaction requirement that accompanied warranty law as it originally developed does not come without costs. Warranties create a fixed, per se standard for determining whether coverage exists in situations where the occurrence (or non-occurrence) of an event is agreed by the parties to have relevance to whether the insurer should be obligated to reimburse the insured for a loss. In circumstances where parties with equal sophistication (such as a large, commercial insured and an insurer) insert a warranty in a policy, one might assume that these parties by their agreement desire to avoid the sometimes costly inquiries into whether the breach of a warranty materially increased the risk of loss, or whether a particular breach contributed to the loss, or whether the statement made into a warranty is substantially true. By inserting provisions in policies that are intended to avoid these kinds of costly determinations, the cost of coverage should be reduced, and this is something for which particular insureds may wish to bargain. However, where statutory or judicial regulation declares that warranties must be treated as representations, insureds are prevented from bargaining for these savings.

As Professor Abraham has observed, the old rule that warranties must be literally satisfied can be viewed as "a relatively inexpensive method of guarding against adverse selection and moral hazard."[66] With respect to moral hazard, for example, if warranties are interpreted as affirmative rather than promissory, the insured suffers no cost if the insured chooses after the insurance policy is issued to cease a risk-reducing practice, the existence of which the insured "warranted" in the policy. But if warranties must be strictly satisfied, the insured has a powerful incentive to continue with the risk-reducing practice, because failing to do so will bar coverage regardless of the cause of a future loss. No costly inquiries are required to determine the presence of coverage: either the condition that was warranted is in existence or it is not, and coverage will turn on this yes-no answer.

A similar point can be made with respect to adverse selection. Realizing that an offer of insurance tends to attract a disproportionate number of high-risk insureds, an insurer might insist that insureds warrant in exchange for a premium reduction that the risk-producing condition will be controlled or eliminated. Thus, higher-risk

---

[65] Powell v. Time Ins. Co., 382 S.E.2d 342, 348 (W.Va. 1989).

[66] Kenneth S. Abraham, *Insurance Law and Regulation: Cases and Materials* 11 (1990).

insureds will not agree to the warranty, and they will pay a higher premium, as they should. Higher-risk insureds who warrant that the condition will be controlled or eliminated lose their coverage if they do not deliver on their commitment. But if the harsh effects of warranties are mitigated by judicial or statutory means, this kind of inexpensive risk classification by insurers is not feasible.

Given the extensive regulation of the warranty defense, it must be assumed that those who make public policy believe that the instances of insurer use of warranties to gain advantages over unsophisticated insureds greatly outweigh the circumstances in which insurers use warranties to reduce costs for the benefit of all policyholders. Whether this belief is a correct assessment of what transpires in insurance markets is a debatable point.

[f]   The Distinction Between Warranties and Coverage Provisions

The distinction between warranties and representations has long been an important one. However, now that legislatures regulate warranty provisions in so many states, the distinction that now has importance is that between coverage provisions and warranties. Under the most common kind of warranty-regulating statutes, a breach of warranty is grounds for avoiding the policy only if the breach is material in some sense. But noncompliance with a coverage provision is a defense regardless of materiality. Thus, in response to statutes that regulate the warranty defense, insurers have been more inclined to write policy provisions in language of coverage rather than in language of warranty.

One might view insurers' utilization of language of coverage, which presumably creates a per se rule (the insured either falls within or outside the coverage depending on whether the circumstance on which coverage turns is present), as an effort to recover the advantages of the now-abandoned rule that warranties must be strictly satisfied. Because warranties can no longer be used effectively to control moral hazard and adverse selection or to support risk classification efforts, insurers now employ language of coverage to secure these advantages.

The distinction between a coverage provision and a warranty is not an easy one to articulate. A warranty is in the nature of a promise that certain conditions exist or will continue to exist. A coverage provision is a clause that purports to define which risks are covered, as opposed to those which are not. The confusion arises from the fact that conditions precedent are typically viewed as coverage provisions: no coverage exists because a condition to coverage never occurred. Before examining the nature of the distinction further, it is helpful to examine a case where the significance of the distinction is apparent.

In *Charles, Henry & Crowley, Co. v. Home Insurance Co.*,[67] the insured, a jewelry firm, possessed a "Jewelers' Block Policy" insuring against loss due to theft from the firm's display windows. One provision in the policy stated that it was a "condition of this insurance precedent to any recovery hereunder that the values of property displayed will not exceed" an amount specified in the proposal form attached to the policy. A loss was suffered from the display windows while the value

---

[67] 212 N.E.2d 240 (Mass. 1965).

on display exceeded the specified maximums. The trial court treated the insured's representation that the displayed jewelry would not exceed the specified sums as a representation or warranty, which under Massachusetts statutory law, would not avoid coverage if the insurer's risk was not materially increased. Finding no such increase in risk, the court entered a judgment for the insured.

On appeal, the court said that the statute applied "only to representations and warranties and does not apply to conditions precedent expressly within the terms of a policy."[68] In this case, the court said that the policy's language was language of condition:

> [A] statement made in an application for a policy of insurance may become a condition of the policy rather than remain a warranty or representation if: (1) the statement made by the insured relates essentially to the insurer's intelligent decision to issue the policy; and (2) the statement is made a condition precedent to recovery under the policy, either by using the precise words "condition precedent" or their equivalent. . . . Both tests are met in the instant case.[69]

Thus, the statute requiring the insurer to show an increase of risk did not apply, and the lower court's judgment for the insured was reversed.[70]

Efforts have been made to articulate a distinction between a condition, a coverage provision, and a warranty, but these efforts often add little clarity to the problem. For example, the Couch treatise states that conditions "call for the performance of some event after the terms of the contract have been agreed upon before the contract shall take effect . . . whereas a warranty is such that its breach forfeits an existing contract and contains no element that an event shall happen or act be done, after the agreement is made in form, before it shall take effect as a contract."[71] This distinction obfuscates the meaning of condition. Under basic contract law principles, the fact that a contractual duty is conditioned does not mean that a contract is not in "effect"; rather, the contract is fully effective, but the nonoccurrence of the condition to the duty simply means that the performance is not owing at the present time. If the condition does not occur, the duty will be suspended; and if after a period of time it becomes clear that the condition cannot occur in a timely fashion, the conditioned duty is discharged. The discharge of a duty under an existing contract — which is precisely what happens when a condition to a duty does not occur — is indistinguishable in legal effect from what the Couch treatise calls the "forfeiture of an existing contract."

Actually, the Couch treatise is probably attempting to state the distinction between conditions precedent and conditions subsequent. If a condition precedent is not satisfied, the conditioned duty, although in existence, is not yet due and owing (and when it becomes clear the condition can never be satisfied, the duty is discharged); if a condition subsequent is not satisfied, the conditioned duty, which existed and

---

[68] 212 N.E.2d at 241–42.

[69] 212 N.E.2d at 242.

[70] See also Benton Casing Service, Inc. v. Avemco Ins. Co., 379 So. 2d 225 (La. 1979); Edmonds v. United States, 642 F.2d 887 (1st Cir. 1981) (explaining *Charles*).

[71] 7 COUCH 2d § 36:47, at 478.

was due and owing, is discharged. Nonsatisfaction of a condition subsequent very much resembles the forfeiture of an existing contract. But not all condition subsequents are warranties. An insurance contract might provide that the insurer's duty to pay proceeds is discharged if the insured fails to file a claim within twelve months of the loss. The insured does not "warrant" that a claim will be timely filed, but the insurer's duty — which is due and owing as soon as the covered loss occurs — will be discharged if a claim is not timely filed.

Part of the reason for the confusion in attempting to distinguish warranties from conditions is that warranties do have an element of condition in them. In fact, Professor Patterson wrote that "every warranty creates a condition,"[72] but this observation clears little of the confusion. Warranties can be duties on the part of the insured, such as "I warrant that I will not (meaning I promise that I will not) display jewelry in the window exceeding a value of x dollars." If the insured breaches the duty, the insurer's duty to pay proceeds will be discharged (under the theory that a duty is a constructive condition to the other side's duty of performance, and nonsatisfaction of this constructive condition discharges the other party's duty to perform). Whether or not the warranty is a duty, it can also be a condition: "The insured warrants that (meaning that the insurer's duty to pay proceeds is expressly conditioned on the fact that) jewelry exceeding a value of x dollars will not be displayed in the window." Failure to satisfy strictly the express condition has the same effect of nonsatisfaction of a constructive condition: the insurer's duty to perform is discharged. The legal effect of the nonsatisfaction of conditions to coverage is identical: the insurer's duty to perform is discharged.

To distinguish between warranty-conditions and other kinds of conditions, Professor Patterson articulated a distinction between conditions relating to "potential causes" (warranties) and conditions relating to "actual causes" (coverage provisions). More specifically, according to Professor Patterson, a coverage provision has one or more characteristics: (1) it deals with actual causes of loss, as distinguished from potential causes of loss; (2) it deals with the existence of facts that determine whether an insured event has occurred, instead of facts that affect the risk that an insured event will occur; (3) it identifies the risk, instead of ameliorating the risk; (4) it determines the scope of coverage according to the cause of loss, instead of suspending coverage irrespective of the cause of loss. Warranty provisions, in contrast, involve potential causes of loss, facts that affect the risk that an insured event will occur, amelioration of risk, and suspending coverage without regard to cause.[73]

The framework which Professor Patterson (who was once the Deputy Superintendent of Insurance of New York) developed eventually made its way into section 3106 of the New York Insurance Code:

> The term "warranty" . . . means any provision of an insurance contract which has the effect of requiring, as a condition of the taking effect of such contract or as a condition precedent of the insurer's liability thereunder, the existence

---

[72] Patterson, note 10, *supra,* at 275.
[73] *Id.* at 272–283.

of a fact which tends to diminish, or the nonexistence of a fact which tends to increase, the risk of the occurrence of any loss, damage or injury within the coverage of the contract.[74]

Under this statute, a provision in a policy stating that it is a condition to coverage that the premises be protected by an automatic sprinkler is a warranty, because the presence or absence of a sprinkler deals with a potential cause of loss only. However, a provision in a policy conditioning coverage on the loss being caused by flood is a coverage provision, because it deals with an actual cause of loss, as opposed to a potential cause.

The significance of this distinction rests in the following proposition: warranties are subject to mitigating statutes, but coverage provisions are not. Thus, categorization is extremely important to outcomes in cases. But categorizing even common provisions is difficult and perplexing. For example, insurance policy forms make widespread use of the term "condition." Does this automatically convert all such provisions into coverage provisions? Sometimes policies refer to a series of provisions with the title "Warranties and Other Conditions." When similar provisions are grouped together and the categorization turns on subtle differences in wording, much confusion is inevitable. Indeed, it is difficult to imagine a layperson understanding in any meaningful way the distinction between warranty and coverage, or otherwise having a sense of how the insured's rights under the policy are affected.

If coverage provisions remove insurers from the reach of statutes regulating the warranty defense, one might expect that insurers would always explicitly draft in terms of coverage rather than in terms of warranty. However, coverage provisions do not always secure the insurer's underwriting objectives. Consider the situation where an insurer is willing to cover a building for loss by fire, but the insurer does not want to provide the coverage if the insured stores paper products on the premises. The insurer might draft in terms of coverage: "the insurer will pay for loss due to fire, except that no coverage exists if the fire is caused by paper products stored on the premises at the time of loss."[75] The insurer will bear the burden of establishing the applicability of the exclusion, but this burden may be difficult to carry if the building is completely destroyed by fire. There could be multiple causes, any one of which contributed to the loss. To avoid these difficulties, the insurer might prefer that the insured warrant that paper products will never be stored on the premises. In this event, all the insurer will need to demonstrate is that the warranty was breached. Mitigation doctrines are likely to require the insurer to establish materiality of the breach, but this burden may be easier to carry than the burden of establishing the actual cause of loss, as the coverage provision articulated above would require.

_____

[74] N.Y. Ins. Law § 3106.

[75] In the Patterson terminology, this provision is drafted in terms of actual cause. If the provision were drafted to read "the insurer will pay for loss due to fire, except that no coverage exists if paper products are stored on the premises," the provision would involve a "potential cause," and under the terms of the New York statute quoted above, the provision would constitute a warranty.

§ 102   Insured's Misrepresentation

[a]   A General Rule

A representation is a statement, either oral or written, made by the insured to the insurer which forms at least part of the basis on which the insurer decides to enter into the contract. If a representation (1) is untrue or misleading, (2) is material to the risk, and (3) is relied upon by the insurer in agreeing to issue the policy at a specified premium, the insurer can void the policy or refuse a claim for payment of proceeds on account of the misrepresentation (unless the policy has become incontestable). The misrepresentation defense in insurance law is simply a variant of the more general contract law principle that allows an injured party to void a contract when that party's assent to the bargain is induced by the fraudulent or material misrepresentation of the other contracting party, and the injured party relies on the misrepresentation in question.[1]

To establish the defense of misrepresentation, most courts insist only on the existence of the three elements identified above and do not require intent to commit the misrepresentation.[2] A minority of courts, however, add the requirement that the insured must have made the misrepresentation with intent to defraud.[3]

The Fifth Circuit recently explained Texas law in this way:

> A misrepresentation defense under Texas law requires a showing that "the misrepresentation was made willfully with the intent to deceive or to induce the insurance company to issue the policy." An applicant for insurance cannot willfully intend to deceive its potential insurer unless it actually, not constructively, knows that what it misrepresents is untrue, especially when the allegedly untrue statement was one of opinion. Further, Texas law holds that even a material misrepresentation in an insurance application does not defeat recovery if it is made innocently and in good faith. A good faith standard implies

---

[1] See generally *Restatement (Second) of Contracts* §§ 159-173 (1981).

[2] See, e.g., Methodist Medical Center of Ill. v. American Medical Sec. Inc., 38 F.3d 316 (7th Cir. 1994) (applying Illinois law); Coots v. United Employers Federation, 865 F.Supp. 596 (E.D. Mo. 1994); Clemons v. American Cas. Co., 841 F.Supp. 160 (D.Md. 1993); Berger v. Manhattan Life Ins. Co., 805 F.Supp. 1097 (S.D. N.Y. 1992); Worley v. State Farm Mut. Auto. Ins. Co., 432 S.E.2d 244 (Ga. Ct. App. 1993); Curtis v. American Community Mut. Ins. Co., 610 N.E.2d 871 (Ind. Ct. App. 1993); Evora v. Henry, 559 A.2d 1038 (R.I. 1989); Martell v. Universal Underwriters Life Ins. Co., 564 A.2d 584 (Vt. 1989); Continental Assur. Co. v. Carroll, 485 So. 2d 406 (Fla. 1986); Guardian Life Ins. Co. v. Tillinghast, 512 A.2d 855 (R.I. 1986); Clark v. Alabama Farm Bur. Mut. Cas. Ins. Co., 465 So. 2d 1135 (ALa. Ct. App. 1984); Evans v. Occidental Life Ins. Co., 455 N.E.2d 678 (Ohio Ct.App. 1982). See generally Banks McDowell, *The Misrepresentation Defense in Insurance: A Problem for Contract Theory,* 16 Conn. L. Rev. 513 (1984).

[3] E.g., Parsaie v. United Olympic Life Ins. Co., 29 F.3d 219 (5th Cir. 1994) (applying Texas law); Middlesex Mut. Assur. Co. v. Walsh, 590 A.2d 957 (Conn. 1991) (extending rule that innocent misrepresentations are insufficient to void life insurance policy to automobile liability policy); Burnham v. Bankers Life & Cas. Co., 470 P.2d 261 (Utah 1970); Kuhns v. New York Life Ins. Co., 147 A. 76 (Pa. 1929); Commercial Bank v. American Bonding Co., 187 S.W. 99 (Mo. Ct. App. 1916).

subjectivity; an objective standard could not fit within a test that allowed innocent misrepresentations.[4]

Many of these cases, like the Fifth Circuit case noted above,[5] have involved representations of opinions, which are incapable of being misrepresented in the absence of an intention to do so. This has led some courts to mistakenly assume that intent is an element of the misrepresentation defense, when, as discussed in more detail in a following subsection, showing intent to mislead is simply one aspect of proving the untruth of a statement of opinion.

[b] Representation versus Warranty

The essence of the warranty-representation distinction was stated by one court as follows: "A warranty in insurance enters into and is part of the contract, and must be literally true to permit a recovery on the policy while a representation is not part of the contract but an inducement thereto. A representation must relate to a material matter, and is only required to be substantially true."[6]

Thus, a representation is not a term of the contract. If a representation is explicitly incorporated into the written contract, it becomes a warranty. Because a representation is not a contract term, it does not "bind" the insured as does a warranty. Suppose, for example, an insured warrants that he or she will never pilot an airplane, and the insured is made to understand that breaching this warranty absolutely voids the coverage. If a loss occurs while the warranty is being breached, no coverage results. However, if the insurer asks the applicant whether the applicant has ever piloted an airplane and the applicant answers "no," a truthful answer, this answer by itself will not prevent the applicant, once insured, from taking flying lessons, becoming a pilot, and flying aircraft. The insurer may have assumed that the answer "no" meant that there was little chance the applicant would become a pilot, but this was an uncertainty the insurer took into account when deciding to issue the policy. The truthful answer did not commit the applicant to any particular kind of conduct in the future.

Moreover, because a warranty and a representation differ as to their binding effect, a breach of warranty has a potentially different effect than a misrepresentation. As explained by one court, "[t]he difference in law between a warranty and a false representation is that breach of a warranty voids the contract, irrespective of its gravity, while a false representation will void the contract when it is shown to have been made . . . either with knowledge of its falsity or recklessly, without any knowledge as to whether it was true or false, such representation being of a nature

---

[4] Enserch Corp. v. Shand Morahan & Co., 952 F.2d 1485, 1496 (5th Cir. 1992) (citation omitted).

[5] In *Enserch*, the application for insurance asked the insured to state if it knew of any circumstances that might give rise to claims against the insured, a corporation. Attorneys for the insured had 36 corporate officers respond to a poll; none listed the circumstances that would later give rise to the lawsuit underlying the case. 952 F.2d at 1490.

[6] Whitehead v. Fleet Towing Co., 442 N.E.2d 1362, 1365 (Ill. App. Ct. 1982). See also Sanford v. Federated Guar. Ins. Co., 522 So. 2d 214 (Miss. 1988). For further discussion, see § 101[e], *supra*.

that would reasonably tend to influence the action of the insurer in accepting or declining the risk or in fixing the amount of premium to be paid."[7] The circumstances under which a misrepresentation will void coverage are discussed in the subsections which follow.

[c] The Requirement That the Representation Be Untrue or Misleading

In a contest between insurer and insured, courts tend to favor the insured, typically the weaker of the two parties. Consistent with this attitude, courts interpret representations whenever possible in a manner that sustains the policy's validity. This preference manifests itself in several ways. It is often said that the insured cannot misrepresent a fact about which the insured has no knowledge, meaning that an insured who is ignorant about information cannot misrepresent it.[8] Another oft-stated principle is that if a representation is "substantially" correct, the policy will not be voided and the insurer will not be given a defense to a claim for proceeds.[9] Misrepresentations are thus distinct from warranties or express conditions, which must be strictly satisfied. A misrepresentation can be viewed as a corollary of contract law's constructive condition, which requires not strict compliance but only substantial performance for its satisfaction. Where a misrepresentation is innocent or merely negligent, the insistence on mere substantial accuracy has much to commend it. If an insurer asks an applicant whether he or she has ever been injured and the applicant forgets to mention a childhood injury that had no permanent effect on the applicant's health, a court should conclude that the representation was substantially correct. Similarly, a representation that an applicant has not seen a physician for a specified period of time will not void the policy if the only visits were for minor illnesses unrelated to the illness in question.

Courts also tend to treat representations as pertaining to opinion rather than fact. This also assists in maintaining the validity of contracts in the face of an insurer's claim that a misrepresentation has occurred. For example, if the insurer asks the applicant whether he or she is in good health and the applicant replies "yes" in circumstances where, unknown to the applicant, he or she is suffering from a terminal illness, the court will probably conclude that no misrepresentation has occurred. The court will construe the insurer's question as follows: "Do you believe that you are in good health?" The applicant committed no misrepresentation when the

---

[7] Walker v. Fireman's Fund Ins. Co., 234 P. 542, 547 (Or. 1925), *approved in* Kentner v. Gulf Ins. Co., 686 P.2d 339 (Or. 1984).

[8] See, e.g., Miller v. Republic Nat'l Life Ins. Co., 789 F.2d 1336 (9th Cir. 1986); Perault v. Time Ins. Co., 633 So. 2d 263 (La. Ct. App. 1993); Callaway v. Sublimity Ins. Co., 858 P.2d 888 (Or. Ct. App. 1993); Estate of Rivera v. North Am. Co. for Life & Health Ins., 635 A.2d 598 (N.J. Super. Ct. App. Div. 1993); Northern Life Ins. Co. v. Ippolito Real Estate Partnership, 624 N.E.2d 1266 (Ill. App. Ct. 1993); Carroll v. Jackson Nat'l Life Ins. Co., 405 S.E.2d 425 (S.C. Ct. App. 1991).

[9] See, e.g., Sohn v. New York Indem. Co., 172 N.E. 57 (Ill. 1930); Holtzclaw v. Bankers Mut. Ins. Co., 448 N.E.2d 55 (Ind. Ct. App. 1983); Whitehead v. Fleet Towing Co., 442 N.E.2d 1362 (Ill. App. Ct. 1982); National Life & Acc. Ins. Co. v. Vaughan, 32 So. 2d 490 (La. Ct. App. 1947).

applicant said "yes," because the applicant actually believed he or she was in good health.[10] A misrepresentation would have occurred had the applicant known of the illness, for then the deliberately deceptive statement would have constituted a misrepresentation of the applicant's opinion.

The inability of some courts to distinguish between representations of fact and representations of opinion has generated a minority rule that intent is an element of the misrepresentation defense.[11] It is correct to assert that a misrepresentation of opinion can be demonstrated *only* by showing that the insured when making the statement intended to deceive the insurer. Without such intent, no false or incorrect statement has occurred; without such intent, the belief of the applicant is accurately stated. This, however, does not mean that intent is an element of the misrepresentation defense. All that the misrepresentation defense requires is that a false representation be made. With a statement of fact, this is established by showing inaccuracy; with a statement of belief, this is established by showing that the belief was not held by the insured, meaning that the insured made the statement with intent to deceive the insurer. In most cases where courts have said that intent is an element of the defense of misrepresentation, the representations at issue were representations of belief, not of fact.[12]

Thus, if the insured states his or her opinion on the value of property being insured and the statement is, objectively speaking, inaccurate, a misrepresentation has not occurred *unless* the insured intentionally misstated the property's value. Similarly, if an insured represents what he or she intends to do in the future and then fails to take this action, the insurer does not have a basis for voiding the policy *unless* the insurer can establish that at the time of the representation the insured did not intend to do the stated act. Such a representation is a statement about a present state of mind, not a promise that an event will come about in the future. If the insurer feels strongly about the represented conduct, the insurer should obtain a promissory warranty from the insured or make the existence of a certain state of facts a condition to the policy's coverage.

A classic case illustrating the fact-opinion distinction is *Cushing Bryant v. The Ocean Insurance Co.*[13] Plaintiffs procured a policy of insurance on a ship and cargo

---

[10] See City Nat'l Bank & Trust Co. v. Jackson Nat'l Life Ins., 804 P.2d 463 (OkLa. Ct. App. 1990); Gatlin v. World Service Life Ins. Co., 616 S.W.2d 606 (Tenn. 1981); Suravitz v. Prudential Ins. Co., 91 A. 495 (Pa. 1914); but see Leach v. Millers Life Ins. Co., 400 F.2d 179 (5th Cir. 1968) (requiring that insured be in good health on the date of the delivery of the policy as a condition precedent to liability).

[11] See note 1, *supra*, and cited cases.

[12] See, e.g., World Service Life Ins. Co. v. Bodiford, 492 So. 2d 457 (Fla. Dist. Ct. App. 1986); Gasque v. Voyager Life Ins. Co., 344 S.E.2d 182 (S.C.App. 1986); Continental Assur. Co. v. Carroll, 459 So. 2d 443 (Fla. Dist. Ct. App. 1984), *opinion vacated*, 485 So. 2d 406 (Fla. 1986). Because of the general confusion in this area, cases can be found holding where the representation appeared to be one of belief that intent was not an element of the defense. See Continental Assur. Co. v. Carroll, 495 So. 2d 406 (Fla. 1986); Evans v. Occidental Life Ins. Co., 455 N.E.2d 678 (Ohio Ct.App. 1982).

[13] 39 Mass. 200 (1839). For a more recent case that explicitly recognizes the distinction, see Stewart v. Mutual of Omaha Ins. Co., 817 P.2d 44, 47-48 (Ariz. Ct. App. 1991). For a case where the judges divided on the question of whether the insured "knowingly" made a false statement of belief, see Time Ins. Co. v. Bishop, 425 S.E.2d 489 (Va. 1993).

to be sailed to New Orleans. The insurer offered evidence that prior to contracting the agent for the insureds represented that "he was then taking in paving stones for ballast, and should fill up with hay for New Orleans." However, the cargo was in fact exclusively paving stones, which increased the risks of the voyage. The insurer did not offer evidence that at the time of the representation the plaintiffs were not taking in paving stones or that at that time of the representation the vessel was fully loaded with paving stones. Also, the insurer offered no evidence that the plaintiffs at the time of the representation did not expect or intend to take in a cargo of hay, or that at the time of the representation the plaintiffs intended to defraud the insurer. The insurer's argument was simply that it relied on the representation and the plaintiffs "were bound to make it good." The trial court refused to admit the offered evidence, ruling that the representation was not one of fact but was one of intention, and that the representation of intention would not void the policy unless fraudulently made.

The trial court's judgment was affirmed on appeal. The court explained that a misrepresentation of fact would void a policy, whether made intentionally, mistakenly, or negligently, if the insurer were "thereby led into an error, and computes the risk upon false grounds." But the court said the representation in issue was one of "expectation or belief," meaning it was only a statement that plaintiffs *intended* to ship hay, a statement which may have been correct at the time it was made. A representation of intention, the court said, could void a policy only if it were fraudulently made. The court held that under the common law the evidence was inadmissible. However, the court also said that even if admitted the evidence would not help the insurer: "It would only prove the declaration of an intention of the plaintiffs previous to the policy, and as it was not afterwards inserted in the policy the defendants must be presumed to have taken upon themselves the risk of any change of intention; otherwise they would have required a warranty."

[d] Materiality

Whether a misrepresentation is material depends on a number of factors, including "when the misrepresentation is made, the terms of the insurance contract and applicable statutes, and the nature of the misrepresentation."[14] At common law, a representation is material if it induces a reasonable insurer to enter into a contract that it would otherwise have refused, or to accept a lower premium that it would otherwise have required.[15] In at least sixteen states, the essence of this standard has been statutorily codified. One typical formulation is as follows:

> Misrepresentations, omissions, concealment of facts, and incorrect statements shall not prevent a recovery under the policy or contract unless: (1) fraudulent; (2) material either to the acceptance of the risk or to the hazard assumed by the insurer; or (3) the insurer in good faith would either not have issued the policy or contract or would not have issued a policy or contract in as large an amount or at the premium rate as applied for or would not have provided

---

[14] Bryant v. Nationwide Mut. Fire Ins. Co., 313 S.E.2d 803, 807 (N.C. Ct. App. 1984).

[15] See, e.g., Bush v. Mayerstein-Burnell Financial Services, Inc., 499 N.E.2d 755 (Ind. App. 1986); Crewse v. Shelter Mut. Ins. Co., 706 S.W.2d 35 (Mo. Ct. App. 1985).

coverage with respect to the hazard resulting in the loss if the true facts had been known to the insurer as required either by the application for the policy or contract or otherwise.[16]

The logic of the materiality requirement is simple: it is upon material representations that insurers can be expected to rely. Insurers will not be induced to enter into contracts by immaterial representations, and thus such representations have no legal significance. Thus, to a large extent the materiality requirement overlaps with the reliance requirement: the insurer cannot rely on the presence or absence of facts about which it made no inquiry. Stated otherwise, if an insurer fails to inquire about some fact or circumstance, that fact or circumstance cannot be material to the insurer's decision about whether to issue a policy or on what terms a policy should be issued.[17] On the other hand, if the insurer inquires into a particular matter when soliciting the application, it is more probable than not that the subject matter of the inquiry is material to the risk.[18] The insurer must, of course, ask questions that elicit the information they seek; if the insurer's questions are worded in such a manner that an insured can give an honest, responsive answer that does not disclose information the insurer considers relevant, the insurer cannot later deny coverage on the grounds of misrepresentation.[19] Whatever the test, the burden of establishing materiality rests upon the insurer.[20]

Having said this much, the fact remains that most standards of materiality have considerable play in the joints. One issue concerns the *quality* of the standard for misrepresentation: should the test be how a reasonable insurer would respond to the misrepresentation, or how this particular insurer responds to misrepresentations of the kind in question? In most jurisdictions, the test for materiality is objective: the inquiry is whether *a reasonable insurer* under similar circumstances would be so induced.[21] However, some formulations of the materiality doctrine use a subjective

---

16 See, e.g., Fla. Stat. Ann. § 627.409; Del. Code tit. 18 § 2711; W. Va. Code § 32-6-7. See generally Farnham, *Application Misrepresentation and Concealment in Property Insurance: The Elusive Elements of the Defense,* 20 Forum 299 (1985); see generally Annot., *Failure to Disclose Terminal Illness as Basis for Life Insurer's Avoidance of High-Risk, High-Premium Policy Requiring No Health Warranties or Proof of Insurability,* 42 A.L.R.4th 158 (1985).

17 See, e.g., Allstate Ins. Co. v. Shirah, 466 So. 2d 940 (Ala. 1985); Stewart-Smith Haidinger, Inc. v. Avi-Truck, Inc., 682 P.2d 1108 (Alaska 1984).

18 See Tharrington v. Sturdivant Life Ins. Co., 443 S.E.2d 797 (N.C. Ct. App. 1994) (in life insurance, written questions and answers relating to health are material as a matter of law).

19 See Waxse v. Reserve Life Ins. Co., 809 P.2d 533 (Kan. 1991) (insured did not misrepresent his condition when failing to disclose prior positive test for HIV); Schneider v. Minnesota Mut. Life Ins. Co., 806 P.2d 1032 (Mont.; 1991) (alcoholism is not material to risk because insurer did not ask about it).

20 See Pederson v. Chrysler Life Ins. Co., 677 F.Supp. 472 (N.D. Miss. 1988); Glens Falls Ins. Co. v. Long, 195 S.E.2d 887 (Va. 1973); Transamerican Ins. Co. v. Austin Farm Center, Inc., 354 N.W.2d 503 (Minn. Ct. App. 1984).

21 See, e.g., Penn Mutual Life Ins. Co. v. Mechanics' Savings Bank & Trust Co., 72 F. 413 (6th Cir. 1896); Burnham v. Bankers Life & Cas. Co., 277, 470 P.2d 261 (Utah 1970); Oakes v. Blue Cross Blue Shield, Inc., 317 S.E.2d 315 (Ga. Ct. App. 1984); Haynes v.

test: whether *this particular insurer,* had it known the truth about the misrepresented fact, would have charged a higher premium or refused the insurance.[22]

As between the two tests, the objective test is more consistent with general contract law, the rules of which are generally premised on what a reasonable person in the shoes of the contracting party would believe the other party's manifestations mean in the context presented. The subjective test improves upon the objective test in a case where the insurer knew of the misrepresentation when it was made but issued the policy anyway and a reasonable insurer would not have issued the policy in the same circumstances. Obviously, it would be unfair to allow an insurer who issued a policy with full knowledge of the misrepresentation to avoid the policy on the grounds of the misrepresentation, and the subjective test avoids this result.[23] Yet if the objective test is applied in the same situation, one should conclude that the reliance element of the misrepresentation defense has not been met: the insurer who knows of a misrepresentation and issues the policy anyway has not relied on the misrepresentation, regardless of what test of materiality is used.

The subjective test of materiality can make a difference when the insurer has stricter underwriting standards than most other insurers. For example, in *Goodwin v. Investors Life Insurance Company,*[24] the insured, an applicant for life insurance, failed to disclose in response to a question on the application the fact that his drivers license had been suspended and he had had two or more moving violations and accidents within the past two years. After the policy was issued, the insured died in an accident during a pre-arranged race in which he was driving seventy miles-per-hour in a thirty-five-mile-per-hour zone. The insurer refused to pay the claim, and the insured's beneficiary sued. The insurer argued that the misrepresentation was material, and the insurer's evidence showed that had it known the true facts, the policy would have been issued had a much higher premium. Plaintiff urged that an objective test of materiality be used, and presented evidence that not all life insurance companies inquire into an applicant's driving record. The court, however, opted for a subjective test of materiality, giving great weight to the insurer's option to have stricter underwriting standards:

Missouri Property Ins. Placement Facility, 641 S.W.2d 497 (Mo. Ct. App. 1982); Sentry Indem. Co. v. Brady, 264 S.E.2d 702 (Ga. Ct. App. 1980).

[22] See Goodwin v. Investors Life Ins. Co. of N. Am., 419 S.E.2d 766 (N.C. 1992); Imperial Cas. & Indem. Co. v. Sogomonian, 198 Cal.App.3d 169 (Cal. Ct. App. 1988); Fagen v. National Home Life Assur. Co., 473 So. 2d 918 (La. Ct. App. 1985). Compare William R. Vance, *Handbook on the Law of Insurance* 407 (3d ed. Anderson 1951) (appearing to state a subjective test) with 18 COUCH 2d § 69:120, at 162 (1983) (stating a clear preference for an objective test). To some extent, the subjective test of materiality duplicates the reliance element of misrepresentation, under which the insurer must prove it was induced to underwrite the risk in reliance upon the misrepresentation. See, e.g., New York Life Ins. Co. v. Kuhlenschmidt, 33 N.E.2d 340 (Ind. 1941); Bryant v. Nationwide Mut. Fire Ins. Co., 313 S.E.2d 803 (N.C. Ct. App. 1984); 7 *Wigmore on Evidence* § 1946 (Chadbourn Rev. 1978).

[23] This is consistent with general contract law principles, under which a party who knows the other side means something other than what the words spoken objectively convey cannot hold the other party to the objectively manifested meaning. See *Restatement (Second) of Contracts* § 21 (1981).

[24] 419 S.E.2d 76 (N.C. 1993).

> [T]he question of applicant's driving record is related to determining an actuarially sound premium. Investors chose to ask the question and had guidelines for determining what rate would be charged according to how the question was answered and what information an investigation revealed. The insurance industry is highly competitive and that competition will determine what rates will be charged and what questions a company can afford to ask, or fail to ask, and remain in business.[25]

In these circumstances, the insured's false representation was material, and the insurer was held entitled to a directed verdict.[26]

A second issue concerns the *quantity* of materiality required to provide a defense to the insured, regardless of whether the test is objective or subjective. Most formulations are less than specific on whether the insurer, to establish the defense, must demonstrate that it would not have issued any contract at all to the insured had an accurate disclosure been made, or whether the insurer need only show that the fact misrepresented was relevant to the risk and would have altered the premium charged or the amount of coverage offered. Clearly, this can make a difference; the latter of the two formulations might allow the insurer to escape coverage when it would have issued a policy, albeit at a higher premium or with more restrictions on coverage, had the true facts been disclosed to the insurer.[27]

Notwithstanding the absence of cohesion in the principles in various jurisdictions that serve to define materiality, there is some consensus on what constitutes a material misrepresentation. To some extent, it is fair to say that we know what is material when we see it. Because it is a matter of "common knowledge" that drivers aged sixteen to twenty-four are substantially greater risks than drivers age twenty-five or older, an Illinois court held that the insured's failure to disclose that she had a twenty-year-old son residing in her household who also drove her car was a misrepresentation that materially affected the risk assumed by the insurer.[28] An Indiana Court held that the insured's failure to reveal, in response to a question in the application, her prior diagnosis for severe cervical ectropion (which was not discovered during the insurer's underwriting due to the applicant's intervening change of name) was a material misrepresentation which barred her recovery under a health

---

[25] 419 S.E.2d at 769-70.

[26] 419 S.E.2d at 770.

[27] See Zulcosky v. Farm Bur. Life Ins. Co. of Mich., 520 N.W.2d 366 (Mich. Ct. App. 1994) (notwithstanding 1959 Michigan Supreme Court precedent, subsequent cases have inquired only into whether the insurer would have rejected the application altogether had the true facts been known, and have not focused on whether the insurer would have been entitled to charge an increased premium but for the misrepresentation); Greves v. Ohio St. Life Ins. Co., 821 P.2d 757, 763-65 (Ariz. Ct. App. 1991).

[28] Ratliff v. Safeway Ins. Co., 628 N.E.2d 937 (Ill. App. Ct. 1993). See also Small v. Prudential Life Ins. Co., 617 N.E.2d 80 (Ill. App. Ct. 1993) (insured's failure to disclose three recent hospitalizations for major depressive disorder was material, and provided insurer valid defense to coverage under life insurance policy where insured died from cardiac arrest caused by a ruptured aneurysm). See also Annot., *Fire Insurance: Failure to Disclose Prior Fires Affecting Insured's Property as Ground for Avoidance of Policy,* 4 A.L.R.5th 117 (1991).

insurance policy for a hysterectomy.[29] A Pennsylvania court held that an insurance agent's failure to disclose on his own application for errors and omissions coverage that he had been advised he would be sued for his failure to secure proper coverage for one of his clients was held material, thereby justifying the agent's insurer in rescinding policies that had been issued earlier.[30] A Vermont court held that an insured's affirmative answer to a question asking whether his aircraft had passed an annual inspection in the last twelve months in circumstances where the aircraft had not been inspected at all constituted a material misrepresentation that voided the insured's liability policy and his coverage for damages arising out of the aircraft's crash.[31]

[e] Reliance

Another element of the misrepresentation defense is that the insurer rely on the misrepresentation when issuing the policy. The essence of reliance is inducement: the insurer must be induced by the misrepresentation to issue the policy to the insured.[32] Reliance is closely related to materiality: if a statement is material, it can often be inferred that the insurer relied upon it. Insurers will not rely upon immaterial statements, and in those circumstances cannot assert misrepresentation as a defense. The reliance requirement also prevents the insurer from defending based upon a misrepresentation where the insurer had knowledge of the true facts or the falsity of the applicant's statements.[33] If the insurer investigates and learns the true facts before issuing the policy, the insurer obviously did not rely on the representation in issuing the policy.

In some situations, the reliance requirement has been deemed not satisfied if the insured revealed enough information to put the insurer on notice of a possible misstatement and the insurer acted unreasonably in not pursuing the matter.[34] In

---

[29] Curtis v. American Community Mut. Ins. Co., 610 N.E.2d 871 (Ind. Ct. App. 1993).

[30] A.G. Allebach, Inc. v. Hurley, 540 A.2d 289 (Pa. Super. Ct. 1988).

[31] McAllister v. Avemco Ins. Co., 528 A.2d 758 (Vt. 1987).

[32] See, e.g., Mayes v. Massachusetts Mut. Life Ins. Co., 608 S.W.2d 612 (Tex. 1980); Adams v. National Cas. Co., 307 P.2d 542 (Okla. 1957); American Fire & Cas. Co., Inc. v. Archie, 409 So. 2d 854 (ALa. Ct. App. 1982).

[33] See, e.g., Union Ins. Exch. Inc. v. Gaul, 393 F.2d 151 (7th Cir. 1968); Chitsey v. National Lloyd's Ins. Co., 698 S.W.2d 766 (Tex. Ct. App. 1985); John Hancock Life Ins. Co. v. Cronin, 51 A.2d 2 (N.J.Eq. 1947). Usually, the insurer does not have a duty to investigate facts presented to it in an application. See Old Southern Life Ins. Co. v. Spann, 472 So. 2d 987 (Ala. 1985); Aetna Ins. Co. v. Rodriguez, 496 N.E.2d 1321 (Ind. Ct. App. 1986).

[34] See Hardy v. Prudential Ins. Co. of Am., 763 P.2d 761, 770-71 (Utah 1988); Hardy v. Integon Life Ins. Corp., 355 S.E.2d 241 (N.C. Ct. App. 1987); Stewart-Smith Haidinger, Inc. v. Avi-Truck, Inc., 682 P.2d 1108 (Alaska 1984); Tannenbaum v. Provident Mut. Life Ins. Co., 386 N.Y.S.2d 409 (N.Y. App. Div. 1976), aff'd, 364 N.E.2d 1122 (N.Y. 1977); American Policyholders' Ins. Co. v. Portale, 212 A.2d 668 (N.J. Super. Ct. App. Div. 1965). See also Centrust Mortgage Corp. v. PMI Mortgage Ins. Co., 800 P.2d 37, 43 (Ariz. Ct. App. 1991) (discussing rules, but holding that even if insurer had duty of inquiry, it could not reasonably have been expected to discover the true facts).

many of these cases, the insurer failed to take any steps at all to investigate the apparent misstatement. In other cases, the insurer commenced an inquiry into the possible misstatement but did not pursue the matter far enough, and the court held that the insurer had not demonstrated its reliance on the misstatement. Other cases hold that the insurer's negligent failure to investigate will not preclude the insurer's right to rely upon representations made by the insured.[35]

The reliance requirement probably emerged in cases where the insured's misrepresentation, although material, was innocent or negligent. It makes sense to impose a duty on the insurer to investigate the applicant's representation if it appears, for example, that the applicant may have innocently misunderstood a question on the application. The insurer who knows the truth of the misrepresented statement cannot rely on the misrepresentation for a defense; by the same token, the insurer who knows or has reason to know that the insured may have given a mistaken, materially inaccurate answer cannot hold the insured to that answer.[36]

[f] Intent and Its Relation to Materiality and Reliance

As noted earlier,[37] most courts do not require intent to commit the misrepresentation as an element of the defense of misrepresentation. Where the alleged misrepresentation is one of opinion and not as fact, intent to mislead must be demonstrated under the reasoning that one cannot misrepresent one's belief without intending deception, but this does not mean that intent is an element of the defense of misrepresentation.[38] Thus, it is fair to say that in most jurisdictions the insurer will possess a good defense to coverage, whether or not the misrepresentation was intentional, if a misrepresentation is material (and the reliance test is also met).[39] Although one can find judicial pronouncements that an immaterial but fraudulent misrepresentation will void a policy,[40] these pronouncements are rare. More importantly, no court appears to have voided an insurance contract because an insured fraudulently misrepresented an immaterial fact. Some courts purporting to adhere to the rule that a fraudulent misrepresentation will void the policy irrespective of the representation's materiality have reintroduced what is in effect a materiality requirement by demanding that the misrepresentation affect the risk or influence the insurer's judgment.[41]

---

[35] See, e.g., Omaha Nat'l Bank v. Manufacturers Life Ins. Co., 332 N.W.2d 196 (Neb. 1983) (insurer's reliance on statement in application is improper only if so utterly unreasonable that there could be no justifiable reliance); Burger v. Nationwide Mut. Ins. Co., 632 P.2d 1381 (Or. Ct. App. 1981).

[36] See Omaha Nat'l Bank v. Manufacturers Life Ins. Co., 332 N.W.2d 196 (Neb. 1983). Compare Kraus v. Prudential Ins. Co., 799 F.2d 502 (9th Cir. 1986) (court holds, applying Oregon law, that an insurer has no duty to investigate an insurance application which is "incomplete on its face" unless the omissions are so obviously material that reliance on the incomplete application would be reckless).

[37] See § 102[a], *supra.*

[38] See § 102[c].

[39] See, e.g., Bankers Life & Cas. Co. v. Long, 266 So. 2d 780 (ALa. Ct. App. 1972); Elfstrom v. New York Life Ins., 432 P.2d 731 (Cal. 1967).

[40] See New York Life Ins. Co. v. McLaughlin, 26 A.2d 108 (Vt. 1942).

[41] See Northwestern Mut. Life Ins. Co. v. Yoe's Executor, 154 S.W.2d 559 (Ky. 1941); Fitzgerald v. Metropolitan Life Ins. Co., 98 A. 498 (Vt. 1916).

Immaterial representations, whether or not intentional, should not provide the insurer with a basis for voiding a policy. Suppose an insurer asks the applicant for a policy of an automobile insurance whether her teenage son, who is to be a driver of the vehicle, has successfully completed a driver's education course. The applicant answers, "Yes, he completed a course at the Sebring Driver's School," which is widely perceived as an outstanding driver's school. In fact, her son completed driver's education at the local high school, but she intentionally misrepresented the source of his education in the mistaken belief that this fact would lower her premium. It is important to the insurer that the applicant's son passed driver's education; precisely where he took the course is unimportant to the insurer. If the insurer later tried to void the policy on the ground that the applicant misrepresented where her son took driver's education, the insurer should not be excused from its contract obligations.

[g]   Misrepresentation of Age in Life Insurance

The life insurance cases involving misrepresentation of age do not comport entirely with the common understanding of the reliance requirement — or, for that matter, the materiality requirement. Consider a case where the applicant for life insurance misstates his or her age on the application as 37 when it is actually 47.[42] The applicant presumably misstated the age to secure a lower premium, although the possibility that the misstatement was an honest error cannot be casually dismissed. The age of the applicant was material to the risk, and the insurer no doubt relied upon it when issuing the policy at a given premium. The insurer might require medical examinations for applicants age 45 and over; the misrepresentation might have enabled the applicant to evade such an exam. If the insurer can show from an autopsy that the medical examination would have revealed the condition that contributed to the insured's death and that the insurer would not have issued the policy on account of this discovery, it seems fair that the insurer should be allowed to void the coverage. However, if the insured dies in an accident and no indication exists that if the insurer had known the correct age it would have refused coverage altogether, it seems unfair to allow the insurer to void the coverage in its entirety. Most state statutes now provide that if the age of an insured has been misstated, the benefit payable is limited to that which the premium would have purchased at the proper age[43] — a result which would not necessarily occur if the common law misrepresentation principles were applied. However, in life insurance, unlike property insurance, it is relatively easy to recalculate what the premium would have been if the insured risk had been correctly described to the insurer. Also, if in the foregoing example the insurer claims it does not write insurance to applicants over age 45 and thus the policy should be void, this result would be permitted by the statute; it is the same as scaling the benefits down to zero.

This kind of statute does not exist in the liability or property insurance area. Letting the insured preserve coverage if the misrepresentation is discovered after

---

[42] See, e.g., New York Life Ins. Co. v. Hollender, 237 P.2d 510 (Cal. 1937); Funchess v. U.S. Life Ins. Co., 430 N.Y.S.2d 77 (N.Y. App. Div. 1980); New York Life Ins. Co. v. Kay, 251 So. 2d 544 (Fla. Dist. Ct. App. 1971).

[43] E.g., Va. Code § 38.2-3306; Wash. Rev. Code Ann. § 48.23.180.

the loss by paying the difference between the premium the insurer charged and the premium the insurer would have charged if it had known of the representation is disadvantageous to the insurer and to other policyholders. The insurer loses the benefit of the interest on the amount of extra premium that should have been paid. Also, if the insured is not found out, the insurer has actually been underwriting a higher risk without receiving a premium for it, which distorts the rate structure. These disadvantages exist regardless of the kind of insurance involved, but with life insurance it is perhaps easier to discover the misrepresentation, and the procedure for reducing the benefits payable is certainly simpler. With property and liability insurance, the more complicated calculation does not lend itself to easy post-loss adjustment.

[h] Statutory Regulation

As noted earlier,[44] statutes in many states prescribe the elements of the misrepresentation defense. For the most part, these statutes either codify or modify the common law materiality test. One typical formulation requires that the representation, to be material, actually increase the risk of loss.[45] Sometimes the increasing-the-risk requirement is combined with an alternative test: that the representation be made with "intent to deceive."[46] Such a formulation suggests that an immaterial but intentional misrepresentation would be a ground for avoiding the contract. However, courts have uniformly held that under such statutes an intentional but immaterial misrepresentation is not a basis for avoiding the policy.[47] A material but innocent misrepresentation is ordinarily considered grounds for avoiding the policy, but an occasional decision has required both materiality *and* intent to be shown.[48]

Another formulation requires that the matter misrepresented actually contribute to the loss before it constitutes a ground for defense.[49] Absent statutory regulation, the misrepresentation ordinarily need not causally contribute to the loss for the coverage to be invalid.[50] This kind of statute makes it very difficult for the insurer

---

[44] See § 101[e], *supra.*

[45] E.g., Ill. Rev. Stat. ch. 73, § 154; Minn. Stat. § 60A.08; Mass. Stat. ch. 175, § 186.

[46] E.g., Mass. Stat. ch. 175, § 186; Ill. Stat. ch. 73, § 766; Wash. Stat. § 48.18.090.

[47] See, e.g., American Indem. Co. v. Elespuru, 302 F. Supp. 878 (D.C. Mont. 1969); Campbell v. Prudential Ins. Co., 155 N.E.2d 9 (Ill. 1958).

[48] See Murphy v. Continental Cas. Co., 269 So. 2d 507 (La. Ct. App. 1972). This result was also reached in Massachusetts Mut. Life Ins. Co. v. Manzo, 560 A.2d 1215, 1231 (N.J. Super. Ct. App. Div. 1989), but the decision was later reversed by the New Jersey Supreme Court. See Massachusetts Mut. Life Ins. Co. v. Manzo, 584 A.2d 190 (N.J. 1991).

[49] See, e.g., Kan. Stat. Ann § 40-418; Mo. Rev. Stat. §§ 376.580, 377.340; Okla. Stat. Ann. tit. 36, § 2515 (life insurance only). In Arkansas, the rule has been adopted by judicial decision. See National Old Line Ins. Co. v. People, 506 S.W.2d 128 (Ark. 1974), *discussed in* D.F. Adams, *Misrepresentation and Procurement of Insurance: The Arkansas Law,* 4 U. Ark. Little Rock L.J. 17 (1981).

[50] See Darnell v. Auto-Owners Ins. Co., 369 N.W.2d 243 (Mich. Ct. App. 1985); Wickersham v. John Hancock Mut. Life Ins., 318 N.W.2d 456 (Mich. 1982); but see National Old Line Ins. Co. v. People, 506 S.W.2d 128 (Ark. 1974) (interpreting Arkansas statute imposing materiality requirement as requiring a "causal relation" between applicant's misrepresentation and the loss).

to defeat coverage on the grounds of misrepresentation. In many situations the misrepresentation will have no causal relationship to the loss or the insurer will be unable to prove the relationship by a preponderance of the evidence. Moreover, the statute has the potential to work injustice. Imagine two identically situated applicants for life insurance, both suffering from a serious ailment of which each is aware. *A* discloses the illness and is refused coverage; *B* misrepresents himself or herself as being in good health and receives coverage. If both lose their lives in an automobile accident, *A's* beneficiaries will receive no proceeds because *A* was refused coverage, but *B's* beneficiaries will, in effect, be rewarded for *B's* dishonesty since the misrepresentation did not contribute to the loss.[51]

[i]   The Obligation to Correct Misrepresentations

Representations speak not only at the time of their utterance but also at the time of the policy's effectiveness. Thus, the insured has an obligation to correct a representation made on an application that becomes incorrect prior to the policy's effective date, just as an insured has an obligation to disclose a fact brought to his or her attention that was not revealed to the insurer earlier. The United States Supreme Court stated in *Stipcich v. Metropolitan Life Insurance Co.*:[52]

> [E]ven the most unsophisticated person must know that in answering the questionnaire and submitting it to the insurer he is furnishing the data on the basis of which the company will decide whether, by issuing a policy, it wishes to insure him. If, while the company deliberates, he discovers facts which make portions of his application no longer true, the most elementary spirit of fair dealing would seem to require him to make a full disclosure. If he fails to do so the company may, despite its acceptance of the application, decline to issue a policy. . . .[53] The *Stipcich* rule has been applied in numerous cases, particularly those involving life insurance.[54]

If the newly acquired information in the insured's possession is simply a variant of information already submitted on the application, it is not necessary for the insured to reveal the information to the insurer. For example, in *Seidler v. Georgetown Life Insurance Co.*,[55] a 1980 Illinois case, information about the applicant's health made available to the insurer revealed that the applicant had a history of heart and cardiovascular disease. Before the policy was issued, the applicant had a mild heart attack and was hospitalized twice. These incidents were not reported to the insurer. Five months after the policy was issued, the insured died

---

[51] Fred S. Six & Todd Thompson, *Misrepresentation in the Application for Life Insurance: Lies in the Eyes of the Beholder*, 52 Ins. Counsel J. 282, 287 (1985).

[52] 277 U.S. 311, 48 S.Ct. 512, 72 L.Ed. 895 (1928).

[53] 277 U.S. at 316.

[54] See, e.g., Massachusetts Mut. Life Ins. Co. v. O'Brien, 5 F.3d 1117 (7th Cir. 1993) (life insurance); MacKenzie v. Prudential Ins. Co. of Am., 411 F.2d 781 (6th Cir. 1969) (life insurance); Lawyers Title Ins. Corp. v. First Federal Sav. Bank & Trust, 744 F.Supp. 778 (E.D. Mich. 1990) (mortgage title insurance); Western Fire Ins. Co. v. Moss, 298 N.E.2d 304 (Ill. App. Ct. 1973) (property and liability insurance policy on boat held invalid; accident after application date, where policy's term was retroactive to application date, was not disclosed).

[55] 402 N.E.2d 666 (Ill. App. Ct. 1980).

of acute heart failure. The insurer denied coverage, but the court said the policy was not invalidated by the nondisclosures. The court vacated a summary judgment issued for the insurer, holding that if the insured's heart difficulties were merely a continuation of a health condition previously known by the insurer, the coverage would not be invalidated. A material question of fact existed as to whether the heart difficulties were part of the earlier described heart condition.

The court in *Seidler*, in vacating the summary judgment for the insurer, conceded the applicant's duty to disclose all relevant changed conditions under the *Stipcich* principle, but also recognized a duty on the part of the insurer to ask again about the insured's health before the policy's delivery. The court held that which duty outweighed the other depended on whether the undisclosed condition was a newly-contracted disease or merely a manifestation of the pre-existing, already identified condition.[56] This analysis suggests another possible rule for dealing with changed conditions after application but before delivery: Changed, undisclosed conditions do not invalidate coverage unless the insurer inquires prior to the delivery of the policy about whether the insured's health has changed since the application. This kind of rule would alter the understanding that insurers are entitled to rely on statements made in the application, and would impose an additional, and not cost-free, step in the process of contract formation. Life and health insurers who place a "good health" clause in the policy, which purports to condition the policy's effectiveness on the continued "good health" of the insured at the time of the policy's delivery, can be viewed as attempting to gain the benefits of a "follow-up" to the application's inquiry into the insured's health without the costs of actually asking the insured an additional question and processing the insured's response prior to the policy's delivery.[57]

Once the policy is effective, should some new information come to the insured's attention or should an event occur affecting the risk, the insured no longer has an obligation to correct the statement on the application.[58] Events subsequent to the policy's issuance cannot induce the insurer to issue the policy; therefore, the insured has no duty to inform the insurer of such events. Indeed, it is against such events or the risk of changed circumstances that the insured purchases insurance.

The rule that the applicant has a duty to correct information on the application prior to the issuance of the policy has the potential to influence a case more when misrepresentation is involved than when concealment is involved. As discussed in the next section, intent is an element of concealment; thus, failure to disclose a fact that has come to the attention of the insured will not provide the insurer with a defense unless the insurer can establish the insured's bad faith. However, intent is not an element of misrepresentation; therefore, mere failure to correct a prior misrepresentation can provide the insurer with a defense to coverage.

---

[56] 402 N.E.2d at 671.

[57] Good-health clauses is discussed in another section. See § 34[c], *supra*.

[58] See MacKenzie v. Prudential Ins. Co., 411 F.2d 781 (6th Cir. 1969); Waseca Mut. Ins. Co. v. Noska, 331 N.W.2d 917 (Minn. 1983); Estate of Bingham v. Nationwide Life Ins. Co., 638 P.2d 352 (Kan.Ct.App. 1981).

This rule is also important in the context of policy renewals. In the usual case, a policy is renewed on the strength of representations made in the original policy, unless a new application is submitted. Therefore, with regard to the renewal policy's coverage, it would seem that the insured should have a duty to notify the insurer of any material changes in the information given the insurer since the time the original representations were made. If, however, the reissuance of the policy does not depend upon the truth of the representations made the first time the policy was issued, it would follow that such a duty should not be imposed.

[j] How Much Regulation of the Defense is Appropriate?

Just as one might question of whether regulation of the warranty defense is appropriate,[59] one can ask to what extent it is appropriate to regulate the misrepresentation defense. Just as insurers would like to use warranties reduce their exposure in situations where they lack access to information about circumstances that are relevant to risk, insurers ask questions on applications in order to gather information about facts and circumstances that is not readily or easily available to them. By taking the insured's answers at face value, the insurer can make a more informed choice about whether to underwrite the risk. Moreover, this choice can be made at lower cost; rather than expend resources in investigating the applicant, the insurer simply asks questions and gets answers. Of course, if the applicant gives an answer that raises concerns about taking on the risk, the insurer can undertake further investigation or deny the application outright.

If the insurer takes the risk and the insured later suffers a loss, the insurer may do some additional investigation; because relatively few insureds in any given risk pool will suffer loss, the insurer can confine the expenditure of its investigative resources to a relatively few cases, thereby reducing overall costs, which benefits all insureds. If in the course of that inquiry it is discovered that the insured was not forthcoming with entirely accurate answers, the insurer may choose to deny coverage based on misrepresentation. In taking this position, the insurer can be viewed as defending the integrity of its risk classification scheme; in effect, the insurer's position when denying coverage on account of misrepresentation is that this particular insured was a high risk insured that did not belong in this insurer's risk pool (or at least not at the premium charged).

Whenever a legislature constrains the insurer's use of this defense, or whenever a court decides in favor of an insured, the limitation on the misrepresentation defense can be viewed as a decision to require those non-high risk insureds who remain in the pool (and who may choose to join the pool thereafter) to pay slightly more in premium to provide benefits to the insured that the insurer believed was a high-risk insured that should not have been admitted to the pool. When viewed in this way, cases where the misrepresentation defense is raised present a choice between protecting the integrity of insurers' risk classification schemes and extending coverage to persons whose situations evoke much sympathy but who, at the margin, present close questions on whether they were eligible for coverage (either at all or at the premium charged) in the first place.

---

[59] See § 101[e], *supra*.

§ 103   Insured's Concealment

[a]   Overview: Distinguishing Misrepresentation from Concealment

The boundary between misrepresentation and concealment is extremely difficult to draw. State statutes frequently impose requirements for successful assertion of the defenses of misrepresentation or concealment, without making any distinction between the two.[1] Courts tend to use "concealment" in the same sense as "misrepresentation,"[2] and this compounds the confusion. Although the differences between the two defenses may be blurred more often than not, the distinction is essentially grounded in the differences between nondisclosures (concealment) and inaccurate disclosures (misrepresentation).

A nondisclosure is exactly the opposite of a representation. As discussed in the previous section, a representation is a communicated affirmation or denial of a fact material to the risk. Thus, if the insurer asks the applicant for a health insurance policy "how many times have you been hospitalized in the past year?" and the insured says "none" when in fact the insured had been hospitalized once, the insured has misrepresented a fact material to the risk. It might be said that the insured has "concealed" the hospitalization, but what the insured has actually done is to misrepresent the fact through the denial.

Concealment in insurance law is best viewed as the insured's failure, without being asked, to disclose known facts which the insurer would regard as material to the risk. To state an extreme case, an applicant for life insurance submits an application for life insurance without informing the insurer that later in the day the applicant is to be engaged in a duel. The insurer did not ask "are you dueling later today?" or "will you be involved in an abnormally dangerous activity later?" but the reasonable insured should know that an insurer would deem the imminent duel as a fact material to the risk. If the insured should lose the duel, the insurer would later be able to void the coverage on, among other grounds, the fact that the insured concealed a material fact from the insurer.[3]

The foregoing distinction is easy to state but hard to apply. Not surprisingly, the distinction is blurred in the cases; this is of considerable significance since the tests for establishing the defenses of concealment and misrepresentation differ. Sometimes, the facts of cases make the boundary between concealment and misrepresentation unclear. The "partial disclosure" is a good example. For example, suppose the insurer asks the applicant to list all accidents for each of the preceding three years. The applicant lists "one" when in fact the applicant had one in the first year and

---

[1] See, e.g., Ga. Code Ann. § 33-24-7; Tex. Stat. Ann. art. 21.17.

[2] See Merchants Fire Assur. Corp. v. Lattimore, 263 F.2d 232 (9th Cir. 1959); Kozlowski v. Pavonia Fire Ins. Co., 183 A. 154 (N.J.L. 1936).

[3] The example is borrowed from Circuit Judge William H. Taft's opinion in Penn Mutual Life Ins. Co. v. Mechanics' Savings Bank & Trust Co., 72 F. 413, 435 (6th Cir. 1896). But see New York Life Ins. Co. v. Bacalis, 94 F.2d 200 (5th Cir. 1938) (applicant's failure to disclose that he was carrying gun due to fear of being murdered by his former partner, whom he had accused of committing adultery with his wife, was not material concealment; applicant was murdered a few months later by an unknown person).

two in each of the succeeding years, and the policy is later issued. If this is viewed as a concealment on the two subsequent years (by interpreting the question as "how many accidents did you have in 1994? in 1995? in 1996?" and reasoning that the applicant accidentally failed to answer the last two questions), the insured may prevail under the reasoning that he or she answered for only the first year because of an innocent misunderstanding of the question. Intent to deceive, (as discussed below) is an element of the defense of concealment; merely negligently failing to disclose material facts will not give the insurer a good defense. However, if the answer is viewed as a misrepresentation (by interpreting the question as "how many accidents did you have during the period 1994–96?"), the insurer need not show intent to have a good defense, and the misrepresentation of a material fact might void the coverage.[4]

[b]   The General Rule

When applying for an insurance policy and even while the insurance contract is in effect, an insured has an affirmative duty to disclose to the insurer all facts material to the risk. Concealment exists (except with respect to marine risks) when the insured, having knowledge of a fact material to the risk, intentionally declines to disclose the fact. Concealment constitutes a ground for voiding the policy; it provides the insurer with a defense to coverage.[5]

The concealment defense has its roots in the method by which risks were underwritten at Lloyd's Coffee House in London. When the shipper circulated a slip of paper to potential underwriters seeking a commitment to assume part of the risk, the only information for the underwriters was the description of the ship and cargo on the slip. Since the underwriters relied entirely on the applicant for information, a rule developed that the description of the risk should set forth fully and accurately all the facts that would influence the underwriter in deciding whether to accept or reject it; if such facts were withheld by the applicant, whether intentionally or innocently, the resulting contract of insurance was void.[6]

In England, the rule announced first in marine insurance was gradually extended to all insurance.[7] In America, however, courts did not extend the marine insurance rule to other kinds of insurance.[8] In fire, life, and casualty insurance, American

---

[4] This hypothetical is based on Gates v. General Cas. Co. of Am., 120 F.2d 925 (9th Cir. 1941). In the case, the court treated the partial disclosure as concealment, but applied the marine rule on intent and held for the insurer. In the facts of the case, the insurer's question was how many accidents had occurred during a three-year period, and the response to this question should have been viewed as a misrepresentation. See Bertram Harnett, *The Doctrine of Concealment: A Remnant in the Law of Insurance,* 15 Law & Contemp. Probs. 391, 405–06 (1950).

[5] See, e.g., Lighton v. Madison-Onondaga Mut. Fire Ins. Co., 483 N.Y.S.2d 515 (N.Y. App. Div. 1984); Reliance Ins. Co. v. Substation Products Corp., 404 So. 2d 598 (Ala. 1981); State Farm Fire & Cas. Co. v. Jenkins, 305 S.E.2d 801 (Ga. Ct. App. 1983).

[6] Carter v. Boehm, 3 Burrows 1905 (1766).

[7] See Lindenau v. Desborough, 8 Barn. & C. 586, 108 Eng.Rpt. 1160 (1828) ("in all cases of insurance, whether on ships, houses, or lives, the underwriter should be informed of every material circumstances within the knowledge of the assured.")

[8] See Sun Mut. Ins. Co. v. Ocean Ins. Co., 107 U.S. 485, (1883).

courts opted for a rule that required intent to conceal as a prerequisite to the insurer voiding the coverage.[9] The reason usually given for abandoning the marine insurance rule in the other lines was that in marine insurance, the insurer is obliged to rely on the insured's disclosures, but such was not the case in other lines where the underwriter has the ability to examine the risk.[10] Thus, the American rule today is that in nonmarine insurance a nondisclosure of material information will not void the policy unless the insured acted in bad faith in withholding information known to be important to the insurer's evaluation of the risk.[11] In an age when information about ships and their cargoes is readily available and easily communicated, it seems inapt to have a separate rule in marine insurance recognizing innocent concealment as a defense to coverage. Nevertheless, there are no apparent indications that courts are about to alter the rule.

As noted above, the concealment doctrine developed during a time when underwriting procedures were less sophisticated than they are today. In the application, the insurer is free to ask the prospective insured for information regarding any matter the insurer deems material to the risk. Thus, it is not surprising that the United States Supreme Court over fifty years ago in *Stipcich v. Metropolitan Life Insurance Co.*[12] reasoned that the modern practice of requiring the applicant for insurance to answer questions prepared by the insurer justified relaxing the traditional rule that the insured's deliberate failure to disclose facts relevant to the risk makes the insurance contract voidable at the insurer's option. More recently, numerous courts have held that unless the insurer specifically requests information, a prospective insured is under no duty to volunteer it.[13]

The *Stipcich* rule has much to commend it. The insurer, through the application, is free to ask questions on any matter it deems relevant to the risk. It is fair for the insured to presume in the usual case that information not requested by the insurer is immaterial. Basic estoppel concepts also support the *Stipcich* rule: the insurer that has failed to ask the proper questions should be estopped to deny that the insured has concealed material facts that would have caused the insurer to make a different underwriting decision. This rule, if applied on a widespread basis, would eliminate the relevance of the concealment defense in most insurance cases. If concealment is defined as the insured's nondisclosure when no request for information is made by the insurer (and misrepresentation is defined as an inaccurate response to an

---

[9] See, e.g., Jerry V. Carbone, Inc. v. North River Ins. Co., 503 A.2d 885 (N.J. Super. Ct. App. Div. 1986); Matthews v. New York Life Ins. Co., 443 P.2d 456 (Idaho 1968); Gomogda v. Prudential Ins. Co., 501 P.2d 756 (Colo.Ct.App. 1972); Kentner v. Gulf Ins. Co., 673 P.2d 1354 (Or. Ct. App. 1983).

[10] See Hartford Protection Ins. Co. v. Harmer, 2 Ohio St. 452, 59 Am.Dec. 684 (1853).

[11] See Scarburgh Co. v. American Mfrs. Mut. Ins. Co., 435 N.Y.S.2d 997 (N.Y. Sup. Ct. 1979) (higher duty of disclosure in marine insurance than in nonmarine). Because the standard is a subjective one, a person who because of special expertise has knowledge of a material fact must disclose it, even though a layperson would not appreciate the fact's materiality.

[12] 277 U.S. 311, (1928).

[13] See, e.g., Allstate Ins. Co. v. Shirah, 466 So. 2d 940 (Ala. 1985); Block v. Voyager Life Ins. Co., 303 S.E.2d 742 (Ga. 1983); Graham v. Aetna Ins. Co., 132 S.E.2d 273 (S.C. 1963); U.S. Life Credit Ins. Co. v. McAfee, 630 P.2d 450 (Wash. Ct. App. 1981).

inquiry), the circumstances in which concealment could provide the basis for avoiding a policy would be rare.[14]

To summarize the American rule, intentional concealment of a material fact by an applicant for insurance will provide the insurer unaware of that fact with a defense to coverage. In marine insurance only, an applicant's unintentional, good faith failure to disclose a material fact will also provide the insurer unaware of that fact with a defense to coverage. The burden to establish the concealment is on the insurer.[15] A substantial caveat to the American rule is the following: to the extent courts hold that insureds have no duty to volunteer information when insurers make no request for it, the concealment doctrine has no range of operation.

[c] Materiality

The materiality requirement in the defense of concealment closely tracks the materiality requirement in misrepresentation. A material fact is one which would influence the particular insurer in deciding whether to issue the policy at all or whether to issue it only for a certain premium.[16] If the insurer is denied by the nondisclosure the information "it must have deemed necessary to an honest appraisal of insurability," the concealment is material.[17] Absent statutory regulation, it is not essential that the fact contribute to the loss for which the insured seeks to hold the insurer liable or even that the fact affect the risk (though often this will be the case). If an insurer inquires into a particular subject matter, it is conclusively presumed that matters made the subject of inquiry are material.[18]

[d] Intent

Establishing that the insured intentionally concealed a fact is a formidable burden. Sometimes the burden can be carried by inference from the obviously material nature of the information withheld.[19] Insureds sometimes successfully refute the concealment defense on the ground that the insurer led the insured to believe that the information was immaterial because it was not the subject of inquiry in questions asked by the insurer on the application. Insurers sometimes on the application form require the insured to represent affirmatively that all material information has been disclosed. Such a requirement should not, however, impose a greater burden on the

---

[14] For example, if the applicant for life insurance on someone else's life failed to disclose a plan to murder the insured, this vicious concealment of a material fact should still constitute a good defense, despite the insurer's failure to make an inquiry regarding the applicant's plans.

[15] See, e.g., American States Ins. Co. v. Ehrlich, 701 P.2d 676 (Kan. 1985); Treit v. Oregon Auto. Ins. Co., 499 P.2d 335 (Or. 1972); Tsosie v. Foundation Reserve Ins. Co., 427 P.2d 29 (N.M. 1969); Dinkins v. American Nat'l Ins. Co., 154 Cal. Rptr. 775 (Cal. Ct. App. 1979).

[16] See, e.g., American States Ins. Co. v. Ehrlich, 701 P.2d 676 (Kan. 1985); In-Towne Restaurant Corp. v. Aetna Cas. and Sur. Co., 402 N.E.2d 1385 (Mass.App.Ct. 1980).

[17] Clingan v. Vulcan Life Ins. Co., 694 S.W.2d 327, 330 (Tenn. Ct. App. 1985).

[18] See, e.g., Mickelson v. American Family Mut. Ins. Co., 329 N.W.2d 814 (Minn. 1985); Puccia v. Farmers & Traders Life Ins. Co., 428 N.Y.S.2d 78 (N.Y. App. Div. 1980).

[19] See White v. Medico Life Ins. Co., 327 N.W.2d 606 (Neb. 1982); Jones v. United Sav. Life Ins. Co., 486 So. 2d 1110 (La. Ct. App. 1986).

insured to make good faith disclosures than the insured has in the absence of such a representation.

Intent is an element of the defense of concealment, but not of misrepresentation. One court phrased the distinction this way: "While there is authority for the view that the intention is immaterial where the concealment relates to a matter made the subject of a specific inquiry, it seems to be the settled rule that, where no inquiry is made, the concealment must be tainted with a fraudulent intent."[20] Actually, a nondisclosure in response to an inquiry is a misrepresentation; intent is not an element of misrepresentation. Where no inquiry is made, the relevant defense is concealment, and intent is a prerequisite.

[e] A Continuing Obligation

Once the insurance contract is in effect, the insured is no longer obligated to disclose material information that comes to its attention after that point.[21] The logic of this rule is the same as that with the misrepresentation defense: no information can be material unless it might influence the other in the *making* of the contract. However, if the contract is not yet made at the time the insured learns of the information, a duty exists to disclose the information, assuming the information is material to the treasurer's decision on whether to underwrite the risk.

This rule is significant because often a substantial period of time exists between the time of the application and the time the policy becomes effective, due to the time it takes for the insurer to investigate the claim. During this period, the applicant is obligated to reveal material information that comes to the applicant's attention. This is simply a corollary of the rule, discussed in the context of the misrepresentation defense, that if a prior statement to the insurer becomes inaccurate due to an intervening event, the insured is obligated to notify the insurer of this development.[22]

[f] Justifications for Not Disclosing Material Information

Occasionally, circumstances will make it unnecessary for the applicant to disclose material facts known to him. No duty exists to disclose facts known to the other side; it would be highly unfair to allow an insurer to deny coverage for an insured's error when there is simply no way in which the insurer could be prejudiced by the insured's failure to act.[23] Similarly, no duty exists to disclose facts which ought to

---

[20] Kozlowski v. Pavonia Fire Ins. Co., 183 A. 154, 156 (N.J.L. 1936).

[21] See, e.g., Disposable Services, Inc. v. ITT Life Ins. Co., 453 F.2d 218 (5th Cir. 1971), *cert. denied,* 409 U.S. 1023 (1972); Weir v. City Title Ins. Co., 308 A.2d 357 (N.J. Super. Ct. App. Div. 1973).

[22] This rule would not apply in circumstances where the terms of a binding receipt make intervening changes in circumstances, such as the insured's health, irrelevant to the insurer's obligation to issue the policy. See § 33, *supra.*

[23] Wootton v. Combined Ins. Co. of Am., 395 P.2d 724 (Utah 1964) (although wife failed to disclose husband left job because of weak leg, her prior disclosure of husband's affliction held sufficient to put insurer on notice). Compare Schrader v. Prudential Ins. Co., 280 F.2d 355 (5th Cir. 1960) (approving rule, but refusing to apply it where information was located in file of division of insurer not connected to underwriting).

be known to the other side in circumstances where no reason exists to know the other side's lack of knowledge.[24] In these circumstances, allowing the insurer to void coverage for the insured's nondisclosure imposes on the insured the sanction for the insurer's unreasonable conduct. No duty exists to disclose facts when the other side has waived the need for communication.[25] No duty exists to disclose facts relating to a risk excluded or excepted from the coverage; such facts are obviously immaterial.

§ 104 Limitations on the Insurer's Defenses

The following sections discuss limitations on an insurer's assertion of the defenses of breach of warranty, misrepresentation, and concealment.

§ 104A Waiver and Estoppel

The doctrines of waiver and estoppel are often used by courts to limit the defenses that an insurer might assert in a particular case. Defenses based on provisions limiting liability and excluding coverage have been ignored under the authority of the waiver and estoppel doctrines. In the claims processing area, insurers have been held to waive deadlines for the insured giving notice of a claim, paying the premium, and other acts required of the insured. The doctrines of waiver and estoppel have the potential to touch almost any aspect of the relationship of insurer and insured.

Most courts follow the rule that upon being notified of an insured's claim, the insurer may either accept or deny liability; if it chooses to deny liability, all defenses of which the insurer has knowledge at the time of the denial must be asserted or else are waived.[1] However, if the insurer lacks knowledge of the defense at the time of denying liability, the insurer does not waive it.[2] Some courts, however, follow the opposite view and do not require the insurer to raise all possible defenses in its letter to the insured.[3]

---

[24] See L. Smirlock Realty Corp. v. Title Guar. Co., 418 N.E.2d 650 (N.Y. 1981) (insured under no duty to disclose information of record, which was freely available to title insurer); Anne Quinn Corp. v. American Mfrs. Mut. Ins. Co., 369 F. Supp. 1312 (S.D. N.Y. 1973), aff'd, 505 F.2d 727 (2d Cir. 1974) (insureds' failure to disclose alleged practice of overloading ship did not void policy where practice was common in the trade).

[25] See § 25E, supra.

[1] See, e.g., Cotton Belt Ins. Co. v. Hauck, 424 F. Supp. 570 (D.C.Mo. 1976), aff'd, 553 F.2d 102 (1977); General Acc. Ins. Group v. Cirucci, 387 N.E.2d 223 (N.Y. 1979); 16A APPLEMAN § 9260 (1981); 18 COUCH 2d § 71:43 (1983).

[2] See, e.g., Luria Bros. & Co., Inc. v. Alliance Assur. Co., Ltd., 780 F.2d 1082 (2d Cir. 1986); Zurich Co. v. Monarch Co., 230 A.2d 330 (Md. 1967). See also § 25E, supra.

[3] See, e.g., Whiting Corp. v. Home Ins. Co., 516 F. Supp. 643 (D.C.N.Y. 1981); Ladd Constr. Co. v. Ins. Co. of N. Am., 391 N.E.2d 568 (Ill. App. Ct. 1979).

§ 104B   Incontestability

[a]   Overview

Every life insurance contract, whether issued on an individual or group basis, contains an incontestability clause. The clause, often required by state statute, ordinarily provides that after the policy has been in force for two years and "during the lifetime of the insured," the policy's validity will become "incontestable." If a policy becomes incontestable, the insurer has no right to challenge the policy's validity or to assert the policy's invalidity as a defense to an insured's claim for proceeds. In sum, the validity of an incontestable policy is indisputable.

Incontestability clauses first appeared in life insurance policies in the late nineteenth century. In an era where the public's perception of insurers was particularly negative and it was widely assumed, with some justification, that insurers would seek to escape their obligations through the assertion of technical defenses, insurers created the clause to help dispel the general public's fear that insurers would refuse to pay death benefits under life insurance policy due to the insured's errors in the application.[1] If an insurer should decline to pay a death claim, the danger to the insured's beneficiaries was obvious; the insured would not be available to testify about the application, which may have been submitted many, many years earlier. By the early twentieth century, many states had enacted statutes requiring that life insurance policies contain an incontestability clause.[2]

In most situations, the effect of the incontestability clause is to limit defenses available to the insurer. Thus, the clause is primarily for the insured's benefit. Indeed, the presence of the clause would be of great importance to any insured who understood its purposes and the ramifications of its absence from a policy's text: no insured would want a policy which did not eliminate the possibility that after the insured's death, when the insured is not available to testify, the insurer might claim that the insured made a misstatement in the application that voids the coverage, which in turn would force the insured's beneficiaries to commence a lawsuit to recover the proceeds.[3]

Furthermore, at least in theory, the clause does not compromise the insurer's interests because two years, the usual period of contestability, is presumably long enough to enable the insurer to discover any reason that existed when the policy was issued to invalidate the coverage.[4]

---

[1] This history parallels the evolution of the breach of warranty defense and its regulation. See § 101[e], *supra*.

[2] The first such statute was passed in New York in 1906 in the wake of the Armstrong investigation. See § 11, *supra*. For current examples of statutes requiring incontestability clauses, see Cal. Ins. Code § 10113.5; Idaho Code § 41-1905; Ind. Code § 27-1-12-5.

[3] See Powell v. Mutual Life Ins. Co., 144 N.E. 825 (Ill. 1924).

[4] See generally William F. Young, *"Incontestable"—As to What?* 1964 U. Ill. L. Forum 323; Robert Works, *Coverage Clauses and Incontestable Statutes: The Regulation of Post-Claim Underwriting,* 1979 U. Ill. L. Forum 809. See Crow v. Capitol Bankers Life Ins. Co., 891 P.2d 1206 (N.M. 1995) (incontestability clause "protects the insurance company by giving it an adequate window of time in which to investigate an application for life insurance so as to discover any material misrepresentations on the part of the applicant.")

Health insurance policies usually contain incontestability clauses, but they usually lack the broad sweep of the clauses found in life insurance policies. For example, a major medical expense policy in common use today states that "no misstatements, except fraudulent misstatements" made by the insured in the application shall be used to invalidate the policy or to deny a claim after two years of the commencement of coverage.[5] Incontestability clauses do not need to be as broad in health insurance policies because, unlike the situation in life insurance, the insured under a health policy usually survives and is able to testify and take other steps to protect his or her interests when the insurer denies coverage.[6]

In short, the most important advantage of the incontestability clause to the insured is the security the insured acquires against the possibility of a challenge by the insurer to the policy's validity at a later time. In the absence of such clauses, insurers would contest a slightly higher percentage of claims for proceeds than they do presently; this reduction in litigation benefits insureds. Although the incontestability clause causes insurers to pay some claims that have no merit, which means that some insureds pay an unfairly low premium relative to other insureds, this disadvantage is outweighed by the advantages accruing from eliminating the possibility that insurers might make specious challenges to the validity of policies in the distant future.

[b] Scope of Incontestability Clauses

[1] Temporal Scope

The typical incontestability clause has two phrases that determine the provision's temporal scope: the policy must be "in force" for a period of time, and this period must be "during the lifetime of the insured." Both phrases have generated some controversy.

It is uniformly agreed that the insurer may seek not only to invalidate the policy while the insured is living but also to contest the coverage if the insured dies during the two-year period.[7] But what if the insured dies during the two-year period, and the insurer does not contest coverage until after the two-year period? The "during the lifetime of the insured" requirement suggests, by its plain language, that the insured must live through the incontestability period in order for the policy to become incontestable. Under this reading, the incontestability clause never takes effect if the insured dies within the two-year period; the rights and obligations of the parties become fixed at the time of the insured's death.[8] Thus, if the insured dies immediately prior to the expiration of the period of contestability, the two-year anniversary of the policy's issuance passes, and the insurer then announces that it is refusing to pay proceeds because of the insured's misrepresentation on the

---

[5] *Policy Kit* at 104 (IA 5710).

[6] See Taylor v. Metropolitan Life Ins. Co., 214 A.2d 109 (N.H. 1965).

[7] See Friedman v. Prudential Life Ins. Co., 589 F. Supp. 1017 (S.D. N.Y. 1984); Crow v. Capitol Bankers Life Ins. Co., 891 P.2d 1206 (N.M. 1995); Ledley v. William Penn Life Ins. Co., 651 A.2d 92 (N.J. 1995).

[8] See, e.g., Legel v. American Community Mut. Ins. Co., 506 N.W.2d 530 (Mich. Ct. App. 1993).

application, the incontestability clause does not operate to cause the insurer to lose the misrepresentation defense.

There is, however, considerable authority for the proposition that the insured's death does not interrupt the running of the two-year period. These cases for the most part do not involve policies that have the "during the lifetime" terminology in the incontestability clause. Under this line of authority, the insurer which waits until after the incontestability period expires to contest coverage in a situation where the insured did not survive through the period is barred by the clause from denying coverage.[9]

Sometimes disputes have arisen over whether a policy has been "in force" for two years. Most courts measure the two-year period from the policy's "date of issue" a date which is ordinarily explicitly stated in the policy itself.[10] There is some authority, however, which computes the contestability period from an earlier date, which benefits the insured. For example, if a binder is issued and the insurance begins on an earlier date, some courts have used the date of the binder or the date of the application to compute the contestability period.[11] Because it is common to backdate a policy's issue date in order to enable applicants to take advantage of reduced premium rates, using the issue date benefits insureds by causing the period of contestability to expire sooner.

[2]   Coverage versus Validity

Courts uniformly hold that the incontestability clause should be viewed as an agreement by the insurer not to contest the validity of the policy as written. The principle is commonly stated as follows: the incontestability clause will operate to bar defenses based on the policy's *validity* but not defenses pertaining to the policy's *coverage*. Thus, the insurer after the contestability period expires loses the defenses of fraud, misrepresentation, concealment, and breach of warranty. However, the clause does not prevent the insurer from defending an action after the incontestability

---

[9] See, e.g., Bolick v. Prudential Ins. Co. of Am., 249 F.Supp. 735 (D.S.C. 1969); Kocack v. Metropolitan Life Ins. Co., 189 N.E. 677 (N.Y. 1934); Ramsay v. Old Colony Life Ins. Co., 131 N.E. 108 (Ill. 1921).

[10] See, e.g., Yates v. New England Mut. Life Ins. Co., 220 N.W. 285 (Neb. 1928); Hammer v. Investors Life Ins. Co. of N. Am., 473 N.W.2d 884 (Minn. Ct. App. 1991); Guardian Life Ins. Co. of Am., Inc. v. Schaefer, 519 N.E.2d 288 (N.Y. App. 1987). Compare Lloyd v. Franklin Life Ins. Co., 245 F.2d 896 (9th Cir. 1957) (date of issue and policy date are the same).

[11] See, e.g., Holtze v. Equitable Life Assur. Soc'y of U.S., 351 A.2d 139 (Md. 1976); Nationwide Life Ins. Co. v. Ojha, 324 S.E.2d 292 (N.C. Ct. App. 1985). See also Pappageorge v. Federal Kemper Life Assur. Co., 878 P.2d 56 (Colo.Ct.App. 1994) (generally incontestability periods run from effective date; however, when binder has been issued which relates coverage back to date of examination of application, contestable period runs from earlier date; held, relation-back rule not applicable in facts of instant case). In many cases, this reasoning is problematic, in that the binder terminates by its terms upon the issuance of the policy for which the application was made.

period expires on the ground that the loss was not covered under the terms of the policy or was specifically excluded from coverage.[12]

If incontestability clauses took away the insurer's defenses based on coverage, the effect of the clause would be to expand coverage that never existed in the first place. To take two examples, when an insurer denies a claim because the premiums were not paid[13] or because the insured's death resulted from an excepted or non-covered cause,[14] the insurer is denying coverage for a reason other than the policy's invalidity. In such instances, the insurer assumes the validity of the policy and alleges a failure to comply with the policy's terms. Similarly, if the insurer seeks to reform the policy to correct the stated amount of insurance sold the insured, the incontestability clause will not bar the insurer's requested relief. Reformation in this instance does not contest the validity of the policy, but instead seeks merely to correct a scrivener's error.[15]

It is not always, however, a simple matter to determine whether an insurer's defense is based on the policy's validity or on a question of coverage. For example, suppose a disability policy covers any sickness first manifesting itself during the term of the policy. The insured becomes disabled three years after the policy's effective date and one year after the contestability period expires, but the insurer contends that the disabling illness had manifested itself before the policy became effective and thus the disability is not covered. The insurer argues that pre-existing illnesses are not covered by the policy. The insured argues that the insurer, had it investigated more thoroughly, could have raised its objection earlier — and perhaps refused to issue the policy. To allow the insurer to escape liability after the contestability period expires is precisely what the incontestability clause is designed to prevent. Some courts have accepted the insured's argument,[16] while others have sided with the insurer.[17]

[3] Void Ab Initio versus Voidable

The distinction between defenses going to coverage and defenses going to validity is similar to another distinction — that drawn between defenses showing that the contract is void *ab initio* and defenses pursuant to which the contract is voidable. For the insured's fraud or misrepresentation or breach of warranty, the contract is voidable at the insurer's option. If this option is not exercised within the contestability period, the insurer loses the right to invalidate the contract. In contrast, there

---

[12] See, e.g., Fisher v. U.S. Life Ins. Co., 249 F.2d 879 (4th Cir. 1957); Fisher v. Prudential Ins. Co. of Am., 218 A.2d 62 (N.H. 1966); Miller v. Protective Life Ins. Co., 485 So. 2d 746 (ALa. Ct. App. 1986); Searcy v. Fidelity Bankers Life Ins. Co., 656 S.W.2d 39 (Tenn. Ct. App. 1983).

[13] See, e.g., Rogers v. Atlantic Am. Life Ins. Co., 370 S.E.2d 810 (Ga. Ct. App. 1988).

[14] See, e.g., Hebert v. Hughes Tool Co., 539 So. 2d 789 (La. Ct. App. 1989) (incontestability clause was inapplicable where it was determined that policy did not cover employee's heart attack because heart attack was not accident).

[15] See ITT Life Ins. Corp. v. Farley, 783 F.2d 978 (10th Cir. 1986).

[16] See Fischer v. Massachusetts Cas. Ins. Co., 458 F. Supp. 939 (S.D. N.Y. 1978); White v. Massachusetts Cas. Ins. Co., 465 N.Y.S.2d 345 (N.Y. App. Div. 1983).

[17] See Keaton v. Paul Revere Life Ins. Co., 648 F.2d 299 (5th Cir. 1981); Massachusetts Cas. Ins. Co. v. Forman, 516 F.2d 425 (5th Cir. 1975).

are some defenses that the insurer might assert which argue, in essence, that a contractual relationship was never formed. For example, the great weight of authority holds that the defense of lack of insurable interest can be raised after the contestability period expires.[18] A lack of insurable interest makes the contract not merely voidable at the insurer's option but void — in effect, utterly invalid and nonexistent. If the contract never existed in the first place, the incontestability provision of the policy cannot be enforced.

[4] Exceptions versus Conditions

For purposes of applying the incontestability clause, some courts distinguish "exceptions" from "conditions." Most courts prevent an insurer from claiming that the policy is void because of nonsatisfaction of a condition after the policy becomes incontestable. In other words, a defense based on nonsatisfaction of a condition is viewed as a defense based on the policy's validity rather than its coverage. To take a common example, most policies provide that the policy shall not take effect unless the insured is in good health when the policy is delivered and the first premium is paid. Courts often construe such a provision as a condition, meaning that a company cannot defend after the policy becomes incontestable on the ground that the insured was not in good health on the date the policy was delivered.[19] These results have led to confusion in cases where the policy's language is not clearly an exception or a condition.

Until the forms used by insurers were recently clarified, considerable confusion surrounded those cases where the insured's death resulted from suicide after the contestability period expired. Some courts treated suicide as a condition in the following sense: it was a condition to coverage that the death not occur by suicide. Other courts viewed suicide as a limitation upon the coverage of the policy. Results in these cases often turned upon highly technical constructions of the language of the policies.

[c] Incontestability and the Defense of Fraud

Although the incontestability clause generally operates to bar the defense of fraud, this rule is subject to some exceptions. These exceptions are essentially a reaction to the incontestability clause achieving its purposes too well: an insured can willfully, deliberately misrepresent facts on an application, hide the truth for the contestability period, and then have secure coverage. In some situations, this kind of deception, the costs of which ultimately must be borne by all insureds, is too repugnant to be disregarded.

If the insured's fraud is so profound that public policy would be disserved by enforcing the policy, the insurer may be allowed to contest its validity. This is the logic which underlies the principle that if the beneficiary purchases insurance on the life of the insured with the intention of killing the insured, the policy is void ab initio.[20] This principle is essentially an exception to incontestability: taking out

---

[18] See § 47[c], *supra*.

[19] See William R. Vance, *Handbook on the Law of Insurance* (3d ed. Anderson 1951).

[20] See § 52A[e], *supra*.

insurance on the life of another with the secret intention of killing the insured is one of the most serious kinds of concealment imaginable. When the insurer claims that the beneficiary possessed such an intent at the inception of the policy, the insurer is contesting the policy's validity on the basis of fraud and concealment. Yet it is clear that such a defense can be raised by the insurer notwithstanding the passage of the period of contestability.[21] In this instance, a particularly strong public policy trumps the interests promoted by the incontestability clause.

Similarly, if a person applies for insurance by fraudulently impersonating the proposed insured, most courts hold that the incontestability clause will not bar the insurer from contesting coverage.[22] In these circumstances, as with the insurable interest doctrine, the insurer's defense is essentially that the contract is not merely voidable, but void *ab initio*. Since a contractual relationship was never established in the first place, there is no incontestability provision to be enforced.[23]

In a few jurisdictions, statutes explicitly except fraudulent misrepresentations from the applicability of the incontestability clause, or give the insurer the option to narrow the clause in that respect.[24]

The tension between the pro-insured purposes of the incontestability clause and the public policy ramifications of allowing insureds to secure coverage through wilful deceit is well illustrated by *Blue Cross & Blue Shield of Georgia, Inc. v. Sheehan,*[25] a 1994 Georgia decision. The insurer issued a health insurance policy to plaintiff in May 1990. In his application, plaintiff had provided false answers to several questions, including a denial that he had been diagnosed as HIV-positive. The insurer reserved the right to require plaintiff to submit to a physical exam, but the insurer did not do so. Plaintiff filed no claims under the policy until November 1992, at which time the insurer investigated plaintiff and discovered the fraudulent answers on his application. The policy contained a statutorily-required incontestability clause:

> Two years after this Contract is issued, no false statements which might have been in your application can be used to void the Contract. Also, after these same two years, no claim can be denied because of any false statement on your application.

Three years after the effective date of the policy, the insurer notified the plaintiff that it was rescinding the policy on account of the fraudulent misrepresentations on the application.

---

[21] See Columbian Mut. Life Ins. Co. v. Martin, 136 S.W.2d 52 (Tenn. 1940); Henderson v. Life Ins. Co. of Va., 179 S.E. 680 (S.C. 1935).

[22] See, e.g., Obartuch v. Security Mut. Life Ins. Co., 114 F.2d 873 (7th Cir. 1940); Strawbridge v. New York Life Ins. Co., 504 F. Supp. 824 (D.C.N.J. 1980); Maslin v. Columbian National Life Ins. Co., 3 F. Supp. 368 (S.D. N.Y. 1932).

[23] See, e.g., Obartuch v. Security Mutual Life Ins. Co., 114 F.2d 873 (7th Cir. 1940); Wood v. New York Life Ins. Co., 336 S.E.2d 806 (Ga. 1985).

[24] See, e.g., N.J. Stat. § 17B:26-5; Md. Ann. Code, art. 48A, § 441; 40 Pa. Stat. § 753. For a case interpreting and applying the New Jersey statute, see Paul Revere Life Ins. Co. v. Haas, 644 A.2d 1098 (N.J. 1994).

[25] 450 S.E.2d 228 (Ga. Ct. App. 1994).

The court held that the insurer was barred by the incontestability clause from rescinding the policy. The court explained:

> The insurer's inability to rescind the policy based on the applicant's fraud is contrary to traditional principles of contract law and may at first blush seem unjust. It becomes more understandable, however, if we focus on the behavior of the insurer rather than the insured, and remember that the purpose of the incontestability clause is not only to protect the expectations of insureds (an interest which admittedly would not be compelling in any case involving an alleged fraud on the part of an insured), but also to encourage the insurer to be diligent in performing its duty to investigate within a specified period, and to penalize it if it does not.[26]

Because the insurer did not investigate plaintiff's application as it had a right to do, it could not now contest the policy.

The result in *Sheehan* conforms to the literal language of the contract, but one can reasonably wonder whether the legislatively-mandated constraints on insurers contesting coverage for deceit represent good public policy. The insurer could have done more investigation, but doing so with respect to every applicant, which is what would be required to protect against fraud, would increase administrative costs and hence the premiums charged all insureds. As discussed earlier, insureds under health policies need incontestability clauses less, and health insurers, unlike life insurers, can expect fraud to be revealed in claims the insured is likely to file during the contestability period. As *Sheehan* shows, the incontestability clause increases moral hazard in order to gain some protection against post-claim underwriting by insurers. Whether this is the appropriate adjustment of the competing interests in this situation can be doubted. At a time when controlling health care costs is a national imperative,[27] the insured's successful transfer to the insurer of the substantial costs of his illness through fraud is troublesome, unless, as the court suggested, one recalls one of the fundamental premises of the incontestability clause: it is better to endure the occasional fraud than to prolong the time during which an insurer can initiate a controversy over the validity of the coverage.

[d] Troublespots

Incontestability clauses raise special problems in two areas: reinstating the lapsed policy and group insurance.

[1] Reinstatement and Renewal

Before a lapsed policy is reinstated, the insured is almost always required to present new evidence of insurability. If the policy is reinstated due to the fraud or misrepresentation of the insured, most courts hold that with respect to the new evidence presented the contestability period runs again from the date of the reinstatement. However, defenses based on facts relevant to the initial issuance of

---

[26] 450 S.E.2d at 229.

[27] See § 64[c][1], *supra*.

the policy and that were barred by the running of the first contestability period remain barred.[28]

There is some authority for the rule that a reinstatement cannot be contested if the time limits in the incontestability clause in the original contract have now expired,[29] but statutory changes in at least some of these jurisdictions have reversed some of these results,[30] and the future vitality of this minority position is in doubt. There is also some old authority for the view that reinstatement creates a new contract which makes all of the terms in the contract contestable once again,[31] but one must wonder whether this line of authority has any remaining vitality in light of the better-reasoned majority view.

The majority approach has much logic behind it. As to new representations that may be false or fraudulent, the insurer should have a new period of time to investigate and determine their truth. Yet, the fact remains that only one insurance policy was issued; reinstatement of a policy is not the formation of a new contract, but is simply the putting back in effect of the original coverage. Therefore, defenses arising out of circumstances relevant to the policy's inception and now barred should remain barred notwithstanding the subsequent reinstatement of the policy after its lapse. Some states have enacted statutes which codify the prevailing approach.[32]

Renewal of a policy, such as a group policy issued to an employer where the employees are the certificate holders, raises a similar set of considerations. Because the incontestability period runs from the date of the policy's issuance, subsequent renewals of the same policy should not be treated as subsequent issuances, which then cause a new contestability period to commence. This answer should not be changed even if some changes are made in the policy's coverage upon renewal.[33] Otherwise, a one-year term renewable insurance policy would always be contestable.

[2] Group Insurance

As noted above, the incontestability clause usually contains certain exceptions; for example, the insurer does not lose the right to contest coverage if the insured refuses to pay a premium when due after the contestability period expires. Obviously, the clause has other implicit exceptions as well. The insurer can always argue that a particular event — the event alleged to be insured — never occurred, even if this allegation is being made after the period of incontestability expires.

---

[28] See Spencer v. Kemper Investors Life Ins. Co., 764 P.2d 408 (Colo.Ct.App. 1988); New York Life Ins. Co. v. Burris, 174 Miss. 658, 165 So. 116 (1936); Annot., *Insurance: Incontestable Clause As Affected By Reinstatement of Policy*, 23 A.L.R.3d 743 (1969).

[29] See Chavis v. Southern Life Ins. Co., 347 S.E.2d 425 (N.C. 1986); Burnham v. Bankers Life & Cas. Co., 470 P.2d 261 (Utah 1970); New York Life Ins. Co. v. Dandridge, 149 S.W.2d 45 (Ark. 1941).

[30] See Ark.Stat.An. § 66-3324; Utah Code Annot. § 31A-22-403(3).

[31] See Jefferson Standard Life Ins. Co. v. Bomchel, 194 So. 156 (Ala. 1940); Umans v. New York Life Ins. Co., 156 N.E. 721 (Mass. 1927).

[32] See, e.g., Wash. Rev. Code § 48.23.270; Utah Code Ann. § 31A-22-403(3); Ark. Stat. Ann. § 66-3324.

[33] See Bonitz v. Traveler's Ins. Co., 372 N.E.2d 254 (Mass. 1978); Halstead Consultants, Inc. v. Continental Cas. Co., 891 P.2d 926 (Ariz. Ct. App. 1994).

For many years, the leading case explaining the distinction between claims that are contestable and those that are not was *Metropolitan Life Insurance Co. v. Conway,*[34] a 1930 New York decision written by then-Chief Judge Cardozo. The Superintendent of Insurance of New York had refused to approve an aviation rider which limited the insured's recovery to the payment of the cash reserve if the insured's death occurred due to specified aviation activities. The Superintendent concluded that the rider was inconsistent with the incontestability clause required under New York law, but the court disagreed with that conclusion:

> The provision that a policy shall be incontestable after it has been in force during the lifetime of the insured for a period of two years is not a mandate as to coverage, a definition of the hazards to be borne by the insurer. It means only this, that within the limits of the coverage the policy shall stand, unaffected by any defense that it was invalid in its inception, or thereafter became invalid by reason of a condition broken.[35]

Thus, *Conway* drew a distinction between the insurer's defenses based on a policy's coverage and defenses going to the policy's "validity at its inception." The former could always be asserted, regardless of the incontestability clause, but the latter could only be asserted during the period of contestability.

Although easy to state, the distinction drawn in *Conway* was difficult to apply. This was starkly apparent in group insurance. As explained in *Crawford v. Equitable Life Assurance Society of United States,*[36] a 1973 Illinois Supreme Court decision:

> With individual life insurance the policy identifies a specific individual by name, and it is relatively easy to distinguish between a question of coverage (the death of the insured or his death from some specific cause) and a question of validity created by antecedent misrepresentations on the part of the insured. In the case of group life insurance, however, the master policy undertakes to provide insurance for a collection of unnamed persons defined only in terms of membership in a class, such as the employees of a certain company. To ascertain whether a person is insured necessitates a determination of whether he is in fact a member of the class. To the extent that the determination is based upon information furnished by the employer or by an employee or alleged employee, the question whether coverage exists tends to become intertwined with the question whether the coverage was obtained by false representations.[37]

The confusion in the group insurance setting has led to widely inconsistent results in the cases where the coverage versus validity-at-inception distinction has been applied.

At first glance, most people would probably conclude under the logic of *Conway* that eligibility in a group insurance plan is a matter that is always contestable: the insured is either eligible, and hence covered, or not. Whether someone fits the definition of "insured" in a group plan seems much like whether a death under an

---

[34] 169 N.E. 642 (N.Y. 1930).

[35] 169 N.E. at 642.

[36] 305 N.E.2d 144 (Ill. 1973).

[37] 305 N.E.2d at 149.

accidental death benefit plan resulted from an "accident" and is therefore covered, or whether an person named "John Smith" who seeks insurance under a health insurance policy issued to "John Smith" is the same "John Smith" the policy purports to cover. All of these matters seem to be the kinds of questions which do not become incontestable after two years.

Yet in *Simpson v. Phoenix Mutual Life Insurance Co.,*[38] a 1969 New York decision, the court seemed to abandon *Conway* in concluding that a defense based on eligibility is subject to the incontestability clause. In *Simpson,* the insurer issued a group policy through the trustees of the cemetery-funeral services association. Simpson was an officer and attorney for a cemetery association that was a participating employer. He completed an enrollment card and was included in the list submitted to the insurer. He never satisfied, however, the eligibility provision that required him to work thirty hours per week at the employer's place of business. Over two years later, he was killed by a robber. The court held that the incontestability clause bars claims, even those related to the scope of coverage and the risks assumed, if the relevant facts could have been discovered at the time the contract was formed. Because the insurer could have discovered that the certificate holder did not work thirty hours a week as required by the employer's group policy's eligibility criterion, the insurer was barred from asserting the defense of ineligibility after the contestability period expired.

In stark contrast to *Simpson* is *Crawford v. Equitable Life Assurance Society of United States,*[39] mentioned above. Plaintiff, the president of his company, enrolled his employees in a group insurance plan purchased by an association to which his company belonged. The master policy purported to cover only "full time employees" whose schedules called for no less than thirty-two hours of work per week. Plaintiff enrolled his wife in the group, falsely representing that she worked thirty-two hours per week for his company. The insurer made no inquiry into these representations; only when the insurer saw on the wife's death certificate that her occupation was "housewife" did the insurer investigate further. Upon ascertaining the wife's true employment status, the insurer denied coverage.

Plaintiff contended that the insurer's claim that the deceased wife was not eligible for coverage was incontestable due to the passage of over two years from the time the policy was issued. The court rejected plaintiff's claim, reasoning that it was not the misrepresentations that were decisive, and thus it was not the policy's validity that was at issue. Rather, eligibility was a question of coverage, and the insurer could raise the question of coverage at any time regardless of what prior representations had been made. Moreover, the court expressed concern that if eligibility were incontestable after the expiration of two years, applicants could misrepresent their eligibility, obtain coverage, and thus impose a burden on the pool of insureds who meet the underwriting requirements.

Finally, the court in *Crawford* noted that if the insured's eligibility status changed after the expiration of the contestability period and the insurer received no notice,

---

[38] 247 N.E.2d 655 (N.Y. 1969).
[39] 305 N.E.2d 144 (Ill. 1973).

there would be no way for the insurer to resist a claim for coverage after a loss had occurred. Termination of employment should not be a defense that the insurer loses because of the contestability period, and eligibility, in the court's view, should not be treated differently. The court specifically rejected the discoverability test of *Simpson*: insisting that the insurer investigate applications for group insurance to determine eligibility, or be at risk of providing coverage for ineligible certificate holders after the expiration of the contestability period, would greatly increase the costs of marketing group insurance, which would diminish the principal advantage of group insurance for all parties, including insureds.

The issue faced by the courts in *Simpson* and *Crawford* is a close one, and courts have divided roughly equally between the two positions. Many courts follow the logic of *Simpson*,[40] while other courts adhere to the logic of *Crawford*.[41]

Neither answer is so compelling as to be obviously correct. Notwithstanding the considerable criticism of the approach followed in *Crawford* , the analysis of that case makes much sense. Compared to the employer who purchases a policy of group insurance and often administers it, the insurer lacks easy access to the information needed to verify insured's eligibility, and the employer has incentives to stretch the coverage by including as many employees on the eligibility list as possible. On-going monitoring by the insurer of employee eligibility would add much administrative cost, which ultimately increases premiums. Moreover, because full-time employment is normally the proxy for more detailed medical underwriting by the insurer, including ineligible employees within the coverage when the incontestability period has run goes to the heart of the actuarial soundness of the risk pool.

On the other hand, fraud, misrepresentation, concealment, and breach of warranty also go to the heart of the actuarial soundness of the risk pool. Incontestability clauses take away these defenses because the insurer has at its disposal the ability to determine these issues at the inception of the coverage, and eligibility should, arguably, be treated no differently. Moreover, many certificate holders and their beneficiaries rely on group coverage as the cornerstone of their insurance protection. An inadvertent error about the number of hours the certificate needs to work to be eligible for coverage should not be assertable by the insurer many years after the inception of coverage, to the detriment of the beneficiaries, when the situation could have been easily clarified earlier on. In other words, the public policy promoted by incontestability clauses — that insureds obtain certainty in their coverage after the expiration of a specified period of time — is just as strong when the issue is

---

[40] See, e.g., Bonitz v. Travelers Ins. Co., 372 N.E.2d 254 (Mass. 1978); Hulme v. Springfield Life Ins. Co., 565 P.2d 666 (Okla. 1977); Freed v. Bankers Life Ins. Co., 216 N.W 2d 357 (Iowa 1974); Cragun v. Bankers Life Co., 497 P.2d 641 (Utah 1972); Halstead Consultants, Inc. v. Continental Cas. Co., 891 P.2d 926 (Ariz. Ct. App. 1994); Groll v. Safeco Life Ins. Co., 566 A.2d 269 (Pa. Super. Ct. 1989). See also Rapak v. Companion Life Ins. Co., 424 S.E.2d 486 (S.C. 1992) (insurer cannot contest certificate holder's eligibility for group life policy after two years based on statements of certificate holder).

[41] See, e.g., General Am. Life Ins. Co. v. Charleville, 471 S.W.2d 231 (Mo. 1971) (applying Arkansas law); Fisher v. Prudential Ins. Co. of Am., 218 A.2d 62 (N.H. 1966); Home Life Ins. Co. v. Regueira, 313 So. 2d 438 (Fla. Dist. Ct. App. 1975).

eligibility under a group insurance policy as it is when fraud, warranty, or the other defenses are involved.

The issue is close, and it is doubtful that either approach will attain clear supremacy over the other.

§ 104C   Divisibility or Severability

The concept of divisibility is a basic doctrine of contract law. The essence of the principle is that under some circumstances a breach of part of a contract will not prevent the breaching party from enforcing the rest of the contract. In contract law, "[i]f the performances to be exchanged under a contract can be apportioned into corresponding pairs of part performances so that the parts of each pair are properly regarded as agreed equivalents," performance of a portion of one's duties will not prevent that party from receiving from the other party the agreed exchange for that portion, despite the nonperformance of other duties under the contract.[1] Under the logic of this principle, the insured's breach of one portion of an insurance contract will not deprive the insured of the full measure of the insurer's promised performance. If a contract is indivisible, a material breach of any part of a contract will deprive the breaching party of the other party's return performance.

Divisibility has frequently proved to be a difficult doctrine for courts to administer. Whether a contract is divisible is a question of the parties' intent, but intent is not always easy to discern. The essence of the doctrine can be illustrated, however, with simple examples. If C agrees to sell D a car for $1000 and a truck for $1500, for some purposes courts will treat the transaction as two contracts — one for a car and one for a truck. The basic contract rule is that a breach of one contract does not entitle the injured party to refuse to perform a separate contract with the breaching party. The divisibility concept essentially enables pairs of performances in a single contract to be treated as separate contracts: if C delivers the car to D but not the truck, D cannot refuse to pay $1000 for the car. However, if C has entered into one contract for the sale of one car, C cannot recover the price of an engine if C delivers only the engine to D; the contract is not divisible into the component parts of the car.

The divisibility or severability question often arises with respect to the risks covered by an insurance policy. As a general rule, if a policy covers three different perils and states three different premiums, and if each premium is attributed expressly or implicitly to the different peril, a breach of warranty or nonsatisfaction of a condition as to one peril is nɔ. i :cessarily good grounds for the insurer to refuse to provide coverage on the other two perils.[2] In logic, the insured is considered to

---

[1] *Restatement (Second) of Contracts* § 240 (1981).

[2] See, e.g., Elias v. Fireman's Ins. Co. of Newark, N.J., 420 S.E.2d 504 (S.C. 1992); Johnson v. South State Ins. Co., 341 S.E.2d 793 (S.C. 1986); Loomis v. Rockford Ins. Co., 45 N.W. 813 (Wis. 1890). See also Merced Cty. Mut. Fire Ins. Co. v. State, 284 Cal. Rptr. 680 (Cal. Ct. App. 1991) (issues relating to validity of endorsement are severable from main policy; insurer may seek rescission without seeking rescission of the main policy).

own three different policies for three different perils — even though the coverage is stated within the parameters of one written contract.

The difficulty is presented when one policy states one premium but covers several different perils. Courts reach diverse results in this situation, but some generalizations are possible. If the contract states that a misrepresentation or breach of warranty will invalidate the entire policy, courts tend to treat the contract as indivisible. If the misrepresentation or breach of warranty on one subject of the policy materially increases the risk of loss with regard to the other subjects, courts tend to treat the contract as indivisible. If the contract does not specify that the entire policy will be voided by a misrepresentation or breach of warranty, and if the misrepresentation or breach does not affect all the subjects, the contract may be deemed divisible.

Consumer's Money Order Corporation of America, Inc. v. New Hampshire Insurance Co.,[3] a 1964 Missouri case, is illustrative. The insurance policy covered the plaintiff's losses of money, securities, and other property by robbery "outside the premises while being conveyed by a messenger." An endorsement was added extending the coverage to "property in unattended automobiles" subject to a condition that automobiles be fitted with an alarm to be maintained in good order and to be set "on" at all times. On the day of the loss in question, cold temperatures prevented the plaintiff's employee from turning the lock on the alarm to the "on" position. After making a collection of money at a liquor store, the employee returned to the car and found it would not start. While standing outside the car and looking inside the hood, he was robbed. The insurer moved for a directed verdict, claiming that the coverage was suspended due to the noncompliance with the warranty that the alarm be operable. The plaintiff claimed that the warranty's terms were not applicable to robberies outside the car.

The court reasoned that "[i]f the character of the risks assumed is such that what affects the risk on one item does not affect the risk on the others the parties must have intended that the policy should be regarded as severable and divisible, and any warranty the breach of which could only affect one item will be deemed directed to that item and not to the policy as a whole."[4] Thus, the warranty, the court concluded, related only to loss by robbery from unattended vehicles, which was not the situation in the case. Therefore, the trial court did not err in refusing to direct a verdict for the insurer.

Another application of the divisibility doctrine is evident in the rule followed by a minority of courts that fraud or misrepresentation by the insured will only void those portions of the policy tainted by the fraud.[5] Thus, in *Johnson v. South State Insurance Company,*[6] a 1986 South Carolina case, the court held that the insured's fraudulent statements on the proof of loss regarding the contents of her house destroyed by fire only voided the contents coverage; the coverages for loss of the

---

[3] 386 S.W.2d 674 (Mo. Ct. App. 1964).

[4] 386 S.W.2d at 677.

[5] See Kerr v. State Farm Fire & Cas. Co., 552 F.Supp. 992 (D.S.C. 1982), *aff'd in part and rev'd on other grounds,* 731 F.2d 227 (4th Cir. 1984); Fratto v. Northern Ins. Co., 242 F.Supp. 262 (W.D. Pa. 1965), *aff'd,* 359 F.2d 842 (3d Cir. 1966).

[6] 341 S.E.2d 793 (S.C. 1986).

dwelling and additional living expenses, which were not affected by the fraud, were not invalidated. The underlying logic of cases such as *Johnson* is that the policy is divisible, and the insurer's defense is operative only with respect to a portion of the policy. Most courts reject this logic, however, and hold that any fraud or misrepresentation with respect to a portion of the covered property invalidates the entire policy.[7]

The divisibility doctrine is applicable not only to risks, but also to the interests protected by a policy. This issue is usually addressed in the context of litigation over the impact of the so-called "severability of interests" provision which purports to make the coverage apply separately to each insured as its interest may appear. Courts have followed widely divergent approaches in applying the severability of interests clause.

Under one line of authority, the severability of interests clause has the effect of extending coverage to one insured despite the acts of another insured or an exclusion that seems to apply only to another insured.[8] As explained by one court,

> Severability of interests provisions were adopted by the insurance industry to define the extent of coverage afforded by a policy issued to more than one insured . . . Where a policy contains a severability of interests clause, it is a recognition by the insurer that it has a separate and distinct obligation to each insured under the policy, and that the exclusion under the policy as to employees of the insured is confined to the employee of the insured who seeks protection under the policy.[9]

A common fact pattern in which the issue arises involves circumstances like those presented in *Worcester Mutual Insurance Co. v. Marnell,*[10] a 1986 Massachusetts case. The insureds were sued for negligently supervising their minor son, who killed an individual while driving a vehicle he owned while intoxicated. The insureds' homeowners policy explicitly excluded coverage for injuries arising out of the ownership or use of a motor vehicle owned or operated by any insured. The insurer agreed that the minor son was an insured under the policy's omnibus clause, but argued that the motor vehicle exclusion applied and the insurer had no duty to defend the parents under the negligent supervision claim. The court disagreed, reasoning that "the severability of insurance clause . . . requires that each insured be treated as having a separate insurance policy. Thus, the term 'insured' as used in the motor vehicle exclusion refers only to the person claiming coverage under the policy. Since it is undisputed that neither [parent] owned or operated the motor vehicle that struck

---

[7] See Johnson v. South State Ins. Co., *supra,* 341 S.E.2d at 795.

[8] See, e.g., Catholic Diocese of Dodge City v. Raymer, 840 P.2d 456 (Kan. 1992); American Nat'l Fire Ins. Co. v. Estate of Fournelle, 472 N.W.2d 292 (Minn. 1991); American Cast Iron Pipe Co. v. Commerce & Industry Ins. Co., 481 So. 2d 892 (Ala. 1985); Barnette v. Hartford Ins. Group, 653 P.2d 1375 (Wyo. 1982); Lumberman's Mut. Cas. Co. v. Hanover Ins. Co., 645 N.E.2d 35 (Mass.App. 1995); Premier Ins. Co. v. Adams, 632 So. 2d 1054 (Fla. Dist. Ct. App. 1994).

[9] Sacharko v. Center Equities Limited Partnership, 479 A.2d 1219, 1222 (Conn.App.Ct. 1984).

[10] 496 N.E.2d 158 (Mass. 1986).

the intestate, the [exclusion] does not prevent [the insured parents] from obtaining coverage."[11]

There are, however, numerous cases where courts have not applied the severability of interests provision to expand coverage. A leading example is *Chacon v. American Family Mutual Insurance Co.,*[12] a 1990 Colorado decision. In that case, the parents of a ten-year-old boy sought coverage under their homeowner's policy after the boy committed acts of vandalism to school property. The insurer argued that the intentional act exclusion, which said that personal liability coverage would not apply to damage "which is expected or intended by *any* insured," took away the boy's coverage and applied to take away the parents' coverage as well, notwithstanding the presence of a severability of interests clause. The court agreed with the insurer's position, reasoning that the severability of interests clause did not create an ambiguity to be resolved in the insured's favor.[13]

In some respects, *Chacon* is a simple case because the clear language of the exclusion trumped the severability clause. In cases where the language is less clear, the same result can be reached under the reasoning that the claim for which coverage is sought is derivative of another insured's excluded claim, and thus the exclusion subsumes both claims. Thus, where the personal representatives of the decedents' estates brought an action against the homeowner's insurer for the parents of the minor driver whose negligence allegedly caused the deaths, alleging that the insurer had a duty to defend the insured parents against the plaintiff's claim that the parents negligently supervised the minor driver, the court held that the exclusion for losses arising out of the use of an automobile also had the effect of excluding coverage for the parents.[14] Similarly, where a home day-care coverage endorsement had an explicit exclusion for sexual molestation, the court held that, notwithstanding the presence of a severability clause, the exclusion precluded coverage for the insured in an action against the insured alleging that she failed to use due care in supervising the child and negligently failed to prevent her husband's sexual contact with the child.[15]

The divisibility issue also arises whenever a court is asked to decide whether conduct by one insured sufficient to disqualify that person from coverage also bars recovery by innocent coinsureds. In a number of cases, courts have held that the conduct of one coinsured will not bar an innocent coinsured from recovery on the policy,[16] although there are numerous cases to the contrary where the severability

---

[11] 496 N.E.2d at 160-61.

[12] 788 P.2d 748 (Colo. 1990).

[13] 788 P.2d at 752.

[14] See Gorzen v. Westfield Ins. Co., 526 N.W.2d 43 (Mich. Ct. App. 1994).

[15] See Northwest G.F. Mut. Ins. Co. v. Norgard, 518 N.W.2d 179 (N.D. 1994).

[16] See, e.g., Haynes v. Hanover Ins. Cos., 783 F.2d 136 (8th Cir. 1986); Mercantile Trust Co. v. New York Underwriters Ins. Co., 376 F.2d 502 (7th Cir. 1967); Morgan v. Cincinnati Ins. Co., 307 N.W.2d 53 (Mich. 1981); Delph v. Potomac Ins. Co., 620 P.2d 1282 (N.M. 1980); Hildebrand v. Holyoke Mut. Fire Ins. Co., 386 A.2d 329 (Me. 1978); Hosey v. Seibels Bruce Group, South Carolina Ins. Co., 363 So. 2d 751 (Ala. 1978); see section 63A, *supra.*

of interest made no difference.[17] In essence, the pro-coverage cases represent an application of the divisibility doctrine: the policy is divisible according to the number of insureds, and the invalidity of the policy as to one insured will not bar the coverage for other coinsureds.

In short, the doctrines of divisibility and severability are used in some cases to limit the reach of defenses asserted by the insurer.

---

[17] See, e.g., Bryant v. Allstate Ins. Co., 592 F. Supp. 39 (E.D. Ky. 1984); Short v. Oklahoma Farmers Union Ins. Co., 619 P.2d 588 (Okla. 1988); Taryn E.F. v. Joshua M.C., 505 N.W.2d 418 (Wis. Ct. App. 1993). See also § 63A, *supra* for more discussion of this issue.

CHAPTER 11

THE ADDITIONAL DUTIES IN THIRD-PARTY INSURANCE

§ 110 The Insured's Duty to Cooperate and Assist in the Defense

[a] Overview

The primary obligation that the insured owes the insurer in third-party insurance (apart from paying the premium when due) is the duty of cooperation.[1] The duty to cooperate is essentially the flipside of the insurer's duty to defend. The insurer promises in the liability policy to provide the insured with a defense, but the insured simultaneously commits to cooperate with the insurer in making settlements, providing evidence, enforcing subrogation rights, and attending hearings, trials, and depositions. Also, the insured commits not to take any action that would adversely affect the insurer's handling of the claim. The insured's commitment is expressly stated in the policy, but even if it were not, the commitment would be implied; indeed, under general contract law principles, if one party obligates itself to perform a duty that requires some measure of cooperation from the other side, a duty to cooperate is imposed on the other party. In the liability insurance setting, the insured's cooperation is often essential if the insurer is to defend successfully the interests of both insurer and insured. The Illinois Supreme Court explained it this way:

> Typically the insurer has little or no knowledge of the facts surrounding a claimed loss, while the insured has exclusive knowledge of such facts. The insurer is, therefore, dependent on its insured for fair and complete disclosure; hence, the duty to cooperate. While the insured has no obligation to assist the insurer in any effort to defeat recovery of a proper claim, the cooperation clause does obligate the insured to disclose all of the facts within his knowledge and otherwise to aid the insurer in its determination of coverage under the policy. . . . The insurer is entitled, irrespective of whether its duty is to defend or to indemnify, to gain as much knowledge and information as may aid it in its investigation, or as may otherwise be significant to the insurer in determining its liability under the policy and in protecting against fraudulent claims. To hold

---

[1] The duty of cooperation exists in first-party insurance also. For additional discussion of the duty generally, see § 85, *supra.*

(Matthew Bender & Co., Inc.)

(Pub.837)

otherwise effectively places the insurer and the mercy of the insured and severely handicaps it in contesting a claim.[2]

The varieties of an insured's noncooperation run a gamut from the trivial to the substantial. At one extreme, the insured might collude with the third-party claimant for the purpose of maximizing the claimant's recovery, a clear and definite breach of the duty to cooperate. Indeed, a principle purpose of the cooperation clause is the prevention of collusion between the insured and the injured third party.[3] Alternatively, the insured might simply fail to do any of the obligations typically found in a policy. For example, under the typical liability policy, the insured has a duty to send a copy of the complaint to the insurer, inform the insurer of the circumstances of the accident or loss, and notify the insurer of any injured persons or witnesses. In circumstances where the insured fails to do any of the specifically mandated actions and does not respond to any of the insurer's efforts to initiate communications, the insured has failed to cooperate.[4] At the other extreme, the insured's refusal to be interviewed at any time other than a 6:30 a.m. breakfast meeting is an act of intransigence that might be labeled noncooperation. However, the dispute is a trivial one, and no one would contend that the insured's coverage should be voided on this account if the insured otherwise cooperates with the insurer. Between these two extremes, whether the insured's noncooperation constitutes a basis for voiding the coverage can present a difficult question.[5]

Finally, if the insurer requests and does not obtain the insured's cooperation for purposes unrelated to the performance of contractual obligations, the insurer has no defense based on the insured's lack of cooperation. Suppose, for example, the insurer settles a claim against its insured, and the settlement agreement requires a third-party contractor to do repairs. Is the insured obligated to supervise the implementation of the agreement pursuant to the duty to cooperate? A Pennsylvania court said no, reasoning that such a duty is not within the scope of purpose of the policy's cooperation clause because administering a settlement had nothing to do with the defense of the claim.[6] The principle is a simple one; one party to a contract cannot demand extra-contractual performance from the other side.

[b]   The Reciprocal Nature of the Insurer's Duties and the Insured's Duty to Cooperate

Under basic contract law principles, a party may not suspend performance in response to an insignificant or immaterial breach by the other party. This rule is designed to prevent the breaching party from suffering the forfeiture which could

---

[2] Waste Management, Inc. v. International Surplus Lines Ins. Co., 579 N.E.2d 322, 333 (Ill. 1991.)

[3] See Farmer's Cas. Co. v. Green, 390 F.2d 188 (10th Cir. 1968); Watson v. Jones, 610 P.2d 619 (Kan. 1980); American Policyholder's Ins. Co. v. Baker, 409 A.2d 1346 (N.H. 1979); Forest City Grant Liberty Assoc. v. Genro II, Inc., 652 A.2d 948 (Pa. Super. Ct. 1995); Harris v. Prudential Prop. & Cas. Co., 632 A.2d 1380 (Del.Super.Ct. 1993).

[4] See, e.g., Owens v. Allstate Ins. Co., 455 S.E.2d 368 (Ga. Ct. App. 1995).

[5] See, e.g., Annot., *Liability Insurance: Misstatement by Insured, Later Withdrawn or Corrected, as Breach of Co-Operation Clause,* 13 A.L.R.4th 837 (1982).

[6] See Forest City Grant Liberty Assoc. v. Genro II, Inc., 652 A.2d 948 (Pa.Super.Ct. 1994).

occur if the nonbreaching party responded to the trivial breach by suspending his or her entire performance. To state the rule in other words, a nonbreaching party is not entitled to suspend performance upon the other party's breach absent some substantial impairment of the nonbreaching party's rights under the contract.

The essence of this reciprocal relationship is the heart of the law relevant to the duty to cooperate. Courts in most jurisdictions have approved the rule that the insured's breach of the cooperation clause will not relieve the insurer of its obligations under the policy unless the lack of cooperation is substantial or material.[7] It is not enough to show a lack of cooperation; an insubstantial, trivial lack of cooperation has no legal significance. As one court observed, "[f]ailure to cooperate can come about in many ways, some of which may be technical and inconsequential, thereby resulting in no prejudice to the insurance company."[8]

Some courts have added to these requirements the element of intent, meaning that in addition to materiality and prejudice the insurer must show that the insured's noncooperation was willful and intentional.[9] As a matter of contract doctrine, the insured's state of mind should not figure into the evaluation of the insured's satisfaction of its obligations under the contract. Instead, the issue should simply be whether the insured has met whatever threshold of behavior amounts to cooperation. Yet if the insured's contract duty is interpreted as "not deliberately doing anything that would amount to noncooperation," then whether the insured's noncooperation is willful can be an important consideration.[10]

The reciprocal nature of the insured's duty to cooperate vis-a-vis the insurer's duties suggests another question: can the insurer demand the insured's cooperation at the same time it is disavowing coverage? The question is to what extent the insurer's repudiation of its duties to the insured frees the insured from the duty to cooperate.

The answer depends in part on whether one views the insured's duty to cooperate as an obligation the insured owes the insurer with respect to individual claims, or whether it is a broad, overarching duty that exists regardless of how the insurer responds to a particular claim. If the latter, one could reason that the insurer's disavowal of coverage does not affect the insured's general obligation to cooperate.

---

[7] See, e.g., O'Leary v. Lumbermen's Mut. Cas. Co., 420 A.2d 888 (Conn. 1979); Billington v. Interinsurance Exch., 456 P.2d 982 (Cal. 1969).

[8] See, e.g., Miller v. Dilts, 463 N.E.2d 257 (Ind. 1984); see also Murphy v. Clancy, 404 N.E.2d 287 (Ill. App. Ct. 1980), aff'd in part and rev'd in part sub nom., Murphy v. Urso, 430 N.E.2d 1079 (Ill. 1981).

[9] See, e.g., Bowyer v. Thomas, 423 S.E.2d 906 (W.Va. 1992); Thrasher v. U.S. Liab. Ins. Co., 225 N.E.2d 503 (N.Y. 1967).

[10] See, e.g., Mount Vernon Fire Ins. Co. v. 170 E. 106th St. Realty Corp., 622 N.Y.S.2d 758 (N.Y. Sup. Ct. 1995) (insurer lacked noncooperation defense because it did not provide "sufficient evidence from which it may be inferred that [the insured's] failure to remain in touch with the insurer can be clearly ascribed to willfulness rather than simply to carelessness"); Atlantic Mut. Ins. Co. v. Struve, 621 N.Y.S.2d 5 (N.Y. Sup. Ct. 1994) ("[insured's] obstinate refusal to accept legal representation at [insurer's] expense and insistence on representing herself graphically demonstrate her willful obstructionism".

If the former, the insurer's assertion that it owes no duties to the insured with respect to a particular claim means that the insured should be excused from its contract obligations to the insurer with respect to that claim (although, of course, as long as the insured continues to claim coverage for the claim the prudent insured should not fail to cooperate). Because most liability policies define the insured's duty to cooperate with respect to what the insured must do when a claim is made, it makes sense to interpret the insured's duty severally, that is, with respect to each claim. In essence, the street should be two-way: the insured's breach of the duty to cooperate with respect to claim X should not give the insurer a right to deny coverage on claim Y; and the insurer's breach of the duty to defend with respect to claim E should not entitle the insured to decline to cooperate with respect to claim F.

To illustrate how the issue might arise, suppose the insured submits a claim brought against it to the insurer for a defense. The insurer denies coverage, and the insured files a declaratory judgment action against the insurer seeking to establish coverage. In that action, the insurer requests documents from the insured relevant to the issue, and the insured declines to do so on the grounds of privilege. The insurer then asserts lack of cooperation as a defense to coverage under the reasoning that the insured must provide information to the insurer to allow it to determine whether coverage exists or not. The tension inherent in this situation is well illustrated by a 1992 New Jersey case involving essentially the foregoing situation.[11] The court stated that the "duty to cooperate should be limited to situations where insurers actually conduct or pay for the defense of underlying claims and actions. To afford the defendant insurers access to confidential defense information would enable them to both demand cooperation from their insured in the defense of underlying actions while at the same time allowing them to disavow coverage. Such a result is an anomaly."[12] The court then retreated to some extent: "Nevertheless, plaintiffs cannot totally avoid application of the cooperation clauses of the policies on the insurers' refusal to defend."[13] The court noted that the insured and insurer had a common interest in defeating plaintiffs' claims, and that this common interest required disclosing such information as would permit the insurer to reach a decision on the coverage issue, including some information prepared by the insureds at their attorneys' direction in the underlying action but not the attorneys' work product.[14]

As long as the question of coverage is unresolved and the insurer has not rejected the possibility of coverage, the insured, it would seem, must cooperate with the insurer in providing the insured with needed information, subject to the caveat that the insured need not disclose privileged information. Once, however, the insurer denies coverage, it would seem that the insured's obligation to cooperate further with the insurer with regard to the claim in question ends.[15] Presumably, of course, the

---

[11] See In re Environmental Ins. Declaratory Judgment Actions, 612 A.2d 1338 (N.J. Super. Ct. App. Div. 1992).

[12] 612 A.2d at 1342.

[13] Id.

[14] 612 A.2d at 1342-43.

[15] See Wolff v. Royal Ins. Co. of Am., 472 N.W.2d 233 (S.D. 1991) ("insurer's denial of coverage must be unjustified before policy provisions, such as a cooperative clause, are considered waived"); Arizona Prop. & Cas. Ins. Guar. Fund v. Helme, 735 P.2d 451 (Ariz.

insured will do whatever is necessary to continue to demonstrate to the insurer that coverage exists (and if the insurer changes its mind and provides coverage, the insured's duty to cooperate is resurrected). The legal significance of the demise of the duty to cooperate on account of the insurer's denial of coverage is that the insurer cannot thereafter assert acts by the insured after the denial of coverage as an independent basis for denying coverage.[16] This approach views the obligation imposed by the policy to cooperate as one that is severable in the sense that the insurer's denial of a claim excuses the insured's further cooperation with respect to that claim. With respect to all other claims and potential claims, the insurer and insured continue to owe reciprocal duties to each other under the policy.

Notwithstanding the foregoing, the insured's relief from the duty to cooperate does not give the insured a license to disregard the insurer's interests in other respects. For example, the subrogation clause and the general duty to cooperate prohibit an insured from settling the victim's claim without the insurer's consent.[17] If the insurer unjustifiably refuses to defend, the insurer's breach obviously excuses the insured from its obligation to consult with the insurer before settling the claim with the victim. If later the insurer is found to have breached the duty to defend, the insurer should be estopped to assert that the insured breached the duty to cooperate by settling without the insurer's consent and is for that reason not entitled to coverage. But the excuse from the duty to cooperate does not give the insured the right to settle the claim on whatever terms the insured desires; an unreasonable settlement (such as one that involves collusion with the victim followed by the insured's assignment of rights against the insurer to the victim) should be vulnerable to attack by the insurer.

One way to explain this result is that the insured retains a duty to act in good faith independent of the duty to cooperate, and being excused from the duty to cooperate does not justify the insured in acting other than in good faith. Another way to explain it is to hold that the insurer's breach excuses to some extent, but not fully, the insured's duty to cooperate. In the words of one court:

> We do not hold that the insurer's anticipatory repudiation [of its duty to defend] eliminates the insured's duty of cooperation so that the insured may enter into any type of [settlement] agreement or take any type of action that may protect him from financial ruin. We hold only that once the insurer commits an anticipatory breach of its policy obligations, the insured need not wait for the sword to fall and financial disaster to overtake. The insurer's breach narrows the insured's obligations under the cooperation clause and permits him to take reasonable steps to save himself. Among those steps is making a reasonable settlement with the claimant. So long as that settlement agreement is neither

---

1987) (en banc) ("once an insurer breaches any duty to its insured, the insured is no longer fully bound by the cooperation clause.")

16 Compare S.G. v. St. Paul Fire & Marine Ins. Co., 460 N.W.2d 639 (Minn. Ct. App. 1990) (where insurer had denied coverage, even though insurer would later agree to provide defense under reservation of rights, insured's settlement with claimants was not breach of duty to cooperate).

17 See § 96[g], *supra*.

fraudulent, collusive, nor otherwise against public policy, the insured has not breached the cooperation clause.[18]

Either way, the insurer's breach of the duty to defend gives the insured more freedom to respond to the claim and insulates the insured to some extent from having to account to the insurer for his or her actions.

[c] Materiality and Prejudice

At a minimum, the insurer cannot refuse to provide coverage unless the insured has committed a material breach of the noncooperation clause. Some courts couple the requirement of materiality with a requirement that the insurer be prejudiced by the insured's noncooperation.[19] In many cases, the prejudice requirement adds nothing to the materiality requirement. If a breach is immaterial, the insurer will not be prejudiced. Similarly, in most instances where the breach is material, the insurer will suffer some sort of adverse, prejudicial consequence. This led one court to state that "[t]he 'test for determining what is material and substantial with respect to an insured's alleged failure to cooperate' amounts to a 'requirement of prejudice to the insurer.' "[20]

There is a difference, however, between materiality and prejudice. A material breach is basically the equivalent of insubstantial performance; conversely, when one substantially performs his or her duty, no material breach occurs. If, for example, the insured promises to show up for trial and does not do so, a material breach occurs. Complete nonperformance of an undertaking is virtually always a material breach. Yet it does not follow that the insured's failure to show up for trial prejudices the insurer's interests. If the third party's case for liability is overwhelming and nothing in the circumstances suggests a defense to liability, the material breach of the duty of cooperation does not prejudice the insurer. Thus, the existence of prejudice may be relevant to whether the insured's noncooperation is material; if the insurer is prejudiced, it is likely that a material breach occurred. Similarly, lack of prejudice points toward a conclusion that the insured's noncooperation was immaterial. However, the presence or absence of prejudice is not determinative on the question of materiality.

---

18 Arizona Prop. & Cas. Ins. Guar. Fund. v. Helme, 735 P.2d 451, 460 (Ariz. 1987) (en banc).

19 See, e.g., Bowyer v. Thomas, 423 S.E.2d 906 (W.Va. 1992); Pickwick Park Ltd. v. Terra Nova Ins. Co., 602 A.2d 515 (R.I. 1992); Darcy v. Hartford Ins. Co., 554 N.E.2d 28 (Mass. 1990); Miller v. Dilts, 463 N.E.2d 257 (Ind. 1984); State Farm Mut. Auto. Ins. Co. v. Porter, 272 S.E.2d 196 (Va. 1980); Clemmer v. Hartford Ins. Co., 587 P.2d 1098 (Cal. 1978); Travelers Ins. Co. v. Godsey, 273 A.2d 431 (Md. 1971); Kurz v. Collins, 95 N.W.2d 365 (Wis. 1959); Pruyn v. Agricultural Ins. Co., 42 Cal. Rptr.2d 295 (Cal. Ct. App. 1995); Forest City Grant Liberty Assoc. v. Genro II, Inc., 652 A.2d 948 (Pa. Super. Ct. 1995); Eldin v. Farmers Alliance Mut. Ins. Co., 890 P.2d 823 (N.M.Ct.App. 1994); Templin v. Grange Mut. Cas. Co., 611 N.E.2d 944 (Ohio Ct.App. 1992); Riffe v. Peeler, 684 S.W.2d 539 (Mo. Ct. App. 1984).

20 See, e.g., Farmers Cas. Co. v. Green, 390 F.2d 188 (10th Cir. 1968); Hurston v. Georgia Farm Bureau Mut. Ins. Co., 250 S.E.2d 886 (Ga. Ct. App. 1978); Broussard v. Broussard, 84 So. 2d 899 (La. Ct. App. 1956).

Home Indemnity Co. v. Reed Equipment Co.,[21] a 1980 Alabama case, is illustrative. The insured did not advise the insurer for eleven months after an accident of the existence of a wheel that allegedly came off the insured's vehicle and caused the accident. The insurer, lacking access to all the relevant information, attributed the loss to another cause. The insured in *Reed Equipment* surely committed a material breach: the insured deliberately concealed from the insurer obviously relevant evidence about the cause of an accident upon which a third party's claim was based. The court said that to the extent the wheel, which was stored by the insured under lock and key during this period, was evidence adverse to the insurer's defense of its insured, the evidence was neither more nor less damaging later than it was immediately after the accident. Under these circumstances, the insurer could not show prejudice from the insured's lack of cooperation.

Cases like *Reed Equipment,* at first glance, seem unfair to the insurer. After all, the insured's concealment was only marginally less offensive than an insured's collusion with a third party to maximize the probability of the third party's recovery. Yet results in these kinds of cases are easier to understand if viewed, not as pro-insured or anti-insurer results, but as pro-victim results. The court in *Reed Equipment,* by refusing to acquiesce in the insurer's request to be discharged from liability, provided the victim with access to sufficient funds to reimburse the injury suffered in the accident. Thus, it can be said that the prejudice requirement, which limits somewhat the number of insurers whose duties will be discharged by the insured's noncooperation, is primarily designed to protect the interests of third parties. As stated by one court, "public policy requires that, where the rights of an injured third party have intervened subsequent to the issuance of the contract of insurance, the insurer should not be freed from liability to such third party, on the ground of noncooperation of the insured in having made a false statement, unless the insurer has been harmed thereby."[22]

What, then, is necessary to constitute the "harm" or "prejudice" which will void the insurer's obligation to the insured, thereby denying the victim access to insurance proceeds to reimburse the victim's injury? It is not enough for the insurer to contend that it would have had more evidence if the insured had cooperated to resist the third party's claim. Instead, the insurer's ability to contest the merits of the case must be compromised by the insured's noncooperation.[23] One court defined prejudice as an act by the insured that affects a jury or causes a jury to render a verdict against the insured.[24] By these formulations, it is not necessary for the insurer to show that a pro-insurer outcome would have occurred but for the insured's noncooperation, although such a showing would certainly establish prejudice. In effect, the insurer is entitled to a "fair determination of its liability," and if the insured's noncooperation precludes this fair determination, the insurer has suffered prejudice.[25]

---

[21] 381 So. 2d 45 (Ala. 1980). This case is also discussed in § 85[c], *supra.*

[22] Kurz v. Collins, 95 N.W.2d 365, 371 (Wis. 1959).

[23] Anderson v. Kemper Ins. Co., 340 N.W.2d 87 (Mich. Ct. App. 1983).

[24] See, e.g., Harleysville Ins. Co. v. Rosenbaum, 351 A.2d 197 (Md.Ct.App. 1976).

[25] See Schauf v. Badger State Mut. Cas. Co.,153 N.W.2d 510, 514 (Wis. 1967).

[d] Burden of Proof

In most jurisdictions, if the insurer raises lack of cooperation as a defense to coverage, the burden is on the insurer to prove the breach.[26] Similar to the principles which require the insurer to inform the insured of a deficiency in a proof of loss, so as to give the insured a chance to correct it, before using the deficiency as a basis for denying coverage, the insurer must act reasonably to try to bring about the insured's cooperation.[27]

In a few jurisdictions, however, when the insurer raises the defense, the burden is placed on the insured to demonstrate cooperation. If, for example, the claimed lack of cooperation is the insured's absence from trial, the burden is on the insured to establish that the absence was excused or justified.[28] By putting the burden on the insured, what courts are actually doing is presuming the existence of prejudice by virtue of the insured's act or neglect. Some kinds of acts are viewed by some courts as constituting prejudice per se; only if the insured can persuade the factfinder that no prejudice resulted in the particular case will the insurer not be discharged from liability. But this shift of burden to the insured has consequences for the victim of the insured's acts. As one court has stated, "[t]he rationale for imposing this heavy burden [on the insurer] is to protect an innocent injured party, who may well have relied upon the fact that the insured had adequate coverage, from being penalized for the imprudence of the insured, over whom he or she has no control."[29]

[e] Common Instances of Noncooperation

[1] Insured's Absence from Trial or Other Proceeding

Much litigation over the insured's alleged failure to fulfill the duty to cooperate concerns situations where the insured failed to present himself at a trial or other judicial proceeding. Some courts follow a strict rule and hold that the insured's willful failure to testify voids the policy for breach of the cooperation clause.[30] Refusal to participate is unquestionably a material breach of the duty to cooperate, but it does not necessarily follow that the insurer's interests will be prejudiced by the breach. Moreover, the per se rule has the additional detrimental effect of denying coverage to the victim of the insured's negligence where the insured lacks sufficient personal assets to reimburse the victim's loss. At the other extreme, requiring the

---

[26] See, e.g., Shelter Mut. Ins. Co. v. Page, 873 S.W.2d 534 (Ark. 1994); M.F.A. Mutual Ins. Co. v. Cheek, 363 N.E.2d 809 (Ill. 1977); Garcia v. Abrams, 471 N.Y.S.2d 161 (N.Y. App. Div. 1983).

[27] See, e.g., Bowyer v. Thomas, 423 S.E.2d 906 (W.Va. 1992); American Guar. & Liab. Ins. Co. v. Chandler Mfg. Co., 467 N.W.2d 226 (Iowa 1991); Darcy v. Hartford Ins. Co., 554 N.E.2d 28 (Mass. 1990); Mount Vernon Fire Ins. Co. v. 170 E. 106th St. Realty Corp., 622 N.Y.S.2d 758 (N.Y. Sup. Ct. 1995).

[28] See, e.g., O'Leary v. Lumbermen's Mut. Cas. Co., 420 A.2d 888 (Conn. 1979); Western Mut. Ins. Co. v. Baldwin, 137 N.W.2d 918 (Iowa 1965).

[29] Mount Vernon Fire Ins. Co. v. 170 E. 106th St. Realty Corp., 622 N.Y.S.2d 758, 760 (N.Y. Sup. Ct. 1995).

[30] See State Farm Mut. Auto. Ins. Co. v. Davies, 310 S.E.2d 167 (Va. 1983); Watson v. Jones, 610 P.2d 619 (Kan. 1980).

insurer to show that the judgment would have been different if the insured had cooperated places an onerous burden on insurers.

The mid-range solution favored by most courts seems more appropriate: when the insurer establishes that the insured's willful failure to appear at the trial deprived the insurer of evidence that would have made a jury issue of the insured's liability and would have supported a verdict in the insured's favor, the insurer has carried its burden of proving prejudice.[31] Thus, the insured's absence is not enough, standing alone, to establish material, substantial noncooperation. In addition, the insurer has the burden to establish that it made timely and diligent efforts to secure the insured's participation.[32] As one court stated, "[t]he insurer must prove it acted in good faith and attempted to secure the attendance and testimony of its assured at the trial and that the assured's failure to appear and testify at trial was due to an intentional refusal to cooperate despite timely and diligent efforts by the insurer."[33] Simply sending letters to the insured reminding him of the time to appear in court is not enough. Indeed, one court has gone so far as to impose a duty on the insurer, the fulfillment of which is a prerequisite to disclaiming coverage, to make some effort to determine the insured's whereabouts when the insured fails to show up for a trial.[34]

[2] Making False Statements to the Insurer

If the insured deliberately makes a false statement of material fact to the insurer after a loss occurs, some courts have held that the conduct constitutes a breach of the cooperation clause which discharges the insurer's liability under the policy.[35] Other courts, however, continue to insist upon the insurer's showing that the false statement was material and prejudicial to the insurer. Undoubtedly, making false statements to the insurer constitutes a breach of the cooperation clause. As one court stated, "[i]t is obviously true that an insured has not 'cooperated' with the insurer, if he deliberately induces the insurer to plead what he believes to be false, even though he later recants."[36] Not all false statements, however, adversely affect the insurer's interests. Noncooperation affecting credibility, for example, is not

---

[31] See State Farm Mut. Auto. Ins. Co. v. Davies, 310 S.E.2d 167 (Va. 1983). See also Hendrix v. Jones, 580 S.W.2d 740 (Mo. 1979).

[32] See, e.g., Shelter Mut. Ins. Co. v. Page, 873 S.W.2d 534 (Ark. 1994); O'Leary v. Lumbermen's Mut. Cas. Co., 420 A.2d 888 (Conn. 1979); Riffe v. Peeler, 684 S.W.2d 539 (Mo. Ct. App. 1984); Banner Cas. Co. v. Nationwide Ins. Co., 454 N.Y.S.2d 264 (N.Y.Civ.Ct. 1982); Murphy v. Clancy, 404 N.E.2d 287 (Ill. App. Ct. 1980). See generally Annot., *Liability Insurance: Failure or Refusal of Insured to Attend Trial or to Testify as Breach of Co-Operation Clause,* 9 A.L.R.4th 218 (1981).

[33] See Watson v. Jones, 610 P.2d 619, 625 (Kan. 1980).

[34] See O'Leary v. Lumbermen's Mut. Cas. Co., 420 A.2d 888 (Conn. 1979).

[35] See, e.g., Fine v. Bellefonte Underwriters Ins. Co., 725 F.2d 179 (2d Cir.), *on remand,* 589 F. Supp. 438 (S.D. N.Y. 1984), *aff'd,* 758 F.2d 50 (2d Cir. 1985), *cert. denied,* 469 U.S. 874 (1985) (discussed in § 82[d], *supra*); Samson v. Transam. Ins. Co., 636 P.2d 32 (Cal. 1981); Quintin v. Miller, 417 A.2d 941 (Vt. 1980) (willful misrepresentation regarding claim constitutes noncooperation, which voids policy and relieves insurer of duty to defend).

[36] Farm Bureau Mut. Auto. Ins. Co. v. Bascom, 287 F.2d 73, 75 (2d Cir. 1961).

necessarily prejudicial.[37] Also, a false statement, if subsequently corrected, is usually not a basis for voiding the policy for breach of the cooperation clause.[38]

[3] Collusion

Collusion between the insured and the third-party victim is perhaps the worst kind of noncooperation. Third-party insurance provides a temptation for such collusion. In many situations, the insured has the ability to help a friend recover a judgment against the insured through favorable testimony or other acts of noncooperation. The insurer, of course, must first establish the collusion. If the insurer is able to do so, the policy should be invalid without any further showing from the insurer.[39] Collusion is obviously a material breach, and the prejudice to the insurer's interest inheres in the insured's conduct. As stated by one court, "[w]e have no doubt that a deliberate misleading of the insurer by the insured in collaboration with the claimant to make it appear that the claimant was free from negligence or assumption of the risk when in fact he clearly had been negligent or clearly had assumed the risk, would be a fraudulent violation of the obligation to cooperate that would excuse the insurer from liability under its contract to indemnify its insured . . . .' '[40]

In the intrafamily situation, the desire for the insured-tortfeasor to assist the plaintiff-family member is most intense.[41] Courts must be particularly alert in such situations to the possibility of collusion. Of course, the mere fact of the relationship is not enough to infer collusion.[42]

[f] Noncooperation and Compulsory Insurance

When insurance is compulsory, as is the case with automobile liability insurance in most states, the rules concerning noncooperation are altered somewhat. The purpose of compulsory liability insurance statutes is to protect third parties; acknowledging the noncooperation defense in this situation has the effect of denying coverage to a victim of someone else's negligence. The public interest in this area is so strong that normally lack of cooperation on the part of the insured is not a defense to a third party's action where the insurance is compulsory.[43] This result

---

[37] See Williams v. Alabama Farm Bureau Mut. Cas. Ins. Co., 416 So. 2d 744 (Ala. 1982); State Farm Mut. Auto. Ins. Co. v. McSpadden, 411 N.E.2d 121 (Ill. App. Ct. 1980) (insurer cannot claim reliance on insured's false statements when insurer knew that insured had strong motive to falsify facts and circumstantial evidence points toward falsification).

[38] See, e.g., Wheeler v. Lumbermen's Mut. Cas. Co., 5 F.Supp. 193 (D.Me. 1933); M.F.A. Mut. Ins. Co. v. Cheek, 363 N.E.2d 809 (Ill. 1977).

[39] See, e.g., Travelers Ins. Co. v. Godsey, 273 A.2d 431 (Md. 1971) (despite acknowledgment of statute requiring prejudice to be shown); Schaefer v. Northern Assur. Co. of Am., 513 N.W.2d 615 (Wis. Ct. App. 1994); Hurston v. Georgia Farm Bureau Mut. Ins. Co., 250 S.E.2d 886 (Ga.App. 1978).

[40] Travelers Ins. Co. v. Godsey, 273 A.2d 431, 434 (Md. 1971).

[41] See Dietz v. Hardware Dealers Mut. Fire Ins. Co., 276 N.W.2d 808 (Wis. 1979); Upshaw v. Great American Indemnity Co., 112 So. 2d 125 (La. Ct. App. 1959).

[42] See Home Indem. Co. v. Reed Equipment Co., 381 So. 2d 45, 48 (Ala. 1980), *quoted in* Williams v. Alabama Farm Bureau Mut. Cas. Ins. Co., 416 So. 2d 744 (Ala. 1982).

[43] See Coburn v. Fox, 389 N.W.2d 424 (Mich. 1986); Annot., *Failure To Give Notice, Or Other Lack Of Co-peration By Insured, As Defense To Action Against Compulsory Liability Insurer By Injured Member Of The Public,* 31 A.L.R.2d 645 (1953).

may appear to be anti-insurer, but it is actually more pro-victim. Requiring coverage when the insured breaches the duty to cooperate creates some amount of upward pressure on premiums, since insurers must pay some claims for which they would otherwise have been discharged because of the insured's noncooperation. These increased costs are minimal, however, particularly given the beneficial effect of providing coverage for more victims of accidents.

Noncooperation should be available as a defense to coverage in compulsory liability insurance if the insured and victim are conspiring against the insurer. In such a case, it does not contravene public policy for the insurer to deny coverage altogether. It is as much the victim who has forfeited an entitlement to coverage as the insured. In addition, it is arguable that the noncooperation defense should not be precluded with respect to liability coverages exceeding the statutory minimum.

§ 111   The Insurer's Duty to Defend

[a]   Source of the Duty

The insurer under a liability insurance policy, in addition to assuming a duty to indemnify the insured in the event the insured incurs a liability to a third party, assumes a duty of defending the insured in a lawsuit brought by a third party alleging liability within the policy's coverage.[1] The source of this duty is contractual; the insurer undertakes to defend covered claims by the language of the policy itself. Often the insurer promises to defend any suit against an insured alleging damage within the scope of the policy "even if the suit is groundless, false, or fraudulent."[2] Thus, liability insurance is in a real sense "litigation insurance" as well.[3] Consistent with the rules pertaining to the duty to indemnify, the insured, to establish entitlement to a defense, must carry the burden of establishing that the complaint's allegations are within coverage. Once this burden is carried, the duty to defend is owed, unless the insurer can carry the burden of establishing that the facts fall within an applicable exclusion.[4]

As between the duty to pay proceeds and the duty to defend, the more expansive duty is the duty to defend.[5] The insurer is contractually obligated to defend even

---

[1] Occasionally, liability policies are "indemnity-only," meaning the insurer will pay any resulting judgment but the insured is obligated to provide and pay for the defense. This type of policy is sometimes purchased by large companies which have the means to finance their own defenses, and even then only in circumstances where the insurer is confident that the insured will undertake defenses competently and with appropriate sensitivity to costs.

[2] This particular phrase is in the current version of the standard homeowner's form. See *Policy Kit* at 29 (ISO Form HO 00 03 04 91).

[3] See International Paper Co. v. Continental Cas. Co., 320 N.E.2d 619 (N.Y. 1974).

[4] See Commercial Union Ins. Co. v. Albert Pipe & Supply Co., 484 F. Supp. 1153 (S.D. N.Y. 1980); but see Lanoue v. Fireman's Fund Am. Ins. Co., 278 N.W.2d 49 (Minn. 1979).

[5] See Gulf Chem. & Metallurgical Corp. v. Associated Metals & Minerals Corp., 1 F.3d 365 (5th Cir. 1993); Hartford Acc. & Indem. Co. v. Gulf Ins. Co., 776 F.2d 1380 (7th Cir. 1985); Pacific Indem. Co. v. Linn, 590 F. Supp. 643 (E.D. Pa. 1984), *aff'd*, 766 F.2d 754 (3d Cir. 1985); Newell-Blais Post No. 443, Veterans of Foreign Wars, Inc. v. Shelby Mut.

meritless suits that fall within the coverage; presumably, the plaintiff's claims in meritless suits will be defeated, and the insurer will therefore not incur any obligation to provide indemnification. However, before the merits are decided, the insurer must provide and pay for the insured's defense. In effect, the insured receives "coverage" for the defense itself, even though no duty to indemnify will ever exist in that situation.

The same point can be made by thinking about the conditions which apply to the insurer's duties to defend and to indemnify. The duty to indemnify exists as soon as the contract is formed, but the duty is a conditional one: the insurer's duty to pay proceeds is not due and owing until the insured's liability, which basically depends on how the law applies to the facts, is established. The duty to defend is not similarly conditioned: the duty to defend exists as soon as the claim within coverage is filed, regardless of whether the law of negligence would find liability in the circumstances. Because the duty to indemnify is conditioned and the duty to defend is not subject to the same or a similar condition, the duty to defend is broader.

It is possible, therefore, that the insurer could be required to defend an action as to which there is no obligation to pay proceeds, because the obligation to defend arises anytime an action is filed against the insured in which the allegations of the third party would bring the claim, *if successful*, within coverage. As stated by one court,

> The test is not the ultimate proof of the allegations but rather whether sufficient facts are stated so as to invoke coverage under the policy. The duty to defend arises not from the probability of recovery but from its possibility, no matter how remote. Any doubt as to whether the allegations state a claim covered by the policy must be resolved in favor of the insured as against the insurer.[6]

Perhaps the best way to understand the distinction between the duty to defend and the duty to indemnify is to think of the duty of defense as being keyed to coverage, instead of to liability. Even if a claim is groundless, the insurer must defend it provided the claim is within coverage. The duty to defend has nothing to do with the actual merits of a claim, and thus the duty to defend does not depend upon liability. (By the same token, where the allegations as a matter of law fall outside the coverage, there is no duty to defend.)[7] Therefore, a general rule might be stated as follows: The insurer has a duty to defend any lawsuit alleging claims against its insured for which, if liability were later established, the insurer would be required to pay damages on behalf of the insured.

Ins. Co., 487 N.E.2d 1371 (Mass. 1986); Aetna Cas. & Sur. Co. v. Pitrolo, 342 S.E.2d 156 (W.Va. 1986); Colon v. Aetna Life & Cas. Ins. Co., 484 N.E.2d 1040 (N.Y. 1985). For a decision bluntly rejecting the insurer's efforts to link together the duty to defend and the duty to indemnify, see Bankers Trust Co. v. Old Republic Ins. Co., 7 F.3d 93 (7th Cir. 1993).

6 See, e.g., George Muhlstock & Co. v. American Home Assur. Co., 502 N.Y.S.2d 174, 178 (N.Y. App. Div. 1986).

7 See, e.g., Brooklyn Law School v. Aetna Cas. & Sur. Co., 849 F.2d 788 (2d Cir. 1988); Ledford v. Gutoski, 877 P.2d 80 (Or. 1994) (en banc); J.C. Penney Cas. Ins. Co. v. M.K., 804 P.2d 689 (Cal. 1991) (en banc); Technicon Elecs. Corp. v. American Home Assur. Co., 542 N.E.2d 1048 (N.Y. 1989).

It is important also to recognize that the insurer has not only a duty but also a right to defend an action against an insured that falls within the coverage. Consider, for example, the relevant language from the standard homeowner's form:

> If a claim is made or a suit is brought against an "insured" for damages because of "bodily injury" or "property damage" caused by an "occurrence" to which this coverage applies, we will:. . . .

> 2. Provide a defense at our expense by counsel of our choice, even if the suit is groundless, false or fraudulent. We may investigate and settle any claim or suit that we decide is appropriate. Our duty to settle or defend ends when the amount we pay for damages resulting from the "occurrence" equals our limit of liability.[8]

The foregoing clause requires that the claim against the insured be within coverage; thus, if the plaintiff brings a claim against the insured for, for example, breach of contract, the insurer has no duty to defend the action. If a covered claim is made against the insured, the insurer will pay for the defense. The insurer also grants to itself the right to settle any claim as it deems appropriate; by this language, the decision to settle a case which the insurer defends belongs to the insurer, although an insurer which disregards the insured's interests affected by any settlement may incur additional liabilities to the insured.[9] Finally, the duty to defend is not unlimited; when the policy limits are exhausted by "paying damages," the insurer's duty to defend ends.

The current version of the CGL is even more explicit about the insurer's right to defend: "We will have the right and duty to defend any 'suit' seeking those damages [that the insured becomes legally obligated to pay because of 'bodily injury' or 'property damage' to which this insurance applies]. We may at our discretion investigate any 'occurrence' and settle any claim or 'suit' that may result."[10]

There are significant reasons why the insurer desires to defend the insured against covered claims. Only if the insurer controls the defense can the insurer be confident that groundless claims will be defeated, the costs of defending valid claims will be controlled and contained, and collusion between the insured and the victim will not occur.[11] In particular, the insurer will usually do a better job of managing litigation than the insured, particularly when it comes to selecting and monitoring defense counsel, making judgments about the value of claims, and other facets of defending a lawsuit. These advantages have meaning not only for the insurer, whose indemnity obligation may ultimately depend on how well the defense obligation is performed, but also for the insured, who benefits both in terms of a lower premium for coverage when defense costs are managed and sometimes in terms of favorable judgments, secured through the contribution of skilled attorneys who specialize in insurance defense.[12]

---

[8] *Policy Kit* at 29 (ISO Form HO 03 04 91).

[9] See § 111[f], *infra*.

[10] *Policy Kit* at 309 (ISO Form CG 00 01 10 93).

[11] Charles Silver, *Does Insurance Defense Counsel Represent the Company or the Insured?*, 74 Tex.L.Rev. 1583, 1595-96 (1994).

[12] *Id.* at 1596-98.

In most cases, the insured welcomes the insurer's provision of the defense and willingly assists the insurer in bringing the defense to a successful conclusion. In some cases, however, the insured's interest in how the defense is conducted becomes adverse or potentially adverse to the insurer's; these problems are discussed in a subsequent section.[13]

[b] To Whom Is the Duty Owed?

The short answer to the question "to whom is the duty owed?" is the named insured and any additional insureds. The perplexing aspect of this answer concerns the situation where someone contends that he or she, a defendant in a lawsuit, is an insured and therefore entitled to a defense but the circumstances suggest that the defendant does not enjoy the status of an insured under the policy in question. In most jurisdictions, if the victim alleges incorrectly that the defendant is an insured (such as an additional insured on a policy of insurance issued to someone else), the allegations of the complaint are not dispositive, and the insurer is not obligated to provide a defense if the insurer can establish, through extrinsic evidence, that the defendant is not the insurer's insured.[14] As a practical matter, this means that until the insurer establishes, either by declaratory judgment or otherwise, that the defendant is not an insured, the insurer has a duty to defend noninsureds who are alleged to be insureds.[15] The logic of these cases is that the insurer's obligation is to defend any allegations within coverage. In many situations, the insurer should have little difficulty determining the defendant's status as either an insured or a noninsured; when the facts showing the nonexistence of coverage are clear, the insurer should be able to easily extricate itself from the defense.

This answer is beyond serious dispute. The insurer's duty to defend is owed only to *insureds*; because a stranger to the insurer paid no premiums for coverage, the stranger should not be entitled to a defense, even if the allegations of the complaint assert that the stranger is within the coverage. To take an extreme case, if the insurer were obligated to provide a defense *anytime* the defendant is alleged to be an insured, insurers would be obligated to provide defenses to car thieves who subsequently had accidents simply because the victim alleged that the thief had constructive permission to use the car. Few insureds, let alone insurers, would desire this result.

As a practical matter, few reasons exist for an injured third party to claim that a stranger to the insurer is an insured. One possible reason is to extract a nominal settlement from the insurer, which may choose to make a minimal payment to avoid the costs of removing itself from the lawsuit. At least a minimum amount of investigation and discovery would be needed to establish the grounds on which the insurer could refuse to defend the insured. It would seem, however, that the sanctions available under the rules of procedure should deter the filing of frivolous claims that the defendant is an insured of some insurer.

---

[13] See § 114, *infra*.

[14] See, e.g., Texaco, Inc. v. Hartford Acc. & Indem., 453 F. Supp. 1109 (E.D. Okla. 1978); McCarty v. Parks, 564 P.2d 1122 (Utah 1977).

[15] See Colon v. Aetna Life and Cas. Ins. Co., 494 N.E.2d 1040 (N.Y. 1985); Holland Am. Ins. Co. v. National Indem. Co., 454 P.2d 383 (Wash. 1969).

In a few situations, however, whether the defendant is an insured can be the subject of a reasonable dispute. As suggested above, the victim might claim that the defendant had permission to operate the insured's vehicle and was therefore an insured, while the insurer (and perhaps the insured) claim that the defendant had no such permission and therefore was not an insured. Where the defendant's status as an insured depends on the development of additional facts which are expected to be clarified in the underlying action, some courts have held that the insurer does not breach its duty to defend by denying a defense provided the insurer later reimburses the insured for defense costs in the event the defendant is subsequently found to be an insured.[16] This approach, which has been applied by some courts in other situations where coverage is disputed,[17] eliminates the possibility that a person who is not an insured will receive a free defense he or she does not deserve.

Yet when the insurer refuses to provide a defense, the defendant who must fund a defense from his or her own resources may find the costs of litigation to be beyond his or her means. In the situation where the insurer turns out to have been mistaken and denies a defense that its insured deserves, the insured in the meantime may have suffered considerable financial stress. It may be better, however, to subject a few insureds to this risk, realizing that insureds who deserve a defense will later be reimbursed for defense costs, rather than require all insurers to defend all defendants who assert, often incorrectly, that they are entitled to a defense. It is unrealistic to expect that insurers will be able to recoup defense expenditures from defendants who were not insureds; to the extent some of these expenditures are uncollectible, all insureds in the insurer's pool end up subsidizing a small number of non-insureds, and these costs must be absorbed by all insureds in the form of increased premiums.

Although there is no perfect solution, most insureds would probably prefer the answer that allows an insurer to discharge its defense obligation by subsequently reimbursing defense costs in situations where the defendant's status as an insured is doubtful and it later turns out that the insured should have received a defense. As a practical matter, insurers should be expected to withhold the defense only when the defendant's status is extremely doubtful; insurers would prefer to control the defense if possible, and unreasonably disregarding their contractual obligations to their insureds could expose insurers to liability for bad faith conduct in many jurisdictions.

[c]   The Tests for Whether The Insurer Must Defend a Particular Claim

In any contract, reciprocal rights and duties come into existence as soon as the contract is formed. However, most duties in contracts, including insurance contracts, are not unbounded, and the duty to defend is no exception. The insurer's duty is to defend claims within coverage. It is evident from this statement that some claims do not trigger the duty to defend and that some standards are therefore needed to determine whether the duty is owed in a particular case.

---

[16] See, e.g., Cincinnati Ins. Co. v. Vance, 730 S.W.2d 521 (Ky. 1987); Granite State Ins. Corp. v. Mountain States Telephone & Telegraph Co., 573 P.2d 506 (Ariz. Ct. App. 1977).
[17] See § 114, *infra*.

[1] The General Rule

The starting point for determining whether the duty to defend exists is an examination of the allegations of the complaint against the insured. If the complaint states claims which, if proved, would make the insured liable to pay damages for a loss within coverage, the insurer must defend the suit.[18] One court stated the proposition this way:

> In determining whether there is a duty to defend, the point of departure is the allegations of the complaint in the action brought against the insured. If the allegations in the underlying action are, on their face, within the compass of the risk covered by the policy, the insurer is obliged to assume the defense of the action.[19]

The allegations of the complaint, however, do not tell the entire story. The allegations-of-the-complaint test is valid as an *inclusionary* standard, meaning that every complaint which makes allegations within coverage gives rise, at least presumptively, to a duty to defend. But the allegations-of-the-complaint test is not valid as an *exclusionary* standard.[20] In other words, it is not correct that if the complaint's allegations do not state a claim within coverage, no duty to defend exists. Instead, the insurer sometimes has a duty to defend even though no claim within coverage was clearly alleged in the complaint. Several situations in which the allegations of the complaint are not dispositive on whether a duty to defend exists are discussed in the following subsections.

[2] Evidence Extrinsic to the Complaint

The allegations in the plaintiff's complaint are not dispositive if the insurer learns from extrinsic information that coverage probably exists. Suppose, for example, that the plaintiff's complaint alleges that the insured-defendant intentionally battered the plaintiff. These allegations are outside coverage, and standing alone do not give rise to the duty to defend. Nevertheless, if the insurer becomes aware of evidence tending to show that the insured negligently, rather than intentionally, injured the plaintiff, the insurer will have a duty to defend, even if the complaint does not plead all of

---

18 See, e.g., Farrell Lines, Inc. v. Insurance Co. of N. Am. 789 F.2d 300 (5th Cir. 1986); Milbank Ins. Co. v. Garcia, 779 F.2d 1446 (10th Cir. 1985); White Mountain Cable Constr. Co. v. Transamerica Ins. Co., 631 A.2d 907 (N.H. 1993); Lusalon, Inc. v. Hartford Acc. & Indem. Co., 511 N.E.2d 595 (Mass. 1987); Jostens, Inc. v. Mission Ins. Co., 387 N.W.2d 161 (Minn. 1986); Waste Management of Carolinas, Inc. v. Peerless Ins. Co., 340 S.E.2d 374 (N.C. 1986); Gross v. Lloyds of London Ins. Co., 358 N.W.2d 266 (Wis. 1984); Millers Mut. Fire Ins. Co. v. Ed Bailey, Inc., 647 P.2d 1249 (Idaho 1982); Horace Mann Ins. Co. v. Maine Teachers Ass'n, 449 A.2d 358 (Me. 1982); Parker v. Hartford Fire Ins. Co., 278 S.E.2d 803 (Va. 1981); Hogan v. Midland Nat'l Ins. Co., 476 P.2d 825 (Cal. 1970); American States Ins. Co. v. Maryland Cas. Co., 628 A.2d 880 (Pa. Super. Ct. 1993); Luyties Pharmacal Co. v. Frederic Co., Inc., 716 S.W.2d 831 (Mo. Ct. App. 1986). See generally David S. Garbett, *Duty to Defend Clause in a Liability Insurance Policy: Should the Exclusive Pleading Test Be Replaced?* 36 U. Miami L. Rev. 235 (1982).

19 George Muhlstock & Co. v. American Home Assur. Co., 502 N.Y.S.2d 174, 178 (N.Y. App. Div. 1986).

20 See R. Keeton, *Insurance Law: Basic Text* 464 (1971).

the facts needed to bring the claim within coverage.[21] As stated by one court, "[w]here the insurer knows or could reasonably ascertain facts that, if proven, would be covered by its policy, the duty to defend is not dismissed because the facts alleged in a third-party complaint appear to be outside coverage, or within a policy exception to coverage."[22] This rule is sensible: an insurer should not be allowed to escape its obligations by ignoring true facts, simply because the plaintiff failed to allege them.

The converse of the foregoing rule is not correct. Insurers are not allowed to refuse to defend when the complaint makes allegations within coverage simply because the insurer has knowledge of extrinsic evidence showing that the complaint's allegations are incorrect or untrue. For example, suppose that the complaint alleges that the insured negligently operated his or her car, thereby causing injury to the plaintiff in an accident on January 3 at 2:00 a.m. The true facts are that the insured was asleep at home, with the car locked in the garage on January 3 at 2:00 a.m. Even though the insurer has extrinsic information that the allegations of the complaint are incorrect, this does not mean the insurer can refuse to defend. The insurer's commitment to its insured is to defend even groundless claims asserted within the coverage.[23] The plaintiff's claim may be utterly without merit, but if the complaint makes allegations within coverage, the insurer is obligated to defend them. Under this same logic, if the complaint against the insured alleges a loss due to negligence and the insured admits he or she acted willfully in causing the loss, the insurer is still obligated to defend the suit.[24] This claim, too, is within coverage, and therefore the insurer must defend it. With regard to this specific example, it is possible that the insured's willful conduct injuring the victim was in self-defense,[25] and many

---

[21] See, e.g., Rhodes v. Chicago Ins. Co., Civ. of Interstate Nat'l Corp., 719 F.2d 116 (5th Cir. 1983); U.S. Fid. & Guar. Co. v. Louis A. Roser Co., 585 F.2d 932 (8th Cir. 1978); National Fire & Marine Ins. Co. v. Picazio, 583 F. Supp. 624 (D.Conn. 1983); Metcalfe Bros., Inc. v. American Mut. Liab. Ins. Co., 484 F. Supp. 826 (W.D. Va. 1980); Saylin v. California Ins. Guar. Ass'n, 224 Cal. Rptr. 493 (Cal. Ct. App. 1986); Commercial Union Ins. Co. v. Henshall, 553 S.W.2d 274 (Ark. 1977); City of Palo Alto v. Pacific Indem. Co., 230 Cal. Rptr. 210 (Cal. Ct. App. 1986).

[22] Waste Management of Carolinas, Inc. v. Peerless Ins. Co., 340 S.E.2d 374, 377 (N.C. 1986).

[23] See, e.g., Trizec Properties, Inc. v. Biltmore Constr. Co., 767 F.2d 810 (11th Cir. 1985); Afcan v. Mutual Fire, Marine & Inland Ins. Co., 595 P.2d 638 (Alaska 1979); Truchinski v. Cashman, 257 N.W.2d 286 (Minn. 1977); Employer's Fire Ins. Co. v. Beals, 240 A.2d 397 (R.I. 1968); City of Palo Alto v. Pacific Indem. Co., 230 Cal. Rptr. 210 (Cal. Ct. App. 1986); Green Bus Lines v. Consolidated Mut. Ins. Co., 426 N.Y.S.2d 981 (N.Y. App. Div. 1980).

[24] See Aetna Ins. Co. v. Janson, 377 N.E.2d 296 (Ill. App. Ct. 1978); Dochod v. Central Mut. Ins. Co., 264 N.W.2d 122 (Mich. Ct. App. 1978). But see Saylin v. California Ins. Guar. Ass'n, 224 Cal. Rptr. 493 (Cal. Ct. App. 1986) (where facts "reveal that potential liability does not exist under the policy, the insurer, at its own risk, may refuse to defend the suit"); Liberty Mut. Ins. Co. v. Metzler, 586 N.E.2d 897 (Ind. Ct. App. 1992) (insurer may refuse to defend when its own independent investigation reveals a claim patently outside the risks covered, but insurer does so at its own peril).

[25] See Preferred Mut. Ins. Co. v. Thompson, 491 N.E.2d 688 (Ohio 1986).

courts hold that intentional acts in self-defense are covered by policies of liability insurance.[26]

Although most courts hold that an insurer that has knowledge that the complaint's allegations of a loss within coverage are incorrect or untrue must still defend the insured, there is a line of authority pointing to a different answer in some situations. Under these cases, if an insurer through extrinsic evidence establishes that *no coverage* exists, the insurer is not obligated to provide a defense.[27] This principle is illustrated by the rule, discussed above, concerning inaccurate allegations that a defendant is the insurer's insured. Most courts do not require the insurer to defend a stranger even though the complaint alleges that the defendant is the insurer's insured. Once the insurer establishes that the defendant enjoys no coverage, the insurer can withdraw from the defense. This logic applies to other kinds of claims as well: if the undisputed facts show that the insured, under any possible interpretation of the facts, has no coverage for the liability in question, most courts allow the insurer to withdraw from the defense.[28] A situation where the undisputed facts show no coverage for the possible liability is, of course, distinguishable from a situation where the undisputed facts show that the insured has no liability for a claim within coverage. In the latter instance, it is the insurer's duty to defend and presumably file the appropriate motion (such as a motion to dismiss or motion for summary judgment) to bring the case to an end in the insured's favor.

In many cases, however, the insurer's attempt to withdraw raises additional problems, because the defendant will often want to contest the insurer's opinion that no coverage exists. This creates a conflict of interest between insurer and insured, a problem discussed in more detail below.[29]

[3] Ambiguous Claims

Another situation in which the insurer ordinarily has a duty to defend even though the complaint's allegations do not clearly state a claim within coverage is where the plaintiff's claims are ambiguous. Doubts regarding the existence of a claim within coverage are resolved in the insured's favor.[30] Actually, this is nothing more

---

26 See § 63C[c], *supra*.

27 See Haarstad v. Graff, 517 N.W.2d 582 (Minn. 1994); Kepner v. Western Fire Ins. Co., 509 P.2d 222 (Ariz. 1973); Gray v. Zurich Ins. Co., 419 P.2d 168 (Cal. 1966); Montrose Chem. Corp. v. Superior Court, 10 Cal. Rptr.2d 687 (Cal. Ct. App. 1992), *aff'd*, 861 P.2d 1153 (Cal. 1993); Millers Mut. Ins. Ass'n of Ill. v. Ainsworth Seed Co., 552 N.E.2d 254 (Ill. App. Ct. 1989); Cincinnati Ins. Co. v. Mallon, 409 N.E.2d 1100 (Ind. Ct. App. 1980); Keeton, note 20, *supra,* at 467–68 (arguing that if the insurer can show that an "unnecessary allegation" giving rise to coverage is false, the insurer should be allowed to prove facts contrary to the allegation and withdraw from the duty to defend).

28 See § 111[e][1], *infra*.

29 See § 114, *infra*.

30 See, e.g., Trizec Properties v. Biltmore Constr. Co., 767 F.2d 810 (11th Cir. 1985); Howard v. Russell Stover Candies, Inc., 649 F.2d 620 (8th Cir. 1981); St. Paul Fire & Marine Ins. Co. v. Sears, Roebuck & Co., 603 F.2d 780 (9th Cir. 1979); Robinson v. Utica Mut. Ins. Co., 585 S.W.2d 593 (Tenn. 1979). See also National Grange Mut. Ins. Co. v. Continental Cas. Ins. Co., 650 F. Supp. 1404 (S.D. N.Y. 1986) (ambiguity of pollution exclusion, insurer held to have duty to defend).

than an application of common principles of insurance contract interpretation. Suppose, for example, the accident victim sues the insured in tort but the victim's complaint takes no position one way or another on some point determinative of coverage. Perhaps the insured's policy was in effect for a one-year period expiring October 31, 1995; the victim alleges that the insured injured the victim during the fall of 1995, but the date of the injury is not alleged. The exact date of the injury may not be a critical fact in the underlying action between the victim and the insured-defendant, but the date is a crucial fact on the question of whether the insured's liability, if any, is covered. Most courts resolve all doubts in the insured's favor: the insurer will be required to defend as long as there is potential coverage.

In the situation where the plaintiff's claims are ambiguous, some courts not only have required the insurer to defend but also have imposed an affirmative obligation on the insurer to investigate the claims to determine whether coverage might exist.[31] This affirmative obligation derives from "the modern acceptance of notice pleading and of the plasticity of pleadings in general."[32] Once a complaint is filed, it is highly probable that most insurers would proceed immediately to investigate coverage issues suggested by ambiguous claims, whether a duty to do so is imposed on them or not. Even in the prelitigation stage after notice of an event that might give rise to liability is received, the prudent insurer would begin to investigate the circumstances of the loss. Because most insurers will investigate coverage issues irrespective of the existence of the duty, imposing such a duty on the insurer does not entail any sort of substantial burden.

Some courts have approved a narrower view of the insurer's obligation in these circumstances, and this view is discussed below.[33]

[4] Complaint Containing Claims Within Coverage and Claims Outside Coverage

A third situation in which the duty to defend exists although the allegations of the complaint are not decisive on the question of coverage is where the plaintiff's complaint contains some claims within coverage and some claims outside coverage. A typical example is the following: suppose the plaintiff alleges in the first count that the defendant-insured negligently struck the plaintiff and caused injury; in the second count, plaintiff alleges that the defendant-insured intentionally struck the plaintiff and caused injury. The first count is within coverage, but the second count is outside coverage. Notwithstanding some disagreement in the decided cases over how the insurer may discharge its duty to defend in this situation, it is uniformly held that joining causes of actions outside coverage with causes of action inside coverage does not defeat the duty to defend.[34] It may be, for example, that the

---

[31] See, e.g., American States Ins. Co. v. Aetna Life & Cas. Co., 379 N.E.2d 510 (Ind. Ct. App. 1978); Fresno Economy Import Used Cars, Inc. v. U.S. Fid. & Guar. Co., 142 Cal. Rptr. 681 (Cal. Ct. App. 1977).

[32] Waste Management of Carolinas, Inc. v. Peerless Ins. Co., 340 S.E.2d 374, 378 (N.C. 1986).

[33] See § 111[f], *infra*.

[34] See, e.g., Foreman v. Continental Cas. Co., 770 F.2d 487 (5th Cir. 1985); Trizec Properties, Inc. V. Biltmore Constr. Co., 767 F.2d 810 (11th Cir. 1985); Sauer v. Home

plaintiff's action arises out of a situation where the defendant did act intentionally, and the only reason for the negligence count is plaintiff's effort to reach insurance proceeds. The insurer's obligation, however, is to defend even *groundless* claims within coverage, and the duty is triggered even when the only reason a claim within coverage exists is the creativity of the complaint's drafter. When, however, it is established that the underlying facts will only support a claim that falls outside the coverage (that is, that the insured has no coverage for the claim in question), the insurer, under the reasoning discussed earlier,[35] is entitled to withdraw from the defense, provided that this will not prejudice the represented party.

The situation is more difficult if the complaint alleges a claim outside coverage (such as battery), but the alleged facts also seem to support an unalleged claim of negligence. Under some authorities, no duty to defend exists in such a situation because the complaint does not allege a claim within coverage.[36] This conclusion seems appropriate only in those cases where no possibility exists that the complaint could be amended to allege negligence. For example, if the nature of the plaintiff's alleged injuries are such that they could not have been negligently inflicted (as is the case if the plaintiff is a victim of malicious prosecution), it follows that the insured has no right to a defense.[37]

In other circumstances, however, denying the insured a defense simply because the pleader did not separate out the negligence claim is unfair to the insured. In *Gray v. Zurich Insurance Co.,*[38] a 1966 California decision, the insurer refused to defend the insured because the plaintiff's complaint sought damages for an intentional tort. The court said, however, that one must look not just to the pleading but also to the "potential liability" created by the suit. The court noted that the plaintiff's complaint could have been amended to allege negligence or the insured's intentional infliction of injury might have been in self-defense. Therefore, the insurer owed the insured a defense, notwithstanding the absence of a specific allegation within coverage in the complaint.

The analysis in a case like *Gray* is much like looking for the "lesser included offense" in criminal law. One court offered the example of a complaint alleging willful entry and seeking punitive damages for the violation. Without amending the complaint, the plaintiff could also recover ordinary damages for nonwillful entry. The insurer, therefore, has a duty to defend despite the existence of a policy exclusion for intentional wrongdoing.[39] Most courts follow this reasoning, and hold

---

Indem. Co., 841 P.2d 176 (Alaska 1992); Preferred Mut. Ins. Co. v. Thompson, 491 N.E.2d 688 (Ohio 1986); Jostens, Inc. v. CNA Ins. Continental Cas. Co., 336 N.W.2d 544 (Minn. 1983); Fidelity & Cas. Co. of N.Y. v. Mobay Chem. Corp., 625 N.E.2d 151 (Ill. App. Ct. 1992); Voorhees v. Preferred Mut. Ins. Co., 588 A.2d 417 (N.J. Super. Ct. App. Div. 1991); Oweiss v. Erie Ins. Exch., 509 A.2d 711 (Md.Ct.App. 1986); Harold S. Schwartz & Associates, Inc. v. Continental Cas. Co., 705 S.W.2d 494 (Mo. Ct. App. 1985); Garden Sanctuary, Inc. v. Insurance Co. of N. Am., 292 So. 2d 75 (Fla. Dist. Ct. App. 1974).

[35] See § 111[c][2], *supra.*

[36] See Harbin v. Assur. Co. of Am., 308 F.2d 748 (10th Cir. 1962).

[37] See Aetna Cas. & Sur. Co. v. Freyer, 411 N.E.2d 1157 (Ill. App. Ct. 1980).

[38] 419 P.2d 168 (Cal. 1966).

[39] See Ferguson v. Birmingham Fire Ins. Co., 460 P.2d 342 (Or. 1969).

that if the facts alleged create a possibility of coverage even though the legal theory alleged by the plaintiff does not fall within coverage, the insured is entitled to a defense. This result is consistent with the general rule, discussed earlier, that the insurer which learns of evidence suggesting that the plaintiff's claim is within coverage has a duty to defend, even though the complaint asserts no claim within coverage.

In the situation where the complaint alleges claims both within and outside coverage and the claims involve common issues, a strong likelihood exists that the insurer and insured will have differing interests. If the plaintiff's complaint alleges both negligent and intentional conduct, the insurer and the insured have a common interest to the extent the action is defended on the grounds that no tort occurred at all. However, if a tort occurred, the insured desires that the tort be characterized as negligent so that coverage exists, while the insurer desires that the tort be characterized as intentional so that no coverage exists. Similarly, if the complaint seeks both compensatory damages (within coverage) and punitive damages (outside coverage in many jurisdictions), the insurer lacks the economic stake to resist the punitive damages count. These conflicts are discussed in a later section.[40] As explained more fully there, when a conflict arises, most courts require that the insured be given the option to choose counsel and to conduct his or her own defense, with the cost of the defense being paid by the insurer. In effect, this answer transforms the duty to defend into a duty to pay the costs of the defense.

If the claims inside and outside coverage do not involve common issues, the insurer still has a duty to defend the insured on the covered claims. The insurer, however, has no duty to defend the unrelated claims outside coverage. If the claims do not involve common issues, the chances of a conflict of interest in the manner in which the defense is conducted are remote. In the usual case, the insured will designate and pay for the insured's own counsel to handle the claims outside coverage, and the attorney designated by the insurer will cooperate with the insured's attorney in presenting the defense.

A particular kind of complaint asserting claims both within and outside coverage is the complaint that seeks both damages and injunctive relief. As one would expect from the foregoing principles, it is well settled in this circumstance that the insurer has a duty to defend.[41] If the complaint against the insured seeks *only* injunctive relief, a more difficult situation is presented. Because the insurance policy only purports to provide indemnification in the event a monetary award is assessed against the insured, it would seem that the insurer has no duty to defend a suit seeking injunctive relief.[42] However, some courts, primarily in cases involving insureds who have allegedly released pollutants into the environment thereby

---

[40] See § 114, *infra*.

[41] See, e.g., Buckeye Union Ins. v. Liability Solvents & Chemicals Co., 477 N.E.2d 1227 (Ohio Ct.App. 1984); Jostens, Inc. v. CNA Ins. Continental Cas. Co., 336 N.W.2d 544 (Minn. 1983); Prudential Prop. & Cas. Ins. Co. v. Lawrence, 724 P.2d 418 (Wash. Ct. App. 1986); Garden Sanctuary, Inc. v. Insurance Co. of N. Am., 292 So. 2d 75 (Fla. Dist. Ct. App. 1974).

[42] See Aetna Cas. & Sur. Co. v. Hanna, 224 F.2d 499 (5th Cir. 1955); School Dist. of Shorewood v. Wausau Ins. Cos., 488 N.W.2d 82 (Wis. 1992).

causing damage, have rejected this reasoning. For example, in *United States Aviex Co. v. Travelers Insurance Co.*[43] the court held that the insurer was obligated to defend a suit seeking a mandatory cleanup of contaminated water. The court reasoned that the plaintiff could have cleaned up the water itself and then sought damages from the insured. Since that kind of suit would have required the insurer to defend, the court reasoned that the insurer should defend the suit requiring the insured to clean the water.[44] It has also been held that an insurer must provide a defense to the insured in equitable actions where the court possesses the authority to award damages as a remedy.[45]

If the allegation of a covered claim brings a complaint that would otherwise be outside the coverage within the scope of the insurer's obligation to defend, the possibility exists that a plaintiff might add a negligence count to what is otherwise a set of allegations completely outside the coverage. In many situations, the plaintiff's hope is that once the insurer is brought into the suit the plaintiff will be able to negotiate a settlement on terms more favorable than if the defendant were not represented by counsel appointed by the insurer. Sometimes a court will disregard the "allegations of the complaint" rule in these circumstances. In support of its holding that the insurer was not obligated to provide a defense, a California court opined that "[w]e do not sanction relabeling child molestation as negligence in order to secure insurance coverage for the plaintiff's injuries."[46]

Some courts have approved a narrower view of the insurer's obligation when covered and noncovered claims are combined in the same complaint, and this view is discussed in the next subsection.

[5] Narrowing the Duty When a Fact Issue Dispositive of Coverage Will Not Be Resolved in the Underlying Action

As the prior discussion indicates, the general rule is that the insurer is obligated to defend an action against its insured whenever the complaint alleges a claim for which, if liability were later established, the insurer would be required to pay damages on behalf of the insured. From the insurer's perspective, a problem with this rule in some cases is that the facts suggest the claim falls outside the coverage, but the allegations nevertheless state groundless, albeit covered claims. If the insurer provides the defense and it later turns out when the case is over and the true facts are known that the claim was outside the coverage, the insured has received at the insurer's expense a defense to which the insured had no entitlement.[47]

---

[43] 336 N.W.2d 838 (Mich. Ct. App. 1983).

[44] For more discussion of this issue, see § 65[f], *supra*.

[45] See Haines v. St. Paul Fire & Marine Ins. Co., 428 F. Supp. 435 (D.Md. 1977).

[46] Horace Mann Ins. Co. v. Barbara B., 846 P.2d 792, 799 (Cal. 1993). Compare Allstate Ins. Co. v. Atwood, 572 A.2d 154, 157 (Md. 1990) ("Where the allegations in the tort suit against the insured obviously constitute a patent attempt to recharacterize, as negligent, an act that is clearly unintentional, we believe that a declaratory judgment action prior to the trial of the tort case is permissible.")

[47] This assumes, of course, that the insurer does not obtain reimbursement of the defense costs from the insured. As a practical matter, recovery of these costs will be difficult in many situations. Moreover, whether the insurer even has a right to seek reimbursement is

No one suggests that the solution to this difficulty is to declare that the insurer's obligation to defend the insured evaporates in such circumstances. Rather, the question is whether the insurer can withhold a defense in these circumstance until the coverage issue is resolved, with the insurer then reimbursing the insured for defense costs incurred in the event the coverage issue is subsequently resolved in the insured's behavior. The leading case approving the position that the insurer can fulfill the duty to defend when the claim is subsequently demonstrated to be within coverage by reimbursing the insured for defense costs is *Burd v. Sussex Mutual Insurance Co.*,[48] a 1970 New Jersey decision. In *Burd*, the insured inflicted a shotgun wound on a third-party. The insured was convicted for atrocious assault and battery; in a civil action, the victim sued the insured for damages resulting from the insured's intentional wrongdoing and the insured's negligence. The insurer refused to defend on the grounds that the insured's conduct fell within the intentional act exclusion. The insured then defended the suit with his own counsel, and a general verdict was entered for the victim in the amount of $8,500. The insured subsequently sued the insurer to recover the amount of the judgment and the insured's defense costs. The insurer claimed that the insured's criminal conviction was binding on the issue of whether the insured had intentionally injured the victim. The insured argued that the insured, having refused to defend the civil action, could not challenge the claim that the victim's injuries were negligently inflicted. The trial court held that the insurer was precluded from challenging the negligence allegation and did not, as a result, reach the insurer's contention that the criminal conviction was determinative on the applicability of the intentional act exclusion.

The court began its analysis by observing that the duty to defend is not necessarily linked to the allegations of the complaint:

> The insured says the carrier is obligated to defend an action whenever the complaint alleges a basis in liability within the covenant to pay. This is the general approach. [Citations omitted.] But when coverage, i.e., the duty to pay, depends upon a factual issue which will not be resolved by the trial of the third party's suit against the insured, the duty to defend may depend upon the actual facts and not upon the actual allegations of the complaint.[49]

In the instant case, the complaint alleged both intentional conduct and negligence, and the court observed that as a result the insurer and insured have conflicting interests in how the insured's defense should be presented.[50] This meant that the insured necessarily had the right to determine how the defense to the underlying claim should be presented:

---

controversial. For a debate over whether insurers should have a right to reimbursement of defense costs when it is subsequently determined that the claim against the insured was outside the coverage, see Richard Giller, *Insurer's Right to Seek Reimbursement of Defense Costs: A National Perspective*, 17 Ins. Litig. Rptr. 132 (1995); Brent E. Johnson, *A Policyholder's Perspective: A Reply to Richard Giller*, 17 Ins. Litig. Rtpr. 252 (1995); Richard Giller, *A Further Explanation as to Why Insurers Are Entitled to Seek Reimbursement of Defense Costs*, 17 Ins. Litig. Rptr. 319 (1995).

[48] 267 A.2d 7 (N.J. 1970).

[49] 267 A.2d at 9.

[50] 267 A.2d at 10.

There may be cases in which the interests of the carrier and the insured coincide so that the carrier can defend such an action with complete devotion to the insured's interest. But if the trial will leave the question of coverage unresolved so that the insured may later be called upon to pay, or if the case may be so defended by a carrier as to prejudice the insured thereafter upon the issue of coverage, the carrier should not be permitted to control the defense.[51]

Because the insurer could not control the defense, it would be anomalous to estop the insurer from disputing coverage because it refused to defend:

In such circumstances the carrier should not be estopped from disputing coverage because it refused to defend. On the contrary the carrier should not be permitted to assume the defense if it intends to dispute its obligation to pay a plaintiff's judgment, unless of course the insured expressly agrees to that reservation. This is not to free the carrier from its covenant to defend, but rather to translate its obligation into one to reimburse the insured if it later adjudged that the claim was one within the policy covenant to pay.[52]

The court recognized that a proceeding where the insurer and insured could "fight out their differences" was necessary, and that this declaratory judgment proceeding could occur either before the trial in the underlying action or after it, as the parties decided. It was not inappropriate to wait until after the trial in the underlying action, as having the declaratory judgment action earlier "could lead to unnecessary litigation."[53]

Significantly, the court in *Burd* acknowledged that the insurer could have undertaken the defense pursuant to a reservation of rights, provided the insured agreed to proceed in that manner.[54] But the import of *Burd* was that the insurer was not required to follow this course. Where the underlying action would not resolve the coverage issue, under *Burd* the insurer is entitled to withhold a defense without being subsequently estopped to contest coverage. The court observed that if the insured prevails in the underlying action, it will not be clear whether the groundless claim was one for an intentional wrong or a negligent wrong, and "[i]n that situation the carrier may fairly be required to reimburse the insured for the cost of the successful defense even though the carrier would not have had to pay the judgment if the case had gone against the insured on a finding of intentional injury."[55]

The circumstance that created the difficulty in *Burd* was the conflict of interest between the insurer and insured by virtue of the combination of covered claims and uncovered claims in one complaint. This conflict, which is treated in more detail in a later section,[56] can be resolved by requiring the insurer to appoint independent counsel for the insured (or perhaps pay the expenses of counsel selected by the insured) to defend the insured in the underlying action, with the understanding that

---

[51] *Id.*

[52] *Id.*

[53] 267 A.2d at 11.

[54] See § 114[c][3], *infra.*

[55] 267 A.2d at 12.

[56] See § 114, *infra.*

fact findings in the underlying action will not be binding on the insurer in the coverage action.[57] This answer, obviously, requires the insurer sometimes to pay for defenses where none is warranted. The *Burd* court, however, resolved the conflict by allowing the insurer to withhold the defense while remaining obligated to reimburse defense costs if coverage were subsequently found to exist for the claim in question. In effect, the court resolved the conflict by narrowing the duty to defend. This approach has been followed in other situations, such as where the defendant's status as an insured is uncertain,[58] or where the question is whether the insurer's policy was in force at the time of the occurrence in question and this fact question will not be resolved in the underlying action.[59]

From the insured's perspective, the answer favored by cases like *Burd* is less problematic if the insured has the financial means to underwrite a defense until the coverage issues are resolved. Thus, large businesses and corporations with substantial litigation budgets may not feel any particular adverse effect from the rule. But the same cannot be said for small businesses and most individuals. Those without the financial resources to underwrite a defense may be unable to purchase an adequate defense. In some situations, this could result in settlements or judgments in excess of a claim's true value (as could result if the insured is unable to afford a lawyer with expertise in a particular area and the counsel retained incorrectly assesses a claim's value). Yet insurers likewise have a stake in controlling a defense, given that a weak defense may result in the insurer have a large indemnity obligation in the event the claim is later found to be within coverage.

Although no known source of data allows these observations to be tested empirically, it would seem that most insurers provide a defense whenever it appears that coverage is possible; this is because insurers want to control the defense and reduce their own (and their insured's) indemnity exposure if possible. By this same analysis, it would seem that insurers are likely to deny a defense only when they, rightly or wrongly, are very certain that the claim is outside coverage. Of course, the harsh situations for insureds are those where the insurer is very certain, but very wrong, about the absence of coverage. What the *Burd* approach does is trade this harshness in a few cases for the savings generated from reducing the circumstances in which the insurer provides free defenses for noncovered claims. Further

---

[57] This should be the result when independent counsel is appointed, given that the insurer is not a party to the underlying action and is not in privity with the insured for purposes of issue preclusion.

[58] See § 111[b], *supra*.

[59] In Hartford Acc. & Indem. Co. v. Aetna Life & Cas. Ins. Co., 483 A.2d 402 (N.J. 1984), the suit against the insured, a pharmaceutical company, alleged the insured's negligence with respect to warnings that should have been made about uses of a particular drug. Aetna refused to defend the action against its insured, alleging that the policy had expired before the injury in question. The court concluded that Aetna had a factual basis for disputing coverage and that the fact questions determinative of coverage would not be resolved in the underlying action. In these circumstances, the court held that Aetna did not breach its duty to defend by not providing a defense, but that if it later were demonstrated that coverage did exit, the insurer could fulfill its burden by reimbursing the insured for its defense costs. 483 A.2d at 407-08.

observations on the conflict of interest issue which gives rise to cases like *Burd* are discussed in a later section.[60]

[d] Triggering the Duty to Defend: When Does the Duty Exist?

Because the essence of the duty to defend is providing the insured with a defense in litigation where the insured's potential liability is at issue, most courts hold that the duty to defend begins when the insurer has notice of the litigation.[61] Notice of the litigation, however, should be viewed as the *latest* time at which the duty to defend is triggered. Some courts take a broader view of the duty to defend, reasoning that it extends to any effort to protect the interests of the insured against claims filed or that may be filed by third parties. Under this analysis, the duty to defend exists in the prelitigation stage as well.[62]

Plainly, the insurer cannot do anything to prejudice the insured's interests before litigation begins. Moreover, if an insurer, after receiving notice of a claim but before litigation is commenced, takes steps on the insured's behalf to settle the claim or otherwise dispose of it without litigation, the insurer owes the insured a duty to act on the insured's behalf in good faith and with due care, so as to protect and not impair the insured's interests. This suggests that the duty to defend may exist as early as the time the insurer receives notice of even a potential claim against the insured.[63]

A duty to defend also might arise sometime after the original complaint is filed. For example, if the first complaint containing no claims within coverage is amended to include a new allegation within the coverage, or if facts surface after litigation commences showing that the claim is within coverage, the insurer's duty to defend will come into existence.[64]

At the same time the insurer has a duty to defend, the insured may have counterclaims against the plaintiff or cross-claims against other parties. Insureds may wish for their insurers to prosecute such claims, but the duty to defend does not require the insurer to do so.[65] A different answer might be appropriate if a counterclaim or cross-claim were so intertwined with plaintiff's claim that prosecuting the affirmative claim for relief was tantamount to defending, and was the only effective way to defend, against the plaintiff's claim.[66]

---

[60] See § 114, *infra.*

[61] See Hoyt v. St. Paul Fire & Marine Ins. Co., 607 F.2d 864 (9th Cir. 1974).

[62] See, e.g., Pacific Indem. Co. v. Linn, 766 F.2d 754 (3d Cir. 1985); Harborside Refrigerated Services, Inc. v. IARW Ins. Co., 759 F.2d 829 (11th Cir. 1985); Sterilite Corp. v. Continental Cas. Co., 458 N.E.2d 338 (Mass.App. 1983); Miller v. Elite Ins. Co., 161 Cal. Rptr. 322 (Cal. Ct. App. 1980).

[63] See, e.g., Samson v. Transamerica Ins. Co., 636 P.2d 32 (Cal. 1981); Sorenson v. Kruse, 293 N.W.2d 56 (Minn. 1980); Gray v. Zurich Ins. Co., 419 P.2d 168 (Cal. 1966).

[64] See, e.g., Journal Publishing Co. v. General Cas. Co., 210 F.2d 202 (9th Cir. 1954); Lee v. Aetna Cas. & Sur. Co., 178 F.2d 750 (2d Cir. 1949); Great Am. Ins. Co. v. McKemie, 259 S.E.2d 39 (Ga. 1979); Oweiss v. Erie Ins. Exch., 509 A.2d 711 (Md.Ct.App. 1986).

[65] See, e.g., National Cas. Ins. Co. v. City of Mt. Vernon, 515 N.Y.S.2d 267 (N.Y. App. Div. 1987); Goldberg v. American Home Assur. Co., 439 N.Y.S.2d 2 (N.Y. App. Div. 1981); Osborne v. Hartford Acc. & Indem. Co., 476 S.W.2d 256 (Tenn. Ct. App. 1971).

[66] See, e.g., Towne Realty, Inc. v. Zurich Ins. Co., 534 N.W.2d 886 (Wis. Ct. App. 1995).

[e] Premature Termination of the Duty to Defend

Once the duty to defend is triggered, ordinarily the insurer is bound to provide the defense at least until a final judgment or settlement is entered in the plaintiff's action against the insured-defendant. In some extraordinary circumstances, however, the duty can be prematurely terminated. For example, if the insured commits a material breach of the duty of cooperation, the insurer is entitled to suspend its performance under the duties both to defend and indemnify.[67] Courts also allow withdrawal if the insurer subsequently determines that its initial assumption of the defense was not warranted,[68] or if the insurer subsequently discovers facts that negate coverage.

[1] Discovery of Facts That Negate Coverage

When the insurer undertakes a defense in a situation where the allegations are ambiguous, the possibility exists that at a later time it will become clear that no coverage exists under any plausible set of facts. In that situation, the insurer is entitled to withdraw from the defense, so long as doing so will not prejudice the insured's interests.[69] This rule was stated by Judge Hand in *Lee v. Aetna Casualty & Surety Co.*:[70] "If the plaintiff's complaint against the insured alleged facts which would have supported a recovery covered by the policy, it was the duty of the defendant to undertake the defense, until it could confine the claim to a recovery that the policy did not cover."[71] Because the insurer is always obligated to defend groundless claims within coverage, it is essential that no claim within coverage remain for the insurer to be entitled to withdraw.

For example, if the ambiguity is that the date of the loss is uncertain and thus it is not clear whether the coverage exists, and the parties proceed to stipulate that the date of loss was not when the policy was in effect, the insurer is entitled to withdraw, since there is no longer a possibility under any set of facts that coverage can exist. Similarly, if the complaint alleges claims within coverage and claims outside coverage, and the claims within coverage are withdrawn from the litigation, the insurer is no longer obligated to provide a defense. As one court has explained, "the insurer need not defend if the third party complaint can by no conceivable theory raise a single issue which could bring it within the policy coverage. Hence the obligation to defend does not mature if the policy was not in force at the time

---

[67] See § 110, *supra*.

[68] See, e.g., Manny v. Estate of Anderson, 574 P.2d 36 (Ariz. 1977); Cobb v. Empire Fire and Marine Ins. Co., 488 So. 2d 349 (La. Ct. App. 1986); Oweiss v. Erie Ins. Exch., 509 A.2d 711 (Md.Ct.App. 1986).

[69] See Pacific Indem. Co. v. Linn, 766 F.2d 754 (3d Cir. 1985); Harborside Refrigerated Servs. v. IARW Ins. Co., 759 F.2d 829 (11th Cir. 1985); Sears, Roebuck & Co. v. Reliance Ins. Co., 654 F.2d 494 (7th Cir. 1981); Lee v. Aetna Cas. & Sur. Co., 178 F.2d 750 (2d Cir. 1949); Steyer v. Westvaco Corp., 450 F. Supp. 384 (D.Md. 1978); Waller v. Truck Ins. Exch., 1995 WL 516406 (Cal. 1995); Worcester Ins. Co. v. Dairyland Ins. Co., 555 A.2d 1050 (Me. 1989); Sturges Mfg. Co. v. Utica Mut. Ins. Co., 332 N.E.2d 319 (N.Y. 1975); Saylin v. California Ins. Guar. Ass'n, 224 Cal. Rptr. 493 (Cal. Ct. App. 1986).

[70] 178 F.2d 750 (2d Cir. 1949).

[71] 178 F.2d at 753.

of the alleged occurrence or if the nature of the alleged intentional tort compels a finding of intentional wrongdoing such as malicious prosecution."[72] It has also been held that when the insured is sued for negligence in connection with injuries inflicted on the plaintiff, and the insured is convicted of the criminal charge of battery in connection with the same incident on which the plaintiff's complaint is based, the conduct is outside the coverage of the insurance policy and the insurer need not provide a defense.[73]

Even if entitled to withdraw, the insurer cannot do so if the insured will be prejudiced. For example, if the attempted withdrawal is very close to trial and the court is unwilling to grant a continuance, the insurer should be obligated to continue with the defense. Otherwise, extraordinary hardship to the defendant could result due to its prior reliance on the assistance of the insurer.[74] The decisions and rationales offered by courts when addressing the question of withdrawal of counsel are diverse. For example, in *Raymond v. Monsanto Co.*,[75] the insurer was not allowed to withdraw from the defense even though the trial was scheduled to begin in six months. The court concluded that it would be difficult for new counsel to assume the defense and acquire the same competence and understanding of the issues as the existing counsel.

If the insurer prematurely withdraws, the insurer commits a breach of contract and is liable for the resulting damages. In the ordinary case, this means that the insurer would be liable at least for the attorneys' fees incurred by the insured to replace the counsel the insurer was obligated to provide. Moreover, if the premature withdrawal prevented the insured from having an adequate defense and an excess judgment results, the insurer may be held liable for the judgment.

[2] Terminating the Duty to Defend by Paying the Policy Limits

A particularly troublesome issue concerns the relationship between the duty to indemnify and the duty to defend.[76] Insurers and insureds differ sharply in their assessment of this relationship, and judicial support can be found for both points of view.

Insurers sometimes argue that the duty to defend only exists as long as the duty to indemnify remains unsatisfied. In other words, once the insurer fulfills its duty to indemnify by paying the policy limits, the duty to defend is discharged, even if litigation remains pending against the insured. Insureds take a different approach: proceeding from the premise that the duty to defend and the duty to indemnify are separate and independent, insureds argue that it is impossible to satisfy one duty

---

[72] Gray v. Zurich Ins. Co., 419 P.2d 168, 176 n.15 (Cal. 1966).

[73] See Shelter Mut. Ins. Co. v. Bailey, 513 N.E.2d 490 (Ill. App. Ct. 1987). But see Patrons Mut. Ins. Ass'n v. Harmon, 732 P.2d 741 (Kan. 1987) (conviction of voluntary manslaughter was not dispositive on question of insured's intent to kill spouse in coverage action).

[74] See Fireman's Fund Ins. Co. v. Chasson, 24 Cal. Rptr. 726 (Cal. Ct. App. 1962).

[75] 329 F. Supp. 247 (D.N.H. 1971).

[76] See generally Eric J. Van Vugt, *Termination of the Insurer's Duty to Defend by Exhaustion of Policy Limits*, 44 Ins. Counsel J. 254 (1977); Annot., *Liability Insurer's Duty To Defend Action Against An Insured After Insurer's Full Performance Of Its Payment Obligations Under Policy*, 27 A.L.R.3d 1057 (1969).

by performing the other. The widely recognized principle that the duty to defend is broader than the duty to indemnify [77] buttresses this conclusion: if the duty to defend is broader, it necessarily follows that the duty cannot be satisfied by simply paying the policy's proceeds to a claimant, to the insured, or to the court.

Because the duty to defend is created by contract, the language of the policy is extremely important to determining the effect of discharging the duty to indemnify on the duty to defend. In commercial liability insurance, where this issue has arisen most often, the relevant language of the CGL has undergone many changes through the years, changes which are important to understanding the scope of judicial pronouncements on the effect of paying the policy limits on the insurer's duty to defend.

Prior to 1966, liability insurance policies typically did not contain language which purported to limit the duty to defend once the policy limits had been paid. In addition, the clauses defining the insurer's duty to defend were usually in a different section of the policy than clauses defining the insurer's duty to indemnify. Thus, many courts construing language from the pre-1966 commercial liability forms held that the duty to defend was separate from and broader than the duty to indemnify, and that the duty to defend was not discharged by advance payment of the policy proceeds.[78] How far these precedents extended, however, was not easy to determine. Many of the cases involved a situation where the insurer attempted to pretermit its duty to defend by tendering the policy limits without making any effort whatever to investigate or protect the insured's interests. Some of the cases involved what fairly can be described as bad faith conduct by the insurer.[79] Because of the peculiar circumstances of many of the cases, it was not clear that the decisions could fairly be read as endorsing the broad proposition that the insurer's duty to defend persisted after the policy limits had been paid to fulfill the insurer's indemnity obligation.

With respect to the pre-1966 language, a separate line of cases developed where courts held that the insurer's duty to defend terminated when the insurer paid the policy limits.[80] The leading case in this line of authority is *Lumbermen's Mutual Casualty Co. v. McCarthy,*[81] a 1939 New Hampshire decision. In *McCarthy,* the

---

[77] See § 111[a], *supra.*

[78] See, e.g., American Cas. Co. v. Howard, 187 F.2d 322 (4th Cir. 1951); Liberty Mut. Ins. Co. v. Pacific Indem. Co., 557 F. Supp. 986 (W.D. Pa. 1983); Simmons v. Jeffords, 260 F. Supp. 641 (E.D. Pa. 1966); National Cas. Co. v. Insurance Co. of N. Am., 230 F. Supp. 617 (N.D. Ohio 1964); Travelers Indem. Co. v. East, 240 So. 2d 277 (Miss. 1970); St. Paul Fire & Marine Ins. Co. v. Thompson, 433 P.2d 795 (Mont. 1967); Maine Bonding & Cas. Co. v. Centennial Ins. Co., 667 P.2d 548, *aff'd,* 693 P.2d 1296 (Or. Ct. App. 1983); Palmer v. Pacific Indem. Co., 254 N.W.2d 52 (Mich. Ct. App. 1977).

[79] See Anchor Cas. Co. v. McCaleb, 178 F.2d 322 (5th Cir. 1949); National Cas. Co. v. Ins. Co. of N. Am., 230 F. Supp. 617 (N.D. Ohio 1964); Travelers Indem. Co. v. East, 240 So. 2d 277 (Miss. 1970).

[80] See, e.g., ACandS, Inc. v. Aetna Cas. and Sur. Co., 764 F.2d 968 (3d Cir. 1985); Allstate Ins. Co. v. Montgomery Trucking Co., 328 F. Supp. 415 (N.D. Ga. 1971); Lumbermen's Mut. Cas. Co. v. McCarthy, 8 A.2d 750 (N.H. 1939).

[81] 8 A.2d 750 (N.H. 1939).

insurer defended two actions against its insured arising from an automobile accident until one reached judgment and resulted in an award exceeding the policy limits. The insurer paid the judgment up to its limits, and then sought to withdraw from the defense of the second action. The court allowed the insurer to withdraw:

> [I]t seems to us that the primary obligation imposed upon the insurer was to pay the insured's legal liability for damages on account of the contingencies specified, and that the other provisions were dependent thereon and designed to implement that primary obligation. . . . [U]pon performance of its duties of payment its duty to defend ceases to exist and the further defense of any action pending thereafter must be conducted and may be controlled by the insured.[82]

The full import of *McCarthy'* s holding was (and remains) less than clear. The ambiguity was created by the court's statement that the insurer could not avoid its obligation to investigate, settle, and defend the lawsuit by simply tendering the proceeds to the insured nor could the insurer withdraw from the defense in a manner that prejudiced the insured's rights.[83] Thus, courts following *McCarthy* typically refused to permit an insurer to avoid its duty to defend by paying the policy limits before effecting a settlement.[84] Only a few courts permitted the insurer to withdraw from the defense by merely tendering the policy limits to the insured or to a court.[85]

In 1966, the standard CGL form was revised to provide that the insurer "shall not be obligated to pay any claim or judgment or to defend any suit after the applicable limit of the Company's liability has been exhausted by the payment of judgment or settlements."[86] If the drafters of the 1966 revision intended to enable insurers to discharge their duty to defend by paying the policy limits into court, the literal language of the revision did not accomplish this result. The revision's literal language provides that only if the insurer pays the proceeds pursuant to *judgment* or *settlement* is the insurer discharged from its duties. The effect of this language is to discharge the duty to defend once *prior claims* have exhausted the policy limits. If a recovery in earlier litigation exhausts the policy limits, the insurer, under this language, has no duty to defend subsequent litigation. Also, under the literal language, if the insurer is simultaneously defending multiple suits against the insured, and one of the suits goes to judgment or settlement causing the policy limits to be exhausted, the insurer could withdraw from the defense of the other pending litigation.

Most courts have applied the language of the 1966 revision literally, and have allowed the insurer to refuse to defend only if the full amount of proceeds are paid

---

[82] 8 A.2d at 752.

[83] *Id.*

[84] See, e.g., Simmons v. Jeffords, 260 F. Supp. 641 (E.D. Pa. 1966); Sutton Mut. Ins. Co. v. Rolph, 244 A.2d 186 (N.H. 1968); Liberty Mut. Ins. Co. v. Mead Corp., 131 S.E.2d 534 (Ga. 1963).

[85] See, e.g., Denham v. La Salle-Madison Hotel Co., 168 F.2d 576 (7th Cir. 1948), *cert. denied,* 335 U.S. 871 (1948); Commercial Union Ins. Co. v. Adams, 231 F. Supp. 860 (S.D. Ind. 1964); National Union Ins. Co. v. Phoenix Assur. Co., 301 A.2d 222 (D.C. 1973).

[86] *Policy Kit (1985)* at 267 (CK 809-2).

pursuant to a judgment or settlement.[87] Under these decisions, mere tender of the policy limits prior to judgment or settlement does not terminate the duty to defend. Because the claim must be settled or a final judgment must be reached, the insurer is, in effect, required to defend the claim (except in the multiple claim situation, noted above). These decisions, like the older cases, view the duty to defend and the duty to pay proceeds as being independent from one another, at least when the duty to indemnify has not been discharged in prior litigation during the policy's term.[88]

Nevertheless, there is some authority for the proposition that the insurer can terminate its defense of the insured once policy limits are exhausted, even if the insurer is in the midst of providing a defense.[89] The rationale for such a result is that the insurer and insured have the freedom to contract with each other. If the insurer gives clear notice to the insured that the insurer may be relieved of its duty to defend simply by tendering the policy limits for settlement, insureds should understand that they are purchasing only an indemnity policy. Insureds would then be able to purchase additional or separate coverage providing for an unlimited defense.[90]

Although involving slightly different language in the policy form, *Anderson v. United States Fidelity & Guaranty Co.,*[91] a 1986 Georgia Court of Appeals decision, illustrates the approach that treats the duty to defend as being separate from the duty to indemnify notwithstanding an insurer's effort to tie the duty to defend to the duty to indemnity. The insured was the defendant in several suits filed by parties allegedly injured in a multiple-vehicle collision involving the insured. Three claims were settled by the insurer, and the insurer sought to be discharged from its duty to defend the insured by paying the balance of the coverage into the registry of the trial court. The policy stated: "In addition to our limit of liability, we will pay all defense costs we incur. Our duty to settle or defend ends when our limit of liability for this coverage has been exhausted." The court said that this language contained "no intimation . . . that [the insurer's] duty to defend may be satisfied merely by paying into court the applicable policy limits. To read the policy otherwise would render

---

[87] See, e.g., Utah Power & Light Co. v. Federal Ins. Co., 711 F. Supp. 1544 (D.Utah 1989); Stanley v. Cobb, 624 F. Supp. 536 (E.D. Tenn. 1986); Landando v. Bluth, 292 F. Supp. 975 (N.D. Ill. 1968); Samply v. Integrity Ins. Co., 476 So. 2d 79 (Ala. 1985); Conway v. Country Cas. Ins. Co., 442 N.E.2d 245 (Ill. 1982); Ursprung v. Safeco Ins. Co., 497 S.W.2d 726 (Ky. 1973); National Union Ins. Co. v. Phoenix Assur. Co., 301 A.2d 222 (D.C. 1973); Travelers Indem. Co. v. East, 240 So. 2d 277 (Miss. 1970); Thaler v. American Ins. Co., 614 N.E.2d 1021 (Mass.App.Ct. 1993).

[88] See, e.g., Samply v. Integrity Ins. Co., 476 So. 2d 79 (Ala. 1985); Kocse v. Liberty Mut. Ins. Co., 387 A.2d 1259 (N.J. Super. Ct. App. Div. 1978); Oda v. Highway Ins. Co., 194 N.E.2d 489 (Ill. App. Ct. 1963).

[89] See Commercial Union Ins. Co. v. Pittsburgh Corning Corp., 789 F.2d 214 (3d Cir. 1986); Gross v. Lloyds of London Ins. Co., 358 N.W.2d 266 (Wis. 1984); Batdorf v. Transamerica Title Ins. Co., 702 P.2d 1211 (Wash. Ct. App. 1985) (policy language making it absolutely clear insurer has the right to withdraw from the defense).

[90] See Gross v. Lloyds of London Ins. Co., 358 N.W.2d 266 (Wis. 1984); Novak v. American Family Mut. Ins. Co., 515 N.W.2d 504 (Wis. Ct. App. 1994).

[91] 339 S.E.2d 660 (Ga. Ct. App. 1986).

a near nullity a most significant protection afforded by the policy—that of defense." The court rejected the insurer's argument that the term "exhaust" included paying into the court the policy limits; instead, the court interpreted that term "to mean the payment either of a settlement or of a judgment wholly depleting the policy amount."[92]

By the early 1980s, the CGL had been revised in relevant part to read as follows: "Our right and duty to defend end when we have used up the applicable limit of insurance in the payment of judgments or settlements under Coverages A [bodily injury and property damage liability] or B [personal and advertising injury or liability] or medical expenses under Coverage C."[93] This language remains that which is in common use in commercial liability forms today.[94] This language is more straightforward than the 1966 revision, but it does not appear to make any material change in the substance of the provision as revised in 1966.

Under any standard that allows an insurer to withdraw at some point from providing a defense upon paying the policy proceeds to someone, if the insured would suffer prejudice due to adverse timing of the withdrawal in a pending case, it would seem that the insurer's withdrawal should not be permitted.[95] This rule is consistent with the principle applicable to gratuitous undertakings generally; even when someone undertakes to perform an act or service voluntarily and without obligation, the act or service must be performed non-negligently; that is, the volunteer will be held liable for the consequences of negligently performing the undertaking, even though the performance was purely voluntary and gratuitous.

Currently, the question of whether the duty to defend can be discharged by fulfilling the duty to indemnify is a confused one in insurance law. Defense costs remain a large portion of insurance company payments, and insurers will no doubt continue in the future to search for ways to reduce their potential liability, including termination of the duty to defend once a stated amount of defense costs has been incurred. In the meantime, courts will grapple with the scope of the insurers' duties, and the issue will remain controversial.[96]

[f] Disclaiming Coverage

In the event the insurer concludes that a duty to defend is not owed because the claim against the insured is outside the coverage, the insurer needs to disclaim coverage. This is ordinarily accomplished by written notice to the insured. The notice must have sufficient specificity to enable the insured to understand the grounds for the disclaimer,[97] and the disclaimer must be sent as soon as reasonably

---

[92] 339 S.E.2d at 661.

[93] *Policy Kit* (1987) at 294 (ISO Form CG 00 01 11 85).

[94] See *Policy Kit* at 309 (ISO Form CG 00 01 10 93).

[95] See, e.g., Gibson v. Preferred Risk Mut. Ins. Co., 456 S.E.2d 248 (Ga. Ct. App. 1995).

[96] For a pro-insurer assessment of the cases, see Zulkey & Pollard, *The Duty to Defend After Exhaustion of Policy Limits,* 27 For the Defense 21 (June, 1985).

[97] See, e.g., Sauer v. Home Indem. Co., 841 P.2d 176 (Alaska 1992) (insurer that does not explain basis for denying coverage should be precluded from later arguing that coverage under the policy did not exist); General Acc. Ins. Group v. Cirucci, 387 N.E.2d 223 (N.Y. 1979); Allstate Ins. Co. v. Keillor, 511 N.W.2d 702 (Mich. Ct. App. 1993), *aff'd,* 537 N.W.2d 589 (Mich. 1995).

possible after the insurer learns of the basis for it.[98] In some states, the obligation to provide prompt notice of the disclaimer of coverage is imposed by statute.[99] A late disclaimer can have the same effect as failing to issue a disclaimer: the insurer waives policy defenses.[100] Although it has been held that an insurer cannot omit from a disclaimer grounds for denying coverage that it knows (or should know in the reasonable discharge of its investigation), and then later offer these other grounds as additional bases for denying coverage,[101] most courts have held that coverage defenses are not waived by a failure to assert them in a disclaimer.[102] The logic of the cases adhering to the majority rule is that finding a waiver in circumstances where a coverage defense is omitted from a denial letter would be inconsistent with established waiver principles, which require a knowing and voluntary relinquishment of a right.

[g]   Standard of Conduct: The Duty of Care

An insurer undertaking to defend the insured must perform with "due care."[103] The attorney must meet the standard of care and the ethical responsibilities that apply to every attorney in every representation. If the attorney fails to make a reasonable effort to investigate the plaintiff's claim, to discover key evidence, to answer the complaint, to take a timely appeal, or to present a key defense, and the insured is damaged as a result of the insurer's or the attorney's negligence, the insured has an action for the damages resulting from the breach, just as a client has an action against its attorney for malpractice any time the attorney breaches the professional standard of care. Damages flowing from the breach of the duty of care may include the entire amount of any excess judgment against the insured.

Although there is no doubt that the attorney who represents the insured owes duties to the insured, whether the attorney also owes duties to the insurer is a more difficult question, one that has engendered considerable controversy. These matters are taken up in a later section.[104]

---

[98] See, e.g., Whitney v. Continental Ins. Co., 595 F.Supp. 939 (D.Mass. 1984); Sauer v. Home Indem. Co., 841 P.2d 176 (Alaska 1992); Allstate Ins. Co. v. Macaluso, 628 N.Y.S.2d 701 (N.Y. App. Div. 1995).

[99] See, e.g., Cal. Ins. Code § 554; Fla. Stat. Ann. § 627.426.

[100] See, e.g., Griggs v. Bertram, 443 A.2d 163 (N.J. 1982); Public Serv. Mut. Ins. Co. v. Overlook Terrace Corp., 619 N.Y.S.2d 18 (N.Y. App. Div. 1994); Reis v. Aetna Cas. & Sur. Co., 387 N.E.2d 700 (Ill. App. Ct. 1978).

[101] See Armstrong v. Hanover Ins. Co., 289 A.2d 669 (Vt. 1971).

[102] See, e.g., Waller v. Truck Ins. Exch., 1995 WL 516406 (Cal. 1995); Schiff Assoc. v. Flack, 417 N.E.2d 84 (N.Y. 1980); Alta Cal. Regional Ctr. v. Fremont Indem. Co., 30 Cal. Rptr. 841 (Cal. Ct. App. 1994); Terre Haute First Nat'l Bank v. Pacific Employers Ins. Co., 634 N.E.2d 1336 (Ind. Ct. App. 1993); Tobi Engineering v. Nationwide Mut. Ins. Co., 574 N.E.2d 160 (Ill. App. Ct. 1991). McLaughlin v. Connecticut Gen. Life Ins. Co., 565 F.Supp. 434 (N.D. Cal. 1983), provided support for a waiver rule, but this case was disapproved by the *Waller* decision. For discussion of the California cases and an argument against an automatic waiver rule, see Cheryl Byer Berg & Philip A. O'Connell Jr., *Waiver and Estoppel Without Waste*, 17 Ins. Litig. Rptr. 13 (1995).

[103] See, e.g., Maine Bonding & Cas. Co. v. Centennial Ins. Co., 693 P.2d 1796 (Or. 1985); Spencer v. Aetna Life & Cas. Co., 611 P.2d 149 (Kan. 1980).

[104] See § 114, *infra*.

[h]   Remedies for Breach of the Duty to Defend

Because the duty to defend is a contract duty, an insured can recover compensatory damages for the insurer's breach of its duty to defend. These damages include (1) attorney's fees and costs expended in defending the underlying action, (2) consequential damages naturally arising from the insurer's failure to defend, and (3) sometimes the attorney's fees incurred in the action against the insurer to enforce the insurer's defense obligation.

[1]   Attorney's Fees and Other Costs Incurred in Defending the Underlying Action

If the insurer unjustifiably refuses to defend the victim's suit against the insured, the insured will probably hire counsel to provide a defense. Hiring defense counsel is tantamount to "covering"; the insurer promises to provide a service, but when the insurer fails to do so, the insured is free to go to the market and purchase a substitute service. Having already paid for the insurer's service with the insurance premium, the insured is entitled to have the costs of cover fully reimbursed by the insurer. The substitute purchase must be a reasonable one; thus, the insured is entitled to recover the "reasonable" attorney's fees incurred in defending the lawsuit. The insured can also recover other costs incidental to the defense, such as witness fees, court costs, investigation costs, and costs of appeals.[105]

In addition to recovering attorney's fees and related costs, the insured is entitled to recover consequential damages. Under contract law principles, these damages must be foreseeable at the time of contracting and must naturally arise from the breach.[106] For example, the insurer knows that defense costs can be substantial and that many insureds lack the personal resources to pay these fees. Thus, it is foreseeable that if the insurer breaches the duty to defend, the insured may have to borrow money in order to pay for counsel. The interest on the loan and other charges incidental to the borrowing of the money should be recoverable from the insurer as a consequential damage. Any damages that can be linked in this manner to the insurer's breach of the duty to defend are recoverable from the insurer.

[2]   Excess Judgment

Subject to some important qualifications discussed below, the insurer is not liable for an excess judgment against the insured after the insurer has breached the duty to defend. Presumably the attorney hired by the insured will provide the same quality of representation as the attorney that the insurer would have provided. If this is so, the amount of the judgment in the underlying action against the insured should be the same, regardless of who provides the insured's defense. Therefore, it cannot be said that the insurer's refusal to defend the insured is the cause of any excess judgment; that is, any excess judgment that results does not "naturally arise" from the breach. The same is true if the insured settles the case for an amount exceeding

---

[105] See, e.g., Tibbs v. Great Am. Ins. co., 755 F.2d 1370 (9th Cir. 1985); United States Fid. & Guar. Co. v. Copfer, 400 N.E.2d 298 (N.Y. 1979); Alabama Farm Bur. Mut. Cas. Ins. Co. v. Moore, 349 So. 2d 1113 (Ala. 1977); Amato v. Mercury Cas. Co., 23 Cal. Rptr.2d 73 (Cal. Ct. App. 1993).

[106] See Hadley v. Baxendale, 9 Ex. 341, 156 Eng.Rep. 145 (1854).

the policy limits after the insurer breaches the duty to defend. The settlement is presumably a fair reflection of the value of the plaintiff's claim, and in theory this settlement value should not increase if the insurer breaches the duty to defend.

This rule must be qualified in several respects. First, if the attorney appointed by the insurer to defend the insured withdraws from the defense just a few days before trial, and the insured is forced to hire counsel at the last minute to provide the defense, it is a likely consequence of this kind of breach of the duty to defend that a larger judgment would be entered against the insured than if the attorney familiar with the case had tried it.[107] If an excess judgment results in these circumstances, it can be argued that the judgment resulted from the insurer's breach of the duty to defend and should be recoverable as consequential damages by the insured. In the language of the rule from the law of contract remedies, it was foreseeable to both parties at the time of contracting that if the insurer breached its duty in this way such damages could result.

Similarly, if the insurer leads the insured to believe that it will provide a defense, the insured reasonably relies on the insurer's manifested intent by not securing counsel, and the insurer fails to defend the suit which directly results in the entry of a default judgment exceeding the policy limits, the entire judgment should be the responsibility of the insurer, absent some other fact that makes it unfair for the insurer to bear this burden. Whether the insured has a responsibility to avoid damages resulting from breach of the insurer's duty to defend by hiring counsel is discussed below.[108] Apart from whatever reliance the insurer induced, if the insurer knew at the time of contracting that the insured lacked the financial means to retain an attorney and that a default judgment would probably be entered in excess of the policy limits if the insurer did not perform its duty, a court should award damages for breach of the duty to defend equal to the entire judgment.

Some courts, however, depart from the approach outlined above (i.e., that the insurer is not liable for any excess judgment for breaching the duty to defend in the absence of special circumstances). These courts simply allow the insured to recover the full amount of any settlement and excess judgment attributable to claims within coverage.[109] The logic underlying this alternative view is that insurers will not be deterred from deliberately breaching the duty to defend unless damages greater than the cost of defense are available for the aggrieved insured. At least one court, however, has reasoned that an excess judgment is the natural and proximate result of a breach of the duty to defend.[110] Another theory of awarding the entire judgment is estoppel, and this is discussed in one of the following subsections.[111] Those cases involving settlements exceeding the policy limits are also discussed below.[112]

---

[107] See Beckwith Machinery Co. v. Travelers Indem. Co., 638 F. Supp. 1179 (W.D. Pa. 1986).

[108] See § 111[h], *infra*.

[109] See, e.g., Newhouse v. Citizens Sec. Mut. Ins. Co., 501 N.W.2d 1 (Wis. 1993); Sauer v. Home Indem. Co., 841 P.2d 176 (Alaska 1992); Stockdale v. Jamison, 330 N.W.2d 389 (Mich. 1982); Reiss v. Aetna Cas. & Sur. Co., 387 N.E.2d 700 (Ill. App. Ct. 1978).

[110] See Newhouse v. Citizens Sec. Mut. Ins. Co., 501 N.W.2d 1 (Wis. 1993).

[111] See § 111[g][6], *infra*.

[112] See § 111[g][5], *infra*.

[3]   Attorney's Fees in the Insured's Action Against the Insurer or the Insurer's Declaratory Judgment Action

It is also foreseeable that if the insurer breaches the duty to defend, the insured will not only have to hire an attorney to defend the underlying suit but will also have to bring a suit against the insurer to recoup these damages. The insured may argue that the attorney's fees expended in bringing the suit against the insurer should be recoverable as damages for the insurer's breach of the duty to defend. This argument is troublesome because American courts require each party in litigation to bear its own attorney's fees, absent extraordinary circumstances. In contract law generally, the aggrieved party suing on the contract must bear his or her own attorney's fees; it is understood that requiring the plaintiff to bear his or her own attorney's fees means, as a practical matter, that the plaintiff will not net the full measure of the defendant's promised performance and that the plaintiff's expectations under the contract will inevitably be disappointed to some extent.

Under the traditional view, the insured suing the insurer for breach of its duties under the contract stands on no different footing than the typical contract plaintiff. The insured must bear his or her own expenses in prosecuting the action.[113] Yet because the insurance industry is vested with the responsibility to protect the public interest, and because the insured-insurer relationship in the liability setting has fiduciary overtones, the argument for allowing the recovery of attorney's fees in the insured's action against the insurer to enforce the duty to defend is stronger than in many other situations. Some courts credit these concerns and allow the insured to recover attorney's fees incurred in prosecuting the action against the insurer if the insurer is found to have wrongfully refused to defend the insured.[114] Some courts insist, as a prerequisite to the insured's recovery of attorneys' fees, that the insurer must have acted in bad faith in refusing to provide coverage.[115] This gloss is consistent with the exception to the American rule of attorneys' fees: normally each side must bear its own fees, but an exception to this rule exists when the plaintiff's suit is vexatious or brought in bad faith. It is consistent with the American rule to permit the insured to recover attorneys' fees in circumstances where the insurer's bad faith conduct causes the insured to incur these expenses.

The same issue exists when the insurer institutes a declaratory judgment action to determine whether it has a duty to defend, and courts are split on this question. Some courts, giving weight to the rule that each party is to bear its own costs of litigation and attorneys' fees, hold that the insured must fund whatever defense the

---

[113] See, e.g., Steptore v. Masco Constr. Co., 643 So. 2d 1213 (La. 1994); Johnson v. General Mut. Ins. Co., 246 N.E.2d 713 (N.Y. 1969); Reis v. Aetna Cas. & Sur. Co., 387 N.E.2d 700 (Ill. App. Ct. 1978).

[114] See, e.g., Missouri Terrazzo Co. v. Iowa Nat'l Mut. Ins. Co., 740 F.2d 647 (8th Cir. 1984); Montgomery Ward & Co. v. Pacific Indem. Co., 557 F.2d 51 (3d Cir. 1977); Cunniff v. Westfield, Inc., 829 F. Supp. 55 (E.D. N.Y. 1993); Beckwith Machinery Co. v. Travelers Indem. Co., 638 F. Supp. 1179 (W.D. Pa. 1986); Government Employees Ins. Co. v. Taylor, 310 A.2d 49 (Md. 1973); Lanoue v. Fireman's Fund Am. Ins. Co., 278 N.W.2d 49 (Minn. 1979).

[115] See, e.g., Farmers Ins. Exch. v. Call, 712 P.2d 231 (Utah 1985); Union Mut. Fire Ins. Co. v. Inhabitants of Topsham, 441 A.2d 1012 (Me. 1982).

insured wishes to make to the insurer's declaratory judgment action.[116] Other jurisdictions hold that the insured can recover attorneys' fees if the insurer is found to have a duty to defend.[117]

[4]   Tort Damages

The criticism of confining insureds who are aggrieved by the insurer's breach of the duty to defend to those damages allowed by contract law is that insurers will not be deterred from breaching the duty to defend. If the only damages for which the insurer can anticipate being held liable are the costs the insured incurs in hiring the counsel that the insurer did not provide, which is a cost the insurer would have incurred had it performed its duty, the insurer has few reasons not to breach the promise it made the insured. It is true that if the insured hires his or her own counsel, the insurer will lose control over the defense. Also, the attorney hired by the insured may be less effective and might be more expensive. While these consequences will drive up the insurers' costs somewhat, it is likely that some insureds will choose not to pursue the insurer for breach of its duty in a subsequent action, due to the costs of prosecuting the action, the time required for such a lawsuit, and the anxiety. If enough insureds walk away from their claims against the insurer, the insurer in the long run might profit from not performing its duty to defend, assuming the insurer does not lose its clientele as a result of the poor service it provides its insureds.[118]

One court, apparently dissatisfied with the compensatory and deterrent capabilities of traditional contract remedies in the insurance setting, has taken a broad view of the duty to defend and has held that breach of the duty sounds in tort.[119] Other courts have reached substantially the same result by labeling the breach as bad faith conduct for which extra-contractual damages are available.[120] The supposed advantage of this approach is that it broadens the damages that the insured can recover for breach of the duty to defend. Tort law allows a broader range of consequential damages to be recovered; in particular, damages for emotional distress or mental anguish are available in tort, but not in contract. Also, egregious torts may entitle the aggrieved party to punitive damages, which are rarely awarded in contract. The availability of tort law remedies, it is assumed, will deter insurers from breaching the duty to defend. Also, the extra recovery in tort provides a fund out of which the insured's attorney can be reimbursed, which means that the insured is more likely to have his or her contract expectations fulfilled.

---

[116] See, e.g., Atlantic Mut. Ins. Co. v. Judd Co., 380 N.W.2d 122 (Minn. 1986); Tuell v. State Farm Fire & Cas. Co., 477 N.E.2d 70 (Ill. App. Ct. 1985).

[117] See, e.g., Paxton & Vierling Steel Co. v. Great Am. Ins. Co., 497 F. Supp. 573 (D.Neb. 1980); Aetna Cas. & Sur. Co. v. Pitrolo, 342 S.E.2d 156 (W.Va. 1986); Farmers Ins. Co. v. Rees, 638 P.2d 580 (Wash. 1982); Hegler v. Gulf Ins. Co., 243 S.E.2d 443 (S.C. 1978); SCSC Corp. v. Allied Mut. Ins. Co., 533 N.W.2d 603, 616-17 (Minn. 1995).

[118] See generally Annot., *Insurer's Tort Liability for Consequential or Punitive Damages for Wrongful Failure or Refusal to Defend Insured*, 20 A.L.R.4th 23 (1983).

[119] See Smith v. American Family Mut. Ins. Co., 294 N.W.2d 751 (N.D. 1980).

[120] See, e.g., Tibbs v. Great Am. Ins. Co., 755 F.2d 1370 (9th Cir. 1985); State Farm Fire and Cas. Co. v. Prize, 684 P.2d 524 (N.M.Ct.App. 1984).

On the other hand, critics of the tort approach observe that the damages available in tort are so broad that the mere availability of the remedy causes some insurers entitled to refuse to defend to forgo that right to avoid the possibility of an extracontractual judgment. To the extent the availability of tort remedies "over-deters" a large number of insurers, the costs incurred by insurers rise, which translates into higher premiums for all insureds.[121]

[5]   Liability for the Insured's Settlement of the Underlying Action

Some courts hold that when the insurer unjustifiably refuses to provide the insured with a defense, the insured proceeds to defend the lawsuit, and the insured then terminates the lawsuit by entering into a reasonable settlement agreement with the plaintiff, the insurer is responsible for the amount of the settlement (up to the policy limits[122]), even though the insurer has no control over it.[123] The logic of this remedy is that the insurer had the right to control the defense and the settlement negotiations; when the insurer chose not to defend, it did so at its own risk. Part of this risk was the possibility that the insured might settle the lawsuit.

From the insurer's perspective, this result can be quite worrisome. Consider the situation where the plaintiff alleges claims both within and outside coverage. If the insurer fulfills its duty to defend and a final judgment is nevertheless entered against the insured, the insurer will not be precluded or estopped from declining to pay that portion of the judgment outside the coverage.[124] Similarly, if the suit is settled, it follows that the insured should pay for that portion of the settlement attributable to the claim outside the coverage.[125] Extending from this analysis, it can be argued that if the insurer wrongfully fails to defend and then the insured settles the suit for a large sum, the insurer, because it is not obligated to indemnify the claim outside coverage, should be allowed to contest coverage, show that the only valid claim against the insured was the one outside coverage, and thereby establish that it had no duty to indemnify.[126] The insurer would still be liable for damages directly attributable to breach of the duty to defend.

---

[121] For a more detailed criticism of the intrusion of tort remedies into contract cases, see John E. Benedict, Comment, *Tort Remedies for Breach of Contract: The Expansion of Tortious Breach of the Implied Covenant of Good Faith and Fair Dealing into the Commercial Realm,* 86 Colum. L. Rev. 368 (1986).

[122] Normally, the remedy for breach of the duty to settle preceded by a breach of the duty to defend cannot exceed the policy limits. See § 112[g], *infra.*

[123] See, e.g., Bunge Corp. v. London & Overseas Ins. Co., 394 F.2d 496 (2d Cir. 1968); Employers Mut. Liab. Ins. Co. v. Hendrix, 199 F.2d 53 (4th Cir. 1952); Gladstone v. D.W. Ritter Co., 508 N.Y.S.2d 880 (N.Y. Sup. Ct. 1986).

[124] See Garden Sanctuary, Inc. v. Insurance Co. of N. Am., 292 So. 2d 75 (Fla. Dist. Ct. App. 1974).

[125] The insured has little leverage over the insurer if the facts clearly show that the claim is outside coverage. All the insurer need do to induce the insured to contribute its fair portion of the settlement is to offer the following alternative, which is within the insurer's rights: the insurer will continue the defense until obtaining a declaratory judgment that no coverage exists or until facts are adduced in discovery clearly demonstrating that no coverage exists for the events in question, at which point the insurer will withdraw completely from the defense.

[126] See Servidone Constr. Corp. v. Security Ins. Co., 477 N.E.2d 441 (N.Y. 1985); Oweiss v. Erie Ins. Exch., 509 A.2d 711 (Md.Ct.App. 1986).

Despite the foregoing, the fact remains that if insurers are allowed to later contest coverage when they fail without good cause to provide a defense, insurers will have few reasons to defend the insured in lawsuits where the existence of the duty to defend is arguable. The insured who has to retain counsel and pay the costs of defense is likely to suffer financial hardship; to terminate the accumulation of defense costs, the insured may choose to settle at a sum exceeding the "fair" value of the plaintiff's claim. This may actually benefit the insurer in an important respect: the insurer who breaches the duty to defend will definitely be liable for attorney's fees, and the early settlement reduces the amount of those expenses.[127]

The debate is a close one, but it makes sense to conclude that the insurer that refuses to defend does so at its own risk, meaning that the insurer bears the risk that the insured might settle the lawsuit, even for a sum exceeding the policy limits.[128] This will undoubtedly cause insurers to provide some indemnification where there is no duty to do so, but this is a reasonable price to pay in exchange for the insured saving the insurer costs of defense by entering into settlements. Moreover, the insurer that desires to avoid this risk need only fulfill its duty to defend.

The rule that the insurer is responsible for the costs of settlement after the insurer has breached the duty to defend is subject to the following qualification: If the insurer can establish that the settlement paid by the insured was unreasonably excessive in the circumstances or that the settlement was accompanied by collusion between the insurer and insured (which is per se unreasonable), the insurer should not be required to pay the settlement amount, despite its breach of the duty to defend. In that instance, the insurer should still be required to answer for the direct consequences of its breach of the duty to defend, specifically, the reasonable defense costs. Of course, if it later turns out that no coverage existed in the circumstances and that the insurer did not act improperly in refusing to provide a defense, the insurer would not be liable to the insured for either the settlement amount or the defense costs.

-----

[127] Courts concurring with this viewpoint have sometimes offered ill-conceived reasons for the same answer. Some courts have argued that the insurer's breach excuses the insured's duty to comply with the policy; it is true that the insurer's breach excuses the insured's noncompliance with claims processing requirements, but it does not follow that the insured receives coverage — which is in effect imposing an additional duty on the insurer. Other courts have claimed that the insured cannot easily prove that the insured's damages are causally related to the insurer's breach of the duty to defend. In most cases, no causal relationship exists anyway; if this is a concern, it is a simple matter to require the insurer to show the absence of a causal relationship. See Alan D. Windt, 1 *Insurance Claims and Disputes*, § 4.37, at 266-70 (3d ed. 1995).

[128] If an insurer is liable for the entire amount of a default judgment, including the excess portion, in the event of a breach of the duty to defend, see § 112[f], *infra*, it is consistent to make the insurer liable for the entire amount of a judgment entered by settlement after the insurer breaches the duty to defend. On the other hand, if the insurer's liability in the case of a default judgment is limited to the policy limits, see *id.*, it is consistent to limit the insurer's liability for a judgment entered by settlement to the policy limits.

[6] Breach of the Duty to Defend as an Estoppel to the Insurer's Denial of Coverage

If the insurer breaches the duty to defend, some courts have held that the insurer is estopped to deny coverage.[129] In other words, the insurer that refuses to defend the insured does so at its own risk. If it is subsequently determined that the insurer should have provided a defense, the insurer is then estopped to take the position that it owes no obligation to the insured to indemnify the loss.

In many cases, this rule has no practical effect. The insurer's duty is to defend claims asserted within coverage. If the insurer refuses to defend and it is later established that the insurer should have defended, and if the basis for that conclusion is that the plaintiff's claims were within coverage, it follows that the insurer has a duty to indemnify. The only effect of the estoppel rule in that situation is to take away an argument that the insurer will surely lose — that the loss was not covered by the policy's terms. In other situations, however, estopping the insurer to deny coverage has the potential to expand the insurer's obligation beyond that which the insurer assumed under the policy.

Suppose, for example, that the plaintiff's complaint is ambiguous on a point determinative of coverage, but the insurer refuses to defend, ignoring the rule that a duty is owed in this setting. The insured arranges his or her own defense, and during discovery it is determined that facts on the point determinative of coverage are adverse to the insured. The case goes to trial, and a judgment is entered against the insured. The insured then brings an action against the insurer, claiming that the insurer breached the duty to defend; the insurer asserts that no duty was owed because the plaintiff's claim was outside the coverage, citing the evidence adduced during discovery determinative on that point. Under the rule that breaching the duty to defend estops the insurer to deny coverage, the insurer cannot assert that no duty was owed. If the court determines that the insurer should have defended the ambiguous claim until the evidence determinative of coverage was discovered, the insurer will be obligated to pay the insured's judgment even though no coverage existed.[130]

The same scenario can unfold in a case where the plaintiff asserts claims against the insured both within and outside coverage. The insurer that wrongfully refuses to defend will be estopped to deny coverage. If the jury gives a verdict for the insured on the claim within coverage and a verdict for the plaintiff on the claim outside coverage, the insurer estopped to deny coverage because of breaching the duty to defend will be required to indemnify the insured for liability outside the coverage.[131] Had the insurer provided a defense and the same judgment been entered,

---

[129] See, e.g., Gray v. Zurich Ins. Co., 419 P.2d 168 (Cal. 1966); Novak v. Insurance Administration Unlimited, Inc., 414 N.E.2d 258 (Ill. App. Ct. 1980). See also Riverside Ins. Co. v. Kolonich, 329 N.W.2d 528 (Mich. Ct. App. 1982).

[130] This was the argument made by the insured, and rejected by the court, in Burd v. Sussex Mut. Ins. Co., 267 A.2d 7 (N.J. 1970), discussed in § 110[c][5], *supra*.

[131] But see Harold S. Schwartz & Associates, Inc. v. Continental Cas. Co., 705 S.W.2d 494 (Mo. Ct. App. 1985) (suggesting that where the complaint alleges claims both inside and outside coverage and the insurer breaches its duty to defend, the insurer's liability should be limited to defense costs for claims covered by the policy, assuming it is possible to segregate the costs for covered and noncovered claims).

the insured would have paid for all damages attributable to the claim outside coverage,[132] just as the insured would have paid any judgment in excess of the policy limits when the insurer fully performs its duties.

Because the estoppel rule has the potential to create coverage where none exists, some courts decline to follow it.[133] Under the estoppel rule, an insurer that breaches the duty to defend is obligated to pay the attorney's fees and other expenses incidental to defending the suit plus the amount of the judgment against the insured within the policy limits, whether or not the ultimate judgment against the insured is based on a claim within the policy's coverage. Courts refusing to follow this rule reason that when the insurer unjustifiably refuses to defend, it is not likely, absent extraordinary circumstances, that the insurer's breach contributes to the size of the judgment. Since the insurer's breach does not cause the judgment to be entered against the insured, the amount of that judgment does not naturally arise from the breach, and the insurer is therefore not responsible for it.

At first glance, it might seem that estopping the insurer to deny coverage when it unjustifiably refuses to defend puts the insurer in an impossible dilemma. If the insurer refuses to defend, it runs the risk of being held liable for damages for breach of the duty to defend and may be estopped to deny coverage. Yet it is well settled that if the insurer undertakes to defend the action, it will be estopped to deny coverage by virtue of performing its defense duty.[134] The answer is that the insurer is not on the horns of a dilemma because these are not the insurer's only alternatives. There are mechanisms that enable an insurer to perform its duty to defend without giving up the right to contest coverage later. The insurer can undertake the defense pursuant to a reservation of rights, which means the insurer undertakes the defense but reserves the right to contest coverage at a later time. Moreover, the insurer can file a separate declaratory judgment action in which it asks the court to determine that no coverage exists under the policy.[135]

Indeed, it is the availability of these procedural alternatives that provides the best reason for estopping the insurer to deny coverage when it breaches the duty to defend.[136] If the insurer's obligation to defend is unclear, the insurer is free in a declaratory judgment action to litigate the question of coverage. In the meantime, the insured receives the defense for which it bargained. One possible problem with this solution is that if a judgment is returned against the insured before the coverage question is determined, the insurer who pays proceeds and then is found to owe no obligations will have provided a defense where none was owed, and will probably

---

[132] Garden Sanctuary, Inc. v. Insurance Co. of N. Am., 292 So. 2d 75 (Fla. Dist. Ct. App. 1974).

[133] See Burd v. Sussex Mut. Ins. Co., 267 A.2d 7 (N.J. 1970); Saline Cty. Agr. Ass'n v. Great Am. Ins. Co., 494 N.E.2d 1278 (Ill. App. Ct. 1986); NAWCAS Benevolent Auxiliary v. Levin, 162 S.E.2d 738 (Ga. Ct. App. 1968).

[134] See § 114, infra; Safeco Ins. Co. v. Ellinghouse, 725 P.2d 217 (Mont. 1986); Transamerica Ins. Group v. Chubb and Son, Inc., 554 P.2d 1080 (Wash. Ct. App. 1976).

[135] See § 114[c][4], infra.

[136] See, e.g., Equity General Ins. Co. v. C&A Realty Co., 715 P.2d 768 (Ariz. Ct. App. 1985); Nandorf, Inc. v. CNA Ins. Cos., 479 N.E.2d 988 (Ill. App. Ct. 1985); but see Fireman's Fund Ins. Co. v. Rairigh, 475 A.2d 509 (Md.Ct.App. 1984).

be unable to recoup the costs of the defense from the insured. The insurer, however, is in a better position to bear this risk than the typical insured is able to assume a defense obligation that an insurer is not performing. Thus, although the alternative procedures are not mandatory, it is fair to hold that the insurer who refuses to defend under a reservation of rights or without seeking a declaratory judgment does so at its own risk. If it is later determined that the insurer should have defended, the insurer should not be allowed to deny an obligation to pay proceeds.

[7]   Other Consequences of Breaching the Duty to Defend

If the insurer breaches the duty to defend, the breach will have consequences beyond simply giving the insured a claim for damages.[137] Upon the insurer's breach, the insured has the right to assume control of the defense. The insurer cannot complain that the defense was not conducted properly or in a manner different from that which the insurer would have used. The insured can enter into a settlement with the plaintiff and hold the insurer responsible at least for the settlement within the policy limits and perhaps for more, as discussed above, despite the fact that the policy gives the insurer the right to control the settlement. The insured is also relieved of its obligations to the insurer in claims processing, including requirements for filing a proof of loss, giving notice of the loss, or forwarding papers of the lawsuit. The insured is also excused from the obligation to cooperate with the insurer. These results all follow from a basic principle of contract law: when one party commits a material breach of its duties under a contract, the aggrieved party's obligations to the breaching party are discharged.

[i]   The Insured's Duty to Mitigate Damages When the Insurer Breaches the Duty to Defend

In contract law, technically speaking there is no duty to mitigate damages. The victim of a breach is never liable to the breaching party for failing to mitigate damages. Rather, the contract rule is that a party who fails to take reasonable steps to mitigate damages loses the right to recover damages that these reasonable steps would have avoided. Thus, if the buyer of goods agrees to meet the seller's truck at 1:00 p.m. to take delivery of goods, the buyer does not appear at 1:00 p.m., the seller appears with a truck and leaves it running while awaiting the buyer's appearance, and the truck's engine overheats, the seller cannot recover the damage caused by the overheating of the truck's engine. These damages could have been avoided had the seller acted reasonably by shutting off the truck's engine when it began to overheat. In some situations, the victim of a breach is expected to take affirmative steps to find a substitute for the promisor's nonperformance. If these affirmative but reasonable steps are not taken, the aggrieved party cannot recover for the damages that could have been avoided.[138]

The insurer's breach of the duty to defend brings these issues to the fore. On the one hand, it is a foreseeable consequence of the insurer's refusal to provide any

---

[137] See State Farm Fire & Cas. Co. v. Prize, 684 P.2d 524 (N.M. 1984).

[138] See E. Allan Farnsworth, *Contracts* 858–63 (1982). This hypothetical is based on Virtue v. Bird, 3 Keble 766, 84 Eng.Rep. 1000 (1677) (plaintiff's horse overheated and died while waiting for defendant to show up and receive goods).

defense that a default judgment will be entered, perhaps in excess of the policy limits. Yet the insured could avoid this consequence of the insured's breach by hiring his or her own counsel. Indeed, the insurer might contend that the default judgment arises not from the insurer's breach but from the insured's failure to take reasonable steps in the aftermath of the insurer's breach. Accordingly, if the insurer refuses to defend, and the insured takes no action on the insured's own behalf and allows a default judgment to be entered, the insurer is likely to assert when the insured or the insured's assignee sues for breach of the duty to defend that the insured should have taken affirmative steps to hire counsel to provide a defense, thereby avoiding the damages associated with the entry of the default judgment.

Thus, on the one hand, it would seem that the insured who is wrongfully refused a defense by the insurer should hire counsel to provide a defense. Standing idly by and allowing a default judgment to be entered is not a reasonable response to the insurer's breach.[139] If this view is accepted, the insured cannot recover in damages from the insurer for breach of the duty to defend those damages that could have been avoided by hiring counsel. If hiring counsel would have prevented part or all of the judgment from being entered, the insured is personally liable for this amount. Most courts, however, have rejected this viewpoint and have held that when the insurer refuses to defend, the insurer assumes the risk that the insured will hire no attorney at all and allow a default judgment to be entered. The majority rule is that the insurer is responsible for the default judgment up to the policy limits.[140] The logic apparently underlying this rule is that it is foreseeable at the time of contracting that the insured will be unable to provide his or her own defense if the insurer fails to do so. The logic underlying allowing recovery for the default judgment up to the policy limits but not in excess thereof is not readily apparent. The entire amount of the judgment is the consequence of the insurer's breach, not just the portion within the policy limits. Although contract law is ill-disposed to award consequential damages (i.e., damages exceeding the breaching party's promised performance, otherwise described as the "loss of bargain") which could have been avoided by arranging a substitute transaction (i.e., "cover"),[141] the entire amount of the default judgment is a consequential damage,[142] not just the portion exceeding the policy limits. Courts are no doubt uncomfortable making an insurer liable for an amount determined by whatever damage figure the plaintiff happens to plead, but as a matter of contract

---

[139] See La Rotunda v. Royal Globe Ins. Co., 408 N.E.2d 928 (Ill. App. Ct. 1980); Cornwell v. Safeco Ins. Co., 346 N.Y.S.2d 59 (N.Y. App. Div. 1973).

[140] See, e.g., Western Cas. & Sur. Co. v. Herman, 405 F.2d 121 (8th Cir. 1968); Greer v. Northwestern Nat'l Ins. Co., 743 P.2d 1244 (Wash. 1987) (en banc); Medical Protective Co. v. Davis, 581 S.W.2d 25 (Ky. Ct. App. 1979). Compare Maynard v. Sauseda, 329 N.W.2d 774 (Mich. Ct. App. 1982) (insurer is liable for entire default judgment including excess), *vacated,* 338 N.W.2d 189 (Mich. 1983), *after remand,* 343 N.W.2d 590 (Mich. Ct. App. 1983) (insurer is liable for entire default judgment, limited by the extent to which the insured has assets not exempt from legal process).

[141] See Unif. Comm. Code § 2-715(a).

[142] The "loss of bargain' when the insurer does not defend is the cost of the defense. For another view of this general issue, see Allan D. Windt, 1 *Insurance Claims and Disputes: Representation of Insurance Companies and Insureds,* § 4.35, at 258-63 (3d ed. 1995).

law, there is no in-between answer. Either the insured should arrange for a defense when the insurer declines to do so, in which case a default judgment is avoided in its entirety, or the insured has no such obligation, in which case the foreseeable consequence of the breach is the entry of a default judgment in the amount of plaintiff's claim.

[j]   "Defense Within Limits" Policies

In recent years, available data suggest that an increasing percentage of total payments made by insurers are chargeable to the costs of defense; concomitantly, a smaller percentage of total insurer outlays go directly to reimburse loss.[143] In response to this trend, the Insurance Services Office, an insurance industry-supported organization which prepares policy forms, proposed in the mid-1980s that the CGL policy be revised to include the cost of a legal defense against third-party claimants within the policy's aggregate dollar limits.[144] The proposal would not have applied to the personal liability coverage of homeowners and private individuals, but successful implementation in the commercial lines would probably have encouraged extension of the proposed program to consumer lines as well.[145]

The first version of the proposal would have included all defense costs within the general policy limits; in other words, every dollar spent on an insured's defense would be deducted from the insured's policy coverage, thereby leaving less coverage available in the event a judgment was rendered against the insured. A later version would have entitled the insured to use fifty percent of a policy's aggregate limits before deducting defense expenses from the coverage. Thus, if the insured's policy limits were $100,000, the insured would be entitled to the first $50,000 in defense costs without any deduction from the policy limits; all defense expenses thereafter would be deducted dollar-for-dollar from the $100,000 policy limits. Under this proposal, once $150,000 in defense costs were accumulated, the insured would have no coverage left for any resulting judgment. Under either version, the purpose of the proposal was to contain defense costs by discharging the insurer's duty to indemnify once defense costs surpass a designated amount. The ISO eventually withdrew the proposal when the market for liability insurance eased and a number of regulators expressed doubts about the approach.[146]

---

[143] Various ISO studies through the years have pegged the percentage of expenditures for defense costs at between 36 and 41 percent of all payments by insurers; in other words, the amount paid by insurers for claims is more, but not much more, that what insurers pay for defense costs.

[144] For a discussion of the ISO's proposals and the potential problems they raised, see Daniel Dorsch, *Insurance Defense Costs and the Legal Defense Cost Containment Program: Is the Free Ride Over?* 53 Ins. Counsel J. 580 (1986); James K. Killelea, *Format of Liability Insurance Policies,* 296 PLI/Lit 229 (1985) (reprinting ISO, "Legal Defense Cost Containment" (pamphlet)).

[145] Defense within limits policies have been utilized for directors and officers and professional liability risks for some time, but these policies are typically indemnity policies where the insurer has no duty to defend the insured. The policy reimburses defense costs as part of the total limits of liability. Shaun M. Baldwin, *Legal and Ethical Considerations for "Defense Within Limits" Policies,* 61 Def. Couns. J. 89 (1994). Such a policy is to be distinguished from a defense within limits policy where the insurer also has the duty to defend.

[146] See Baldwin, *supra* note 145, at 89-90.

If a proposal like the ISO's were ever implemented, it would raise a number of intriguing, difficult questions about the duty to defend: Will excess insurance be triggered as soon as defense costs are expended? Will the insured have a greater right to control the defense if every activity of defense counsel directly reduces the coverage available for indemnity? Is the burden on the insurer to settle the case greater, since continuing to try the case could increase what the insured pays out of the insured's own personal assets? Will the insured acquire control over the designation of defense counsel? If the insurer is found to have breached one of these duties in bad faith, will the insurer become liable for the entire judgment, which means the policy will actually tend to increase insurers' obligations? These questions lack easy, ready answers. It is not inconceivable, however, that a future proposal linking together the duties to defend and indemnify might be made, and if such a proposal were adopted, these questions would soon be presented to insurance defense counsel.[147]

§ 112   Settlement Obligations

Liability insurance policies routinely create a contractual duty to defend, but do not by their terms create a duty to settle. Instead, the typical language reserves to the insurer a privilege to settle, or not to settle, as the insurer in the exercise of its discretion sees fit. For example, the standard homeowner's form states: "We may investigate and settle any claim or suit that we decide is appropriate."[1] The CGL form states: "We may at our discretion investigate any 'occurrence' and settle any claim or 'suit' that may result."[2] This privilege may even extend to allowing the insurer to settle claims without the insured's consent, even when the claim is fully within the deductible.[3] Notwithstanding the expansive language establishing the insurer's privilege to settle, the insurer's discretion is limited in substantial ways by court-made rules. Although the insurer is entitled to exercise its own judgment, it owes an obligation to the insured to exercise good faith and to maintain a due regard for the insured's interests. Because these obligations may require an insurer in some situations to respond to a settlement offer affirmatively, it is often said that the insurer owes the insured a "duty to settle."

At the same time the usual policy language gives considerable discretion to the insurer, the insured is subject to some constraints. For example, the insured is usually prohibited from settling any claims, voluntarily assuming any liability, or interfering in any legal proceedings or settlement negotiations without the insurer's consent.

---

[147] There has been some litigation over the few defense within limits policies that have been in force. For discussion of these cases, see Baldwin, *supra* note 145.

[1] *Policy Kit* at 29 (ISO Form HO 00 03 04 91).

[2] *Policy Kit* at 309 (ISO Form CG 00 01 19 93).

[3] See, e.g., Shuster v. South Broward Hosp. Dist. Physicians' Professional Liab. Ins. Trust, 591 So. 2d 174 (Fla. 1992); Western Polymer Technology, Inc. v. Reliance Ins. Co., 38 Cal. Rptr.2d 78 (Cal. Ct. App. 1995); Casualty Ins. Co. v. Town & Country Pre-School Nursery, Inc., 498 N.E.2d 1177 (Ill. App. Ct. 1986); Orion Ins. Co. v. General Elec. Co., 493 N.Y.S.2d 397 (N.Y.Sup.Ct 1985).

One purpose of these restrictions is to prevent the insured from entering into collusive settlement agreements with third parties in, perhaps, deliberate disregard of the insurer's interests. Another purpose is to give the insurer the ability to control all aspects of the defense (including settlement) so that the insurer, which should be expected to have more expertise in processing litigation than insureds, can manage the lawsuit in the most cost-effective manner.

Normally, the question is whether the insurer has respected the insured's rights when considering a settlement offer from the plaintiff, and this subject is the primary focus of this section. However, sometimes the issue is whether the insured has violated its obligation to the insurer by settling a case without the insurer's consent. This is considered in the next subsection.

[a]   Insured's Settlement Without Insurer's Consent

As noted in the discussion of the duty to defend, an insured need not obtain the insurer's consent to settle the plaintiff's claim in circumstances where the insurer has breached the duty to defend.[4] Absent those circumstances, the insured's voluntary settlement with the plaintiff excuses the insurer's obligations under the policy, including the obligation to pay the amount of the settlement. The logic is that by settling without the insurer's consent, the insured has breached the duty of cooperation owed the insurer.[5]

It has been held, however, that the insured's voluntary settlement does not discharge the insurer unless the insurer could demonstrate that it had been substantially prejudiced by the settlement.[6]

Courts have also struggled with the situation where the insured enters into a voluntary settlement with the plaintiff and assigns the insured's rights under the policy to the plaintiff in exchange for the plaintiff's covenant not to execute against the insured's personal assets. Some courts, apparently concerned about the collusive aspects of such arrangements, have held that the assignee cannot recover against the insurer because the insured was not obligated to pay damages to the plaintiff pursuant to a judgment.[7] If the settlement is reasonable, other courts decline to bar the assignee's claim, at least where the insurer has refused to provide a defense.[8]

---

[4] See § 111[h][5], *supra*.

[5] See, e.g., Augat, Inc. v. Liberty Mut. Ins. Co., 571 N.E.2d 357 (Mass. 1991); United Services Auto. Ass'n v. Morris, 741 P.2d 246 (Ariz. 1987) (en banc).

[6] See, e.g., Hernandez v. Gulf Group Lloyds, 875 S.W.2d 691 (Tex. 1994); Roberts Oil Co. v. Transamerica Ins. Co., 833 P.2d 222 (N.M. 1992). See also Bantz v. Bongard, 864 P.2d 618 (Idaho 1993) (involving uninsured motorist coverage).

[7] See, e.g., Hitt v. Cox, 737 F.2d 421 (4th Cir. 1984); Stubblefield v. St. Paul Fire & Marine Ins. Co., 517 P.2d 262 (Or. 1973).

[8] See, e.g., Foremost Cty. Mut. Ins. Co. v. Home Indem. Co., 897 F.2d 754 (5th Cir. 1990); Jones v. Southern Marine & Aviation Underwriters, Inc., 888 F.2d 358 (5th Cir. 1989); State Farm Mut. Auto. Ins. Co. v. Paynter, 593 P.2d 948 (Ariz. Ct. App. 1979).

[b]   The Standard for Determining the Nature of the Insurer's Duty to Settle

The difficulty of articulating the scope of the duty to settle stems from two factors. First, the typical liability insurance policy gives the insurer a privilege, not a duty to settle. Thus, to the extent the insurer does in fact have a duty to settle, exactly where it comes from is not self-evident. Second, once a duty of some sort is acknowledged, it is apparent that the duty is not absolute, meaning no one seriously suggests that an insurer must accept any and all settlement offers. Whether to accept a settlement offer is largely a question of judgment, but it is nevertheless necessary to articulate a boundary that distinguishes between the proper and improper exercise of judgment.

[1]   The Reasonable-Offer Test

Many courts have described the insurer's obligation by reference to the concept of "good faith and fair dealing."[9] Under this test, if the insurer acts in good faith and deals fairly when responding to a settlement offer, the insurer has complied with its duty to settle. Bad faith conduct is more than making a mistake in judgment or failing to predict correctly the outcome of the litigation between plaintiff and insured. Rather, bad faith connotes some sort of intentional, reckless, or otherwise improper disregard of the legitimate interests and expectations of the insured in the circumstances.[10] One court explained it this way: "it is not bad faith for an insurer to refuse to settle an injured's claim within the policy limits when the question of policy coverage is fairly debatable and when the grounds for the refusal, if determined in the insurer's favor, would wholly defeat the indemnity responsibility of the insurer to its insured."[11] The underlying premise of this standard is that insurers sometimes make mistakes in judgment, but reasonable insurers do not act without appropriate regard for the interests of the insureds on whose behalf they have undertaken to act in defense of a third party's claim.

Another test often found in the reported cases, although not as frequently as the "good faith" test, is the "due care" standard. Under the due care test, if the insurer is not negligent in deciding to accept a settlement offer within the policy limits, the insurer has fulfilled its duty.[12] This test, which draws heavily from tort law, asks whether the insurer's conduct conforms with what is expected of a reasonable insurer in the same circumstances. This test implies that a mere "accident" in the outcome of the plaintiff's suit against the insured does not establish the insurer's breach of its obligation to the insured. Hindsight alone is not enough to hold the insurer liable.

---

[9] See, e.g., Mowry v. Badger State Mut. Cas. Co., 385 N.W.2d 171 (Wis. 1986); Short v. Dairyland Ins. Co., 334 N.W.2d 384 (Minn. 1983); Kooyman v. Farm Bur. Mut. Ins. Co., 315 N.W.2d 30 (Iowa 1982); Fireman's Fund Ins. Co. v. Security Ins. Co., 367 A.2d 864 (N.J. 1976). See generally Kent D. Syverud, *The Duty to Settle,* 76 Va. L. Rev. 1113 (1990); Thomas B. Alleman, *The Reasonable Thing to Do: The Insurer's Duty to Settle Claims Against Its Insured,* 50 UMKC L. Rev. 251 (1982).

[10] See § 25G, *supra.*

[11] Mowry v. Badger State Mut. Cas. Co., 385 N.W.2d 171, 181 (Wis. 1986).

[12] See, e.g., Robertson v. Hartford Accident & Indem. Co., 333 F. Supp. 739 (D.Or. 1970); Aetna Cas. & Sur. Co. v. Kornbluth, 471 P.2d 609 (Colo.Ct.App. 1970).

Whether any practical distinction exists between the good faith and due care tests is not readily apparent. With the distinctions being so obscure, in most jurisdictions the standards have coalesced. For example, in *Crisci v. Security Insurance Co.*,[13] the California Supreme Court stated that whether an insurer has acted in bad faith is determined by considering "whether a prudent insurer without policy limits would have accepted the settlement offer."[14]

Various other formulations exist for the amount of deference the insurer should give the insured's interests when responding to a settlement offer. These tests are best understood as efforts by courts to give more content to the elusive concepts of "good faith," "due care," and "reasonableness." Some courts have stated that the insurer must give "equal consideration" or "fair" consideration to the insured's interests.[15] This test gives little guidance to insurers; at what point the insurer has given ample consideration to the insured's interests such that it can be said that the insurer is acting "fairly" or with "equal" regard for the insured is not capable of easy measurement. Other courts have stated that the insurer must give paramount weight to the insured's interests, even at the expense of its own.[16] When the insurer's deference to the insured's interests has moved to a level that can be described as "paramount weight" is also difficult to ascertain.

If the "good faith" and "due care" tests coalesce, and if one agrees that the differences among these tests and the other formulations are subtle, it is fair to describe all of these assorted tests under the label of the "reasonable-offer" test.[17] Under this test, the issue is simply whether an insurer under a policy with no limits would accept the offer; in fact, a number of courts have articulated the insurer's duty to settle in virtually identical language.[18] This formulation is clearer by virtue of its simplicity: the insurer's duty is to its insured, and the insurer should protect the insured's interests, even if it means sacrificing its own. Moreover, as discussed more fully in a later section,[19] dual representation is not easy when the insurer's and the insured's interests conflict, as is often the case when a settlement offer is received from the plaintiff. In some situations, it is simply not possible to protect fully the

---

[13] 426 P.2d 173 (Cal. 1967).

[14] 426 P.2d at 176. See also Bollinger v. Nuss, 449 P.2d 502 (Kan. 1969).

[15] See, e.g., National Farmers Union Property & Cas. Co. v. O'Daniel, 329 F.2d 60 (9th Cir. 1964); Hartford Acc. & Indem. Co. v. Foster, 528 So. 2d 255 (Miss. 1988); Bollinger v. Nuss, 449 P.2d 502 (Kan. 1969). Compare Allstate Ins. Co. v. Campbell, 639 A.2d 652 (Md. 1994) (court declines to extend tort of bad faith failure to settle to situation where insurer initially declines settlement offer but thereafter settles and secures full release of insured).

[16] See, e.g., Lieberman v. Employers Ins., 419 A.2d 417 (N.J. 1980); Tyger River Pine Co. v. Maryland Cas. Co., 170 S.E. 346 (S.C. 1933).

[17] See Kenneth S. Abraham, *Distributing Risk: Insurance, Legal Theory, and Public Policy* 191- 92 (1986) (describing "reasonable-offer test" as "[a]n insurer must accept any offer within the limits of coverage that a reasonable party responsible for the entire amount of any subsequent judgment would accept.")

[18] See, e.g., Voccio v. Reliance Ins. Co., 703 F.2d 1 (1st Cir. 1983); Herges v. Western Cas. & Surety Co., 408 F.2d 1157 (8th Cir. 1969); Davis v. Cincinnati Ins. Co., 288 S.E.2d 233 (Ga. Ct. App. 1982); Davy v. Public Nat'l Ins. Co., 5 Cal. Rptr. 488 (Cal. Ct. App. 1960).

[19] See § 114, *infra*.

interests of both insurer and insured. The reasonable-offer test is designed to ensure that the insurer does not sacrifice the insured's interest in order to pursue its own.

The reasonable-offer test is premised on the assumption that some settlement offers should be accepted by an insurer and others should be rejected. Thus, for the insurer to fulfill the duty to settle, the insurer must give "appropriate" deference to the insured's interests. This test contemplates that the insurer can permissibly reject some settlement offers, even if it turns out in hindsight that the insured would have been better served by accepting the offer. Thus, a judgment against the insured in excess of the settlement offer, or in excess of the policy limits, does not automatically mean that the insurer has breached the duty to settle.

[2]   The Strict Liability Alternative

The reasonable-offer test necessarily requires a court to make subjective judgments about whether an insurer's response to a settlement offer was appropriate in the circumstances. In other words, the test is necessarily interested in determining whether the insurer was "at fault" in responding to a settlement offer. Although the test allows any factor relevant to the reasonableness of the insurer's conduct to be considered, the test's flexibility is a recipe for inconsistent and unpredictable results. Some commentators have therefore suggested a "no-fault" approach to measuring the insurer's conduct. Under this proposed test, an insurer is strictly liable for the amount of any judgment against the insured whenever the insurer has rejected a settlement offer within policy limits.[20]

At first glance, the strict liability test appears to be very pro-plaintiff and anti-insurer, even implying that the insurer has a duty to accept all settlement offers within the policy limits. But that is not what the strict liability rule contemplates. Unreasonable settlement offers within the policy limits should be rejected; if a jury returns a verdict below the amount of the offer, the insurer's reasonableness in refusing to settle is vindicated, and the insurer is better off as a result of having rejected the offer (unless, of course, litigation costs exceed the differential between the jury verdict and the plaintiff's offer). If the verdict turns out to equal the amount of the settlement offer, it is apparent that the plaintiff's offer was reasonable and should have been accepted, but the insurer will pay the same amount in proceeds when it indemnifies the insured for the judgment. If a verdict exceeds the settlement offer, the strict liability rule infers that the offer should have been accepted, and the insurer will be liable for the excess judgment, including that portion which exceeds the policy limits.

Thus, the difference between the strict liability and the reasonable-offer tests is that under the strict liability test (and not under the reasonable-offer test), insurers will be liable for excess judgments in circumstances where it was reasonable for them to reject the settlement offer. Where a plaintiff's settlement offer is close to the line between a reasonable offer and an unreasonable offer, the reasonable-offer test creates hurdles for the insured who bears the burden of establishing that the

---

[20] For a court's discussion of the test even though the court did not adopt it, see Crisci v. Security Ins. Co. of New Haven, Conn., 426 P.2d 173 (Cal. 1967). For a detailed analysis of the strict liability test, see Abraham, *supra* note 17, at 193-95.

nearly-reasonable offer was in fact unreasonable. Under the reasonable-offer tests insurers, knowing that insureds will have difficulty carrying their burden of establishing the reasonableness of the offer, should be more inclined to reject settlement offers that are close to the line. If, however, under a strict liability test, insureds no longer have the burden of establishing the unreasonableness of the insurer's conduct, insurers may be more inclined to accept settlement offers that are close to the line between reasonable and unreasonable offers.[21]

Plaintiffs, realizing the pro-settlement pressure that a strict liability rule places on insurers, should be more inclined to make policy-limits settlement offers, since the rejection of any such offer makes the insurer automatically liable for the total amount of any excess judgment. Stated otherwise, whenever a plaintiff makes a settlement offer at or within the policy limits during the litigation, the liability limits of the policy become irrelevant.[22] This, in turn, may result in insurers settling more cases where coverage is marginally more dubious or the insured's liability marginally less clear. In theory, one should expect a strict liability standard, to the extent it is more pro-plaintiff, to encourage more litigation against insured defendants, although this effect seems too indirect to be substantial.

The precise extent of any of these effects is unknown, but the uncertainty of these effects, when combined with the relative comfort courts have with standards like "reasonableness" and "good faith," has discouraged any court from adopting a strict liability standard to date.[23] No court has come closer to adopting a strict liability rationale than the West Virginia Supreme Court in *Shamblin v. Nationwide Mutual Insurance Co.,*[24] a 1990 decision. There, the court adopted what it called "a hybrid negligence-strict liability standard,"[25] which the court explained as follows:

> [W]herever there is a failure on the part of an insurer to settle within policy limits where there exists the opportunity to so settle and where such settlement within policy limits would release the insured from any and all personal liability, that the insurer has prima facie failed to act in its insured's best interest and that such failure to so settle prima facie constitutes bad faith towards its insured.
>
> In other words, it will be the insurer's burden to prove by clear and convincing evidence that it attempted in good faith to negotiate a settlement, that any failure to enter into a settlement where the opportunity to do so existed was based on a reasonable and substantial grounds, and that it accorded the interests and rights of the insured at least as great a respect as

---

[21] See Abraham, *supra* note 17, at 194-95.

[22] See Kent D. Syverud, The Duty to Settle, 76 Va. L. Rev. 1113, 1168-70 (1990).

[23] For an example of a court that was tempted to adopt the strict liability approach but ultimately declined to do so, see Rova Farms Resort, Inc. v. Investors Ins. Co. of Am., 323 A.2d 495 (N.J. 1974). Although California decisions, particularly Johansen v. California State Auto. Ass'n Inter-Ins. Bur., 538 P.2d 744 (Cal. 1975), are sometimes described as "strict liability" decisions (see, e.g., Mowry v. Badger State Mut. Cas. Co., 385 N.W.2d 171 (Wis. 1986)), the California decisions, read closely, follow the reasonable-offer approach.

[24] 396 S.E.2d 766 (W.Va. 1990).

[25] 396 S.E.2d at 776.

its own. Whether an insurer demonstrates that it comported with this very strong obligation of good faith to its insured must necessarily turn on the facts of each case, as the factual scenarios are as varied and endless as the imagination.[26]

This approach automatically shifts the burden of proof to the insurer whenever an insurer declines to settle within policy limits and a judgment is rendered against the insured. Yet it is far from clear that any of these tests would generate results that significantly vary from the outcomes under the reasonable offer test.[27]

[c] Source of the Insurer's Obligation: Tort or Contract?

The insurer's obligation to accept a reasonable settlement offer ultimately devolves from the fact that the insurer's interests in responding to a settlement offer may not be the same as the insured's interests. If the plaintiff seeks damages beyond the policy limits but is willing to settle for a sum close to or at the policy limits, the insured is very interested in attempting to arrange a settlement on those terms. Such a settlement protects the insured from the risk of an excess judgment. Yet the insurer considering settling at or near the policy limits would be no worse off, except for the costs of litigation, if the case were tried and an excess judgment entered; moreover, trying the case and investing the costs of litigation at least gives the insurer a chance of obtaining a zero- or low-dollar judgment. Imposing on the insurer a duty to use good faith or due care in settling the lawsuit counterbalances, at least in theory, the insurer's incentive in some situations to ignore the insured's interests when considering settlement offers.

Because the duty to settle is implied from the relationship of the parties and is not explicitly set forth in the policy of insurance, the source of the duty is unclear. On the one hand, it is argued that the duty cannot be a contract duty because it does not appear in the contract. Instead, the duty must be imposed by law, and this suggests that the duty sounds in tort. It is sometimes said that contract duties are imposed by agreement and tort duties are imposed by law.[28] This formulation is an overgeneralization because some tort duties arise out of contractual relationships, but the rubric explains why some courts have been inclined to the view that the duty to settle is a tort duty.

---

[26] 396 F.2d at 766.

[27] See Alan O. Sykes, *"Bad Faith" Refusal to Settle by Liability Insurers: Some Implications for the Judgment-Proof Problem*, 23 J. Legal Stud. 77 (1994).

[28] See, e.g., Findley v. Time Ins. Co., 573 S.W.2d 908 (Ark. 1978) ("[A]n insurance company, in addition to its liability on the contract, may also be liable to its insured in tort for breach of an implied duty to deal fairly and in good faith with the insured in the settlement of a claim under the policy."); Grand Sheet Metal Prods. Co. v. Protection Mut. Ins. Co., 375 A.2d 428 (Conn.Super.Ct. 1977) ("the duty violated arises not from the terms of the insurance contract but is a duty imposed by law, the violation of which is a tort"); Mauldin v. Sheffer, 150 S.E.2d 150 (Ga. Ct. App. 1966) ("[I]n order to maintain an action ex delicto because of a breach of duty growing out of a contractual relation the breach must be shown to have been a breach of a duty imposed by law and not merely the breach of a duty imposed by the contract itself.').

Another explanation of the conclusion that the duty to settle sounds in tort rather than contract springs from the nature of the obligation owed the insured by the insurer. When the insurer undertakes to defend the insured, a fiduciary relationship is created. This devolves in part from the attorney-client relationship that the contract creates, and in part from the observation that the insurance industry is vested with protecting the public interest. Breaches of fiduciary duties can be remedied in tort;[29] thus, it follows that the duty to settle, since it is based on a fiduciary relationship, must sound in tort.

The implications concluding that the duty to settle sources in tort are basically twofold. First, the range of damages that is available in tort exceeds that which is available in contract. Tort law is not subject to the limitations on consequential damages found in contract law. Moreover, for egregious violations of duty, tort law approves the award of punitive damages, whereas contract law typically will not award punitive damages in the absence of the existence of an independent tort. Although nonpecuniary damages have been awarded relatively infrequently for breach of the duty to settle,[30] the possibility that such damages might be awarded ought to deter some insurer misconduct. Second, the statute of limitations is often shorter for tort actions.[31]

Although most courts have agreed with the analysis that the duty to settle sounds in tort, this choice is hardly inevitable. The duty to defend is plainly contractual in origin, and one way to defend a lawsuit is to settle it. Settlement negotiations are part and parcel of the defense of a lawsuit, and it thus seems that the duty to settle is merely a subpart of the contractually-based duty to defend. As such, the duty to settle sounds in contract, not in tort.[32]

In response to this analysis, some argue that the references to "due care" and "good faith" in determining whether the duty to settle is breached demonstrates that the duty to settle sounds in tort. If the duty to settle is not breached unless the insurer negligently refuses the settlement offer, the duty, it is argued, must be tort-based,

---

[29] See, e.g., Moore v. Regents of Univ. of Cal., 793 P.2d 479 (Cal. 1990); Destefano v. Grabrian, 763 P.2d 275 (Colo. 1988)(Quinn, C.J. concurring); Broadway Nat'l Bank v. Barton-Russell Corp., 585 N.Y.S.2d 933 (N.Y. Sup. Ct. 1992); Restatement (Second) of Torts, § 874 cmt. b (1979) ("A fiduciary who commits a breach of his duty as a fiduciary is guilty of tortious conduct to the person for whom he should act."); 2 Dan B. Dobbs, Law of Remedies: Damages-Equity-Restitution, § 10.4, at 668 (2d ed. 1993) ("[A] breach of fiduciary relationship . . . can amount to a tort.")

[30] See Kenneth S. Abraham, Distributing Risk: Insurance, Legal Theory and Public Policy 192 (1986) ("In fewer than ten of the hundreds of reported cases on settlement over the last fifteen years have [nonpecuniary] damages been awarded, and in those cases the egregious conduct of the insurer actually deserved the label bad faith.") The most prominent duty-to-settle case in which an award of nonpecuniary damages was upheld is Crisci v. The Security Ins. Co. of New Haven, Conn., 426 P.2d 173 (Cal. 1967). See Annot., Emotional or Mental Distress as Element of Damages for Liability Insurer's Wrongful Refusal to Settle, 57 A.L.R.4th 801 (1987).

[31] 3 Am. Jur. Trials § 21 (1965).

[32] See Equity General Ins. Co. v. C&A Realty Co., 715 P.2d 768 (Ariz. 1985) (failing to consider settlement offers is a breach of the duty to defend).

since negligence is a creature of tort. However, the use of the tort law's terminology to decide whether the insurer has performed its obligation does not prove the source of the duty. Instead, contract law simply borrowed the language of tort for determining when the contract duty is breached. Contract law is no-fault law, in that contract law cares only if promises are performed and does not concern itself, for the most part, with the reasons for the nonperformance. Nothing prohibits defining the contours of contract duties by reference to the language of tort, and that is the situation with the duty to settle.

Regardless, there are several reasons for the relative attractiveness of treating the duty to settle as being grounded in tort. First, the extra damages recoverable in tort can help compensate the insured's attorney, and thus help give the insured a full remedy for the insurer's breach of the duty to settle, unimpaired by the transaction costs of securing the remedy. Second, without the availability of tort remedies, plaintiffs' attorneys will be reluctant to take suits on behalf of insureds, and it is unlikely that the insureds would find representations of a quality routinely available to insurers. Third, unless the insurer is liable for extracontractual damages, the insurer has little incentive to perform its contract obligations. If the most that contract will award is the cost of performing the contract obligations, insurers will refuse to perform at all in some of the cases, knowing that some insureds will not take the time or trouble to pursue the contract remedies.

Whether the advantages attributed to the tort remedies exist or are worth pursuing is not uniformly accepted. As for the lack of deterrence of the contract remedy, nothing inherent in the contract remedy limits damages to the value of the insurer's promised performance. Contract law has always allowed consequential damages that naturally arise from the breach and that are foreseeable. Excess judgments from declining to settle are well within this zone of recovery. The extracontractual recovery may help reimburse the insured for the cost of legal representation, but it does so at the cost of overdeterring the insurer, which will be more likely to settle frivolous claims to avoid the chance of an excess judgment, which will be followed by an increase in premiums for all insureds.

[d] Insurer Conduct Constituting Breach of the Duty to Settle

In most jurisdictions, the insurer cannot be liable for breaching the duty to settle unless a settlement offer is made by the plaintiff.[33] Without a settlement offer, it is not possible for the insurer to have breached its duty. Yet under the logic that settlement is but one way of defending a suit, one could argue that the insurer has an affirmative duty to investigate the possibility of settlement in circumstances where such a resolution of the litigation seems appropriate. Some courts have suggested the existence of this broader obligation.[34]

No precise formula exists for what kinds of insurer conduct constitute breach of the duty to settle. Courts have listed numerous factors relevant to the determination

---

[33] See, e.g., Seward v. State Farm Mut. Auto. Ins. Co., 392 F.2d 723 (5th Cir. 1968); Davis v. Nationwide Mut. Fire Ins. Co., 370 So. 2d 1162 (Fla. Dist. Ct. App. 1979).

[34] See, e.g., Coleman v. Holecek, 542 F.2d 532 (10th Cir. 1976); Maine Bonding v. Centennial Ins. Co., 693 P.2d 1296 (Or. 1985); Rova Farms Resort, Inc. v. Investors Ins. Co., 323 A.2d 495 (N.J. 1974).

of whether a breach has occurred, such as the extent to which the insurer attempted to induce the insured to contribute to the settlement, failed to follow the advice of its attorney, failed to take account of the strength of the plaintiff's case, or induced the insured to reject the offer by misrepresenting the facts. Also, whether the insurer informed the insured of all settlement offers and the amount of financial exposure for the insured from the refusal to settle are relevant factors.[35]

[e] The Mechanics of Handling Settlement Offers

Under the typical liability insurance policy, the insurer is free to exercise its own judgment regarding whether to enter into a settlement. Unless the policy explicitly prohibits settlement, the insurer can settle a lawsuit despite the insured's request that it not do so, even if the claim is fully within the deductible portion of the policy.[36] Moreover, the policy typically prohibits the insured from entering into settlement agreements on his or her own: the policy's language will prohibit the insured from voluntarily assuming any liability, settling any claims, incurring any expenses, or interfering in any legal proceedings or negotiations for settlement without the insurer's consent. The insurer, however, is not at liberty to release claims that the insured may have against the plaintiff.[37]

In professional liability insurance, however, insureds typically have more leeway in the settlement process. Such policies sometimes contain a settlement clause permitting the insured to refuse to consent to a settlement. This is for the benefit of the professional — such as the lawyer or physician — who prefers that a claim of professional competence not appear to be conceded via the lawsuit's settlement without a full trial. In exchange for this ability to interfere with the insurer's settlement plans, the policy also expressly limits the insurer's liability if an excess judgment is subsequently entered.

Although the insurer typically has discretion to settle the claim, even when the settlement involves the expenditure of the insured's own funds, a settlement offer exceeding the policy limits must be handled with great delicacy, lest the attorney fail to serve the insured's interests fully. At a minimum, when a settlement offer exceeding the policy limits is received, the insurer should do several things: (1) take steps to try to get the settlement offer reduced, as that would benefit the insured;

---

[35] See, e.g., Ging v. American Liberty Ins. Co., 423 F.2d 115 (5th Cir. 1970); Kaudern v. Allstate Ins. Co., 277 F. Supp. 83 (D.N.J. 1967); Brown v. Guarantee Ins. Co., 319 P.2d 69 (Cal. Ct. App. 1957); William M. Shernoff, Stanford M. Gage, & Harvey R. Levine, *Insurance Bad Faith Litigation* § 3.04, at 3-16 to 3-24 (1986).

[36] See, e.g., Marginian v. Allstate Ins. Co., 481 N.E.2d 600 (Ohio 1985); Employer's Surplus Line Ins. Co. v. Baton Rouge, 362 So. 2d 561 (La. 1978); Olson v. Union Fire Ins. Co., 118 N.W.2d 318 (Neb. 1962); Casualty Ins. Co. v. Town & Country Pre-School Nursery, Inc., 498 N.E.2d 1177 (Ill. App. Ct. 1986); Orion Ins. Co., Ltd. v. General Elec. Co., 493 N.Y.S.2d 397 (N.Y. Sup. Ct. 1985); see generally Seymour Kurland & David F. Simon, *The Insured's Duty to Tender a Deductible in Settlement,* 47 Ins. Counsel J. 552 (1980); Hal Grossman, Note, *Insured's Right to Refuse to Settle,* 33 Rutgers L. Rev. 1199 (1981) (discussing Lieberman v. Employers Ins. of Wausau, 419 A.2d 417 (N.J. 1980).

[37] See, e.g., Woodstock v. Evanoff, 550 P.2d 1132 (Wyo. 1976); Berlant v. McAllister, 480 P.2d 126 (Utah 1971).

(2) use reasonable diligence to determine the facts upon which a good faith decision to settle or not settle can be reached; (3) where the likelihood of liability exceeding the policy limits exists, inform the insured of this possibility and of the company's adverse interest so that the insured can take steps to protect the insured's own interests; (4) inform the insured of any settlement offers received and the progress of settlement negotiations.[38] If informed of the offer, the insured might choose to make up the difference to avoid the risk of a higher judgment.

If the insurer is defending the lawsuit under a reservation of rights (which means that the insurer reserves the right to later contest coverage in the event a judgment is entered against the insured or the lawsuit is settled on terms involving payment to the plaintiff), it is ordinarily the insured who pays the amount of any settlement or judgment. Thus, in this situation, the ultimate choice of whether to settle belongs not to the insurer, but to the insured, regardless of the language of the policy.[39] Otherwise, the insurer would be taking inconsistent positions: it would be asserting its right under the policy to control settlement, while simultaneously taking the position (or preparing to do so) that it has no obligations under the policy (and concomitantly no rights either) with respect to the particular claim.

If the insurer is defending the lawsuit, the insurer cannot refuse to settle the lawsuit because it believes no coverage exists. Refusing to settle puts the insured at risk of an excess judgment. In this situation, it is more appropriate for the insurer to settle the action against the insured subject to a reservation of rights to seek indemnification from the insured should the nonexistence of coverage later be established.[40] Alternatively, if the action against the insured can be stayed, the insurer can commence a declaratory judgment action to establish coverage.

If the insurer has unjustifiably refused to defend the lawsuit, the insurer has committed a material breach. Normally, the insured cannot settle lawsuits on its own, but because of the insurer's prior material breach, the insured need no longer comply with its obligations to the insured, and it is not essential that the insured have the insurer's permission to enter into a settlement. Thus, if the settlement is reasonable, the insurer is responsible for it.[41] If the settlement is for a claim outside the coverage, a difficult situation is presented; this problem is discussed in an earlier section.[42]

[f] Remedies for Breach of the Duty to Settle

Whether the duty to settle sounds in tort or contract, it is clear that the insured can recover damages in excess of the policy limits if the insurer breaches this duty.

---

[38] See, e.g., North River Ins. Co. v. St. Paul Fire & Marine Ins. Co., 600 F.2d 721 (8th Cir. 1979); Mowry v. Badger State Mut. Cas. Co., 385 N.W.2d 171 (Wis. 1986); Boston Old Colony Ins. Co. v. Gutierrez, 386 So. 2d 783 (Fla. 1980); Koppie v. Allied Mut. Ins. Co., 210 N.W.2d 844 (Iowa 1973); Roberie v. Southern Farm Bur. Cas. Ins. Co., 194 So. 2d 713 (La. 1967).

[39] See Tank v. State Farm & Cas. Co., 715 P.2d 1133 (Wash. 1986).

[40] See, e.g., Johansen v. California State Auto. Ass'n Inter-Ins. Bur., 538 P.2d 744, (Cal. 1975); see § 111[g][6], *supra.*

[41] See Isadore Rosen & Sons, Inc., v. Security Mut. Ins. Co., 291 N.E.2d 380 (N.Y. 1972); § 111[g][6], *supra.*

[42] See § 111[g][6], *supra.*

Suppose, for example, that the insured has a liability insurance policy with limits of $100,000. A claim is filed against the insured in the amount of $500,000. The insurer defends the suit. The plaintiff offers to settle the litigation against the insured for $80,000. If this offer is accepted, the insurer would pay the entire judgment. However, if the settlement is declined, the parties proceed to trial, and a $500,000 judgment is entered, the insurer will only pay $100,000 of the judgment, leaving the remaining $400,000 to the insured to pay out of the insured's own pocket. Understandably, the insured is often eager for the insurer to accept a settlement offer within the policy limits, since this eliminates the possibility that the insured will have to contribute personally to the judgment. Alternatively, rather than pay $80,000, the insurer may be tempted to reject the settlement offer and proceed to trial on the merits, hoping that a zero verdict will be entered.

Courts do not permit insurers to gamble with the fortunes of the insureds they defend. Yet insurers are not obligated to accept all settlement offers within the policy limits, as there are some cases where a vigorous defense is to be preferred over paying ransom for the relief from the irritation of a nonmeritorious lawsuit. The difficult task is articulating a standard which distinguishes settlement offers which should be accepted from those which should be rejected: the reasonable-offer test, discussed above, usually serves to determine the scope of the insurer's duty to settle.

If the insurer breaches the duty to settle, the insured is entitled to damages exceeding the policy limits, and this is true whether the duty sounds in tort or contract. Under the tort theory, the excess judgment is a proximate result of the insurer's breach of duty. Under the contract theory, a judgment exceeding the policy limits is a foreseeable, naturally arising consequential damage for which contract law should provide a remedy. Tort law, however, can give a broader range of consequential damages, including damages for mental distress suffered by the insured due to the insurer's refusal to settle, and in particularly egregious circumstances will make available punitive damages, which are almost never available in contract.

[g] Effect of Breaching the Duty to Defend on the Duty to Settle

Because the source of the duty to settle is uncertain, its relationship to the duty to defend is equally uncertain. In the typical situation where both duties are at issue, the insurer refuses to defend and consequently refuses to respond to any settlement offer made by the plaintiff. As discussed earlier,[43] most courts hold that the insurer which breaches its duty to defend is responsible for any reasonable settlement negotiated by the insured to the extent of the policy limits. Why not make the insurer liable for the entire settlement, even that over the policy limits? The analysis must be that the insurer's breach of the duty to defend does not "cause" a settlement exceeding the policy limits, and therefore the insurer is not responsible for any settlement exceeding those limits. An insurer that "relinquishes" the duty to defend by allowing the insured to select his or her own counsel, with the expenses to be paid by the insurer, still owes a duty to settle and must participate in the defense to the extent of evaluating any settlement offers.[44] However, the duty to defend is

---

[43] See § 111[g][5], *supra*.

[44] See Orion Ins. Co. v. General Elec. Co., 493 N.Y.S.2d 397 (N.Y.Sup.Ct 1985).

independent from the duty to settle, because the insurer that breaches the duty to defend does not simultaneously breach the duty to settle.

A slightly different approach reaching the same result holds that the insurer has no duty to settle until it assumes the defense of the insured. This was the essence of the Oregon Supreme Court's decision in *Farris v. United States Fidelity and Guaranty Co.,*[45] a case where the insurer refused to defend the insured and the insureds settled the suit prior to trial:

> Assuming, but not deciding, that a cause of action for failure to settle within the policy limits is one in tort, it is our opinion that the rationale of such an action has no application to the present situation and that the present action is not one in tort. In an action for failure to settle within the policy limits, the insurance company is charged with acting in a fiduciary capacity as an attorney in fact representing the insured's interest in litigation. . . . In the present case, defendant did not undertake this fiduciary duty to represent the insured's interest in the litigation — it refused it. It did not, in the course of representing plaintiffs, violate its fiduciary duty arising out of sole control of the settlement. It never undertook any fiduciary duty by purporting to act in the interests of the insured.[46]

In this case, and others like it,[47] the insurer would be liable for the costs of defense and, under the duty to indemnify, the amount of the judgment up to the policy limits. However, under this approach, the insurer is not liable for any portion of the excess judgment.

Other courts have viewed the situation differently. As noted earlier, courts have held that an insurer that refuses to consider a settlement offer because of a good faith belief in noncoverage is liable for the excess judgment.[48] Some of these cases treat the duty to defend as being intertwined with the duty to settle; a breach of the duty to defend, if accompanied by inaction in response to the plaintiff's settlement offers, is tantamount to a breach of the duty to settle. The effect of this analysis is to give the insured extracontractual damages for the insurer's breach of the duty to defend.[49]

Whether one approach has merit over the other depends on one's assessment of what amount of liability needs to be imposed on insurers to obtain optimal deterrence of insurers contemplating breach of the duties to defend and settle. If one believes that the present system, on the whole, underdeters, one would favor the broader remedial approach, which would treat breaching the duty to defend as a simultaneous breach of the duty to settle (assuming a settlement offer were submitted by the plaintiff, which is likely to be the case) and would make tort remedies available. If one believes that this level of deterrence is not needed, one would be content with

---

[45] 587 P.2d 1015 (Or. 1978).

[46] 587 P.2d at 1018–19.

[47] See, e.g., Gordon v. Nationwide Mut. Ins. Co., 285 N.E.2d 849 (N.Y. 1972); Landie v. Century Indem. Co., 390 S.W.2d 558 (Mo. Ct. App. 1965).

[48] See § 112[e], *supra.*

[49] See Luke v. American Family Mut. Ins. Co., 476 F.2d 1015 (8th Cir. 1972); see § 111[g][5], *supra.*

the more limited remedy of reimbursing the insured's expenses in conducting the defense and requiring the insurer to pay for any judgment or settlement up to the policy limits.

[h]   A Duty to Mitigate?

It is a basic principle of contract law that an aggrieved party cannot recover damages for consequences of a breach that the aggrieved party could have avoided through reasonable measures. From the insurer's perspective, an excess judgment following the insurer's refusal to settle is not caused by the insurer's breach; rather, the insured should have mitigated damages by accepting the settlement offer, thereby eliminating the possibility of an excess judgment. Two problems exist with this argument.[50]

First, the insured surrenders control of settlement to the insurer and actually promises in the policy not to enter into settlements without the insurer's consent. If the insured settled a lawsuit without the insurer's consent, the insurer could claim that its obligations were discharged by the insured's breach. A party to a contract is not required to jeopardize its own rights by breaching a contractual undertaking in order to mitigate damages. Any other result would virtually empower insurers to reject settlement offers without fear of being held liable for excess judgments, and this would effectively vitiate the benefits of recognizing such a duty. Second, mitigation will not be feasible for insureds who lack the financial resources to pay a settlement out of personal assets. Many insureds fall into this category, and this is foreseeable to the insurer at the time of contracting. For these reasons, the insurer should not in the usual case be allowed to prevail on a claim that it owes no damages for breach of the duty to settle due to the insured's failure to mitigate damages.

§ 113   The Insurer's Duty with Regard to Appeals

The duty to defend does not end with the termination of proceedings in the trial court. If the insured prevails in the trial court and the unsuccessful plaintiff appeals a judgment given for the insured, it is the insurer's obligation to defend that appeal.[1] In short, the insurer's duty to defend is not over until the plaintiff has exhausted any post-trial options and the case finally reaches its end.

If a judgment adverse to the insured is rendered in the trial court, courts have used various standards to articulate the insurer's obligation in these circumstances. Notwithstanding some loose language in some decisions,[2] no court imposes on the

---

[50] Compare § 111[h], *supra.*

[1] See, e.g., Commerce & Indus. Ins. Co. v. Bank of Hawaii, 832 P.2d 733 (Haw. 1992) (insurer's duty to defend insured continues until the conclusion of the litigation); Travelers Indem. Co. v. East, 240 So. 2d 277 (Miss. 1970).

[2] In fairness, one must note that sometimes it is not necessary to the decision for a court to be more precise. For example, Chrestman v. United States Fid. & Guar. Co., 511 F.2d 129 (5th Cir. 1975), has been cited as exemplar of a "minority" approach that only requires "reasonable grounds" for an insurer to be obligated to appeal. See Guarantee Abstract & Title Co. v. Interstate Fire & Cas. Co., 618 P.2d 1195, 1200 (Kan. 1980). Yet a close reading of

insurer an obligation to prosecute an appeal on the insured's behalf when it would clearly be futile to do so.[3] The common sense inherent in this position is obvious; no doubt there is some insured somewhere who would insist that a jury's determination that the insured was negligent in connection with a traffic accident be appealed all the way to the United States Supreme Court. No insured should be able to insist on such a clearly wasteful course of action. On the other hand, it makes sense that the insurer should have a duty to appeal a judgment adverse to the insured when the insured's interests would be furthered or assisted. In other words, some kind of rule of reason must be articulated, for there are situations where the insurer should prosecute an appeal.

One of the first decisions to discuss the issue in detail, *Hawkeye-Security Insurance Co. v. Indemnity Insurance Co.*[4] a 1958 Tenth Circuit decision, articulated a "fraud or bad faith" standard to determine when the insurer's failure to prosecute an appeal would constitute a breach of the duty to defend. The insurer refused to follow appointed counsel's advice to prosecute an appeal of a judgment adverse to the insured, and the Tenth Circuit held this fact alone was not enough to make the insurer liable, but that the insurer would be liable if it acted fraudulently or in bad faith. This decision, if it means that the insurer satisfies its obligation as long as it does not commit fraud or similar egregious, tortious conduct, requires relatively little of the insurer to fulfill its obligation to the insured.

Most courts, sometimes citing *Hawkeye-Security*,[5] turn the bad faith standard around and hold that the insurer does not have an absolute obligation to prosecute an appeal, even when an excess judgment is rendered, but does have a duty of good

---

Chrestman shows that the court, in finding insufficient grounds for imposing a duty on the insurer to appeal, reasoned that the insured had not even shown, at the very least, "reasonable grounds," meaning that the insured could not even clear the lowest of the hurdles that one might use as a threshold.

[3] For an interesting twist on the usual fact pattern, see Youngman v. CNA Ins. Co., 585 A.2d 511 (Pa. Super. Ct. 1991) (insured, a member of school board, appealed in his official capacity a judgment rendered against school board collectively, even though judgment imposed no liability on insured and board voted 8-1 not to appeal adverse judgment; held, appeal by insured, when board voted against appeal, was outside scope of that member's duties, and thus the appeal was outside the coverage; "where the insured appeals, the rendered judgment, and not the allegations of the complaint, govern the insurer's duty regarding the appeal regardless of the allegations in the complaint.") One case might be read as authority for the view that the insurer's duty to appeal, when requested, is absolute. In Palmer v. Pacific Indem. Co., 254 N.W.2d 52 (Mich. Ct. App. 1977), a malpractice insurer declined to appeal an adverse excess judgment against its insured, and the court held that the insurer breached its duty to defend: "an insurance company will be expected to proceed with an appeal, if requested by an insured, if it writes a broad 'duty to defend' clause into its insurance contracts. . . . The insured is entitled to be defended by the insurer at both the trial level as well as the appellate level unless otherwise specifically set forth in the contract of insurance." 254 N.W.2d at 55. The court rejected the insurer's contention that its duty to appeal would exist only if there were reasonable grounds for the appeal.

[4] 260 F.2d 361 (10th Cir. 1958).

[5] See Guarantee Abstract & Title Co. v. Interstate Fire & Cas. Co., 618 P.2d 1195 (Kan. 1980).

faith and fair dealing which means that the insurer is obligated to prosecute some appeals in some situations in order to fulfill its duties to the insured.[6]

Other courts articulate the standard differently, holding that where there appear "reasonable grounds" for appeal, the insurer's duty to defend extends to appealing a judgment adverse to the insured.[7] Whether this test necessarily leads to different results from the good faith and fair dealing standard is not obvious. If the finding of reasonable grounds presupposes a good faith inquiry, the tests are probably the same. Yet if one views "reasonable grounds" as something equivalent to a basis for bringing an appeal that is not frivolous, it would seem that one could almost always find a "reasonable ground" for appeal, even though it is clearly futile and an exercise of poor judgment to pursue it.[8]

The heart of the test, and some courts have used language which embraces this idea, is that the insurer's obligation to appeal a judgment adverse to the insured is measured by whether the appeal can reasonably be expected to advance, presumably in some substantial, non-incidental way, the interests of the insured.[9] This idea embraces the expectation that the insurer will evaluate the case in a good faith manner and will deal fairly with the insured's interests, and also acknowledges that the insurer's duty to appeal is not absolute.

Whatever test one favors, it would seem that the same test should determine whether an insurer has an obligation to pursue other kinds of post-judgment relief,

---

[6] See, e.g., Guarantee Abstract & Title Co. v. Interstate Fire & Cas. Co., 618 P.2d 1195 (Kan. 1980) (also approving *Hawkeye-Security*); Aetna Ins. Co. v. Borrell-Bigby Elec. Co., 541 So. 2d 139 (Fla. Dist. Ct. App. 1989). Cf. Reichert v. Continental Ins. Co., 290 So. 2d 730 (La. Ct. App. 1974) (though approving "minority" view, states that majority of jurisdictions employ test of good faith and fair dealing, and cites *Hawkeye-Security* for this position).

[7] See, e.g., Chrestman v. United States Fid. & Guar. Co., 511 F.2d 129 (5th Cir. 1975) ("[a]t the very least" reasonable grounds is the test); Crist v. Insurance Co. of N. Am., 529 F. Supp. 601 (D. Utah 1982); Ursprung v. Safeco Ins. Co. of Am., 497 S.W.2d 726 (Ky. 1973); Jenkins v. Insurance Co. of N. Am., 272 Cal. Rptr. 7 (Cal. Ct. App. 1990); Reichert v. Continental Ins. Co., 290 So. 2d 730 (La.App. 1974); Fidelity Gen. Ins. Co. v. Aetna Ins. Co., 278 N.Y.S.2d 787 (N.Y. App. Div. 1967); Kaste v. Hartford Acc. & Indem. Co., 170 N.Y.S.2d 614 (N.Y. App. Div. 1958).

[8] See Cathay Mortuary (Wah Sang), Inc. v. United Pac. Ins. Co., 582 F. Supp. 650 (N.D. Cal. 1984) (court discusses different approaches and declines to choose among different tests; however, finds "general consensus" among all decisions that insurer has duty to appeal when there are "reasonable grounds"; finds insurer breached its duty in instant case because insurer "plainly had very strong grounds for appeal.")

[9] See Truck Ins. Exch. of Farmers Ins. Group v. Century Indem. Co., 887 P.2d 455 (Wash. Ct. App. 1995) (duty to appeal exists where "there are reasonable grounds to believe a substantial interest of the insured may be served or protected thereby"); Reichert v. Continental Ins. Co., 290 So. 2d 730 (La. Ct. App. 1974) (approving "reasonable grounds" test, but also states that "[w]here there appears reasonable grounds that a substantial interest of the insured may be served or protected by appeal, insurer owed the duty to appeal.")

such as a motion for a new trial or a motion for a judgment notwithstanding the verdict.[10]

§ 114 Conflicts of Interest

[a] Overview

Conflicts between the interests of insurers and insureds are inevitable in insurance. In first-party insurance, once a loss has occurred, the insurer may wish to pay less in proceeds than the insured demands. This conflict, however, is no different than what can arise in any contractual relationship. A contract is formed to advance each party's interests, but sometimes disputes arise during the contract's performance because one party's expectations about the other's performance are disappointed. The phrase "conflict of interest" as used in the professional responsibility context refers to more than the ordinary situation where one party to a contract has different expectations than the other. It also means more than the mere fact that the interests of the clients diverge. In the professional responsibility context, and in the liability insurance context as well, a conflict of interest occurs whenever one lawyer has multiple clients and the representation of one is or would be rendered less effective by reason of his or her representation of another.[1]

---

[10] See Cathay Mortuary (Wah Sang), Inc. v. United Pac. Ins. Co., 582 F. Supp. 650 (N.D. Cal. 1984); Truck Ins. Exch. of Farmers Ins. Group v. Century Indem. Co., 887 P.2d 455 (Wash. Ct. App. 1995).

[1] For additional discussion of these issues, see generally Charles Silver & Kent Syverud, *The Professional Responsibilities of Insurance Defense Lawyers,* 45 Duke L.J. 255 (1995); Charles Silver, *Does Insurance Counsel Represent the Company or the Insured?,* 72 Tex. L. Rev. 1583 (1994); Douglas R. Richmond, *Walking a Tightrope: The Tripartite Relationship Between Insurer, Insured, and Insurance Defense Counsel,* 73 Neb. L. Rev. 265 (1994); Debra A. Winiarski, *Walking the Fine Line: A Defense Counsel's Perspective,* 28 Tort & Ins. L. J. 596 (1993); Karen O. Bowdre, *Conflicts of Interest Between Insurer and Insured: Ethical Traps for Unsuspecting Defense Counsel,* 17 Am. J. Trial Advocacy 101 (1993); William T. Barker, "The Right and Duty to Defend": Conflicts of Interest and Insurer Control of the Defense, in A.B.A. Sec. Tort & Ins. Prac., *Litigating the Coverage Claim: Denial of Coverage & Duty to Defend* (1992), at 195; Richard L. Neumeier, *Serving Two Masters: Problems Facing Insurance Defense Counsel and Some Proposed Solutions,* 77 Mass. L. Rev. 66 (1992); William T. Barker, *When Does the Insurer Lose the Right to Control the Defense?,* 58 Def. Couns. J. 469 (1991); Robert E. O'Malley, *Ethics Principles for the Insurer, the Insured, and Defense Counsel: The Eternal Triangle Reformed,* 66 Tul. L. Rev. 511 (1991); Thomas V. Murray & Diane M. Bringus, *Insurance Defense Counsel: Conflicts of Interest,* Fed'n Ins. & Corp. Couns. Q. 283 (1991); William T. Barker et al., *Is an Insurer a Fiduciary to Its Insureds?,* 25 Tort & Ins. L. J. 1 (1989); Eric M. Holmes, *A Conflict-of-Interest Roadmap for Insurance Defense Counsel: Walking an Ethical Tightrope Without a Net,* 26 Willamette L. Rev. 1 (1989); Brooke Wunnicke, *The Eternal Triangle: Standards of Ethical Representation by the Insurance Defense Lawyer, For the Def.,* Feb. 1989; Michael A. Berch & Rebecca White Berch, *Will the Real Counsel for the Insured Please Rise?,* 19 Ariz. St. L. J. 27 (1987); John K. Morris, *Conflicts of Interest in Defending Under Liability Insurance Policies: A Proposed Solution,* 1981 Utah L. Rev. 457.

In liability insurance, conflicts between the insurer's and the insured's interests have serious implications. The insurer promises to defend the insured against claims within coverage; pursuant to this undertaking, the insurer appoints an attorney to represent the insured's interest (and simultaneously, at least at the outset, the insurer's common interest in defeating or minimizing the insured's liability on the plaintiff's claim). When the attorney undertakes to represent the insured's interests, a fiduciary relationship, which does not exist in ordinary first-party insurance, enters the picture; the attorney's fiduciary obligation to the insured, which exists independently of the liability insurance contract between insurer and insured, requires zealous representation of the insured's interests. As explained by Mallen and Smith, "[t]he intrusion of the insurance contract does not alter the fact that the relationship with the insured is that of attorney and client. Defense counsel owes the same unqualified loyalty as if he had been personally retained by the insured."[2] Yet the attorney is retained and paid by the insurer, which may influence the attorney to represent the insured's interests inadequately when the insured's interests conflict with those of the insurer.

When addressing the problem of conflicts of interest in liability insurance, it is helpful to keep two things distinct: the duties of the insurer under the insurance contract, and the duties of the attorney, appointed by the insurer to represent the insured, to the client. The insurer owes the insured a duty to defend the insured against any claims asserted against the insured within the policy's coverage. The insurer typically designates and pays an attorney to provide this defense to the insured. Once the attorney commences the representation of the insured, the attorney, irrespective of the contract between insurer and insured, owes fiduciary duties to the insured, just as any attorney owes these duties to the client. If the insurer fails to provide a defense to the insured, the insurer may be held liable for breach of the contractual duty to defend. If the attorney fails to protect the interests of the client(s), the attorney could be found to have violated the attorney's ethical obligations and to have committed malpractice.

The nub of the problem for the attorney is that the attorney has two masters: the insurer who retains the attorney, pays the bills, and probably expects the attorney not to do anything that impairs the insurer's interest; and the insured for whom the attorney appears, who probably has a similar, albeit sometimes conflicting expectation based on his or her payment of premiums. The relationship between insurer and insured is governed by the liability insurance contract; the relationship between the insurer and the attorney is governed by a retainer agreement, if one exists; the relationship between attorney and insured is governed by those two parties' understanding of the scope of the representation, but this understanding is affected greatly by both the liability contract and, if one exists, the retainer agreement. In addition, the law of agency, the law of professional responsibility, and the general principles of contract law and insurance law that regulate the liability insurance contract overlay the entirety of these relationships.[3] This tripartite relationship has

---

[2] Ronald E. Mallen & Jeffrey M. Smith, *Legal Malpractice,* § 23.3, at 365 (1989).

[3] For further discussion of these relationships, and in particular the role the retainer agreement can play in affecting them, see generally Silver, *supra* note 1; Silver & Syverud, *supra* note 1.

often been described as a tightrope that the attorney must traverse at considerable peril. But it is important to recognize that just because an attorney has multiple clients with divergent interests, it does not follow that the attorney has conflicting interests. Mallen and Smith have summarized the issue this way:

> The test is whether there is actual adversity so that the competent representation of one client dictates that the attorney contend for that client which his duty to the other client requires him to oppose. The conflict between the clients may also be recognized by its consequences, that is, the representation of one client is rendered less effective because of the representation of the interests of the other. Conflicting interests interfere with the obligation of undivided loyalty which prohibits the attorney from subordinating the interest of one client to that of the other.[4]

Conflicts between insurer and insured can arise in virtually countless ways, but some are more common than others. Consider, for example, the following: (A) Because liability insurance is designed to pay for a third party's loss caused by the insured, the insured may desire to assist the third party in recovering proceeds, perhaps out of a sense of moral obligation or because the third party is a friend or relative. (B) The insurer may be interested in pursuing a litigation strategy that would establish a precedent to guide other cases in which the insurer — but not the insured — has a stake. The absence of a shared interest in the long-run implications of the outcome of the insured's case may lead to conflicting ideas on how the litigation should be conducted. (C) Even if the insurer decides to provide coverage and pay some proceeds, a conflict exists between insured and insurer when the potential liability exceeds the policy limits and settlement offers are made by the plaintiff within the policy limits. (D) When the insurer undertakes the defense, the insured may prefer tactical choices that the insurer believes to be unsound. For example, insurers may prefer prompt settlements of some claims for economic reasons, but the insured for personal reasons, such as professional reputation or a belief that the claim is unjustified, may oppose settlement. (E) After the representation has begun, the attorney appointed by the insurer may discover information that is adverse to one of the parties vis-a-vis the other. For example, the attorney may discover from information supplied by the insured a basis for the insurer denying coverage. If the information is revealed to the insurer, the insured's interests are damaged; yet if the information is concealed, the insurer's interests are compromised.

The foregoing are the more common conflicts, but others exist as well.[5] These situations present the attorney defending the insured with extremely difficult, sometimes intractable, choices.[6] Unfortunately, there are few clear answers, and this creates further problems, as succinctly and powerfully explained by Professors Silver and Syverud:

---

[4] Mallen & Smith, *supra* note 2, § 23.12 at 393-94.

[5] For another catalogue of possible conflicts, see Silver & Syverud, *supra* note 1, at 266-67.

[6] See Winiarski, *supra* note 1, at 610 ("It is impossible to set forth bright-line rules regarding the recognition and handling of all potential problems that may arise in the tripartite relationship.") See generally Ronald E. Mallen, *Insurance Counsel: The Fine Line between Professional Responsibility and Malpractice,* 45 Ins. Counsel J. 244 (1978).

Insurance defense lawyers are integral parts of the engine that drives civil litigation, and the rules that govern their conduct are both extraordinarily vague and often wrong. The rules fail to provide clear and defensible answers to the most basic questions, such as whether an attorney-client relationship exists between the insurance company and the lawyer retained to handle the lawsuit against the insured. Consequently, the rules are almost entirely unhelpful when more complicated questions arise. The obvious danger is that insurance defense lawyers will act improperly, even when they attempt to adhere to the law.[7]

[b]   The Basic Alternatives: To Whom Is Loyalty Owed?

When the attorney represents both the insured and the insurer (as in the case when the attorney appears on behalf of the insured and is retained and paid by the insurer), the attorney can conduct the representation in one of three ways: giving absolute loyalty to the insurer; giving absolute loyalty to the insured; or representing the interests of both parties.

[1]   The Dual Representation Model

The American Bar Association's *Code of Professional Responsibility* adopts a "dual representation" standard.[8] The attorney who appears for the insured when retained by the insurer represents both clients and owes a duty of loyalty to each. Disciplinary Rule 5-105(C) states that

a lawyer may represent multiple clients if it is obvious that the attorney can adequately represent the interest of each and if each consents to the representation after full disclosure of the possible effect of such representation on the exercise of the attorney's independent professional judgment on behalf of each.

Consent is obviously a critical aspect of the dual representation model. Some courts have concluded that the insured's purchase of a liability policy containing a provision authorizing the insurer to control the defense constitutes consent by the insured to dual representation.[9] Otherwise, the consent occurs when the insured agrees to the insurer's offer of the defense in a particular case, assuming the offer is accompanied by the insurer's full disclosure to the insured of the potential effects of the joint representation.[10]

Ethical Consideration 5-15 states that "[a] lawyer should never represent in litigation multiple clients with different interests" and adds that few situations exist

---

[7] Silver & Syverud, *supra* note 1, at 263.

[8] One of the earliest, and perhaps the first, articulation of the dual representation model is found in ABA Formal Opinion 282 (ABA Comm. on Professional Ethics, Formal Op. 282 (1950)), which accepted "unequivocally that a lawyer may ethically undertake the dual representation of the insurer and the insured in the defense of a third party action against the insured." Yet even this early opinion contained language which suggested a different approach for some cases. The opinion also stated that the "essential point of ethics involved is that the lawyer so employed shall represent the insured as his client with undivided fidelity." *Id.* at 2.

[9] See Brohawn v. Transamerica Ins. Co., 347 A.2d 842 (Md. 1975); Houston Gen. Ins. Co. v. Superior Court, 166 Cal. Rptr. 904 (Cal. Ct. App. 1980).

[10] The consent issue is discussed in great detail in Silver & Syverud, *supra* note 1, at 313-31.

where a lawyer "would be justified in representing in litigation multiple clients with potentially differing interests." If such a representation were undertaken and it became clear later that differing interests existed, the lawyer would be required to withdraw from the representation. Ethical Consideration 5-17 identifies "insurer and insured" as a typically recurring situation where "potentially differing interests" may be involved, and then observes: "Whether a lawyer can fairly and adequately protect the interests of multiple clients in these and similar situations depends upon an analysis of each case." Rule 1.7 of the *ABA Model Rules of Professional Conduct* reiterates the foregoing; it states that an attorney cannot represent parties with adverse interests[11] unless the lawyer "reasonably believes the representation will not be adversely affected" and the clients consent after full disclosure. One court explained the issue as follows: "Although a lawyer may ethically in some circumstances, and with his client's consent, limit the objectives of his representation [citing Model Rule 1.2(c)], this can never authorize the attorney to engage in dual legal representation entailing professional decisions on his part which stand to benefit one client at the expense of another [citing Model Rule 1.7]."[12] In other words, Rule 1.7 "permits representation in conflict situations only when there is both fully counseled client consent *and* a reasonable belief on the part of the lawyer that the conflict is not insurmountable. In practice, this means that in some cases client consent will not suffice, and indeed should not even be sought."[13]

Although the framework of the Code and the Model Rules contemplates dual representation, both the Code and the Rules make clear that the attorney's exercise of his or her own independent judgment must not be compromised. Model Rule 1.8(f) provides as follows:

> A lawyer shall not accept compensation for representing a client from one other than the client unless:
>
> (1) The client consents after consultation;
>
> (2) There is no interference with the lawyer's independence of professional judgment or with the client-lawyer relationship; and
>
> (3) Information relating to the representation of a client is protected as required by Rule 1.6.

This rule, by its terms, appears to apply to insurance defense counsel,[14] and the rule makes no distinction between defense counsel selected by the insurer or the

---

[11] Rule 1.7 categorizes conflicts into two situations: those where representing one client "will be directly adverse to another client" and those where "the representation of that client may be materially limited by the lawyer's responsibilities to another client or to a third person, or by the lawyer's own interests."

[12] Hartford Acc. & Indem. Co. v. Foster, 528 So. 2d 255, 269 (Miss. 1988).

[13] Geoffrey C. Hazard, Jr. & W. William Hodes, *The Law of Lawyering: A Handbook on the Model Rules of Professional Conduct* § 1.7:301, at 246.1 (1994).

[14] See Rule 1.7, comment 10 ("A lawyer may be paid from a source other than the client, if the client is informed of that fact and consents and the arrangement does not compromise the lawyer's duty of loyalty to the client. See Rule 1.8(f). For example, when an insurer and its insured have conflicting interests in a matter arising from a liability insurance agreement,

insured. By its terms, Rule 1.8(f) acknowledges that dual representation is possible and permissible if the necessary consent is obtained, the insured's interests are protected, and the insurer does not interfere with the attorney's exercise of his or her own independent professional judgment.

The importance of the attorney making his or her own professional judgments is underscored by DR 5-107(B), which provides: "A lawyer shall not permit a person who recommends, employs, or pays him to render legal services to another to direct or regulate his professional judgment in rendering such legal services."[15]

To assist the insurance defense counsel in working through the dual representation "minefield," the American Bar Association National Conference of Lawyers and Liability Insurers issued in 1969 and the ABA House of Delegates approved in 1972 a set of "Guiding Principles" for lawyers and liability insurers in furnishing a defense to insureds. The Principles stated that the insurer "has the right to have counsel of its own choice" to defend the insurer and "so long as no conflict of interests exist" to defend the insured. If a conflict arises, the insurer should inform the insured of the conflict and invite the insured "to retain his own counsel at his own expense." For the toughest questions, the Principles did not attempt to provide an answer. For example, regarding the situations where the insured refuses to consent to dual representation or if the full protection of the separate interests cannot occur in a common defense, the Principles merely stated that "the insurance company or the insured should seek other procedures to resolve the coverage question."[16] In 1980, the ABA withdrew its approval of the principles, apparently because of their antitrust ramifications as a trade agreement.[17]

To summarize the dual representation approach, when the interests of the insurer and insured do not differ, the attorney treats the insurer and insured, in essence, as co-clients. Recognizing that an attorney who represents an insured pursuant to the insurer's obligation to defend has two clients (the insured and the insurer) provides legitimacy to the insurer's desire to control the defense of the insured.[18] When an

---

and the insurer is required to provide special counsel for the insured, the arrangement should assure the special counsel's professional independence.") It is possible, however, to argue that Model Rule 1.8(f) applies to one-client representations in which a third party is paying the bill, not to dual- or joint-client representations, such as that undertaken by insurance defense counsel. In this regard, it is significant that the sentence beginning with "for example" in comment 10 to Rule 1.7 refers to the situation where the insured has independent counsel paid for by the insurer, which is not a dual-representation situation. I am grateful to Professor Silver for his perspective on this issue; for more discussion, see generally Silver, *supra* note 1.

15 Model Rule 5.4(c) is substantially identical to DR 5-107(B). Again, however, it can be argued that this and the related rules speak to one-client, third-party-payor situations, and not joint representations. See note 14 *supra*.

16 The Guiding Principles are reprinted at 49 Ins. Counsel J. 358 (1972).

17 Geoffrey C. Hazard, Jr. & Susan P. Koniak, *The Law and Ethics of Lawyering* 646 (1990).

18 See Silver, *supra* note 1, at 1586. As explained by Professor Silver, if the insurer is a client, the insurer has a right, no less than that enjoyed by any other co-client, to instruct the attorney on how to conduct the defense. If the insurer is not a client of the appointed counsel, the insurer's ability to control the defense is in doubt.

attorney represents multiple clients, it is a breach of the attorney's relationship with a client if the attorney subordinates that client's interests to the interests of one or more of the other clients.[19] Thus, under the dual representation model, an attorney who has reason to believe that he or she cannot serve one client without compromising the interests of another cannot, without both clients' informed consent, continue to represent both. Unfortunately, there is no consensus on what happens after it is apparent that continued joint representation is no longer possible.

[2]   What Happens When Dual Representation Is No Longer Possible?

When an insured withholds his or her consent for continued dual representation in the face of a potential conflict of interest, or if an actual conflict between insurer and insured makes dual representation impossible, there is a consensus that defense counsel cannot continue with the joint representation. Beyond this observation, there is disagreement among courts and commentators.

Under one point of view, the defense attorney must withdraw from representing either the insurer or the insured and cannot thereafter counsel either party with regard to the subject matter of the pending litigation.[20] This position draws heavily on the principle that in dual representation the attorney cannot take an action that would benefit one client's interests at the expense of the other client's interests, or which, stated otherwise, would subordinate one client's interests to the other's.

A different point of view essentially ratchets the withdrawal solution one additional notch: if dual representation becomes impossible due to an insurmountable conflict, the attorney assumes a duty of undivided loyalty to the insured. That is, an attorney provided by the insurer to represent the insured owes the insured the same allegiance that would be owed if the attorney had been retained by the insured directly.[21] In such circumstances, it is as if the "dual representation" model changes into a "one-client" model when an irreconcilable conflict is confronted. In other words, an attorney may undertake a joint representation when there is no conflict, but the attorney must favor the insured absolutely if a conflict emerges.

In the one-client, undivided-loyalty-to-the-insured model, the insurer discharges its duties under the liability insurance contract with its insured by providing counsel

---

19 See, e.g., Parsons v. Continental Nat'l Am. Group, 550 P.2d 94 (Ariz. 1976); Brohawn v. Transamerica Ins. Co., 347 A.2d 842 (Md. 1975).

20 See, e.g., Lieberman v. Employers Ins. of Wausau, 419 A.2d 417 (N.J. 1980); Brohawn v. Transamerica Ins. Co., 347 A.2d 842 (Md. 1975); Employers Cas. Co. v. Tilley, 496 S.W.2d 552 (Tex. 1973); Safeco Ins. Co. of Am. v. Barnes, 891 P.2d 682 (Or.App. 1995); Ranger Cty. Mut. Ins. Co. v. Guin, 704 S.W.2d 813 (Tex. Ct. App. 1985). The most thoroughly-reasoned defenses of this position have been provided by Professors Silver and Syverud and attorney-commentator William Barker. See articles cited at note 1, *supra*.

21 See, e.g., New York State Urban Dev. Corp. v. VSL Corp., 738 F.2d 61 (2d Cir. 1984); Doe v. Allstate Ins. Co., 653 So. 2d 371 (Fla. 1995); Hartford Acc. & Indem. Co. v. Foster, 528 So. 2d 255 (Miss. 1988); 69th St. and 2d Ave. Garage Assoc. v. Ticor Title Guar. Co., 622 N.Y.S.2d 13 (N.Y.Sup. 1995); Feliberty v. Damon, 527 N.E.2d 261 (N.Y. App. Div. 1988); Nandorf, Inc. v. CNA Ins. Cos., 479 N.E.2d 988 (Ill. App. Ct. 1985); Bogard v. Employers Cas. Co., 210 Cal. Rptr. 578 (Cal. Ct. App. 1985). See generally Charles W. Wolfram, *Modern Legal Ethics* § 8.4.2, at 430 (1986).

for the insured who is instructed to conduct the defense without regard to the insurer's interests. How the insurer discharges its duties under the approach which calls for the attorney's withdrawal from the defense is less clear. One answer has the insurer appoint a new attorney to undertake a dual representation, but this will not make the conflict disappear. Indeed, if the conflict is not resolved in some way,[22] it is likely that continued efforts to undertake a dual representation will continue to fail. Another answer has the insurer withhold the defense under the reasoning that the insured has breached his or her duty to cooperate in the conduct of the defense. In some circumstances, this answer will be the correct one, but it is an answer that the insurer gives at some risk,[23] and the consequences of being wrong will be worrisome to any insurer.[24] In some situations, the court may refuse to permit defense counsel to withdraw under the reasoning that withdrawal is prejudicial to the insured, and in this circumstance the only option available to the insurer, short of declining to pay for a defense altogether with whatever attendant consequences that decision might have, is to provide for the expenses of independent counsel for the insurer.[25]

Whether the withdrawal approach or the one-client approach is favored by the precedents is a subject of dispute among commentators.[26] What is certain is that strong authority exists for each.

[3] Assessing The Dual Representation and One-Client Models

Although the dual representation model contemplates that the attorney will not be beholden to one party to the exclusion of the interests of the other, there is

----

[22] Of course, if the conflict were resolvable, withdrawal should not have occurred in the first place. What might happen, however, is that the insured may change his or her mind, and decide that having a defense is preferable to insisting that the defense be conducted in a particular way. Yet the insured is unlikely to reach this conclusion without being provided with additional information about the consequences of insisting that the defense be conducted in a certain way. From one perspective, this information will be an objective presentation of logical consequences; from another perspective, this information will amount to threatened withholdings of benefits under the policy to which the insured is entitled as a matter of contract right. Moreover, as discussed earlier, some conflicts are not subject to waiver. The fundamental problem is that it is difficult to make a conflict disappear.

[23] See § 110, *supra*.

[24] See § 111, *supra* (discussing consequences of breaching the duty to defend).

[25] See Silver & Syverud, *supra* note 1, at 341.

[26] See, e.g., Winiarski, *supra* note 1, at 597 ("Under either the dual or single client views, however, virtually all courts and commentators are in agreement that defense counsel's primary loyalty, should a conflict develop between the insured and the insurer, is to the insured."); Silver & Syverud, *supra* note 1, at 337 ("[the primary client rule] appears to be a minority view"); 1 Allan D. Windt, *Insurance Claims and Disputes: Representation of Insurance Companies and Insureds,* § 4.22, at 226-30 (3d ed. 1995) (identifying six lines of authority on the question of the insurer's obligation when there is a conflict of interest between insurer and insured). Windt argues in favor of giving the insurer, in the absence of the insured's consent to some other solution, "a choice between hiring independent counsel to control the defense or allowing the insured to select private counsel (to be paid for by the insurer) to control the defense." He rejects forcing the latter alternative on the insurer. *Id.,* at 229.

unavoidable tension in any joint representation situation if only one of the parties is paying the expenses. If, as stated by Model Rule 1.8(f), the attorney's independent judgment is not subject to interference by the party paying the expenses (i.e., the insurer), it follows that an insurer may not substitute its judgment for the attorney's with regard to how much discovery to undertake, which and how many experts are to be retained, etc. By the same token, an attorney appointed to represent the insured need not and should not proceed as if the defense budget is unlimited. At some point, the marginal benefit of additional legal services is zero, and the insurer should not have to pay for unnecessary legal services. In the gray area where the additional service may be useful but is not obviously so, the insured has an incentive to receive the service because the marginal cost to the insured is zero; but the insurer may well have a different perspective, given that minimizing the costs of defense will be a priority for the insurer. In short, some degree of adversity is inherent in the relationship between insurer and insured.

It has been suggested that scope of the attorney's obligation should be defined by reference to what the attorney would be asked to do if the defendant had no insurance.[27] This test, however, risks depriving the insured of the benefits for which he or she contracted: the insured may well have purchased the liability policy because the insured did not want to be in the position of having a defense limited by the scant resources he or she had available to contribute to a defense. The better view is that the insured is entitled to have all necessary steps taken to provide a fully adequate defense; the fact that this fully adequate defense may cost more than even the policy limits is irrelevant. But the tension between the insurer's interests and the insured's, a tension inherent in one party paying the bills for another party's defense, does not disappear. Moreover, defining the components of a "fully adequate" defense, much like defining "good faith" or the elements of effective assistance of counsel under the Sixth Amendment, is not without difficulty.

Yet tension alone does not create a conflict of interest, and dual representation does not automatically give rise to conflicting interests. Indeed, the mere possibility that interests of multiple clients might conflict at some time in the future is not enough to automatically preclude dual representation. But the attorney must be ever mindful of the possibility that a conflict will arise and must also heed the possibility that the attorney's loyalty to either client might be impaired. If in doubt about his or her ability to zealously represent both clients, the attorney should err on the side of not undertaking or continuing with a dual representation.[28]

The dual representation model becomes more attractive if one assumes some or all of the following: that (a) the liability contract gives the insurer the right to name itself as a co-client with the insured, (b) the liability insurance contract gives the insurer the right to control all aspects of the defense and the attorney has no obligation to obey the insured's instructions with regard to any aspect of it, (c) the liability

27 See Neumeier, *supra* note 1, at 79 ("the best approach is to determine what counsel would do to defend the claim if there were no insurance, the insured was likely to pay any judgment, and the attorney expected to be paid by the insured.")

28 Mallen & Smith, *supra* note 2, at 394. For a more elaborate discussion of how the attorney should respond to conflicts from the perspective of two scholars who support the dual representation model, see Silver & Syverud, *supra* note 1, at 326-61.

insurance contract allows the insurer to settle claims notwithstanding the insured's objections, and (d) the insurer owes no fiduciary duties to the insured.[29] In that event, the attorney's obligations to the insured are softened, and it becomes easier to resolve situations where the interests of insurer and insured are adverse in ways that do not require the expensive remedy of appointing independent counsel for the insured. This approach, in effect, gives the insurer the ability to control, within the context of a dual representation, how counsel will conduct the insured's defense. Interestingly, giving the insurer undivided loyalty from the outset of the representation with respect to settlement negotiations was urged by Professor (now Judge) Keeton a number of years ago.[30] Although this view has not been adopted in recent cases,[31] the proposal continues to have strong advocates.[32] In short, when the attorney represents less than all of the insured's interests, a substantial part (not all) of the inherent tension between insurer and insured disappears; if the insured has no right to insist that certain of his or her interests be protected, there is less to be weighed in the balancing.

The other way to escape the difficulties of dual representation is to abandon it whenever actual conflicts exist or potential conflicts appear insurmountable, and opt for a one-client model. Much of the support for this model has its roots in critiques of the dual representation model, where the attendant issues are thought by many observers to be more complex than the model's advocates concede.

First, it is suggested that the dual representation model gives no guidance on how conflicts that arise in the insurer-insured setting should be resolved. What happens under this standard, as a practical matter, is that conflicts are resolved on an ad hoc basis; different courts provide different solutions to similar problems.[33] Second, the model gives, it is argued, insufficient weight to the fact that most defense attorneys who practice insurance defense work do so on a large-volume basis. Although this no doubt creates cost-saving efficiencies, the close economic and personal relationships that tend to develop between defense counsel and insurers inevitably lead to the diminished emphasis on the insured's interests in some cases. The attorney's relationship with the insured is usually one of short duration and is limited to one specific lawsuit.[34] One court explained it this way: "Even the most optimistic view of human nature requires us to realize that an attorney employed by an insurance

---

[29] Some commentators would disagree with all of the foregoing propositions, some would support all of them in total, and others would argue that there is some measure of merit to all of the foregoing propositions but that circumstances in particular cases prevent their unqualified endorsement.

[30] See Robert E. Keeton, *Liability Insurance and Responsibility for Settlement*, 67 Harv. L. Rev. 1136, 1169-72 (1954).

[31] See, e.g., Hartford Acc. & Indem. Co. v. Foster, 528 So. 2d 255, 272 (Miss. 1988).

[32] See Silver & Syverud, *supra* note 1, at 296-301. Compare Barker, *Litigating Coverage*, *supra* note 1, at 311 (contending that defense counsel may not advise either party on whether to settle).

[33] John K. Morris, *Conflicts of Interest in Defending Under Liability Insurance Policies: A Proposed Solution*, 1981 Utah L. Rev. 457, 462.

[34] *Id.* at 463. For more discussion of this point, including the opposing view, see § 114[c][6][ii], *infra*.

company will slant his efforts, perhaps unconsciously, in the interest of his real client — the one who is paying his fee and from whom he hopes to receive future business — the insurance company."[35] Third, the insured who purchases liability insurance buys a *full* defense to claims asserted against the insured that are within coverage. If the attorney also serves someone with a potentially differing interest, the insured has not received the product for which the insured paid. Although the typical liability policy gives the insurer the "right and duty to defend," requires the insured to cooperate with the insurer, and in some instances allows the insurer to make settlements as it deems expedient, its language does not explicitly allow the attorney representing the insured to compromise the insured's interests in favor of the insurer's.

The problems of dual representation are avoided, it is argued, if the lawyer's only actual client is the insured. In other words, from the moment the attorney establishes an attorney-client relationship with the insured, the attorney's sole client is the insured, even if the attorney is appointed by and has his or her bills paid by an insurer.[36] There is no possibility of a conflict between two clients if the attorney has only one client. How, then, does one describe the relationship between attorney and insurer if the relationship is not one of attorney-client? Clearly, the relationship is at least contractual, because the attorney and insurer agree that the attorney will perform services for a third party, the insured, who is in a contractual relationship with the insurer. To the extent the insured has contractual obligations to the insurer (such as the duty to cooperate), the attorney should seek to make sure that those contractual obligations are fulfilled, but these duties presumably are not owed by the attorney to the insurer, and in no sense are grounded in a fiduciary relationship of attorney and client.[37]

Under the dual representation model, as is the case with any multiple-client representation, at a certain point it can become impossible to dodge or finesse a conflict of interest. When a reckoning is required, withdrawing from the representation only postpones the reckoning; in the end, someone's interests must be favored. Giving undivided loyalty to the insurer's interests is not a realistic alternative. The attorney has appeared in the litigation on the insured's behalf, and acting solely in the insurer's interests would impair the interests of the client of record. Moreover, giving undivided loyalty to the insurer's interests is impossible to square with the insurer's contractual obligations to its insured. At a minimum, when dual representation is no longer feasible, the attorney owes an absolute duty of loyalty to the insured.[38]

---

[35] United States Fid. & Guar. Co. v. Lewis A. Roser Co., 585 F.2d 932, 938 n. 5 (8th Cir. 1978). See also Bogard v. Employers Cas. Co., 210 Cal. Rptr. 578 (Cal. Ct. App. 1985) ("in reality, the insurer's attorneys may have closer ties with the insurer and a more compelling interest in protecting the insurer's position, whether or not it coincides with what is best for the insured.")

[36] See, e.g., Atlanta Int'l Ins. Co. v. Bell, 475 N.W.2d 294 (Mich. 1991).

[37] See Winiarski, *supra* note 1, at 597.

[38] See, e.g., Zieman Mfg. Co. v. St. Paul Fire & Marine Ins. Co., 724 F.2d 1343 (9th Cir. 1983); United States Fid. & Guar. Co. v. Louis A. Roser Co., 585 F.2d 932 (8th Cir. 1978); Outboard Marine Corp. v. Liberty Mut. Ins. Co., 536 F.2d 730 (7th Cir. 1976); Cardin v.

Even this answer, notwithstanding its considerable deference to the insured's interests, fails to satisfy all of the critics. The problem with the undivided loyalty standard, it is argued, is that one can never be certain that undivided loyalty is actually given. If the insurer selects the attorney and pays the bill, the attorney is inevitably under some pressure to please the insurer, and this may cause the attorney to elevate the insurer's interests over the insured's even if the insured is nominally the sole client.

One answer to this criticism is to allow the insured to select the insured's own attorney, who is then paid by the insurer. With respect to conflicts over the issue of coverage, most courts have held that when the insurer's and insured's interests conflict, the insured is entitled to reject counsel appointed by the insurer, select his or her own attorney, and control the defense with the insurer bearing the costs.[39] This one-client view also appears to be endorsed by what is at this writing the most recent tentative draft of the *Restatement of the Law Governing Lawyers*, but the absence of a definitive statement in the rather nuanced draft leaves upon the possibility that subsequent drafts might change course and give support to the dual-representation model.[40]

From the insurer's perspective, allowing the insured to select counsel whose loyalty runs only to the insured is problematic for several reasons. First, the insurer loses control of the defense; when the insurer loses control of the defense, costs of defense are likely to increase. Insurers tend to compensate attorneys at a lower rate than do private parties. The additional costs of paying for independent counsel must be recouped ultimately through premiums, and this redounds to the detriment of all

---

Pacific Employers Ins. Co., 745 F. Supp. 330 (D.Md. 1990); Atlanta Int'l Ins. Co. v. Bell, 475 N.W.2d 294 (Mich. 1991) (plurality opinion); Feliberty v. Damon, 527 N.E.2d 261 (N.Y. 1988); Tank v. State Farm & Cas. Co., 715 P.2d 1133 (Wash. 1986); Siebert Oxidermo, Inc. v. Shields, 446 N.E.2d 332 (Ind. 1983); Norman v. Insurance Co. of N. Am., 239 S.E.2d 902 (Va. 1978).

[39] See, e.g., Universal Underwriters Ins. Co. v. East Central Ala. Ford-Mercury, Inc., 574 So. 2d 716 (Ala. 1990); United Services Auto. Ass'n v. Morris, 741 P.2d 246 (Ariz. 1987) (en banc); Prahm v. Rupp Constr. Co., 277 N.W.2d 389 (Minn. 1979); Fulton v. Woodford, 545 P.2d 979 (Ariz. 1976); Three Sons, Inc. v. Phoenix Ins. Co., 257 N.E.2d 774 (Mass. 1970); Insurance Co. of Pa. v. Protective Ins. Co., 592 N.E.2d 117 (Ill. App. Ct. 1992); McGee v. Superior Court, 221 Cal. Rptr. 421 (Cal. Ct. App. 1985); Dryden Mut. Ins. Co. v. Michaud, 495 N.Y.S.2d 509 (N.Y. App. Div. 1985). This answer also has much support in secondary authorities. See, e.g., Morris, *supra* note 1; Bowdre, *supra* note 1; O'Malley, *supra* note 1; Winiarski, *supra* note 1. But see Silver, *supra* note 1 (urging dual representation model).

[40] See *Restatement (Third) of the Law Governing Lawyers,* §§ 209, 215 (Tentative Draft No. 4, 1991). For analysis of the tentative draft and citation to other commentators' views, see Silver, *supra* note 1, at 1588-89. Although, as Professor Silver points out, the draft does not explicitly repudiate the dual representation model, the absence of any affirmative approval of dual representation is significant, given the notoriety of conflicts in insurance defense and the fact that insurance is discussed in other sections of the draft *Restatement. Id.,* n. 24. The fact that § 215 of the draft uses the headings "Lawyer's Obligation to Third Persons" and "Fee Payment by a Third Person" and in the illustrations treats the insured as a client and the insurer as a third-party payor strongly suggests that the draft *Restatement* endorses the one-client model. Winiarski, *supra* note 1, at 598 n.10.

insureds. In the end, insureds pay the cost of eliminating the conflict through transfer of control of the defense from insurer to insured. In addition, the ability of insureds to choose counsel as experienced in insurance defense is questionable. Less-experienced counsel are likely to be less efficient, which increases costs still further. Furthermore, even if the insured chooses personal counsel, it is possible that the attorney, hoping to secure future business from the insurer, may opt to conduct the litigation in a way that will impress the insurer. This may mean subordinating the insured's interests to those of the insurer.

[4] A Concluding Thought

The debate over the proper responsibilities and obligations of insurance defense counsel appears, in some ways, to be nothing less than a struggle for the soul of liability insurance. From one perspective (labeled here as the "cost-minimization perspective"), the primary purpose of liability insurance is to indemnify insureds against judgments they may incur to third parties for certain kinds of wrongs. Indeed, if indemnity-only insurance could be successfully marketed and sold, this kind of insurance would be the preferred method of fulfilling this primary purpose.

The fatal problem, however, with indemnity-only insurance is one of moral hazard. Except for the limits of the policy, the insurer's obligation is virtually unbounded because the insured has no incentive to minimize the amount of a judgment; the insured's only incentive (except for collateral matters having to do with the reputational loss, encouraging future litigation, etc. that might accompany losing a lawsuit to a plaintiff) is to ensure that the liability does not exceed the policy limits. Thus, the only way an insurer can control its exposure within policy limits is to control the defense of the claim; through control of litigation tactics, choice of counsel, and settlement, the insurer is able to assert downward pressure on its indemnity exposure, presumably to such an extent that the indemnity savings will offset the costs of providing and controlling the defense. Also, by reducing its indemnity obligations across many cases, the insured is able to keep premiums lower for insureds.

Under the cost-minimization perspective, the extent of the defense provided by the insurer should be limited to whatever is efficiently expended to keep the indemnity obligation in check. Also, this perspective contends that insureds prefer limited defenses because premiums are thereby reduced; this assumes, of course, that insureds value lower premiums more than the other interests (e.g., reputational, effect on encouraging other suits, etc.) that a fuller, more expansive defense of a lawsuit might serve.

From the perspective labeled here as the "interest-protection perspective," the insured purchases liability insurance for two reasons: to be protected from the financial calamity associated with a judgment for damage caused a third party; and to be protected from the financial costs associated with both defending against the third-party's claim and protecting in the litigation all of the insured's interests implicated by the claim. From the interest-protection perspective, the insured purchases insurance so that the insured will have the same legal representation he or she would have enjoyed if he or she had hired an attorney directly. Under this perspective, it is assumed that the insured is represented by an attorney whose loyalty is absolute. This does not preclude joint representation as long as the insurer's and insured's interests coalesce, but when a conflict develops, the attorney's loyalty runs solely to the insured. In sum, the persepctive holds that insured purchases full indemnity for covered claims within coverage; and the insured also purchases a full, unlimited defense for these claims.

Adherents to the cost-minimization perspective fear, with considerable justification, that the interest-protection perspective will be too costly. Just as health insurance encourages consumption of medical services,[41] liability (or litigation) insurance encourages the consumption of legal services. Just as the provision of health care needs to be managed in the 1990s, so does, it is argued, the consumption of legal services when a third-party pays the bill. The principle is simple: when the marginal cost of additional services is little or nothing, more of those services will be consumed than if the consumer bears a portion (or all) of those costs. Indeed, adherents of the cost-minimization perspective reason that insureds should have the opportunity to buy streamlined, reduced-coverage policies at a lower cost (i.e., Chevrolets) because not all insureds desire to pay for a luxury version of defense-cost coverage (i.e., Cadillacs). But the lower-cost product cannot even be made available if insurers are not allowed, as a default rule, to control defenses in ways that sometimes run counter to the preferences and interests of insureds (i.e., Chevrolets cannot be sold if courts require insurers to include all of the features of Cadillacs).

Although this assessment is debatable, the cost-minimization perspective appears to be at odds with the weight of commentary and authority; this conventional wisdom expects counsel who represent insureds to subordinate the insurers' interests when those interests come into conflict with the interests of insureds. This conventional wisdom may be driven to a large extent by current liability insurance forms and the process through which these forms are marketed. Notwithstanding long-used provisions that give the insurer the right to control the defense and settle claims as the insurer sees fit, these forms do not clearly manifest to insureds an intention by insureds to provide something less than a defense of all of the insured's interests, and agents and brokers do not routinely inform insureds when policies are sold that the insurer's defense obligation is subject to significant limitations. This may overstate the indefiniteness of current forms and the marketing process, but the opening appears large enough to permit courts to use other well-established insurance law doctrines, such as pro- insured interpretive principles and the doctrine of reasonable expectations, to define the nature of the insurer's (and hence the attorney's) obligations to insureds in more expansive ways than the cost-minimization perspective prefers. This implies that the cost-minimization perspective is not so much contrary to immutable principles of agency and professional responsibility law as it is inconsistent with what most reasonable consumers believe they are purchasing when the insurer promises to provide the insured with a defense against claims asserted by third parties.

A very different picture emerges, however, if one favors a four-corners, literal reading of insurance contracts,[42] and uses this interpretive approach to trump

---

[41] See § 64[c], *supra*.

[42] See § 25A, *supra*.

arguments that expand an insurer's obligations beyond plain language. When this narrower understanding of the insurer's contractual obligations is combined with the thesis that an attorney and client can agree to limit the scope of representation, what the insured is entitled to expect from defense counsel is greatly reduced, and the framework for managing particular conflicts becomes much different than the one provided by the one-client model.

[c] Managing Conflicting Interests

As discussed in the preceding section, the question "to whom is loyalty owed" has no simple answer that is satisfying in all respects. Further insights into the difficulties presented by the tripartite relationship can be gained by analyzing the alternative ways of managing conflicting interests created by a disagreement between an insurer and insured over coverage.

[1] The "Do Nothing" Alternative

One option when a conflict arises is to proceed with the defense and ignore the conflict. In the situation where the insured and insurer have differing views about how the defense should be conducted in circumstances where coverage may hang in the balance, the "do nothing" alternative would have the attorney appointed by the insurer proceed with the defense and leave the question of coverage until a later time. If the plaintiff does not prevail in the action against the insured, the coverage question with respect to the duty to indemnify need not be resolved. Only if the insurer is inclined to argue that it was not obligated to defend the insured and that the insured should reimburse the insurer for the costs of defense is a second round of litigation possible. To rationalize the proposition that this approach does not adversely impact the insured, one must argue that fact-findings in the underlying action tending to show the nonexistence of coverage are not binding on the insured in the coverage action. As the court in *Ferguson v. Birmingham Fire Insurance Co.*[43] reasoned, the insured should be estopped by a fact-finding in the underlying action only if the interests of insurer and insured are identical. This is not the case if a conflict of interest exists. If the insurer cannot gain any collateral estoppel advantage from the result in the underlying action, it can be argued that no reason exists for the attorney selected by the insurer to conduct the litigation in a manner that impairs the insured's interest when a conflict exists.

The "do nothing" alternative, however, is not a viable solution. The attorney appointed by the insurer to represent the insured cannot continue with the defense while purporting to ignore the conflict and competently serve both clients. For example, in settlement negotiations, particularly if it appears possible that a judgment after trial could exceed the policy limits, it is impossible for the attorney to serve both clients' interests fully. If the insurer has a coverage defense, the attorney must make choices at trial and during depositions that will have ramifications for that defense. In short, the conflict of interest never fully disappears, and it simply cannot be ignored.

Thus, if the insurer assumes the defense, the attorney does nothing to deal with the conflict, and the insurer continues with the defense under circumstances in which

---

[43] 460 P.2d 342 (Or. 1969).

it possessed knowledge of facts giving rise to a defense to coverage on the policy, it is universally held that the insurer waives any claim that no coverage exists under the policy.[44] Strictly speaking, it may be that collateral estoppel, properly applied, does not bar the insurer from relitigating fact issues decided in the plaintiff's suit against the insured because of the absence of a true identity of interests.[45] The estoppel that prevents the insurer from denying coverage, however, is not one based on the identity of interests in the action where fact questions are decided. Rather, the estoppel to deny coverage is based on the unfairness inherent in the insurer continuing to represent the insured in circumstances where tactical choices purportedly made on the insured's behalf have direct ramifications for the insurer's interests. If the insurer does nothing to guard against the unfairness likely in such circumstances, the insurer should be estopped to deny coverage in the event the insured is found liable to the plaintiff.

[2]   The "Abandon the Insured" Alternative

In many settings where conflicts of interest arise, the appropriate solution is for the attorney to withdraw. This, of course, provides a solution for the attorney who was appointed as defense counsel. What, however, about the insurer's contractual obligations to the insured to provide a defense? One possible answer is that the insured's unwillingness to waive the conflict constitutes a breach of the duty of cooperation, which discharges the insurer from its obligations under the contract. Breach of cooperation can discharge the insurer's obligations under the policy,[46] but, under the conventional wisdom, an insured's insistence that the insurer not subordinate the insured's legitimate interests in order to pursue its own is not likely to be held by many courts to constitute a breach of the insured's duty of cooperation. Another possible answer is that whenever the insurer cannot control a defense because of a conflict of interest, the insurer has no duty to defend, and the insured must provide a defense at his or her own expense. In the insurance setting, this is often an impractical solution. The difficulty with this answer is that the insurer is obligated to provide a defense, and the mere fact that a conflict arises does not mean that the contractual duty disappears.[47] But appointing another attorney to replace

---

[44] See, e.g., Knox-Tenn Rental Co. v. Home Ins. Co., 2 F.3d 678 (6th Cir. 1993); Peavey Co. v. M/V ANPA, 971 F.2d 1168 (5th Cir. 1992); Pitts By and Through Pitts v. American Sec. Life Ins. Co., 931 F.2d 351 (5th Cir. 1991); Steptore v. Masco Constr. Co., 643 So. 2d 1213 (La. 1994); First United Bank of Bellevue v. First Am. Title Ins. Co., 496 N.W.2d 474 (Neb. 1993); American Home Assur. Co. v. Ozburn-Hessey Storage Co., 817 S.W.2d 672 (Tenn. 1991); Parsons v. Continental Nat'l Am. Group, 550 P.2d 94 (Ariz. 1976); Employers Cas. Co. v. Tilley, 496 S.W.2d 552 (Tex. 1973); Dryden Mut. Ins. Co. v. Michaud, 495 N.Y.S.2d 509 (N.Y. App. Div. 1985).

[45] See Spears v. State Farm Fire & Cas. Ins., 725 S.W.2d 835 (Ark. 1987); American Cas. Co. v. Corum, 885 P.2d 726 (Or. Ct. App. 1994); Cluett v. Medical Protective Co., 829 S.W.2d 822 (Tex. Ct. App. 1992); Insurance Co. of N. Am. v. Whatley, 558 So. 2d 120 (Fla.App. 1990); Wear v. Farmers Ins. Co. of Wash., 745 P.2d 526 (Wash. Ct. App. 1987). See also Progressive Cas. Ins. Co. v. Morris, 603 N.E.2d 1380 (Ind. Ct. App. 1992) (collateral estoppel binds insurer to results of litigation to which its insured was a party as long as insurer had notice and opportunity to control the earlier action).

[46] See § 110, *supra.*

[47] See Hamilton v. State Farm Mut. Ins. Co., 511 P.2d 1020, *aff'd,* 523 P.2d 193 (Wash. Ct. App. 1974).

the attorney who has withdrawn does nothing to resolve the conflict. Assuming a conflict does not give the insurer a right to abandon the insured, an answer that involves something more than withdrawal must be found. But articulating precisely what constitutes this "something more" is no easy feat, and articulating an answer that is not controversial is impossible. The range of possible solutions is discussed in the subsections that follow.

[3]　The Nonwaiver Agreement and Reservation of Rights Notice

If the insurer undertakes to defend the insured (or perhaps even begins to investigate the claim), the possibility exists that the insured might contend that the insurer waived its right to contest coverage or is estopped to deny that coverage exists. To protect itself against the possibility that a waiver or estoppel argument will be asserted, insurers often enter into a nonwaiver agreement with, or send a reservation of rights notice to, the insured.

A nonwaiver agreement is a contract between the insured and insurer in which the insurer agrees to continue with the defense, while the insured agrees that the insurer shall have the right to contest any issues relating to coverage in the event the insured is found liable in the underlying action. In effect and often in form, it is a reservation of rights letter to which the insured has consented. The reasons for using a nonwaiver agreement were explained by one court:

> In many instances, the validity of policy defenses requires protracted investigation. . . . If coverage is not determined at the time the claimant files suit, both the insured and the carrier are at a disadvantage. If the insurance company fails to provide a defense, the claimant may enter a default judgment against the insured. If, however, the company affords representation without some understanding with the insured, the carrier may later be estopped to assert an otherwise valid coverage defense. . . . From the insured's standpoint, the prospect of a default judgment is unacceptable, as is the perhaps unnecessary expense of retaining competent counsel on short notice.
>
> To accommodate the concerns of both the insured and the carrier, the practice of using a nonwaiver agreement has developed. . . . Through this device, the carrier informs the insured of various factors which cast doubt on coverage, reserves the right to assert those matters at a later date, but agrees to provide a defense in the interim. This practice not only serves the interests of the parties to the insurance policy but is helpful to claimants and the courts as well because the claimant's tort litigation may proceed expeditiously. Indeed, in most instances, the coverage issues are amicably resolved along with the tort claims. It is unlikely that such settlements would be reached if the carrier could not reserve its right to ultimately disclaim liability.[48]

The nonwaiver agreement attempts to solve the problem of potential or actual adversity in the dual representation situation by securing, in effect, the consent of all parties to the joint representation despite the existence of a potential or actual conflict.

---

[48] Draft Systems, Inc. v. Alspach, 756 F.2d 293, 296 (3d Cir. 1985).

The nonwaiver agreement is, however, not a perfect solution. First, if the attorney submits the document to the insured with a recommendation that it be signed, the attorney may be hurting the client's interests, because it may be in the insured's best interests to demand that the insurer concede the existence of coverage immediately. Furthermore, the validity of the agreement depends upon whether both clients understand the nature of all potential conflicts, and this depends on whether the insured has received a full explanation. There is little cause for confidence that a full explanation can be given by an attorney who has two clients with adverse interests. Second, the nonwaiver agreement does not eliminate the conflict. For example, in settlement negotiations on the claim in the underlying action, the insurer may be reluctant to settle the case because it knows it will have a second chance to escape payment if it raises the coverage question in a subsequent action by the insured on the policy. A nonwaiver agreement allows joint representation; it does not solve conflicts. Third, the insured may refuse to sign the nonwaiver agreement. If this happens, some insurers send a reservation of rights notice, but this approach is not without problems of its own.

A reservation of rights notice is simply a unilateral notice sent by the insurer to the insured stating that the insurer reserves the right to contest coverage despite its undertaking to investigate the claim and defend the insured. The basic purpose of a reservation of rights notice is to eliminate the possibility that the insurer will meet the argument that it waived its right to deny coverage or to withdraw from the defense simply because it undertook to defend the insured. In this respect, the reservation of rights is weaker than the nonwaiver agreement because the reservation, unlike the agreement, does not demonstrate the insured's consent to the insurer's conditional representation.

When coverage is questionable, most courts favor an insurer defending the insured under a reservation of rights, and perhaps seeking a declaratory judgment[49] to determine the insurer's obligations.[50] In many situations, the representation will proceed without difficulty. As explained by one court, "[m]erely because the insurer and the insured have divergent interests when the insurer seeks to defend under a reservation of rights does not necessarily mean that appointed counsel also has conflicting interests. If appointed counsel makes it clear at the outset of his engagement that he is going to be involved only in the defense of the liability claim, not in coverage issues, and that his client is the insured, not the insurer, conflicts should be rare."[51] However, other courts have held that it is always a conflict of interest for the insurer to represent the insured under a reservation of rights.[52] When the

---

[49] This is discussed in the next subsection.

[50] See, e.g., Commercial Union Ins. Co. v. International Flavors & Fragrances, 822 F.2d 267 (4th Cir. 1987); Cay Divers, Inc. v. Raven, 812 F.2d 866 (3d Cir. 1987); Montrose Chem. Corp. v. Superior Court, 861 P.2d 1153 (Cal. 1993); First United Bank of Bellevue v. First Am. Title Ins. Co., 496 N.W.2d 474 (Neb. 1993).

[51] CHI of Alaska, Inc. v. Employers Reins. Corp., 844 P.2d 1113, 1116 (Alaska 1993).

[52] See, e.g., Fireman's Fund Ins. Co. v. Waste Management of Wisconsin, Inc., 777 F.2d 366 (7th Cir. 1985); New York State Urban Dev. Corp. v. VSL Corp., 738 F.2d 61 (2d Cir. 1984); Continental Ins. Co. v. Bayless & Roberts, Inc., 608 P.2d 281 (Alaska 1980); American Home Assur. Co. v. Weissman, 434 N.Y.S.2d 410 (N.Y. App. Div. 1981); but see McGough

insurer reserves the right to contest coverage, a possibility exists that the insurer might be less interested in offering the insured a full defense, since it might later protect itself by prevailing on the coverage question.[53] If this argument is credited, the only way the conflict can be resolved is for the insured to select his or her own counsel and have the insurer pay the bill. Yet even here, the attorney selected by the insured would know that the insurer is paying the bill, and this attorney, to impress the insurer and perhaps obtain future business, may conduct the defense in a manner that favors the insurer's interests.

One court has dealt with the perceived problems of an insurer representing the insured under a reservation of rights by imposing an "enhanced" duty of good faith on the insurer in such a situation. In *Tank v. State Farm Fire & Casualty Co.*,[54] the Washington Supreme Court opined:

> We have stated that the duty of good faith of an insurer requires fair dealing and equal consideration for the insured's interests. . . . We find, however, that the potential conflicts of interest between insurer and insured inherent in [a defense under reservation of rights] mandate an even higher standard: an insurance company must fulfill an enhanced obligation to its insured as part of its duty of good faith. Failure to satisfy this enhanced obligation may result in liability of the company, or retained defense counsel, or both.[55]

The court said that this "enhanced" obligation could be met by the insurer's fulfillment of specific criteria: thoroughly investigating the plaintiff's claim; retaining competent defense counsel for the insured; fully informing the insured of all developments relevant to the coverage and the progress of the lawsuit; refraining from doing anything that would demonstrate a greater concern for the insurer's financial interest than the insured's; and conducting the defense with absolute loyalty to the insured. In addition, the court imposed distinct obligations on defense counsel representing the insured. Defense counsel is required to give absolute loyalty to the insured, to keep the insured fully informed of developments, including any settlement offers, and to inform the insured of conflicts and to resolve them in the insured's favor.[56]

Ultimately, whether one is comfortable with a reservation of rights approach depends on one's opinion about the ability of attorneys designated by insurers to serve insureds loyally. If one refuses to presume that attorneys who appear on behalf of insureds can give undivided loyalty to the insured, the reservation of rights is not a correct answer. If one discounts the possibility that an attorney who has a close working relationship with the insurer and whose compensation comes from the insurer will inevitably be subject to subtle influences to favor the insurer, the reservation of rights approach provides an answer to the conflict. The reservation of rights

---

v. Insurance Co. of N. Am., 691 P.2d 738 (Ariz. 1984) (insured has no right to require the insurer to provide defense without reserving rights).

[53] See State v. Dowd, 858 S.W.2d 307 (Mo. Ct. App. 1993).

[54] 715 P.2d 1133 (Wash. 1986).

[55] 715 P.2d at 1137.

[56] 715 P.2d at 1137–38. *Tank* was approved and adopted in L & S Roofing Supply Co. v. St. Paul Fire & Marine Ins. Co., 521 So. 2d 1298 (Ala. 1987).

approach has the added benefit of relieving the insurer of the obligation to pay for separate counsel for the insured and thereby surrender control of the defense; such a drastic response would be reserved for special circumstances, such as where two parties are covered by the same insurer or where proof of certain facts would shift liability from the insurer to the insured.[57]

If a reservation of rights approach is viewed as an appropriate resolution of the conflict of interest, the reservation of rights notice must be given promptly to the insured — "within a reasonable time" or "as soon as practical." Failure to transmit the reservation of rights notice in a timely manner will render the reservation ineffective.[58] Furthermore, the reservation of rights must inform the insured of all of the potential defenses to coverage that the insurer has identified in its analysis of the claim; potential defenses known to the insurer but omitted might be considered waived.[59] This does not, however, preclude the insurer from supplementing its reasons for denying coverage should new information be discovered that adds to the insurer's coverage defenses.[60] If the insurer seeks to enter into a nonwaiver agreement and the insured refuses, the insurer will probably send a reservation of rights notice. Some courts have held that the subsequent sending of the reservation after unsuccessful efforts to achieve a nonwaiver agreement has no effect unless the insured consents to it. Consent will be found in the insured's silence only if the reservation of rights letter advises the insured of the right to reject the insurer's defense of the case under the reservation and secure his or her own attorney.[61] Other courts have held that the insured's failure to respond to the reservation of rights letter constitutes acquiescence to its terms.[62]

[4]   Declaratory Judgment

Another approach for resolving the conflict of interest is the declaratory judgment action in which the insurer and insured are separately represented and the coverage or obligation-to-defend question is presented directly.[63] Assuming the declaratory judgment action reaches judgment first, the conflict is eliminated. Bifurcation of the underlying action and the coverage questions avoids the problems of defending under a reservation of rights. It also avoids the situation that can arise if the plaintiff recovers and the insurer pays the proceeds to the plaintiff; if the coverage issues are subsequently decided adversely to the insured, the insurer may not be able to

---

57 See Pekin Ins. Co. v. Home Ins. Co., 479 N.E.2d 1078 (Ill. App. Ct. 1985).

58 See, e.g., Allstate Ins. Co. v. Gross, 265 N.E.2d 736 (N.Y. 1970).

59 See, e.g., Intel Corp. v. Hartford Acc. & Indem. Co., 952 F.2d 1551 (9th Cir. 1991); Canadian Ins. Co. of Cal. v. Rusty's Island Chip Co., 42 Cal. Rptr. 505 (Cal. Ct. App. 1995); American States Ins. Co. v. National Cycle, Inc., 631 N.E.2d 1292 (Ill. App. Ct. 1994).

60 See, e.g., State Farm Fire & Cas. Co. v. Finney, 770 P.2d 460 (Kan. 1989).

61 See Merchant's Indem. Corp. v. Eggleston, 179 A.2d 505 (N.J. 1962).

62 See Pacific Indem. Co. v. ACEL Delivery, Inc., 485 F.2d 1169 (5th Cir. 1973), *cert. denied*, 415 U.S. 921 (1974); see generally Diamond Service Co. v. Utica Mut. Ins. Co., 476 A.2d 648 (D.C. 1984).

63 See, e.g., Clemens v. Wilcox, 392 N.W.2d 863 (Minn. 1986); Mowry v. Badger State Mut. Cas. Co., 385 N.W.2d 171 (Wis. 1986); Pekin Ins. Co. v. Home Ins. Co., 479 N.E.2d 1078 (Ill. App. Ct. 1985); Richmond v. Georgia Farm Mut. Ins. Co., 231 S.E.2d 245 (Ga. Ct. App. 1976).

recoup proceeds already paid. Moreover, the insurer is saved the cost of defending the tort action.

It has been held, however, that a declaratory judgment action cannot be commenced until a liability is imposed on the insured in the underlying action.[64] The difficulty with this view is that the primary purpose of the declaratory judgment action is to enable the insurer to avoid the costs of defense for a claim outside coverage; but if the declaratory judgment action is not appropriate until after the insurer incurs these costs, the advantage of the procedure is lost. In essence, these courts reason that judicial machinery should not be invoked until it is clear that the insured has suffered a loss, i.e., a judgment of liability in the underlying action. Where coverage is uncertain, the insurer should defend the underlying action, rather than having the system of justice bear the costs of a declaratory judgment action when whether the insured owes liability to anyone remains unresolved.

In that event, it is as beneficial for the insurer to defend the action under a reservation of rights, which means the insurer's defense obligation is performed, while allowing the insurer to save its coverage defenses for later determination. If, of course, the underlying action results in a judgment of no liability, the need for the declaratory judgment action is eliminated. Also, if the judgment turns out to be very small, the insurer may elect to pay it rather than incur the costs of seeking the declaratory judgment.

One difficulty with the declaratory judgment alternative is that the action, like any civil lawsuit, could take a long time. Some courts look favorably upon requests to expedite the declaratory judgment action or delay the tort action for a reasonable period of time, assuming the requests are made well in advance of the time the tort action is set for trial.

A further difficulty arises out of the considerable uncertainty in the cases regarding what issues may appropriately be considered in the declaratory judgment action. A number of cases have held that a declaratory judgment should not be entered if it depends on the resolution of fact questions that are at issue in the underlying action.[65] This holding is variously justified: the insured should not be

---

[64] See, e.g., Central Sur. & Ins. Corp. v. Anderson, 445 S.W.2d 514 (Tex. 1969). See also Country Ins. Co. v. Agricultural Development, Inc., 695 P.2d 346 (Idaho 1984) (insurer should not bring declaratory judgment action after assuming insured's defense under reservation of rights when action would involve questions of negligence and proximate cause).

[65] See, e.g., Morris v. Farmers Ins. Exch., 771 P.2d 1206 (Wyo. 1989); St. Paul Fire & Marine Ins. Co. v. Pryeski, 438 A.2d 282 (Md. 1981); Allstate Ins. Co. v. Novak, 313 N.W.2d 636 (Neb. 1981); California Ins. Guar. Ass'n v. Superior Court, 283 Cal. Rptr. 104 (Cal. Ct. App. 1991). See also American Motorist Ins. Co. v. Artra Group, Inc., 659 A.2d 1295 (Md. 1995) (whether insured had duty to indemnify could be determined in declaratory judgment action where, inter alia, no issues to be determined in underlying action were intertwined with coverage issue); United States Fid. & Guar. Ins. Co. v. Jiffy Cab Co., 637 N.E.2d 1167 (Ill. App. Ct. 1994) (declaratory judgment action was not premature; coverage issue was "wholly separable" from issues involved in underlying action). Compare Allstate Ins. Co. v. Conde, 595 So. 2d 1005 (Fla. Dist. Ct. App. 1992) (insurer could bring declaratory judgment action to resolve disputed factual issues determinative of coverage that were raised by alternative, mutually exclusive allegations against its insured).

required to try the fact questions twice; trying two lawsuits is not an efficient use of judicial resources; the insured does not receive the full measure of the defense that the insured purchased; and the holding in the declaratory judgment action might collaterally estop the parties in the underlying action on certain fact questions.[66]

From the insurer's perspective, the declaratory judgment has other potential disadvantages. First, the declaratory judgment procedure can increase the insurer's expenses. If the insurer loses the declaratory judgment action, the insurer will probably have to pay the insured for its defense costs incurred in defending the action. If the tort action is ultimately settled prior to resolution of the declaratory judgment action — and many such claims will be disposed of in this manner, any expenses incurred in the declaratory judgment proceeding were, in hindsight, unnecessary. Second, the third-party victim may discover evidence in the declaratory judgment action adverse to the insured's interests; this information would eventually be discovered anyway, but the timing of the discovery could adversely affect settlement of the underlying action. Third, the insured is more likely to become a hostile adversary to the insurer as a result of the insurer's filing an action against the insured.[67]

[5] Joint Lawsuit to Determine Coverage and the Validity of the Plaintiff's Claim

Most of the objections to the separate declaratory judgment approach can be met by combining the liability question and the coverage question into one lawsuit. The insurer is allowed to defend the insured, but the insurer is also made a party to the suit in which the tort claim against the insured is being adjudicated. The insurer in this action is entitled to argue that the claim is outside coverage; the insured would be expected to argue that the loss was within the coverage.

One problem with this approach is that the insured does not get the full defense for which the insured bargained. On the one hand, the insured must defend against the victim's claim, while on the other hand the insured must attempt to hold the insurer responsible for it. Similarly, the insurer must take inconsistent positions: in the underlying action, the insurer defends the insured, but in the coverage action, the insurer argues that it has no obligation to the insured.[68] These objections, it would seem, are substantially met if the insured is allowed to choose his or her own attorney, who is then reimbursed by the insurer. The insured receives an unconstrained defense, and all of the issues are settled in one proceeding.

One problem from the insurer's perspective that this approach cannot solve involves the insurer's reluctance to appear before the jury in its own name. The presence of the insurance company in the action arguably has the potential to inflate the amount recovered by the plaintiff and perhaps even cause a pro-plaintiff verdict where one would not otherwise occur.

---

[66] See, e.g., Stout v. Grain Dealers Mut. Ins. Co., 307 F.2d 521 (4th Cir. 1962); All-Star Ins. Corp. v. The Steel Bar, Inc., 324 F. Supp. 160 (N.D. Ind. 1971).

[67] For further discussion of the pros and cons of the declaratory judgment action from the insurer's perspective, see Robert S. Treece & Richard D. Hall, *When Do You File a Declaratory Judgment Action?* 53 Ins. Counsel J. 396 (1986).

[68] See Western Fire Ins. Co. v. Persons, 393 N.W.2d 234 (Minn. Ct. App. 1986).

[6]   Separate or Independent Counsel for Insured

When the insurer and insured encounter a conflict that cannot be reconciled, and when no other procedure seems adequate or appropriate, the remaining alternative is for the insurer to supply separate or independent counsel for the insured. This alternative is itself a collection of various related options.

[i]   The Separate Counsel Approach

When a conflict of interest arises, some courts require the insurer to hire separate counsel for the insured, who participates in the defense of the action with the attorney designated by the insurer.[69] Other courts contemplate that the insurer will advise the insured to select private counsel, to be paid by the insurer, and that such counsel can assist the counsel selected by the insurer in defending the insured.[70] This latter approach is usually followed when the complaint against the insured alleges claims both within and outside coverage or when the complaint seeks damages exceeding the policy limits. The separate counsel for the insured represents the insured's interests, and presumably ensures that the defense is conducted in a manner than does not impair the insured's interests.

The weakness of the separate counsel approach is that it does nothing to resolve the conflict of interest. The approach offers no explanation for how tactical decisions in the defense of the action are made. Ultimately, someone must have control of the defense. Merely allowing the insured's attorney input into decisions does not ensure that the choices made will be in the insured's interest. Control of the lawsuit remains with the insurer; ultimate decision-making authority cannot be divided between two parties.

[ii]   Independent Counsel for Insured

An alternative to the separate counsel approach has the insurer designate independent counsel for the insured, relinquish control of the defense, and authorize the attorney appointed for the insured to make all decisions on behalf of the insured without supervision by the insurer.[71] The independent counsel is instructed not to seek to further the insurer's interests and is asked by the insurer not to consider or comment on any questions of coverage. The underlying, fundamental premise is that the attorney retained to represent the insured in the underlying action owes undeviating allegiance to the insured.[72] Stated otherwise, the attorney's retention is "limited to defending the liability claim."[73] The insurer simply pays the fees of

---

[69] See Bogard v. Employers Cas. Co., 210 Cal. Rptr. 578 (Cal. Ct. App. 1985).

[70] See, e.g., Western Cas. & Sur. Co. v. Herman, 405 F.2d 121 (8th Cir. 1968); Employers' Fire Ins. Co. v. Beals, 240 A.2d 397 (R.I. 1968).

[71] See, e.g., United States Fidelity & Guar. Co. v. Louis A. Roser Co., 585 F.2d 934 (8th Cir. 1978); American Motorists Ins. Co. v. Trane Co., 544 F.Supp. 669 (W.D. Wis. 1982), aff'd, 718 F.2d 842 (7th Cir. 1983); Transamerica Ins. Co. v. Keown, 451 F. Supp. 397 (D.N.J. 1978); Public Serv. Mut. Ins. Co. v. Goldfarb, 425 N.E.2d 810 (N.Y. 1981). See generally Annot., *Duty of Insurer to Pay for Independent Counsel When Conflict of Interest Exists Between Insured and Insurer,* 50 A.L.R.4th 932 (1986).

[72] See Farmers Ins. Co. v. Vagnozzi, 675 P.2d 703 (Ariz. 1983).

[73] Mallen & Smith, *supra* note 2, § 23.16, at 402. For a proposed set of guiding principles based on the premise that the attorney has an absolute duty of loyalty to the insured within

the counsel, and the attorney has no attorney-client relationship with the insurer. One rationale for this answer is that the insurer's contractual right to control the defense is lost whenever the insurer is subject to a conflict of interest or divided loyalties.[74]

One potential difficulty with this approach is that the attorney chosen by the insurer may, despite the insurer's instructions, be unable to give undivided loyalty to the insured. Attorneys who defend insureds for insurance companies often develop strong personal and professional relationships with the insurer, and this may make it difficult for the attorney to make a hard decision on behalf of the insured that is contrary to the insurer's interests. One court explained it this way in the context of automobile liability insurance: "Lawyers employed to defend motor vehicle cases generally are specialists who have for many years depended upon the insurance industry for their livelihood. To suggest that they forget the client who employs them and affords them a living in favor of an isolated client they may never again represent, or even see, has only an idealistic image to support it."[75] Moreover, the insured may not trust the insurer to designate an attorney. Because of this potential difficulty, some courts go one additional step and allow the insured to designate the attorney who will represent the insured. The inability of insurer and insured to agree on counsel is, by this analysis, also a conflict of interest; since the insurer promises to give the insured a full defense, this duty can be satisfied, it is argued, only by allowing the insured to choose an attorney who will give undivided allegiance to the insured and to reimburse the insured for these expenses.[76] From the insurer's perspective, however, the assumption that attorneys selected by insurers to represent insureds will not discharge their duties ethically belies reality. One court has described the suggestion that lawyers cannot maintain complete loyalty to insureds, even when the interests of insurer and insured are not entirely coterminous, as "impertinent, if not scandalous."[77] In addition, insurers have a more practical objection to letting the insured choose his or her own attorney: giving the insured

the scope of defending the liability claim, see O'Malley, *supra* note 1, at 521- 25. Compare Lysick v. Walcom, 65 Cal. Rptr. 406 (Cal. Ct. App. 1968) (parties may create a relationship in which the attorney owes no duty to the insured in matters of settlement; thus, if attorney fails to protect insured's interests in settlement, insured's action is against the insurer, not the attorney).

[74] See Orion Ins. Co. v. General Elec. Co., 493 N.Y.S.2d 397 (N.Y. Sup. Ct. 1985).

[75] Hartford Acc. & Indem. Co. v. Foster, 528 So. 2d 255, 271-72 (Miss. 1988). This court ultimately held, however, in favor of the dual representation model: "[i]t is the attorney's ethical obligation to have undiluted loyalty to both clients. It is just as repugnant ethically to ask him to ignore the interest of his insurance carrier client as it would be the other way around." 528 So. 2d at 272.

[76] See, e.g., Illinois Masonic Med. Ctr. v. Turegum Ins. Co., 522 N.E.2d 611 (Ill. App. Ct. 1988); Baron v. Home Ins. Co., 492 N.Y.S.2d 50 (N.Y. Sup. Ct. 1985).

[77] Siebert Oxidermo, Inc. v. Shields, 430 N.E.2d 401 (Ind. Ct. App. 1982), *aff'd,* 446 N.E.2d 332 (Ind. 1983). See also Federal Ins. Co. v. X-Rite, Inc., 748 F. Supp. 1223, 1229 (W.D. Mich. 1990) ("The Court is unable to conclude that Michigan law professes so little confidence in the integrity of the bar of this state.")

(Matthew Bender & Co., Inc.)   (Pub.837)

free rein in choosing an attorney may increase costs without improving the quality of the representation.[78]

Various methods of designating the attorney for the insured are possible. For example, the insurer could submit a list of attorneys to the insured, who would then choose one; or the insured could submit a list of attorneys to the insurer who would then select one;[79] or the insured could select any attorney he or she desires.[80] Some insurers have begun to put clauses in their policies giving them the right to participate in the selection of counsel in the event a conflict arises, and these clauses have been enforced.[81] Where the insured has the right to designate independent counsel, this choice must be exercised reasonably.[82] As one court explained, the insured is obligated to select a competent attorney, and one who is "willing to engage in ethical billing practices susceptible to review at a standard stricter than that of the market place."[83] Moreover, the insurer is obligated only to pay the reasonable expenses of independent counsel, not all expenses.[84] Regardless of the specific procedure employed, the basic concept is for the insurer to reserve all coverage defenses to itself, while at the same time the insured receives a full defense to the claim asserted in the liability action.[85]

This was the solution approved in *San Diego Navy Federal Credit Union v. Cumis Insurance Society, Inc.,*[86] a 1984 California decision. In *Cumis,* the insureds tendered the defense of an action seeking $750,000 in general and $6.5 million in punitive damages to their insurer. The insurer accepted the defense and retained counsel to defend the action, but the insurer notified the insureds that it was reserving the right to deny coverage at a later date since the insureds' policy did not cover punitive damages. After receiving this letter, the insureds retained independent counsel and submitted a claim to the insurer for the fees and costs so incurred. The insurer agreed to pay two invoices for fees, but refused thereafter to make additional payments. The trial court ruled that the insurer was required to pay the legal fees and costs incurred as a result of hiring independent counsel, and the appellate court

---

[78] See Hartford Acc. & Indem. Co. v. Foster, 528 So. 2d 255, 269 (Miss. 1988) ("Because the company is footing the bill for the defense, and will be obligated to pay any judgment rendered (if it does not settle the case), it is clearly entitled to select the attorney and conduct the defense.")

[79] See New York State Urban Development Corp. v. VSL Corp., 738 F.2d 61 (2d Cir. 1984).

[80] See, e.g., Ladner v. American Home Assur. Co., 607 N.Y.S.2d 296 (N.Y. Sup. Ct. 1994).

[81] See, e.g., New York State Urban Development Corp. v. VSL Corp, 738 F.2d 61 (2d Cir. 1984); Butler v. Maryland Cas. Co., 147 F. Supp. 391 (D.C. La. 1956); Keithan v. Massachusetts Bonding & Ins. Co., 267 A.2d 660 (Conn. 1970); Ricciardi v. Bernasconi, 253 A.2d 487 (N.J. 1969).

[82] See, e.g., CHI of Alaska, Inc. v. Employers Reins. Corp., 844 P.2d 1113 (Alaska 1993).

[83] See Center Foundation v. Chicago Ins. Co., 278 Cal. Rptr. 13, 20-21 (Cal. Ct. App. 1991).

[84] See, e.g., Boyd Bros. Transp. Co. v. Fireman's Fund Ins. Cos., 729 F.2d 1407 (11th Cir. 1984); Prahm v. Rupp Constr. Co., 277 N.W.2d 389 (Minn. 1979); Maryland Cas. Co. v. Peppers, 355 N.E.2d 30 (Ill. 1976).

[85] See also Fireman's Fund v. Waste Management of Wis., 777 F.2d 366 (7th Cir. 1985).

[86] 208 Cal. Rptr. 494 (Cal. Ct. App. 1984).

affirmed. The court reasoned that if the insurer must pay for the cost of defense, and if the insured is entitled to control the defense in the event of a conflict, it follows that the insurer must pay for a defense conducted by independent counsel.

The court in *Cumis* recognized that the conflict between the interests of insurer and insured was inescapable:

> Although issues of coverage under the policy are not actually litigated in the third party suit, this does not detract from the force of these opposing interests as they operate on the attorney selected by the insurer, who has a dual agency status. Here, it is uncontested that the basis for liability, if any, might rest on conduct excluded by the terms of the insurance policy. [The attorneys] will have to make certain decisions at the trial of the [underlying] action which may either benefit or harm the insureds. For example, [they] will have to seek or oppose special verdicts, the answers to which may benefit the insureds by finding nonexcluded conduct, and harm either [the insurer's] position on coverage or the insureds by finding excluded conduct. These decisions are numerous and varied. Each time one of them must be made, the lawyer is placed in the dilemma of helping one client concerning insurance coverage and harming the other.[87]

The court understood that the same problems exist in settlement: "On the advisability of settlement, [the attorneys] represented clients with conflicting interests. No matter how honest the intentions, counsel cannot discharge inconsistent duties."[88] The court also noted that the attorney appointed by the insurer to defend the insured depends upon the insurer for future business, and that the attorney might be tempted to shape the insured's defense so as to place the risk of loss on the insured.

As a result, the court held that the Canons of Ethics at a minimum require counsel appointed by the insurer to explain to the insured the full implications of joint representation whenever the insurer reserves its right to deny coverage at a later date. According to the court, if the insured does not consent to the continued representation (and, as noted above, it is difficult to understand why the insured would consent), the insurer must pay the reasonable cost of independent counsel hired by the insured.

Cumis implicitly rejected the concept of an independent counsel selected by the insurer to serve solely the insured's interests.[89] In many jurisdictions, it is assumed that the conflict can be resolved by the insurer reserving its rights to deny coverage yet retaining control over the litigation by hiring counsel for the sole purpose of defending the insured in the underlying suit. However, *Cumis* assumes that the attorney's ongoing relationship with the insurer creates an incentive to favor the carrier, an incentive which cannot be overcome simply by telling the attorney to take only the insured's interests into account. After *Cumis,* then, the insurer has

---

[87] 208 Cal. Rptr. at 498–99.

[88] 208 Cal. Rptr. at 499.

[89] See Federal Ins. Co. v. X-Rite, Inc., 748 F. Supp. 1223, 1227 (W.D. Mich. 1990) ("*Cumis* is representative of a growing body of case law which would give the insured an absolute right to choose counsel where a conflict exists"; court ultimately rejects *Cumis* approach).

something of a dilemma: if the insurer continues to represent the insured without sending a reservation of rights letter, the insurer will be held to have waived the right to contest coverage. On the other hand, if the insurer reserves rights, it runs the substantial risk of losing control of the defense. In fact, extending from the logic of *Cumis,* if the insurer reserves its rights, it arguably should not be able to retain any right to participate in the selection of counsel and must instead surrender this right to the insured.

Subsequent decisions in California have limited the effect of *Cumis.* In *McGee v. Superior Court,* [90] decided only one year later, the court held that the rule of *Cumis* applies only when the insurer's reservation of rights is "based on the nature of the insured's conduct, which as developed at trial would affect the determination of coverage." [91] The holding of *McGee,* which had the effect of narrowing the reach of *Cumis,* [92] was subsequently codified by the California legislature. Section 2860 of the California Civil Code states in pertinent part: [93]

> (a) If the provisions of a policy of insurance impose a duty to defend upon an insurer and a conflict of interest arises which creates a duty on the part of the insurer to provide independent counsel to the insured, the insurer shall provide independent counsel to represent the insured . . .

> (b) For purposes of this section, a conflict of interest does not exist as to allegations or facts in the litigation for which the insurer denies coverage; however, when an insurer reserves its rights on a given issue and the outcome of that coverage issue can be controlled by counsel first retained by the insurer for the defense of the claim, a conflict of interest may exist. No conflict of interest shall be deemed to exist as to allegations of punitive damages or be deemed to exist solely because an insured is sued for an amount in excess of the insurance policy limits.

Thus, so-called "*Cumis* counsel" is required in circumstances where the manner in which the insurer's retained counsel defends the action will affect the underlying coverage dispute between insurer and insured. [94] Similarly, when the insured refuses

---

[90] 221 Cal. Rptr. 421 (Cal. Ct. App. 1985).

[91] 221 Cal. Rptr. at 423.

[92] See 221 Cal. Rptr. at 423 ("petitioner asserts that whenever an insurer proposes to provide a defense under a reservation of rights based on noncoverage, there is a conflict of interest between the insurer and the insured which gives counsel selected and paid by the insurer to represent the insured a conflict of interest disqualifying him or her from representing the insured. Taken out of context, there is some language in the rather wordy *Cumis* opinion that might be so understood. However, that is not the holding of the *Cumis* decision. Nor could it be.")

[93] The requirements of the statute have been the subject of further litigation. See, e.g., Western Polymer Tech. Inc. v. Reliance Ins. Co., 38 Cal. Rptr.2d 78 (Cal. Ct. App. 1995) (neither statute nor case law provides that independent counsel's control of defense prevents insurer from exercising right under policy to settle claim as insurer deems expedient); Handy v. First Interstate Bank of Cal., 16 Cal. Rptr.2d 770 (Cal. Ct. App. 1993) (arbitration of *Cumis* counsel fees under statute was improper).

[94] See, e.g., Golden Eagle Ins. Co. v. Foremost Ins. Co., 25 Cal. Rptr.2d 242, 256 (Cal. Ct. App. 1993).

to consent to a settlement in excess of the policy limits in circumstances where the insurer favors the settlement, a conflict exists.[95] Some courts, however, stress that independent counsel should not be appointed until there is an "actual" conflict of interest, as opposed to an "appearance" of a conflict of interest.[96] A California appellate court decision endorsed this same idea in 1988: "[N]ot every reservation of rights creates a conflict of interest; rather, the existence of a conflict depends upon the grounds on which the insurer is denying coverage. . . If the reservation of rights arises because of coverage questions which depend upon the insured's own conduct, a conflict exists . . . On the other hand, where the reservation of rights is based on coverage disputes which have nothing to do with the issues being litigated in the underlying action, there is no conflict of interest requiring independent counsel."[97] Moreover, it has been held that the right to independent counsel is a right belonging to the insured, which the insured may assert or waive, as he or she chooses.[98]

To summarize, many courts now hold that when the interests of the insurer and insured conflict and the insured is unwilling to accept joint representation, the insured is entitled to independent counsel who will participate and protect his or her interests in the underlying action, all at the expense of the insurer.[99] Some courts go further and hold that if the insured is unwilling to accept joint representation in the conflict situation, the insured can select his or her own counsel, to be paid for by the insurer, and this counsel is allowed to control the defense.[100] Other courts have held that the choice of counsel can be retained by the insurer, and that the insured is not entitled to designate the counsel, although the insurer must exercise the selection in good faith.[101]

---

[95] Id., 25 Cal. Rptr.2d at 258.

[96] See, e.g., Mutual Serv. Cas. Ins. Co. v. Luetmer, 474 N.W.2d 365 (Minn. Ct. App. 1991) (stating that insurer wished to be informed of progress of litigation in main action while also litigating a declaratory judgment action on the question of coverage did not establish actual conflict of interest).

[97] Foremost Ins. Co. v. Wilks, 253 Cal. Rptr. 596, 601-02 (Cal. Ct. App. 1989).

[98] See McGee v. Superior Court, 221 Cal. Rptr. 421 (Cal. Ct. App. 1985).

[99] See CHI of Alaska, Inc. v. Employers Reins. Corp., 844 P.2d 1113 (Alaska 1993); Prashker v. United States Guar. Co., 136 N.E.2d 871 (N.Y. 1956); San Diego Navy Fed. Credit Union v. Cumis Ins. Soc'y, Inc., 208 Cal. Rptr. 494 (Cal. Ct. App. 1984); Annot., *Duty Of Insurer To Pay Independent Counsel When Conflict Of Interest Exists Between Insured and Insurer,* 50 A.L.R. 4th 932 (1987).

[100] See, e.g., Steyer v. Westvaco Corp., 450 F. Supp. 384 (D.Md. 1978); Maryland Cas. Co. v. Peppers, 355 N.E.2d 24 (Ill. 1976); Brohawn v. Transamerica Ins. Co., 347 A.2d 842 (Md. 1975). The possible parallel between the costs of defense counsel and health-insurance reimbursement of physicians' services should not be overlooked. In health care, one can surrender the choice of physician in exchange for a lower health insurance premium (i.e., enroll in an HMO), or one can retain the choice of physician but pay more for the insurance and probably also be subject to some kind of post-utilization review.

[101] See, e.g., Federal Ins. Co. v. X-Rite, Inc., 748 F. Supp. 1223 (W.D. Mich. 1990).

[d]　Particular Conflicts and Their Resolution

[1]　Claims Exceeding the Policy Limits

When a plaintiff-victim makes a claim against the insured in excess of the policy limits, a potential conflict of interest between insurer and insured automatically exists.[102] The insured desires to avoid an excess judgment and thus has an incentive to settle the case within the policy limits, if possible. The insurer, on the other hand, will not be responsible for the excess judgment and thus does not share the insured's special concern for settling the case within policy limits. Since the insurer's exposure is limited, the insurer is more likely to be willing to litigate the case in the hope of securing a zero-liability judgment. For the insured, the possibility of an excess judgment may make litigation an unacceptably risky strategy.

One of the leading cases in this area is *Lysick v. Walcom*,[103] a 1968 California decision. The insured's liability policy had limits of $10,000. The insurer refused to settle a lawsuit against the insured, and a judgment of $225,000 was entered against the insured. The insured charged the insurer with breach of the duty to settle and the attorney with malpractice. The insurer settled the insured's claim against it, but the attorney chose to litigate the malpractice claim. He prevailed in the trial court, but the appellate court reversed the verdict. The court said that the attorney owed both the insurer and insured a "high duty of care" and that this duty was breached when the attorney failed to communicate with the insured concerning settlement negotiations and failed to insist that the insurer pay the full policy limits in settlement.[104]

The inadequacies of the dual representation approach are apparent in *Lysick*. If the attorney had insisted that the insurer pay the full policy limits, the attorney would have been making a request to the insurer contrary to the insurer's interests. Making such a demand upon the insurer could expose the insurer to a bad faith claim if the insurer chose to refuse it. In such a situation, it is simply not possible for a single attorney to serve the interests of both clients fully. Under the ethical rules, if the insured had consented to the attorney's representation despite the conflict and with a full understanding of the conflict, the dual representation (but not, of course, the failure to communicate) would have been permissible. However, this solution does not confront the fact that the insured contracts for a full defense, and the insurer's

---

[102] Compare Hartford Acc. & Indem. Co. v. Foster, 528 So. 2d 255 (Miss. 1988) ("a damage claim beyond policy limits in and of itself presents no ethical problem to the lawyer employed to defend the case, because his employment is for one of two purposes: either win the case outright, or keep the damages as low as possible. Everything he does in fulfillment of either objective must of necessity benefit both clients"; when, however, a coverage question is presented, defense counsel "is presented with an ethical question up front"); Blanchard v. State Farm Fire & Cas. Co., 2 Cal. Rptr.2d 884 (Cal. Ct. App. 1991) (conflict of interest requiring appointment of independent counsel for insured does not exist solely because insured is sued for amount in excess of policy limits).

[103] 65 Cal. Rptr. 406 (Cal. Ct. App. 1968).

[104] 65 Cal. Rptr. at 416–17.

duty to the insured is not fulfilled if the attorney does not give undivided loyalty to the insured's interests.[105]

One answer suggested by Professor (now Judge) Keeton is that the insurer make clear to the insured that, with respect to settlement, the only duties owed by counsel are to the insurer.[106] This eliminates the conflict with respect to settlement, and would have presumably saved the attorney in *Lysick* much grief. One criticism of this approach is that settling a lawsuit is simply one aspect of defending it; that is, settlement negotiations are logically indistinct from other aspects of trial preparation. If the insured must obtain independent counsel at his or her own expense to obtain settlement advice, the insured is not receiving a full defense. Moreover, it is debatable whether an attorney's retention should be capable of limitation to such an extent that so fundamental an aspect of representation — counsel and advice about settlement — could be removed from the attorney's obligation. Last but not least, Model Rule 1.2(a) provides that "[a] lawyer shall abide by a client's decision whether to accept an offer of settlement of a matter." This rule, by its terms, appears to leave little room for an attorney to choose to conduct (or conclude) the defense in disregard of the client's wishes regarding settlement.

Those who agree with Professor Keeton would emphasize the distinction between a duty to obey the client's settlement wishes and a duty to take care of the client's interests with regard to settlement. In other words, if the contract between attorney and client explicitly removes advice and counsel with regard to settlement issues from the representation, the attorney owes no duty of care with regard to settlement. Moreover, this view preserves consistency with the provisions of the standard liability policy that give control of settlement decisions to the insurer.[107]

If one concludes that defense counsel cannot conduct a dual representation where a settlement conflict exists and that it is impermissible for the insurer and appointed counsel to abandon the insured on the issue of settlement, the only remaining solution is for the attorney in settlement negotiations to act as if the attorney has only one client — the insured. Only if the attorney gives undivided loyalty to the insured will the insured receive the full measure of the defense for which the insured paid a premium. The insurer may refuse to settle, with all the risk that this judgment entails. The attorney must be left unconstrained to advise the insured of the implications of the insurer's refusal, that this gives rise to potential claims against the insurer, and that the insured should consider consulting with independent counsel about pursuing these claims. The attorney cannot represent the insured in asserting these claims, as the prior representation of the insurer will give the attorney information and knowledge that could not be revealed without breaching the duty of confidentiality owed the insurer.

---

[105] For an explanation of how one court envisions the duty to settle being fulfilled while dual representation is maintained, see Hartford Acc. & Indem. Co. v. Foster, 528 So. 2d 255, 271 (Miss. 1988).

[106] Keeton, *supra* note 30, at 1168-1171; see also § 112, *supra*.

[107] For more recent discussions advocating the Keeton solution, see Silver & Syverud, *supra* note 1; William T. Barker, *Defense Attorneys and Policy Limits Settlement Offers: Another View*, 1990 Bad Faith L. Rep. 141.

[2] Insured's Noncooperation

The preceding section considered the conflict created when a claim exceeds the policy limits. What if the claim is worth much less than the policy limits, and the insured does not wish to settle?[108] That was the situation in *Rogers v. Robson, Masters, Ryan, Brumund & Belom,*[109] a 1979 Illinois decision. The insured, a physician, was represented by a law firm appointed by the insurer; the insurance policy allowed the insurer to settle suits against the insured without the insured's consent. The firm, following the insurer's instructions but without informing the physician, settled the suit against him for a nominal sum, obtaining from the plaintiff an express denial that the doctor had done anything wrong. The insured, however, did not want to settle, and he sued the insurer for breach of contract and the firm for malpractice. His claim against the insurer was dismissed on the ground that the insurer simply exercised a right given to it by the contract, but the court allowed the suit against the law firm to go forward under the reasoning that the firm had violated a duty it owed the insured.

Professor Silver finds irony in *Rogers*: the court held that the firm violated a professional duty by failing to consult with the insured about a matter that the insured had no contractual right to control.[110] Stated otherwise, the decision in *Rogers* assumes that the insured has a right to refuse to settle, and this right trumps whatever right the insurer has to direct that a settlement occur. This means, necessarily, that the attorney appointed by the insurer must refuse to settle if the insured says no to the settlement. Professor Silver finds this outcome to be anomalous, and his critique is a thoughtful one.[111]

Yet the attorney who has appeared in the underlying litigation for the insured cannot, it would seem, take a position in the litigation that the client believes is utterly inconsistent with the client's interests.[112] If the insured's conduct in *Rogers* seemed irrational, one need only change the facts slightly to make the insured's position more sympathetic: Suppose, for example, the insured's liability policy has a deductible of $2500, and the insurer reaches an agreement to settle a claim against the insured, in circumstances where the insured believes he or she has no liability whatever, for $3500; the insurer demands that the insured contribute the amount of the deductible, and the insured refuses, believing the claim to be groundless. An insurer that wishes to dispose of the case probably should pay the entire $3500 and be rid of the suit, but most contracts do not require this answer, given that the price of the policy assumes that the insured will pay any liability up to the amount of the

---

[108] See generally Annot., *Liability of Insurer to Insured for Settling Third-Party Claim Within Policy Limits Resulting in Detriment to Insured,* 18 A.L.R.5th 474 (1993).

[109] 392 N.E.2d 1365 (Ill. App. Ct. 1979), *aff'd,* 407 N.E.2d 47 (Ill. 1980).

[110] Silver, *supra* note 1, at 1593.

[111] *Id.* at 1593-96.

[112] See Neumeier, *supra* note 1, at n. 22 ("an attorney can never act contrary to the express instructions of the client.")

deductible and that the insurer will have the right to control the defense and settlement.[113]

To sort through this quandary, consider first the same claim made in circumstances where the defendant has no insurance; the defendant retains an attorney to defend the claim, with the attorney's fee being paid by the defendant. In those circumstances, the attorney, whose bill is paid by the defendant, cannot take a position in the litigation that the defendant believes is against the defendant's interests.[114] The attorney who finds the client's settlement position and other strategic choices to be bizarre, eccentric, or uniquely strange must, after failing to persuade the client to a more sensible course, either abide by the client's wishes or withdraw from the representation, provided this can be accomplished without prejudicing the client's interests.

The question becomes, then, whether the presence of third-party payment by a liability insurer changes this answer. One answer is to say that the analysis does not change when the attorney's fee is paid by a third party. In other words, the attorney owes absolute allegiance to the insured, and the attorney's options when confronted with an insured who favors a bizarre litigation strategy from which the insured cannot be dissuaded are either to continue with the defense on the client's terms or to withdraw. Withdrawal, of course, is an unsatisfactory answer if the attorneys selected by the insurer repeatedly reach the same conclusion, and each decides to withdraw.

Another answer is to conclude that the contract between insurer and insured modifies what would otherwise be an absolute duty owed by the attorney to adhere to the insured's wishes regarding how the litigation should be conducted. These limits come from two parts of the typical liability insurance policy: first, the insured's relinquishment to the insurer of the right to control the litigation and to veto the insurer's wishes as to settlement; and second, the insured's promise to cooperate with the insurer in the undertaking of the defense. An issue, of course, may be present as to whether the insured understood at the time of contracting that he or she was relinquishing to the insurer rights clients otherwise have to control the choices made in litigation in which the client is a party.

Assuming, however, that the insured is not unreasonably surprised by the contract provisions which constrain what the insured can demand by way of a defense, there is something to be said for finding in the contract a limitation on appointed counsel's obligation to conduct the litigation at all times in a manner demanded by the insured, particularly where what the insured demands is unreasonable or contrary to what a reasonable person would do in the same circumstances. Yet this cannot be easily

---

[113] Some professional liability policies now have what are called "hammer clauses," which specify the procedure to be followed if the insured declines to settle in circumstances where the insurer desires to settle. These clauses attempt to hold the insured personally liable for any excess judgment over the amount for which the case could be settled. Winiarski, *supra* note 1, at 600.

[114] The comments to Model Rule 1.2 contemplate that the client has control over the purposes of the representation and decisions that affect the client's substantive rights. Decisions involving tactics and trial strategy are the lawyer's responsibility.

reconciled with the principle that an attorney who represents a client must promote what the client, not some third party, believes are the client's best interests. As one court has stated, "[a] contract which authorized any dilution of the ethical obligation of an attorney to the client would be void as against public policy."[115]

The most recent tentative draft of the proposed *Restatement of the Law Governing Lawyers*[116] addresses this issue by recognizing the insurer's ability to constrain the defense in circumstances where only the insurer will be liable for any resulting judgment. Section 215 reiterates that an attorney's independent professional judgment cannot be diminished by the fact that a third party, i.e., an insurer, pays the attorney's fees. However, comment d allows for some third-party control in some circumstances:

> With the consent of the client, however, limitations on the scope of the lawyer's representation of the client may be imposed by the third person, if they are reasonably necessary to limit the financial burden on the third person, if they nonetheless provide effective representation to the client, and if the client agrees to the limitations with appropriate understanding of them.

One of the illustrations following this comment, illustration four, elaborates with an example from liability insurance: In defending a suit where the claim is within the policy limits, the attorney urges that more depositions be taken. In particular, the attorney opines that doubling the number of depositions at a cost of $5000 would increase the insured's chances of prevailing by 20 percent. The illustration states:

> If the insurance contract confers authority on the Insurer to make such decisions, Lawyer may rely on Insurer's judgment and direction that taking depositions would not be worth the cost.

> Just as there are limits to client consent in § 202, there are limits to the restrictions on scope of the representation permitted under this Section. In general, unless the third person who is paying the lawyer bears substantially all of the consequences of the result in litigation, the third person may not direct or restrict the lawyer's decision.

This illustration recognizes that the insurer, which has a right to control the defense, may make decisions that may be influenced by cost concerns, but the illustration suggests that this right exists only when the insurer will be the party liable for any judgment. If the insurer defends under a reservation of rights or if the claim exceeds the policy limits, the illustration contemplates, implicitly, that the insurer may not base defense decisions on cost concerns.[117]

Beyond the problems presented by the insured who does not wish to settle when it is appropriate to do so and by the insured who has unusual ideas about how the defense should be conducted, most insurance defense counsel at one time or another must deal with the insured-defendant who is unobservant with regard to the insured's obligations to cooperate with the insurer. If the inattentiveness constitutes noncooperation, the attorney is faced with a dilemma. The attorney must protect the client's

---

[115] Hartford Acc. & Indem. Co. v. Foster, 528 So. 2d 255, 268 (Miss. 1988).

[116] Tentative Draft No. 4 (1991).

[117] See Winiarski, *supra* note 1, at 605- 06.

interests and must not favor the insurer in the representation. This suggests that the attorney must endure the situation until the attorney-client relationship is terminated by the insured or by the court.

Not all acts of noncooperation constitute a breach of the policy; some acts of noncooperation are so insignificant as to have no ramifications for the contract between insurer and insured. Moreover, one should not assume that all acts of noncooperation are actually adverse to the insurer's interests or materially impair the attorney or insurer's ability to reach a successful resolution of the litigation.[118] Indeed, even the insured's failure to cooperate with the insurer by, for example, being available to assist in the defense, etc., may not necessarily give rise to a conflict of interest with respect to the effort to oppose the plaintiff's claim: the question is whether the insured's absence or other noncooperation makes it impossible to prepare a defense. Thus, it may be that the attorney can continue with the defense even when there is a high degree of dissonance between insured and insurer, recognizing that whether the coverage continues in the face of the insured's noncooperation is an issue to be handled by separate counsel for both insurer and insured, with the attorney appointed in the underlying action being barred from ascending into either role.

Yet at a certain point, it may become clear that the insured's noncooperation constitutes a breach of contract and an interference with fundamental interests of the insurer. If the insurer's and the insured's interests become hopelessly adverse to the point that it is impossible to prepare an effective defense for the insured, one answer is to conclude that the attorney cannot continue to represent both clients and has no alternative but to withdraw from the defense of both.

Not all instances in which the insured and insurer have different objectives in trying a lawsuit constitute a conflict of interest. This distinction was explained in *Roussos v. Allstate Insurance Co.,*[119] a 1995 Maryland decision. The insured wanted the insurer to pay for an attorney of the insured's own choice because, among other reasons, the insured, believing herself to have been unjustly sued as a result of an automobile accident, did not want to the plaintiff to recover anything in circumstances where the insurer was inclined to settle in order to minimize the litigation. As explained by the court,

> Although these objectives are not identical, they are simply not adverse. . . . Despite the fact that Allstate stated in a letter to Roussos that it believed her to be "legally liable" for Baxley's damages, each would have benefitted greatly if, at trial, Roussos were found not to have been negligent. An insurer's right to control the litigation against its insured is essential to protect the insurer's financial interest in the outcome of the suit. . . . We decline to extend an insurer's duty to provide independent counsel to a situation where the insured merely disagrees with the manner in which he or she is to be defended. . . . In sum, there was no conflict of interest . . . .[120]

---

118 See § 110, *supra.*

119 655 A.2d 40 (Md.Ct.App. 1995).

120 655 A.2d at 44-45. Compare 69th Street & 2nd Ave. Garage Associates, L.P. v. Ticor Title Guar. Co., 622 N.Y.S.2d 13 (N.Y. App. Div. 1995) (insured, who needed quick

In *Roussos*, the policy provided that Allstate would defend the suit and choose the counsel, and that Allstate "may settle any claim or suit if we believe it is proper." The insured's insistence upon selecting her own counsel at the insurer's expense was costly, because by not letting Allstate control the defense, the insured breached the duty to cooperate she owed the insurer, which excused the insurer's obligation to pay for any judgment against her.[121]

The court in *Roussos* recognized, however, that there are other situations where a conflict of interest is presented and a different analysis is required.[122] For example, when the attorney's planned defense, if successful, would leave the insured personally exposed for the victim's loss, the unfairness of allowing the attorney to assert the defense is evident. Similarly, if the plaintiff alleges the insured's negligence, the attorney should not be allowed to defend on the ground that the insured intentionally caused the loss, a defense which, if successful, would establish noncoverage.[123] In the final analysis, if the insurer insists upon asserting a defense that is plainly contrary to the insured's interests, it is impossible for the attorney to continue to represent both the insured and the insurer. In such circumstances, allowing the insured to retain independent counsel paid for by the insurer and relinquishing control of the defense to the insured is the best answer.

Another set of difficult problems is created when the insured does not agree with the tactical choices of the attorney hired to represent the insured because of a feeling of moral obligation to the plaintiff. Sometimes the insured does not wish a particular defense to be asserted because that defense will impair the third party's ability to recover; for example, the insured may feel a moral responsibility to assist the victim and is unwilling to approve a procedural defense that will defeat the victim's claim. A variation on this example involves the insured who opposes the attorney's plan to seek dismissal of the plaintiff's complaint because a friend or relative will lose the ability to recover insurance proceeds. Some courts have approved the attorney's conduct in securing a dismissal on a legally valid ground, noting that any other course ignores the unfairness of the insured's collusion with the victim.[124] Other courts, however, have refused to allow attorneys to file motions, seek dismissal, submit interrogatories, and take other steps to defend the claim without the insured's approval of the planned action.[125] Again, the basic conflict is between the insurer's right to control the defense and the insured's right, as a client, to have the defense conducted in whatever manner the insured thinks is in his or her best interest.

---

resolution of underlying action, and insurer, who could proceed leisurely with detriment, had "divergent interests" which amounted to "crucial conflict of interests between them.")

[121] 655 A.2d at 45.

[122] 655 A.2d at 44 (where complaint involves covered and noncovered claims; where insured is exposed to a potential excess judgment).

[123] See Crum v. Anchor Cas. Co., 119 N.W.2d 703 (Minn. 1963) (attorneys assert exclusive remedy provision of workers' compensation act as defense to plaintiff's claim, even though insured had no separate workers' compensation coverage; held, attorney could not take position adverse to client).

[124] See Buchanan v. Buchanan, 160 Cal. Rptr. 577 (Cal. Ct. App. 1979).

[125] See, e.g., DeGraw v. State Sec. Ins. Co., 351 N.E.2d 302 (Ill. App. Ct. 1976); Reynolds v. Maramorosch, 144 N.Y.S.2d 900 (N.Y. Sup. Ct. 1955).

One step beyond the situation where the insured feels a sense of moral responsibility for the victim is the situation in which the insured and the plaintiff are involved in a collusive scheme to defraud the insurer. Collusion between the insured and the third-party plaintiff is the most flagrant kind of noncooperation. If the attorney suspects collusion, it is not an appropriate response for the attorney to impugn the integrity of the insured at trial.[126] Indeed, such action would be directly contrary to the interests of the insured. If the insurer concludes that collusion must be raised as a defense, it is impossible for the attorney to continue to represent the interests of both the insurer and the insured and the attorney has no alternative except to withdraw from the representation. Indeed, if the insured is attempting to commit a fraud on the insurer, Model Rule 1.2(d) prohibits the insured's attorney from assisting the insured.[127] Where continuing in the representation would cause the attorney to violate Model Rule 1.2(d), the rules themselves require the attorney to withdraw from the defense.

Again, the best solution here is for the attorney to give undivided loyalty to the insured. If the insured wishes certain tactical choices to be made, ultimately it is the attorney's responsibility to the client to respect those choices. If the insured wishes to commit fraud or otherwise assist the third party, it is not the attorney's responsibility to assist in these efforts. Indeed, no attorney can assist in perpetrating a fraud; if the attorney becomes aware that the he or she is being used to perpetrate a fraud, it is the attorney's obligation to withdraw.[128]

[3] Disclosure of Information by Insured Inconsistent with Insurer's Obligation

A fundamental premise of the attorney-client relationship is the attorney's obligation to maintain the confidentiality of communications and disclosures by his or her client to the attorney. An attorney who represents an insured or insurer is subject to the same confidentiality obligation. Anytime an attorney has multiple clients, the possibility exists that the attorney will learn from one client information that is adverse to the interests of the other.

---

[126] See Montanez v. Irizarry-Rodriguez, 641 A.2d 1079 (N.J.Super. 1994.)

[127] Model Rule 1.2(d) provides in relevant part: "A lawyer shall not counsel a client to engage, or assist a client, in conduct that the lawyer knows is criminal or fraudulent." See also Model Rule 1.16(a)(1) (requiring a lawyer to withdraw from the representation where fraud is involved); Model Rule 4.1 ("In the course of representing a client a lawyer shall not knowingly . . . (b) fail to disclose a material fact to a third person when disclosure is necessary to avoid assisting a criminal or fraudulent act by a client, unless disclosure is prohibited by Rule 1.6.")

[128] See Clemens v. Wilcox, 392 N.W.2d 863 (Minn. 1986). In *Montanez, supra* note 126, the court indicated that the attorney, if he or she believed the insured intended to testify falsely, could seek the court's permission to withdraw from the defense. See 641 A.2d at 1985. This may give the insurer notice that the cooperation clause is being breached, which is contrary to the insured's interests, but this is preferable to direct participation in the commission of a fraud. The requirement that the attorney withdraw in these circumstances elevates the value in attorneys not participating in frauds over the value of attorneys maintaining absolute loyalty to their clients. For a more detailed discussion of this issue, see Silver & Syverud, *supra* note 1.

In the multiple-client situation where the clients have a common interest and a common goal in the litigation, information communicated by one client to the attorney to promote the common goal is not entitled to confidentiality with respect to other clients. Indeed, there is no need for confidentiality between co-defendants when the information promotes joint interests. If, however, the information communicated by, for example, the insured affects the insured's coverage, the confidentiality of this information must be maintained, and the information may not be disclosed to the insurer.[129]

The consequences of failing to adhere to this principle are starkly illustrated by *Parsons v. Continental National American Group,*[130] a 1976 Arizona decision. The insured, a 14-year-old who was charged with assault and battery, was defended by counsel appointed by the insurer pursuant to a reservation of rights. The attorney obtained a confidential psychiatric file about the insured as well as communications from the insured that confirmed that the insured's acts against the plaintiff were willful and therefore within the scope of the intentional act exclusion. The insurer declined a settlement offer of $22,500, and a judgment was entered against the insured for $50,000; the policy limits were $25,000. In the coverage action, the court held that the insured was estopped from asserting the intentional acts exclusion since the evidence upon which it relied to deny coverage was obtained in violation of defense counsel's duty of confidentiality.[131]

Recognizing that the tripartite relationship does not allow the attorney to compromise the insured's interests, the question is what action the attorney should take in circumstances where disclosures create a conflict, or where such disclosures are anticipated. If the discovery could be anticipated, the dual representation approach would require disclosure of the potential conflict to the insured and withdrawal from the defense unless the insured consents to the joint representation: "There is reason for concern if the conflict of interests is reasonably apparent at the time of counsel's involvement. A mere diversity of interests between the clients does not create conflicting interests. Yet, even representation of divergent interests should only proceed where there has been adequate disclosure and consent."[132] Thus, for example, if the attorney suspects that the insurer may enjoy a defense of late notice, the attorney should advise the insured of the possible defense and the attorney's obligation to gather and communicate to the insurer any information about it. Unless consent to joint representation is forthcoming, the attorney should withdraw from the defense. If the insured does not consent to the joint representation, the only alternatives that avoid repetition of the scenario are for independent counsel to be appointed and paid for by the insurer, or for the insured to be allowed to choose his or her own independent counsel whose expenses are paid by the insurer.

---

[129] See, e.g., Parsons v. Continental Nat'l Am. Group, 550 P.2d 94 (Ariz. 1976); American Mut. Liab. Ins. Co. v. Superior Court, 113 Cal. Rptr. 561 (Cal. Ct. App. 1974). For a more detailed discussion of this issue, see Silver & Syverud, *supra* note 1, at 341-61. See also Geoffrey C. Hazard, Jr. & W. William Hodes, *The Law of Lawyering: A Handbook on the Model Rules of Professional Conduct* § 1.7:304, at 250.1-.2 (1994).

[130] 550 P.2d 94 (Ariz. 1976).

[131] 550 P.2d at 98.

[132] Mallen & Smith, *supra* note 2, at § 23.12, p. 393.

It may be, however, that the attorney will have no advance notice that information adverse to the insurer is about to be revealed by the insured. Suppose, for example, the insured informs the attorney of his or her fraud in inducing the insurer to issue the policy. This information would provide a basis for denying policy coverage; the lawyer cannot disclose the information to the insurer without violating the confidences of the client, the insured. The attorney who violates this obligation to the client may be disciplined under the ethical rules, may be sued for malpractice, and can cause the insurer to lose its coverage defenses.[133] As explained by one court, "[w]e emphasize that the attorney who represents the insured owes him an undeviating allegiance whether compensated by the insurer or the insured and cannot act as an agent of the insurance company by supplying information detrimental to the insured."[134] The attorney also has clients with utterly inconsistent interests, and it is not possible to get permission for joint representation without disclosing the confidential information. Under such circumstances, it has been held that the attorney's only recourse is to withdraw from the representation.[135] This answer is not perfect. If the insurer appoints a new attorney to conduct the insured's defense, the conflict will inevitably arise again, forcing the second attorney to withdraw. But the alternative, allowing the insured to retain independent counsel at the insurer's expense, is worse in this situation, for it would enable the insured to succeed in perpetrating a fraud upon the insurer.

[4]　Common Issue Cases

An extremely difficult problem is presented when the claim against the insured and the question of coverage involve the same facts or issues. If a fact or issue involved in the underlying litigation necessarily determines both the insured's liability to the plaintiff and the existence of coverage, a conflict of interest would exist if determining the fact or resolving the issue would adversely affect either the insurer or the insured.

A common example is the situation where the complaint alleges the insured's negligence, but the facts suggest that an intentional tort, which is outside the coverage, may have occurred.[136] The insured wishes one of two outcomes: the insured is not liable because no tort occurred, or the insured was negligent and this liability is covered by the policy. The insurer wishes one of two outcomes: the insured is not liable because no tort occurred, or the insured acted with intent and has no coverage. On only one of the defensive strategies are the insurer's and insured's interests aligned. If an outcome in the underlying tort action on the nature

---

[133] See *ABA Code of Professional Responsibility,* DR 4-101; CHI of Alaska, Inc. v. Employers Reins. Corp., 844 P.2d 1113 (Alaska 1993); Parsons v. Continental Nat'l American Group, 550 P.2d 94 (Ariz. 1976). But see Shafer v. Utica Mut. Ins. Co., 289 N.Y.S. 577 (N.Y. App. Div. 1936) (counsel acted properly in disclosing information to insurer that enabled insurer to deny liability).

[134] Farmers Ins. Co. of Ariz. v. Vagnozzi, 675 P.2d 703, 708 (Ariz. 1983).

[135] See, e.g., State Farm Mut. Auto. Ins. Co. v. Walker, 382 F.2d 548 (7th Cir. 1967); Mortiz v. Medical Protective Co., 428 F. Supp. 865 (W.D. Wis. 1977); Parsons v. Continental Nat'l Am. Group, 550 P.2d 94 (Ariz. 1976).

[136] See, e.g, Fireman's Fund Ins. v. Waste Management of Wisconsin, 777 F.2d 366 (7th Cir. 1985); Klein v. Salama, 545 F. Supp. 175 (E.D. N.Y. 1983).

of the insured's liability is binding with regard to coverage, the attorney representing the insured is faced with an intractable conflict of interest.[137]

Another common example is the situation where the plaintiff's complaint seeks small compensatory damages (which are covered) but large punitive damages (in a jurisdiction where punitive damages are not covered).[138] Even if the insurer defends the action under a reservation of rights, the insurer, unconcerned about the compensatory damage claims, may provide a less than vigorous defense to the allegations in the complaint which, if proved, would support an imposition of punitive damages. Indeed, whenever the insurer offers to defend its insured while disclaiming coverage for punitive damages sought by the plaintiff, the interests of the insurer and insured do not coincide.[139]

Some courts have held that the existence of such a conflict eliminates the duty to defend.[140] These cases draw support from the language in liability policies giving the insurer the right to control the defense; if the insured seeks to deny the insurer this contract right, the insured fails to cooperate, and thus forfeits the coverage. The opposing view emphasizes the insurer's contractual undertaking to provide a defense to the insured for claims within coverage; discharging the insurer from all its obligations has the effect of depriving the insured of what the insured paid for. The better view is that the existence of the conflict does not eliminate the duty to defend, but merely transforms it into an obligation to assume the costs of defense: the insured is entitled to a defense by an attorney of his or her own choosing, whose reasonable fee is to be paid by the insurer.[141]

[5] Multiple Insureds with Conflicting Interests

A conflict of interest problem also exists whenever two or more insureds are named as defendants in the same lawsuit and the insureds' interests do not coincide. If, for example, one insured has a defense that is detrimental to another, it is not possible for one attorney to represent both insureds. In such a situation, it is well settled that the insurer must hire a separate counsel for each insured with a conflicting interest.[142]

---

[137] See, e.g., State Farm Fire & Cas. Co. v. Pildner, 321 N.E.2d 600 (Ohio 1974); Burd v. Sussex Mut. Ins. Co., 267 A.2d 7 (N.J. 1970); Employers' Fire Ins. Co. v. Beals, 240 A.2d 397 (R.I. 1968); Utica Mut. Ins. Co. v. Cherry, 358 N.Y.S.2d 519 (N.Y. App. Div. 1974), aff'd, 343 N.E.2d 758 (N.Y. 1975).

[138] See Public Serv. Mut. Ins. Co. v. Goldfarb, 425 N.E.2d 810 (N.Y. 1981); see also § 65[g], supra.

[139] See Nandorf, Inc. v. CNA Ins. Cos., 479 N.E.2d 988 (Ill. App. Ct. 1985); Parker v. Agricultural Ins. Co., 440 N.Y.S.2d 964 (N.Y. Sup. Ct. 1981).

[140] See, e.g., Glens Falls Ins. Co. v. American Oil Co., 254 A.2d 658 (Md. 1969); Williams v. Farmers Mut. of Enumclaw, 423 P.2d 518 (Or. 1969).

[141] See, e.g., Public Service Mut. Ins. Co. v. Goldfarb, 425 N.E.2d 810 (N.Y. 1981); Brohawn v. Transamerica Ins. Co., 347 A.2d 842 (Md. 1975); American Employers' Ins. Co. v. Crawford, 533 P.2d 1203 (N.M. 1975).

[142] See, e.g., Bituminous Ins. Cos. v. Pennsylvania Mfr.'s Ass'n Ins. Co., 427 F. Supp. 539 (E.D. Pa. 1976); First Ins. Co. of Hawaii, Inc. v. State, 665 P.2d 648 (Haw. 1983); Sorenson v. Krusen, 293 N.W.2d 56 (Minn. 1980); Spindle v. Chubb/Pacific Indem. Group, 152 Cal. Rptr. 776 (Cal. Ct. App. 1979). Cf. Lehto v. Allstate Ins. Co., 36 Cal. Rptr.2d 814

The answer to the conflict in the multiple-insured situation is straightforward and beyond controversy. The more difficult problem, at least in some circumstances, is determining whether a conflict of interest exists; in other words, the greatest risk in such situations is that the attorney will not recognize the conflict. But complicating the landscape is the fact that conflicts do not automatically arise from mere differences in potential liability. Also, the mere fact that one insured has a defense that the other one does not possess does not necessarily constitute a conflict, even though in that situation the insured without a defense would hope that the defense would fail, so that one more defendant might exist to pay any subsequent judgment. On the other hand, a contested issue which will determine which of several defendants is liable gives rise to a conflict. If one insured has a potential claim against another insured which the first insured's attorney would pursue in the absence of a joint representation, a conflict exists. Also, when one insured has cross-claims against another arising out of the occurrence, a conflict of interest clearly exists.[143]

The problem of multiple insureds with conflicting interests can arise in other ways too numerous to canvass here. *Rawlings v. Apodaca,*[144] a 1986 Arizona Supreme Court decision, illustrates an interesting version of one of these patterns. The Rawlingses, whose dairy hay barn was damaged by a fire, believed that the fire had been started by negligent trash burning by the Apodacas, who lived nearby. Farmers Insurance Company (Farmers) provided the Rawlingses with $10,000 coverage for their hay barn. The Rawlingses promptly filed a claim with Farmers, and when the fire investigators for Farmers appeared, they indicated their desire to pursue a claim against the Apodacas. The investigators assured the Rawlingses that they would have access to their investigation report, and the Rawlingses did not proceed with the investigation themselves.

As it turned out, the Apodacas were insured by Farmers under a liability policy with $100,000 limits. This, of course, created a conflict between insureds: Farmers insured a small portion of the Rawlingses' loss as their first-party insurer, but Farmers was potentially responsible for a larger portion of the loss as the Apodacas' third-party insurer. Farmers then declined to forward the report to the Rawlingses, and did not inform the Rawlingses that they were the liability insurer for the Apodacas. The trial court ultimately found that Farmers attempted to prevent Rawlingses' suit against the Apodacas and that it did so to protect its own interests, without fair consideration to the loss that the Rawlingses would incur. Because Farmers "pursued this objective by deceit, nondisclosure, reneging on promises, violation of industry custom and deliberate attempts to obfuscate," the trial court ruled, and the Supreme Court affirmed, that Farmers committed a tort through its violation of the covenant of good faith and fair dealing.[145] When faced with the

(Cal. Ct. App. 1995) (discussing insurer's obligations in situation where plaintiff offered to release one of two insureds from liability in exchange for payment of policy limits).

[143] See, e.g., Sorenson v. Kruse, 293 N.W.2d 56 (Minn. 1980); Rowell v. Transpacific Life Ins. Co., 156 Cal. Rptr. 679 (Cal. Ct. App. 1979); Rimar v. Continental Cas. Co., 376 N.Y.S.2d 309 (N.Y. App. Div. 1975).

[144] 726 P.2d at 565 (Ariz. 1986).

[145] 726 P.2d at 577.

conflicting interests between the insureds, Farmers should have represented each insured independently. Independent counsel should have been appointed for the Apodacas, and the fire investigation report, because it was prepared by Farmers in its status as the Rawlingses' insurer, should have been made available to the Rawlingses.

[6]   Insured's Counterclaims

Some problems closely related to the conflict of interest questions are raised when an insured has counterclaims against the tortfeasor. The typical fact pattern involves an insured who out of the same transaction or occurrence possesses a claim that must be asserted as a compulsory counterclaim in the plaintiff's action. Under a liability policy, the insurer is only obligated to defend claims brought against the insured. Therefore, the insurer is not required to assume the cost of prosecuting a counter-claim on behalf of the insured, assuming that the counterclaim does not constitute a part of the defense of the plaintiff's claim. However, if the insurer settles the underlying action against the insured, the stipulated judgment will bar claims that the insured should have asserted in the action as compulsory counterclaims.

Many courts are reluctant to apply the compulsory counterclaim rule. However, to avoid its potential barring effect the insurer should advise the insured of the existence of the counterclaim and allow the insured to get separate counsel to pursue it. If the claim has been asserted as a compulsory counterclaim, and the insurer wants to settle the underlying claim, permission to sever the claim should be secured from the court, along with an order that settlement of plaintiff's claim will not affect the counterclaim. If the insurer, through the attorney, fails to advise the insured of the compulsory counterclaim, one of two things might happen. The court might choose to ignore the compulsory counterclaim bar by invoking the rule of excuse by inadvertence, oversight, or neglect. If this course is not followed, the alternative is to enforce the bar and give the insured a cause of action against the insurer.

Obviously, the insurer cannot direct the insured to ignore the existence of a counterclaim or to give it up, because the counterclaim does not belong to the insurer. Failure to advise the insured of the counterclaim is, however, conducting the defense in a manner that prejudices the insured's rights.[146] Moreover, the insurer must protect the counterclaim when conducting the defense of the lawsuit.[147] Thus, failure to advise the insured of the existence of the counterclaim and of the insured's need to hire counsel to prosecute it should be treated as a breach of defense counsel's obligations to the insured.

§ 115   Problems of Primary versus Excess Coverage

In recent years, the relationship between primary and excess insurers has raised difficult questions in a variety of situations. The primary insurer is the insurer responsible for providing the first layer of insurance coverage. The excess insurer or insurers provide layers of coverage beyond the policy limits of the primary

---

146 See Rothtrock v. Ohio Farmers Ins. Co., 43 Cal. Rptr. 716 (Cal. Ct. App. 1965).

147 See Barney v. Aetna Cas. & Sur. Co., 230 Cal. Rptr. 215 (Cal. Ct. App. 1986).

insurer's policy. Normally, the excess policy is rated based on the assumption that primary layers of coverage exist; the excess policy typically requires that certain levels of underlying coverage be maintained in force. However, it is sometimes not obvious whether a particular policy is intended as excess or primary coverage; this issue, when it arises, is resolved through application of "other insurance" clauses, a problem discussed in an earlier section.[1]

If it is clear that one policy is primary and another is excess, problems can arise when an insured is sued by a third party on a claim within coverage. Take, for example, the problem of settlement. It was noted earlier that the insurer has the right to control the settlement, but when a claim is made exceeding the policy limits, the insurer has a special obligation to take the insured's interests into account, since the insured stands to bear the expense of any judgment or settlement exceeding the policy limits. A similar problem exists when excess coverage is involved: the insurer controlling the litigation is putting at risk the insurance commitment of the excess carrier. The essential question in primary-excess insurer relations is what duties are owed by the primary insurer to the excess insurer.

[a] Some "Guiding Principles"

To deal with these problems, two insurance organizations and some unaffiliated insurers promulgated in 1974 a set of norms titled "Guiding Principles for Insurers of Primary and Excess Coverages." In essence, the Principles state that the primary insurer should promptly investigate all claims even if it appears that the policy limits will be exhausted, should attempt settlement where it appears desirable, should notify the excess insurer if an excess judgment seems likely, should inform the excess insurer if a settlement is possible but the primary is unwilling to settle due to the appraisal of liability, should not seek contribution from the excess carrier for settlements within the primary's limits, and should consult with the excess carrier regarding appeals. The Principles also state that the excess carrier should not attempt to coerce the primary insurer to settle within the primary policy limits.[2]

The Principles leave numerous questions open. For example, they do not state who, as between the primary and excess insurer, is responsible for reviewing the issue of liability, to what extent the excess carrier can or should participate in settlement negotiations, when the primary's duty to notify the excess carrier of liability exceeding the primary's limits arises, or to what extent the primary insurer has a duty to determine whether excess coverage exists.[3] Because of these ambiguities, many insurers — particularly excess carriers who thought the Principles diminished their judicially recognized rights and created new liabilities — refused to approve the Principles. The inability of the insurers to agree on a statement of the norms governing the relationships of primary and excess insurers is indicative of the confusion currently existing in this area.

---

[1] See § 97, *supra.*

[2] The Guiding Principles are set forth in Harold E. Hardies, *Guiding Principles (and Principals) in Primary and Excess Problems,* 1977 Ins. L.J. 469.

[3] Cozen & Dey, "Rights and Duties of Primary and Excess Carriers — A Nuts and Bolts Appraisal," in Defense Research Institute, *Rights and Duties of Primary and Excess Carriers* 11 (1984).

[b]   The Primary Insurer's Duty and Its Source

As a general rule, a primary insurer owes an excess insurer the same good faith or due care duty it owes its insured in processing, defending, and settling a claim.[4] Just as courts variously describe the standard of care that the insurer owes its insured, courts variously articulate the standard of care the primary insurer owes the excess carrier. Some courts use good faith, some use due care, and some state that the primary insurer must give the excess carrier's interests at least as much weight as its own. Clear differences among these standards are not readily apparent, and the standards tend to coalesce in most cases.

The source of the primary insurer's obligation to the excess carrier is not contract, because the primary and excess carrier have no contractual relationship with each other. Most courts ground the duty in the doctrine of legal (or equitable) subrogation, although a few courts treat the duty as one originating in tort law. The subrogation theory is most easily understood by considering the example of a primary carrier that unreasonably fails to accept a settlement offer within the primary carrier's policy limits, and a judgment reaching into the excess coverage results. The excess insurer will pay the insured's loss exceeding the limits of primary coverage, pursuant to the legal compulsion of the excess insurer's contract with the insured. The excess insurer is then subrogated to the insured's rights, if any, against third parties. One of the insured's rights is a claim against the primary insurer for breach of the duty to settle, a right which the primary insurer owes the insured. Thus, the excess carrier, in the status of a subrogee, is entitled to assert the insured's claim against the primary carrier. Through this logic, the primary carrier effectively owes a duty to the excess carrier.[5]

Under the equitable subrogation theory, the excess insurer, as the insured's subrogee, is subject to any defenses the primary insurer could raise against the insured. Thus, in the foregoing illustration, if the primary carrier and the insured agree that a case brought by a third party should be tried and not settled, and if an excess judgment is subsequently entered, the insurer has a good defense against the insured's claim that the insurer breached the duty to settle, and this would effectively preclude the excess insurer's action.[6]

---

[4] See, e.g., Kivi v. Nationwide Mut. Ins. Co., 695 F.2d 1285 (11th Cir. 1983); Peter v. Travelers Ins. Co., 375 F. Supp. 1347 (C.D.Cal. 1974). See generally Michael D. Gallagher & Edward C. German, *Resolution of Settlement Conflicts Among Insureds, Primary Insurers, and Excess Insurers: Analysis of the Current State of the Law and Suggested Guidelines for the Future,* 61 Neb. L. Rev. 284 (1982); Annot., *Liability Insurance: Excess Carrier's Right of Action Against Primary Carrier For Improper Or Inadequate Defense of Claim,* 49 A.L.R.4th 304 (1986). See also Annot., *Reinsurer's Liability for Primary Liability Insurer's Failure to Compromise or Settle,* 42 A.L.R.4th 1072 (1985).

[5] See, e.g., Puritan Ins. Co. v. Canadian Universal Co., 775 F.2d 76 (3d Cir. 1985); North River Ins. Co. v. St. Paul Fire & Marine Ins. Co., 600 F.2d 721 (8th Cir. 1979); Portland General Elec. Co. v. Pacific Indem. Co., 579 F.2d 514 (9th Cir. 1978); Vencill v. Continental Cas. Co., 433 F. Supp. 1371 (S.D. W.Va. 1977); Commercial Union Assur. Cos. v. Safeway Stores, Inc., 610 P.2d 1038 (Cal. 1980); Centennial Ins. Co. v. Liberty Mut. Ins. Co., 404 N.E.2d 759 (Ohio 1980); Continental Cas. Co. v. Reserve Ins. Co., 238 N.W.2d 862 (Minn. 1976).

[6] See Puritan Ins. Co. v. Canadian Universal Co., 775 F.2d 76 (3d Cir. 1985).

Some courts, however, reason that the primary carrier's duty to the excess carrier is based on the relationship the insurers have in providing coverage to the insured. The duty is simply implied by law: the primary carrier can foresee that the excess carrier might be harmed by negligent performance of its undertakings for its insured, and thus the excess carrier is within the zone of entities to whom the primary carrier owes a duty.[7]

[c] Allocating Defense Costs Between Primary and Excess Carrier

Courts have had tremendous difficulty with the questions of whether and to what extent excess insurers should be required to share in the cost of defense.[8] As one might expect, liability policies rarely speak to the question. Thus, whatever obligations do exist arise out of equitable principles.[9] This is essentially an "other insurance" clause issue, and the defense cost obligation is allocated, generally speaking, in accordance with the principles used to allocate the indemnity obligation.[10]

If the settlement or judgment is within the primary carrier's limits, the excess carrier generally is not obligated to pay for a portion of the defense.[11] However, if the settlement or judgment exceeds the primary limits, the excess carrier has some obligation under the duty to defend. Some cases require the excess insurer to assume the defense obligation altogether.[12] Other cases have held that excess carriers are liable for a pro rata share of the defense costs based on the proportion of the entire judgment the excess carrier pays, even though the primary carrier's obligation to defend continues after the policy limits are exhausted.[13] Recently, some courts have applied a pro rata or "equitable" division of defense cost obligations between the

---

[7] See, e.g., Vencill v. Continental Cas. Co., 433 F. Supp. 1371 (S.D. W.Va. 1977).

[8] See generally James R. Sutterfield, *Relationships between Excess and Primary Insurers: The Excess Judgment Problem,* 52 Ins. Counsel J. 638 (1985); Joseph A. Bergadano & Jeffrey C. Seymour, *Duty of Defense Counsel to The Excess Insurance Carrier,* 20 Forum 489 (1985); Edward C. German & Michael D. Gallagher, *Allocation of the Duties of Defense Between Carriers Providing Coverage to the Same Insured,* 47 Ins. Counsel J. 224 (1980); Annot., *Allocation of Defense Costs Between Primary and Excess Insurance Carriers,* 19 A.L.R.4th 107 (1983).

[9] See American Auto Ins. Co. v. Seaboard Sur. Co., 318 P.2d 84 (Cal. Ct. App. 1957); see generally Hix, Kurlander & Farrugia, "Allocation of Defense Costs Between Primary and Excess Carriers," in Defense Research Institute, *Rights and Duties of Primary and Excess Carriers* 52 (1984).

[10] See § 97 *supra.*

[11] See, e.g., Federated Mut. Ins. Co. v. Pennsylvania Nat'l Mut. Ins. Co., 480 F. Supp. 599 (E.D. Tenn. 1979), *aff'd mem.,* 659 F.2d 1080 (6th Cir. 1981); Hartford Acc. & Indem. Co. v. Superior Court, 29 Cal. Rptr.2d 32 (Cal. Ct. App. 1994); Nabisco, Inc. v. Transport Indem. Co., 192 Cal. Rptr. 207 (Cal. Ct. App. 1983).

[12] See, e.g., Valentine v. Aetna Ins. Co., 564 F.2d 292 (9th Cir. 1977); Bettenburg v. Employers Liab. Assur. Corp., Ltd., 350 F. Supp. 873 (D.Minn. 1972); National Union Ins. Co. v. Phoenix Assur. Co., 301 A.2d 222 (D.C. 1973).

[13] See, e.g., Signal Cos. v. Harbor Ins. Co., 612 P.2d 889 (Cal. 1980); Celina Mut. Ins. Co. v. Citizens Ins. Co., 349 N.W.2d 547 (Mich. Ct. App. 1984); Aetna Cas. & Sur. Co. v. Market Ins. Co., 296 So. 2d 555 (Fla. Dist. Ct. App. 1974).

primary and excess insurer for claims continuing after the primary insurer's limits have been exhausted.[14]

---

[14] See, e.g., Schulman Investment Co. v. Olin Corp., 514 F. Supp. 572 (S.D. N.Y. 1981); American Fid. Ins. Co. v. Employees Mut. Cas. Co., 593 P.2d 14 (Kan.Ct.App. 1979).

Part D

SOME REMAINING MATTERS

(Matthew Bender & Co., Inc.)

(Pub.837)

CHAPTER 12

GROUP INSURANCE

§ 120 Overview: The Nature of Group Insurance

The purposes of the first group life insurance policies were macabre. In the early nineteenth century, slave traders named themselves the beneficiaries under insurance on the lives of shiploads of slaves being transported from Africa to America. A few decades later, group insurance was obtained on the lives of Chinese laborers being transported from China to Panama to work on the Panama Canal. The history of modern group insurance, however, began with the efforts of Montgomery Ward and Company to secure a policy of group life insurance for its employees. The plan that the Company negotiated became the model for several plans which commenced in 1911 and 1912: the employer obtains a policy of insurance on the lives of its employees; the employer is not the beneficiary; the employees are allowed to designate the beneficiaries; the employer pays the premium; and the lives of all employees are insured regardless of insurability. The Montgomery Ward plan called for employees to make contributions toward the premium paid by the employer, but this is not an essential feature of group insurance.

Initially, some insurers objected to the practice of group underwriting by their competitors. These insurers were troubled by the lack of evaluation of each individual applicant's insurability. They also argued that the lower rates made possible by group underwriting were unfairly discriminatory. The NAIC, however, lent its approval to the group marketing concept when it developed a standard definition of group insurance in 1917, and the challenges initially made to group insurance never gained momentum.[1]

It was not until after World War II that group insurance became a dominant feature of the insurance marketplace. In fact, since 1971, group life insurance in force has more than tripled. Today, virtually every employee receives some kind of group insurance fringe benefit. At the end of 1993, nearly $4.5 trillion worth of group life insurance was in force in the United States, accounting for roughly 40 percent of all life insurance in force. Approximately 90 percent of health insurance is provided on a group basis.[2]

---

[1] See Muriel L. Crawford, *Law and the Life Insurance Contract* 448–50 (7th ed. 1994).

[2] The life insurance data is provided by the American Council of Life Insurance in its *1994 Life Insurance Fact Book,* at page 28. One source sets the health insurance figure at 87%; see Comptroller General of the United States, *Economic Implications of the Fair Insurance Practices Act* (Apr. 6, 1984), at 19, a. For other sources, see § 64[c], *supra.*

(Matthew Bender & Co., Inc.)   (Pub.837)

Group underwriting is much less prominent in property and liability insurance. In life, health, and accident insurance, the incidence of risk for individuals is a function of age, occupation, and physical well-being. If a particular group (such as an employer's workforce) participates in a group plan in sufficiently high numbers, problems of adverse selection based on health can be avoided. With employees, for example, the fact that an individual is healthy enough to be employed is a fairly good indicator that the individual is in reasonably good health. In property insurance, the individual properties within any given group of properties are likely to be exposed to very different kinds of risks, which makes individual underwriting more appropriate. Similarly, the kinds of liabilities which a group of individuals is likely to incur are likely to vary, whereas the risk of death for members of a particular group is at any given age are likely to be equal. Also, the market for property and liability insurance is much more saturated than that for personal insurance. In contrast, no limits exist on the amount of life insurance one can purchase on one's own life, since the principle of indemnity is not operative to the same extent as in property and liability insurance. For these reasons, group insurance is confined largely to personal insurance, but in this area it has become the most important method of marketing insurance.[3]

In many respects, the distinction between insurance marketed to groups and insurance marketed to individuals is inconsequential. Most principles of insurance law apply with equal force in both settings. However, group insurance, because of the unique manner in which it is marketed, is subject to some special rules having little or no relevance to individual insurance. These special rules are discussed in this chapter.

§ 121 The Tripartite Contract: Problems of Agency

Unlike the typical contract between an individual insured and the insurer, a group insurance policy involves three parties — the insurer, the group representative, and the certificate holders. The group representative (usually the employer)[1] secures the policy for the benefit of a group of individuals somehow associated with the representative (usually employees). Thus, the group representative is actually an intermediary between the insurer and the actual insureds — the individuals who receive the coverage and the benefits of the insurance.

The group representative's status as an intermediary presents a perplexing question: whether the group representative is the agent for the insurer or the insured. Courts have reached different results when deciding this question; the answer seems

---

[3] However, in 1987, the NAIC approved the "Group Personal Lines Property and Casualty Insurance Model Act." Nat'l Ass'n of Ins. Commissioners, *Model Laws, Regulations and Guidelines,* vol. 1, at 423-1 (1987). This reflects some increase in interest in group insurance in the property and liability lines.

[1] Sometimes, a small employer will belong to an association of employers; the association then serves as the group representative of a policy for the benefit of all employees of member employers. Also, employer associations also set up separate trusts for the purpose of administering group insurance; in this instance, the trustee serves as the group representative.

to depend on the situation. Many courts have concluded that because the group representative is not appointed by the insurer to serve as its agent and does not act solely for the insurer's benefit, the group representative is not the insurer's agent, but is instead the agent for members of the group.[2] Following this analysis, the insurer is not bound by the knowledge of the group representative or by its representations. This seems appropriate, since the certificate holders are the actual insureds and recipients of the benefits of the policy (or the ones entitled to designate the beneficiary). The group representative ordinarily seeks these benefits on the insureds' behalf, and thus seems to act as the insureds' agent, not the insurer's.

However, the foregoing result has the potential to work hardship on the certificate holder if the group representative through oversight or neglect fails to include a particular person among the list of covered insureds. If the group representative is not the insurer's agent, the group representative's negligence cannot be imputed to the insurer and the insured might be denied coverage on that basis. The insured would have a claim against the group representative in most situations, but no guarantee exists that the claim will be reducible to a judgment. Cognizant of the potential hardship to the beneficiaries of the insurance by virtue of the act of an intermediary over which the insured has no control, a number of courts have held that the group representative is the agent of the insurer rather than the insured.[3]

Sometimes the determination that the group representative serves as the insurer's agent is defended by resort to principles of agency law. One of the touchstones of an agency relationship is the principal's right to control the activities of the agent. The insured typically has no control over the activities of the group representative. Consequently, some courts have concluded that the group representative is the insurer's agent, not the insureds'. The logic of this analysis is unimpressive, since the insurer has no right to control the group representative's activities in administering the policy either. The results, however, sometimes avoid the insured suffering a forfeiture, such as where the insured's premium is paid by a deduction from salary administered and forwarded by the group representative and where the group representative failed to pay the premium on the insured's behalf.[4]

---

[2] E.g., First Nat'l Bank of Anson Cty. v. Nationwide Ins. Co., 278 S.E.2d 507 (N.C. 1981); Kilbourn v. Henderson, 577 N.E.2d 1132 (Ohio Ct.App. 1989); Phelps v. Elgin Academy, 260 N.E.2d 864 (Ill. App. Ct. 1970); Couch v. Connecticut Gen. Life Ins. Co., 216 So. 2d 72, 73 (Fla. Dist. Ct. App. 1968). See also Credeur v. Continental Assur. Co., 502 So. 2d 214 (La. Ct. App. 1987) (school board not agent of insurer).

[3] E.g., Clauson v. Prudential Ins. Co. of Am., 195 F. Supp. 72, 80 (D.Mass. 1961), aff'd, 296 F.2d 76 (1st Cir. 1961); Elfstrom v. New York Life Ins. Co., 432 P.2d 731 (Cal. 1967); Pacific Standard Life Ins. Co. v. Tower Indus., Inc., 12 Cal. Rptr.2d 524 (Cal. Ct. App. 1992) (employer was group life insurer's agent and fiduciary in performing administrative function of notifying employees of their conversion rights); Soileau v. Time Ins. Co., 486 So. 2d 307 (La. Ct. App. 1986); Steward v. City of Mt. Vernon, 497 N.E.2d 939 (Ind. Ct. App. 1986); Legler v. Meriwether, 391 S.W.2d 599 (Mo. Ct. App. 1965). Cf. Nidiffer v. Clinchfield R. Co., 600 S.W.2d 242 (Tenn. Ct. App. 1980) (in selecting insurer, employer was not acting as agent for employees; therefore, employer not liable for breach of fiduciary duty when premiums doubled as a result of transfer of group policy to new insurer).

[4] See generally 1 APPLEMAN § 43.25 (1981).

In the final analysis, whether or not the group representative is the insurer's or the insureds' agent is a factual question to be resolved on a case-by-case basis.[5] It is conceivable that for some purposes, the group representative might be the insurer's agent, but for other purposes, the group representative might be the agent of all the certificate holders. One court explained it this way: "when an employer takes action to procure group coverage for its employees — e.g., when the employer selects a group insurer, negotiates for new coverage or changes in existing coverage, and obtains applications from the employees to be submitted to the insurer — the employer acts as an agent of the employees . . . However, once the policy is issued, when the employer performs duties necessary to make the group policy effective or applicable to individual employees, the employer becomes the insurer's agent."[6] One court outlined several factors that should be examined to determine whether an employer administering a group insurance plan is the insurer's agent: whether the task in question was expressly delegated to the employer by the insurer; whether the insurer supervises and controls the employer's performance of the task; and whether there is any evidence of collusion between the employer and employee to defraud the insurer.[7]

The diversity of results regarding the question of for whom the intermediary is an agent gives rise to some special problems when a premium is not paid. As noted earlier, failure to pay a premium when due allows the insurer to terminate the coverage.[8] The rule in group insurance is the same, except that the peculiar tripartite nature of the contract leads to variance from the general principle in some circumstances. If the policy is non-contributory (meaning that the employer pays the premium in its entirety without contribution by the employee), there is no basis for finding a contractual relationship between the insurer and the employee.[9] Thus, with respect to non-contributory plans courts generally hold that the failure of the employer to pay the premium for an employee terminates the employee's coverage under the policy.[10] The same result follows where the employee under a contributory policy fails to make a required contribution and the employer therefore makes no premium payment on the employee's behalf.[11] However, some courts have found coverage where the employee had made contributions that the employer failed to forward to the insurer.[12] The logic underlying these decisions is that the employer

---

[5] See Paulson v. Western Life Ins. Co., 636 P.2d 935 (Or. 1981).

[6] See, e.g., Miles v. Great Southern Life Ins. Co., 398 S.E.2d 772, 774 (Ga. Ct. App. 1990).

[7] See Kirkpatrick v. Boston Mut. Life Ins. Co., 473 N.E.2d 173 (Mass. 1985).

[8] See § 71[a], *supra*.

[9] See Abbiati v. Buttura & Sons, Inc., 639 A.2d 988 (Vt. 1994); Watson v. Pilot Life Ins. Co., 741 S.W.2d 342 (Tenn. Ct. App. 1987).

[10] See, e.g., Massachusetts Mut. Life Ins. Co. v. De Salvo, 482 P.2d 380 (Colo. 1971); Hampton v. Metropolitan Ins. Co., 528 S.W.2d 17 (Mo. Ct. App. 1975).

[11] See, e.g., Manning v. Western Airlines, 354 P.2d 568 (Utah 1960); Rivers v. State Capital Life Ins. Co., 96 S.E.2d 431 (N.C. 1957).

[12] See, e.g., Norby v. Bankers Life Co., 231 N.W.2d 665 (Minn. 1975); New York Life Ins. Co. v. Love, 428 P.2d 364 (Colo. 1967). See generally Annot., *Termination of Employee's Individual Coverage Under Group Policy For Nonpayment Of Premiums*, 22 A.L.R.4th 321 (1983).

is the insurer's agent for the purpose of the collection of premiums, and the employer's negligence in this undertaking should be attributable to the insurer. Occasionally, group policies provide that a mistake made by the employer in paying the premium will not void the coverage, and such a provision is, of course, enforceable.

It is fair to ask why the agency issues remain so murky in the group insurance setting. After all, what prevents the insurer from putting explicit requirements in the master policy regarding how the policyholder shall administer the policy, giving the policyholder explicit, actual authority to perform these administrative tasks on the insurer's behalf, and providing that the policyholder will indemnify the insurer for any unauthorized acts that cause damage to the insurer? As noted in the discussion of actual versus apparent authority in an earlier section,[13] it is quite difficult for a principal (the insurer) to limit the creation of apparent authority in its agents. That being so, the insurer in many cases will have a difficult time avoiding liability to certificate holders in circumstances where the employer's or policyholder's errors or omissions in administering the group plan resulted in a certificate holder's facially plausible claim to coverage.

Moreover, if an insurer sought a right of indemnity against an employer or other policyholder for the insurer's liability resulting from the policyholder's errors or omissions in administering the plan, it is probable that the policyholder would take its group insurance business to some other insurer, specifically one that does not hold policyholders liable for their mistakes in administering group insurance plans. Thus, in the final analysis, it may be more efficient for insurers to factor into the rates charged policyholders for group plans a sum sufficient to protect the insurer against the risk that errors or omissions by plan administrators will result in liabilities to certificate holders in situations where coverage would not otherwise exist.

§ 122   Special Problems of Contract Interpretation

[a]   The Problem of Multiple Documents

Unlike the typical individual policy which is evidenced by one document (including attachments), group insurance can be evidenced by several distinct documents: the primary contract between the group representative and the insurer (often called the "master policy"); the certificate given to each insured; and an enrollment form (or application) filled out by the insured. Typically, the master policy is a long document with substantial detail; in contrast, the certificate is often a one- or two-page document listing the essential, material aspects of the coverage.

Although it is often said that courts look at all of these documents together when deciding a question of coverage,[1] courts usually look first to the master policy.[2] If

---

[13] See § 35[b], *supra*.

[1] See, e.g., Paul v. Insurance Co. of N. Am., 675 S.W.2d 481 (Tenn. Ct. App. 1984); Morrison Assur. Co. Inc. v. Armstrong, 264 S.E.2d 320 (Ga. Ct. App. 1980); Fryer v. Kaiser Found. Health Plan, Inc., 34 Cal. Rptr. 688 (Cal. Ct. App. 1963); All States Life Ins. Co. v. Kelso, 195 So. 460 (Ala. Ct. App. 1940). See also Manz v. Continental Am. Life Ins. Co.,

the group representative is viewed as the insured's agent, it follows that knowledge of the terms of the master policy is imputed to the insured.[3] Under this logic, many courts have held that the failure to include a policy term in the certificate provided the insured — which is practically speaking the only document the insured in a group insurance policy ever sees — does not negate the term in the master policy. Instead, the term in the master policy controls.[4] In a number of these cases, courts have emphasized language in the certificate or other explanatory material given the certificate holder that explicitly conditions the coverage upon the substance of the master policy.[5] A few courts have even extended this logic to the situation where the master policy conflicts with a term in the certificate and have held the master policy controlling,[6] although the weight of authority is decidedly in favor of holding the certificate controlling in such circumstances.

Thus, when the master policy is unclear, or when the master policy conflicts with a term in the certificate, most courts hold that the language of the certificate is controlling and negates unclear or contradictory language in the master policy. The logic of these decisions is that the insured cannot be reasonably expected to have knowledge of the details of the master policy. The certificate provided the insured is implicitly (or even explicitly) represented to be an accurate description of the coverage, and the insured is entitled to rely upon it.[7] In particular, when a policy exclusion is contained in the master policy but is omitted from the certificate, benefits booklet, or other explanatory materials provided the insured, most courts hold that the policy exclusion is unenforceable.[8]

---

849 P.2d 549 (Or. Ct. App. 1993) ("a certificate of insurance provided under a group plan is part of the insurance contract, along with the master policy.")

[2] See, e.g., Mannschreck v. Connecticut Gen. Life Ins. Co., 263 N.W.2d 849 (Neb. 1978); Sahlin v. American Cas. Co., 436 P.2d 606 (Ariz. 1968); Riske v. National Cas. Co., 67 N.W.2d 385, 388 (Wis. 1954).

[3] See Standard of Am. Life Ins. Co. v. Humphreys, 519 S.W.2d 64 (Ark. 1975).

[4] See, e.g., Fontenot v. Global Marine, Inc., 703 F.2d 867 (5th Cir. 1983); Boyd v. Travelers Ins. Co., 421 S.W.2d 929 (Tex. Ct. App. 1967).

[5] See, e.g., Shenandoah Life Ins. Co. v. French, 373 S.E.2d 718 (Va. 1988); Chrysler Corp. v. Hardwick, 1 N.W.2d 43 (Mich. 1941); Morrison Assur. Co., v. Armstrong, 264 S.E.2d 320 (Ga. Ct. App. 1980).

[6] See, e.g., Standard of Am. Life Ins. Co. v. Humphreys, 519 S.W.2d 64 (Ark. 1975).

[7] See, e.g., Hale v. Life Ins. Co., 750 F.2d 547 (6th Cir. 1984), *appeal after remand,* 795 F.2d 22 (6th Cir. 1986); Davis v. Crown Life Ins. Co., 696 F.2d 1343 (11th Cir. 1983); Life Ins. Co. v. Lee, 519 F.2d 475 (6th Cir. 1975); Fittro v. Lincoln Nat'l Life Ins. Co., 757 P.2d 1374 (Wash. 1988) (en banc); Romano v. New England Mut. Life Ins. Co., 362 S.E.2d 334 (W.Va. 1987); General Motors Acceptance Corp. v. Martinez, 668 P.2d 498 (Utah 1983); Martin v. Crown Life Ins. Co., 658 P.2d 1099 (Mont. 1983); Martin v. Oklahoma Farmers Union, 622 P.2d 1078 (Okla. 1981); Hofeld v. Nationwide Life Ins. Co., 322 N.E.2d 454 (Ill. 1975); Riske v. National Cas. Co., 67 N.W.2d 385 (Wis. 1954).

[8] See, e.g., Hale v. Life Ins. Co. of N. Am., 750 F.2d 547 (6th Cir. 1984); Linn v. North Idaho Dist. Med. Serv. Bur., Inc., 638 P.2d 876 (Idaho 1981); Lecker v. General Am. Life Ins. Co., 525 P.2d 1114 (Haw. 1974); Blue Cross & Blue Shield of Md., Inc., v. Chestnut Lodge, Inc., 567 A.2d 147 (Md.Ct.App. 1989); Domke v. Farmers & Mechanics Savings Bank, 363 N.W.2d 898 (Minn. Ct. App. 1985). For additional discussion, see Annot., *Group*

Krauss v. Manhattan Life Insurance Co.,[9] a 1983 Second Circuit case, is indicative of the willingness of courts to construe coverage broadly where the certificate and master policy conflict. Hyman Krauss, a part-time officer of a printing company, was insured under a group life plan provided by the employer through a trust to which the employer belonged. The master policy, which was delivered to the trust fund's principal place of business, provided for a maximum of $25,000 coverage for part-time employees, but this limitation was never brought to Krauss's attention. None of the application forms inquired as to Krauss's full-time or part-time status. A certificate was issued to Krauss which stated his coverage at $100,000, and the employer paid premiums for Krauss based on that amount of coverage. When he died, the insurer tendered only $25,000 to Krauss's wife, the beneficiary; the insurer claimed that this sum was the maximum owed under the policy. Under the circumstances of the case, the court held that the insurer was estopped to deny that Krauss's beneficiary was entitled to $100,000 in coverage.

In addition to the principal documents (the master policy, the certificate, and the enrollment form), it is common for the insurer when it advertises a group insurance plan or upon the plan's effective date to explain the coverage through promotional booklets or other literature. Often these materials are deliberately cast in simplified language. If the supplementary materials appear to give more coverage than actually provided by the terms of the master policy or appear to diminish certain prerequisites to coverage, the insureds may develop expectations at odds with the actual coverage. In numerous cases, insureds have claimed under the doctrines of waiver or estoppel that the supplementary writings prevent the insurer from denying that coverage is restricted or that certain prerequisites to coverage have not been met. Courts are uniform in their willingness to entertain the claims of waiver and estoppel; the outcomes in the particular cases depend on the precise circumstances involved.[10]

[b]   The "Actively at Work" Problem

Insurers, whether marketing group or individual coverage, desire insureds who meet specific eligibility requirements. With individual policies, the medical examination is typically the means by which the insurer determines the applicant's eligibility. However, group insurers cannot engage in the same kinds of investigation and hope to achieve the economies essential to the reduced rates charged for group policies. To substitute for the detailed underwriting of individual policies, group insurers typically require that individuals enrolled in the policy be "actively employed" or "full-time employees" at the policy's effective date. It is probable that a person employed at the policy's effective date is in good health; a person who is ill at home and thus unable to work is not the kind of risk that the insurer wishes to underwrite.

Insurance: Binding Effects Of Limitations On Or Exclusions Of Coverage Contained In Master Group Policy But Not In Literature Given Individual Insureds, 6 A.L.R.4th 835 (1981).

[9] 700 F.2d 870 (2d Cir. 1983).

[10] See § 25E, *supra*; see generally Annot., *Group Insurance: Waiver Or Estoppel On Basis Of Statements In Promotional Or Explanatory Literature Issued To Insureds,* 36 A.L.R.3d 541 (1971).

The actively-at-work requirement has led to considerable litigation over what constitutes "active employment" or "full-time employment." *Estate of Bingham v. Nationwide Life Insurance Co.*[11] is illustrative. Bingham had a heart attack on August 24, 1977, and was hospitalized until September 27. He recuperated at home, occasionally taking a call from the office, until October 26, when he started spending half-days at the office. On November 1, Bingham's employer allowed the existing group life insurance plan to expire and arranged for a Nationwide policy to replace the existing policy. An enrollment card was signed for Bingham while he was away; on November 7, Bingham signed a card himself, on which he represented that on the date of signature he was "actively at work . . . on a full-time basis." He also represented that he worked "at least the number of hours in [his] employer's normal work week, but not less than 30 hours per week" and that "[d]uring the past four weeks" he had "not been absent from work on account of [his] own sickness or injury." On November 16, Bingham suffered a fatal heart attack.

The insured denied coverage to Bingham on the ground that he did not meet the full-time employment requirement. The policy defined an eligible person as one who is "regularly employed" or who subsequent to the policy's effective date "had been regularly employed . . . not less than one month." "Regular employment" was defined as being "continuously employed by the Policyholder for at least 30 hours each week." By any literal reading, Bingham did not meet these requirements. On the policy's effective date, he had only worked at the office five half-days and had only "occasionally" worked at home when taking a telephone call. On the date of his death, he had only worked nine full days. The court overcame the insurer's argument by reasoning that the policy's requirements on active employment were intended only to exclude part-time employees. Bingham was a full-time, "regularly employed" employee even though he had been substantially unavailable for work prior to his death due to illness.

Most courts agree that active and full-time employment does not require regular, continuous employment at a particular place.[12] Thus, a schoolteacher who has no instructional responsibilities during the summer should be considered "regularly employed" for purposes of coverage if the policy's effective date falls in the middle of the summer recess and the teacher is not physically present at the school where he or she is employed. Also, one who has a temporary, non-serious illness on the policy's effective date is usually treated as being covered as of the effective date on the ground that the policy's requirements are not intended to exclude from

---

[11] 638 P.2d 352 (Kan.Ct.App. 1981), *aff'd per curiam, as modified,* 646 P.2d 1048 (Kan. 1982).

[12] See, e.g., Great-West Life Assur. Co. v. Levy, 382 F.2d 357 (10th Cir. 1967) (insured, who sold insurance agency but continued in capacity of consultant, was full-time employee even though he did not work at office); Cody v. Remington Elec. Shavers, Div. of Sperry-Rand Corp., 427 A.2d 810 (Conn. 1980); 1 APPLEMAN § 44, at 122-30 (1991 Supp.) Compare Smith v. New England Mut. Life Ins. Co., 827 P.2d 635 (Haw. 1992) (provision in group life policy requiring three months of continuous active service must be read in conjunction with definition of employee, so that coverage is effective only after three months of continuous service as full-time employee).

coverage individuals with minor ailments.[13] However, in cases where the group member suffers from a serious illness and is unable to perform the employer's customary work, courts usually refuse coverage.[14] Moreover, when an employee is on strike, laid off, or otherwise not actively working on the effective date of the insurance, the employee is not covered.[15] The court in *Bingham* took a more extreme pro-insured view than do most courts, but the decision illustrates the proclivity for courts to find coverage in close cases.[16]

Whether an employee is actively at work can also raise a problem with the incontestability clause. This problem is discussed in an earlier section.[17]

§ 123 Special Problems of Risk Control

One of the advantages of marketing insurance to groups instead of individuals is that the per-risk marketing costs are substantially reduced, which translates into cheaper insurance for each insured. These savings are obtained, however, at the cost of forgoing individualized risk assessment. For example, a medical examination is rarely a prerequisite in group life insurance. Since group insurance necessarily involves less thorough appraisal of each underwritten risk, a greater likelihood exists that high-risk individuals will make up a disproportionate percentage of the pool of insureds, due to the operation of the principle of adverse selection.

To counteract the impact of adverse selection, insurers use various techniques to limit their exposure. Most group insurance is sold in the employment setting, and this is for good reason: employed people tend to constitute lower risks in health and life insurance, the principal group insurance areas, than non-workers. To assure

---

[13] See, e.g., Morris v. Mutual Benefit Life Ins. Co., 258 F. Supp. 186 (N.D. Ga. 1966); Augusta v. John Hancock Mut. Life Ins. Co., 170 N.Y.S.2d 908 (N.Y. Sup. Ct. 1958); 1 APPLEMAN § 44, at 136–46 (1991 Supp.).

[14] See, e.g., Elsey v. Prudential Ins. Co., 262 F.2d 432 (10th Cir. 1958); Commercial Ins. Co. v. Burnquist, 105 F. Supp. 920 (N.D. Iowa 1952); Smith v. Founders Life Assur., 333 S.E.2d 5 (Ga. Ct. App. 1985); Blum v. Prudential Ins. Co. of Am., 309 A.2d 905 (N.J.Super.Ct.Law Div. 1973), aff'd, 333 A.2d 277 (N.J. Super. Ct. App. Div. 1975); Boyer v. Travelers Ins. Co., 61 P.2d 925 (Cal. 1936); but see Lincoln Nat'l Life Ins. Co. v. Commonwealth Corrugated Container Corp., 327 S.E.2d 98 (Va. 1985) (employee in hospital at time group policy became effective, and who died five days later in hospital, was "actively at work.")

[15] See, e.g., Cudd v. John Hancock Mut. Life Ins. Co., 310 S.E.2d 830 (S.C. Ct. App. 1983); cf. Sheller-Globe Corp. v. Sheller, 413 N.E.2d 318 (Ind. Ct. App. 1980) (vacation pay period at end of termination did not constitute "active work" for purposes of calculating termination date).

[16] *Bingham'* s extreme interpretation of the full-time employment requirement is weak. Yet the result in that case is correct: the successor insurer should, in most situations, be required to step into the shoes of the prior insurer and assume its liabilities as they exist on the date of succession. Unfortunately, the court in *Bingham* did not rest the decision on this basis. See Robert H. Jerry, II, *Recent Developments in Kansas Insurance Law: A Survey, Some Analysis, and Some Suggestions,* 32 Kan. L. Rev. 287, 291–94 (1984).

[17] See § 104B[d], *supra.*

securing the underwriting objectives, a typical group insurance policy will require that a certain percentage of an eligible membership (e.g., 80 percent of the employees in an identified work force) enroll in the group before coverage begins. Similarly, by restricting coverage to those employees actually at work on the policy's effective date or who return to work within a few days, the insurer excludes from coverage any employee incapacitated by illness or injury.[1] Policies often prescribe a waiting period for coverage for those employees who are not at work on or immediately following the policy's effective date.[2] Thus, an employee who recovers might secure the coverage, but an employee who remains ill is excluded.

Insurer efforts to counter adverse selection have another impact that should not be overlooked. Group policies — particularly in health insurance — tend to cover the healthiest, fittest groups in society. This is simply because cheaper rates can be offered to these groups. The phenomenon reflects nothing more than the normal operation of market forces. This means that those most prone to illness and disability — the unemployed and the working poor whose employers do not provide health insurance coverage — are least likely to have group insurance, and these people are least able to afford the more expensive insurance marketed on an individual basis. This means that the most disadvantaged in society are the least likely to have insurance and thus are the least likely to have access to medical care. This problem, which has no easy solution, will become increasingly obvious as prices in the health care industry continue to rise.

§ 124　Termination and Modification

An individual can be insured under a group policy only if that person is a member of the group. Thus, if the person ceases to be a member of the group which is insured, most policies provide that the insurance coverage terminates.[1] Policies often provide, however, certain continuity provisions, and sometimes limited continuity is required by statute in the case of health insurance. Typically, if the certificate holder has made a contribution for a certain period of coverage and if that person's status as a member of the group terminates in the middle of the period, the coverage does not cease until the expiration of the last period for which the certificate holder made a contribution. Also, as is the case with most health insurance, when the group policy covers expenses incurred while the policy is in force, expenses incurred after the policy's termination, even if for an injury or illness suffered before the policy's termination, are not covered.[2]

[1] See, e.g., Helland v. Metropolitan Life Ins. Co., 488 F.2d 496 (9th Cir. 1973); Schulman v. Federated Life Ins. Co., 268 S.E.2d 704 (Ga. Ct. App. 1980); Rabinovitz v. Travelers Ins. Co., 105 N.W.2d 807 (Wis. 1960).

[2] See, e.g., Marriot v. Pacific Nat'l Life Assur. Co., 467 P.2d 981 (Utah 1970).

[1] See, e.g., Hamilton v. Travelers Ins. Co., 752 F.2d 1350 (8th Cir. 1985); Bartulis v. Metropolitan Life Ins. Co., 218 N.E.2d 225 (Ill. App. Ct. 1966).

[2] See, e.g., Forbau v. Aetna Life Ins. Co., 876 S.W.2d 132 (Tex. 1994); Howard v. Blue Cross & Blue Shield of Neb., 494 N.W.2d 99 (Neb. 1993); Altiere v. Blue Cross & Blue Shield of Ala., 551 So. 2d 290 (Ala. 1989); Fraker v. Sentry Life Ins. Co., 23 Cal. Rptr.2d 372 (Cal. Ct. App. 1993); Hebert v. Red Simpson, Inc., 544 So. 2d 751 (La. Ct. App. 1989).

In some cases, however, courts have held that the insurer's obligation to pay proceeds extends after the termination of the policy. Much depends on the particular circumstances. If the insurer has led the insured to believe, either through an ambiguity in the policy or through some representation, that the benefits exceed the coverage stated in the policy, some courts have held the insurer liable even after the termination. For example, in *Lutsky v. Blue Cross Hospital Service, Inc.*[3] the insured incurred medical expenses while a policy with a "lifetime maximum" of $1 million in coverage was in force. During the insured's treatment, the policy was replaced with another one, issued by the same insurer, which specified a lifetime maximum of $25,000 for the insured's particular kind of treatment. Despite the facts that the policy specified the insurer's right to terminate or modify the coverage at any time and that the policy only covered expenses incurred while the policy was in force, the court held that the insurer was obligated to provide coverage under the original policy with the higher limits. The ambiguity in the policy coupled with the unfairness to the insured led the court to hold that the insured was entitled to coverage past the termination of the original policy.

Whether a group representative has any liability to the certificate holder for modifying or terminating a group policy depends on the situation. If the plan is non-contributory (meaning the employer makes all premium payments) and the group representative gratuitously undertakes to manage the group insurance plan, most courts hold that the group representative is not liable to the certificate holder for failure to keep the policy in force and for modifying the insurance without giving notice to the certificate holder.[4] In contrast, if the plan is contributory (meaning the employee makes at least some of the premium payments) courts have held group representatives to a duty of good faith and due care in administering the policy and in notifying the employee of information relevant to the policy.[5]

In this same connection, most courts hold that the insurer and the group representative can jointly decide to terminate coverage or amend the policy.[6] Unless there is a provision in the policy to the contrary, the individual members of the group cannot prevent cancellation or termination.[7] However, a minority of courts hold, usually in cases involving contributory policies, that the certificate holders must consent to termination or modification of the coverage.[8] Even if the insureds' consent is not required, notice to the insureds usually is: most courts hold that the insurer is obligated to give notice to the insureds of any change in the coverage, whether termination or modification, before the change is effective. The purpose

---

[3] 695 S.W.2d 870 (Mo. 1985).

[4] See, e.g., Massachusetts Mut. Life Ins. Co. v. De Salvo, 482 P.2d 380 (Colo. 1971); Couch v. Connecticut General Life Ins. Co., 216 So. 2d 72 (Fla. Dist. Ct. App. 1968); see also Bell v. New York Life Ins. Co., 190 N.E.2d 432 (Ind. Ct. App. 1963).

[5] See, e.g., Estate of Saffles v. Reliance Universal, Inc., 701 S.W.2d 821 (Tenn. Ct. App. 1985); Paul Revere Life Ins. Co. v. Gardner, 438 N.E.2d 317 (Ind. Ct. App. 1982).

[6] See, e.g., Massachusetts Mut. Life Ins. Co. v. Nails, 549 So. 2d 826 (La. 1989); Lister v. American United Life Ins. Co., 797 P.2d 832 (Colo.Ct.App. 1990).

[7] See Guardian Life Ins. Co. v. Zerance, 479 A.2d 949 (Pa. 1984).

[8] See, e.g., Clayton v. National Elec. Products Corp., 219 A.2d 595 (Pa. 1966); Blue Cross-Blue Shield v. Jackson, 172 So. 2d 804 (ALa. Ct. App. 1965).

of this requirement is to enable each insured to take measures to secure appropriate insurance to compensate for the change in coverage.[9] If, however, the certificate holder's participation in the group plan is being canceled on account of that person's failure to make a premium payment when due, notice of cancellation is not required.[10]

Sometimes a group representative, such as an employer, will switch insurers in order to obtain a more favorable price or better coverage. This switch involves terminating one policy and establishing coverage under another. However, if the new policy contains a waiting period or some provision designed to exclude coverage of pre-existing illnesses or disabilities, a gap in coverage may exist. For example, assume that an employee, while the prior insurance policy was in effect, suffered a heart attack and was prevented from continuing work. If the new policy covers employees actively at work on its effective date, the ill employee faces this situation: the former coverage terminates and the employee is ineligible for the new policy. Although there are cases to the contrary,[11] ordinarily the new insurer assumes the rights and obligations of the former company as they exist on the date of succession.[12]

§ 125   Assignments; Changing the Beneficiary; Standing to Sue

As is the case with individual policies of insurance, the certificate holder in group life insurance normally has the right to designate the beneficiary and to change that designation at any time.[1] However, unlike individual policies of insurance, the certificate holder usually does not have the power to assign the policy. Normally, the master policy will have a clause prohibiting assignment.

---

[9] See, e.g., Chavez v. American Life & Cas. Ins. Co. 872 P.2d 366 (N.M. 1994) ("a majority of states require that notice of cancellation or change in policy be given to the employee certificate holder in a group contributory insurance policy"); Newton v. United Chambers Ins. Plans, 485 So. 2d 1147 (Ala. 1986); Freeman v. Bonnes Trucking, Inc., 337 N.W.2d 871 (Iowa 1983); Fassio v. Montana Physicians' Serv., 553 P.2d 998 (Mont. 1976); Ogden v. Continental Cas. Co., 494 P.2d 1169 (Kan. 1972). In Life Ins. Co. of Ark. v. Ashley, 824 S.W.2d 393 (Ark. 1992), the certificate holder who was killed 88 days after his group life insurance terminated was covered by individual insurance because he was not given proper notice of his right to convert to individual insurance; thus, the original 31-day conversion period was extended by the court to 91 days, and his death fell within this period. But see Mueller v. Healthplus, Inc., 589 A.2d 439 (D.C. 1991) ("Ordinarily, notice to the employee of cancellation of a group insurance policy is only required if it is expressly specified in the insurance contract.")

[10] See, e.g., Chavez v. American Life & Cas. Ins. Co. 872 P.2d 366 (N.M. 1994). See also Annot., *Termination of Employee's Individual Coverage Under Group Policy For Nonpayment Of Premiums,* 22 A.L.R.4th 321 (1983).

[11] See, e.g., Continental Cas. Co. v. Equitable Life Assur. Soc'y, 418 N.E.2d 1298 (N.Y. 1981) (two carriers required to share coverage); Harrod v. Sun Life Assur. Co., 176 S.E. 53 (Ga. Ct. App. 1934).

[12] See, e.g., Pacific Mut. Life Ins. Co. v. American Guar. Life Ins. Co., 722 F.2d 1498 (9th Cir. 1984); Northeastern Life Ins. Co. v. Gaston, 470 S.W.2d 128 (Tex. Ct. App. 1971); Micallef v. Travelers Ins. Co., 234 N.Y.S.2d 134 (N.Y.Civ.Ct. 1962).

[1] See 1 APPLEMAN § 45, at 144 (1981).

If the certificate holder dies and the insurer for some reason refuses to pay the proceeds, several possibilities exist regarding who might assert the certificate holder's claim against the insurer: the beneficiary (in the case of life insurance); the certificate holder's legal representative (the estate); the certificate holder (in the case of injury or disability covered by group accident or health insurance); or the group representative (acting as a trustee for the certificate holder). Courts have recognized the standing of each of the foregoing parties to assert claims against the insurer in the group insurance context.[2]

§ 126 Legislation Affecting Group Insurance

In 1917, the NAIC adopted model legislation defining group life insurance and specifying minimum standards.[1] This model act was substantially revised in 1956, and has been amended periodically since that time. The model legislation requires that a group insurance plan conform to one of several descriptions, each of which is structured around a particular kind of group. The various descriptions involve groups of employees, creditors or debtors, employee organizations or labor unions, associations, credit unions, and trusts for the benefit of employers, employees, or labor unions. The model statute also prescribes certain provisions that the policies must contain. In 1983, the NAIC adopted model legislation defining group health insurance and specifying minimum standards.[2] This act is substantially similar to the model act for group life insurance. All states have adopted some kind of statutory regulation of both group life and group health insurance. Most states have adopted some kind of statute patterned on the NAIC model act for group life insurance, and several states have followed the NAIC model for group health insurance.

In 1986, significant legislation was enacted by Congress concerning the continuity of group health insurance benefits. As discussed in an earlier section,[3] in recent years the number of Americans without any health insurance coverage has increased and the problems of access to health care have mounted. Those who are not covered by an employer-provided group health plan often cannot afford the high cost of privately marketed health insurance; thus, large groups of Americans — the unemployed, many self-employed persons, the working poor, and people who are between jobs — lack any kind of health insurance, which is often tantamount to lacking health care access. Dependents on employer-provided health care plans often lose coverage due to loss of the dependency status (due to divorce, death of the insured, etc.), and some insureds who change jobs discover that they cannot meet the underwriting requirements of the new employer's health insurance carrier.

---

[2] See, e.g., Steele v. General Am. Life Ins. Co., 535 P.2d 948 (Kan. 1975) (beneficiary); Knox v. Cuna Mut. Ins. Soc'y, 213 So. 2d 667 (Ala. 1968) (member and group representative); Russ v. Group Health, Inc., 356 N.Y.S.2d 193 (N.Y. Sup. Ct. 1974) (certificate holder); Bauer v. Bates Lumber Co., 503 P.2d 1168 (N.M.App. 1972) (estate).

[1] See NAIC, "Group Life Insurance Definition and Group Health Insurance Standard Provisions Model Act," III *Model Laws, Regulations, and Guidelines* at 565-1 (1993).

[2] See NAIC, "Group Health Insurance Definition and Group Health Insurance Standard Provisions Model Act," I *Model Laws, Regulations, and Guidelines* at 100-1 (1993).

[3] See § 64[c], *supra.*

To address at least part of the problem, Congress passed as part of the massive Consolidated Omnibus Budget Reconciliation Act of 1985 ("COBRA") requirements for group health insurance plans regarding continuity of coverage. The legislation amended the Internal Revenue Code to deny the business tax deduction for a group health plan which failed to include a continuation option for a widowed spouse and dependent children, a divorced or separated spouse and dependent children, and a Medicare-ineligible spouse and dependent children. Denying the deduction for failing to comply with the requirements effectively required virtually all group health plans to contain the continuation option. Congress later amended the law and substituted, effective with tax years beginning after January 1, 1989, a tax in place of the forfeiture of the tax deduction.[4]

Under COBRA, so called "qualified beneficiaries" must be offered the option to continue health insurance coverage for up to three years at group rates without meeting any physical examination or insurability requirement. The option is to be offered during a period, which must last at least 60 days, beginning at the time the individual otherwise would lose coverage under the group health plan. Coverage can be canceled during the three-year period if the employer ceases to provide any group health plan to employees, the beneficiary does not pay the premiums of the individual policy or becomes covered under another group policy or Medicare, or in some other circumstances. The premium payment on the individual coverage is to be paid by the beneficiary, but the premium cannot exceed 102 percent of the premium charged the employer and employee under the group health insurance. At the end of the continuation period, the insured is to be offered the right to convert to an individual plan, at normal individual rates, without evidence of insurability, if such an option is generally offered to beneficiaries of the group plan.[5]

COBRA has improved the health insurance coverage of many Americans. To illustrate the operation of the statute, consider the following example. The spouse of an insured under group health insurance incurs a disability that will require years of ongoing medical care and expenses. The disabled person has no insurance of his or her own; for a time, the person's medical expenses are reimbursed since the person is a dependent under the spouse's group plan. The insured spouse subsequently changes jobs, but the new insurer will not insure the disabled spouse for medical expenses incurred by the preexisting disability. The disabled person cannot obtain insurance in the private market either, due to the preexisting illness exclusion. (The same result would occur if the spouses were divorced after the one spouse was disabled.) COBRA makes it possible for the disabled spouse to purchase ongoing health insurance coverage for at least three years at group rates, and thereafter at individual rates (assuming all beneficiaries have the option to convert to individual coverage). But for the statute, the insured would have no coverage and perhaps no way to obtain needed, expensive medical care.[6]

---

[4] See 26 U.S.C. § 4980B(a).

[5] For more detail about COBRA, see 26 U.S.C. § 4980B; see also Roberta Casper Watson, *Cobra Health Continuation Benefits*, C840 ALI-ABA 241 (Sept. 9, 1993).

[6] The NAIC has also promulgated a model regulation on the continuity problem. See NAIC, "Group Coverage Discontinuance and Replacement Model Regulation," I *Model Laws,*

Notwithstanding the importance of COBRA in making health insurance more widely available, it falls far short of addressing all of the difficult problems in the availability of health insurance. As noted above, the option to convert to an individual plan after the period of continuation benefits expires is not guaranteed, and COBRA does not assist those who cannot obtain, for whatever reason, the initial health insurance policy. Moreover, it appears that COBRA has had at least one perverse effect. The availability of continuation benefits under COBRA has encouraged some employers to impose waiting periods which delay the effective date of health insurance coverage for new employees. In other words, employers who wish to reduce the cost of providing a group health policy find it easier to delay coverage for new employees under the reasoning that new employees are entitled under COBRA to continue their coverage under the insurance provided by prior employers. But COBRA continuation benefits are not available to those who are entering the workforce for the first time. Where benefits are available, the cost must be shouldered entirely by the employee, which will often make the coverage prohibitively expensive, particularly in areas with high medical costs and correspondingly high premiums under the group plan. Because COBRA is not a complete or even perfect solution to the complex problems of health care access, it is likely that future historians will consider COBRA an important step along a long path toward universal access to health insurance.

Regulations, and Guidelines at 110-1 (1992). This regulation, which has been adopted by statute or administrative regulation in about twenty states, is not nearly as broad, however, as the newly enacted federal legislation. Other states have adopted their own legislation as well. See also Annot., *Group Insurance: Construction, Application, And Effect Of Policy Provision Extending Conversion Privilege To Employee After Termination of Employment,* 32 A.L.R.4th 1037 (1984); Annot., *Medical Care Insurance: Right of Insured Under Individual Policy to Coverage Afforded by Group Policy From Which He Directly Transferred on Termination of His Employment,* 66 A.L.R.3d 1192 (1975) (discussing whether insured under individual medical care insurance policy, procured under conversion option of employer's group policy, is entitled to same coverage afforded by the group policy).

CHAPTER 13

AUTOMOBILE INSURANCE

§ 130 Overview

One of the most significant developments of the twentieth century is the widespread ownership and use of automobiles and other vehicles. During roughly the first half of the century, nearly one million Americans lost their lives in automobile accidents.[1] In 1992, 40,300 people died on the nation's highways; this large number is actually a substantial decline from the 56,300 highway deaths that occurred in 1972. In 1992, over 5.4 million personal injuries and $98 billion in economic loss were suffered in the 31.8 million auto accidents that occurred in the United States.[2] Because Americans crash their cars into other vehicles, property, and persons so frequently, automobile insurance in many respects has both a history and a set of governing principles of its own. These special principles are briefly explored in this chapter.

§ 131 The History of Automobile Accident Compensation

Under the common law tort system, the liability of one person to another is based on fault. Thus, as a prerequisite to recovery from the third party who caused an injury or loss, the plaintiff-accident victim must establish that the defendant negligently caused the victim's injury or loss. An equally important practical prerequisite to the plaintiff's suit is that the defendant be worth suing — that is, that the defendant have personal assets or insurance sufficient to pay any resulting judgment. If these prerequisites are not met, the person injured in an automobile accident must look to his or her own resources — either first-party insurance or personal assets — for relief from the loss.

---

[1] U.S. Dep't of Commerce, Bureau of the Census, Historical Statistics of the United States 719 (1975).

[2] The data is supplied by the National Safety Council and the Insurance Information Institute. In terms of the death rate per 100 million miles driven, the decline in fatalities has been extraordinary — from 2.68 deaths per 100 million miles in 1983 to 1.80 deaths in 1992, a decline of 33% in one decade. Undoubtedly, the decline in drunken driving, increased use of seat belts, child restraints, and motorcycle helmets, and safer vehicles have contributed to this dramatic decline. See Insurance Information Institute, *The Fact Book 1994: Property/ Casualty Insurance Facts* 87 (1994).

(Matthew Bender & Co., Inc.)
(Pub.837)

Early in the twentieth century, some observers took the position that the fault system of assessing liability and remedying loss was an inefficient mechanism for dealing with the consequences of automobile accidents. One of the first commentaries was a 1919 article in the *Minnesota Law Review,* which set forth a proposal to reduce the high costs of litigation by eliminating negligence as an issue in motor vehicle accident cases. The article's author also recommended spreading the costs of compensating auto accident victims through statutorily mandated insurance coverage.[1]

The proposal that victims of automobile accidents be compensated by their own insurer without regard to their own fault was hardly radical. In property, fire, accident, and health insurance, injured parties have always been allowed to recover without regard to their own fault (as long as the loss was not intentionally self-inflicted). For example, if an insured negligently loses a diamond ring, negligently drops a lighted match into a sofa causing its destruction, negligently operates a car and hits a tree, or smokes cigarettes and develops a smoking-related disease that leads to his or her hospitalization, the insurer will reimburse the insured's economic loss, even though the insured arguably should bear some measure of responsibility for it. Moreover, some losses for which third parties should be held responsible are compensated only by first-party insurers. For example, if a third party burns down the insured's house or if a third party negligently injures the insured and causes health care expenses to be incurred, the insured with first-party coverage is entitled to reimbursement from his or her own insurer, whether or not the third party is ultimately held responsible for the loss. The insured, instead of looking to the negligent third party or that party's insurer for reimbursement, deals with his or her own insurer on a first-party basis and is reimbursed by that insurer for the loss. If the insurer asserts subrogation rights, the loss will fall on the third party causing the loss, but if the third party is financially irresponsible, the insurer, instead of the injured party, will not be compensated.

Although the proposal had the advantage of ensuring that more victims of automobile accidents would be compensated for their injuries, the proposal was highly detrimental to the victim who would be able to recover more under the traditional common law recovery than under the mandatory first-party coverage. For this reason, states were initially unwilling to embrace the proposal's no-fault concept.

States were, however, attracted to the idea of compulsory liability insurance. In 1925, Massachusetts became the first state to address the problem of motorists being unable to answer for the harm caused by their negligence in a systematic way.[2] The

---

[1] See Ernest C. Carman, *Is a Motor Vehicle Accident Compensation Act Advisable,* 4 Minn. L. Rev. 1 (1919). Carman urged mandatory first-party coverage for all motorists. He also urged mandatory "compensation insurance" which would pay the losses of persons injured by the motorist, whether or not the motorist was negligent. Where multiple policies applied, he proposed that the loss be shared by pro rata by the insurers according to premiums paid.

[2] In 1925, the same year the Massachusetts statute was enacted, Connecticut enacted a statute that authorized the State Commissioner of Motor Vehicles to require the operator and/or owner of a vehicle involved in an accident to establish financial responsibility. Alan I. Widiss, *Uninsured and Underinsured Motorist Insurance* (1995), § 1.2.

statute enacted by the Massachusetts legislature, which became effective in 1927, required every person registering a motor vehicle in the state either to show a certificate stating that the person has liability insurance, to produce a bond, or to deposit cash, stock, or bonds as security for the payment of judgments. The purpose of this statute was to remedy the problem of the defendant who lacked the personal resources to compensate the victims of his or her negligence.[3] In other words, if the victim of an accident possessed a valid claim against the negligent motorist, the victim would be guaranteed reimbursement by the third party's insurer.

The Massachusetts statute was an important step forward in providing relief for victims of auto accidents, but the statute contained many gaps. Before the liability insurer would be required to pay proceeds, it was necessary for the injured party to establish the insured-tortfeasor's liability. Thus, the purpose of the statute was not as much to compensate victims as it was to ensure solvent defendants. If, for example, the injured party were contributorily negligent (comparative negligence principles would not receive widespread application until forty years later), the injured third party would obtain no reimbursement.

Another weakness in the compulsory liability insurance statutes was the relatively low compulsory coverage. At this early time (and even today), the limits of most liability policies were very low, meaning that the financial resources available for paying the injured party's loss were restricted. Moreover, many such statutes did not apply to out-of-state drivers, many of whom caused accidents to the state's residents but who could not be held financially responsible for the loss. Similarly, the mandatory liability coverages were available to protect victims of accidents occurring in the insured's state, but no coverage was required if the insured were injured in an accident in another state. Furthermore, the compulsory liability insurance statutes did not address the problem of the hit-and-run driver. If the tortfeasor could not be located or identified, the compulsory liability coverage was of no avail. Finally, despite the mandatory nature of the statutes, not all operators of vehicles purchased the insurance, and some owners let their policies lapse. Under the compulsory liability statutes, if a person were injured by an uninsured motorist who lacked sufficient personal resources to pay the judgment, the victim of the accident would be uncompensated.

Many states followed Massachusetts's lead and enacted compulsory liability insurance statutes. Some states enacted alternative — and often less effective — statutes to deal with the same problem. Some forced drivers involved in accidents to prove their financial responsibility or else give up their license and vehicle registration. Taking uninsured motorists off the road was a good idea for the future, but penalizing the irresponsible driver provided no economic redress for the person already injured by that driver. Fortunately, most states adopted, often in conjunction with compulsory liability insurance statutes, legislation that required the owner of a vehicle to prove financial responsibility or the existence of valid insurance at the time of vehicle registration.

Despite the beneficial effects of the compulsory liability insurance and financial responsibility statutes, it became clear by the late 1940s that the statutes did not

---

[3]*No-Fault and Uninsured Motorist Automobile Insurance* § 4.00[3], at 4–5 (1986).

provide a complete answer to the problem of financially irresponsible motorists. Some motorists continued to lack coverage altogether, exclusions or policy breaches eliminated coverage in some instances, and occasionally the tortfeasor was an unidentified hit-and-run motorist.

Several states, however, took action to address the problem of the uninsured or hit-and-run motorist. These states enacted — and five states still have today — "unsatisfied judgment fund" laws. These statutes enabled the uncompensated motorist who was legally entitled to recover damages from an uninsured or hit-and-run motorist to recover from a state fund to which insurers and vehicle owners were required to contribute.[4] In effect, the funds resembled insurance companies managed by the state government. Like an insurance policy, each fund had a limit of liability; the fund's proceeds were not intended to make each claimant whole.[5] One weakness with such funds, which has existed since they were first established, is that they provide no coverage for accidents outside the jurisdiction of the fund. Thus, a resident of a state with an unsatisfied judgment fund, unless some other kind of insurance is purchased, has no coverage for losses caused by an uninsured motorist in an accident outside the state.

After the first unsatisfied judgment funds were created, insurers quickly sensed that the coverage provided by the funds could be provided by the insurers themselves as endorsements to liability policies. Spurred by the prospect of other states setting up such funds and preempting the business, insurers began to market uninsured motorist insurance, and the remaining states eventually enacted statutes requiring that such coverage be offered to motorists.

Under uninsured motorist coverage, if the insured can establish that an uninsured third party was legally responsible for the insured's injury, the insured's own insurer is required to reimburse the insured's loss. Thus, uninsured motorist insurance is a kind of first-party coverage: the insured pays a premium to his or her own insurer for coverage in the event a financially irresponsible person is legally responsible for the insured's injury. If the insurer can establish that no tort occurred or that the tortfeasor was immune from liability, the insurer is not obligated under uninsured motorist coverage to pay proceeds to the insured-victim. In addition, the insured's contributory negligence can be asserted by the insurer as an offset to the insured's recovery.[6]

These statutory changes were extremely important, but none altered the underlying fault-premise of the liability system. The doctrines of contributory negligence and assumption of risk prevented many victims from recovering anything for their injuries. In the late 1920s and early 1930s, over half the states enacted "guest statutes," which prohibited a gratuitous passenger from recovering damages from the driver without showing something more than ordinary negligence (such as gross negligence or wanton conduct). Since 1970, these statutes have been declared

---

[4] See CCH Auto. Ins. Law Rptr. ¶ 1000, at 1012 (1986). See 2 Irvin E. Schermer, *Automobile Liability Insurance* § 23.01, at 23.2 (2d rev. ed. 1989).

[5] For a detailed study of unsatisfied judgment fund laws, see G. Victor Hallman, *Unsatisfied Judgment Funds* (1968).

[6] NO-FAULT TREATISE § 1.30.

unconstitutional in many states, but guest statutes still exist in a handful of states, and they preclude tort recovery by many passengers in those jurisdictions.[7] Moreover, in some jurisdictions, some kinds of defendants enjoy immunity from suit in tort. These immunities — primarily the governmental, charitable, interspousal, and parent-child — have been eroded substantially in recent years, but where they still exist, tort recovery is precluded.[8]

As states experimented with repairs of the fault-system for relieving the victims of automobile accidents, a number of studies on the overall effectiveness of the fault system were underway, and various commentators critically analyzed the tort-liability system and suggested changes in it.[9] A study under the auspices of Columbia University was the principal basis for a no-fault plan adopted in Saskatchewan, Canada, in 1946. The distinctive feature of the Saskatchewan plan was its provision for mandatory first-party protection for victims of automobile accidents.[10] In 1965, then-Professor Robert Keeton and Professor Jeffrey O'Connell published an important book that comprehensively analyzed both the limitations of the traditional liability system and the pros and cons of no-fault. The book also contained a model no-fault plan.[11] In 1970, the Department of Transportation released a study critical of the traditional liability system and supporting no-fault. The DOT study confirmed what previous studies had determined: compensation for accident victims rarely bore a fair relation to accident losses; counsel fees and litigation costs reduced recoveries; payment usually occurred long after the injury; and court dockets were overloaded with automobile cases. The DOT study also revealed that liability insurance was becoming increasingly difficult to obtain, that companies were more carefully screening applicants in order to increase profits, and that many more motorists were driving without liability insurance.[12]

In Massachusetts, the problems discussed in the studies were particularly severe; in fact, Massachusetts residents paid the highest automobile liability insurance premiums in the nation. In 1971, the Massachusetts legislature responded by enacting the first no-fault statute in the United States.[13] This statute contained the two key components of modern no-fault legislation: (1) compulsory first-party coverage for personal losses, such as medical and funeral expenses, lost earnings,

---

[7] *Id.,* § 1.10[4] at 1-15 to 1-16.

[8] *Id.,* § 1.10[4] at 1-17 to 1-18.

[9] See, e.g., Albert A. Ehrenzweig, *"Full Aid" Insurance for the Traffic Victim* (1954); Robert E. Keeton & Jeffrey O'Connell, *Basic Protection for the Traffic Victim: A Blueprint for Reforming Automobile Insurance* (1965).

[10] See Keeton & O'Connell, note 9, *supra,* at 140–48.

[11] See Robert E. Keeton & Jeffrey O'Connell, *Basic Protection for the Traffic Victim* (1965).

[12] U.S. Dep't of Transportation, *Economic Consequences of Automobile Accident Injuries,* Volumes I and II (1970).

[13] In 1972, the National Conference of Commissioners on Uniform State Laws proposed model no-fault legislation. See 14 U.L.A. 35 (1990). The Model Act, titled the "Uniform Motor Vehicle Accident Reparations Act," has been adopted in substantially the form of the model only in Kentucky. Ky. Rev. Stat. Ann. §§ 304.39-010 to 304.39-340. Even at that, the Kentucky statute contains many variations and deletions, as well as additions, to the Model Act.

and personal services, without regard to fault; (2) a limitation upon the right of a victim of someone else's negligence to sue and recover damages from that person in a tort action.

A number of states followed Massachusetts' approach, while another group of states enacted the first component of no-fault, the mandatory first-party coverage element, but not the second. This approach is sometimes called "add-on no-fault," but in the view of some this approach is not no-fault at all because there is no modification of the underlying tort liability system.[14] By 1975 twenty-six states, the District of Columbia, and Puerto Rico had adopted some kind of no-fault legislation,[15] although fifteen of these states were add-on no-fault jurisdictions.[16]

In some respects, it is fair to say that what happened in the 1970s with respect to first-party coverage was the most important development of the period. In addition to the fifteen states that mandated the purchase of first-party coverage for medical and hospital expenses, four other states mandated that such coverage be offered to purchasers of automobile liability insurance.[17] In addition, regardless of the statutory mandates, insurers offered this coverage as optional benefits in all states by 1974.[18] Those who purchased such coverage, either because it was mandated or because they desired the optional coverage, and their families could recover some benefits merely by showing that they were injured in an automobile accident and that they had the insurance. In the looser sense of the term, this was "no-fault" coverage, although it was not widely recognized as such; most considered it merely a supplemental coverage that provided a first-party protection, as if it were simply health insurance for injuries arising out of auto accidents. This coverage is called "medical payments insurance," or "MedPay" insurance. MedPay, while similar to the first-party coverages required under no-fault law (usually called "Personal Injury Protection" or "PIP" benefits), differs in some respects.[19] The most significant difference is one of breadth: MedPay typically covers medical and hospital expenses, but PIP ordinarily covers these expenses plus funeral expenses, lost wages, and other economic losses.

By the 1990s, no-fault's first generation of experience was over, and the experience was mixed. Widely varied interpretations of the success of no-fault's first

---

[14] See Ruth Gastel, *No-Fault Auto Insurance,* Insurance Information Institute III Abstracts (April 1995) ("in its strictest form, no-fault applies only to state laws that both provide for the payment of no-fault first-party benefits and restrict the right to sue.")

[15] *Id.,* § 4.30 at 4-21 to 4-25. For discussion of the effect of these statutes, see U.S. Dep't of Transportation, *Compensating Auto Accident Victims: A Follow-Up Report on No-Fault Auto Insurance Experiences* (1985); Alan I. Widiss et al., *No-Fault Automobile Insurance in Action: The Experiences in Massachusetts, Florida, Delaware and Michigan* (1977); Willis P. Rokes, *No-Fault Insurance* (1971); American Bar Association, Special Committee on Automobile Insurance Legislation, *Automobile No-Fault Insurance* (Feb. 1978); All-Industry Research Advisory Committee, *Automobile Injuries and Their Compensation in the United States* (1979).

[16] Robert H. Joost, *Automobile Insurance and No-Fault* (2d ed. 1992), at § 1.1 at pp. 1-3.

[17] *Id.,* at § 1.1 at pp. 1-3.

[18] *Id.,* § 1.9, at p. 23 n. 53.

[19] See Joost, *supra* note 16, at § 1.9, pp. 23-24.

twenty years are now offered, and the current debate over how to deal with the losses incurred in automobile accident is no less intense.

§ 132   The Current Landscape for Compensating Automobile Accident Injuries

[a]   The Traditional System

[1]   Overview

The traditional method of compensating auto accident victims uses the tort liability system to remedy an injured person's economic and non-economic losses, and the premise of the tort system is that the person responsible for causing the victim's injury should be held responsible for the loss. Thus, the victim's injuries are compensated through whatever liability insurance or personal assets the tortfeasor possesses, as complemented by whatever first-party insurance the victim has. The traditional system also relies upon uninsured and underinsured coverages to fill in reimbursement gaps created by tortfeasors who lack insurance or other means to compensate the victims of their torts. Also, the traditional system is not inconsistent with first-party coverage, i.e. MedPay; ordinarily, however, the insurer that provides first-party coverage seeks to preserve a subrogation right against the tortfeasor.

[2]   The Liability Insurance Component

Currently, forty-two states and the District of Columbia require every person registering a motor vehicle in the state to present a certificate stating that he or she has liability insurance in at least a specified minimum amount. These statutes provide victims of automobile accidents with access to funds to cover their loss by requiring each vehicle owner in the state to have "security" for any judgments that may be registered against the owner of the vehicle arising out of the vehicle's operation.[1] The statutes typically state minimum coverages that every policy of motor vehicle liability insurance issued in a state must contain. In Kansas, for example, the statute requires that the policy provide liability coverage of not less than $25,000 for bodily injury to or death of one person in any one accident, a limit not less than $50,000 for bodily injury to or death of two or more persons in any one accident, and a limit no less than $10,000 for harm to or destruction of property of others in any one accident.[2] Someone who purchases the minimum coverage would be said to have a liability policy with coverage of "25/50/10," which refers to the amounts of coverage purchased for "bodily injury to one person/bodily injury per occurrence/property damage per occurrence."

[3]   Financial Responsibility Requirements

Compulsory liability insurance statutes typically dovetail into, or are coterminous with, statutes that require the owner of the motor vehicle to demonstrate financial

---

[1] See Insurance Information Institute, *The Fact Book 1994: Property/Casualty Insurance Facts* 117-18 (1994).

[2] Kan. Stat. Ann. § 40-3107.

responsibility. These statutes typically function in one of two ways. Under one orientation, the statute seeks to impose financial responsibility for accidents that occurred in the past. The other orientation attempts to ensure that the owner of a vehicle will be financially responsible for future accidents.

Financial responsibility statutes that are oriented toward the past typically operate in one of three ways. Under one form of the statute, if an accident involving personal or property damage of a specified severity occurs, the owner of each vehicle involved in the accident, regardless of fault, is obligated to demonstrate financial responsibility. This requirement is typically fulfilled by filing a certificate of insurance covering the owner and operator of the vehicle, by posting a bond, or by depositing money or securities with a governmental entity. If a person subject to the act fails to demonstrate financial responsibility, the person's driving privileges and sometimes the vehicle's registration are suspended. A second form of the statute requires the suspension of the licenses and registrations of a tortfeasor who fails to satisfy a judgment arising out of an automobile accident. A variant of this form states that the tortfeasor's licenses and registrations are suspended upon the presentation to the administrator of a final judgment against the tortfeasor. A third form requires that a tortfeasor demonstrate financial responsibility after being convicted for violating a traffic law.

Regardless of how they operate, these kinds of financial responsibility statutes suffer from the substantial disadvantage that their requirements are not triggered until after a loss has occurred. If the owner cannot establish his or her financial responsibility after an accident, the owner's driver's license and perhaps vehicle registration are subject to suspension. If the owner cannot produce appropriate insurance, the owner is required to deposit cash or securities as a condition to retention of his or her license. Once a license is suspended, the license can be restored only if the owner can produce an effective insurance policy and show that any past judgment against the owner arising out of an accident has been satisfied. Suspensions continue until any outstanding judgment is satisfied and proof of financial responsibility is provided. The theory of this kind of statute is that the owner-tortfeasor will be pressured to pay damages owed as a result of a past accident in order to obtain the privilege of driving, but no guarantee exists that a victim injured in an accident will ever be reimbursed for the loss.

To address this potential problem, most financial responsibility statutes follow the second orientation, which seeks to guarantee that owners of vehicles will be financially responsible for future accidents. This is accomplished through certification provisions, which require the owner of a vehicle to produce evidence of financial responsibility as a prerequisite to being allowed to register the vehicle or to renew its registration. Although liability insurance is mandatory, somewhere between five and twenty percent of the vehicles operated on the highways today are not covered by valid policies of liability insurance.[3] In some areas of the country, particularly where insurance is more expensive, the percentage of uninsured motorists is higher. For example, a study in California undertaken by that state's

---

[3] See Alan I. Widiss, *Uninsured and Underinsured Motorist Insurance (1995)*, § 1.12 (summarizing recent studies).

insurance department showed that 27.8 percent of vehicles in the state are uninsured (about 5.8 million motorists), and the percentage was as high as 37 percent in Los Angeles County.[4]

[4]   Observations

Few would seriously suggest that the traditional liability system is perfect. No enforcement mechanism can assure that 100 percent of the motorists in any given state have liability insurance, even if it is compulsory. Uninsured and underinsured motorist benefits can help fill these gaps,[5] but because UM and UIM coverage allows an insured to recover from his or her own insurer to the extent the insured could recover in tort against the uninsured (or underinsured) motorist, valid defenses to the insured's claim will prevent the insured from receiving compensation for his or her loss.

To some extent, MedPay benefits can help when liability insurance falls short (and MedPay benefits are important for the circumstance where the insured causes his or her own injury and there is no other responsible party). This, however, only serves to raise another issue: the traditional liability system requires risk-averse people to "double insure." One must purchase liability insurance to protect oneself from the consequences of one's own negligence, and the cost of this coverage will be, in theory, a function of the likelihood that the insured will cause someone else a loss. But it is not possible to rely on other people to do the same; thus, it is also necessary to purchase sufficient first-party coverage to guard against being injured by someone else, and the cost of this coverage will be a function of how many people in one's vicinity are probably driving without coverage.

One of the important reasons this system survives in so many jurisdictions is that it is understood by most people. Auto accidents are almost always the result of someone's negligence, and the notion that the negligent party should be responsible for the loss is a powerful one, as is the related idea that "my premiums" should not be determined by the poor driving habits of other people. Yet it is no small irony that in the American legal system the idea that an injured party should be reimbursed for loss without regard to his or her fault is actually more important than the fault-based mechanism for recovering damages found in tort law. All first-party insurance is essentially "no-fault" coverage: an individual who negligently starts a fire that burns down his or her house recovers under the individual's own fire insurance policy; a person whose negligent operation of his or her auto results in a one-car accident will be covered for both the personal injury and property damage, assuming the person purchased the correct coverages; a person who incurs medical expenses because of deliberate (e.g., excessive smoking or drinking) or negligent (e.g., standing on the top step of a ladder and falling off) acts is protected by his or her health insurance. Overall, the number of situations in which an individual looks to a third party as his or her primary source of relief is actually quite small relative to all compensable losses that occur in our society.

---

[4] Ruth Gastel, *supra* § 131 note 14.

[5] See § 134, *infra*.

[b] Add-on No-Fault

In eleven jurisdictions (in addition to the true no-fault states discussed below), statutes require that insureds be given an opportunity to purchase first-party no-fault benefits that provide compensation for economic loss suffered as a result of an auto accident. These statutes do not limit the right to sue in tort. However, individuals who recover no-fault benefits cannot recover those benefits a second time in a lawsuit against the tortfeasor.[6] In some of these jurisdictions, the insurer has a subrogation right against the tortfeasor to the extent of the payment of first-party benefits.[7] Where a subrogation right does not exist, the assumption is that the system will produce some cost savings in circumstances where a person's losses are less than the amount of no-fault coverage; obviously, such a person has no incentive to bring a suit against the tortfeasor. In two of the eleven jurisdictions,[8] the motorist is required to purchase the no-fault benefits; in the other nine states,[9] the purchase of the benefits is optional.

[c] True No-Fault

During the 1970s, sixteen states mandated no-fault benefits and established thresholds for the right to bring a tort action against the person causing the injury. The amount of the benefits varied, as did the thresholds. All of the plans but one had monetary thresholds; under these plans, if the injured party had medical expenses above a certain amount, the person could sue a third party in tort, but if the expenses were below the threshold, the person could not pursue a tort remedy. Some of the plans combined a monetary threshold with a verbal threshold, under which a person could also sue if he or she suffered an injury of a particular type (such as a broken weight-bearing bone, permanent disfigurements, etc.).[10]

Through the years, some states modified their no-fault laws, and some statutes were repealed.[11] As of 1995, thirteen states[12] and Puerto Rico have true no-fault laws, meaning statutes that mandate the purchase of first-party benefits and place some restrictions on tort suits. Five of the thirteen states[13] use verbal thresholds

---

[6] Joost, *supra* § 131 note 16, at §§ 2:19, 5.01; Gastel, *supra* § 131 note 14.

[7] *Id.*, § 5.01.

[8] The two are Delaware and Oregon. Joost, *supra*. § 131 note 16, § 5.1.

[9] In addition to Delaware and Oregon, the other nine add-on jurisdictions are Arkansas, the District of Columbia, Maryland, New Hampshire, South Dakota, Texas, Virginia, Washington, and Wisconsin. *Id.*

[10] See Joost, *supra* note 16. See generally Annot., *What Constitutes Sufficiently Serious Personal Injury, Disability, Impairment, or the Like to Justify Recovery of Damages Outside of No-Fault Automobile Insurance Coverage*, 33 A.L.R.4th 767 (1984).

[11] Nevada repealed its no-fault statute in 1980, Georgia repealed its no-fault statute in 1991, and Connecticut repealed its no-fault statute in 1993. Pennsylvania repealed its no-fault statute in 1984, but then reenacted a choice no-fault statute, discussed below, in 1990. See Ruth Gastel, *supra* § 131 note 14.

[12] The thirteen states are Colorado, Florida, Hawaii, Kansas, Kentucky, Massachusetts, Michigan, Minnesota, New Jersey, New York, North Dakota, Pennsylvania, and Utah. See Ruth Gastel, *supra* § 131 note 14.

[13] The five are Florida, Michigan, New Jersey, New York, and Pennsylvania. *Id.*

for the right to sue in tort, and the remainder use a monetary threshold. Also, three of the states,[14] as discussed below, allow motorists to reject the limitation on tort actions and thereby retain the right to sue for injuries suffered in automobile accidents.

While it can be said that twenty-three states, the District of Columbia, and Puerto Rico are no-fault jurisdictions, only ten of these jurisdictions unconditionally require that all the motorists in the state surrender the right to sue in tort. Three states make the limitation on the right to sue in tort possible, but do not require it. In the remaining jurisdictions, the first-party no-fault benefits are optional, and the right to sue in tort is not affected, except to the extent that a person who collects first-party benefits cannot recover the same benefits twice.

As for the thirteen true no-fault jurisdictions, the extent to which the tort system is replaced with no-fault principles depends on the level of the thresholds. Some states adopted relatively low thresholds in their statutes; for example, in the 1973 Kansas statute, the victim must have suffered an injury that caused medical expenses of at least $500 to be incurred or that consisted "in whole or in part of permanent disfigurement, a fracture of a weightbearing bone, a compound, comminuted, displaced or compressed fracture, loss of a body member, permanent injury within reasonable medical probability, permanent loss of a bodily function or death."[15] The thresholds were in the alternative, and the monetary threshold was relatively easy to meet. Moreover, many states did not increase their thresholds for many years, and a decade or more of inflation substantially eroded their impact. For example, it was not until 1987 that Kansas raised its threshold to $2000. At the opposite extreme is a state like Hawaii, where the threshold, called the "medical rehabilitation limit," is adjusted annually and which was set at $10,000 in 1992.[16] Obviously, a high threshold prevents a relatively larger number of tort claims from being litigated.

The kinds of benefits that no-fault policies provide on a first-party basis vary from state to state, but most benefits fall into one of five categories: (1) the insured's loss of income, wages, or earnings; (2) the value of personal services that the insured would ordinarily have performed for his or her family; (3) the survivors' loss, based on the income, wages, or earnings that a deceased insured would have provided; (4) medical, health-related, and rehabilitation expenses; and (5) funeral expenses. These benefits are commonly called "personal injury protection" benefits, or "PIP benefits."

All no-fault statutes permit insurers to insert some exclusions in the policies. For example, only injuries "arising out of the use" of a vehicle[17] need be covered, and benefits are payable only to "covered persons." A common exclusion eliminates coverage for persons who failed to purchase a required policy in circumstances where the policy would have provided coverage for the injury in question. The obvious purpose of such an exclusion is to encourage people to purchase no-fault

---

[14] The three are Kentucky, New Jersey, and Pennsylvania.

[15] Kan. Stat. Ann. § 40-3117 (1974).

[16] See Haw. Rev. Stat. § 431:10C-308.

[17] See Annot., *What Constitutes "Motor Vehicle" for Purposes of No-Fault Insurance,* 73 A.L.R.4th 1053 (1989).

coverage and to prevent the insurance industry generally from having to reimburse losses for which additional premiums should have been collected. Statutes also routinely permit exclusions for injuries suffered while intentionally attempting to inflict injury on another, while fleeing the police, while under the influence of alcohol, etc.[18]

Most no-fault statutes also give the insurer that pays no-fault benefits a subrogation right against the tortfeasor.[19] Thus, if the insured's injuries are sufficiently serious that the insured has an action in tort against the third-party who caused the injury, the insurer is entitled to be reimbursed out of the insured's recovery to the extent the judgment duplicates PIP benefits paid. In situations where subrogation is available and is asserted, the burden of paying the no-fault benefits actually falls on the tortfeasor's liability insurer. If the insured's injuries are such that no action in tort can be brought against the third-party, the insurer has no subrogation right — since the insured has no right against the tortfeasor to which the insurer can be subrogated.

Most no-fault statutes do not mandate first-party coverage for property damage. Currently, only Michigan and Delaware require the insurer to issue no-fault coverage for property damage caused by their insured motorists arising out of the use, operation, or maintenance of the vehicle. Thus, for the most part, American no-fault is limited to personal injury losses.[20]

The constitutionality of no-fault statutes has been challenged in several states on a variety of grounds, usually due process and equal protection. With only a very few exceptions, courts have upheld no-fault statutes against these constitutional challenges.[21]

[d]   Choice Systems

Nothing precludes putting a no-fault and traditional tort system side-by-side in the same state, as discussed in more detail below. No state currently has an ambitious choice system in place, but three states (Kentucky, New Jersey, and Pennsylvania) give motorists the opportunity to surrender their right to sue in tort in exchange for lower premiums or higher benefits. In Kentucky, the statute requires each motorist to purchase no-fault insurance unless the motorist affirmatively rejects no-fault and the limitation on tort suits; however, any motorist rejecting no-fault must maintain minimum amounts of liability insurance.[22] Under the New Jersey statute, each automobile owner must maintain specified no-fault coverage. However, each owner then is asked to choose between (a) retaining the right to sue in tort for all accidental

---

[18] See *No-Fault and Uninsured Motorist Automobile Insurance* § 10.00 et seq.

[19] See *id.* § 14.70, at 14-38 to 14-42.

[20] See *id.* § 13.00 et seq.

[21] See generally *id.* § 3.00 et seq., at 3-1 to 3-36; 1 Schermer, § 11.01–11.14, at 11-1 to 11-39; Josephine Y. King, *Constitutionality of No-Fault Jurisprudence,* 1982 Utah L. Rev. 797. In 1972, the Illinois Supreme Court held the Illinois statute unconstitutional on the ground that it did not apply to all types of motor vehicles, see Grace v. Howlett, 283 N.E.2d 474 (Ill. 1972), and Illinois does not currently have a no-fault statute.

[22] Joost, *supra* § 131 note 16, § 8.22.

injuries, and (b) giving up the right to sue in tort unless the injury is "serious," as defined in the statute (i.e., the verbal threshold). If no choice is made, the insured is treated as having elected the verbal threshold.[23] The Pennsylvania statute is like the New Jersey statute, except that the option which surrenders a portion of the right to sue in tort (called the "limited tort option" as opposed to the "full tort option") can sue for all medical and other economic losses, but cannot claim pain and suffering unless the injuries fall within the statute's definition of "serious injury" or other described condition.[24]

[e]　Possible Future Developments

[1]　Perceptions of the Current System

The record of the first generation of no-fault statutes passed in the 1970s is mixed. A summary of developments since 1980 illustrates the absence of consensus on the effectiveness of no-fault: Nevada repealed its statute in 1980; the District of Columbia enacted a no-fault statute in 1983; Pennsylvania repealed its true no-fault law in 1984 and replaced it with an add-on no-fault statute, and then replaced this statute with a choice statute in 1990; New Jersey amended its no-fault statute in 1984 and 1989, converting it into a choice statute; Georgia repealed its no-fault statute in 1991; and Connecticut repealed its no-fault statute in 1993. California will have a public referendum on no-fault on the ballot during the March 1996 presidential primary election. Texas is considering converting from an add-on no-fault state to a true no-fault state. Modifications to the Michigan no-fault law, which would have capped PIP benefits in order to reduce rising premiums, passed the legislature in 1993 but failed to survive a voter referendum in 1994. In 1994, a bill to repeal the Massachusetts no-fault law passed that state's Senate but failed in its House.[25]

When auto insurance premiums increase, the tendency is to blame whatever compensation system is in existence in the particular jurisdiction.[26] In jurisdictions that have tried to increase benefits without generating cost-savings somewhere in the system (i.e., by imposing stringent-enough restrictions on the right to sue in tort), premiums have increased, and this has led some to conclude that no-fault does not work. But the available evidence indicates that where no-fault has been implemented with sensitivity to the need to pay for additional first-party benefits through savings somewhere in the system, no-fault has succeeded.[27] Where no-fault has failed to

[23] *Id.* § 8.23.

[24] *Id.,* § 8.24.

[25] See Ruth Gastel, *supra* § 131 note 14.

[26] For example, a number of developments in tort law, such as the abrogation of charitable and familial immunities, the repeal or invalidation of guest statutes, and the widespread adoption of comparative negligence (which means more people recover at least some damages, instead of being absolutely barred by the doctrine of contributory negligence) all serve to increase liability and hence the cost of liability insurance. See Joost, *supra* § 131 note 16, 1994 supp. at 10.

[27] For a detailed evaluation of no-fault's economic impact, see Stephen J. Carroll, James S. Kakalik, Nicholas M. Pace & John L. Adams, *No-Fault Approaches to Compensating People Injured in Automobile Accidents* (1991) (RAND study); U.S. Dep't of Transp., *Compensating Auto Accident Victims: A Follow-Up Report on No-Fault Auto Insurance*

achieve the promised cost savings, it is fair to conclude, as Professor O'Connell and some of his recent collaborators write, that "the economic shortcomings of no-fault laws are not inherent, but rather result from the politically driven character of many state no-fault laws: such laws are crafted to preserve too many full-scale tort claims — above defined thresholds of either dollar losses or verbally described severe injuries — payable in addition to no-fault claims."[28]

Regardless of the economic advantages of properly implemented no-fault plans, it is unlikely that any comprehensive no-fault scheme which involves total or near-total abrogation of the right to sue in tort for auto accident injuries will be able to muster, at least for the foreseeable future, the political majorities needed to enact it. To address no-fault's perceived shortcomings and to accommodate the political realities any no-fault proposal must confront, proposals for a second generation of no-fault systems have been offered in recent years.

[2] Second-Generation No-Fault Proposals

In an important article published in 1986,[29] Professor Jeffrey O'Connell and his collaborator Robert Joost offered a plan that would give automobile owners a choice between no-fault and traditional insurance. Although they believed the optimal system would mandate the complete elimination of tort liability in auto accidents and would substitute no-fault benefits in its place, they conceded that political pressures in each state's legislature will never permit the tort system to be totally abrogated for auto accident claims. Therefore, they proposed that each state allow the two systems to compete side by side; ultimately, the better system will prevail as automobile owners "vote" with their preferences.

O'Connell and Joost urged the enactment of statutes that would do essentially the following: (1) consumers must choose to purchase either no-fault coverage or traditional liability insurance; (2) no-fault insureds would be barred from suing another motorist in tort to recover for injuries suffered in an auto accident; (3) no-fault insureds would be declared uninsured motorists for purposes of all uninsured motorist policies sold in the state; (4) anyone who opts for the traditional liability and UM coverage would be deemed to have waived his or her right to sue a no-fault insured, and to have elected to recover from his or her UM policy any tort damages resulting from an accident with a no-fault insured; (5) an insurer would be authorized to sell no-fault insurance if its policy provides a high ceiling on no-fault benefits (e.g., $500,000) to each insured named in the policy and to each relative of a named insured living in the same household; and (6) a motorist satisfies the state's financial

Experiences (1985). For a lively exchange on the pros and cons of no-fault, compare Elizabeth M. Landes, _Insurance, Liability, and Accidents: A Theoretical and Empirical Investigation of the Effect of No-Fault Accidents_, 25 J.Law & Econ. 49 (1982) (arguing that no-fault increases accidents) with O'Connell & Levmore, _A Reply to Landes: A Faulty Study of No-Fault's Effect on Fault?_, 48 Mo. L. Rev. 649 (1983).

28 Jeffrey O'Connell, Stephen Carroll, Michael Horowitz, Allan Abrahamse, & Daniel Kaiser, _The Costs of Consumer Choice for Auto Insurance in States Without No-Fault Insurance_, 54 Md. L. Rev. 281, 282 (1995).

29 See Jeffrey O'Connell & Robert H. Joost, _Giving Motorists a Choice Between Fault and No-Fault Insurance_, 72 Va. L. Rev. 61 (1986).

responsibility requirements if he or she maintains either (a) no-fault insurance with a high established limit on benefits or (b) motor vehicle insurance that promises to pay tort damages, up to a specified limit, to persons injured by the fault of the insured, and that promises to reimburse the insured for damages attributable to the fault of an uninsured, a hit-and-run, or a no-fault insured motorist.[30] In subsequent articles, Professor O'Connell, writing with a number of other collaborators, refined the choice proposal and drafted model legislation for its enactment.[31]

In 1992 the Bush administration proposed[32] a federal statute that would (a) give motorists the option of purchasing PIP coverages at the financial responsibility levels required by state law for liability for personal injury; (b) prohibit persons electing such PIP coverage from suing or being sued for pain-and-suffering damages suffered in auto accidents; (c) allow, however, PIP-electing motorists to claim tort damages against any motorist for economic loss exceeding the PIP limits, except in cases where the injury was caused by a tortfeasor's alcohol or drug abuse; (d) allow tort insureds injured by a PIP-electing insured to claim against their own insurer for both economic and non-economic loss (under coverage to-be-termed "tort maintenance coverage") just as they do today under UM coverage, and to claim against PIP-electing insureds for economic loss exceeding the amount of their tort maintenance coverage.[33]

Under either the 1986 O'Connell-Joost proposal or the 1992 Bush proposal, automobile owners could choose whether to stay in the tort-based system or move to a no-fault system. Proponents of the systems believed that those who moved to the no-fault system would have reduced premiums, increased coverage, or both, and as the benefits became more obvious, more people would elect into the no-fault system.[34]

---

[30] *Id.* at 80–81.

[31] See Jeffrey O'Connell, *A Draft Bill to Allow Choice Between No-Fault and Fault-Based Auto Insurance,* 27 Harv. J. on Legis. 143 (1990); Jeffrey O'Connell & Robert H. Joost, *A Model Bill Allowing Choice Between Auto Insurance Payable With and Without Regard to Fault,* 51 Ohio St. L.J. 947 (1990); Jeffrey O'Connell, Stephen Carroll, Michael Horowitz & Allan Abrahamse, *Consumer Choice in the Auto Insurance Market,* 52 Md. L. Rev. 1016 (1993) (hereafter "O'Connell 1993"; Jeffrey O'Connell, Stephen Carroll, Michael Horowitz, Allan Abrahamse & Daniel Kaiser, *The Costs of Consumer Choice for Auto Insurance in States Without No-Fault Insurance,* 54 Md. L. Rev. 281 (1995).

[32] The proposal was made at the urging, and with the participation of Jeffrey O'Connell and Michael Horowitz. O'Connell 1993 at 1062 n. 45.

[33] *Id.* at 1026.

[34] There are other ways to fashion choice system, and these are detailed in Robert H. Joost, *supra* § 131 note 16, §§ 8.4-8.11. Except for the common law restriction on assigning tort rights and duties in exchange for a consideration, a choice system could develop without authorizing legislation. See *id.,* § 8.2. One could imagine an insured transferring his or her present or future right to sue a auto accident tortfeasor to an insurer (which could then recover damages for any economic or non-economic loss suffered by the insured) in exchange for the insurer's promises (a) to reimburse the insured's economic loss without regard to fault and (b) to defend against whatever claim the other person injured in the accident might bring against the insured, as well as pay any resulting judgment obtained by that person. The obvious problem is that personal injury claims are not assignable before the claim is

A different kind of no-fault proposal that attracted considerable attention in the early 1990s was author Andrew Tobias's proposed "pay-at-the-pump" no-fault plan for automobile insurance in California. The proposal, as it evolved, would finance a true no-fault system by adding a 25-cent-per-gallon surcharge to the price of gasoline, a $141 per vehicle auto-registration surcharge, and a surcharge on bad drivers to finance a first-party compensation system.[35] Similar pay-at-the pump proposals have been made in about a half-dozen other states. The obvious advantage of such a plan is its relatively easy administration; the infrastructure used to collect gasoline taxes could be adapted to collect the per-gallon premiums. In addition to reducing litigation costs, the proposal would affect marketing of auto policies drastically, eliminating entirely the need for agents in this line of insurance.

The pay-at-the-pump proposal has, thus far, made little headway in California, in no small measure because of the combined opposition of trial lawyers, insurance agents, and the oil industry. Beyond the obvious stakes these groups have in defeating the proposal, there are a number of aspects of pay-at-the-pump that are problematic. Absent a mechanism to identify bad drivers and charge them more, which adds a bureaucratic mechanism to the proposal which defeats a part of its advantage of simplicity, pay-at-the-pump ignores some of the most important factors in assessing the likelihood that a driver will be involved in an accident. The proposal gives great weight to miles driven as a rating factor, and perhaps too little weight to the factor of traffic density, which is strongly associated with the frequency of accidents. Moreover, rural drivers who must travel longer distances (not to mention businesses with large transportation expenses) will pay more for insurance than urban drivers who travel shorter distances (but who face the higher risks associated with greater traffic density). The owners of low-mileage vehicles will subsidize the owners of high-mileage vehicles. The Tobias proposal also made no-fault benefits excess over available health insurance; to the extent the cost savings in auto insurance are transferred to higher health insurance premiums, no net savings result. Although less of a problem in large states like California, a pay-at-the-pump proposal would no doubt encourage residents near state boundaries to purchase gasoline in adjacent states where no surcharge is assessed. Although pay-at-the-pump may be capable of modification to address these concerns, it is doubtful that enough support for the proposal can be marshaled to overcome those who for these and other reasons will oppose it.

---

adjudicated or reduced to judgment, and this rule would probably need to be superseded by statute before an insurer would consider entering into such an arrangement with an insured. Opponents of this kind of voluntary choice model must grapple with its close similarity to arrangements in first-party insurance of unquestioned validity: in current MedPay or UM coverages, the insurer pays its own insured for a loss, and then is subrogated to the insured's rights against the tortfeasor. One might observe that subrogation is limited to the amount of the insurer's payment and thus serves the contribution-and-indemnity function, unlike the situation where a personal injury claim is assigned in exchange for the promise of no-fault benefits. See Joost, *supra* note 16, at § 8.2. But the arrangements are more similar than they are different.

35 See Ruth Gastel, *Proposition 103 and Related Issues, Insurance Information Institute Report* (March 1995).

[3] Applying No-Fault Beyond the Motor Vehicle Setting: Neo-No-Fault Proposals

Despite the mixed results for automobile accident no-fault compensation systems, no-fault will continue to play an important role in accident compensation for the foreseeable future. In addition to no-fault automobile insurance, which now exists in roughly half the country, all states have some kind of workers' compensation system, which is a kind of no-fault insurance. Employees receive first-party benefits for their occupational injuries without having to prove someone else's fault. Despite the shortcomings of the workers' compensation system, no one seriously advocates returning to a fault-based system for compensating workplace injuries. In those settings where it is relatively easy to determine that an accident has caused an injury (such as the automobile and the employment contexts), no-fault is a viable option to the traditional tort-liability insurance system.

In many areas where the traditional tort system needs reform, however, no-fault's usefulness is limited. For example, in medical malpractice, where tort reform has long been hotly debated, pure no-fault may not be a viable alternative. Medical accidents do occur, but it is often difficult to distinguish the medical accident from the injury caused by disease, which should not be compensated through the tort system. Obviously, insurers cannot be expected to pay for all of the economic loss of every patient whose health declines after receiving medical care.[36] The same difficulty exists in product liability insurance. Insurers should not be expected to compensate a consumer for economic loss every time the consumer is injured while using a product; some consumers should be compensated, but it would be extremely expensive and questionable social policy to require the insurers of chair manufacturers to compensate consumers for their economic loss every time one falls off a chair while using it as a ladder.[37]

A "cousin" of no-fault, however, has the potential to provide substantial advantages in medical malpractice, product liability, and other similar problem areas. The prototype for this so-called "neo-no-fault" approach [38] to compensating accident victims is a system of athletic insurance currently in existence in most states. Devised by Professor O'Connell, the system involves a school entering into a contract with its insurer providing that if a student-athlete is catastrophically injured (e.g.,

---

[36] For more discussion of no-fault in the health care setting, see Eleanor D. Kinney, *Malpractice Reforms in the 1990s: Past Disappointments, Future Success?*, 20 J. Health Pol. Pol'y & L. 99 (1995); Jeffrey O'Connell, Phillip A. Bock, & Stewart Petoe, *Blending Reform of Tort Liability and Health Insurance: A Necessary Mix,* 79 Cornell L. Rev. 1303 (1994); Jeffrey O'Connell, *Must Health and Disability Insurance Subsidize Wasteful Injury Suits?,* 41 Rutgers L. Rev. 1055 (1989).

[37] See Jeffrey O'Connell, *Offers That Can't Be Refused: Foreclosure of Personal Injury Claims by Defendants' Prompt Tender of Claimants' Net Economic Losses,* 77 Nw. U. L. Rev. 589 (1982); *Alternative Medical Liability Act: Hearing Before the Subcomm. on Health of the House Comm. on Ways and Means,* 98th Cong., 2d Sess. (1984).

[38] See Jeffrey O'Connell, *A "Neo No-Fault" Contract in Lieu of Tort: Preaccident Guarantees of Postaccident Settlement Offers,* 73 Cal. L. Rev. 898 (1985); Jeffrey O'Connell, *An Alternative to Abandoning Tort Liability: Elective No-Fault Insurance for Many Kinds of Injuries,* 60 Minn. L. Rev. 501 (1976).

paraplegia), the school will offer payment for medical expenses and other economic loss — both present and future — all of which will be paid for by the insurance policy. The athlete (through his or her parent or guardian) can decide whether to accept the payment. If the payment is accepted, the athlete waives the right to sue for additional compensation.[39]

In theory, nothing prevents prospective defendants on any tort claim, including the accident on the athletic field, from offering to settle the plaintiff's claim by paying the plaintiff's present and future economic loss. Thus, a fair question is whether the neo-no-fault system for compensating athletic injuries really adds anything to the status quo. The answer is found in the "practice" rather than the "theory." A tort defendant rarely offers to pay the plaintiff's economic loss for fear that such a favorable settlement offer, particularly if made early in the litigation, will encourage the plaintiff to assume that a larger offer will be forthcoming later. This leads to the plaintiff assuming a more aggressive posture in litigation, which causes additional expenses to accumulate for both sides. The neo-no-fault approach used for catastrophic athletic contest injuries guarantees that a full economic loss offer will be made, an offer with which many, and perhaps most, injured persons would be satisfied.

The athletic injury compensation system requires the insured-school to make the economic loss offer to the injured athlete, but this is not unfair. As is the case with automobile accidents or occupational injuries, the insured "event" is clearly demarcated. This sort of system would not work as well in some other settings. Requiring, for example, physicians and health care providers to always offer a full economic loss settlement whenever they are subject to a tort claim is problematic. Catastrophic claims that are not accidental are unlikely to arise on the athletic field, but a catastrophic loss in the medical arena could be the result of illness, not an accident. Indeed, if consumers knew that the health care provider would be compelled to make a full-economic-loss settlement offer whenever sued for malpractice, many consumers who were merely ill would allege that a medical accident caused their condition to worsen. To meet this objection, a variation on the athletic injury version of neo-no-fault gives the defendant an *option* as to whether to make the full-economic-loss offer of settlement. If such an offer is made, the plaintiff is required to accept it. In effect, the defendant is guaranteed that a generous, reasonable offer of settlement will be accepted.

An objection to the variation is that injured plaintiffs should not be compelled to accept full-economic-loss settlement offers. The objection actually has two aspects. First, it is argued that plaintiffs should have the option to sue in tort, taking their chances that the jury might award pain and suffering damages in addition to economic loss compensation or, at the other extreme, nothing at all. The response is that this right to choose is less important than making sure that more victims of accidents are fully compensated. Second, it is argued that some kinds of serious injuries — such as accidentally rendering a person infertile — do not involve economic loss, and neo-no-fault does not fairly compensate this kind of seriously injured plaintiff. This objection is a substantial one; one response is that in a country

---

[39] See National Law Journal, Nov. 18, 1985, p. 22, c. 1.

where compensation dollars are scarce, the first priority should be remedying economic loss, and that some harsh results must be tolerated (as they are in workers' compensation) until the problem of inadequate compensation for economic loss is met more satisfactorily.

For many, the foregoing responses to the objections are unsatisfactory. Thus, to meet squarely the objection that plaintiffs should not be compelled to accept offers of full payment for all present and future economic loss, yet another variation on neo-no-fault provides that the plaintiff can choose whether to accept the defendant's settlement offer. The plaintiff who refuses such an offer and sues in tort is subject to a cap on the amount of damages for noneconomic loss that can be recovered. In other words, the cap is triggered only when a settlement offer is made and refused. The advantage of this alternative is that it provides an incentive for defendants to make full-economic-loss settlement offers and for plaintiffs to accept such offers at an early stage of the litigation.

A fair observation on the neo-no-fault proposals — particularly the last one discussed — is that these proposals more closely resemble modifications in the way tort claims are litigated rather than the full-fledged no-fault systems that exist for automobile accident claims in many states. However, the common thread that ties all of the no-fault and neo-no-fault proposals together is the following premise: our society — and particularly victims of accidents — is better off if accident victims are paid prompt, full compensation for their economic loss in exchange for giving up their right to seek the traditional tort recovery through litigation.

For the foreseeable future, consumers, business groups, the insurance industry, and others will continue to scrutinize the tort system and to consider the possibility of some kind of no-fault method for reimbursing injuries. The tort system of liability is premised on the notion that holding people liable for their negligence will deter negligent and intentional conduct. Whether or not the likelihood of tort liability deters intentional conduct, it is highly unlikely that the tort system will be abandoned for intentional claims. However, the assumption that tort liability deters negligent conduct is of questionable validity. Currently, much loss caused by negligent conduct is compensated outside the tort-liability system through first-party insurance, government insurance (particularly disability under Social Security), and self-insurance. Many accidents where no one is at fault occur, and these are compensated entirely outside the tort-liability system. The enormous transaction costs of the tort-liability system, where it is applicable, will continue to fuel interest in first-party compensation systems that do not depend on establishing the negligence of a third party.

§ 133 Compulsory Liability Insurance and Financial Responsibility Insurance: Some Additional Issues

[a] The Problem of Intentional Conduct

In liability insurance generally, the insurer does not provide coverage for the liability of its insured for intentional harm inflicted upon a third party. As a general rule, public policy does not favor allowing an insured to escape the consequences of intentional acts by shifting liability for those acts to the insurer.[1]

In automobile insurance, however, the public policy favoring victim compensation sometimes trumps the public policy in favor of requiring willful perpetrators of injury to compensate their victims out of their own resources. This preference is evident in *Wheeler v. O'Connell,*[2] a 1937 Massachusetts case. The insured driver was stopped by a policeman for a traffic violation. As the policeman stood on the car's running board, the driver pushed him off, causing the policeman injury. The policeman obtained a civil judgment against the driver for "wilful wanton and reckless behavior." Even though there was no negligence or even gross negligence, the court found the driver's insurer responsible for the insured's liability. The court stated:

> The purpose of the compulsory motor vehicle liability insurance is not, like ordinary insurance, to protect the owner or operator alone from loss, but rather is to provide compensation to persons injured through the operation of the automobile insured by the owner. . . . [I]f the purpose of the statute is to compensate the injured party rather than to save the operator of the vehicle from loss it is difficult to see why an injured person's rights should be affected by the fact that the operator's conduct was wilful, . . . as distinguished from negligent. The evil intended to be remedied is as certainly present in the one case as in the other.[3]

The court specifically stated that the policy favoring protection of third parties overrode the policy against indemnifying a person from liability resulting from intentional conduct: "The statute itself is declaratory of public policy applicable to compulsory insurance and supersedes any rule of public policy which obtains in ordinary insurance law."[4]

The logic of *Wheeler* was followed in *State Farm Fire & Casualty Co. v. Tringali,*[5] a 1982 Ninth Circuit case, where the insured intentionally drove his car against a stationary motorcycle on which the injured passenger was sitting. In construing the Hawaii compulsory automobile insurance statute as requiring coverage for liability intentionally caused, the court stated:

> From the viewpoint of the victim, the mental state of the insured is irrelevant. The common objection to insuring one's self against liability for deliberately wrongful acts has little force in this context. Where compulsory automobile liability insurance statutes use the terms "accident" or "accidental" we should, if possible, read those terms in a way that does not exclude intentional acts of, or even intentional wrongs done by, the insured. An event is accidental if it is neither expected nor intended from the viewpoint of the person who is injured.[6]

---

[1] See §§ 63–63C, *supra.*

[2] 9 N.E.2d 544 (Mass. 1937).

[3] 9 N.E.2d at 546.

[4] 9 N.E.2d at 547.

[5] 686 F.2d 821 (9th Cir. 1982).

[6] 686 F.2d at 824.

The basic notion is that in the compulsory insurance context whether an act is intentional should be viewed from the victim's viewpoint, not the insured's; this has the effect of making compensation available to the victim, at least up to the amount of the statutorily-mandated benefits, in situations where the usual application of the intentional act exclusion would prevent it.[7]

The interest in victim compensation does not always, however, trump the public interest in requiring those who commit intentional torts to bear personally the costs of their misconduct. In a 1995 Pennsylvania case,[8] the court held that the insured's liability policy did not provide coverage in circumstances where the insured, who was intoxicated, drove to the rental home where his wife, from whom he was separated, was living, twice drove his truck into the rear of his wife's vehicle, drove across the lawn when his wife came out of the house and struck her, and thereafter drove his truck into the wall of the house three times. The court rejected the contention that the insured's voluntary intoxication rendered his acts unintentional,[9] and then held that it violated public policy to provide coverage for the intentional acts. Other courts have followed the same reasoning,[10] which demonstrates an absence of consensus on how far liability insurers should be expected to support the goal of victim compensation in circumstances where their insureds' behavior has not comported with the minimum needed to have a right to the policy's coverage.

[b] The Effect of the Insured's Bankruptcy on Victim Compensation

State compulsory insurance and financial responsibility laws typically withdraw driving privileges from a person against whom a judgment has been entered as a result of the person's negligent operation of a motor vehicle unless the judgment has been satisfied. In *Perez v. Campbell*,[11] the United States Supreme Court held that the Arizona financial responsibility act was unconstitutional to the extent it required payment of a tort judgment as a condition of restoration of driving privileges. The court reasoned that the statute impaired the objective of the Bankruptcy Act in giving debtors a "fresh start" by providing creditors with leverage for collecting judgments discharged in bankruptcy. Section 525 of the Bankruptcy Act[12] codified *Perez*, making clear Congress's intent that bankrupts not be deprived of their fresh start by governmental discrimination against them through the denial of privileges solely on account of their bankruptcy. The effect of *Perez* and section 525, in circumstances where the state statute requires a tort judgment to be satisfied

---

[7] See Hudson v. State Farm Mut. Ins. Co., 569 A.2d 1168 (Del. 1990); South Car. Farm Bur. Mut. Ins. Co. v. Mumford, 382 S.E.2d 11 (S.C. 1989); Mosely v. West Am. Ins. Co., 743 S.W.2d 854 (Ky. Ct. App. 1987); Martin v. Chicago Ins. Co., 361 S.E.2d 835 (Ga. Ct. App. 1987).

[8] See State Farm Mut. Auto. Ins. Co. v. Martin, 660 A.2d 66 (Pa. Super. Ct. 1995).

[9] See § 63C[d], *supra*.

[10] See, e.g., Sullivan v. Equity Fire & Cas. Co., 889 P.2d 1285 (OkLa. Ct. App. 1995) (object intentionally thrown from insured's car which struck and fractured plaintiff's arm).

[11] 402 U.S. 637 (1971).

[12] 11 U.S.C. § 525.

as a condition to having driving privileges restored, is to allow drivers to circumvent the penalties of the state financial responsibility statute by declaring bankruptcy.[13]

In response to *Perez* and section 525, some states amended their financial responsibility statutes to condition the restoration of driving privileges on showing proof of future financial responsibility.[14] For example, after *Perez,* Ohio amended its financial responsibility statute[15] to provide that the driving privileges of a person who had not satisfied a tort judgment against him or her would be suspended for seven years or until "such judgment is stayed, or satisfied in full . . . *and* upon such person's filing with the registrar of motor vehicles evidence of financial responsibility."[16] This change corrected the flaw recognized by *Perez* by allowing a stay of a judgment, which occurs in bankruptcy, to have the same effect as satisfying the judgment. Thus, it was no longer a prerequisite to obtaining driving privileges that the judgment be satisfied. However, the statute did set as a prerequisite to obtaining driving privileges that the motorist demonstrate future financial responsibility by either purchasing liability insurance, posting a bond, or posting cash or securities. This raised another question: whether the requirement to show proof of future responsibility was imposed solely because the debtor failed to satisfy a debt dischargeable in bankruptcy. This question was specifically left undecided in *Perez,*[17] but the Sixth Circuit took it up in *Duffey v. Dollison.*[18]

In *Duffey,* the Sixth Circuit held that the Ohio statute was valid insofar as it required a judgment debtor whose debt has been discharged in bankruptcy to furnish proof of future financial responsibility prior to restoration of driving privileges suspended prior to bankruptcy, as long as the statute is applied equally to bankrupts and nonbankrupts. The court reasoned that the statute neither provided creditors leverage for collecting damages nor did it coerce bankrupts into reaffirming discharged debts, the problems that the Supreme Court in *Perez* perceived in the Arizona statute. Although *Duffey* has been criticized,[19] the opposite result in *Duffey* would have allowed a driver with an unsatisfied judgment to go through bankruptcy and then have driving privileges restored without having to demonstrate financial responsibility. The Ohio statute, as the Sixth Circuit noted, did not require bankrupts to do anything to regain driving privileges beyond that required of anyone who has an unsatisfied tort judgment for any reason whatever. Thus, in upholding the statute, the Sixth Circuit made it impossible for a driver to take bankruptcy and thereby avoid

---

[13] See, e.g., Weaver v. O'Grady, 350 F. Supp. 403 (S.D. Ohio 1972).

[14] See, e.g., Nev. Rev. Stat. § 485.302; N.H. Rev. Stat. Ann. § 264.12; Tenn. Code Ann. § 55-12-108.

[15] The Ohio statute is a security type of statute; the motorist can have one accident (or "one bite") before being required to demonstrate financial responsibility.

[16] Ohio Rev. Code Ann. § 4509.40 (emphasis added).

[17] The Court noted that "the validity of the limited requirement that some drivers post evidence of financial responsibility for the future in order to regain driving privileges is not questioned here." Perez v. Campbell, 402 U.S. 637, 642, (1971).

[18] 734 F.2d 265 (6th Cir. 1984).

[19] See Douglass G. Boshkoff, *Bankruptcy-Based Discrimination,* 66 Am. Bankr. L.J. 387 (1992).

the financial obligations relating to the operation of motor vehicles. More recent decisions have followed the analysis of *Duffey*.[20]

[c] Insurer's Defense Against Insured

In all kinds of insurance, including liability insurance, the insurer's obligations to the insured are conditioned on the insured's performance of certain acts, such as giving notice of loss, cooperating with the insurer, and not committing misrepresentations in the application. When liability insurance is compulsory, however, the insurer's claim that it has no obligations because of the insured's breach of contract could result in financial loss to the innocent victim of the insured's negligent conduct, the very person the compulsory insurance scheme is designed to protect. Thus, legislatures typically provide in the financial responsibility and compulsory liability insurance statutes that defenses which would ordinarily discharge the insurer from its obligations cannot be used to prevent the payment of proceeds to the injured third party.[20] Insurers, to avoid bearing all of the risk of the insured's noncooperation, failure to give notice of loss, and other acts or omissions, typically insert in their policies a provision entitling them to reimbursement from the insured of any claims paid to third parties in circumstances where the insured's act or neglect would ordinarily have relieved the insurer of its obligation to pay.

Farmers Insurance Exchange v. Anderson,[22] a recent Michigan case, illustrates well the competing considerations in this area.[23] The insured under a policy of automobile liability insurance with coverage exceeding the statutory minimums did not disclose in the application that her son, whose driving license had been revoked, would be operating her vehicle. The son, driving without a license and while intoxicated, caused an accident which killed the driver of the other vehicle. The court applied the Michigan statute in question according to its terms, and held that once an accident inflicting injury upon a third party occurs, the policy's coverage becomes absolute, even in the face of insurer defenses such as fraud or misrepresentation. Prior to that time, however, the insurer can declare a policy void on those grounds.[24] Thus, under this statutory scheme, automobile liability policies are voidable until a third party acquires a stake in the policy's benefits; at that point, the insurer's ability to avoid providing coverage becomes greatly constrained. As for optional excess coverage, the court held that the statute did not deprive insurers of these defenses, but that these defenses would not be available even as to excess coverages if the fraud or misrepresentation "could have been ascertained easily by the insurer at the time the contract of insurance was entered into."[25]

---

[20] See, e.g., In re Duke, 167 B.R. 324 (D.R.I. 1994); Holder v. State of Wis. Dep't of Transp., 40 B.R. 847 (E.D. Wis. 1984). *Duffey* was reaffirmed and applied in Norton v. Tennessee Dep't of Safety, 867 F.2d 313 (6th Cir. 1989).

[21] See, e.g., N.C. Gen. Stat. § 21-279.21(f)(1); Neb. Rev. Stat. § 60-538.

[22] 520 N.W.2d 686 (Mich. Ct. App. 1994).

[23] See also State Auto Prop. & Cas. Ins. Co. v. Gibbs, 444 S.E.2d 504 (S.C. 1994); Continental Western Ins. Co. v. Clay, 811 P.2d 1202 (Kan. 1991); Odum v. Nationwide Mut. Ins. Co., 401 S.E.2d 87 (N.C. Ct. App. 1991).

[24] 520 N.W.2d at 688-89. To the same effect, although involving a binder, see Strickler v. Huffine, 618 A.2d 430 (Pa. Super. Ct. 1992).

[25] 520 N.W.2d at 689.

§ 134   Uninsured and Underinsured Motorist Insurance

[a]   Purpose

The tort liability system does not always work efficiently to reimburse fully the victims of torts. One weakness of the system is that a person injured by one who lacks either assets to pay a judgment or insurance will not be compensated for his or her loss. The primary way of remedying this gap in protection for victims of automobile accidents is uninsured motorist ("UM") coverage, which is now required or required to be offered by statutes in forty-nine states.[1]

Under this coverage, a person injured by an uninsured motorist will be compensated by his or her own insurer in an amount equal to what the uninsured tortfeasor's liability insurer would have paid if the tortfeasor had carried liability insurance. Generally the coverage pays for personal injury but not property damage. In about eighteen states, UM coverage is mandatory; each policy of liability insurance offered in the state must contain a UM endorsement. In most of the remaining states, the insurer is required to offer the coverage, but the insured has the privilege to either reject it or select lower limits.[2]

The same analysis applies to underinsured motorist insurance, except that the concern is not with the tortfeasor having no liability insurance but is instead with the tortfeasor having too little liability insurance to compensate the victim for his or her loss. In approximately twenty-five jurisdictions UM protection is now supplemented with underinsured motorist protection.[3]

[b]   Nature of Uninsured Motorist Coverage

[1]   Four Elements of Coverage

The typical UM statute requires each automobile liability policy issued in the state to provide for or offer a minimum amount of compensation for bodily injuries received by the insured in an accident caused by an uninsured motorist. The minimum UM coverage required to be provided or offered varies from state to state. Generally, the insured is required to provide or offer coverage with minimums no less than those required under the compulsory liability insurance. In most states, UM coverage may be rejected or lower policy limits selected. In some states, the rejection is valid only if in writing. Although the rejection provisions may seem contrary to the purpose of the statute, the logic is that the insured who wishes to cover these potential costs directly (perhaps under a health insurance policy) can do so and not pay the premium required for the UM endorsement.[4]

Normally the UM statute will contain a definition of the term "uninsured vehicle." For example, in Virginia, the statute defines uninsured vehicle as a vehicle for which

---

[1] See Alan I. Widiss, *Uninsured and Underinsured Motorist Insurance (1995),* § 2.1 at 21. A minority (approximately 17) of the states require UM insurance to be sold with liability policies, and most states simply require that it be offered. *Id.,* § 2.5.

[2] See *Id.,* Appendix B, at 400-01.

[3] See *id.,* Appendix B, at 400-01.

[4] See *No-Fault and Uninsured Motorist Automobile Insurance* § 23.10.

there is no liability policy as required by law, or no bond, cash, or securities given in lieu thereof, or the owner of which is not qualified as a self-insurer.[5] Most statutes grant the right of subrogation to the insurer who pays benefits under the UM coverage. Also, most statutes specifically require that the insured be legally entitled to recover from the uninsured tortfeasor.[6] In other words, the insured must establish that he or she has a substantive right to recover damages from the uninsured motorist. Also, the insured must prove the amount of damages, just as if the action were being brought against the uninsured motorist.[7]

[2] The "Legally Entitled" Requirement and Immunity

If for some reason the tortfeasor is immune from liability to the insured, a difficult question can arise as to whether the insured has been injured by an "uninsured" motorist. Immunities can be either substantive or procedural. If the insured has no cause of action against the tortfeasor because of the existence of the immunity, the insured is normally not considered "legally entitled" to damages from the tortfeasor.[8] For example, in the states that still recognize some vestige of the parent-child immunity,[9] if a parent is injured by the negligence of the minor child-motorist, or vice versa, the injured person is usually not entitled to uninsured motorist benefits.[10] Prior to the abrogation of the doctrine of interspousal immunity, the same result was ordinarily reached when a spouse-motorist injured the other spouse in an auto accident; the spouse-motorist was not an uninsured motorist in relation to the injured spouse.[11] In a number of cases, courts have held that the scheme of exclusive remedies under a state workers' compensation statute bars a claimant's recovery under an uninsured motorist policy when the negligent motorist is a coemployee or the employer, due to the coemployee's or employer's statutory immunity from suit.[12] It has been held that an insured from a non-no-fault state injured in an

---

[5] Va. Code § 46.2-705.

[6] See Widiss, *supra* note 1, at §§ 7-1 to 7-15.

[7] See, e.g., State Farm Mut. Auto. Ins. Co. v. Kelly, 380 S.E.2d 654 (Va. 1989); Silvers v. Horace Mann Ins. Co., 378 S.E.2d 21 (N.C. 1989); Lee v. Saliga, 373 S.E.2d 345 (W.Va. 1988); Riccio v. Prudential Prop. & Cas. Ins. Co., 531 A.2d 717 (N.J. 1987). The same requirement applies for underinsured protection. See, e.g., Roller v. Stonewall Ins. Co., 801 P.2d 207 (Wash. 1990) (en banc). Cf. Annot., *Insured's Recovery of Uninsured Motorist Claim Against Insurer as Affecting Subsequent Recovery Against Tortfeasors Causing Injury,* 3 A.L.R.5th 746 (1992).

[8] See, e.g., Markham v. State Farm Mut. Auto. Ins. Co., 464 F.2d 703 (10th Cir. 1972); Allstate Ins. Co. v. Boynton, 486 So. 2d 552 (Fla. 1986); York v. State Farm Fire and Cas. Co., 414 N.E.2d 423 (Ohio 1980); Sayan v. United Serv. Auto. Ass'n, 716 P.2d 895 (Wash. Ct. App. 1986); Boyd v. Wright, 422 So. 2d 529 (La. Ct. App. 1982).

[9] Most states have abrogated or limited the doctrine. See § 136C, note 3, *infra.*

[10] Markham v. State Farm Mut. Auto. Ins. Co., 464 F.2d 703 (10th Cir. 1972).

[11] See, e.g., Patrons Mut. Ins. Ass'n v. Norwood, 647 P.2d 1335 (Kan. 1982); Aitken v. State Farm Mut. Auto. Ins. Co., 404 So. 2d 1040 (Miss. 1981). See generally Patty Ferraiolo, Note, *Uninsured Motorist Coverage and Interspousal Immunity,* 57 Chi.-Kent L. Rev. 297 (1981). (As for the two jurisdictions cited, Kansas abrogated interpousal immunity in Flagg v. Loy, 734 P.2d 1183 (Kan. 1987), and Mississippi abrogated the immunity in Burns v. Burns, 518 So. 2d 1205 (Miss. 1988).)

[12] See, e.g., Medders v. United States Fid. & Guar. Co., 623 So. 2d 979 (Miss. 1993) (coemployee); Stuhlmiller v. Nodak Mut. Ins. Co., 475 N.W.2d 136 (N.D. 1991) (coemployee);

accident with another motorist in a no-fault state was not legally entitled to recover noneconomic damages that were below the threshold for a tort claim under the law of the no-fault state.[13] One of the reasons urged in support of this rule is that allowing the insured to recover uninsured motorist benefits where the tortfeasor is immune from liability would frustrate the insurer's subrogation rights.[14]

In some recent cases, however, there is authority that finds coverage notwithstanding the fact that the tortfeasor has some degree of immunity.[15] For example, it has been held that where a school district had limited liability (i.e., a limited immunity) under state law, the insured, one of a number of persons injured in an auto accident caused by a vehicle operated and insured by the school district, was "legally entitled to collect" from the school district.[16] If the tortfeasor is immune due to a personal or procedural defense, the insured is usually considered "legally entitled" to damages.[17] Note, however, that the substance-procedure distinction is amorphous in this context. For example, it has been held that the interspousal immunity is a procedural bar only, and the UM insurer is therefore obligated to pay benefits to the spouse of the insured.[18] The statute of limitations would seem to be a procedural bar, one which is personal to the insured, and numerous cases so hold.[19] But in some states, the running of the statute of limitations has been treated as a substantive bar and has relieved the UM insurer from providing coverage.[20]

In short, this is an area where the precedents of the particular jurisdiction where the dispute arises must be evaluated.

[3] Exclusions

Statutes often authorize insurers to insert particular exclusions in the UM coverages. For example, many statutes authorize the exclusion of farm-type tractors and off-road vehicles (such as dune buggies, golf carts, and dirt bikes) from the definition of insured vehicle.[21] Thus, a hiker on a sand dune who is hit by an

---

State Farm Mut. Auto. Ins. Co. v. Royston, 817 P.2d 118 (Haw. 1991) (employer); State Farm Mut. Auto. Ins. Co. v. Webb, 562 N.E.2d 132 (Ohio 1990) (coemployee).

[13] See Kurent v. Farmers Ins. of Columbus, Inc., 581 N.E.2d 533 (Ohio 1991); Berardi, U.S.A., Ltd. v. Employers Mut. Cas. Co., 526 A.2d 515 (R.I. 1987).

[14] See Allstate Ins. Co. v. Boynton, 486 So. 2d 552 (Fla. 1986).

[15] See State Farm Mut. Auto. Ins. Co. v. Baldwin, 764 F.2d 773 (11th Cir. 1985); Karlson v. City of Oklahoma, 711 P.2d 72 (Okla. 1985). See generally Alan I. Widiss, *Uninsured Motorist Coverage: Observations on Litigating Over When a Claimant Is "Legally Entitled to Recover,"* 68 Iowa L. Rev. 397 (1983).

[16] See Gabriel v. Minnesota Mut. Fire & Cas. Co., 506 N.W.2d 73 (N.D. 1993). To the same effect in different settings is Michigan Millers Mut. Ins. Co. v. Bourke, 607 So. 2d 418 (Fla. 1992); State Farm Mut. Auto. Ins. Co. v. Estate of Braun, 793 P.2d 253 (Mont. 1990).

[17] 2 Schermer, *Automobile Liability Insurance,* § 24.01, at 24-2.

[18] See Allstate Ins. Co. v. Elkins, 396 N.E.2d 528 (Ill. 1979).

[19] See, e.g., Booth v. Fireman's Fund Ins. Co., 218 So. 2d 580 (La. 1969) (superseded by statute as stated in Bond v. Commercial Union Assur. Co., 407 So. 2d 401 (La. 1981); Schulz v. Allstate Ins. Co., 244 N.E.2d 546 (Ohio Ct.App. 1968).

[20] See Brown v. Lumbermen's Mut. Cas. Co., 204 S.E.2d 829 (N.C. 1974); Bocek v. Inter-Ins. Exch., 369 N.E.2d 1093 (Ind. Ct. App. 1977).

[21] See, e.g., N.C. Gen. Stat. § 20-279.21(4); Cal. Ins. Code § 11580.2(b)(2). See generally Alan I. Widiss, *supra* note 1, §§ 8.4, 8.10.

uninsured dune buggy could not recover uninsured motorist benefits under his or her own policy. Another common exclusion exists for vehicles driven by nonpermissive users.[22] To take another example, the occupant of an otherwise insured vehicle who is injured in an accident while the vehicle is operated negligently by a nonpermissive user would not be entitled to uninsured motorist benefits under his or her own policy. Insurers also insert exclusions in UM coverages that are not specifically prohibited by law, as insurers will do with any policy; whether such exclusions contravene the policy of the statute is often controversial, as the subsequent discussion of the hit-and-run exclusion illustrates.[23]

The possible exclusions in UM coverage are so numerous that complete discussion of all of them is not possible here.[24] However, one exclusion has recently generated particular controversy: the exclusion that denies coverage to an insured injured by an uninsured motorist while the insured is occupying a vehicle owned by the insured but not listed on the insurance policy under which benefits are sought. This exclusion, commonly called the "other vehicle" exclusion, has been declared invalid in a number of jurisdictions.[25] The logic underlying this line of cases is that the UM statute establishes a public policy allowing injured insureds to recover damages they would have been entitled to recover if the tortfeasor had maintained liability insurance. Accordingly, the statute should be liberally construed to promote this purpose, and exclusions that narrow the zone of coverage by disqualifying a class of insureds from benefits should be narrowly interpreted or ignored. Moreover, since the benefit is designed for the protection of persons and not vehicles, the purchase of one policy should be enough to entitle the insured to coverage.

In support of the exclusion, however, it is argued that the purpose of UM coverage is to protect insured motorists from uninsured motorists, not to protect uninsured motorists from uninsured motorists, and a number of courts have agreed.[26] The problem with this argument is that the injured motorist is not uninsured; the injured motorist has simply failed to purchase coverage on the additional vehicle in which he or she was injured. Nevertheless, the exclusion has the effect of encouraging persons to insure all vehicles, which is a good thing with respect to liability insurance. In other words, insurers have a legitimate interest in avoiding the additional and sometimes unreasonable risk of the insured driving another vehicle

---

[22] See Alan I. Widiss, *supra* note 1, § 4.20.

[23] See § 134[b][4], *infra*. In Keeler v. Farmers and Merchants Ins. Co., 724 S.W.2d 307 (Mo. Ct. App. 1987), the court held that a UM policy covered injury intentionally inflicted by a third party and any effort to exclude such coverage would be invalid.

[24] For a much fuller treatment, see generally Alan I. Widiss, *supra* note 1. For a recent annotation on a related question, see Annot., *Uninsured or Underinsured Motorist Insurance: Validity and Construction of Policy Provision Purporting to Reduce Recovery by Amount of Social Security Disability Benefits or Payments Under Similar Disability Benefits Law,* 24 A.L.R.5th 766 (1994).

[25] See, e.g., Calvert v. Farmers Ins. Co., 697 P.2d 684 (Ariz. 1985); Welch by Richards v. State Farm Mut. Auto. Ins. Co., 361 N.W.2d 680 (Wis. 1985); Lindahl v. Howe, 345 N.W.2d 548 (Iowa 1984).

[26] See Herrick v. Liberty Mut. Fire Ins. Co., 274 N.W.2d 147 (Neb. 1979) (upholding exclusion).

not described in the policy, and exclusions which encourage insureds to purchase coverage on all vehicles they own should be favored.[27] At the same time the exclusion encourages insurance coverage to be purchased, it prevents the stacking of benefits across multiple policies, which, at least in theory, helps keep premiums low.

In some states, legislatures have settled the issue, although not the controversy, by explicitly authorizing the "other vehicle" exclusion.[28]

[4]   Hit-and-Run Accidents

A particularly vexing problem in UM coverage is the "hit-and-run" accident, where the negligent driver flees the scene of the accident and neither the driver nor the vehicle's owner can be found. On the one hand, the policy of maximizing coverage for the victims of accidents would seem to favor the broadest coverage possible: anytime a third party causes an accident and leaves the scene, the uninsured motorist insurer should provide coverage. On the other hand, if no restrictions are put on the coverage, any insured could claim that an accident was the result of an unknown third party's negligence and thus receive proceeds even though the loss was entirely the fault of the insured.[29]

Legislatures and courts vary widely in how the competing interests outlined above are balanced. Several state statutes require that the insured's vehicle have a "physical contact" with the hit-and-run driver.[30] Other state statutes reject the physical contact requirement.[31] A third group of state statutes require that uninsured motorist coverages provide protection for the victims of hit-and-run drivers, but the statutes do not specifically require or proscribe physical contact as a prerequisite to coverage.[32] In these states, courts have been asked to interpret the statutes, and the courts have reached divergent results. Courts in at least eighteen states have declared that the statutes do not require physical contact and that policies requiring such contact are contrary to the statute and are void as against public policy.[33] In at least fifteen other states, courts have declined to follow this reasoning and have upheld policies in which the insurer has limited uninsured motorist coverage to situations where the physical contact is evident.[34]

---

[27] See Safeco Ins. Co. v. Hubbard, 578 S.W.2d 49 (Ky. 1979).

[28] See, e.g., Cal. Ins. Code § 11580.2(c)(6); Kan. Stat. Ann. § 40-284(e)(1).

[29] For a more detailed discussion, see Alan I. Widiss, *supra* note 1, §§ 9.1 to 9.13.

[30] See, e.g., Cal. Ins. Code § 11580.2(b)(1); Miss. Code Ann. § 83-11-103.

[31] See, e.g., Mo. Stat. § 379.203 (entitlement to UM benefits "exists whether or not physical contact was made between the uninsured motor vehicle and the insured or the insured's motor vehicle.")

[32] See, e.g., R.I. Gen. Laws § 27-7-2.1; N.J. Stat. Ann. § 17:28-1.1.

[33] See, e.g., Streitweiser v. Middlesex Mut. Assur. Co., 593 A.2d 498 (Conn. 1991); Lanzo v. State Farm Mut. Auto. Ins. Co., 524 A.2d 47 (Me. 1987); Pin Pin H. Su v. Kemper Ins. Cos., 431 A.2d 416 (R.I. 1981); State Farm Mut. Auto. Ins. Co. v. Abramowicz, 386 A.2d 670 (Del. 1978); State Farm Fire and Cas. Co. v. Lambert, 285 So. 2d 917 (Ala. 1973).

[34] See, e.g., Mayfield v. Allied Mut. Ins. Co., 436 N.W.2d 164 (Neb. 1989); Moritz v. Farm Bur. Mut. Ins. Co., 434 N.W.2d 624 (Iowa 1989); Hayne v. Progressive Northern Ins. Co., 339 N.W.2d 588 (Wis. 1983); Said v. Auto Club Ins. Ass'n, 393 N.W.2d 598 (Mich. Ct. App. 1986); Empire Mut. Ins. Co. v. Zelin, 502 N.Y.S.2d 20 (N.Y. App. Div. 1986); Bonis v. Commercial Union Ins. Co., 482 So. 2d 1017 (La. Ct. App. 1986).

The debate is a vigorous one. Those who oppose the physical contact requirement make several points. Giving the term "hit-and-run" a narrow, literal meaning is inconsistent with the public policy underlying uninsured motorist statutes which is to broaden the coverage provided to victims of automobile accidents.[35] Moreover, the term "hit-and-run" is now used colloquially to refer to any accident where the negligent perpetrator flees the scene, regardless of whether a physical touching occurs. Under principles of interpretation, then, it does not follow that a touching is required. Opponents of the physical contact doubt that requiring physical contacts will significantly reduce fraudulent claims, since the insured bent on fraud can create the evidence of contact in many situations.[36] Finally, the physical contact requirement creates an indefensible anomaly: the less vigilant driver who does not avoid another motorist has a physical contact and obtains coverage, but the vigilant, defensive driver who manages to avoid an increased hazard (such as a massive head-on accident) but nevertheless suffers a less-serious accident not involving physical contact with the other motorist has no coverage.[37]

Those who favor the requirement urge, first, that the term "hit-and-run" has a literal, discernible meaning. A "hit" is required, and a hit involves a touching. A miss is simply not a hit. Second, not requiring a physical contact gives an incentive for fraudulent claims; the insured who falls asleep and drives off the road is likely to seek a recovery from the insurer by claiming that an unknown third party ran the insured off the road.[38] Third, insurers are ordinarily free to contract with the insureds on whatever terms they desire. Nothing prohibits limiting uninsured motorist coverage to where a physical touching is evident; the insured is always free to secure first-party coverages for the "miss-and-run" cases.

The problem is further complicated by the fact that hit-and-run accidents occur in a variety of ways, and not all of them involve the direct contact of the unknown motorist crashing his or her vehicle into the insured's vehicle. In fact, the hit-and-run cases run the gamut from no contact at one extreme to devastating contact at the other.

At the "no contact" extreme is the relatively common situation where the tortfeasor swerves into the insured's path, causing the insured to take evasive action, which results in a contact between the insured's vehicle and another vehicle or a fixed object. In these situations, the tendency of courts is to deny coverage.[39] The

---

[35] See, e.g., Pin Pin H. Su v. Kemper Ins. Cos., 431 A.2d 416 (R.I. 1981); Simpson v. Farmers Ins. Co., 592 P.2d 445 (Kan. 1979); Brown v. Progressive Mut. Ins. Co., 249 So. 2d 429 (Fla. 1971).

[36] See De Mello v. First Ins. Co., 523 P.2d 304 (Haw. 1974).

[37] See Streitweiser v. Middlesex Mut. Assur. Co., 593 A.2d 498, 502 (Conn. 1991).

[38] See, e.g., Travelers Indem. Co. v. Reddick, 308 N.E.2d 454 (Ohio 1974); Ely v. State Farm Mut. Auto. Ins. Co., 268 N.E.2d 316 (Ind. Ct. App. 1971); Smith v. Allstate Ins. Co., 456 S.W.2d 654 (Tenn. 1970). One answer to this argument is that fraudulent claims are not easy to manufacture given modern techniques of accident investigation.

[39] See, e.g., Hammon v. Farmers Ins. Co., 707 P.2d 397 (Idaho 1985); Rohret v. State Farm Mut. Auto. Ins. Co., 276 N.W.2d 418 (Iowa 1979); Ward v. Consolidated Underwriters, 535 S.W.2d 830 (Ark. 1976); Said v. Auto Club Ins. Ass'n, 393 N.W.2d 598 (Mich. Ct. App. 1986); Empire Mut. Ins. Co. v. Zelin, 502 N.Y.S.2d 20 (N.Y. App. Div. 1986); Bonis v.

obvious concern in these situations is that the insured will claim that an unknown motorist caused an accident when in truth no such motorist existed. Suppose an insured falls asleep, drives off the road, and suffers an accident. If the insured suffers injury but lacks accident or health insurance, the insured may be inclined to assert that a driver of another car forced the insured off the road, thereby enabling him or her to obtain UM benefits under the insured's own policy. Thus, because of the insurer's vulnerability to feigned claims, most courts hold that swerving to avoid an unknown vehicle is not a physical contact.

This result is, however, troubling in one kind of case: unknown motorist is attempting to pass a truck in no-passing zone; the oncoming motorist, the insured, swerves to avoid a head-on collision, but in successfully doing so loses control and has an accident. These were the facts in *Lowing v. Allstate Insurance Co.*,[40] a 1993 case before the Arizona Supreme Court. The Arizona statute did not address the problem of the unidentified motorist. In striking down a policy's physical contact requirement, the court observed:

> Commentators agree that the physical contact requirement was created by insurance companies to prevent fraudulent claims by insureds who negligently damage their vehicles and invent a "phantom" vehicle in an attempt to recover from their insurer. The contact requirement, however, is both too broad and too narrow to accomplish this goal. As one commentator noted, if twenty witnesses will swear that an accident occurred as claimed by the injured insured, it is simply arbitrary to deny coverage in the absence of physical contact under the rubric of fraud prevention. Conversely, if there are not witnesses to an insured's own negligence, he or she can easily claim physical contact when there was none, and create the evidence to corroborate such a claim.[41]

The court's observation goes to the heart of the matter, explaining also why some states have by statute require coverage to be provided in the absence of physical contact if a 'disinterested witness' saw the incident. Under such a statutory regimen, one hopes, of course, that the truck or other vehicle being passed at the time of the accident does not drive on.

An intermediate case some distance from the "no contact" extreme is the situation where the insured's vehicle hits a piece of debris lying in the roadway, which results in an accident. The debris may be a piece of an automobile, such as a tire fragment, a piece of metal, or a bolt, or nonvehicular debris. The insured will argue that an unknown motorist left the debris in the highway when it fell off his or her car, and that this is a physical contact between the other motorist's vehicle and the insured's vehicle. The insurer may argue that it is just as likely that the debris fell off a garbage truck, and this is hardly the direct physical contact that the policy contemplates; this argument has more force if the debris is not vehicular. Where motorists hit vehicular debris of unknown origin on the road and have an accident as a result, most courts

---

Commercial Union Ins. Co., 482 So. 2d 1017 (La. Ct. App. 1986); Inter-Insurance Exch. v. Lopez, 47 Cal. Rptr. 834 (Cal. Ct. App. 1965).

[40] 859 P.2d 724 (Ariz. 1993) (en banc).

[41] 859 P.2d at 730.

have not been inclined to allow coverage because of the absence of a direct causal connection between the uninsured vehicle and the insured's vehicle.[42] If vehicular debris in the roadway does not create coverage, it must follow that non-vehicular debris left in the roadway, presumably because it fell off a vehicle, that subsequently causes an accident also does not create coverage.[43] For the most part, these cases reason that what is covered by the policy is direct automobile-to-automobile contacts, not situations where a part of vehicle or nonvehicular debris has an incidental contact with the insured's vehicle.

Another step along the continuum toward coverage is a case where a piece of a vehicle detaches (or a piece of nonvehicular debris falls off a vehicle) and while in motion after the separation hits the insured's vehicle, causing an accident. In some of these cases, a physical contact has been recognized. This is but a step away from direct collision; the only fact missing is that the vehicle part (or the load) is not attached to the rest of the vehicle at the time of the contact. The dangers of fraudulent claims are substantially reduced in these instances,[44] but in most of these cases coverage has been denied.[45] Some cases have also that the physical contact resulting from an object intentionally discharged from the uninsured vehicle fails to satisfy the physical contact requirement.[46]

One court, however, appeared to draw a distinction between vehicular debris and nonvehicular debris in this situation, and found coverage when vehicular debris was involved. In *Allstate Insurance Co. v. Killakey,*[47] a tire and rim from an unidentified vehicle fell off, cross the median, and hit another vehicle, causing a fatal accident. A number of witnesses saw the driver of the unidentified vehicle stop, put on a spare,

---

[42] See, e.g., State Farm Mut. Auto. Ins. Co. v. Norman, 446 S.E 2d 720 (W.Va. 1994) (tire); Yutkin v. United States Fid. & Guar. Co., 497 N.E.2d 471 (Ill. App. Ct. 1986) (tire fragment); Kersten v. Detroit Auto. Inter-Ins. Exch., 267 N.W.2d 425 (Mich. Ct. App. 1978) (tire assembly); Blankenbaker v. Great Central Life Ins. Co., 281 N.E.2d 496 (Ind. Ct. App. 1972) (tire assembly).

[43] Kern v. Nevada Ins. Guar. Ass'n, 856 P.2d 1390 (Nev. 1993) (unknown slippery substance on pavement that also caused five other cars to have accident); Wynn v. Doe, 180 S.E.2d 95 (S.C. 1971) (slick chemical substance on highway); Smith v. Great Am. Ins. Co., 272 N.E.2d 528 (N.Y. 1971) (snow and ice which had detached from unidentified vehicle); Barnes v. Nationwide Mut. Ins. Co., 230 Cal. Rptr. 800 (Cal. Ct. App. 1986) (box of dinette chairs).

[44] See Illinois Nat'l Ins. Co. v. Palmer, 452 N.E.2d 707 (Ill. App. Ct. 1983).

[45] See, e.g., Smith v. Great Am. Ins. Co., 272 N.E.2d 528 (N.Y. 1971) (snow dislodged from passing vehicle results in accident); Utica Mut. Ins. Co. v. Tucker, 505 N.Y.S.2d 992 (N.Y. Sup. Ct. 1986) (rimless tire of unknown origin crashed through windshield of auto as it drove under overpass); Government Employees Ins. Co. v. Goldschlager, 355 N.Y.S.2d 9 (N.Y. App. Div. 1974) (wheel came off unidentified vehicle, bounced across road, and struck insured's vehicle).

[46] See, e.g., Mazon v. Farmers Ins. Exch., 491 P.2d 455 (Ariz. 1971) (stone thrown by unknown person in unidentified auto hit insured in eye while driving vehicle); Fisher v. Clarendon Nat'l Ins. Co., 437 S.E.2d 344 (Ga. Ct. App. 1993) (insured truck driver who was shot by unknown person in another vehicle is not entitled to benefits under uninsured motorist coverage).

[47] 580 N.E.2d 399 (N.Y. 1991).

and drive on. The court explained that " 'physical contact' occurs within the meaning of the statute, when the accident originates in collision with an unidentified vehicle, or an integral part of an unidentified vehicle."[48] The court then explained:

> The remedy for distinguishing between valid and fraudulent hit-and-run claims should rest on the proof that there was, indeed, an unidentified vehicle and that physical contact with the vehicle caused an accident, not on artificial distinctions between accidents involving a vehicle and those which may involve parts which undeniably come from it. The burden of proving a claim when only a part of a vehicle is involved, however, is necessarily substantial; to establish that the claim originated in collision . . ., the claimant must prove that the detached part, in an unbroken chain of events, caused the accident.[49]

That test was easily met in *Killakey*, given the circumstances of the accident.

Closely related to a piece of the vehicle or its load falling off and hitting the insured's vehicle is the situation where the unknown motorist's vehicle kicks up a piece of highway debris which hits the insured's vehicle and causes an accident. In some of these cases, a physical contact has been found to exist.[50] In other cases, however, no physical contact has been recognized.[51] In many of these cases, the facts no doubt influence the outcome. If a stone thrown by a vehicle's tires penetrates the windshield and kills the insured, a court may be more inclined to find a physical contact than in a case with less dramatic facts.

Yet another step along the continuum is the situation where the uninsured tortfeasor hits one vehicle and propels that vehicle into the insured's vehicle. In the chain reaction accident, most courts hold that a physical contact has occurred for purposes of the uninsured motorist coverage.[52] Once one begins equating intermediate contact with direct physical contact, it becomes difficult to draw lines. It is not easy for courts that find a physical contact in the chain reaction situation to explain the absence of coverage where a wheel comes off the unknown motorist's vehicle and hits the insured's vehicle.

---

[48] 580 N.E.2d at 399.

[49] 580 N.E.2d at 399.

[50] See, e.g., Hill v. Citizens Ins. Co., 403 N.W.2d 147 (Mich. Ct. App. 1986) (rock kicked up by unidentified vehicle which struck and killed passenger in car held physical contact); Illinois Nat'l Ins. Co. v. Palmer, 452 N.E.2d 707 (Ill. App. Ct. 1983); Allied Fid. Ins. Co. v. Lamb, 361 N.E.2d 174 (Ind. Ct. App. 1977) (rock kicked up by unidentified vehicle which struck and killed passenger in car held physical contact); Barfield v. Insurance Co. of N. Am., 443 S.W.2d 482 (Tenn.App. 1968) (stone kicked up by passing automobile that went through windshield held physical contact).

[51] See, e.g., Masler v. State Farm Mut. Auto. Ins. Co., 894 S.W.2d 633 (Ky. 1995). See also Bruce v. Rogers Oil Tool Serv., Inc., 556 So. 2d 922 (La. Ct. App. 1990) (upholding jury instruction that object on roadway which was propelled into insured vehicle would not constitute physical contact upheld).

[52] See, e.g., Hartford Acc. and Indem. Co. v. LeJeune, 499 N.E.2d 464 (Ill. 1986); Hoyle v. Carroll, 646 S.W.2d 161 (Tenn. 1983); Spaulding v. State Farm Mut. Ins. Co., 202 S.E.2d 653 (S.C. 1974); In re Application of New York City Health and Hospitals Corp., 506 N.Y.S.2d 644 (N.Y. Sup. Ct. 1986); Inter-Ins. Exch. v. Lopez, 47 Cal. Rptr. 834 (Cal. Ct. App. 1965).

In the final analysis, most policies provide coverage to insureds who suffer bodily injury in hit-and-run accidents, but they also require that the hit-and-run vehicle make physical contact with the insured or the vehicle the insured occupied. Such a requirement raises two issues: first, whether a physical contact occurred in the particular circumstances; and second, whether the relevant state statute specifying the scope of uninsured motorist coverage invalidates the policy's physical contact requirement.

[c] Nature of Underinsured Coverage

There are two models of underinsured motorist ("UIM") insurance in the statutes. Under one type of statute, if the injured person possessed liability insurance in excess of the liability insurance carried by the tortfeasor, and if the injured person's loss exceeds the limits of the tortfeasor's coverage, the injured person's own insurance picks up the difference. In effect, underinsured motorist coverage protects an insured against injury caused by a tortfeasor with very low amounts of liability insurance: the insured who is injured by another driver is provided with coverage as though the insured were injured by a driver with policy limits equal to the insured's own. The focus of this kind of statute is not so much on reimbursing the insured in full for his or her loss, as it is making sure that the insured has first-party protection equal at least in amount to the amount of liability insurance that the insured has purchased.

A different approach to UIM coverage makes the amount of the insured's liability coverage an add-on to the amount of the tortfeasor's liability coverage if the tortfeasor's coverage is inadequate to reimburse the insured's loss. Thus, this type of arrangement focuses less on "topping off" the tortfeasor's liability insurance, and focuses more on providing resources to compensate the injured victim. Of course, since this kind of UIM coverage is broader, it should cost more than a "topping-off" UIM coverage.[53]

UIM coverage is mandatory in a few states (about four), is included unless the insured specifically rejects the coverage in writing in most states (about twelve), and the coverage is optional in the remaining states (about nine).[54]

In effect, what the "topping-off" statutes do is cap the UIM recovery at the amount of the UM recovery, i.e., what the insured would recover if the tortfeasor had no insurance. This capping is accomplished through what is essentially a set-off that the UM carrier gets for any amounts paid by the tortfeasor or the tortfeasor's liability insurer to the insured-victim. To illustrate, suppose an insured suffers actual damages in excess of $500,000. The tortfeasor has a $100,000 liability insurance policy, and the insured has $250,000 in underinsured motorist benefits. The insured, after receiving $100,000 from the tortfeasor, would like to claim $250,000 from the insured's own insurer. The insurer, however, will set off from the $250,000 the $100,000 the insured received from the tortfeasor's insurer, even though the insured's damages greatly exceed $350,000. Statutes in twelve states expressly

---

[53] See generally Alan I. Widiss, *supra* note 1, § 32.2.

[54] See Alan I. Widiss, *supra* note 1, § 32.4; *No-Fault and Uninsured Motorist Automobile Insurance* § 30.30.

authorize the setoffs; in the absence of such statutory authorization, most states hold that setoff provisions in the policies are invalid.[55]

§ 135 Property Coverage in Automobile Insurance

Most people who purchase insurance for any liability they might incur while operating their vehicle also purchase property coverage for their automobile. (If a vehicle has very little value and the vehicle is not security for a mortgagee who loaned the insured money to purchase it, the insured may elect not to insure the vehicle for property damage. Of course, if the vehicle is later destroyed, the owner must bear this loss directly.) Of course, if a third-party is at fault in an accident which causes damage to the automobile, that third party (or its insurer) will ultimately pay for the damage to the automobile. However, in the event the negligent third party is uninsured and without other financial means, or in the event the insured is at fault in causing damage to his or her own automobile, or in the event the damage to the auto is no one's fault (as if, for example, the auto is destroyed in a hailstorm), an insured's first-party property insurance coverage on an auto will reimburse the loss. As discussed in a previous section,[1] the insured will be limited by the contract to recovery the cost to repair or replace the vehicle, or the vehicle's actual cash value, whichever is less and subject to the policy's limits. Also, the insurer who pays for the loss will have a subrogation right against any third party that is legally responsible for the loss.

Automobile property insurance coverage is of two types: collision coverage and comprehensive coverage. Collision coverage protects the insured against damage to the insured vehicle caused by the vehicle's upset or its impact with another vehicle or object. Often collision is defined by reference to a number of causes that do not constitute collision, such as fire, theft, hail, windstorm, vandalism, or flood. The other kind of coverage, comprehensive coverage, protects the insured against damage to the insured caused by perils which are not collisions, such as the perils just enumerated. Collision and comprehensive coverages are intended to be exclusive and non-duplicative of each other.[2]

There are, of course, situations that do not fit neatly into either the collision category or the comprehensive category. For example, if a windstorm causes a truck to veer off the road and hit a tree, is the loss under the collision or the comprehensive coverage? If a hailstorm breaks out the windshield while the vehicle is moving and the driver hits a tree as a result, is the loss under the collision or the comprehensive coverage? Numerous other situations can be imagined. If the insured has both comprehensive and collision coverage, the uncertainty has no practical significance. But if the insured has either collision or comprehensive coverage and not both, how one perceives the cause of the loss will be determinative of the coverage.

---

[55] *Id.* § 30.50, at 30-37 to 30-43.

[1] See § 93, *supra.*

[2] See, e.g., Huntington Nat'l Bank v. Hawkins, 642 N.E.2d 436 (Ohio Ct.App. 1994) (definitions applicable to liability and collision sections of policy are not applicable to comprehensive coverage).

A few cases illustrate the difficulty.[3] In a 1979 North Carolina case,[4] the insured had comprehensive coverage on his truck but not collision coverage. While the truck was transporting a load of gravel across a bridge, the bridge collapsed, causing the truck to slide into a river, with ensuing damage. The insurer argued that the accident was a loss by collision and therefore outside the coverage; the insured argued that the loss was within the comprehensive coverage. Noting that ambiguities are interpreted in the insured's favor, the court held that the loss was not a collision and was covered under the comprehensive coverage.[5] In a 1981 Arizona case,[6] the insured, who was driving a motor home, claimed that he swerved to avoid hitting a gray, four-legged four-feet-high animal that crossed its path, and that he heard a "thump," presumably caused by the vehicle's impact with the animal, before the motor home left the pavement, rolled over, and was severely damaged. There was no blood or hair of an animal found on or near the motor home. The insureds had allowed their collision coverage to lapse, and only carried comprehensive coverage on the motor home. The policy stated that loss caused by "colliding with birds or animals" was not loss caused by collision, and thus was covered under the comprehensive coverage. The trial court directed a verdict for the insured, reasoning that swerving to avoid an animal was covered under the policy. On appeal, the court held that if there were no impact between the motor home and the animal, then no collision had occurred, and thus the damage would have resulted from the vehicle's upset, which would constitute a collision. Accordingly, the court remanded the case to the trial court because the proper fact issue — whether there was an impact between the animal and the vehicle — had not been submitted to the jury.[7]

There are a number of approaches that one can use in deciding cases where uncertainty exists as to whether the loss falls within the comprehensive or the collision coverage. One approach is to treat comprehensive coverage as covering those losses that occur when the vehicle is not being operated, and collision coverage as pertaining to all other losses. This approach needs other distinguishing criteria when a "comprehensive-type" peril combines with a collision to produce a loss. For example, if a tree falls on a car, it makes little sense to have different results simply because the car is moving at the time of the loss in one case and is stationary in

---

[3] For examples other than those discussed in the text, see Gargallo v. Nationwide Gen. Ins. Co., 598 N.E.2d 1219 (Ohio Ct.App. 1991) (shopping cart's contact with car was not "collision" and was within "comprehensive" coverage); Bekermus v. State Farm Mut. Ins. Co., 545 N.Y.S.2d 799 (N.Y. Sup. Ct.App. Div. 1989) (insured whose auto struck object in road, causing puncture in oil pan, loss of oil, and immediate engine seizure, was entitled to recover under collision coverage). See also Simpsonville Wrecker Serv., Inc. v. Empire Fire & Marine Ins. Co., 793 S.W.2d 825 (Ky. Ct. App. 1989) (cargo transportation policy held to provide coverage for damage to crane which, while being transported on bed of trailer, hit overpass and suffered damage, even though no "collision" occurred between truck or trailer and overpass).

[4] Allison v. Iowa Mut. Ins. Co., 258 S.E.2d 489 (N.C. Ct. App. 1979).

[5] 258 S.E.2d at 492.

[6] Rodemich v. State Farm Mut. Auto. Ins. Co., 637 P.2d 748 (Ariz.App. 1981).

[7] 637 P.2d at 750-51. The interpretive approach utilized by the court in *Rodemich* was harshly criticized by the Arizona Supreme Court in Darner Motor Sales, Inc. v. Universal Underwriters Ins. Co., 682 P.2d 388 (Ariz. 1984) (en banc).

another. Another approach distinguishes among risks that involve the vehicle's operation and risks that do not: a tree falling on the car is non-operational (even if the car is being operated), and is thus within the comprehensive coverage; but a loss that requires the vehicle's operation to produce the loss is within the collision coverage (as is the case if a bridge falls under the weight of a truck, because the truck's operation is necessary to the bridge's collapse). This distinction is artificial in some situations; it may be that the vehicle's operation was what was necessary to put the vehicle in a location where a non-operational risk could produce the loss. Yet another approach gives greater weight to causation analysis: if the vehicle's operation was a substantial contributing cause of the loss, the loss is treated as being a collision, but if the vehicle's operation is not a substantial contributing cause, the vehicle's loss is treated as being within the comprehensive coverage. This last approach is difficult to apply, but may be truest to the intended distinction between the two kinds of coverage.

§ 136   Other Issues in Automobile Insurance

§ 136A   What Constitutes "Use" of an Automobile

Most automobile insurance policies purport to cover losses "arising out of the ownership, maintenance, or use of an insured vehicle." Although this phrase reads so as to "provide" coverage, it is designed to limit coverage to certain kinds of events. In other words, although the phrase is styled as a primary definition of coverage, it has the potential to defeat coverage if applied in a restrictive manner.[1]

Because the problem is basically one of interpretation, the decisions on what constitutes "use" of a vehicle are not uniform. The cases basically take one of two approaches. Some courts limit the coverage to losses occurring when the vehicle is being used as a vehicle, meaning while the vehicle's controls are being manipulated for the purpose of propelling the vehicle.[2] Other courts take a broader view of "use," requiring only that the vehicle be employed for some purpose, even if not the ordinary purposes for which vehicles are used.[3] Most cases where vehicles are used for purposes unrelated to transportation are decided in the insurers' favor,[4] but

---

[1] For more discussion, see Alan I. Widiss, *Uninsured and Underinsured Motorist Insurance (1995)*, §§ 11.1 to 11.5; Annot., *Automobile Liability Insurance: What Are Accidents or Injuries "Arising Out of Ownership, Maintenance, or Use" of Insured Vehicle*, 15 A.L.R.4th 10 (1982).

[2] See, e.g., Indemnity Ins. Co. of N. Am. v. Metropolitan Cas. Ins. Co., 166 A.2d 355 (N.J. 1960).

[3] See, e.g., State Farm Mut. Auto. Ins. Co. v. Allstate Ins. Co., 175 S.E.2d 478 (W.Va. 1970).

[4] See, e.g., National Farmer's Union Prop. & Cas. Co. v. Gibbons, 338 F. Supp. 430 (D.N.D. 1972) (top of the car was used as a gun rest; a deflected bullet went through the top of the car injuring an occupant; loss did not arise out of use); Coletrain v. Coletrain, 121 S.E.2d 89 (S.C. 1961) (a woman's hand was injured when her husband slammed a taxi's door on it; held covered, as he was using the vehicle); PEMCO Ins. Co. v. Schlea, 817 P.2d 878

there are notable exceptions.[5]

At a minimum, the "arising out of the use" terminology contemplates some sort of sequential relationship between the vehicle's use and the loss. This relationship is described in various ways: "One is that the vehicle need not be the proximate cause of the injury in the legal sense, but 'the events giving rise to the claim must arise out of, and be related to, its use.' Another is that the injury be a 'natural and reasonable incident or consequence of the use of the [automobile] for the purposes shown by the declarations . . . [and not] directly caused by some independent act, or intervening cause wholly disassociated from, independent of and remote from the use of the [automobile].' "[6] The insistence that some sort of sequential relationship exist between the use and the loss imparts into these cases the rules on causation, which were discussed in a previous section.[7] For example, in *Pecos Valley Cotton Oil, Inc. v. Fireman's Fund Insurance Co.*,[8] a 1986 Tenth Circuit decision, the court held that an automobile policy did not cover injuries suffered while unloading seed from a truck (which under the policy constituted "use" of the truck) into a seed pit because the "efficient and predominant" cause of the loss was a faulty weld on the seed pit door, not the unloading of the truck.

Two contrasting cases illustrate the issues raised by the "arising out of the use" terminology. In *Farm Bureau Mutual Insurance Co. v. Evans*,[9] a 1981 Kansas case, three persons were sitting in the back seat of a station wagon parked at a bonfire party. During the party, one of the persons, with the help of the other two, allegedly threw an "M-80," a small explosive device in the fireworks genre, out of the rear

---

(Wash. Ct. App. 1991) (abduction and rape of insured in automobile her assailant had taken from co-worker did not arise out of the "use" of vehicle); Leverette v. Aetna Cas. & Sur. Co., 276 S.E.2d 859 (Ga. Ct. App. 1981) (insured stood on the vehicle trying to pick plums and fell off; loss does not arise out of use).

[5] See Perry v. State Farm Mut. Auto. Ins. Co., 506 F. Supp. 130 (D. Minn. 1980) (insured and two sons were towing an antique, uninsured Model A Ford behind the insured van; insured was steering the Model A when a police officer stopped the cars; as the insured exited the Model A, he was fatally shot by the police officer; held arising out of use of van); Lawver v. Boling, 238 N.W.2d 514 (Wis. 1976) (insured, in making repairs to his barn, rigged a lift by connecting a wooden platform to a rope, placing the rope through a pulley, and then tying the rope to the back of his truck; when the truck moved forward or backward, the platform was raised or lowered; rope broke, causing injury to the insured's son-in-law; court held that the loss arose out of the use of the truck, since it is reasonable to expect a farming vehicle to be put to uses beyond transportation); Merchants Co. v. Hartford Ins. Co., 192 So. 566 (Miss. 1940) (insured used several large poles to get his truck out of a ditch; poles were left beside road; plaintiff's car struck the poles at night; loss arose out of use of truck, since the dangerous situation had its origin in the use of the truck); Liberty Mut. Ins. Co. v. O'Rourke, 298 A.2d 725 (N.J.Super.Ct.Ch.Div. 1973) (insured's car stalled; neighbors attempted to restart it by priming the carburetor with gas; explosion ensued, injuring the insured's son; court held that coverage existed, because the repairs were necessary for the continuation of the journey).

[6] Pacific Indem. Co. v. Truck Ins. Exch., 76 Cal. Rptr. 281, 283 (Cal. Ct. App. 1969).

[7] See § 67, *supra.*

[8] 780 F.2d 892 (10th Cir. 1986).

[9] 637 P.2d 491 (Kan.App. 1981).

of the station wagon. The M-80 landed in a glass of beer held by a woman at the party; the ensuing explosion caused her substantial injuries. The trial court concluded that the automobile policies provided coverage for the woman's injuries because "the automobile was being used as a shelter, a reasonable incident of its use and one reasonably contemplated by the parties to the insurance contract."[10] The appeals court reversed. The court insisted that some causal connection exist between the use of the vehicle and the injury. In *Evans,* the court found no such causal connection — the vehicle "did not causally contribute to Karen's injuries anymore than it would have if one of the occupants . . . had shot her with a firearm."[11] Plaintiff contended that the vehicle provided a shelter that made it easier to light the M-80, but the court said this causation was too remote to support a finding of coverage.

In contrast, in *Hartford Accident & Indemnity Co. v. Civil Service Employees Insurance Co.,*[12] a 1973 California case, a sufficient nexus between the vehicle and the injury was found. The insured parked her car in front of her guest-passenger's home, and the passenger started to alight from the vehicle. The insured's male scottie dog had been riding in the back seat. While the passenger sat on the right front seat and started to open the door in order to leave the car, the dog, also attempting to alight from the car, jumped from the back seat to the front seat over the passenger's right shoulder and bit the passenger beside her right eye and on her right arm.

The insured possessed homeowner's liability coverage and automobile liability coverage. The homeowner's policy purported to be excess insurance to the extent of collectible automobile insurance; the issue was whether the passenger's injuries were covered under the automobile liability policy. The trial court held that the automobile policy did not cover the loss because the loss arose out of the ownership of a dog, not out of the use of an automobile. The appeals court disagreed: "The term [use] is not confined to motion on the highway, but extends to any activity in utilizing the insured vehicle in the manner intended or contemplated by the insured."[13] Because the transportation of pets in family vehicles is common, the court was disposed to conclude that the passenger's injuries arose out of the use of the vehicle.

The factual patterns that give rise to the issue of whether the loss arises out of the vehicle's use are virtually endless. A relatively common situation in the reported cases involves altercations between people who have just been involved in an automobile accident.[14] In *Foss v. Cignarella,*[15] a 1984 New Jersey case, Foss's car was sideswiped when Cignarella attempted to pass Foss on the left by driving in the expressway's median. Both drivers brought their cars to a stop on the road's

---

[10] 637 P.2d at 493–94.

[11] 637 P.2d at 494.

[12] 108 Cal. Rptr. 737 (Cal. Ct. App. 1973).

[13] 108 Cal. Rptr. at 741, *quoting* Pacific Indem. Co. v. Truck Ins. Exch., 76 Cal. Rptr. 281 (Cal. Ct. App. 1969).

[14] See generally Annot., *Injury or Death Caused by Assault as Within Coverage of No-Fault Motor Vehicle Insurance,* 44 A.L.R.4th 1010 (1985).

[15] 482 A.2d 954 (N.J.Super.Ct.Law Div. 1984).

shoulder, but Foss's car bumped Cignarella's car in the rear. Cignarella became enraged, ran up to Foss's vehicle, stabbed Foss in the chest while he was seated in the car with the door closed but the window partially open, and then drove away. Foss suffered no injuries from the accident; he later sought a recovery from Cignarella's insurer for the injuries arising from the stabbing. The court said that the injuries did not arise from the use of the vehicle:

> This act of Cignarella, however reprehensible and unfortunate, was not causally connected with his operation of the automobile. . . . [The fact that but for the use of the auto and the accident Cignarella would not have assaulted Foss] is not the substantial nexus required between the use of the insured vehicle and the injury to impose liability upon the insurer. . . . Unlike debris being thrown from, or falling out of, a moving vehicle, the commission of an assault with a weapon by one driver involved in an automobile accident upon the driver of the other vehicle, is such an uncommon and bizarre occurrence that neither the insurer nor the insured would consider it to be a natural and reasonable consequence of the use of the insured vehicle.[16]

There are cases to the contrary, however. In *Government Employees Insurance Co. v. Novak,*[17] a 1984 Florida case, the court held that when a driver was attacked and shot while sitting in a car by a person to whom she refused entry into the vehicle, she was entitled to personal injury protection benefits under the insurance policy covering the automobile on the ground that the loss arose out of the vehicle's use. A similar holding was reached in another Florida case, *Allstate Insurance Co. v. Gillespie,*[18] where the insured while sitting in the car was attacked by a person enraged at the manner in which the insured was driving. In attempting to repel the attack, the insured produced a gun which, during a struggle over it, discharged and injured the attacker. The attacker sued the insured for his injuries, and the court held that the insurer was obligated to provide the insured a defense because the incident was "inexorably tied to [the insured's] use of his automobile."[19]

One source of controversy is whether the act of loading or unloading a vehicle constitutes use of the vehicle. In the *Hartford Accident* case discussed above, the car was stopped and the dog, which bit the passenger, was being "unloaded." Most courts, like *Hartford Accident,* have interpreted the loading or unloading of a vehicle to be a use of that vehicle, and liability incurred during the loading or unloading

---

[16] 482 A.2d at 957. See also Baber v. Fortner, 412 S.E.2d 814 (W.Va. 1991) (intentional shooting from inside of cab of stationary truck was not an act "arising out of the ownership, maintenance, operation, or use" of the vehicle); State Farm Mut. Auto. Ins. Co. v. Nolen, 857 S.W.2d 37 (Tenn.App. 1993) (insured's disabled vehicle was being towed after it ran off road; insured was given ride in police officers' patrol car; during ride, insured, who was later found mentally ill, shot and killed both officers; held, officers' deaths did not arise out of ownership or maintenance of insured's vehicle); Day v. State Farm Mut. Ins. Co., 396 A.2d 3 (Pa. Super. Ct. 1978). But see Chapman v. Allstate Ins. Co., 211 S.E.2d 876 (S.C. 1975) (injury when woman fell from a moving vehicle while trying to resist the amorous advances of the driver held covered; loss arose out of the use of the vehicle).

[17] 453 So. 2d 1116 (Fla. 1984).

[18] 455 So. 2d 617 (Fla. Dist. Ct. App. 1984).

[19] 455 So. 2d at 619.

process is therefore covered.[20] Some courts have reached the opposite conclusion, however, holding that the mere loading or unloading of a vehicle does not constitute using the vehicle.[21] The loading-unloading dispute involves not only cargo but also human beings. In the typical case, the disembarking of a passenger from the vehicle arises out of the vehicle's use,[22] but not all courts agree.[23]

Losses related to the use of vehicles to transport guns appear in a large number of cases. When guns are accidentally discharged inside moving or motionless vehicles while an occupant of the vehicle is handling the gun, coverage is usually disallowed on the ground that no causal connection exists between discharge of the gun and the vehicle's use.[24] If the gun discharges inside a vehicle due to movement or operation of the vehicle, coverage is usually allowed.[25] When guns are discharged while loading them into or out of vehicles or onto or off gun racks permanently attached to the vehicle, most courts conclude that the discharge arises out of the vehicle's use.[26] The logic is that loading or unloading cargo is a normal, expectable

---

[20] See, e.g., Pepsi-Cola Bottling Co. v. Indemnity Ins. Co. of N. Am., 318 F.2d 714 (4th Cir. 1963); Truck Ins. Exch. v. Home Ins. Co., 841 P.2d 354 (Colo.Ct.App. 1992); Greentree Assoc. v. U.S. Fid. & Guar. Co., 607 A.2d 175 (N.J. Super. Ct. App. Div. 1992).

[21] See, e.g., Florida Crushed Stone Co. v. Commercial Standard Ins. Co., 432 So. 2d 690 (Fla. Dist. Ct. App. 1983).

[22] See National Indem. Co. v. Farmers Home Mut. Ins. Co., 157 Cal. Rptr. 98 (Cal. Ct. App. 1979) (after exiting from a parked car, a small child was hit by an oncoming car; held covered, because the insured's negligent failure to supervise the child when alighting from the car caused the loss).

[23] See Shoreland Early Childhood Ctr., Inc. v. Alexander, 616 N.E.2d 274 (Ohio Ct.App. 1992) (child, hit by oncoming car after he had disembarked from insured teacher's car and was crossing street, was unloaded, because act of unloading that child was finished even though other children were being unloaded; therefore, exclusion for loading and unloading of insured's automobile did not apply); Preferred Risk Mut. Ins. Co. v. United States Fid. & Guar. Co., 395 N.E.2d 1180 (Ill. App. Ct. 1979) (child, disembarking from a Sunday school bus to retrieve her brother, who was hit by a police car while crossing the street was not covered, since the bus had not begun to take the children home). See generally Annot., *Risks Within "Loading and Unloading" Clause of Motor Vehicle Liability Insurance Policy,* 6 A.L.R.4th 686 (1981).

[24] See, e.g., Hartford Fire Ins. Co. v. State Farm Mut. Auto. Ins. Co., 574 S.W.2d 265 (Ark. 1978); National Family Ins. Co. v. Boyer, 269 N.W.2d 10 (Minn. 1978); American Liberty Ins. Co. v. Soules, 258 So. 2d 872 (Ala. 1972); State Farm Mut. Auto. Ins. Co. v. Smith, 691 P.2d 1289 (Idaho Ct.App. 1984).

[25] See, e.g., Southeastern Fid. Ins. Co. v. Stevens, 236 S.E.2d 550 (Ga. Ct. App. 1977); State Farm Mut. Auto. Ins. Co. v. Partridge, 514 P.2d 123 (Cal. 1973).

[26] See, e.g., Kohl v. Union Ins. Co., 731 P.2d 134 (Colo. 1986); Travelers Ins. Co. v. Aetna Cas. & Sur. Co., 491 S.W.2d 363 (Tenn. 1973); Toler v. Country Mut. Ins. Co., 462 N.E.2d 909 (Ill. App. Ct. 1984). See also Transamerica Ins. Group v. United Pac. Ins. Co., 593 P.2d 156 (Wash. 1979), *overruled on other grounds,* State v. Olsen, 893 P.2d 629 (Wash. 1995) (taking gun off gun rack is not unloading, but is within use of vehicle and therefore insurer is liable). But see Morari v. Atlantic Mut. Fire Ins. Co., 468 P.2d 564 (Ariz. 1970); Aetna Cas. & Sur. Co. v. Safeco Ins. Co., 163 Cal. Rptr. 219 (Cal. Ct. App. 1980) (loading gun in motionless vehicle does arise out of use of vehicle, but no causal link exists between loading and the resulting injury; thus, injury not excluded under homeowner's policy).

use of a vehicle; thus, the discharge of a weapon, which is typically viewed as normal cargo, which results in injury to a passenger constitutes use of the vehicle. In one case, a shotgun on a pickup truck's gun rack discharged while the truck was parked and motionless and while the gun was not being handled, killing a person who was outside the truck and approaching it, but who was not an occupant of the truck and had no intent to become an occupant. The court held that the claimant's death did not arise out of the use of the insured truck.[27] In cases where a vehicle has been used as a gun rest for the purpose of firing a weapon, the courts split.[28] A closely related situation involves the discharge of fireworks and firecrackers inside vehicles; courts usually hold that this is not use of the vehicle.[29] However, when the fireworks or projectiles are thrown from inside a moving vehicle, courts sometimes hold that the loss arises out of the use of the vehicle.[30] The same is true when guns are fired from inside moving vehicles.[31]

---

[27] See State Farm Mut. Auto. Ins. Co. v. Powell, 318 S.E.2d 393 (Va. 1984). See also Cameron Mut. Ins. Co. v. Ward, 599 S.W.2d 13 (Mo. Ct. App. 1980) (injury caused when gun discharges when not being handled while car is at rest and door of car is shut does not arise out of use).

[28] Compare Fidelity & Cas. Co. v. Lott, 273 F.2d 500 (5th Cir. 1960) (allowing coverage), with National Farmers Union Prop. and Cas. Co. v. Gibbons, 338 F. Supp. 430 (D.N.D. 1972) (no coverage); Norgaard v. Nodak Mut. Ins. Co., 201 N.W.2d 871 (N.D. 1972) (no coverage). See also Topole v. Edison, 464 So. 2d 406 (La. Ct. App. 1985) (injury caused by boy firing gun while standing in bed of motionless truck does not arise out of use of vehicle).

[29] See, e.g., Morari v. Atlantic Mut. Fire Ins. Co., 468 P.2d 564 (Ariz. 1970); Speziale v. Kohnke, 194 So. 2d 485 (La. Ct. App. 1967).

[30] See, e.g., Home Ins. Co. v. Towe, 441 S.E.2d 825 (S.C. 1994); National Am. Ins. Co. v. Insurance Co. of N. Am., 140 Cal. Rptr. 828 (Cal. Ct. App. 1977); Valdes v. Smalley, 303 So. 2d 342 (Fla. Dist. Ct. App. 1974); Westchester Fire Ins. Co. v. Continental Ins. Co., 312 A.2d 664 (N.J. Super. Ct. App. Div. 1973), aff'd, 319 A.2d 732 (N.J. 1974) (drawing distinction between throwing stick out of car, which does arise out of use, and throwing fireworks and other inherently dangerous objects out of car, which is usually not covered).

[31] See, e.g., State Farm Mut. Auto. Ins. Co. v. Davis, 937 F.2d 1415 (9th Cir. 1991) (applying California and Tennessee law); Continental Western Ins. Co. v. King, 415 N.W.2d 876 (Minn. 1987). But see Ruiz v. Farmers Ins. Co., 865 P.2d 762 (Ariz. 1993) (in car-to-car shooting, bodily injury sustained by insured does not arise out of use of uninsured motor vehicle); Taylor v. Phoenix Ins. Co., 622 So. 2d 506 (Fla. Dist. Ct. App. 1993) (unprovoked firing of automatic weapon at insured's vehicle while both vehicles were being driven on Florida interstate highway does not arise out of use of vehicle); Sciascia v. American Ins. Co., 443 A.2d 1118 (N.J.Super.Ct.Law Div. 1982), aff'd, 459 A.2d 1198 (N.J. Super. Ct. App. Div. 1983) (firing gun from inside moving vehicle does not constitute use of vehicle). Given the recent increase in drive-by shootings and similar random acts of gun violence committed from vehicles, it is not frivolous to ask whether these kinds of occurrences involve "expected" uses of vehicles, at least for purposes of insurance coverage. Two different answers are suggested by the majority and dissenting opinions in Pemco Ins. Co. v. Schlea, 817 P.2d 878 (Wash. Ct. App. 1991), where the majority held that abduction and rape of the insured in an automobile her assailant had taken from a co-worker did not arise out of the 'use' of the vehicle. The majority observed that "[k]idnapping, assault, and rape are not motoring risks against which the parties intended to insure." 817 P.2d at 880. The dissent responded: "While using a vehicle as a means of transporting a victim and as a place to commit a rape is not either a 'reasonable,' or 'traditional' use of an automobile, it is . . . a use nonetheless." Id.

Courts that extend the use of vehicle to the operation of loading and unloading cargo soon confront an additional problem: determining when the process of unloading is complete. Under the "comes to rest" test, the process of unloading is finished when the article is independent of the vehicle and begins to move toward its final destination.[32] Under the "completion of the delivery" test, unloading is finished when all of the operations necessary to complete the delivery of an object have terminated.[33] The "completion of the delivery" test has two variations. Under one formulation, delivery is not complete until the cargo is delivered to its ultimate destination;[34] another formulation inquires into whether commercial delivery has been accomplished.[35] A third test frames the issue in terms of causation, and asks whether "a sufficient causal nexus" exists between the activities relating to an accident and the use of the vehicle.[36]

Although the differences among the tests may seem slight, fact patterns like that in *Estes Co. v. Employers Mutual Casualty Co.,*[37] a 1980 Illinois case, demonstrate the significance of the distinctions. A concrete supplier was delivering concrete to a building construction site. To get the concrete to the forms, the concrete was poured by the driver of a ready-mix truck into a bucket connected to an overhead crane which lifted the concrete to the forms. The crane was operated by the contractor's workmen. As one filled bucket was being swung from the concrete truck over to the forms, the crane hit a high-tension wire, causing injury to the contractor's employees. The issue was whether the concrete supplier's insurance policy on the truck covered the employees' injuries. The contractor argued that the loss arose out of the unloading of the concrete truck. The court said no. The concrete never came to rest, and it was unclear when complete delivery occurred. The court reasoned that the unloading was completed when the concrete truck finished its handling of the concrete and the material was placed in the hands of the receiver at the designated reception point. Commercial delivery had occurred, even though further transportation of the concrete was necessary.

A simple set of facts like that presented in *American Family Mutual Insurance Co. v. Shelter Mutual Insurance Co.,*[38] a 1988 Missouri case, is also revealing on the importance of the test applied. Two men were carrying a transmission from the bed of a pickup truck, the insured vehicle, to a body shop at the residence of the truck owner. When they had carried the transmission some 20 to 35 feet down the

---

[32] See American Auto. Ins. Co. v. American Fid. & Cas. Co., 235 P.2d 645 (Cal. Ct. App. 1951).

[33] See Entz v. Fidelity & Cas. Co., 412 P.2d 382 (Cal. 1966); August A. Busch & Co. v. Liberty Mut. Ins. Co., 158 N.E.2d 351 (Mass. 1959).

[34] See St. Paul Mercury Ins. Co. v. Huitt, 336 F.2d 37 (6th Cir. 1964).

[35] See Liberty Mut. Ins. Co. v. Johnson, Drake & Piper, Inc., 390 F.2d 410 (8th Cir. 1968).

[36] See Mission Ins. Co. v. Aid Ins. Serv., 585 P.2d 240 (Ariz. 1978); Viani v. Aetna Ins. Co., 501 P.2d 706 (Idaho 1972), *overruled on other grounds,* Sloviaczek v. Estate of Puckett, 565 P.2d 564 (Idaho 1977); American Family Mut. Ins. Co. v. Shelter Mut. Ins. Co., 747 S.W.2d 174 (Mo. Ct. App. 1988); Celina Mut. Ins. Co. v. Citizens Ins. Co., 355 N.W.2d 916 (Mich. Ct. App. 1984).

[37] 402 N.E.2d 613 (Ill. 1980).

[38] 747 S.W.2d 174 (Mo. Ct. App. 1988).

driveway, one of the men fell to the ground, and the transmission fell on his hand, causing a hand injury. The court considered each of the various tests for determining whether the accident occurred in the process of unloading the truck. Under the "come to rest" test, presumably loading was finished when the transmission was lifted from the bed of the truck, immediately prior to the commencement of the walk down the driveway (although one could argue that continual motion in the process of loading would mean that the "rest" had not occurred). Under the complete operation test, the unloading was still underway because the transmission was not yet at its final destination. The court, however, applied the "substantial causal nexis" test, and held that the unloading was still underway at the time of the accident because without the use of the truck the transmission would not have been on the premises. The court said it did not matter if the unloading were not the proximate cause of the accident,[39] although if the evidence showed that the injured person tripped and fell over a large crack in the driveway, it is fair to wonder whether the loss would have been covered under the insurance policy on the truck.[40]

In automobile liability policies, the "arising out of the use" language serves as an affirmative grant of coverage. In other liability policies, insurers often exclude coverage through the "arising out of the use" terminology.[41] For example, losses arising out of the use of an automobile are specifically excluded by the homeowners' policy; the assumption is that insureds will acquire automobile insurance to cover their liability for automobile-related losses. *Auto-Owners Insurance Co. v. Transamerica Insurance Co.,*[42] a 1984 South Dakota case, is illustrative. Auto-Owners had issued a mobile homeowner's insurance policy to the insured, an employee of an electric company. The insured entered the premises of his employer to do some repair work on the axle of his go-cart. He drained the gasoline from the cart, tipped it on end, and began welding. Because combustible material was present on the premises, he put a fire extinguisher close to his work. While welding, some gas ignited, starting a fire. The insured deployed the extinguisher, but because it was a CO_2 extinguisher it simply caused the gasoline-fed fire to spread. The employer obtained a judgment against the insured for the resulting damage. Auto-Owners claimed that its policy did not cover the loss due to the exclusion for loss "arising out of the ownership, maintenance, operation, use, loading or unloading of . . . any

---

[39] 747 S.W.2d at 178.

[40] For other examples, see Fiscus Motor Freight, Inc. v. Universal Sec. Ins. Co., 770 P.2d 679 (Wash. Ct. App. 1989) ("loading and unloading" clause held ambiguous in auto policy and interpreted to provide coverage, where truck driver's companion fell into fertilizer pit during course of fertilizer delivery); Merit Ins. Co. v. Parent Bdlg. Materials, Inc., 531 N.E.2d 1015 (Ill. App. Ct. 1988) (stack of plasterboard toppled and fell day after being unloaded from delivery vehicle; held, injuries arose out of "loading and unloading" of delivery vehicle within meaning of policy).

[41] The same distinction can be made with respect to the loading versus unloading distinction. See Travelers Ins. Co. v. Aetna Life & Cas. Co., 571 N.E.2d 1383 (Mass. 1991) (wheelchair client fell down porch steps while being transported to adult day-care center; held, client was being "loaded" into van when accident occurred; automobile policy provided coverage and general business liability policy did not.

[42] 357 N.W.2d 519 (S.D. 1984).

recreational motor vehicle owned by any insured, if the bodily injury or property damage occurs away from the residence premises." The court reasoned that the welding of the go-cart was maintenance, and but for the maintenance the fire would not have occurred, and thus the damages were excluded from the policy.

Some policies use the term "occupying" to limit the coverage: these policies provide coverage for losses occurring while the insured is occupying the vehicle.[43] For example, in *Kantola v. State Farm Insurance Co.,*[44] a 1979 Ohio case, the issue was whether a minor child was "occupying" a school bus when he was struck by a car while crossing the street in front of the bus after being discharged from the bus. The insurance policy for the bus defined "occupying" to mean "in, or upon or entering into or alighting from." The court construed "alighting from" to mean reaching a place of safety. Thus, the child was still alighting from the bus — and therefore occupying it — when hit while crossing the street in front of the bus.[45] However, in *Marcilionis v. Farmers Insurance Co.,*[46] a 1994 Oregon case, the plaintiff, who was in the middle of the street picking up the keys to his uncle's car when he was struck and injured by an uninsured motorist, was not "occupying" his uncle's car at the time he was injured.[47] In these cases, much depends on the proximity of the claimant to the vehicle through which coverage is sought as well as the presence, if any, of intervening causal factors.[48]

Although less common, there have been cases where the question has been whether the insured was "operating" the vehicle for the purpose of the automobile insurance coverage. In *Farm Bureau General Insurance Co. v. Riddering,*[49] a 1988 Michigan case, the insured, who had coverage under both an automobile and a homeowner's policy, was the front-seat passenger in a car being driven by someone else. The five people in the car were leaving a party; the insured appeared to be fairly

---

[43] See Annot., *What Constitutes Occupancy of Motor Vehicle for Purposes of No-Fault Automobile Insurance Coverage,* 35 A.L.R.4th 364 (1985).

[44] 405 N.E.2d 744 (Ohio Mun. 1979).

[45] Compare Evangelinos v. Trans World Airlines, Inc., 550 F.2d 152 (3d Cir. 1977) (while forming a line in front of the departure gate in the Athens airport, passengers were fired upon by two terrorists; court held passengers were in course of "embarking" on the aircraft and therefore were covered under the Warsaw Convention liability limits of $75,000 per passenger); see also Day v. Trans World Airlines, Inc., 528 F.2d 31 (2d Cir. 1975), *cert. denied,* 429 U.S. 890, (1976). See generally Annot., *What Constitutes "Entering" or "Alighting From" Vehicle Within Meaning of Insurance Policy, or Statute Mandating Insurance Coverage,* 59 A.L.R.4th 149 (1988).

[46] 871 P.2d 470 (Or. 1994).

[47] The plaintiff, while driving the car at 3:00 a.m., noticed a woman waving at him to pull over to the curb. Plaintiff, who was deaf, stopped the car and tried unsuccessfully to communicate with her. She then unexpectedly entered the auto, grabbed the keys from the ignition, exited the auto, and began running down the street. Plaintiff left the car and ran after her; as he caught up with her, she threw the keys into the street. After searching for the keys, he found them; while in the act of picking them up, he was hit by an speeding motorist.

[48] For other examples, see State Farm Mut. Auto. Ins. Co. v. Cookinham, 604 A.2d 563 (N.H. 1992) (friend of insured who was leaning on insured's vehicle at time she was struck by another vehicle was "occupying" the vehicle for purposes of UM coverage).

[49] 432 N.W.2d 404 (Mich. Ct. App. 1988).

intoxicated. At some point during the drive, the insured, apparently deciding that the group should go somewhere other than where the driver was taking them, grabbed the top of the steering wheel for about thirty seconds and turned it sharply to the left, thereby causing the car to leave the roadway and crash, with serious consequences, into a tree. One issue in the case was whether the insured was "operating" the vehicle, thereby relieving the homeowner's insurer from responsibility and placing the ultimately liability on the automobile insurance policy. The court held that the insured was not "operating the vehicle," noting that operation involves more than steering; it also involves using the gas and brake pedals and other switches, etc. that make a car move. The insured clearly interfered with the operation of the car, which made the homeowner's insurer responsible for the defense of the claim and any ultimate indemnification.[50] Other courts that have considered similar facts have divided on the operation issue, with some holding that the passenger's interference with the driving constitutes "operation"[51] and others saying that it does not.[52]

§ 136B　What Constitutes "Ownership"

Automobile policies typically limit their coverage to vehicles that are "owned" and deny coverage for certain losses occurring in "nonowned" vehicles. Whether a person is an owner of a vehicle can be highly controversial.[1] Most courts hold that the term "owner" in an automobile liability insurance policy includes only persons who are able to give permission to use the vehicle and who have the right and power to control it.

Kelly v. Aetna Casualty & Surety Co.,[2] a 1983 Washington case, is illustrative. United Services Automobile Association (USAA) issued a general automobile liability policy to Dr. George Schneider; this policy covered him for damages arising out of the ownership or use of an owned automobile identified in the policy. An accident occurred while Dr. Schneider's 21-year-old son Kenneth was operating another vehicle; the plaintiff, a passenger in the vehicle, was injured. The car involved in the accident was not listed in Dr. Schneider's policy as an owned vehicle. The car's title, however, mistakenly listed Dr. Schneider as the owner of the vehicle. In a suit brought by the injured passenger against Dr. Schneider, Dr. Schneider obtained a summary judgment on the ground that he had no control over the vehicle involved in the accident. After plaintiff obtained a $848,000 judgment against Kenneth, USAA paid its policy limits of $100,000 to the plaintiff. Plaintiff then

---

50 432 N.W.2d at 407-08.

51 See, e.g., United States Fid. & Guar. Co. v. Hokanson, 584 P.2d 1264 (Kan.Ct.App. 1978); State Farm Mut. Auto. Ins. Co. v. Larsen, 377 N.E.2d 1218 (Ill. App. Ct. 1978).

52 See, e.g., West Bend Mut. Ins. Co. v. Milwaukee Mut. Ins. Co., 384 N.W.2d 877 (Minn. 1986); State Farm Mut. Auto. Ins. Co. v. White, 655 P.2d 599 (Or. Ct. App. 1982); West Am. Ins. Co. v. Silverman, 378 So. 2d 28 (Fla. Dist. Ct. App. 1979).

1 See generally Annot., *What Constitutes Ownership of Automobile Within Meaning of Automobile Insurance Owner's Policy,* 36 A.L.R.4th 7 (1985).

2 670 P.2d 267 (Wash. 1983).

proceeded to sue Aetna Casualty and Surety Company, Dr. Schneider's umbrella carrier, for the rest of the judgment. Aetna denied coverage, contending that the car involved in the accident was not owned by Dr. Schneider and therefore the policy provided no coverage for the accident, and the trial court agreed. The appeals court affirmed, holding that neither the USAA nor the Aetna policy provided coverage.

With respect to the petitioner's argument that Aetna was bound by USAA's decision after the accident to add the vehicle to the USAA policy retroactive to before the accident, the court observed that USAA's decision to pay the policy limits was not contractually required. USAA provided coverage for drivers operating vehicles owned by the insured with the insured's permission. The son had permission to drive the car, but the vehicle was not an "owned vehicle" for purposes of the coverage at the time of the accident. The court reasoned that the term "owner" includes only those persons who are able to give permission for the vehicle's use and have the right to control the vehicle. Dr. Schneider lacked such a right; he was only listed as legal owner to secure the loan he made to Kenneth to purchase the car.

Usually, as in *Kelly,* it is necessary to establish that the vehicle is owned in order to have coverage. Occasionally, however, it is essential to coverage that the plaintiff establish that the automobile is "not owned." In *Simon v. Lumbermens Mutual Casualty Co.,*[3] a 1981 New York case, Karen, a Rhode Island resident, owned a car on which she possessed insurance. Karen's sister, who lived with her father in New York, was driving the car with Karen's permission when she struck Karen's infant daughter. The daughter and her father brought a negligence action against Karen and her sister, hoping that the father's policy would be declared excess insurance coverage. The policy promised to pay on behalf of any insured damages arising out of the use of an owned or nonowned automobile, provided the use of any nonowned automobile was with the permission of the vehicle's owner. The coverage was basically identical to that in *Kelly.* The sister, because she lived in her father's household, qualified as an insured. She also had permission from Karen to use the car. The question, then, was whether the vehicle was a nonowned vehicle, which was defined in the policy as an "automobile . . . not owned by or furnished for the regular use of either the named insured or any relative, other than a temporary substitute automobile." Thus, it was essential to establish that the vehicle was not furnished for the sister's regular use. Because the sister had exclusive use of the vehicle for a six-week period before the accident, the court concluded that she had regular use of the vehicle and thus the car was not a nonowned vehicle. Therefore, the insurer was held not liable for the judgment entered against Karen and her sister.

The ownership issue can also surface where conditional sales are involved. For example, in *Beatty v. Western Pacific Insurance Co.,*[4] the insured sold his car to Scott, but the insured retained title to the car until he received the remaining money. The insured left his policy in force for two weeks, and during this period Scott, while operating the vehicle, was involved in an accident. The party injured by Scott in the accident sought to recover under the insured's policy, arguing that the vehicle

---

[3] 436 N.Y.S.2d 139 (N.Y. Sup. Ct. 1981).
[4] 445 P.2d 325 (Wash. 1968).

was still owned by the insured and that Scott's use of the vehicle was with his permission. The court rejected this argument: "where possession of the automobile has been transferred pursuant to the conditional sales agreement, the conditional vendor no longer owns the vehicle in such a sense as will enable him to give or withhold his consent to the use of the vehicle by the vendee, and that the vendor retains title for security purposes rather than for purposes of dominion over the vendee's possession and use of the car."[5]

§ 136C　The Family (or Household) Exclusion

The "family exclusion" or "household exclusion" clause is sometimes found in the liability coverages of an automobile insurance policy. This provision states that no coverage exists for "any obligation . . . for bodily injury to the insured or any member of the family of the insured residing in the same household of the insured." The purpose of the clause is to eliminate the insurer's liability under the liability coverages when one family member's negligence causes injury to another family member. The insurance industry's main concern is the risk of familial collusion. If one family member is injured in an accident caused by the negligence of another family member, and if the injured person sues a relative in tort, the relationship between the parties could lead to collusion: the negligent family member has an incentive to assist the injured family member in securing a judgment and recovering the proceeds of insurance.

Fear about possible collusion between plaintiff and insured-defendant is a recurring theme in tort and insurance law. For example, nine states have "guest statutes" which provide that the owner or operator of a motor vehicle is not liable for the injury or death of a passenger in the vehicle being transported without payment unless the operator is guilty of something more than mere negligence. In effect, the statutes create a zone of immunity from liability for owners or operators of motor vehicles under certain circumstances. The principal rationale for the statutes is that negligent operators are inclined to assist their injured passengers in obtaining recoveries from the operators' insurers. In a much larger number of states, the statutes have been successfully challenged on the ground that the risk of collusion is an inadequate rationale for denying coverage to innocent guest passengers injured in automobile accidents.[1] In the final analysis, the guest statutes protect insurance companies, not generous hosts, against lawsuits filed by negligently injured guests.[2]

Fear of collusion is the underpinning of the intrafamily immunities. Both the doctrine of interspousal immunity and the doctrine of parent-child immunity have been abrogated or significantly limited in most states.[3] To the extent it is a state's

---

[5] 445 P.2d at 331.

[1] E.g., Whitworth v. Bynum, 699 S.W.2d 194 (Tex. 1985); Malan v. Lewis, 693 P.2d 661 (Utah 1984); Johnston v. Stoker, 685 P.2d 539 (Utah 1984).

[2] See Thompson v. Hagan, 523 P.2d 1365 (Idaho 1974).

[3] A recent note states that 14 of the 43 states that initially adopted some form of parental immunity have abrogated the doctrine completely. In 25 of the remaining 29 states, the doctrine has been significantly limited. See Craig E. Hansen, Note, *An Indiana Approach to*

policy to limit these immunities and to allow tort claims to be asserted in the intrafamily setting in order to provide compensation for victims, the household exclusion frustrates the state's purpose by allowing insurers to deny coverage in situations where the tort claim is asserted.[4]

It is not surprising, then, that considerable hostility exists to the household exclusion clause. Most jurisdictions that have addressed the validity of the exclusion after the adoption of mandatory automobile liability insurance statutes have invalidated it either entirely or to the extent of statutorily-mandated coverage.[5] but there are several decisions to the contrary.[6] The public policy opposing the validity

the Emerging Passive Parent Action, 29 Val. U. L. Rev. 1299 nn. 8-10 (1995). Another recent note states that 39 jurisdictions have totally abrogated interspousal immunity and 9 others have abrogated it in special circumstances, leaving only three states that retain it for negligent torts. Daniel T. Barker, Note, *Interspousal Immunity and Domestic Torts: A New Twist on the "War of the Roses,"* 15 Am. J. Trial Advoc. 625 n. 3 (1992).

[4] Sometimes the scope of the intrafamily immunity is articulated as a function of the insurance coverage. In some jurisdictions, intrafamily immunity exists unless there is insurance coverage. This allows the injured family member to recover the limits of the family insurance coverage in damages. The existence of insurance determines whether an immunity exists. Critics of this approach claim that it constitutes nothing more than insurance company-bashing for the purpose of helping victims who did not purchase sufficient first-party insurance.

[5] See, e.g., State Farm Mut. Auto. Ins. Co. v. Wolfe, 638 F. Supp. 1247 (D.Haw. 1986); Nation v. State Farm Ins. Co., 880 P.2d 877 (Okla. 1994) (void as to minimum amount of statutorily-mandated coverage; see cases cited at 881 n.5); National Cty. Mut. Fire Ins. Co. v. Johnson, 879 S.W.2d 1 (Tex. 1993) (void as to minimum amount of mandated coverage); Halpin v. American Family Mut. Ins. Co., 823 S.W.2d 479 (Mo. 1992) (en banc) (void as to minimum amount of statutorily-mandated coverage); State Farm Auto. Ins. Co. v. Alexander, 583 N.E.2d 309 (Ohio 1992); Farmers Ins. Exch. v. Young, 832 P.2d 376 (Nev. 1992) (void as to minimum amount of statutorily-mandated coverage); Stepho v. Allstate Ins. Co., 383 S.E.2d 887 (Ga. 1989) (void as to minimum amount of statutorily-mandated coverage); State Farm Mut. Auto. Ins. Co. v. Wagamon, 541 A.2d 557 (Del. 1988); Farmers Ins. Exch. v. Call, 712 P.2d 231 (Utah 1985) (void as to minimum amount of statutorily-mandated coverage); Allstate Ins. Co. v. Wyoming Ins. Dep't, 672 P.2d 810 (Wyo. 1983); Transamerica Ins. Co. v. Royle, 656 P.2d 820 (Mont. 1983); Mutual of Enumclaw Ins. Co. v. Wiscomb, 643 P.2d 441 (Wash. 1982); Dewitt v. Young, 625 P.2d 478 (Kan. 1981); Bishop v. Allstate Ins. Co., 623 S.W.2d 865 (Ky. 1981) (void as to minimum amount of statutorily-mandated coverage); Arceneaux v. State Farm Mut. Auto. Ins. Co., 550 P.2d 87 (Ariz. 1976) (void as to minimum amount of statutorily-mandated coverage). See also Allstate Ins. Co. v. Anzalone, 462 N.Y.S.2d 738 (N.Y. Sup. Ct. 1983) (exclusion invalid as to household members other than spouse). See generally Annot., *Validity, Under Insurance Statutes, of Coverage Exclusion for Injury to or Death of Insured's Family or Household Members,* 52 A.L.R.4th 18 (1988).

[6] See, e.g., Rich v. Allstate Ins. Co., 445 S.E.2d 249 (W.Va. 1994); State Farm Mut. Auto. Ins. Co. v. Hildebrand, 502 N.W.2d 469 (Neb. 1993); Allstate Ins. Co. v. Feghali, 814 P.2d 863 (Colo. 1991) (en banc); Shannon v. Shannon, 442 N.W.2d 25 (Wis. 1989); Allstate Ins. Co. v. Boles, 481 N.E.2d 1096 (Ind. 1985); Faraj v. Allstate Ins. Co., 486 A.2d 582 (R.I. 1984); Walker v. American Family Mut. Ins. Co., 340 N.W.2d 599 (Iowa 1983); Severs v. Country Mut. Ins. Co., 434 N.E.2d 290 (Ill. 1982). See also Principal Cas. Ins. Co. v. Blair, 500 N.W.2d 67 (Iowa 1993) (household exclusion in homeowner's policy is valid); State

of the household exclusion is one favoring compensation of accident victims. Compulsory liability insurance statutes provide that every owner of a motor vehicle shall continuously provide insurance against loss resulting from liability imposed by law for bodily injury, death, or damage to property suffered by *any person,* subject only to the specified, express exclusions permitted by the statute. Every time an exclusion is authorized, an insured is uninsured to the extent of the exclusion. If the family exclusion is enforced, the people most seriously disadvantaged are those who are most commonly exposed to the potential negligence of named insureds.[7]

Moreover, if the family exclusion is enforced, whether liability insurance is available to help reimburse a loss often turns on random choices and events. The court in *Farmers Insurance Group v. Reed,*[8] a 1985 Idaho decision, gave several examples. Suppose a father is driving a van filled with household members, distant cousins who are not household members, and friends. If the passengers suffer injury in an accident caused by the father's negligence, the friends and distant relatives have coverage under the father's liability policy, but the household members do not, even though everyone rode in the same vehicle. If a son or daughter who is away at college takes the wheel of the van, everyone in the van is immediately covered, but if the mother or child living at home takes the wheel, coverage disappears for household members. When a family friend takes the wheel, coverage reappears.

An even more stark example is the following: two families, who are next-door neighbors, plan a trip to an amusement park in two cars, one owned by each family. At the outset of the trip, the children of the two families are intermingled in each car; that is, some children ride with their own parent, and the other children ride with the neighbor. Both cars are involved in an accident in which each driver is negligent. In this situation, the liability insurers will compensate only those injured children or spouses who, by some quirk of fate, happened to climb into the car without an immediate family member at the wheel.

In defense of the exclusion, one might argue that the inequities outlined above are no worse than those which can occur anytime an uninsured motorist causes an accident. Through the quirk of fate of being hit by an uninsured motorist, the injured victim, depending on what coverage he or she has purchased, may well receive more or less compensation than the victim injured by a motorist with liability insurance. Also, any of these disparities in coverage would be reduced if each family obtained first-party medical coverage for their own losses. If sufficient first-party insurance existed and the injured party were willing to forego recoveries for noneconomic losses, the injured party would be, arguably, fully reimbursed. Furthermore, in defense of the exclusion, the right to sue a family member in tort is not the same

---

Farm Mut. Auto. Ins. Co. v. Ballmer, 899 S.W.2d 523 (Mo. 1995) (en banc) (because a defense is not mandated by financial responsibility statute, insurer has no duty to defend child-driver against lawsuit brought by her mother for death of another child in accident).

[7] See Farmers Ins. Exch. v. Call, 712 P.2d 231 (Utah 1985). For a decision of a deeply divided court where the various opinions explore the issue from different perspectives, see Nation v. State Farm Ins. Co., 880 P.2d 877 (Okla. 1994).

[8] See Farmers Ins. Group v. Reed, 712 P.2d 550 (Idaho 1985).

thing as, and need not be coextensive with, the right to recover from an insurance company for those injuries. If the possibility of collusion is greater where the assets to be reached by the plaintiff's claim are those of the insurer instead of those of the plaintiff's spouse, it is not unfair to allow the insurer to protect itself through the household exclusion.[9]

§ 136D   Stacking of Automobile Insurance Benefits

[a]   Overview

Stacking is a term that refers to obtaining for a single loss insurance proceeds from duplicate coverages. If an insured is allowed to stack coverages, the insured is allowed to recover for damages received a sum up to the stated limit of each policy that provides coverage. Under the principle of indemnity, an insured is allowed to recover from insurance no more than the loss. However, the policy limits of available insurance coverages often are less than the injuries suffered by an insured or a victim of the insured's conduct. If more policies can be reached for coverage, it is more likely that the victim will receive compensation for his or her injuries.

Courts throughout the country have considered in a variety of contexts whether stacking should be permitted, and the results in these cases vary widely. Several considerations have the potential to be determinative. The most important factor is whether a state statute prohibits stacking or allows a policy to prohibit it. If the legislature speaks explicitly to the matter, none of the other considerations has relevance. Absent a clear legislative mandate, other factors can be important. First, the purpose of the legislative scheme is important. Many courts credit the expressed or implicit desire of legislatures to broaden coverage to victims of automobile accidents; this policy cuts in favor of stacking. Second, if the insured pays additional insurance premiums for additional insurance coverages, the insured probably expects additional coverages, and these reasonable expectations figure importantly in many decisions. Third, if the policy language is ambiguous, it will be interpreted against the insurer, and this will cut in favor of stacking.

It is impossible in a few pages to comprehensively relate the law of stacking. In the next few subsections, the most important points will be briefly addressed. For a more detailed overview, other discussions are helpful.[1] For specific answers to particular questions, it is necessary to probe the law of the particular jurisdiction.

---

[9] See Allstate v. Boles, 481 N.E.2d 1096 (Ind. 1985); see § 95[d], *supra,* discussing difference between right to recover in tort and right to recover from insurer.

[1] An excellent overview of stacking is Nicholas P. Terry, "Stacking of Benefits," in *No-Fault and Uninsured Motorist Automobile Insurance* §§ 33.00 to 33.300, at 33-1 to 33-92. See also Annot., *Combining Or "Stacking" Of "No Fault" or Personal Injury Protection (PIP) Coverages In Automobile Liability Policy Or Policies,* 29 A.L.R.4th 12 (1984); Annot., *Combining or "Stacking" Uninsured Motorist Coverages Provided In Policies Issued By Different Insurers To Different Insureds,* 28 A.L.R.4th 362 (1984); Annot., *Combining or "Stacking" Uninsured Motorist Coverages Provided In Separate Policies Issued By Same Insurer To Same Insured,* 25 A.L.R.4th 6 (1983); Annot., *Combining or "Stacking" Medical Payment Provisions Of Automobile Liability Policy Or Policies Issued By One Or More*

[b]   Liability Insurance

In liability insurance, stacking is not permitted if the victim of the insured's tort would recover more than the damages. Under the principle of indemnity, double recovery is not permitted. Regardless, insurers have thought about this possibility, and liability policies therefore contain other insurance clauses, which purport to limit each insurer's responsibility to a portion of the victim's loss. These clauses are discussed in more detail in another section.[2] If the insured's liability exceeds the total limits of all the policies, the insured is usually allowed the full coverage of each policy.

However, this last principle can be altered by statute. In Kansas, for example, insurers are authorized to insert the following exclusion in automobile liability coverages: "if two or more vehicle liability policies apply to the same accident, the total limits of liability under all such policies shall not exceed that of the policy with the highest limits of liability."[3] Under this kind of statute, also found in other states,[4] the insured accomplishes nothing by purchasing additional separate liability coverages. In the event of a judgment against the insured, each insurer will simply share a portion of the loss, as calculated by the other insurance clauses, and the insured will personally bear the judgment to the extent it exceeds the policy with the highest limits. The insured who wishes additional coverage should not purchase a separate policy, but should increase the limits of his or her own policy or purchase umbrella coverage.

Stacking is more commonly an issue in uninsured motorist coverage and the PIP coverages of no-fault insurance.

[c]   Uninsured Motorist Insurance

To understand stacking in the uninsured motorist setting, it is essential as a preliminary matter to understand some of the terminology of stacking cases. First, "stacking" itself is an unfortunate term in that it implies a duplication of benefits. Some courts and commentators refer to "pyramiding" and "aggregating" benefits, but the term "stacking" is most commonly used. Second, many cases make a distinction between one policy providing multiple coverages and the situation where multiple policies apply to a particular incident. In the first situation, stacking is often called "intrapolicy stacking," while in the second situation, stacking is often labeled "interpolicy stacking."[5]

Third, some cases distinguish "named insureds" from "occupancy insureds." An "occupancy insured" is one whose claim for coverage is based on the fact that the

---

Insurers To Different Insureds, 25 A.L.R.4th 66 (1983); Annot., *Combining Or "Stacking" Uninsured Motorist Coverages Provided In Single Policy Applicable To Different Vehicles Of Individual Insured,* 23 A.L.R.4th 12 (1983); Annot., *Combining or "Stacking" Uninsured Motorist Coverages Provided In Policies Issued By Different Insurers To Same Insured,* 21 A.L.R.4th 211 (1983).

  2 See § 97, *supra.*

  3 Kan. Stat. Ann. § 40-3107(i)(5).

  4 E.g., Wash. Rev. Code Ann. § 48.22.030.

  5 See Taft v. Cerwonka, 433 A.2d 215 (R.I. 1981).

insured occupied the vehicle that was insured and was hit by an uninsured motorist. A "named insured" is one who is the owner of the policy and whose coverage is therefore not limited to being in any particular location when the uninsured motorist causes injury. Named insureds have more opportunities to stack, since they have the potential of being covered under more policies in any given incident. When the named insured attempts to stack his or her own policies, that kind of stacking is sometimes referred to as "horizontal stacking." When the named insured seeks to add onto his or her own policy coverage under someone else's policy (in the named insured's status as an occupancy insured on that other policy), the phrase "vertical stacking" is often used.

When the insured is injured by an uninsured motorist, the stacking issue can arise in a variety of ways. Professor Nicolas Terry has devised a straightforward scheme for categorizing the stacking issue.[6] First, the insured may have been a passenger in a vehicle the insured did not own. In that event, the insured may seek to recover from both the insured's own policy (as a named insured) and the policy of the driver of the vehicle (as an occupancy insured). This kind of stacking is called "interpolicy vertical stacking." Second, the insured may have two separate policies on two different vehicles; the insured, if injured in one of the insured's vehicles, may seek to recover under both policies. This is called "interpolicy horizontal stacking." Third, the insured may have paid multiple premiums under one policy for multiple vehicles; if injured in one of the vehicles, the insured may seek multiple recoveries under the uninsured motorist coverage. This is called "intrapolicy horizontal stacking." It should be noted that in any of the three foregoing situations, the insured may not have even been in a vehicle when injured; if injured as a pedestrian, the insured may seek to recover under multiple policies.

Fourth, sometimes a claimant seeks to stack multiple policies owned by someone else. If a guest in an automobile suffers injury when an uninsured motorist hits the vehicle in which the guest was riding, the guest may seek to recover as an occupancy insured against the driver's policy and may seek to stack other policies which the driver owns on other vehicles. This can be called "interpolicy horizontal stacking by an occupancy insured." If in the same situation the claimant seeks coverages under one policy the host has on multiple vehicles, one would have "intrapolicy horizontal stacking by an occupancy insured."

When stacking is allowed, the purpose is not to enable the claimant to recover more than the loss. Indeed, no jurisdiction allows recovery in excess of the loss, even when the jurisdiction takes a liberal approach to stacking. Instead, if the insured's loss exceeds the coverage of one policy, the insured attempts and may be allowed to stack coverages until the loss is fully reimbursed.

Several clauses in uninsured motorist coverages may seek to prevent stacking. The most common kind of clause, which is sometimes authorized or required by statute, simply states that the insured's recovery is limited to the minimum statutory coverage, regardless of how many policies or coverages apply to the accident. These clauses usually are conclusive on the question of stacking, whether intrapolicy or

---

[6] See *No-Fault and Uninsured Motorist Automobile Insurance* § 33.00, at 33-7 to 33-8.

interpolicy stacking, except in the situation where the insurer inserts such a clause in the absence of a legislative directive on its permissibility. Some courts in such a situation have held that the antistacking clause is invalid in that it violates the policy of the statute. The logic of these cases is that the uninsured motorist statute requires each automobile policy to contain at least a minimum amount of uninsured motorist protection; if stacking is prohibited, the statutory purpose is frustrated.[7]

Occasionally, the policy will contain an "other insurance" clause. If the policy contains an excess other insurance clause, the policy seeks to transfer the entire liability to any other insurance that is applicable. If the policy contains a pro rata other insurance clause, the policy seeks to transfer only a portion of the liability to other applicable insurance, under the logic that the applicable coverages should share the liability on a pro rata basis. These clauses are targeted at interpolicy stacking.

Finally, it should be noted that uninsured motorist coverages often require that other kinds of benefits received by the claimant, such as workers' compensation benefits and no-fault insurance benefits, may be used by the insurer to set off what is owed under the uninsured motorist coverage.[8] Most jurisdictions do not allow such setoffs, largely because it reduces the likelihood that the victim of an auto accident will be fully reimbursed for his or her loss,[9] but there is a much authority to the contrary.[10]

[d] No-Fault Coverages

The same sort of issues confronted in the uninsured motorist setting appear when an insured seeks to recover under multiple applicable no-fault coverages. Courts seem most receptive to multiple recoveries when multiple premiums have been paid, but this result is by no means uniform. Beyond this weak generalization, courts vary widely from state to state regarding when no-fault stacking is allowed.[11]

---

[7] See, e.g., Allstate Ins. Co. v. Morgan, 575 P.2d 477 (Haw. 1978); Keel v. MFA Ins. Co., 553 P.2d 153 (Okla. 1976). This argument, it would seem, is more persuasive with interpolicy stacking than with intrapolicy stacking. But see Lundy v. Aetna Cas. & Sur. Co., 458 A.2d 106 (N.J. 1983).

[8] See Alan I. Widiss, *Uninsured and Underinsured Motorist Insurance (1995),* §§ 14.1 to 14.8.

[9] See, e.g., Brunmeier v. Farmers Ins. Exch., 208 N.W.2d 860 (Minn. 1973); State Farm Mut. Auto. Ins. Co. v. Cahoon, 252 So. 2d 619 (Ala. 1971).

[10] See Alan I. Widiss, *supra* note 7, at § 14.1 ("There is a clear split of judicial authority among these decisions.")

[11] *See No-Fault and Uninsured Motorist Automobile Insurance* § 33.30, at 33-79 to 33-82.

CHAPTER 14

REINSURANCE

§ 140 Overview

In the first chapter of this book, the manner in which individuals and companies attempt to manage risk through the insurance mechanism was explained. Insurers also confront risk and are desirous of taking steps to manage it. In modern times, risks in a single building, ship, or airplane can run to the millions of dollars. Some exposures — such as the risk of loss due to hurricanes or earthquakes — affect many insureds at one time. Few insurers could handle claims of this magnitude without impairing and perhaps threatening their financial solvency. To help manage the risks that insurers face, insurers have developed the reinsurance mechanism.[1] For those who once joked that reinsurance was 'a mystery not worth the solving,'[2] there is no joke to be made anymore. Although reinsurance did not become important until the last half of the twentieth century, it is now a vital ingredient in how risk is transferred and distributed in insurance markets around the world.

[a] Definition

Reinsurance is essentially a form of insurance for insurance companies; insurance business is transferred from one insurer to another. Reinsurance should not be confused with the situation where one insured takes out two or more policies covering the same risk with two or more insurers. Also, reinsurance should not be confused with the situation where the insured cancels one policy and substitutes another for it. Reinsurance is not a separate line or branch of the insurance business. Rather, it is a special kind of insurance transaction. It occurs in all lines of the private insurance system — personal, property, and liability. Reinsurance exists only where a primary insurer becomes a "reinsured" by entering into a contract with another insurer, the "reinsurer." By securing reinsurance, the primary insurer does not

---

[1] For detailed treatments of reinsurance, see Graydon S. Staring, *Law of Reinsurance* (1993); Robert W. Strain, ed., *Reinsurance* (1980). For some briefer overviews, see Patrick L. Brockett, Robert C. Witt & Paul R. Aird, *An Overview of Reinsurance and the Reinsurance Markets,* 9 J. Ins. Reg. 432 (1991); Insurance Information Institute, *Reinsurance: Fundamentals and Current Issues* (1983); Reinsurance Facilities Corporation, *A Contemporary Guide to Reinsurance* (1979).

[2] Henry T. Kramer, "The Nature of Reinsurance," in Strain, *supra* note 1, at 1 (making point that reinsurance has become very important in recent decades).

discharge any of its liability to its insureds. In fact, the insured is rarely aware that reinsurance transactions have occurred.

The business of reinsurance has developed some special terminology. The company originally writing the insurance is called the "primary insurer" or sometimes the "ceding insurer," the "direct writer," or the "reinsured." The portion of the risk which the primary insurer retains is called the "net retention" or the "net line." The act of transferring the risk is called "ceding," and the portion of the risk passed to the reinsurer is called the "cession." An insurer that assumes reinsurance may in turn cede to another insurer a portion of the exposure reinsured. This transaction is called a "retrocession" and the second reinsurer is known as a "retrocessionaire."

[b]   Types of Reinsurance Arrangements and Coverage

Two basic kinds of reinsurance arrangements exist, although within these two categories there are many variations. "Facultative" reinsurance involves the primary insurer entering into an agreement for the reinsurance of a particular risk. The reinsurance can be written on a pro rata or an excess basis; the root word "faculty" denotes that the reinsurer has choice of accepting or rejecting any risk proposed and of demanding whatever premium it thinks appropriate. Compared to treaty reinsurance, facultative reinsurance is more cumbersome because the primary insurer must submit a proposal to the reinsurer in sufficient detail to enable the reinsurer to investigate the risk and make an underwriting decision. Also, each time the primary insurer desires reinsurance, it must enter the reinsurance market and negotiate the terms of coverage, the premium, and the commission. Facultative reinsurance is sometimes also called "street" reinsurance.

Most reinsurance is "treaty" reinsurance. The treaty arrangement, sometimes called "automatic reinsurance," involves a commitment of a reinsurer to assume part of the risk of the primary insurer, either on a pro rata or an excess basis, for a stated period. The reinsurer is obligated to accept a portion of all of the risks that meet the requirements agreed to by the parties, as opposed to providing reinsurance directly for a particular risk. The primary insurer may or may not be obligated to cede risks. Provisions exist for renewing or terminating the reinsurance, but the distinguishing aspect of the treaty is that a commitment to reinsure exists, which is not the case when facultative arrangements are used.

In both facultative or treaty reinsurance, two kinds of coverages exist. *Pro rata reinsurance,* sometimes called "quota share" reinsurance, means that losses, premiums, and expenses are divided pro rata by the primary insurer and the reinsurer. For example, the primary insurer may retain sixty percent of the risk and transfer forty percent. If any loss occurs, whether large or small, the primary insurer is liable for sixty percent of the loss and the reinsurer is liable for forty percent.

A special kind of pro rata reinsurance is "surplus" reinsurance. Under surplus reinsurance, the reinsurer agrees to cover a share of the risk that varies with the size of the exposure. For example, the treaty might specify that losses under $50,000 are covered in full by the primary insurer, that the first $50,000 of losses between $50,000 and $250,000 is paid by the direct insurer and the rest by the reinsurer, and that losses exceeding $250,000 are paid 20 percent by the direct insurer and 80 percent by the reinsurer.

Excess reinsurance, which should not be confused with surplus reinsurance, involves a commitment of the reinsurer to pay a part of a claim after the primary insurer's coverage is exhausted. Thus, once a certain threshold is reached, the reinsurer commits to pay any additional losses. The reinsurer is liable only when the loss exceeds the primary insurer's specified retention. A special type of excess reinsurance is "catastrophe" reinsurance. This label simply denotes the situation where the primary insurer retains a very large amount of risk. Although the retention amounts are high, the limits of the reinsurance coverage are also typically very high. These policies operate in the multimillion-dollar ranges: the primary insurer may retain $50 million worth of risk, but losses above $50 million up to $500 million may be covered by the reinsurance.

The term "fronting contract" refers to a contract in which reinsurers underwrite all of the risk on a policy issued by a direct insurer or "fronting company." The fronting company receives a small percentage of the total premium in exchange for its services. The purpose of this arrangement is to permit a reinsurer to write coverage that it cannot do so directly. Sometimes the term "fronting policy" is used to describe a large primary policy; in this situation, the insurer is entitled to indemnity from the insured, which means the insured retains the risk (or, it might be said, functions as the reinsurer on a policy issued to cover its own risks). Such policies may be written in order to enable the insured to qualify for excess insurance or to meet other contractual commitments that the insured may have. Also, at times such policies may be written for illegal or unethical purposes, such as for the purpose of evading state regulation or taxation. Although "fronting" has a pejorative connotation in most usages, fronting in insurance is often highly appropriate, although there are no doubt some fronting arrangements which, though legal, should probably be prohibited.

Another aspect of the fronting arrangement is the use of "captive" insurance companies. Sometimes insureds or groups of insureds (typically commercial enterprises) believe, rightly or wrongly, that they can obtain insurance less expensively and more efficiently through insurance companies that they own and control. In the usual arrangement, the insured organizes a captive insurer offshore, usually in Bermuda or one of the various Caribbean islands; this enables the captive to be organized with a minimum of regulatory oversight and hassle. Because the captive will not be admitted to do business in any state, the captive cannot issue insurance. However, a company that is already admitted to a particular state or states in which it is desired that the captive do business will be used as the fronting company. The front will reinsure the entire risk with the captive and may even provide some other services, such as underwriting and adjustment of claims.

§ 141 Purposes

Reinsurance serves several purposes, of which a few of the important ones will be sketched here.[1]

First, reinsurance permits an insurer to transfer large risks that it is unable to manage or which are simply too risky to another insurer. For example, an insurer that has a portfolio of coverage faces the risk that a large number of small losses of an unexpected, unexceptional nature may occur, thereby exceeding the insurer's capacity to pay for them without suffering a loss. Also, the insurer faces the risk that a single catastrophic event, the precise timing of which is uncertain (e.g., an earthquake) may occur with devastating consequences to the insurer's balance sheet. For either of these risks, an insurer can seek reinsurance to protect against these contingencies.

Second, reinsurance increases an insurer's capacity to write policies. When the primary insurer purchases reinsurance, it reduces the size of its potential losses, which reduces the size of the reserves it must maintain. Insurers, however, are not as interested in reducing reserves as they are in increasing their business. An insurer with the minimum allowable level of reserves and surplus (the amount an insurer is required to maintain in excess of reserves to meet unexpected losses) could not take on new business or enter new fields. However, reinsurance provides a solution: the insurer could write the coverage, transfer the risk to a reinsurer, and receive a commission from the reinsurer. The primary insurer adds no new liabilities, but its surplus increases by the amount of the commission. This increased surplus enables the primary insurer to write and retain additional coverage. Another way to view this transaction is that some of the excess capacity of the reinsurer is utilized by the business-garnering efforts of the primary insurer; in essence some excess capacity is transferred from the reinsurer to the primary insurer. For the small insurer who wants to grow, reinsurance is an important way to take on new business beyond its means and simultaneously increase its capacity.

Third, just as reinsurance enables an insurer to take on new business, reinsurance can also be used to enable an insurer to leave a particular kind of business quickly. An insurer that wants to rid itself of a particular kind of coverage can solicit reinsurance for all of the insurance the carrier has written, which effectively takes the insurer out of the business and makes the reinsurer the insurer for all of the risks.

A fourth purpose of reinsurance is to stabilize insurers' profits and losses. Through reinsurance, the maximum losses on policies can be kept to manageable levels, and cumulative losses over a period of time can be kept within a designated limit. This, in turn, stabilizes insurer profits. To illustrate, suppose an insurer knows that over a period of time one out of every 1,000 homes will be destroyed by fire. If each home is valued at $100,000, it is enough to cover the risk (ignoring administrative expenses and profits) that the insurer collect $100 from each homeowner-insured as a premium. The insurance would be priced at $1 for each $1,000 of each home's value. Suppose one of the homes is valued at $200,000. The insurer who adheres

---

[1] See generally Robert A. Baker, "The Purpose of Reinsurance," in Strain, *supra* note 1, at 33-49.

to its pricing structure will collect $200 in premiums, which means that from the 1,000 homeowner-insureds the insurer collects $100,100 (999 times $100 plus one times $200). If the one home of the 1,000 which happens to be destroyed by fire is the $200,000 home, the insurer will have collected insufficient premiums to pay the loss. One answer, of course, is to refuse to provide coverage for any home over $100,000. Another answer is reinsurance: by transferring some of the risk of loss to another insurer, the primary insurer obtains the certainty that it could cover a loss to any of the insured homes, even to those that have value above the norm. This stabilizes the insurer's losses and profits. This example also illustrates the link between reinsurance and capacity. The reinsurance mechanism enables the insurer with limited reserves to underwrite the $200,000 home, which, in the absence of reinsurance, it could not accept as a risk.

§ 142 Legal Issues Involving Reinsurance

The number of reported appellate cases involving reinsurance issues is relatively small.[1] Nevertheless, it is clear that for many purposes, the ordinary principles of insurance law apply to reinsurance contracts, such as the rules governing the interpretation of contracts and insurance policies.[2] There are, however, a number of issues where the peculiar nature of reinsurance requires additional analysis, and a few of those matters are discussed in this section.[3]

[a] Insurable Interest

The doctrine of insurable interest applies to reinsurance just as it does to any insurance contract. Therefore, the primary insurer is not entitled to contract for reinsurance exceeding the limits of the policies ceded to the reinsurer. Similarly, the reinsurer cannot provide coverage for risks beyond the scope of the coverage provided by the primary insurer. As stated by one court, "the nature of the risk covered by the reinsurance is defined and circumscribed by the risk covered in the primary insurer's policy with its own insured. The reinsured risk 'must be the same as that covered by the original insurance policy.' "[4] If the primary insurer has an insurable interest in the subject matter of the insurance, the primary insurer can reinsure this risk.

---

[1] See Sumitomo Marine & Fire Ins. Co. v. Cologne Reins. Co. of Am., 552 N.E.2d 139 (N.Y. 1990) ("This appeal calls upon us to resolve a question of reinsurance law—a field in which differences have often been settled by handshakes and umpires, and pertinent precedents of this court are few in number.")

[2] See Justice v. Stuyvesant Ins. Co., 265 F. Supp. 63 (S.D. W.Va. 1967).

[3] For more detailed discussion of legal issues involving reinsurance, see 13A APPLEMAN §§ 7681–7707, at 479–594 (1976); 19 COUCH 2d §§ 80:1–80:78, at 621–686 (1983). For discussion of reinsurance regulation, see John C. Gurley, *Regulation of Reinsurance in the United States,* 19 Forum 72 (1983).

[4] Ott v. All-Star Ins. Corp., 299 N.W.2d 839, 847 (Wis. 1981), *quoting* 19 COUCH 2d § 80:51, at 947 (1968).

[b] Insolvency of the Primary Insurer

Early reinsurance contracts, like most liability policies of the early twentieth century, were contracts of indemnity; thus, the reinsurer was required to pay for a loss only if the primary insurer was required to pay proceeds. This situation was to be distinguished from a liability arrangement, where the reinsurer would be obligated to pay proceeds as soon as the primary insurer's liability were established.

The distinction was an important one in situations where the primary insurer became insolvent. Under the liability arrangement, the reinsurer would be obligated to pay proceeds despite the primary insurer's insolvency; but that would not be true if the arrangement were one of indemnity. In a 1937 case, the United States Supreme Court enforced an indemnity arrangement, and held that the reinsurer need not pay proceeds where the primary insurer was insolvent and had not paid proceeds.[5]

As a result of this decision and others following it, most states passed statutes that required reinsurance contracts to contain an insolvency clause,[6] much like that which would also be required in liability policies.[7] Thus, if the primary insured became insolvent, the proceeds of reinsurance would be paid to the receiver, liquidator, or other trustee for the primary insurer.[8] As with other insolvency clauses, this requirement forced reinsurers to perform their policies and prevented reinsurers from reducing their obligations because of the fortuitous circumstances of the primary insurer's insolvency.[9]

Some state statutes permit what is called a "cut-through" clause, which allows the reinsurer to obligate itself directly the insured under a specified policy or to all of the primary insurer's insureds.[10] When such a clause is present, the insured may bring suit directly against the reinsurer.[11] Also, the reinsurer may make direct payment notwithstanding the insolvency of the primary insurer,[12] although there appears to be some authority for disregarding the cut-through clauses in case of insolvency.[13] This makes the reinsurance proceeds an asset of the insured, rather

---

[5] See Fidelity & Deposit Co. of Md. v. Pink, 302 U.S. 224 (1937). See also Arrow Trucking Co. v. Continental Ins. Co., 465 So. 2d 691 (La. 1985).

[6] See, e.g., N.Y.Ins. Law § 1308(a)(2)(A)(i); Mo. Rev. Stat. § 375.246.

[7] See § 97[d][5], *supra*.

[8] See Annot., *Primary Insurer's Insolvency as Affecting Excess Insurer's Liability,* 85 A.L.R.4th 729 (1991).

[9] See, e.g., Ainsworth v. General Reins. Corp., 751 F.2d 962 (8th Cir. 1985); Wyoming Ins. Guar. Ass'n v. Allstate Indem. Co., 844 P.2d 464 (Wyo. 1992); Ascherman v. General Reins. Corp., 228 Cal. Rptr. 1 (Cal. Ct. App. 1986); Prince Carpentry, Inc. v. Cosmopolitan Mut. Ins. Co., 479 N.Y.S.2d 284 (N.Y. Sup. Ct. 1984); Eastern Eng. & Elevator Co., Inc. v. American Re-Ins. Co., 455 A.2d 1235 (Pa. Super. Ct. 1983); Semple & Hall, *Liquidations and Reinsurance: Liability of Reinsurers When Property and Casualty Insurers Become Insolvent,* 5 J. of Ins. Reg. 156 (1986).

[10] See, e.g., N.Y.Ins.Law § 1308(2)(B).

[11] In the absence of a cut-through clause, an insured in a direct action jurisdiction may still be able to proceed against the reinsurer directly. See Ott v. All-Star Ins. Corp., 299 N.W.2d 839 (Wis. 1981).

[12] Kramer, *supra* note 2, at 18-19.

[13] See Graydon S. Staring, *supra* note 1, at § 19.3, p. 6.

than an asset of all the insolvent insurer's creditors. Reinsurers would prefer, all things being equal, not to include cut-through clauses in their policies, but mortgagees who are the original insureds sometimes insist upon these arrangements so that the credit they extend is fully secured.[14]

[c]   Reinsurer's Defenses and the Duty of Utmost Good Faith

In many respects, the relationship between primary insurer and reinsurer tracks that of the original insured and the primary insurer. The primary insurer and reinsurer have a duty to deal with each other in good faith, and the reinsurer will have available to it the defense of misrepresentation, breach of warranty, fraud, or concealment in circumstances where the primary insurer's acts or neglect give rise to the defense. The reinsurer may have a defense to liability where the primary insurer, after entering into the contract of reinsurance, authorizes without the reinsurer's permission the original insured to do some act which increases the risk of loss. In this instance, the primary insurer has breached a duty owed the reinsurer, and the reinsurer may be able to void the policy.

Although the precise contours of the duty of good faith in reinsurance are not obvious, good faith has particular significance in these kinds of transactions. In the words of a person who made most of his career in reinsurance, "[i]t is the position of reinsurers that their contracts are those of 'utmost good faith.' Utmost good faith contracts of any kind are so delicate in character and so susceptible of abuse that unusual precautions must be observed by both parties in their implementation."[15] The business of reinsurance often involves considerable oral exchange of information between primary insurer and reinsurer, and the reliability of this information is very important.[16] The resemblance of the customary practices to how business used to be conducted at the Lloyd's Coffee House of old is unmistakable.[17] The strict law of warranty which applied to the old transactions at Lloyd's[18] probably has something in common with the duty of "utmost good faith" which applies in reinsurance,[19] Both doctrines have the effect of ratcheting up the expectations contracting parties can reasonably possess with regard to the accuracy of information shared by the other party.

[d]   Rights of Original Insured Against Reinsurer

The primary insurer is, of course, liable in a proper case to the original insured regardless of the existence of reinsurance. Also, the reinsurer has the power to

---

[14] See Kramer, *supra* note 2, at 18-19; James D. Koehnen, "Administration and Maintenance of Business in Force," in Strain, *supra* note 2, at 508- 10.

[15] Henry Kramer, *supra* note 2, at 9.

[16] For a description of this process, see Old Reliable Fire Ins. Co. v. Castle Reins. Co., 665 F.2d 239 (8th Cir. 1981). Another court after describing the process of risk underwriting in reinsurance labeled it a "swift, seemingly almost casual process of contract formation." Sumitomo Marine & Fire Ins. Co. v. Cologne Reins. Co. of Am., 552 N.E.2d 139, 142 (N.Y. 1990).

[17] See § 13B[b], *supra*.

[18] See § 101, *supra*.

[19] See Kenneth S. Abraham, *Insurance Law and Regulation: Cases and Materials* 735 (2d ed. 1995).

assume liability to the original insured. However, absent the creation of a contractual relationship between the original insured and the reinsurer, no privity of contract exists between the original insured and reinsurer. Moreover, the contract of reinsurance rarely explicitly creates rights in favor of the original insured. Accordingly, the original insured ordinarily has no cause of action against the reinsurer, even when the primary insurer has become insolvent.[20]

However, in some situations, direct actions by the original insured against the reinsurer have been permitted. If the reinsurer is a party to a third-party beneficiary contract or where the reinsurer has assumed the primary insurer's liabilities, the original insured often enjoys a direct action against the reinsurer.[21] In determining whether the reinsurance agreement is intended to benefit the original insured or whether the reinsurer has assumed the primary insurer's liabilities, the language of the contract between the primary insurer and the reinsurer must be examined.[22]

[e] "Following the Fortunes"

The usual role of the reinsurer is to "follow the fortunes" of the primary insurer as if the reinsurer were a party to the original insurance. As the phrase suggests, the idea is that the reinsurer is to accept whatever settlements the primary insurer makes and participate and pay according to the reinsurance arrangement the appropriate share of whatever judgments are entered that trigger the primary insurer's liability. Difficulties can arise in determining exactly what "fortunes" the reinsurer agreed to "follow," in that the reinsurer's obligation to participate in whatever payments the primary insurer makes is not unlimited. If, for example, the primary insurer settles or pays a claim that is outside the coverage of the underlying policy, the reinsurer need not participate in paying the claim.[23] Also, if the reinsurance contract requires that a particular amount of underlying insurance be maintained and this does not occur, the reinsurer need not contribute to a claim that falls below the amount of coverage that was to be obtained but exceeds the amount of underlying insurance that was actually in force.[24] These limitations will be set forth in the reinsurance contract, and the precise language of the contract can be important.[25] As one court has explained, if there is an ambiguity in what a settlement

---

[20] See, e.g., Reid v. Ruffin, 469 A.2d 1030 (Pa. 1983); Ascherman v. General Reins. Corp., 228 Cal. Rptr. 1 (Cal. Ct. App. 1986); Prince Carpentry, Inc. v. Cosmopolitan Mut. Ins. Co., 479 N.Y.S.2d 284 (N.Y. Sup. Ct. 1984); Schuylkill Products, Inc. v. H. Rupert & Sons, Inc., 451 A.2d 229 (Pa. Super. Ct. 1982).

[21] See, e.g., American Re-Insur. Co. v. Insurance Comm'n of Cal., 696 F.2d 1267 (9th Cir. 1983); American Ins. Co. v. North Am. Co. for Prop. & Cas. Ins., Inc. 697 F.2d 79 (2d Cir. 1982); Arrow Trucking Co. v. Continental Ins. Co., 465 So. 2d 691 (La. 1985); Fontenot v. Marquette Cas. Co., 235 So. 2d 631 (La. Ct. App. 1970), *aff'd in part and rev'd on other grounds,* 247 So. 2d 572 (La. 1971); Ott v. All-Star Ins. Corp., 299 N.W.2d 839 (Wis. 1981); David P. Schack, Comment, *Reinsurance and Insurer Insolvency: The Problem of Direct Recovery by the Original Insured or Injured Claimant,* 29 UCLA L. Rev. 872 (1982).

[22] See Ascherman v. General Reins. Corp., 228 Cal. Rptr. 1 (Cal. Ct. App. 1986).

[23] See Graydon S. Staring, *law of Reinsurance (1993),* § 18.1 at 3.

[24] See Michigan Millers Mut. Ins. Co. v. North Am. Reins. Corp., 452 N.W.2d 841 (Mich. Ct. App. 1990).

[25] *Id.* at 4-6. See, e.g., Bellefonte Reins. Co. v. Aetna Cas. & Sur. Co., 903 F.2d 910 (2d Cir. 1990) (interpreting clause providing that settlements "shall be binding on the reinsurer"

covers, a "follow the fortunes" clause "may obligate a reinsurer to contribute to a settlement even though it might encompass excluded items."[26]

; Calvert Fire Ins. Co. v. Yosemite Ins. Co., 573 F. Supp. 27 (E.D. N.C. 1983) (applying "follow the settlements"); Insurance Co. of N. Am. v. United States Fire Ins. Co., 322 N.Y.S.2d 520 (N.Y. Sup. Ct. 1971), aff'd, 348 N.Y.S.2d 122 (N.Y. App. Div. 1973) (interpreting "pay as may be paid.")

[26] American Ins. Co. v. North Am. Co. for Prop. & Cas. Ins., Inc., 697 F.2d 79, 80 (2d Cir. 1982). See also Unigard Sec. Ins. Co. v. North River Ins. Co., 762 F. Supp. 566 (S.D. N.Y. 1991), aff'd in part and rev'd in part, 4 F.3d 1049 (2d Cir. 1993).

Table of Cases

[References are to Sections]

[References are to Sections]

[References are to Sections]

[References are to Sections]

[References are to Sections]

[References are to Sections]

[References are to Sections]

[References are to Sections]

Bogard v. Employers Cas. Co. (1985) . . . . .
114[2] n21, [3] n35, [6][i] n69

Bohna v. Hughes, Thorsness, Gantz, Powell & Brundin (1992) . . . . 91 n17; 96[4][i] n91

Bolick v. Prudential Ins. Co. of Am. (1969) . .
104B[1] n9

Boling v. New Amsterdam Cas. Co. (1935) . .
25G n8

Bolivar Cty. Bd. of Supervisors v. Forum Ins. Co. (1986) 81 n32

Bolle v. Hume (1993) 25A n19

Bollinger v. Nuss (1969) . . . 112[1] ns14, 15

Bolz v. Security Mut. Life Ins. Co. (1986) . . .
71 n13

Bond v. Commercial Union Assur. Co. (1981)
. . . . 134[2] n19

Bonis v. Commercial Union Ins. Co. (1986) . .
134[4] ns34, 39

Bonitz v. Traveler's Ins. Co. (1978) . . . . . .
104B[1] n33, [2] n40

Bonny v. Society of Lloyd's (1993) . . . . . .
13B n12

Boone v. Lowry (1983) . . . . . 85[2][c] n21

Boos v. National Fed. of State High School Ass'ns (1995) 25A n25

Booska v. Hubbard Ins. Agency, Inc. (1993) . .
32 n21; 35[2][ii] ns35, 44

Booth v. Fireman's Fund Ins. Co. (1969) . . .
134[2] n19

Borgen v. Economy Preferred Ins. Co. (1993)
. . . . 84 n11

Borman v. State Farm Fire & Casualty Co. (1994)
. . . . 63A n15

Borserine v. Maryland Cas. Co. (1940) . . . . .
96 n18

Boseman v. Connecticut General Life Ins. Co. (1937) 36 n21

Boston Camping Distributor Co. v. Lumbermens Mut. Cas. Co. (1972) 31 n12

Boston Ins. Co. v. Pendarvis (1967) . . 51 n29

Boston Ins. Co. v. Read (1948) 31 n22

Boston Old Colony Ins. Co. v. Gutierrez (1980)
. . . . 112[2][e] n38

Boston-Old Colony Ins. Co. v. Warr (1972) . .
93[5][e] n55

Bough Constr. Co. v. Mission Ins. Co. (1988)
. . . . 81 n36

Bourne v. Haynes (1962) . . . . . 52A[4] n39

Bourque v. Duplechin (1976) 84 n38

Bowers v. Bowers (1982) 52A n23

Bowes v. North Carolina Farm Bur. Mut. Ins. Co. (1975) 66 ns10, 12

Bowler v. Fidelity & Cas. Co. (1969) . . . . .
64[2][b] n49

Bowman v. Zenith Life Ins. Co. (1978) . . . .
43 n6

Bowyer v. Thomas (1992) . . . 110 n9, n19, n27

Boyd v. Aetna Ins. Co. (1960) . . 62B[1] n32

Boyd v. Travelers Ins. Co. (1967) . . . 122 n4

Boyd v. Wright (1982) . . . . 134[2] n8

Boyd Bros. Transp. Co. v. Fireman's Fund Ins. Cos. (1984) . . . . 114[6][ii] n84

Boyer v. Travelers Ins. Co. (1936) . . 122 n14

Boyle v. Orkin Exterminating Co. (1991) . . .
12 n8

Bradshaw v. Fireman's Fund American Life Ins. Co. (1984) . . . . 64[1] n29

Brakeman v. Potomac Ins. Co. (1977) . . . . .
81 n36

Braman v. Mutual Life Ins. Co. (1934) . . . . .
35[4] n103

Brand v. International Investors Ins. Co. (1974)
. . . . 71 n29

Brand v. Monumental Life Ins. Co. (1981) . . .
71 n36

Brander v. Nabors (1978) . . . 62A[4][e] ns63, 64

Braner v. Southern Trust Ins. Co. (1985) . . . .
93[5][e] n53

Brant v. GEICO Gen. Ins. Co. (1993) . . . . .
35[2][ii] n34

Brassil v. Maryland Casualty Co., ... 25G

Breeding v. Massachusetts Indem. & Life Ins. Co. (1982) 25I n5

Brendle v. Shenandoah Life Ins. Co. (1985) . .
64[2] n37

Brethren Mut. Ins. Co. v. Filsinger (1983) . . .
83 n17

Brewster v. Michigan Millers Mutual Ins. Co. (1993) . . . . 42[1] n18

Brewton v. Alabama Farm Bureau Mut. Cas. Ins. Co., Inc. (1985) . . . . 42[3][c] n48

Briggs v. United Services Life Ins. Co. (1962)
. . . . 36 n13

Brindis v. Mutual Life Ins. Co. of N.Y. (1990)
. . . . 63B n1

Brinkman v. Aid Ins. Co. (1988) 82 n5

Bristol v. Commercial Union Life Ins. Co. of Am. (1989) . . . . 35[3] n99

Bristol v. Metropolitan Life Ins. Co. (1954) . .
64[1] n18

Britton v. Wooten (1991) 53E n9

Broadway Nat'l Bank v. Barton-Russell Corp. (1992) . . . . 112[2][c] n29

Brockton v. Southern Life and Health Ins. Co. (1989) 43 n8

Brohawn v. Transamerica Ins. Co. (1975) . . .
114[1] ns9, 19, [2] n20, [4] n141, [6][ii] n100

Broidy v. State Mut. Life Assur. Co. (1951) . .
35[4] n104

[References are to Sections]

[References are to Sections]

C

C & C Tile Co. v. Independent School Dist. (1972)
. . . . 96[4][i] n90

C&J Fertilizer, Inc. v. Allied Mut. Ins. Co. (1975)
. . . . 25D n5, 25f

C. Douglas Wilson & Co v. Insurance Co. of N.
Am. (1979) 61 n1

Cabrini Medical Ctr. v. KM Ins. Brokers (1988)
. . . . 35[2][iii] n51

Cafey v. Caffey (1981) . . . . . . 42[1] n36

Cairns v. Grinnell Mut. Reins. Co. (1987) . . .
25C

Calder Race Course, Inc. v. Hialeah Race Course,
Inc. (1980) . . . . 97[3] n38

Calfarm Ins. Co. v. Deukmejian (1989) . . . .
22 n15

California Ins. Guar. Ass'n v. Superior Court
(1991) . . . . 114[4] n65

California League of Independent Ins. Producers v.
Aetna Cas. & Sur. Co. (1959) . . . .
21[4] ns63, 66

California Physician's Service v. Garrison (1946)
. . . . 12 n4

California Union Ins. Co. v. Landmark Ins. Co.
(1983) 65 n67

Callaway v. Sublimity Ins. Co. (1993) . . . . .
102 n8

Calnon v. Fidelity-Phenix Fire Ins. Co. (1925)
. . . . 93 n25

Calocerinos & Spina Consulting Engineers,
P.C. v. Prudential Reins. Co. (1994) . . . .
62A[4][e] n67

Calvert v. Farmers Ins. Co. (1985) . . . .
134[3] n25

Calvert Fire Ins. Co. v. Yosemite Ins. Co. (1983)
. . . . 142 n25

Calvert Ins. Co. v. Western Ins. Co. (1989) . .
63C n17

Cameron Mut. Ins. Co. v. Bouse (1982) . . . .
35[1] n15

Cameron Mut. Ins. Co. v. Ward (1980) . . . .
136A n27

Camilla Feed Mills, Inc. v. St. Paul Fire & Marine
Ins. Co. (1949) . . . . 62B[2] n39

Campbell v. Allstate Ins. Co. (1963) . . . . . .
81 n36

Campbell v. Hartford Fire Ins. Co. (1976) . . .
101 n21

Campbell v. Prudential Ins. Co. (1958) . . . . .
102 n47

Canadian Ins. Co. of Cal. v. Rusty's Island Chip
Co. (1995) . . . . 114[3] n59

Canadian Radium & Uranium Corp. v. Indem. Ins.
Co. of N. Am. (1952) . . . . . 65[f][5] n92

Canadyne-Georgia Corp. v. Continental Ins. Co.
(1993) 81 n32

Canal Ins. Co. v. Savannah Bank & Trust Co.
(1987) 52B n6

Cannon v. Southland Life Ins. Co. (1971) . . .
33 n12

Canyon Country Store v. Bracey (1989) . . . .
82 ns5, 14; 84 n8

Capitol Life Ins. Co. v. Porter (1986) . . . . .
52A n15

Capone, In re Estate of (1987) 52A

Capps v. Klebs (1978) 96 n19

Card v. Commercial Cas. Ins. Co. (1936) . . .
51 n26

Cardin v. Pacific Employers Ins. Co. (1990) . .
114[3] n38

Cardone v. Empire Blue Cross & Blue Shield
(1995) 61 n6

Cargill, Inc. v. Commercial Union Ins. Co. (1989)
. . . . 97[4] n75

Cargill, Inc. v. Commercial Union Insurance Co.
(1989) . . . . 97[4] n76

Caribou Four Corners, Inc. v. Truck Ins. Exch.
(1971) 97 n18

Carle Place Plaza Corp. v. Excelsior Ins. Co.
(1988) 52B n4

Carlin v. Crum & Forster Ins. Co. (1993) . . .
82 n15

Carlson v. Mutual Serv. Ins. (1993) . . 32 n33

Carlton v. Wilson (1984) 53D n1

Carmouche v. CNA Ins. Cos. (1988) . . . . . .
64[4] n87

Carney Through Carney v. Lone Star Life Ins. Co.
(1989) 32 n16

Carolina Production Maintenance, Inc. v. United
States Fidelity and Guar. Co. (1992) . . . .
35[2][ii] n35

Carparts Distribution Center, Inc. v. Automobive
Wholesalers' Ass'n of New England (1994)
. . . . 24[b] n46

Carpenter v. Besco Corp. (1986) 62A

Carper; State v., (1989) . . . . . . 64[2] n64

Carriers Ins. Co. v. American Policyholders Ins.
Co. (1979) . . . . . 97[2] n31, [6][e] n60

Carroll v. CUNA Mut. Ins. Soc'y (1995) . . .
63B n54

Carroll v. CUNA Mutual Insurance Society (1995)
. . . . 64[1] n12

Carroll v. Jackson Nat'l Life Ins. Co. (1991)
. . . . 102 n8

Carrothers v. Knights of Columbus (1973) . . .
64[1] n20

Carroway v. Johnson (1965) . . . .
65[f][7][g] n131

Carter v. Boehm, 3 Burrows 1905 (1905) . . .
103 n6

[References are to Sections]

[References are to Sections]

[References are to Sections]

[References are to Sections]

[References are to Sections]

[References are to Sections]

F

[References are to Sections]

[References are to Sections]

G

[References are to Sections]

[References are to Sections]

[References are to Sections]

[References are to Sections]

[References are to Sections]

[References are to Sections]

[References are to Sections]

[References are to Sections]

[References are to Sections]

J

[References are to Sections]

K

[References are to Sections]

[References are to Sections] ·

[References are to Sections]

[References are to Sections]

[References are to Sections]

[References are to Sections]

[References are to Sections]

[References are to Sections]

 (Pub.837)

[References are to Sections]

[References are to Sections]

O

[References are to Sections]

[References are to Sections]

[References are to Sections]

[References are to Sections]

[References are to Sections]

[References are to Sections]

S

[References are to Sections]

[References are to Sections]

[References are to Sections]

Spencer v. Kemper Investors Life Ins. Co. (1988) . . . . 104B[1] n28

Sperling v. Liberty Mut. Ins. Co. (1973) . . . . 93[3] n34

Sperry v. Springfield Fire & Marine Ins. Co. (1886) . . . . 62B[1] n31

Speziale v. Kohnke (1967) 136A n29

Spezialetti v. Pacific Employers Ins. Co. (1985) 63A n14

Sphere Drake Ins. Co. v. Bank of Wilson (1993) 93 n18

Sphere Drake Ins. Co. v. Ross (1992) 67 n44

Spindle v. Chubb/Pacific Indem. Group (1979) . . . . 114[5] n142

Spirt v. TIAA (1984) . . . . . . 24[5][6] n12

Splish Splash Waterslides, Inc. v. Cherokee Ins. Co. (1983) . . . . 42[1] n17

Springfield Fire & Marine Ins. Co. v. Wade (1902) . . . . 62B[1] n31

Sprouse v. North River Ins. Co. (1986) . . . . 53A[2] n29

Sroga v. Lund (1961) . . . . . . 35[2][iii] n52

St. John's Regional Health Ctr. v. American Cas. Co. (1992) . . . . 97[3] n69

St. Joseph Light & Power Co. v. Zurich Ins. Co. (1983) . . . . 93[5][e] n51

St. Julian v. Financial Indem. Co. (1969) . . . 71 n4

St. Paul Fire & Mar. Ins. Co. v. Parzen (1983) . . . . 62A[4][e] n56

St. Paul Fire & Mar. Ins. Co. v. Smith (1967) . . . . 93[5][e] n55

St. Paul Fire & Marine Ins. Co. v. Albany Cty. Sch. Dist. No. 1 (1988) 61 n1

St. Paul Fire & Marine Ins. Co. v. Barry (1978) . . . . 21[5] n89

St. Paul Fire & Marine Ins. Co. v. Cumiskey (1983) 63A n1

St. Paul Fire & Marine Ins. Co. v. Glassing (1994) . . . . 96[1] n47

St. Paul Fire & Marine Ins. Co. v. Pryeski (1981) . . . . 114[4] n65

St. Paul Fire & Marine Ins. Co. v. Sears, Roebuck & Co. (1979) . . . . 111[3] n30

St. Paul Fire & Marine Ins. Co. v. Thompson (1967) . . . . 111[2] n78

St. Paul Fire & Marine Ins. Co. v. Warwick Dyeing Corp. (1994) . . . . . 65[f][6] n95

St. Paul Fire & Marine Ins. Co. v. W.P. Rose Supply Co. (1973) 96 n17

St. Paul Fire & Marine Insurance Co. v. Barry, ... 21[5]

St. Paul Ins. Cos. v. Talladega Nursing Home, Inc. (1979) 63C n21

St. Paul Mercury Ins. Co. v. Huitt (1964) . . . 97[1] n66; 136A n34

St. Paul-Mercury Indem. Co. v. Rutland (1955) 65 n24

Standard Accident Insurance Co. v. Christy. . . 67[1]

Standard Life & Accident Ins. Co. v. Pylant (1982) 52A n16

Standard Mut. Ins. Co. v. Boyd (1983) . . . . 85[2][c] n25

Standard of Am. Life Ins. Co. v. Humphreys (1975) 122 ns3, 6

Standard Venetian Blind Co. v. American Empire Ins. Co. (1983) 25A n31; 32 n29; 25A n12; 32

Stanley v. Cobb (1986) . . . . . . 111[2] n87

Starcher v. Reserve Ins. Co. (1980) 71 ns37, 38

Starkman v. Sigmond (1982) . . . 53A[1] n26

State v. (see name of defendant)

State Auto. Mut. Ins. Co. v. Youler (1990) . . 81 n16

State Auto Prop. & Cas. Ins. Co. v. Gibbs (1994) . . . . 133 n23 ; 51 n 16

State Compensation Fund v. Industrial Comm'n of Ariz. (1983) 61 n1

State Dep't of Env. Protection v. Signo Trading Int'l, Inc. (1992) . . . . 65[f][7] n121

State ex rel. (see name of relator)

State Farm Auto. Ins. Co. v. Alexander (1992) 136C n5

State Farm Fire & Cas. Co. v. Caldwell (1994) 63C n53

State Farm Fire & Cas. Co. v. Compupay, Inc. (1995) 63C n51

State Farm Fire & Cas. Co. v. Davis (1993) . . 63C n45

State Farm Fire & Cas. Co. v. Finney (1989) . . . . 114[3] n60

State Farm Fire & Cas. Co. v. Jenkins (1985) 63C n6

State Farm Fire & Cas. Co. v. Jenkins (1983) 103 n5

State Farm Fire & Cas. Co. v. Martin (1994) 51 ns8, 19

State Farm Fire & Cas. Co. v. Morgan (1988) 63C n70

State Farm Fire & Cas. Co. v. Muth (1973) . . 63C n5

State Farm Fire & Cas. Co. v. Nycum (1991) 63C n47

State Farm Fire & Cas. Co. v. Pildner (1974) . . . . 114[4] n137

State Farm Fire & Cas. Co. v. Prize (1984) . . 111[7] n137

[References are to Sections]

[References are to Sections]

[References are to Sections]

(Matthew Bender & Co., Inc.)

[References are to Sections]

[References are to Sections]

V

[References are to Sections]

W

[References are to Sections]

[References are to Sections]

[References are to Sections]

INDEX

[References are to pages.]

A

ACCIDENTAL DEATH
Benefits, generally . . . § 64[a][1]
Definition of accident . . . § 64[a][1]
Distinguishing intentional acts from accidents . . . §§ 63B[d], 63C[d]
Driving while intoxicated . . . § 63B[d]
Drug use . . . § 63B[d]
Intentional conduct of insured . . . § 63B
Means and results distinguished . . . § 63B[d]
Suicide . . . § 63B[a]
Time limits . . . § 64[a][2]
Unlawful acts related to death . . . § 63B[b]

ACCIDENT INSURANCE
Amount payable . . . § 94
Casualty insurance . . . § 13A[c]
Combination with health policy . . . § 13A[c]
Motor vehicles (See AUTOMOBILE INSURANCE)

ADVERSE SELECTION
And AIDS . . . § 24[b]

ADVICE
Agent's duty to provide . . . § 35[f][2][ii]

AGENCY/AGENT (See also INTERMEDIARIES)
Actual authority . . . § 35[b], [c]
Apparent authority . . . § 35[b], [c]
By estoppel . . . § 35[b]
General principles . . . § 35[b]

AGENTS
Defined . . . § 35[e]
Duty of care . . . § 35[f][2][i]
Duty of insurer that fails to pay proceeds . . . . § 35[f][4]
Duty to advise . . § 35[f][2][ii]; see also Explain, duty to
Duty to procure insurance . . . § 35[f][2][iii]
Insolvent insurers, and . . . § 35[f][2][iv]
Liability of . . . § 35[f]
Liability to third parties . . . § 35[f][3]
Versus brokers . . . 35[e]

AIDS . . . § 24[b]
Statutes regulating coverage . . . § 22[e]

ALL-RISK COVERAGE
Advantage to insured . . . § 60A
Definition of term . . . § 13D[b]
Language of policy . . . § 13D[b]
Scope . . . § 60A
Specified-risk differentiated . . . §§ 13D[b], 60A

AMERICANS WITH DISABILITIES ACT . . . § 24[b]

ANNUITIES
Insurance role . . . § 13A[3]

ANTI-REBATE STATUTES . . . § 20

APPEALS
Duty of insurer . . . § 113

APPLICATIONS
Errors in preparation . . . § 35[c][3]
Evaluation . . . §§ 13C[iv], 30
Group insurance enrollment form . . . § 122[a]
Insurer's duty to respond . . . § 32[a]
Offer and acceptance doctrine . . . § 31[a]
Solicitation by insurer . . . § 13C[a][i]
Submittal process . . . §§ 13C[a], 30

APPRAISAL PROCEEDINGS
Resolution of insurer-insured dispute . . § 83[a]

ARBITRATION
Enforcement of agreements . . . § 84[a]
Resolution of insurer-insured dispute . . . § 83
Statutory procedures . . . § 83

ASSIGNED RISK PLAN . . . § 22[e]

ASSIGNMENT
Generally . . . § 52B
Beneficiary rights/privileges . . . § 52A[3]
Free assignability . . . § 45[b]
Group insurance . . . § 125
Insurable interest requirement . . . § 45
Insurer's consent . . . § 52B[c]
Life insurance policy . . . § 52B[d]
Mortgage insurance . . . § 53A
Property insurance policy . . . § 52B[1]
Right to receive proceeds . . . § 52B

ATTORNEYS
American Bar Association 'Guiding Principles' . . . § 114[b]
Conflict of interest (See CONFLICT OF INTEREST)
Discovery of adverse information . . § 114[d][3]
Dual representation approach . . § 114[b], [d][1]
Fees (See ATTORNEY'S FEES)
Independent counsel for insured . . § 114[5][ii]

T

U

V

W